Nissan Pick-ups Automotive Repair Manual

by Rik Paul, Ken Freund and John H Haynes

Member of the Guild of Motoring Writers

Models covered:

Nissan/Datsun pick-ups 1980 through 1996

Pathfinder 1987 through 1995

Does not include diesel engine information

(12Y15 - 72030)
(771)

ABCDE
FGHIJ
2

Haynes Publishing Group
Sparkford Nr Yeovil
Somerset BA22 7JJ England

Haynes North America, Inc
861 Lawrence Drive
Newbury Park
California 91320 USA

Acknowledgements

We are grateful for the help and cooperation of the Nissan Motor Company, Ltd. for assistance with technical information, certain illustrations and vehicle photos. Nissan also supplied the vehicle shown on the rear cover.

A book in the **Haynes Automotive Repair Manual Series**

Printed in the USA

ISBN 1 56392 198 7

Library of Congress Catalog Card Number 96-76645

93-416

Contents

1988 Nissan King Cab model D21 pick-up

About this manual

Its purpose

The purpose of this manual is to help you get the best value from your vehicle. It can do so in several ways. It can help you decide what work must be done, even if you choose to have it done by a dealer service department or a repair shop; it provides information and procedures for routine maintenance and servicing; and it offers diagnostic and repair procedures to follow when trouble occurs.

It is hoped that you will use the manual to tackle the work yourself. For many simpler jobs, doing it yourself may be quicker than arranging an appointment to get the vehicle into a shop and making the trips to leave it and pick it up. More importantly, a lot of money can be saved by avoiding the expense the shop must pass on to you to cover its labor and overhead costs. An added benefit is the sense of satisfaction and accomplishment that you feel after having done the job yourself.

Using the manual

The manual is divided into Chapters. Each Chapter is divided into numbered Sections, which are headed in bold type between horizontal lines. Each Section consists of consecutively numbered paragraphs.

At the beginning of each numbered section you will be referred to any illustrations which apply to the procedures in that section. The reference numbers used in illustration captions pinpoint the pertinent Section and the Step within that section. That is, illustration 3.2 means the illustration refers to Section 3 and Step (or paragraph) 2 within that Section.

Procedures, once described in the text, are not normally repeated. When it is necessary to refer to another Chapter, the reference will be given as Chapter and Section number i.e. Chapter 1/16). Cross references given without use of the word "Chapter" apply to Sections and/or paragraphs in the same Chapter. For example, "see Section 8" means in the same Chapter.

Reference to the left or right side of the vehicle is based on the assumption that one is sitting in the driver's seat, facing forward.

Even though extreme care has been taken during the preparation of this manual, neither the publisher nor the author can accept responsibility for any errors in, or omissions from, the information given.

NOTE

A Note provides information necessary to properly complete a procedure or information which will make the steps to be followed easier to understand.

CAUTION

A Caution indicates a special procedure or special steps which must be taken in the course of completing the procedure in which the **Caution** is found which are necessary to avoid damage to the assembly being worked on.

WARNING

A Warning indicates a special procedure or special steps which must be taken in the course of completing the procedure in which the **Warning** is found which are necessary to avoid injury to the person performing the procedure.

Introduction to the Datsun/Nissan pick-ups and Pathfinder

The Datsun/Nissan pick-up truck and Pathfinder vehicles are conventional front engine/rear wheel drive layout with four-wheel drive (4WD) available on some models.

The inline four-cylinder or V6 engines used in these vehicles are equipped with either a carburetor or throttle body fuel injection. The engine drives the rear wheels through either a four or five-speed manual or automatic transmission via a driveshaft and solid rear axle. On 4WD models, a transfer case and driveshaft are used to drive the front wheels through independent driveaxles.

Front suspension is independent, featuring torsion bars, with power-assisted steering available on later models. Leaf springs are used in the rear on pick-up models, while Pathfinders have coil springs.

Brakes are power assisted discs at the front and self-adjusting drum or discs at the rear.

Vehicle identification numbers

Modifications are a continuing and unpublicized part of vehicle manufacturing. Since spare parts manuals and lists are compiled on a numerical basis, the individual vehicle numbers are essential to correctly identify the component required.

Vehicle Identification Number (VIN)

The VIN is very important because it's used for title and registration purposes. The VIN is stamped into a metal plate fastened to the dashboard close to the windshield on the driver's side of the vehicle **(see illustration)**. It contains valuable information such as where and when the vehicle was manufactured, the model year and the body style.

Vehicle identification plate

This metal plate, attached to the right side of the engine compartment, contains important information including the vehicle type, engine type, displacement and maximum horsepower as well as the chassis serial number.

Vehicle chassis serial number

The vehicle chassis serial number is found on the vehicle identification plate and is also stamped on the right front frame rail, adjacent to the engine.

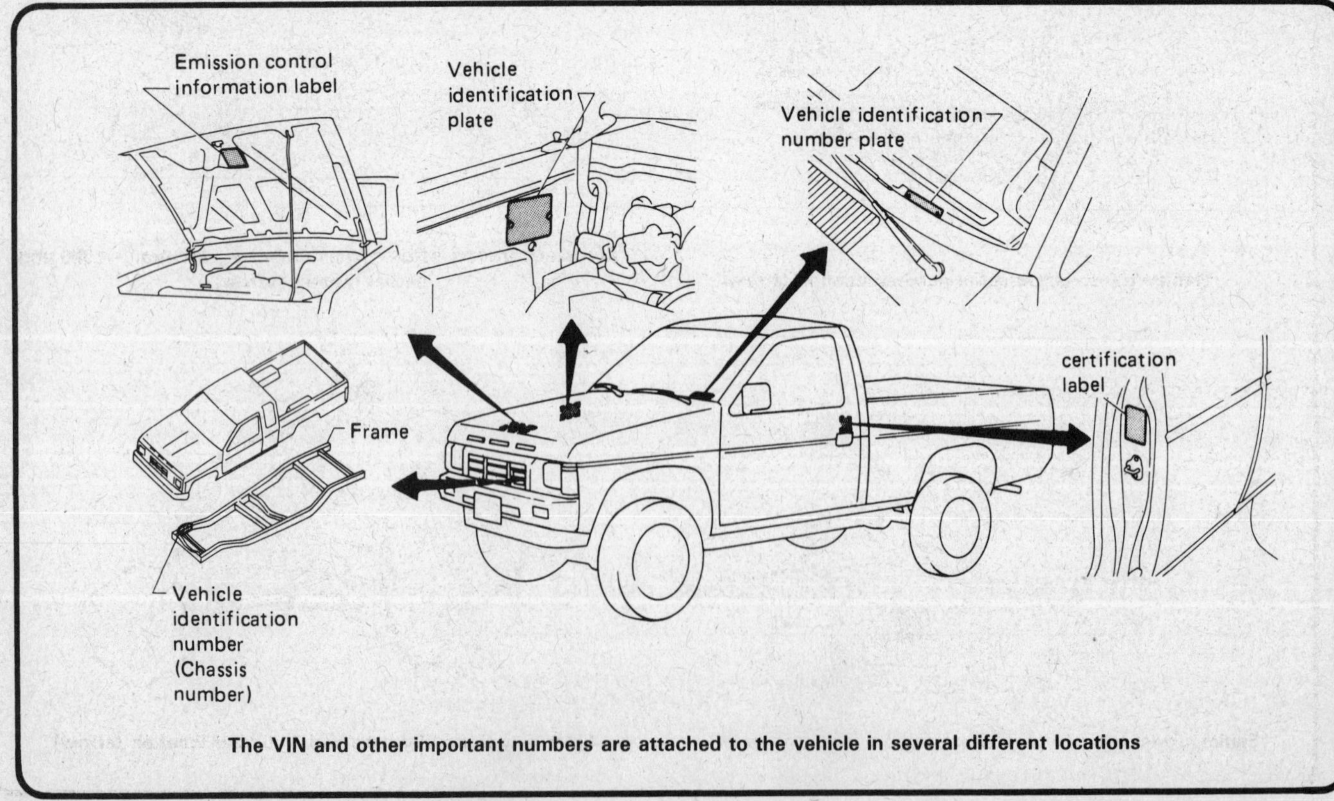

The VIN and other important numbers are attached to the vehicle in several different locations

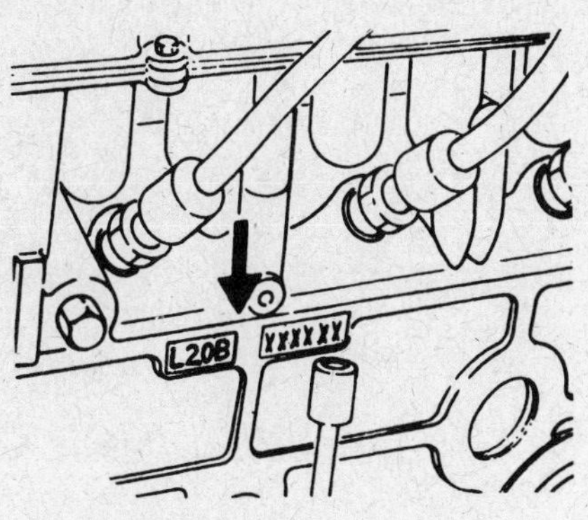

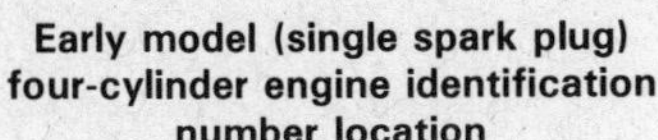

Early model (single spark plug) four-cylinder engine identification number location

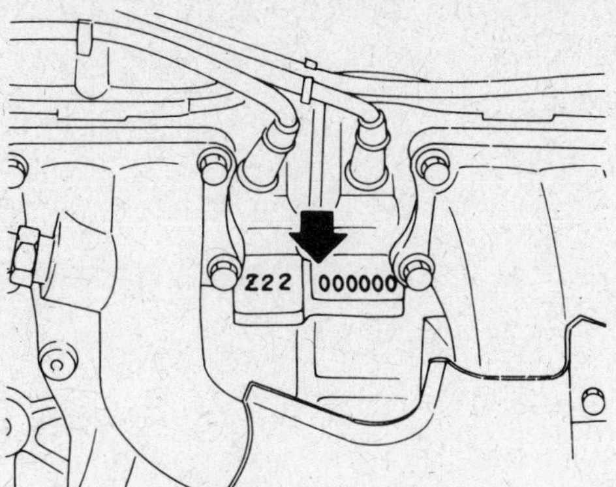

Later model (dual spark plug) four-cylinder engine identification number location

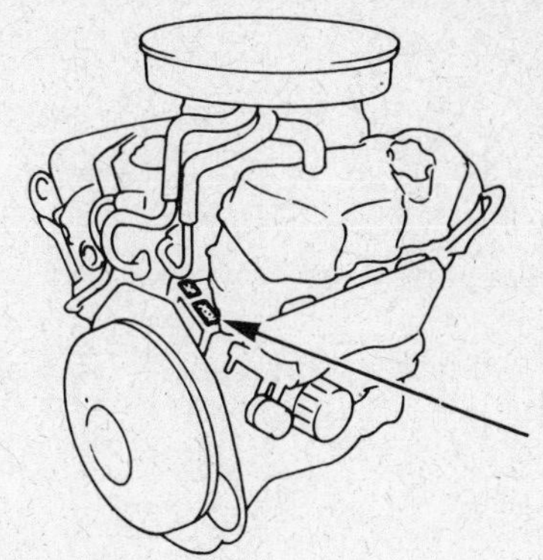

V6 engine identification number location

Engine identification numbers

The engine identification number on four-cylinder engines through 1990 is stamped on a pad on the right side of the block **(see illustrations).** On 1991 and later four-cylinder engines, the number is on the left side of the block, at the rear. On the V6 engine, the ID number is found on the rear side of the block, just below the right cylinder head **(see illustration)**.

Manual transmission serial number

The manual transmission serial number is located on a pad on the top side of the clutch housing.

Automatic transmission serial numbers

On 1990 and earlier models, the automatic transmission serial number is located on a tag on the right side of the transmission case **(see illustration)**. On 1991 and later models, the number is on the right side of the rear extension housing.

Transfer case serial number (4WD models)

The transfer case serial number is located on the right side of the case, either on the front or top of the case **(see illustrations)**.

Vehicle Emission Control Information label

The Vehicle Emission Control Information label is attached to the underside of the hood.

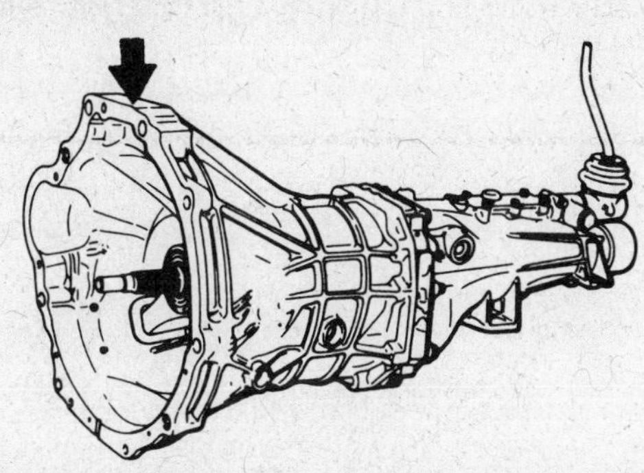

Manual transmission serial number location (arrow)

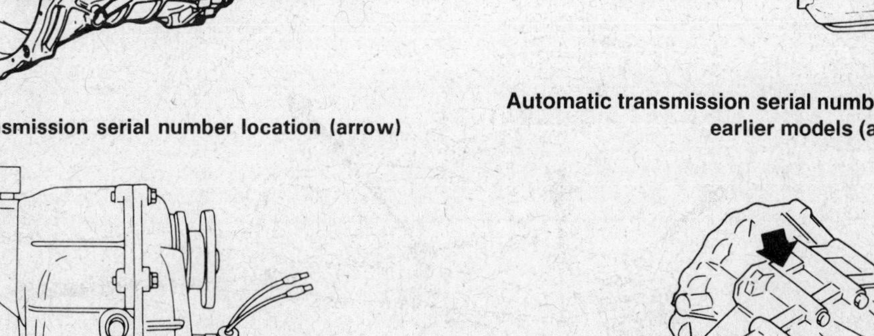

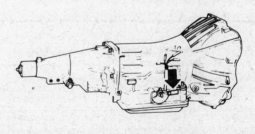

Automatic transmission serial number tag location – 1990 and earlier models (arrow)

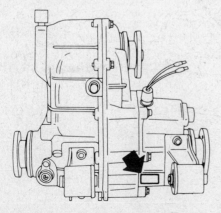

Earlier model transfer case serial number location (arrow)

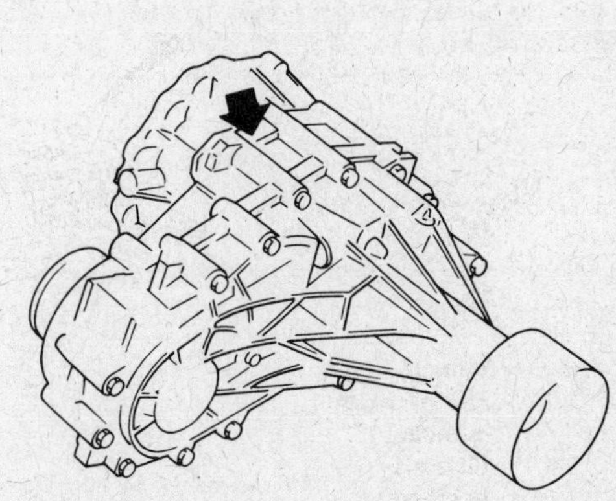

Later model transfer case serial number location (arrow)

Buying parts

Replacement parts are available from many sources, which generally fall into one of two categories – authorized dealer parts departments and independent retail auto parts stores. Our advice concerning these parts is as follows:

Retail auto parts stores: Good auto parts stores will stock frequently needed components which wear out relatively fast, such as clutch components, exhaust systems, brake parts, tune-up parts, etc. These stores often supply new or reconditioned parts on an exchange basis, which can save a considerable amount of money. Discount auto parts stores are often very good places to buy materials and parts needed for general vehicle maintenance such as oil, grease, filters, spark plugs, belts, touch-up paint, bulbs, etc. They also usually sell tools and general accessories, have convenient hours, charge lower prices and can often be found not far from home.

Authorized dealer parts department: This is the best source for parts which are unique to the vehicle and not generally available elsewhere (such as major engine parts, transmission parts, trim pieces, etc.).

Warranty information: If the vehicle is still covered under warranty, be sure that any replacement parts purchased – regardless of the source – do not invalidate the warranty!

To be sure of obtaining the correct parts, have engine and chassis numbers available and, if possible, take the old parts along for positive identification.

Maintenance techniques, tools and working facilities

Maintenance techniques

There are a number of techniques involved in maintenance and repair that will be referred to throughout this manual. Application of these techniques will enable the home mechanic to be more efficient, better organized and capable of performing the various tasks properly, which will ensure that the repair job is thorough and complete.

Fasteners

Fasteners are nuts, bolts, studs and screws used to hold two or more parts together. There are a few things to keep in mind when working with fasteners. Almost all of them use a locking device of some type, either a lockwasher, locknut, locking tab or thread adhesive. All threaded fasteners should be clean and straight, with undamaged threads and undamaged corners on the hex head where the wrench fits. Develop the habit of replacing all damaged nuts and bolts with new ones. Special locknuts with nylon or fiber inserts can only be used once. If they are removed, they lose their locking ability and must be replaced with new ones.

Rusted nuts and bolts should be treated with a penetrating fluid to ease removal and prevent breakage. Some mechanics use turpentine in a spout-type oil can, which works quite well. After applying the rust penetrant, let it work for a few minutes before trying to loosen the nut or bolt. Badly rusted fasteners may have to be chiseled or sawed off or removed with a special nut breaker, available at tool stores.

If a bolt or stud breaks off in an assembly, it can be drilled and removed with a special tool commonly available for this purpose. Most automotive machine shops can perform this task, as well as other repair procedures, such as the repair of threaded holes that have been stripped out.

Flat washers and lockwashers, when removed from an assembly, should always be replaced exactly as removed. Replace any damaged washers with new ones. Never use a lockwasher on any soft metal surface (such as aluminum), thin sheet metal or plastic.

Fastener sizes

For a number of reasons, automobile manufacturers are making wider and wider use of metric fasteners. Therefore, it is important to be able to tell the difference between standard (sometimes called U.S. or SAE) and metric hardware, since they cannot be interchanged.

All bolts, whether standard or metric, are sized according to diameter, thread pitch and length. For example, a standard 1/2 — 13 x 1 bolt is 1/2 inch in diameter, has 13 threads per inch and is 1 inch long. An M12 — 1.75 x 25 metric bolt is 12 mm in diameter, has a thread pitch of 1.75 mm (the distance between threads) and is 25 mm long. The two bolts are nearly identical, and easily confused, but they are not interchangeable.

In addition to the differences in diameter, thread pitch and length, metric and standard bolts can also be distinguished by examining the bolt heads. To begin with, the distance across the flats on a standard bolt head is measured in inches, while the same dimension on a metric bolt is sized in millimeters (the same is true for nuts). As a result, a standard wrench should not be used on a metric bolt and a metric wrench should not be used on a standard bolt. Also, most standard bolts have slashes radiating out from the center of the head to denote the grade or strength of the bolt, which is an indication of the amount of torque that can be applied to it. The greater the number of slashes, the greater the strength of the bolt. Grades 0 through 5 are commonly used on automobiles. Metric bolts have a property class (grade) number, rather than a slash, molded into their heads to indicate bolt strength. In this case, the higher the number, the stronger the bolt. Property class numbers 8.8, 9.8 and 10.9 are commonly used on automobiles.

Strength markings can also be used to distinguish standard hex nuts from metric hex nuts. Many standard nuts have dots stamped into one side, while metric nuts are marked with a number. The greater the number of dots, or the higher the number, the greater the strength of the nut.

Metric studs are also marked on their ends according to property class (grade). Larger studs are numbered (the same as metric bolts),

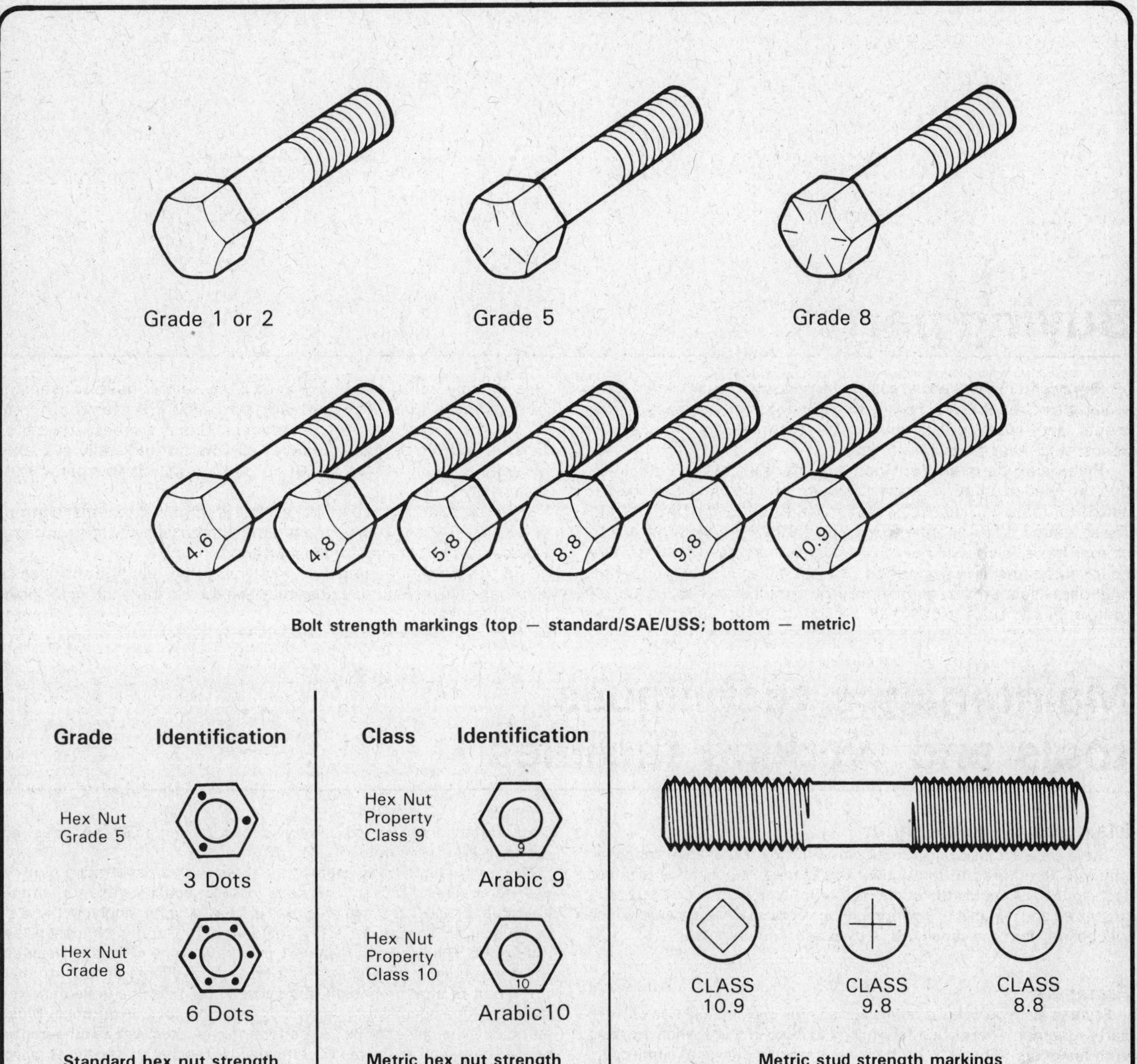

Bolt strength markings (top — standard/SAE/USS; bottom — metric)

Standard hex nut strength markings

Metric hex nut strength markings

Metric stud strength markings

while smaller studs carry a geometric code to denote grade.

It should be noted that many fasteners, especially Grades 0 through 2, have no distinguishing marks on them. When such is the case, the only way to determine whether it is standard or metric is to measure the thread pitch or compare it to a known fastener of the same size.

Standard fasteners are often referred to as SAE, as opposed to metric. However, it should be noted that SAE technically refers to a non-metric *fine thread* fastener only. Coarse thread non-metric fasteners are referred to as USS sizes.

Since fasteners of the same size (both standard and metric) may have different strength ratings, be sure to reinstall any bolts, studs or nuts removed from your vehicle in their original locations. Also, when replacing a fastener with a new one, make sure that the new one has a strength rating equal to or greater than the original.

Tightening sequences and procedures

Most threaded fasteners should be tightened to a specific torque value (torque is the twisting force applied to a threaded component such as a nut or bolt). Overtightening the fastener can weaken it and cause it to break, while undertightening can cause it to eventually come loose. Bolts, screws and studs, depending on the material they are made of and their thread diameters, have specific torque values, many of which are noted in the Specifications at the beginning of each Chapter. Be sure to follow the torque recommendations closely. For fasteners not assigned a specific torque, a general torque value chart is presented here as a guide. These torque values are for dry (unlubricated) fasteners threaded into steel or cast iron (not aluminum). As was previously mentioned, the size and grade of a fastener determine the amount of torque that can safely be applied to it. The figures listed here are approximate

Metric thread sizes	Ft-lb	Nm/m
M-6	6 to 9	9 to 12
M-8	14 to 21	19 to 28
M-10	28 to 40	38 to 54
M-12	50 to 71	68 to 96
M-14	80 to 140	109 to 154
Pipe thread sizes		
1/8	5 to 8	7 to 10
1/4	12 to 18	17 to 24
3/8	22 to 33	30 to 44
1/2	25 to 35	34 to 47
U.S. thread sizes		
1/4 – 20	6 to 9	9 to 12
5/16 – 18	12 to 18	17 to 24
5/16 – 24	14 to 20	19 to 27
3/8 – 16	22 to 32	30 to 43
3/8 – 24	27 to 38	37 to 51
7/16 – 14	40 to 55	55 to 74
7/16 – 20	40 to 60	55 to 81
1/2 – 13	55 to 80	75 to 108

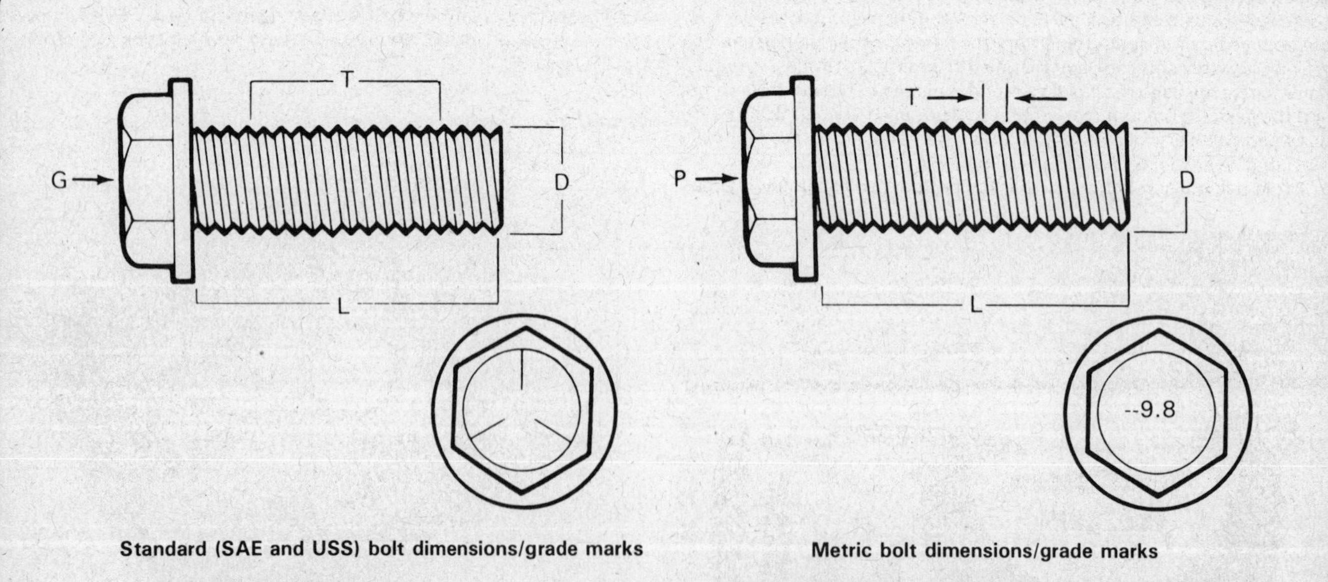

Standard (SAE and USS) bolt dimensions/grade marks

G Grade marks (bolt strength)
L Length (in inches)
T Thread pitch (number of threads per inch)
D Nominal diameter (in inches)

Metric bolt dimensions/grade marks

P Property class (bolt strength)
L Length (in millimeters)
T Thread pitch (distance between threads in millimeters)
D Diameter

for Grade 2 and Grade 3 fasteners. Higher grades can tolerate higher torque values.

Fasteners laid out in a pattern, such as cylinder head bolts, oil pan bolts, differential cover bolts, etc., must be loosened or tightened in sequence to avoid warping the component. This sequence will normally be shown in the appropriate Chapter. If a specific pattern is not given, the following procedures can be used to prevent warping.

Initially, the bolts or nuts should be assembled finger-tight only. Next, they should be tightened one full turn each, in a criss-cross or diagonal pattern. After each one has been tightened one full turn, return to the first one and tighten them all one-half turn, following the same pattern. Finally, tighten each of them one-quarter turn at a time until each fastener has been tightened to the proper torque. To loosen and remove the fasteners, the procedure would be reversed.

Component disassembly

Component disassembly should be done with care and purpose to help ensure that the parts go back together properly. Always keep track of the sequence in which parts are removed. Make note of special characteristics or marks on parts that can be installed more than one way, such as a grooved thrust washer on a shaft. It is a good idea to lay the disassembled parts out on a clean surface in the order that they were removed. It may also be helpful to make sketches or take instant photos of components before removal.

When removing fasteners from a component, keep track of their locations. Sometimes threading a bolt back in a part, or putting the washers and nut back on a stud, can prevent mix-ups later. If nuts and bolts cannot be returned to their original locations, they should be kept in a compartmented box or a series of small boxes. A cupcake or muffin tin is ideal for this purpose, since each cavity can hold the bolts and nuts from a particular area (i.e. oil pan bolts, valve cover bolts, engine mount bolts, etc.). A pan of this type is especially helpful when working on assemblies with very small parts, such as the carburetor, alternator, valve train or interior dash and trim pieces. The cavities can be marked with paint or tape to identify the contents.

Whenever wiring looms, harnesses or connectors are separated, it is a good idea to identify the two halves with numbered pieces of masking tape so they can be easily reconnected.

Gasket sealing surfaces

Throughout any vehicle, gaskets are used to seal the mating surfaces between two parts and keep lubricants, fluids, vacuum or pressure contained in an assembly.

Many times these gaskets are coated with a liquid or paste-type gasket sealing compound before assembly. Age, heat and pressure can sometimes cause the two parts to stick together so tightly that they are very difficult to separate. Often, the assembly can be loosened by striking it with a soft-face hammer near the mating surfaces. A regular hammer can be used if a block of wood is placed between the hammer and the part. Do not hammer on cast parts or parts that could be easily damaged. With any particularly stubborn part, always recheck to make sure that every fastener has been removed.

Avoid using a screwdriver or bar to pry apart an assembly, as they can easily mar the gasket sealing surfaces of the parts, which must remain smooth. If prying is absolutely necessary, use an old broom handle, but keep in mind that extra clean up will be necessary if the wood splinters.

After the parts are separated, the old gasket must be carefully scraped off and the gasket surfaces cleaned. Stubborn gasket material can be soaked with rust penetrant or treated with a special chemical to soften it so it can be easily scraped off. A scraper can be fashioned from a piece of copper tubing by flattening and sharpening one end. Copper is recommended because it is usually softer than the surfaces to be scraped, which reduces the chance of gouging the part. Some gaskets can be removed with a wire brush, but regardless of the method used, the mating surfaces must be left clean and smooth. If for some reason the gasket surface is gouged, then a gasket sealer thick enough to fill scratches will have to be used during reassembly of the components. For most applications, a non-drying (or semi-drying) gasket sealer should be used.

Hose removal tips

Warning: *If the vehicle is equipped with air conditioning, do not disconnect any of the A/C hoses without first having the system depressurized by a dealer service department or an air conditioning specialist.*

Hose removal precautions closely parallel gasket removal precautions. Avoid scratching or gouging the surface that the hose mates against or the connection may leak. This is especially true for radiator hoses. Because of various chemical reactions, the rubber in hoses can bond itself to the metal spigot that the hose fits over. To remove a hose, first loosen the hose clamps that secure it to the spigot. Then, with slip-joint pliers, grab the hose at the clamp and rotate it around the spigot. Work it back and forth until it is completely free, then pull it off. Silicone or other lubricants will ease removal if they can be applied between the hose and the outside of the spigot. Apply the same lubricant to the inside of the hose and the outside of the spigot to simplify installation.

As a last resort (and if the hose is to be replaced with a new one anyway), the rubber can be slit with a knife and the hose peeled from the spigot. If this must be done, be careful that the metal connection is not damaged.

If a hose clamp is broken or damaged, do not reuse it. Wire-type clamps usually weaken with age, so it is a good idea to replace them with screw-type clamps whenever a hose is removed.

Tools

A selection of good tools is a basic requirement for anyone who plans to maintain and repair his or her own vehicle. For the owner who has few tools, the initial investment might seem high, but when compared to the spiraling costs of professional auto maintenance and repair, it is a wise one.

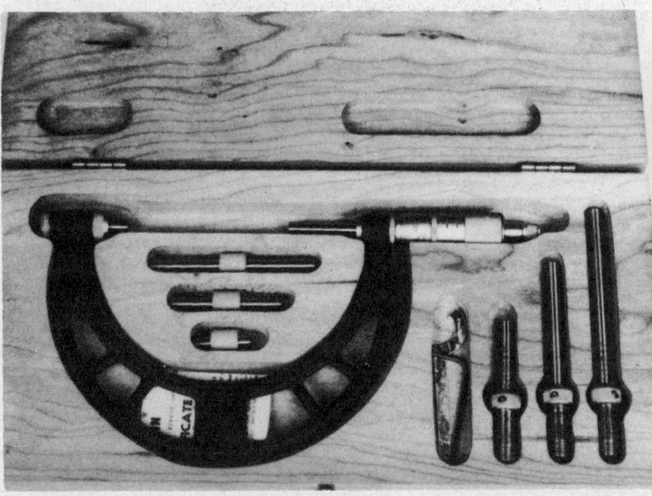

Micrometer set

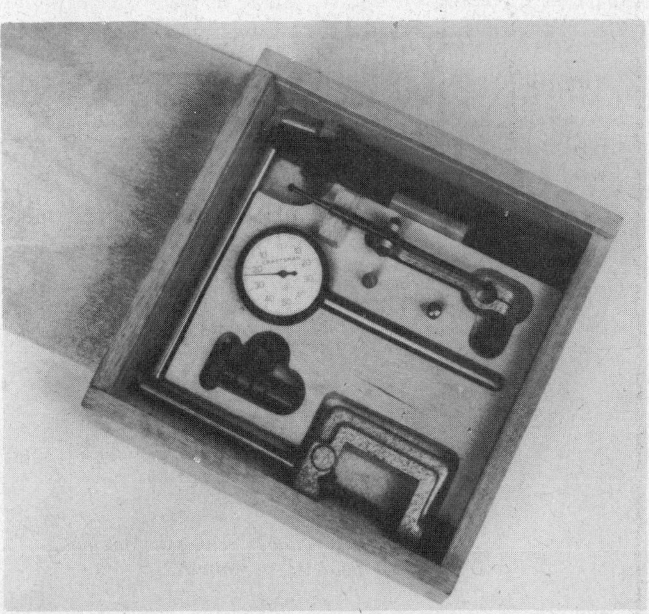

Dial indicator set

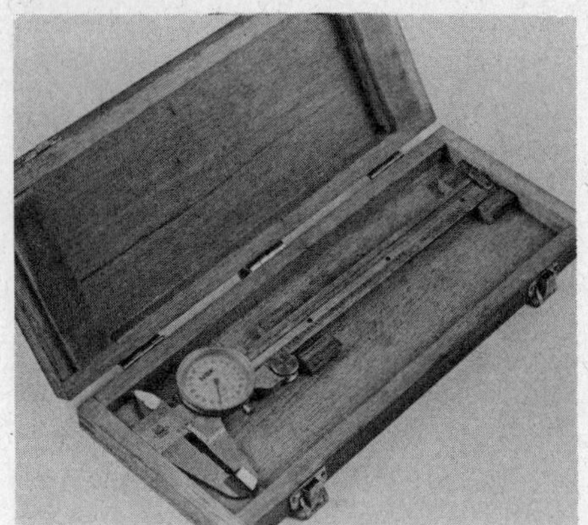

Dial caliper

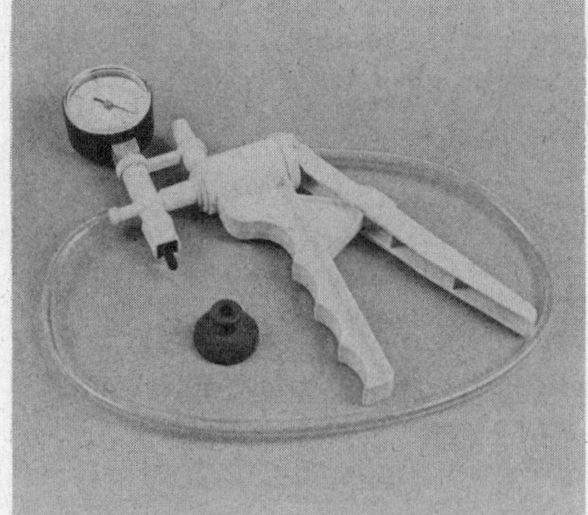

Hand-operated vacuum pump

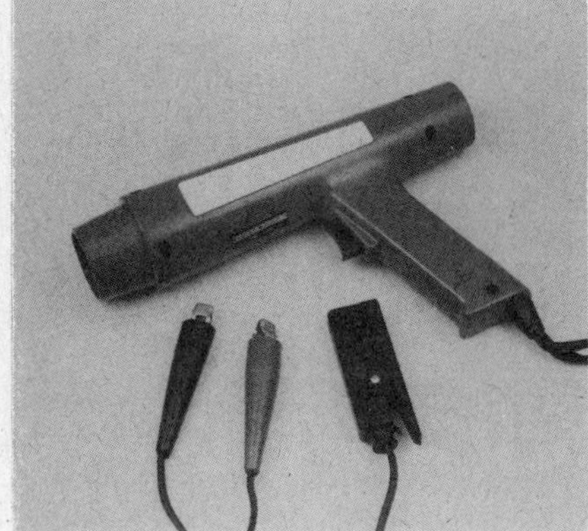

Timing light

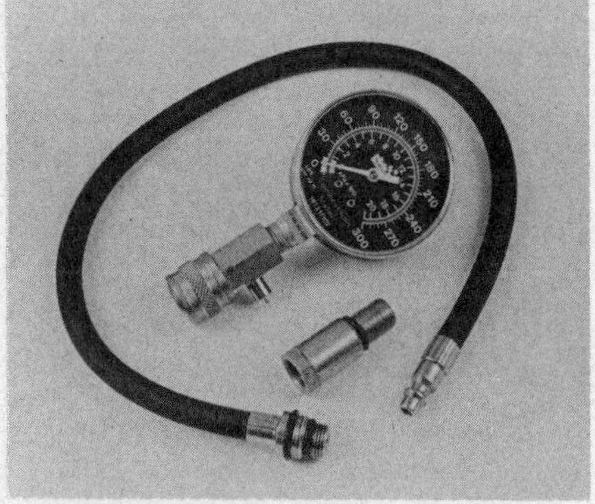

Compression gauge with spark plug hole adapter

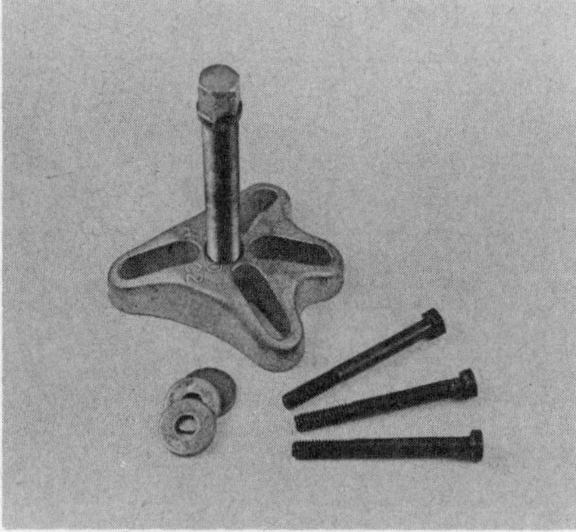

Damper/steering wheel puller

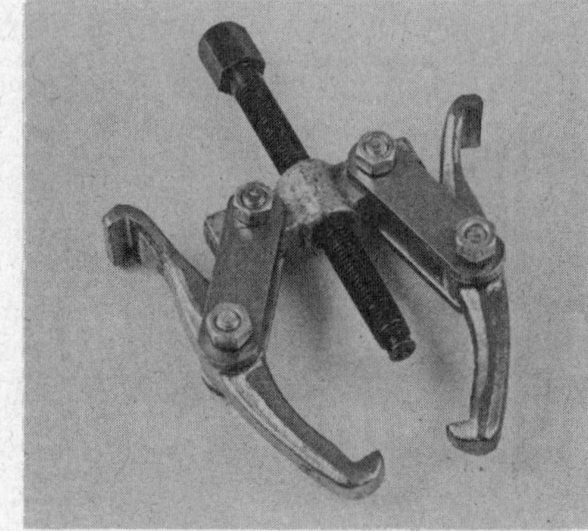

General purpose puller

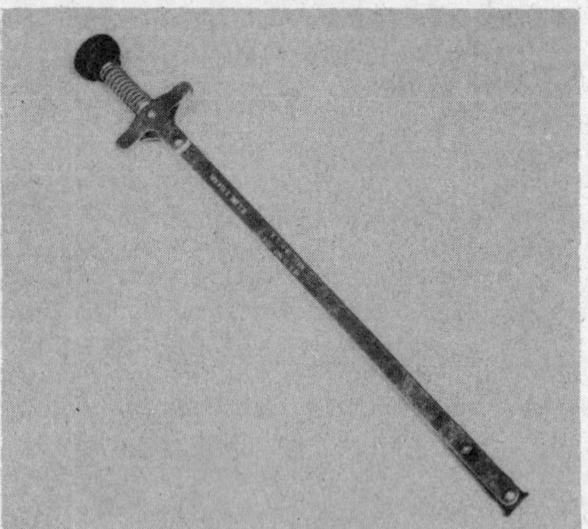

Hydraulic lifter removal tool

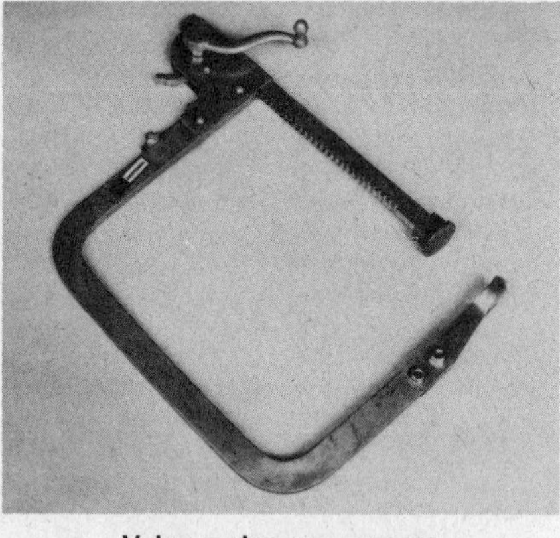

Valve spring compressor

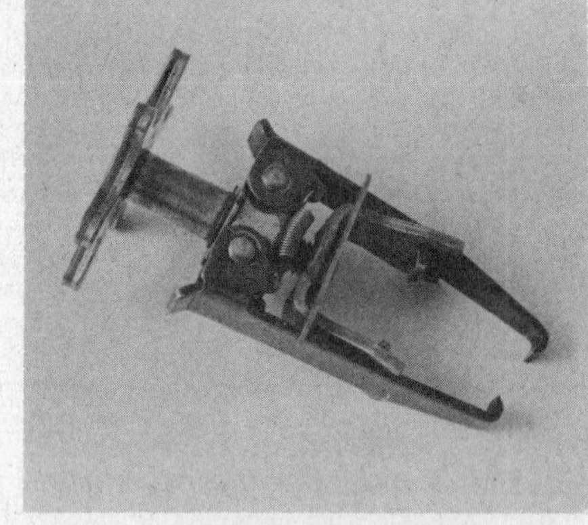

Valve spring compressor

Ridge reamer

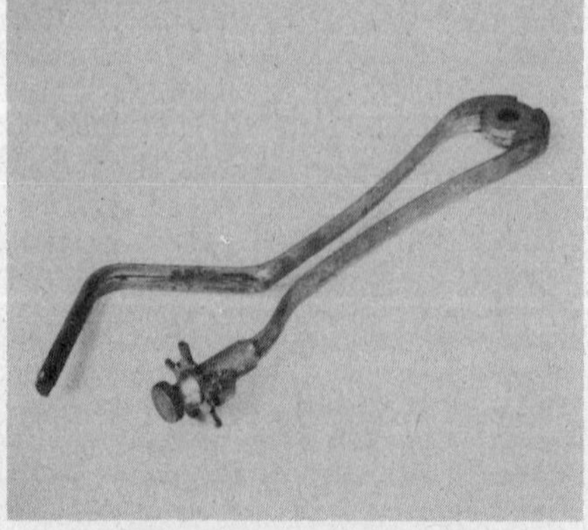

Piston ring groove cleaning tool

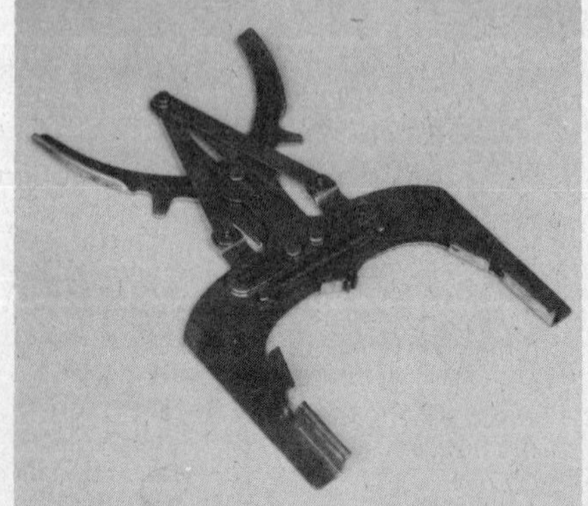

Ring removal/installation tool

Ring compressor

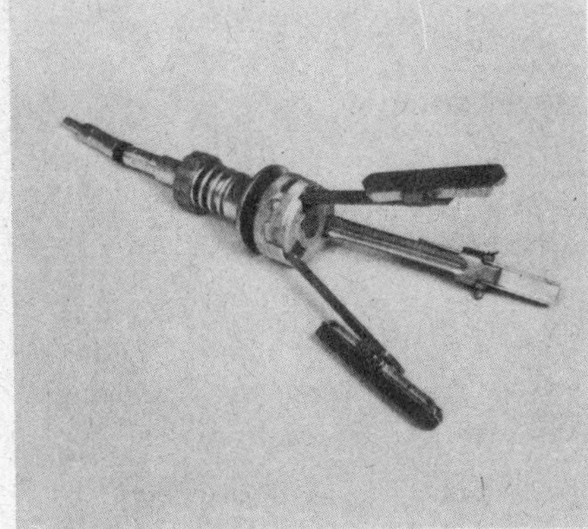
Cylinder hone

Brake hold-down spring tool

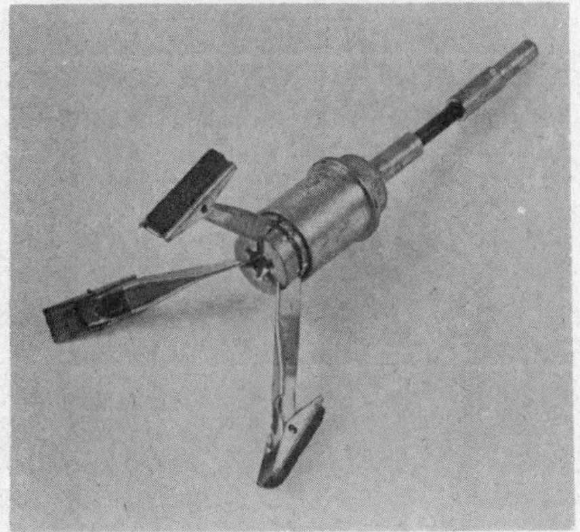
Brake cylinder hone

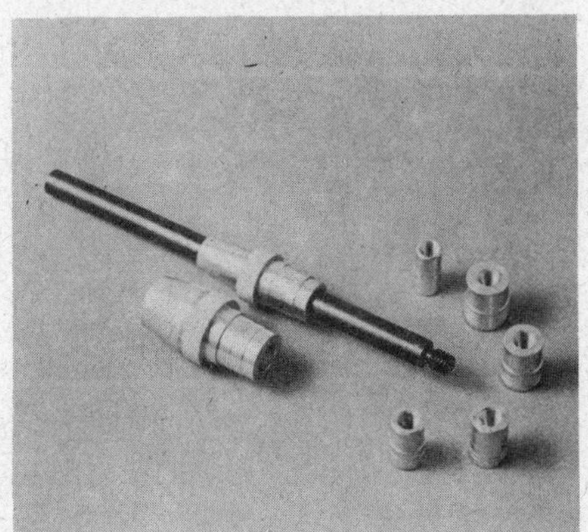
Clutch plate alignment tool

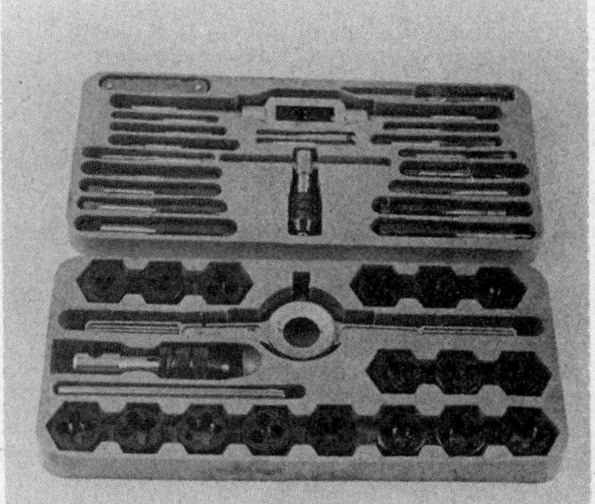
Tap and die set

To help the owner decide which tools are needed to perform the tasks detailed in this manual, the following tool lists are offered: *Maintenance and minor repair, Repair/overhaul* and *Special*.

The newcomer to practical mechanics should start off with the maintenance and minor repair tool kit, which is adequate for the simpler jobs performed on a vehicle. Then, as confidence and experience grow, the owner can tackle more difficult tasks, buying additional tools as they are needed. Eventually the basic kit will be expanded into the repair and overhaul tool set. Over a period of time, the experienced do-it-yourselfer will assemble a tool set complete enough for most repair and overhaul procedures and will add tools from the special category when it is felt that the expense is justified by the frequency of use.

Maintenance and minor repair tool kit

The tools in this list should be considered the minimum required for performance of routine maintenance, servicing and minor repair work. We recommend the purchase of combination wrenches (box-end and open-end combined in one wrench). While more expensive than open end wrenches, they offer the advantages of both types of wrench.

Combination wrench set (1/4-inch to 1 inch or 6 mm to 19 mm)
Adjustable wrench, 8 inch
Spark plug wrench with rubber insert
Spark plug gap adjusting tool
Feeler gauge set
Brake bleeder wrench
Standard screwdriver (5/16-inch x 6 inch)
Phillips screwdriver (No. 2 x 6 inch)
Combination pliers — 6 inch
Hacksaw and assortment of blades
Tire pressure gauge
Grease gun
Oil can
Fine emery cloth
Wire brush
Battery post and cable cleaning tool
Oil filter wrench
Funnel (medium size)
Safety goggles
Jackstands (2)
Drain pan

Note: *If basic tune-ups are going to be part of routine maintenance, it will be necessary to purchase a good quality stroboscopic timing light and combination tachometer/dwell meter. Although they are included in the list of special tools, it is mentioned here because they are absolutely necessary for tuning most vehicles properly.*

Repair and overhaul tool set

These tools are essential for anyone who plans to perform major repairs and are in addition to those in the maintenance and minor repair tool kit. Included is a comprehensive set of sockets which, though expensive, are invaluable because of their versatility, especially when various extensions and drives are available. We recommend the 1/2-inch drive over the 3/8-inch drive. Although the larger drive is bulky and more expensive, it has the capacity of accepting a very wide range of large sockets. Ideally, however, the mechanic should have a 3/8-inch drive set and a 1/2-inch drive set.

Socket set(s)
Reversible ratchet
Extension — 10 inch
Universal joint
Torque wrench (same size drive as sockets)
Ball peen hammer — 8 ounce
Soft-face hammer (plastic/rubber)
Standard screwdriver (1/4-inch x 6 inch)
Standard screwdriver (stubby — 5/16-inch)
Phillips screwdriver (No. 3 x 8 inch)
Phillips screwdriver (stubby — No. 2)

Pliers — vise grip
Pliers — lineman's
Pliers — needle nose
Pliers — snap-ring (internal and external)
Cold chisel — 1/2-inch
Scribe
Scraper (made from flattened copper tubing)
Centerpunch
Pin punches (1/16, 1/8, 3/16-inch)
Steel rule/straightedge — 12 inch
Allen wrench set (1/8 to 3/8-inch or 4 mm to 10 mm)
A selection of files
Wire brush (large)
Jackstands (second set)
Jack (scissor or hydraulic type)

Note: *Another tool which is often useful is an electric drill motor with a chuck capacity of 3/8-inch and a set of good quality drill bits.*

Special tools

The tools in this list include those which are not used regularly, are expensive to buy, or which need to be used in accordance with their manufacturer's instructions. Unless these tools will be used frequently, it is not very economical to purchase many of them. A consideration would be to split the cost and use between yourself and a friend or friends. In addition, most of these tools can be obtained from a tool rental shop on a temporary basis.

This list primarily contains only those tools and instruments widely available to the public, and not those special tools produced by the vehicle manufacturer for distribution to dealer service departments. Occasionally, references to the manufacturer's special tools are inluded in the text of this manual. Generally, an alternative method of doing the job without the special tool is offered. However, sometimes there is no alternative to their use. Where this is the case, and the tool cannot be purchased or borrowed, the work should be turned over to the dealer service department or an automotive repair shop.

Valve spring compressor
Piston ring groove cleaning tool
Piston ring compressor
Piston ring installation tool
Cylinder compression gauge
Cylinder ridge reamer
Cylinder surfacing hone
Cylinder bore gauge
Micrometers and/or dial calipers
Hydraulic lifter removal tool
Balljoint separator
Universal-type puller
Impact screwdriver
Dial indicator set
Stroboscopic timing light (inductive pick-up)
Hand operated vacuum/pressure pump
Tachometer/dwell meter
Universal electrical multimeter
Cable hoist
Brake spring removal and installation tools
Floor jack

Buying tools

For the do-it-yourselfer who is just starting to get involved in vehicle maintenance and repair, there are a number of options available when purchasing tools. If maintenance and minor repair is the extent of the work to be done, the purchase of individual tools is satisfactory. If, on the other hand, extensive work is planned, it would be a good idea to purchase a modest tool set from one of the large retail chain stores. A set can usually be bought at a substantial savings over the individual tool prices, and they often come with a tool box. As additional tools are needed, add-on sets, individual tools and a larger tool box can be purchased to expand the tool selection. Building a tool set gradually allows the cost of the tools to be spread over a longer period of time and gives the mechanic the freedom to choose only those tools that will actually be used.

Tool stores will often be the only source of some of the special tools that are needed, but regardless of where tools are bought, try to avoid cheap ones, especially when buying screwdrivers and sockets, because they won't last very long. The expense involved in replacing cheap tools will eventually be greater than the initial cost of quality tools.

Care and maintenance of tools

Good tools are expensive, so it makes sense to treat them with respect. Keep them clean and in usable condition and store them properly when not in use. Always wipe off any dirt, grease or metal chips before putting them away. Never leave tools lying around in the work area. Upon completion of a job, always check closely under the hood for tools that may have been left there so they won't get lost during a test drive.

Some tools, such as screwdrivers, pliers, wrenches and sockets, can be hung on a panel mounted on the garage or workshop wall, while others should be kept in a tool box or tray. Measuring instruments, gauges, meters, etc. must be carefully stored where they cannot be damaged by weather or impact from other tools.

When tools are used with care and stored properly, they will last a very long time. Even with the best of care, though, tools will wear out if used frequently. When a tool is damaged or worn out, replace it. Subsequent jobs will be safer and more enjoyable if you do.

Working facilities

Not to be overlooked when discussing tools is the workshop. If anything more than routine maintenance is to be carried out, some sort of suitable work area is essential.

It is understood, and appreciated, that many home mechanics do not have a good workshop or garage available, and end up removing an engine or doing major repairs outside. It is recommended, however, that the overhaul or repair be completed under the cover of a roof.

A clean, flat workbench or table of comfortable working height is an absolute necessity. The workbench should be equipped with a vise that has a jaw opening of at least four inches.

As mentioned previously, some clean, dry storage space is also required for tools, as well as the lubricants, fluids, cleaning solvents, etc. which will soon become necessary.

Sometimes waste oil and fluids, drained from the engine or cooling system during normal maintenance or repairs, present a disposal problem. To avoid pouring them on the ground or into a sewage system, pour the used fluids into large containers, seal them with caps and take them to an authorized disposal site or recycling center. Plastic jugs, such as old antifreeze containers, are ideal for this purpose.

Always keep a supply of old newspapers and clean rags available. Old towels are excellent for mopping up spills. Many mechanics use rolls of paper towels for most work because they are readily available and disposable. To help keep the area under the vehicle clean, a large cardboard box can be cut open and flattened to protect the garage or shop floor.

Whenever working over a painted surface, such as when leaning over a fender to service something under the hood, always cover it with an old blanket or bedspread to protect the finish. Vinyl covered pads, made especially for this purpose, are available at auto parts stores.

Booster battery (jump) starting

Certain precautions must be observed when using a booster battery to start a vehicle.

a) Before connecting the booster battery, make sure the ignition switch is in the Off position.
b) Turn off the lights, heater and other electrical loads.
c) Your eyes should be shielded. Safety goggles are a good idea.
d) Make sure the booster battery is the same voltage as the dead one in the vehicle.
e) The two vehicles MUST NOT TOUCH each other!
f) Make sure the transmission is in Neutral (manual) or Park (automatic).
g) If the booster battery is not a maintenance-free type, remove the vent caps and lay a cloth over the vent holes.

Connect the red jumper cable to the *positive* (+) terminals of each battery.

Connect one end of the black jumper cable to the *negative* (–) terminal of the booster battery. The other end of this cable should be connected to a good ground on the vehicle to be started, such as a bolt or bracket on the engine block **(see illustration)**. Use caution to ensure that the cable will not come into contact with the fan, drivebelts or other moving parts of the engine.

Start the engine using the booster battery, then, with the engine running at idle speed, disconnect the jumper cables in the reverse order of connection.

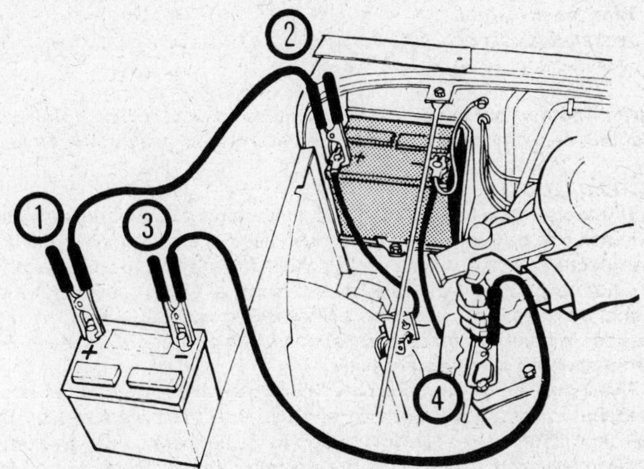

Make the booster battery cable connections in the numerical order shown (note that the negative cable of the booster battery is NOT attached to the negative terminal of the dead battery)

Jacking and towing

Jacking

The jack supplied with the vehicle should be used only for raising the vehicle when changing a tire or placing jackstands under the frame. **Warning:** *Never work under the vehicle or start the engine while the jack is being used as the only means of support.*

The vehicle should be on level ground with the wheels blocked and the transmission in Park (automatic) or Reverse (manual). On 4WD models, the transfer case must be in the 2H, 4H or 4L position (never in Neutral).

If a tire must be changed, remove the hub cap (if equipped), loosen the lug nuts one-half turn and leave them in place until the wheel is raised off the ground. Place the jack under the side of the vehicle in the indicated position **(see illustrations)**.

Operate the jack slowly and carefully until the wheel is raised off

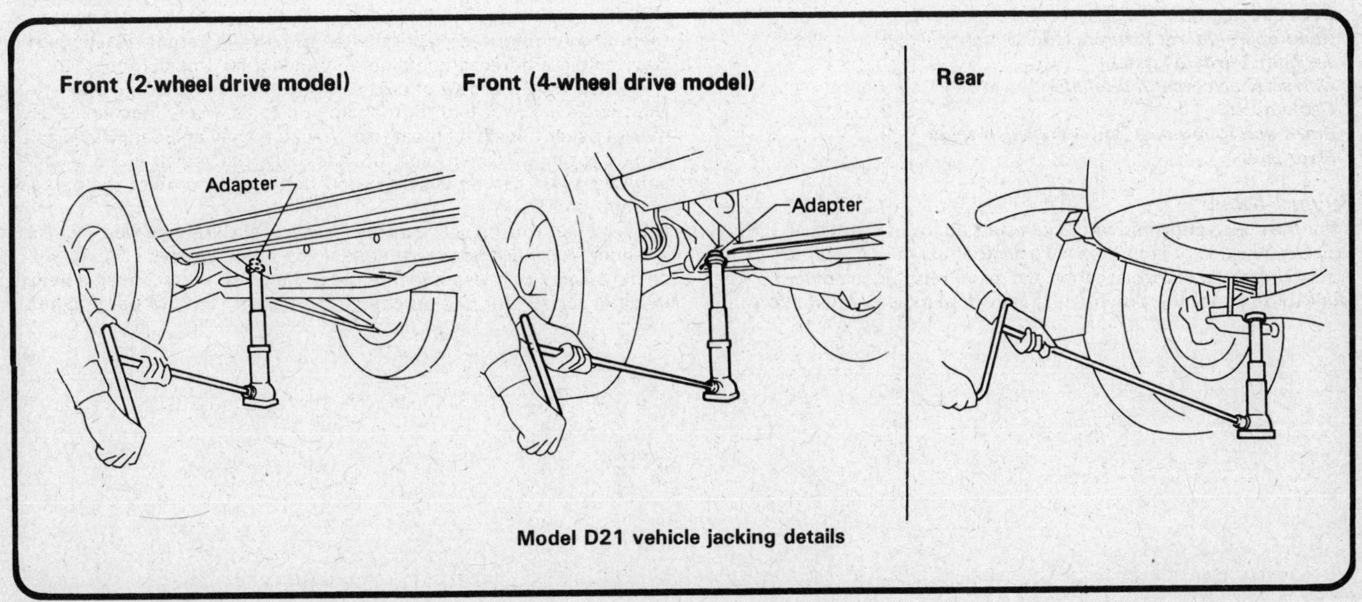

Model D21 vehicle jacking details

the ground. Finish removing the lug nuts, then remove the tire and install the spare. Install the lug nuts and tighten them until they're snug, but wait until the wheel is on the ground to tighten them with the wrench. Lower the vehicle, remove the jack and tighten the lug nuts in a criss-cross pattern. Turn the wrench clockwise.

Towing

These vehicles can be towed with all four wheels on the ground, as long as speeds don't exceed 30 mph and the distance is less than 40 miles, otherwise transmission damage can result. If it's necessary to tow the vehicle at higher speeds and/or for a greater distance, remove the driveshaft(s).

Towing equipment specifically designed for this purpose should be used and should be attached to the main structural members of the vehicle, not the bumper or brackets.

Safety is a major consideration when towing and all applicable state and local laws must be obeyed. A safety chain must be used when towing.

While towing, the parking brake should be released and the transmission must be in Neutral. On 4WD models, the control lever should be in Neutral and free running hubs should be in the Free position. The steering must be unlocked (ignition switch in the Off position). Remember that power steering and power brakes won't work with the engine off!

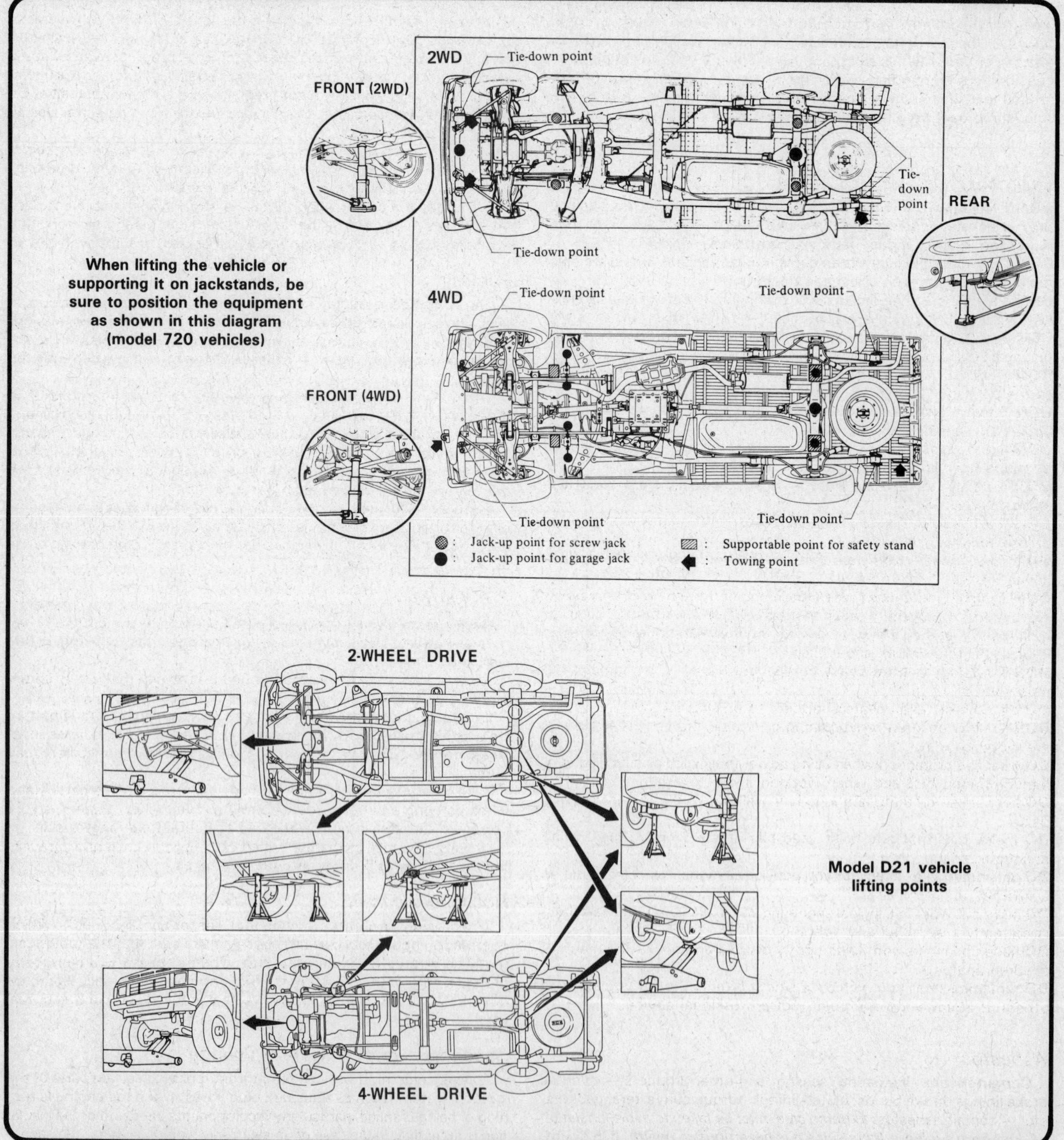

When lifting the vehicle or supporting it on jackstands, be sure to position the equipment as shown in this diagram (model 720 vehicles)

Model D21 vehicle lifting points

Safety first!

Regardless of how enthusiastic you may be about getting on with the job at hand, take the time to ensure that your safety is not jeopardized. A moment's lack of attention can result in an accident, as can failure to observe certain simple safety precautions. The possibility of an accident will always exist, and the following points should not be considered a comprehensive list of all dangers. Rather, they are intended to make you aware of the risks and to encourage a safety conscious approach to all work you carry out on your vehicle.

Essential DOs and DON'Ts

DON'T rely on a jack when working under the vehicle. Always use approved jackstands to support the weight of the vehicle and place them under the recommended lift or support points.
DON'T attempt to loosen extremely tight fasteners (i.e. wheel lug nuts) while the vehicle is on a jack — it may fall.
DON'T start the engine without first making sure that the transmission is in Neutral (or Park where applicable) and the parking brake is set.
DON'T remove the radiator cap from a hot cooling system — let it cool or cover it with a cloth and release the pressure gradually.
DON'T attempt to drain the engine oil until you are sure it has cooled to the point that it will not burn you.
DON'T touch any part of the engine or exhaust system until it has cooled sufficiently to avoid burns.
DON'T siphon toxic liquids such as gasoline, antifreeze and brake fluid by mouth, or allow them to remain on your skin.
DON'T inhale brake lining dust — it is potentially hazardous (see *Asbestos* below)
DON'T allow spilled oil or grease to remain on the floor — wipe it up before someone slips on it.
DON'T use loose fitting wrenches or other tools which may slip and cause injury.
DON'T push on wrenches when loosening or tightening nuts or bolts. Always try to pull the wrench toward you. If the situation calls for pushing the wrench away, push with an open hand to avoid scraped knuckles if the wrench should slip.
DON'T attempt to lift a heavy component alone — get someone to help you.
DON'T rush or take unsafe shortcuts to finish a job.
DON'T allow children or animals in or around the vehicle while you are working on it.
DO wear eye protection when using power tools such as a drill, sander, bench grinder, etc. and when working under a vehicle.
DO keep loose clothing and long hair well out of the way of moving parts.
DO make sure that any hoist used has a safe working load rating adequate for the job.
DO get someone to check on you periodically when working alone on a vehicle.
DO carry out work in a logical sequence and make sure that everything is correctly assembled and tightened.
DO keep chemicals and fluids tightly capped and out of the reach of children and pets.
DO remember that your vehicle's safety affects that of yourself and others. If in doubt on any point, get professional advice.

Asbestos

Certain friction, insulating, sealing, and other products — such as brake linings, brake bands, clutch linings, torque converters, gaskets, etc. — contain asbestos. *Extreme care must be taken to avoid inhalation of dust from such products since it is hazardous to health.* If in doubt, assume that they *do* contain asbestos.

Fire

Remember at all times that gasoline is highly flammable. Never smoke or have any kind of open flame around when working on a vehicle. But the risk does not end there. A spark caused by an electrical short circuit, by two metal surfaces contacting each other, or even by static electricity built up in your body under certain conditions, can ignite gasoline vapors, which in a confined space are highly explosive. Do not, under any circumstances, use gasoline for cleaning parts. Use an approved safety solvent.

Always disconnect the battery ground (–) cable *at the battery* before working on any part of the fuel system or electrical system. Never risk spilling fuel on a hot engine or exhaust component.

It is strongly recommended that a fire extinguisher suitable for use on fuel and electrical fires be kept handy in the garage or workshop at all times. Never try to extinguish a fuel or electrical fire with water.

Fumes

Certain fumes are highly toxic and can quickly cause unconsciousness and even death if inhaled to any extent. Gasoline vapor falls into this category, as do the vapors from some cleaning solvents. Any draining or pouring of such volatile fluids should be done in a well ventilated area.

When using cleaning fluids and solvents, read the instructions on the container carefully. Never use materials from unmarked containers.

Never run the engine in an enclosed space, such as a garage. Exhaust fumes contain carbon monoxide, which is extremely poisonous. If you need to run the engine, always do so in the open air, or at least have the rear of the vehicle outside the work area.

If you are fortunate enough to have the use of an inspection pit, never drain or pour gasoline and never run the engine while the vehicle is over the pit. The fumes, being heavier than air, will concentrate in the pit with possibly lethal results.

The battery

Never create a spark or allow a bare light bulb near a battery. They normally give off a certain amount of hydrogen gas, which is highly explosive.

Always disconnect the battery ground (–) cable *at the battery* before working on the fuel or electrical systems.

If possible, loosen the filler caps or cover when charging the battery from an external source (this does not apply to sealed or maintenance-free batteries). Do not charge at an excessive rate or the battery may burst.

Take care when adding water to a non maintenance-free battery and when carrying a battery. The electrolyte, even when diluted, is very corrosive and should not be allowed to contact clothing or skin.

Always wear eye protection when cleaning the battery to prevent the caustic deposits from entering your eyes.

Household current

When using an electric power tool, inspection light, etc., which operates on household current, always make sure that the tool is correctly connected to its plug and that, where necessary, it is properly grounded. Do not use such items in damp conditions and, again, do not create a spark or apply excessive heat in the vicinity of fuel or fuel vapor.

Secondary ignition system voltage

A severe electric shock can result from touching certain parts of the ignition system (such as the spark plug wires) when the engine is running or being cranked, particularly if components are damp or the insulation is defective. In the case of an electronic ignition system, the secondary system voltage is much higher and could prove fatal.

Conversion factors

Length (distance)					
Inches (in)	X 25.4	= Millimetres (mm)	X 0.0394	= Inches (in)
Feet (ft)	X 0.305	= Metres (m)	X 3.281	= Feet (ft)
Miles	X 1.609	= Kilometres (km)	X 0.621	= Miles
Volume (capacity)				
Cubic inches (cu in; in^3)	X 16.387	= Cubic centimetres (cc; cm^3)	X 0.061	= Cubic inches (cu in; in^3)
Imperial pints (Imp pt)	X 0.568	= Litres (l)	X 1.76	= Imperial pints (Imp pt)
Imperial quarts (Imp qt)	X 1.137	= Litres (l)	X 0.88	= Imperial quarts (Imp qt)
Imperial quarts (Imp qt)	X 1.201	= US quarts (US qt)	X 0.833	= Imperial quarts (Imp qt)
US quarts (US qt)	X 0.946	= Litres (l)	X 1.057	= US quarts (US qt)
Imperial gallons (Imp gal)	X 4.546	= Litres (l)	X 0.22	= Imperial gallons (Imp gal)
Imperial gallons (Imp gal)	X 1.201	= US gallons (US gal)	X 0.833	= Imperial gallons (Imp gal)
US gallons (US gal)	X 3.785	= Litres (l)	X 0.264	= US gallons (US gal)
Mass (weight)				
Ounces (oz)	X 28.35	= Grams (g)	X 0.035	= Ounces (oz)
Pounds (lb)	X 0.454	= Kilograms (kg)	X 2.205	= Pounds (lb)
Force				
Ounces-force (ozf; oz)	X 0.278	= Newtons (N)	X 3.6	= Ounces-force (ozf; oz)
Pounds-force (lbf; lb)	X 4.448	= Newtons (N)	X 0.225	= Pounds-force (lbf; lb)
Newtons (N)	X 0.1	= Kilograms-force (kgf; kg)	X 9.81	= Newtons (N)
Pressure				
Pounds-force per square inch (psi; lbf/in^2; lb/in^2)	X 0.070	= Kilograms-force per square centimetre (kgf/cm^2; kg/cm^2)	X 14.223	= Pounds-force per square inch (psi; lbf/in^2; lb/in^2)
Pounds-force per square inch (psi; lbf/in^2; lb/in^2)	X 0.068	= Atmospheres (atm)	X 14.696	= Pounds-force per square inch (psi; lbf/in^2; lb/in^2)
Pounds-force per square inch (psi; lbf/in^2; lb/in^2)	X 0.069	= Bars	X 14.5	= Pounds-force per square inch (psi; lbf/in^2; lb/in^2)
Pounds-force per square inch (psi; lbf/in^2; lb/in^2)	X 6.895	= Kilopascals (kPa)	X 0.145	= Pounds-force per square inch (psi; lbf/in^2; lb/in^2)
Kilopascals (kPa)	X 0.01	= Kilograms-force per square centimetre (kgf/cm^2; kg/cm^2)	X 98.1	= Kilopascals (kPa)
Torque (moment of force)				
Pounds-force inches (lbf in; lb in)	X 1.152	= Kilograms-force centimetre (kgf cm; kg cm)	X 0.868	= Pounds-force inches (lbf in; lb in)
Pounds-force inches (lbf in; lb in)	X 0.113	= Newton metres (Nm)	X 8.85	= Pounds-force inches (lbf in; lb in)
Pounds-force inches (lbf in; lb in)	X 0.083	= Pounds-force feet (lbf ft; lb ft)	X 12	= Pounds-force inches (lbf in; lb in)
Pounds-force feet (lbf ft; lb ft)	X 0.138	= Kilograms-force metres (kgf m; kg m)	X 7.233	= Pounds-force feet (lbf ft; lb ft)
Pounds-force feet (lbf ft; lb ft)	X 1.356	= Newton metres (Nm)	X 0.738	= Pounds-force feet (lbf ft; lb ft)
Newton metres (Nm)	X 0.102	= Kilograms-force metres (kgf m; kg m)	X 9.804	= Newton metres (Nm)
Power				
Horsepower (hp)	X 745.7	= Watts (W)	X 0.0013	= Horsepower (hp)
Velocity (speed)				
Miles per hour (miles/hr; mph)	X 1.609	= Kilometres per hour (km/hr; kph)	X 0.621	= Miles per hour (miles/hr; mph)
Fuel consumption*				
Miles per gallon, Imperial (mpg)	X 0.354	= Kilometres per litre (km/l)	X 2.825	= Miles per gallon, Imperial (mpg)
Miles per gallon, US (mpg)	X 0.425	= Kilometres per litre (km/l)	X 2.352	= Miles per gallon, US (mpg)

Temperature

Degrees Fahrenheit = (°C x 1.8) + 32

Degrees Celsius (Degrees Centigrade; °C) = (°F - 32) x 0.56

**It is common practice to convert from miles per gallon (mpg) to litres/100 kilometres (l/100km), where mpg (Imperial) x l/100 km = 282 and mpg (US) x l/100 km = 235*

Automotive chemicals and lubricants

A number of automotive chemicals and lubricants are available for use during vehicle maintenance and repair. They include a wide variety of products ranging from cleaning solvents and degreasers to lubricants and protective sprays for rubber, plastic and vinyl.

Cleaners

Carburetor cleaner and choke cleaner is a strong solvent for gum, varnish and carbon. Most carburetor cleaners leave a dry-type lubricant film which will not harden or gum up. Because of this film it is not recommended for use on electrical components.

Brake system cleaner is used to remove grease and brake fluid from the brake system where clean surfaces are absolutely necessary. It leaves no residue and often eliminates brake squeal caused by contaminants.

Electrical cleaner removes oxidation, corrosion and carbon deposits from electrical contacts, restoring full current flow. It can also be used to clean spark plugs, carburetor jets, voltage regulators and other parts where an oil-free surface is desired.

Demoisturants remove water and moisture from electrical components such as alternators, voltage regulators, electrical connectors and fuse blocks. It is non-conductive, non-corrosive and non-flammable.

Degreasers are heavy-duty solvents used to remove grease from the outside of the engine and from chassis components. They can be sprayed or brushed on, and, depending on the type, are rinsed off either with water or solvent.

Lubricants

Motor oil is the lubricant formulated for use in engines. It normally contains a wide variety of additives to prevent corrosion and reduce foaming and wear. Motor oil comes in various weights (viscosity ratings) from 5 to 80. The recommended weight of the oil depends on the season, temperature and the demands on the engine. Light oil is used in cold climates and under light load conditions. Heavy oil is used in hot climates and where high loads are encountered. Multi-viscosity oils are designed to have characteristics of both light and heavy oils and are available in a number of weights from 5W-20 to 20W-50.

Gear oil is designed to be used in differentials, manual transaxles and other areas where high-temperature lubrication is required.

Chassis and wheel bearing grease is a heavy grease used where increased loads and friction are encountered, such as for wheel bearings, balljoints, tie rod ends and universal joints.

High temperature wheel bearing grease is designed to withstand the extreme temperatures encountered by wheel bearings in disc brake equipped vehicles. It usually contains molybdenun disulfide (moly), which is a dry-type lubricant.

White grease is a heavy grease for metal to metal applications where water is a problem. White grease stays soft under both low and high temperatures (usually from −100°F to +190°F), and will not wash off or dilute in the presence of water.

Assembly lube is a special extreme pressure lubricant, usually containing moly, used to lubricate high-load parts such as main and rod bearings and cam lobes for initial start-up of a new engine. The assembly lube lubricates the parts without being squeezed out or washed away until the engine oiling system begins to function.

Silicone lubricants are used to protect rubber, plastic, vinyl and nylon parts.

Graphite lubricants are used where oils cannot be used due to contamination problems, such as in locks. The dry graphite will lubricate metal parts while remaining uncontaminated by dirt, water, oil or acids. It is electrically conductive and will not foul electrical contacts in locks such as the ignition switch.

Moly penetrants loosen and lubricate frozen, rusted and corroded fasteners and prevent future rusting or freezing.

Heat-sink grease is a special electrically non-conductive grease that is used for mounting HEI ignition modules where it is essential that heat be transferred away from the module.

Sealants

RTV sealant is one of the most widely used gasket compounds. Made from silicone, RTV is air curing, it seals, bonds, waterproofs, fills surface irregularities, remains flexible, doesn't shrink, is relatively easy to remove, and is used as a supplementary sealer with almost all low and medium temperature gaskets.

Anaerobic sealant is much like RTV in that it can be used either to seal gaskets or to form gaskets by itself. It remains flexible, is solvent resistant and fills surface imperfections. The difference between an anaerobic sealant and an RTV-type sealant is in the curing. RTV cures when exposed to air, while an anaerobic sealant cures only in the absence of air. This means that an anaerobic sealant cures only after the assembly of parts, sealing them together.

Thread and pipe sealant is used for sealing hydraulic and pneumatic fittings and vacuum lines. It is usually made from a teflon compound, and comes in a spray, a paint-on liquid and as a wrap-around tape.

Chemicals

Anti-seize compound prevents seizing, galling, cold welding, rust and corrosion in fasteners. High temperature anti-seize, usually made with copper and graphite lubricants, is used for exhaust system and manifold bolts.

Anaerobic locking compounds are used to keep fasteners from vibrating or working loose, and cure only after installation, in the absence of air. Medium strength locking compound is used for small nuts, bolts and screws that you expect to be removing later. High strength locking compound is for large nuts, bolts and studs which you don't intend to be removing on a regular basis.

Oil additives range from viscosity index improvers to chemical treatments that claim to reduce internal engine friction. It should be noted that most oil manufacturers caution against using additives with their oils.

Gas additives perform several functions, depending on their chemical makeup. They usually contain solvents that help dissolve gum and varnish that build up on carburetor and intake parts. They also serve to break down carbon deposits that form on the inside surfaces of the combustion chambers. Some additives contain upper cylinder lubricants for valves and piston rings, and others chemicals to remove condensation from the gas tank.

Miscellaneous

Brake fluid is specially formulated hydraulic fluid that can withstand the heat and pressure encountered in brake systems. Care must be taken that this fluid does not come in contact with painted surfaces or plastics. An opened container should always be resealed to prevent contamination by water or dirt.

Weatherstrip adhesive is used to bond weatherstripping around doors, windows and trunk lids. It is sometimes used to attach trim pieces.

Undercoating is a petroleum-based tar-like substance that is designed to protect metal surfaces on the underside of the vehicle from corrosion. It also acts as a sound-deadening agent by insulating the bottom of the vehicle.

Waxes and polishes are used to help protect painted and plated surfaces from the weather. Different types of paint may require the use of different types of wax and polish. Some polishes utilize a chemical or abrasive cleaner to help remove the top layer of oxidized (dull) paint on older vehicles. In recent years many non-wax polishes that contain a wide variety of chemicals such as polymers and silicones have been introduced. These non-wax polishes are usually easier to apply and last longer than conventional waxes and polishes.

Troubleshooting

Contents

This Section provides an easy reference guide to the more common problems that may occur during the operation of your vehicle. Various symptoms and their probable causes are grouped under headings denoting components or systems, such as Engine, Cooling system, etc. They also refer to the Chapter and/or Section that deals with the problem.

Remember that successful troubleshooting isn't a mysterious 'black art' practiced only by professional mechanics, it's simply the result of knowledge combined with an intelligent, systematic approach to a problem. Always use a process of elimination starting with the simplest solution and working through to the most complex — and never overlook the obvious. Anyone can run the gas tank dry or leave the lights on overnight, so don't assume that you're exempt from such oversights.

Finally, always establish a clear idea why a problem has occurred and take steps to ensure that it doesn't happen again. If the electrical system fails because of a poor connection, check all other connections in the system to make sure they don't fail as well. If a particular fuse continues to blow, find out why – don't just go on replacing fuses. Remember, failure of a small component can often be indicative of potential failure or incorrect functioning of a more important component or system.

Engine and performance

1 Engine will not rotate when attempting to start

1 Battery terminal connections loose or corroded. Check the cable terminals at the battery; tighten cable clamp and/or clean off corrosion as necessary (see Chapter 1).
2 Battery discharged or faulty. If the cable ends are clean and tight on the battery posts, turn the key to the On position and switch on the headlights or windshield wipers. If they won't run, the battery is discharged.
3 Automatic transmission not engaged in park (P) or Neutral (N).
4 Broken, loose or disconnected wires in the starting circuit. Inspect all wires and connectors at the battery, starter solenoid and ignition switch (on steering column).
5 Starter motor pinion jammed in flywheel ring gear. If manual transmission, place transmission in gear and rock the vehicle to manually turn the engine. Remove starter (Chapter 5) and inspect pinion and flywheel (Chapter 2) at earliest convenience.
6 Starter solenoid faulty (Chapter 5).
7 Starter motor faulty (Chapter 5).
8 Ignition switch faulty (Chapter 13).
9 Engine seized. Try to turn the crankshaft with a large socket and breaker bar on the pulley bolt.

2 Engine rotates but will not start

1 Fuel tank empty.
2 Battery discharged (engine rotates slowly). Check the operation of electrical components as described in previous Section.
3 Battery terminal connections loose or corroded. See previous Section.
4 Fuel not reaching carburetor or fuel injector. Check for clogged fuel filter or lines and defective fuel pump. Also make sure the tank vent lines aren't clogged (Chapter 4).
5 Choke not operating properly (Chapter 1).
6 Faulty distributor components. Check the cap and rotor (Chapter 1).
7 Low cylinder compression. Check as described in Chapter 2.
8 Valve clearances not properly adjusted (Chapter 1).
9 Water in fuel. Drain tank and fill with new fuel.
10 Defective IC ignition unit (Chapter 5).
11 Dirty or clogged carburetor jets or fuel injector. Carburetor out of adjustment. Check the float level (Chapter 4).
12 Wet or damaged ignition components (Chapters 1 and 5).
13 Worn, faulty or incorrectly gapped spark plugs (Chapter 1).
14 Broken, loose or disconnected wires in the starting circuit (see previous Section).
15 Loose distributor (changing ignition timing). Turn the distributor body as necessary to start the engine, then adjust the ignition timing as soon as possible (Chapter 1).
16 Broken, loose or disconnected wires at the ignition coil or faulty coil (Chapter 5).
17 Timing belt or chain failure or wear affecting valve timing (Chapter 2).

3 Starter motor operates without turning engine

1 Starter pinion sticking. Remove the starter (Chapter 5) and inspect.
2 Starter pinion or flywheel/driveplate teeth worn or broken. Remove the inspection cover on the left side of the engine and inspect.

4 Engine hard to start when cold

1 Battery discharged or low. Check as described in Chapter 1.
2 Fuel not reaching the carburetor or fuel injectors. Check the fuel filter, lines and fuel pump (Chapters 1 and 4).
3 Choke inoperative (Chapters 1 and 4).
4 Defective spark plugs (Chapter 1).

5 Engine hard to start when hot

1 Air filter dirty (Chapter 1).
2 Fuel not reaching carburetor or fuel injectors (see Section 4). Check for a vapor lock situation, brought about by clogged fuel tank vent lines.
3 Bad engine ground connection.
4 Choke sticking (Chapter 1).
5 Defective pick-up coil in distributor (Chapter 5).
6 Float level too high (Chapter 4).

6 Starter motor noisy or engages roughly

1 Pinion or flywheel/driveplate teeth worn or broken. Remove the inspection cover on the left side of the engine and inspect.
2 Starter motor mounting bolts loose or missing.

7 Engine starts but stops immediately

1 Loose or damaged wire harness connections at distributor, coil or alternator.
2 Intake manifold vacuum leaks. Make sure all mounting bolts/nuts are tight and all vacuum hoses connected to the manifold are attached properly and in good condition.
3 Insufficient fuel flow (see Chapter 4 for the fuel pump testing procedure).

8 Engine 'lopes' while idling or idles erratically

1 Vacuum leaks. Check mounting bolts at the intake manifold for tightness. Make sure that all vacuum hoses are connected and in good condition. Use a stethescope or a length of fuel hose held against your ear to listen for vacuum leaks while the engine is running. A hissing sound will be heard. A soapy water solution will also detect leaks. Check the intake manifold gasket surfaces.
2 Leaking EGR valve or plugged PCV valve (see Chapters 1 and 6).
3 Air filter clogged (Chapter 1).
4 Fuel pump not delivering sufficient fuel (Chapter 4).
5 Leaking head gasket. Perform a cylinder compression check (Chapter 2).
6 Timing chain or belt worn or (Chapter 2).
7 Camshaft lobes worn (Chapter 2).
8 Valve clearance out of adjustment (Chapter 1). Valves burned or otherwise leaking (Chapter 2).
9 Ignition timing out of adjustment (Chapter 1).
10 Ignition system not operating properly (Chapters 1 and 5).
11 Thermostatic air cleaner not operating properly (Chapter 1).
12 Choke not operating properly (Chapters 1 and 4).
13 Dirty or clogged injectors. Carburetor dirty, clogged or out of adjustment. Check the float level (Chapter 4).
14 Idle compensator not operating properly (Chapter 4).
15 Idle speed out of adjustment (Chapter 1).

9 Engine misses at idle speed

1 Spark plugs faulty or not gapped properly (Chapter 1).
2 Faulty spark plug wires (Chapter 1).
3 Wet or damaged distributor components (Chapter 1).
4 Short circuits in ignition, coil or spark plug wires.

5 Sticking or faulty emissions systems (see Chapter 6).
6 Clogged fuel filter and/or foreign matter in fuel. Remove the fuel filter (Chapter 1) and inspect.
7 Vacuum leaks at intake manifold or hose connections. Check as described in Section 8.
8 Incorrect idle speed (Chapter 1) or idle mixture (Chapter 4).
9 Incorrect ignition timing (Chapter 1).
10 Low or uneven cylinder compression. Check as described in Chapter 2.
11 Choke not operating properly (Chapter 1).
12 Clogged or dirty fuel injectors (Chapter 4).

10 Excessively high idle speed

1 Sticking throttle linkage (Chapter 4).
2 Choke opened excessively at idle (Chapter 4).
3 Idle speed incorrectly adjusted (Chapter 1).
4 Defective BCDD or FICD system (Chapter 6).
5 Valve clearances incorrectly adjusted (Chapter 1).
6 Dash pot out of adjustment (Chapter 4).

11 Battery will not hold a charge

1 Alternator drivebelt defective or not adjusted properly (Chapter 1).
2 Battery cables loose or corroded (Chapter 1).
3 Alternator not charging properly (Chapter 5).
4 Loose, broken or faulty wires in the charging circuit (Chapter 5).
5 Short circuit causing a continuous drain on the battery (Chapter 13).
6 Battery defective internally.
7 Faulty regulator (Chapter 5).

12 Alternator light stays on

1 Fault in alternator or charging circuit (Chapter 5).
2 Alternator drivebelt defective or not properly adjusted (Chapter 1).

13 Alternator light fails to come on when key is turned on

1 Faulty bulb (Chapter 13).
2 Defective alternator (Chapter 5).
3 Fault in the printed circuit, dash wiring or bulb holder (Chapter 13).

14 Engine misses throughout driving speed range

1 Fuel filter clogged and/or impurities in the fuel system. Check fuel filter (Chapter 1) or clean system (Chapter 4).
2 Faulty or incorrectly gapped spark plugs (Chapter 1).
3 Incorrect ignition timing (Chapter 1).
4 Cracked distributor cap, disconnected distributor wires or damaged distributor components (Chapter 1).
5 Defective spark plug wires (Chapter 1).
6 Emissions system components faulty (Chapter 6).
7 Low or uneven cylinder compression pressures. Check as described in Chapter 2.
8 Weak or faulty ignition coil (Chapter 5).
9 Weak or faulty ignition system (Chapter 5).
10 Vacuum leaks at intake manifold or vacuum hoses (see Section 8).
11 Dirty or clogged carburetor or fuel injector (Chapter 4).
12 Leaky EGR valve (Chapter 6).
13 Carburetor out of adjustment (Chapter 4).
14 Idle compensator not operating properly (Chapter 4).
15 Idle speed out of adjustment (Chapter 1).

15 Hesitation or stumble during acceleration

1 Ignition timing incorrect (Chapter 1).
2 Ignition system not operating properly (Chapter 5).
3 Dirty or clogged carburetor or fuel injector (Chapter 4).
4 Low fuel pressure. Check for proper operation of the fuel pump and for restrictions in the fuel filter and lines (Chapter 4).
5 Carburetor out of adjustment (Chapter 4).

16 Engine stalls

1 Idle speed incorrect (Chapter 1).
2 Fuel filter clogged and/or water and impurities in the fuel system (Chapter 1).
3 Choke not operating properly (Chapter 1).
4 Damaged or wet distributor cap and wires.
5 Emissions system components faulty (Chapter 6).
6 Faulty or incorrectly gapped spark plugs (Chapter 1). Also check the spark plug wires (Chapter 1).
7 Vacuum leak at the carburetor, intake manifold or vacuum hoses. Check as described in Section 8.
8 Valve clearances incorrect (Chapter 1).

17 Engine lacks power

1 Incorrect ignition timing (Chapter 1).
2 Excessive play in distributor shaft. At the same time check for faulty distributor cap, wires, etc. (Chapter 1).
3 Faulty or incorrectly gapped spark plugs (Chapter 1).
4 Air filter dirty (Chapter 1).
5 Spark timing control system not operating properly (Chapter 6).
6 Faulty ignition coil (Chapter 5).
7 Brakes binding (Chapters 1 and 10).
8 Automatic transmission fluid level incorrect, causing slippage (Chapter 1).
9 Clutch slipping (Chapter 8).
10 Fuel filter clogged and/or impurities in the fuel system (Chapters 1 and 4).
11 EGR system not functioning properly (Chapter 6).
12 Use of sub-standard fuel. Fill tank with proper octane fuel.
13 Low or uneven cylinder compression pressures. Check as described in Chapter 2.
14 Air leak at carburetor or intake manifold (check as described in Section 8).
15 Dirty or clogged carburetor jets or malfunctioning choke (Chapters 1 and 4).

18 Engine backfires

1 EGR system not functioning properly (Chapter 6).
2 Ignition timing incorrect (Chapter 1).
3 Thermostatic air cleaner system not operating properly (Chapter 6).
4 Anti-backfire valve not operating properly (Chapter 4).
5 Vacuum leak (refer to Section 8).
6 Valve clearances incorrect (Chapter 1).
7 Damaged valve springs or sticking valves (Chapter 2).
8 Intake air leak (see Section 8).
9 Carburetor float level out of adjustment (Chapter 4).
10 BCDD or FICD system not operating properly (Chapter 6).

19 Engine surges while holding accelerator steady

1 Intake air leak (see Section 8).
2 Fuel pump not working properly (Chapter 4).
3 Fault in secondary ignition system, no spark to exhaust side plugs.

20 Pinging or knocking engine sounds when engine is under load

1 Incorrect grade of fuel. Fill tank with fuel of the proper octane rating.
2 Ignition timing incorrect (Chapter 1).

3 Carbon build-up in combustion chambers. Remove cylinder head(s) and clean combustion chambers (Chapter 2).
4 Incorrect spark plugs (Chapter 1).

21 Engine diesels (continues to run) after being turned off

1 Idle speed too high (Chapter 1).
2 Ignition timing incorrect (Chapter 1).
3 Incorrect spark plug heat range (Chapter 1).
4 Intake air leak (see Section 8).
5 Carbon build-up in combustion chambers. Remove the cylinder head(s) and clean the combustion chambers (Chapter 2).
6 Valves sticking (Chapter 2).
7 BCDD or FICD system not operating properly (Chapter 6).
8 Valve clearance incorrect (Chapter 1).
9 EGR system not operating properly (Chapter 6).
10 Fuel shut-off system not operating properly (Chapter 6).
11 Check for causes of overheating (Section 27).

22 Low oil pressure

1 Improper grade of oil.
2 Oil pump regulator valve not operating properly (Chapter 2).
3 Oil pump worn or damaged (Chapter 2).
4 Engine overheating (refer to Section 27).
5 Clogged oil filter (Chapter 1).
6 Clogged oil strainer (Chapter 2).
7 Oil pressure gauge not working properly (Chapter 2).

23 Excessive oil consumption

1 Loose oil drain plug.
2 Loose bolts or damaged oil pan gasket (Chapter 2).
3 Loose bolts or damaged front cover gasket (Chapter 2).
4 Front or rear crankshaft oil seal leaking (Chapter 2).
5 Loose bolts or damaged rocker arm cover gasket (Chapter 2).
6 Loose oil filter (Chapter 1).
7 Loose or damaged oil pressure switch (Chapter 2).
8 Pistons and cylinders excessively worn (Chapter 2).
9 Piston rings not installed correctly on pistons (Chapter 2).
10 Worn or damaged piston rings (Chapter 2).
11 Intake and/or exhaust valve oil seals worn or damaged (Chapter 2).
12 Worn valve stems.
13 Worn or damaged valves/guides (Chapter 2).

24 Excessive fuel consumption

1 Dirty or clogged air filter element (Chapter 1).
2 Incorrect ignition timing (Chapter 1).
3 Incorrect idle speed (Chapter 1).
4 Low tire pressure or incorrect tire size (Chapter 11).
5 Fuel leakage. Check all connections, lines and components in the fuel system (Chapter 4).
6 Choke not operating properly (Chapter 1).
7 Dirty or clogged carburetor jets or fuel injectors (Chapter 4).

25 Fuel odor

1 Fuel leakage. Check all connections, lines and components in the fuel system (Chapter 4).
2 Fuel tank overfilled. Fill only to automatic shut-off.
3 Charcoal canister filter in Evaporative Emissions Control system clogged (Chapter 1).
4 Vapor leaks from Evaporative Emissions Control system lines (Chapter 6).

26 Miscellaneous engine noises

1 A strong dull noise that becomes more rapid as the engine accelerates indicates worn or damaged crankshaft bearings or an unevenly worn crankshaft. To pinpoint the trouble spot, remove the spark plug wire from one plug at a time and crank the engine over. If the noise stops, the cylinder with the removed plug wire indicates the problem area. Replace the bearing and/or service or replace the crankshaft (Chapter 2).
2 A similar (yet slightly higher pitched) noise to the crankshaft knocking described in the previous paragraph, that becomes more rapid as the engine accelerates, indicates worn or damaged connecting rod bearings (Chapter 2). The procedure for locating the problem cylinder is the same as described in Paragraph 1.
3 An overlapping metallic noise that increases in intensity as the engine speed increases, yet diminishes as the engine warms up indicates abnormal piston and cylinder wear (Chapter 2).To locate the problem cylinder, use the procedure described in Paragraph 1.
4 A rapid clicking noise that becomes faster as the engine accelerates indicates a worn piston pin or piston pin hole. This sound will happen each time the piston hits the highest and lowest points in the stroke (Chapter 2). The procedure for locating the problem piston is described in Paragraph 1.
5 A metallic clicking noise coming from the water pump indicates worn or damaged water pump bearings or pump. Replace the water pump with a new one (Chapter 3).
6 A rapid tapping sound or clicking sound that becomes faster as the engine speed increases indicates "valve tapping" or improperly adjusted valve clearances. This can be identified by holding one end of a section of hose to your ear and placing the other end at different spots along the rocker arm cover. The point where the sound is loudest indicates the problem valve. Adjust the valve clearance (Chapter 1).
7 A steady metallic rattling or rapping sound coming from the area of the timing chain cover indicates a worn, damaged or out-of-adjustment timing chain. Service or replace the chain and related components (Chapter 2).

Cooling system

27 Overheating

1 Insufficient coolant in system (Chapter 1).
2 Drivebelt defective or not adjusted properly (Chapter 1).
3 Radiator core blocked or radiator grille dirty and restricted (Chapter 3).
4 Thermostat faulty (Chapter 3).
5 Fan not functioning properly (Chapter 3).
6 Radiator cap not maintaining proper pressure. Have cap pressure tested by gas station or repair shop.
7 Ignition timing incorrect (Chapter 1).
8 Defective water pump (Chapter 3).
9 Improper grade of engine oil.
10 Inaccurate temperature gauge (Chapter 13).

28 Overcooling

1 Thermostat faulty (Chapter 3).
2 Inaccurate temperature gauge (Chapter 13).

29 External coolant leakage

1 Deteriorated or damaged hoses. Loose clamps at hose connections (Chapter 1).
2 Water pump seals defective. If this is the case, water will drip from the weep hole in the water pump body (Chapter 3).
3 Leakage from radiator core or header tank. This will require the radiator to be professionally repaired (see Chapter 3 for removal procedures).
4 Engine drain plugs or water jacket freeze plugs leaking (see Chapters 1 and 2).

5 Leak from coolant temperature switch (Chapter 3).
6 Leak from damaged gaskets or small cracks (Chapter 2).
7 Damaged head gasket. This can be verifed by checking the condition of the engine oil as noted in Section 30.

30 Internal coolant leakage

Note: *Internal coolant leaks can usually be detected by examining the oil. Check the dipstick and inside the rocker arm cover for water deposits and an oil consistency like that of a milkshake.*

1 Leaking cylinder head gasket. Have the system pressure tested or remove the cylinder head (Chapter 2) and inspect.
2 Cracked cylinder bore or cylinder head. Dismantle engine and inspect (Chapter 2).
3 Loose cylinder head bolts (tighten as described in Chapter 2).
4 Timing cover broken or cracked.
5 Intake manifold gasket leaking (V6).

31 Abnormal coolant loss

1 Overfilling system (Chapter 1).
2 Coolant boiling away due to overheating (see causes in Section 27).
3 Internal or external leakage (see Sections 29 and 30).
4 Faulty radiator cap. Have the cap pressure tested.
5 Cooling system being pressurized by engine compression. This could be due to a cracked head or block or leaking head gasket(s).

32 Poor coolant circulation

1 Inoperative water pump. A quick test is to pinch the top radiator hose closed with your hand while the engine is idling, then release it. You should feel a surge of coolant if the pump is working properly (Chapter 3).
2 Restriction in cooling system. Drain, flush and refill the system (Chapter 1). If necessary, remove the radiator (Chapter 3) and have it reverse flushed or professionally cleaned.
3 Loose water pump drivebelt (Chapter 1).
4 Thermostat sticking (Chapter 3).
5 Insufficient coolant (Chapter 1).

33 Corrosion

1 Excessive impurities in the water. Soft, clean water is recommended. Distilled or rainwater is satisfactory.
2 Insuffiecient antifreeze solution (refer to Chapter 1 for the proper ratio of water to antifreeze).
3 Infrequent flushing and draining of system. Regular flushing of the cooling system should be carried out at the specified intervals as described in (Chapter 1).

Clutch

Note: *All clutch related service information is located in Chapter 8, unless otherwise noted.*

34 Fails to release (pedal pressed to the floor – shift lever does not move freely in and out of Reverse)

1 Clutch contaminated with oil. Remove clutch plate and inspect.
2 Clutch plate warped, distorted or otherwise damaged.
3 Diaphragm spring fatigued. Remove clutch cover/pressure plate assembly and inspect.
4 Leakage of fluid from clutch hydraulic system. Inspect master cylinder, operating cylinder and connecting lines.
5 Air in clutch hydraulic system. Bleed the system.
6 Insufficient pedal stroke. Check and adjust as necessary.
7 Piston seal in operating cylinder deformed or damaged.
8 Lack of grease on pilot bushing.

35 Clutch slips (engine speed increases with no increase in vehicle speed)

1 Worn or oil soaked clutch plate.
2 Clutch plate not broken in. It may take 30 or 40 normal starts for a new clutch to seat.
3 Diaphragm spring weak or damaged. Remove clutch cover/pressure plate assembly and inspect.
4 Flywheel warped (Chapter 2).
5 Debris in master cylinder preventing the piston from returning to its normal position.
6 Clutch hydraulic line damaged.

36 Grabbing (chattering) as clutch is engaged

1 Oil on clutch plate. Remove and inspect. Repair any leaks.
2 Worn or loose engine or transmission mounts. They may move slightly when clutch is released. Inspect mounts and bolts.
3 Worn splines on transmission input shaft. Remove clutch components and inspect.
4 Warped pressure plate or flywheel. Remove clutch components and inspect.
5 Diaphragm spring fatigued. Remove clutch cover/pressure plate assembly and inspect.
6 Clutch linings hardened or warped.
7 Clutch lining rivets loose.

37 Squeal or rumble with clutch engagad (pedal released)

1 Improper pedal adjustment. Adjust pedal free play.
2 Release bearing binding on transmission shaft. Remove clutch components and check bearing. Remove any burrs or nicks, clean and relubricate before reinstallation.
3 Pilot bushing worn or damaged.
4 Clutch rivets loose.
5 Clutch plate cracked.
6 Fatigued clutch plate torsion springs. Replace clutch plate.

38 Squeal or rumble with clutch disengaged (pedal depressed)

1 Worn or damaged release bearing.
2 Worn or broken pressure plate diaphragm fingers.

39 Clutch pedal stays on floor when disengaged

1 Binding linkage or release bearing. Inspect linkage or remove clutch components as necessary.
2 Linkage springs being over extended. Adjust linkage for proper free play. Make sure proper pedal stop (bumper) is installed.

Manual transmission

Note: *All manual transmission service information is located in Chapter 7, unless otherwise noted.*

40 Noisy in Neutral with engine running

1 Input shaft bearing worn.
2 Damaged main drive gear bearing.
3 Insufficient transmission oil (Chapter 1).
4 Transmission oil in poor condition. Drain and fill with proper grade oil. Check old oil for water and debris (Chapter 1).
5 Noise can be caused by variations in engine torque. Change the idle speed and see if noise disappears.

41 Noisy in all gears

1 Any of the above causes, and/or:
2 Worn or damaged output gear bearings or shaft.

42 Noisy in one particular gear

1 Worn, damaged or chipped gear teeth.
2 Worn or damaged synchronizer.

43 Slips out of gear

1 Transmission loose on clutch housing.
2 Stiff shift lever seal.
3 Shift linkage binding.
4 Broken or loose input gear bearing retainer.
5 Dirt between clutch lever and engine housing.
6 Worn linkage.
7 Damaged or worn check balls, fork rod ball grooves or check springs.
8 Worn mainshaft or countershaft bearings.
9 Loose engine mounts (Chapter 2).
10 Excessive gear end play.
11 Worn synchronizers.

44 Oil leaks

1 Excessive amount of lubricant in transmission (see Chapter 1 for correct checking procedures). Drain lubricant as required.
2 Side cover loose or gasket damaged.
3 Rear oil seal or speedometer oil seal damaged.
4 To pinpoint a leak, first remove all built-up dirt and grime from the transmission. Degreasing agents and/or steam cleaning will achieve this. With the underside clean, drive the vehicle at low speeds so the air flow will not blow the leak far from its source. Raise the vehicle and determine where the leak is located.

45 Difficulty engaging gears

1 Clutch not releasing completely.
2 Loose or damaged shift linkage. Make a thorough inspection, replacing parts as necessary.
3 Insufficient transmission oil (Chapter 1).
4 Transmission oil in poor condition. Drain and fill with proper grade oil. Check oil for water and debris (Chapter 1).
5 Worn or damaged striking rod.
6 Sticking or jamming gears.

46 Noise occurs while shifting gears

1 Check for proper operation of the clutch (Chapter 8).
2 Faulty synchronizer assemblies. Measure baulk ring-to-gear clearance. Also, check for wear or damage to baulk rings or any parts of the synchromesh assemblies.

Automatic transmission

Note: *Due to the complexity of the automatic transmission, it's difficult for the home mechanic to properly diagnose and service. For problems other than the following, the vehicle should be taken to a reputable mechanic.*

47 Fluid leakage

1 Automatic transmission fluid is a deep red color, and fluid leaks should not be confused with engine oil which can easily be blown by air flow to the transmission.
2 To pinpoint a leak, first remove all built-up dirt and grime from the transmission. Degreasing agents and/or steam cleaning will achieve this. With the underside clean, drive the vehicle at low speeds so the air flow will not blow the leak far from its source. Raise the vehicle and determine where the leak is located. Common areas of leakage are:
- a) Fluid pan: tighten mounting bolts and/or replace pan gasket as necessary (Chapter 1).
- b) Rear extension: tighten bolts and/or replace oil seal as necessary.
- c) Filler pipe: replace the rubber oil seal where pipe enters transmission case.
- d) Transmission oil lines: tighten fittings where lines enter transmission case and/or replace lines.
- e) Vent pipe: transmission overfilled and/or water in fluid (see checking procedures, Chapter 1).
- f) Speedometer connector: replace the O-ring where speedometer cable enters transmission case.

48 General shift mechanism problems

Chapter 7 deals with checking and adjusting the shift linkage on automatic transmissions. Common problems which may be caused by out of adjustment linkage are:
- a) Engine starting in gears other than P (park) or N (Neutral).
- b) Indicator pointing to a gear other than the one actually engaged.
- c) Vehicle moves with transmission in P (Park) position.

49 Transmission will not downshift with the accelerator pedal pressed to the floor

Chapter 7 deals with adjusting the kickdown switch to enable the transmission to downshift properly.

50 Engine will start in gears other than Park or Neutral

Chapter 7 deals with adjusting the Neutral start switch installed on automatic transmissions.

51 Transmission slips, shifts rough, is noisy or has no drive in forward or Reverse gears

1 There are many probable causes for the above problems, but the home mechanic should concern himself only with one possibility; fluid level.
2 Before taking the vehicle to a shop, check the fluid level and condition as described in Chapter 1. Add fluid, if necessary, or change the fluid and filter if needed. If problems persist, have a professional diagnose the transmission.

Driveshaft

Note: *On 2WD models refer to Chapter 8, unless otherwise specified, for service information. On 4WD models, refer to Chapter 9.*

52 Leaks at front of driveshaft

Defective transmission rear seal. See Chapter 7 for replacment procedure. As this is done, check the splined yoke for burrs or roughness that could damage the new seal. Remove burrs with a fine file or whetstone.

53 Knock or clunk when transmission is under initial load (just after transmission is put into gear)

1 Loose or disconnected rear suspension components. Check all mounting bolts and bushings (Chapters 1 and 11).

2 Loose driveshaft bolts. Inspect all bolts and nuts and tighten them securely.
3 Worn or damaged universal joint bearings. Replace driveshaft (Chapter 8).
4 Worn sleeve yoke and mainshaft spline.
5 Defective center bearing or insulator.

54 Metallic grating sound consistent with vehicle speed

Pronounced wear in the universal joint bearings. Replace U-joints or driveshafts, as necessary.

55 Vibration

Note: *Before blaming the driveshaft, make sure the tires are perfectly balanced and perform the following test.*

1 Install a tachometer inside the vehicle to monitor engine speed as the vehicle is driven. Drive the vehicle and note the engine speed at which the vibration (roughness) is most pronounced. Now shift the transmission to a different gear and bring the engine speed to the same point.
2 If the vibration occurs at the same engine speed (rpm) regardless of which gear the transmission is in, the driveshaft is NOT at fault since the driveshaft speed varies.
3 If the vibration decreases or is eliminated when the transmission is in a different gear at the same engine speed, refer to the following probable causes.
4 Bent or dented driveshaft. Inspect and replace as necessary.
5 Undercoating or built-up dirt, etc. on the driveshaft. Clean the shaft thoroughly.
6 Worn universal joint bearings. Replace the U-joints or driveshaft as necessary.
7 Driveshaft and/or companion flange out of balance. Check for missing weights on the shaft. Remove driveshaft and reinstall 180° from original position, then recheck. Have the driveshaft balanced if problem persists.
8 Loose driveshaft mounting bolts/nuts.
9 Defective center bearing, if so equipped.
10 Worn transmission rear bushing (Chapter 7).

56 Scraping noise

Make sure the dust cover on the sleeve yoke isn't rubbing on the transmission extension housing.

57 Whining or whistling noise

Defective center bearing, if so equipped.

Rear axle and differential

Note: *For differential servicing information on 2WD models, refer to Chapter 8, unless otherwise specified. On 4WD models, refer to Chapter 9.*

58 Noise — same when in drive as when vehicle is coasting

1 Road noise. No corrective action available.
2 Tire noise. Inspect tires and check tire pressures (Chapter 1).
3 Front wheel bearings loose, worn or damaged (Chapter 1).
4 Insufficient differential oil (Chapter 1).
5 Defective differential.

59 Knocking sound when starting or shifting gears

Defective or incorrectly adjusted differential.

60 Noise when turning

Defective differential.

61 Vibration

See probable causes under Driveshaft. Proceed under the guidelines listed for the driveshaft. If the problem persists, check the rear wheel bearings by raising the rear of the vehicle and spinning the wheels by hand. Listen for evidence of rough (noisy) bearings. Remove and inspect (Chapter 8).

62 Oil leaks

1 Pinion oil seal damaged (Chapter 8).
2 Axleshaft oil seals damaged (Chapter 8).
3 Differential cover leaking. Tighten mounting bolts or replace the gasket as required.
4 Loose filler or drain plug on differential (Chapter 1).
5 Clogged or damaged breather on differential.

Transfer case (4WD models)

Note: *Refer to Chapter 9 for 4WD system service and repair information.*

63 Gear jumping out of mesh

1 Incorrect control lever free play.
2 Interference between the control lever and the console.
3 Play or fatigue in the transfer case mounts.
4 Internal wear or incorrect adjustments.

64 Difficult shifting

1 Lack of oil.
2 Internal wear, damage or incorrect adjustment.

65 Noise

1 Lack of oil in transfer case.
2 Noise in 4H and 4L, but not in 2H indicates cause is in the front differential or front axle.
3 Noise in 2H, 4H and 4L indicates cause is in rear differential or rear axle.
4 Noise in 2H and 4H but not in 4L, or in 4L only, indicates internal wear or damage in transfer case.

Brakes

Note: *Before assuming a brake problem exists, make sure the tires are in good condition and inflated properly, the front end alignment is correct and the vehicle is not loaded with weight in an unequal manner. All service procedures for the brakes are included in Chapter 10, unless otherwise noted.*

66 Vehicle pulls to one side during braking

1 Defective, damaged or oil contaminated brake pad on one side. Inspect as described in Chapter 1. Refer to Chapter 10 if replacement is required.
2 Excessive wear of brake pad material or disc on one side. Inspect and repair as necessary.
3 Loose or disconnected front suspension components. Inspect and tighten all bolts securely (Chapters 1 and 11).
4 Defective caliper assembly. Remove caliper and inspect for stuck

piston or damage.
5 Brake pad to rotor adjustment needed. Inspect automatic adjusting mechanism for proper operation.
6 Scored or out of round rotor.
7 Loose caliper mounting bolts.
8 Incorrect wheel bearing adjustment.

67 Noise (high-pitched squeal)

1 Front brake pads worn out. This noise comes from the wear sensor rubbing against the disc. Replace pads with new ones immediately!
2 Glazed or contaminated pads.
3 Dirty or scored rotor.
4 Bent support plate.

68 Excessive brake pedel travel

1 Partial brake system failure. Inspect entire system (Chapter 1) and correct as required.
2 Insufficient fluid in master cylinder. Check (Chapter 1) and add fluid – bleed system if necessary.
3 Air in system. Bleed system.
4 Excessive lateral rotor play.
5 Brakes out of adjustment. Check the operation of the automatic adjusters.
6 Defective check valve. Replace valve and bleed system.

69 Brake pedal feels spongy when depressed

1 Air in brake lines. Bleed the brake system.
2 Deteriorated rubber brake hoses. Inspect all system hoses and lines. Replace parts as necessary.
3 Master cylinder mounting nuts loose. Inspect master cylinder bolts (nuts) and tighten them securely.
4 Master cylinder faulty.
5 Incorrect shoe or pad clearance.
6 Defective check valve. Replace valve and bleed system.
7 Clogged reservoir cap vent hole.
8 Deformed rubber brake lines.
9 Soft or swollen caliper seals.
10 Poor quality brake fluid. Bleed entire system and fill with new approved fluid.

70 Excessive effort required to stop vehicle

1 Power brake booster not operating properly.
2 Excessively worn linings or pads. Check and replace if necessary.
3 One or more caliper pistons seized or sticking. Inspect and rebuild as required.
4 Brake pads or linings contaminated with oil or grease. Inspect and replace as required.
5 New pads or linings installed and not yet seated. It'll take a while for the new material to seat against the rotor or drum.
6 Worn or damaged master cylinder or caliper assemblies. Check particularly for frozen pistons.
7 Also see causes listed under Section 69.

71 Pedal travels to the floor with little resistance

Little or no fluid in the master cylinder reservoir caused by leaking caliper piston(s) or loose, damaged or disconnected brake lines. Inspect entire system and repair as necessary.

72 Brake pedal pulsates during brake application

1 Wheel bearings damaged, worn or out of adjustment (Chapter 1).
2 Caliper not sliding properly due to improper installation or obstructions. Remove and inspect.
3 Rotor not within specifications. Remove the rotor and check for excessive lateral runout and parallelism. Have the rotors resurfaced or replace them with new ones. Also make sure that all rotors are the same thickness.
4 Out of round rear brake drums. Remove the drums and have them turned or replace them with new ones.

73 Brakes drag (indicated by sluggish engine performance or wheels being very hot after driving)

1 Output rod adjustment incorrect at the brake pedal.
2 Obstructed master cylinder compensator. Disassemble master cylinder and clean.
3 Master cylinder piston seized in bore. Overhaul master cylinder.
4 Caliper assembly in need of overhaul.
5 Brake pads or shoes worn out.
6 Piston cups in master cylinder or caliper assembly deformed. Overhaul master cylinder.
7 Rotor not within specsifications (Section 72).
8 Parking brake assembly will not release.
9 Clogged brake lines.
10 Wheel bearings out of adjustment (Chapter 1).
11 Brake pedal height improperly adjusted.
12 Wheel cylinder needs overhaul.
13 Improper shoe to drum clearance. Adjust as necessary.

74 Rear brakes lock up under light brake application

1 Tire pressures too high.
2 Tires excessively worn (Chapter 1).
3 Defective NLSV valve.

75 Rear brakes lock up under heavy brake application

1 Tire pressures too high.
2 Tires excessively worn (Chapter 1).
3 Front brake pads contaminated with oil, mud or water. Clean or replace the pads.
4 Front brake pads excessively worn.
5 Defective master cylinder or caliper assembly.

Suspension and steering

Note: *All service procedures for the suspension and steering systems are included in Chapter 11, unless otherwise noted.*

76 Vehicle pulls to one side

1 Tire pressures uneven (Chapter 1).
2 Defective tire (Chapter 1).
3 Excessive wear in suspension or steering components (Chapter 1).
4 Front end alignment incorrect.
5 Front brakes dragging. Inspect as described in Section 73.
6 Wheel bearings improperly adjusted (Chapter 1).
7 Wheel lug nuts loose.
8 Worn upper or lower link or tension rod bushings.

77 Shimmy, shake or vibration

1 Tire or wheel out of balance or out of round. Have them balanced on the vehicle.
2 Loose, worn or out of adjustment wheel bearings (Chapter 1).
3 Shock absorbers and/or suspension components worn or damaged. Check for worn bushings in the upper and lower links.
4 Wheel lug nuts loose.
5 Incorrect tire pressures.

6 Excessively worn or damaged tire.
7 Loosely mounted steering gear housing.
8 Steering gear improperly adjusted.
9 Loose, worn or damaged steering components.
10 Damaged idler arm.
11 Worn balljoint.

78 Excessive pitching and/or rolling around corners or during braking

1 Defective shock absorbers. Replace as a set.
2 Broken or weak leaf springs and/or suspension components.
3 Worn or damaged stabilizer bar or bushings.
4 Worn or damaged upper or lower links or bushings.

79 Wandering or general instability

1 Improper tire pressures.
2 Worn or damaged upper and lower link or tension rod bushings.
3 Incorrect front end alignment.
4 Worn or damaged steering linkage or upper or lower link.
5 Improperly adjusted steering gear.
6 Out of balance wheels.
7 Loose wheel lug nuts.
8 Worn rear shock absorbers.
9 Fatigued or damaged rear leaf springs.

80 Excessively stiff steering

1 Lack of lubricant in power steering fluid reservoir, where appropriate (Chapter 1).
2 Incorrect tire pressures (Chapter 1).
3 Lack of lubrication at balljoints (Chapter 1).
4 Front end out of alignment.
5 Steering gear out of adjustment or lacking lubrication.
6 Improperly adjusted wheel bearings.
7 Worn or damaged steering gear.
8 Interference of steering column with turn signal switch.
9 Low tire pressures.
10 Worn or damaged balljoints.
11 Worn or damaged steering linkage.
12 See also Section 79.

81 Excessive play in steering

1 Loose wheel bearings (Chapter 1).
2 Excessive wear in upper or lower link or tension rod bushings (Chapter 1).
3 Steering gear improperly adjusted.
4 Incorrect front end alignment.
5 Steering gear mounting bolts loose.
6 Worn steering linkage.

82 Lack of power assistance

1 Steering pump drivebelt faulty or not adjusted properly (Chapter 1).
2 Fluid level low (Chapter 1).
3 Hoses or pipes restricting the flow. Inspect and replace parts as necessary.
4 Air in power steering system. Bleed system.
5 Defective power steering pump.

83 Steering wheel fails to return to straight-ahead position

1 Incorrect front end alignment.
2 Tire pressures low.
3 Steering gears improperly engaged.
4 Steering column out of alignment.
5 Worn or damaged balljoint.
6 Worn or damaged steering linkage.
7 Improperly lubricated idler arm.
8 Insufficient oil in steering gear.
9 Lack of fluid in power steering pump.

84 Steering effort not the same in both directions (power system)

1 Leaks in steering gear.
2 Clogged fluid passage in steering gear.

85 Noisy power steering pump

1 Insufficient oil in pump.
2 Clogged hoses or oil filter in pump.
3 Loose pulley.
4 Improperly adjusted drivebelt (Chapter 1).
5 Defective pump.

86 Miscellaneous noises

1 Improper tire pressures.
2 Insufficiently lubricated balljoint or steering linkage.
3 Loose or worn steering gear, steering linkage or suspension components.
4 Defective shock absorber.
5 Defective wheel bearing.
6 Worn or damaged upper or lower link or tension rod bushing.
7 Damaged leaf spring.
8 Loose wheel lug nuts.
9 Worn or damaged rear axleshaft spline.
10 Worn or damaged rear shock absorber mounting bushing.
11 Incorrect rear axle end play.
12 See also causes of noises at the rear axle and driveshaft.
13 Worn or damaged driveaxle joints (4WD models).

87 Excessive tire wear (not specific to one area)

1 Incorrect tire pressures.
2 Tires out of balance. Have them balanced on the vehicle.
3 Wheels damaged. Inspect and replace as necessary.
4 Suspension or steering components worn (Chapter 1).

88 Excessive tire wear on outside edge

1 Incorrect tire pressure.
2 Excessive speed in turns.
3 Front end alignment incorrect (excessive toe-in).

89 Excessive tire wear on inside edge

1 Incorrect tire pressure.
2 Front end alignment incorrect (toe-out).
3 Loose or damaged steering components (Chapter 1).

90 Tire tread worn in one place

1 Tires out of balance. Have them balanced on the vehicle.
2 Damaged or buckled wheel. Inspect and replace if necessary.
3 Defective tire.

Chapter 1 Tune-up and routine maintenance

Contents

Specifications

Recommended lubricants and fluids

Engine oil	
Type	API SF or SG
Viscosity	See accompanying chart
Automatic transmission fluid	Dexron II automatic transmission fluid (ATF)
Manual transmission oil	
Type	API GL-4
Viscosity	See accompanying chart
Differential oil	
Type	API GL-5
Viscosity	See Manual transmission oil chart
Transfer case oil (4WD models)	
Through 1990	API GL-5
1991 and later	DEXRON II automatic transmission fluid (ATF)
Power steering fluid	Dexron II ATF
Brake fluid	DOT 3
Clutch fluid	DOT 3 brake fluid
Coolant	Mixture of good quality ethylene glycol based antifreeze and water, in at least a 50/50 ratio (but not to exceed a 70/30 ratio of antifreeze to water)
Manual steering gear oil	API GL-4 (see Manual transmission oil chart for correct weight)

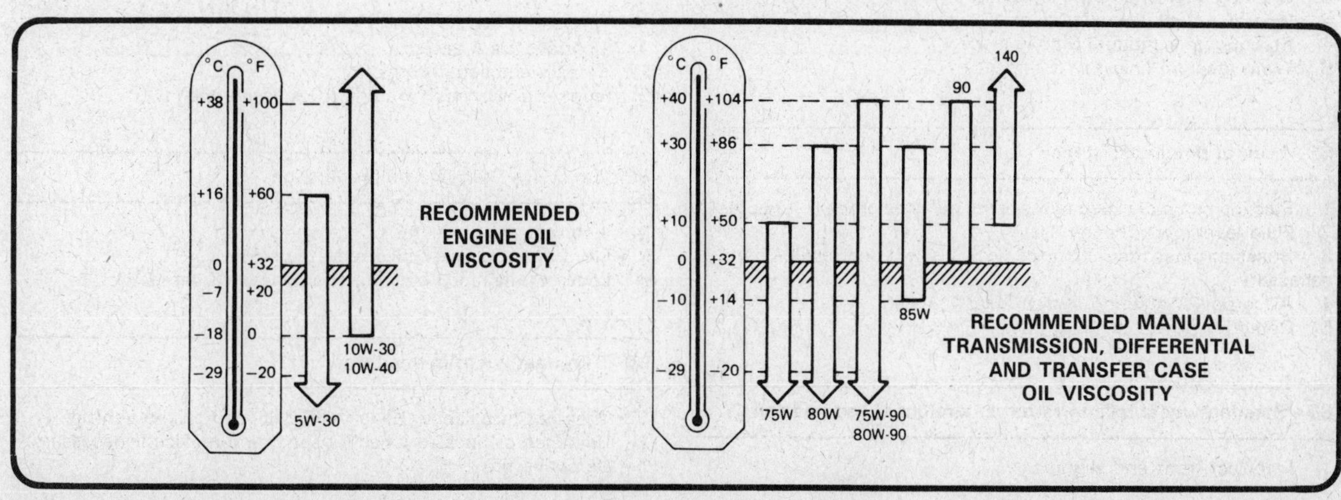

Recommended lubricants and fluids (continued)

Chassis components	Chassis grease
Hood and door hinges	Engine oil
Hood latch assembly	
Pivots and spring anchor	Engine oil
Release pawl	Chassis grease
Key lock cylinders	WD-40 Spray lubricant or equivalent

Lubricant and fluid capacities

Engine oil (approximate capacity)		
1980	Quarts	Liters
With new filter	4-1/2	4.3
Without new filter	4	3.8
1981 and 1982		
With new filter		
2WD	4-5/8	4.4
4WD	4-1/2	4.2
Without new filter		
2WD	4-1/2	3.9
4WD	3-7/8	3.7
1983 through 1985		
With new filter		
2WD	4-3/8	4.1
4WD	4-1/2	4.3
Without new filter		
2WD	3-7/8	3.6
4WD	4	3.8
1986 on		
Four-cylinder engine		
2WD	4	3.8
4WD		
Through 1990	4-1/2	4.1
1991 and later	3-1/2	3.3
V6 engine		
2WD	4-1/4	4.1
4WD	3-5/8	4.0
Coolant (approximate capacity)		
1980	9-1/4	8.75
1981	10-1/2	9.9
1982	10	9.5
1983 through 1985		
Manual transmission	10	9.5
Automatic transmission	10-3/4	10.2
1986 through 1990		
Four-cylinder engine	9-1/4	8.75
V6 engine	11	10.4
1991 and later		
Four-cylinder engine		
2WD	8-5/8	8.1
4WD	9-1/2	9.0
V6 engine		
2WD	11-3/8	10.7
4WD	12-3/8	11.7
Transmission (approximate capacity)		
1980 through 1983		
Manual transmission		
Four-speed	3-5/8 pt	1.7 liters
Five-speed	4-1/2 pt	2.0 liters
Automatic transmission	5-7/8 qt	5.5 liters
1984 and 1985		
Manual transmission	4-1/2 pt	2.1 liters
Automatic transmission	5-7/8 pt	5.5 liters
1986 through 1989		
Four-cylinder engine		
2WD		
Manual transmission	4-1/4 pt	2.0 liters
Automatic transmission	7-3/8 qt	7.0 liters
4WD		
Manual transmission	5-1/8 pt	2.4 liters
Automatic transmission	7-3/8 qt	7.0 liters
V6 engine		
2WD		
Manual transmission	5-1/8 pt	2.4 liters
Automatic transmission	7-3/8 qt	7.0 liters

4WD		
Manual transmission	7-5/8 pt	3.6 liters
Automatic transmission	7-3/8 qt	7.0 liters
1990 on		
Manual transmission FS5W71C		
2WD	4-1/4 pt	2.0 liters
4WD	8-1/2 pt	4.0 liters
Manual transmission FS5R30A		
2WD	5-1/8 pt	2.4 liters
4WD	7-5/8 pt	3.6 liters
Automatic transmission		
2WD	8-3/8 qt	7.9 liters
4WD	9 qt	8.5 liters
Transfer case oil		
1980 through 1985	1-1/2 qt	1.4 liters
1986 on	2-3/8 qt	2.2 liters
Rear differential oil		
1980 through 1985		
US	2-5/8 pt	1.25 liters
Canada	3-1/8 pt	1.5 liters
Dual wheel models	2-3/4 pt	1.3 liters
1986 on		
H190	3-1/8 pt	1.5 liters
C200	2-3/4 pt	1.3 liters
Dual wheel models	5-7/8 pt	2.8 liters
Front differential oil		
1980 through 1985	2-1/8 pt	1.0 liter
1986 on		
R180A	2-3/4 pt	1.3 liters
R200A	3-1/8 pt	1.5 liters

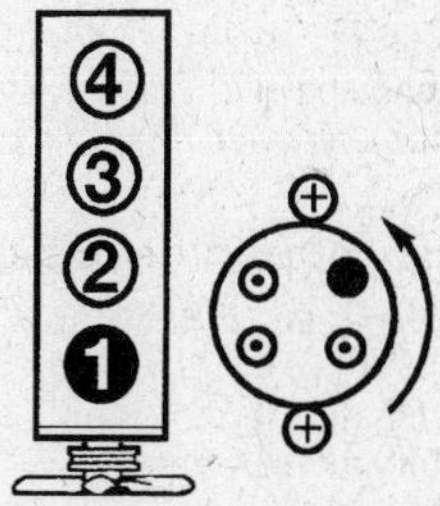

All 4-cylinder engines except Z-series

1990 and later V6 engines

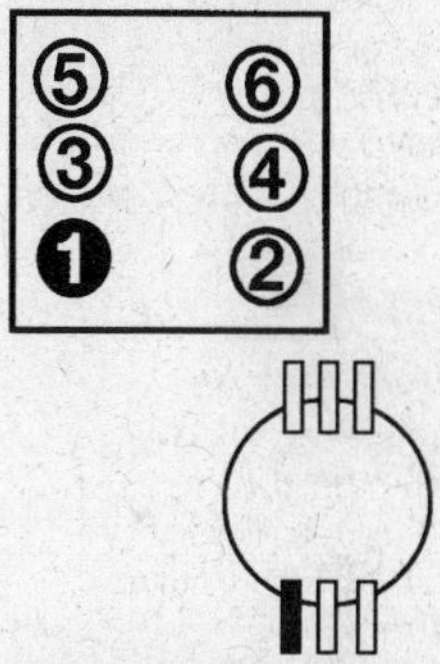

1989 and earlier V6 engines

Cylinder location and distributor rotation

1

Tune-up data

Spark plug type		
1980		
US (standard)	BP6ES-11	
Canadian (standard) and US (optional)	BP6ES	
1981 through 1985		
Intake side	BPRS6ES	
Exhaust side	BPRS5ES	
1986 through 1989		
Four-cylinder engine	BPRS5ES	
V6 engine	BPRS5ES-11	
1990 on		
V6	BKR6EY	
KA24E	ZFR5E-11	
Spark plug gap		
1980	0.039 to 0.043 in (1.0 to 1.1 mm)	
1981 through 1989		
Four-cylinder engine	0.031 to 0.035 in (0.8 to 0.9 mm)	
V6 engine	0.039 to 0.043 in (1.0 to 1.1 mm)	
1990 on		
Four-cylinder	0.040 (1.0 mm)	
V6	0.031 - .035 (0.8 to 0.9 mm)	
Valve clearances		
1980	**HOT engine**	**COLD engine**
Intake	0.010 in (0.25 mm)	0.007 in (0.17 mm)
Exhaust	0.012 in (0.30 mm)	0.009 in (0.24 mm)
1981 through 1989		
Intake	0.012 in (0.30 mm)	0.008 in (0.21 mm)
Exhaust	0.012 in (0.30 mm)	0.009 in (0.24 mm)
1990 on	hydraulic	
Firing order		
Four-cylinder engine	1-3-4-2	
V6 engine	1-2-3-4-5-6	

Ignition timing and idle speed

Note: *Automatic transmission equipped models should be checked with the shift lever in Drive.*

1980	
US Federal and Canadian Cab/chassis models	12 ± 2-degrees BTDC/600 ± 100 rpm
California	
Heavy duty models	10 ± 2-degrees BTDC/600 ± 100 rpm*
All others	12 ± 2-degrees BTDC/600 ± 100 rpm*
Canadian (except Cab/chassis models)	12-degrees BTDC/600 rpm

Tune-up data (continued)

Ignition timing and idle speed	
1981	
Manual transmission	
2WD	5 ± 2-degrees BTDC/650 ± 100 rpm*
4WD	5 ± 2-degrees BTDC/800 ± 100 rpm*
Automatic transmission	5 ± 2-degrees BTDC/650 ± 100 rpm
1982	
2WD (all)	3 ± 2-degrees BTDC/650 ± 100 rpm*
4WD	3 ± 2-degrees BTDC/800 ± 100 rpm*
1983 on	Refer to the *Emission Control Information label* in the engine compartment
Distributor cap carbon terminal length	
1980 (all) and 1981 4WD	0.470 in (12 mm)
All others	0.390 in (10 mm)

** Ignition timing should be checked with the distributor vacuum advance hose disconnected and plugged*

Drivebelt deflection

	Four-cylinder engine	V6 engine
Alternator		
Through 1990	3/8 to 7/16 in	1/4 to 5/16 in
1991 and later	21/32 in	15/32 in
Power steering pump		
Through 1990	25/64 to 15/32 in	7/16 to 1/2 in
1991 and later	19/32 in	21/32 in
A/C compressor		
Through 1990	7/32 to 25/64 in	3/8 to 7/16 in
1991 and later	5/8 in	5/8 in

Radiator cap pressure rating

11 to 14 psi

Clutch pedal

Height	
1980 through 1983	6.73 to 6.79 in (171 to 172 mm)
1984 and 1985	7.05 to 7.44 in (179 to 189 mm)
1986 on	
Four-cylinder engine	9.29 to 9.69 in (236 to 246 mm)
V6 engine	8.94 to 9.33 in (227 to 237 mm)
Free play	
1980 through 1983	0.040 to 0.200 in (1 to 5 mm)
1984 and 1985	0.040 to 0.120 in (1 to 3 mm)
1986 on	0.039 to 0.059 in (1 to 1.5 mm)

Brake pedal

Height	
1980 through 1983	6.61 to 6.85 in (168 to 174 mm)
1984 and 1985	6.93 to 7.32 in (176 to 186 mm)
1986 on	
Manual transmission	8.23 to 8.62 in (209 to 219 mm)
Automatic transmission	8.35 to 8.74 in (212 to 222 mm)
Free play	
1980 through 1983	0.040 to 0.200 in (1 to 5 mm)
1984 and 1985	0.012 to 0.039 in (0.3 to 1.0 mm)
1986 on	0.039 to 0.118 in (1.0 to 3.0 mm)
Depressed height	Over 3-1/4 in (82 mm) (4.72 in/120 mm on 1986 and later models)

Brakes

Brake pad wear limit	5/64 in (2 mm)
Rear brake shoe lining wear limit	1/16 in (1.5 mm)

Torque specifications

	Ft-lbs
Automatic transmission pan bolts	4.3
Spark plugs	14 to 22
Engine oil drain plug	
Through 1990	18
1991 and later	22 to 29
Rocker arm nuts	12 to 16
Rocker pivot locknuts	12 to 16
Manual transmission	
Check/fill plug	18 to 25
Drain plug	18 to 25

	Ft-lbs
Differential	
Check/fill plug	
Through 1990	60
1991 and later	43
Drain plug	
Through 1990	60
1991 and later	
Front	29 to 43
Rear	43 to 72
Transfer case check/fill and drain plugs	22
Carburetor mounting nuts	9 to 13
Throttle body mounting nuts (fuel-injected models)	
Through 1992	9 to 13
1993 and later	
Step 1	6.5 to 8.0
Step 2	13 to 16
Oxygen sensor	
Four-cylinder engine	
Through 1990	13 to 17
1991 and later	30 to 37
V6 engine	30 to 37

(Specifications continued on next page)

Engine compartment components — 1981 and later model four-cylinder engines (typical)

1 Wiper motor
2 Carburetor
3 Heater hose
4 EGR valve
5 VVT valve
6 PCV valve
7 Accelerator cable
8 Rocker cover
9 Engine oil dipstick
10 Brake booster check valve
11 Steering column
12 Clutch master cylinder
13 Brake booster
14 Exhaust manifold
15 Brake master cylinder
16 Coolant reservoir
17 Inlet air duct (connects to the air cleaner)
18 Charcoal canister
19 Ignition coils
20 Steering gear
21 Distributor
22 Engine oil filler cap
23 Spark plug wires
24 Water pump and crankshaft pulley
25 Fan shroud
26 EAI (air induction) tubes
27 Intake manifold
28 Radiator
29 Alternator
30 Air induction valve case
31 Battery
32 Fusible links
33 Windshield washer tank
34 AB valve
35 Vacuum switch
36 Boost control unit
37 Altitude compensator

Specifications (continued)

Wheel lug nuts	Ft-lbs
Single steel wheels	
1980	
2WD	65
4WD	97
1981 and 1982	97
1983 on	87 to 108
Dual steel wheels (all)	166 to 203
Aluminum wheels	
1984 and 1985	58 to 72
1986 on	87 to 108
Front wheel hub nuts (2WD)	25 to 29

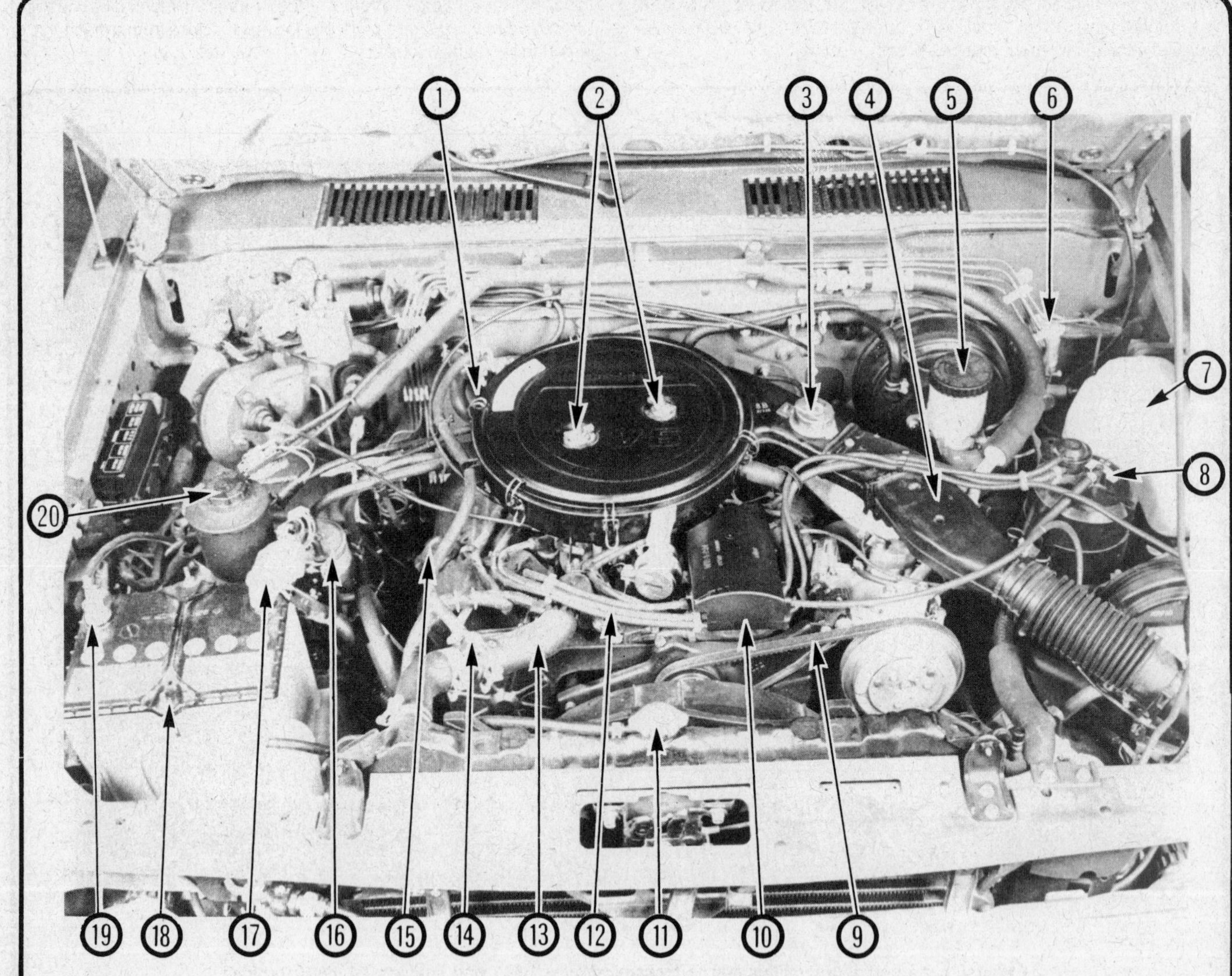

Engine compartment components — V6 engine (typical)

1. *Air cleaner housing spring clips*
2. *Air cleaner housing wing nuts*
3. *Thermostatic air cleaner vacuum motor*
4. *Air cleaner snorkel flexible duct*
5. *Brake fluid reservoir*
6. *Clutch fluid reservoir*
7. *Windshield washer fluid reservoir*
8. *EEC system charcoal canister*
9. *A/C compressor drivebelt*
10. *Distributor*
11. *Radiator cap*
12. *Spark plug wires*
13. *Upper radiator hose*
14. *Air valve*
15. *Engine oil filler cap*
16. *Fuel filter*
17. *Positive (+) battery cable*
18. *Battery hold-down clamp*
19. *Negative (–) battery cable*
20. *Power steering fluid reservoir/dipstick*

1 Introduction

This Chapter is designed to help the home mechanic maintain the Datsun/Nissan pick-up/Pathfinder with the goals of maximum performance, economy, safety and reliability in mind.

Included is a master maintenance schedule (page 1–10), followed by procedures dealing specifically with each item on the schedule. Visual checks, adjustments, component replacement and other helpful items are included. Refer to the accompanying illustrations of the engine compartment and the underside of the vehicle for the locations of various components.

Servicing your vehicle in accordance with the planned mileage/time maintenance schedule and the step-by-step procedures should result in maximum reliability and extend the life of your vehicle. Keep in mind that it's a comprehensive plan – maintaining some items but not others at the specified intervals will not produce the same results.

As you perform routine maintenance procedures, you'll find that many can, and should, be grouped together because of the nature of the procedures or because of the proximity of two otherwise unrelated components or systems.

For example, if the vehicle is raised for chassis lubrication, you should inspect the exhaust, suspension, steering and fuel systems while you're under the vehicle. When you're rotating the tires, it makes good sense to check the brakes since the wheels are already removed. Finally, let's suppose you have to borrow or rent a torque wrench. Even if you only need it to tighten the spark plugs, you might as well check the torque of as many critical fasteners as time allows.

The first step in this maintenance program is to prepare yourself before the actual work begins. Read through all the procedures you're planning to do, then gather up all the parts and tools needed. If it looks like you might run into problems during a particular job, seek advice from a mechanic or experienced do-it-yourselfer.

Underside view of four-cylinder engine/transmission — 1981 and later model 4WD (typical)

1 Idler arm
2 Alternator
3 Oil pump
4 Front differential forward mounting crossmember
5 Crankshaft pulley
6 Front differential forward mounting insulator
7 Stabilizer bar
8 Distributor
9 Cross rod
10 Steering gear
11 Left tension rod
12 Engine mounting insulator and bracket
13 Side rod
14 Knuckle arm
15 Knuckle
16 Left driveaxle
17 Left lower link
18 Front differential
19 Left torsion bar
20 Front exhaust pipe
21 Front driveshaft
22 Manual transmission drain plug
23 Transmission
24 Front differential rear mounting crossmember
25 Right torsion bar
26 Clutch operating cylinder
27 Suspension crossmember
28 Right driveaxle
29 Right lower link
30 Knuckle
31 Knuckle arm
32 Right tension rod
33 Side rod
34 Engine mounting insulator and bracket
35 Oil pan

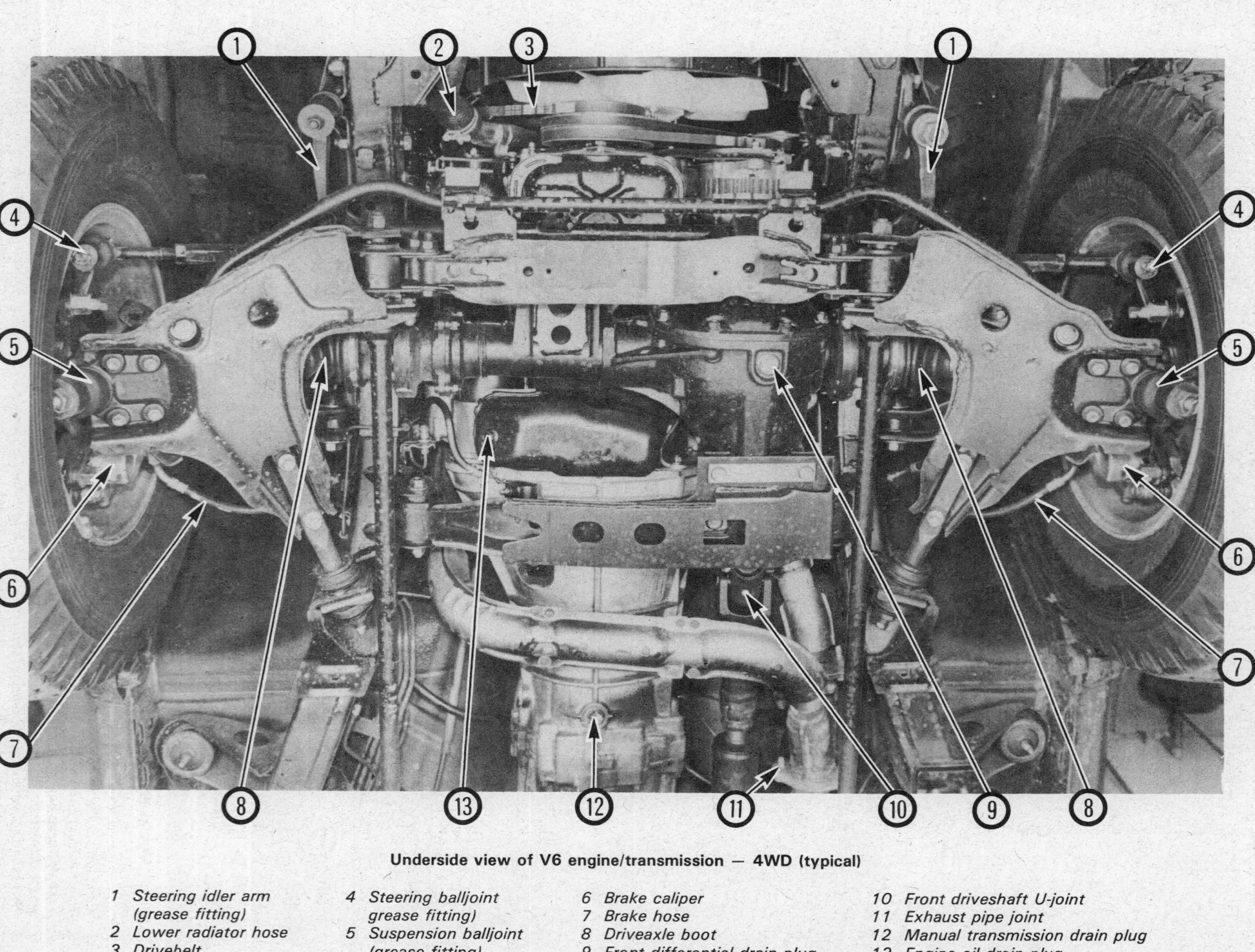

Underside view of V6 engine/transmission — 4WD (typical)

1 Steering idler arm (grease fitting)
2 Lower radiator hose
3 Drivebelt
4 Steering balljoint grease fitting)
5 Suspension balljoint (grease fitting)
6 Brake caliper
7 Brake hose
8 Driveaxle boot
9 Front differential drain plug
10 Front driveshaft U-joint
11 Exhaust pipe joint
12 Manual transmission drain plug
13 Engine oil drain plug

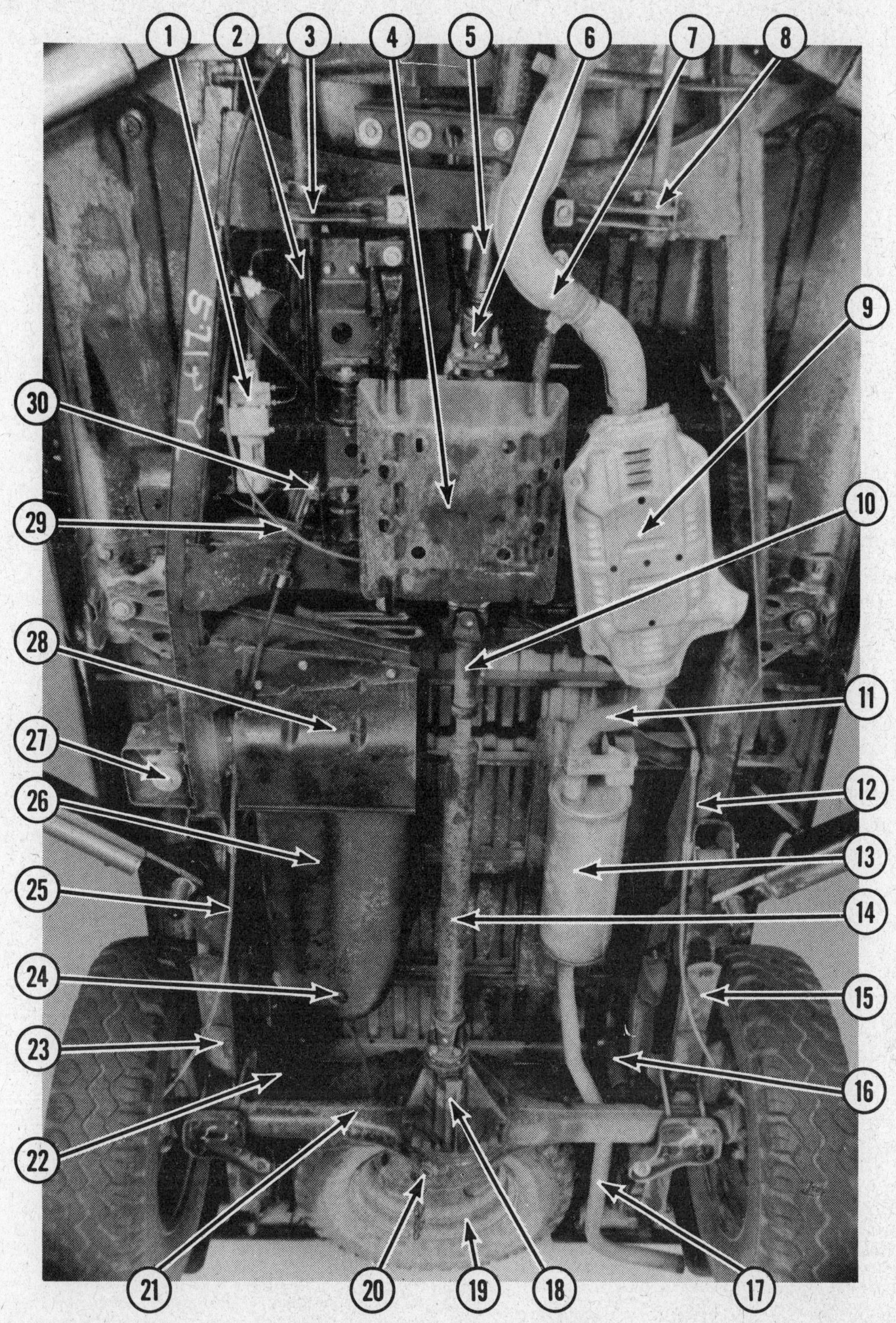

Underside view of components at the rear of the vehicle — 1981 and later 4WD models (typical)

1 Load sensing valve
2 Fuel and vent lines
3 Right torsion bar anchor arm
4 Transfer case and rock guard
5 Front driveshaft
6 Driveshaft universal joint (spider assembly)
7 Front exhaust pipe
8 Left torsion bar anchor arm
9 Catalytic converter
10 Driveshaft sleeve yoke
11 Center tube
12 Left rear parking brake cable
13 Muffler
14 Rear driveshaft
15 Left leaf spring
16 Left shock absorber
17 Tailpipe
18 Rear differential
19 Spare tire
20 Rear differential drain plug
21 Rear axle
22 Rear shock absorber
23 Right leaf spring
24 Fuel tank drain plug
25 Right rear parking brake cable
26 Fuel tank
27 Electric fuel pump
28 Fuel tank shield
29 Speedometer cable
30 Parking brake balance lever

2 Nissan pick-up and Pathfinder Maintenance schedule

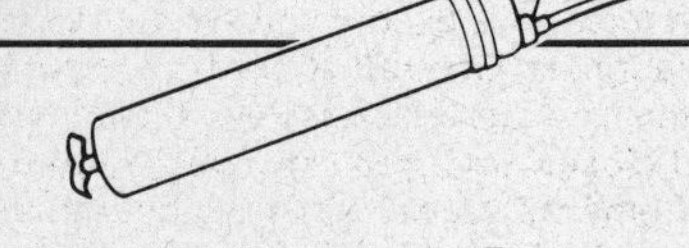

The following maintenance intervals are based on the assumption that the vehicle owner will be doing the maintenance or service work, as opposed to having a dealer service department do the work. Although the time/mileage intervals are based on factory recommendations, most have been shortened to ensure, for example, that such items as lubricants and fluids are checked/changed at intervals that promote maximum engine/driveline service life. Also, subject to the preference of the individual owner interested in keeping his or her vehicle in peak condition at all times and with the vehicle's ultimate resale in mind, many of the maintenance procedures may be performed more often than recommended in the following schedule. We encourage such owner initiative.

When the vehicle is new it should be serviced initially by a factory authorized dealer service department to protect the factory warranty. In many cases the initial maitenance check is done at no cost to the owner — check with your dealer service department for more information.

Every 250 miles or weekly, whichever comes first

Check the engine oil level (Section 4)
Check the coolant level (Section 4)
Check the windshield washer fluid level (Section 4)
Check the brake and clutch fluid levels (Section 4)
Check the automatic transmission fluid level (Section 5)
Check the power steering fluid level (Section 6)
Check the tires and tire pressures (Section 7)

Every 7500 miles or 12 months, whichever comes first

All items listed above plus:
Check and service the battery (Section 8)
Check the cooling system (Section 9)
Inspect and, if necessary, replace the windshield wiper blades (Section 10)
Inspect and, if necessary, replace all underhood hoses (Section 11)
Check/adjust the brake pedal (Section 12)
Change the engine oil and filter (Section 13)*

Every 15,000 miles or 12 months, whichever comes first

All items listed above plus:
Have a dealer service department or repair shop check the mixture ratio (1980 models only)
Check and adjust the valve clearances (four-cylinder engine only) (Section 14)
Lubricate the chassis components (Section 15)
Inspect the suspension and steering components (Section 16)*
Check the driveshaft(s) (Section 17)
Inspect the exhaust system (Section 18)*
Check the clutch pedal height and free play (Section 19)
Check the manual transmission oil level (Section 20)*
Check the transfer case oil level (Section 21)*
Check the differential oil level (Section 22)*
Rotate the tires (Section 23)
Check the brakes (Section 24)*
Check the fuel system (Section 25)
Check the thermostatic air cleaner (Section 26)
Check and, if necessary, adjust the engine drivebelts (Section 27)
Check the seatbelts (Section 28)
Replace the spark plugs (1980 models only) (Section 45)
Have the front end alignment checked (especially if abnormal tire wear is evident)

Every 30,000 miles or 24 months, whichever comes first

All items listed above plus:
Replace the air filter and PCV filter (Section 29)
Replace the fuel filter (Section 30)
Replace the Air Induction Valve filter (Section 31)
Replace the air pump filter (1980 models only) (Section 32)
Replace the charcoal canister filter (Section 33)
Check the carburetor choke operation (Section 34)
Check the carburetor/throttle body mounting nut torque (Section 35)
Check the throttle pedal and cable (carburetor equipped vehicles only) (Section 36)
Check and, if necessary, adjust the engine idle speed (Section 37)
Change the transfer case oil (Section 38)
Change the manual transmission oil (Section 39)
Change the rear axle differential oil (Section 40)*
Change the automatic transmission fluid (Section 41)**
Check and repack the front wheel bearings (2WD models only) (Section 42)
Service the cooling system (drain, flush and refill) (Section 43)
Check and, if necessary, replace the PCV valve (Section 44)
Replace the spark plugs (Section 45)
Check/replace the spark plug wires (Section 46)
Check/replace the distributor cap and rotor (Section 47)
Check and, if necessary, adjust the ignition timing (Section 48)
Replace the oxygen sensor (1985 California models only) (Section 49)

Every 50,000 miles or 24 months, whichever comes first

Replace the oxygen sensor (1985 49-state models only) (Section 49)

Every 60,000 miles or 24 months, whichever comes first

Replace the oxygen sensor (all 1986 and later models) (Section 49)
Replace the timing belt (V6 engine only) (Chapter 2, Part B)

* This item is affected by "severe" operating conditions as described below. If your vehicle is operated under severe conditions, perform all maintenance indicated with an asterisk (*) at 3000 mile/3 month intervals. Severe conditions are indicated if you mainly operate your vehicle under one or more of the following:

Driving in dusty areas
Towing a trailer
Idling for extended periods and/or low speed operation
When outside temperatures remain below freezing and most trips are less than four miles in length

** If operated under one or more of the following conditions, change the automatic transmission fluid every 15,000 miles:

In heavy city traffic where the outside temperature regularly reaches 90°F (32°C) or higher
In hilly or mountainous terrain
Frequent trailer pulling

3 Tune-up general information

The term *tune-up* is used in this manual to represent a combination of individual operations rather than one specific procedure.

If, from the time the vehicle is new, the routine maintenance schedule is followed closely and frequent checks are made of fluid levels and high wear items, as suggested throughout this manual, the engine will be kept in relatively good running condition and the need for additional work will be minimized.

More likely than not, however, there will be times when the engine is running poorly due to lack of regular maintenance. This is even more likely if a used vehicle, which has not received regular and frequent maintenance checks, is purchased. In such cases, an engine tune-up will be needed outside of the regular routine maintenance intervals.

The first step in any tune-up or diagnostic procedure to help correct a poor running engine is a cylinder compression check. A compression check (see Chapter 2 Part C) will help determine the condition of internal engine components and should be used as a guide for tune-up and repair procedures. If, for instance, a compression check indicates serious internal engine wear, a conventional tune-up will not improve the performance of the engine and would be a waste of time and money. Because of its importance, the compression check should be done by someone with the right equipment and the knowledge to use it properly.

The following procedures are those most often needed to bring a generally poor running engine back into a proper state of tune.

Minor tune-up

Check all engine related fluids
Clean and check the battery (Section 8)
Check and adjust the drivebelts (Section 27)
Replace the spark plugs (Section 44)
Check the cylinder compression (Chapter 2)
Inspect the distributor cap and rotor (Section 46)
Inspect the spark plug and coil wires (Section 45)
Replace the air and PCV filters (Section 28)
Check and adjust the idle speed (Section 36)
Check and adjust the ignition timing (Section 47)
Replace the fuel filter (Section 29)
Replace the Air Induction Valve filter (Section 30)
Check the PCV valve (Section 43)
Adjust the valve clearances (Section 14)
Check and service the cooling system (Section 42)
Replace the air pump filter (1980 models only) (Section 32)
Have a dealer service department or repair shop check the mixture ratio (1980 models only)

Major tune-up

All items listed under Minor tune-up plus . . .
Check the vacuum advance system (Chapter 6 — Spark Timing Control System)
Check the EGR system (Chapter 6)
Check the charging system (Chapter 5)
Check the ignition system (Chapter 5)
Check the fuel system (Section 25 and Chapter 4)
Replace the spark plug wires, distributor cap and rotor (Sections 46 and 47)

4 Fluid level checks

Note: *The following are fluid level checks to be done on a 250 mile or weekly basis. Additional fluid level checks can be found in specific maintenance procedures which follow. Regardless of how often the fluid levels are checked, watch for puddles under the vehicle — if leaks are noted, make repairs immediately.*

1 Fluids are an essential part of the lubrication, cooling, brake, clutch and windshield washer systems. Because the fluids gradually become depleted and/or contaminated during normal operation of the vehicle, they must be periodically replenished. See *Recommended lubricants and fluids* at the beginning of this Chapter before adding fluid to any of the following components. **Note:** *The vehicle must be on level ground when fluid levels are checked.*

Engine oil

Refer to illustrations 4.4a, 4.4b, 4.4c, 4.4d, 4.4e and 4.6

2 The engine oil level is checked with a dipstick that extends through a tube and into the oil pan at the bottom of the engine.

3 The oil level should be checked before the vehicle has been driven, or about 15 minutes after the engine has been shut off. If the oil is checked immediately after driving the vehicle, some of the oil will remain in the upper engine components, resulting in an inaccurate reading on the dipstick.

4 Pull the dipstick from the tube **(see illustrations)** and wipe all the oil from the end with a clean rag or paper towel. Insert the clean dipstick

4.4a On 1980 2WD models, the engine oil dipstick is located on the right (passenger) side of the engine (arrow), while . . .

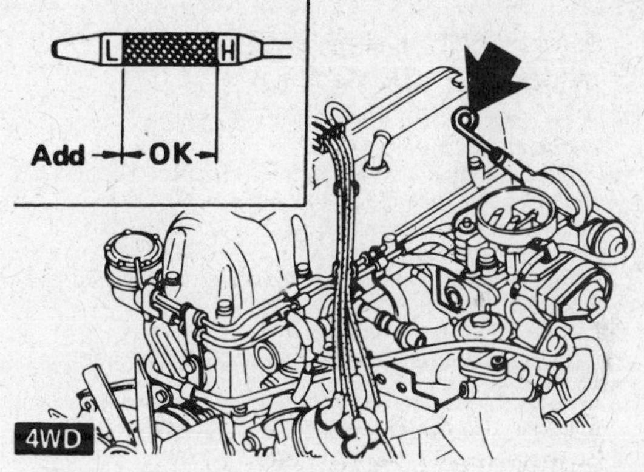

4.4b . . . on 4WD models, it's located on the left (driver's) side

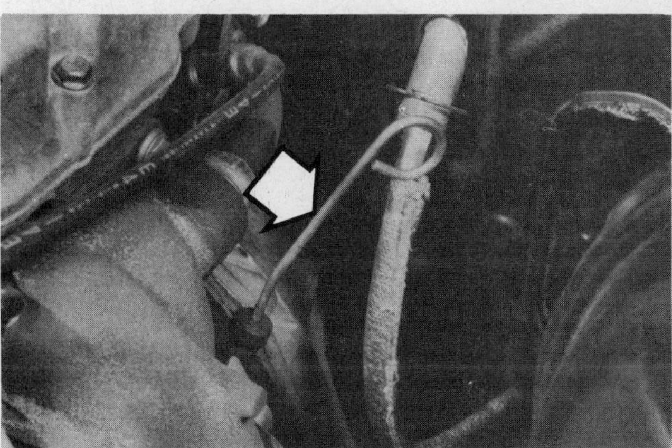

4.4c On eight spark plug four-cylinder engines, the oil dipstick is located on the left (driver's) side, near the rear of the engine

1

4.4d On the V6 engine, the oil dipstick is located at the rear of the engine compartment, next to the brake booster

4.6 On the V6 engine, the oil filler cap is located on the right side rocker arm cover

4.8 The coolant level must be kept between the two marks on the side of the reservoir – coolant is added after removing the cap

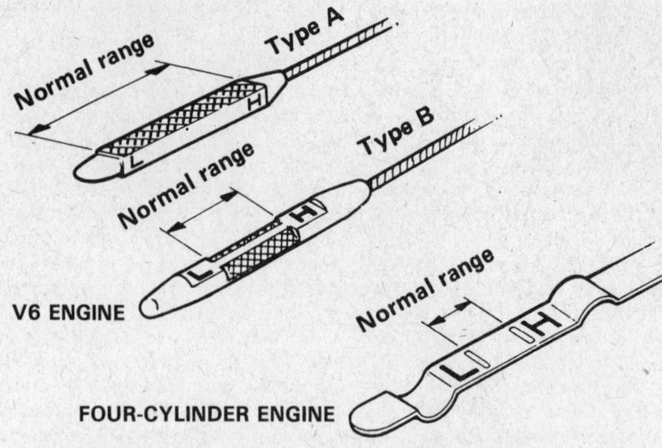

4.4e The engine oil dipstick may be marked in one of several different ways, but the correct level will be obvious when looking at it

all the way back into the tube, then pull it out again. Note the oil at the end of the dipstick. Add oil as necessary to keep the level between the L (low) mark and the H (high) mark on the dipstick **(see illustration)**.

5 Don't overfill the engine by adding too much oil since this may result in oil fouled spark plugs, oil leaks or oil seal failures.

6 Oil is added to the engine after removing a threaded cap from the rocker arm cover **(see illustration)**. An oil can spout or funnel may help to reduce spills.

7 Checking the oil level is an important preventive maintenance step. A consistently low oil level indicates oil leakage through damaged seals, defective gaskets or past worn rings or valve guides. If the oil looks milky in color or has water droplets in it, the cylinder head gasket(s) may be blown or the head(s) or block may be cracked. The engine should be checked immediately. The condition of the oil should also be checked. Whenever you check the oil level, slide your thumb and index finger up the dipstick before wiping off the oil. If you see small dirt or metal particles clinging to the dipstick, the oil should be changed (Section 13).

Engine coolant

Refer to illustration 4.8

Warning: *Don't allow antifreeze to come in contact with your skin or painted surfaces of the vehicle. Flush contaminated areas immediately with plenty of water. Don't store new coolant or leave old coolant lying around where it's accessible to children or pets – they're attracted by its sweet taste. Ingestion of even a small amount of coolant can be fatal! Wipe up garage floor and drip pan coolant spills immediately. Keep antifreeze containers covered and repair leaks in your cooling system immediately.*

8 All vehicles covered by this manual are equipped with a pressurized coolant recovery system. A white plastic coolant reservoir located in the engine compartment is connected by a hose to the radiator filler neck **(see illustration)**. If the engine overheats, coolant escapes through a valve in the radiator cap and travels through the hose into the reservoir. As the engine cools, the coolant is automatically drawn back into the cooling system to maintain the correct level.

9 The coolant level in the reservoir should be checked regularly. **Warning:** *Do not remove the radiator cap to check the coolant level when the engine is warm.* The level in the reservoir varies with the temperature of the engine. When the engine is cold, the coolant level should be at or slightly above the MIN mark on the reservoir. Once the engine has warmed up, the level should be at or near the MAX mark. If it isn't, allow the engine to cool, then remove the cap from the reservoir and add a 50/50 mixture of ethylene glycol-based antifreeze and water.

10 Drive the vehicle and recheck the coolant level. If only a small amount of coolant is required to bring the system up to the proper level, water can be used. However, repeated additions of water will dilute the antifreeze and water solution. In order to maintain the proper ratio of antifreeze and water, always top up the coolant level with the correct mixture. An empty plastic milk jug or bleach bottle makes an excellent container for mixing coolant. Do not use rust inhibitors or additives.

11 If the coolant level drops consistently, there may be a leak in the

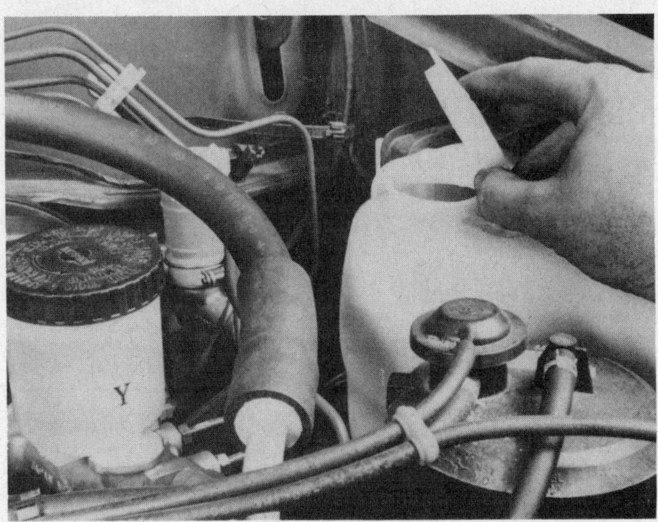

4.14 The windshield washer fluid level must be near the top of the reservoir — fluid can be added after removing the cap (be sure to close it securely when you're done)

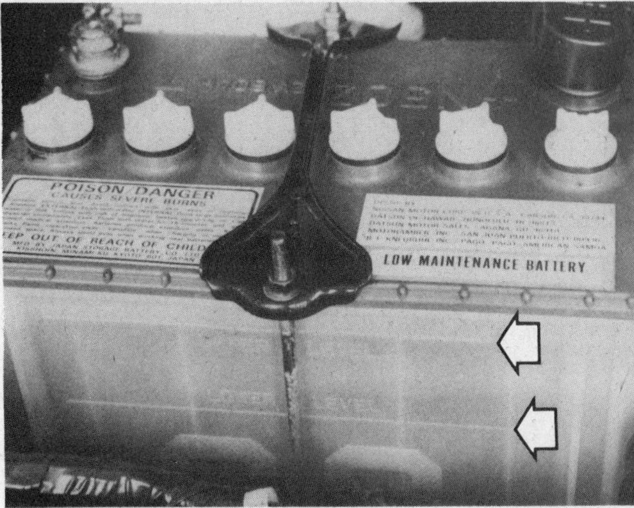

4.17 On original equipment batteries, the electrolyte level can be checked without removing the cell caps — it must be maintained between the marks on the case (arrows)

system. Inspect the radiator, hoses, filler cap, drain plugs and water pump (see Section 9). If no leaks are noted, have the radiator cap pressure tested by a service station.

12 If you have to remove the radiator cap, wait until the engine has cooled, then wrap a thick cloth around the cap and turn it to the first stop. If coolant or steam escapes, let the engine cool down longer, then remove the cap.

13 Check the condition of the coolant as well. It should be relatively clear. If it's brown or rust colored, the system should be drained, flushed and refilled. Even if the coolant appears to be normal, the corrosion inhibitors wear out, so it must be replaced at the specified intervals.

Windshield washer fluid

Refer to illustration 4.14

14 Fluid for the windshield washer system is stored in a plastic reservoir located on the driver's side of the engine compartment **(see illustration)**. If necessary, refer to the underhood component illustration(s) at the beginning of this Chapter to locate the reservoir.

15 In milder climates, plain water can be used in the reservoir, but it should be kept no more than 2/3 full to allow for expansion if the water freezes. In colder climates, use windshield washer system antifreeze, available at any auto parts store, to lower the freezing point of the fluid. Mix the antifreeze with water in accordance with the manufacturer's directions on the container. **Caution:** *Don't use cooling system antifreeze — it will damage the vehicle's paint.*

16 To help prevent icing in cold weather, warm the windshield with the defroster before using the washer.

Battery electrolyte

Refer to illustration 4.17

17 To check the electrolyte level in the battery, remove all of the cell caps. If the level is low, add *distilled* water until it's above the plates. Original equipment batteries are translucent so the electrolyte level can be checked by looking at the side of the case **(see illustration)**. Most aftermarket replacement batteries have a split-ring indicator in each cell to help you judge when enough water has been added — don't overfill the cells!

Brake and clutch fluid

Refer to illustrations 4.19a and 4.19b

18 The brake master cylinder is mounted on the front of the power booster unit in the engine compartment. The clutch cylinder used on manual transmissions is mounted adjacent to it on the firewall.

19 The fluid inside is readily visible. The level should be between the MIN and MAX marks on the reservoirs **(see illustration)**. If a low level is indicated, be sure to wipe the top of the reservoir cover with a clean rag to prevent contamination of the brake and/or clutch system before

4.19a The brake fluid level should be kept near the upper mark on the reservoir — it's translucent so the cap doesn't have to be removed to check the level

4.19b The clutch fluid level should be kept between the MIN and MAX marks on the reservoir

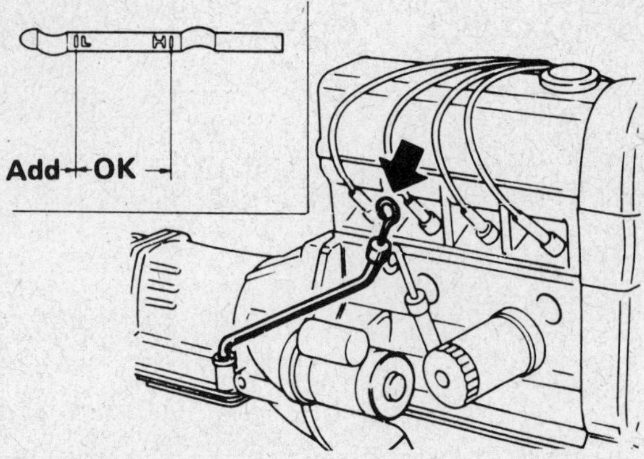

5.3 The automatic transmission fluid dipstick on 1980 models is located on the right (passenger) side of the engine, near the rear

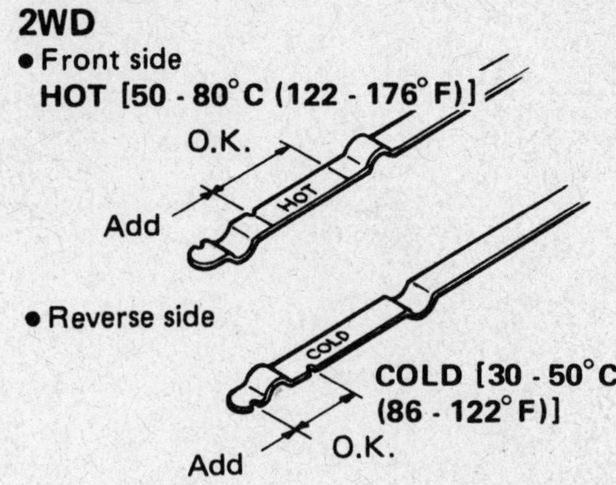

5.6a The automatic transmission dipstick on 2WD models is marked like this, while . . .

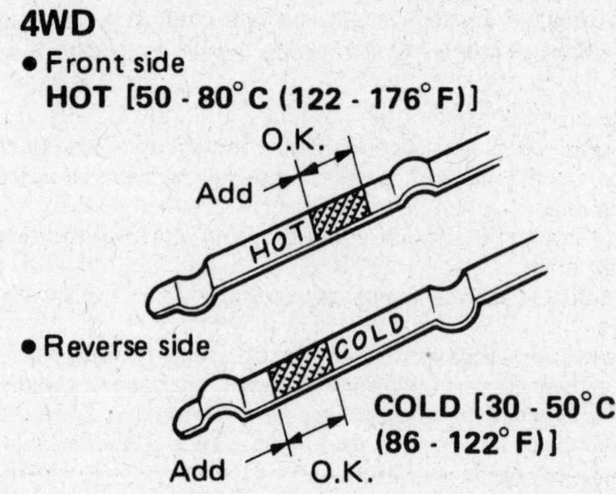

5.6b . . . on 4WD models it looks like this (typical)

removing the cover.

20 When adding fluid, pour it carefully into the reservoir to avoid spilling it onto surrounding painted surfaces. Be sure the specified fluid is used, since mixing different types of brake fluid can cause damage to the system. See *Recommended lubricants and fluids* at the front of this Chapter or your owner's manual. **Warning:** *Brake fluid can harm your eyes and damage painted surfaces, so be very careful when handling or pouring it. Don't use brake fluid that's been standing open or is more than one year old. Brake fluid absorbs moisture from the air. Excess moisture can cause a dangerous loss of brake efficiency.*

21 At this time the fluid and master cylinder can be inspected for contamination. The system should be drained and refilled if deposits, dirt particles or water droplets are seen in the fluid.

22 After filling the reservoir to the proper level, make sure the cover is on tight to prevent fluid leakage.

23 The brake fluid level in the master cylinder will drop slightly as the pads and the brake shoes at each wheel wear down during normal operation. If the master cylinder requires repeated additions to keep it at the proper level, it's an indication of leakage in the brake system, which should be corrected immediately. Check all brake lines and connections (see Section 24 for more information).

24 If, upon checking the master cylinder fluid level, you discover one or both reservoirs empty or nearly empty, the brake system should be bled (Chapter 9).

5 Automatic transmission fluid level check

Refer to illustrations 5.3, 5.6a and 5.6b

1 The automatic transmission fluid level should be carefully maintained. Low fluid level can lead to slipping or loss of drive, while overfilling can cause foaming and loss of fluid.

2 With the parking brake set, start the engine, then move the shift lever through all the gear ranges, ending in Park. The fluid level must be checked with the vehicle level and the engine running at idle. **Note:** *Incorrect fluid level readings will result if the vehicle has just been driven at high speeds for an extended period, in hot weather in city traffic, or if it has been pulling a trailer. If any of these conditions apply, wait until the fluid has cooled (about 30 minutes).*

3 With the transmission at normal operating temperature, remove the dipstick from the filler tube. The dipstick is located at the rear of the engine compartment on the passenger's side **(see illustration)**.

4 Carefully touch the fluid at the end of the dipstick to determine if it's cool (86 to 122°F) or hot (123 to 176°F). Wipe the fluid from the dipstick with a clean rag and push it back into the filler tube until the cap seats.

5 Pull the dipstick out again and note the fluid level.

6 If the fluid felt cool, the level should be within the COLD range (between the cutouts) **(see illustrations)**. If the fluid was hot, the level should be within the HOT range (between the upper cutout and the upper line on the dipstick).

7 On earlier models, the dipstick probably won't have a COLD and HOT range. Instead, it'll be marked with an L (for low) and an H (for high). The fluid level should be between the H mark and 1/4-inch below the mark with the transmission fluid at normal operating temperature (hot) **(see illustration 5.3)**.

8 If additional fluid is required, add it directly into the tube using a funnel. It takes about one pint to raise the level from the L mark to the H mark with a hot transmission, so add the fluid a little at a time and keep checking the level until it's correct.

9 The condition of the fluid should also be checked along with the level. If the fluid at the end of the dipstick is a dark reddish-brown color, or if it smells burned, it should be changed. If you are in doubt about the condition of the fluid, purchase some new fluid and compare the two for color and smell.

6 Power steering fluid level check

Refer to illustration 6.5

1 Unlike manual steering, the power steering system relies on fluid which may, over a period of time, require replenishing.

2 The fluid reservoir for the power steering pump is located on the pump body at the front of the engine. On vehicles with a V6 engine, the reservoir is separate from the pump and is mounted behind the battery.

3 For the check, the front wheels should be pointed straight ahead and the engine should be off. The engine and power steering fluid should be cold.

4 Use a clean rag to wipe off the reservoir cap and the area around it. This will help prevent any foreign matter from entering the reser-

6.5 Check the power steering fluid level on the dipstick after twisting off the cap (V6 engine shown)

voir during the check.

5 Twist off the cap – it has a dipstick attached to it **(see illustration)**.

6 Wipe off the fluid with a clean rag, reinsert the dipstick, then withdraw it and note the fluid level. The level should be within the range marked on the dipstick. Never allow the fluid level to drop below the lower range mark.

7 If additional fluid is required, pour the specified type directly into the reservoir, using a funnel to prevent spills.

8 If the reservoir requires frequent fluid additions, all power steering hoses, hose connections and the power steering pump should be carefully checked for leaks.

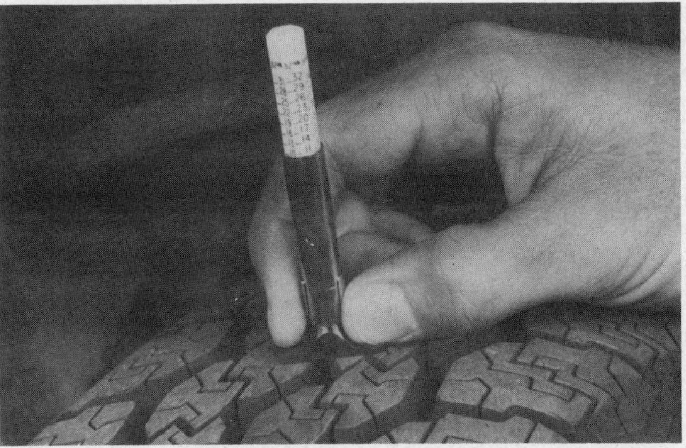

7.2 A tire tread depth indicator should be used to monitor tire wear – they're available at auto parts stores and service stations and cost very little

7 Tire and tire pressure checks

Refer to illustrations 7.2, 7.3, 7.4a, 7.4b and 7.8

1 Periodic inspection of the tires may spare you the inconvenience of being stranded with a flat tire. It can also provide you with vital information regarding possible problems in the steering and suspension systems before major damage occurs.

2 The original tires on this vehicle are equipped with wear indicator bars that will appear when tread depth reaches a predetermined limit, usually 1/16-inch, but they don't appear until the tires are worn out. Tread wear can be monitored with a simple, inexpensive device known as a tread depth indicator **(see illustration)**.

3 Note any abnormal tread wear **(see illustration)**. Tread pattern ir-

Condition	Probable cause	Corrective action	Condition	Probable cause	Corrective action
Shoulder wear	• Underinflation (both sides wear) • Incorrect wheel camber (one side wear) • Hard cornering • Lack of rotation	• Measure and adjust pressure. • Repair or replace axle and suspension parts. • Reduce speed. • Rotate tires.	Feathered edge Toe wear	• Incorrect toe	• Adjust toe-in.
Center wear	• Overinflation • Lack of rotation	• Measure and adjust pressure. • Rotate tires.	Uneven wear	• Incorrect camber or caster • Malfunctioning suspension • Unbalanced wheel • Out-of-round brake drum • Lack of rotation	• Repair or replace axle and suspension parts. • Repair or replace suspension parts. • Balance or replace. • Turn or replace. • Rotate tires.

7.3 This chart will help you determine the condition of your tires, the probable cause(s) of abnormal wear and the corrective action necessary

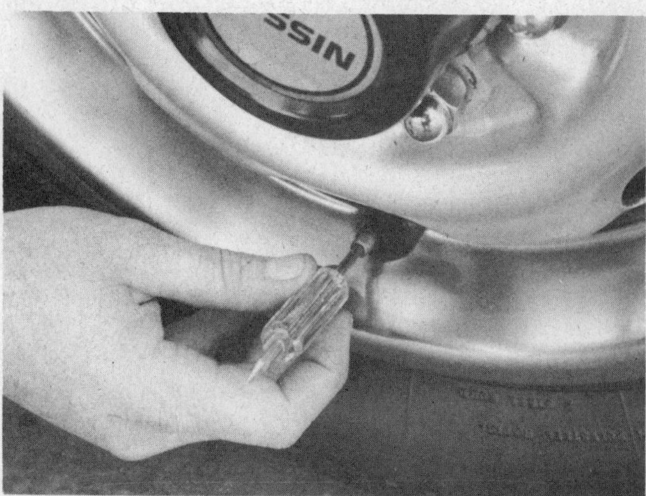

7.4a If a tire loses air on a steady basis, check the valve core first to make sure it's snug (special inexpensive wrenches are commonly available at auto parts stores)

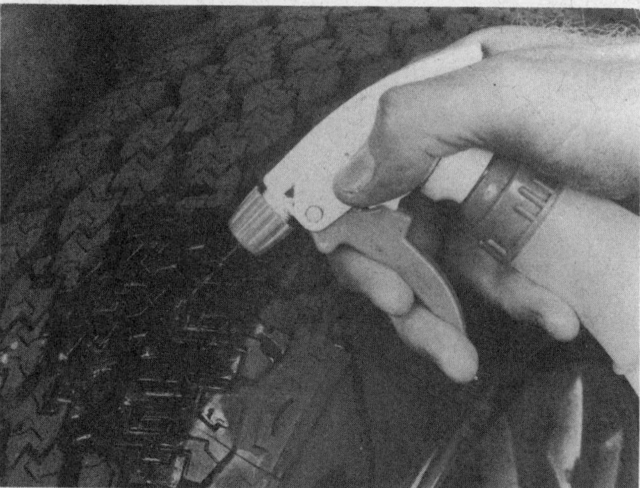

7.4b If the valve core is tight, raise the corner of the vehicle with the low tire and spray a soapy water solution on the tread as the tire is slowly turned – slow leaks will cause small bubbles to appear

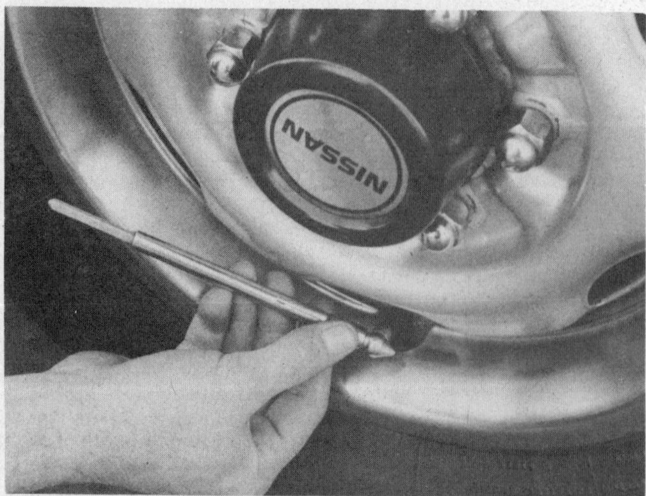

7.8 To extend the life of your tires, check the air pressure at least once a week with an accurate gauge (don't forget the spare!)

8.1 Tools and materials required for battery maintenance

1 ***Face shield/safety goggles*** — *When removing corrosion with a brush, the acidic particles can easily fly up into your eyes*
2 ***Baking soda*** — *A solution of baking soda and water can be used to neutralize corrosion*
3 ***Petroleum jelly*** — *A layer of this on the battery posts will help prevent corrosion*
4 ***Battery post/cable cleaner*** — *This wire brush cleaning tool will remove all traces of corrosion from the battery posts and cable clamps*
5 ***Treated felt washers*** — *Placing one of these on each post, directly under the cable clamps, will help prevent corrosion*
6 ***Puller*** — *Sometimes the cable clamps are very difficult to pull off the posts, even after the nut/bolt has been completely loosened. This tool pulls the clamp straight up and off the post without damage*
7 ***Battery post/cable cleaner*** — *Here is another cleaning tool which is a slightly different version of number 4 above, but it does the same thing*
8 ***Rubber gloves*** — *Another safety item to consider when servicing the battery; remember that's acid inside the battery!*

regularities such as cupping, flat spots and more wear on one side than the other are indications of front end alignment and/or balance problems. If any of these conditions are noted, take the vehicle to a tire shop or service station to correct the problem.

4 Look closely for cuts, punctures and embedded nails or tacks. Sometimes a tire will hold air pressure for a short time or leak down very slowly after a nail has embedded itself in the tread. If a slow leak persists, check the valve stem core to make sure it's tight **(see illustration)**. Examine the tread for an object that may have embedded itself in the tire or for a ''plug'' that may have begun to leak (radial tire punctures are repaired with a plug that's installed in a puncture). If a puncture is suspected, it can be easily verified by spraying a solution of soapy water onto the puncture area **(see illustration)**. The soapy solution will bubble if there's a leak. Unless the puncture is unusually large, a tire shop or service station can usually repair the tire.

5 Carefully inspect the inner sidewall of each tire for evidence of brake fluid leakage. If you see any, inspect the brakes immediately.

8.6 The battery cable clamp bolts should be kept tight to avoid problems

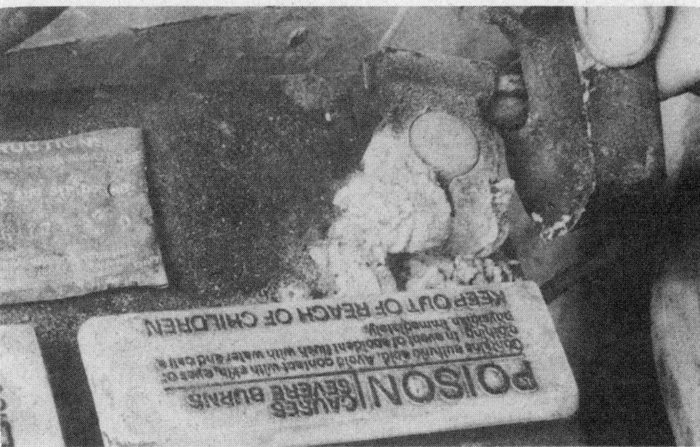

8.7a Battery terminal corrosion usually appears as light, fluffy powder

8.7b Removing the cable from a battery post with a wrench — sometimes a special battery pliers is required for this procedure if corrosion has caused deterioration of the nut hex (always remove the ground cable first and hook it up last!)

8.7c Regardless of the type of tool used to clean the battery posts, a clean, shiny surface should be the result

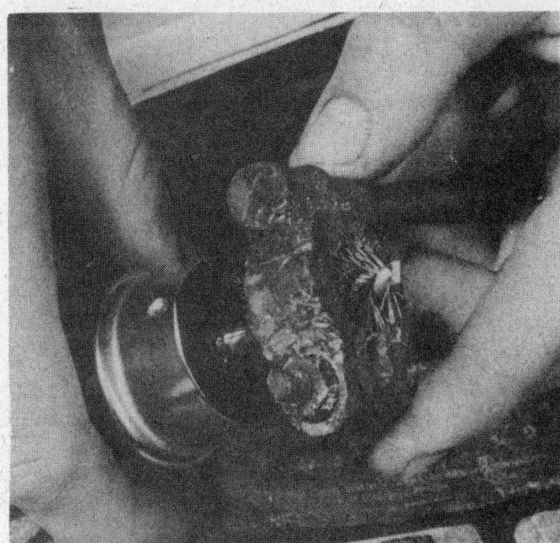

8.7d When cleaning the cable clamps, all corrosion must be removed (the inside of the clamp is tapered to match the taper on the post, so don't remove too much material)

6 Correct air pressure adds miles to the lifespan of the tires, improves mileage and enhances overall ride quality. Tire pressure cannot be accurately estimated by looking at a tire, especially if it's a radial. A tire pressure gauge is essential. Keep an accurate gauge in the vehicle. The pressure gauges attached to the nozzles of air hoses at gas stations are often inaccurate.

7 Always check tire pressure when the tires are cold. Cold, in this case, means the vehicle has not been driven over a mile in the three hours preceding a tire pressure check. A pressure rise of four to eight pounds is not uncommon once the tires are warm.

8 Unscrew the valve cap protruding from the wheel or hubcap and push the gauge firmly onto the valve stem **(see illustration)**. Note the reading on the gauge and compare the figure to the recommended tire pressure shown on the placard on the glove compartment door. Be sure to reinstall the valve cap to keep dirt and moisture out of the valve stem mechanism. Check all four tires and, if necessary, add enough air to bring them up to the recommended pressure.

9 Don't forget to keep the spare tire inflated to the specified pressure (refer to your owner's manual or the tire sidewall).

8 Battery check and maintenance

Refer to illustrations 8.1, 8.6, 8.7a, 8.7b, 8.7c and 8.7d

Warning: *Several precautions must be followed when checking and servicing the battery. Hydrogen gas, which is highly flammable, is always present in the battery cells. so keep lighted tobacco and all other open flames and sparks away from the battery. The electrolyte in the cells is actually dilute sulfuric acid, which will cause injury if splashed on your skin or in your eyes. It'll also ruin clothes and painted surfaces. When removing the battery cables, always detach the negative cable first and hook it up last!*

Check

1 Battery maintenance is an important procedure which will help ensure that you aren't stranded because of a dead battery. Several tools are required for this procedure **(see illustration)**.

2 On vehicles equipped with a conventional battery, the electrolyte level should be checked every week (see Section 4).

3 If the vehicle is equipped with a battery electrolyte level warning light, the electrolyte should still be visually checked on a regular basis to make sure all cells are full.

4 On some models a sealed maintenance-free battery is used. Unlike a conventional battery, it has no removable cell caps and is completely sealed except for a small vent hole. Because of its sealed design, water cannot be added to the cells.

5 Periodically clean the top and sides of the battery. Remove all dirt and moisture. This will help prevent corrosion and ensure that the battery doesn't become partially discharged by leakage through moisture and dirt. Check the case for cracks and distortion.

6 Check the tightness of the battery cable bolts **(see illustration)** to ensure good electrical connections. Inspect the entire length of each cable, looking for cracked or abraded insulation and frayed conductors.

7 If corrosion, which usually appears as white, fluffy deposits, is evident, remove tha cables from the terminals, clean them with a battery brush and reinstall them **(see illustrations)**. Corrosion can be kept to a minimum by applying a layer of petroleum jelly to the terminals

after the cables are in place.

8 Make sure the battery carrier is in good condition and the hold-down clamp is tight. If the battery is removed, make sure that nothing is in the bottom of the carrier when it's reinstalled and don't overtighten the clamp nuts.

9 A temperature-compensated hydrometer is built into the top of maintenance-free batteries. It gives an indication of the electrolyte level and the battery's state of charge. If a blue dot is seen in the indicator window on top of the battery, the battery is properly charged. If the indicator is transparent, the battery should be recharged from an external source and the charging system should be checked (Chapter 5).

10 The freezing point of electrolyte depends on its specific gravity. Since freezing can ruin a battery, it should be kept in a fully charged state to protect against freezing.

11 If you frequently have to add water to a conventional battery and the case has been inspected for cracks that could cause leakage, but none are found, the battery is being overcharged; the charging system should be checked as described in Chapter 5.

12 If any doubt exists about the battery state of charge, a hydrometer should be used to test it by withdrawing a little electrolyte from each cell, one at a time.

13 The specific gravity of the electrolyte at 80 °F will be approximately 1.270 for a fully charged battery. For every 10 °F that the electrolyte temperature is above 80 °F, add 0.04 to the specific gravity. Subtract 0.04 if the temperature is below 80 °F.

14 A specific gravity reading of 1.240 with an electrolyte temperature of 80 °F indicates a half-charged battery.

15 Some of the common causes of battery failure are:

- a) Accessories, especially headlights, left on overnight or for several hours.
- b) Slow average driving speeds for short intervals.
- c) The electrical load of the vehicle being more than the alternator output. This is very common when several high draw accessories are being used simultaneously (such as radio/stereo, air conditioning, window defoggers, lights, etc.).
- d) Charging system problems such as short circuits, slipping drivebelt, defective alternator or faulty voltage regulator.
- e) Battery neglect, such as loose or corroded terminals or loose battery hold-down clamp.

Battery charging

16 In winter when heavy demand is placed upon the battery, it's a good idea to occasionally have it charged from an external source.

17 When charging the battery, the negative cable should be disconnected. The charger leads should be connected to the battery *before* the charger is plugged in or turned on. If the leads are connected to the battery terminals after the charger is on, a spark could occur and the hydrogen gas given off by the battery could explode!

18 The battery should be charged at a low rate of about 4 to 6 amps, and should be left on for at least three or four hours. A trickle charger charging at the rate of 1.5 amps can be safely used overnight.

19 Special rapid boost charges which are claimed to restore the power of the battery in a short time can cause serious damage to the battery plates and should only be used in an emergency situation.

20 The battery should be left on the charger only until the specific gravity is brought up to a normal level. On maintenance-free batteries, continue to charge only until the blue dot is seen in the indicator window. Don't overcharge the battery! **Note:** *Some battery chargers will automatically shut off after the battery is fully charged, making it unnecessary to keep a close watch on the state of charge.*

21 When disconnecting the charger, unplug it before disconnecting the charger leads from the battery.

9 Cooling system check

Refer to illustration 9.4

1 Many major engine failures can be attributed to a faulty cooling system. If the vehicle is equipped with an automatic transmission, the cooling system also cools the transmission fluid, prolonging transmission life.

2 The cooling system should be checked with the engine cold. Do this before the vehicle is driven for the day or after it has been shut off for at least three hours.

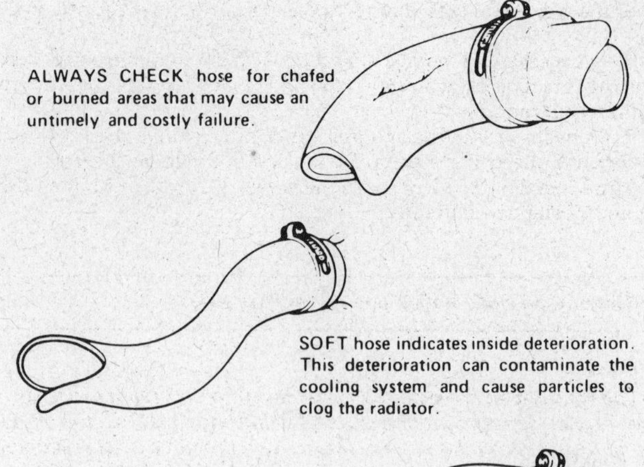

ALWAYS CHECK hose for chafed or burned areas that may cause an untimely and costly failure.
SOFT hose indicates inside deterioration. This deterioration can contaminate the cooling system and cause particles to clog the radiator.

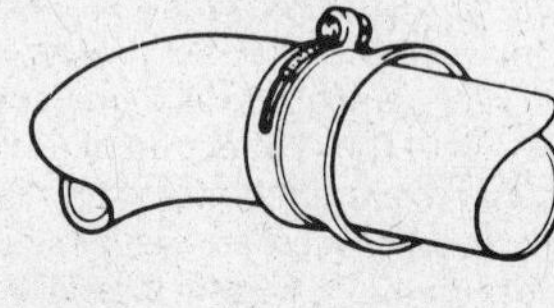

HARDENED hose can fail at any time. Tightening hose clamps will not seal the connection or stop leaks.

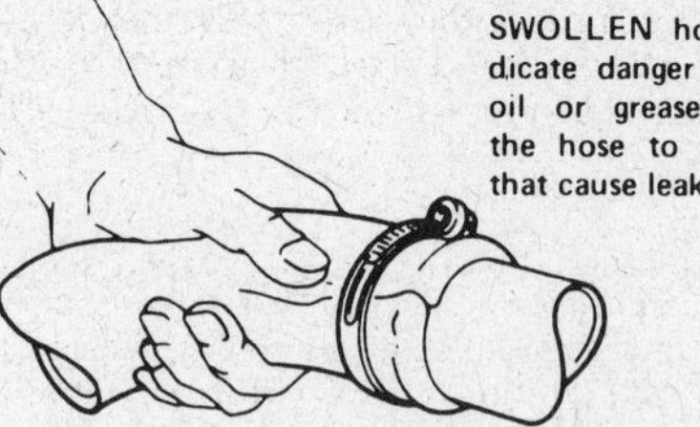

SWOLLEN hose or oil soaked ends indicate danger and possible failure from oil or grease contamination. Squeeze the hose to locate cracks and breaks that cause leaks.

9.4 Hoses, like drivebelts, have a habit of failing at the worst possible time — to prevent the inconvenience of a blown radiator or heater hose, inspect them carefully as shown here

3 Remove the radiator cap by turning it counterclockwise until it reaches a stop. If you hear a hissing sound (indicating there's still pressure in the system), wait until it stops. Now press down on the cap with the palm of your hand and continue turning until it can be removed. Thoroughly clean the cap, inside and out, with clean water. Also clean the filler neck on the radiator. All traces of corrosion should be removed. The coolant inside the radiator should be relatively transparent. If it's rust colored, the system should be drained and refilled (Section 43). If the coolant level is not up to the top, add additional antifreeze/coolant mixture (see Section 4).

4 Carefully check the large upper and lower radiator hoses along with the smaller diameter heater hoses which run from the engine to the firewall. Inspect each hose along its entire length, replacing any hose that's cracked, swollen or deteriorated. Cracks may become more apparent if the hose is squeezed **(see illustration)**. Regardless of condition, it's a good idea to replace hoses with new ones every two years.

5 Make sure that all hose connections are tight. A leak in the cooling system will usually show up as white or rust colored deposits on the areas adjoining the leak. If wire-type clamps are used at the ends of the hoses, it may be a good idea to replace them with more secure screw-type clamps.

6 Use compressed air or a soft brush to remove bugs, leaves, etc. from the front of the radiator or air conditioning condenser. Be careful not to damage the delicate cooling fins or cut yourself on them.

7 Every other inspection, or at the first indication of cooling system problems, have the cap and system pressure tested. If you don't have a pressure tester, most gas stations and repair shops will do this for a minimal charge.

10 Wiper blade inspection and replacement

Refer to illustrations 10.1 and 10.2

1 The wiper blade is removed by depressing the release tab at the

end of the wiper arm **(see illustration)** and pulling the blade out of the arm.

2 If it's necessary to remove the rubber element from the blade, compress the retaining clips at the end of the blade and slide the element out **(see illustration)**.

3 If it's necessary to replace the wiper arm, remove the cover and nut securing the wiper arm to the linkage and detach the arm.

4 When installing the wiper arm, be sure it's lined up with the other arm and positioned correctly on the shaft.

11 Underhood hose check and replacement

General

1 **Caution:** *Replacement of air conditioning hoses must be left to a dealer service department or air conditioning shop that has the equipment to depressurize the system safely. Never remove air conditioning components or hoses until the system has been depressurized.*

2 High temperatures in the engine compartment can cause the deterioration of the rubber and plastic hoses used for engine, accessory and emission systems operation. Periodic inspection should be made for cracks, loose clamps, material hardening and leaks. Information specific to the cooling system hoses can be found in Section 9.

3 Some, but not all, hoses are secured to the fittings with clamps. Where clamps are used, check to be sure they haven't lost their tension, allowing the hose to leak. If clamps aren't used, make sure the hose has not expanded and/or hardened where it slips over the fitting, allowing it to leak.

Vacuum hoses

4 It's quite common for vacuum hoses, especially those in the emissions system, to be color coded or identified by colored stripes molded into them. Various systems require hoses with different wall thicknesses, collapse resistance and temperature resistance. When replacing hoses, be sure the new ones are made of the same material.

5 Often the only effective way to check a hose is to remove it completely from the vehicle. If more than one hose is removed, be sure to label the hoses and fittings to ensure correct installation.

6 When checking vacuum hoses, be sure to include any plastic T-fittings in the check. Inspect the fittings for cracks and the hose where it fits over the fitting for distortion, which could cause leakage.

7 A small piece of vacuum hose (1/4-inch inside diameter) can be used as a stethoscope to detect vacuum leaks. Hold one end of the hose to your ear and probe around vacuum hoses and fittings, listening for the "hissing" sound characteristic of a vacuum leak. **Warning:** *When probing with the vacuum hose stethoscope, be very careful not to come into contact with moving engine components such as the drivebelts, cooling fan, etc.*

Fuel hose

Warning: *There are certain precautions which must be taken when inspecting or servicing fuel system components. Work in a well ventilated area and don't allow open flames (cigarettes, appliance pilot lights, etc.) or bare light bulbs near the work area. Mop up any spills immediately and don't store fuel soaked rags where they could ignite. On vehicles equipped with fuel injection, the fuel system is under pressure, so if any fuel lines are to be disconnected, the pressure in the system must be relieved first (see Chapter 4 for more information).*

8 Check all rubber fuel lines for deterioration and chafing. Check carefully for cracks in areas where the hose bends and where it's attached to fittings.

9 High quality fuel line, usually identified by the word *Fluroelastomer* printed on the hose, should be used for fuel line replacement. **Warning:** *Never, under any circumstances, use unreinforced vacuum line, clear plastic tubing or water hose for fuel lines!*

10 Spring-type clamps are commonly used on fuel lines. They often lose their tension over a period of time, and can be "sprung" during removal. Replace all spring-type clamps with screw clamps whenever a hose is replaced.

Metal lines

11 Sections of metal line are often used for fuel line between the fuel pump and carburetor or fuel injection unit. Check carefully to be sure the line has not been bent or crimped and look for cracks.

12 If a section of metal fuel line must be replaced, only seamless steel tubing should be used, since copper and aluminum tubing don't have the strength necessary to withstand normal engine vibration.

13 Check the metal brake lines where they enter the master cylinder and brake proportioning unit (if used) for cracks in the lines and loose fittings. Any sign of brake fluid leakage means an immediate thorough inspection of the brake system should be done.

12 Brake pedal check and adjustment

Refer to illustration 12.1

1 Brake pedal height is the distance the pedal sits away from the floor **(see illustration)**. The distance should be as specified (see the

1

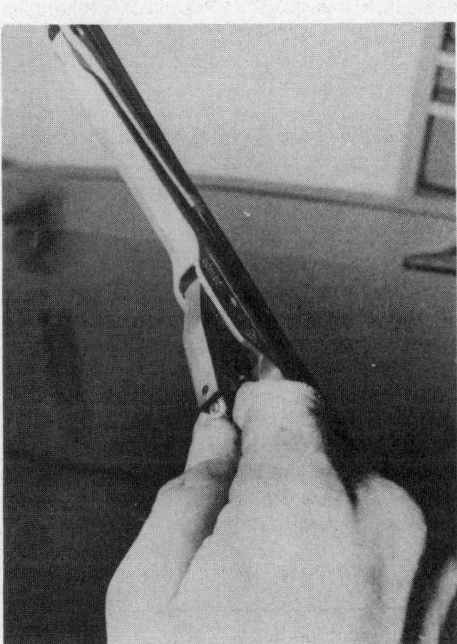

10.1 The wiper blade is removed by depressing the release tab and pulling it off

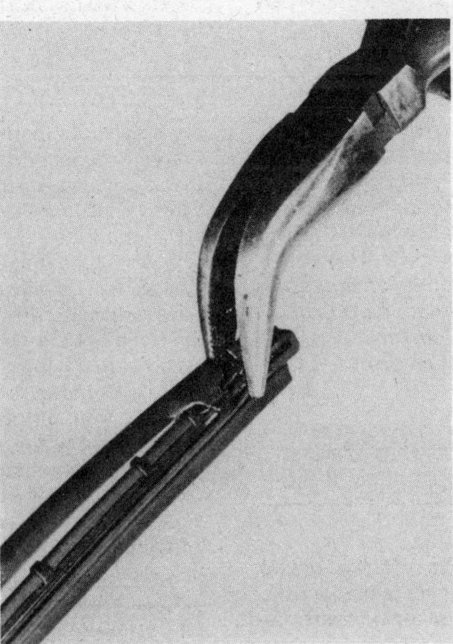

10.2 If necessary, the wiper blade element can be removed by squeezing the retaining clips with pliers

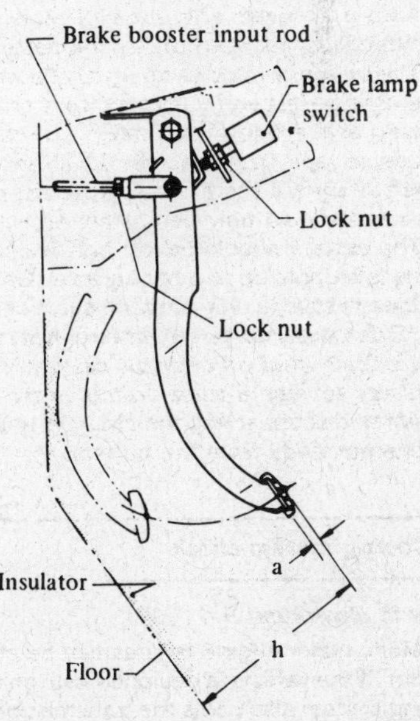

12.1 The brake pedal should be periodically inspected for correct height (h) and free play (a)

Specifications). If the pedal height is not within the specified range, loosen the locknut on the brake light switch located in the bracket to the rear of the brake pedal and turn the switch in or out until the pedal height is correct. Retighten the locknut.
2 The free play is the pedal slack, or the distance the pedal can be depressed before it begins to have any effect on the brakes (distance a in illustration 12.1). It should be as specified. If it isn't, loosen the locknut on the brake booster input rod, to which the brake pedal is attached. Turn the input rod until the free play is correct, then retighten the locknut.

13 Engine oil and filter change

Refer to illustrations 13.3, 13.9, 13.11, 13.14 and 13.18

1 Frequent oil changes are the most important preventive maintenance procedures that can be done by the home mechanic. As engine oil ages, it becomes diluted and contaminated, which leads to premature engine wear.
2 Although some sources recommend oil filter changes every other oil change, the minimal cost of an oil filter and the fact that it's easy to install dictate that a new filter be used every time the oil is changed.
3 Gather all necessary tools and materials before beginning this procedure **(see illustration)**.
4 You should have plenty of clean rags and newspapers handy to mop up any spills. Access to the underside of the vehicle is greatly improved if the vehicle can be lifted on a hoist, driven onto ramps or supported by jackstands. **Warning:** *Do not work under a vehicle which is supported only by a bumper, hydraulic or scissors-type jack!*
5 If this is your first oil change, get under the vehicle and familiarize yourself with the locations of the oil drain plug and the oil filter. The engine and exhaust components will be warm during the actual work, so note how they're situated to avoid touching them when working under the vehicle.
6 Warm the engine to normal operating temperature. If the new oil or any tools are needed, use the warm-up time to obtain everything necessary for the job. The correct oil for your application can be found in *Recommended lubricants and fluids* at the beginning of this Chapter.
7 With the engine oil warm (warm engine oil will drain better and more built-up sludge will be removed with it), raise and support the vehicle. Make sure it's safely supported!
8 Move all necessary tools, rags and newspapers under the vehicle. Set the drain pan under the drain plug. Keep in mind that the oil will initially flow from the pan with some force; position the pan accordingly.
9 Being careful not to touch any of the hot exhaust components, use a wrench to remove the drain plug near the bottom of the oil pan **(see illustration)**. Depending on how hot the oil is, you may want to wear gloves while unscrewing the plug the final few turns.

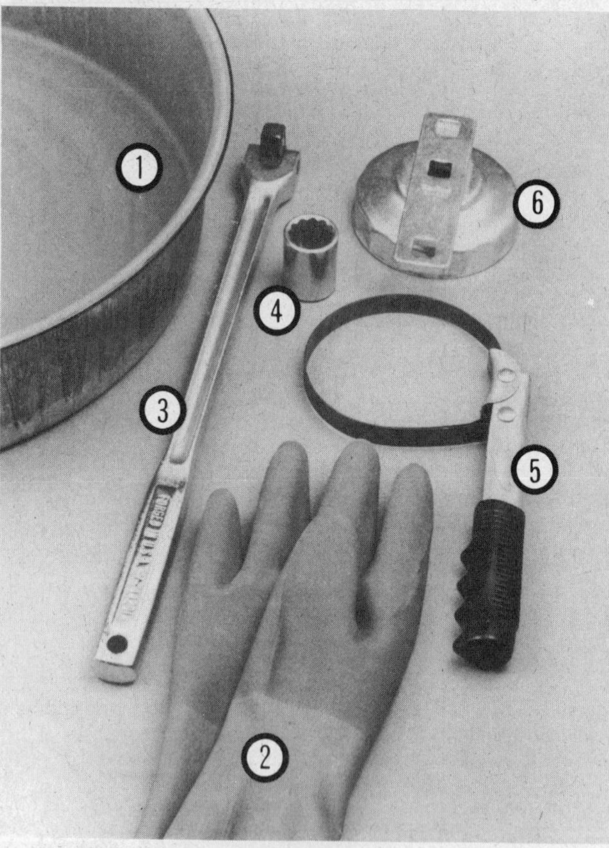

13.3 These tools are required when changing the engine oil and filter

1 **Drain pan** — *It should be fairly shallow in depth, but wide in order to prevent spills*
2 **Rubber gloves** — *When removing the drain plug and filter it is inevitable that you will get oil on your hands (the gloves will prevent burns)*
3 **Breaker bar** — *Sometimes the oil drain plug is pretty tight and a long breaker bar is needed to loosen it*
4 **Socket** — *To be used with the breaker bar or a ratchet (must be the correct size to fit the drain plug)*
5 **Filter wrench** — *This is a metal band-type wrench, which requires clearance around the filter to be effective*
6 **Filter wrench** — *This type fits on the bottom of the filter and can be turned with a ratchet or breaker bar (different size wrenches are available for different types of filters)*

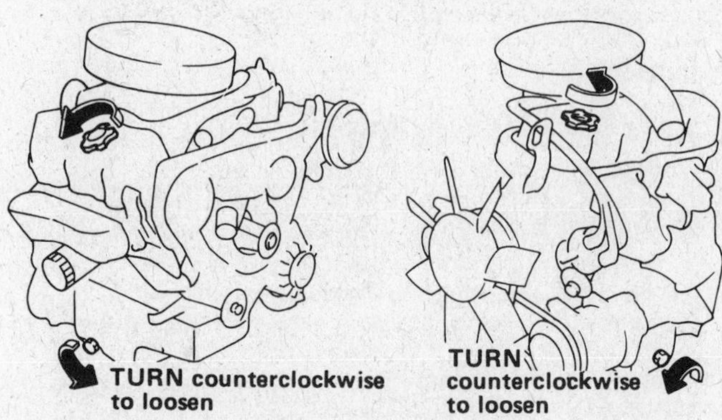

13.9 Engine oil drain plug locations (left — V6 engine; right — four-cylinder engines)

13.11 Be sure to clean the drain plug to remove any metal particles clinging to it!

10 Allow the old oil to drain into the pan. It may be necessary to move the pan as the oil flow slows to a trickle.
11 After all the oil has drained, wipe off the drain plug with a clean rag. Small metal particles may cling to the plug and would immediately contaminate the new oil **(see illustration)**.
12 Clean the area around the drain plug opening and reinstall the plug. Tighten the plug securely with the wrench. If a torque wrench is available, use it to tighten the plug.
13 Move the drain pan into position under the oil filter.
14 Use the filter wrench to loosen the oil filter **(see illustration)**. Chain or metal band filter wrenches may distort the filter canister, but it doesn't matter since the filter will be discarded anyway.
15 Completely unscrew the old filter. Be careful; it's full of oil. Empty the oil inside the filter into the drain pan.
16 Compare the old filter with the new one to make sure they're the same type.
17 Use a clean rag to remove all oil, dirt and sludge from the area where the oil filter mounts to the engine. Check the old filter to make sure the rubber gasket isn't stuck to the engine. If the gasket is stuck to the engine, remove it.
18 Apply a light coat of clean oil to the rubber gasket on the new oil filter **(see illustration)**.
19 Attach the new filter to the engine, following the tightening directions printed on the filter canister or packing box. Most filter manufacturers recommend against using a filter wrench due to the possibility of overtightening and damage to the seal.
20 Remove all tools, rags, etc. from under the vehicle, being careful not to spill the oil in the drain pan, then lower the vehicle.
21 Move to the engine compartment and locate the oil filler cap.
22 If an oil can spout is used, push the spout into the top of the oil can and pour the fresh oil through the filler opening. A funnel may also be used.
23 Pour three or four quarts of fresh oil into the engine. Wait a few minutes to allow the oil to drain into the pan, then check the level on the oil dipstick (see Section 4 if necessary). If the oil level is above the L mark, start the engine and allow the new oil to circulate.
24 Run the engine for only about a minute and then shut it off. Immediately look under the vehicle and check for leaks at the oil pan drain plug and around the oil filter. If either one is leaking, tighten it a little more.
25 With the new oil circulated and the filter now completely full, recheck the level on the dipstick and add more oil as necessary.
26 During the first few trips after an oil change, make it a point to check frequently for leaks and correct oil level.
27 The old oil drained from the engine cannot be reused in its present state and should be disposed of. Oil reclamation centers, auto repair shops and gas stations will normally accept the oil, which can be refined and used again. After the oil has cooled it can be poured into a container (capped plastic jugs or bottles, milk cartons, etc.) for transport to a disposal site.

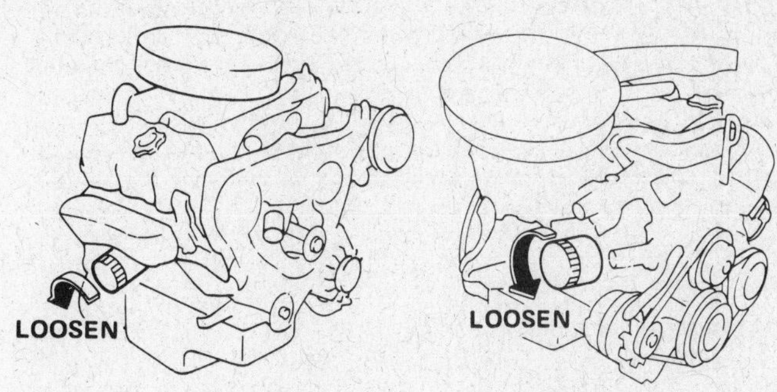

13.14 Oil filter locations (left — V6 engine; right — four-cylinder engines)

13.18 Lubricate the oil filter gasket with clean engine oil before installing the filter on the engine

14 Valve clearance adjustment (four-cylinder engines only)

1 Although the valves can be adjusted with the engine cold, it's better to adjust them with the engine hot. If they're adjusted cold they should be rechecked once the engine has warmed up and readjusted if necessary to conform to the hot engine specifications.

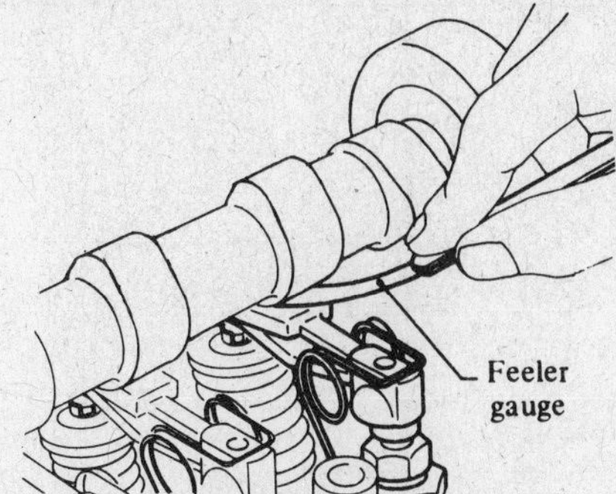

14.5 On 1980 models, measure the valve clearance by inserting a feeler gauge between the heel of the cam lobe and the rocker arm

2 Start the engine and allow it to reach normal operating temperature, then turn the engine off.
3 Remove the rocker arm cover as described in Chapter 2.

1980 models

Refer to illustrations 14.5, 14.9 and 14.11

4 Rotate the crankshaft until the number one (front) camshaft lobe points straight up. This can be done with a ratchet and socket on the crankshaft pulley bolt at the front of the engine — turn the crankshaft *clockwise*. Removing the spark plugs makes this easier. Another method is to use the ignition key to operate the starter in short bursts. If this is done, the ignition coil wire should be disconnected from the distributor cap and grounded on the engine to prevent the engine from starting.
5 The valve clearance is measured by inserting the specified size feeler gauge between the heel of the cam lobe and the rocker arm **(see illustration)**. You should feel a slight amount of drag when the feeler gauge is moved back and forth.
6 If the gap is too large or too small, loosen the rocker pivot locknut and turn the rocker pivot to obtain the correct gap.
7 Once the gap has been set, hold the rocker pivot in position with one wrench and retighten the locknut with another.
8 Recheck the valve clearance. Sometimes it'll change slightly when the pivot locknut is tightened. If so, readjust it until it's correct.

9 With the camshaft in this position the number 1, 3, 5, and 7 valves can be adjusted using the procedure just described **(see illustration)**.
10 Rotate the camshaft until the number one cam lobe is pointing straight down. In this position the number 2, 4, 6 and 8 valves can be adjusted in the same manner.
11 After all valves have been adjusted, check the torque on the rocker pivot locknuts **(see illustration)**. A special adapter, available from import auto parts stores, is required for this check.
12 After all valves have been adjusted, reinstall the rocker arm cover.

1981 and 1982 models

Refer to illustrations 14.14 and 14.18

13 Rotate the crankshaft until the number one (front) camshaft lobe points straight down. This can be done with a ratchet and socket on the crankshaft bolt at the front of the engine. Turn the crankshaft *clockwise*. Removing the spark plugs makes this easier. Another method is to use the ignition key to operate the starter in short bursts. If this is done, the ignition coil wire should be disconnected from the distributor cap and grounded on the engine to prevent the engine from starting.
14 The valve clearance is measured by inserting the specified size feeler gauge between the end of the valve stem and the adjusting screw **(see illustration)**. You should feel a slight amount of drag when the feeler gauge is moved back and forth.
15 If the gap is too large or too small, loosen the locknut and turn the adjusting screw to obtain the correct gap.
16 Once the gap has been set, hold the screw in position with a screw-driver and retighten the locknut.
17 Recheck the valve clearance. Sometimes it'll change slightly when the locknut is tightened. If so, readjust it until it's correct.
18 With the camshaft in this position, the number 1, 4, 6 and 7 valves can be adjusted using the procedure just described **(see illustration)**.
19 Rotate the camshaft until the number one cam lobe is pointing straight up. In this position the number 2, 3, 5 and 8 valves can be adjusted in the same manner.
20 After all valves have been adjusted, reinstall the rocker arm cover.

1983 and later models

Refer to illustration 14.22

21 Run the engine until normal operating temperature is reached. Remove the rocker arm cover from the engine as described in Chapter 2.
22 Position the number one piston at top dead center (TDC) on the

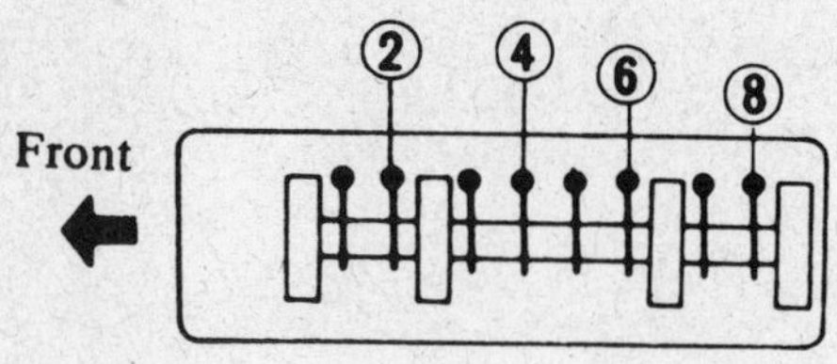

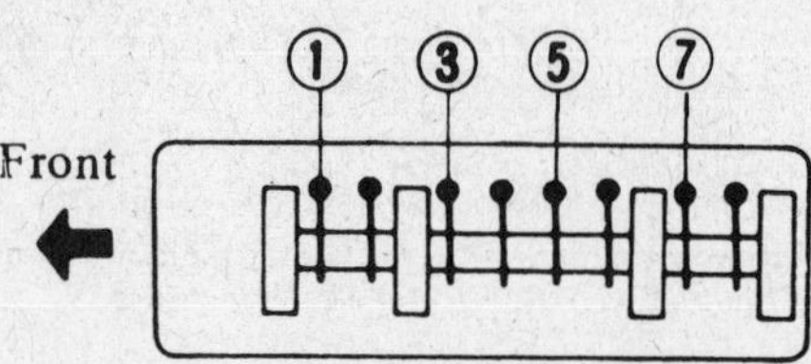

14.9 With the number one cam lobe pointing UP, the valves in the upper illustration (1, 3, 5 and 7) can be adjusted, while the valves in the lower illustration (2, 4, 6 and 8) can be adjusted when the number one cam lobe is pointing DOWN (1980 models only)

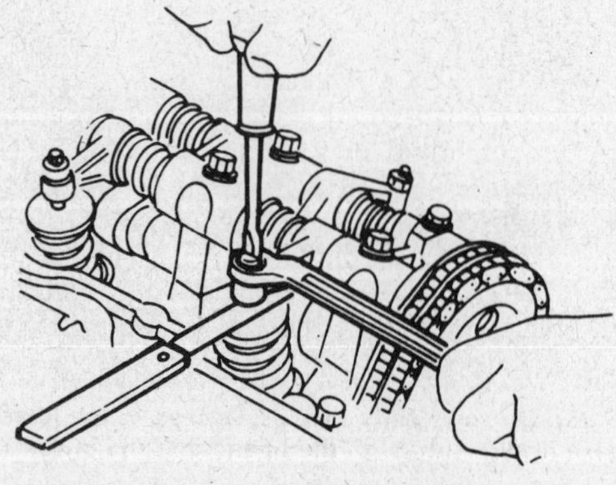

14.14 on 1981 and 1982 models, valve clearance is adjusted by inserting a feeler gauge between the adjusting screw and valve stem and turning the screw

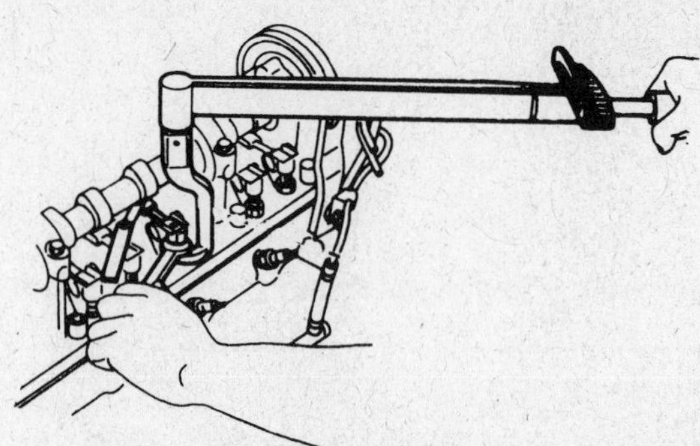

14.11 Correct tightening of the rocker arm pivot locknut on 1980 models requires a special adaptor (available through dealer parts departments and import auto parts stores)

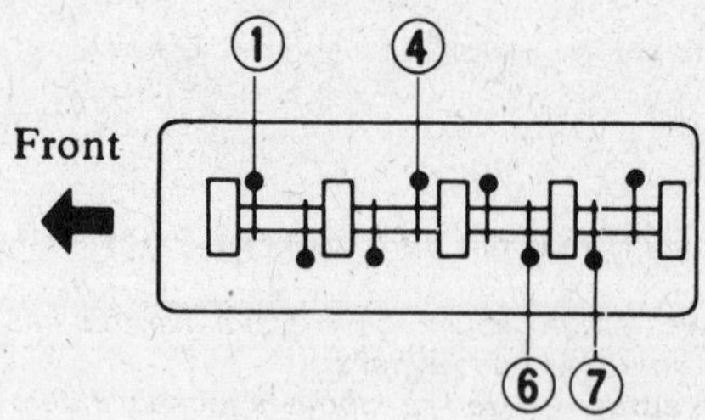

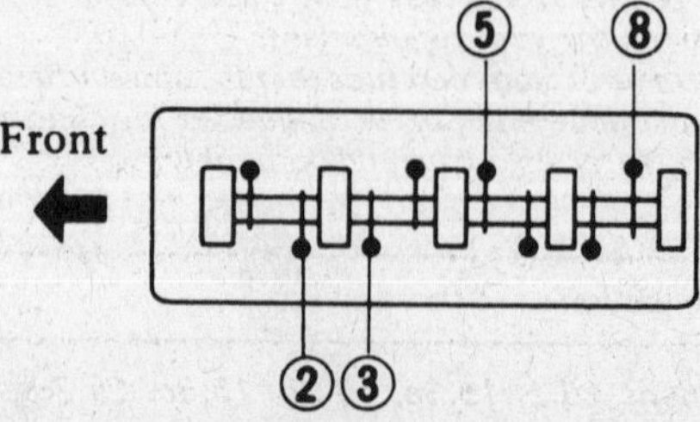

14.18 When the number one cam lobe is pointing DOWN, the valves shown in the top illustration (1, 4, 6 and 7) can be adjusted; the valves shown in the lower illustration (2, 3, 5 and 8) can be adjusted when the number one cam lobe is pointing UP (1981 and 1982 models)

compression stroke (see Chapter 2). The valve clearances for valves 1, 2, 4 and 6 can now be checked **(see illustration)**.

23 Insert a 0.012-inch (0.30 mm) feeler gauge between the valve stem and the adjusting screw. If the feeler gauge fits between the stem and screw with a slight amount of drag, the clearance is correct.

24 If adjustment is required, loosen the adjusting screw locknut and carefully loosen or tighten the adjusting screw until you feel a slight drag on the feeler gauge as it's withdrawn from between the valve stem and screw.

25 Hold the adjusting screw and tighten the locknut securely. Recheck the clearance to make sure it didn't change.

26 Turn the crankshaft one complete revolution (360°) clockwise so the number four piston is at TDC on the compression stroke. Verify this by checking where the distributor rotor is pointing. Adjust the number 3, 5, 7 and 8 valves **(see illustration 14.22)**.

27 Install the rocker arm cover.

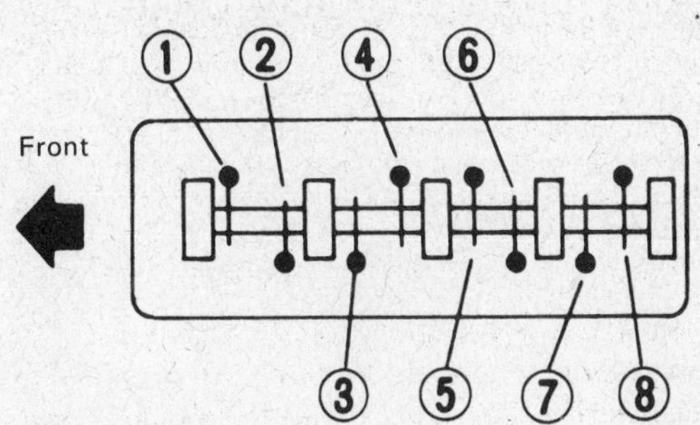

14.22 On 1983 and later models use this diagram to locate the valves

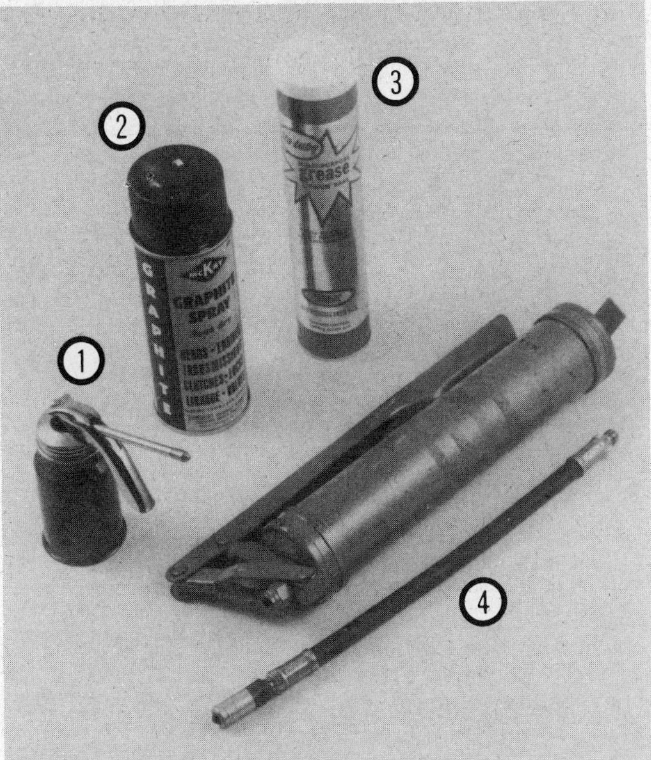

15.1 Materials required for chassis and body lubrication

1 ***Engine oil*** *— Light engine oil in a can like this can be used for door and hood hinges*
2 ***Graphite spray*** *— Used to lubricate lock cylinders*
3 ***Grease*** *— Grease, in a variety of types and weights, is available for use in a grease gun. Check the Specifications for your requirements*
4 ***Grease gun*** *— A common grease gun, shown here with a detachable hose and nozzle, is needed for chassis lubrication. After use, clean it thoroughly!*

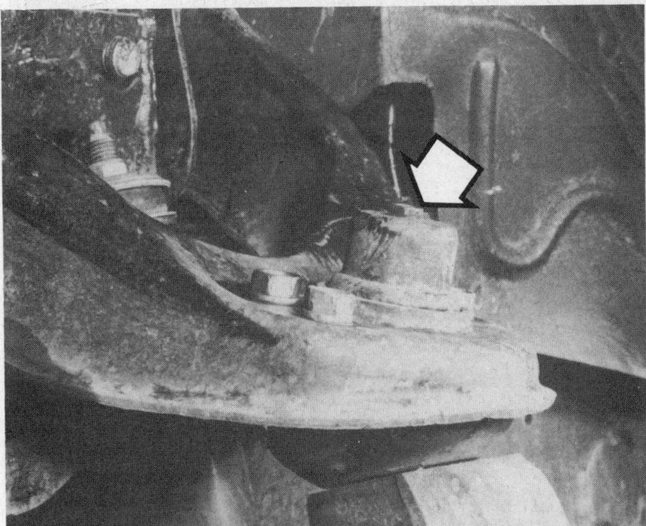

15.3a The upper suspension balljoints usually have plugs installed in the grease fitting holes

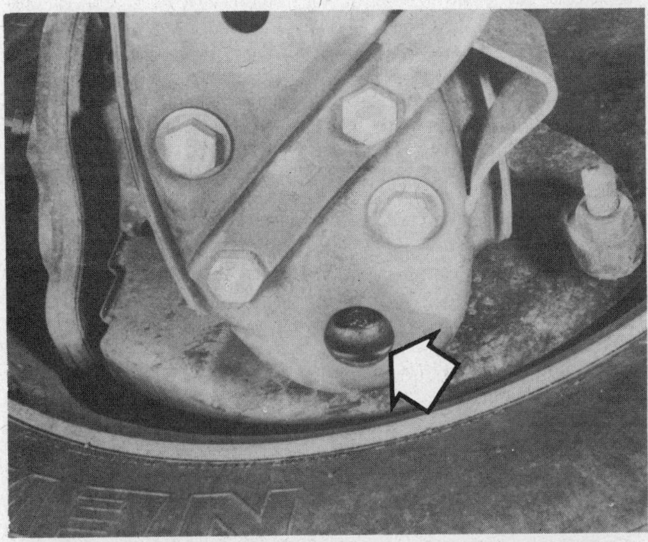

15.3b On some early models, access to the lower balljoint grease fitting is through the opening in the lower link (arrow)

15 Chassis lubrication

Refer to illustrations 15.1, 15.3a, 15.3b, 15.3c, 15.3d and 15.3e

1 A grease gun and cartridge filled with the recommended grease are the only items required for chassis lubrication other than some clean rags and equipment needed to raise and support the vehicle safely **(see illustration)**.

2 There are several points on the vehicle's suspension, steering and drivetrain components that must be periodically lubricated with lithium based multi-purpose grease. Included are the upper and lower suspension balljoints, the swivel joints on the steering linkage and, on 4WD models, the front and rear driveshafts.

3 The grease point for each upper suspension balljoint is on top of the balljoint **(see illustration)** and is accessible by removing the front wheel and tire. Access to the lower suspension balljoint grease point is through the hole in the bottom of the lower link **(see illustration)**. The steering linkage swivel joints are designed to be lubricated **(see**

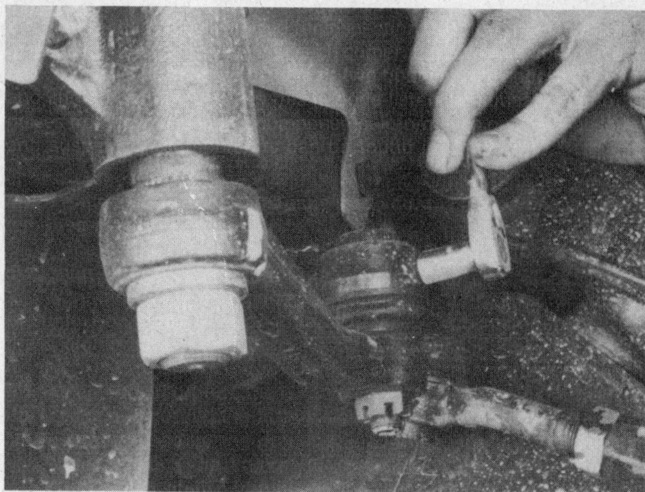

15.3c Each suspension and steering joint is equipped with a plug — a small socket or wrench can be used to remove the plugs so grease fittings can be installed

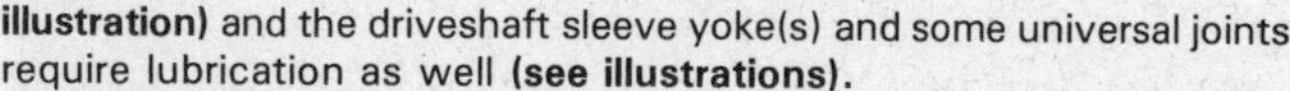

illustration) and the driveshaft sleeve yoke(s) and some universal joints require lubrication as well **(see illustrations).**

4 For easier access under the vehicle, raise it with a jack and place jackstands under the frame. Make sure the vehicle is safely supported on the stands!

5 If grease fittings aren't already installed, the plugs will have to be removed and fittings screwed into place.

6 Force a little of the grease out of the gun nozzle to remove any dirt, then wipe it clean with a rag.

7 Wipe the grease fitting and push the nozzle firmly over it. Squeeze the trigger on the grease gun to force grease into the component. Both the balljoints and swivel joints should be lubricated until the rubber reservoir is firm to the touch. Don't pump too much grease into the fittings or it could rupture the reservoir. If the grease seeps out around the grease gun nozzle, the fitting is clogged or the nozzle isn't seated all the way. Resecure the gun nozzle to the fitting and try again. If necessary, replace the fitting.

8 Wipe excess grease from the components and the grease fittings.

9 While you're under the vehicle, clean and lubricate the parking brake cable along with the cable guides and levers. This can be done by smearing some of the chassis grease onto the cable and its related parts with your fingers.

10 Lower the vehicle to the ground for the remaining body lubrication process.

11 Open the hood and rear gate and smear a little chassis grease on the latch mechanisms. Have an assistant pull the release knob from inside the vehicle as you lubricate the cable at the latch.

12 Lubricate all the hinges (door, hood, hatch) with a few drops of light engine oil to keep them in proper working order.

13 The key lock cylinders can be lubricated with spray-on graphite, which is available at auto parts stores.

16 Suspension and steering check

1 Whenever the front of the vehicle is raised for any reason, it's a good idea to visually check the suspension and steering components for wear.

2 Indications of steering or suspension problems include excessive play in the steering wheel before the front wheels react, excessive swaying around corners or body movement over rough roads and binding at some point as the steering wheel is turned.

3 Before the vehicle is raised for inspection, test the shock absorbers by pushing down agressively at each corner. If the vehicle doesn't come back to a level position within one or two bounces, the shocks are worn and should be replaced. As this is done listen for squeaks and other noises from the suspension components. Information on shock absorber and suspension components can be found in Chapter 11.

15.3d Some driveshafts have a grease fitting on the sleeve yoke (arrow)

15.3e Some universal joints have a grease fitting hole — use a screwdriver to remove the plug (arrow)

4 Raise the front end of the vehicle and support it on jackstands. Make sure it's safely supported!

5 Crawl under the vehicle and check for loose bolts, broken or disconnected parts and deteriorated rubber bushings on all suspension and steering components. Look for grease or fluid leaking from around the steering gear assembly and shock absorbers. If equipped, check the power steering hoses and connections for leaks.

6 The balljoint seals should be checked at this time. This includes not only the upper and lower suspension balljoints, but those connecting the steering linkage parts as well. After cleaning around the balljoints, inspect the seals for cracks and damage.

7 Grip the top and bottom of each wheel and try to move it in and out. It won't take a lot of effort to be able to feel any play in the wheel bearings. If the play is noticeable it would be a good idea to adjust it right away or it could confuse further inspections.

8 Grip each side of the wheel and try rocking it laterally. Steady pressure will, of course, turn the steering, but back and forth pressure will reveal a loose steering joint. If some play is felt it would be easier to get assistance from someone so while one person rocks the wheel from side to side, the other can look at the joints, bushings and connections in the steering linkage. On models equipped with a steering gearbox there are eight places where the play may occur. The two outer balljoints on the tie-rods are the most likely, followed by the two inner joints on the same rods, where they join to the center rod. Any play in them means replacement of the tie-rod end. Next are two swivel bushings, one at each end of the center gear rod. Finally, check the steering gear arm balljoint and the one on the idler arm which supports

17.9 Damage to the front driveaxle boots (arrows) can quickly lead to failure of the constant velocity joints (4WD models only)

the center rod on the side opposite the steering box. This unit is bolted to the side of the frame member and any play calls for replacement of the bushings.

9 To check the steering box, first make sure the bolts holding the steering box to the frame are tight. Then get another person to help examine the mechanism. One should look at, or hold onto, the arm at the bottom of the steering box while the other turns the steering wheel a little from side to side. The amount of lost motion between the steering wheel and the gear arm indicates the degree of wear in the steering box mechanism. This check should be carried out with the wheels first in the straight ahead position and then at nearly full lock on each side. If the play only occurs noticeably in the straight ahead position then the wear is most likely in the worm and/or nut. If it occurs at all positions, then the wear is probably in the sector shaft bearing. Oil leaks from the unit are another indication of such wear. In either case the steering box will need removal for closer examination and repair.

10 Moving to the vehicle interior, check the play in the steering wheel by turning it slowly in both directions until the wheels can just be felt turning. The steering wheel free play should be less than 1-3/8 inch (35 mm). Excessive play is another indication of wear in the steering gear or linkage.

11 Following the inspection of the front, a similar inspection should be made of the rear suspension components, again checking for loose bolts, damaged or disconnected parts and deteriorated rubber bushings.

17 Driveshaft check

Refer to illustration 17.9

1 Raise the rear of the vehicle and support it securely on jackstands. Block the front wheels. The transmission should be in Neutral.

2 Crawl under the vehicle and visually inspect the driveshaft. Look for dents and cracks in the tube. If any are found, the driveshaft must be replaced (Chapter 8).

3 Check for oil leakage at the front and rear of the driveshaft. Leakage where the driveshaft enters the transmission indicates a defective rear transmission seal. Leakage where the driveshaft enters the differential indicates a defective pinion seal. For these repair operations refer to Chapters 7 and 8 respectively.

4 While still under the vehicle, have an assistant turn the rear wheel so the driveshaft will rotate. As it does, check for binding, noise and excessive play in the U-joints. On Long Bed and King Cab models, listen for noise from the center bearing, indicating it's worn or damaged. Refer to Chapter 8 to correct any problems.

5 The universal joints can also be checked with the driveshaft motionless, by gripping both sides of the joint and attempting to twist it. Any movement at all in the joint is a sign of considerable wear. Lifting up on the shaft will also indicate movement in the universal joints.

6 Check the driveshaft mounting bolts at both ends to make sure they're tight.

7 On 4WD models, the above driveshaft checks should be repeated on all driveshafts. In addition check for grease leakage around the sleeve yoke, indicating failure of the yoke seal.

8 Check for leakage where the driveshafts connect to the transfer case.

9 At the same time, check for looseness in the joints of the front driveaxles. Also check the CV joint boots for damage, leaks and tight clamps **(see illustration)**. Oil leakage at the differential junction indicates a defective side oil seal. Leakage at the wheel side indicates a defective front hub seal. For servicing of all 4WD system components, refer to Chapter 9.

18 Exhaust system check

1 With the engine cold (at least three hours after the vehicle has been driven), check the complete exhaust system from the manifold to the end of the tailpipe. Be careful around the catalytic converter, which may be hot even after three hours. The inspection should be done with the vehicle on a hoist to permit unrestricted access. If a hoist isn't available, raise the vehicle and support it securely on jackstands.

2 Check the exhaust pipes and connections for signs of leakage and/or corrosion indicating a potential failure. Make sure that all brackets and hangers are in good condition and tight.

3 Inspect the underside of the body for holes, corrosion, open seams, etc. which may allow exhaust gases to enter the passenger compartment. Seal all body openings with silicone sealant or body putty.

4 Rattles and other noises can often be traced to the exhaust system, especially the hangers, mounts and heat shields. Try to move the pipes, mufflers and catalytic converter. If the components can come in contact with the body or suspension parts, secure the exhaust system with new brackets and hangers.

19 Clutch pedal height and free play check and adjustment

Refer to illustration 19.2

1 On vehicles equipped with a manual transmission, the clutch pedal height and free play must be correctly adjusted.

2 The height of the clutch pedal is the distance the pedal sits off the floor **(see illustration)**. The distance should be as specified. If the

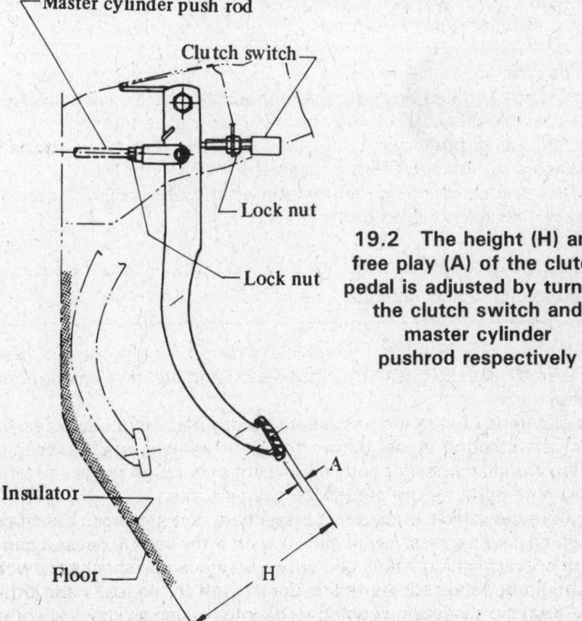

19.2 The height (H) and free play (A) of the clutch pedal is adjusted by turning the clutch switch and master cylinder pushrod respectively

1

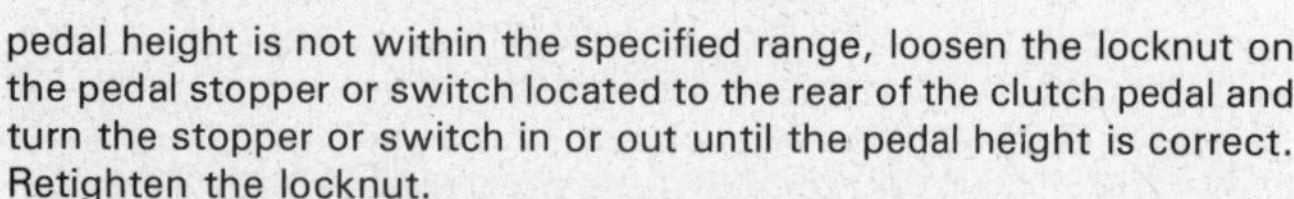
20.1 The manual transmission check/fill and drain plugs are accessible from under the vehicle — a 1/2-inch drive extension will fit into the square hole in the plug

pedal height is not within the specified range, loosen the locknut on the pedal stopper or switch located to the rear of the clutch pedal and turn the stopper or switch in or out until the pedal height is correct. Retighten the locknut.

3 The free play is the pedal slack, or the distance the pedal can be depressed before it begins to have any effect on the clutch (A in illustration 19.2). The distance should be as specified. If it isn't, loosen the locknut on the clutch master cylinder pushrod, turn the pushrod until the free play is correct, then retighten the locknut.

20 Manual transmission oil level check

Refer to illustration 20.1

1 Manual transmissions don't have a dipstick. The oil level is checked by removing a plug from the side of the transmission case **(see illustration)**. Locate the plug and use a rag to clean the plug and the area around it. If the vehicle is raised to gain access to the plug, be sure to support it safely on jackstands — DO NOT crawl under the vehicle when it's supported only by a jack!

2 With the engine and transmission cold, remove the plug. If lubricant immediately starts leaking out, thread the plug back into the transmission — the level is correct. If it doesn't, completely remove the plug and reach inside the hole with your little finger. The level should be even with the bottom of the plug hole.

3 If the transmission needs more lubricant, use a syringe or small pump to add it through the plug hole.

4 Thread the plug back into the transmission and tighten it securely. Drive the vehicle, then check for leaks around the plug.

21 Transfer case oil level check

Refer to illustration 21.1

1 The transfer case oil level is checked by removing a plug from the side of the case **(see illustration)**. Remove the rock guard, then locate the plug and use a rag to clean the plug and the area around it. If the vehicle is raised to gain access to the plug, be sure to support it safely on jackstands — DO NOT crawl under the vehicle when it's supported only by a jack!

2 With the engine and transfer case cold, remove the plug. If lubricant immediately starts leaking out, thread the plug back into the case — the level is correct. If it doesn't, completely remove the plug and reach inside the hole with your little finger. The level should be even with the bottom of the plug hole.

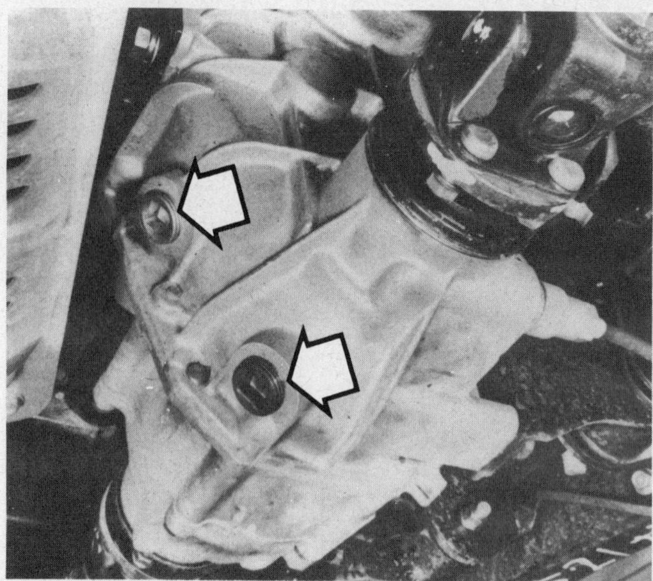

21.1 Remove the transfer case rock guard for access to the check/fill (upper) and drain (lower) plugs

3 If more oil is needed, use a syringe or small pump to add it through the opening.

4 Thread the plug back into the case and tighten it securely. Drive the vehicle, then check for leaks around the plug. Install the rock guard.

22 Differential oil level check

Refer to illustrations 22.2 and 22.3

1 The differential has a check/fill plug which must be removed to check the oil level. If the vehicle is raised to gain access to the plug, be sure to support it safely on jackstands — DO NOT crawl under the vehicle when it's supported only by a jack.

2 Remove the oil check/fill plug from the differential **(see illustrations)**.

22.2 Front differential check/fill and drain plug locations (arrows)

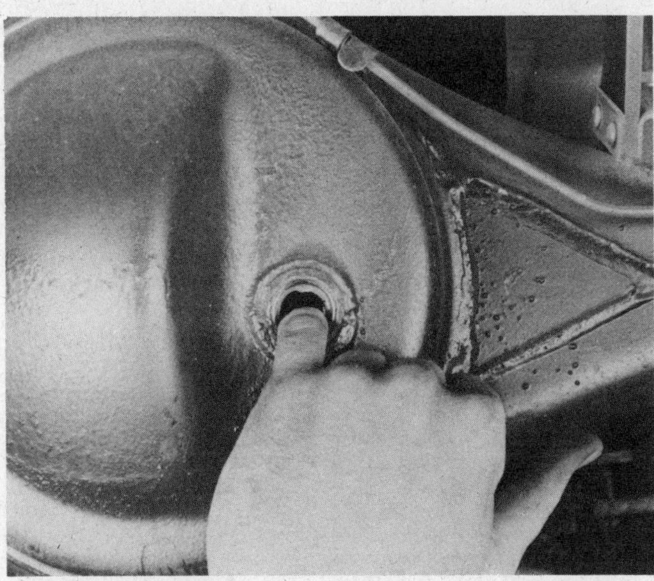

22.3 Use your finger as a dipstick to make sure the oil level is even with the bottom of the hole

3 The oil level should be at the bottom of the plug opening **(see illustration)**. If not, use a syringe to add the recommended lubricant until it just starts to run out of the opening. On some models a tag is located in the area of the plug and contains information regarding lubricant type, particularly on models equipped with a limited slip differential.
4 Install the plug and tighten it securely.

23 Tire rotation

Refer to illustration 23.2

1 The tires should be rotated at the specified intervals and whenever uneven wear is noticed.
2 Refer to the accompanying illustration for the preferred tire rotation pattern.
3 Refer to the information in *Jacking and towing* at the front of this manual for the proper procedures to follow when raising the vehicle and changing a tire. If the brakes are to be checked, don't apply the parking brake as stated. Make sure the tires are blocked to prevent the vehicle from rolling as it's raised.
4 Preferably, the entire vehicle should be raised at the same time. This can be done on a hoist or by jacking up each corner and then lowering the vehicle onto jackstands placed under the frame rails. Always use four jackstands and make sure the vehicle is safely supported.
5 After rotation, check and adjust the tire pressures as necessary and be sure to check the lug nut tightness.
6 For additional information on the wheels and tires, refer to Chapter 11.

24 Brake check

Refer to illustrations 24.6, 24.12, 24.14 and 24.16

Note: *For detailed photographs of the brake system, refer to Chapter 10.*

Warning: *Brake system dust contains asbestos, which is hazardous to your health. DO NOT blow it out with compressed air and DO NOT inhale it. DO NOT use gasoline or solvents to remove the dust. Use brake system cleaner or denatured alcohol only!*

1 In addition to the specified intervals, the brakes should be inspected every time the wheels are removed or whenever a defect is suspected.
2 To check the brakes, the vehicle must be raised and supported securely on jackstands.

Disc brakes

3 Disc brakes are used on the front wheels. Extensive rotor damage

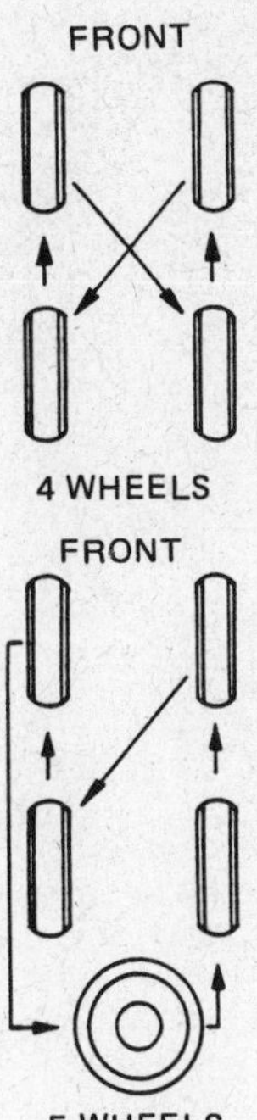

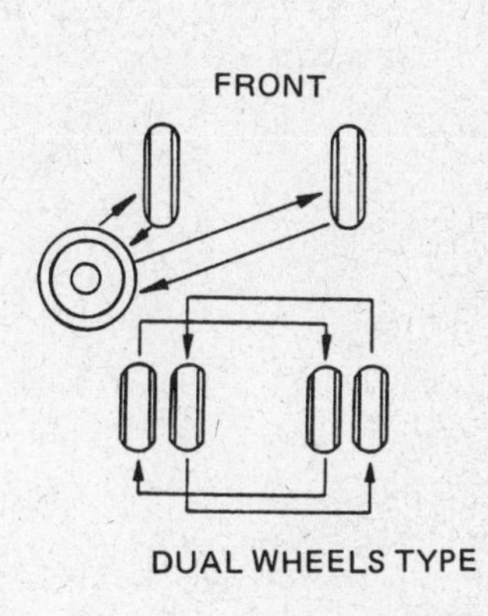

Do not include the T-type spare and small tire in the tire rotation.

23.2 Tire rotation diagram

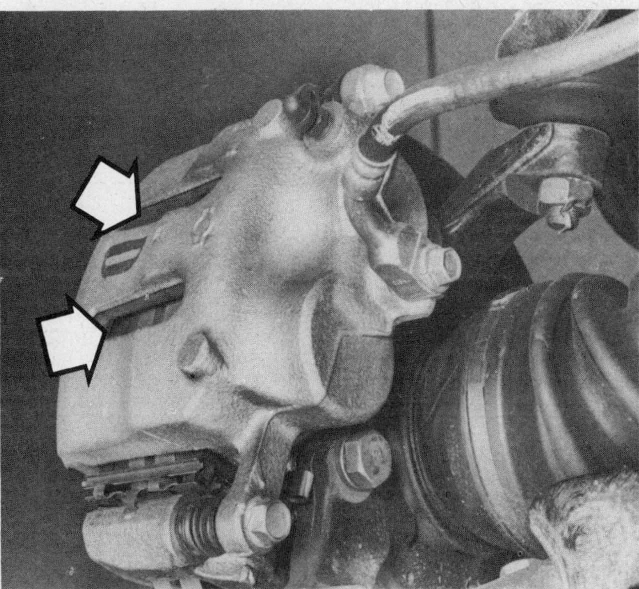

24.6 The disc brake pads are visible through the openings in the caliper (arrows)

can occur if the pads are allowed to wear beyond the specified limit.
4 Raise the vehicle and support it securely on jackstands, then remove all four wheels (see *Jacking and Towing* at the front of the manual if necessary).
5 The disc brake calipers, which contain the pads, are visible with the wheels removed. There's an outer pad and an inner pad in each caliper. All four pads should be inspected.
6 Each caliper has openings, which will allow you to inspect the pads **(see illustration)**. If the pad material has worn to about 5/64-inch or less, the pads should be replaced.
7 If you're unsure about the exact thickness of the remaining lining material, remove the pads for further inspection or replacement (refer to Chapter 10).
8 Before installing the wheels, check for leakage and/or damage

24.12 The rear brake drums can be removed by screwing bolts into the threaded holes in each drum

(cracks, splitting, etc.) around the brake hose connections. Replace the hose or fittings as necessary, referring to Chapter 10.
9 Check the condition of the rotor. Look for score marks, deep scratches and burned spots. If these conditions exist, the hub/rotor assembly should be removed for servicing (Section 42 – 2WD models only).

Drum brakes

10 On rear brakes, remove the drum by pulling it off the axle and brake assembly. If it's stuck, make sure the parking brake is released, then squirt penetrating oil into the joint between the hub and drum. Allow the oil to soak in and try to pull the drum off again.
11 If the drum still can't be pulled off, the brake shoes will have to be adjusted. This is done by first removing the dust cover from the backing plate. With the cover removed, use a small screwdriver to turn the star wheel, which will move the brake shoes away from the drum.
12 As a last resort, thread a bolt into each of the holes in the drum and tighten the bolts a little at a time to force the drum off **(see illustration)**.
13 With the drum removed, be careful not to touch any brake dust (see the **Warning** at the beginning of this Section).
14 Note the thickness of the lining material on both the front and rear brake shoes. If the material has worn away to within 1/16-inch of the recessed rivets or metal backing, the shoes should be replaced **(see illustration)**. The shoes should also be replaced if they're cracked, glazed (shiny surface) or contaminated with brake fluid.
15 Make sure that all the brake assembly springs are connected and in good condition.
16 Check the brake components for signs of fluid leakage. Carefully pry back the rubber cups on the wheel cylinders located at the top of the brake shoes with your finger **(see illustration)**. Any leakage is an indication that the wheel cylinders should be overhauled immediately (Chapter 10). Also check brake hoses and connections for leakage.
17 Wipe the inside of the drum with a clean rag and brake cleaner or denatured alcohol. Again, be careful not to breath the asbestos dust.
18 Check the inside of the drum for cracks, score marks, deep scratches and hard spots, which will appear as small discolorations. If imperfections cannot be removed with fine emery cloth, the drum must be taken to a machine shop equipped to turn the drums.
19 If after the inspection process all parts are in good working condition, reinstall the brake drum.
20 Install the wheels and lower the vehicle.

Parking brake

21 The parking brake operates from a hand lever and locks the rear brake system. The easiest, and perhaps most obvious method of periodically checking the operation of the parking brake assembly is to park the vehicle on a steep hill with the parking brake set and the transmission in Neutral. If the parking brake cannot prevent the vehicle from rolling within 6 to 10 clicks, it's in need of adjustment (see Chapter 10).

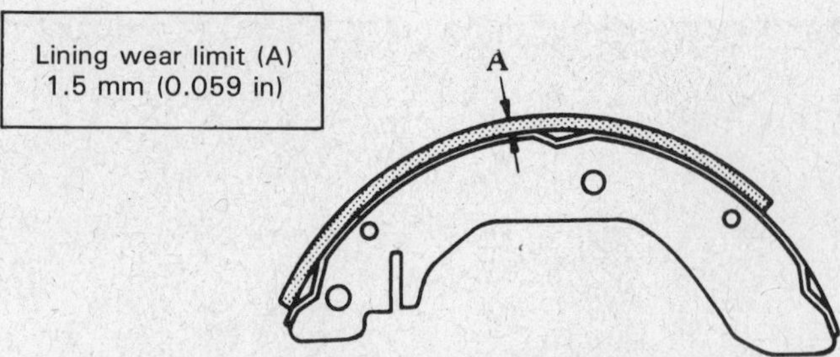

24.14 The rear brake shoe lining thickness (A) is measured from the outer surface of the lining to the metal shoe

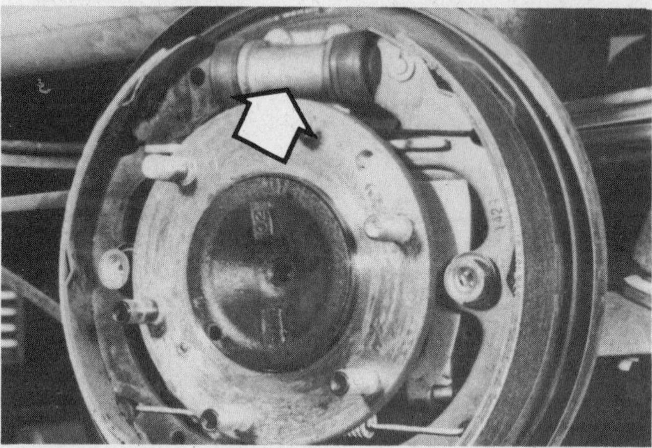

24.16 Whenever the brake drum is off, the wheel cylinder (arrow) should be checked for leaking brake fluid

25 Fuel system check

Warning: *There are certain precautions to take when inspecting or servicing the fuel system components. Work in a well ventilated area and don't allow open flames (cigarettes, appliance pilot lights, etc.) in the work area. Mop up spills immediately and don't store fuel soaked rags where they could ignite. On fuel injection equipped models the fuel system is under pressure. No components should be disconnected until the pressure has been relieved (see Chapter 4).*

1 On most models the main fuel tank is located at the rear of the vehicle.
2 The fuel system should be checked with the vehicle raised on a hoist so the components underneath the vehicle are readily visible and accessible.
3 If the smell of gasoline is noticed while driving or after the vehicle has been in the sun, the system should be thoroughly inspected immediately.
4 Remove the gas tank cap and check for damage, corrosion and an unbroken sealing imprint on the gasket. Replace the cap with a new one if necessary.
5 With the vehicle raised, check the gas tank and filler neck for punctures, cracks and other damage. The connection between the filler neck and the tank is especially critical. Sometimes a rubber filler neck will leak due to loose clamps or deteriorated rubber, problems a home mechanic can usually rectify. **Warning:** *Do not, under any circumstances, try to repair a fuel tank yourself (except rubber components). A welding torch or any open flame can easily cause the fuel vapors to explode if the proper precautions are not taken!*
6 Carefully check all rubber hoses and metal lines leading away from the fuel tank. Look for loose connections, deteriorated hoses, crimped lines and other damage. Follow the lines to the front of the vehicle, carefully inspecting them all the way. Repair or replace damaged sections as necessary.
7 If a fuel odor is still evident after the inspection, refer to Chapter 6 and check the EEC system.

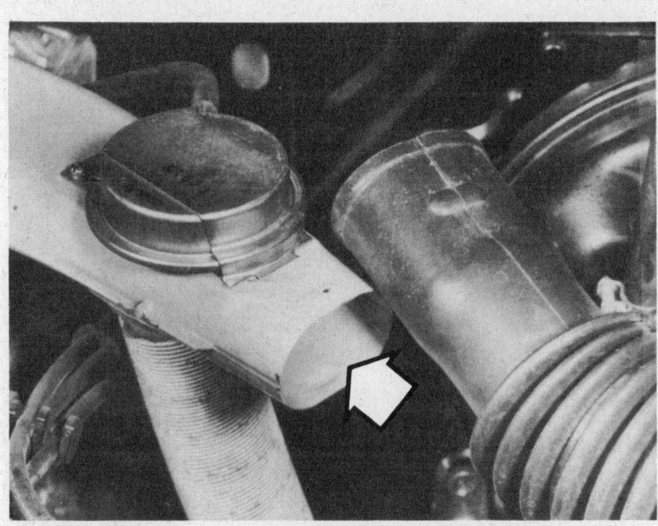

26.4 Remove the flexible air duct from the air cleaner so you can look directly into the end of the snorkel at the air control valve

26 Thermostatic air cleaner check

Refer to illustrations 26.4 and 26.5

1 All models are equipped with a thermostatically controlled air cleaner, which draws air to the carburetor from different locations depending on engine temperature.

2 This is a simple visual check. However, if access is tight, a small mirror may have to be used.

3 Open the hood and find the air control valve on the air cleaner assembly. It's located inside the long snorkel portion of the metal air cleaner housing.

4 If there's a flexible air duct attached to the end of the snorkel, disconnect it so you can look through the end of the snorkel and see the air control valve inside **(see illustration)**. A mirror may be needed if you can't safely look directly into the end of the snorkel.

5 The check should be done when the engine and outside air are cold. Start the engine and watch the air control valve, which should move up and close off the snorkel air passage. With the valve closed, air can't enter through the end of the snorkel, but instead enters the air cleaner through the hot air duct attached to the exhaust manifold **(see illustration)**.

6 As the engine warms up to operating temperature, the valve should open to allow air through the snorkel end. Depending on outside air temperature, this may take 10 to 15 minutes. To speed up the check you can reconnect the snorkel air duct, drive the vehicle and then check

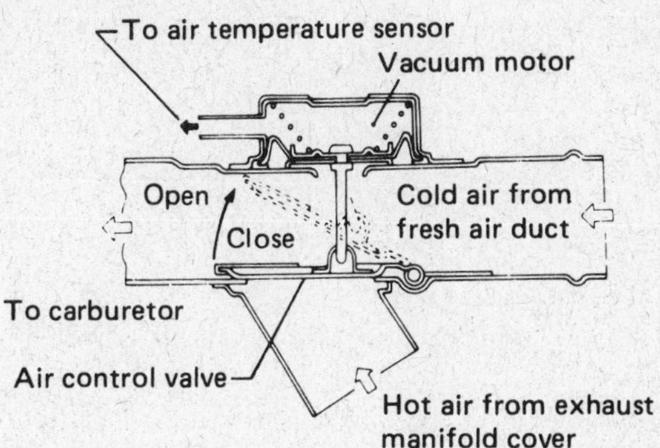

26.5 When the engine is cold, the air control valve should move to the up position and close off the snorkel opening – as the engine warms up, the valve will move back down to open the passage

the position of the valve.

7 If the thermostatic air cleaner isn't operating properly, see Chapter 6 for more information.

27 Drivebelt check, adjustment and replacement

Refer to illustrations 27.3, 27.4, 27.5a, 27.5b, 27.6a and 27.6b

1 The drivebelts, or V-belts as they are often called, are located at the front of the engine and play an important role in the overall operation of the engine and accessories. Due to their function and material make-up, the belts are prone to failure after a period of time and should be inspected and adjusted periodically to prevent major engine damage.

2 The number of belts used on a particular vehicle depends on the accessories installed. Drivebelts are used to turn the alternator, power steering pump, water pump and air conditioning compressor. Depending on the pulley arrangement, more than one of the components may be driven by a single belt.

3 With the engine off, locate the drivebelts at the front of the engine. Using your fingers (and a flashlight, if necessary), move along the belts checking for cracks and separation of the belt plies. Also check for fraying and glazing, which gives the belt a shiny appearance **(see illustration)**. Both sides of each belt should be inspected, which means you'll have to twist each belt to check the underside. Check the pulleys for nicks, cracks, distortion and corrosion.

4 The tension of each belt is checked by pushing on it at a distance halfway between the pulleys. Push firmly with your thumb and see how much the belt moves (deflects) **(see illustration)**. A rule of thumb is that if the distance from pulley center-to-pulley center is between 7 and 11 inches, the belt should deflect 1/4-inch. If the belt travels between pulleys spaced 12-to-16 inches apart, the belt should deflect 1/2-inch.

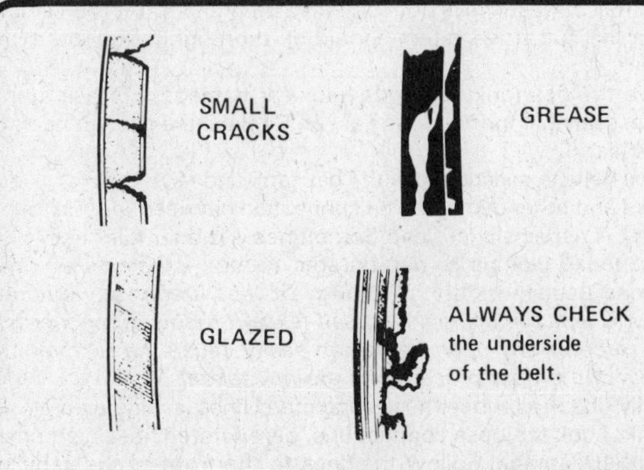

27.3 Here are some of the more common problems associated with drivebelts (check the belts very carefully to prevent an untimely breakdown)

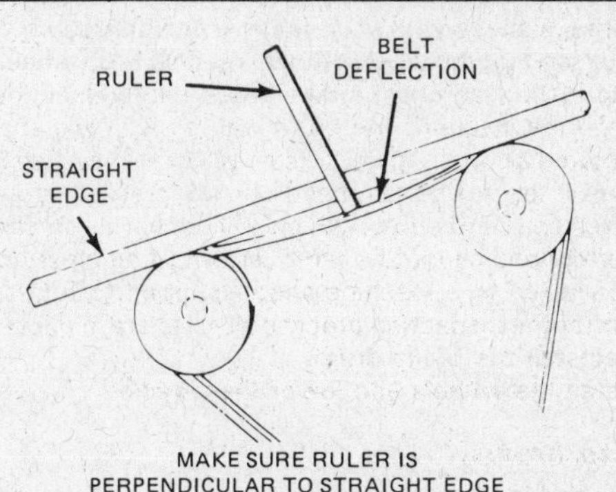

27.4 Measuring drivebelt deflection with a straightedge and ruler

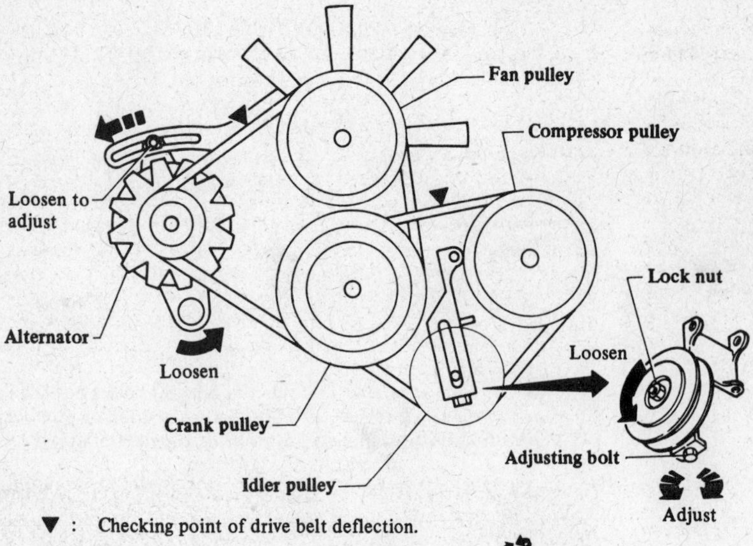

Fan pulley
Compressor pulley
Loosen to adjust
Alternator
Loosen
Crank pulley
Idler pulley
Lock nut
Loosen
Adjusting bolt
Adjust

▼ : Checking point of drive belt deflection.

27.5a Typical later model four-cylinder engine drivebelt adjustment points

Water pump pulley
Power steering pump pulley
Compressor pulley
Alternator pulley
Crank pulley

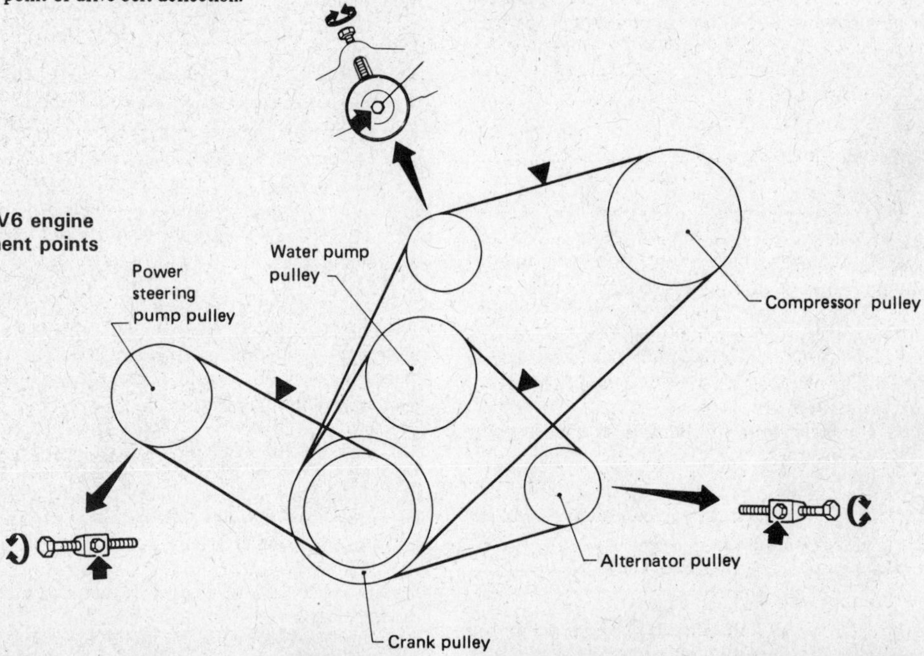

27.5b Typical V6 engine drivebelt adjustment points

27.6a On some components, drivebelt adjustment is simplified – all you have to do is loosen the mounting bolt (arrow) . . .

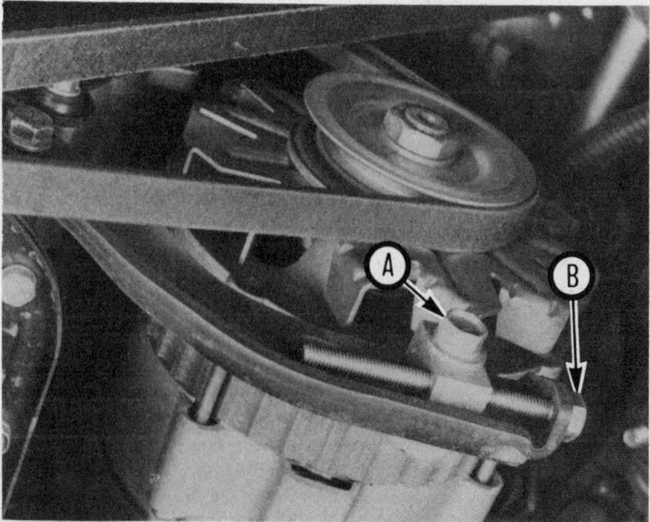

27.7b . . . and the lock bolt (A), then turn the adjusting bolt (B) until the belt tension is correct (V6 engine shown)

5 If adjustment is needed, either to make the belt tighter or looser, it's done by moving the belt-driven accessory on the bracket **(see illustrations)**.

6 Each component usually has an adjusting bolt and a pivot bolt. Both bolts must be loosened slightly to enable you to move the component. Some components have an adjusting bolt that can be turned to change the belt tension after the mounting bolt is loosened **(see illustrations)**. Others are equipped with an ilder pulley that must be moved to change the belt tension.

7 After the two bolts have been loosened, move the component away from the engine to tighten the belt or toward the engine to loosen the belt. Hold the accessory in position and check the belt tension. If it's correct, tighten the two bolts until just snug, then recheck the tension. If the tension is correct, tighten the bolts.

8 You may have to use some sort of pry bar to move the accessory while the belt is adjusted. If this must be done to gain the proper leverage, be very careful not to damage the component being moved or the part being pried against.

9 To replace a belt, follow the above procedures for drivebelt adjustment but slip the belt off the pulleys and remove it. Since belts tend to wear out more or less at the same time, it's a good idea to replace all of them at the same time. Mark each belt and the corresponding pulley grooves so the replacement belts can be installed properly.

10 Take the old belts with you when purchasing new ones in order to make a direct comparison for length, width and design.

11 Adjust the belts as described earlier in this Section.

28 Seatbelt check

1 Check the seatbelts, buckles, latch plates and guide loops for any obvious damage or signs of wear.

2 Make sure the seatbelt reminder light comes on when the key is turned on.

3 The seatbelts are designed to lock up during a sudden stop or impact, yet allow free movement during normal driving. The retractors should hold the belt against your chest while driving and rewind the belt when the buckle is unlatched.

4 If any of the above checks reveal problems with the seatbelt system, replace parts as necessary.

29 Air filter and PCV filter replacement

Refer to illustrations 29.3 and 29.6

1 At the specified intervals, the air filter should be replaced with a new one. A thorough program of preventive maintenance would also call for the filter to be inspected periodically between changes, especially if the vehicle is often driven in dusty conditions.

2 The air filter is located inside the air cleaner housing, which is mounted on top of the carburetor or throttle body.

3 Remove the wing nuts that hold the top plate to the air cleaner body, release the clips and lift it off **(see illustration)**.

4 Lift the air filter out of the housing. If it's covered with dirt, it should be replaced.

5 Wipe the inside of the air cleaner housing with a rag.

6 Pull out the old PCV filter (if equipped) and press the new one into the housing **(see illustration)**.

7 Place the old filter (if in good condition) or the new filter (if replacement is necessary) into the air cleaner housing.

8 Reinstall the top plate on the air cleaner and tighten the wing nuts, then snap the clips into place.

30 Fuel filter replacement

Warning: *Gasoline is extremely flammable, so extra safety precautions must be observed when working on the fuel system. DO NOT smoke or allow open flames or bare light bulbs near the vehicle. Also, don't perform fuel system maintenance procedures in a garage where a natural gas type appliance, such as a water heater or clothes dryer, is present.*

1 This job should be done with the engine cold (after sitting at least three hours). Place a metal container, rags or newspapers under the filter to catch spilled fuel.

Carburetor equipped models

With mechanical fuel pump

2 The fuel filter is located in the right front corner of the engine compartment, next to the battery. **Warning:** *Before attempting to remove the fuel filter, disconnect the negative cable from the battery and position it out of the way so it can't accidentally contact the battery post.*

3 To replace the filter, loosen the clamps and slide them down the hoses, past the fittings on the filter.

4 Carefully twist and pull on the hoses to separate them from the filter. If the hoses are in bad shape, now would be a good time to replace them with new ones.

5 Pull the filter out of the clip and install the new one, then hook up the hoses and tighten the clamps securely. Start the engine and check carefully for leaks at the filter hose connections.

29.3 Disengage the spring clips and remove the wing nuts to detach the air cleaner top plate

29.6 On models so equipped, pull the PCV filter out of the housing inside the air cleaner

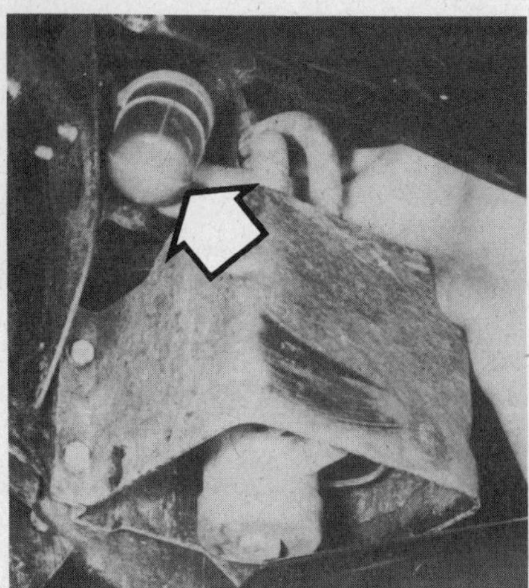

30.6 On carburetor equipped models with an electric fuel pump, the fuel filter (arrow) is mounted on top of the frame rail on the right side, next to the fuel pump

30.10 Fuel injected models have a canister type filter, located in the engine compartment (V6 engine shown)

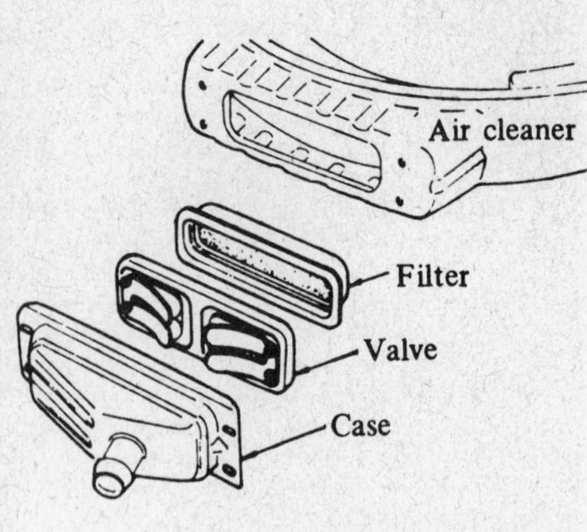

31.1 Early model Air Induction Valve filter and reed valve component layout

With electric fuel pump

Refer to illustration 30.6

Warning: *The fuel pump on these models is mounted on the right (passenger side) frame rail, above the front spring shackle, near the fuel tank, and is very difficult to remove! Since it's mounted lower than the tank, gasoline will run out of the fuel lines when they're disconnected at the filter. To prevent this, which is a very unsafe situation, siphon all of the fuel out of the tank or run the tank dry before replacing the filter.*

6 After the tank has been emptied, note how the filter is installed, then pull it out of the clip, loosen the clamps and slide them down the hoses, past the fittings on the filter **(see illustration)**.

7 Carefully twist and pull on the hoses to separate them from the filter. If the hoses are in bad shape, now would be a good time to replace them with new ones.

8 Connect the hoses to the new filter and install it in the clip. Make sure the filter is properly oriented — fuel filters usually have an arrow on the canister that indicates the direction of fuel flow. Start the engine and check carefully for leaks at the filter hose connections.

Fuel injected models

Refer to illustration 30.10

9 Depressurize the fuel system (Chapter 4).

10 To replace the filter, loosen the clamps and slide them down the hoses, past the fittings on the filter **(see illustration)**.

11 Note how the filter is installed (which end is facing up) so the new filter doesn't get installed backwards. Carefully twist and pull on the hoses to separate them from the filter. If the hoses are in bad shape, now would be a good time to replace them with new ones.

12 Loosen the clamp bolt and remove the filter.

13 Install the new filter in the clamp and tighten the bolt. Make sure the filter is properly oriented — fuel filters usually have an arrow on the canister that indicates the direction of fuel flow.

14 Connect the hoses to the new filter and tighten the clamps securely.

15 Start the engine and check carefully for leaks at the filter hose connections.

31 Air Induction Valve (AIV) filter replacement

Early models

Refer to illustration 31.1

1 Remove the screws that retain the AIV case to the air cleaner housing **(see illustration)**.

2 One of two methods can be used to gain access to the filter: either loosen the air induction tube nuts at the exhaust manifold and tube brackets so the tubes and case can be moved away from the air cleaner housing, or remove the air cleaner housing.

3 Pry the old filter out of the air cleaner housing.

4 Press the new filter into position.

5 Reinstall the valve case on the air cleaner and tighten the air induction tube nuts (if loosened).

Later models

Refer to illustrations 31.6a and 31.6b

6 Later models have a remote AIV filter located in a separate housing. Remove the housing cover nuts or bolts, lift the cover off and remove the filter **(see illustrations)**.

7 Install the new filter and reinstall the cover.

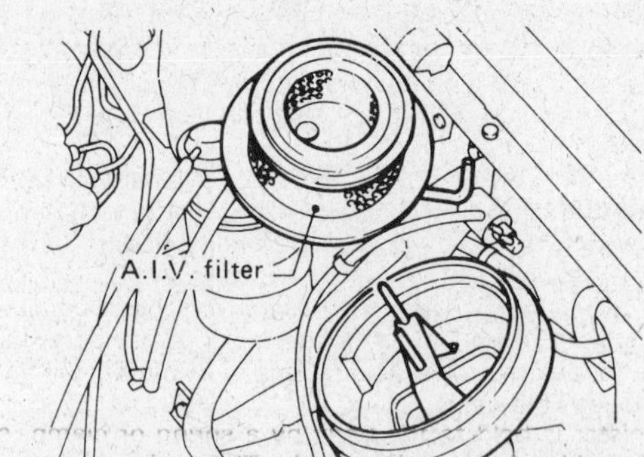

31.6a On later models, remove the Air Induction Valve remote filter housing for access to the filter (four-cylinder engine shown)

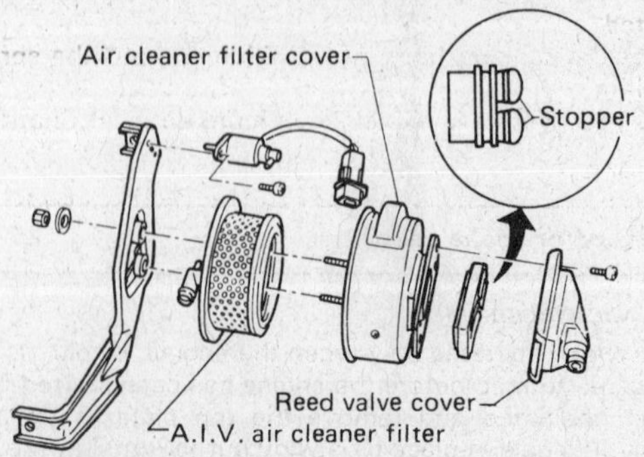

31.6b V6 engine Air Induction Valve filter installation details

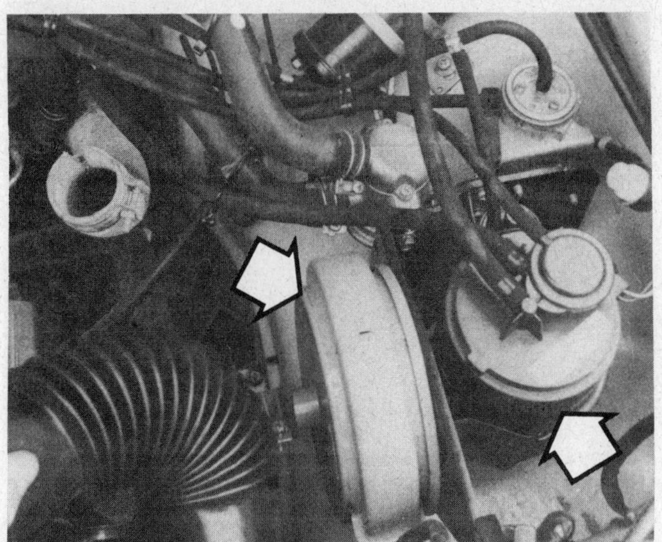

32.1 The air pump filter (left arrow) is located next to the charcoal canister (right arrow) (1980 models only)

34.3 With the air cleaner removed, the choke plate (arrow) is visible at the top of the carburetor

32 Air pump filter replacement (1980 models only)

Refer to illustration 32.1

1 Remove the rubber air hose from the air pump filter housing **(see illustration)**.
2 Disconnect the filter housing from the bracket.
3 The filter is part of the lower section of the housing. Separate the housing sections and replace the housing filter section with a new one.

33 EEC system charcoal canister filter replacement

1 The function of the EEC system is to draw fuel vapors from the fuel tank, store them in a charcoal canister and burn them during normal engine operation.
2 The filter at the bottom of the charcoal canister should be replaced at the specified intervals. If, however, a fuel odor is detected, the canister, filter and system hoses should immediately be inspected (Chapter 6).
3 To replace the filter, locate the canister in the engine compartment. It has several hoses running out of the top of it. If necessary, refer to the underhood component illustrations(s) at the beginning of this Chapter to locate the canister.
4 The canister is held to the body by a spring or clamp, secured around the outside of the canister body. The canister is removed by lifting it out of the mount, freeing it from the spring or clamp.
5 Turn the canister upside-down and pull the old filter from the bottom of the canister.
6 Push the new filter into the bottom of the canister, making sure it's seated.
7 Place the canister back into position and pull the spring around it to hold it.
8 The EEC system is explained in more detail in Chapter 6.

34 Carburetor choke check

Refer to illustration 34.3

1 The choke operates only when the engine is cold, so this check should be performed before the engine has been started for the day.
2 Open the hood and remove the top plate of the air cleaner assembly. It's held in place by a wing nut (or nuts) at the center and several spring clips around the edge. If any vacuum hoses must be disconnected, tag them to ensure reinstallation in their original positions.
3 Look at the center of the air cleaner housing. You'll notice a flat plate at the carburetor opening **(see illustration)**.
4 Have an assistant press the throttle pedal to the floor. The plate should close completely. Start the engine while you watch the plate at the carburetor. Don't position your face near the carburetor, as the engine could backfire, causing serious burns! When the engine starts, the choke plate should open slightly.
5 Allow the engine to continue running at an idle speed. As the engine warms up to operating temperature, the plate should slowly open, allowing more air to enter through the top of the carburetor.
6 After a few minutes, the choke plate should be completely open to the vertical position. Blip the throttle to make sure the fast idle cam disengages.
7 You'll notice that engine speed corresponds to the plate opening. With the plate closed, the engine should run at a fast idle speed. As the plate opens and the throttle is moved to disengage the fast idle cam, the engine speed will decrease.
8 With the engine off and the throttle held half-way open, open and close the choke several times. Check the linkage to see if it's hooked up correctly and make sure it doesn't bind.
9 If the choke or linkage binds, sticks or works sluggishly, clean it with choke cleaner (an aerosol spray available at auto parts stores). If the condition persists after cleaning, replace the troublesome parts.
10 Visually inspect all vacuum hoses to be sure they're securely connected and look for cracks and deterioration. Replace as necessary.
11 If the choke fails to operate normally, but no mechanical causes can be found, refer to Chapter 4 and check the choke electrical circuits.

35 Carburetor/throttle body mounting nut torque check

1 The carburetor or TBI unit is attached to the top of the intake manifold by several bolts or nuts. The fasteners can sometimes work loose from vibration and temperature changes during normal engine operation and cause a vacuum leak.
2 If you suspect that a vacuum leak exists at the bottom of the carburetor or throttle body, obtain a two-foot length of fuel line hose. Start the engine and place one end of the hose next to your ear as you probe around the base with the other end. You'll hear a hissing sound if a leak exists (be careful of hot or moving engine components).
3 Remove the air cleaner assembly, tagging each hose that's disconnected with a piece of numbered tape to make reassembly easier.
4 Locate the mounting nuts or bolts at the base of the carburetor or throttle body. Decide what special tools or adapters will be necessary, if any, to tighten the fasteners.
5 Tighten the nuts or bolts to the specified torque. Don't overtighten them, as the threads could strip.

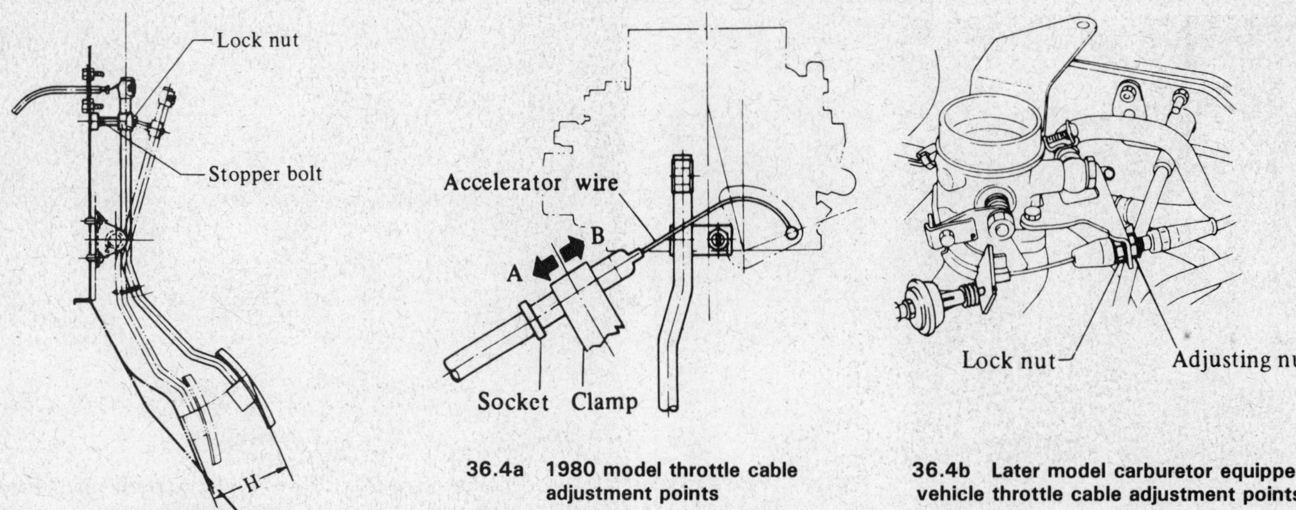

36.2 Throttle pedal adjustment is made by turning the stopper bolt at the top of the shaft

36.4a 1980 model throttle cable adjustment points

36.4b Later model carburetor equipped vehicle throttle cable adjustment points

6 If, after the nuts or bolts are properly tightened, a vacuum leak still exists, the carburetor or throttle body must be removed and a new gasket installed. See Chapter 4 for more information.
7 After tightening the fasteners, reinstall the air cleaner and return all hoses to their original positions.

36 Throttle pedal and cable check and adjustment (carburetor equipped vehicles only)

Refer to illustrations 36.2, 36.4a and 36.4b

1 With the engine off, depress the throttle pedal several times to make sure the linkage is operating smoothly. Also, see if the pedal is returning to its original position when released.
2 Check the height (H) of the throttle pedal **(see illustration)**. It should be about 4-5/8 inch (118 mm) from the floor. If the height isn't correct, loosen the locknut and turn the pedal stopper bolt until it is, then retighten the locknut.
3 Have an assistant depress the throttle pedal all the way several times while you look into the carburetor to make sure the throttle valve is opening completely when the pedal is depressed and closing all the way when the pedal is released.
4 If the throttle cable must be adjusted use the following procedure **(see illustrations)**:

a) Prior to adjustment, release the automatic choke mechanism by holding the choke open with your fingers while you pull the throttle lever on the carburetor up by hand.
b) On 1980 models, set the throttle lever in the fully closed position and loosen the throttle cable retaining clamp. Slowly pull the socket on the cable housing away (direction A) from the throttle lever until the lever is about to move. This is the zero play point. Move the socket back (direction B) toward the throttle lever 3/64 to 1/16-inch (1 to 1.5 mm) and tighten the clamp.
c) On 1981 and later models, loosen the throttle cable locknut and make sure the throttle lever on the carburetor is in the fully closed position. Tighten the adjusting nut until the throttle lever is about to move, which is the zero play point. From this position, unscrew the adjusting nut one to two turns so the cable play is 1/16 to 3/32-inch (1 to 2.5 mm).
d) Following adjustment, repeat the checks described in Step 1.

37 Idle speed check and adjustment

Refer to illustrations 37.5, 37.8, 37.11a, 37.11b and 37.11c

1 Engine idle speed is the speed at which the engine operates when no throttle pedal pressure is applied. The idle speed is critical to the performance of the engine itself, as well as many engine sub-systems.
2 A hand-held tachometer must be used when adjusting idle speed to get an accurate reading. The exact hook-up for these meters varies with the manufacturer, so follow the particular directions included.
3 Set the parking brake and block the wheels. Be sure the transmission is in Neutral (manual transmission) or Park (automatic transmission).
4 Turn off the air conditioner (if equipped), the headlights and any other accessories during this procedure.
5 On 1986 and later models, attach a cable harness adapter (available from your dealer – special tool number EG11150000) between the ignition coil primary terminals and the harness connector **(see illustration)**. Connect a tachometer to the adapter harness.

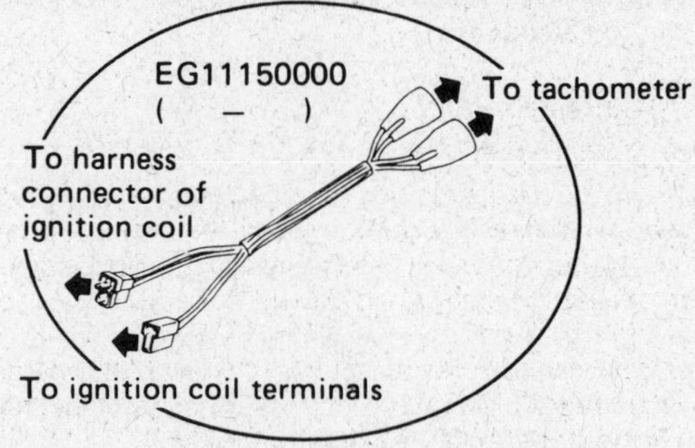

37.5 On 1986 and later models, an adapter harness must be installed as shown before adjusting the idle speed

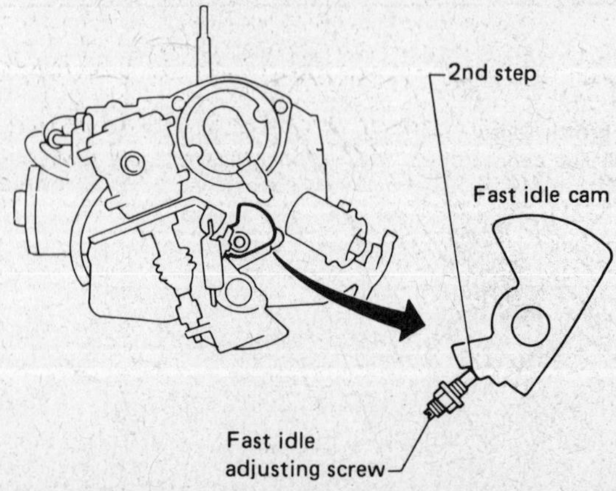

37.8 When setting the fast idle speed on later carburetor equipped models, make sure the adjusting screw is on the 2nd step of the cam as shown

37.11a Typical early model carburetor idle speed screw location (arrow) (1981 model shown)

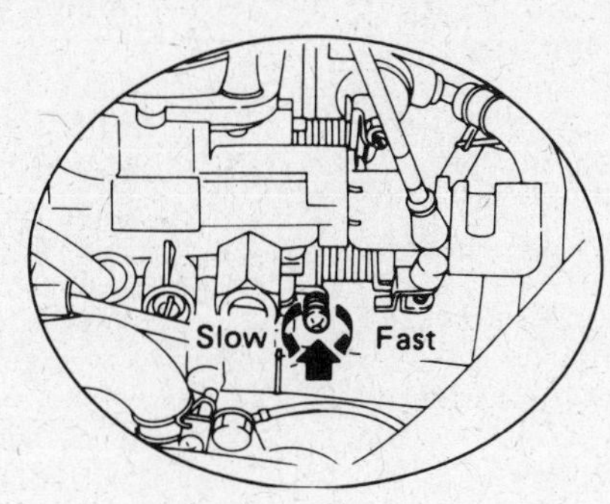

37.11b 1986 and later four-cylinder engine idle speed adjustment screw location

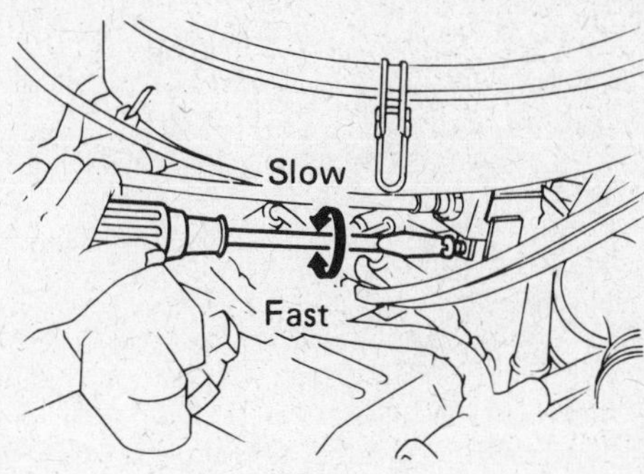

37.11c V6 engine idle speed adjustment screw location

6 Start the engine and allow it to reach normal operating temperature.
7 Open the hood and run the engine at about 2000 rpm for approximately three minutes, then allow it to idle again for about one minute.
8 On 1984 and later models, make sure the carburetor fast idle arm is on the 2nd step of the fast idle cam **(see illustration)**.
9 On automatic transmission equipped vehicles, have an assistant shift to Drive while keeping the brake pedal firmly depressed. Place manual transmission equipped vehicles in Neutral.
10 Check the engine idle speed with the tachometer and compare it to the VECI label.
11 If the idle speed is not correct, turn the idle speed adjusting screw (clockwise for faster, counterclockwise for slower) until the idle speed is correct **(see illustrations)**.

1990 and later models

Refer to illustrations 37.12a, 37.12b, 37.12c and 37.12d

12 On 1990 and later vehicles equipped with the MPFI systems, if the idle speed is not correct, disable the fuel injection components that specifically control the idle system before proceeding with the adjustment. For more information concerning the fuel injection system, refer to Chapters 4 and 6.

a On V6 engines, disconnect the AAC valve electrical harness **(see illustration)**. On KA24E engines, disconnect the throttle sensor harness connector **(see illustration)**.
b Check the ignition timing (see Section 48).
c Adjust the engine idle speed by turning the adjustment screw **(see illustrations)**.
d Reconnect the AAC valve (V6 engine) or the throttle sensor (KA24E engine) and run the engine at approximately 2,000 rpms for a few minutes.
e If the engine still will not idle properly, have the CO mixture checked at a dealership service department.

13 After adjustment, shift the automatic transmission into Park and turn the engine off.

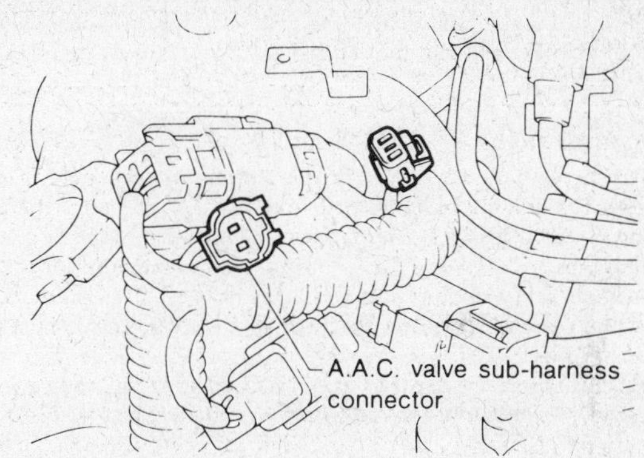

37.12a Disconnect the AAC valve harness connector before adjusting the idle speed

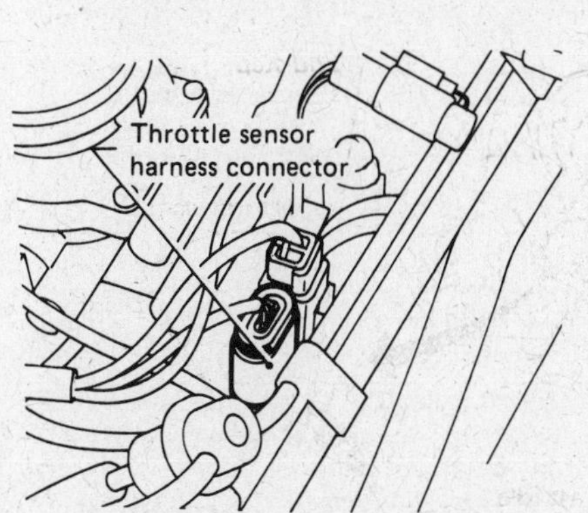

37.12b Disconnect the throttle sensor harness connector before adjusting the idle speed

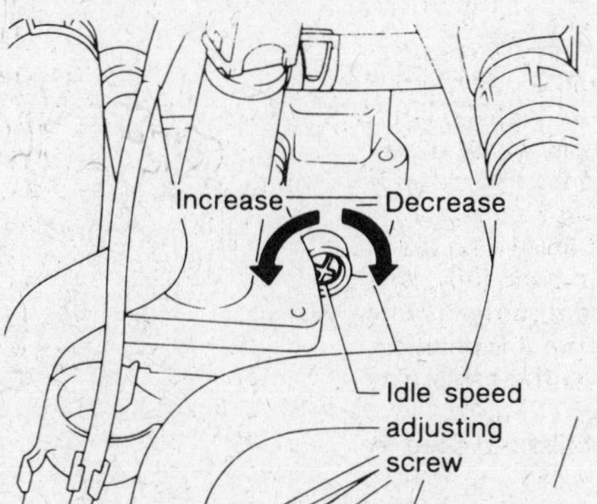

37.12c Location of the idle speed adjusting screw on the V6 engine

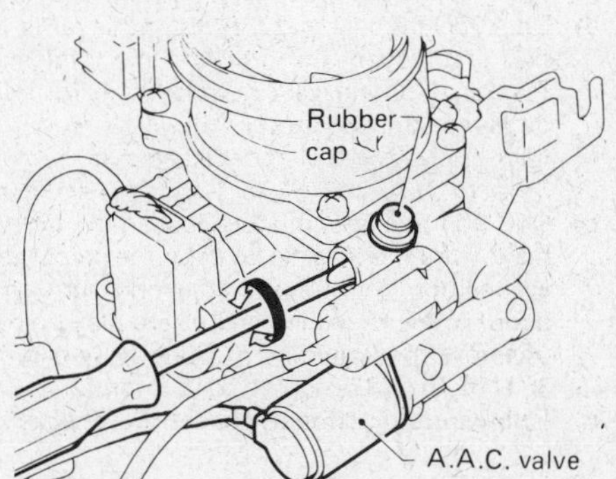

37.12d Location of the idle speed adjusting screw on the KA24E engine

38 Transfer case oil change

1 Drive the vehicle for at least 15 minutes in 4WD to warm up the oil in the case.
2 Raise the vehicle and support it securely on jackstands. Remove the rock guard.
3 Move a drain pan, rags, newspapers and a breaker bar or ratchet (to fit
the square drive hole in the transfer case plugs) under the vehicle.
4 Remove the check/fill plug **(see illustration 21.1)**.
5 Remove the drain plug from the lower part of the case and allow the old oil to drain completely.
6 Carefully clean and install the drain plug after the case is completely drained. Tighten the plug to the specified torque.
7 Fill the case with the specified lubricant until it's level with the lower edge of the filler hole.
8 Install the check/fill plug and tighten it securely.
9 Install the rock guard, then lower the vehicle.
10 Check carefully for leaks around the drain plug after the first few miles of driving.

39 Manual transmission oil change

Refer to illustration 39.3

1 Drive the vehicle for a few miles to thoroughly warm up the transmission oil.
2 Raise the vehicle and support it securely on jackstands.
3 Move a drain pan, rags, newspapers and a 1/2-inch drive breaker bar or ratchet with an extension under the vehicle. With the drain pan and newspapers in position under the transmission, use the ratchet and extension to loosen the drain plug located in the bottom of the transmission case **(see illustration)**.

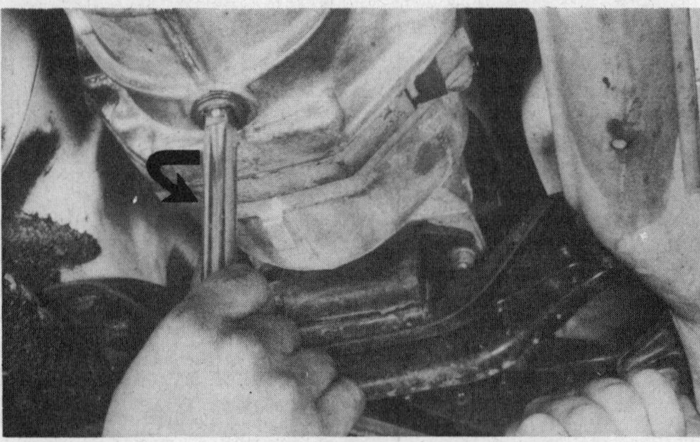

39.3 Use a ratchet and extension to remove the manual transmission drain plug

4 Once loosened, carefully unscrew it with your fingers until you can remove it from the transmission. Allow all of the oil to drain into the pan. If the plug is too hot to touch, use the wrench to remove it.
5 If the transmission is equipped with a magnetic drain plug, see if there are bits of metal clinging to it. If there are, it's a sign of excessive internal wear, indicating that the transmission should be carefully inspected in the near future. If the transmission isn't equipped with a magnetic drain plug, allow the oil in the pan to cool, then feel with your hands along the bottom of the drain pan for debris.
6 Clean the drain plug, then reinstall it in the transmission and tighten it to the specified torque.
7 Remove the transmission oil check/fill plug (see Section 20). Using a hand pump or syringe, fill the transmission with the correct amount and grade of oil (see the Specifications), until the level is just at the bottom of the plug hole.
8 Reinstall the check/fill plug and tighten it securely.

40 Differential oil change

Note: *The following procedure can be used for the rear differential as well as the front differential used on 4WD vehicles.*

1 Drive the vehicle for several miles to warm up the differential oil, then raise the vehicle and support it securely on jackstands.
2 Move a drain pan, rags, newspapers and a 1/2-inch drive breaker bar or ratchet with an extension under the vehicle.
3 With the drain pan under the differential, use the breaker bar or ratchet and extension to loosen the drain plug. It's the lower of the two plugs **(see illustrations 22.2 and 22.3)**.
4 Once loosened, carefully unscrew it with your fingers until you can remove it from the case.
5 Allow all of the oil to drain into the pan, then replace the drain plug and tighten it to the specified torque.
6 Feel with your hands along the bottom of the drain pan for any metal bits that may have come out with the oil. If there are any, it's a sign of excessive wear, indicating that the internal components should be carefully inspected in the near future.
7 Remove the differential check/fill plug located above the drain plug. Using a hand pump, syringe or funnel, fill the differential with the correct amount and grade of oil (see the Specifications) until the level is just at the bottom of the plug hole.
8 Reinstall the plug and tighten it securely.
9 Lower the vehicle. Check for leaks at the drain plug after the first few miles of driving.

41 Automatic transmission fluid change

1 At the specified time intervals, the transmission fluid should be drained and replaced. Since the fluid should be hot when it's drained, drive the vehicle for 15 or 20 minutes before proceeding.
2 Before beginning work, purchase the specified transmission fluid (see *Recommended lubricants and fluids* at the front of this Chapter).
3 Other tools necessary for this job include jackstands to support the vehicle in a raised position, a drain pan capable of holding at least eight pints, newspapers and clean rags.
4 Raise the vehicle and support it securely on jackstands.
5 With a drain pan in place, remove the rear and side transmission fluid pan mounting bolts. Be careful not to burn yourself on anything- it may be wise to wear gloves.
6 Loosen the front pan bolts approximately four turns, but don't remove them.
7 Carefully pry the transmission pan loose with a screwdriver, allowing the fluid to drain. Be very careful not to damage the pan or transmission gasket surfaces! Save the fluid so you can estimate how much new fluid to add to the transmission.
8 Remove the remaining bolts, pan and gasket. Carefully clean the gasket surface of the transmission to remove all traces of the old gasket and sealant.
9 Drain the fluid from the transmission pan, clean it with solvent and dry it with compressed air.
10 Apply a thin layer of RTV sealant to the transmission case side of the new gasket.
11 Make sure the gasket surface on the transmission pan is clean, then apply a thin layer of RTV sealant to it and position the new gasket on the pan. Put the pan in place against the transmission, install the bolts and, working around the pan, tighten each bolt a little at a time until the final torque figure is reached.
12 Lower the vehicle and add new automatic transmission fluid through the filler tube (Section 5). The amount should be equal to the amount of fluid that was drained (you don't want to overfill it).
13 With the transmission in Park and the parking brake set, run the engine at a fast idle, but don't race it.
14 Move the gear selector through each range and back to Park, then check the fluid level (Section 5). Add more fluid as required.
15 Check under the vehicle for leaks during the first few miles of driving.

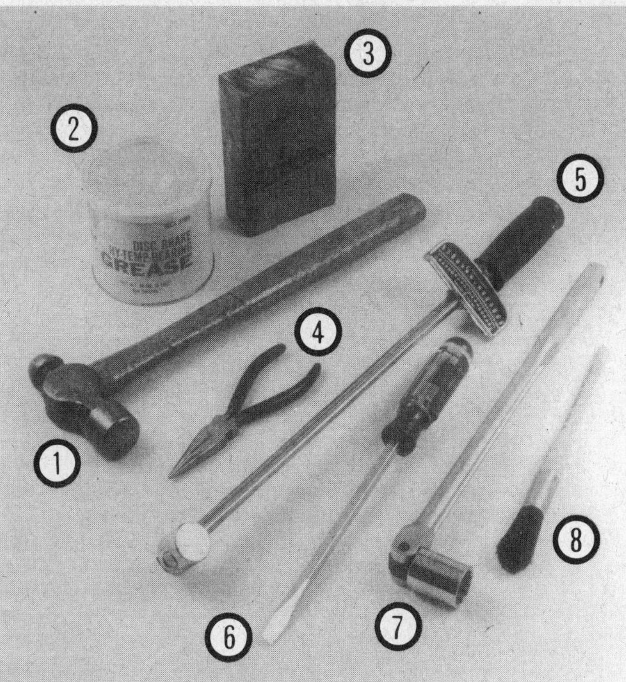

42.1 Tools and materials needed for front wheel bearing maintenance

1 **Hammer** – *A common hammer will do just fine*
2 **Grease** – *High-temperature grease that is formulated specially for front wheel bearings should be used*
3 **Wood block** – *If you have a scrap piece of 2x4, it can be used to drive the new seal into the hub*
4 **Needle-nose pliers** – *Used to straighten and remove the cotter pin in the spindle*
5 **Torque wrench** – *This is very important in this procedure; if the bearing is too tight, the wheel won't turn freely – if it's too loose, the wheel will "wobble" on the spindle. Either way, it could mean extensive damage.*
6 **Screwdriver** – *Used to remove the seal from the hub (a long screwdriver would be preferred)*
7 **Socket/breaker bar** – *Needed to loosen the nut on the spindle if it's extremely tight*
8 **Brush** – *Together with some clean solvent, this will be used to remove old grease from the hub and spindle*

42.6 Pry off the dust cap with a screwdriver

42 Front wheel bearing check, repack and adjustment (2WD models only)

Refer to illustrations 42.1, 42.6, 42.7, 42.11 and 42.15

1 In most cases the front wheel bearings will not need servicing until the brake pads are changed. However, the bearings should be checked whenever the front of the vehicle is raised for any reason. Several items, including a torque wrench and special grease, are required for this procedure **(see illustration)**.

2 With the vehicle securely supported on jackstands, spin each wheel and check for noise, rolling resistance and free play.

3 Grasp the top of each tire with one hand and the bottom with the other. Move the wheel in-and-out on the spindle. If there's any noticeable movement, the bearings should be checked and then repacked with grease or replaced if necessary.

4 Remove the wheel(s).

5 Fabricate a wood block to slide between the brake pads to keep them separated. Remove the brake caliper (Chapter 10) and hang it out of the way on a piece of wire.

6 Pry the dust cap out of the hub using a screwdriver or hammer and chisel **(see illustration)**.

7 Straighten the bent ends of the cotter pin, then pull the cotter pin out of the adjusting nut cap **(see illustration)**. Discard the cotter pin and use a new one during reassembly.

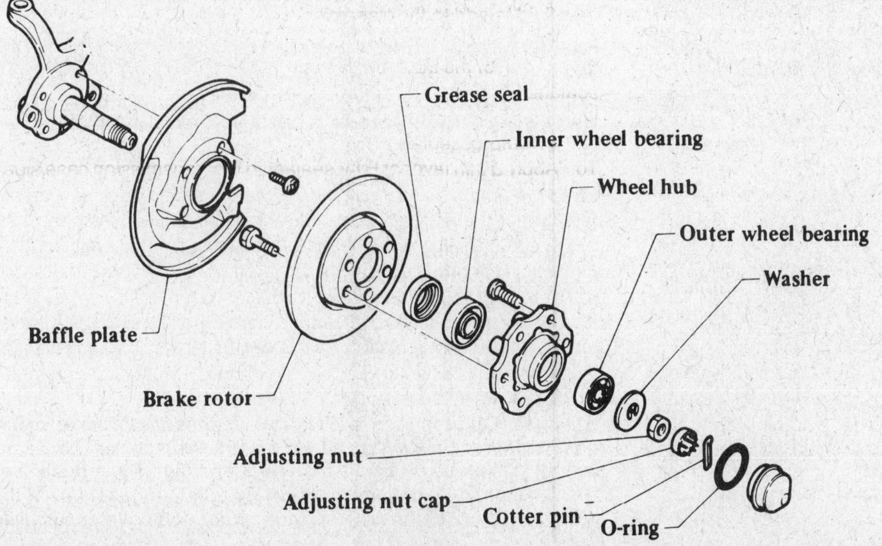

42.7 Front wheel bearing components – exploded view

42.11 Use a large screwdriver to pry the grease seal from the rear of the hub

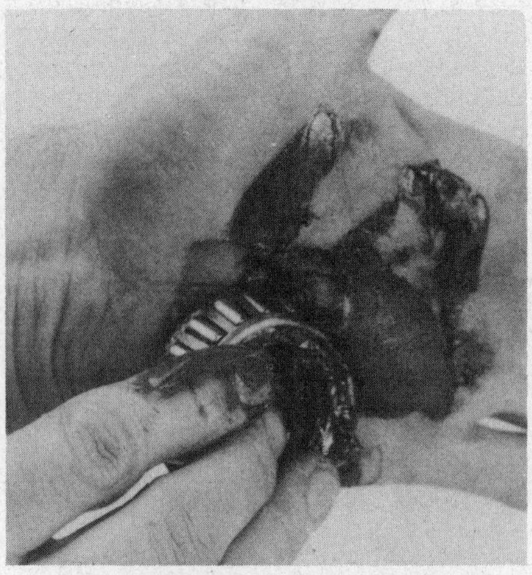

42.15 Work clean grease into each bearing until it's full

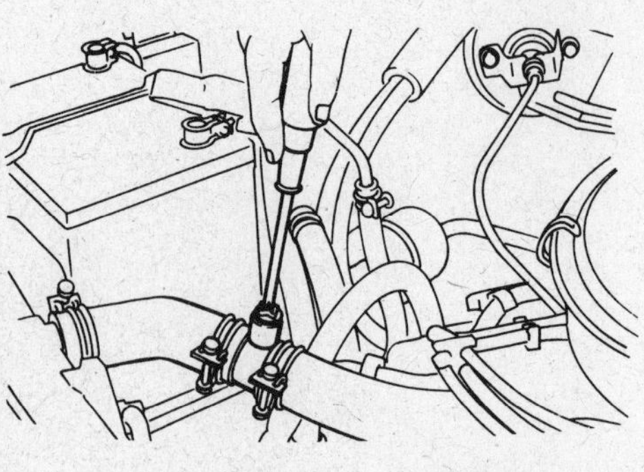

43.4 On V6 engines, open the air valve with a screwdriver to facilitate draining of the coolant from the radiator and engine

8 Remove the adjusting nut and washer from the end of the spindle.
9 Pull the hub out slightly, then push it back into its original position. This should force the outer wheel bearing off the spindle enough so it can be removed.
10 Pull the hub off the spindle.
11 Use a screwdriver to pry the grease seal out of the rear of the hub **(see illustration)**. As this is done, note how the seal is installed.
12 Remove the inner wheel bearing from the hub.
13 Use solvent to remove all traces of the old grease from the bearings, hub and spindle. A small brush may prove helpful; however make sure no bristles from the brush embed themselves inside the bearing rollers. Allow the parts to air dry.
14 Carefully inspect the bearings for cracks, heat discoloration, worn rollers, etc. Check the bearing races inside the hub for wear and damage. If the bearing races are defective, the hubs should be taken to a machine shop with the facilities to remove the old races and press new ones in. Note that the bearings and races come as matched sets and old bearings should never be installed on new races.
15 Use high-temperature front wheel bearing grease to pack the bearings. Work the grease completely into the bearings, forcing it between the rollers, cone and cage from the back side **(see illustration)**.
16 Apply a thin coat of grease to the spindle at the outer bearing seat, inner bearing seat, shoulder and seal seat.
17 Put a small quantity of grease behind each bearing race inside the hub. Using your finger, form a dam at these points to provide for extra grease and to keep thinned grease from flowing out of the bearing.
18 Place the grease-packed inner bearing into the rear of the hub and put a little more grease outside of the bearing.
19 Place a new seal over the inner bearing and tap the seal evenly into place with a hammer and block of wood until it's flush with the hub.
20 Carefully place the hub assembly onto the spindle and push the grease-packed outer bearing into position.
21 Install the washer and adjusting nut. Tighten the nut slightly (only 27 ft-lbs of torque).
22 Spin the hub in a forward direction to seat the bearings and remove any grease or burrs which could cause excessive bearing play later.
23 Check to see that the tightness of the nut is still approximately 27 ft-lbs. Spin the hub in both directions several turns, then recheck the torque again (it must be 27 ft-lbs.).
24 Loosen the nut exactly 45-degrees (1/8 turn), no more.
25 Install the adjusting nut cap and see if the hole in the spindle is aligned with the slot in the cap. If the nut must be turned to align them, turn it clockwise only! Install a new cotter pin.
26 Bend the ends of the cotter pin until they're flat against the nut. Cut off any extra length which could interfere with the dust cap.
27 Make sure the O-ring is in place, then install the dust cap, tapping it into place with a hammer.
28 Place the brake caliper near the rotor and carefully remove the wood spacer. Install the caliper (Chapter 10).
29 Install the tire/wheel assembly on the hub and tighten the lug nuts.
30 Grasp the top and bottom of the tire and check the bearings in the manner described earlier in this Section.
31 Lower the vehicle.

43 Cooling system servicing (draining, flushing and refilling)

See illustration 43.4

Warning: *Antifreeze is a corrosive and poisonous solution, so be careful not to spill any of the coolant mixture on the vehicle's paint or your skin. If you do, rinse it off immediately with plenty of clean water. Consult local authorities regarding proper disposal of antifreeze before draining the cooling system. In many areas, reclamation centers have been established to collect used oil and coolant mixtures.*

1 Periodically, the cooling system should be drained, flushed and refilled to replenish the antifreeze mixture and prevent formation of rust and corrosion, which can impair the performance of the cooling system and cause engine damage. When the cooling system is serviced, all hoses and the radiator cap should be checked and replaced if necessary.
2 Apply the parking brake and block the wheels. If the vehicle has just been driven, wait several hours to allow the engine to cool down before beginning this procedure.
3 Once the engine is completely cool, remove the radiator cap. Place the heater temperature control in the maximum heat position.
4 Move a large container under the radiator drain to catch the coolant, then unscrew the drain plug (a pair of pliers may be required to turn it). If your vehicle has a V6 engine, use a screwdriver to loosen the air valve installed in the upper radiator hose (turn it counterclockwise as far as possible) **(see illustration)**.
5 After the coolant stops flowing out of the radiator, move the container under the engine block drain plug (on four-cylinder engines it's at the left-rear corner of the block; on the V6 engine it's behind the alternator). On 1990 and later V6 engines the drain plugs are located near the alternator (left side) and the engine mount (right side). Remove the plug and allow the coolant in the block to drain.
6 While the coolant is draining, check the condition of the radiator hoses, heater hoses and clamps (refer to Section 9 if necessary).
7 Replace any damaged clamps or hoses.
8 Once the system is completely drained, flush the radiator with fresh water from a garden hose until it runs clear at the drain. The flushing action of the water will remove sediments from the radiator but will not remove rust and scale from the engine and cooling tube surfaces.
9 These deposits can be removed with a chemical cleaner. Follow the procedure outlined in the manufacturer's instructions. If the radiator is sev-

Common spark plug conditions

NORMAL

Symptoms: Brown to grayish-tan color and slight electrode wear. Correct heat range for engine and operating conditions.
Recommendation: When new spark plugs are installed, replace with plugs of the same heat range.

WORN

Symptoms: Rounded electrodes with a small amount of deposits on the firing end. Normal color. Causes hard starting in damp or cold weather and poor fuel economy.
Recommendation: Plugs have been left in the engine too long. Replace with new plugs of the same heat range. Follow the recommended maintenance schedule.

CARBON DEPOSITS

Symptoms: Dry sooty deposits indicate a rich mixture or weak ignition. Causes misfiring, hard starting and hesitation.
Recommendation: Make sure the plug has the correct heat range. Check for a clogged air filter or problem in the fuel system or engine management system. Also check for ignition system problems.

ASH DEPOSITS

Symptoms: Light brown deposits encrusted on the side or center electrodes or both. Derived from oil and/or fuel additives. Excessive amounts may mask the spark, causing misfiring and hesitation during acceleration.
Recommendation: If excessive deposits accumulate over a short time or low mileage, install new valve guide seals to prevent seepage of oil into the combustion chambers. Also try changing gasoline brands.

OIL DEPOSITS

Symptoms: Oily coating caused by poor oil control. Oil is leaking past worn valve guides or piston rings into the combustion chamber. Causes hard starting, misfiring and hesitation.
Recommendation: Correct the mechanical condition with necessary repairs and install new plugs.

GAP BRIDGING

Symptoms: Combustion deposits lodge between the electrodes. Heavy deposits accumulate and bridge the electrode gap. The plug ceases to fire, resulting in a dead cylinder.
Recommendation: Locate the faulty plug and remove the deposits from between the electrodes.

TOO HOT

Symptoms: Blistered, white insulator, eroded electrode and absence of deposits. Results in shortened plug life.
Recommendation: Check for the correct plug heat range, over-advanced ignition timing, lean fuel mixture, intake manifold vacuum leaks, sticking valves and insufficient engine cooling.

PREIGNITION

Symptoms: Melted electrodes. Insulators are white, but may be dirty due to misfiring or flying debris in the combustion chamber. Can lead to engine damage.
Recommendation: Check for the correct plug heat range, over-advanced ignition timing, lean fuel mixture, insufficient engine cooling and lack of lubrication.

HIGH SPEED GLAZING

Symptoms: Insulator has yellowish, glazed appearance. Indicates that combustion chamber temperatures have risen suddenly during hard acceleration. Normal deposits melt to form a conductive coating. Causes misfiring at high speeds.
Recommendation: Install new plugs. Consider using a colder plug if driving habits warrant.

DETONATION

Symptoms: Insulators may be cracked or chipped. Improper gap setting techniques can also result in a fractured insulator tip. Can lead to piston damage.
Recommendation: Make sure the fuel anti-knock values meet engine requirements. Use care when setting the gaps on new plugs. Avoid lugging the engine.

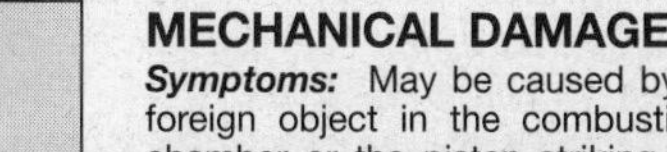

MECHANICAL DAMAGE

Symptoms: May be caused by a foreign object in the combustion chamber or the piston striking an incorrect reach (too long) plug. Causes a dead cylinder and could result in piston damage.
Recommendation: Repair the mechanical damage. Remove the foreign object from the engine and/or install the correct reach plug.

44.1 The PCV valve screws into the intake manifold (arrow) (1982 model shown)

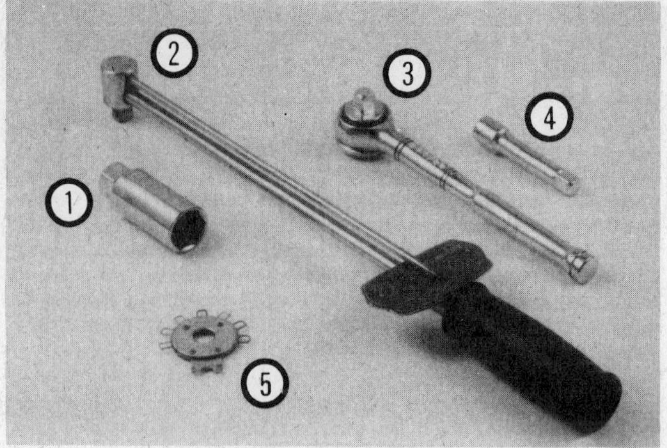

45.2 Tools required for changing spark plugs

1 ***Spark plug socket*** *– This will have special padding inside to protect the spark plug's porcelain insulator*
2 ***Torque wrench*** *– Although not mandatory, using this tool is the best way to ensure the plugs are tightened properly*
3 ***Ratchet*** *– Standard hand tool to fit the spark plug socket*
4 ***Extension*** *– Depending on model and accessories, you may need special extensions and universal joints to reach one or more of the plugs*
5 ***Spark plug gap gauge*** *– This gauge for checking the gap comes in a variety of styles. Make sure the gap for your engine is included.*

erely corroded, damaged or leaking, it should be removed (Chapter 3) and taken to a radiator repair shop.

10 Remove the overflow hose from the coolant recovery reservoir. Drain the reservoir and flush it with clean water, then reconnect the hose.

11 Reinstall and tighten the radiator drain plug. Install and tighten the block drain plug.

12 Slowly add new coolant (a 50/50 mixture of water and antifreeze) to the radiator until it's full. Add coolant to the reservoir up to the lower mark. Close the air valve in the upper radiator hose (V6 engine only).

13 Leave the radiator cap off and run the engine in a well-ventilated area until the thermostat opens (coolant will begin flowing through the radiator and the upper radiator hose will become hot).

14 Turn the engine off and let it cool. Add more coolant mixture to bring the level back up to the lip on the radiator filler neck.

15 Squeeze the upper radiator hose to expel air, then add more coolant mixture if necessary. Replace the radiator cap.

16 Start the engine, allow it to reach normal operating temperature and check for leaks.

44 PCV valve check and replacement

Refer to illustration 44.1

1 On all models the PCV valve threads into the intake manifold and is connected by a rubber hose and metal tube to the crankcase **(see illustration)**.

2 When purchasing a replacement PCV valve, make sure it's the correct one for your vehicle.

3 Remove the air cleaner.

4 Loosen the clamp securing the hose to the PCV valve and disconnect the hose from the valve.

5 Unscrew the valve from the intake manifold.

6 Compare the old valve with the new one to make sure they're the same.

7 Screw the new valve into the manifold and connect the hose to it.

8 More information on the PCV system can be found in Chapter 6.

45 Spark plug replacement

Refer to illustrations 45.2, 45.5a, 45.5b, 45.6 and 45.10

1 Replace the spark plugs with new ones at the intervals recommended in the Routine maintenance schedule. Four plugs are used in 1980 four-cylinder engines, while later model four-cylinder engines require eight plugs (two per cylinder). V6 engines, obviously, have six plugs.

2 In most cases, the tools necessary for spark plug replacement include a spark plug socket which fits onto a ratchet (spark plug sockets are padded inside to prevent damage to the porcelain insulators on the new plugs), various extensions and a gap gauge to check and adjust the gaps on the new plugs **(see illustration)**. A special plug wire removal tool is available for separating the wire boots from the spark plugs, but it isn't absolutely necessary. A torque wrench should be used to tighten the new plugs.

3 The best approach when replacing the spark plugs is to purchase the new ones in advance, adjust them to the proper gap and replace them one at a time. When buying the new spark plugs, be sure to obtain the correct plug type for your particular engine. This information can be found on the Emission Control Information label located under the hood and in the factory owner's manual. If differences exist between the plug specified on the emissions label and in the owner's manual, assume the emissions label is correct.

4 Allow the engine to cool completely before attempting to remove any of the plugs. While you're waiting for the engine to cool, check the new plugs for defects and adjust the gaps.

5 The gap is checked by inserting the proper thickness gauge between the electrodes at the tip of the plug **(see illustration)**. The gap between the electrodes should be the same as the one specified on the Emissions Control Information label. The wire should just slide between the electrodes with a slight amount of drag. If the gap is incorrect, use the adjuster on the gauge body to bend the curved side electrode slightly until the proper gap is obtained **(see illustration)**. If the side electrode is not exactly over the center electrode, bend it with the adjuster until it is. Check for cracks in the porcelain insulator (if any are found, the plug shouldn't be used).

6 With the engine cool, remove the spark plug wire from one spark plug. Pull only on the boot at the end of the wire $ don't pull on the wire. A plug wire removal tool should be used if available **(see illustration)**.

7 If compressed air is available, use it to blow any dirt or foreign material away from the spark plug hole. A common bicycle pump will also work. The idea here is to eliminate the possibility of debris falling into the cylinder as the spark plug is removed.

8 Place the spark plug socket over the plug and remove it from the engine by turning it in a counterclockwise direction.

9 Compare the spark plug to those shown in the accompanying photos to get an indication of the general running condition of the engine.

10 Thread one of the new plugs into the hole until you can no longer turn it with your fingers, then tighten it with a torque wrench (if available) or the

45.5a Spark plug manufacturers recommend using a wire type gauge when checking the gap – if the wire does not slide between the electrodes with a slight drag, adjustment is required

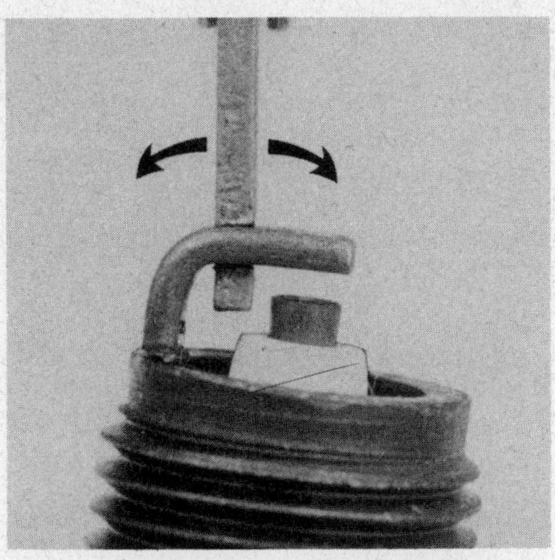

45.5b To change the gap, bend the *side* electrode only, as indicated by the arrows, and be very careful not to crack or chip the porcelain insulator surrounding the center electrode

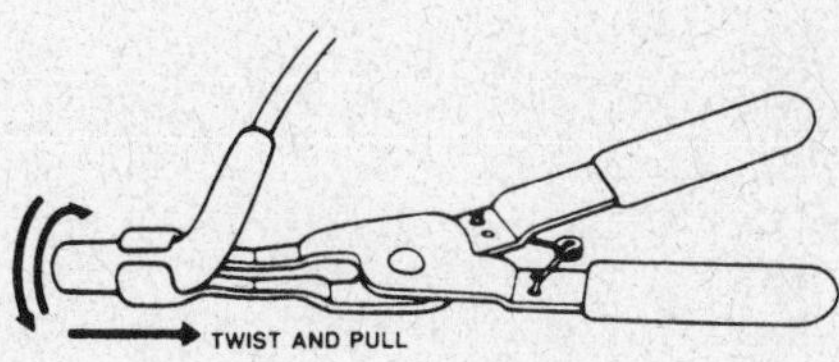

45.6 When removing the spark plug wires, pull only on the boot and twist it back-and-forth

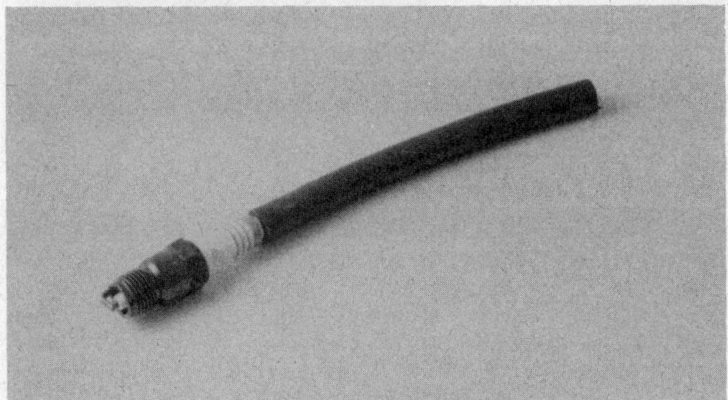

45.10 A length of 3/16-inch ID rubber hose will save time and prevent damaged threads when installing the spark plugs

ratchet. It might be a good idea to slip a short length of rubber hose over the end of the plug to use as a tool to thread it into place **(see illustration)**. The hose will grip the plug well enough to turn it, but will start to slip if the plug begins to cross-thread in the hole – this will prevent damaged threads and the accompanying repair costs.

11 Before pushing the spark plug wire onto the end of the plug, inspect it following the procedures outlined in Section 46.

12 Attach the plug wire to the new spark plug, again using a twisting motion on the boot until it's seated on the spark plug.

13 Repeat the procedure for the remaining spark plugs, replacing them one at a time to prevent mixing up the spark plug wires.

46 Spark plug wire check and replacement

1 The spark plug wires should be checked at the recommended intervals and whenever new spark plugs are installed in the engine.

2 The wires should be inspected one at a time to prevent mixing up the order, which is essential for proper engine operation.

3 Disconnect the plug wire from one spark plug. To do this, grab the rubber boot, twist slightly and pull the wire free. Do not pull on the wire itself, only on the rubber boot **(see illustration 45.6)**.

4 Check inside the boot for corrosion, which will look like a white crusty powder. Push the wire and boot back onto the end of the spark plug. It should be a tight fit on the plug. If it isn't, remove the wire and use a pair of pliers to carefully crimp the metal connector inside the boot until it fits securely on the end of the spark plug.

5 Using a clean rag, wipe the entire length of the wire to remove any built-up dirt and grease. Once the wire is clean, check for holes, burned areas, cracks and other damage. Don't bend the wire excessively or the conductor inside might break.

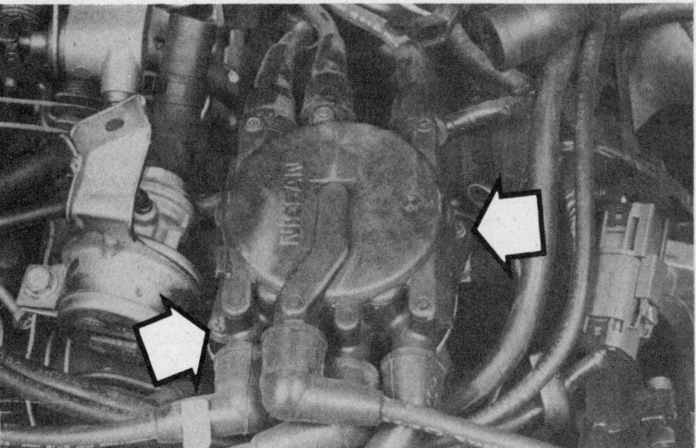

47.2 On later models, the distributor cap is held in place by two screws (arrows)

6 Disconnect the wire from the distributor cap. Again, pull only on the rubber boot. Check for corrosion and a tight fit in the same manner as the spark plug end. Reattach the wire to the distributor cap.

7 Check the remaining spark plug wires one at a time, making sure they are securely fastened at the distributor and the spark plug when the check is complete.

8 If new spark plug wires are required, purchase a new set for your specific engine model. Wire sets are available pre-cut, with the rubber boots already installed. Remove and replace the wires one at a time to avoid mix-ups in the firing order. The wire routing is extremely important, so be sure to note exactly how each wire is situated before removing it.

47 Distributor cap and rotor check and replacement

Refer to illustrations 47.2, 47.4, 47.5 and 47.8

Note: *It's common practice to install a new distributor cap and rotor whenever new spark plug wires are installed.*

1 Although the breakerless distributor used on these vehicles requires much less maintenance than a conventional distributor, periodic inspections should be performed at the intervals specified in the routine maintenance schedule and whenever any work is performed on the distributor.

2 Disconnect the ignition coil wire(s) from the coil(s), then unsnap the spring clips or loosen the screws that hold the cap to the distributor body **(see illustration)**. Detach the distributor cap and wires.

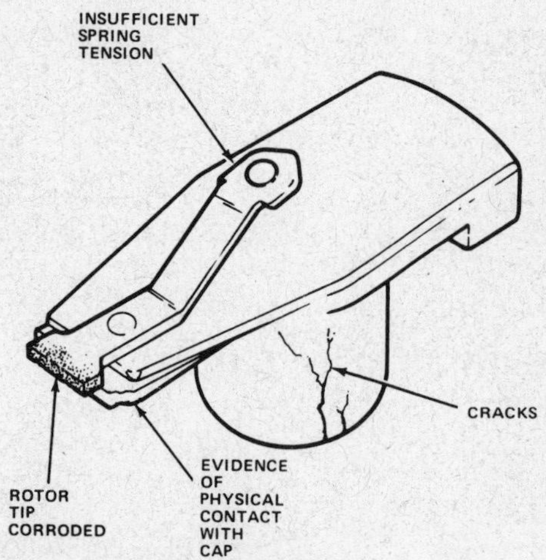

47.4 The ignition rotor should be checked for wear and corrosion as indicated here (if in doubt about its condition, buy a new one)

47.5 Later model distributor rotors are retained by a bolt (arrow) – don't try to pry off the rotor until the bolt has been loosened!

3 Place the cap, with the spark plug and coil wires still attached, out of the way. Use a length of wire or rope to secure it, if necessary.

4 The rotor is now visible on the end of the distributor shaft. Check it carefully for cracks and carbon tracks. Make sure the center terminal spring tension is adequate (not all models) and look for corrosion and wear on the rotor tip **(see illustration)**. If in doubt about its condition, replace it with a new one.

5 If replacement is required, detach the rotor from the shaft and install a new one. On 1980 models, the rotor can simply be pulled off the shaft. On later models, the rotor is retained on the shaft by a single screw **(see illustration)**.

6 Check the wire connections at the IC unit (on 1980 models this is the unit on the outside of the distributor body with a wiring connector attached to it; on 1981 and later models, it's inside the distributor, with two or three wires leading to it). Make sure they're clean and tight. Also check the wires to make sure they aren't cracked or broken.

7 While the distributor cap is off, check the air gap as described in Chapter 5.

8 Check the distributor cap for carbon tracks, cracks and other damage. Closely examine the terminals on the inside of the cap for excessive corrosion and damage **(see illustration)**. Slight deposits are normal. Again, if in doubt about the condition of the cap, replace it with a new one.

9 When replacing the cap, simply transfer the spark plug and coil wires, one at a time, from the old cap to the new cap. Be very careful not to mix up the wires!

10 Reattach the cap to the distributor, then tighten the screws or reposition the spring clips to hold it in place.

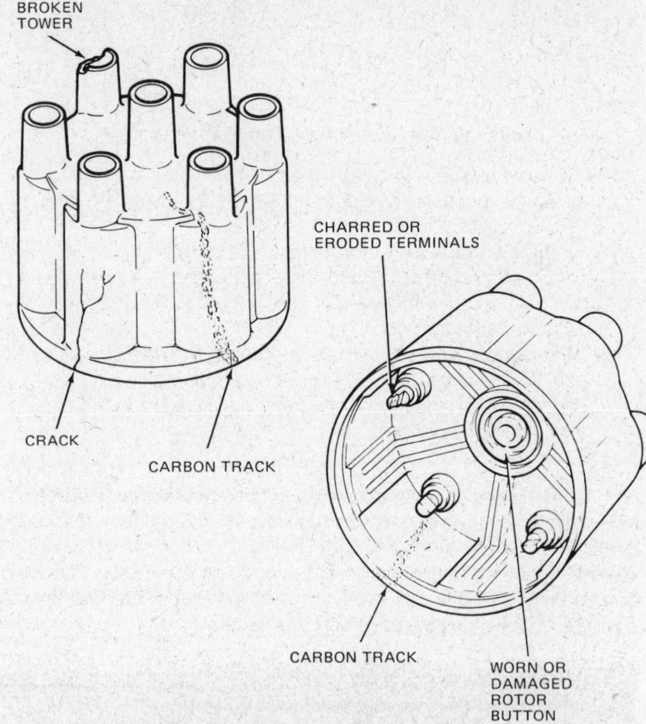

47.8 Shown here are some of the common defects to look for when inspecting the distributor cap (if in doubt about its condition, install a new one)

48 Ignition timing check and adjustment

Refer to illustrations 48.1, 48.2, 48.4 and 48.11

Note: *Ignition timing on 1990 and later models is controlled electronically by the E.C.U. and cannot be altered by the home mechanic. Additional information can be found in Chapter 6.*

1 The proper ignition timing setting for your vehicle is printed on the VECI label located on the underside of the hood. It can also be found in the Specifications section at the beginning of this Chapter. If there are any discrepancies between the figures, the VECI label should be considered correct. Some special tools will be required for this procedure **(see illustration)**.

2 On four-cylinder engines, locate the timing plate on the front of the engine, near the crankshaft pulley **(see illustration)**. The 0 mark is Top Dead Center (TDC). To locate which mark the notch in the pulley must line up with for the timing to be correct, count back from the 0 mark the number of degrees BTDC (Before Top Dead Center) noted in the Specifications. Normally each mark on the timing plate equals 5 degrees, so if your vehicle Specifications call for 6-degrees BTDC, you should make a mark with white paint or chalk at the 5 mark on the timing plate.

3 Locate the timing notch in the pulley and mark it with a dab of paint or chalk so it'll be visible under the strobe light. To locate the notch it may be necessary to have an assistant temporarily turn the ignition off and on in short bursts to turn the crankshaft. Warning: Stay clear of all moving engine components if the engine is turned in this manner!

4 On the V6 engine, the timing mark scale is on the vibration damper and the timing indicator (pointer) is stationary, attached to the engine **(see illustration)**. Highlight the pointer and the appropriate mark on the vibration damper with chalk or white paint (refer to the Emissions Control Information label).

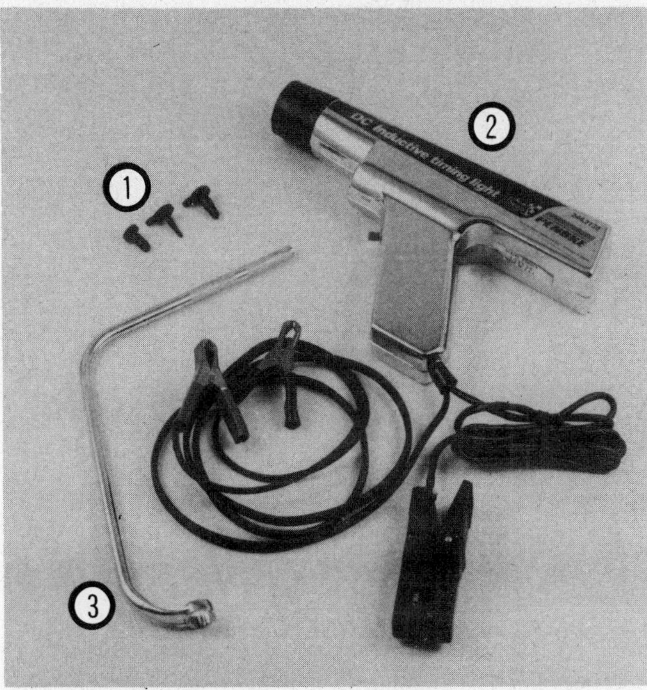

48.1 Tools needed to check and adjust the ignition timing

1 ***Vacuum plugs*** – *Vacuum hoses will, in most cases, have to be disconnected and plugged. Molded plugs in various shapes and sizes are available for this.*
2 ***Inductive pick-up timing light*** – *Flashes a bright concentrated beam of light when the number one spark plug fires. Connect the leads according to the instructions supplied with the light.*
3 ***Distributor wrench*** – *On some models, the hold-down bolt for the distributor is difficult to reach and turn with conventional wrenches or sockets. A special wrench like this must be used.*

5 Connect a tachometer according to the manufacturer's instructions and make sure the idle speed is correct. Adjust it if necessary as described in Section 37.

6 Allow the engine to reach normal operating temperature. Be sure the air conditioner, if equipped, is off. On 1980 models, disconnect the hose from the air injection pipe assembly and securely plug the pipe opening.

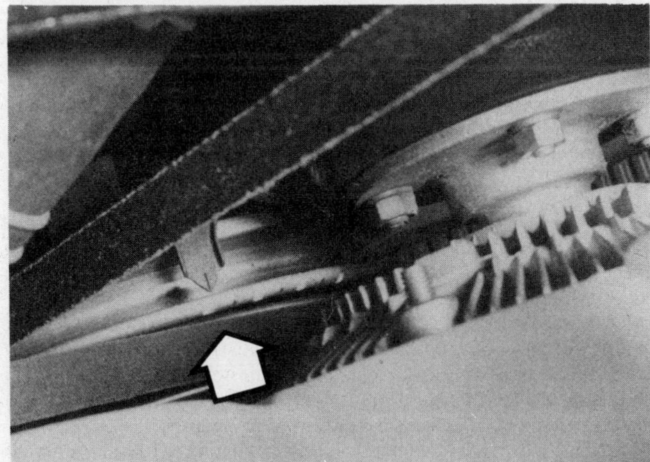

48.4 On the V6 engine, the timing marks are on the vibration damper and a pointer is attached to the engine

48.2 When setting the ignition timing, the crankshaft pulley notch (marked with white paint) should align with the specified notch or point on the timing plate (four-cylinder engines)

On some models, as noted in the Specifications or on the VECI label, you must disconnect the distributor vacuum advance hose and plug it.

7 With the ignition switch off, connect the pick-up lead of the timing light to the number one spark plug wire. On four-cylinder engines, it's the front one. On V6 engines it's the first spark plug on the right side as viewed from the driver's seat. Use either a jumper lead between the wire and plug or an inductive-type pick up. Don't pierce the wire or attempt to insert a wire between the boot and plug wire. Connect the timing light power leads according to the manufacturer's instructions.

8 Make sure the wiring for the timing light is clear of all moving engine components, then start the engine. Race the engine two or three times, then allow it to idle for a minute.

9 Point the flashing timing light at the timing marks, again being careful not to come in contact with moving parts. The marks you highlighted should appear stationary. If the marks are in alignment, the timing is correct. If the marks aren't aligned, turn off the engine.

10 On 1980 models, loosen the distributor mounting bolt until the distributor can be rotated. On later models, loosen the adjusting bolts (indicated by the long slots they're mated with) which are separate from the distributor mounting bolts.

11 Start the engine and slowly rotate the distributor either left or right until the timing marks are aligned **(see illustration)**.

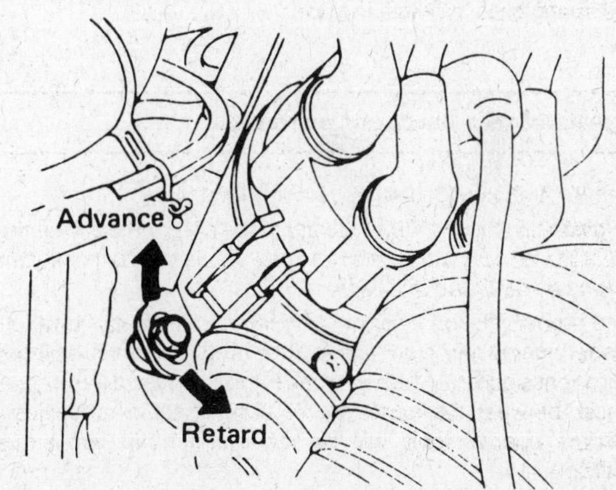

48.11 Ignition timing is adjusted by turning the distributor slightly as needed

1

12 Shut off the engine and tighten the distributor mounting/adjusting bolts, being careful not to move the distributor.
13 Restart the engine and recheck the timing to make sure the marks are still in alignment.
14 Disconnect the timing light.
15 Race the engine two or three times, then allow it to run at idle. Recheck the idle speed with the tachometer. If it has changed from the correct setting readjust it.
16 Drive the vehicle and listen for "pinging" noises. They'll be noticeable when the engine is hot and under load (climbing a hill, accelerating from a stop). If you hear engine pinging, the ignition timing is too far advanced (Before Top Dead Center). Reconnect the timing light and turn the distributor to move the mark 1-degrees or 2-degrees in the retard direction (counterclockwise). Road test the vehicle again to check for proper operation.
17 To keep "pinging" at a minimum, yet still allow you to operate the vehicle at the specified timing setting, use gasoline of the same octane at all times. Switching fuel brands and octane levels can decrease performance and economy, and possibly damage the engine.

49 Oxygen sensor replacement

1 The oxygen (exhaust gas) sensor, used on all 1984 and later models, should be replaced at the specified intervals.
2 The sensor is threaded into the exhaust manifold and can be identified by the wires attached to it. Replacement consists of disconnecting the wire harness and unthreading the sensor from the manifold. Tighten the new sensor to the specified torque, then reconnect the wire harness.

Chapter 2 Part A Four-cylinder engines

Contents

Specifications

All engines

Cylinder numbers (front-to-rear)	1–2–3–4
Firing order	1-3-4-2
Displacement	
L20B (1980)	1952 cc
Z20 (1984 and 1985)	1952 cc
Z22 (1981 through 1983)	2187 cc
Z24 (1984 and 1985)	2389 cc
Z24i (1986 on)	2389 cc
KA24E	2389 cc
Valve clearances	See Chapter 1

L20B engine (1980)

Camshaft

Journal diameter	1.8877 to 1.8883 in (47.949 to 47.962 mm)
Bearing inner diameter	1.8898 to 1.8904 in (48.000 to 48.016 mm)
Bearing oil clearance	0.0015 to 0.0026 in (0.038 to 0.067 mm)
Runout limit	0.002 in (0.05 mm)
End play	0.008 in (0.2 mm)
Lobe height	
Intake	1.5866 to 1.5886 in (40.30 to 40.35 mm)
Exhaust	1.5866 to 1.5886 in (40.30 to 40.35 mm)

Oil pump

Rotor tip clearance	
Standard	Less than 0.0047 in (0.12 mm)
Limit	0.0079 in (0.20 mm)
Outer rotor-to-body clearance	
Standard	0.0059 to 0.0083 in (0.15 to 0.21 mm)
Limit	0.0197 in (0.5 mm)
Rotor end clearance	Less than 0.0024 in (0.06 mm)
Body-to-straightedge clearance	Less than 0.0012 in (0.03 mm)

Torque specifications

	Ft-lbs
Cylinder head bolts	51 to 61
Cylinder head-to-front cover bolts	3 to 6
Front cover-to-block bolts	
6 mm	3 to 7
8 mm	7 to 12
Chain guide and tensioner bolts	4.3 to 7.2
Crankshaft pulley bolt	87 to 116
Manifold bolts/nuts	9 to 12
Camshaft sprocket bolt	87 to 116
Camshaft thrust plate bolts	4.3 to 7.2
Rocker arm cover bolts	7 to 12
Oil strainer mounting bolts	7 to 12
Oil pump mounting bolts	8 to 11
Oil pan mounting bolts	4.3 to 7.2
Flywheel/driveplate-to-crankshaft bolts	101 to 116

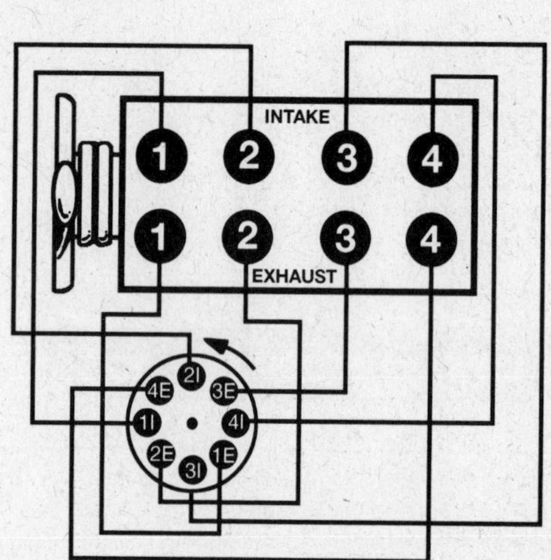

Spark plug wiring for the Z24i four-cylinder engine

NAPS-Z engine (1981 on)

Camshaft

Journal diameter	1.2967 to 1.2974 in (32.935 to 32.955 mm)
End play	0.008 in (0.2 mm)
Cam lobe height	1.5148 to 1.5168 in (38.477 to 38.527 mm)
Cam lobe wear limit	0.0098 in (0.25 mm)
Camshaft runout (one-half TIR @ center journal)	0.008 in (0.2 mm)
Bearing inside diameter	1.2992 to 1.3002 in (33.000 to 33.025 mm)
Bearing oil clearance	0.0018 to 0.0035 in (0.045 to 0.090 mm)

Oil pump

Rotor tip clearance	
Standard	Less than 0.0047 in (0.12 mm)
Limit	0.0079 in (0.20 mm)
Outer rotor-to-body clearance	
Standard	0.0059 to 0.0083 in (0.15 to 0.21 mm)
Limit	0.0197 in (0.50 mm)
Rotor end clearance	Less than 0.0024 in (0.06 mm)
Body-to-straightedge clearance	Less than 0.0012 in (0.03 mm)

Torque specifications

	Ft-lbs
Camshaft sprocket bolt	87 to 116 12 to 16
Chain guide and tensioner bolts	4.5 to 7
Crankshaft pulley bolt	87 to 116 12 to 16
Cylinder head bolts	
Z22 engine	
1981 and 1982	51 to 58
1983	58 to 65

Torque specifications (continued)	Ft-lbs
Cylinder head bolts	
Z20 and Z24 engines	
Step 1	22
Step 2	58
Step 3	Loosen all bolts
Step 4	22
Step 5	58
Exhaust manifold bolts/nuts	12 to 15
Flywheel/driveplate-to-crankshaft bolts	101 to 116
Rocker arm cover bolts	0.7 to 2.2
Front cover-to-block bolts	
6 mm	3 to 7
8 mm	7 to 12
Intake manifold bolts/nut	12 to 15
Oil pan mounting bolts	3.5 to 5
Oil pump mounting bolts	8 to 11
Valve rocker assembly mounting bolts	11 to 18

All 4-cylinder engines except Z-series

Cylinder location and distributor rotation

KA24E engine (1990 on)

Camshaft

Journal diameter	1.2967 to 1.2974 in (32.935 to 32.955 mm)
End play	0.008 in (0.2 mm)
Cam lobe height	1.7653 to 1.7728 in (44.839 to 45.029 mm)
Cam lobe wear limit	0.0098 in (0.25 mm)
Camshaft runout (one-half TIR @ center journal)	0.0008 in (0.02 mm)
Bearing inside diameter	1.2992 to 1.3002 in (33.000 to 33.025 mm)
Bearing oil clearance	0.0018 to 0.0035 in (0.045 to 0.090 mm)

Oil pump

Rotor tip clearance	
Standard	Less than 0.0047 in (0.12 mm)
Limit	0.0079 in (0.20 mm)
Outer rotor-to-body clearance	
Standard	0.0059 to 0.0083 in (0.15 to 0.21 mm)
Limit	0.0197 in (0.50 mm)
Rotor end clearance	Less than 0.0024 in (0.06 mm)
Body-to-straightedge clearance	Less than 0.0012 in (0.03 mm)

Torque specifications	Ft-lbs
Camshaft sprocket bolt	87 to 116
Chain guide and tensioner bolts	5.1 to 9.0
Crankshaft pulley bolt	87 to 116
Cylinder head bolts	
Step 1	22
Step 2	58
Step 3	Loosen all bolts completely
Step 4	22
Step 5	54 to 61
Exhaust manifold bolts/nuts	12 to 15
Flywheel-to-crankshaft bolts	105 to 112
Driveplate-to-crankshaft bolts	69 to 76
Intake manifold bolts/nuts	12 to 15
Oil pan mounting bolts	3.5 to 5.0
Oil pump mounting bolts	8 to 11
Rocker arm cover bolts	2.9 to 5.8
Valve rocker assembly mounting bolts	27 to 30

1 General information

This Part of Chapter 2 is devoted to in-vehicle repair procedures for the four-cylinder engines. All information concerning engine removal and installation and engine block and cylinder head overhaul can be found in Part C of this Chapter.

The following repair procedures are based on the assumption that the engine is installed in the vehicle. If the engine has been removed from the vehicle and mounted on a stand, many of the steps outlined in this Part of Chapter 2 will not apply.

The Specifications included in this Part of Chapter 2 apply only to the procedures contained in this Part. Part C of Chapter 2 contains the Specifications necessary for cylinder head and engine block rebuilding.

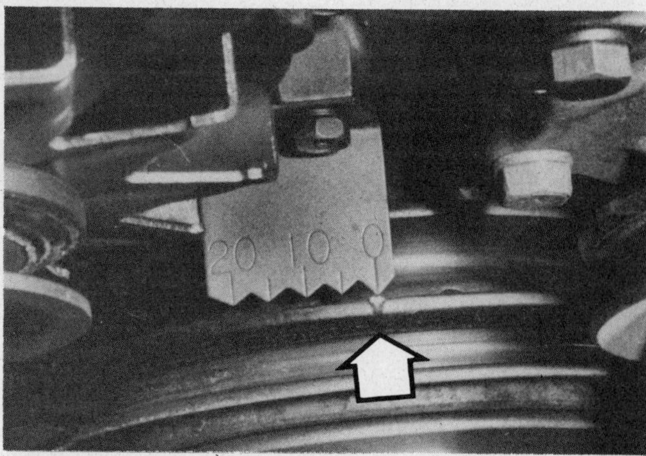

3.5a **The number one piston is at TDC on the compression stroke when the notch in the crankshaft pulley is aligned with the 0 on the timing plate and the rotor is pointing at the number one spark plug terminal in the distributor cap**

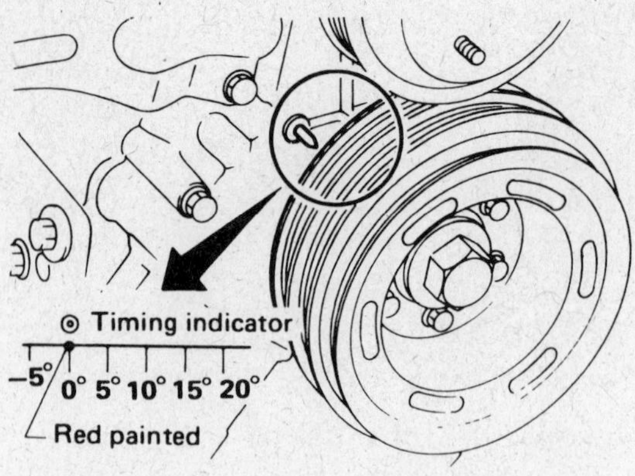

3.5b **Timing mark designations on the KA24E engine**

In 1980, the first year of the 720 Series pick-up, the truck came equipped with the L20B engine, a carry-over from the 620 Series. In 1981 the NAPS-Z engine was introduced to the pick-up line. Both types are four-cylinder OHC inline engines.

The cast iron engine block contains the four cylinder bores and acts as a rigid support for the five main bearing crankshaft. The machined cylinder bores are surrounded by water jackets to dissipate heat and control operating temperature.

The cylinder head is aluminum and incorporates wedge-type combustion chambers. In the NAPS-Z engines, two spark plugs are used for each cylinder to burn the fuel/air mixture with greater efficiency.

Two valves per cylinder are mounted at a slight angle in the cylinder head and are actuated by a rocker arm in direct contact with the camshaft. Double springs are installed on each valve.

The camshaft is driven by a roller chain from the front of the crankshaft. Chain tension is controlled by a tensioner, which is operated by oil and spring pressure. The rubber shoe type tensioner controls vibration and tension of the chain.

The pistons are a special aluminum casting with struts to control thermal expansion. There are two compression rings

and one oil control ring. The piston pin is a hollow steel shaft which is fully floating in the piston and a press fit in the connecting rod. The pistons are attached to the crankshaft by forged steel connecting rods.

The distributor, which is mounted on the left-hand side of the engine block, is driven by a helical gear mounted on the front of the crankshaft. The oil pump, which is mounted low on the right-hand side of the block is on a common centerline with the distributor and is driven by the same helical gear.

The crankshaft, which is made of special forged steel, has internal oil passages to provide lubrication to the main and connecting rod bearings. Oil is delivered, via the filter and pressure relief valve, to the main oil gallery from which it passes to the main bearing journals and then to the connecting rod bearing journals through holes in the crankshaft. Oil throw off from the connecting rod lower ends, as well as a jet hole drilled through each connecting rod into the lower end, provides lubrication for the pistons and connecting rod upper ends. At the top of the engine, galleries drilled in the camshaft supports provide oil for the five bearings, while a pipe that runs along the length of the camshaft, delivers oil to each cam pad surface, to provide lubrication for the rocker arm and pivot.

2 Repair operations possible with the engine in the vehicle

Many major repair operations can be accomplished without removing the engine from the vehicle.

Clean the engine compartment and the exterior of the engine with some type of pressure washer before any work is done. It'll make the job easier and help keep dirt out of the internal areas of the engine.

Remove the hood to improve access to the engine as repairs are performed (refer to Chapter 12 if necessary).

If vacuum, exhaust, oil or coolant leaks develop, indicating a need for gasket or seal replacement, the repairs can generally be made with the engine in the vehicle. The oil pan gasket, cylinder head gasket, intake and exhaust manifold gaskets, engine front cover gaskets and the crankshaft oil seals are accessible with the engine in place.

Exterior engine components, such as the water pump, the starter motor, the alternator, the distributor and the fuel system components, as well as the intake and exhaust manifolds, can be removed for repair with the engine in place.

Since the cylinder head can be removed without pulling the engine, camshaft and valve component servicing can also be accomplished with the engine in the vehicle.

Replacement of, repairs to or inspection of the timing chain and sprockets and the oil pump are all possible with the engine in place.

In extreme cases caused by a lack of necessary equipment, repair or replacement of piston rings, pistons, connecting rods and rod bearings is possible with the engine in the vehicle. However, this practice is not recommended because of the cleaning and preparation work that must be done to the components involved.

3 Top Dead Center (TDC) for number one piston – locating

Refer to illustration 3.5a and 3.5b

1 Top Dead Center (TDC) is the highest point in the cylinder that each piston reaches as it travels up-and-down when the crankshaft turns. Each piston reaches TDC on the compression stroke and again on the exhaust stroke, but TDC generally refers to piston position on the compression stroke. The timing marks on the pulley installed on the front of the crankshaft are referenced to the number one piston at TDC on the compression stroke.

2 Positioning the piston(s) at TDC is an essential part of many procedures such as rocker arm removal, camshaft and timing chain/sprocket removal and distributor removal.

3 In order to bring any piston to TDC, the crankshaft must be turned using one of the methods outlined below. When looking at the front of the engine, normal crankshaft rotation is clockwise. **Warning:** *Before beginning this procedure, be sure to place the transmission in Neutral. Also, detach the coil wire from the center terminal of the distributor cap and ground in on the block with a jumper wire.*

a) The preferred method is to turn the crankshaft with a large socket and breaker bar attached to the crankshaft pulley hub bolt threaded into the front of the crankshaft.

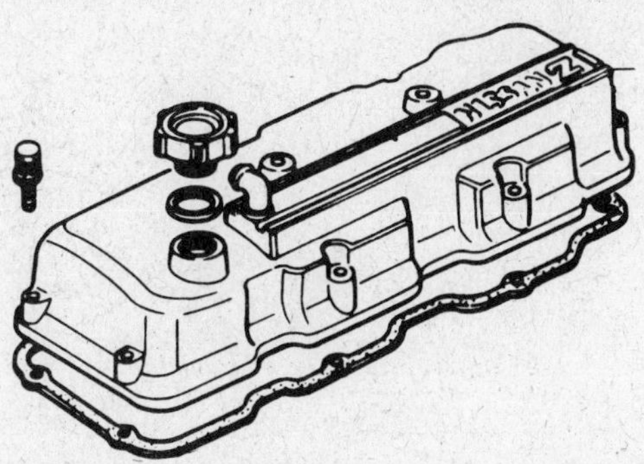

4.4 Rocker arm cover and related components – exploded view

b) A remote starter switch, which may save some time, can also be used. Attach the switch leads to the solenoid terminals. Once the piston is close to TDC, use a socket and breaker bar as described in the previous paragraph.

c) If an assistant is available to turn the ignition switch to the Start position in short bursts, you can get the piston close to TDC without a remote starter switch. Use a socket and breaker bar as described in Paragraph a) to complete the procedure.

4 Note the position of the terminal for the number one spark plug wire on the distributor cap. Use a felt-tip pen or chalk to make a mark on the distributor body directly under the terminal. Detach the cap from the distributor and set it aside.

5 Turn the crankshaft (see Paragraph 3 above) until the notch in the crankshaft pulley is aligned with the 0 on the timing plate (located at the front of the engine) **(see illustrations)**.

6 Look at the distributor rotor – it should be pointing directly at the mark you made on the distributor body. If the rotor is pointing at the terminal for the number four spark plug, the number one piston is at TDC on the exhaust stroke.

7 To get the piston to TDC on the compression stroke, turn the crankshaft one complete turn (360-degrees) clockwise. The rotor should now be pointing at the mark on the distributor. When the rotor is pointing at the number one spark plug wire terminal in the distributor cap and the ignition timing marks are aligned, the number one piston is at TDC on the compression stroke.

8 After the number one piston has been positioned at TDC on the compression stroke, TDC for any of the remaining pistons can be located by turning the crankshaft 180-degrees at a time and following the firing order.

4 Rocker arm cover – removal and installation

Refer to illustration 4.4 and 4.9

1 Remove the air cleaner (Chapter 4).

2 Remove the spark plug wires from all spark plugs and remove the wire supports from the rocker arm cover. Don't disconnect the wires from the supports.

3 On 1981 and later models, disconnect the brake booster vacuum hose and position it out of the way.

4 Remove the rocker arm cover mounting bolts **(see illustration)**.

5 Remove the rocker arm cover. **Caution:** *If the cover is stuck to the head, bump the end with a block of wood and a hammer to jar it loose. If that doesn't work, try to slip a flexible putty knife between the head and cover to break the gasket seal. Don't pry at the cover to-head joint or damage to the sealing surfaces may occur, leading to oil leaks in the future.*

6 The mating surfaces of the head and rocker arm cover must be perfectly clean when the cover is installed. Use a gasket scraper to remove all traces of sealant and old gasket material, then clean the mating surfaces with lacquer thinner or acetone. If there's sealant or oil on the mating surfaces when the cover is installed, oil leaks may develop.

7 Apply a continuous bead of sealant to the cover-to-head mating surface of the cover. Be sure to apply it to the inside of the mounting bolt holes.

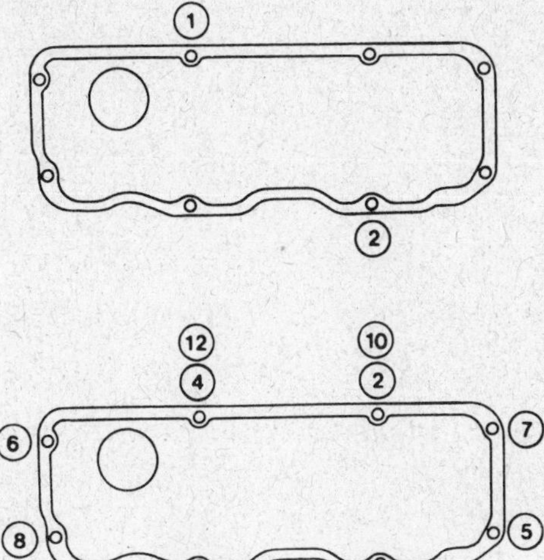

4.9 On KA24E engines, tighten bolts 1 and 2 to 2.2 ft-lbs on Step 1 then tighten ALL the bolts to 5.1 to 7.2 ft-lbs in the order shown in Step 2

8 Place the new gasket in position on top of the cylinder head, then place the rocker arm cover on the gasket. While the sealant is still wet, install the mounting bolts and tighten them to the specified torque.

9 Complete the installation by reversing the removal procedure **(see illustration)**.

5 Rocker arm assembly (1980 models) – removal and installation

Refer to illustrations 5.3, 5.4a and 5.4b

1 Remove the rocker arm cover as described in Section 4.

2 The crankshaft must be turned until the cam lobe contacting the rocker arm to be removed is pointing straight up. This can be done by operating the starter in short bursts or by turning the large bolt in the front of the crankshaft with a socket attached to a breaker bar.

3 Remove the valve rocker spring **(see illustration)**.

5.3 Removing the valve rocker spring (L20B engine)

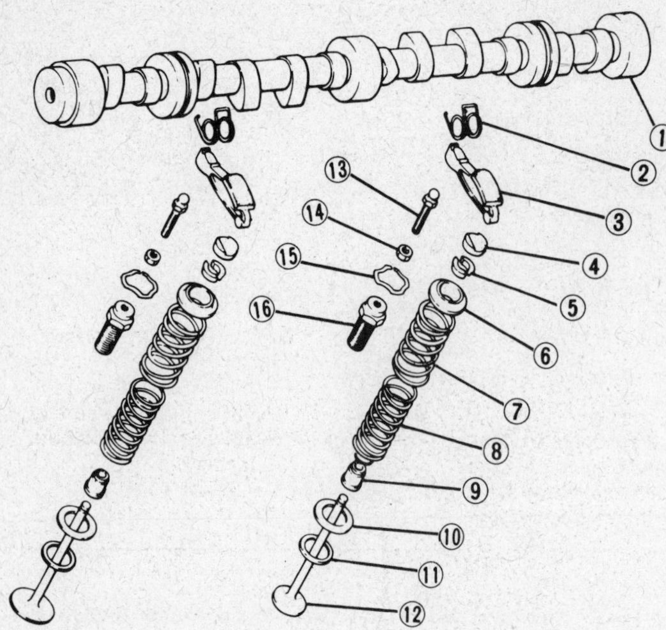

5.4a Camshaft and valve train components – exploded view (L20B engine)

1 Camshaft
2 Valve rocker spring
3 Rocker arm
4 Valve rocker guide
5 Valve keepers
6 Valve spring retainer
7 Outer valve spring
8 Inner valve spring
9 Valve guide oil seal
10 Outer valve spring seat
11 Inner valve spring seat
12 Valve
13 Valve rocker pivot
14 Rocker pivot locknut
15 Rocker spring retainer
16 Rocker pivot bushing

4 Loosen the rocker pivot locknut **(see illustration)**. Then use a screwdriver to depress the valve spring so the rocker arm can be lifted off **(see illustration)**. **Caution:** *Don't lever the screwdriver against the machined surfaces of the cam lobes.*

5 If more than one rocker arm is being removed, be sure to keep them in order so they can be reinstalled in their original positions on the cylinder head.

6 The valve rocker guides can be lifted off the valves, but be sure to keep them in order.

7 Inspect the contact surfaces of the rocker arms, rocker guides and rocker pivots for damage and excessive wear. Replace as necessary.

8 To replace the rocker pivot, loosen the pivot locknut and unscrew the pivot from the bushing **(see illustration 5.4a)**. Don't remove the pivot bushing from the cylinder head.

9 Prior to installation, apply a dab of grease to the contact surfaces of the rocker arms, rocker guides and rocker pivots.

10 Installation is the reverse of the removal procedure. Adjust the valve clearances first to the Cold specifications and then the Hot specifications as detailed in Chapter 1.

6 Valve rocker assembly (1981 and later models) – removal and installation

1 Remove the rocker arm cover as described in Section 4.

2 The valve rocker assembly is held to the cylinder head by ten mounting bolts. The bolts should be loosened 1/4-turn at a time, working toward the center from both ends. Loosen the bolts until they're free of the cylinder head, but don't remove them from the valve rocker assembly.

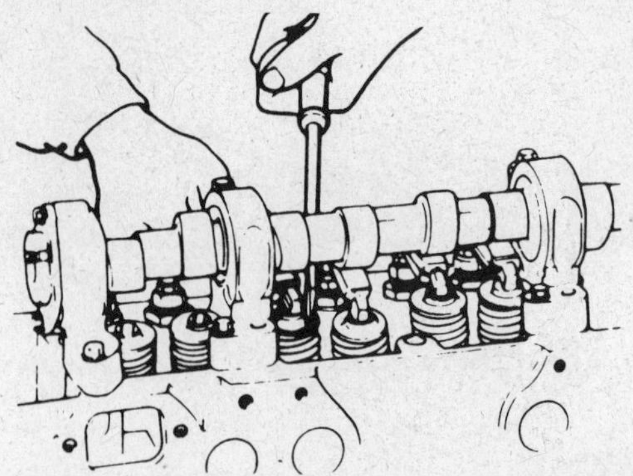

5.4b To remove the rocker arms on 1980 models (L20B engine), a screwdriver positioned as shown can be used to depress each valve spring

3 Once all mounting bolts are loose, lift the valve rocker assembly off the cylinder head.

4 If the valve rocker assembly must be disassembled for inspection or replacement of parts, refer to Section 7. If the valve rocker assembly isn't going to be disassembled, don't remove the four bolts at either end of the assembly (it'll come apart if the bolts are removed).

5 When installing the valve rocker assembly, first tighten the bolts until they're finger tight, working in from both ends. Continue to tighten the bolts 1/4-turn at a time until they're all at the specified torque.

7 Valve rocker assembly (1981 and later models) – disassembly and reassembly

Refer to illustrations 7.5a, 7.5b, 7.5c, 7.5d and 7.6

1 If not previously done, remove all of the valve rocker assembly mounting bolts except the two on either end.

2 While holding the assembly together, carefully remove the two bolts from one end of the assembly and allow the springs to expand.

3 Remove the components from the shafts, noting the installed order. Don't mix up the rocker arms; they must be installed in their original locations.

4 If the valve rocker assembly shafts are excessively worn, damaged or scored, they should be replaced with new ones.

5 To reassemble the rocker arm assembly, hold one of the end brackets and insert both shafts into it. Line up the bolt holes and insert the two end bolts. The intake shaft has a slit on the front surface to identify it, while the exhaust shaft has no identification mark. Both rocker shafts should be assembled so the punch marks on the front are at the top **(see illustration)**. Also, be sure the brackets are in their original locations. To ensure this, identification marks are provided on the cylinder head, as well as each bracket **(see illustration)**.

6 Install the valve rocker assembly components on the shafts in the correct order, compressing the springs as needed until the remaining end bracket can be installed along with the two mounting bolts. For convenience sake the remainder of the mounting bolts can also be installed **(see illustration)**.

8 Camshaft – removal and installation

1980 models (L20B engine)

Refer to illustrations 8.4, 8.6 and 8.13

1 Remove the rocker arm cover as described in Section 4.

2 Remove the rocker arms as described in Section 5.

3 Bring the number one piston to TDC by referring to Section 3, if necessary.

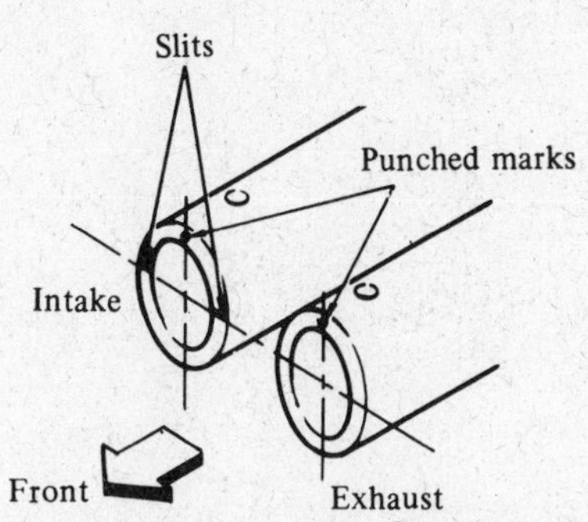

7.5a When installed, the rocker shaft with the slits should be on the intake side and the punch marks on both shafts should be in the 12 o'clock position (on top) (NAPS-Z engine shown)

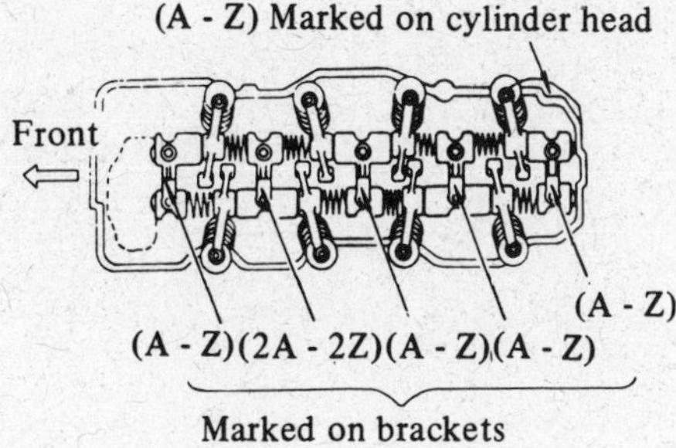

7.5b To ensure the valve rocker assembly brackets are installed in their correct positions, identification marks are provided on both the brackets and the cylinder head (NAPS-Z engine shown)

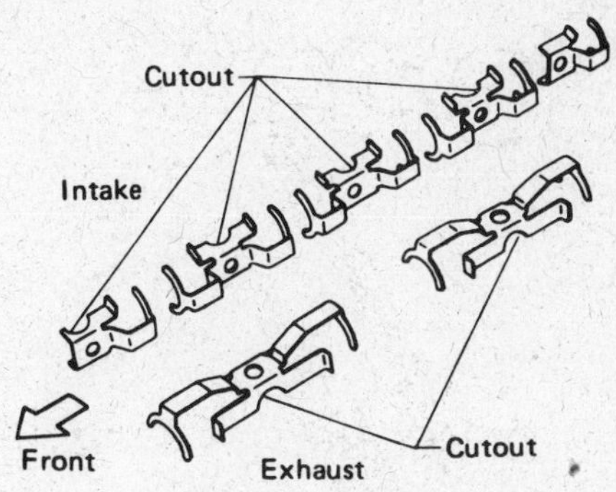

7.5c On KA24E engines, be sure to install the retainers with the cutouts facing out

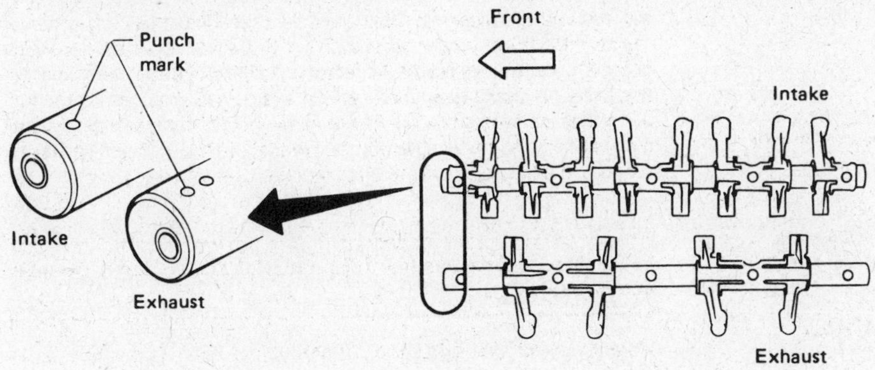

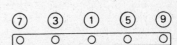

7.5d On KA24E engines, the punch marks face up and toward the front

7 3 1 5 9

8 4 2 6 10

7.6 Tighten the rocker arm assembly starting inside and work your way to the outside bolts

4 If you intend to remove the camshaft only, without disassembly of the cylinder head, DO NOT alter the timing sprocket position in relationship to the timing chain! Mark both the timing chain and the camshaft sprocket to preserve the original installed position of the two **(see illustration)**. The chain must be reinstalled on the camshaft sprocket in the exact same relationship. If a major overhaul is being done, then the sprocket/chain relationship doesn't have to be maintained.

5 Before removing the camshaft sprocket, cut a piece of wood 10 inches long, 3/4 inch thick, 1-1/2 inches wide at the top and approximately 1-inch wide at the bottom.

6 Now remove the camshaft sprocket bolt and fuel pump drive cam, if equipped **(see illustration)**. A rod can be positioned through the camshaft to keep it from turning while the bolt is loosened.

7 Insert the piece of wood into the timing case (small end down) until it's wedged between the two runs of the chain. Be sure it's wedged securely in place. The timing chain must not be allowed to separate from the crankshaft sprocket, as it would necessitate removal of the front cover in order to reinstall the timing chain.

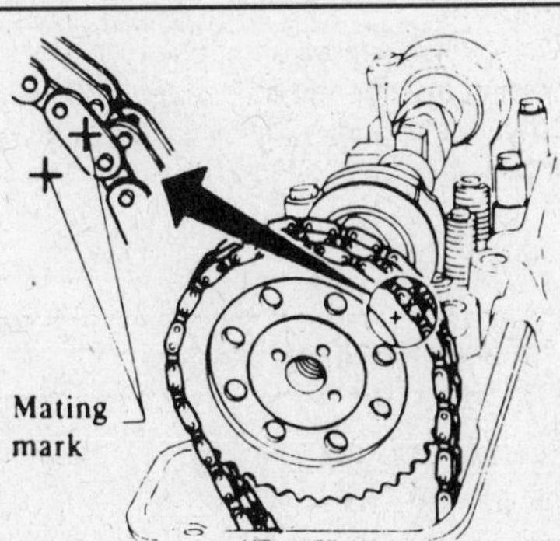

8.4 Prior to removing the timing chain from the camshaft sprocket, marks should be made to ensure correct installation

8.6 On models equipped with a mechanical fuel pump, a fuel pump drive cam is installed with the camshaft sprocket bolt

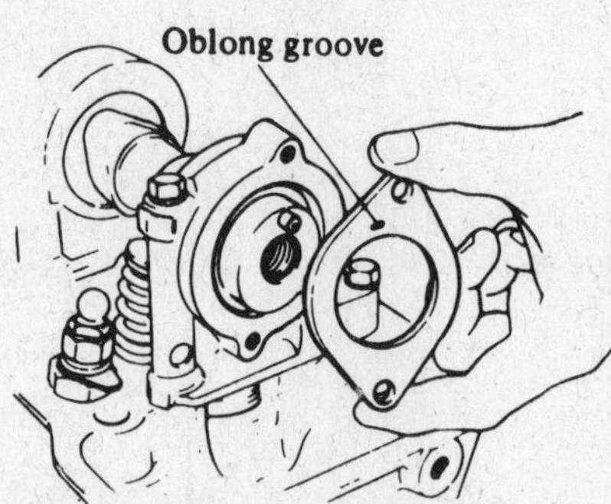

8.13 On 1980 models (L20B engine), the camshaft sprocket thrust plate must be installed with the oblong groove on top and facing out

8 Carefully remove the camshaft sprocket from the camshaft and work the chain off it until the sprocket can be removed. The chain can be left resting on the piece of wood.
9 Remove the bolts and detach the camshaft thrust plate.
10 Note the position of the small dowel pin in the end of the camshaft, then remove the pin. Carefully pull the camshaft out of the cam towers. Support it so the lobes don't scratch or nick the bearing surfaces. **Caution:** *DO NOT loosen the cam bearing tower mounting bolts! They are align bored after installation and must be left in place.*
11 Camshaft, rocker arm and cam bearing inspection instructions can be found in Section 9.
12 Prior to installing the camshaft, apply a coat of moly-base grease or engine assembly lube to the camshaft bearing surfaces, then carefully install the camshaft in the head. Turn it until the dowel pin is positioned correctly.
13 Reinstall the thrust plate with the oblong groove facing the front of the engine **(see illustration)**.
14 With the piece of wood still in place, carefully work the timing chain over the camshaft sprocket and attach the sprocket to the end of the camshaft with the cam dowel located in the number one sprocket hole. Be sure the marks made on the chain and sprocket during removal line up.
15 Carefully remove the piece of wood and install the fuel pump drive cam, if equipped, and camshaft sprocket bolt. Tighten the bolt to the specified torque.
16 Reinstall the rocker arms.
17 Adjust the valve clearances to the Cold specifications as described in Chapter 1.
18 Reinstall the rocker arm cover.

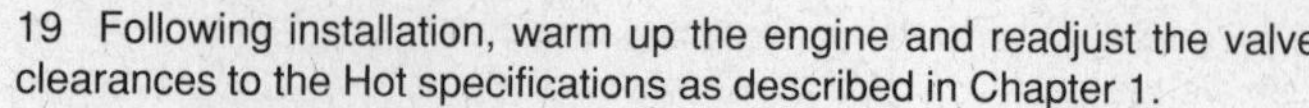

19 Following installation, warm up the engine and readjust the valve clearances to the Hot specifications as described in Chapter 1.

1981 and later models (NAPS-Z engine and KA24E engine)

Refer to illustrations 8.25, 8.27 and 8.31

20 Remove the rocker arm cover as described in Section 4.
21 Remove all spark plugs.
22 Bring the number one piston to TDC by referring to Section 3, if necessary.
23 If you intend to remove the camshaft only, without disassembly of the cylinder head, DO NOT alter the timing sprocket position in relationship to the timing chain! Mark both the timing chain and the camshaft sprocket to preserve the original installed position of the two. The chain must be reinstalled on the camshaft sprocket in the exact same relationship. If a major overhaul is being done, then the sprocket/chain relationship doesn't have to be maintained.
24 Before removing the camshaft sprocket, cut a piece of wood 10 inches long, 3/4 inch thick, 1-1/2 inches wide at the top and approximately 1-inch wide at the bottom.
25 Now remove the camshaft sprocket bolt and fuel pump drive cam, if equipped. A rod can be inserted through the camshaft sprocket to keep it from turning while the bolt is broken loose **(see illustration)**. In order to remove the bolt, the rubber plug located in front of it must be removed first.
26 Insert the piece of wood into the timing case (small end down) until it's wedged between the two runs of the chain. Be sure it's wedged securely in place. The timing chain must not be allowed to separate from the crankshaft sprocket, as it would necessitate removal of the front cover in order to reinstall the timing chain.
27 Carefully remove the camshaft sprocket from the camshaft and work the chain off it until the sprocket can be removed. The chain can be left resting on the piece of wood **(see illustration)**.
28 Remove the valve rocker assembly as described in Section 6.
29 Note the position of the small dowel pin in the end of the camshaft, then lift out the cam.
30 Camshaft, rocker arm and cam bearing inspection instructions can be found in Section 9.
31 When installing the camshaft, lubricate the bearing surfaces with moly-base grease or engine assembly lube **(see illustration)** and place it in the head. Turn it until the dowel pin is positioned the same way it was before removal.
32 Reinstall the valve rocker assembly. Tighten the mounting bolts finger tight only. Temporarily tighten the two center bolts to 14 ft-lbs.
33 With the piece of wood still in place, carefully work the timing chain over the camshaft sprocket and attach the sprocket to the end of the camshaft, with the cam dowel pin located in the number two sprocket hole. Be sure the marks made on the chain and sprocket during removal line up.

8.25 Keep the camshaft from turning by inserting an extension bar through one of the camshaft holes and resting the bar against the rocker arm shaft pedestal

8.27 A piece of wood, cut to the dimensions listed in the text, must be used to hold the timing chain in place while the camshaft sprocket is off

8.31 The camshaft bearing surfaces should be lubricated prior to installation of the camshaft

34 Carefully remove the piece of wood, then install the fuel pump drive cam (if equipped) and camshaft sprocket bolt. Tighten the bolt to the specified torque. Apply sealant to the rubber plug and reinstall it in the cylinder head.

35 Tighten the valve rocker assembly bolts to the specified torque.

36 Adjust the valve clearances to the Cold specifications as described in Chapter 1.

37 Reinstall the rocker arm cover and spark plugs.

38 Following installation, warm up the engine and readjust the valve clearances to the Hot specifications as described in Chapter 1.

9 Camshaft, bearings and rocker arms – inspection

The camshaft, bearing surface and rocker arm inspection procedures are identical to the procedures for the equivalent components in the V6 engine, so refer to Chapter 2, Part B, Section 15, for instructions and illustrations. Be sure to refer to the Specifications here in Part A. Note that Paragraphs 5 through 8 can be ignored, since the four-cylinder engines don't have lifters.

10 Valve springs and seals – replacement in vehicle

Refer to illustrations 10.4 and 10.7

Note: *Broken valve springs and defective valve stem seals can be replaced without removing the cylinder head. Two special tools and a compressed air source are normally required to perform this operation, so read through this Section carefully and rent or buy the tools before beginning the job. If compressed air isn't available, a length of nylon rope can be used to keep the valves from falling into the cylinder during this procedure.*

1 Refer to Section 3 and remove the rocker arm cover. On 1980 models, remove the camshaft (Section 8). On 1981 and later models, remove the valve rocker assembly (Section 6).

2 Remove the spark plug from the cylinder with the defective component. If all of the valve stem seals are being replaced, all of the spark plugs should be removed. On engines with two plugs per cylinder, remove one of the plugs from each cylinder.

3 Turn the crankshaft until the piston in the affected cylinder is at top dead center on the compression stroke (refer to Section 3 for instructions). If you're replacing all of the valve stem seals, begin with cylinder number one and work on the valves for one cylinder at a time. Move from cylinder-to-cylinder following the firing order sequence (1-3-4-2).

4 Thread an adapter into the spark plug hole and connect an air hose from a compressed air source to it **(see illustration)**. Most auto parts stores can supply the air hose adapter. **Note:** *Many cylinder compression gauges utilize a screw-in fitting that may work with your air hose quick-disconnect fitting.*

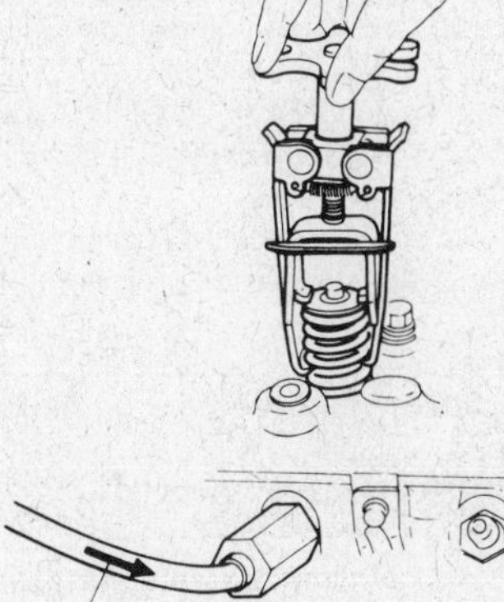

10.4 Compressed air can be used to hold the valves shut as the springs are compressed . . .

5 Apply compressed air to the cylinder. The valves should be held in place by the air pressure. If the valve faces or seats are in poor condition, leaks may prevent the air pressure from retaining the valves - refer to the alternative procedure below.

6 If you don't have access to compressed air, an alternative method can be used. Position the piston at a point just before TDC on the compression stroke, then feed a long piece of nylon rope through the spark plug hole until it fills the combustion chamber. Be sure to leave the end of the rope hanging out of the engine so it can be removed easily. Use a large breaker bar and socket to rotate the crankshaft in the normal direction of rotation until slight resistance is felt.

7 Stuff shop rags into the cylinder head holes to prevent parts and tools from falling into the engine, then use a valve spring compressor to compress the spring. Remove the keepers with small needle-nose pliers or a magnet **(see illustration)**.

8 Remove the valve, spring retainer and valve springs, then remove the umbrella type guide seal. **Note:** *If air pressure fails to hold the valve in the closed position during this operation, the valve face or seat is probably damaged. If so, the cylinder head will have to be removed for additional repair operations.*

9 Wrap a rubber band or tape around the top of the valve stem so the valve won't fall into the combustion chamber, then release the air pressure. **Note:** *If a rope was used instead of air pressure, turn the crankshaft slightly in the direction opposite normal rotation.*

10 Inspect the valve stem for damage. Rotate the valve in the guide and check the end for eccentric movement, which would indicate that the valve is bent.

11 Move the valve up-and-down in the guide and make sure it doesn't bind. If the valve stem binds, either the valve is bent or the guide is damaged. In either case, the head will have to be removed for repair.

12 Reapply air pressure to the cylinder to retain the valve in the closed position, then remove the tape or rubber band from the valve stem. If a rope was used instead of air pressure, rotate the crankshaft in the normal direction of rotation until slight resistance is felt.

13 Lubricate the valve stem with engine oil and install a new valve guide oil seal. A special tool is needed for the intake valve seals – refer to Section 11 in Part C.

14 Install the springs in position over the valve. Make sure the narrow pitch end of the outer spring is against the cylinder head.

15 Install the valve spring retainer. Compress the valve springs and position the keepers in the groove. Apply a small dab of grease to the inside of each keeper to hold it in place if necessary. Remove the pressure from the spring tool and make sure the keepers are seated.

16 Disconnect the air hose and remove the adapter from the spark plug hole. If a rope was used in place of air pressure, pull it out of the cylinder.

17 Install the camshaft (1980 models) or the valve rocker assembly (1981 and later models).

18 Install the spark plug(s) and hook up the wire(s).

10.7 . . . and the keepers (arrow) are removed

11.9 BPT valve, air injection gallery pipe, EGR valve, EGR passage and AB valve locations (left-to-right) (1980 models only)

19 Refer to Section 4 and install the rocker arm cover.
20 Start and run the engine, then check for oil leaks and unusual sounds coming from the rocker arm cover area.

11 Intake manifold – removal and installation

1980 models (L20B engine)

Refer to illustrations 11.9 and 11.18

Note: *The intake and exhaust manifolds on this engine share a common gasket. To prevent air leaks and possible damage to the valves, the gasket must be replaced whenever either manifold is removed – the manifolds must be removed and installed together. The engine must be completely cool when this procedure is done.*

1 Disconnect the negative battery cable from the battery.
2 Drain the cooling system.
3 Remove the air cleaner.
4 Disconnect the fuel and vacuum lines from the carburetor. Plug the fuel lines immediately to prevent fuel leakage and to keep dirt from entering the lines. Mark all lines and hoses before removal to ensure correct installation.
5 Disconnect all hoses from the intake manifold.
6 Unplug all wiring connectors leading to the carburetor.
7 Disconnect the brake booster hose from the intake manifold.
8 Disconnect the hoses from the fuel/vacuum tube assembly attached to the front of the cylinder head. Then remove the mounting bolts and detach the assembly. **Note:** *The hoses should be plugged after disconnection.*
9 Disconnect the hoses from the EGR and BPT valves **(see illustration)**.
10 Remove the BPT valve and bracket.
11 Disconnect the hose that attaches to the air injection gallery pipes.
12 Remove the rear engine lift bracket.
13 Remove the EGR valve, along with the EGR passage it's attached to.
14 Remove the anti-backfire (AB) valve and bracket located behind the carburetor.
15 Remove the duct that runs between the exhaust manifold and air cleaner.
16 Raise the front of the truck and support it on jackstands.
17 Disconnect the front exhaust pipe from the exhaust manifold.
18 Remove the EGR tube **(see illustration)**.
19 Remove the heat shield from the exhaust manifold.
20 Remove the mounting bolts and detach the manifold from the engine complete with carburetor and other attached components. If the manifold must be replaced, the components can be transferred directly to the new manifold prior to installation.

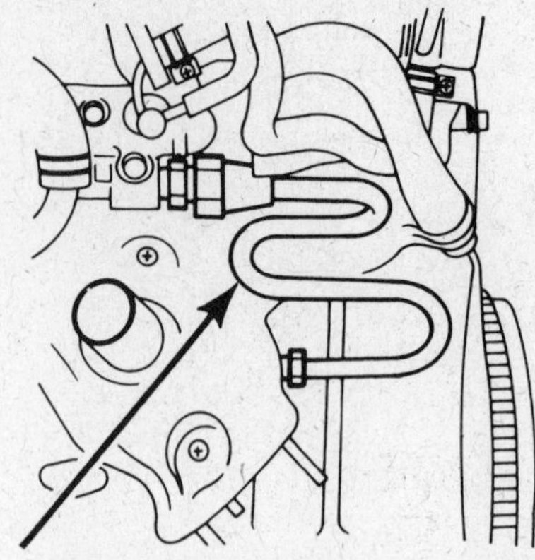

11.18 Location of the EGR tube (arrow), positioned under the intake manifold on 1980 models

21 Remove the exhaust manifold, complete with air injection pipes and injectors. If the manifold must be replaced, transfer them directly to the new manifold prior to installation.
22 Remove the manifold gasket.
23 Before installing the manifolds, stuff clean, lint-free rags in the engine ports and remove all traces of the old gasket and sealant with a scraper. Clean the mating surfaces with lacquer thinner or acetone.
24 Begin installation by placing the new gasket in position on the engine and reinstalling the exhaust manifold. Be sure the chamfered side of each washer faces the engine and tighten the mounting bolts only until they support the manifold. The bolts that are common to both manifolds should be finger tight only!
25 Place the intake manifold in position against the cylinder head and install the remaining bolts, again tightening them only enough to support the manifold.
26 Once both manifolds are installed, the mounting bolts can be tightened to the specified torque (work from the center toward the ends and work up to the final torque in three or four steps).
27 The remainder of installation is the reverse of the removal procedure.
28 Fill the radiator with coolant, start the engine and check for leaks. Also check and adjust the idle speed and throttle linkage as described in Chapter 1.

1981 and later models (NAPS-Z engine and KA24E engine)

Refer to illustration 11.36

29 Disconnect the negative battery cable from the battery.
30 Drain the cooling system.
31 Remove the air cleaner.
32 Disconnect the brake booster vacuum hose where it joins the metal pipe.
33 Disconnect all vacuum lines from the carburetor or throttle body and intake manifold. Mark them before removal to ensure correct installation.
34 Disconnect the rubber fuel hoses where they connect to the metal lines below the intake manifold. **Warning:** *On fuel injected vehicles, the fuel system pressure must be relieved before loosening any fittings or disconnecting any lines! Refer to Chapter 4 for instructions.*
35 Disconnect the vacuum lines leading to the VVT and EGR tubes.
36 Disconnect the EGR exhaust pipe from the EGR valve, and the PCV tube from the PCV valve **(see illustration)**.
37 Disconnect the throttle cable from the carburetor or throttle body.
38 Disconnect any wire harnesses leading to the carburetor or throttle body and intake manifold.
39 Remove the upper radiator hose.
40 Disconnect the battery ground cable from the lower thermostat housing bolt.
41 Disconnect the heater hose from the underside of the intake manifold.
42 Disconnect the hose from the PCV valve.
43 Remove the intake manifold mounting bolts and detach the manifold from the engine complete with carburetor/throttle body, EGR valve and other components. If the manifold must be replaced, the components can be transferred directly to the new manifold prior to installation.

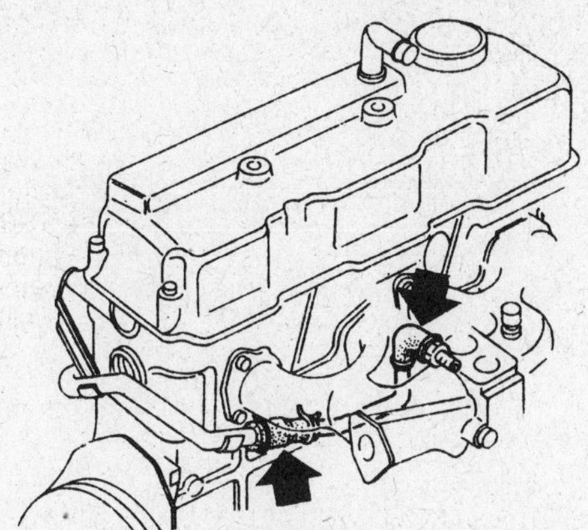

11.36 Location of the PCV tubes on 1981 and later models

44 Before installing the manifold, stuff clean, lint-free rags in the engine ports and remove all traces of the old gasket and sealant with a scraper. Clean the mating
surfaces with lacquer thinner or acetone.
45 Place a new intake manifold gasket in position on the manifold and loosely install the lower manifold mounting bolts and washers. Be sure the chamfered side of each washer is facing the engine. Place the manifold in position against the cylinder head and install the remaining mounting bolts.
46 Tighten the mounting bolts in three or four steps to the specified torque. Work from the center out toward the ends.
47 The remainder of installation is the reverse of the removal procedure.
48 Fill the radiator with coolant, start the engine and check for leaks. Also check and adjust the idle speed as described in Chapter 1.

12 Exhaust manifold – removal and installation

1980 models (L20B engine)

Since the exhaust manifold shares a common gasket with the intake manifold, and the gasket must be replaced when either manifold is removed, both manifolds should always be removed together. Refer to Section 11 for the procedure.

1981 and later models (NAPS-Z engine and KA24E engine)

Refer to illustration 12.4

1 Remove the air induction pipes and valve case, if equipped.
2 Remove the duct that runs between the exhaust manifold and air cleaner.
3 Remove the heat shield.
4 Disconnect the EGR tube from the rear of the exhaust manifold **(see illustration)**.
5 Raise the front of the vehicle and support it on jackstands.
6 Disconnect the front exhaust pipe from the exhaust manifold.
7 Remove the spark plug wires from the exhaust side spark plugs for access to the exhaust manifold bolts/nuts.
8 Remove the bolts and nuts that retain the exhaust manifold to the cylinder head.
9 Detach the exhaust manifold.
10 Before installing the manifold, remove all traces of the old gasket with a scraper. Clean the mating surfaces with lacquer thinner or acetone.
11 Place a new exhaust manifold gasket in position on the cylinder head then hold the manifold in place and install the mounting bolts/nuts finger tight.
12 Tighten the mounting bolts/nuts, in three or four steps, to the specified torque. Work from the center of the manifold out toward the ends to prevent distortion of the manifold.

12.4 Location of the air induction tubes (left) and EGR tube (right) at the exhaust manifold (1981 and later models) (NAPS-Z shown)

13 Install the remaining components. The remainder of installation is the reverse of the removal procedure.
14 Start the engine and check for exhaust leaks between the manifold and cylinder head and between the manifold and exhaust pipe.

13 Cylinder head – removal

1980 models (L20B engine)

Refer to illustration 13.10

1 Remove the intake and exhaust manifolds as described in Section 11.
2 Remove the upper radiator hose.
3 Remove the thermostat housing.
4 Disconnect the heater hose from the fitting on the right rear corner of the cylinder head.
5 Disconnect the spark plug wires from the spark plugs and position them out of the way, then remove the spark plugs.
6 Remove the fuel pump.
7 Remove the bolt that retains the battery ground cable and front engine lifting bracket to the cylinder head.
8 Remove the rocker arm cover.
9 Bring the number one piston to TDC (see Section 3) and remove the camshaft sprocket – be sure to follow the procedure in Section 8.
10 Using a new head gasket, outline the cylinders and bolt pattern on a piece of cardboard. be sure to indicate the front of the engine for reference. Punch holes at the bolt locations. Loosen the ten cylinder head bolts in 1/4-turn increments until they can be removed by hand. Be sure to follow the recommended sequence **(see illustration)**. Store the bolts in the

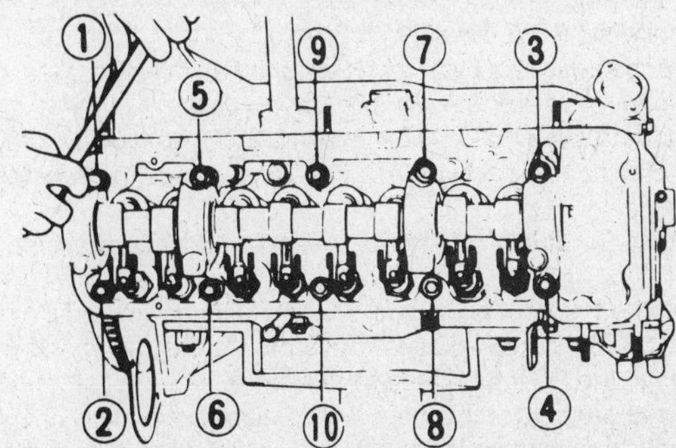

13.10 Cylinder head bolt LOOSENING sequence (1980 L20B engine) – a 10 mm Allen head socket will be needed to loosen/tighten the bolts

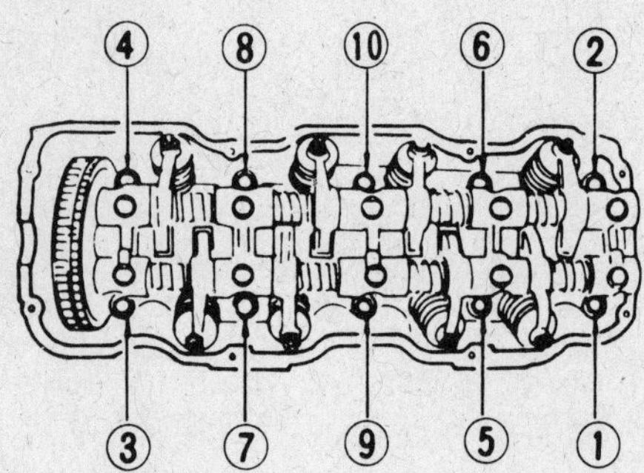

13.26a Cylinder head bolt LOOSENING sequence (1981 and later models)

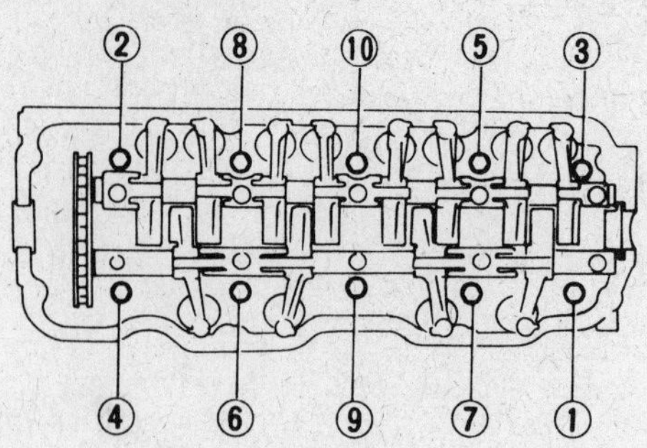

13.26b Cylinder bolt LOOSENING sequence (KA24E engine)

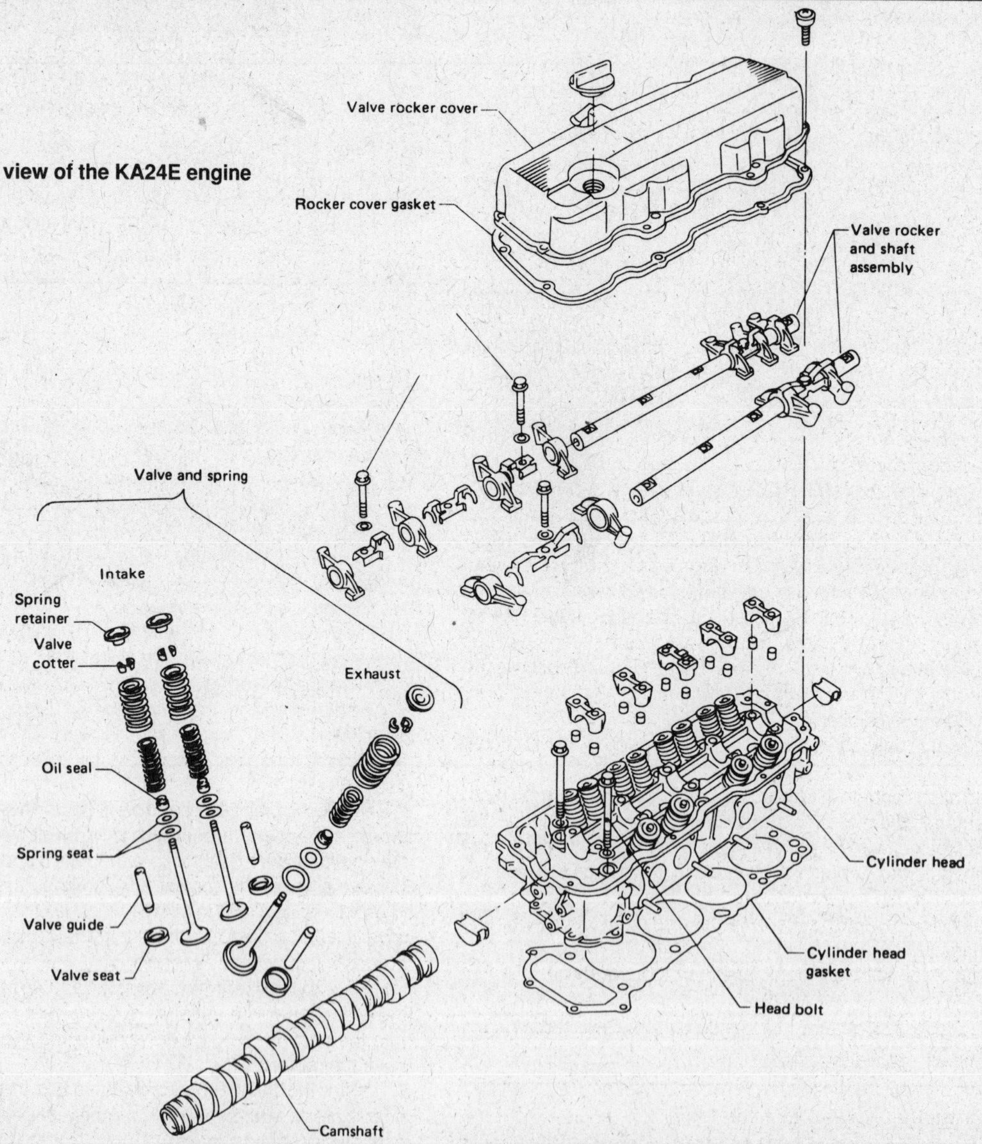

14.2 Exploded view of the KA24E engine

cardboard holder as they're removed – this will ensure that they're reinstalled in their original locations.

11 Remove the small bolts that attach the cylinder head to the front cover.

12 Lift the head off the engine. If it's stuck, DO NOT pry between the head and block – damage to the mating surfaces will result! To dislodge the head, position a block of wood against it and strike the wood block with a hammer. The timing chain should be left in place, resting on the wooden wedge.

13 Remove the cylinder head gasket. Place the head on a block of wood to prevent damage.

14 Refer to Part C for cylinder head inspection procedures.

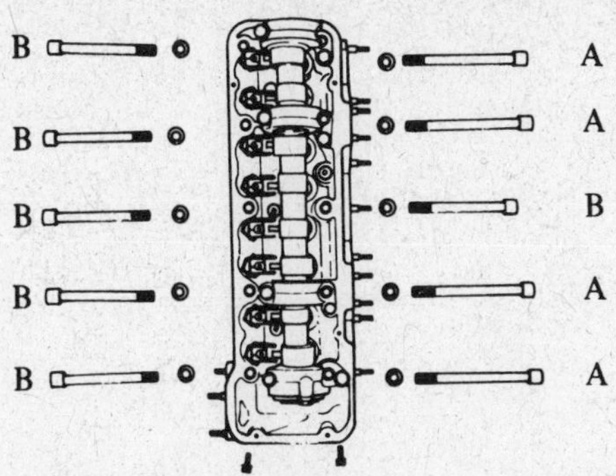

14.5 On 1980 models, two different length head bolts are used – make sure they're installed in the correct holes!

1981 and later models (NAPS-Z engine and KA24E engine)

Refer to illustration 13.26a and 13.26b

15 Drain the cooling system. Refer to Chapter 1, if necessary.
16 Remove the air cleaner and, if equipped, the power steering pump and idler pulley.
17 Disconnect the spark plug wires from the spark plugs and remove the brackets from the rocker arm cover. The spark plug wires do not have to be removed from the brackets.
18 Remove the air induction pipes and valve case, if equipped.
19 Remove the intake manifold as described in Section 11.
20 Remove the VVT valve and bracket from the firewall in the engine compartment. If equipped.
21 If equipped, remove the EGR pipe that runs behind the cylinder head.
22 Remove the mechanical fuel pump from the right front corner of the cylinder head, if equipped.
23 Detach the exhaust manifold from the cylinder head.
24 Remove the rocker arm cover.
25 Bring the number one piston to TDC (see Section 3) and remove the camshaft sprocket. Be sure to use the procedure described in Section 8.
26 Using a new head gasket, outline the cylinders and bolt pattern on a piece of cardboard. be sure to indicate the front of the engine for reference. Punch holes at the bolt locations. Loosen the ten cylinder head bolts in 1/4-turn increments until they can be removed by hand. Be sure to follow the recommended sequence **(see illustrations)**. Make several passes through the sequence to slowly release the tension. Store the bolts in the cardboard holder as they're removed – this will ensure that they're reinstalled in their original locations.
27 Remove the small bolts that attach the cylinder head to the front cover.
28 Lift the head off the engine. If it's stuck, DO NOT pry between the head and block – damage to the mating surfaces will result! To dislodge the head, position a block of wood against it and strike the wood block with a hammer. The timing chain should be left in place, resting on the wooden wedge.
29 Remove the cylinder head gasket. Place the head on a block of wood to prevent damage.
30 Refer to Part C for cylinder head inspection procedures.

14 Cylinder head – installation

Refer to illustrations 14.2, 14.5, 14.6a and 14.6b

1 The mating surfaces of the cylinder head and block must be perfectly clean when the head is installed. Use a gasket scraper to remove all traces of carbon and old gasket material, then clean the mating surfaces with lacquer thinner or acetone. If there's oil on the mating surfaces when the head is installed, the gasket may not seal correctly and leaks could develop. When working on the block, stuff the cylinders with clean shop rags to keep out debris. Use a vacuum cleaner to remove any debris that falls into the cylinders.

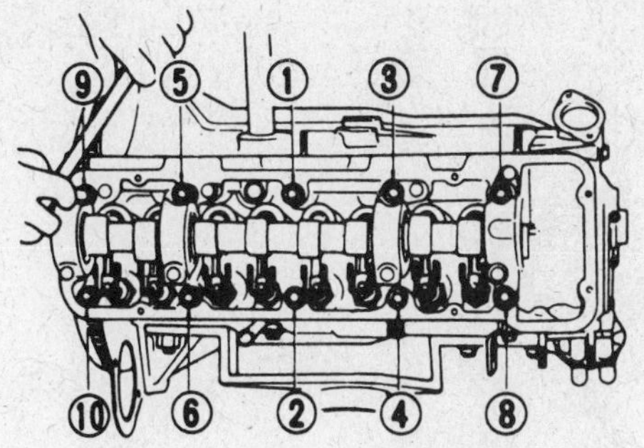

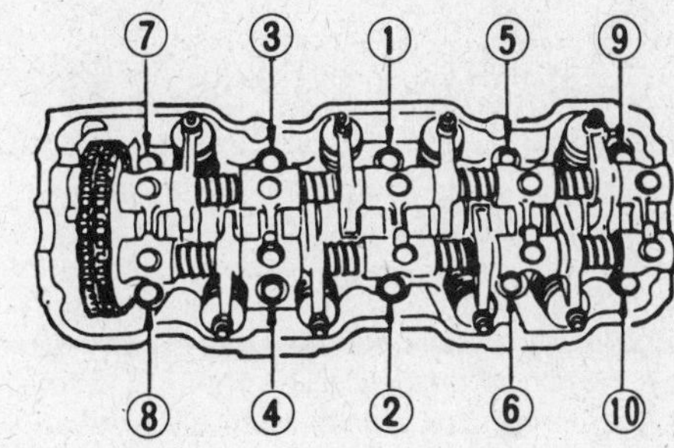

14.6a Cylinder head bolt TIGHTENING sequence (top – 1980 models; bottom – 1981 and later models)

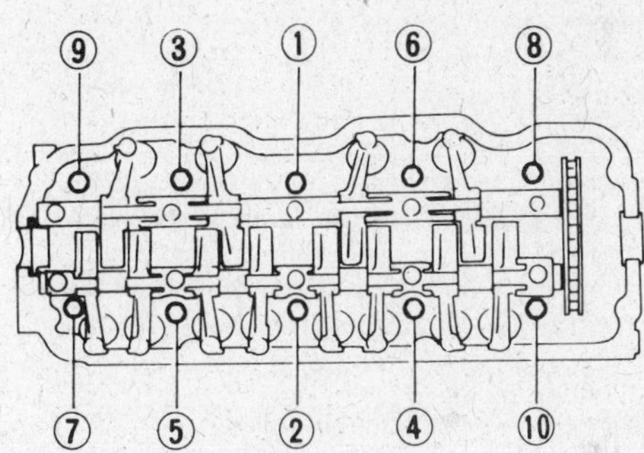

14.6b Cylinder head bolt TIGHTENING sequence for the KA24E engine

2 Check the block and head mating surfaces for nicks, deep scratches and other damage **(see illustration)**. If damage is slight, it can be removed with a file; if it's excessive, machining may be the only alternative.
3 Use a tap of the correct size to chase the threads in the head bolt holes. Mount each bolt in a vise and run a die down the threads to remove corrosion and restore the threads. Dirt, corrosion, sealant and damaged threads will affect torque readings.
4 Place the gasket in place over the engine block dowel pins. Make sure the number one piston is still at TDC, then carefully lower the cylinder head onto the engine, over the dowel pins and the gasket. Be careful not to move the gasket.
5 Install the cylinder head mounting bolts. Note that the bolts on 1980 models are two different lengths – make sure they're installed in the correct holes **(see illustration)**.
6 Tighten the bolts in 1/4-turn increments, following the recommended sequence **(see illustrations)**, until the specified torque is reached. On 1984 and later engines, follow the five step procedure outlined in the torque specifications.
7 Install the camshaft sprocket as described in Section 8.
8 The remainder of the installation procedure is the reverse of the removal procedure.

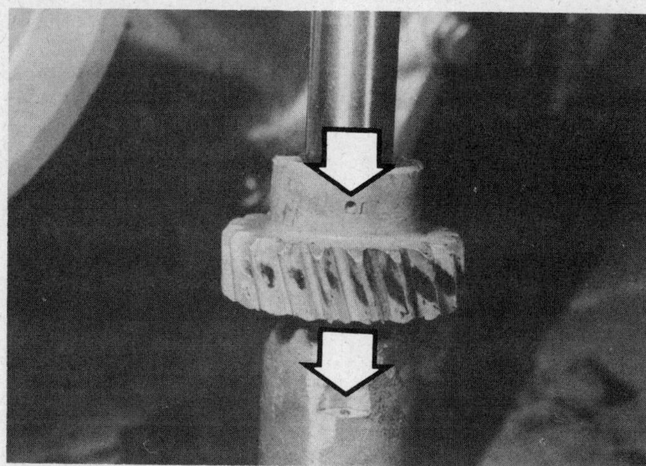

15.10 When installing the oil pump, the punch mark on the side of the spindle should be aligned with the pump's oil hole (arrows)

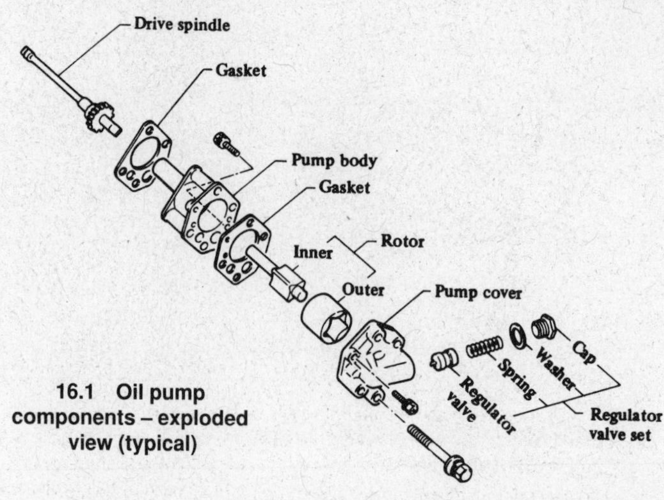

16.1 Oil pump components – exploded view (typical)

9 Fill the radiator with coolant, start the engine and check for leaks. Be sure to recheck the coolant level once the engine has warmed up to operating temperature. Also check and adjust the idle speed as described in Chapter 1.
10 Readjust the valve clearances to the Hot specifications as described in Chapter 1.

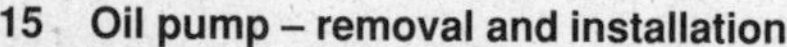

15 Oil pump – removal and installation

Refer to illustrations 15.10

1 Position the number one piston at TDC on the compression stroke. Refer to Section 3 if necessary.
2 Remove the distributor cap and mark the position of the rotor in relation to the distributor body.
3 Raise the front of the truck and support it with jackstands.
4 Remove the splash shields from the underside of the engine compartment.
5 Drain the engine oil.
6 On 4WD models, support the front differential with a jack. Then remove the differential mounting crossmember in order to gain enough clearance for removal of the oil pump.
7 Remove the pump-to-cover bolts and withdraw the oil pump/driveshaft assembly.
8 If the oil pump must be inspected or overhauled, refer to Section 16.
9 Prior to installation, make sure that the number one piston is still at TDC.
10 Fill the pump body with engine oil to prime it and align the punch mark on the driveshaft with the oil hole below the drive gear **(see illustration)**.
11 Install a new gasket and insert the pump into the recess in the engine front cover.
12 Tighten the oil pump mounting
bolts and check that the rotor is still aligned with the mark made on the distributor body. If it isn't, repeat the oil pump installation procedure.
13 Fill the engine with the proper quantity and grade of engine oil (refer to Chapter 1, if necessary).
14 Finally, check the ignition timing as described in Chapter 1.

16 Oil pump – inspection

Refer to illustrations 16.1 and 16.4

1 Remove the pump, then unbolt the cover and pull out the inner and outer rotors **(see illustration)**.
2 Remove the pressure regulator valve cap and washer and extract the spring and valve.

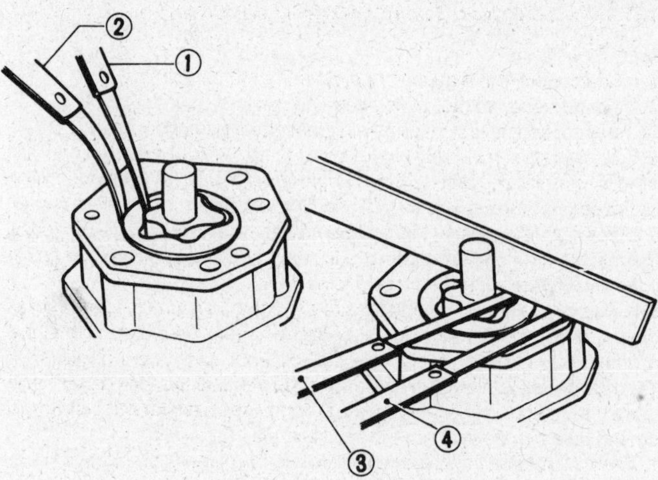

16.4 Feeler gauges are used to check the oil pump's rotor tip clearance (1) outer rotor-to-body clearance (2) rotor end clearance (3) and body-to-straightedge clearance (4)

3 Clean the pump components with solvent and dry them with compressed air, if available.
4 Check all components for excessive wear and score marks. Insert the rotors into the pump body with the marked ends facing IN and check the rotor clearances in the following manner **(see illustration)**:

a) Check the clearance between the lobes on the inner and outer rotors (1 in illustration 16.4).
b) Check the clearance between the outer rotor and the body (2 in illustration 16.4).
c) Check the rotor end clearance with a straightedge and feeler gauges (3 in illustration 16.4).
d) Again, using the straightedge placed across the body, check the clearance between the body and the straightedge (4 in illustration 16.4).

5 If the clearances aren't as specified, replace the pump. The inner and outer rotors are only supplied as matched sets. If the oil pump body is worn or damaged, replace the complete pump assembly.
6 Check the condition of the pressure regulator valve and spring. The sliding surface of the valve must not be damaged or worn. Replace it if necessary.

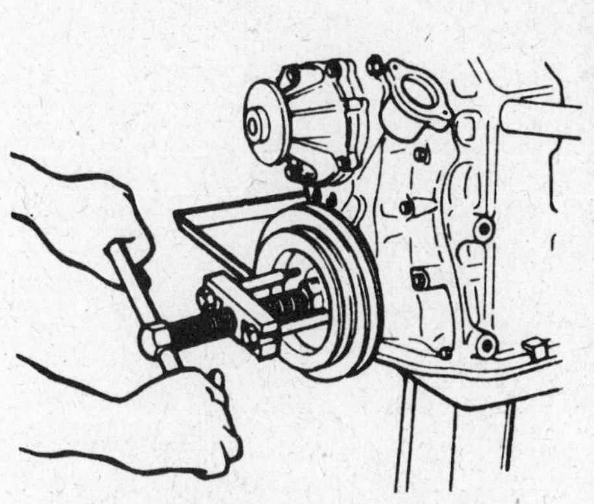

17.6 A puller such as the one shown here may have to be used to remove the crankshaft pulley.

18.2 After removing the crankshaft pulley, carefully pry the seal (arrow) out of the front cover – don't scratch or nick the crankshaft or oil leaks will develop!

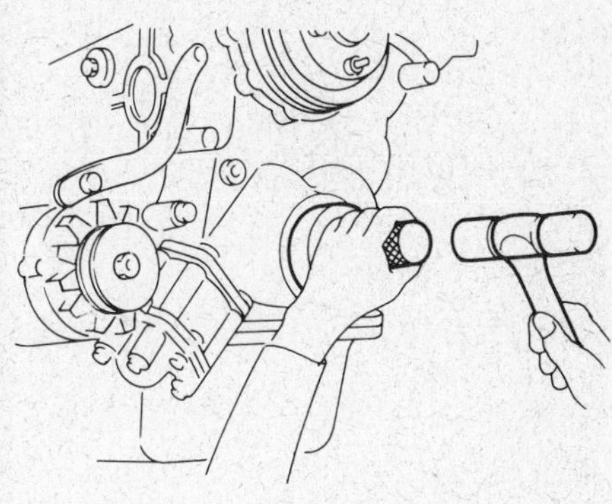

18.3 Install the new seal with a large socket or section of pipe and a hammer

17 Crankshaft pulley – removal and installation

Refer to illustration 17.6

1 Disconnect the negative battery cable from the battery.
2 Remove the radiator and shroud (Chapter 3).
3 Unbolt the lower front cover or skidplate (if equipped).
4 Remove the drivebelts (Chapter 1).
5 On manual transmission equipped models, put the transmission in High gear and apply the parking brake. On automatics, remove the starter and wedge a large screwdriver in the ring gear teeth. Remove the pulley mounting bolt. They're usually very tight, so use a six-point socket and a 1/2-inch drive breaker bar.
6 Use a puller to remove the pulley from the crankshaft **(see illustration)**. Do not use a gear puller that applies force to the outer edge of the pulley!
7 Installation is the reverse of removal. Be sure to apply moly-base grease or clean engine oil to the seal contact surface on the pulley hub before installing the pulley on the crankshaft.
8 Tighten the pulley bolt to the specified torque.

18 Front crankshaft oil seal – replacement

Refer to illustrations 18.2 and 18.3

1 Remove the pulley (Section 17).
2 Carefully pry the oil seal out of the front cover **(see illustration)** with a seal removal tool or screwdriver. Don't scratch the cover bore or damage the crankshaft in the process (if the crankshaft is damaged the new seal will end up leaking).
3 Clean the bore in the cover and coat the outer edge of the new seal with engine oil or multi-purpose grease. Using a socket with an outside diameter slightly smaller than the outside diameter of the seal, carefully drive the new seal into place with a hammer **(see illustration)**. If a socket isn't available, a short section of large diameter pipe will work. Check the seal after installation to be sure that the spring didn't pop out of place.
4 Reinstall the pulley.
5 The parts removed to gain access to the pulley can now be reinstalled.
6 Run the engine and check for leaks.

19 Front cover – removal and installation

Refer to illustrations 19.14a, 19.14b and 19.16

1 Drain the coolant from the engine and radiator (Chapter 1).
2 Remove the fan and radiator as described in Chapter 3.
3 Drain the engine oil.
4 Remove the distributor as described in Chapter 5.
5 Remove the oil pump as described in Section 15.
6 Remove the water pump as described in Chapter 3.
7 Remove the upper alternator adjusting bolt. Then remove the bolts that attach the alternator adjusting arm to the front cover and detach the adjusting arm.
8 Disconnect the hoses from the fuel/vacuum pipe assembly attached to the front cover, then remove the pipe assembly.
9 If equipped, disconnect the air conditioning compressor from the bracket and position it out of the way. Remove the compressor bracket and idler pulley. **Warning:** *Don't disconnect the hoses from the compressor unless the system has been evacuated!*
10 If equipped with power steering, remove the pump from the bracket and position it out of the way. The hydraulic hoses should not be disconnected from the pump.
11 Remove the water inlet from the right side of the front cover.
12 Since the front cover is sandwiched between the cylinder head and the oil pan, the oil pan must be removed in order to remove the front cover. Refer to Section 21 for this procedure.
13 Remove the crankshaft pulley (Section 17).
14 Remove the mounting bolts that attach the front cover to the block and cylinder head and detach the front cover. If it doesn't come off easily, careful tapping with a soft-face hammer will help **(see illustrations)**.

19.14a When removing the front cover, be careful not to bend or damage the front part of the cylinder head gasket (arrow)

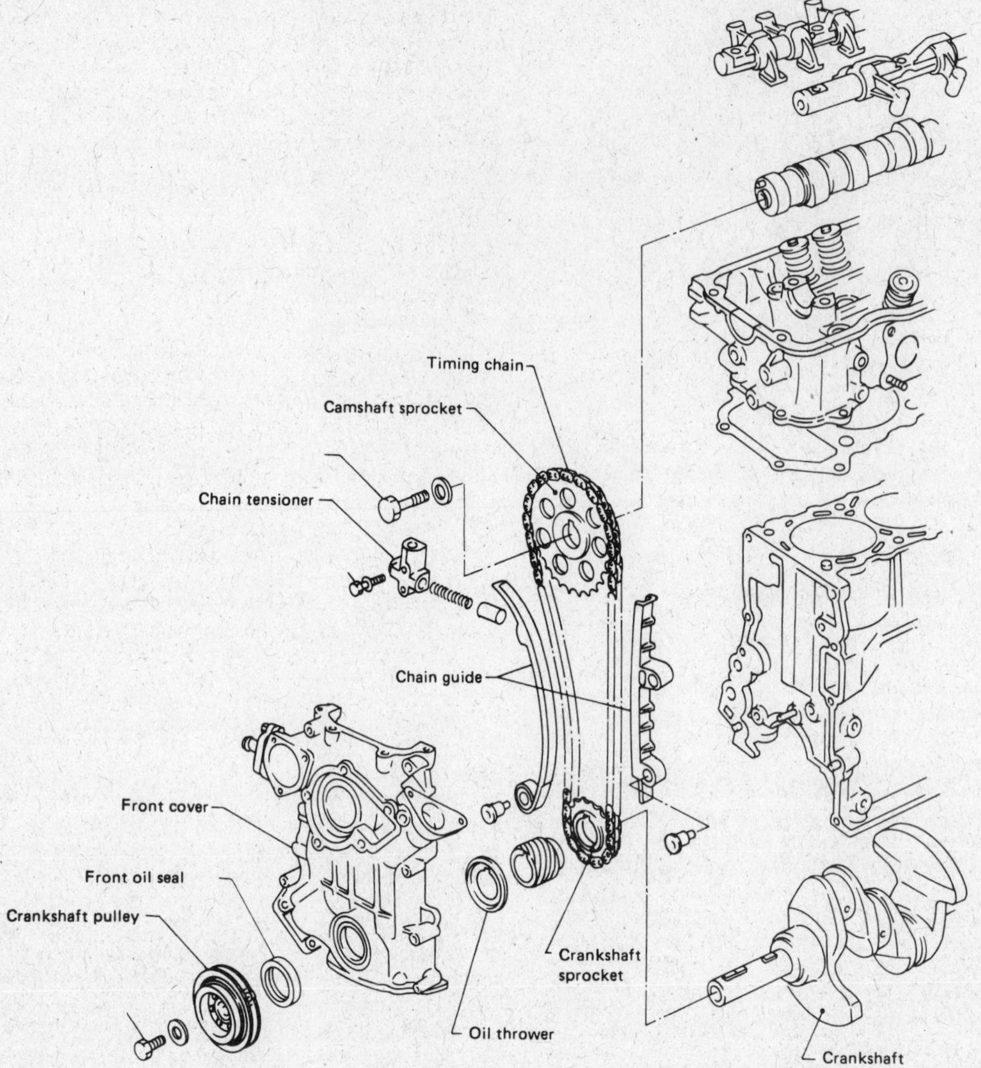

19.14b Exploded view of the front cover on the KA24E engine

15 Install a new seal in the front cover by referring to Section 18.
16 Place the new gaskets in position on the cover, then apply RTV sealant to the points shown in the accompanying illustration.
17 Apply a small amount of grease to the oil seal lip, then place the front cover in position on the block and install the mounting bolts. Tighten them in several steps to the specified torque.
18 The remainder of installation is the reverse of the removal procedure.

20 Timing chain and sprockets – removal and installation

Refer to illustrations 20.2, 20.5, 20.12, 20.14a, 20.14b, 20.14c, 20.15a, 20.15b, 20.16a and 20.16b

Removal

1 Remove the front cover (Section 19)
2 Remove the bolts that attach the chain tensioner and chain guides to the block, then remove them **(see illustration)**.
3 Remove the camshaft sprocket bolt and detach the sprocket (see Section 8 if necessary).
4 Remove the timing chain from the camshaft and crankshaft sprockets.
5 Remove the oil thrower, the oil pump drive gear and the timing chain sprocket from the end of the crankshaft. The sprocket will most likely require the use of a puller **(see illustration)**. Note that three Woodruff keys are used for these components.
6 Examine the teeth on both the crankshaft sprocket and the camshaft sprocket for wear. Each tooth forms an inverted V. If worn, the side of each tooth under tension will be slightly concave in shape when compared with the other side of the tooth (i.e. one side of the inverted V will be concave when compared with the other). If the teeth appear to be worn, the sprockets must be replaced with new ones.

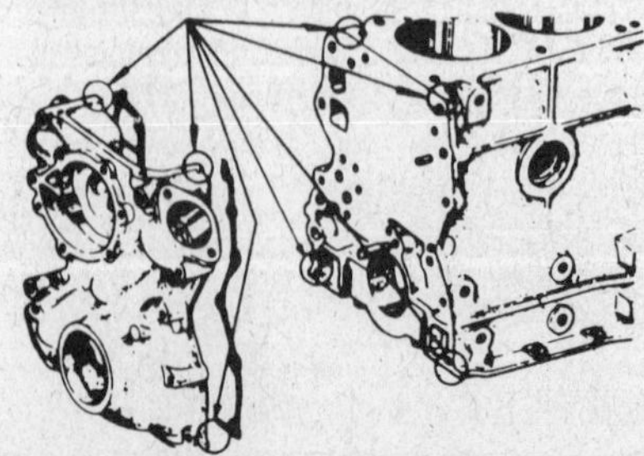

19.16 Prior to installing the front cover and gasket, RTV sealant should be applied to the points shown here

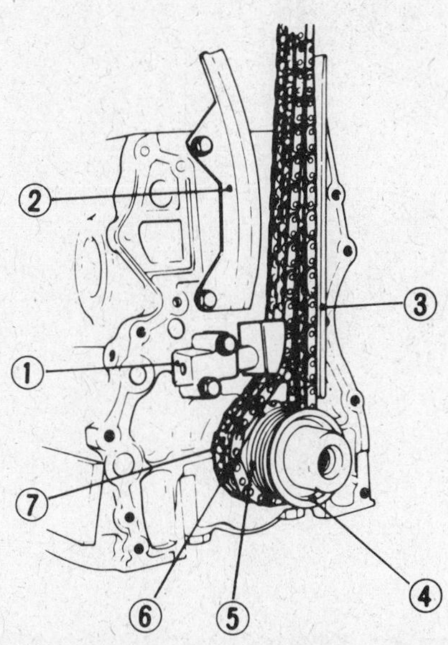

20.2 Timing chain and related components

1 Chain tensioner
2 Slack side chain guide
3 Tension side chain guide
4 Oil thrower
5 Oil pump drive gear
6 Crankshaft sprocket
7 Timing chain

7 The chain should be replaced with a new one if the sprockets are worn or if the chain is loose. It's a good idea to replace the chain at about 30,000 miles (48,000 km) and at lower mileage if the engine is stripped down for a major overhaul. The rollers on a very badly worn chain may be slightly grooved. To avoid future difficulty, if there's any doubt at all about the chain's condition, replace it with a new one.

8 Reattach the camshaft sprocket to the camshaft and check the end play with a dial indicator. The end play should not exceed 0.008-inch (0.2 mm).

9 Examine the components of the chain tensioner and guides. Replace any items that are worn or damaged.

Installation

10 To begin the installation, turn the camshaft until the number one (front) cylinder valves are closed (equivalent to number one piston at TDC), then turn the crankshaft until the number one piston is at TDC.

11 Bolt the two timing chain guides to the block.

12 Install the sprocket, oil pump/distributor drive gear and the oil thrower on the front of the crankshaft. Make sure the timing marks on the sprocket are visible from the front **(see illustration)**.

13 **Note:** *Don't turn the crankshaft or camshaft until the timing chain is installed, otherwise the valves will contact the piston crowns.*

14 Engage the camshaft sprocket in the upper loop of the timing chain, then engage the chain with the teeth of the crankshaft sprocket and bolt the camshaft sprocket to the camshaft. Note the following:

a) The keyway in the crankshaft sprocket should be on top.
b) The timing marks (bright link plates) on the chain should align with the marks on the two sprockets and be positioned on the right side when viewed from the front **(see illustrations)**.

2A

20.5 A puller such as the one shown here will be needed to remove the crankshaft sprocket

20.12 Prior to installing the timing chain, make sure the Woodruff key is pointing up and the timing mark on the crankshaft sprocket is visible (arrows)

20.14a On 1980 models (L20B engine), the bright timing chain link should be aligned with the number one timing mark

20.14b On 1981 and later models, the bright link should be aligned with the number two mark, and the camshaft dowel pin should be in the number two hole (arrows) (NAPS-Z engine shown)

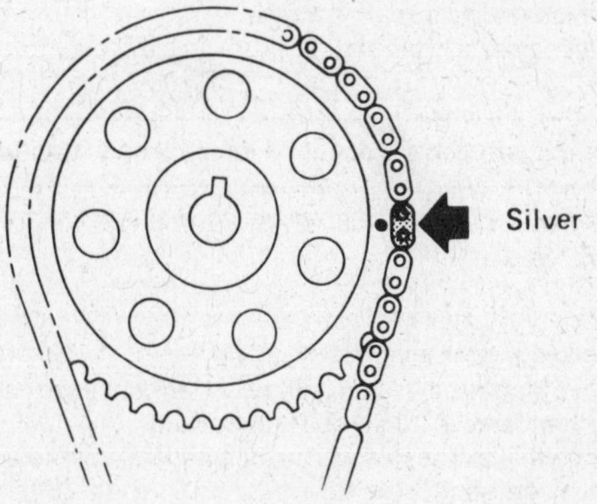

20.14c On KA24E engines, align the silver link with the mark on the camshaft sprocket

20.14d On all models, the lower bright chain link should be aligned with the timing mark on the crankshaft sprocket

20.15a Location of the thrust plate groove and camshaft sprocket notch used for judging timing chain wear (arrow)

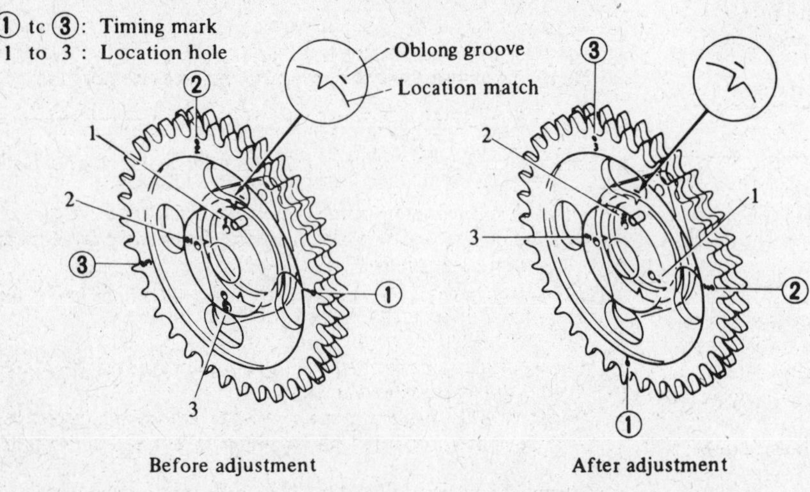

20.15b On 1980 models (L20B engine), if the camshaft sprocket notch is to the left of the thrust plate's oblong groove, the timing chain is stretched and the next sprocket hole and timing mark combination should be used

20.16a When installing the timing chain, the slack side chain guide should be adjusted in as far as possible

- c) The dowel pin in the front of the camshaft should be in the number one sprocket hole on 1980 models. On 1981 and later models, it should be in the number two hole in the camshaft sprocket.

15 When reinstalling a used chain on 1980 models, it should be checked for excessive wear as follows.

- a) With the number one piston at TDC on the compression stroke, see if the notch in the camshaft sprocket (with the chain correctly engaged) appears to the left of the engraved line on the thrust plate **(see illustration)**. If it does, disengage the camshaft sprocket from the chain and move the sprocket around so that when it's remeshed with the chain it'll locate with the camshaft dowel pin in the number two hole. If this adjustment doesn't correct the chain slack, repeat the operation with the number three hole in the camshaft sprocket engaged with the dowel pin. If the number two or three sprocket hole must be used, then the number two or three timing mark must be used to position the chain **(see illustration)**. If this adjustment procedure still doesn't correct or compensate for the slackness in the timing chain, then the chain must be replaced.
- b) When the timing is satisfactory, tighten the camshaft sprocket bolt to the specified torque.

16 Install the chain tensioner assembly on the engine block. Adjust the position of the chain guide above the tensioner so there is no space between the tensioner body and the tensioner plunger unit **(see illustrations)**.

17 Reinstall the front cover, referring to Section 19 as needed.

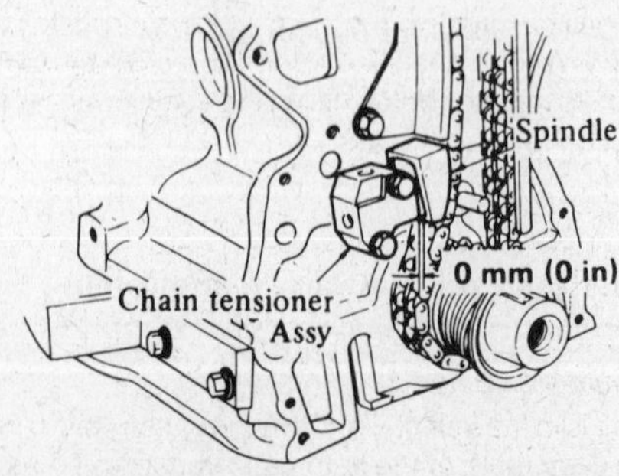

20.16b With a new chain and the chain guides properly installed, there should be no clearance between the chain tensioner body and plunger

22.2 To hold the flywheel stationary while the mounting bolts are loosened, insert a long screwdriver through the starter motor opening and engage it with the flywheel teeth

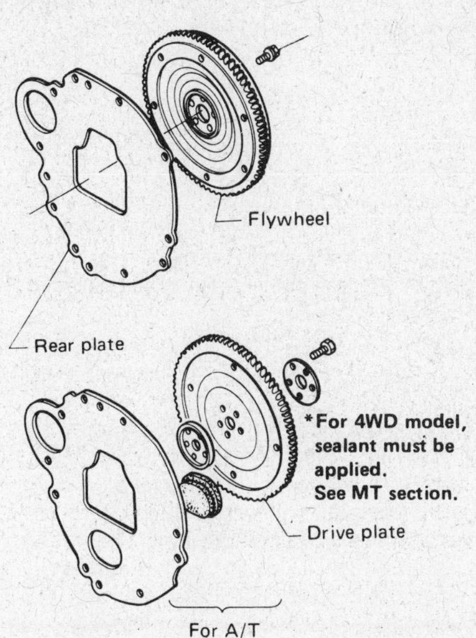

22.4 Exploded view of flywheel/driveplate components

21 Oil pan – removal and installation

1 Drain the engine oil.
2 Raise the front of the vehicle and support it on jackstands placed under the frame.
3 Remove the splash shield, if equipped.
4 On 2WD models, remove the front crossmember.
5 On 4WD models, remove the front differential as described in Chapter 9. Then disconnect the engine and transmission mounts and lift the engine slightly with an engine hoist. **Warning:** *Do not place any part of your body under the engine/transmission when it's off the mounts!* Place wood blocks under the mounts to help support the engine.
6 On 1980 2WD models, remove the idler arm mounting bolts and lower the idler arm and cross rod to provide clearance for the oil pan.
7 Remove the bolts and detach the oil pan. Don't pry between the block and pan or damage to the sealing surfaces may result and oil leaks could develop. Use a block of wood and a hammer to dislodge the pan if it's stuck.
8 Use a scraper to remove all traces of old gasket material and sealant from the block and oil pan. Clean the gasket sealing surfaces with lacquer thinner or acetone and make sure the bolt holes in the block are clean.
9 Check the oil pan flange for distortion, particularly around the bolt holes. If necessary, place the pan on a block of wood and use a hammer to flatten and restore the gasket surface.
10 Before installing the oil pan, apply a thin coat of RTV sealant to the flange. Attach the new gasket to the pan (make sure the bolt holes are aligned).
11 Position the oil pan against the engine block and install the mounting bolts. Tighten them to the specified torque in a criss-cross pattern.
12 Wait at least 30 minutes before filling the engine with oil, then start the engine and check the pan for leaks.

22 Flywheel/driveplate – removal and installation

Refer to illustrations 22.2 and 22.4

1 If the engine is in the vehicle, remove the clutch cover and clutch disc as described in Chapter 8, or the automatic transmission as described in Chapter 7.
2 Flatten the lockplate tabs (if used) and remove the bolts that secure the flywheel/driveplate to the crankshaft rear flange. Be careful, the flywheel is very heavy and should not be dropped. If the crankshaft turns as the bolts are loosened, wedge a screwdriver in the starter ring gear teeth **(see illustration)**.
3 Detach the flywheel/driveplate from the crankshaft flange.
4 Unbolt and remove the engine rear plate **(see illustration)**. Now is a good time to check the engine block rear core plug for leakage.
5 If the teeth on the flywheel/driveplate starter ring gear are badly worn, or if some are missing, install a new flywheel or driveplate.
6 Refer to Chapter 8 for the flywheel inspection procedure.
7 Before installing the flywheel/driveplate, clean the mating surfaces.
8 If removed, reinstall the rear plate.
9 Position the flywheel/driveplate against the crankshaft, using a new spacer, if equipped, and insert the mounting bolts. Use Loc-tite on the bolts.
10 Tighten the bolts in a criss-cross pattern to the specified torque.
11 The remainder of installation is the reverse of removal.

23 Rear crankshaft oil seal – replacement

1 The rear crankshaft oil seal can be replaced without removing the oil pan or crankshaft.
2 Remove the transmission (Chapter 7).
3 If equipped with a manual transmission, remove the pressure plate and clutch disc (Chapter 8).
4 Remove the flywheel or driveplate (Section 22).
5 Using a seal removal tool or a large screwdriver, carefully pry the seal out of the block. Don't scratch or nick the crankshaft in the process!
6 Clean the bore in the block and the seal contact surface on the crankshaft. Check the crankshaft surface for scratches and nicks that could damage the new seal lip and cause oil leaks. If the crankshaft is damaged, the only alternative is a new or different crankshaft.
7 Apply a light coat of engine oil or multi-purpose grease to the outer edge of the new seal. Lubricate the seal lip with moly-base grease.
8 The seal lip must face toward the front of the engine. Carefully work the seal lip over the end of the crankshaft and tap the seal in with a hammer and punch until it's seated in the bore.
9 Install the flywheel or driveplate.
10 If equipped with a manual transmission, reinstall the clutch disc and pressure plate.
11 Reinstall the transmission as described in Chapter 7.

24 Engine mounts – replacement

Refer to illustrations 24.3, 24.6a and 24.6b

Warning: *Don't position any part of your body under the engine when the engine mounts are unbolted!*

1 Engine mounts are non-adjustable and seldom require service. Periodically they should be inspected for hardness and cracks in the rubber and separation of the rubber from the metal backing.

2 To replace the engine mounts with the engine in position, in the vehicle, use the following procedure.

3 Loosen the nuts and bolts that retain the front mounting insulator to the engine mount bracket and frame. Do this on both sides **(see illustration)**.

4 Next, the weight of the engine must be taken off the engine mounts. This can be done from beneath using a jack and wooden block positioned under the oil pan (after removing the crossmember [2WD] or front differential [4WD]), or from above by removing the air cleaner and using an engine hoist attached to the two engine brackets. The engine should be raised slowly and carefully, while keeping a constant check on clearances around the engine to prevent anything from binding or breaking. Pay particular attention to areas such as the fan, ignition coil wires, vacuum lines leading to the engine and rubber hoses and ducts.

5 Raise the engine just enough to provide adequate room to remove the mounting insulator.

6 Remove the nuts and bolts retaining the insulator, then lift it out, noting how it's installed **(see illustrations)**.

7 Installation is the reverse of removal, but be sure the insulator is installed in the same position it was in before removal.

24.3 Location of the nut and bolts (arrows) attaching the engine mount to the mount bracket and frame

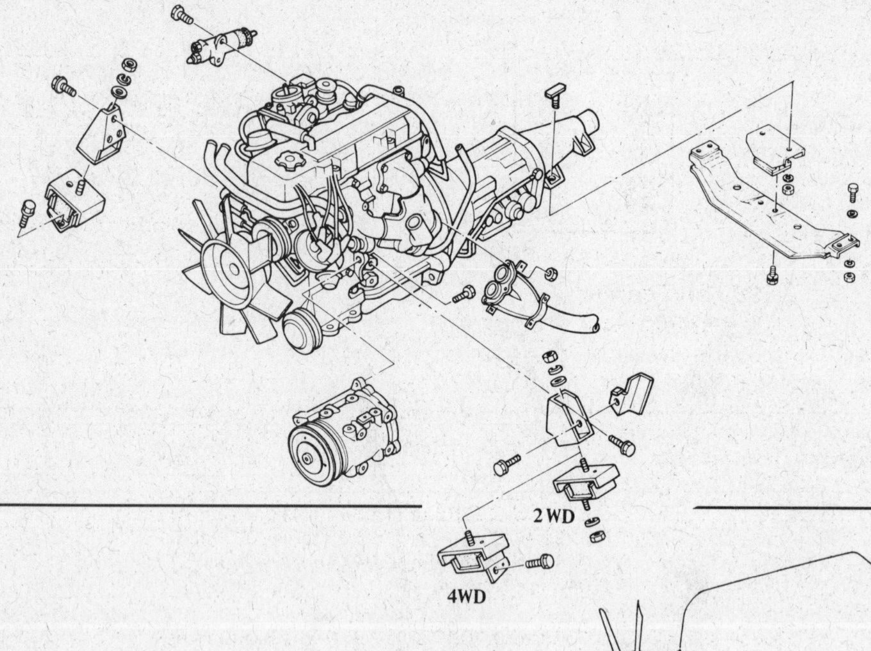

24.6a Exploded view of the NAPS-Z engine mounts (earlier models)

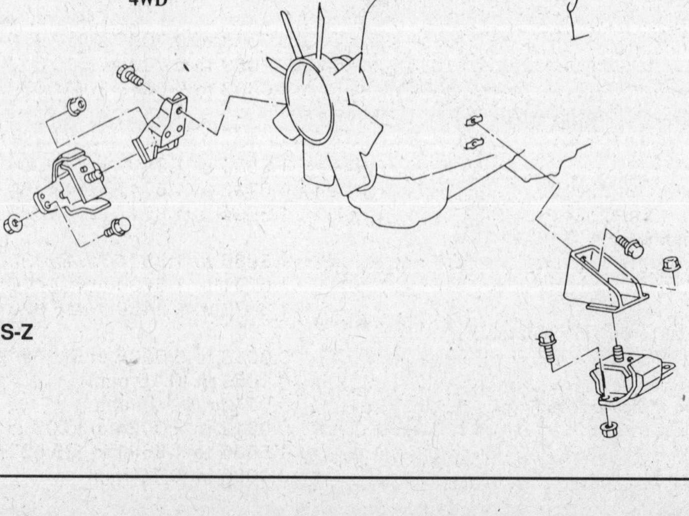

24.6b Exploded view of the NAPS-Z engine mounts (later models)

Chapter 2 Part B V6 engine

Contents

Specifications

General

Displacement	181 cu in (2960 cc)
Compression ratio	9.0 : 1
Firing order	1-2-3-4-5-6
Cylinder numbers (front-to-rear)	
Right (passenger) side	1-3-5
Left (driver's) side	2-4-6

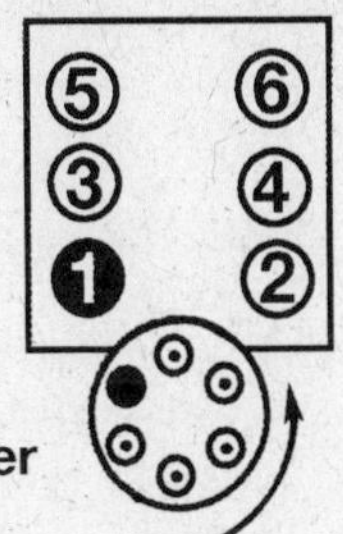

1990 and later V6 engines

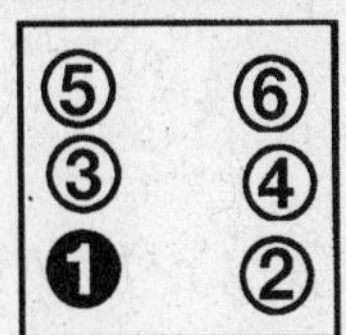

1989 and earlier V6 engines

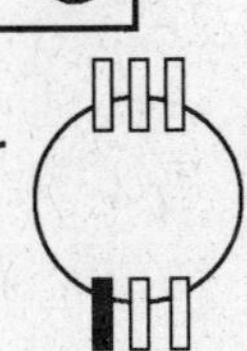

Cylinder location and distributor rotation

Camshaft and related components

Lifters	
Outside diameter	0.6278 to 0.6282 in (15.947 to 15.957 mm)
Guide bore diameter	0.6299 to 0.6304 in (16.000 to 16.013 mm)
Lifter-to-guide clearance	0.0017 to 0.0026 in (0.043 to 0.066 mm)
Lifter movement limit	0.040 in (1.0 mm)
Rocker arms and shafts	
Shaft outside diameter	0.7078 to 0.7087 in (17.979 to 18.000 mm)
Rocker arm bore diameter	0.7089 to 0.7098 in (18.007 to 18.028 mm)
Rocker arm-to-shaft clearance	0.0003 to 0.0019 in (0.007 to 0.049 mm)
Camshaft	
Bearing inside diameter	
Front bearing	1.8898 to 1.8907 in (48.000 to 48.025 mm)
Rear bearing	1.6732 to 1.6742 in (42.500 to 42.525 mm)
All others	1.8504 to 1.8512 in (47.000 to 47.025 mm)
Camshaft journal outside diameter	
Front journal	1.8866 to 1.8874 in (47.920 to 47.940 mm)
Rear journal	1.6701 to 1.6709 in (42.420 to 42.440 mm)
All others	1.8472 to 1.8480 in (46.920 to 46.940 mm)
Bearing oil clearance (journal-to-bearing clearance)	
Standard	0.0018 to 0.0035 in (0.045 to 0.090 mm)
Limit	0.0059 in (0.15 mm)
Camshaft runout limit (total indicator reading)	0.004 in (0.10 mm)
Camshaft end play	0.0012 to 0.0024 in (0.03 to 0.06 mm)
Lobe height	1.5566 to 1.5641 in (39.537 to 39.727 mm)
Lobe wear limit	0.0059 in (0.15 mm)

Oil pump

Body-to-outer gear clearance	0.0043 to 0.0079 in (0.11 to 0.20 mm)
Inner gear-to-crescent clearance	0.0047 to 0.0091 in (0.12 to 0.23 mm)
Outer gear-to-crescent clearance	0.0083 to 0.0126 in (0.21 to 0.32 mm)
Housing-to-inner gear clearance	0.0020 to 0.0035 in (0.05 to 0.09 mm)
Housing-to-outer gear clearance	0.0020 to 0.0043 in (0.05 to 0.11 mm)

Torque specifications

	Ft-lbs *(unless otherwise noted)*
Rocker arm cover screws	8.4 to 26.4 in-lbs
Rocker arm shaft bolts	13 to 16
Intake manifold bolts	
Step 1	2.2 to 3.6
Step 2	12 to 14
Intake manifold nuts	
Step 1	2.2 to 3.6
Step 2	17 to 20
Exhaust manifold mounting nuts	13 to 16
Exhaust manifold-to-pipe mounting nuts/bolts	20 to 27
Vibration damper mounting bolt	90 to 98
Camshaft pulley bolt	58 to 65
Timing belt tensioner locking nut	32 to 43
Camshaft retaining bolt	58 to 65
Cylinder head bolts	
Step 1	22
Step 2	43
Step 3	Loosen all bolts
Step 4	22
Step 5	40 to 47
Flywheel/driveplate mounting bolts*	72 to 80
Oil pan mounting bolts	61 to 70 in-lbs
Oil pump mounting bolts	61 to 70 in-lbs
Oil pump regulator cap	29 to 51
Oil strainer-to-pump bolts	12 to 15
Oil strainer bracket bolts	3 to 6

* *Apply Loc-tite to the threads prior to installation*

1 General information

This Part of Chapter 2 is devoted to in-vehicle repair procedures for the V6 engine. All information concerning engine removal and installation and engine block and cylinder head overhaul can be found in Part C of this Chapter.

The following repair procedures are based on the assumption that the engine is installed in the vehicle. If the engine has been removed from the vehicle and mounted on a stand, many of the steps outlined in this Part of Chapter 2 will not apply.

The Specifications included in this Part of Chapter 2 apply only to the procedures contained in this Part. Part C of Chapter 2 contains the Specifications necessary for cylinder head and engine block rebuilding.

The 60-degree V6 has a cast iron block and aluminum crossflow heads with a camshaft in each head. The block has thin walled sections for light weight. A "cradle frame" main bearing casting — the main bearing caps are cast as a unit, with a bridge, or truss, connecting them — supports the cast ductile iron crankshaft.

Both camshafts are driven off the front of the crankshaft by a cog belt. A spring loaded tensioner, adjusted by an eccentric type locknut, maintains belt tension. Each camshaft actuates two valves per cylinder through hydraulic lifters and shaft-mounted forged aluminum rocker arms.

Each cast aluminum three-ring piston has two compression rings and a three-piece oil control ring. The piston pins are pressed into forged steel connecting rods. The flat-topped pistons produce a 9.0:1 compression ratio.

The distributor, which is mounted on the front of the left cylinder head, is driven by a helical gear on the front of the left camshaft. The water pump, which is bolted to the front of the block, is driven off the crankshaft by a drivebelt and pulley. The gear type oil pump is mounted on the front of the crankshaft.

From the oil pump, oil travels through the filter to the main oil gallery, from which it is routed either directly to the main bearings, crankshaft, connecting rod bearings and pistons and cylinder walls or to the cylinder heads.

2 Repair operations possible with the engine in the vehicle

Many major repair operations can be accomplished without removing the engine from the vehicle.

Clean the engine compartment and the exterior of the engine with some type of pressure washer before any work is done. It'll make the job easier and help keep dirt out of the internal areas of the engine.

Remove the hood, if necessary, to improve access to the engine as repairs are performed (refer to Chapter 12 if necessary).

If vacuum, exhaust, oil or coolant leaks develop, indicating a need for gasket or seal replacement, the repairs can generally be made with the engine in the vehicle. The intake and exhaust manifold gaskets, oil pan gasket, crankshaft oil seals and cylinder head gaskets are all accessible with the engine in place.

Exterior engine components, such as the intake and exhaust manifolds, the oil pan, the oil pump, the water pump, the starter motor, the alternator, the distributor and the fuel system components can be removed for repair with the engine in place.

Since the cylinder heads can be removed without pulling the engine, valve component servicing can also be accomplished with the engine in the vehicle. Replacement of the timing belt and pulleys is also possible with the engine in the vehicle.

In extreme cases caused by a lack of necessary equipment, repair or replacement of piston rings, pistons, connecting rods and rod bearings is possible with the engine in the vehicle. However, this practice is not recommended because of the cleaning and preparation work that must be done to the components involved.

3 Top Dead Center (TDC) for number one piston — locating

Refer to illustrations 3.6a, 3.6b and 3.7

1 Top Dead Center (TDC) is the highest point in the cylinder that each piston reaches as it travels up-and-down when the crankshaft turns. Each piston reaches TDC on the compression stroke and again

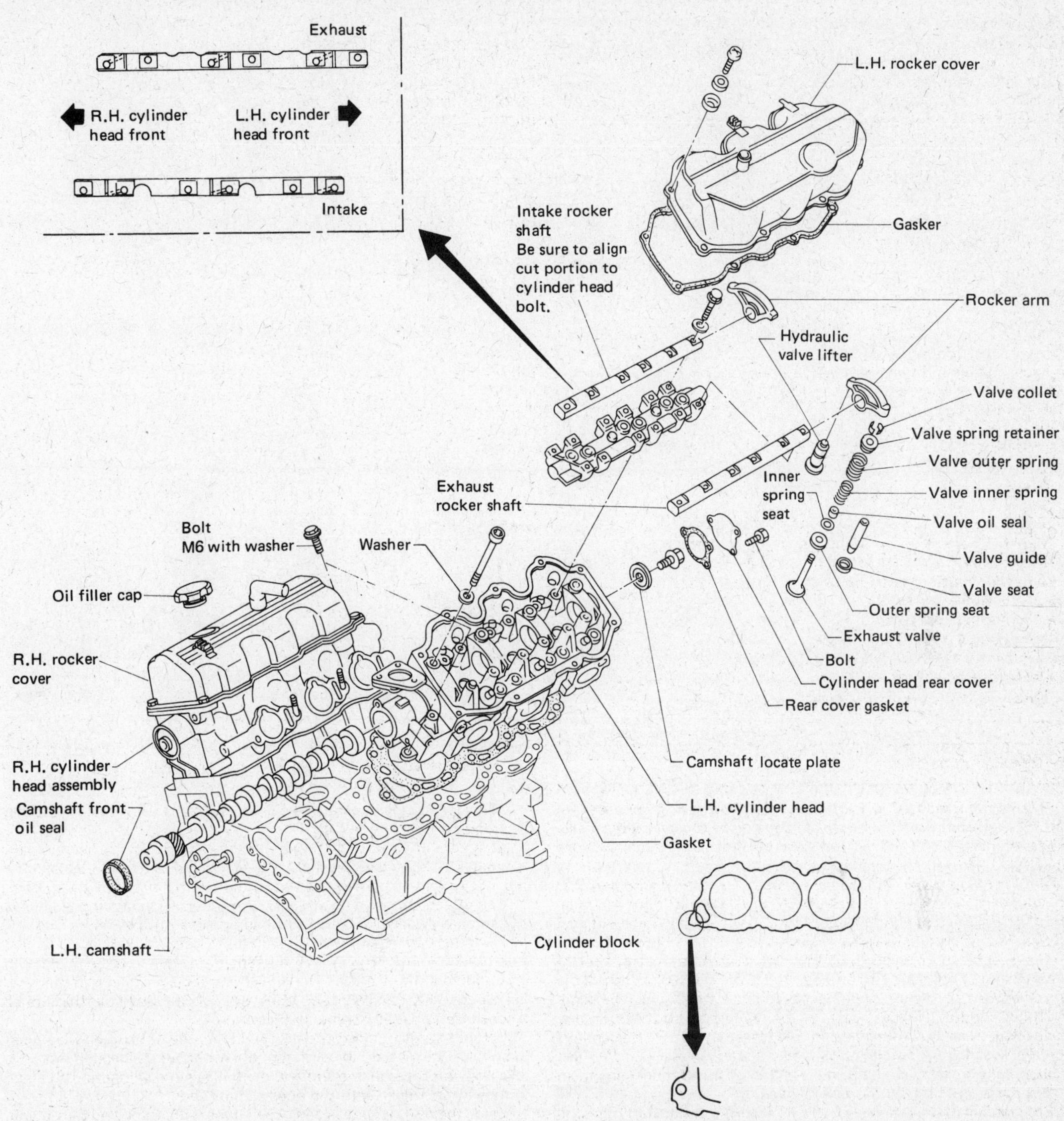

Cylinder head, camshaft and rocker arm components — exploded view

on the exhaust stroke, but TDC generally refers to piston position on the compression stroke. The timing marks on the vibration damper installed on the front of the crankshaft are referenced to the number one piston at TDC on the compression stroke.

2 Positioning the piston(s) at TDC is an essential part of many procedures such as rocker arm removal, valve timing, timing belt and pulley replacement and distributor removal.

3 In order to bring any piston to TDC, the crankshaft must be turned using one of the methods outlined below. When looking at the front of the engine, normal crankshaft rotation is *clockwise*. **Warning:** *Before beginning this procedure, be sure to place the transmission in Neutral. Also, detach the coil wire from the center terminal of the distributor cap and ground it on the block with a jumper wire.*

a) The preferred method is to turn the crankshaft with a large socket and breaker bar attached to the vibration damper bolt threaded into the front of the crankshaft.

b) A remote starter switch, which may save some time, can also be used. Attach the switch leads to the S (switch) and B (battery) terminals on the starter motor. Stay clear of moving engine parts as this is done. Once the piston is close to TDC, use a socket and breaker bar as described in the previous paragraph.

c) If an assistant is available to turn the ignition switch to the Start position in short bursts, you can get the piston close to TDC without a remote starter switch. Use a socket and breaker bar as described in Paragraph a) to complete the procedure.

4 Make a mark on the distributor housing directly below the number

3.6a The timing indicator pointer and vibration damper timing marks (arrows) are located low on the front of the engine

one spark plug wire terminal on the distributor cap.

5 Remove the distributor cap as described in Chapter 1.

6 Turn the crankshaft (see Paragraph 3 above) until the 0 (zero) degree line on the vibration damper is aligned with the timing indicator pointer (**see illustrations**). The timing indicator and vibration damper are located low on the front of the engine, near the pulley that turns the drivebelts.

7 The rotor should now be pointing directly at the mark on the distributor housing (**see illustration**). If it isn't, the piston is at TDC on the exhaust stroke.

8 To get the piston to TDC on the compression stroke, turn the crankshaft one complete turn (360°) clockwise. The rotor should now be pointing at the mark. When the rotor is pointing at the number one spark plug wire terminal in the distributor cap (which is indicated by the mark on the housing) and the ignition timing marks are aligned, the number one piston is at TDC on the compression stroke.

9 After the number one piston has been positioned at TDC on the compression stroke, TDC for any of the remaining cylinders can be located by turning the crankshaft 120° at a time and following the firing order (refer to the Specifications).

4.3 Items that must be detached to remove the right rocker arm cover include the PCV hose, wiring harness and fuel hoses (arrows)

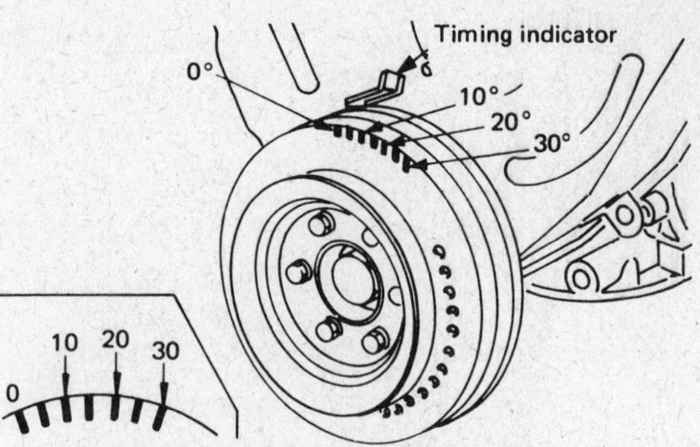

3.6b When the 0 (zero) on the damper is aligned with the timing indicator pointer . . .

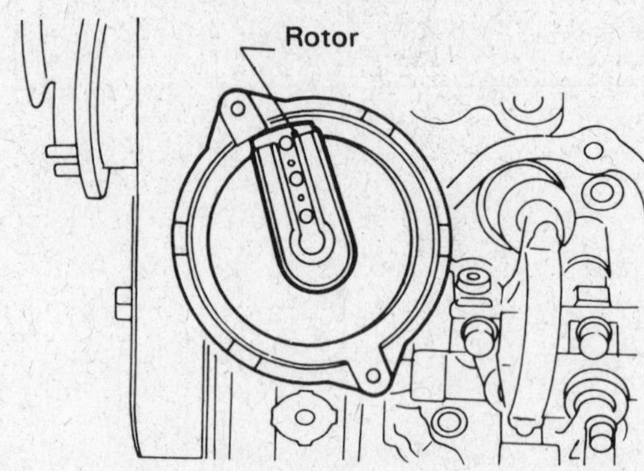

3.7 . . . and the rotor is pointing at the mark on the distributor housing, the number one piston is at TDC on the compression stroke

4 Rocker arm covers – removal and installation

Refer to illustrations 4.3 and 4.8

1 Relieve the fuel system pressure (Chapter 4).

2 Disconnect the negative cable from the battery.

Removal

Right side cover

3 Remove the PCV hose by sliding the hose clamp back and pulling the hose off the fitting on the rocker arm cover **(see illustration)**.

4 Remove the number 1, 3 and 5 spark plug wires from the spark plugs. Mark them clearly with pieces of masking tape to prevent confusion during installation.

5 Remove the wires and fuel hoses attached to the rocker arm cover.

6 Remove the nine rocker arm cover screws and washers.

7 Detach the rocker arm cover. **Caution:** *If the cover is stuck to the head, bump one end with a block of wood and a hammer to jar it loose. If that doesn't work, try to slip a flexible putty knife between the head and cover to break the gasket seal. Don't pry at the cover-to-head joint or damage to the sealing surfaces may occur (leading to oil leaks in the future).*

Left side cover

8 Remove the breather hose from the cover **(see illustration)**.

9 Tag and detach the spark plug wires.

10 Unsnap the wiring brackets from the cover.

11 Remove the nine rocker arm cover screws and lift off the rocker arm cover. Read the **Caution** in Step 7.

Installation

12 The mating surfaces of each cylinder head and rocker arm cover must be perfectly clean when the covers are installed. Use a gasket scraper to remove all traces of sealant and old gasket material, then clean the mating surfaces with lacquer thinner or acetone. If there's sealant or oil on the mating surfaces when the cover is installed, oil leaks may develop.

4.8 Remove the breather hose and the wiring harness (arrows) to detach the left rocker arm cover

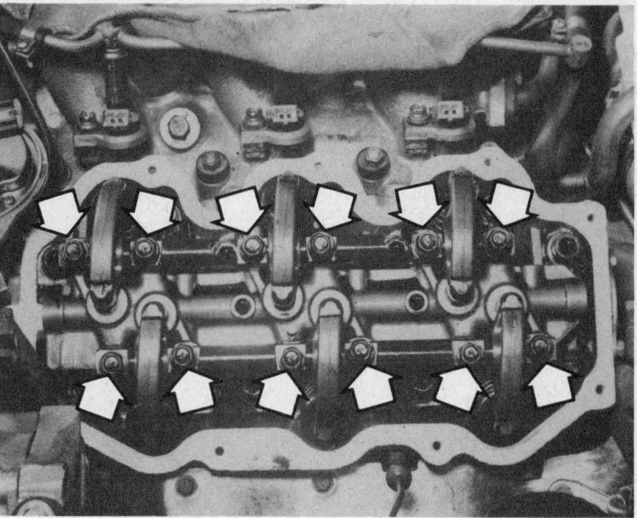

5.2 To remove the rocker arm shaft assemblies, loosen the bolts a little at a time to avoid bending the shaft

5.3 The rocker arm shaft mounting bolts, which are different lengths, must be reinstalled in their original locations – a cardboard box with holes in it will keep the bolts in order

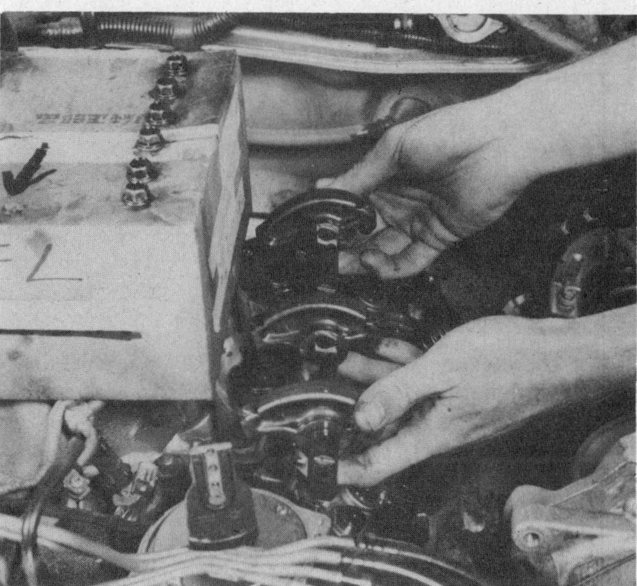

5.4 Remove the rocker arms and shafts as an assembly and keep all of the parts together

13 Clean the mounting screw threads with a die to remove any corrosion and restore damaged threads. Make sure the threaded holes in the head are clean – run a tap into them to remove corrosion and restore damaged threads.
14 The gaskets should be mated to the covers before the covers are installed. Apply a thin coat of RTV sealant to the cover groove, then position the gasket inside the cover and allow the sealant to set up so the gasket adheres to the cover. If the sealant isn't allowed to set, the gasket may fall out of the cover as it's installed on the engine.
15 Carefully position the cover on the head and install the screws.
16 Tighten the screws in three or four steps to the specified torque.
17 The remaining installation steps are the reverse of removal.
18 Start the engine and check carefully for oil leaks as the engine warms up.

5 Rocker arm components – removal and installation

Refer to illustrations 5.2, 5.3 and 5.4

1 Remove the rocker arm cover (Section 4).
2 Loosen the rocker arm shaft retaining bolts **(see illustration)** in two or three stages, working your way from the ends toward the middle of the shafts. **Caution:** *Some of the valves will be open when you loosen the rocker arm shaft bolts and the rocker arm shafts will be under a certain amount of valve spring pressure. Therefore, the bolts must be loosened gradually. Loosening a bolt all at once near a rocker arm under spring pressure could bend the rocker arm shaft.*
3 Remove the rocker arm shaft retaining bolts. The bolts must be kept in order so they can be installed in their original locations. A cardboard box with 12 holes punched in the top can be used to store the bolts in order. Be sure to label the front, left and right sides of the cardboard box **(see illustration)**.
4 Lift off the rocker arm shaft assemblies one at a time and lay them down on a nearby workbench in the same relationship to each other that they're in when installed **(see illustration)**. They must be reinstalled on the same cylinder head. Refer to the exploded view illustration on page 91 if necessary. Refer to Section 15 for the inspection procedures.
5 Installation is the reverse of the removal procedure. Tighten the rocker arm shaft retaining bolts to the specified torque in several steps. Work from the ends of the shafts toward the middle.

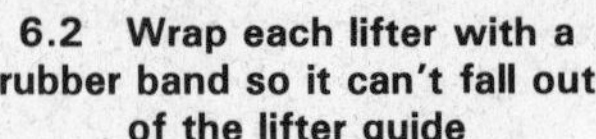

6.2 Wrap each lifter with a rubber band so it can't fall out of the lifter guide

6.3 With the lifters retained by rubber bands, the lifter guide assembly can be removed from the cylinder head

6 Lifters – removal and installation

Refer to illustrations 6.2, 6.3 and 6.5

1 Remove the rocker arm cover (Section 4) and the rocker arm shaft assemblies (Section 5).

2 Secure the lifters by raising them slightly and wrapping a rubber band around each one to prevent them from falling out of the guides **(see illustration). Note:** *If a lifter should fall out of the guide, immediately put it back in its original location.*

3 Remove the hydraulic lifter guide assembly **(see illustration).**

4 Remove the lifters from the bores one at a time. Keep them in order. Each lifter must be reinstalled in its original bore. **Caution:** *Try to avoid turning the lifters upside down. If you turn a lifter upside down, air can become trapped inside and the lifter will have to be bled as follows.*

5 With the lifter in its bore, push down on it **(see illustration).** If it moves more than 0.040-inch (1 mm), air may be trapped inside the lifter.

6 If you think air is trapped inside a valve lifter, reinstall the rocker arm shaft assemblies and rocker arm cover.

7 Bleed air from the lifters by running the engine at 1,000 rpm under no load for about 10 minutes.

8 Remove the rocker arm cover and rocker arm shaft assemblies again. Repeat the procedure in Step 5 once more. If there's still air in the lifter, replace it with a new one.

9 While the lifters are out of the engine, inspect them for wear. Refer to Section 15 for inspection procedures.

10 Installation is the reverse of removal. Be sure to lubricate each lifter with liberal amounts of *clean engine oil* prior to installation.

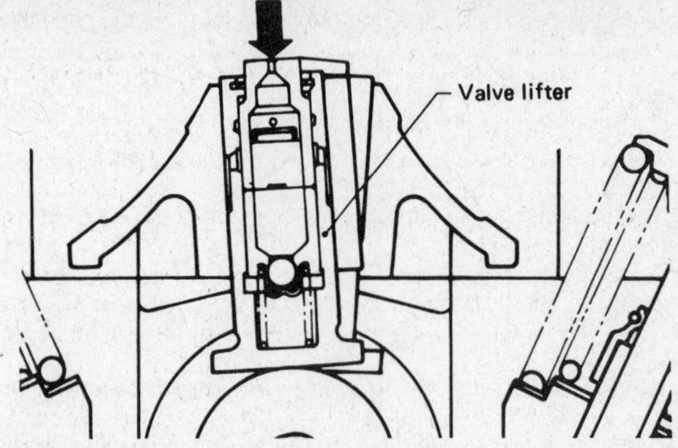

6.5 Depress the valve lifter by hand to see how far it moves

7 Intake manifold – removal and installation

Removal

Refer to illustrations 7.9 and 7.16

1 Release the fuel system pressure (Chapter 4).

2 Disconnect the negative cable from the battery.

3 Drain the cooling system (Chapter 1).

4 Remove the air cleaner (Chapter 4).

5 Remove the throttle body (Chapter 4).

6 Remove the spark plug wires and distributor cap. Be sure to mark the spark plug wires for proper reinstallation.

7 Disconnect the EGR valve (Chapter 6).

8 Remove the air conditioning compressor drivebelt (Chapter 1).

9 Remove the bolts securing the air conditioning idler pulley bracket **(see illustration)** and detach the bracket.

7.9 The air conditioner idler pulley is held in place with three bolts (arrows)

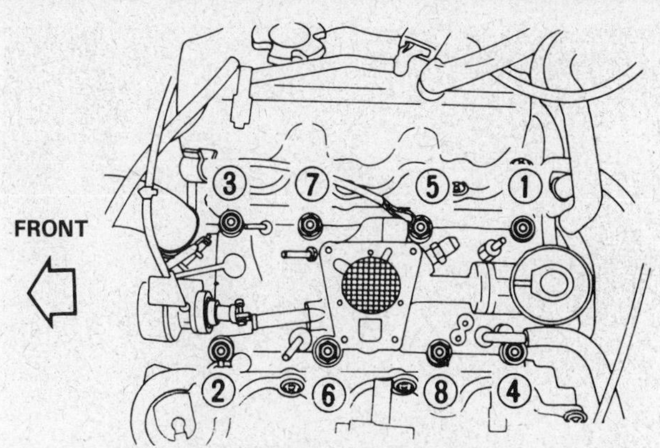

7.16 Loosen the eight intake manifold bolts in the sequence shown here

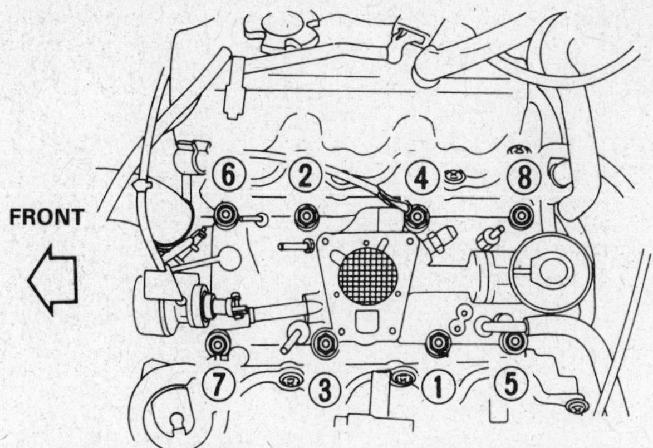

7.23 Intake manifold bolt TIGHTENING sequence

10 Loosen the bypass hose clamp and pry the hose off the thermostat housing.
11 Remove the bolt securing the timing belt cover to the thermostat housing.
12 Remove the upper radiator hose from the thermostat housing.
13 Disconnect the vacuum hoses and wires after labeling them for reinstallation.
14 Remove any remaining hoses, wires or cables attached to the manifold or its components.
15 Disconnect the heater hose from the back of the manifold.
16 Loosen the manifold mounting bolts/nuts in 1/4-turn increments until they can be removed by hand. Follow the recommended sequence **(see illustration)**.
17 The manifold will probably be stuck to the cylinder heads and force may be required to break the gasket seal. **Caution:** *Don't pry between the manifold and the heads or damage to the gasket sealing surfaces may occur, leading to vacuum leaks.*

Installation

Refer to illustration 7.23

Note: *The mating surfaces of the cylinder heads and manifold must be perfectly clean when the manifold is installed. Gasket removal solvents in aerosol cans are available at most auto parts stores and may be helpful when removing old gasket material that's stuck to the heads and manifold (since they're made of aluminum, aggressive scraping can cause damage). Be sure to follow the directions printed on the container.*

18 Use a gasket scraper to remove all traces of sealant and old gasket material, then clean the mating surfaces with lacquer thinner or acetone. If there's old sealant or oil on the mating surfaces when the manifold is installed, oil or vacuum leaks may develop. Use a vacuum cleaner to remove any material that falls into the intake ports in the heads.
19 Use a tap of the correct size to chase the threads in the bolt holes, then use compressed air (if available) to remove the debris from the holes. **Warning:** *Wear safety glasses or a face shield to protect your eyes when using compressed air!*
20 Position the gaskets on the cylinder heads. No sealant is required; however, follow the instructions included with the new gaskets.
21 Make sure all intake port openings, coolant passage holes and bolt holes are aligned correctly.
22 Carefully set the manifold in place. **Caution:** *Don't disturb the gaskets.*
23 Install the bolts/nuts and tighten them to the specified torque following the recommended sequence **(see illustration)**. Work up to the final torque in two steps.
24 The remaining installation steps are the reverse of removal. Start the engine and check carefully for oil and coolant leaks at the intake manifold joints.

8 Exhaust manifolds – removal and installation

1 Remove the air cleaner (Chapter 4).
2 Disconnect the negative cable from the battery.
3 Raise the vehicle and support it securely on jackstands.
4 Working underneath the vehicle, unbolt the exhaust system from the manifold(s) (Chapter 4).

Removal

Right side

Refer to illustrations 8.5 and 8.6

5 Remove the heat shield bolts securing the two heat shield halves to the right exhaust manifold **(see illustration)**.
6 Remove the exhaust manifold mounting nuts in the recommended sequence **(see illustration)**.

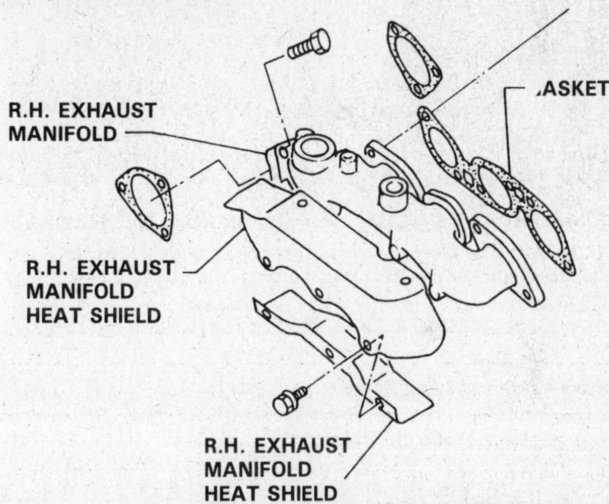

8.5 Right exhaust manifold and related components – exploded view

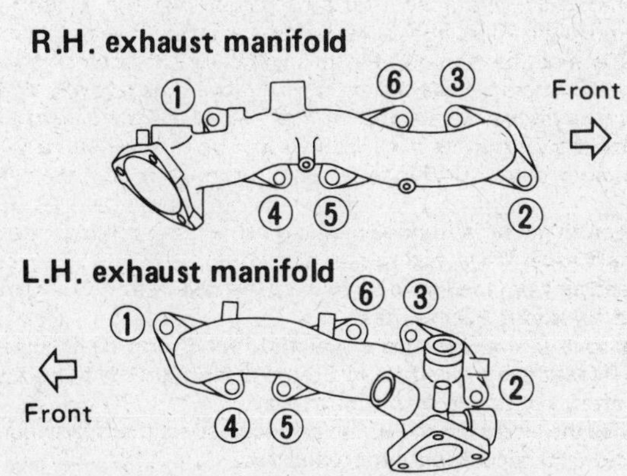

8.6 Exhaust manifold nut LOOSENING sequence

2B

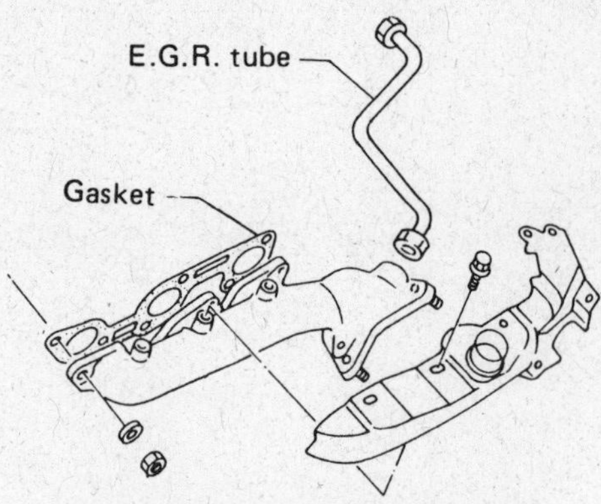

8.8 Left exhaust manifold and related components – exploded view

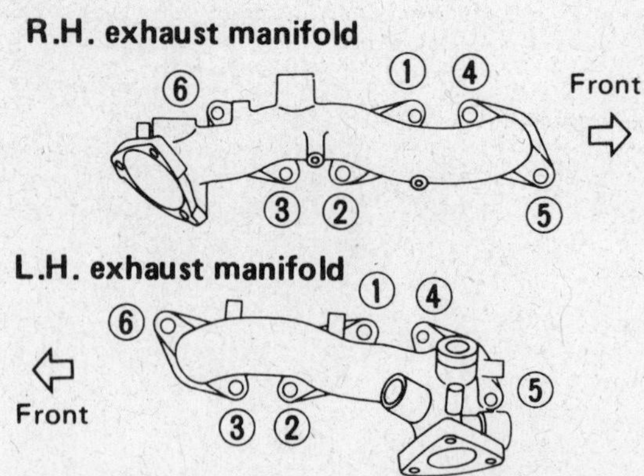

8.14 Exhaust manifold mounting nut TIGHTENING sequence

7 Detach the exhaust manifold by lifting up on the rear, then lift the manifold out of the engine compartment.

Left side

Refer to illustration 8.8

8 Remove the bolts securing the heat shield to the left exhaust manifold **(see illustration)**.
9 Disconnect the EGR tube from the manifold.
10 Working from above – and underneath, when necessary – remove the exhaust manifold nuts, three on top and three on bottom, in the proper sequence **(see illustration 8.6)**.
11 Lift the manifold out the top of the engine compartment.

Installation

Refer to illustration 8.14

12 Prior to installation of either manifold, clean all gasket mating surfaces.
13 Install a new gasket on the studs retaining the manifold to the head.
14 Install the manifold and tighten the nuts in the proper sequence to the specified torque **(see illustration)**.
15 Installation of the remaining components is the reverse of removal.

9 Vibration damper – removal and installation

Refer to illustrations 9.5 and 9.6

1 Disconnect the negative cable from the battery.
2 Remove the fan shroud and fan assembly (Chapter 3).
3 Remove the drivebelts (Chapter 1).
4 Remove the pulley retaining bolts and detach the pulleys. **Caution:** *Before removing the pulleys, mark the location of each one in relation to the vibration damper in order to retain proper timing mark orientation during installation.*

9.5 The large bolt holding the vibration damper in place is very tight, so use a six-point socket and 1/2-inch drive breaker bar to remove it!

9.6 Use the recommended puller to remove the vibration damper – if a puller that applies force to the outer edge is used, the damper may be damaged

5 Remove the starter bolts and push the starter away from the flywheel gear. Wedge a pry bar between the flywheel/driveplate teeth to prevent the crankshaft from turning while loosening the large vibration damper bolt **(see illustration)**.
6 Leave the damper bolt in place to provide the gear puller with something to push against. Use a puller to remove the damper **(see illustration)**. **Caution:** *Don't use a puller with jaws that grip the outer edge of the damper! The puller must be the type shown in the illustration that utilizes bolts to apply force to the damper hub only.*
7 To install the damper, position it on the nose of the crankshaft, align the keyway and install the bolt. Tighten the bolt to the specified torque.
8 The remaining installation steps are the reverse of the removal procedure.

10 Timing belt – check, removal, installation and adjustment

Removal and installation

Refer to illustrations 10.14a, 10.14b, 10.15, 10.16, 10.17, 10.18, 10.20a and 10.20b

1 Relieve the fuel pressure (Chapter 4).
2 Disconnect the negative cable from the battery.
3 Drain the cooling system (Chapter 1).
4 Position the number one piston at TDC on the compression stroke (Section 3).
5 Remove the air cleaner assembly (Chapter 4).

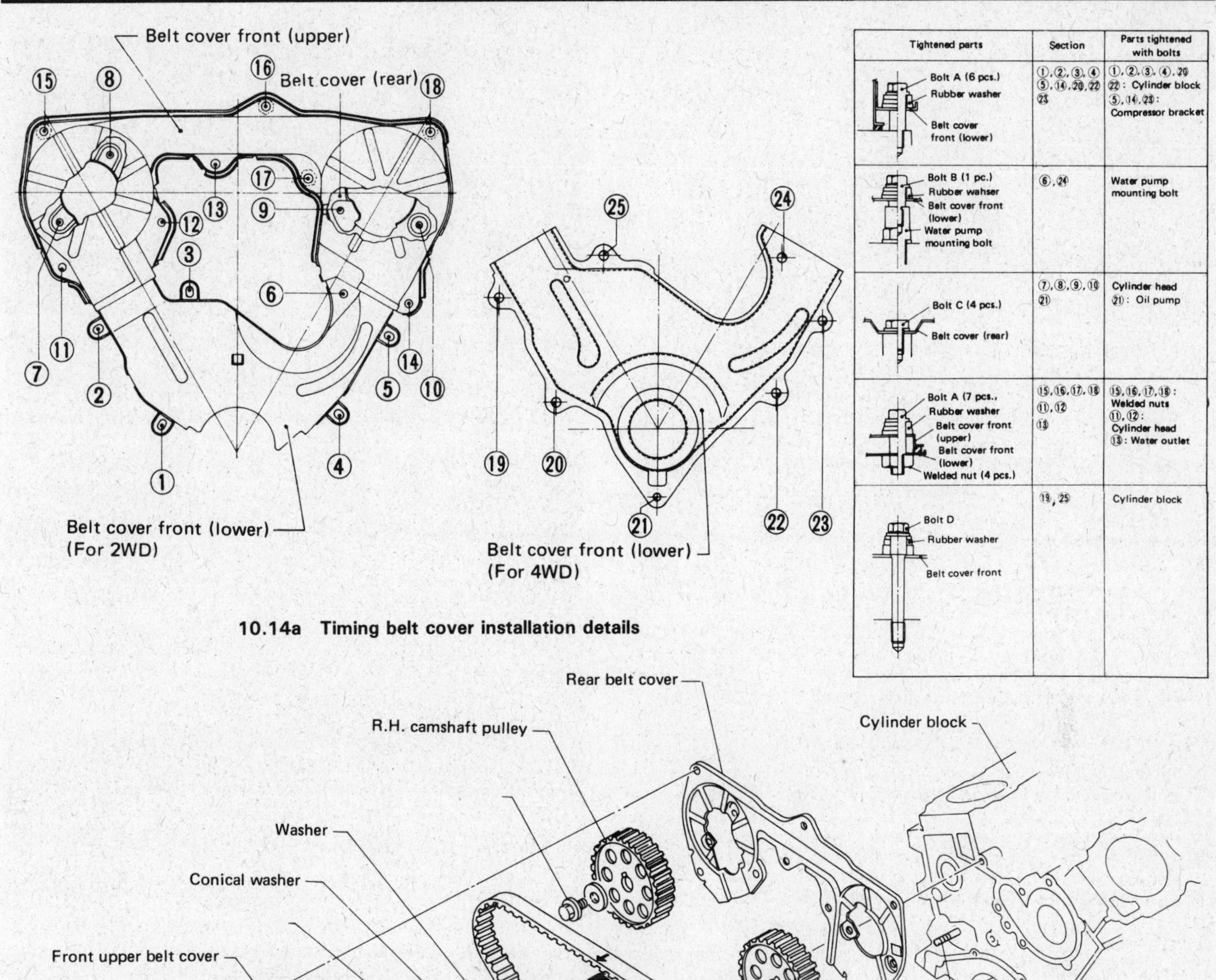

10.14a Timing belt cover installation details

Tightened parts	Section	Parts tightened with bolts
Bolt A (6 pcs.), Rubber washer, Belt cover front (lower)	①, ②, ③, ④, ⑤, ⑭, ⑳, ㉒, ㉓	①, ②, ③, ④, ⑳, ㉒: Cylinder block ⑤, ⑭, ㉓: Compressor bracket
Bolt B (1 pc.), Rubber wahser, Belt cover front (lower), Water pump mounting bolt	⑥, ㉔	Water pump mounting bolt
Bolt C (4 pcs.), Belt cover (rear)	⑦, ⑧, ⑨, ⑩, ㉑	Cylinder head ㉑: Oil pump
Bolt A (7 pcs., Rubber washer, Belt cover front (upper), Belt cover front (lower), Welded nut (4 pcs.)	⑮, ⑯, ⑰, ⑱, ⑪, ⑫, ⑬	⑮, ⑯, ⑰, ⑱: Welded nuts ⑪, ⑫: Cylinder head ⑬: Water outlet
Bolt D, Rubber washer, Belt cover front	⑲, ㉕	Cylinder block

10.14b Timing belt and related components — exploded view

6 Remove the rocker arm covers (Section 4).
7 Loosen the rocker arm shaft mounting bolts (Section 5).
8 Remove all of the drivebelts (Chapter 1).
9 Remove the fan and fan shroud (Chapter 3).
10 Remove the air conditioning compressor idler pulley, if equipped (Chapter 3).
11 Remove the vibration damper (Section 9). **Note:** *Don't allow the crankshaft to rotate during removal of the damper. If the crankshaft moves, the number one piston will no longer be at TDC.*
12 Disconnect the lower radiator hose from the metal pipe and loosen the hose clamp at the other end of the metal pipe.
13 Remove the bolt that attaches the metal pipe to the engine bracket and detach the pipe.
14 Remove the bolts securing the upper and the lower timing belt covers **(see illustrations)**. Note that various types and sizes of bolts are used. They must be reinstalled in their original locations. Mark each

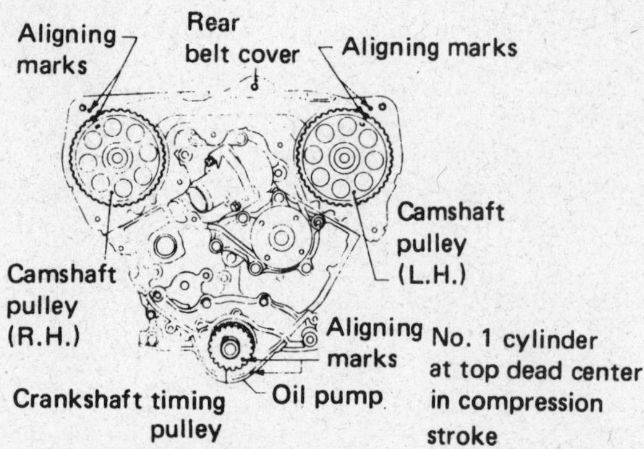

10.15 Once the timing belt cover is off, check all valve timing marks for correct alignment – realign them if necessary before proceeding!

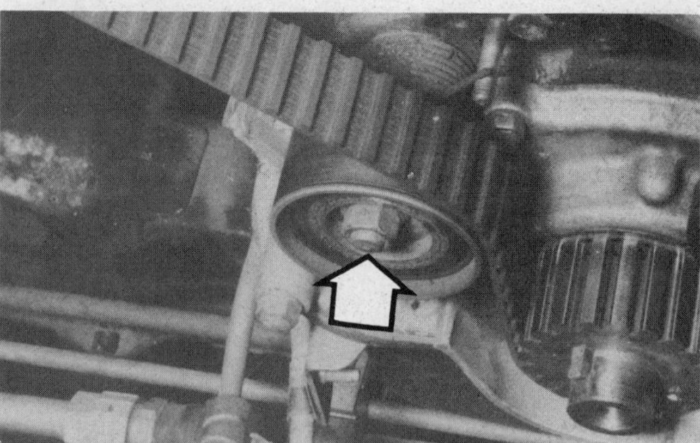

10.16 Loosen the locking nut (arrow) in the middle of the timing belt tensioner

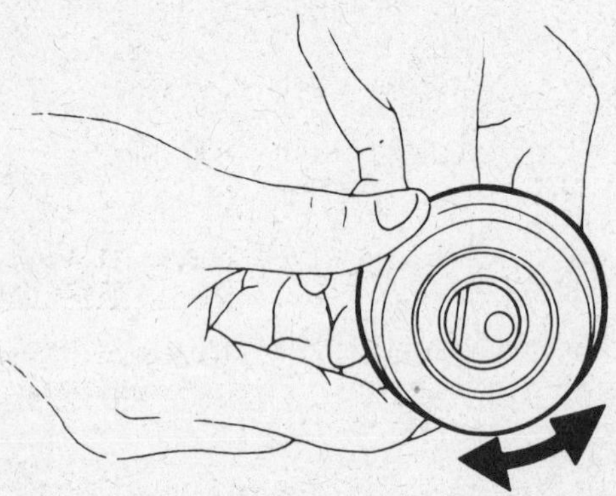

10.17 Check the belt tensioner and spring for wear and damage – the pulley should rotate smoothly

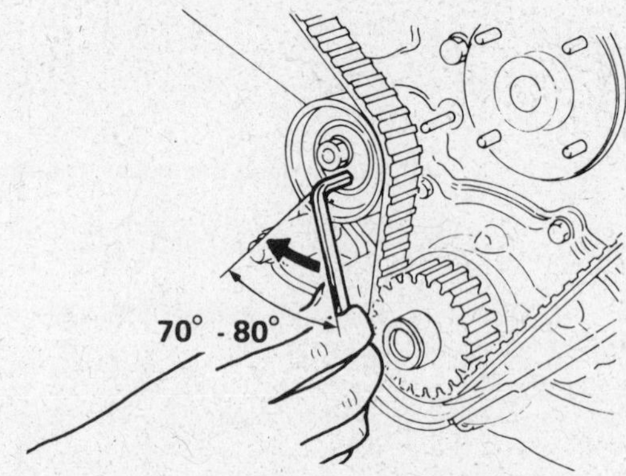

10.18 Turn the tensioner with an Allen wrench to vary timing belt tension

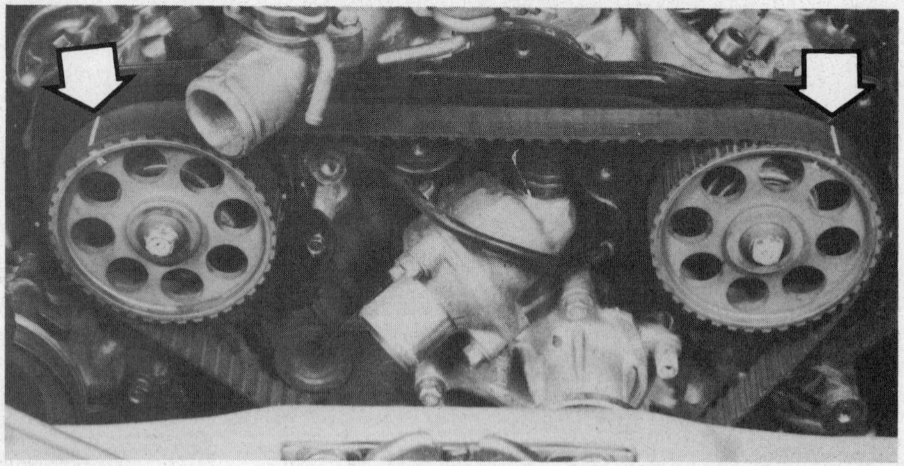

10.20a Align the white marks on the belt (arrows) with the punch marks on the camshaft pulleys and the rear timing belt cover to ensure correct valve timing – this is extremely important – don't continue with belt installation until you're sure it's correct!

bolt or make a sketch to help remember where they go.

15 Confirm that the number one piston is still at TDC on the compression stroke by verifying that the timing marks on all three timing belt pulleys are aligned with their respective stationary alignment marks **(see illustration)**. The stationary marks for the two camshaft pulleys are notches on the rear timing belt cover. The stationary mark for the crankshaft pulley is a notch in the oil pump housing. If the marks don't line up, install the crankshaft damper retaining bolt in the crankshaft and use a wrench to turn the engine over until the timing marks are aligned. DO NOT continue until this has been verified! Remove the damper bolt.

16 Relieve tension on the timing belt by loosening the nut in the middle of the timing belt tensioner **(see illustration)**.

17 Remove the timing belt from the pulleys by sliding it forward. Check the tensioner **(see illustration)**. **Note:** *If the belt is cracked, worn or contaminated with oil or coolant, replace it with a new one.*

18 Prepare to install the timing belt by turning the tensioner clockwise with an Allen wrench and temporarily tightening the locking nut **(see illustration)**.

19 Install the timing belt with the directional arrow pointing forward.

20 Align the factory white lines on the timing belt with the punch mark on each of the camshaft pulleys and the crankshaft pulley. Make sure that all three sets of timing marks are properly aligned **(see illustrations)**. If an arrow appears on the belt, it should face the front belt cover.

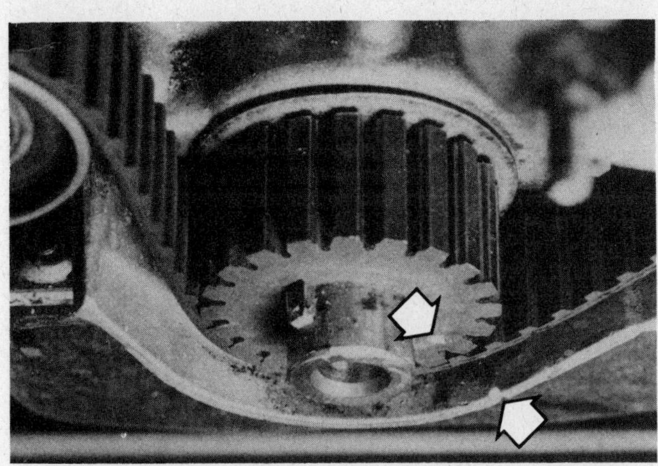

10.20b Make sure the crankshaft pulley mark is aligned with the notch on the oil pump housing (arrows) before releasing the timing belt tensioner

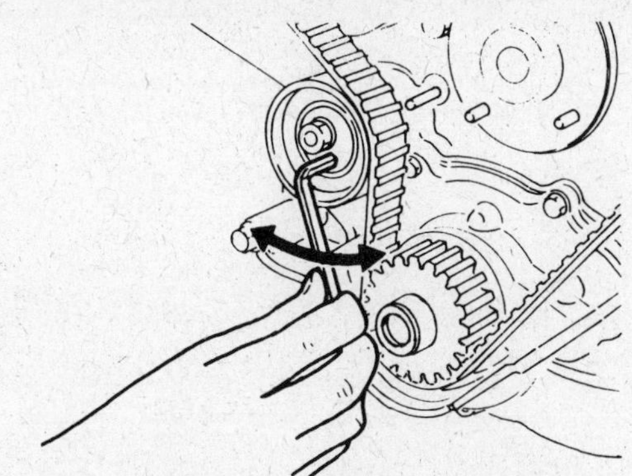

10.22 Use an Allen wrench to turn the tensioner pulley 70° to 80° in a CLOCKWISE direction

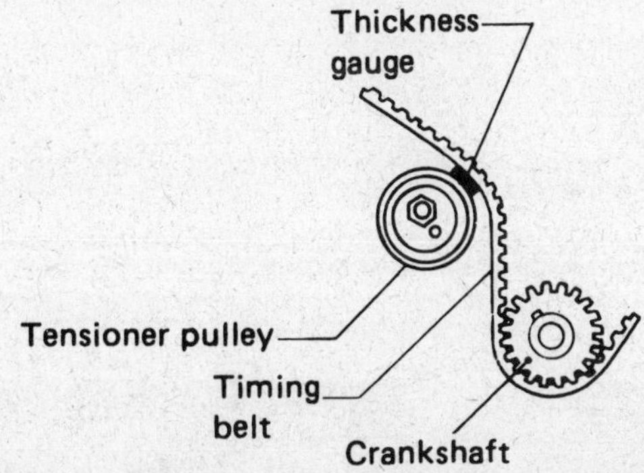

10.27 . . . then turn the crankshaft to move the feeler gauge to the point shown here (it must be exact, so work carefully)

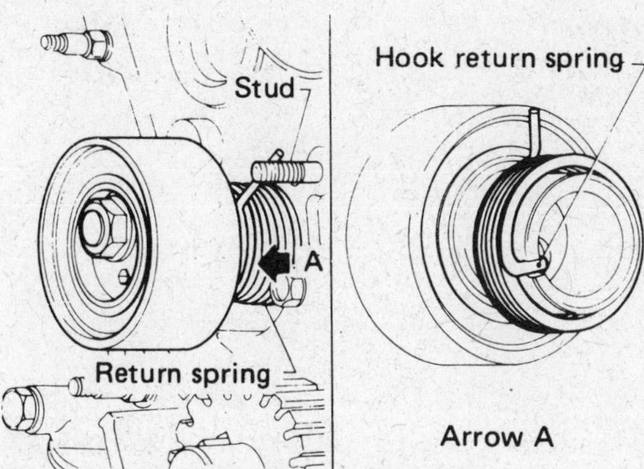

10.21 Belt tensioner spring mounting details (if the stud is removed, use Loc-tite on the threads during installation)

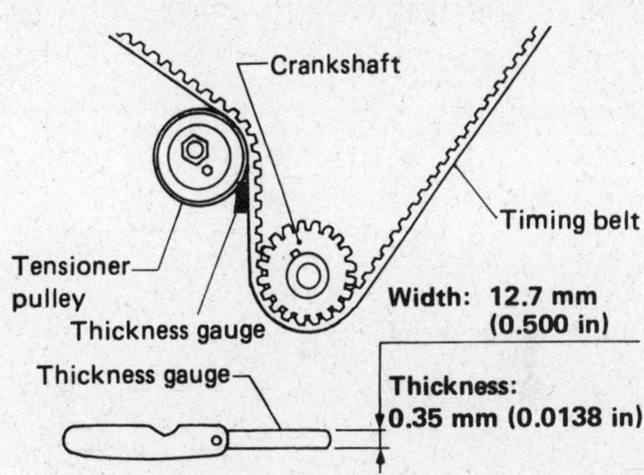

10.26 Position the feeler gauge between the tensioner pulley and the belt as shown here, . . .

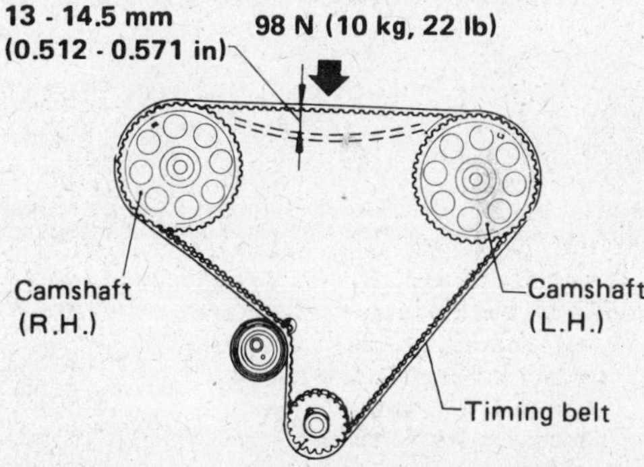

10.31 The deflection of the timing belt is checked exactly half-way between the two camshaft pulleys

Adjustment

Refer to illustrations 10.21, 10.22, 10.26, 10.27 and 10.31

21 If the tensioner was removed, reinstall it and make sure the spring is positioned properly **(see illustration)**. Keep the tensioner steady with the Allen wrench and loosen the locking nut.

22 Using the Allen wrench, swing the tensioner 70° to 80° in a clockwise direction and temporarily tighten the locking nut **(see illustration)**.

23 Install all of the spark plugs.

24 Slowly turn the crankshaft clockwise two or three full revolutions, then return the number one piston to TDC on the compression stroke. **Caution:** *If resistance is felt while turning the crankshaft, it's an indication that the pistons are coming into contact with the valves. Go back over the procedure to correct the situation before proceeding.*

25 Loosen the tensioner locking nut while keeping the tensioner steady with the Allen wrench.

26 Place a 0.0138-inch thick feeler gauge adjacent to the tensioner pulley **(see illustration)**.

27 Slowly turn the crankshaft clockwise until the feeler gauge is between the belt and the tensioner pulley **(see illustration)**.

28 Tighten the tensioner locking nut, keeping the tensioner steady with the Allen wrench.

29 Turn the crankshaft to remove the feeler gauge.

30 Slowly turn the crankshaft two or three revolutions and return the number one piston to TDC.

31 Check the deflection of the timing belt by applying 22 pounds of force midway between the camshaft pulleys **(see illustration)**. The belt should deflect 0.512 to 0.571-inch (13 to 14.5 mm). Readjust the belt if necessary.

32 Install the various components removed during disassembly, referring to the appropriate Sections in this Chapter.

11.3 Use two screwdrivers to pry the crankshaft pulley off . . .

11.4 . . . until the puller jaws will fit behind it – be sure to install the bolt so the puller screw won't damage the threads in the crankshaft nose

11.6 Pry the seal out very carefully with a screwdriver – if the crankshaft is nicked or otherwise damaged, the new seal will leak!

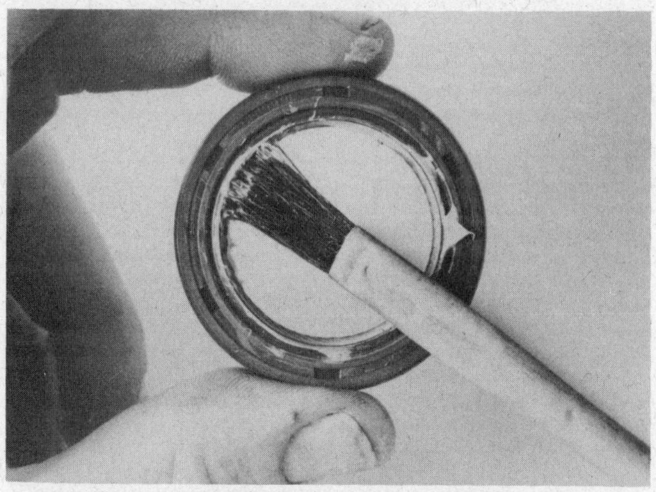

11.7 Apply moly-base grease or assembly lube to the lips of the new seal before installing it (if you apply a small amount of grease to the outer edge, it will be easier to push into the bore)

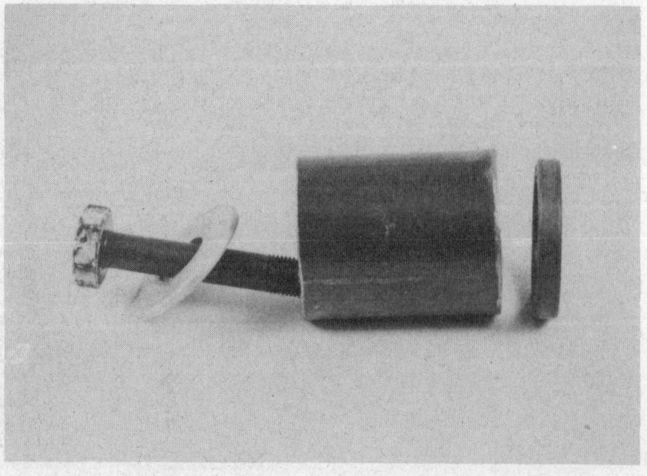

11.8a Fabricate a seal installation tool from a piece of pipe and a large washer . . .

11.8b . . . to push the seal into the bore – the pipe must bear against the outer edge of the seal as the bolt is tightened

11 Front crankshaft oil seal – replacement

Refer to illustrations 11.3, 11.4, 11.6, 11.7, 11.8a and 11.8b

1 Disconnect the negative cable from the battery.
2 Remove the fan shroud and fan assembly (Chapter 3), drivebelts (Chapter 1), pulleys (Section 9), vibration damper (Section 9) and timing belt (Section 10).
3 Wedge two screwdrivers behind the crankshaft pulley **(see illustration)**. Carefully pry the pulley off the crankshaft. Some timing belt pulleys can be pried off easily with screwdrivers. Others are more difficult to remove because corrosion fuses them onto the nose of the crankshaft. If the pulley on your engine is difficult to pry off, don't try to get it all the way off with screwdrivers. Instead, slide it just far enough to grip it with a puller.
4 Once there's enough space between the pulley and the oil pump housing to install a small gear puller, thread the vibration damper bolt into the nose of the crankshaft and install the puller. The bolt provides something solid for the puller screw to push against and protects the crankshaft threads **(see illustration)**.
5 Turn the bolt of the puller until the pulley comes off. Remove the timing belt plate **(see illustration 10.14b)**.
6 Carefully pry the oil seal out with a screwdriver **(see illustration)**. Don't scratch or nick the crankshaft in the process!
7 Before installation, apply a thin coat of assembly lube to the inside of the seal **(see illustration)**.
8 Fabricate a seal installation tool with a short length of pipe of equal or slightly smaller outside diameter than the seal itself. File the end of the pipe that will bear down on the seal until it's free of sharp edges. You'll also need a large washer, slightly larger in diameter than the pipe, on which the bolt head can seat **(see illustration)**. Install the oil seal by pressing it into position with the seal installation tool **(see illustration)**. When you see and feel the seal stop moving, don't turn the bolt any more or you'll damage the seal.
9 Slide the timing belt plate onto the nose of the crankshaft.
10 Make sure the Woodruff key is in place in the crankshaft.
11 Apply a thin coat of assembly lube to the inside of the crankshaft pulley and slide it onto the crankshaft.
12 Installation of the remaining components is the reverse of removal. Tighten all bolts to the specified torque.

12 Camshaft oil seal – replacement

Refer to illustrations 12.3, 12.4, 12.5a, 12.5b and 12.6

1 Disconnect the negative battery cable from the battery.
2 Remove the fan shroud and fan (Chapter 3), drivebelts (Chapter 1), pulley and vibration damper (Section 9) and timing belt (Section 10).
3 Insert a screwdriver through the top hole in the camshaft pulley to lock it in place while loosening the mounting bolt **(see illustration)**.
4 Once the bolt is out, the pulley can be removed by hand. **Note:** *Each pulley is marked with either an R or L* **(see illustration)**. *If you're removing both camshaft pulleys, don't mix them up. They must be installed on the same cam they were removed from.*
5 Carefully remove the old oil seal with a screwdriver. Don't nick or scratch the camshaft in the process **(see illustration)**. Refer to Steps 6, 7 and 8 in Section 11. The same seal installation tool used for the crankshaft seal can be used for both camshaft seals **(see illustration 11.8a)**.

2B

12.3 Insert a screwdriver through the camshaft pulley to hold it while loosening the pulley bolt

12.4 When installing the camshaft timing belt pulleys, note the R and L marks which designate the right and left cylinder heads – don't mix the pulleys up!

12.5a Pry the seal out very carefully with a screwdriver (if the camshaft is nicked or scratched, the new seal will leak!)

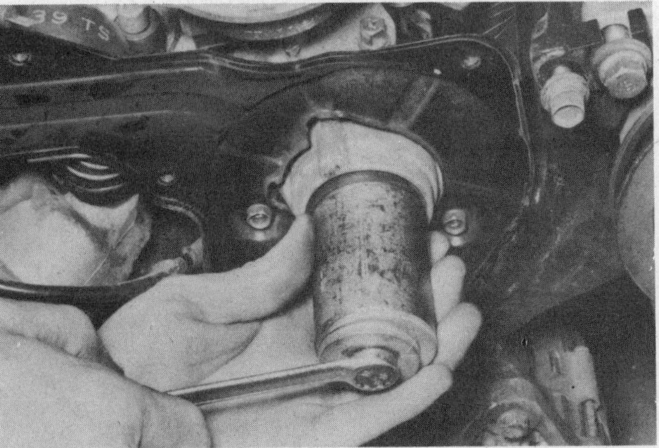

12.5b The same tool you fabricated for installation of the crankshaft front seal can be used to install the camshaft seals

6 Install the pulley. Make sure the R or L mark faces *out*! The side of the pulley with the deep recess must face the engine, which means the shallow recess must face out **(see illustration)**.
7 Insert a screwdriver through the top hole in the camshaft pulley to lock it in place while you tighten the bolt.
8 Installation of the remaining components is the reverse of removal.

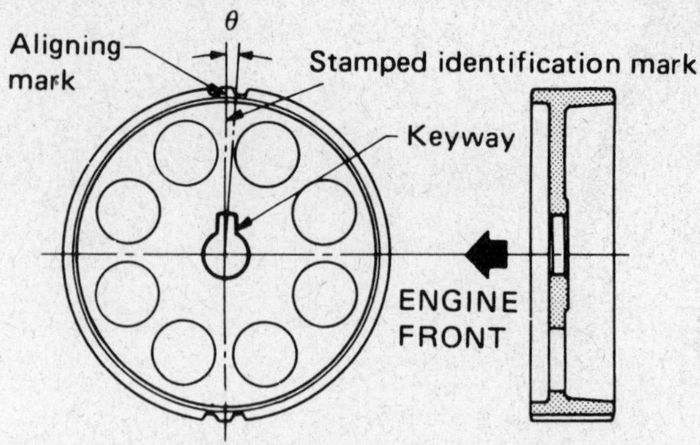

12.6 Make sure the camshaft pulley is installed with the marked side facing OUT!

13 Cylinder heads – removal and installation

Refer to illustrations 13.8, 13.15a, 13.15b, 13.16, 13.29, 13.31a and 13.31b

Note: *Allow the engine to cool completely before beginning this procedure.*

1 Relieve the fuel pressure (Chapter 4).
2 Disconnect the negative cable from the battery.
3 Drain the engine coolant (Chapter 1).
4 Remove the timing belt (Section 10).
5 Remove the throttle body (Chapter 4).
6 Remove the intake manifold (Section 7).
7 Remove the cam pulley(s) (Section 12).
8 Detach the rear timing cover by removing the four bolts **(see illustration)**.

13.8 Remove the four mounting bolts to detach the rear timing belt cover

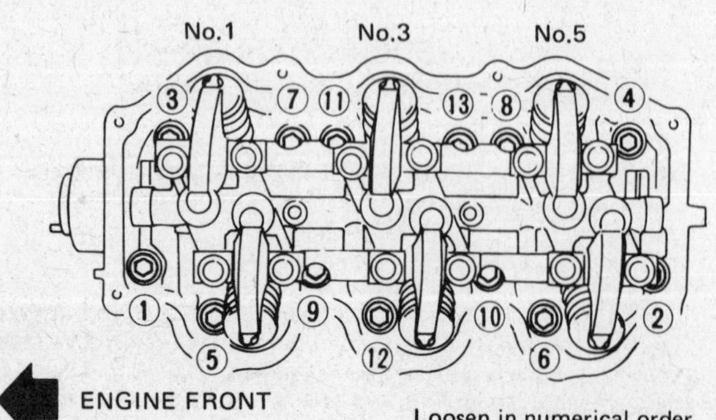

13.15a Cylinder head bolt LOOSENING sequence (loosen the bolts 1/4-turn at a time until they can be removed by hand)

Removal

Left cylinder head

9 Remove the air conditioning compressor from the bracket and set it aside. It may be helpful to secure the compressor with wire to make sure it doesn't move (Chapter 3). DO NOT disconnect any refrigerant lines from the compressor!
10 Remove the distributor (Chapter 5).
11 Remove the alternator and secure it out of the way (Chapter 5).
12 Remove the bolts attaching the air conditioner/alternator bracket to the engine and detach the bracket.
13 Remove the nuts from the exhaust manifold on the left side and slide the manifold away from the cylinder head (Section 8).
14 Remove the rocker arm components (Section 5).
15 Loosen the cylinder head bolts in 1/4-turn increments until they can be removed by hand. Be sure to follow the proper numerical sequence **(see illustration)**. Head bolts must be reinstalled in their original locations. To keep them from getting mixed up, store them in cardboard holders marked to indicate the bolt pattern. Be sure to mark the holders L and R and indicate the front of the engine **(see illustration)**.
16 Remove the small bolt, located at the lower front of the head, securing the head to the block **(see illustration)**.
17 Lift the head off the block. If resistance is felt, dislodge the head by striking it with a wood block and hammer. If prying is required, be very careful not to damage the head or block!

Right cylinder head

18 On vehicles so equipped, unbolt the power steering pump and swing it aside without disconnecting the hydraulic hoses.
19 Remove the exhaust manifold (Section 8).
20 Remove the rocker arm components (Section 5).
21 Remove the cylinder head bolts and keep them in order as described in Step 15.

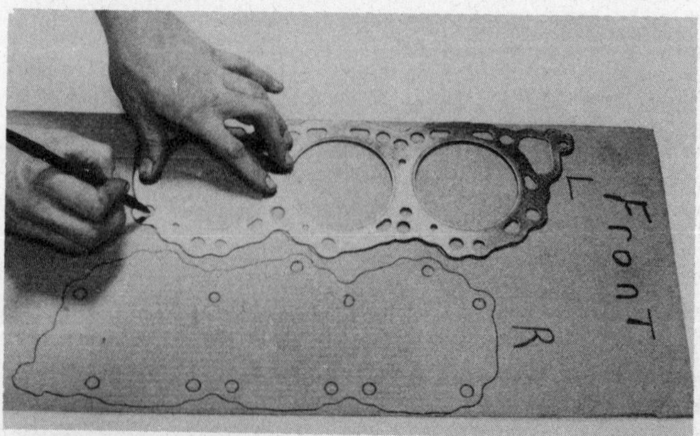

13.15b To avoid mixing up the head bolts, use a new gasket to transfer the hole pattern to a piece of cardboard, punch holes to accept the bolts and push each bolt through the matching hole in the cardboard

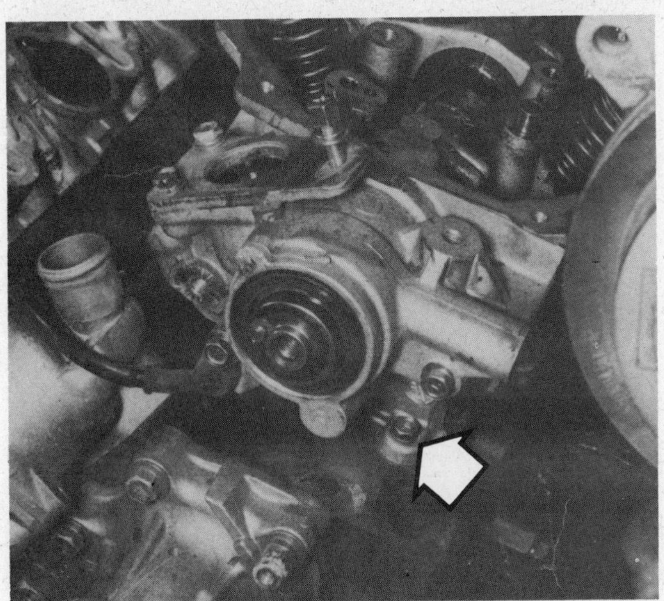

13.16 Remove the small bolt at the front (arrow) before attempting to detach the right side head — the left head has a similar bolt at the rear

13.29 When installing the new gasket, make sure it mates properly with the alignment dowels (arrows)

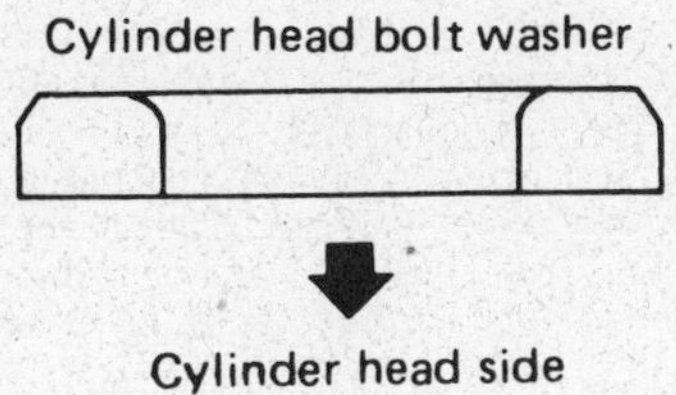

13.31a The washers on the head bolts must be installed with the radiused side against the bolt head

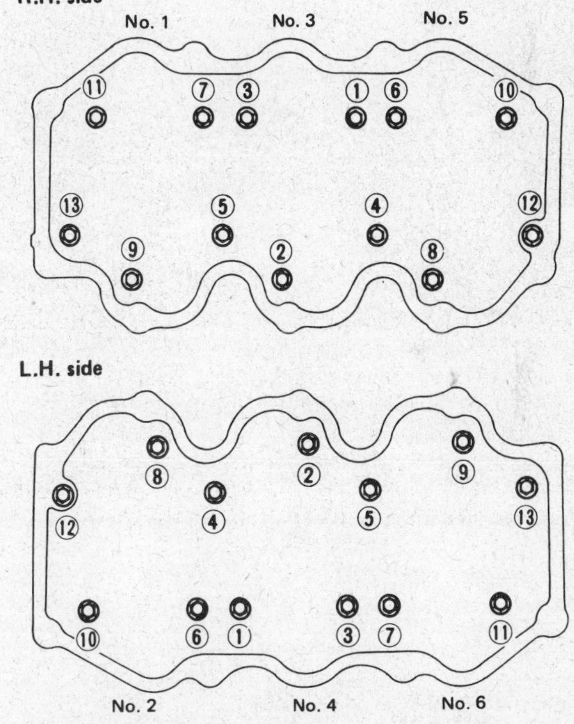

13.31b Cylinder head bolt TIGHTENING sequence (note that bolts 4, 5, 12 and 13 in the sequence are longer than the rest)

22 Remove the small bolt, located at the rear of the head, which secures the cylinder head to the engine block.
23 Lift the head off the engine.
24 If resistance is felt, dislodge the head by striking it with a wood block and hammer. If prying is required, be very careful not to damage the head or block!

Installation

25 The mating surfaces of the cylinder heads and block must be perfectly clean when the heads are installed.
26 Use a gasket scraper to remove all traces of carbon and old gasket material, then clean the mating surfaces wtih lacquer thinner or acetone. If there's oil on the mating surfaces when the heads are installed, the gaskets may not seal correctly and leaks may develop. Use a vacuum cleaner to remove any debris that falls into the cylinders.
27 Check the block and head mating surfaces for nicks, deep scratches and other damage. If damage is slight, it can be removed with a file — if it's excessive, machining may be the only alternative.
28 Use a tap of the correct size to chase the threads in the head bolt holes. Mount each bolt in a vise and run a die down the threads to remove corrosion and restore the threads. Dirt, corrosion, sealant and damaged threads will affect torque readings.
29 Position the new gaskets over the dowel pins in the block **(see illustration)**.
30 Carefully position the heads on the block without disturbing the gaskets.
31 Install the bolts in their original locations and tighten them finger tight. Make sure the washers are in place on the bolts — the radiused side of the washer *must* be against the bolt head, which means the flat side must be against the cylinder head surface **(see illustration)**. Follow the recommended sequence and tighten the bolts in five steps to the specified torque **(see illustration)**. **Caution:** *Bolts 4, 5, 12 and 13 in the sequence are longer than the others — be sure all bolts are in their original installed locations!*
32 The remaining installation steps are the reverse of removal.
33 Change the engine oil and filter (Chapter 1), then start the engine and check carefully for oil and coolant leaks.

14.4 Remove the three camshaft cover plate bolts

14.5a Hold the camshaft lug (arrow) with a large wrench . . .

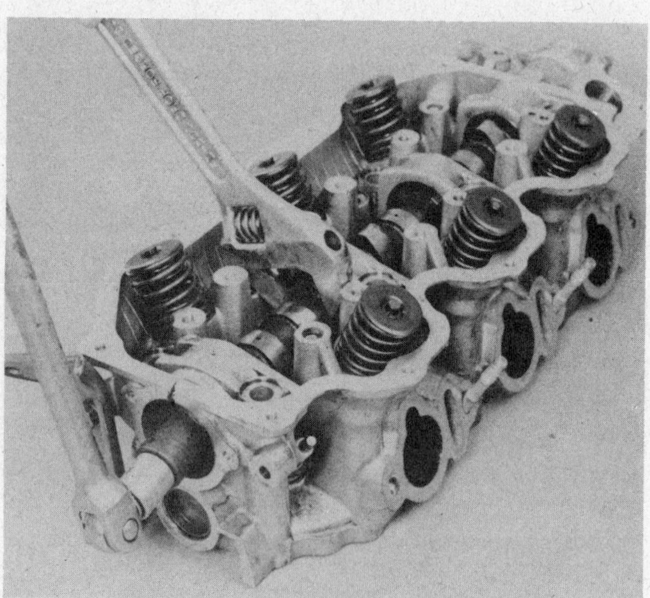
14.5b . . . while loosening the camshaft retaining bolt

14.6 Carefully pry the camshaft oil seal out with a small screwdriver

14 Camshaft – removal and installation

Removal

Refer to illustrations 14.4, 14.5a, 14.5b, 14.6 and 14.7

1 Remove the cylinder head from the engine (Section 13).
2 Remove the valve lifters and lifter guide (Section 6).
3 Remove the rocker arm shafts (Section 5).
4 Remove the bolts and gently pry off the camshaft cover plate **(see illustration)**.
5 Use the holding lug **(see illustration)** to secure the camshaft with a wrench while loosening the retaining bolt **(see illustration)**. Remove the bolt and the locate (thrust) plate.
6 Carefully pry the camshaft oil seal out of the head with a small screwdriver **(see illustration)**. Don't scratch or nick the camshaft in the process!
7 Carefully pull the camshaft out the front of the head using a twisting motion **(see illustration)**. **Caution:** *Don't scratch the bearing surfaces with the cam lobes. Camshaft and bearing inspection is covered in Section 15.*

Installation

Refer to illustrations 14.10 and 14.13

8 Lubricate the camshaft bearing journals and lobes with moly-base grease or engine assembly lube, then install it carefully in the head. Don't scratch the bearing surfaces with the cam lobes!
9 Install the camshaft retaining bolt and tighten it to the specified torque.
10 With the camshaft installed in the head, mount a dial indicator to check the end play **(see illustration)**.
11 Move the camshaft as far as possible to the rear of the head.
12 Zero the dial indicator. Move the cam forward as far as possible.

14.7 Pull the camshaft out the front of the head, using both hands to support it to avoid damage to the bearing surfaces in the head

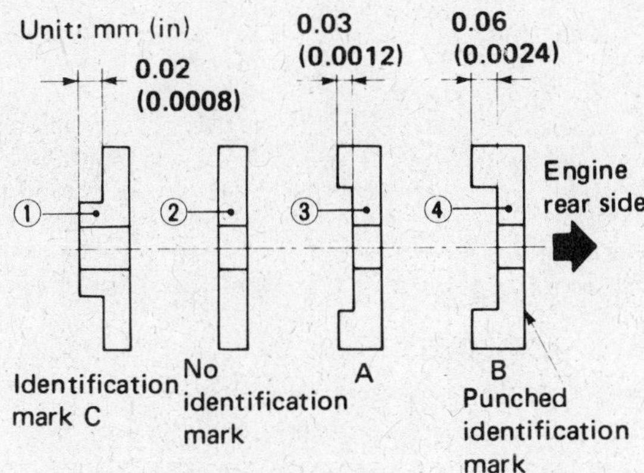

14.13 Camshaft thrust plates are available in different thicknesses

The indicator should read 0.0012 to 0.0024-inch (0.03 to 0.06 mm).
13 End play outside the specified range requires thrust plate replacement. Measure the old plate **(see illustration)** and obtain a new one from your dealer that will produce end play as close to 0.0020-inch (0.05 mm) as possible.

15 Camshaft, lifters, rocker arms and shafts and bearing surfaces - inspection

Refer to illustrations 15.1, 15.2, 15.3, 15.4, 15.5, 15.6, 15.7, 15.10 and 15.11

1 Visually check the camshaft bearing surfaces for pitting, score marks, galling and abnormal wear. If the bearing surfaces are damaged, the head will have to be replaced **(see illustration)**.

2 Measure the outside diameter of each camshaft bearing journal and record your measurements **(see illustration)**. Compare them to the specified journal outside diameter, then measure the inside diameter of each corresponding camshaft bearing and record the measurements. Compare them to the specified camshaft bearing inside diameter. Subtract each cam journal outside diameter from its respective cam bearing bore inside diameter to determine the oil clearance for each bearing. Compare the results to the specified journal-to-bearing clearance. If any of the measurements fall outside the standard specified wear limits, either the camshaft or the head, or both, must be replaced.

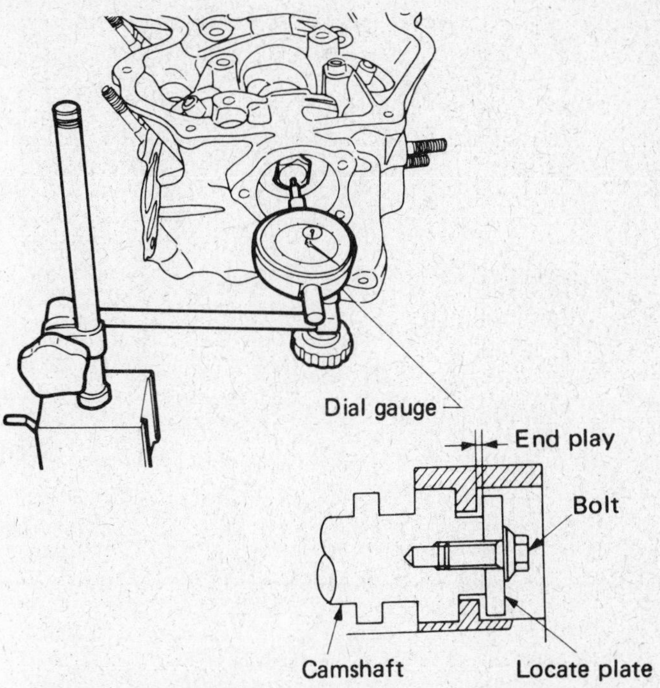

14.10 A dial indicator is needed to check camshaft end play

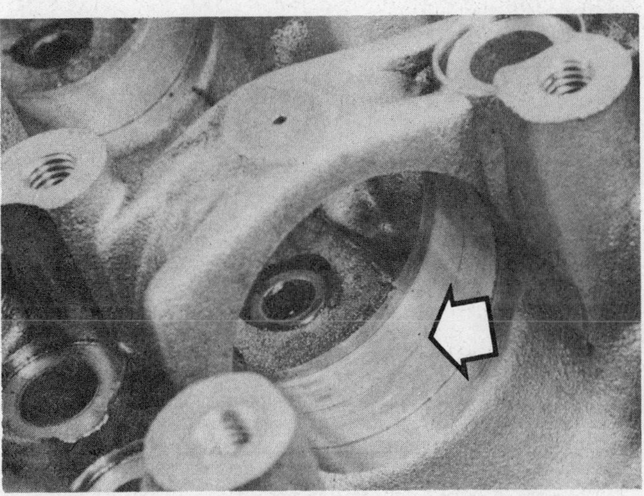

15.1 Inspect the cam bearing surfaces in each head for pits, score marks and abnormal wear – if wear or damage is noted, the head must be replaced

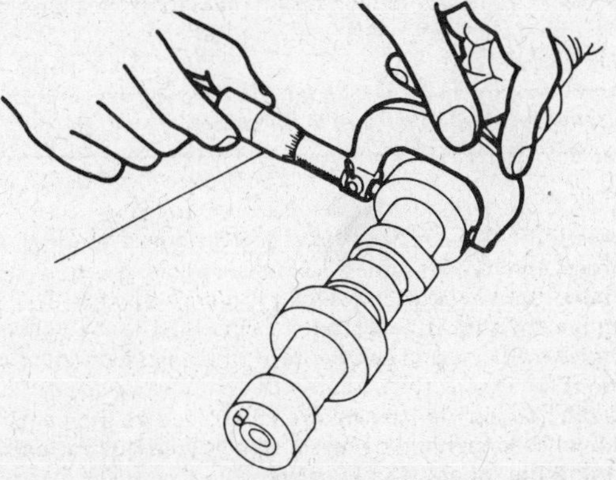

15.2 Measure the outside diameter of each camshaft journal and the inside diameter of each bearing to determine the clearances

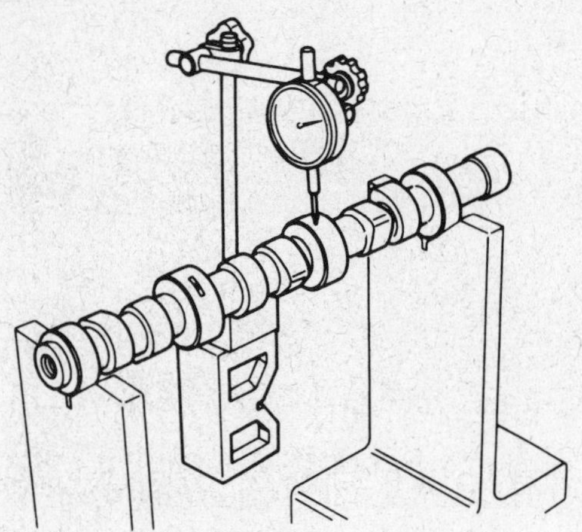

15.3 A dial indicator and V-blocks are needed to check camshaft runout

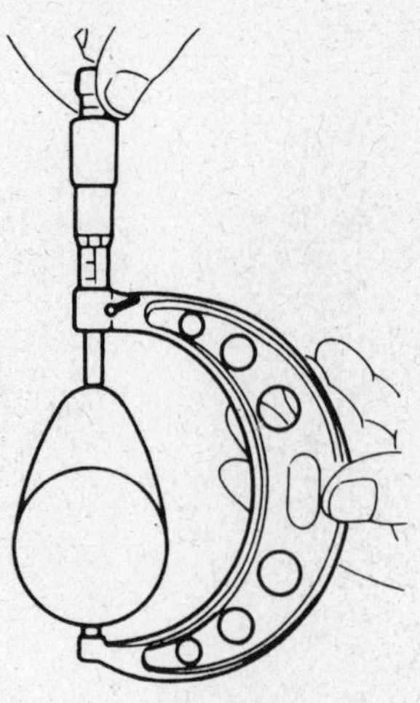

15.4 Measuring cam lobe height with a micrometer

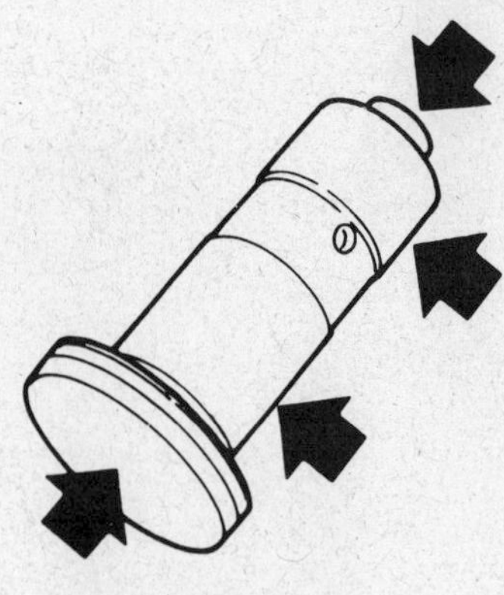

15.5 Check the contact and sliding surfaces of each lifter (arrows) for wear and damage

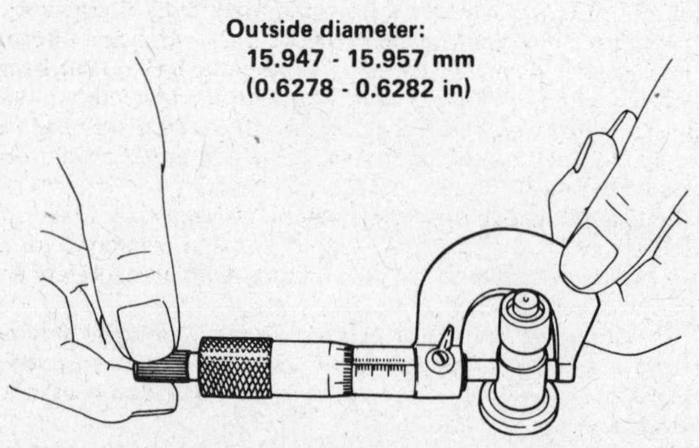

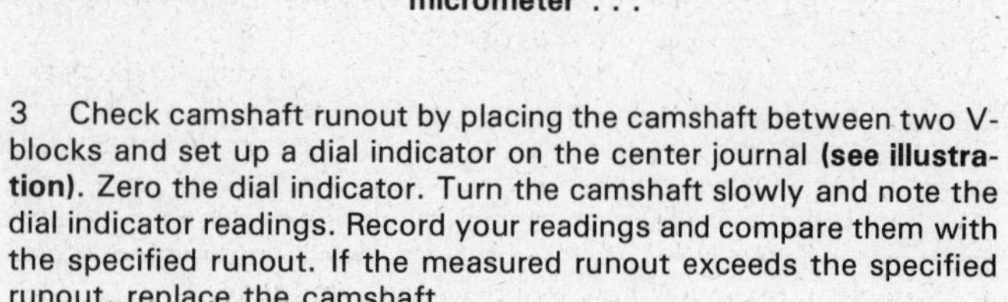

15.6 Measure the outside diameter of each lifter with a micrometer . . .

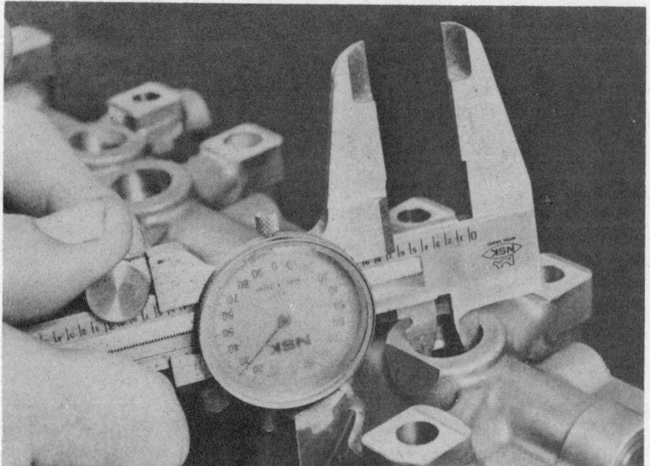

15.7 . . . and the inside diameter of each lifter bore, then subract the lifter diameter to find the lifter-to-guide clearance (compare the results to the Specifications)

3 Check camshaft runout by placing the camshaft between two V-blocks and set up a dial indicator on the center journal **(see illustration)**. Zero the dial indicator. Turn the camshaft slowly and note the dial indicator readings. Record your readings and compare them with the specified runout. If the measured runout exceeds the specified runout, replace the camshaft.

4 Check the camshaft lobe height by measuring each lobe with a micrometer **(see illustration)**. Compare the measurement to the specified cam lobe height. Then subtract the measured cam lobe height from the specified height to compute wear on the cam lobes. Compare it to the specified wear limit. If it's greater than the specified wear limit, replace the camshaft.

5 Inspect the contact and sliding surfaces of each lifter for wear and scratches **(see illustration)**. **Note:** *If the lifter pad is worn, it's a good idea to check the corresponding camshaft lobe, because it will probably be worn too.* **Caution:** *Don't turn the lifters upside down – air can enter and become trapped inside (see Section 6).*

6 Measure the outside diameter of each lifter with a micrometer **(see illustration)** and compare it to the Specifications. If any lifter is worn beyond the specified limit, replace it.

7 Check each lifter bore diameter in the lifter guide assembly **(see illustration)** and compare the results to the Specifications. If any lifter bore is worn beyond the specified limit, the lifter guide assembly must be replaced.

8 Subtract the outside diameter of each lifter from the inside diameter of the lifter bore and compare the difference to the specified clearance. If both the lifter and the bore are within acceptable limits, this measurement should fall within tolerance as well. However, if you buy a new set of lifters alone, or a lifter guide assembly by itself, you may find that this clearance no longer falls within the specified limit.

9 Check the rocker arms and shafts for abnormal wear, pits, galling, score marks and rough spots. Don't attempt to restore rocker arms by grinding the pad surfaces.

10 Measure the outside diameter of the rocker arm shaft at each rocker arm journal **(see illustration)**. Compare the measurements to the specified rocker arm shaft outside diameter.

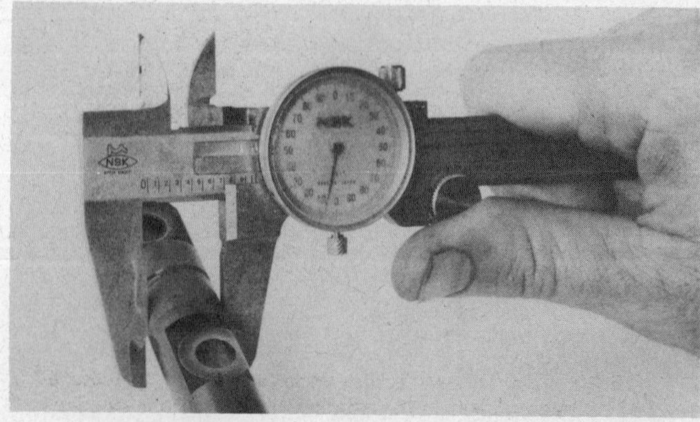

15.10 Measure the rocker arm shaft diameter at each journal where a rocker arm rides on the shaft

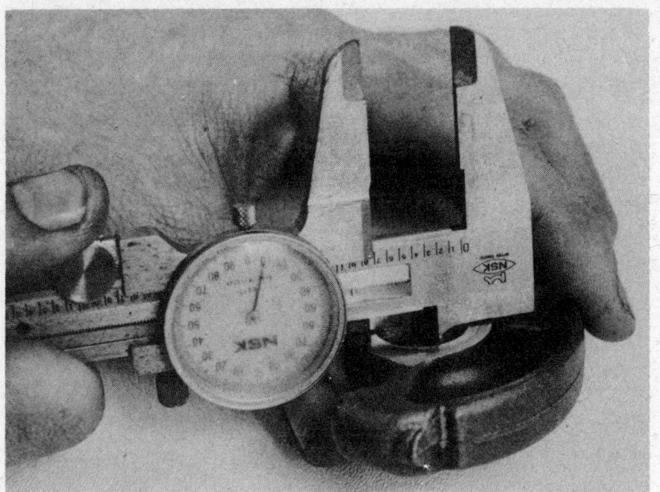

15.11 Measure the inside diameter of each rocker arm bore, subtract the corresponding rocker arm shaft diameter to get the clearance and compare the results to the Specifications

16.19 Apply RTV sealant to the engine block at the oil pump and rear main oil seal retainer junctions (arrows)

11 Measure the inside diameter of each rocker arm with either an inside micrometer or a dial caliper **(see illustration)**. Compare the measurements to the specified rocker arm bore diameter.

12 Subtract the outside diameter of each rocker arm shaft journal from the corresponding rocker arm bore diameter to compute the clearance between the rocker arm shaft and the rocker arm. Compare the measurements to the specified clearance. If any of them fall outside the specified limits, replace either the rocker arms or the shaft, or both.

16 Oil pan – removal and installation

Refer to illustrations 16.19, 16.20 and 16.21

1 Disconnect the negative cable from the battery.
2 Raise the vehicle and support it securely on jackstands.
3 Remove the undercover (belly-pan).
4 Drain the engine oil (Chapter 1).
5 Remove the starter motor (Chapter 5).
6 Remove the braces joining the engine to the bellhousing.
7 Remove the idler arm (Chapter 11).
8 Remove the stabilizer bar bracket bolts (Chapter 11) (2WD models only).
9 Remove the front suspension crossmember from beneath the oil pan (2WD models only).
10 Remove the front differential carrier and mounting bracket (Chapter 9) (4WD models only).
11 Unbolt the transmission mount from the crossmember.
12 Unbolt the exhaust pipes from the manifolds (Chapter 4).
13 Support the engine/transmission securely with a hoist from above or with a jack under the bellhousing. Protect the bellhousing by placing a block of wood on the jack pad. **Warning:** *Be absolutely certain the engine/transmission is securely supported! DO NOT place any part of your body under the engine/transmission – it could crush you if the jack or hoist fails!*
14 Unbolt the engine mounts from the chassis.
15 Carefully lift the engine slightly to provide clearance for oil pan removal. If you encounter any resistance, stop immediately and find out what's hanging up.
16 Remove the bolts and detach the oil pan. Don't pry between the pan and the block or damage to the sealing surfaces may result and oil leaks could develop. If the pan is stuck, dislodge it with a block of wood and a hammer.
17 Use a gasket scraper to remove all traces of old gasket material and sealant from the pan and block. Clean the mating surfaces with lacquer thinner or acetone.
18 Make sure the holes in the block are clean (use a tap to remove any sealant or corrosion from the threads).
19 Apply a small amount of RTV sealant to the oil pump-to-block and rear seal retainer-to-block junctions **(see illustration)**.
20 Apply sealant to the same four points on the new gasket. Be sure to coat both upper and lower surfaces **(see illustration)**.
21 Attach the new gasket to the pan, then position the pan against the block and install the bolts. Tighten the bolts in three or four steps, following the recommended sequence **(see illustration)**.
22 The remaining installation steps are the reverse of removal.

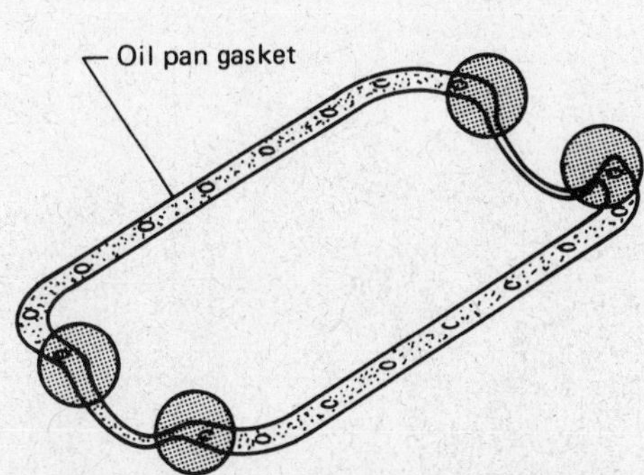

16.20 Appy sealant to the upper and lower surfaces of the oil pan gasket in the shaded areas before installation

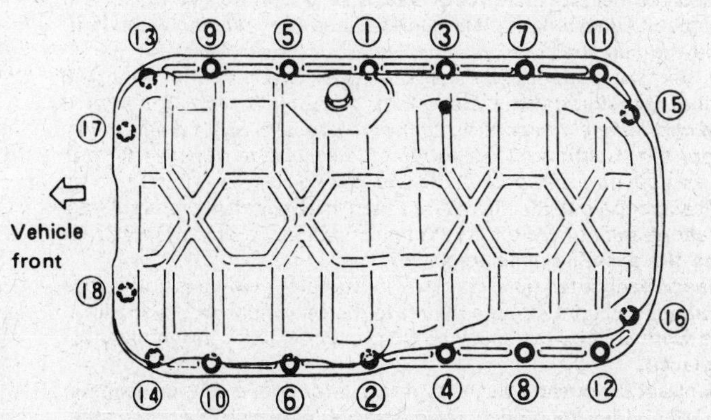

16.21 Oil pan bolt tightening sequence

17.3 Remove the oil pump mounting bolts (arrows) and detach the pump from the engine

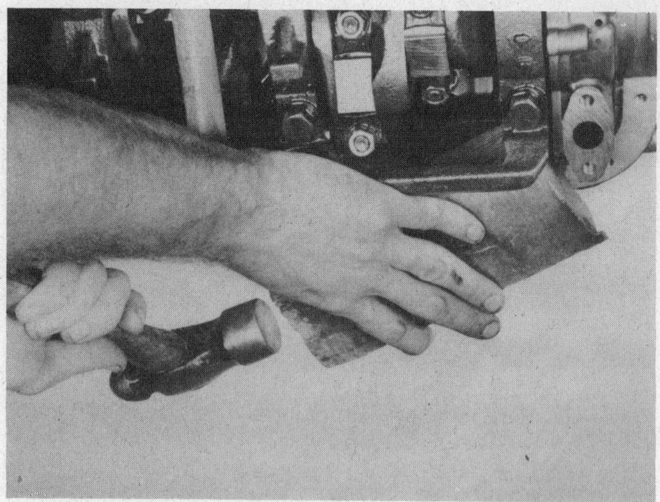

17.4 Use a block of wood and a hammer to gently break the oil pump gasket seal – don't strike the pump body with a steel hammer!

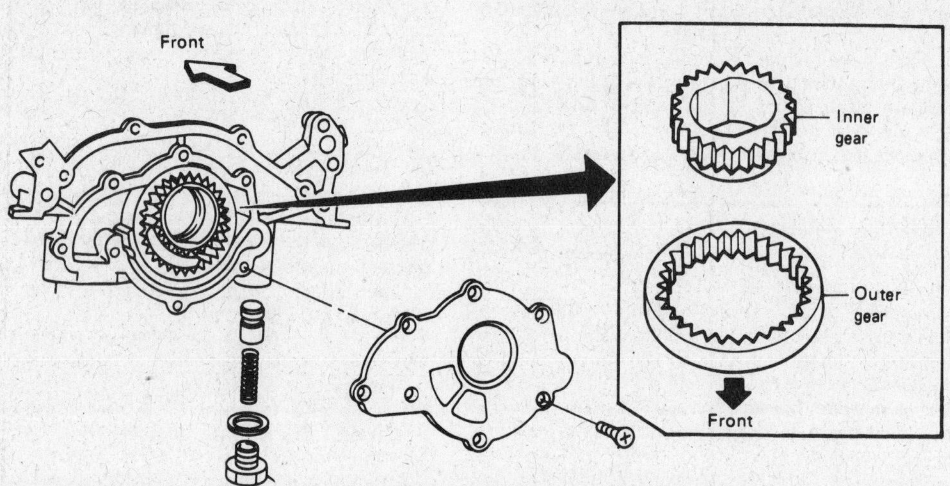

17.7 Oil pump components – exploded view

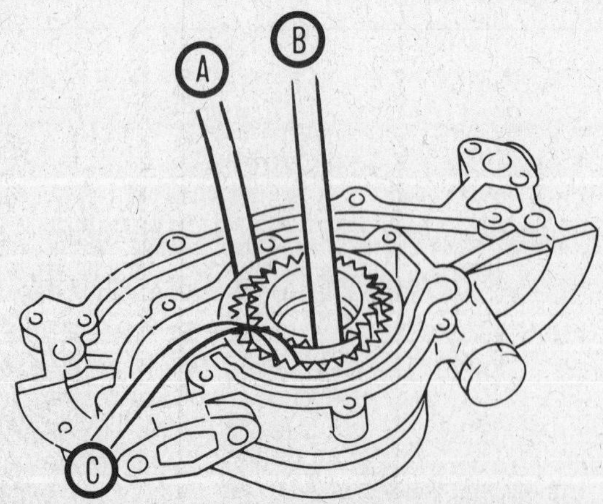

17.10a Use a feeler gauge to check the body-to-outer gear clearance (A), the clearance between the inner gear and crescent (B) and the clearance between the outer gear and crescent (C)

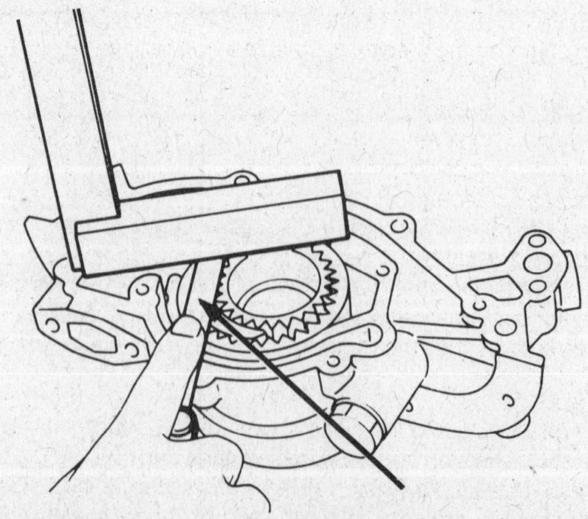

17.10b Check the oil pump housing-to-inner gear and the housing-to-outer gear clearance with a precision straightedge and feeler gauges (arrow)

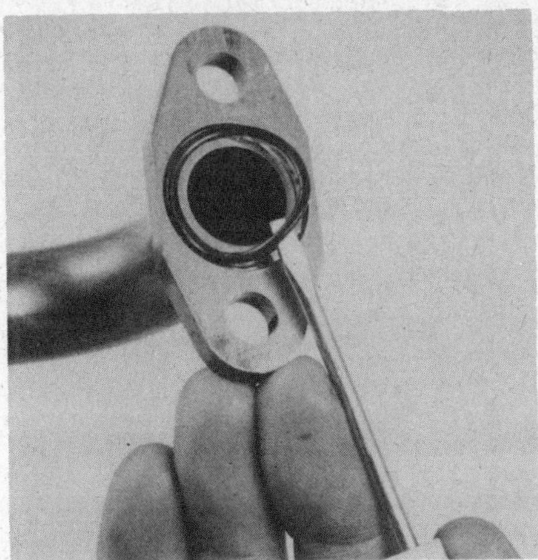

17.13 Before installing the oil strainer, replace the rubber O-ring

18.3 Pry the seal out very carefully with a screwdriver – if the crankshaft is damaged, the new seal will leak!

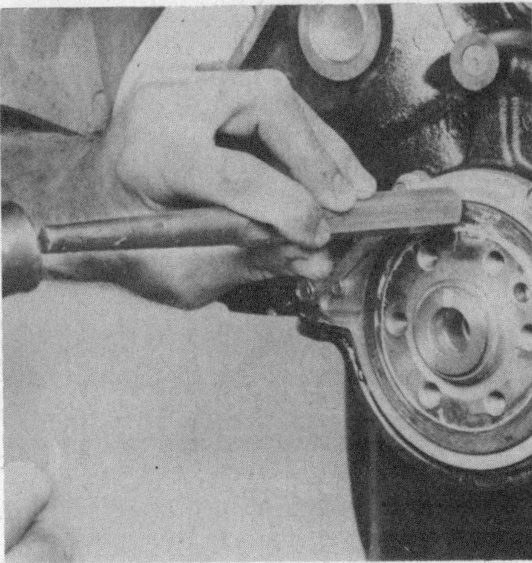

18.6 Once the seal is flush with the retainer face, use a blunt punch (preferably brass) to carefully drive the seal the rest of the way in

17 Oil pump – removal, inspection and installation

Refer to illustrations 17.3, 17.4, 17.7, 17.10a, 17.10b and 17.13

Removal

1 Remove the timing belt and the crankshaft pulley (Sections 10 and 11). Remove the oil pan (Section 16).

2 Remove the bolts and detach the oil pump strainer.

3 Remove the oil pump-to-engine block bolts from the front of the engine **(see illustration)**.

4 Use a block of wood and a hammer to break the oil pump gasket seal **(see illustration)**.

5 Pull forward on the oil pump to remove it from the engine block.

6 Use a scraper to remove old gasket material and sealant from the oil pump and engine block mating surfaces. Clean the mating surfaces with lacquer thinner or acetone.

Inspection

7 Use a large Phillips screwdriver to remove the seven screws holding the front and rear halves of the oil pump together **(see illustration)**.

8 Clean all components with solvent, then inspect them for wear and damage.

9 Remove the oil pressure regulator cap, washer, spring and valve. Check the oil pressure regulator valve sliding surface and valve spring. If either the spring or the valve is damaged, they must be replaced as a set.

10 Check the following clearances with a feeler gauge **(see illustrations)** and compare the measurements to the specified clearances:

Body-to-outer gear
Inner gear-to-crescent
Outer gear-to-crescent
Housing-to-inner gear
Housing-to-outer gear

If any of the clearances are excessive, replace the entire gear set or the entire oil pump assembly.

11 **Note:** *Pack the pump with petroleum jelly to prime it.* Assemble the oil pump and tighten the screws securely. Install the oil pressure regulator valve, spring and washer, then tighten the oil pressure regulator valve cap.

Installation

12 Apply RTV sealant to the oil pump mounting surface.

13 Use new gaskets on all disassembled parts and reverse the removal procedure for installation. Tighten all fasteners securely. **Note:** *Before installing the oil pump strainer, replace the rubber O-ring* **(see illustration)**.

18 Rear crankshaft oil seal – replacement

Refer to illustrations 18.3 and 18.6

1 Remove the transmission (see Chapter 7A for manual transmissions, Chapter 7B for automatics).

2 Remove the flywheel/driveplate (Section 19).

3 Insert a screwdriver between the oil seal and crankshaft, then pry the seal out of the retainer **(see illustration)**. Be very careful not to nick or scratch the crankshaft in the process!

4 Apply moly-base grease to the outer edge and the lips of the new seal.

5 Push the seal onto the crankshaft and gently tap it into the bore with a soft-face hammer.

6 Once the seal face is flush with the seal retainer and the crankshaft flange, very carefully drive the seal the rest of the way into the retainer with the blunt end of a punch. A brass punch is best **(see illustration)**. **Caution:** *Be extremely careful. Take your time and drive the seal gently and evenly into place. Damaging a new seal will result in an oil leak.*

7 The rest of installation is the reverse of removal.

19 Flywheel/driveplate – removal and installation

Refer to illustrations 19.3 and 19.4

1 Raise the vehicle and support it securely on jackstands, then refer to Chapter 7 and remove the transmission.

2 Remove the pressure plate assembly and clutch disc (Chapter 8) (manual transmission equipped vehicles).

3 Use paint to make an alignment mark from the flywheel to the end of the crankshaft for correct alignment during reinstallation **(see illustration)**.

19.3 To ensure proper balance, mark the flywheel/driveplate in relationship to the crankshaft

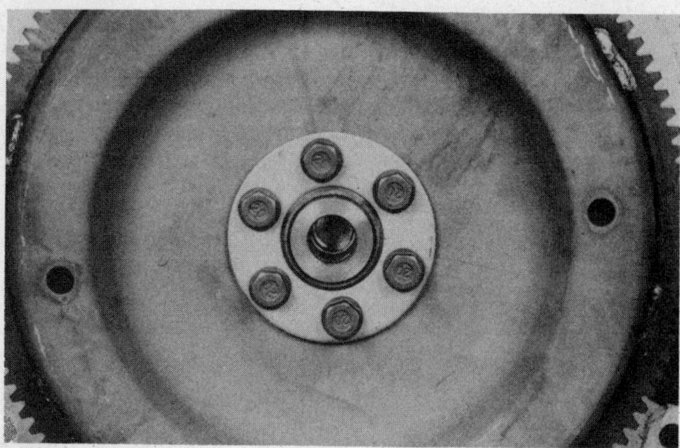

19.4 The flywheel/driveplate bolts are very tight, so use a sixpoint socket and 1/2-inch drive breaker bar to loosen them!

4 Remove the bolts that secure the flywheel to the crankshaft rear flange **(see illustration)**. If difficulty is experienced in removing the bolts due to movement of the crankshaft, wedge a screwdriver through the starter opening to keep the flywheel from turning.

5 Remove the flywheel/driveplate from the crankshaft flange.

6 Clean any grease or oil from the flywheel. Inspect the surface of the flywheel for rivet grooves, burned areas and score marks. Light scoring can be removed with emery cloth. Check for cracked or broken teeth. Lay the flywheel on a flat surface and use a straightedge to check for warpage.

7 Clean the mating surfaces of the flywheel/driveplate and the crankshaft.

8 Position the flywheel/driveshaft against the crankshaft, matching the alignment marks made during removal. Before installing the bolts, apply Loc-Tite to the threads.

9 Wedge a screwdriver through the starter motor opening to keep the flywheel from turning as you tighten the bolts to the specified torque.

10 The remainder of installation is the reverse of the removal procedure.

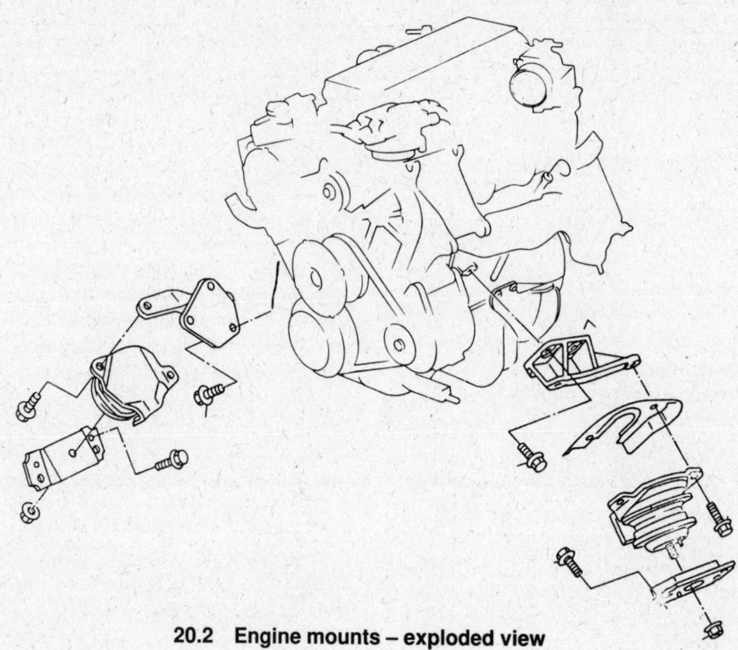

20.2 Engine mounts – exploded view

20 Engine mounts – check and replacement

Refer to illustrations 20.2 and 20.5

1 Engine mounts should be periodically inspected for hardening or cracking of the rubber and separation of the rubber from the metal backing.

2 Replace the front mounts by loosening the nuts and bolts retaining them to the engine mounting bracket and chassis on both sides of the engine **(see illustration)**.

3 Take the weight of the engine off the mounts by placing a jack and wooden block under the oil pan. Carefully raise the engine enough to allow removal of the mount(s). Extreme caution should be exercised during this procedure.

4 If you intend to use the old mounts again, mark them clearly to ensure that they're installed, right side up, on the same side as before. Remove the nuts and bolts retaining the mounts and detach the mounts, noting the correct installed position.

5 Don't loosen the cover on hydraulic type mounts or the fluid will escape (see illustration).

6 Installation is the reverse of the removal procedure.

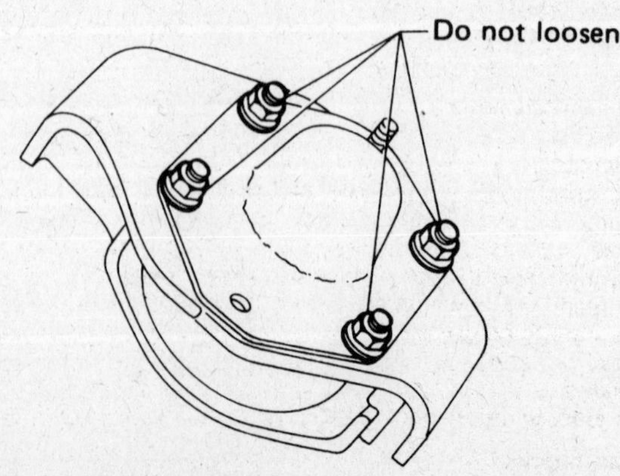

20.5 Don't loosen the cover on hydraulic mounts or the fluid will escape, rendering them useless

Chapter 2 Part C
General engine overhaul procedures

Contents

Specifications

L20B four-cylinder engine (1980)

General

Oil pressure	50 to 60 psi at 3000 rpm
Compression pressure (at 350 rpm)	
Standard	171 psi
Minimum	128 psi

Camshaft

Camshaft	See Chapter 2, Part A

Cylinder head

Warpage limit	0.004 in (0.1 mm)

Valves

Valve stem diameter	
Intake	0.3136 to 0.3142 in (7.965 to 7.980 mm)
Exhaust	0.3128 to 0.3134 in (7.945 to 7.960 mm)
Valve spring free length (intake and exhaust)	
Inner	1.766 in (44.85 mm)
Outer	1.968 in (49.98 mm)
Valve guide height from surface of cylinder head	0.417 in (10.6 mm)
Valve guide inside diameter	0.3150 to 0.3154 in (8.000 to 8.018 mm)
Valve stem-to-guide clearance	
Intake	0.0008 to 0.0021 in (0.101 to 0.053 mm)
Exhaust	0.0016 to 0.0029 in (0.040 to 0.073 mm)
Valve stem end deflection limit	0.008 in (0.2 mm)

Engine block

Deck distortion limit	0.004 in (0.1 mm)
Bore diameter	3.3465 to 3.3484 in (85.000 to 85.050 mm)
Bore taper/out-of-round	Less than 0.0006 in (0.015 mm)
Piston-to-bore clearance	0.0010 to 0.0018 in (0.025 to 0.045 mm)

Pistons and rings

Piston diameter	
Standard	3.3459 to 3.3478 in (84.985 to 85.035 mm)
1st oversize	3.3648 to 3.3667 in (85.465 to 85.515 mm)
2nd oversize	3.3844 to 3.3864 in (85.965 to 86.015 mm)
Piston ring side clearance	
Top compression ring	0.0016 to 0.0029 in (0.040 to 0.073 mm)
Second compression ring	0.0012 to 0.0025 in (0.030 to 0.063 mm)
Piston ring end gap	
Top compression ring	0.0098 to 0.0157 in (0.25 to 0.040 mm)
Second compression ring	0.0059 to 0.0118 in (0.15 to 0.30 mm)
Oil ring	0.0118 to 0.0354 in (0.30 to 0.90 mm)

Crankshaft, connecting rods and main bearings

Connecting rod end play (side clearance)	0.0079 to 0.118 in (0.20 to 0.30 mm)
Crankshaft end play	
Standard	0.0020 to 0.0071 in (0.05 to 0.18 mm)
Limit	0.0118 in (0.3 mm)
Main journal diameter	2.1631 to 2.1636 in (54.942 to 54.955 mm)
Connecting rod journal diameter	1.9670 to 1.9675 in (49.961 to 49.974 mm)
Journal taper/out-of-round limit	0.0004 in (0.01 mm)
Main bearing oil clearance	
Standard	0.008 to 0.0024 in)0.020 to 0.062 mm)
Limit	0.0047 in (0.12 mm)
Connecting rod bearing oil clearance	0.0010 to 0.0022 in (0.025 to 0.055 mm)
Crankshaft runout limit	0.0020 in (0.05 mm)

Torque specifications*

	Ft-lbs
Connecting rod nuts	40
Main bearing cap bolts	40
Transmission-to-engine bolts	35
Driveplate-to-torque converter bolts	35
Clutch-to-flywheel bolts	15
Flywheel/driveplate mounting bolts	110

* **Note:** *Refer to Part A for additional torque specifications.*

Z20, Z22 and Z24 (NAPS-Z) engines (1981 on)

General

Oil pressure	
At idle	10.7 psi
At 3000 rpm	47 to 67 psi
Compression pressure	
Standard	171 psi
Minimum	128 psi

Camshaft and rocker arms

Camshaft and rocker arms	See Chapter 2, Part A

Cylinder head

Warpage limit	0.004 in (0.1 mm)

Valves

Valve stem diameter	
Intake	0.3136 to 0.3142 in (7.965 to 7.980 mm)
Exhaust	0.3128 to 0.3134 in (7.945 to 7.960 mm)
Valve face angle	45° 30'
Valve margin width	
Intake	
Standard	0.051 in (1.3 mm)
Limit	0.020 in (0.5 mm)
Exhaust	
Standard	0.059 in (1.5 mm)
Limit	0.020 in (0.05 mm)
Valve stem end grinding limit	0.020 in (0.5 mm)
Valve spring free length	
Outer spring	1.9594 in (49.77 mm)
Inner spring	1.7362 in (44.10 mm)
Valve spring installed height	
Outer spring	
Standard	1.575 in @ 50.7 lb (40.0 mm @ 23.0 kg)
Limit	1.575 in @ 42.6 lb (40.0 mm @ 19.3 kg)
Inner spring	
Standard	1.378 in @ 24.3 lb (35.0 mm @ 11.0 kg)
Limit	1.378 in @ 19.6 lb (35.0 mm @ 8.9 kg)
Valve spring out-of-square limit	
Outer spring	0.087 in (2.2 mm)
Inner spring	0.075 in (1.9 mm)
Valve guide inside diameter	0.3150 to 0.3157 in (8.000 to 8.018 mm)

Z20, Z22 and Z24 (NAPS-Z) engines (1981 on) (continued)

Valve stem-to-guide clearance	
Intake	0.0008 to 0.0021 in (0.020 to 0.053 mm)
Exhaust	0.0016 to 0.0029 in (0.040 to 0.073 mm)
Valve stem end deflection limit	0.008 in (0.2 mm)
Valve seat	
Angle	45°
Width	
Intake	0.071 to 0.094 in (1.8 to 2.4 mm)
Exhaust	0.059 to 0.075 in (1.5 to 1.9 mm)

Engine block

Deck distortion limit	0.004 in (0.1 mm)
Cylinder bore diameter	
Z22 engine (all)	3.4252 to 3.4272 in (87.000 to 87.050 mm)
Z20 engine	
1984	3.3465 to 3.3484 in (85.000 to 85.050 mm)
1985	
Standard (grade 1)	3.3465 to 3.3468 in (85.000 to 85.010 mm)
Grade 2	3.3468 to 3.3472 in (85.010 to 85.020 mm)
Grade 3	3.3472 to 3.3476 in (85.020 to 85.030 mm)
Grade 4	3.3476 to 3.3480 in (85.030 to 85.040 mm)
Grade 5	3.3480 to 3.3484 in (85.040 to 85.050 mm)
Z24 engine (all)	
Grade 1	3.5039 to 3.5043 in (89.000 to 89.010 mm)
Grade 2	3.5043 to 3.5047 in (89.010 to 89.020 mm)
Grade 3	3.5047 to 3.5051 in (89.020 to 89.030 mm)
Grade 4	3.5051 to 3.5055 in (89.030 to 89.040 mm)
Grade 5	3.5055 to 3.5059 in (89.040 to 89.050 mm)
Cylinder bore taper/out-of-round	Less than 0.0006 in (0.015 mm)
Piston-to-bore clearance	0.0010 to 0.0018 in (0.025 to 0.045 mm)

Pistons and rings

Diameter	
Z22 engine (all)	
Standard	3.4246 to 3.4266 in (86.985 to 87.035 mm)
1st oversize	3.4435 to 3.4455 in (87.465 to 87.515 mm)
2nd oversize	3.4632 to 3.4652 in (87.965 to 88.015 mm)
Z20 engine	
1984	
Standard	3.3451 to 3.3470 in (84.965 to 85.015 mm)
1st oversize	3.3459 to 3.3478 in (84.985 to 85.035 mm)
2nd oversize	3.3648 to 3.3667 in (85.465 to 85.515 mm)
3rd oversize	3.3844 to 3.3864 in (85.965 to 86.015 mm)
1985	
Standard (grade 1)	3.3451 to 3.3455 in (84.965 to 84.975 mm)
Grade 2	3.3455 to 3.3459 in (84.975 to 84.985 mm)
Grade 3	3.3459 to 3.3463 in (84.985 to 84.995 mm)
Grade 4	3.3463 to 3.3466 in (84.995 to 85.005 mm)
Grade 5	3.3466 to 3.3470 in (85.005 to 85.015 mm)
Z24 engine	
1984 and 1988 only	
Standard	3.5026 to 3.5045 in (88.965 to 89.015 mm)
1st oversize	3.5033 to 3.5053 in (88.985 to 89.035 mm)
2nd oversize	3.5222 to 3.5242 in (89.465 to 89.515 mm)
3rd oversize	3.5419 to 3.5439 in (89.965 to 90.015 mm)
1985 through 1987	
Standard (grade 1)	3.5026 to 3.5029 in (88.965 to 88.975 mm)
Grade 2	3.5029 to 3.5033 in (88.975 to 88.985 mm)
Grade 3	3.5033 to 3.5037 in (88.985 to 88.995 mm)
Grade 4	3.5037 to 3.5041 in (88.995 to 89.005 mm)
Grade 5	3.5041 to 3.5045 in (89.005 to 89.015 mm)
Piston ring end gap	
Top compression ring	0.0098 to 0.0157 in (0.25 to 0.40 mm)
Second compression ring	0.0059 to 0.0118 in (0.15 to 0.30 mm)
Oil ring	0.0118 to 0.0354 in (0.30 to 0.90 mm)
Piston ring side clearance	
Top compression ring	0.0016 to 0.0029 in (0.040 to 0.073 mm)
Second compression ring	0.0012 to 0.0025 in (0.030 to 0.063 mm)

Crankshaft, connecting rods and main bearings

Connecting rod end play (side clearance)	
Standard	0.008 to 0.012 in (0.2 to 0.3 mm)
Limit	0.024 in (0.6 mm)
Crankshaft end play	
Standard	0.0020 to 0.0071 in (0.05 to 0.18 mm)
Limit	0.012 in (0.3 mm)

Main bearing journal diameter	2.1631 to 2.1636 in (54.942 to 54.955 mm)
Connecting rod journal diameter	1.9670 to 1.9675 in (49.961 to 49.974 mm)
Journal taper/out-of-round	
Standard	Less than 0.0004 in (0.01 mm)
Limit	0.0012 in (0.03 mm)
Main bearing oil clearance	
Standard	0.0008 to 0.0024 in (0.020 to 0.062 mm)
Limit	0.0047 in (0.12 mm)
Connecting rod bearing oil clearance	
Standard	0.0010 to 0.0022 in (0.025 to 0.055 mm)
Limit	0.0047 in (0.12 mm)
Flywheel runout limit	0.0059 in (0.15 mm)

Torque specifications*

	Ft-lbs
Main bearing cap bolts	36
Connecting rod cap nuts	36

* **Note:** *Refer to Part A for additional torque specifications.*

V6 engine

General

Oil pressure	
At idle	9 psi
At 3200 rpm	53 to 67 psi
Compression pressure at 300 rpm	
Standard	173 psi
Minimum	128 psi
Maximum difference between cylinders	14 psi

Camshaft, lifters and rocker arm components	See Chapter 2, Part B

Cylinder head

Warpage	
Standard	
Through 1990	Less than 0.002 in (0.05 mm)
1991 and later	Less than 0.0012 in (0.03 mm)
Limit	0.004 in (0.10 mm)
Height (nominal)	4.213 ± 0.008 in (107 ± 0.2 mm)

Valves and seats

Valve deflection limit	0.0079 in (0.20 mm)
Valve stem diameter	
Intake	0.2742 to 0.2748 in (6.965 to 6.980 mm)
Exhaust	0.3136 to 0.3138 in (7.965 to 7.970 mm)
Valve guide inside diameter	
Intake	0.2756 to 0.2763 in (7.000 to 7.018 mm)
Exhaust	0.3157 to 0.3154 in (8.000 to 8.018 mm)
Valve stem-to-guide clearance	
Standard	
Intake	0.0008 to 0.0021 in (0.020 to 0.053 mm)
Exhaust	0.0016 to 0.0029 in (0.040 to 0.073 mm)
Limit (intake and exhaust)	0.0039 in (0.10 mm)
Valve margin limit	0.020 in (0.5 mm)
Valve length	
Intake	4.933 to 4.957 in (125.3 to 125.9 mm)
Exhaust	4.890 to 4.913 in (124.2 to 124.8 mm)
Valve stem end grinding limit	0.008 in (0.20 mm)
Valve spring free length	
Inner	1.736 in (44.10 mm)
Outer	2.016 in (51.20 mm)
Valve spring pressure/height	
Inner	0.984 in @ 57.3 lbs (25.0 mm @ 26 Kg)
Outer	1.181 in @ 117.7 lbs (30.0 mm @ 53.4 Kg)
Valve spring out-of-square limit	
Inner	0.075 in (1.9 mm)
Outer	0.087 in (2.2 mm)
Valve spring installed height	
Inner	1.378 in (35.0 mm)
Outer	1.575 in (40.0 mm)
Valve seats	
Angle (intake and exhaust)	45-degrees
Width	
Intake	0.0689 in (1.75 mm)
Exhaust	0.067 in (1.7 mm)

Engine block

Deck distortion	
Standard	Less than 0.0012 in (0.03 mm)
Limit	0.0039 in (0.10 mm)

V6 engine (continued)

Cylinder bore	
Diameter (standard)	
Grade no. 1	3.4252 to 3.4256 in (87.000 to 87.010 mm)
Grade no. 2	3.4256 to 3.4260 in (87.010 to 87.020 mm)
Grade no. 3	3.4260 to 3.4264 in (87.020 to 87.030 mm)
Grade no. 4	3.4264 to 3.4268 in (87.030 to 87.040 mm)
Grade no. 5	3.4268 to 3.4272 in (87.040 to 87.050 mm)
Wear limit	0.0079 in (0.20 mm)
Taper/out-of-round	Less than 0.0006 in (0.015 mm)

Pistons and rings

Piston diameter (A in illustration 17.11)	
Grade no. 1	3.4238 to 3.4242 in (86.965 to 86.975 mm)
Grade no. 2	3.4242 to 3.4246 in (86.975 to 86.985 mm)
Grade no. 3	3.4246 to 3.4250 in (86.985 to 86.995 mm)
Grade no. 4	3.4250 to 3.4254 in (86.995 to 87.005 mm)
Grade no. 5	3.4254 to 3.4258 in (87.005 to 87.015 mm)
Piston-to-bore clearance	
Through 1990	0.0010 to 0.0018 in (0.025 to 0.045 mm)
1991 and later	0.0006 to 0.0014 in (0.015 to 0.035 mm)
Force required to pull 0.0016-inch (0.04 mm) thick feeler gauge past piston in cylinder	0.4 to 3.3 lbs (0.2 to 1.5 Kg)
Piston ring side clearance	
Top compression ring	
Standard	0.0016 to 0.0029 in (0.040 to 0.073 mm)
Limit	0.004 in (0.1 mm)
Second compression ring	
Standard	0.0012 to 0.0025 in (0.030 to 0.063 mm)
Limit	0.004 in (0.1 mm)
Oil control ring	0.0006 to 0.0075 in (0.015 to 0.190 mm)
Piston ring end gap	
Top compression ring	
Standard	0.0083 to 0.0173 in (0.21 to 0.44 mm)
Limit	0.039 in (1.0 mm)
Second compression ring	
Standard	0.0071 to 0.0173 in (0.18 to 0.44 mm)
Limit	0.039 in (1.0 mm)
Oil control ring	0.0079 to 0.0299 in (0.20 to 0.76 mm)

2C

Crankshaft and connecting rods

Connecting rod end play (side clearance)	
Standard	0.0079 to 0.0138 in (0.20 to 0.35 mm)
Limit	0.0157 in (0.40 mm)
Crankshaft end play	
Standard	0.0020 to 0.0067 in (0.05 to 0.17 mm)
Limit	0.0118 in (0.30 mm)
Main journal diameter	
Grade no. 0	2.4790 to 2.4793 in (62.967 to 62.975 mm)
Grade no. 1	2.4787 to 2.4790 in (62.959 to 62.967 mm)
Grade no. 2	2.4784 to 2.4787 in (62.951 to 62.959 mm)
Connecting rod journal diameter	1.9667 to 1.9675 in (49.955 to 49.974 mm)
Journal taper/out-of-round	Less than 0.0002 in (0.005 mm)
Crankshaft runout	Less than 0.0039 in (0.10 mm)
Main bearing oil clearance	
Standard	0.0011 to 0.0022 in (0.028 to 0.055 mm)
Limit	0.0035 in (0.090 mm)
Connecting rod bearing oil clearance	
Standard	0.0006 to 0.0021 in (0.014 to 0.054 mm)
Limit	0.0035 in (0.090 mm)
Main bearings	**Identification color**
Grade no. 0	Black
Grade no. 1	Brown
Grade no. 2	Green
Grade no. 3	Yellow
Grade no. 4	Blue

Torque specifications*

	Ft-lbs
Main bearing cap bolts	67 to 74
Connecting rod cap nuts	
Step 1	10 to 12
Step 2	
With conventional torque wrench	28 to 33
With angle indicating torque wrench	Turn an additional 60 to 65-degrees
Rear oil seal retainer bolts	4.3 to 5.1

* **Note:** *Refer to Part B for additional torque specifications.*

KA24E engine (1990 on)

General

Oil pressure	
At idle	10.7 psi
At 3000 rpm	47 to 67 psi
Compression pressure	
Standard	192 psi
Minimum	142 psi

Camshaft and rocker arms

Camshaft and rocker arms	See Chapter 2, Part A

Cylinder head

Warpage limit	0.004 in (0.1 mm)

Valves

Valve stem diameter	
Intake	0.2742 to 0.2748 in (6.965 to 6.980 mm)
Exhaust	0.3129 to 0.3134 in (7.948 to 7.960 mm)
Valve face angle	45 degrees 30 minutes
Valve margin width	
Intake	
Standard	0.0453 to 0.0571 in (1.15 to 1.45 mm)
Limit	0.020 in (0.5 mm)
Exhaust	
Standard	0.0531 to 0.0650 in (1.35 to 1.65 mm)
Limit	0.020 in (0.5 mm)
Valve stem end grinding limit	0.020 in (0.5 mm)
Valve spring free length	
Intake	
Outer spring	2.2614 in (57.44 mm)
Inner spring	2.1000 in (53.34 mm)
Exhaust	
Outer spring	2.0949 in (53.21 mm)
Inner spring	1.8878 in (47.95 mm)
Valve spring installed height	
Intake – outer spring	
Standard	1.480 in @ 135.8 lb (37.6 mm @ 61.6 kg)
Limit	1.480 in @ 127.7 lb (37.6 mm @ 57.9 kg)
Intake – inner spring	
Standard	1.283 in @ 63.9 lb (32.6 mm @ 29.0 kg)
Limit	1.283 in @ 60.0 lb (32.6 mm @ 27.2 kg)
Exhaust – outer spring	
Standard	1.343 in @ 144.0 lb (34.1 mm @ 65.3 kg)
Limit	1.343 in @ 139.6 lb (34.1 mm @ 63.3 kg)
Exhaust – inner spring	
Standard	1.146 in @ 73.9 lb (29.1 mm @ 33.5 kg)
Limit	1.146 in @ 71.7 lb (29.1 mm @ 32.5 kg)
Valve spring out-of-square limit	
Intake	
Outer spring	0.098 in (2.5 mm)
Inner spring	0.091 in (2.3 mm)
Exhaust	
Outer spring	0.091 in (2.3 mm)
Inner spring	0.083 in (2.1 mm)
Valve guide inside diameter	
Intake	0.2756 to 0.2763 in (7.000 to 7.018 mm)
Exhaust	0.3150 to 0.3157 in (8.000 to 8.018 mm)
Valve stem-to-guide clearance	
Intake	0.0008 to 0.0021 in (0.020 to 0.053 mm)
Exhaust	0.0016 to 0.0028 in (0.040 to 0.070 mm)
Valve stem end deflection limit	0.008 in (0.2 mm)
Valve seat	
Angle	45 degrees
Width	
Intake	0.063 to 0.067 in (1.6 to 1.7 mm)
Exhaust	0.067 to 0.083 in (1.7 to 2.1 mm)

Engine block

Deck distortion limit	0.008 in (0.2 mm)
Cylinder bore diameter	
Grade 1	3.5039 to 3.5043 in (89.000 to 89.010 mm)
Grade 2	3.5043 to 3.5047 in (89.010 to 89.020 mm)
Grade 3	3.5047 to 3.5051 in (89.020 to 89.030 mm)
Cylinder bore taper/out-of-round	Less than 0.0006 in (0.015 mm)
Piston-to-bore clearance	0.0008 to 0.0016 in (0.020 to 0.040 mm)

Pistons and rings

Diameter	
Standard	
Grade 1	3.5027 to 3.5031 in (88.970 to 88.980 mm)
Grade 2	3.5031 to 3.5035 in (88.980 to 88.990 mm)
Grade 3	3.5035 to 3.5039 in (88.990 to 89.000 mm)
1st oversize (0.20 in)	3.5224 to 3.5236 in (89.470 to 89.500 mm)
2nd oversize (0.39 in)	3.5421 to 3.5433 in (89.970 to 90.000 mm)
Piston ring end gap	
Top compression ring	0.0110 to 0.0205 in (0.28 to 0.52 mm)
Second compression ring	0.0177 to 0.0272 in (0.45 to 0.69 mm)
Oil ring	0.0079 to 0.0272 in (0.20 to 0.69 mm)
Piston ring side clearance	
Top compression ring	0.0016 to 0.0031 in (0.040 to 0.080 mm)
Second compression ring	0.0012 to 0.0028 in (0.030 to 0.070 mm)
Oil ring	0.0026 to 0.0053 in (0.065 to 0.135 mm)

Crankshaft, connecting rods and main bearings

Connecting rod end play (side clearance)	
Standard	0.008 to 0.016 in (0.2 to 0.4 mm)
Limit	0.024 in (0.6 mm)
Crankshaft end play	
Standard	0.0020 to 0.0071 in (0.05 to 0.18 mm)
Limit	0.012 in (0.3 mm)
Main bearing journal diameter	
Grade 0	2.5057 to 3.5060 in (63.645 to 63.652 mm)
Grade 1	2.5060 to 2.5064 in (63.652 to 63.663 mm)
Grade 2	2.5064 to 3.5068 in (63.663 to 63.672 mm)
Connecting rod journal diameter	2.3603 to 2.3612 in (59.951 to 59.975 mm)
Journal taper/out-of-round	
Standard	
Through 1990	Less than 0.0004 in (0.01 mm)
1991 and later	0 in (0 mm)
Limit	
Through 1990	0.0012 in (0.03 mm)
1991 and later	0.0004 in (0.01 mm)
Main bearing oil clearance	
Standard	0.0008 to 0.0019 in (0.020 to 0.047 mm)
Limit	0.004 in (0.1 mm)
Connecting rod bearing oil clearance	
Standard	0.0004 to 0.0014 in (0.010 to 0.035 mm)
Limit	0.0035 in (0.09 mm)
Flywheel\driveplate runout limit	0.004 in (0.1 mm)

Torque specifications*

	Ft-lbs
Main bearing cap bolts	36
Connecting rod cap nuts	
First step	10 to 12
Second step	60 to 65 degrees (28 to 33 ft.lbs.)

** Note: Refer to Part A for additional torque specifications.*

1 General information

Included in this portion of Chapter 2 are the general overhaul procedures for the cylinder head(s) and internal engine components.

The information ranges from advice concerning preparation for an overhaul and the purchase of replacement parts to detailed, step-by-step procedures covering removal and installation of internal engine components and the inspection of parts.

The following procedures have been written based on the assumption that the engine has been removed from the vehicle. For information concerning in-vehicle engine repair, as well as removal and installation of the external components necessary for the overhaul, see Part A or B of this Chapter and Section 7 of this Part.

The Specifications included here in Part C are only those necessary for the inspection and overhaul procedures which follow. Refer to Parts A and B for additional Specifications.

2 Cylinder compression check

Refer to illustration 2.4

1 A compression check will tell you what mechanical condition the upper end (pistons, rings, valves, head gaskets) of your engine is in. Specifically, it can tell you if the compression is down due to leakage caused by worn piston rings, defective valves and seats or a blown head gasket. **Note:** *The engine must be at normal operating temperature and the battery must be fully charged for this check. Also, if the engine is equipped with a carburetor, the choke valve must be all the way open to get an accurate compression reading (if the engine's warm, the choke should be open).*

2 Begin by cleaning the area around the spark plugs before you remove them (compressed air should be used, if available, otherwise a small brush or even a bicycle tire pump will work). The idea is to prevent dirt from getting into the cylinders as the compression check is being done. Remove all of the spark plugs from the engine (Chapter 1). On later model four-cylinder engines, remove the spark plugs from one side only.

3 Block the throttle wide open. Detach the coil wire from the distributor cap and ground it on the engine block. Use a heavy jumper wire with alligator clips at both ends to ensure a good ground.

4 With the compression gauge in the number one spark plug hole **(see illustration)**, depress the accelerator pedal all the way to the floor to open the throttle valve. Crank the engine over at least four compression strokes and watch the gauge. The compression should build up quickly in a healthy engine. Low compression on the first stroke, followed by gradually increasing pressure on successive strokes, indicates worn piston rings. A low compression reading on the first stroke, which doesn't build up during successive strokes, indicates leaking valves or a blown head gasket (a cracked head could also be the cause). Record the highest gauge reading obtained.

5 Repeat the procedure for the remaining cylinders and compare the results to the Specifications.

6 Add some engine oil (about three squirts from a plunger-type oil can) to each cylinder, through the spark plug hole, and repeat the test.

7 If the compression increases after the oil is added, the piston rings are definitely worn. If the compression doesn't increase significantly, the leakage is occurring at the valves or head gasket. Leakage past the valves may be caused by burned valve seats and/or faces or warped, cracked or bent valves.

8 If two adjacent cylinders have equally low compression, there's a strong possibility that the head gasket between them is blown. The appearance of coolant in the combustion chambers or the crankcase would verify this condition.

2.4 A compression gauge with a threaded fitting for the spark plug hole is preferred over the type that requires hand pressure to maintain the seal – be sure to open the throttle and choke valves as far as possible during the compression check!

9 If the compression is unusually high, the combustion chambers are probably coated with carbon deposits. If that's the case, the cylinder head(s) should be removed and decarbonized.

10 If compression is way down or varies greatly between cylinders, it would be a good idea to have a leak-down test performed by an automotive repair shop. This test will pinpoint exactly where the leakage is occurring and how severe it is.

3 Engine removal – methods and precautions

If you've decided that the engine must be removed for overhaul or major repair work, several preliminary steps should be taken.

Locating a place to work is extremely important. Adequate work space, along with storage space for the vehicle, will be needed. If a shop or garage isn't available, at the very least a flat, level, clean work surface made of concrete or asphalt is required.

Cleaning the engine compartment and engine before beginning the removal procedure will help keep tools clean and organized.

An engine hoist or A-frame will also be necessary. Make sure the equipment is rated in excess of the combined weight of the engine and accessories. Safety is of primary importance, considering the potential hazards involved in lifting the engine out of the vehicle.

If the engine is being removed by a novice, a helper should be available. Advice and aid from someone more experienced would also be helpful. There are many instances when one person cannot simultaneously perform all of the operations required when lifting the engine out of the vehicle.

Plan the operation ahead of time. Arrange for or obtain all of the tools and equipment you'll need prior to beginning the job. Some of the equipment necessary to perform engine removal and installation safely and with relative ease are (in addition to an engine hoist) a heavy duty floor jack, complete sets of wrenches and sockets as described at the front of this manual, wooden blocks and plenty of rags and cleaning solvent for mopping up spilled oil, coolant and gasoline. If the hoist must be rented, make sure you arrange for it in advance and perform all of the operations possible without it ahead of time. This will save you money and time.

Plan for the vehicle to be out of use for quite a while. A machine shop will be required to perform some of the work the do-it-yourselfer can't accomplish without special equipment. They often have a busy schedule, so it would be a good idea to consult them before removing the engine in order to accurately estimate the amount of time required to rebuild or repair components that may need work.

Always be extremely careful when removing and installing the engine. Serious injury can result from careless actions. Plan ahead, take your time and a job of this nature, although major, can be accomplished successfully.

4 Engine – removal and installation

Refer to illustration 4.40

Warning: *The engine is very heavy, so equipment designed specifically for lifting engines should be used. Never position any part of your body under the engine when it's supported by a hoist – it could shift or fall and cause serious injury or death! Also, the air conditioning system is under high pressure; loosening fittings will cause a sudden discharge of refrigerant, which could cause injuries. Have the system discharged by a service station before disconnecting any hoses or lines.*

1 Read through the Section entitled *Engine removal – methods and precautions* before beginning any work. On 2WD models, the transmission can be removed along with the engine. On 4WD models, the engine should be separated from the transmission and the transmission left in place in the vehicle (make sure the transmission is securely supported).

2 Remove the hood (see Chapter 12 for the correct procedure). Store it in a safe place where it won't be damaged.

3 Remove the air cleaner assembly (see Chapter 4).

4 Disconnect the cables from the battery (negative first, then positive).

5 Drain the coolant from the radiator and engine block (refer to Chapter 1 if necessary).
6 Drain the engine oil.
7 Drain the oil from the transmission. Refer to Chapter 1, if necessary.
8 Remove the upper and lower radiator hoses.
9 Disconnect all wires and vacuum hoses running between the engine and components attached to the body. **Note:** *Before disconnecting or removing wires or hoses, mark them with pieces of tape to identify their installed locations. This will eliminate possible problems and confusion during the installation procedure.*
10 Disconnect the fuel hoses from the mechanical fuel pump, if equipped, and plug them to prevent fuel leakage and the entry of dirt.
11 On 1981 and later models, disconnect the fuel hoses where they attach to the metal lines below the intake manifold.
12 If equipped with air conditioning, remove the A/C compressor from the bracket and secure it out of the way. **Caution:** *Don't disconnect the hoses from the compressor unless the system has been discharged.*
13 If equipped with power steering, remove the power steering pump and secure it out of the way. Leave the hoses connected to the pump.
14 Disconnect the ignition coil wire(s) from the distributor cap.
15 Detach the throttle cable from the carburetor or throttle body (see Chapter 4).
16 Disconnect the brake booster vacuum hose and position it out of the way.
17 Disconnect the heater hoses where they attach to the engine.
18 Remove the VVT valve and bracket, if equipped, from the firewall (see Chapter 6).
19 Raise the front of the truck and support it on jackstands. Apply the parking brake and block the rear wheels.
20 Disconnect the wires from the alternator and starter. On vehicles with a V6 engine, remove the starter (Chapter 5).
21 If equipped with an automatic transmission, disconnect the oil cooler hoses leading from the oil cooler located at the base of the radiator. Allow the fluid to drain into a container.
22 Remove the radiator and shroud. Refer to Chapter 3, if necessary.
23 On 2WD models, detach the speedometer cable from the transmission. Disconnect all wires attached to the transmission.
24 On 4WD models, remove the primary and front driveshafts as described in Chapter 9.
25 On 4WD models, remove the four mounting bolts that attach the front differential to the crossmember, then remove the forward mounting bolt and lower the front differential so it rests on the crossmember.
26 On 2WD models, remove the driveshaft as described in Chapter 8.
27 Disconnect the front exhaust pipe from the exhaust manifold.
28 If equipped with a hydraulic clutch, remove the clutch operating cylinder from the transmission. Refer to Chapter 8 if necessary.
29 Disconnect the parking brake cable and position it out of the way.
30 Disconnect any remaining lines, hoses or wires leading to the engine. Mark them first to avoid confusion during installation.
31 On 2WD models, refer to Chapter 7 and do everything described for transmission removal except removal of the mounting bracket and the engine-to-transmission bolts.
32 On 4WD models, unbolt the transmission from the engine (Chaper 7).
33 On 4WD models with an automatic transmission, unbolt the torque converter from the driveplate (Chapter 7).
34 Attach an engine hoist to the two hoist brackets mounted on the engine. They are located at the corners of the head. Make sure the chain is attached securely with hooks or high quality nuts, bolts and washers. The hook on the hoist should be over the center of the engine with the two lengths of chain the same length so the engine can be lifted straight up.
35 Raise the engine just until all slack is out of the chains.
36 On 4WD models, remove the bolts that attach the rear mounting member of the front differential to the frame.
37 On 1980 2WD models, remove the idler arm mounting bolts and lower the idler arm and cross rod to provide additional clearance for the oil pan.
38 On 2WD models, remove the bolts that attach the transmssion mounting bracket to the body. Then remove the bolts that attach the bracket to the transmission. Remove the damper, if equipped.
39 Remove the bolts that attach the front engine mount bracket to the engine block. **Caution:** *Don't loosen the mount insulator cover nuts (later models). Cover removal results in loss of fluid, which will render the mount useless.*
40 On 4WD models, lift the engine slightly, then move it forward to separate it from the transmission. Check carefully to make sure everything has been disconnected. On 2WD models, tilt the engine/transmission assembly down at the rear to clear the radiator support as you lift it up and out of the engine compartment **(see illustration).**

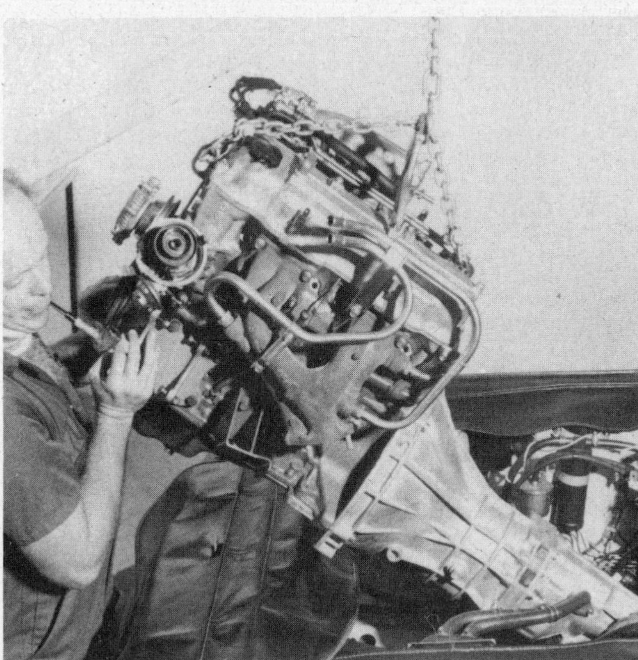

4.40 Be sure the chain is securely attached to the engine brackets and the hoist before lifting the engine

41 To separate the engine from an automatic transmission on 2WD models:

a) Remove the dust cover from the lower half of the torque converter housing.
b) Remove the torque converter-to-driveplate bolts. Access to the bolts can be gained (one at a time), by turning the crankshaft until each bolt comes into view through the lower half of the converter housing.
c) Withdraw the automatic transmission, leaving the driveplate bolted to the crankshaft rear flange.

42 To separate the engine from a manual transmission on 2WD models:

a) Remove the bolts that secure the clutch bellhousing to the engine block.
b) Pull the transmission straight back so its weight doesn't hang up on the input shaft while it's still engaged in the clutch plate.

43 Installation is the reverse of removal. **Note:** *On 4WD models, sealant should be used between the engine and transmission (see Chapter 7).*
44 Tighten all fasteners to the specified torque.
45 Before starting the engine, make sure the oil and coolant levels are correct.
46 Run the engine and check for leaks and proper operation of all accessories, then install the hood and test drive the vehicle.

5 Engine overhaul – general information

Refer to illustration 5.4

It's not always easy to determine when, or if, an engine should be completely overhauled, as a number of factors must be considered.

High mileage is not necessarily an indication that an overhaul is needed, while low mileage doesn't preclude the need for an overhaul. Frequency of servicing is probably the most important consideration. An engine that's had regular and frequent oil and filter changes, as well as other required maintenance, will most likely give many thousands of miles of reliable service. Conversely, a neglected engine may require an overhaul very early in its life.

Excessive oil consumption is an indication that piston rings, valve seals and/or valve guides are in need of attention. Make sure that oil leaks aren't responsible before deciding that the rings and/or guides are bad. Have a cylinder compression or leakdown test performed by an experienced tune-up mechanic to determine the extent of the work required.

If the engine is making obvious knocking or rumbling noises, the connecting rod and/or main bearings may be at fault. Check the oil pressure with a gauge installed in place of the oil pressure sending unit (sometimes called a switch) **(see illustrations – 7.5a for four-cylinder engines, 5.4 for the V6 engine)** and compare it to the Specifications. If it's extremely low, the bearings and/or oil pump are probably worn out.

Loss of power, rough running, excessive valve train noise and high fuel consumption rates may also point to the need for an overhaul, especially if they're all present at the same time. If a complete tune-up doesn't remedy the situation, major mechanical work is the only solution.

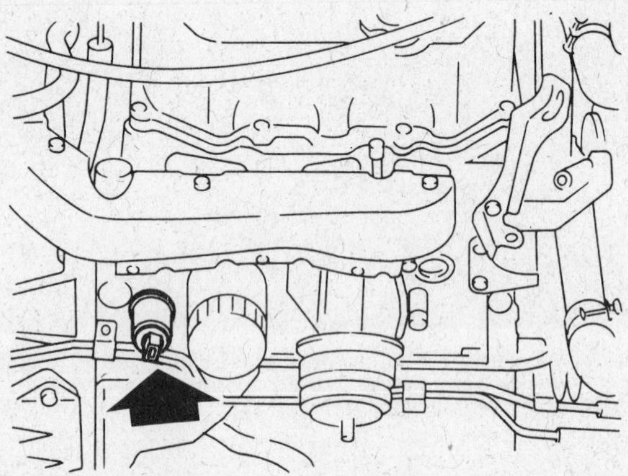

5.4 The oil pressure can be checked by removing the oil pressure switch and installing a pressure gauge in the hole (V6 engine shown)

An engine overhaul involves restoring the internal parts to the specifications of a new engine. During an overhaul, the piston rings are replaced and the cylinder walls are reconditioned (rebored and/or honed). If a rebore is done, new pistons are required. The main and connecting rod bearings are generally replaced with new ones and, if necessary, the crankshaft may be reground to restore the journals. Generally, the valves are serviced as well, since they're usually in less-than-perfect condition at this point. While the engine is being overhauled, other components, such as the distributor, starter and alternator, can be rebuilt as well. The end result should be a like new engine that will give many trouble free miles. **Note:** *Critical cooling system components such as the hoses, drivebelts, thermostat and water pump MUST be replaced with new parts when an engine is overhauled. The radiator should be checked carefully to ensure that it isn't clogged or leaking; if in doubt, replace it with a new one. Also, we don't recommend overhauling the oil pump – install a new one when an engine is rebuilt.*

Before beginning the engine overhaul, read through the entire procedure to familiarize yourself with the scope and requirements of the job. Overhauling an engine isn't difficult, but it is time consuming. Plan on the vehicle being tied up for a minimum of two weeks, especially if parts must be taken to an automotive machine shop for repair or reconditioning. Check on availability of parts and make sure that any necessary special tools and equipment are obtained in advance. Most work can be done with typical hand tools, although a number of precision measuring tools are required for inspecting parts to determine if they must be replaced. Often an automotive machine shop will handle the inspection of parts and offer advice concerning reconditioning and replacement. **Note:** *Always wait until the engine has been completely disassembled and all components, especially the engine block, have been inspected before deciding what service and repair operations must be performed by an automotive machine shop.* Since the block's condition will be the major factor to consider when determining whether to overhaul the original engine or buy a rebuilt one, never purchase parts or have machine work done on other components until the block has been thoroughly inspected. As a general rule, time is the primary cost of an overhaul, so it doesn't pay to install worn or substandard parts.

As a final note, to ensure maximum life and minimum trouble from a rebuilt engine, everything must be assembled with care in a spotlessly clean environment.

6 Engine rebuilding alternatives

The do-it-yourselfer is faced with a number of options when performing an engine overhaul. The decision to replace the engine block, piston/connecting rod assemblies and crankshaft depends on a number of factors, with the number one consideration being the condition of the block. Other considerations are cost, access to machine shop facilities, parts availability, time required to complete the project and the extent of prior mechanical experience on the part of the do-it-yourselfer.

Some of the rebuilding alternatives include:

Individual parts – If the inspection procedures reveal that the engine block and most engine components are in reusable condition, purchasing individual parts may be the most economical alternative. The block, crankshaft and piston/connecting rod assemblies should all be inspected carefully. Even if the block shows little wear, the cylinder bores should be surface honed.

Crankshaft kit – This rebuild package consists of a reground crankshaft and a matched set of pistons and connecting rods. The pistons will already be installed on the connecting rods. Piston rings and the necessary bearings will be included in the kit. These kits are commonly available for standard cylinder bores, as well as for engine blocks which have been bored to a regular oversize.

Short block – A short block consists of an engine block with a crankshaft and piston/connecting rod assemblies already installed. All new bearings are incorporated and all clearances will be correct. The existing camshaft, valve train components, cylinder head(s) and external parts can be bolted to the short block with little or no machine shop work necessary.

Long block – A long block consists of a short block plus an oil pump, oil pan, cylinder head(s), rocker arm cover(s), camshaft and valve train components, timing sprockets and chain or pulleys and belt. All components are installed with new bearings, seals and gaskets incorporated throughout. The installation of manifolds and external parts is all that's necessary.

Give careful thought to which alternative is best for you and discuss the situation with local automotive machine shops, auto parts dealers and experienced rebuilders before ordering or purchasing replacement parts.

7 Engine overhaul – disassembly sequence

Refer to illustrations 7.5a, 7.5b, 7.5c and 7.5d

1 It's much easier to disassemble and work on the engine if it's mounted on a portable engine stand. A stand can often be rented quite cheaply from an equipment rental yard. Before the engine is mounted on a stand, the flywheel/driveplate should be removed from the engine.

2 If a stand isn't available, it's possible to disassemble the engine with it blocked up on a sturdy workbench or on the floor. Be extra careful not to tip or drop the engine when working without a stand.

3 If you're going to obtain a rebuilt engine, all external components must come off first, to be transferred to the replacement engine, just as they will if you're doing a complete engine overhaul yourself. These include:

Alternator and brackets
A/C compressor and brackets
Power steering pump and brackets

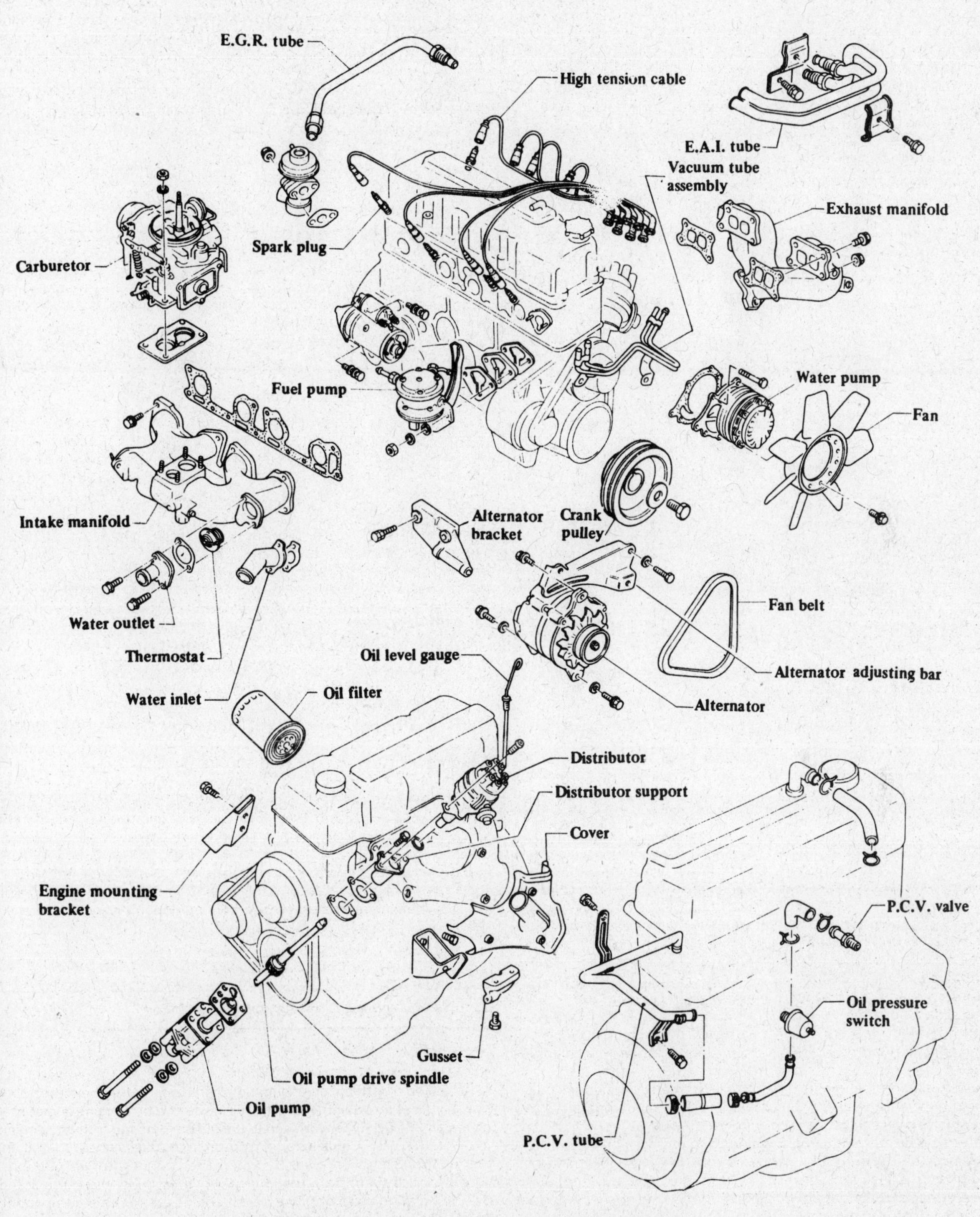

7.5a Four-cylinder engine external components — exploded view (typical)

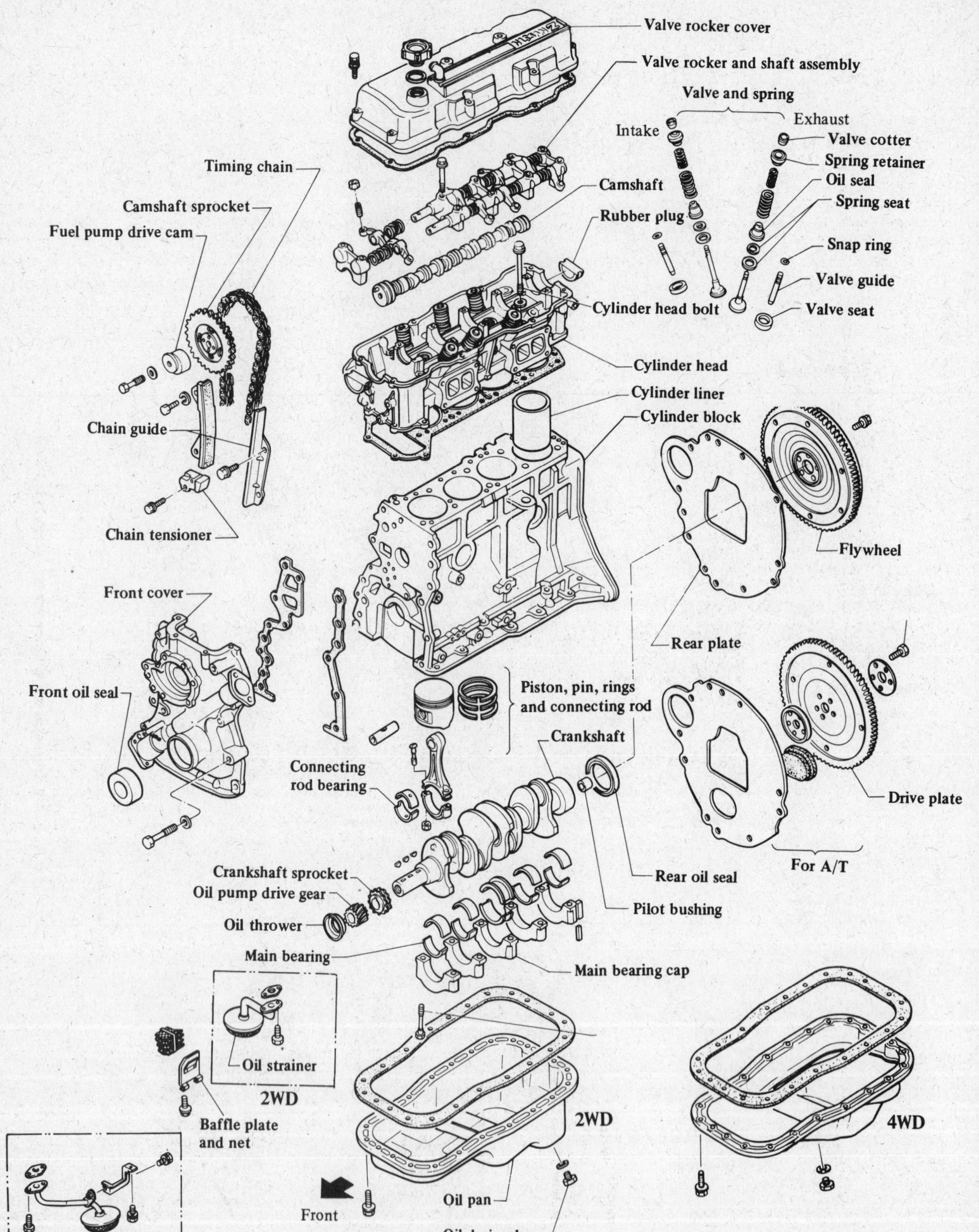

Valve rocker cover
Valve rocker and shaft assembly
Valve and spring
Intake
Exhaust
Valve cotter
Spring retainer
Oil seal
Spring seat
Snap ring
Valve guide
Valve seat
Timing chain
Camshaft
Camshaft sprocket
Rubber plug
Fuel pump drive cam
Cylinder head bolt
Cylinder head
Cylinder liner
Cylinder block
Chain guide
Chain tensioner
Flywheel
Front cover
Rear plate
Front oil seal
Piston, pin, rings and connecting rod
Crankshaft
Connecting rod bearing
Drive plate
For A/T
Rear oil seal
Crankshaft sprocket
Oil pump drive gear
Pilot bushing
Oil thrower
Main bearing
Main bearing cap
Oil strainer
2WD
Baffle plate and net
2WD
4WD
Front
Oil pan
Oil drain plug
Oil strainer
4WD

7.5b Four-cylinder engine internal components — exploded view (typical)

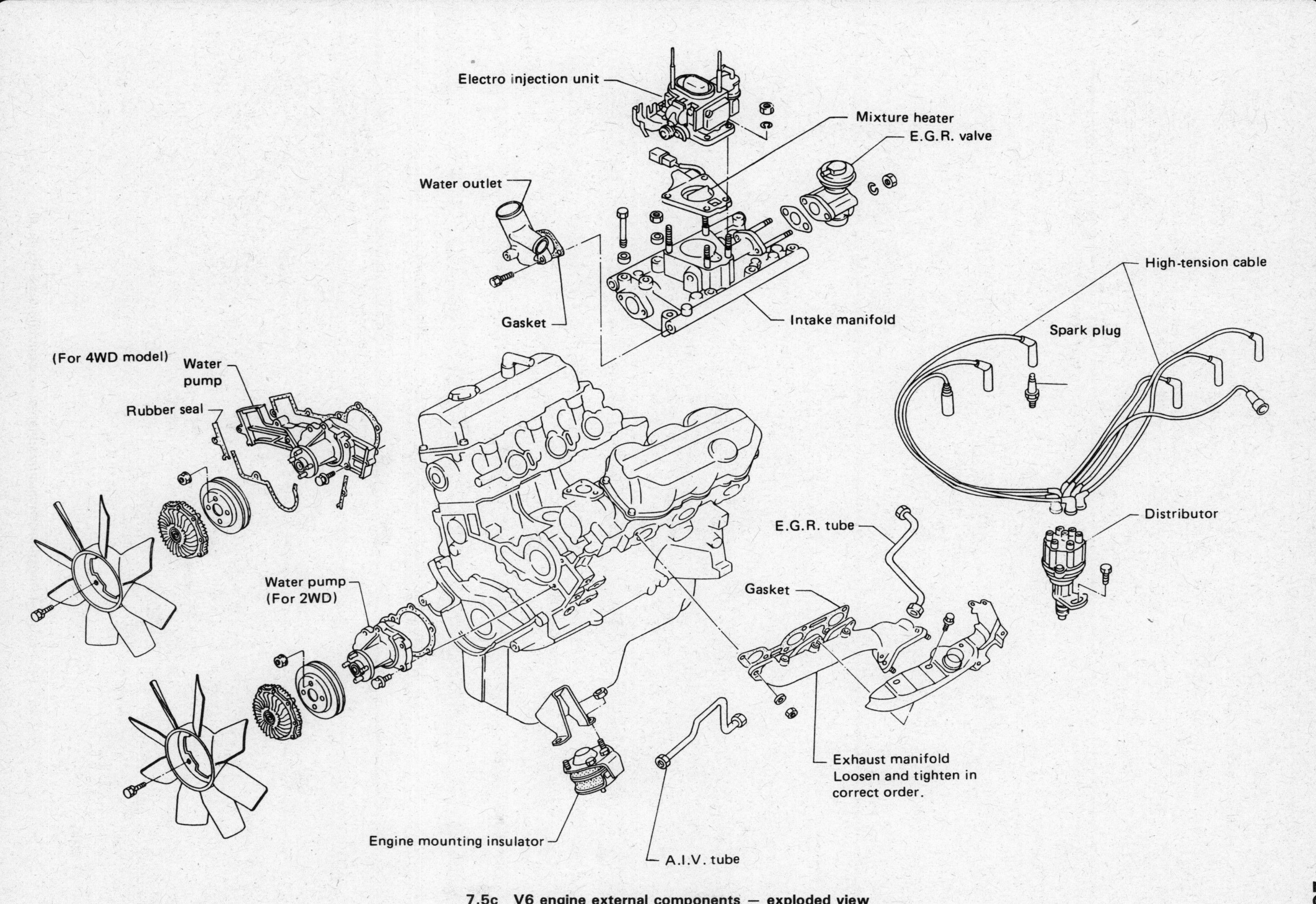

7.5c V6 engine external components — exploded view

Emissions control components
Distributor, spark plug wires and spark plugs
Thermostat and housing cover
Water pump
Fuel injection components or carburetor
Intake/exhaust manifolds
Oil filter
Engine mounts
Clutch and flywheel/driveplate

Note: *When removing the external components from the engine, pay close attention to details that may be helpful or important during installation. Note the installed position of gaskets, seals, spacers, pins, brackets, washers, bolts and other small items.*

4 If you're obtaining a short block, which consists of the engine block, crankshaft, pistons and connecting rods all assembled, then the cylinder head(s), oil pan and oil pump will have to be removed as well. See *Engine rebuilding alternatives* for additional information regarding the different possibilities to be considered.

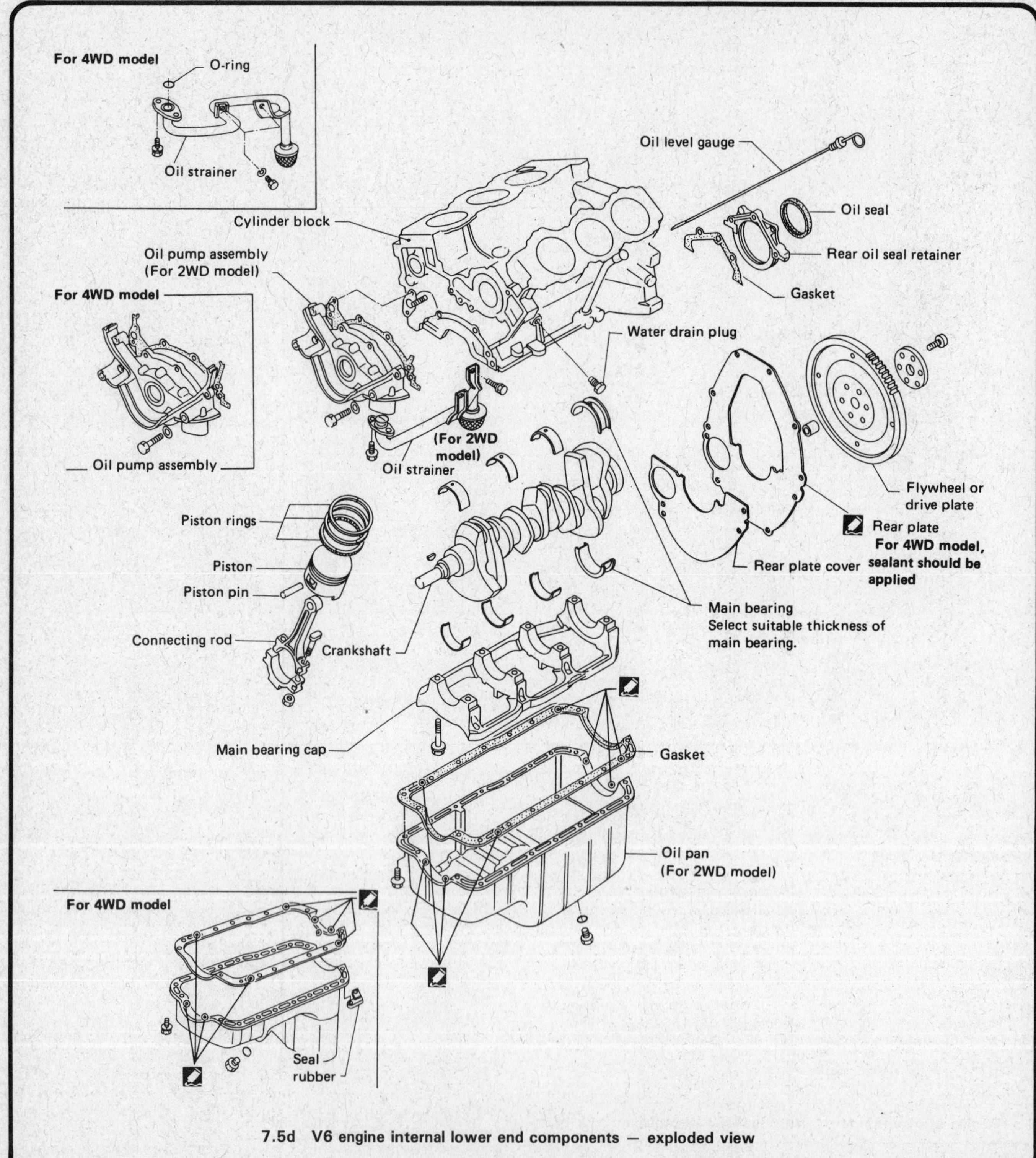

7.5d V6 engine internal lower end components — exploded view

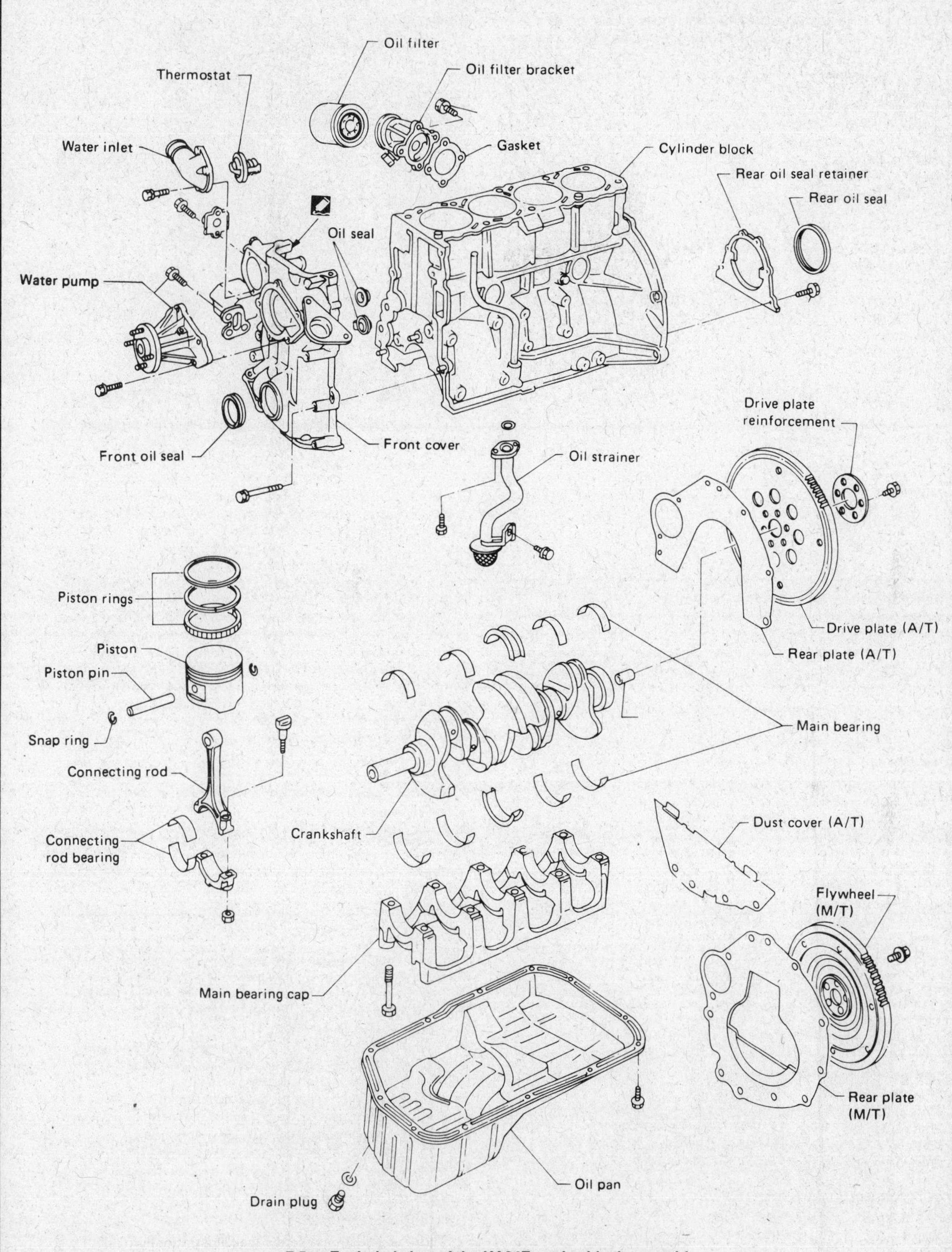

7.5e Exploded view of the KA24E engine block assembly

5 If you're planning a complete overhaul, the engine must be disassembled and the internal components removed in the following order **(see illustrations)**:

Rocker arm cover(s)
Intake and exhaust manifolds
Timing belt cover(s) (V6 engine)
Engine front cover (four-cylinder engines)
Camshaft drive components
Cylinder head(s)
Oil pan
Oil pump
Piston/connecting rod assemblies
Crankshaft and main bearings

6 Before beginning the disassembly and overhaul procedures, make sure the following items are available:

Common hand tools
Small cardboard boxes or plastic bags for storing parts
Gasket scraper
Ridge reamer
Vibration damper puller
Micrometers
Telescoping gauges
Dial indicator set
Valve spring compressor
Cylinder surfacing hone
Piston ring groove cleaning tool
Electric drill motor
Tap and die set
Wire brushes
Oil gallery brushes
Cleaning solvent

8 Cylinder head — disassembly

Refer to illustrations 8.2 and 8.3

Note: *New and rebuilt cylinder heads are usually available for most engines at dealerships and auto parts stores. Due to the fact that some specialized tools are necessary for the disassembly and inspection procedures, and replacement parts may not be readily available, it may be more practical and economical for the home mechanic to purchase replacement head(s) rather than taking the time to disassemble, inspect and recondition the original(s).*

1 Cylinder head disassembly involves removal of the intake and exhaust valves and related components. It's assumed that the rocker arm shaft assemblies and camshaft have been removed from the head. **Caution:** *On 1980 models (L20B engine), DO NOT remove the cam bearing towers from the head! If they're removed, the bearing centers will be misaligned.*

2 Before the valves are removed, arrange to label and store them, along with their related components, so they can be kept separate and reinstalled in the same valve guides they are removed from **(see illustration)**.

8.2 A small plastic bag, with an appropriate label, can be used to store the valve train components so they can be kept together and reinstalled in the correct guide

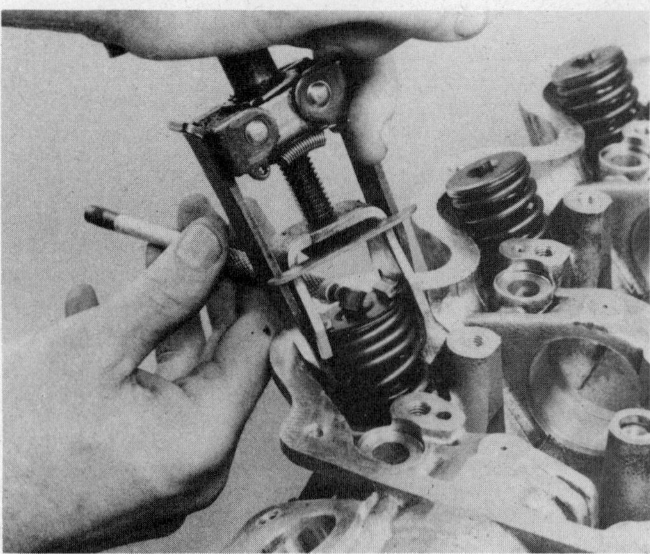

8.3 Use a valve spring compressor to compress the springs, then remove the keepers from the valve stem with a small magnet (V6 engine shown)

3 Compress the springs on the first valve with a spring compressor and remove the keepers **(see illustration)**. Carefully release the valve spring compressor and remove the retainer, the springs and the spring seat. Next, remove the oil seal from the guide, then pull the valve out of the head. If the valve binds in the guide (won't pull through), push it back into the head and deburr the area around the keeper groove with a fine file or whetstone.

4 Repeat the procedure for the remaining valves. Remember to keep all the parts for each valve together so they can be reinstalled in the same locations.

5 Once the valves and related components have been removed and stored in an organized manner, the head should be thoroughly cleaned and inspected. If a complete engine overhaul is being done, finish the engine disassembly procedures before beginning the cylinder head cleaning and inspection process.

9 Cylinder head — cleaning and inspection

Refer to illustrations 9.12, 9.14, 9.17, 9.18 and 9.19

1 Thorough cleaning of the cylinder head(s) and related valve train components, followed by a detailed inspection, will enable you to decide how much valve service work must be done during the engine overhaul.

Cleaning

2 Scrape all traces of old gasket material and sealing compound off the head gasket, intake manifold and exhaust manifold sealing surfaces. Be very careful not to gouge the cylinder head. Special gasket removal solvents that soften gaskets and make removal much easier are available at auto parts stores.

3 Remove all built up scale from the coolant passages.

4 Run a stiff wire brush through the various holes to remove deposits that may have formed in them.

5 Run an appropriate size tap into each of the threaded holes to remove corrosion and thread sealant that may be present. If compressed air is available, use it to clear the holes of debris produced by this operation. **Warning:** *Wear eye protection when using compressed air!*

6 Clean the exhaust and intake manifold stud threads with a wire brush.

7 Clean the cylinder head with solvent and dry it thoroughly. Compressed air will speed the drying process and ensure that all holes and recessed areas are clean. **Note:** *Decarbonizing chemicals are available and may prove very useful when cleaning cylinder heads and valve train components. They are very caustic and should be used with caution. Be sure to follow the instructions on the container.*

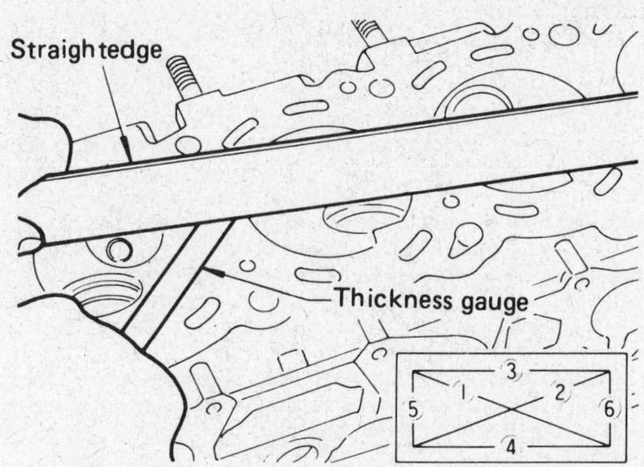

9.12 Check the cylinder head gasket surface for warpage by trying to slip a feeler gauge under the precision straightedge (see the Specifications for the maximum warpage allowed and use a feeler gauge of that thickness)

9.14 A dial indicator can be used to determine the valve stem deflection (move the valve stem as indicated by the arrows)

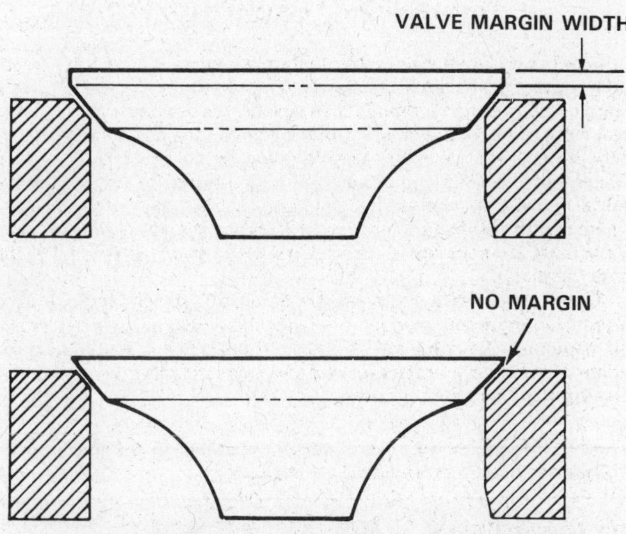

9.17 The margin width on each valve must be as specified (if no margin exists, the valve cannot be reused)

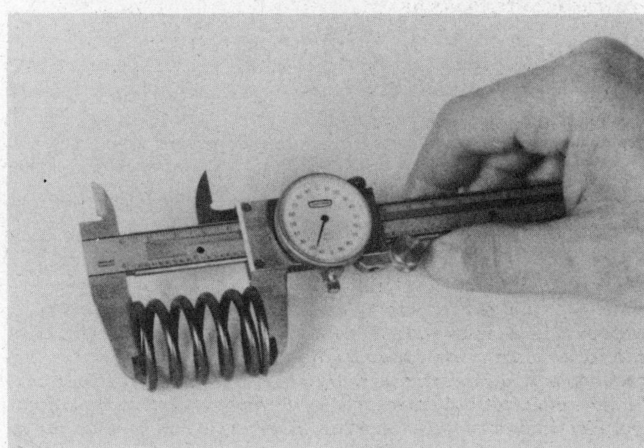

9.18 Measure the free length of each valve spring with a dial or vernier caliper

8 Clean the rocker arms with solvent and dry them thoroughly (don't mix them up during the cleaning process). Compressed air will speed the drying process and can be used to clean out the oil passages.
9 Clean all the valve springs, keepers and retainers with solvent and dry them thoroughly. Do the components from one valve at a time to avoid mixing up the parts.
10 Scrape off any heavy deposits that may have formed on the valves, then use a motorized wire brush to remove deposits from the valve heads and stems. Again, make sure the valves don't get mixed up.

Inspection

Cylinder head

11 Inspect the head very carefully for cracks, evidence of coolant leakage and other damage. If cracks are found, a new cylinder head should be obtained.
12 Using a precision straightedge and feeler gauge, check the head gasket mating surface for warpage **(see illustration)**. If the warpage exceeds the specified limit, the head can be resurfaced at an automotive machine shop. **Note:** *If the V6 engine heads are resurfaced, the intake manifold flanges may also require machining. If the cylinder head is resurfaced, make sure the camshaft rotates freely by hand. If resistance is felt as the cam is turned, replace the head with a new one.*
13 Examine the valve seats in each of the combustion chambers. If they're pitted, cracked or burned, the head will require valve service that's beyond the scope of the home mechanic.
14 Check the valve stem deflection parallel to the rocker arm with a dial indicator attached securely to the head **(see illustration)**. The valve must be in the guide and approximately 1/16-inch off the seat. The total valve stem movement indicated by the gauge needle must be noted. If it exceeds the specified limit, the valve stem-to-guide clearance should be checked by an automotive machine shop (the cost should be minimal).
15 Refer to Part B of Chapter 2 and inspect the camshaft bearing surfaces in the cylinder head.

Valves

16 Carefully inspect each valve face for uneven wear, deformation, cracks, pits and burned areas. Check the valve stem for scuffing and galling and the neck for cracks. Rotate the valve and check for any obvious indication that it's bent. Look for pits and excessive wear on the end of the stem. The presence of any of these conditions indicates the need for valve service by an automotive machine shop.
17 Measure the margin width on each valve **(see illustration)**. Any valve with a margin narrower than 1/32-inch will have to be replaced with a new one.

Valve components

18 Check each valve spring for wear (on the ends) and pits. Measure the free length and compare it to the Specifications **(see illustration)**. Any springs that are shorter than specified have sagged and should not be reused. The tension of all springs should be checked with a special fixture before deciding that they're suitable for use in a rebuilt engine (take the springs to an automotive machine shop for this check).

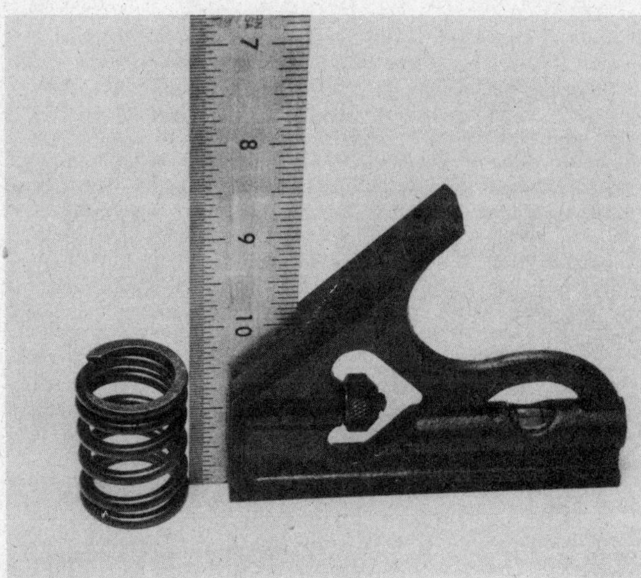

9.19 Check each valve spring for squareness

19 Stand each spring on a flat surface and check it for squareness **(see illustration)**. If any of the springs are distorted or sagged, replace all of them with new parts.
20 Check the spring retainers and keepers for obvious wear and cracks. Any questionable parts should be replaced with new ones, as extensive damage will occur if they fail during engine operation.

Rocker arm components
21 Refer to Section 15 in Part B of Chapter 2 and inspect the rocker arms and related components.
22 If the inspection process indicates that the valve components are in generally poor condition and worn beyond the limits specified, which is usually the case in an engine that's being overhauled, reassemble the valves in the cylinder head and refer to Section 10 for valve servicing recommendations.
23 If the inspection turns up no excessively worn parts, and if the valve faces and seats are in good condition, the valve train components can be reinstalled in the cylinder head without major servicing. Refer to the appropriate Section for the cylinder head reassembly procedure.

10 Valves – servicing

1 Because of the complex nature of the job and the special tools and equipment needed, servicing of the valves, the valve seats and the valve guides, commonly known as a valve job, is best left to a professional.
2 The home mechanic can remove and disassemble each head, do the initial cleaning and inspection, then reassemble and deliver it to a dealer service department or an automotive machine shop for the actual valve servicing.
3 The dealer service department, or automotive machine shop, will remove the valves and springs, recondition or replace the valves and valve seats, recondition or replace the valve guides, check and replace the valve springs, spring retainers and keepers (as necessary), replace the valve seals with new ones, reassemble the valve components and make sure the installed spring height is correct. The cylinder head gasket surface will also be resurfaced if it's warped.
4 After the valve job has been performed by a professional, the head will be in like new condition. When the head is returned, be sure to clean it again before installation on the engine to remove any metal particles and abrasive grit that may still be present from the valve service or head resurfacing operations. Use compressed air, if available, to blow out all the oil holes and passages.

11 Cylinder head – reassembly

Refer to illustrations 11.4, 11.5, 11.6, 11.7 and 11.8
1 Regardless of whether or not the head was sent to an automotive repair shop for valve servicing, make sure it's clean before beginning reassembly.
2 If the head was sent out for valve servicing, the valves and related components will already be in place. Begin the reassembly procedure with Step 8.
3 Install the valve spring seats (where applicable) prior to valve seal installation.
4 Install new seals on each of the valve guides. Intake valve seals require a special tool (Nissan part number KV10107501) or an appropriate size deep socket. Gently tap each intake valve seal into place until it's seated on the guide **(see illustration)**. **Caution:** *Don't hammer on the intake valve seals once they're seated or you may damage them. Don't twist or cock the seals during installation or they won't seal properly on the valve stems.*
5 Apply moly-base grease or engine assembly lube to the first valve and install it in the head. Don't damage the new valve guide oil seal. Set the retainer and keepers in place. Check the installed spring height by lifting up on the retainer until the valve is seated. Measure the distance between the top of the spring seat(s) and the underside of the retainer **(see illustration)**. Compare your measurement to the specified installed height. Add shims, if necessary to obtain the specified height.

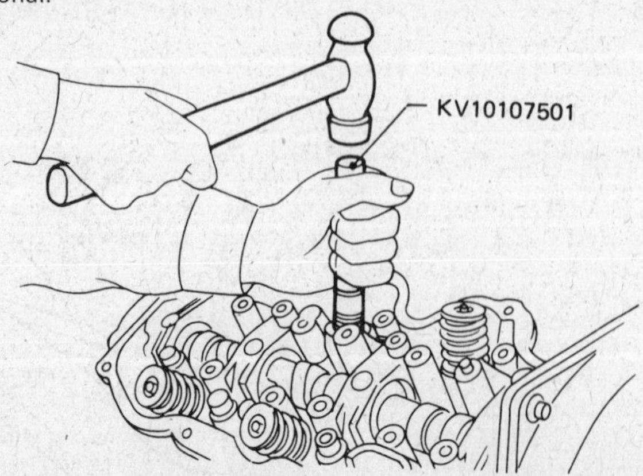

11.4 The intake valve oil seals require a special tool for installation (although a deep socket can be used if the tool isn't available) – don't hammer on the seals once they're seated!

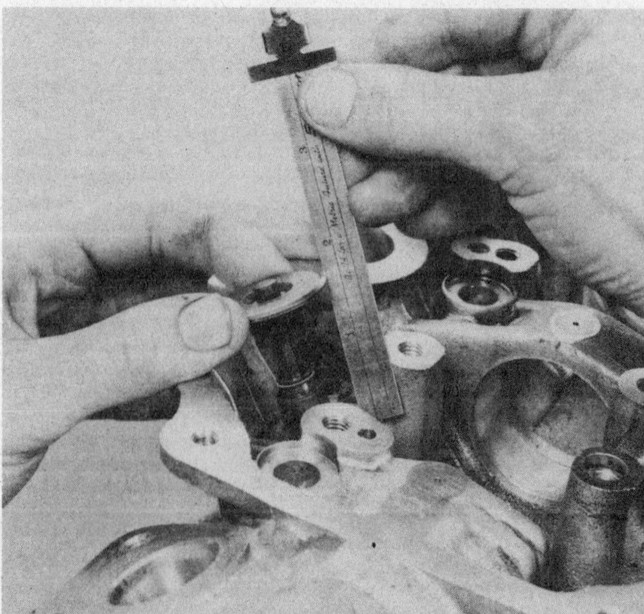

11.5 Check the distance from the top of the spring seat to the underside of the retainer to determine the installed valve spring height

11.6 Make sure each outer valve spring (right) is installed with the narrow pitch end (arrow) against the cylinder head

11.7 Keepers don't always stay in place, so apply a small dab of grease to each one as shown here before installation — it'll hold them in place on the valve stem as the spring is released

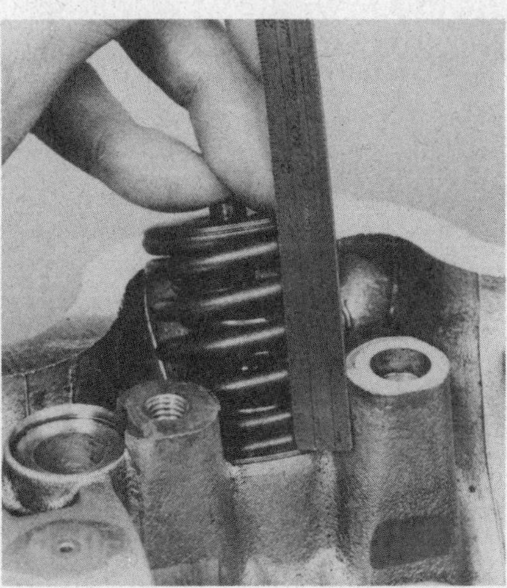

11.8 Double-check the height with the valve springs installed (do this for each valve)

6 Once the correct height is established, remove the keepers and retainer and install the valve springs. **Note:** *The outer spring has a graduated pitch. Install it with the narrow pitch end against the cylinder head* **(see illustration).**

7 Compress the springs and retainer with a valve spring compressor and slip the keepers into place. Release the compressor and make sure the keepers are seated properly in the valve stem groove. If necessary, grease can be used to hold the keepers in place as the compressor is released **(see illustration).**

8 Double-check the installed valve spring height for each valve and compare it to the specified installed height **(see illustration).** If it was correct prior to reassembly, it should still be within the specified limits. If it isn't, you must install more shims until it's correct. **Caution:** *Don't, under any circumstances shim the springs to the point where the installed height is less than specified!*

9 Install the camshaft, rocker arm components and lifters (V6 engine only) as described in Part A or B.

10 On four-cylinder engines, the valves should be adjusted cold (Chapter 1).

11 Store the head in a clean plastic bag until you're ready to install it.

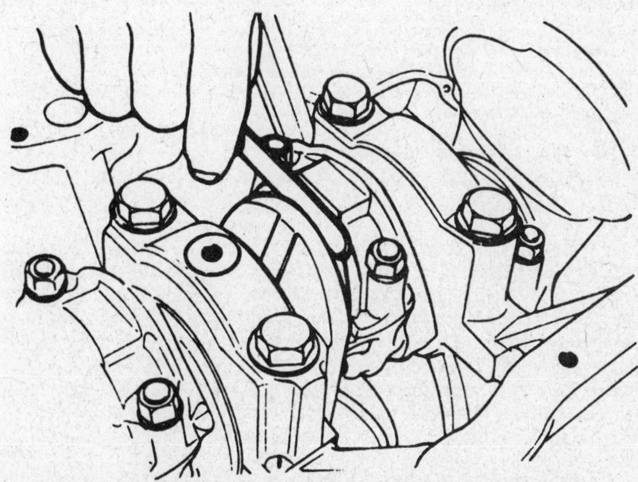

12.3 Check the connecting rod side clearance with a feeler gauge as shown

12 Piston/connecting rod assembly — removal

Refer to illustrations 12.1, 12.3, 12.4, 12.5a and 12.5b

Note: *Prior to removing the piston/connecting rod assemblies, remove the cylinder head(s), the oil pan and the oil pump by referring to the appropriate Sections in Chapter 2, Part A or B.*

1 Completely remove the ridge at the top of each cylinder with a ridge reaming tool **(see illustration).** Follow the manufacturer's instructions provided with the tool. Failure to remove the ridge before attempting to remove the piston/connecting rod assemblies may result in piston breakage.

2 After the cylinder ridges have been removed, turn the engine upside-down so the crankshaft is facing up.

3 Before the connecting rods are removed, check the end play with feeler gauges. Slide them between the connecting rod and the crankshaft throw until the play is removed **(see illustration).** The end play is equal to the thickness of the feeler gauge(s). If the end play exceeds the service limit, new connecting rods will be required. If new rods (or a new crankshaft) are installed, the end play may fall under the specified minimum (if it does, the rods will have to be machined to restore it — consult an automotive machine shop for advice if necessary). Repeat the procedure for the remaining connecting rods.

12.1 A ridge reamer is required to remove the ridge from the top of the cylinder — do this before removing the pistons!

12.4 The connecting rods and caps should be marked to indicate which cylinder they're installed in – if they aren't, mark them with a center punch to avoid confusion during reassembly

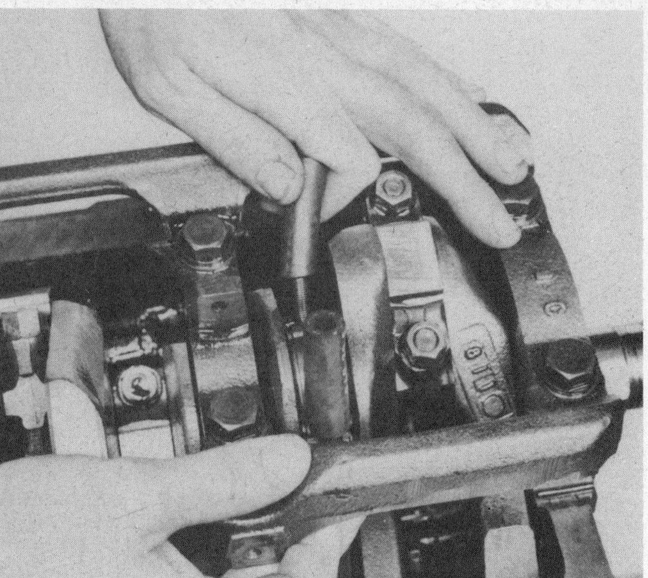

12.5a To prevent damage to the crankshaft journal and cylinder, slip sections of hose over the rod bolts, . . .

12.5b . . . then carefully drive the piston/connecting rod assembly out through the top of the engine with the end of a wooden hammer handle

13.1 Crankshaft end play can be checked with a dial indicator, as shown here, . . .

4 Check the connecting rods and caps for identification marks **(see illustration)**. If they aren't plainly marked, use a small center punch to make the appropriate number of indentations on each rod and cap (1 – 4 or 6, depending on the engine type and cylinder they're associated with).

5 Loosen each of the connecting rod cap nuts 1/2-turn at a time until they can be removed by hand. Remove the number one connecting rod cap and bearing insert. Don't drop the bearing insert out of the cap. Slip a short length of plastic or rubber hose over each connecting rod cap bolt to protect the crankshaft journal and cylinder wall as the piston is removed **(see illustration)**. Push the connecting rod/piston assembly out through the top of the engine **(see illustration)**. Use a wooden hammer handle to push on the upper bearing insert in the connecting rod. If resistance is felt, double-check to make sure that all of the ridge was removed from the cylinder.

6 Repeat the procedure for the remaining cylinders. After removal, reassemble the connecting rod caps and bearing inserts in their respective connecting rods and install the cap nuts finger tight. Leaving the old bearing inserts in place until reassembly will help prevent the connecting rod bearing surfaces from being accidentally nicked or gouged.

13 Crankshaft – removal

Refer to illustrations 13.1, 13.3, 13.4a, 13.4b, 13.4c and 13.5

Note: *The crankshaft can be removed only after the engine has been removed from the vehicle. It's assumed that the flywheel or driveplate, vibration damper, timing chain or belt, oil pan, oil strainer, oil pump (V6 engine), front cover (four-cylinder engine) and piston/connecting rod assemblies have already been removed. The rear main oil seal retainer also must be unbolted and separated from the block before proceeding with crankshaft removal.*

1 Before the crankshaft is removed, check the end play. Mount a dial indicator with the stem in line with the crankshaft and just touching one of the crank throws **(see illustration)**.

13.3 ... or with feeler gauges

13.4a The main bearing caps should be marked so they don't get mixed up – if they aren't, mark them with a center punch (the arrow indicates the front of the engine)

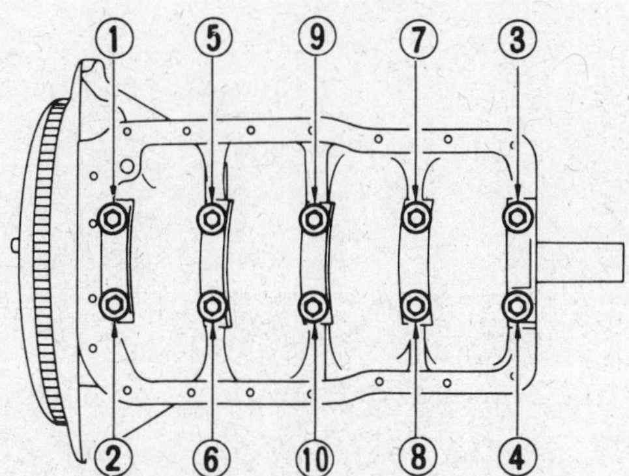

13.4b Main bearing cap bolt LOOSENING sequence – four-cylinder engines

13.4c Main bearing cap bolt LOOSENING sequence – V6 engine

2 Push the crankshaft all the way to the rear and zero the dial indicator. Next, pry the crankshaft to the front as far as possible and check the reading on the dial indicator. The distance that it moves is the end play. If it's greater than specified, check the crankshaft thrust surfaces for wear. If no wear is evident, new main bearings should correct the end play.

3 If a dial indicator isn't available, feeler gauges can be used. Gently pry or push the crankshaft all the way to the front of the engine. Slip feeler gauges between the crankshaft and the front face of the thrust main bearing to determine the clearance **(see illustration)**. The thrust bearing on four-cylinder engines is number three (center), while on the V6 engine it's number four (rear).

4 On four-cylinder engines, check the main bearing caps to see if they're marked to indicate their locations. They should be numbered consecutively from the front of the engine to the rear. If they aren't, mark them with number stamping dies or a center punch. Main bearing caps generally have a cast-in arrow, which points to the front of the engine **(see illustration)**. Loosen the main bearing cap bolts 1/4-turn at a time each in the recommended sequence **(see illustrations)**, until they can be removed by hand.

5 Gently tap the caps with a soft-face hammer, then separate them from the engine block. If necessary, use the bolts as levers to remove the caps. **Note:** *On four-cylinder engines, a special puller may be needed for the rear and center bearing caps* **(see illustration)**. Try not to drop the bearing inserts if they come out with the caps. The main bearing caps on the V6 engine are a one-piece assembly.

6 Carefully lift the crankshaft out of the engine. With the bearing inserts in place in the engine block and main bearing caps or cap assembly, install the caps on the engine block and tighten the bolts finger tight.

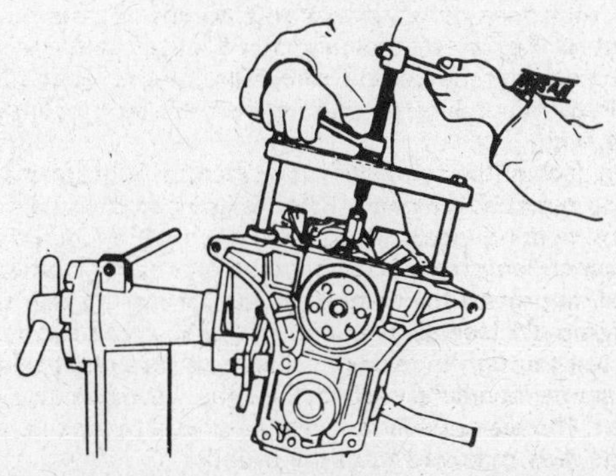

13.5 A special puller may be needed to remove the rear and center main bearing caps on four-cylinder engines – don't try to pry them off!

14.2 Use a gasket scraper to remove all traces of old gasket material and sealant from the block surfaces (gasket removal solvents are available and can make removal of stubborn gaskets much easier)

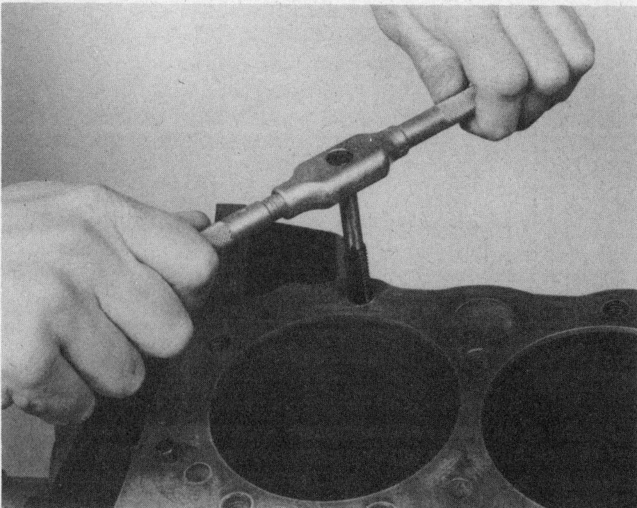

14.7 All bolt holes in the block – particularly the main bearing cap and head bolt holes – should be cleaned and restored with a tap (be sure to remove debris from the holes after this is done)

14 Engine block – cleaning

Refer to illustrations 14.2, 14.7 and 14.9

Note: *The core plugs (also known as freeze or soft plugs) may be difficult or impossible to retrieve if they're driven into the block coolant passages.*

1 Drill a small hole in the center of each core plug and pull them out with an auto body type dent puller.

2 Using a gasket scraper, remove all traces of gasket material from the engine block **(see illustration)**. Be very careful not to nick or gouge the gasket sealing surfaces.

3 Remove the main bearing caps or cap assembly and separate the bearing inserts from the caps and the engine block. Tag the bearings, indicating which cylinder they were removed from and whether they were in the cap or the block, then set them aside.

4 If the engine is extremely dirty it should be taken to an automotive machine shop to be steam cleaned or hot tanked.

5 After the block is returned, clean all oil holes and oil galleries one more time. Brushes specifically designed for this purpose are available at most auto parts stores. Flush the passages with warm water until the water runs clear, dry the block thoroughly and wipe all machined surfaces with a light, rust preventative oil. If you have access to compressed air, use it to speed the drying process and to blow out all the oil holes and galleries. **Warning:** *Wear eye protection when using compresed air!*

6 If the block isn't extremely dirty or sludged up, you can do an adequate cleaning job with hot soapy water and a stiff brush. Take plenty of time and do a thorough job. Regardless of the cleaning method used, be sure to clean all oil holes and galleries very thoroughly, dry the block completely and coat all machined surfaces with light oil.

7 The threaded holes in the block must be clean to ensure accurate torque readings during reassembly. Run the proper size tap into each of the holes to remove any rust, corrosion, thread sealant or sludge and to restore damaged threads **(see illustration)**. If possible, use compressed air to clear the holes of debris produced by this operation. Now is a good time to clean the threads on the head bolts and the main bearing cap bolts as well.

8 Reinstall the main bearing caps or cap assembly and tighten the bolts finger tight.

9 After coating the sealing surfaces of the new core plugs with RTV sealant, install them in the engine block **(see illustration)**. Make sure they're driven in straight and seated properly or leakage could result. Special tools are available for this purpose, but equally good results can be obtained using a large socket, with an outside diameter that will just slip into the core plug, a 1/2-inch drive extension and a hammer.

10 If the engine isn't going to be reassembled right away, cover it with a large plastic trash bag to keep it clean.

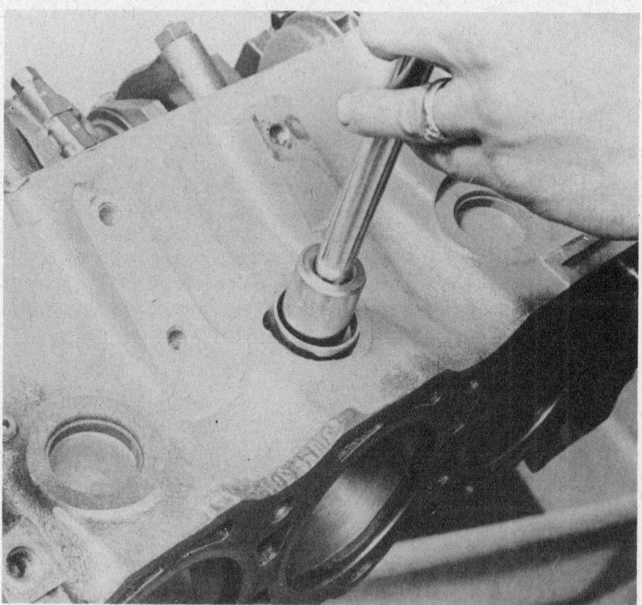

14.9 A large socket on an extension can be used to drive the new core plugs into the bores

15 Engine block – inspection

Refer to illustrations 15.4a, 15.4b, 15.4c, 15.6 and 15.7

1 Before the block is inspected, it should be cleaned as described in Section 14. Double-check to make sure the ridge at the top of each cylinder has been completely removed.

2 Visually check the block for cracks, rust and corrosion. Look for stripped threads in the threaded holes. It's also a good idea to have the block checked for hidden cracks by an automotive machine shop that has the special equipment to do this type of work. If defects are found, have the block repaired, if possible, or replaced.

3 Check the cylinder bores for scuffing and scoring.

4 Measure the diameter of each cylinder at the top (just under the ridge area), center and bottom of the cylinder bore, parallel to the crankshaft axis **(see illustrations)**. Next, measure each cylinder's diameter at the same three locations *across* the crankshaft axis. Compare the results to the Specifications. If the cylinder walls are badly scuffed or scored, or if they're out-of-round or tapered beyond the limits

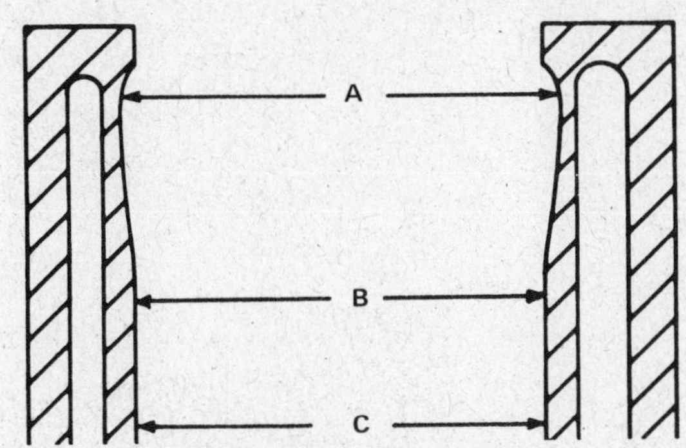

15.4a Measure the diameter of each cylinder just under the wear ridge (A), at the center (B) and at the bottom (C)

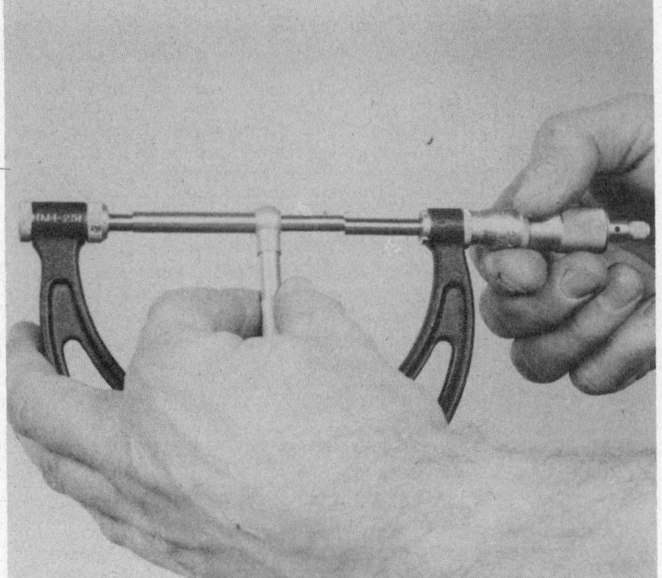

15.4c The gauge is then measured with a micrometer to determine the bore size

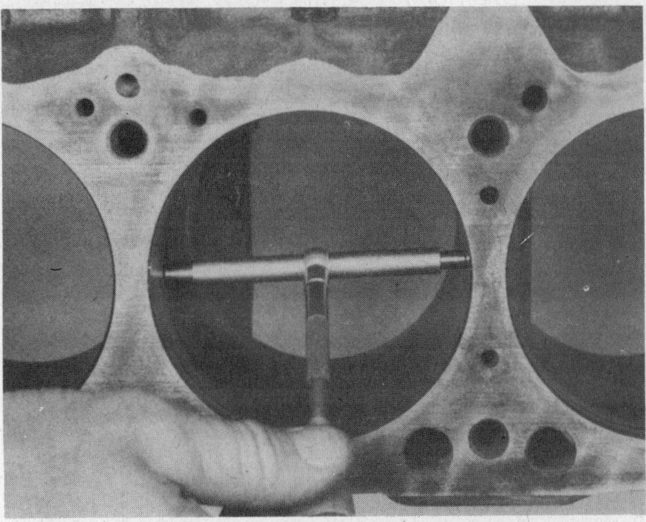

15.4b The ability to "feel" when the telescoping gauge is at the correct point will be developed over time, so work slowly and repeat the check until you're satisfied the bore measurement is accurate

given in the Specifications, have the engine block rebored and honed at an automotive machine shop. If a rebore is done, oversize pistons and rings will be required.

5 If the cylinders are in reasonably good condition and not worn to the outside of the limits, and if the piston-to-cylinder clearances can be maintained properly, then they don't have to be rebored. Honing is all that's necessary (Section 16).

6 Using a precision straightedge and feeler gauge, check the block deck (the surface that mates with the cylinder head[s]) for distortion **(see illustration)**. If it's distorted beyond the specified limit, it can be resurfaced by an automotive machine shop. The amount that can be taken off is determined by the amount taken off the head(s), if resurfacing was done. The total that can be removed (head plus block) cannot exceed 0.008-inch. If it does, new components (block and/or head[s]) will be needed. If the block is replaced, new pistons may also be required — check with a dealer service department.

7 If the block is replaced with a new one, new pistons and rings that match the grade numbers stamped into the block above each cylinder bore **(see illustration)** must also be used.

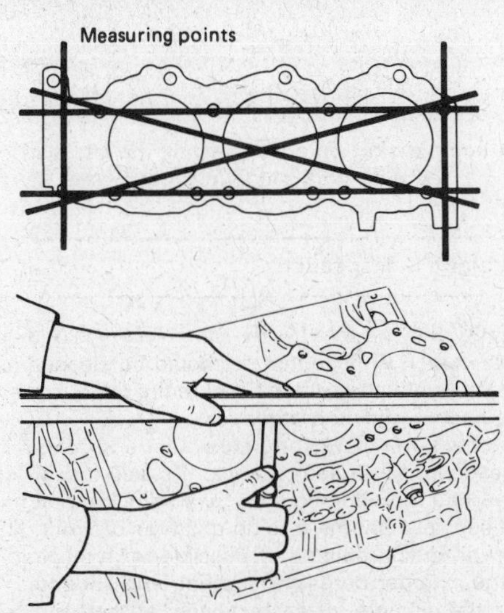

15.6 Check the block deck (both banks on a V6 engine) for distortion with a precision straightedge and feeler gauges

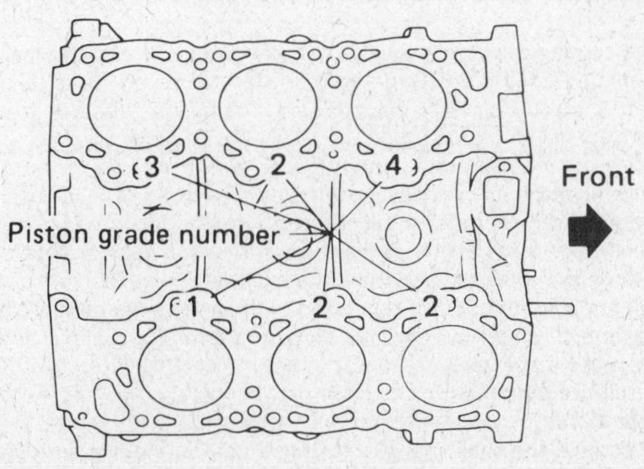

15.7 If the block is replaced, or new pistons are required, be sure to match them up by referring to the grade numbers stamped into the block above each cylinder bore (V6 engine shown)

16.3a A "bottle brush" hone will produce better results if you've never done cylinder honing before

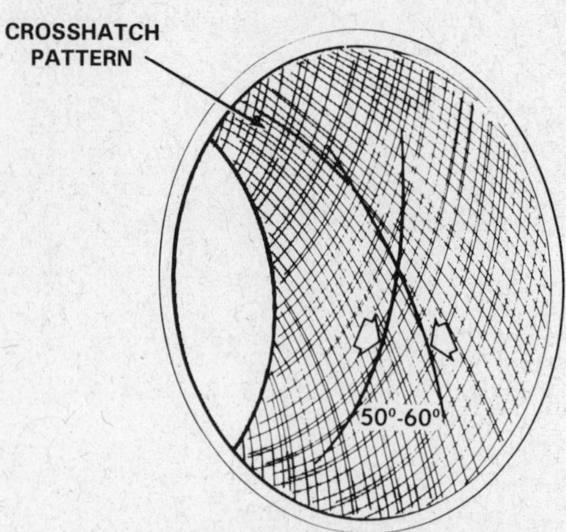

16.3b The cylinder hone should leave a smooth, crosshatch pattern with the lines intersecting at approximately a 60-degree angle

16 Cylinder honing

Refer to illustrations 16.3a and 16.3b

1 Prior to engine reassembly, the cylinder bores must be honed so the new piston rings will seat correctly and provide the best possible combustion chamber seal. **Note:** *If you don't have the tools or don't want to tackle the honing operation, most automotive machine shops will do it for a reasonable fee.*

2 Before honing the cylinders, install the main bearing caps or cap assembly (without bearing inserts) and tighten the bolts to the specified torque.

3 Two types of cylinder hones are commonly available — the flex hone or "bottle brush" type and the more traditional surfacing hone with spring-loaded stones. Both will do the job, but for the less experienced mechanic the "bottle brush" hone will probably be easier to use. You'll also need plenty of light oil or honing oil, some rags and an electric drill motor. Proceed as follows:

a) Mount the hone in the drill motor, compress the stones and slip it into the first cylinder **(see illustration)**. Be sure to wear safety goggles or a face shield!
b) Lubricate the cylinder with plenty of oil, turn on the drill and move the hone up-and-down in the cylinder at a pace that will produce a fine crosshatch pattern on the cylinder walls. Ideally, the crosshatch lines should intersect at approximately a 60° angle **(see illustration)**. Be sure to use plenty of lubricant and don't take off any more material than is absolutely necessary to produce the desired finish. **Note:** *Piston ring manufacturers may specify a smaller crosshatch angle than the traditional 60° — read and follow any instructions included with the new rings.*
c) Don't withdraw the hone from the cylinder while it's running. Instead, shut off the drill and continue moving the hone up-and-down in the cylinder until it comes to a complete stop, then compress the stones and withdraw the hone. If you're using a "bottle brush" type hone, stop the drill motor, then turn the chuck in the normal direction of rotation while withdrawing the hone from the cylinder.
d) Wipe the oil out of the cylinder and repeat the procedure for the remaining cylinders.

4 After the honing job is complete, chamfer the top edges of the cylinder bores with a small file so the rings won't catch when the pistons are installed. **Be very careful not to nick the cylinder walls with the end of the file!**

5 The entire engine block must be washed again very thoroughly with warm, soapy water to remove all traces of the abrasive grit produced during the honing operation. **Note:** *The bores can be considered clean when a white cloth — dampened with clean engine oil — used to wipe them down doesn't pick up any more honing residue, which will show up as gray areas on the cloth.* Be sure to run a brush through all oil holes and galleries and flush them with running water.

6 After rinsing, dry the block and apply a coat of light rust preventive oil to all machined surfaces. Wrap the block in a plastic trash bag to keep it clean and set it aside until reassembly.

17 Piston/connecting rod assembly — inspection

Refer to illustrations 17.4a, 17.4b, 17.5, 17.10 and 17.11

1 Before the inspection process can be carried out, the piston/connecting rod assemblies must be cleaned and the original piston rings removed from the pistons. **Note:** *Always use new piston rings when the engine is reassembled.*

2 Using a piston ring installation tool, carefully remove the rings from the pistons. Be careful not to nick or gouge the pistons in the process.

3 Scrape all traces of carbon from the top of the piston. A hand-held wire brush or a piece of fine emery cloth can be used once the majority of the deposits have been scraped away. Do not, under any circumstances, use a wire brush mounted in a drill motor to remove deposits from the pistons. The piston material is soft and will be eroded away by the wire brush.

4 Use a piston ring groove cleaning tool to remove carbon deposits from the ring grooves. If a tool isn't available, a piece broken off the old ring will do the job. Be very careful to remove only the carbon deposits — don't remove any metal and don't nick or scratch the sides of the ring grooves **(see illustrations)**.

5 Once the deposits have been removed, clean the piston/rod assemblies with solvent and dry them with compressed air (if available). Make sure the oil return holes in the back sides of the piston ring grooves and the oil hole in the lower end of each rod are clear **(see illustration)**.

6 If the pistons and cylinder walls aren't damaged or worn excessively, and if the engine block isn't rebored or replaced, new pistons won't be necessary. However, if new pistons are required, be sure to match them to each cylinder by referring to the grade numbers on the block **(see illustration 15.7)**. Normal piston wear appears as even vertical wear on the piston thrust surfaces and slight looseness of the top ring in its groove. New piston rings, on the other hand, should always be used when an engine is rebuilt.

7 Carefully inspect each piston for cracks around the skirt, at the pin bosses and at the ring lands.

8 Look for scoring and scuffing on the thrust faces of the skirt, holes in the piston crown and burned areas at the edge of the crown. If the skirt is scored or scuffed, the engine may have been suffering from overheating and/or abnormal combustion, which caused excessively high operating temperatures. The cooling and lubrication systems should be checked thoroughly. A hole in the piston crown is an indication that abnormal combustion (preignition) was occurring. Burned areas at the edge of the piston crown are usually evidence of spark knock (detonation). If any of the above problems exist, the causes must

17.4a The piston ring grooves can be cleaned with a special tool, as shown here, . . .

17.4b . . . or a section of a broken ring

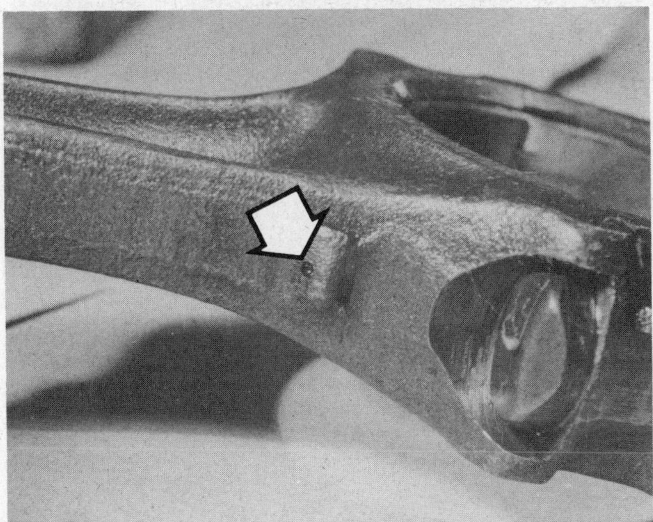
17.5 Make sure the oil hole in the lower end of each connecting rod is clear — if the rods are separated from the pistons, make sure the oil hole is on the correct side when they're reassembled!

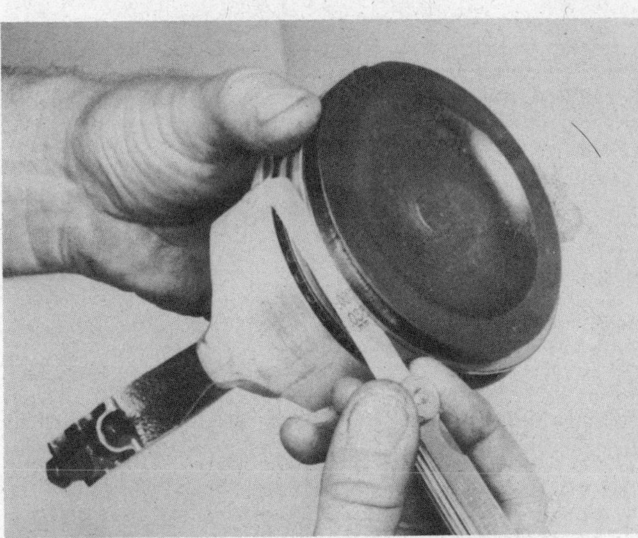
17.10 Check the ring side clearance with a feeler gauge at several points around the groove

be corrected or the damage will occur again.

9 Corrosion of the piston, in the form of small pits, indicates that coolant is leaking into the combustion chamber and/or the crankcase. Again, the cause must be corrected or the problem may persist in the rebuilt engine.

10 Measure the piston ring side clearance by laying a new piston ring in each ring groove and slipping a feeler gauge in beside it **(see illustration)**. Check the clearance at three or four locations around each groove. Be sure to use the correct ring for each groove; they are different. If the side clearance is greater than specified, new pistons will have to be used.

11 Check the piston-to-bore clearance by measuring the bore (see Section 15) and the piston diameter. Make sure the pistons and bores are correctly matched. Measure the piston across the skirt, at a 90° angle to the piston pin, about 13/16-inch up from the lower edge **(see illustration)**. Subtract the piston diameter from the bore diameter to obtain the clearance. If it's greater than specified, the block will have to be rebored and new pistons and rings installed.

12 Check the piston-to-rod clearance by twisting the piston and rod in opposite directions. Any noticeable play indicates excessive wear, which must be corrected. The piston/connecting rod assemblies should be taken to an automotive machine shop to have the pistons and rods

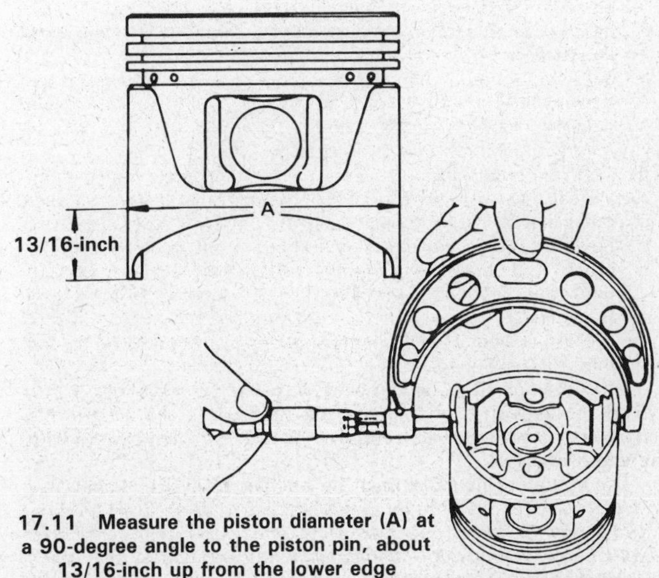

17.11 Measure the piston diameter (A) at a 90-degree angle to the piston pin, about 13/16-inch up from the lower edge

rebored and new pins installed.

13 If the pistons must be removed from the connecting rods for any reason, they should be taken to an automotive machine shop. While they are there have the connecting rods checked for bend and twist, since automotive machine shops have special equipment for this purpose. **Note:** *Unless new pistons and/or connecting rods must be installed, do not disassemble the pistons and connecting rods.*

14 Check the connecting rods for cracks and other damage. Temporarily remove the rod caps, lift out the old bearing inserts, wipe the rod and cap bearing surfaces clean and inspect them for nicks, gouges and scratches. After checking the rods, replace the old bearings, slip the caps into place and tighten the nuts finger tight.

18 Crankshaft – inspection

Refer to illustrations 18.1 and 18.2

1 Clean the crankshaft with solvent and dry it with compressed air (if available). Be sure to clean the oil holes with a stiff brush and flush them with solvent **(see illustration)**. Check the main and connecting rod bearing journals for uneven wear, scoring, pits and cracks. Check the rest of the crankshaft for cracks and other damage.

2 Using a micrometer, measure the diameter of the main and connecting rod journals and compare the results to the Specifications **(see illustration)**. By measuring the diameter at a number of points around each journal's circumference, you'll be able to determine whether or not the journal is out-of-round. Take the measurement at each end of the journal, near the crank throws, to determine if the journal is tapered.

18.1 Check the oil holes in the crankshaft journals to make sure they're clean and smooth – sharp edges here will damage the new bearings!

18.2 Measure the diameter of each crankshaft journal at several points to detect taper and out-of-round conditions

3 Crankshaft runout should be checked also, but large V-blocks and a dial indicator are needed to do it correctly. If you don't have access to them, a machine shop will do it.

4 If the crankshaft journals are damaged, tapered, out-of-round or worn beyond the limits given in the Specifications, have the crankshaft reground by an automotive machine shop. Be sure to use the correct size bearing inserts if the crankshaft is reconditioned.

5 Check the oil seal contact surfaces on both ends of the crankshaft. If they're scratched, nicked or otherwise damaged, the oil seals may leak when the engine is reassembled. Repair may be possible (ask at an automotive machine shop), but a new crankshaft may be required.

6 Refer to Section 19 and examine the main and rod bearing inserts.

19 Main and connecting rod bearings – inspection and main bearing selection

Inspection

1 Even though the main and connecting rod bearings should be replaced with new ones during the engine overhaul, the old bearings should be retained for close examination, as they may reveal valuable information about the condition of the engine.

2 Bearing failure occurs because of lack of lubrication, the presence of dirt or other foreign particles, overloading the engine and corrosion. Regardless of the cause of bearing failure, it must be corrected before the engine is reassembled to prevent it from happening again.

3 When examining the bearings, remove them from the engine block, the main bearing caps, the connecting rods and the rod caps and lay them out on a clean surface in the same general position as their location in the engine. This will enable you to match any bearing problems with the corresponding crankshaft journal.

4 Dirt and other foreign particles get into the engine in a variety of ways. It may be left in the engine during assembly, or it may pass through filters or the PCV system. It may get into the oil, and from there into the bearings. Metal chips from machining operations and normal engine wear are often present. Abrasives are sometimes left in engine components after reconditioning, especially when parts are not thoroughly cleaned using the proper cleaning methods. Whatever the source, these foreign objects often end up embedded in the soft bearing material and are easily recognized. Large particles will not embed in the bearing and will score or gouge the bearing and journal. The best prevention for this cause of bearing failure is to clean all parts thoroughly and keep everything spotlessly clean during engine assembly. Frequent and regular engine oil and filter changes are also recommended.

5 Lack of lubrication (or lubrication breakdown) has a number of interrelated causes. Excessive heat (which thins the oil), overloading (which squeezes the oil from the bearing face) and oil leakage or throw off (from excessive bearing clearances, worn oil pump or high engine speeds) all contribute to lubrication breakdown. Blocked oil passages, which usually are the result of misaligned oil holes in a bearing shell, will also oil starve a bearing and destroy it. When lack of lubrication is the cause of bearing failure, the bearing material is wiped or extruded from the steel backing of the bearing. Temperatures may increase to the point where the steel backing turns blue from overheating.

6 Driving habits can have a definite effect on bearing life. Full throttle, low speed operation (lugging the engine) puts very high loads on bearings, which tends to squeeze out the oil film. These loads cause the bearings to flex, which produces fine cracks in the bearing face (fatigue failure). Eventually the bearing material will loosen in pieces and tear away from the steel backing. Short trip driving leads to corrosion of bearings because insufficient engine heat is produced to drive off the condensed water and corrosive gases. These products collect in the engine oil, forming acid and sludge. As the oil is carried to the engine bearings, the acid attacks and corrodes the bearing material.

7 Incorrect bearing installation during engine assembly will lead to bearing failure as well. Tight fitting bearings leave insufficient bearing oil clearance and will result in oil starvation. Dirt or foreign particles trapped behind a bearing insert result in high spots on the bearing which lead to failure.

Selection (main bearings only)

Refer to illustrations 19.9a, 19.9b, 10.10a, 19.10b, 19.10c, 19.11 and 19.12

8 If the original main bearings are worn or damaged, or if the oil clearances are incorrect (Section 22), the following procedure should be used to select the correct new main bearings for engine reassembly. However, if the crankshaft has been reground, new undersize bearings must be installed – the following procedure should not be used if undersize bearings are required. The automotive machine shop that reconditions the crankshaft will provide or help you select the correct size bearings. Regardless of how the bearing sizes are determined, use the oil clearance, measured with Plastigage (Section 22), as a guide to ensure the bearings are the right size.

9 Locate the main journal grade numbers punched into the oil pan mating surface on the engine block **(see illustrations)**. **Note:** *Late model KA24E engines use only a numeral system to grade main bearings.*

10 If you're working on a four-cylinder engine, be aware that journals 2 and 4 always require a grade B bearing (unless, of course, the crankshaft has been reground). Journals 1, 3 and 5 require different grades (A or B) depending on the grade number on the block **(see illustrations)**.

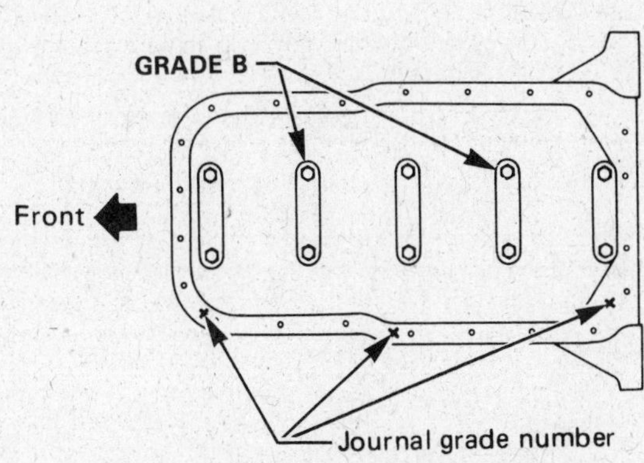

19.9a Main bearing journal grade number locations – four-cylinder engines

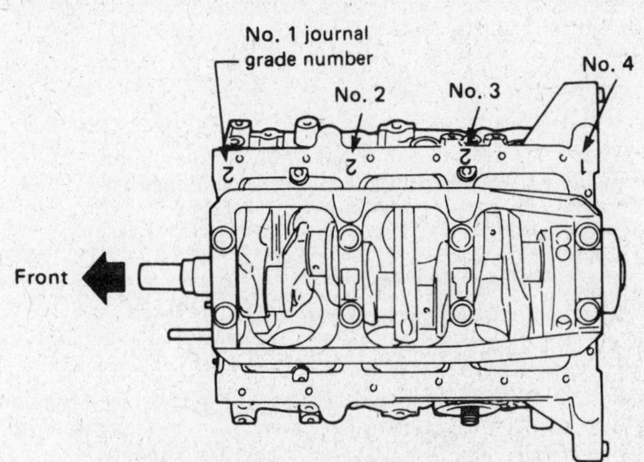

19.9b Main bearing journal grade number locations – V6 engine

No. 1, 3 & 5 main journal grade number	0	Select grade A bearing
	1	Select grade B bearing
For No. 2 & 4 main journals, select grade B bearing.		

19.10a Four-cylinder engine main bearing selection chart

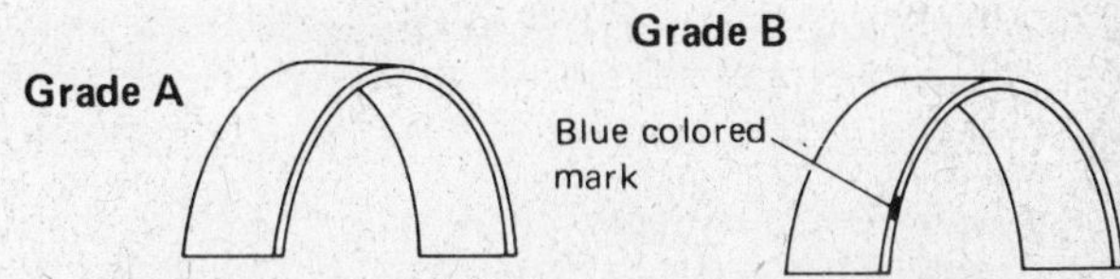

19.10b Grade A bearings are unmarked, while grade B bearings are marked with blue paint on the side

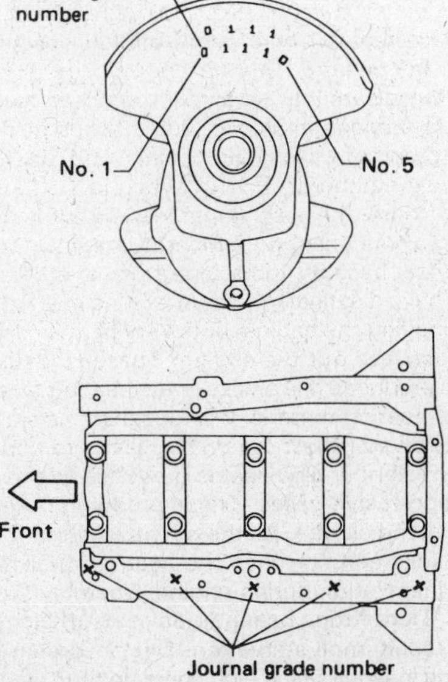

Crankshaft journal grade number \ Main journal grade number	0	1	2
0	0	1	2
1	1	2	3
2	2	3	4

19.10c On KA24E engines, obtain the grade number of the main bearings from the crankshaft and engine block and then follow the chart

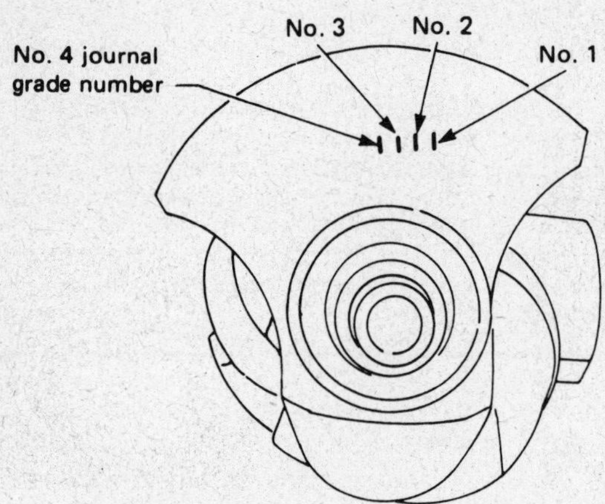

19.11 The V6 engine crankshaft also has grade marks for each main bearing journal (number 1 is the front, number 4 is the rear)

	Main journal grade number		
	0	1	2
	Main bearing grade number		
Crankshaft journal grade number 0	0	1	2
Crankshaft journal grade number 1	1	2	3
Crankshaft journal grade number 2	2	3	4

For example:
Main journal grade number: 1
Crankshaft journal grade number: 2
Main bearing grade number = 1 + 2

19.12 V6 engine main bearing selection chart

11 If you're working on a V6 engine, locate the main journal grade numbers on the crankshaft as well **(see illustration)**.
12 Use the accompanying chart to determine the correct bearings for each main journal **(see illustration)**.
13 Remember, the oil clearance is the final judge when selecting new bearing sizes. If you have any questions or are unsure which bearings to use, get help from a Nissan dealer parts or service department.

20 Engine overhaul – reassembly sequence

1 Before beginning engine reassembly, make sure you have all the necessary new parts, gaskets and seals as well as the following items on hand:

Common hand tools
A 1/2-inch drive torque wrench
Piston ring installation tool
Piston ring compressor
Short lengths of rubber or plastic hose to fit over connecting rod bolts
Plastigage
Feeler gauges
A fine-tooth file
New engine oil
Engine assembly lube or moly-base grease
RTV-type gasket sealant
Thread locking compound

2 In order to save time and avoid problems, engine reassembly must be done in the following general order:

Four-cylinder engines

Piston rings (Part C)
Crankshaft and main bearings (Part C)
Piston/connecting rod assemblies (Part C)
Rear main oil seal (Part C)
Cylinder head (Part A)
Camshaft (Part A)
Rocker arm assembly (Part A)
Timing chain and sprockets (Part A)
Front cover (Part A)
Oil strainer (Part A)
Oil pump (Part A)
Oil pan (Part A)
Intake and exhaust manifolds (Part A)
Rocker arm cover (Part A)
Flywheel/driveplate (Part A)

V6 engine

Piston rings (Part C)
Crankshaft and main bearings (Part C)
Piston/connecting rod assemblies (Part C)
Rear main oil seal/retainer (Part C)
Oil pump (Part B)
Oil pan (Part B)
Cylinder heads (Part B)
Camshafts and lifters (Part B)
Rocker arm assemblies (Part B)
Timing belt and pulleys (Part B)
Timing belt covers (Part B)
Intake and exhaust manifolds (Part B)
Rocker arm covers (Part B)
Engine rear plate
Flywheel/driveplate (Part B)

21 Piston rings – installation

Refer to illustrations 21.3, 21.4, 21.5, 21.9a, 21.9b, 21.11 and 21.12

1 Before installing the new piston rings, the ring end gaps must be checked. It's assumed that the piston ring side clearance has been checked and verified correct (Section 17).
2 Lay out the piston/connecting rod assemblies and the new ring sets so the ring sets will be matched with the same piston and cylinder during the end gap measurement and engine assembly.
3 Insert the top (number one) ring into the first cylinder and square it up with the cylinder walls by pushing it in with the top of the piston **(see illustration)**. The ring should be near the bottom of the cylinder, at the lower limit of ring travel.
4 To measure the end gap, slip feeler gauges between the ends of the ring until a gauge equal to the gap width is found **(see illustration)**. The feeler gauge should slide between the ring ends with a slight amount of drag. Compare the measurement to the Specifications. If the gap is larger or smaller than specified, double-check to make sure you have the correct rings before proceeding.
5 If the gap is too small, it must be enlarged or the ring ends may come in contact with each other during engine operation, which can cause serious damage to the engine. The end gap can be increased by filing the ring ends very carefully with a fine file. Mount the file in a vise equipped with soft jaws, slip the ring over the file with the ends contacting the file face and slowly move the ring to remove material from the ends. When performing this operation, file only from the outside in **(see illustration)**.
6 Excess end gap isn't critical unless it's greater than 0.040-inch. Again, double-check to make sure you have the correct rings for your engine.

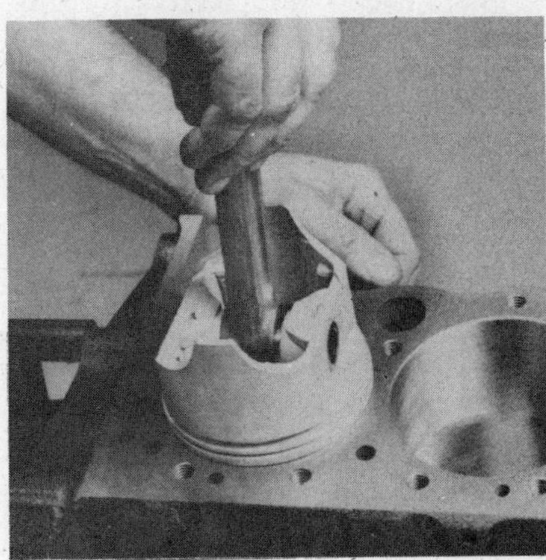

21.3 When checking piston ring end gap, the ring must be square in the cylinder bore (This is done by pushing the ring down with the top of a piston as shown)

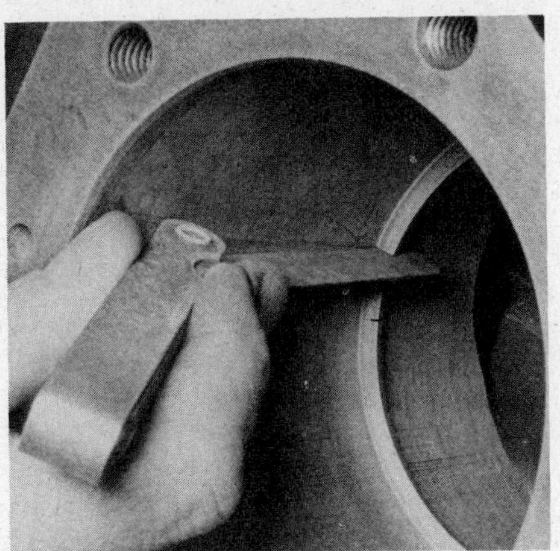

21.4 With the ring square in the cylinder, measure the end gap with a feeler gauge

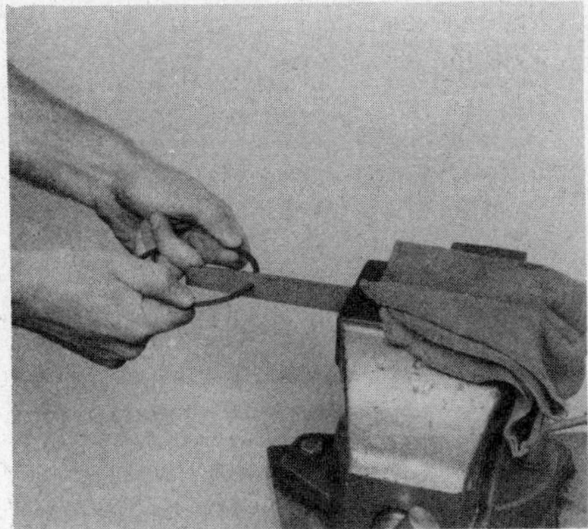

21.5 If the end gap is too small, clamp a file in a vise and file the ring ends (from the outside in only) to enlarge the gap slightly

21.9a Installing the spacer/expander in the oil control ring groove

21.9b DO NOT use a piston ring installation tool when installing the oil ring side rails

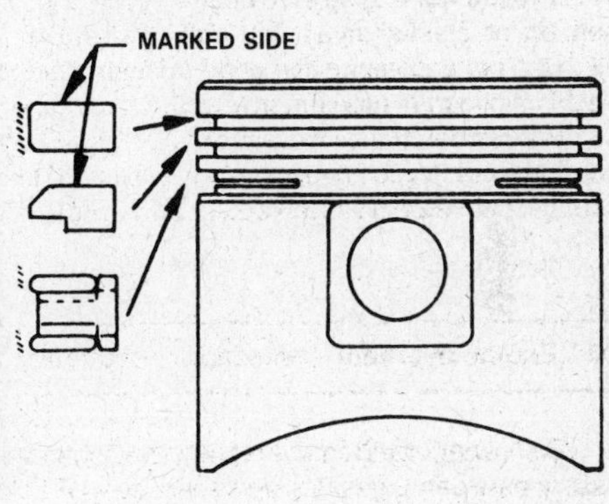

21.11 The piston rings have different shapes, so make sure they aren't mixed up – the marked side must face up!

7 Repeat the procedure for each ring that will be installed in the first cylinder and for each ring in the remaining cylinders. Remember to keep rings, pistons and cylinders matched up.

8 Once the ring end gaps have been checked/corrected, the rings can be installed on the pistons.

9 The oil control ring (lowest one on the piston) is installed first. On most models it's composed of three separate components. Slip the spacer/expander into the groove **(see illustration)**. If an anti-rotation tang is used, make sure it's inserted into the drilled hole in the ring groove. Next, install the lower side rail. Don't use a piston ring installation tool on the oil ring side rails, as they may be damaged. Instead, place one end of the side rail into the groove between the spacer/expander and the ring land, hold it firmly in place and slide a finger around the piston while pushing the rail into the groove **(see illustration)**. Next, install the upper side rail in the same manner.

10 After the three oil ring components have been installed, check to make sure that both the upper and lower side rails can be turned smoothly in the ring groove.

11 The number two (middle) ring is installed next. It's stamped with a mark which must face up, toward the top of the piston. Note: Always follow the instructions printed on the ring package or box – different manufacturers may require different approaches. Do not mix up the top and middle rings, as they have different cross sections **(see illustration)**.

12 Use a piston ring installation tool and make sure the identification mark is facing the top of the piston, then slip the ring into the middle groove on the piston **(see illustration)**. Don't expand the ring any more than is necessary to slide it over the piston.

13 Install the number one (top) ring in the same manner. Make sure the mark is facing up. Be careful not to confuse the number one and number two rings.

14 Repeat the procedure for the remaining pistons and rings.

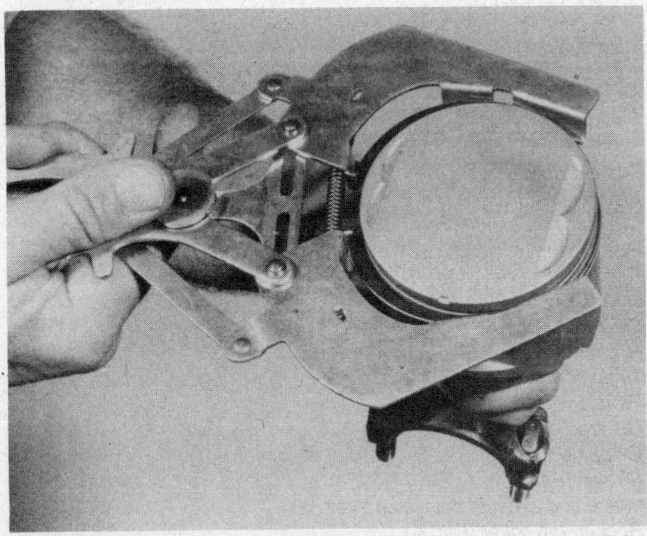

21.12 Install the compression rings with a ring expander

22.2 Make sure the baffle plate and steel net are in place on four-cylinder engines before the crankshaft is installed

22.5 The bearing inserts with the oil groove (arrow) must be installed in the block

22 Crankshaft – installation and main bearing oil clearance check

Refer to illustrations 22.2, 22.5, 22.10, 22.12a, 22.12b, 22.14, 22.19 and 22.24

1 Crankshaft installation is the first major step in engine reassembly. It's assumed at this point that the engine block and crankshaft have been cleaned, inspected and repaired or reconditioned.

2 Position the engine with the bottom facing up. On four-cylinder engines, make sure the steel net and baffle plate are in place in the crankcase **(see illustration)**.

3 Remove the main bearing cap bolts and lift out the caps or cap assembly. Lay the caps out in the proper order to ensure correct installation.

4 If they're still in place, remove the old bearing inserts from the block and the main bearing caps. Wipe the main bearing surfaces of the block and caps with a clean, lint free cloth. They must be kept spotlessly clean!

5 Clean the back sides of the new main bearing inserts and lay the bearing half with the oil groove in each main bearing saddle in the block. Lay the other bearing half from each bearing set in the corresponding main bearing cap. Make sure the tab on each bearing insert fits into the recess in the block or cap. Also, the oil holes in the block must line up with the oil holes in the bearing insert **(see illustration). Caution:** *Do not hammer the bearings into place and don't nick or gouge the bearing faces. No lubrication should be used at this time.*

6 If you're working on a V6 engine, the flanged thrust bearing must be installed in the rear cap and saddle. On four-cylinder engines, the thrust bearing must be installed in the number three (center) cap.

7 Clean the faces of the bearings in the block and the crankshaft main bearing journals with a clean, lint free cloth. Check or clean the oil holes in the crankshaft, as any dirt here can go only one way – straight through the new bearings.

8 Once you're certain the crankshaft is clean, carefully lay it in position in the main bearings.

9 Before the crankshaft can be permanently installed, the main bearing oil clearance ***must*** be checked.

10 Trim several pieces of the appropriate size Plastigage (they must be slightly shorter than the width of the main bearings) and place one piece on each crankshaft main bearing journal, parallel with the journal axis **(see illustration)**.

11 Clean the faces of the bearings in the caps and install the caps in their respective positions (don't mix them up) with the arrows pointing toward the front of the engine. If you're working on a V6 engine, carefully lay the main bearing cap assembly in place. Don't disturb the Plastigage.

12 Following the recommended sequence **(see illustrations)**, tighten the main bearing cap bolts, in three steps, to the specified torque. Don't rotate the crankshaft at any time during this operation!

13 Remove the bolts and carefully lift off the main bearing caps or cap assembly. Keep them in order. Don't disturb the Plastigage or rotate the crankshaft. If any of the main bearing caps are difficult to remove, tap them gently from side-to-side with a soft-face hammer to loosen them.

14 Compare the width of the crushed Plastigage on each journal to the scale printed on the Plastigage container to obtain the main bearing oil clearance **(see illustration)**. Check the Specifications to make sure it's correct.

15 If the clearance is not as specified, the bearing inserts may be the wrong size (which means different ones will be required – see Sec-

22.10 Lay the Plastigage strips (arrow) on the main bearing journals, parallel to the crankshaft centerline

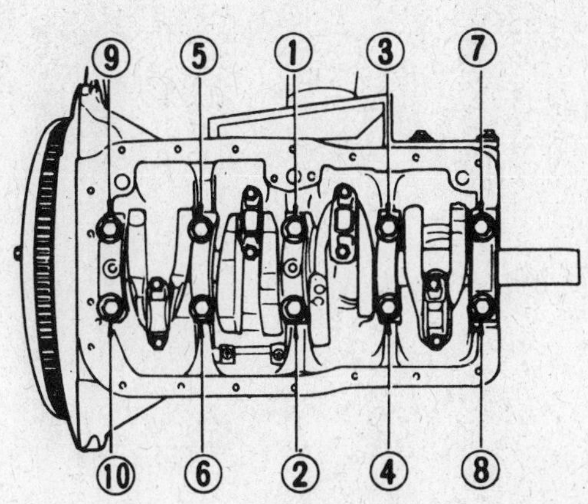

22.12a Main bearing cap bolt TIGHTENING sequence – four-cylinder engine

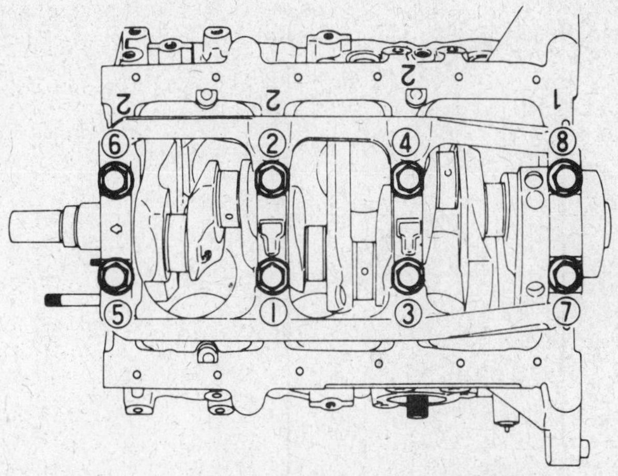

22.12b Main bearing cap bolt TIGHTENING sequence – V6 engine

tion 19). Before deciding that different inserts are needed, make sure that no dirt or oil was between the bearing inserts and the caps or block when the clearance was measured. If the Plastigage is noticeably wider at one end than the other, the journal may be tapered (see Section 18).

16 Carefully scrape all traces of the Plastigage material off the main bearing journals and/or the bearing faces. Don't nick or scratch the bearing faces.

17 Carefully lift the crankshaft out of the engine. Clean the bearing faces in the block, then apply a thin, uniform layer of clean moly-base grease or engine assembly lube to each of the bearing surfaces. Be sure to coat the thrust faces as well.

18 Lubricate the crankshaft surfaces that contact the oil seals with moly-base grease, engine assembly lube or clean engine oil.

19 Make sure the crankshaft journals are clean, then lay the crankshaft back in place in the block. Clean the faces of the bearings in the caps or cap assembly, then apply lubricant to them. Install the caps in their respective positions with the arrows pointing toward the front of the engine. **Note:** *On four-cylinder engines the rear cap must have RTV sealant applied* **(see illustration)**. Install the bolts.

20 Retighten all main bearing cap bolts to the specified torque, following the recommended sequence.

21 On manual transmission equipped models, install a new pilot bearing in the end of the crankshaft (see Chapter 8).

22 Rotate the crankshaft a number of times by hand to check for any obvious binding.

23 Check the crankshaft end play with a feeler gauge or a dial indicator as described in Section 13. The end play should be correct if the crankshaft thrust faces aren't worn or damaged and new bearings have been installed.

24 On four-cylinder engines, install new side seals in the rear main bearing cap after coating them with RTV sealant **(see illustration)**. Don't apply too much sealant.

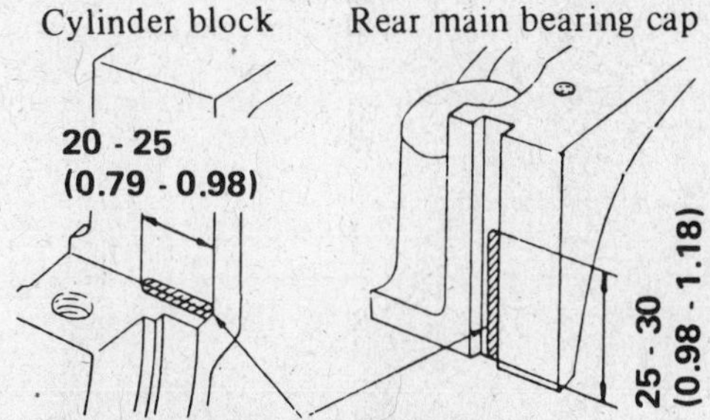

22.19 Apply a small amount of RTV sealant to each side of the rear main bearing cap and block as shown here (four-cylinder engines only)

22.14 Compare the width of the crushed Plastigage to the scale on the container to determine the main bearing oil clearance (always take the measurement at the widest point of the Plastigage); be sure to use the correct scale – inch and metric scales are included

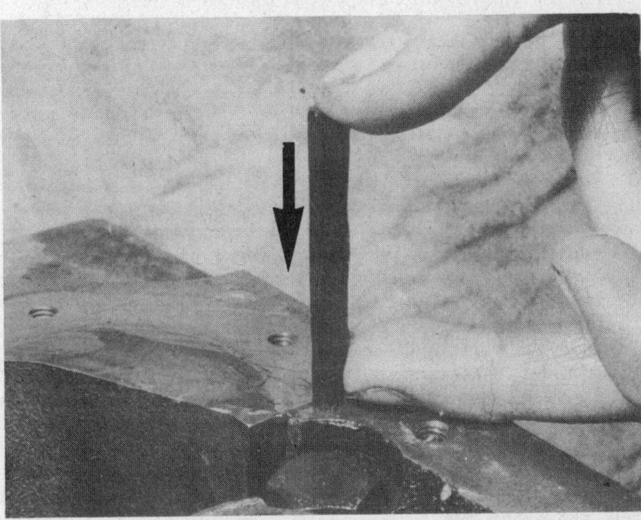

22.24 On four-cylinder engines, install the side seals in the grooves in the rear main bearing cap after coating them with a small amount of RTV sealant

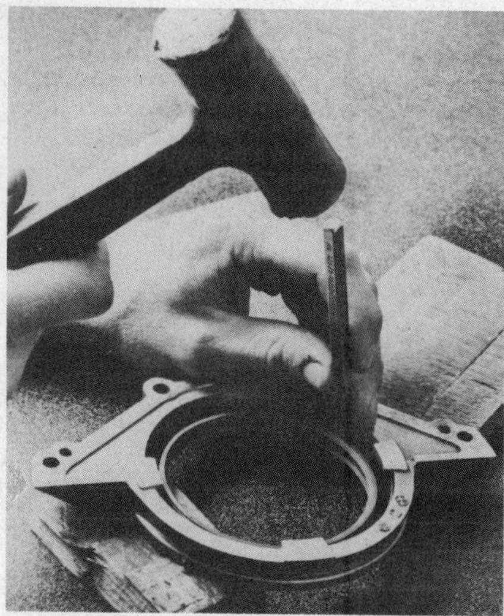

23.6 After removing the retainer from the engine, support it on two blocks of wood and drive the seal out from the back side with a hammer and punch

23.8 Clean the bore, then apply a small amount of grease or oil to the outer edge of the new seal and carefully drive it squarely into the retainer with a block of wood and a hammer – DO NOT damage the seal in the process!

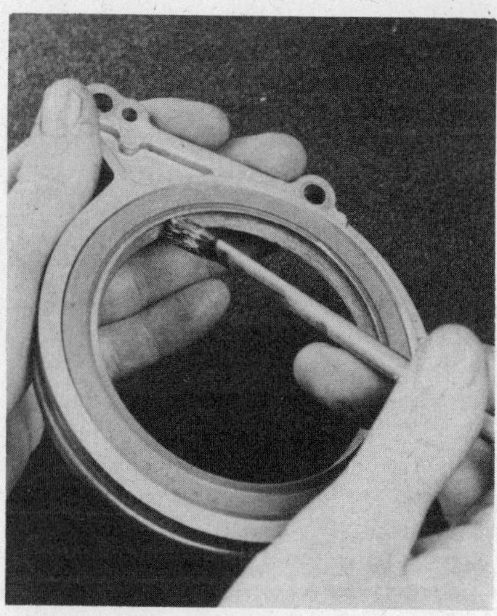

23.9a Apply moly-base grease or clean engine oil to the seal lips , . . .

23 Rear main oil seal installation

Four-cylinder engines

1 Clean the bore in the block and rear main bearing cap and the seal contact surface on the crankshaft. Check the crankshaft surface for scratches and nicks that could damage the new seal lip and cause oil leaks. If the crankshaft is damaged, the only alternative is a new or different crankshaft.

2 Apply a light coat of engine oil or multi-purpose grease to the outer edge of the new seal. Lubricate the seal lip with moly-base grease.

3 Carefully tap the new seal into place with Nissan tool no. KV10105500 or J-25640-01 (if available). The open (spring) side of the seal must face toward the front of the engine. If the special tool isn't available, carefully work the seal lip over the end of the crankshaft and tap the seal in with a hammer and punch until it's seated in the bore.

V6 engine

Refer to illustrations 23.6, 23.8, 23.9a and 23.9b

4 The crankshaft must be installed first and the main bearing cap assembly bolted in place, then the new seal should be installed in the retainer and the retainer bolted to the block.

5 Check the seal contact surface on the crankshaft very carefully for scratches and nicks that could damage the new seal lip and cause oil leaks. If the crankshaft is damaged, the only alternative is a new or different crankshaft.

6 The old seal can be removed from the retainer by driving it out from the back side with a hammer and punch **(see illustration)**. Be sure to note how far it's recessed into the bore before removing it; the new seal will have to be recessed an equal amount. Be very careful not to scratch or otherwise damage the bore in the retainer or oil leaks could develop.

7 Make sure the retainer is clean, then apply a thin coat of engine oil to the outer edge of the new seal. The seal must be pressed squarely into the bore, so hammering it into place isn't recommended. If you don't have access to a press, sandwich the housing and seal between two smooth pieces of wood and press the seal into place with the jaws of a large vise. The pieces of wood must be thick enough to distribute the force evenly around the entire circumference of the seal. Work slowly and make sure the seal enters the bore squarely.

8 As a last resort, the seal can be tapped into the retainer with a hammer. Use a block of wood to distribute the force evenly and make sure the seal is driven in squarely **(see illustration)**.

9 The seal lips must be lubricated with clean engine oil or moly-based grease before the seal/retainer is slipped over the crankshaft and bolted to the block **(see illustration)**. Use a new gasket – and sealant – and make sure the dowel pins are in place before installing the retainer **(see illustration)**.

23.9b . . . and coat the gasket mating surface of the engine block with sealant before installing the seal/retainer assembly

10 Tighten the bolts a little at a time until they're all at the specified torque.

24 Piston/connecting rod assembly – installation and rod bearing oil clearance check

Refer to illustrations 24.3, 24.5a, 25.5b, 24.6, 24.8a, 24.8b, 24.9, 24.11 and 24.13

1 Before installing the piston/connecting rod assemblies, the cylinder walls must be perfectly clean, the top edge of each cylinder must be chamfered, and the crankshaft must be in place.

2 Remove the connecting rod cap from the end of the number one con-

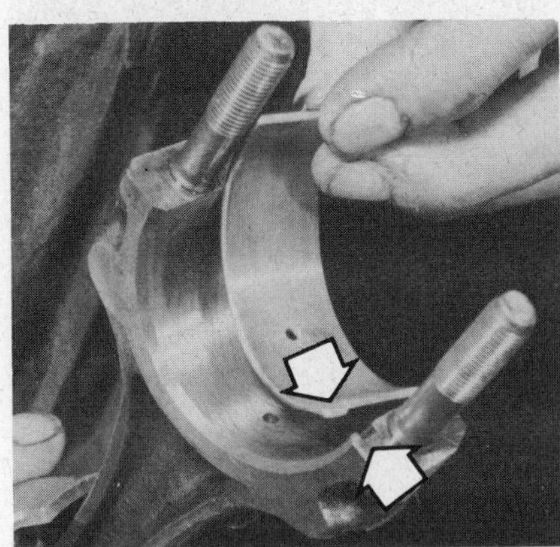

24.3 The tab on each bearing insert must fit into the recess in the rod or cap and the oil holes must line up (arrows)

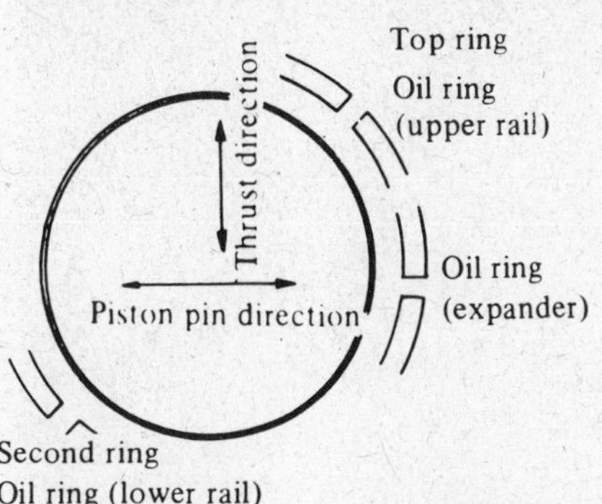

24.5a Stagger the piston ring end gaps as shown here before installing the piston/connecting rod assemblies in the engine

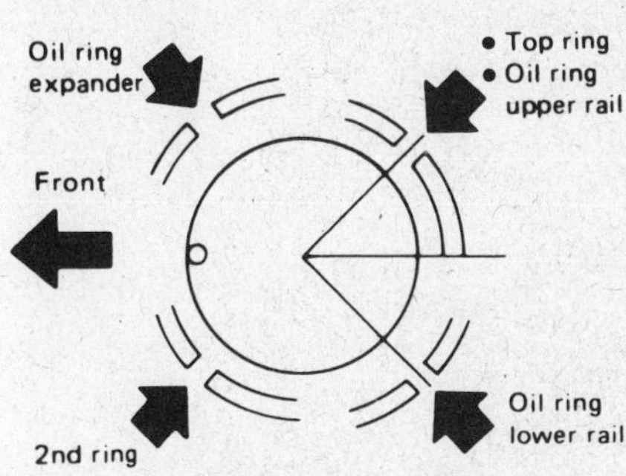

24.5b On 1990 and later engines, stagger the rings according to the above pattern

necting rod. Remove the old bearing inserts and wipe the bearing surfaces of the connecting rod and cap with a clean, lint free cloth. They must be kept spotlessly clean.

3 Clean the back side of the new upper bearing half, then lay it in place in the connecting rod. Make sure the tab on the bearing fits into the recess in the rod **(see illustration)**. Don't hammer the bearing insert into place and be very careful not to nick or gouge the bearing face. Don't lubricate the bearing at this time.

4 Clean the back side of the remaining bearing insert and install it in the rod cap. Again, make sure the tab on the bearing fits into the recess in the cap, and don't apply any lubricant. It's critically important that the mating surfaces of the bearing and connecting rod are perfectly clean and oil free when they're assembled.

5 Position the piston ring gaps at staggered intervals around the piston **(see illustrations)**, then slip a section of plastic or rubber hose over each connecting rod cap bolt.

6 Lubricate the piston and rings with clean engine oil and attach a piston ring compressor to the piston. Leave the skirt protruding to guide the piston into the cylinder. The rings must be compressed until they're flush with the piston **(see illustration)**.

7 Rotate the crankshaft until the number one connecting rod journal is at BDC (bottom dead center) and apply a coat of engine oil to the cylinder walls.

8 With the F mark on the side of the piston (four-cylinder engines) or the dimple on top of the piston (V6 engine) **(see illustrations)** facing the front of the engine, gently insert the piston/connecting rod assembly into the number one cylinder bore and rest the bottom edge of the ring compressor on the engine block. Tap the top edge of the ring compressor to make sure it's contacting the block around its entire circumference.

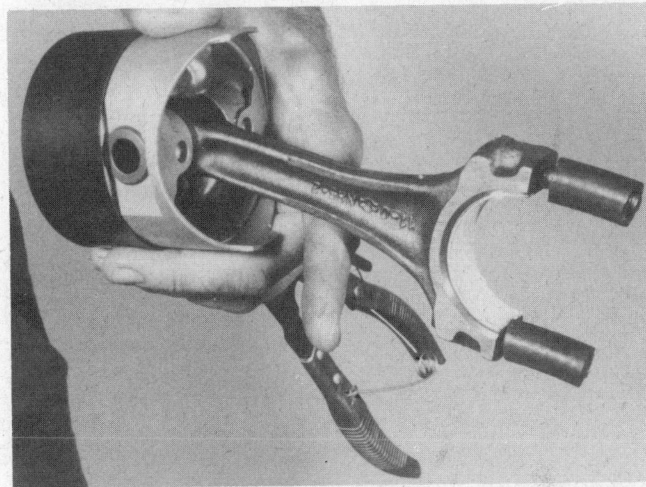

24.6 Slip sections of rubber hose over the rod bolts, then compress the rings with a ring compressor – leave the bottom of the piston sticking out so it'll slip into the cylinder

24.8a The F mark on the side of each piston (four-cylinder engines), . . .

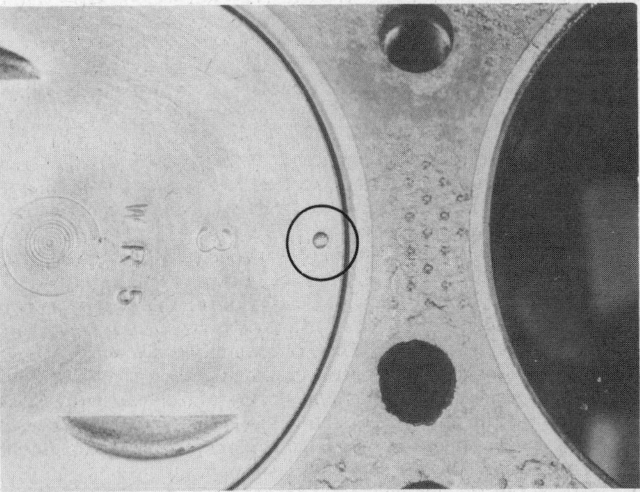

24.8b . . . or the dimple in the top of each piston (V6 engine) must face the FRONT of the engine as the pistons are installed

24.9 Each piston can be gently driven into the cylinder bore with the end of a wooden hammer handle

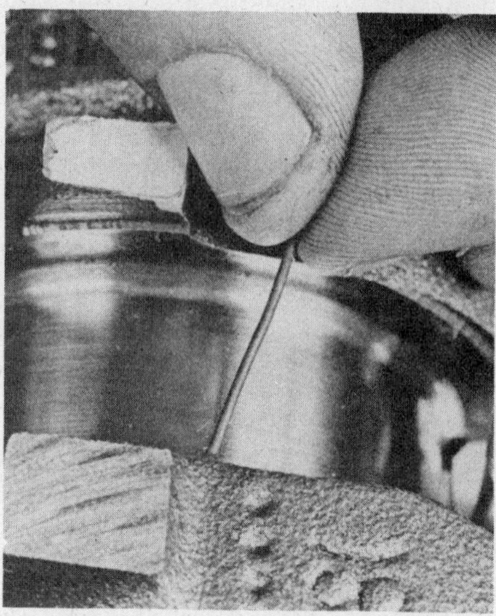

24.11 Lay the Plastigage strips on each rod bearing journal, parallel to the crankshaft centerline

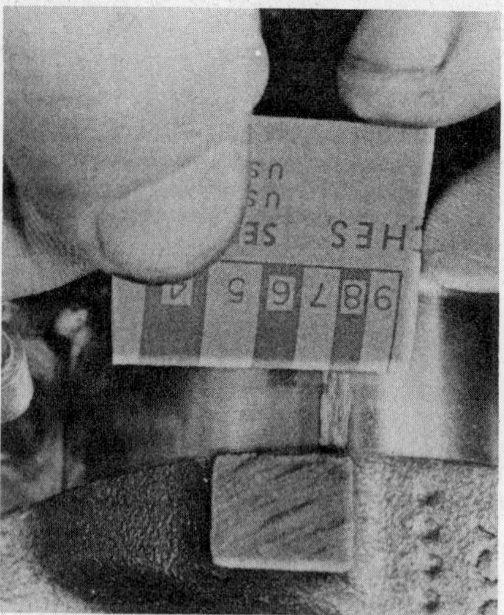

24.13 Measuring the width of the crushed Plastigage to determine the connecting rod bearing oil clearance (be sure to use the correct scale – inch and metric scales are included)

9 Carefully tap on the top of the piston with the end of a wooden hammer handle **(see illustration)** while guiding the end of the connecting rod into place on the crankshaft journal. The piston rings may try to pop out of the ring compressor just before entering the cylinder bore, so keep some downward pressure on the ring compressor. Work slowly, and if any resistance is felt as the piston enters the cylinder, stop immediately. Find out what's hanging up and fix it before proceeding. Do not, for any reason, force the piston into the cylinder, as you might break a ring and/or the piston!

10 Once the piston/connecting rod assembly is installed, the connecting rod bearing oil clearance must be checked before the rod cap is permanently bolted in place.

11 Cut a piece of the appropriate size Plastigage slightly shorter than the width of the connecting rod bearing and lay it in place on the number one connecting rod journal, parallel with the journal axis **(see illustration)**.

12 Clean the connecting rod cap bearing face, remove the protective hoses from the connecting rod bolts and install the rod cap. Make sure the mating mark on the cap is on the same side as the mark on the connecting rod. Install the nuts and tighten them to the specified torque. **Note:** *Use a thin-wall socket to avoid erroneous torque readings that can result if the socket is wedged between the rod cap and nut. Do not rotate the crankshaft at any time during this operation!*

13 Remove the rod cap, being very careful not to disturb the Plastigage. Compare the width of the crushed Plastigage to the scale printed on the Plastigage container to obtain the oil clearance **(see illustration)**. Compare it to the Specifications to make sure the clearance is correct. If the clearance is not as specified, the bearing inserts may be the wrong size (which means different ones will be required). Before deciding that different inserts are needed, make sure that no dirt or oil was between the bearing inserts and the connecting rod or cap when the clearance was measured. Also, recheck the journal diameter. If the Plastigage was wider at one end than the other, the journal may be tapered (refer to Section 18).

14 Carefully scrape all traces of the Plastigage material off the rod journal and/or bearing face. Be very careful not to scratch the bearing – use your fingernail or a credit card. Make sure the bearing faces are perfectly clean, then apply a uniform layer of clean moly-base grease or engine assembly lube to both of them. You'll have to push the piston into the cylinder to expose the face of the bearing insert in the connecting rod – be sure to slip the protective hoses over the rod bolts first.

15 Slide the connecting rod back into place on the journal, remove the protective hoses from the rod cap bolts, install the rod cap and tighten the nuts to the specified torque.

16 Repeat the entire procedure for the remaining piston/connecting rod assemblies. Keep the back sides of the bearing inserts and the inside of the connecting rod and cap perfectly clean when assembling them. Make sure you have the correct piston for the cylinder and that the mark on the piston faces to the front of the engine when the piston is installed. Remember, use plenty of oil to lubricate the piston before installing the ring compressor. Also, when installing the rod caps for the final time, be sure to lubricate the bearing faces adequately.

17 After all the piston/connecting rod assemblies have been properly installed, rotate the crankshaft a number of times by hand to check for any obvious binding.

18 As a final step, the connecting rod end play must be checked. Refer to Section 12 for this procedure. Compare the measured end play to the Specifications to make sure it's correct. If it was correct before disassembly and the original crankshaft and rods were reinstalled, it should still be right. If new rods or a new crankshaft were installed, the end play may be too small. If so, the rods will have to be removed and taken to an automotive machine shop for resizing.

25 Initial start-up and break-in after overhaul

1 Once the engine has been installed in the vehicle, double-check the engine oil and coolant levels.

2 With the spark plugs out of the engine and the ignition system disabled (see Section 2), crank the engine until oil pressure registers on the gauge.

3 Install the spark plugs, hook up the plug wires and restore the ignition system functions (Section 2).

4 Start the engine. It may take a few moments for the gasoline to reach the carburetor or injectors, but the engine should start without a great deal of effort.

5 After the engine starts, it should be allowed to warm up to normal operating temperature. While the engine is warming up, make a thorough check for oil and coolant leaks.

6 Shut the engine off and recheck the engine oil and coolant levels.

7 Drive the vehicle to an area with minimum traffic, accelerate at full throttle from 30 to 50 mph, then allow the vehicle to slow to 30 mph with the throttle closed. Repeat the procedure 10 or 12 times. This will load the piston rings and cause them to seat properly against the cylinder walls. Check again for oil and coolant leaks.

8 Drive the vehicle gently for the first 500 miles (no sustained high speeds) and keep a constant check on the oil level. It is not unusual for an engine to use oil during the break-in period.

9 At approximately 500 to 600 miles, change the oil and filter and retorque the cylinder head bolts.

10 For the next few hundred miles, drive the vehicle normally. Don't pamper it or abuse it.

11 After 2000 miles, change the oil and filter again and consider the engine fully broken in.

3

Chapter 3
Cooling, heating and air conditioning systems

Contents

Specifications

General

Coolant capacity .... See Chapter 1
Radiator cap pressure rating .... See Chapter 1
Thermostat opening temperature
Four-cylinder engine .... 170-degrees F
V6 engine .... 155-degrees F
1990 and later (all engines) .... 170-degrees F

Refrigerant oil

Type .... SUNISO 5GS or equivalent
Capacity
1980 through 1982 .... 5.3 oz/150 ml
1983
York compressor .... 6.3 oz/180 ml
Hitachi compressor .... 5.3 oz/150 ml
1984 .... 8.8 oz/250 ml
1985 on .... 7.0 oz/200 ml

Torque specifications

Torque specifications	Ft-lbs *(unless otherwise noted)*
Water pump bolts	
Four-cylinder engine	
6 mm bolts	35 to 86 in-lbs
8 mm bolts	12
V6 engine	12 to 15
Thermostat housing bolts	12 to 15
Water inlet bolts (V6 engine)	12 to 15
Water outlet bolts	12 to 15
Radiator mounting bolts	26 to 35 in-lbs
Fan-to-water pump bolts	52 to 87 in-lbs
Fan-to-clutch bolts	52 to 87 in-lbs
Air conditioning compressor mounting bracket bolts	
1980 through 1984	33 to 40
1985 on	
Four-cylinder engine	51 to 58
V6 engine	27 to 37
Air conditioning compressor-to-bracket bolts	
1980 through 1984	33 to 40
1985 on	27 to 37

1 Cooling system — general information

Refer to illustration 1.2

The components of the cooling system are the radiator, upper and lower radiator hoses, water pump, thermostat, radiator cap with pressure relief valve and heater hoses.

The principle of the system is that coolant in the bottom of the radiator circulates up through the lower radiator hose to the water pump, where the pump impeller pushes it around the block and heads through the various cast-in passages to cool the cylinder bores, combustion surfaces and valve seats **(see illustration)**. When sufficient heat has been absorbed by the coolant, and the engine has reached operating temperature, the coolant moves from the cylinder head past the now open thermostat into the top radiator hose and into the radiator header tank. The coolant then travels down the radiator tubes where it is rapidly cooled by the natural flow of air as the vehicle moves down the road. A multi-blade fan, mounted on the water pump pulley, assists this cooling action. The coolant now reaches the bottom of the radiator and the cycle is repeated.

When the engine is cold the thermostat remains closed until the coolant reaches a pre-determined temperature (see the Specifications). This assists rapid warm-up.

The system is pressurized by a spring-loaded radiator filler cap, which prevents premature boiling by increasing the boiling point of the coolant. If the coolant temperature goes above this increased boiling point, the extra pressure in the system forces the radiator cap internal spring-loaded valve off its seat and exposes the overflow hose, down which displaced coolant escapes into the coolant recovery reservoir.

The coolant recovery system consists of a plastic reservoir into which the overflow coolant from the radiator flows when the engine is hot. When the engine cools, coolant is drawn back into the radiator from the reservoir and maintains the system at full capacity.

Aside from cooling the engine during operation, the cooling system also provides the heat for the vehicles interior heater and heats the intake manifold. On vehicles equipped with an automatic transmission, the transmission fluid is cooled by a cooler attached to the base of the radiator.

On vehicles equipped with air conditioning systems, a condenser is placed ahead of the radiator.

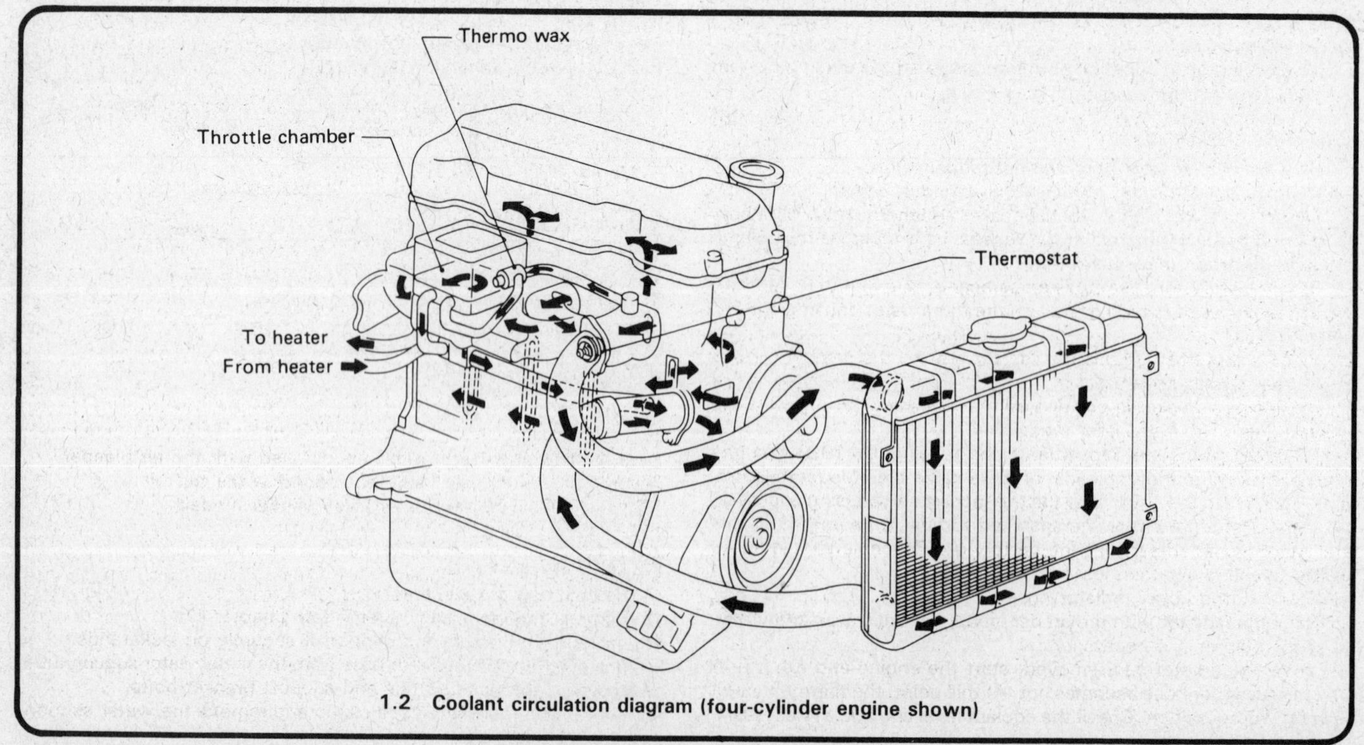

1.2 Coolant circulation diagram (four-cylinder engine shown)

The radiator cooling fan incorporates either a fluid coupling or a fluid/temperature controlled coupling. The latter device comprises an oil-operated clutch and is a coiled bi-metallic thermostat which functions to permit the fan to slip when the engine is below normal operating temperature and does not require the supplementary air flow provided by the fan at normal running speed. At higher engine operating temperature, the fan is locked and rotates at the speed of the water pump pulley. The fan coupling is a sealed unit and requires no periodic maintenance.

Warning: *The radiator cap should not be removed while the engine is hot. The proper way to remove the cap is to wrap a thick cloth around it, rotate the cap slowly counterclockwise to the detent and allow any residual pressure to escape. Do not press the cap down until all hissing has stopped, then push down and twist off.*

2 Antifreeze — general information

1 It is recommended that the cooling system be filled with a water/ethylene glycol based antifreeze solution which will give protection down to at least −20 °F. This provides protection against corrosion and increases the coolant boiling point. When handling antifreeze, take care that it is not spilled on the vehicle paint, since it will cause damage if not removed immediately.

2 The cooling system should be drained, flushed and refilled at least every alternate Fall. The use of antifreeze solutions for periods of longer than two years is likely to cause damage and encourage the formation of rust and scale due to the corrosion inhibitors gradually losing their efficiency.

3 The exact mixture of antifreeze to water which you should use depends upon the relative weather conditions. The mixture should contain at least 50 percent antifreeze, but under no circumstances should the mixture contain more than 70 percent antifreeze.

3 Thermostat — removal and installation

Refer to illustrations 3.5a, 3.5b, 3.9, 3.19 and 3.25

1 The thermostat is a restriction valve which is actuated by a heat sensitive element. It's mounted inside a housing on the left side of the engine (1980 models), at the front of the intake manifold on 1981 and later four-cylinder models, and on V6 models it's on the right-front side of the engine and is designed to open and close at predetermined temperatures to allow coolant to warm up or cool the engine.

2 To remove the thermostat, begin by draining the cooling system (refer to Chapter 1).

Four-cylinder models

3 Remove the air cleaner and upper radiator hose.

4 Remove the bolts that retain the thermostat cover.

5 Lift off the cover along with the gasket and thermostat. Note how the thermostat is positioned in the recess, as it must be replaced in this same position **(see illustration).**

6 Before installation, use a gasket scraper or putty knife to carefully remove all traces of the old gasket on the thermostat housing and the cover.

7 Place a thin bead of silicone sealant around the sealing surface on the thermostat cover.

8 Place a new gasket in position on the housing (1980 models), or on the cover (1981 and later models).

9 Place the thermostat in position in the housing. On 1981 and later models, make sure the air bleeder or jiggle valve is on top **(see illustration).** Then place the cover over the thermostat and housing and install the bolts. Tighten them to the specified torque. On some 1981 and later models, remember that the battery ground cable should be attached to the lower thermostat cover bolt.

10 Reinstall the upper radiator hose.

11 Refill the radiator with the proper mixture of antifreeze and water. Refer to Chapter 1 if necessary.

12 With the radiator cap removed, start the engine and run it until the upper radiator hose becomes hot. At this point, the thermostat will be in the open position. Check the coolant level and add as necessary.

13 Reinstall the radiator cap.

3.5a Correct installed position of the thermostat (1980 models only)

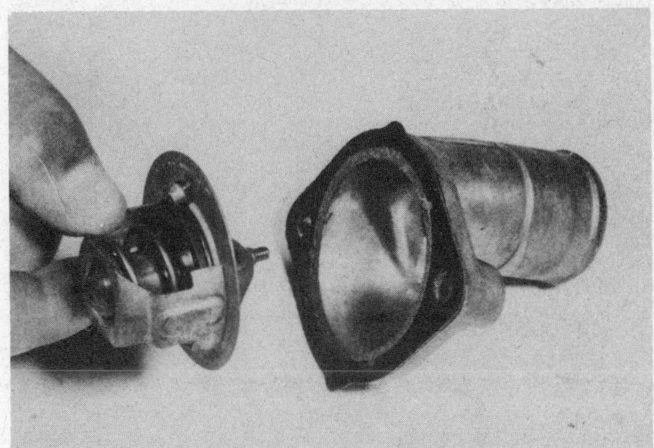

3.5b Correct installed position of the thermostat (1981 and later four-cylinder models)

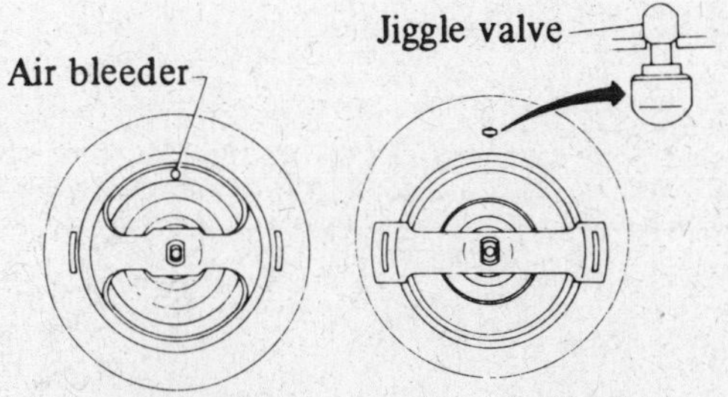

3.9 The thermostat must be installed with the air bleeder or jiggle valve positioned at the top (1981 and later four-cylinder models)

V6 models

14 Remove the fan and shroud.

15 Remove the drivebelts, referring to Chapter 1.

16 Jack up the vehicle and support it securely on jackstands.

17 Remove the lower radiator hose from the metal water suction tube by loosening the hose clamps and support bracket bolts.

18 Loosen the remaining hose clamp and remove the water suction tube from the vehicle.

3

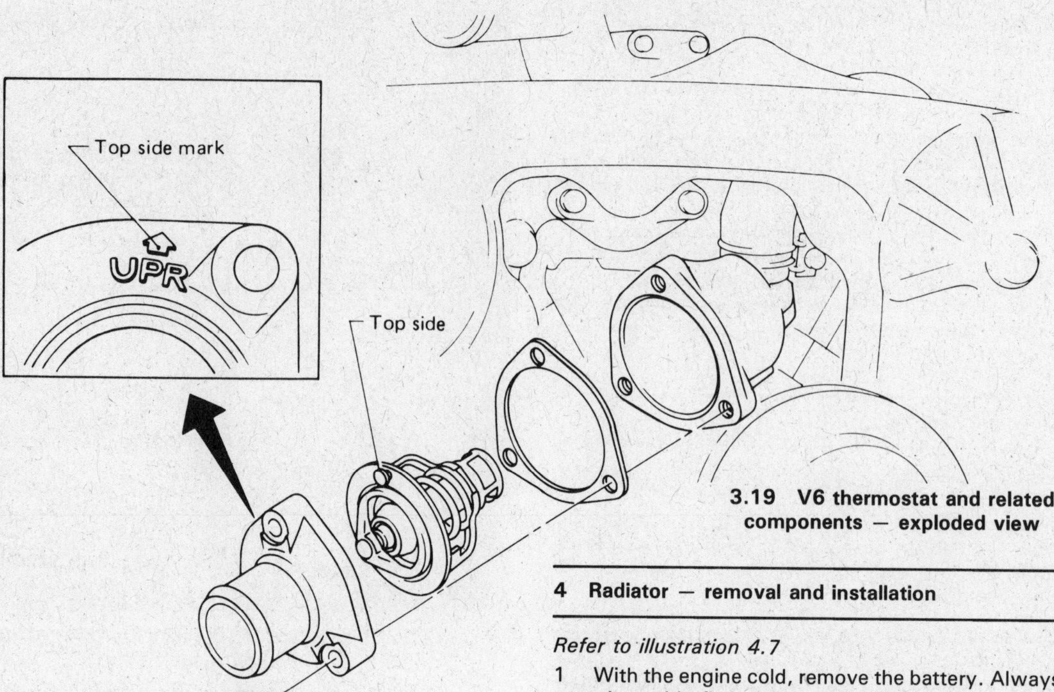

3.19 V6 thermostat and related components — exploded view

19 Remove the three thermostat housing retaining bolts **(see illustration)**.
20 Remove the housing from the engine. If necessary, use a soft-face hammer to tap the housing in order to break the gasket seal.
21 Remove the thermostat from the cavity, carefully noting which end is up.
22 Scrape off all traces of gasket and sealant from the gasket mounting surfaces.
23 Insert the new thermostat into the housing with the spring side in the block. The thermostat should seat in the cavity. The air bleeder must be on top **(see illustration 3.9)**.
24 Apply gasket sealer to both sides of the new gasket and install the gasket on the thermostat housing.
25 Install the thermostat housing onto the block, making sure the arrow on the cover is pointing up **(see illustration)**.
26 Tighten the housing bolts to the proper torque.
27 Reverse the remaining removal procedures, installing new hose clamps if necessary.
28 Refill the cooling system, run the engine and check for leaks and proper thermostat operation.

3.25 Note the arrow on the thermostat housing — it must point up during installation (V6 engine)

4 Radiator — removal and installation

Refer to illustration 4.7

1 With the engine cold, remove the battery. Always disconnect the negative cable first, followed by the positive cable.
2 Remove the undercover (belly pan).
3 Open the drain valve on the underside of the radiator and drain the coolant into a container (see Chapter 1).
4 Remove both the upper and lower radiator hoses.
5 Disconnect the reservoir hose from the radiator filler neck.
6 Remove the screws that attach the shroud to the radiator and slide the shroud toward the engine.
7 If equipped with an automatic transmission, disconnect the cooler hoses from the radiator **(see illustration)**. Place a drip pan to catch the fluid.
8 Remove the bolts that attach the radiator to the body.
9 Lift out the radiator.
10 With the radiator removed, it can be inspected for leaks or damage.

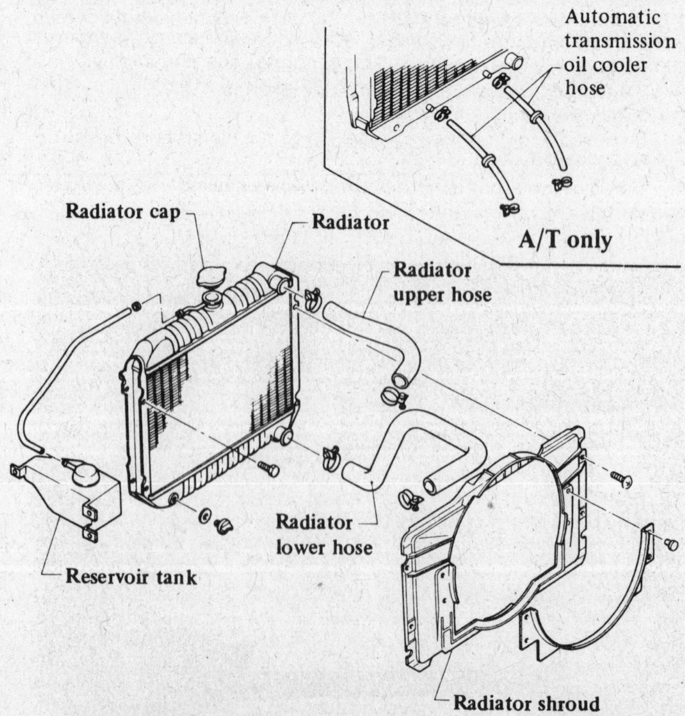

4.7 Exploded views of transmission cooler connections and radiator components (1980 through 1985 models shown)

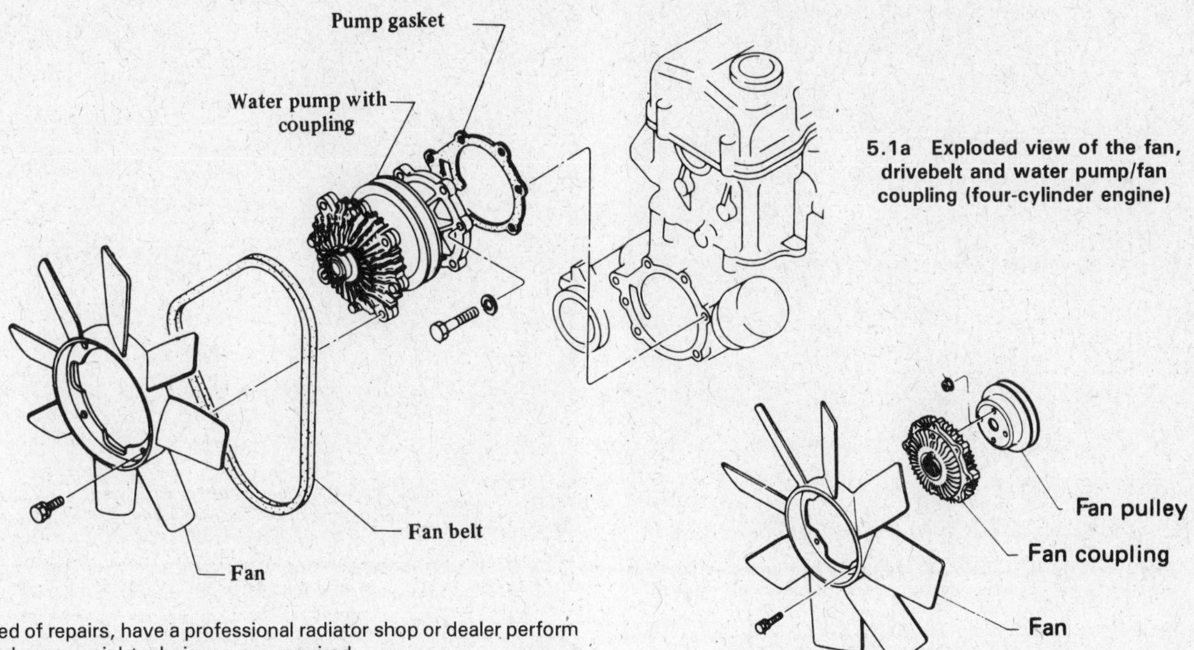

5.1a Exploded view of the fan, drivebelt and water pump/fan coupling (four-cylinder engine)

5.1b Exploded view of V6 engine fan components

If in need of repairs, have a professional radiator shop or dealer perform the work as special techniques are required.

11 Bugs and dirt can be cleaned from the radiator with compressed air and a soft brush. Don't bend the cooling fins as this is done.

12 Installation is the reverse of the removal procedure.

13 After installation, fill the cooling system with the proper mixture of antifreeze and water. Refer to Chapter 1 if necessary.

14 Start the engine and check for leaks. Allow the engine to reach normal operating temperature, indicated by the upper radiator hose becoming hot. Recheck the coolant level and add more if required.

15 On automatic transmission equipped models, check and add fluid as needed.

5 Engine cooling fan and clutch – removal and installation

Refer to illustrations 5.1a, 5.1b and 5.4

1 On four-cylinder models, the fan clutch is integral with the water pump **(see illustration)**. For fan clutch replacement, see Section 8. On V6 engines, the clutch is separate **(see illustration)**.

2 Remove the radiator as described in Section 4.

3 Remove the radiator shroud.

4 Remove the bolts that retain the fan to the clutch and lift off the fan **(see illustration)**.

5 On V6 engines, the fan clutch can now be unbolted from the water pump.

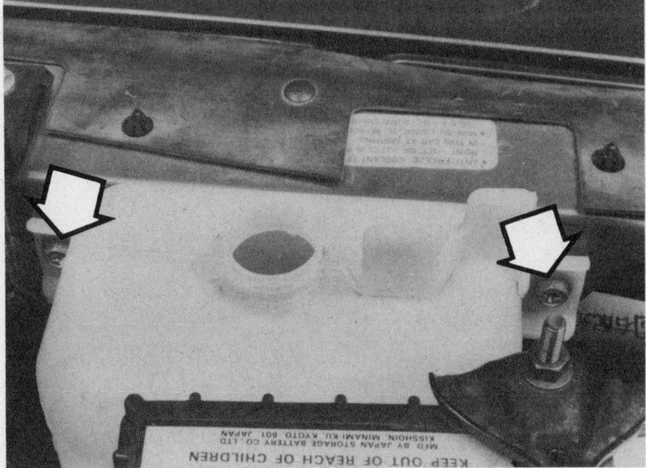

6.2 V6 engine coolant reservoir mounting bolts (arrows)

5.4 If the fan coupling must be replaced, remove the four bolts that attach the fan and coupling (arrows)

6 Coolant reservoir – removal and installation

Refer to illustration 6.2

1 Disconnect the reservoir hose at the radiator neck.

2 Unbolt and lift the reservoir up, then unplug the wiring connector **(see illustration)**.

3 Remove the reservoir from the engine compartment.

4 Drain the coolant into a container. If the reservoir is being replaced, disconnect the hose from the top.

5 Installation is the reverse of the removal procedure.

6 Refill the reservoir with the proper mixture of antifreeze and water. Refer to Chapter 1 if necessary.

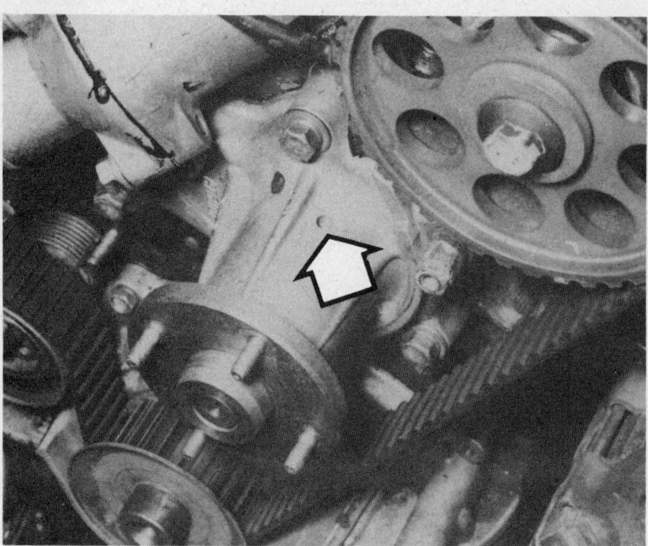

7.4 If coolant is leaking from the weep hole, the water pump seal is damaged or worn and the pump will have to be replaced

7.5 Check the water pump shaft for excessive play and roughness — it should turn smoothly with no play

7 Water pump — check

Refer to illustrations 7.4 and 7.5

1 A failure in the water pump can cause serious engine damage due to overheating.

2 There are three ways to check the operation of the water pump while it is installed on the engine. If the pump is suspect, it should be replaced with a new or rebuilt unit.

3 With the engine running and warmed to normal operating temperature, squeeze the upper radiator hose. If the water pump is working properly, a pressure surge should be felt as the hose is released.

4 Water pumps are equipped with weep or vent holes. If a failure occurs in the pump seal, coolant will leak from this hole. In most cases it will be necessary to use a flashlight to find the hole on the water pump by looking through the space just below the pump to see evidence of leakage **(see illustration).**

5 If the water pump shaft bearings fail there may be a squealing sound at the front of the engine while it is running. Shaft wear can be felt if the water pump pulley is rocked up and down **(see illustration).** Do not mistake drivebelt slippage, which also causes a squealing sound, for water pump failure.

8 Water pump — removal and installation

Refer to illustrations 8.10a, 8.10b and 8.12

1 Disconnect the negative cable at the battery. Place the cable out of the way so it cannot accidentally come in contact with the negative terminal of the battery, as this would once again allow power into the electrical system of the vehicle.

2 Jack up the vehicle and support it securely on jackstands.

3 Drain the cooling system (Chapter 1).

4 Refer to Sections 4 and 5 to remove the fan and shroud.

5 Refer to Chapter 1 and remove the drivebelts.

6 If your vehicle has a four-cylinder engine, skip Steps 7, 8 and 9.

7 Remove the water pump pulley (V6 engine).

8 Refer to Chapter 2B and remove the vibration damper from the crankshaft.

9 Remove the upper and lower timing belt covers (refer to Chapter 2B).

10 Remove the water pump mounting bolts **(see illustrations).**

11 Remove the water pump from the engine block and scrape all gasket and sealant material from the mounting surfaces.

12 Upon installation, apply gasket sealant to both sides of the new

8.10a The small water pump mounting bolts only need to be loosened to remove the pump (four-cylinder engine)

8.10b Remove the six bolts (arrows) retaining the water pump to the engine block (V6 engine)

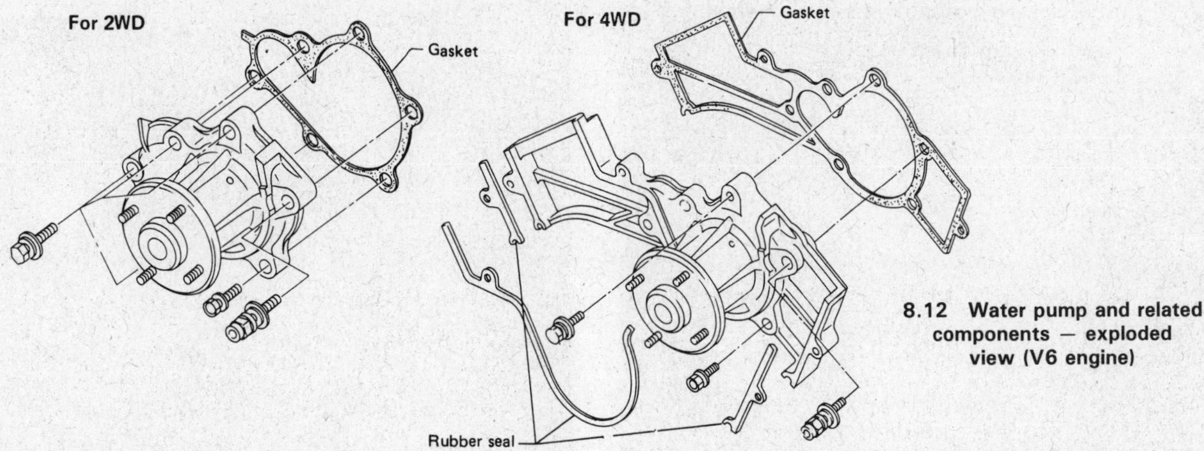

8.12 Water pump and related components – exploded view (V6 engine)

gasket and install it and the water pump on the engine block **(see illustration)**. Note that 2WD and 4WD models differ in the water pump gasket used.
13 Tighten all the water pump bolts, a little at a time, to the specified torque.
14 The remainder of the installation is the reverse of the removal procedure.
15 Adjust the drivebelt to the proper tension. Refer to Chapter 1 if necessary.
16 Fill the cooling system with the proper mixture of antifreeze and water, again referring to Chapter 1 if necessary. Then start the engine and allow it to idle until it reaches normal operating temperature. This is indicated by the upper radiator hose becoming hot. Check around the water pump and radiator for any leaks.
17 Recheck the coolant level and add more if necessary.

9 Coolant temperature sending unit – check and replacement

Check

1 The coolant termperature sending unit provides a variable electrical ground for the coolant temperature gauge.
2 The coolant temperature sending unit is located near the right front corner of the intake manifold.
3 If the gauge does not register, check the electrical fuses. Then unplug the wiring connector from the coolant temperature sending unit and connect a jumper wire between it and a clean electrical ground. Turn the ignition on briefly and the gauge should go to full scale (Hot).
4 If the gauge went to Hot, the sending unit is defective; replace it.
5 If the gauge did not move, the gauge or connecting circuitry is probably faulty.
6 The sending unit may be tested with an ohmmeter by placing it in a pan of water and heating it. At 140°F, resistance should be approximately 70 to 90 ohms and at 212°F, 21 to 24 ohms.

Replacement

7 Allow the engine to cool completely.
8 Drain the coolant (Chapter 1).
9 Unplug the wiring connector from the sending unit.
10 Using an appropriate size deep socket or wrench, unscrew the sending unit from the intake manifold.
11 Install the new unit and tighten it securely. Do not use thread sealer as it may electrically insulate the sending unit.

10 Heating system – general information

The main components of the heating system include the heater unit (which contains the heater core and cable-operated valves) the blower motor, the control assembly (mounted in the dash) and the air ducts which deliver the air to the various outlet locations.

Either outside air or interior (recirculated) air (depending on the settings) is drawn into the system through the blower unit. From there the blower motor forces the air into the heater unit.

The lever settings on the control assembly operate the valves in the heater unit, which determines the mix of heated and outside air by regulating how much air is passed through the heater core. The hotter the setting the more air is passed through the core.

The air ducts carry the heated air from the heater unit to the desired location. Again, valves within the duct system regulate where in the vehicle the air will be delivered.

The heater core is heated by engine coolant passing through it. The heater hoses carry the coolant from the engine to the heater core and then back again.

3

11 Blower unit – removal and installation

1 Disconnect the negative battery cable from the battery.
2 Remove the package tray from under the dash (if equipped).

1980 through 1985 models

Refer to illustration 11.7

3 On models not equipped with air conditioning, remove the heater duct.
4 Disconnect the wiring connector leading to the resistor.
5 Disconnect the air intake door control cable from the blower unit.
6 Remove the blower unit mounting screws and lift the unit out.
7 If the blower unit must be disassembled, refer to the accompanying illustration.
8 Installation is the reverse of the removal procedure. **Note:** *Before*

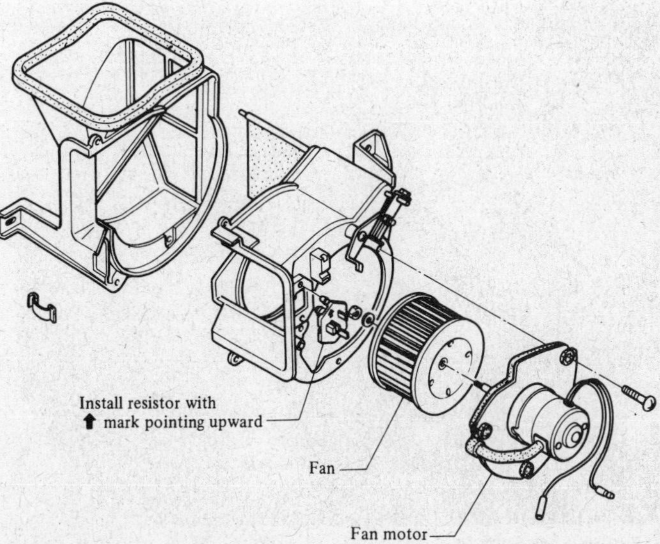

11.7 Exploded view of the heater blower unit

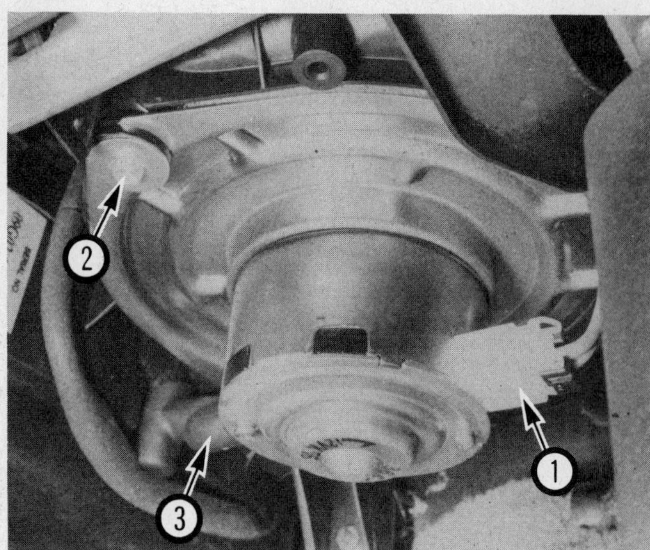

11.9 On 1986 and later models, the heater blower unit is mounted under the glove compartment in the right corner

1 Electrical connector
2 Mounting bolt
3 Hose

12.2 The heater hoses are connected to the heater core fittings behind the engine on the firewall (arrows)

reconnecting the air intake door cable, it must be adjusted by referring to Section 19.

1986 and later models

Refer to illustration 11.9

9 Unplug the electrical connector from the blower unit **(see illustration)**.
10 Disconnect the hose from the blower unit.
11 Remove the three mounting bolts.
12 Lower the blower unit out of the housing.
13 Installation is the reverse of the removal procedure.

12 Heater core – removal and installation

Refer to illustrations 12.2, 12.3, 12.6a, 12.6b, 12.7 and 12.9

1 Drain the coolant into a clean container (see Chapter 1).
2 On models equipped with air conditioning, disconnect the heater hoses at the firewall **(see illustration)**.
3 On models not equipped with air conditioning, remove the heater duct **(see illustration)**. Then disconnect the heater hoses from the heater unit at the point where they enter the vehicle interior through the engine

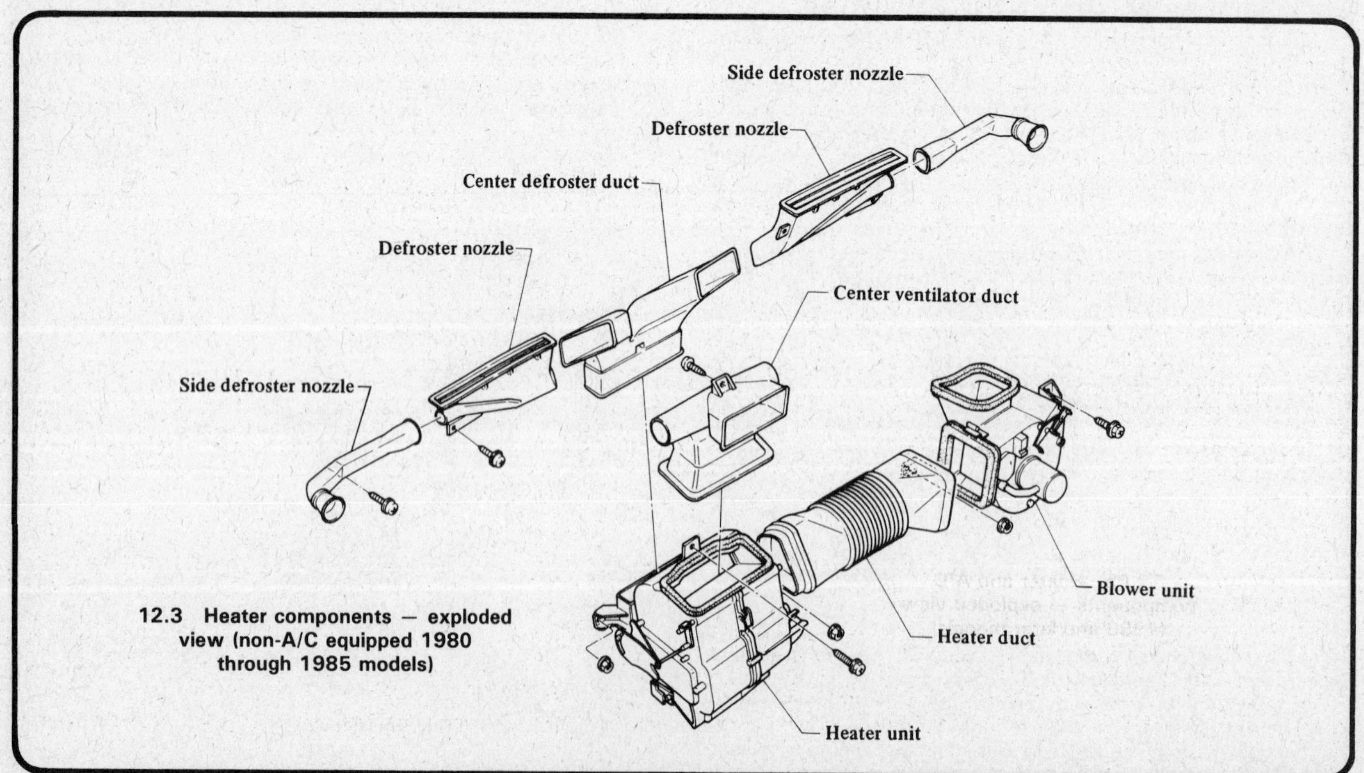

12.3 Heater components – exploded view (non-A/C equipped 1980 through 1985 models)

compartment firewall.

4 Working in the interior, remove the console box if equipped. For additional clearance, remove the package tray from under the dash (1980 through 1985 models).

5 Disconnect the air intake control cable from the blower unit.

6 On models equipped with air conditioning, remove the blower unit as described in Section 11. Then remove the mounting nuts and bolts from the cooling unit **(see illustrations)**.

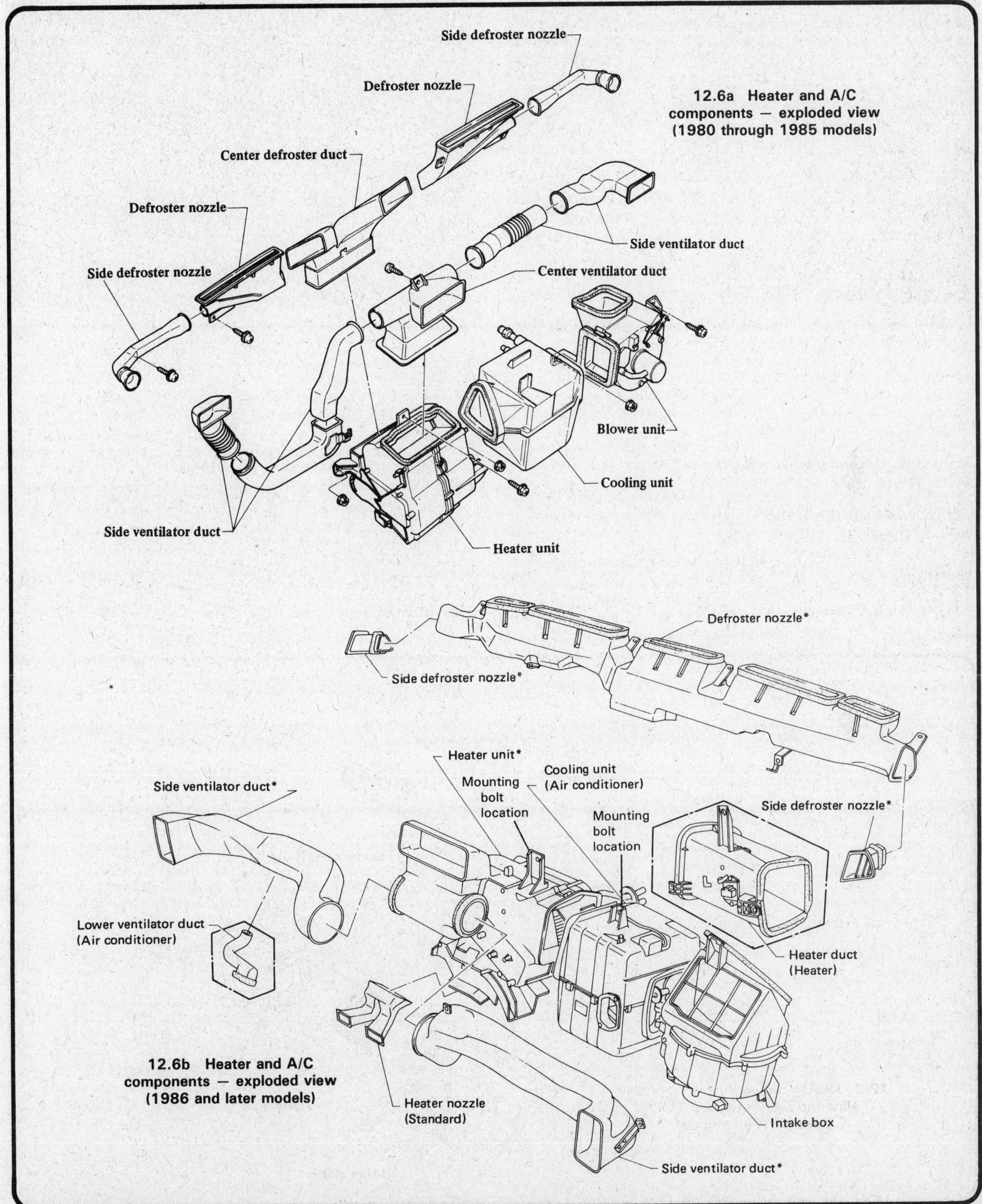

12.6a Heater and A/C components — exploded view (1980 through 1985 models)

12.6b Heater and A/C components — exploded view (1986 and later models)

3

7 Remove the heater unit mounting screws and lift the unit out **(see illustration).**
8 Once removed, the heater/air conditioning control unit can be detached (see Section 19).
9 If the heater unit must be disassembled in order to reach the heater core, disconnect the control rod from the air mix door lever, floor door lever and ventilator door lever, and remove the fasteners that attach the heater unit case halves together **(see illustration). Note:** *During reassembly the control rods must be adjusted as described in Section 19.*

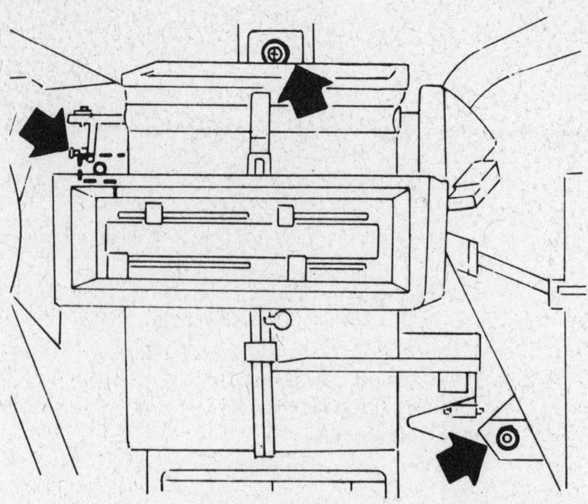

12.7 Location of the heater unit mounting screws (1980 through 1985 models)

13 Air conditioning system – general information

Refer to illustrations 13.3a and 13.3b

Note: *The air conditioning system on 1993 and later models uses the non-ozone depleting refrigerant, referred to as R-134a. The R-134a refrigerant and its lubricating oil are not compatible with the R-12 system and under no circumstances should the two different types of refrigerant and lubricating oil be intermixed. If mixed, it could result in costly compressor failure due to improper lubrication.*

The air conditioning system used in the Datsun/Nissan pick-ups maintains proper temperature by cycling the compressor on and off according to the pressure within the system, and by maintaining a mix of cooled, outside and heated air, using the same blower, heater core and outlet duct system that the heating system uses.

A fast idle control device regulates the engine idle speed when the air conditioner is operating.

The main components of the system include a belt-driven compressor, a condenser (mounted in front of the radiator), an accumulator and an evaporator **(see illustrations).**

The system operates by air (outside or recirculated) entering the evaporator core by the action of the blower, where it receives maximum cooling if the controls are set for cooling. When the air leaves the evaporator, it enters the heater/air conditioner duct assembly and by means of a manually controlled deflector, it either passes through or bypasses the heater core in the correct proportions to provide the desired vehicle temperature.

Distribution of this air into the vehicle is then regulated by a manually-operated deflector, and is directed either to the floor vents, dash vents or defroster vents according to settings. **Warning:** *In view of the toxic nature of the chemicals and gases employed in the system, no part of the system should be disconnected by the home mechanic. Due to the need for specialized discharging and charging equipment, such work should be left to a dealer service department or an automotive air conditioning shop.*

14 Air conditioning system – check and maintenance

Refer to illustration 14.3

1 The following maintenance steps should be performed on a regular basis to ensure that the air conditioner continues to operate at peak efficiency.

a) Check the tension of the A/C compressor drivebelt and adjust it if necessary (refer to Chapter I).
b) Visually inspect the condition of the hoses, looking for any cracks, hardening and other deterioration. **Note:** *Don't remove any hoses until the system has been discharged.*
c) Make sure the fins of the condenser aren't covered with foreign material, such as leaves or bugs. A soft brush and compressed air can be used to remove them.
d) Be sure the evaporator drain is open by slipping a wire into the drain tube occasionally.

2 The A/C compressor should be run about 10 minutes at least once every month. This is especially important to remember during the winter months because long-term non-use can cause hardening of the seals.

3 Due to the complexity of the air conditioning system and the special equipment required to effectively work on it, accurate troubleshooting and repair of the system cannot be done by a home mechanic and should be left to a professional. In any case, due to the toxic nature of the refrigerant, prior to disconnecting any part of the system, the vehicle should be taken to a Nissan dealer or repair shop to have the system discharged. If the system should lose its cooling action, some causes can be diagnosed by the home mechanic. Look for other symptoms of trouble such as those in the following list. In all cases, it's a good idea to have the system serviced by a professional.

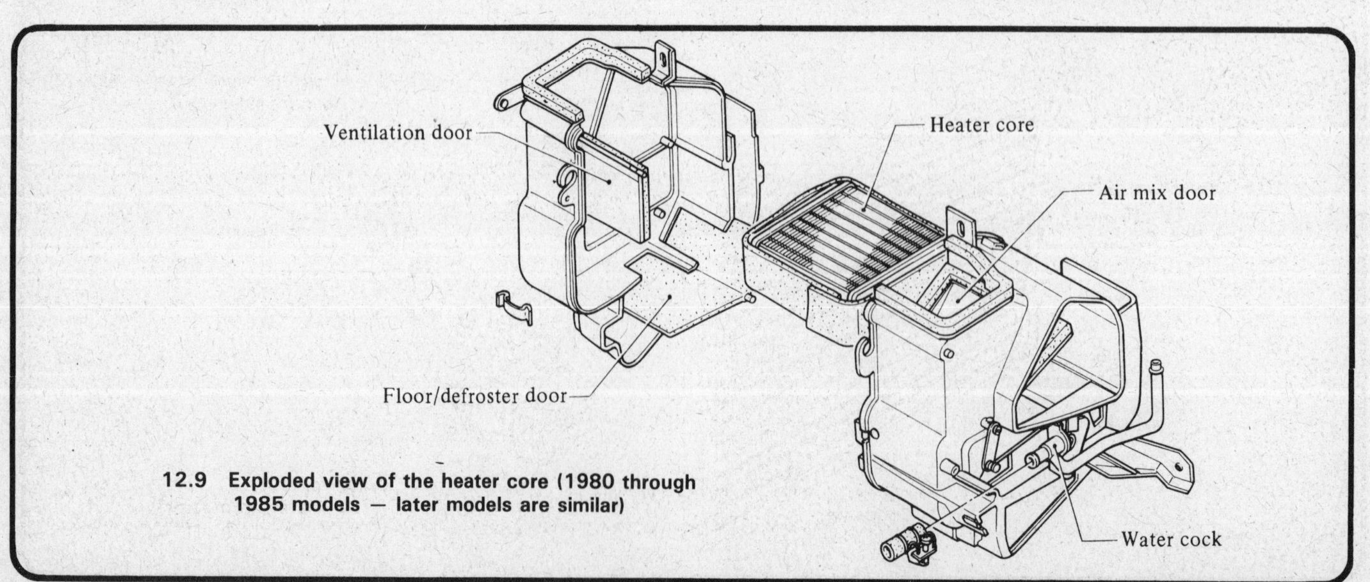

12.9 Exploded view of the heater core (1980 through 1985 models – later models are similar)

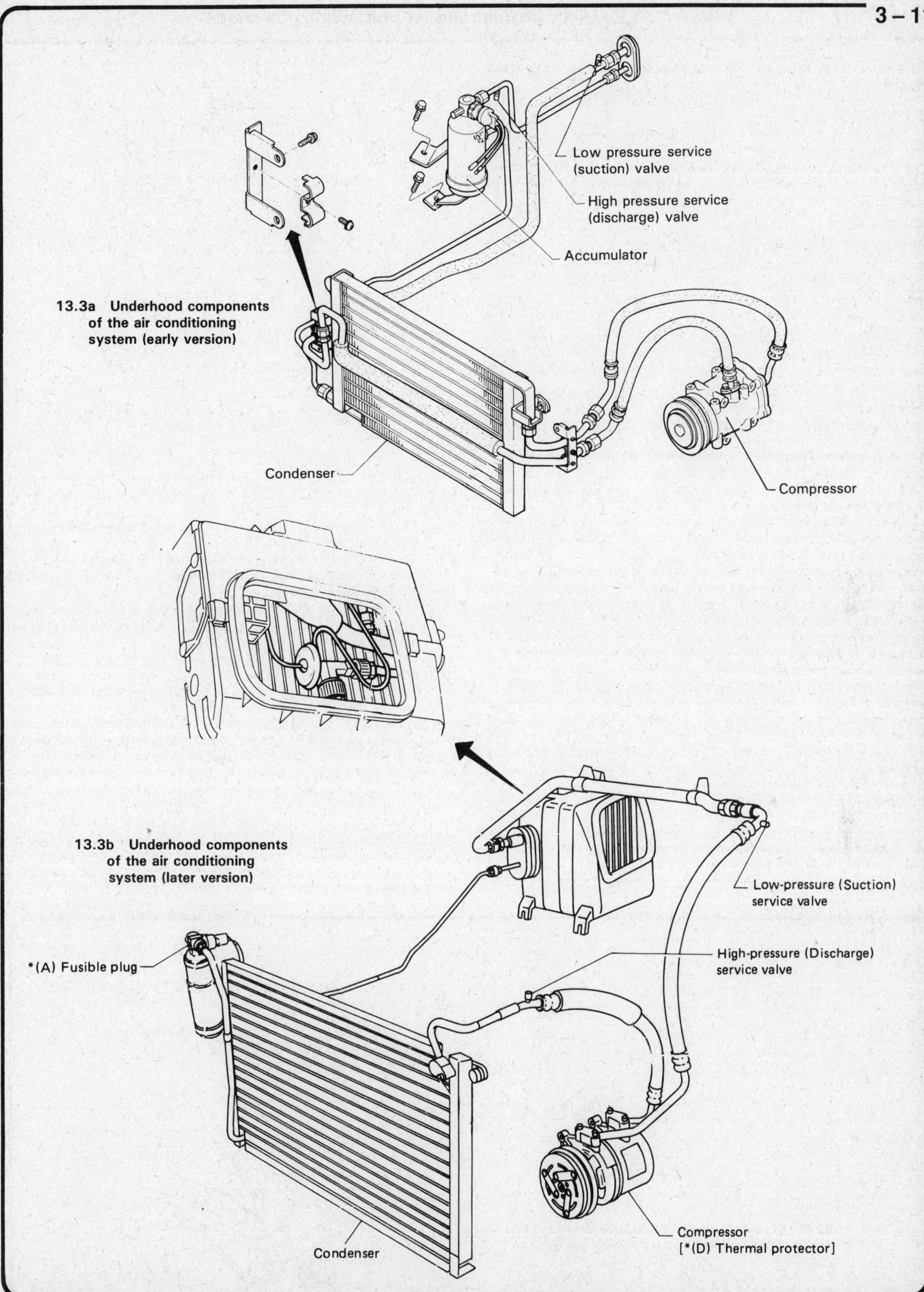

13.3a Underhood components of the air conditioning system (early version)

13.3b Underhood components of the air conditioning system (later version)

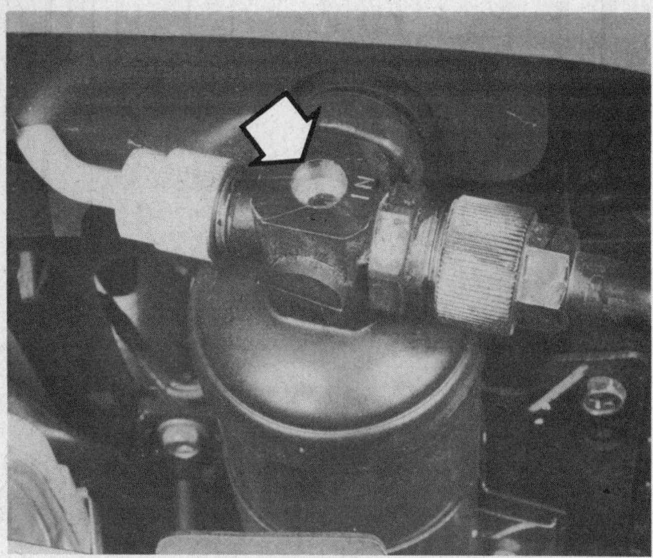

14.3 Top view of accumulator showing sight glass (arrow)

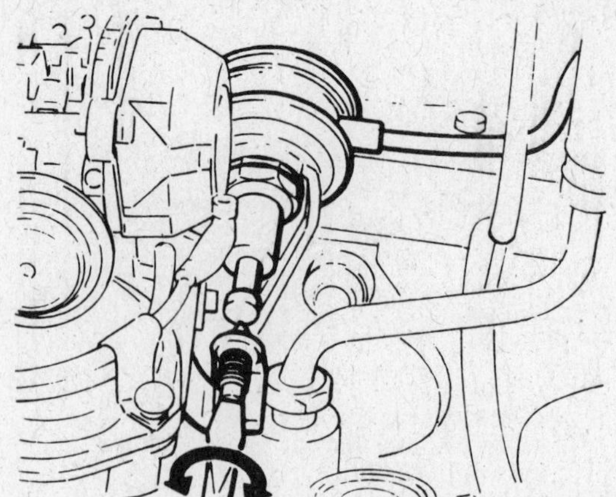

15.4a Location of the fast idle control device adjusting screw (1980 models)

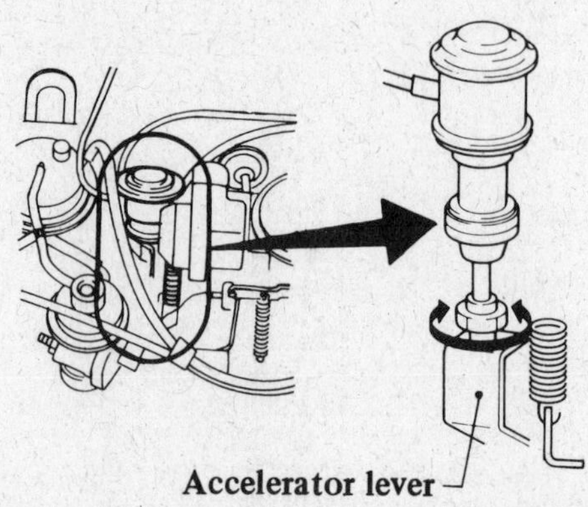

15.4b Location of the fast idle control device adjusting screw (1981 and later carburetor equipped models)

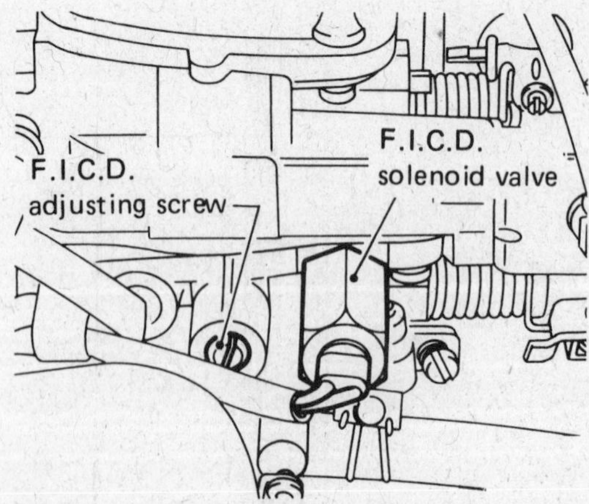

15.5 Fast idle control device – fuel injected models

a) If bubbles appear in the sight glass (located on top of the accumulator **(see illustration)**, this is an indication of either a small refrigerant leak or air in the refrigerant. If air is in the refrigerant, the accumulator is suspect and should be replaced.
b) If the view glass takes on a mist-like appearance or shows many bubbles, this indicates a large refrigerant leak. In such a case, do not operate the compressor at all until the fault has been corrected.
c) Sweating or frosting of the expansion valve inlet indicates that the expansion valve is clogged or defective. It should be cleaned or replaced as necessary.
d) Sweating or frosting of the suction line (which runs between the suction throttle valve and the compressor) indicates that the expansion valve is stuck open or defective. It should be corrected or replaced as necessary.
e) Frosting on the evaporator indicates a defective suction throttle valve, requiring replacement of the valve.
f) Frosting of the high pressure liquid line (which runs between the condenser, accumulator and expansion valve) indicates that either the drier or the high pressure line is restricted. The line will have to be cleared or the accumulator replaced.
g) The combination of bubbles in the sight glass, a very hot suction line and, possibly, overheating of the engine is an indication that either the condenser is not operating properly or the refrigerant is overcharged. Check the tension of the drivebelt and adjust if necessary (Chapter 1). Check for foreign matter covering the fins of the condenser and clean if necessary. Also check for proper operation of the cooling system. If no fault can be found in these checks, the condenser may have to be replaced.

15 Fast idle control device – adjustment

1 Start the engine and allow it to idle until it reaches normal operating temperature.
2 With the air conditioner off check that the idle speed is correctly set, and adjust it if necessary by referring to Chapter 1.
3 Turn the air conditioner on and recheck the idle speed (automatic transmission models should now be placed in the N position).

Carburetor equipped models

Refer to illustrations 15.4a and 15.4b

4 2WD models should be idling at 800 rpm and 4WD models should be idling at 950 rpm. If this isn't the case, the fast idle control device should be adjusted by turning the screw located on the accelerator lever **(see illustrations)**. Do not change the position of the idle speed screw.

Fuel injected models

Refer to illustration 15.5

5 Turn the adjustment screw **(see illustration)** until an idle speed of 850 to 950 rpm is obtained.
6 Following adjustment, depress and release the accelerator pedal several times to make sure the engine speed returns to its proper setting with the air conditioner both on and off.

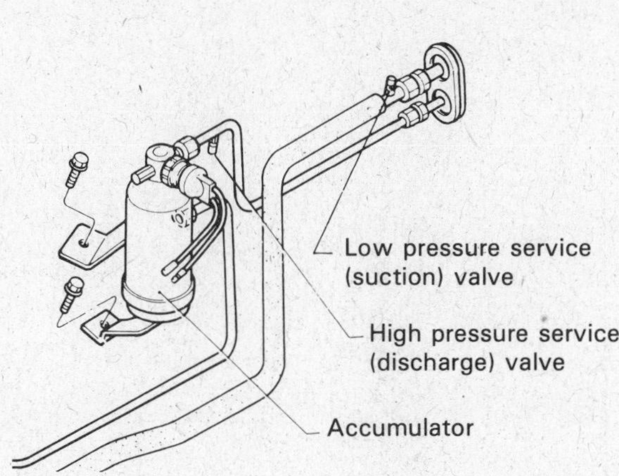

16.5a The A/C accumulator on 1980 through 1985 models is located on the right fender well

16.5b Top view of accumulator (1986 and later models)

1 Line from condenser
2 Outlet line
3 Pressure switch
4 Mounting bracket pinch bolt

16 Air conditioning accumulator – removal and installation

Refer to illustrations 16.5a and 16.5b

Warning: *Prior to disconnecting any air conditioning lines anywhere in the system, the vehicle should be taken to a Nissan dealer or an automotive air conditioning repair shop to have the system depressurized. Due to the toxic nature of the chemicals and gases used in the system, this is not a job for the home mechanic.*

1 Disconnect the negative battery cable from the battery.
2 On 1986 and later models, remove the grille (Chapter 11).
3 Unplug the wires from the pressure switch.
4 Disconnect the refrigerant lines from the accumulator. Use a back-up wrench to keep from twisting the line.
5 Unbolt the accumulator bracket and lift the accumulator out **(see illustrations)**
6 Installation is the reverse of the removal procedure. When reconnecting the hoses be sure that new O-rings are used and that they are installed properly.
7 Once all air conditioning lines have been securely connected the vehicle must once again be taken to a Nissan dealer or repair shop to have the system charged.

17 Air conditioning compressor – removal and installation

Refer to illustrations 17.5, 17.7 and 17.9

Warning: *Prior to disconnecting any air conditioning lines anywhere in the system, the vehicle should be taken to a Nissan dealer or an automotive air conditioning repair shop to have the system depressurized. Due to the toxic nature of the chemicals and gases used in the system, this not a job for the home mechanic.*

1 Operate the compressor, if possible, for about ten minutes at idle speed.
2 The air conditioning controls should be set at maximum cooling and on the high blower speed, with all windows open. This will return the oil within the system to the compressor.
3 Disconnect the negative battery cable from the battery.
4 On 1981 and later models, remove the distributor for clearance. If necessary, refer to Chapter 5.
5 Loosen the bolt at the center of the compressor idler pully and turn the adjusting bolt to loosen the A/C compressor drivebelt **(see illustration).**
6 Remove the drivebelt from the compressor.
7 Disconnect both lines at the compressor **(see illustration).**

17.5 V6 engine A/C idler pulley drivebelt adjuster (loosen A before turning adjuster B)

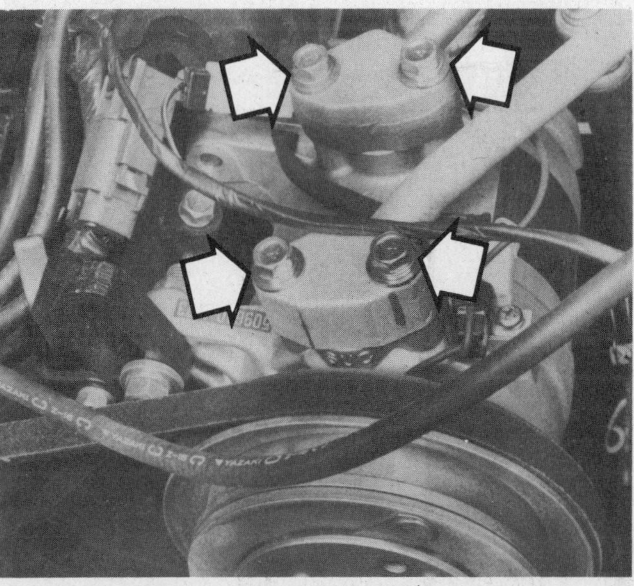

17.7 The V6 engine A/C compressor lines can be detached after removing the bolts (arrows)

3

8 Disconnect all wires attached to the compressor.
9 Remove the bolts that retain the compressor to the bracket and detach the compressor **(see illustration)**.
10 Remove the compressor from the engine compartment. **Note:** *The compressor should not be left on its side or upside-down for more than 10 minutes at a time, as compressor oil could enter the low pressure chambers and cause internal damage. If this should happen, the oil can be expelled from the chambers by positioning the compressor right side up and hand cranking it several times.*
11 Installation is the reverse of the removal procedure. When reconnecting the lines to the compressor be sure to use new O-rings at each connection.
12 Once the compressor and all A/C lines have been securely connected, the vehicle must once again be taken to a Nissan dealer or an air conditioning shop to have the system charged.

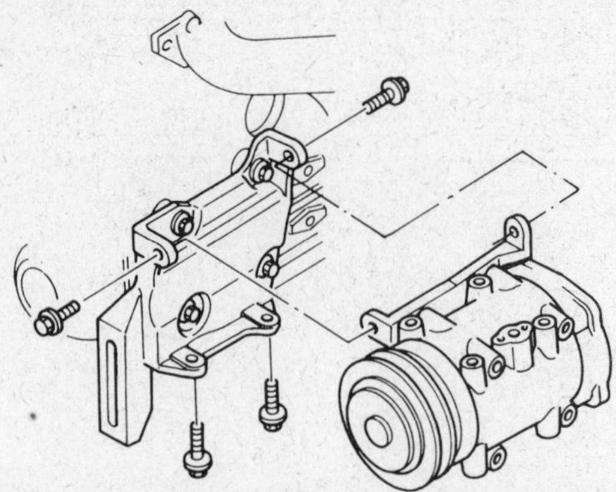

17.9 Mounting arrangement of the A/C compressor and bracket (typical)

18 Air conditioning condenser – removal and installation

Warning: *Prior to disconnecting any air conditioning lines anywhere in the system, the vehicle should be taken to a Nissan dealer or an automotive air conditioning repair shop to have the system depressurized. Due to the toxic nature of the chemicals and gases used in the system, this is not a job for the home mechanic.*

1 Remove the grille as described in Chapter 11 and the optional grille guard if so equipped.
2 Remove the radiator as described in Section 4.
3 Remove the left headlight assembly.
4 Disconnect all tubes and and rubber A/C hoses leading from the condenser.
5 Remove the bolts that hold the condenser to the body and lift out the condenser.
6 If the condenser fins or air passages are clogged with foreign material, such as dirt, insects or leaves, use compressed air and a soft brush to clean the condenser. If the condenser is in need of other repairs, have a professional radiator shop or Nissan dealer perform the work.
7 Installation is the reverse of the removal procedure. When reconnecting the hoses be sure that new O-rings are used and that they are installed correctly.
8 Once all A/C lines have been securely connected, the vehicle must once again be taken to a Nissan dealer or an air conditioning shop to have the system charged.

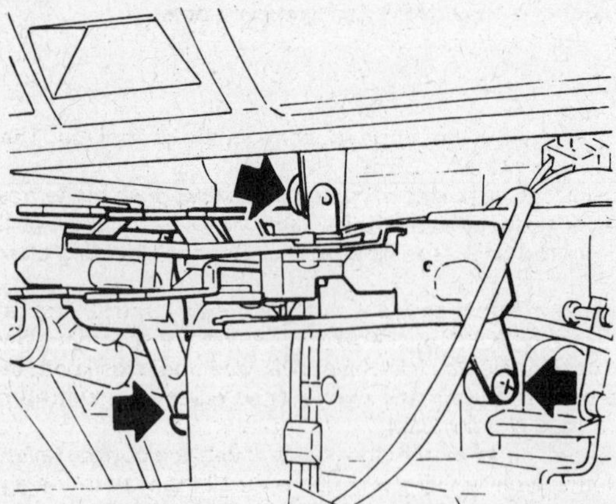

19.4a Location of the heater/air conditioning control unit mounting screws (1980 through 1985 models)

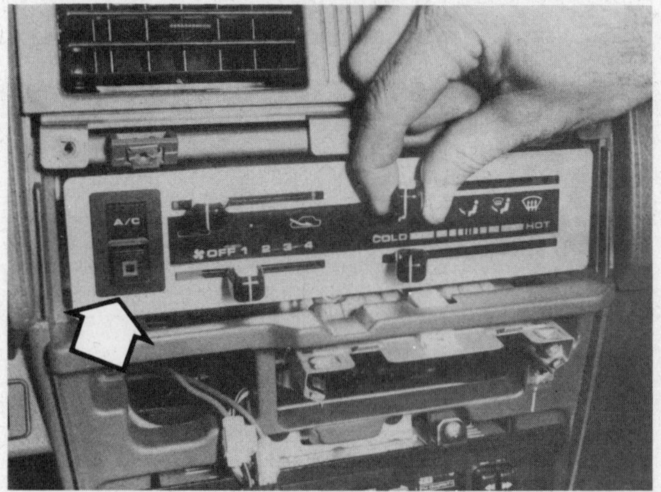

19.3 Pull the control knobs straight off – A/C switch (arrow) pulls straight out (1986 and later models)

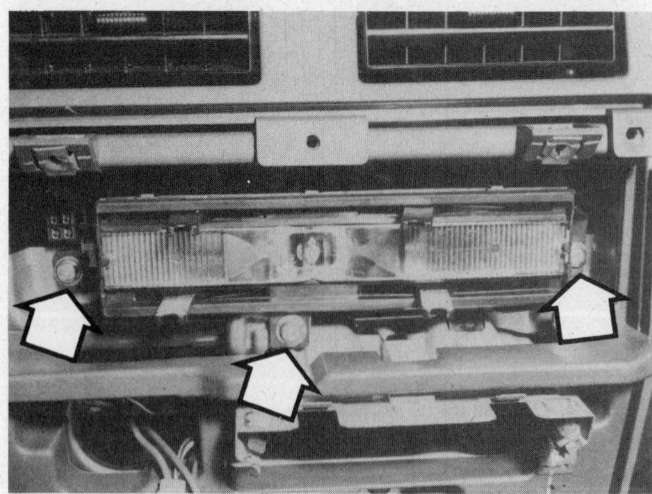

19.4b Remove the screws (arrows) to take out the control assembly (1986 and later models)

19 Heater/A/C control assembly – removal, installation and adjustment

Removal and installation

Refer to illustrations 19.3, 19.4a and 19.4b

1 Disconnect the negative battery cable and remove the package tray from under the dash (if equipped).
2 Disconnect the control cables from the heater unit and the blower unit. **Note:** *The air mix door/water cock control cable on air conditioner equipped models is most easily disconnected with the temperature control lever set in the Cold position.*
3 Detach the knobs from the control levers **(see illustration)** and remove the control unit panel.
4 Remove the heater/A/C control unit mounting screws **(see illustrations)**. Lower the unit from the dash and unplug any wiring harnesses leading to the unit.

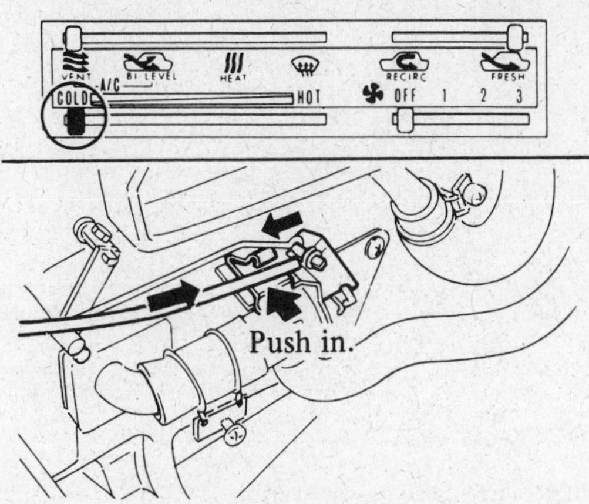

19.8 **Procedure for adjusting the air mix door/water cock cable**

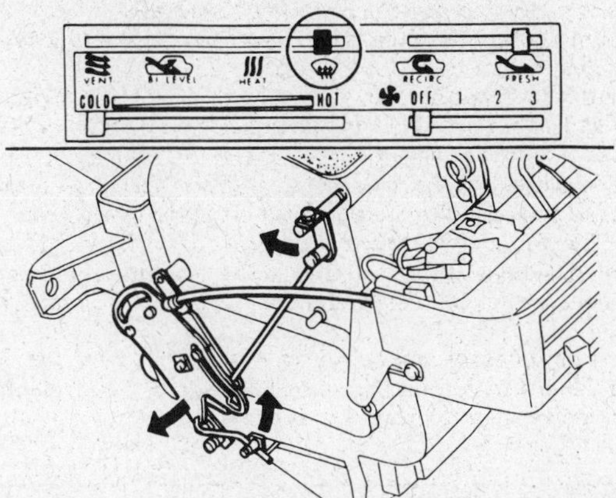

19.9a **Procedure for adjusting the floor door/ventilator door cable**

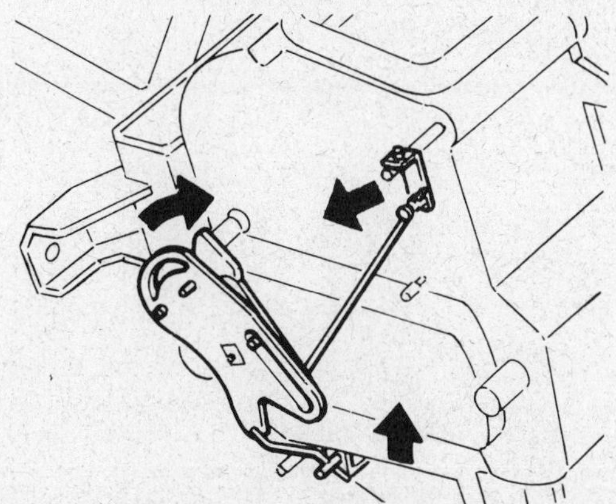

19.9b The side link should be held in the position shown with both the floor door and ventilator door closed before connecting the control rods

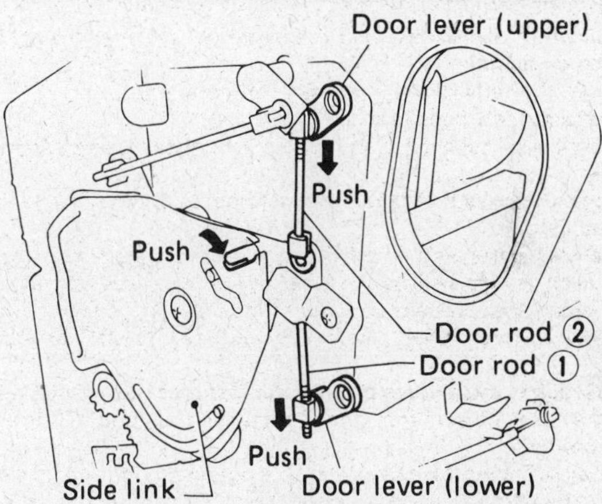

19.12 Procedure for adjusting the ventilator door control rod (1986 and later models)

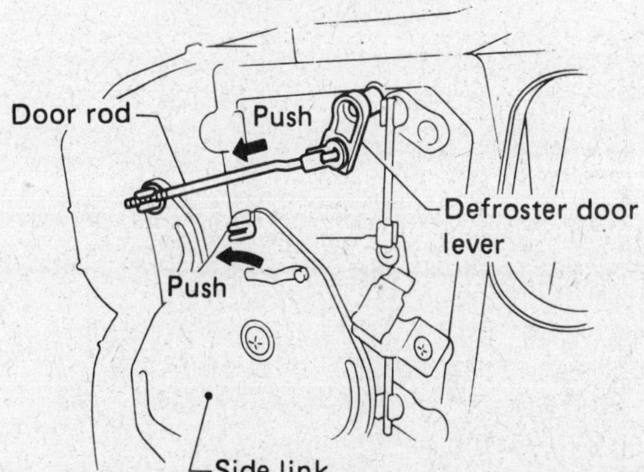

19.13 Procedure for adjusting the defroster door control rod (1986 and later models)

5 The fan switch can be tested by referring to Chapter 13, if necessary. For replacement, it can be detached from the rest of the control unit.

6 Installation is the reverse of the removal procedure. **Note:** *Prior to reconnecting the control cables to the heater and blower units, they must be adjusted as follows.*

Adjustment

1980 through 1985 models

Refer to illustrations 19.8, 19.9a and 19.9b

7 To adjust the air mix door rod, first push the air mix door lever until the air mix door is tilted as far as possible toward the heater core. With the lever held in that position, connect the control rod. The water cock should be closed.

8 To adjust the air mix door/water cock cable, push the temperature control lever to the left, push the cable housing toward the firewall and hold the rod back **(see illustration)**. Snap the holding clamp into place.

9 To adjust the floor door and ventilator door control, first raise the side link all the way in the direction shown in the accompanying illustration. While holding the side link in this position, close both the floor door and ventilator door and connect the respective control rods to the levers **(see illustrations)**.

10 To adjust the air intake door cable, push the control lever to the left, push the cable housing and flap lever all the way to the right and install the holding clamp over the cable.

1986 and later models

Refer to illustrations 19.12, 19.13, 19.14, 19.15, 19.16 and 19.17

11 When adjusting the ventilator door rod and defroster door rod, disconnect the air control cable from the side link first, and then adjust the door rod. Reconnect the air control cable and readjust it.

12 To adjust the ventilator door control rod, move the side link in the direction of the arrow **(see illustration)**. With the upper and lower ventilator door levers held in the direction of the arrow, connect rods 1 and 2 to their corresponding ventilator door levers in that order.

13 To adjust the defroster door control rod, move the side link in the direction of the arrow **(see illustration)**. Connect the rod to the side link while pushing the defroster door lever in the direction of the arrow.

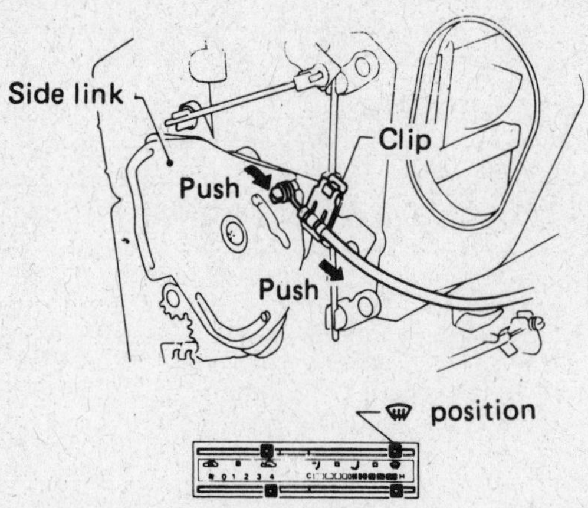

19.14 Procedure for adjusting the air control cable (1986 and later models)

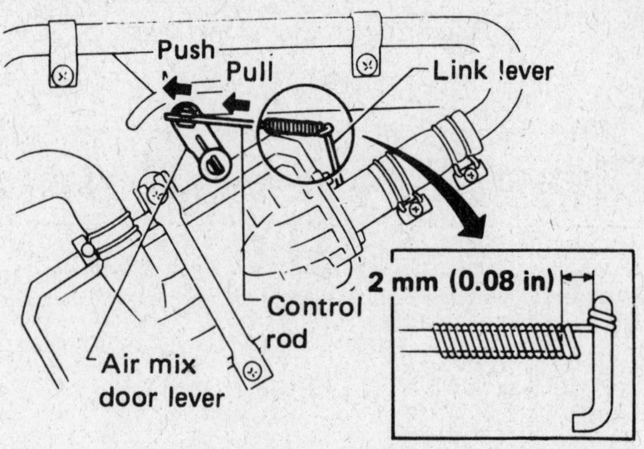

19.15 Procedure for adjusting the water cock control rod (1986 and later models)

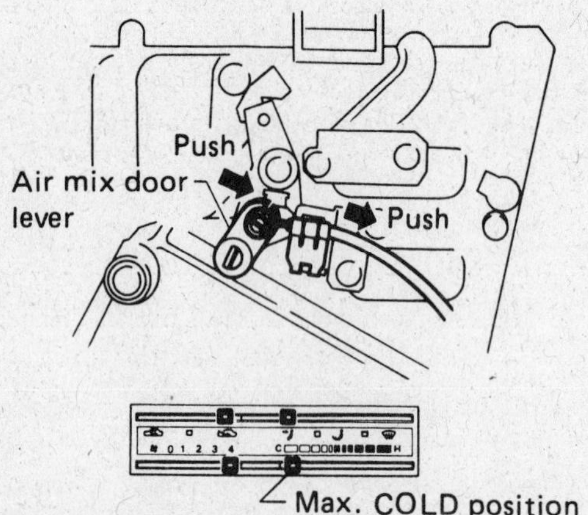

19.16 Procedure for adjusting the temperature control cable (1986 and later models)

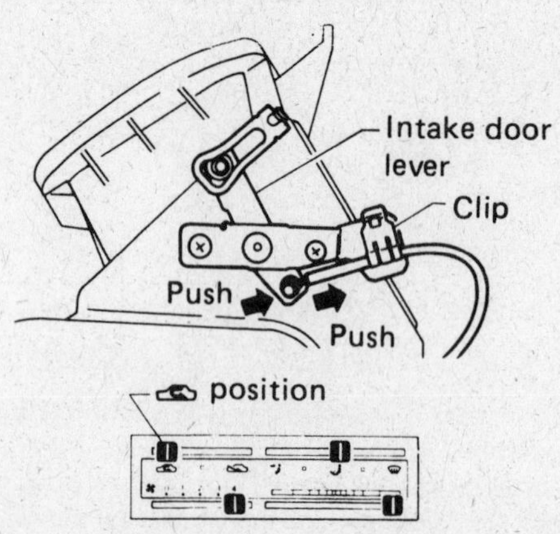

19.17 Procedure for adjusting the intake door control cable (1986 and later models)

14 To adjust the air control cable, push the cable outer case and side link in the direction of the arrow and clamp the cable **(see illustration)**.
15 To adjust the water-cock control rod, first disconnect the temperature control cable from the air mix door lever and then adjust the control rod. Reconnect the temperature control cable and readjust it. Push the air mix door lever in the direction of the arrow **(see illustration)**. Pull the water-cock control rod in the direction of the arrow to provide a clearance of about 0.08-inch between the ends of the rod and link lever and connect the rod to the door lever.
16 To adjust the temperature control cable, push the control to the left **(see illustration)**, push the outer cable and air mix door lever in the direction of the arrows and clamp the cable in position.
17 To adjust the intake door control cable, push the control to the left **(see illustration)**, push the outer cable housing and intake door lever in the direction of the arrow and clamp the cable in position.
18 Check the operation of all the controls, and complete the installation by reversing the disassembly sequence.

Chapter 4 Fuel and exhaust systems

Contents

Specifications

4

Carburetor

Model	
1980 models	DCH340*
1981 through 1983 models	DCR342*
1984 models (Z24 engine)	
California	
Standard	DFP384-3
Heavy duty	DFP384-12
4WD	DFP383-3
49-state	
Standard	DCR384-3
Heavy duty	DCR384-11A
4WD	DCR384-21A
Canada	
Standard	DCR384-5
Heavy duty	DCR384-15
4WD	DCR384-25
1984 models (Z20 engine – all)	DCR342-8
1985 models (Z24 engine)	
California	
2WD – manual transmission	DFP384-5
2WD – automatic transmission	DFP384-6
4WD	DFP384-5
49-state	
2WD – manual transmission	DFP384-7
2WD – automatic transmission	DFP384-8
4WD	DFP384-7

** This is the general model number. Slightly different carburetors are used, depending on vehicle type and geographic location. The specific model number of your carburetor is stamped on it.*

Model	
1985 models (Z24 engine)	
Canada	
2WD – manual transmission	DCR384-7
2WD – automatic transmission	DCR384-8
4WD	DCR384-26
1985 models (Z20 engine – all)	DFP342-11
Automatic choke heater unit resistance	3.7 to 8.9 ohms
Fuel level adjustments	
Top of float-to-inside top of float chamber	0.283 in (7.2 mm)
Float seal-to-needle valve distance	0.051 to 0.067 in (1.3 to 1.7 mm)

Carburetor (continued)

Vacuum break adjustment	
1980 US models	0.0969 to 0.1205 in (2.46 to 3.06 mm)
1980 Canada models	0.102 to 0.126 in (2.6 to 3.2 mm)
1981 through 1983 California models	0.1228 to 0.1465 in (3.12 to 3.72 mm)
1981 through 1983 49-state models	0.1031 to 0.1268 in (2.62 to 3.22 mm)
1984 models	
California	0.1220 to 0.1457 in (3.10 to 3.70 mm)
49-state	
Z24 engine	0.0965 to 0.1201 in (2.45 to 3.0 mm)
Z20 engine	0.1031 to 0.1268 in (2.61 to 3.22 mm)
Canada	
2WD standard	0.0913 to 0.1150 in (2.32 to 2.92 mm)
4WD and heavy duty	0.0965 to 0.1201 in (2.45 to 3.0 mm)
1985 models	
USA	
Z24 engine	0.1339 ± 0.0118 in (3.40 ± 0.30 mm)
Z20 engine	0.1346 ± 0.0118 in (3.42 ± 0.30 mm)
Canada	
2WD standard	0.1031 ± 0.0118 in (2.62 ± 0.30 mm)
4WD and heavy duty	0.1083 ± 0.0118 in (2.75 ± 0.30 mm)
Choke unloader adjustment	
1980 through 1983 models	0.0807 to 0.1122 in (2.05 to 2.85 mm)
1984 and 1985 models	0.0965 ± 0.0157 in (2.45 ± 0.4 mm)
Dashpot adjustment	
1980 models – automatic transmission	1650 to 1850 rpm
1980 Canada models – manual transmission	1900 to 2100 rpm
1981 through 1983 models – automatic transmission	1400 to 1600 rpm
1984 and 1985 models	
Manual transmission	1800 ± 200 rpm
Automatic transmission	1500 ± 200 rpm
Throttle valve interlock opening adjustment	
1980 through 1983 models	0.2906 to 0.3299 in (7.38 to 8.38 mm)
1984 and 1985 models	
Z24 engine	0.3295 ± 0.0197 in (8.37 ± 0.5 mm)
Z20 engine	0.3102 ± 0.0197 in (7.88 ± 0.5 mm)
Fast idle adjustment	
Manual transmission (all models)	0.0319 to 0.0374 in (0.81 to 0.95 mm)
Automatic transmission	
1980 models	0.0402 to 0.0457 in (1.02 to 1.16 mm)
1981 through 1985 models	
California	0.0386 to 0.0441 in (0.98 to 1.12 mm)
49-state	0.0394 to 0.0433 in (1.00 to 1.10 mm)

Fuel injection system

Fast idle inspection and adjustment (TBI systems)	
Clearance G	0.020 to 0.118 in (0.5 to 3.0 mm)
Adjust clearance G	0.031 to 0.047 in (0.8 to 1.2 mm)
Fast idle inspection and adjustment (MPFI systems)(KA24E engine)	
Manual transmission	0.091 in (2.3 mm)
Automatic transmission	0.083 in (2.1 mm)
FICD inspection and adjustment	
Idle speed (A/C off)	
Manual transmission	
Four-cylinder	900 ± 50 rpm
V6	800 ± 50 rpm
Automatic transmission	
Four-cylinder	650 ± 50 rpm
V6	700 ± 50 rpm
Idle speed (A/C on)	900 ± 50 rpm with transmission in Neutral
Dashpot touch speed	
Four-cylinder	1600 to 2000 rpm
V6	1300 to 1500 rpm

Fuel pump

Mechanical pump pressure	3.0 to 3.8 psi
Mechanical pump volume (amount per minute at 1000 rpm)	
1980 models	33.8 fl oz (1000 ml) (35.2 Imp fl oz)
1981 models	57.5 fl oz (1700 ml) (59.8 Imp fl oz)
1982 models	50.7 fl oz (1500 ml) (52.8 Imp fl oz)
Electric pump pressure	
Carburetor	
Through 1983 models	3.1 to 3.8 psi
1984 and 1985 models	2.7 to 3.4 psi
Fuel injection (TBI systems)	36.3 psi

Fuel injection (MPFI systems)	
V6 engine	
With vacuum	34 psi
Without vacuum	43 psi
KA24E	
With vacuum	33 psi
Without vacuum	43 psi
Electric pump volume – carburetor only	47.3 fl oz (1400 ml) (49.3 Imp fl oz) per minute

Torque specifications

	Ft-lbs
Throttle body mounting nuts	
Through 1992	9 to 13
1993	
Step 1	6.5 to 8.0
Step 2	13 to 16
Anti-dieseling solenoid valve mounting bolts	19
Fuel tank drain plug	40
Fuel tank rear bracket mounting bolts	38
Fuel tank mounting bolts	
Through 1990	7
1991 and later	20 to 26
Catalytic converter mounting bolts	
Through 1990	27
1991 and later	
All except V6 Pathfinder	23 to 31
V6 Pathfinder	32 to 41
Front exhaust pipe-to-exhaust manifold bolts	
Through 1990	16
1991 and later	
All except V6 Pathfinder	20 to 27
V6 Pathfinder only	30 to 35

1 Fuel system – general information

Carburetor equipped vehicles

Carburetor equipped versions of this vehicle use a fuel system of conventional design. Simply put, fuel is pumped from the fuel tank, through the fuel lines and fuel filter into the carburetor, where it is mixed with air for combustion. The fuel system, as well as the exhaust system, is interrelated with and works in conjuction with various emissions control systems covered in Chapter 6. Thus, some elements that relate directly to the fuel system and carburetor functions are covered in that chapter.

All carburetors are of the down-draft, two-barrel type. Specific information on the carburetor can be found in Section 9.

Two types of fuel pumps are used. A conventional diaphragm-type, mechanical pump, is attached to the front right side of the cylinder head on earlier models. The operating arm of the pump extends into the cylinder head where it is actuated by an eccentric cam mounted on the front of the camshaft. This eccentric cam, when rotating, moves the operating arm back and forth, providing the pump action.

An electric pump is used on later models. It is mounted to the frame rail on the right underside of the truck.

The fuel tank is located under the rear bed of the truck. Besides the fuel feed line leading to the fuel filter and pump, the tank also has an emission vent hose leading to the charcoal canister, an air ventilation line that connects back into the fuel filler hose and a fuel return hose to route excess fuel back to the tank.

Fuel injected vehicles

Newer vehicles are fuel injected. On these models, fuel is pumped from the fuel tank by an in-tank electric fuel pump through metal fuel lines and a fuel filter to a pair of fuel injectors located inside a throttle body housing mounted on top of the intake manifold. For more information on fuel injected vehicles, see Section 13. **Warning:** *Always relieve the fuel pressure (see Section 14) before attempting to service the components on a fuel injected vehicle.*

2 Fuel filter replacement

Because replacement of the fuel filter is part of the routine maintenance schedule, refer to Chapter 1 for this procedure.

3 Idle speed check and adjustment

Since the idle speed adjustment is an integral part of a tune-up operation, information on this procedure is included in Chapter 1.

4 Fuel lines – repair and replacement

Refer to illustrations 4.1a and 4.1b

Warning: *On fuel injected vehicles, the fuel system pressure must be relieved before disconnecting fuel lines and fittings (see Section 14). Gasoline is extremely flammable, so extra precautions must be taken when working on any part of the fuel system. DO NOT smoke or allow open flames or bare light bulbs near the work area. Also, don't work in a garage where a natural gas appliance such as a water heater or clothes dryer is present. Finally, prior to any operation in which a fuel line line will be disconnected, remove the negative cable from the battery to eliminate the possibility of sparks occurring while fuel vapor is present.*

1 If a section of metal fuel line must be replaced, only brazed seamless steel should be used, as copper or aluminum tubing doesn't have enough durability to withstand normal engine vibrations **(see illustrations)**.

2 If only one section of a metal fuel line is damaged, it can be cut out and replaced with a piece of rubber hose. The rubber hose should be cut four inches (100 mm) longer than the section it's replacing, so there is about two inches of overlap between the rubber and metal tubing at either end of the section. Hose clamps should be used to secure both ends of the repaired section.

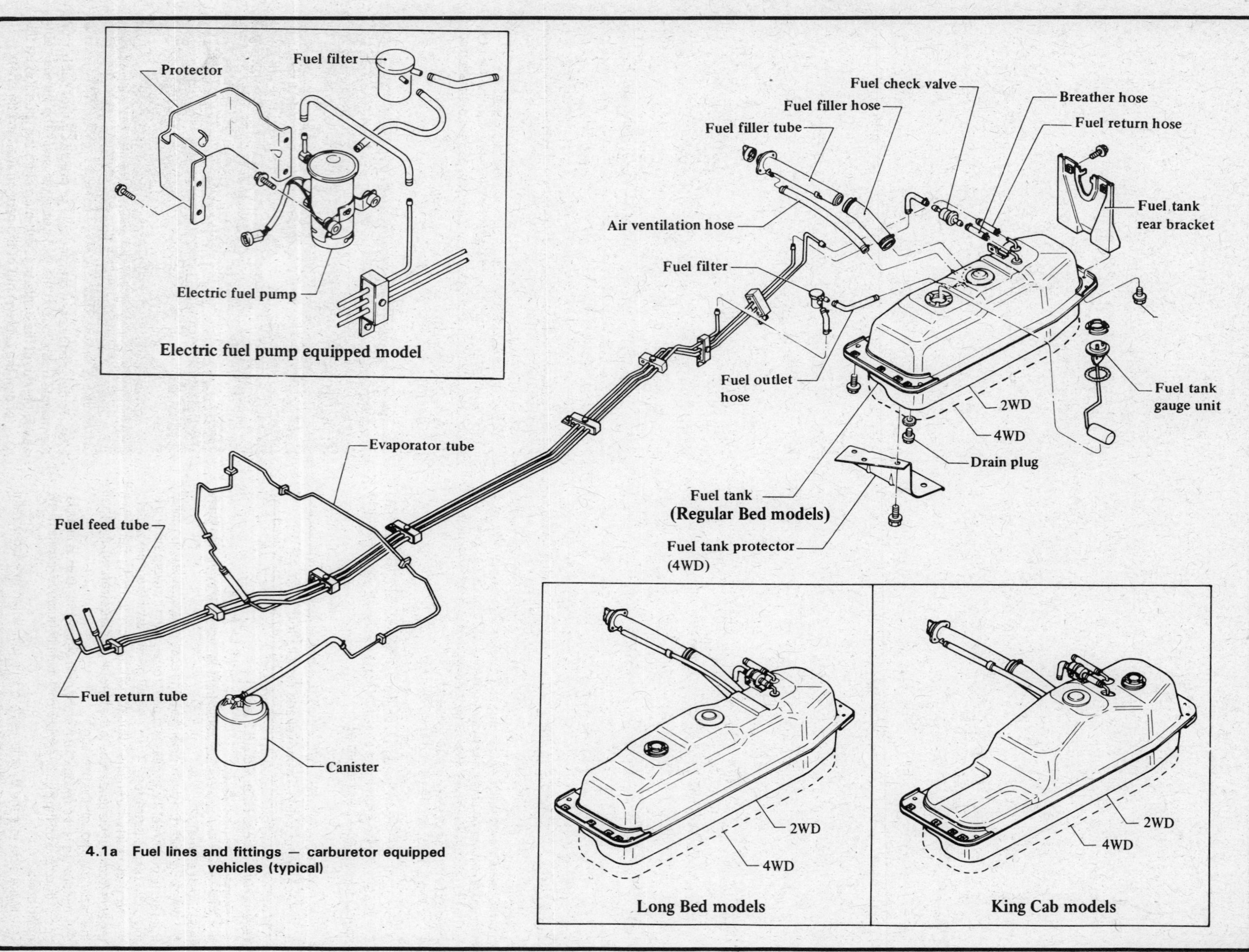

4.1a Fuel lines and fittings — carburetor equipped vehicles (typical)

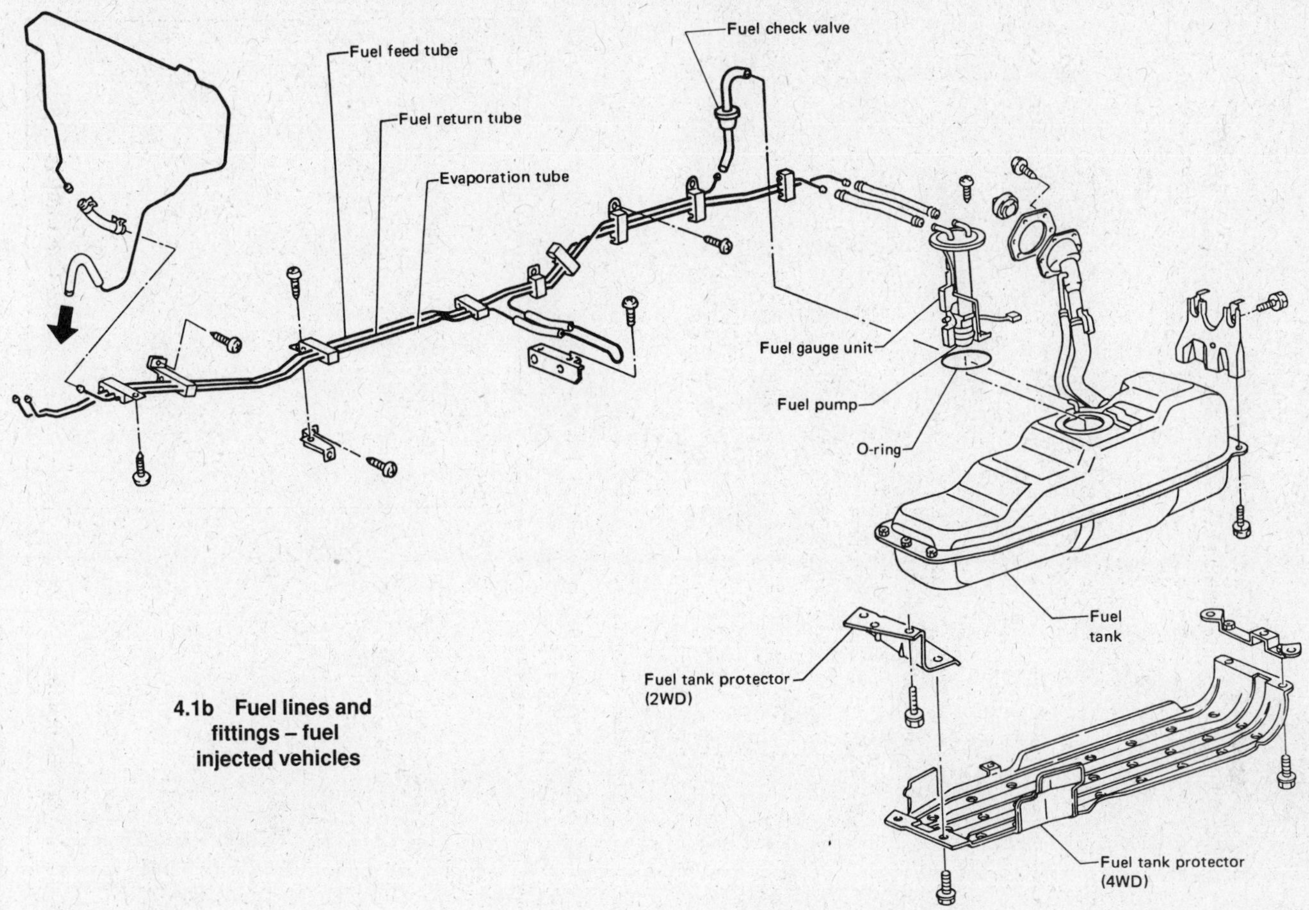

Fuel feed tube
Fuel return tube
Evaporation tube
Fuel check valve
Fuel gauge unit
Fuel pump
O-ring
Fuel tank
Fuel tank protector (2WD)
Fuel tank protector (4WD)

4.1b Fuel lines and fittings – fuel injected vehicles

3 If a section of metal line longer than six inches is being removed, use a combination of metal tubing and rubber hose so that the hose lengths will not be longer than 10-inches. **Warning:** *Never use rubber hose within four inches of any part of the exhaust system!*
4 Always replace O-rings and hose clamps.
5 Do not kink or twist hoses and tubes when installing them.
6 To avoid damage to hoses, do not tighten hose clamps excessively.
7 Always run the engine and check for leaks before driving the vehicle after fuel lines have been serviced.

5 Accelerator cable – removal and installation

Refer to illustrations 5.2a, 5.2b, 5.3 and 5.4

1 Remove the air cleaner.
2 Disconnect the accelerator cable from the carburetor/throttle body **(see illustrations)**.
3 Working under the dash, disengage the accelerator cable nylon collar from the upper end of the accelerator pedal by pushing it toward the end of the cable **(see illustration)**. Then disengage the cable from the pedal.
4 Moving back to the engine compartment, remove the bolts that attach the accelerator cable guide tube to the firewall **(see illustration)**, then pull the cable out through the opening.
5 Installation is the reverse of the removal procedure. During installation of the cable on the pedal, apply a coat of multi-purpose grease to the nylon collar.
6 Make sure that the throttle valve opens fully when the accelerator pedal is fully depressed and returns to idle when released.
7 Adjust accelerator pedal free play by turning the adjusting nut.
8 On automatic transmission models, make sure that the kickdown switch rod is fully pushed in when the accelerator pedal is depressed completely.

5.2a To detach the accelerator cable or cruise control cable from the throttle body, loosen the locknut(s) (arrows) and lift the cable assembly out of the cable bracket, then slide the fitting(s) on the end of the cable(s) out of the cam on the throttle shaft

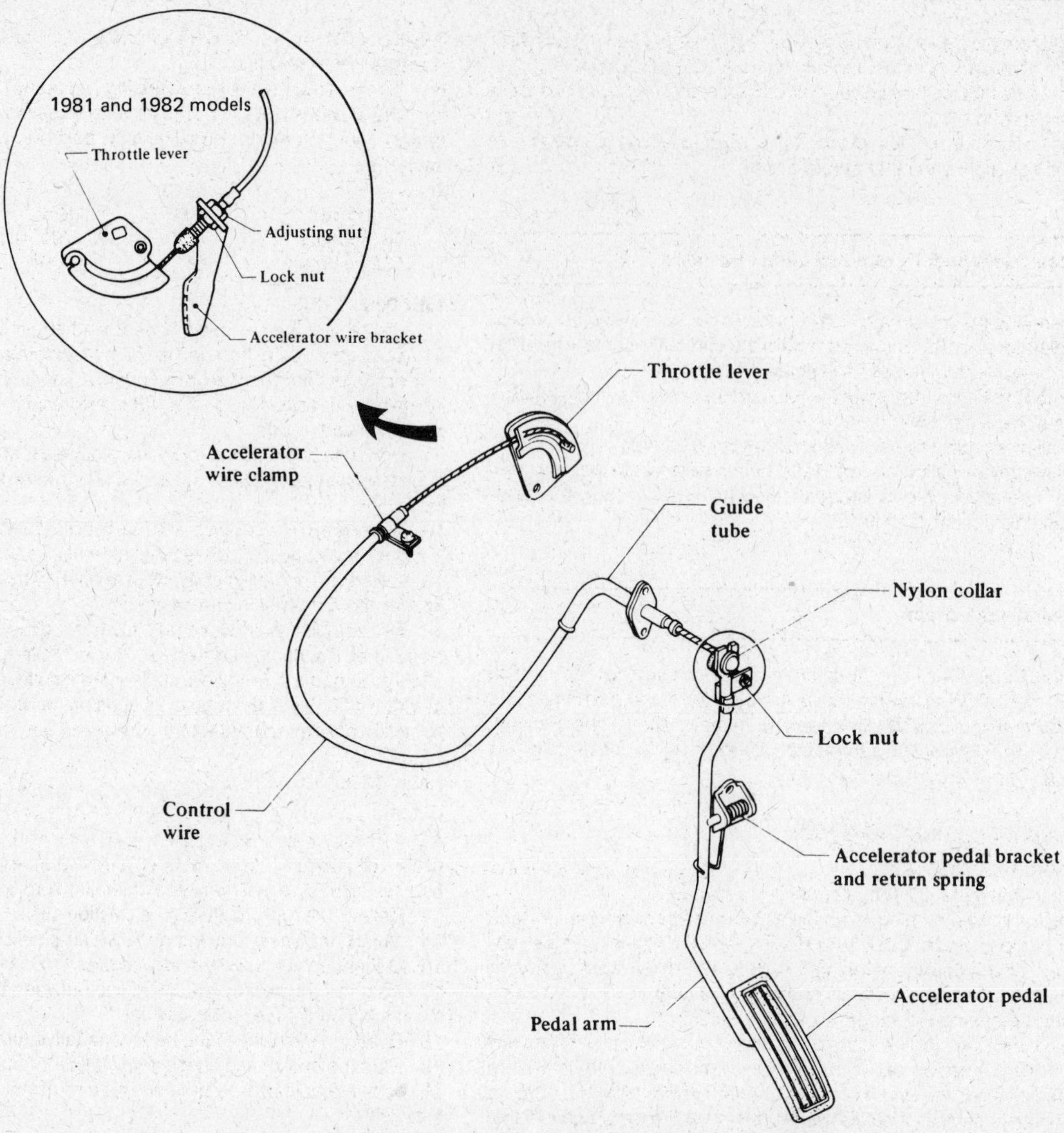

1981 and 1982 models
Throttle lever
Adjusting nut
Lock nut
Accelerator wire bracket

Throttle lever
Accelerator wire clamp
Guide tube
Nylon collar
Lock nut
Control wire
Accelerator pedal bracket and return spring
Accelerator pedal
Pedal arm

5.2b Accelerator pedal and cable components – carburetor equipped vehicles (typical)

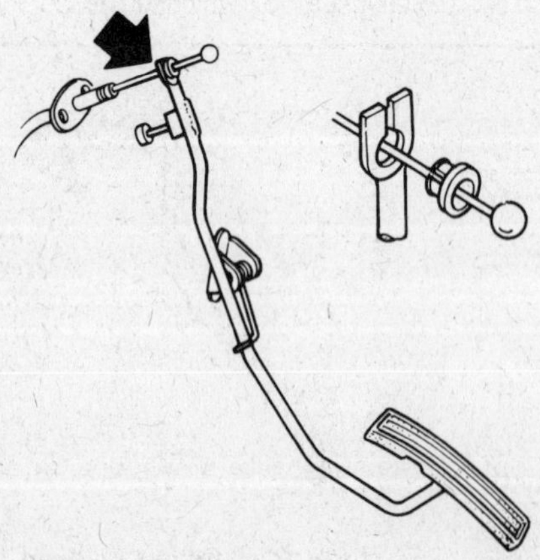

5.3 To disconnect the accelerator cable from the pedal, slide the nylon collar toward the end of the cable and disengage the cable

5.4 To detach the accelerator cable from the engine compartment firewall, remove these two bolts (arrows) (this arrangement is typical of all models)

9 On Automatic Speed Control Device (ASCD) equipped models, first adjust the accelerator cable, then adjust the ASCD cable.
10 Make sure that the throttle cable does not contact any components in close proximity to it.
11 Apply a light coat of multi-purpose grease to all sliding or friction surfaces. Do not apply grease to the wire itself.

6 Accelerator pedal – removal and installation

1 Disengage the accelerator cable nylon collar from the upper end of the accelerator pedal by pushing it toward the end of the cable. Then disengage the cable from the pedal **(see illustration 5.3)**.
2 Remove the bolts that retain the accelerator pedal mounting bracket and lift out the pedal.
3 Installation is the reverse of the removal procedure.
4 Following installation on automatic transmission equipped models, check the operation of the transmission's kickdown switch, adjust it if necessary as described in Chapter 7.

7 Fuel pump – check

Warning: *Gasoline is extremely flammable, so extra precautions must be taken when working on any part of the fuel system. Make sure the engine is cool. Don't smoke or allow open flames or bare light bulbs near the work area. Also, do not work in a garage if a natural gas-type appliance with a pilot light is present.*

Carburetor equipped vehicles

Mechanical pump

1 Check that there is adequate fuel in the fuel tank.
2 With the engine running, examine all fuel lines between the fuel tank and fuel pump for leaks, loose connections, kinks or flattening in the rubber hoses. Do this quickly, before the engine gets hot. Air leaks upstream of the fuel pump can seriously affect the pump's output.
3 Check the pump diaphragm flange for leaks.
4 Disconnect the fuel line at the carburetor. Disconnect the ignition coil wire from the coil and ground it on the engine block (use a jumper wire to prevent sparks) so the engine can be cranked without it firing. Place a clean container such as a coffee can at the end of the detached fuel line and crank the engine for several seconds. There should be a strong spurt of gasoline from the line on every second revolution.
5 If little or no gasoline emerges from the line during engine cranking, then either the line is clogged or the fuel pump is not working properly. Disconnect the fuel line from the pump and blow air through it to be sure the line is clear. If the line is clear then the pump is suspect and needs to be replaced with a new one.
6 A more accurate method of testing fuel pump flow capacity is to perform the previous test using a measuring container and a watch. At 1000 rpm in one minute, the pump should be able to pump the following amounts:

	Fl oz	ml	Imperial fl oz
1980 models	33.8	1000	35.2
1981 models	57.5	1700	59.8
1982 models	50.7	1500	52.8

Electric pump

7 Disconnect the fuel outlet hose from the pump fitting.
8 Connect a rubber hose to the fitting (approximately 1/4-inch/6 mm inside diameter), long enough to reach into a measuring container located in a higher position than the pump. **Note:** *A hose with a smaller diameter will give false test results.*
9 Disconnect the secondary ignition coil wire from the coil to prevent the engine from starting. Use a jumper wire to ground the wire to the engine block.
10 Turn the ignition switch to the Start position and operate the pump for a total of one minute, in 15-second intervals.
11 A normally operating pump will deliver 47.3 fl oz (1400 ml, 49.3 Imp fl oz) into the container in one minute.
12 If little or no fuel emerged from the hose, either the fuel filter or line is clogged or the pump is defective. Remove the fuel filter and blow air through both fuel lines to be sure they are not clogged. Also, replace the fuel filter if not already done. If this does not improve the test results, the pump should be replaced with a new one.

Fuel injected vehicles

Refer to illustration 7.17a, 7.17b and 7.17c

13 With the engine running, check all metal lines and rubber hoses between the fuel tank (inside of which is the electric pump) and the throttle body to make sure that there are no leaks. Turn off the engine.
14 Relieve the fuel pressure (see Section 15).
15 Detach the cable from the negative terminal of the battery.
16 Disconnect the fuel inlet hose at the throttle body.
17 Install a fuel pressure gauge in-line between the fuel inlet hose and the throttle body **(see illustrations)**.
18 Reattach the cable to the battery negative terminal.
19 Start the engine and check the fuel line for fuel leakage.
20 Note the indicated fuel pressure reading. It should be within the specified range.
21 Release the fuel pressure again (see Section 15).
22 Detach the cable from the negative terminal of the battery.
23 Remove the pressure gauge from the fuel line.
24 Reconnect the fuel inlet hose.
25 Attach the cable to the negative terminal of the battery.

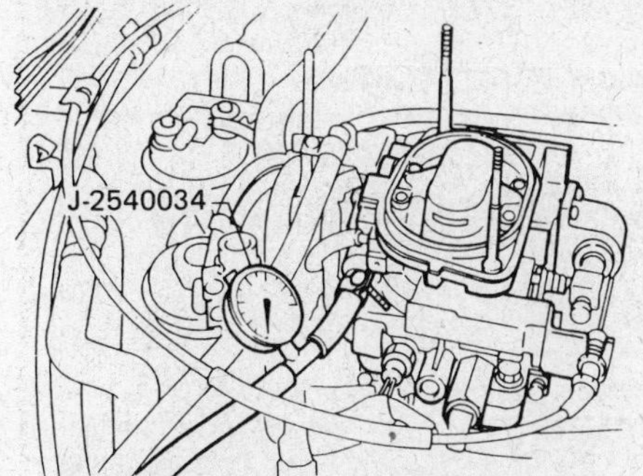

7.17a To check the fuel pressure on fuel injected vehicles,detach the inlet hose from the throttle body and install a pressure gauge between the hose and the throttle body – be sure the hose clamps are tight enough to prevent fuel leakage

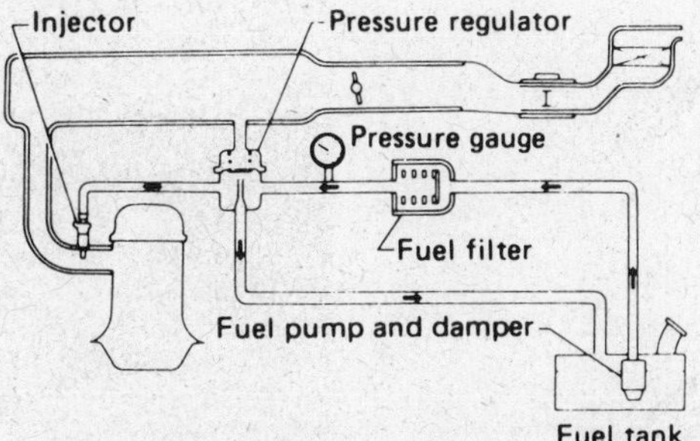

7.17b On KA24E engines, install the pressure gauge between the pressure regulator and the fuel filter. Be sure to record values with the vacuum to the pressure regulator ON and OFF.

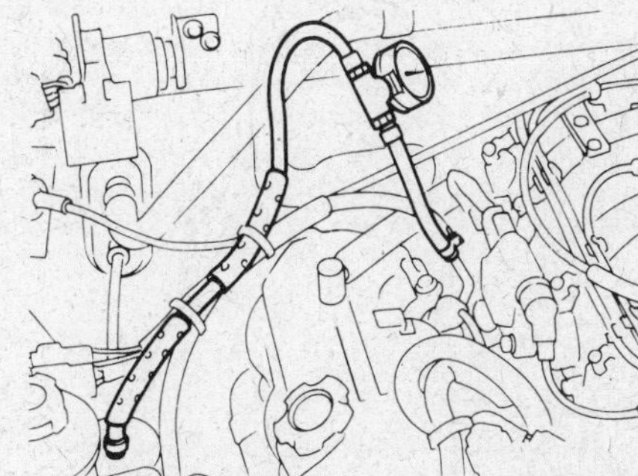

7.17c On MPFI V6 engines, install the pressure gauge between the fuel filter and the fuel tube (engine side). Be sure to record valves with the vacuum to pressure regulator ON and OFF.

4

8.1 On some carbureted vehicles, a mechanical fuel pump is located at the right side of the cylinder head

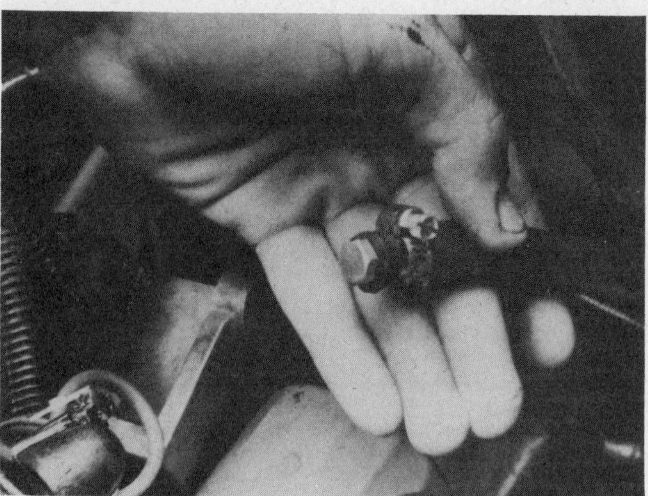

8.2 To plug rubber fuel hoses effectively, insert a bolt into the opening and secure it with a small hose clamp

8.7a On other carbureted vehicles, an electric fuel pump is attached to the frame rail under the right side of the vehicle

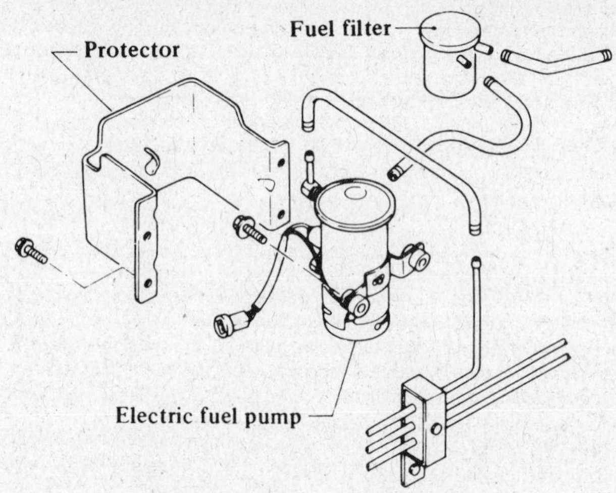

8.7b An exploded view of a typical electric fuel pump assembly on later carbureted vehicles

8 Fuel pump – removal and installation

Refer to illustrations 8.1, 8.2, 8.7a, 8.7b and 8.16

Warning: *Gasoline is extremely flammable, so extra precautions must be taken when working on any part of the fuel system. Make sure the engine is cool. Don't smoke or allow open flames or bare light bulbs near the work area. Also, do not work in a garage if a natural gas-type appliance with a pilot light is present. Remove the cable from the negative terminal of the battery to eliminate the possibility of sparks occurring while fuel vapor is present.*

Carburetor equipped vehicles

Mechanical pump

1 Locate the fuel pump on the front side of the cylinder head **(see illustration)**. Place rags underneath the pump to catch any spilled fuel.

2 Disconnect the fuel lines from the pump. Immediately plug them to prevent the leakage of fuel and the entry of dirt **(see illustration)**.

3 Remove the two nuts that attach the fuel pump to the cylinder head. **Note:** *On some models, the front engine lift bracket may have to be removed for clearance.*

4 Lift the pump from the cylinder head.

5 Installation is the reverse of removal.

Electric pump

Note: *If fuel starvation is occurring, the fuel pump filter may be clogged. See Step 12 below.*

6 If necessary for clearance, raise the right rear corner of the truck and support it on jackstands.

7 Locate the fuel pump on the frame rail, under the right side of the vehicle **(see illustrations)**. Remove the fuel pump protector shield.

8 Place rags or a suitable container under the pump to catch any fuel. Then disconnect the fuel lines from the pump and immediately plug them.

9 Disconnect the wiring connector leading to the pump.

10 Remove the bolts that attach the pump to its bracket and lift the pump off.

11 Installation is the reverse of the removal procedure.

12 Because it is not a portion of the routine maintenance schedule, the following procedure is not contained in Chapter 1. But it should be noted that the electric fuel pump on carbureted vehicles has a replaceable filter which should be inspected at the first sign of any fuel starvation problems or any time the fuel pump is removed.

13 Disconnect the negative cable at the battery.

14 Disconnect and plug the fuel feed line at the fuel pump.

15 Disconnect the ground wire attached to the pump, then remove the fuel pump cover, being careful not to lose the cover magnet or the cover gasket, which are just inside the cover.

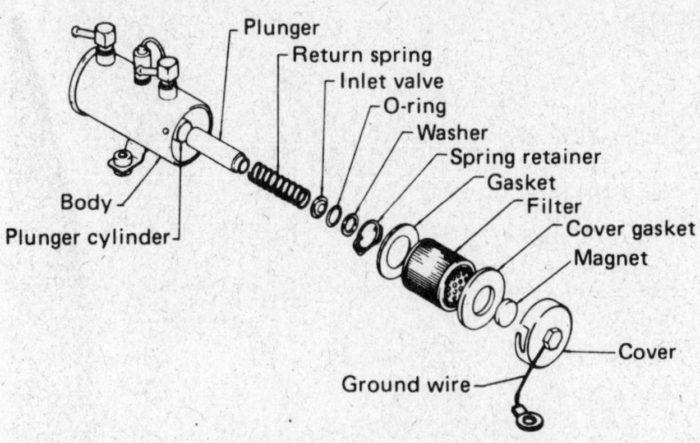

8.16 An exploded view of the electric fuel pump used on carbureted vehicles

16 Slide the filter out of the pump body **(see illustration)** and inspect it for clogging or damage.
17 Reinstall the old filter, or the new one if the inspection indicates a need.
18 Clean the magnet body thoroughly and reinstall it and the cover, along with a new cover gasket. Attach the ground wire and connect the fuel feed hose. After reconnecting the negative battery cable, start the engine and check for leakage around the fuel pump.

Fuel injected vehicles

19 On fuel injected vehicles, the electric fuel pump is mounted in the fuel tank.
20 Relieve the fuel pressure (see Section 14).
21 Disconnect the cable from the negative terminal of the battery.
22 Raise the vehicle and place it securely on jackstands.
23 Remove the fuel tank (see Section 19).
24 Remove the fuel pump/fuel gauge sender unit lock plate by using a hammer and brass punch to turn it clockwise. **Warning:** *Sparks caused by the use of a screwdriver or a punch made of any material other than brass could cause an explosion.*
25 Lift the fuel pump/sender unit assembly from the tank.
26 Separate the fuel pump from the sender unit.
27 Installation is the reverse of removal.

9 Carburetor – general information

The carburetor is a downdraft, two-barrel type. The primary throttle valve is mechanically operated whiie the secondary one is vacuum operated by a diaphragm unit which is actuated by the vacuum in the carburetor venturi.

An electrically assisted, bimetal-type automatic choke is incorporated. This operates a butterfly valve which closes one of the venturi tubes and is synchronized with the primary throttle plate (the latter opens sufficiently to provide a rich mixture and an increased idle speed for easy starting).

For idling and slow running, the fuel passes through the slow running jet, the primary slow air bleed and the secondary slow air bleed. The fuel is finally ejected from the bypass and the idle holes. An anti-dieseling (run-on) solenoid valve is incorporated to ensure that the fuel supply is cut-off when the ignition is switched Off, thus preventing the engine from running-on.

The accelerator pump is synchronized with the throttle valve. During periods of heavy acceleration, the pump, which is of simple piston and valve construction, provides an additional metered quantity of fuel to enrich the normal mixture.

The secondary system provides a mixture for normal driving conditions by means of a main jet and air bleed. On some carburetors, an additional high-speed circuit is incorporated. It consists of a richer jet, richer air bleed and richer nozzle, and allows additional fuel to be drawn into the secondary bore as the air velocity through that bore increases.

A boost controlled deceleration device (BCDD) is incorportated on some models to reduce the hydrocarbons emitted (which tend to occur in excess during engine over-run) when the combustion chamber fuel/air mixture is too lean to permit complete combustion. The BCDD system consists of a vacuum control solenoid valve, and a speed detecting switch and amplifier (manual transmission) or inhibitor switch (automatic transmission). More information on the BCDD is provided in Chapter 6.

On carburetors used on automatic transmission models (and some manual transmission models) a dashpot system is incorporated to reduce the rate at which the primary throttle valve closes when suddenly released. This reduces any tendency for the engine to stall, particularly when cold.

Carburetors used on certain models use an altitude compensator to correct an otherwise too rich mixture which can occur at high altitude.

The float chamber is fed with fuel pumped by the mechanically operated pump on the crankcase or the electric pump (certain models). The level in the chamber is critical and must at all times be maintained as specified.

The air/fuel mixture ratio screw on all 1981 and 1982 models is recessed in the carburetor. The mixture ratio screw on 1980 models is accessible. This adjustment should be checked periodically. Proper adjustment must be done while using special emission sensing equipment, making it impractical for the home mechanic. To have the idle mixture settings checked or readjusted, take your vehicle to a Nissan dealer or other qualified mechanic with the proper equipment.

10 Automatic choke – testing

Refer to illustrations 10.6 and 10.10

Automatic choke mechanism

1 With the engine cold, fully depress the accelerator pedal to close the choke valve.
2 Remove the air cleaner, and push on the choke valve to check for binding.
3 On 1980 models, check that the bi-metal cover index mark is correctly set at the center of the choke housing index mark. The bi-metal cover index mark should not be set in any other position.
4 Make sure the wiring connector leading to the choke mechanism is securely connected. Then start the engine and allow it to warm up to normal temperature. At this point the choke valve should be fully open.
5 If the choke assembly does not operate as described, perform the other checks described in the following sub-sections. If these check out all right, then the bi-metal cover (on 1980 models) or the choke chamber assembly (on 1981 and 1982 models) should be replaced.

Automatic choke heater circuit

6 With the engine off, disconnect the automatic choke wiring connector and attach the leads of a continuity tester to the A and B terminals **(see illustration)**. Do not connect them to any other terminals. If continuity exists, the circuit is functioning properly. If no continuity exists, check for a disconnected or broken wire. An open circuit in the heater unit could also be the problem and should be checked as described in the following sub-section.

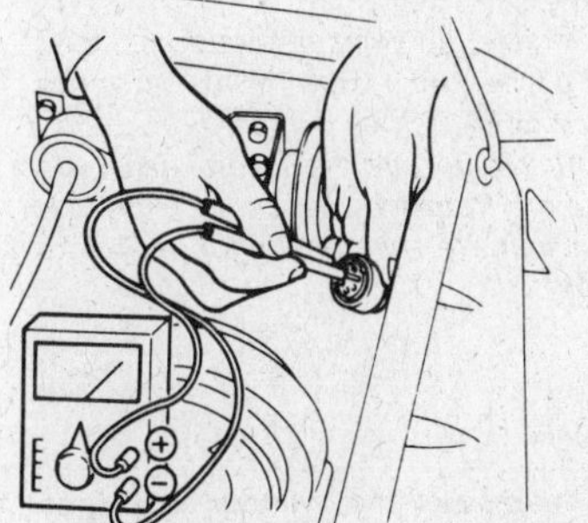

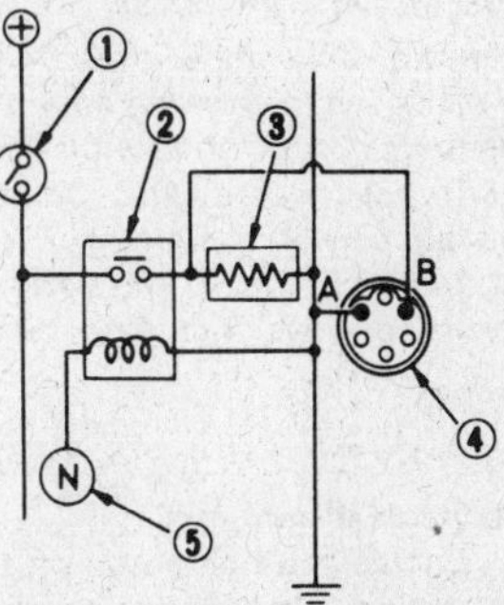

10.6 Identification of terminals A and B for choke heater circuit continuity check

1 Ignition switch
2 Automatic choke relay
3 Automatic choke heater
4 Function test connector
5 Alternator

7 Next, start the engine and connect the leads of a voltmeter to the A and B terminals. A voltmeter reading of 12-volts should be indicated. If the voltmeter reads zero, check for a disconnected or broken wire, an open circuit or faulty choke relay.

Automatic choke heater unit

8 With the automatic choke wiring connector disconnected, attach one lead of an ohmmeter to the connector and the other lead to the carburetor body. A resistance of 3.7 to 8.9 ohms should be indicated. If not, the choke chamber assembly should be replaced.

Automatic choke relay

9 Remove the choke relay, which is mounted next to the parking brake handle under the dash.
10 Attach the leads of a continuity tester to terminals 4 and 5 **(see illustration)**. Continuity should exist.
11 Next, connect the leads to terminals 1 and 2. Again, continuity should exist.
12 Connect the leads to terminals 1 and 3. This time no continuity should be indicated.
13 Now, use jumper wires to connect terminals 4 and 5 to the terminals of a 12-volt battery and again check for continuity between 1 and 2 and then 1 and 3. With power applied, no continuity should exist between 1 and 2, while continuity should now exist between 1 and 3.
14 If the test results are not as described above, replace the relay with a new one.

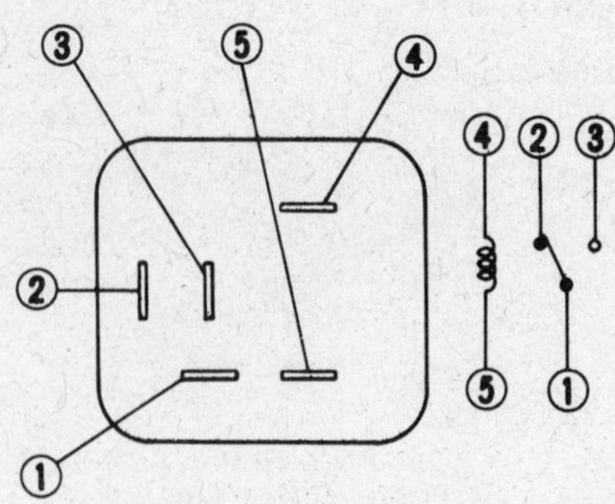

10.10 Identification of choke relay terminals

1 From IG position
2 To automatic choke heater
3 Not used
4 From alternator
5 From ignition switch

11 Carburetor – adjustments

Air/fuel mixture ratio

1 Although the mixture ratio adjusting screw is accessible on 1980 models, the procedure is critical and special equipment is needed to carry it out. On 1981 and 1982 models, the idle mixture ratio adjustment screw is set up at the factory, and then sealed with a steel plug. On 1984 and 1985 vehicles, the air/fuel ratio is adjusted automatically in service by a solenoid mounted on the carburetor body. So, no air-fuel mixture screw is incorporated. For these reasons, we recommend that any mixture ratio adjustments that should be necessary (due to carburetor overhaul, etc.) be done by a Nissan dealer or a repair shop.

Fuel level

Refer to illustrations 11.2 and 11.6

2 With the engine idling, check the level of the fuel in the float chamber by looking at the sight window in the front of the carburetor **(see illustration)**. The fuel level should be at the indicator point (small dot) at the center of the window.

11.2 The fuel level inspection window is located at the front of the carburetor – if the fuel level is correct, it will be at the indicator point (the small dot) in the center of the window

3 If the fuel level is above or below this point, the float must be adjusted, which requires removal of the carburetor.
4 Disconnect the fuel line from the carburetor, and run the engine until it stalls from lack of fuel.
5 Refer to Section 12 and remove the carburetor from the engine, then remove the float chamber cover from the carburetor.
6 Turn the carburetor upside down so that the float comes in contact with the needle valve. Measure the dimension H **(see illustration)**. If this measurement is 0.283-inch (7.2 mm), the top float position is correct. If not, bend the float seat to bring it into proper adjustment.
7 Next, fully raise the float and measure the dimension h in the accompanying figure, between the float seat and the needle valve stem. Proper adjustment is 0.051 to 0.067-inch (1.3 to 1.7 mm). If necessary, bend the float stopper to bring it into proper adjustment.
8 Reinstall the float chamber cover and the carburetor. With the engine idling, again check that the fuel level is at the indicator point on the window.

Vacuum break

Refer to illustration 11.11

9 This mechanism opens the choke valve plate after the engine has been started to provide the correct fuel/air ratio mixture under the prevailing engine operating conditions.
10 The correct setting should be checked and any adjustment carried out in the following manner. Close the choke valve plate completely with the fingers and retain the valve plate in this position using a rubber band connected between the vacuum break lever and carburetor body.

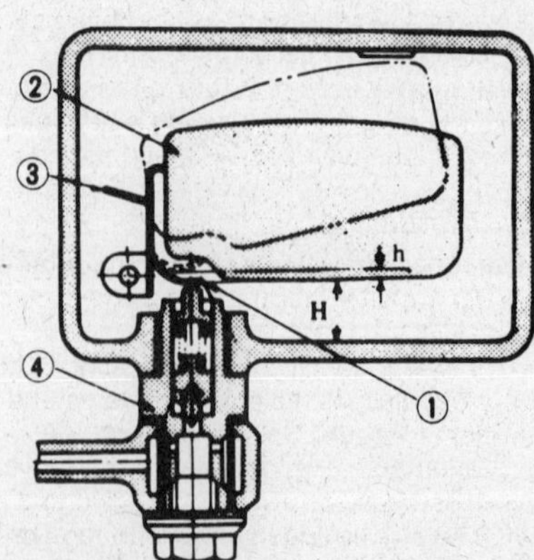

11.6 The carburetor fuel level is adjusted by setting dimensions H and h above to the proper specifications

1 Float seat
2 Float
3 Float stopper
4 Needle valve

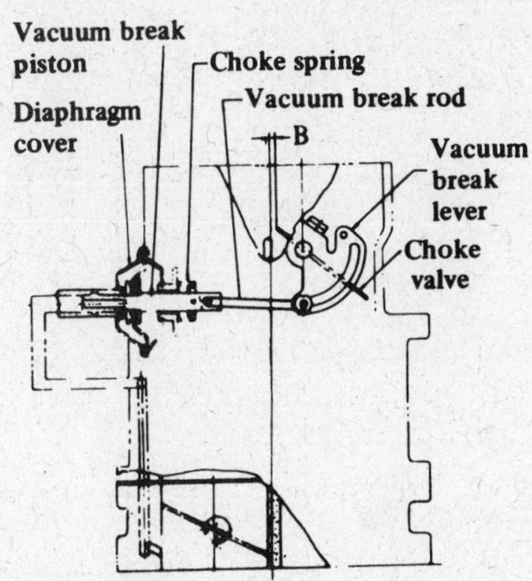

11.11 To adjust the vacuum break, set dimension B

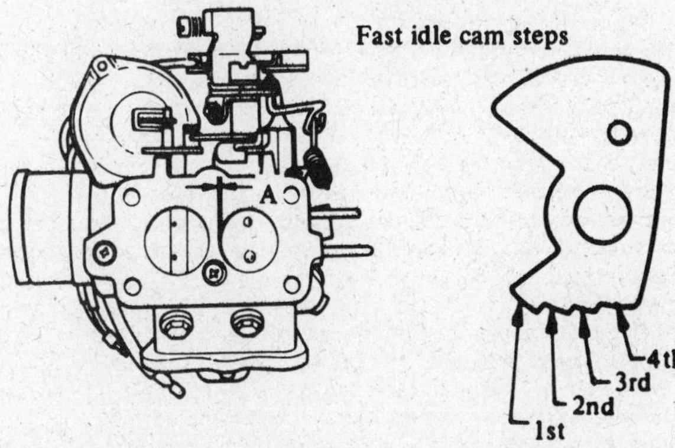

11.20 To adjust the fast idle, set clearance A with the fast idling screw on the second stop of the fast idling cam (1980 through 1983)

11 With a pair of pliers, grip the end of the vacuum diaphragm capsule operating rod and withdraw it as far as it will go without straining it. Now bend the connecting rod (if necessary) to provide a clearance between the edge of the choke valve plate and the carburetor body (distance B) as given in the Specifications **(see illustration)**.

Choke unloader

12 Close the choke valve plate completely with the fingers and retain the valve plate in this position using a rubber band connected between the vacuum break lever and carburetor body.
13 Pull the throttle lever until it is fully open and bend the unloader tongue (if necessary) to provide a clearance between the choke valve and carburetor body as given in the Specifications.

Dashpot adjustment

14 Run the engine to normal operating temperature and check that the idle speed adjustment (Chapter 1) is correct. Also, the air conditioning should be Off.
15 Release the dashpot locknut and then adjust the position of the dashpot so that it just touches the stop plate when the engine is running at the speed indicated in the Specifications.
16 Retighten the locknut without moving the dashpot.
17 Raise the engine speed to about 2000 rpm and suddenly release the accelerator. The engine speed should be reduced to 1000 rpm in approximately three seconds, otherwise the adjustment has been incorrectly carried out or the dashpot is faulty.

Interlock opening of throttle valves

Refer to illustration 11.18

18 Check that when the primary throttle plate is opened 50°, the throttle valve adjust plate is contacting the return plate at point A **(see illustration)**. Open the throttle plate further and check that the locking arm is detached from the secondary throttle arm, allowing the secondary system to function. Bend the connecting lever, if necessary, to obtain the specified distance between the throttle valve and the throttle chamber inner wall.

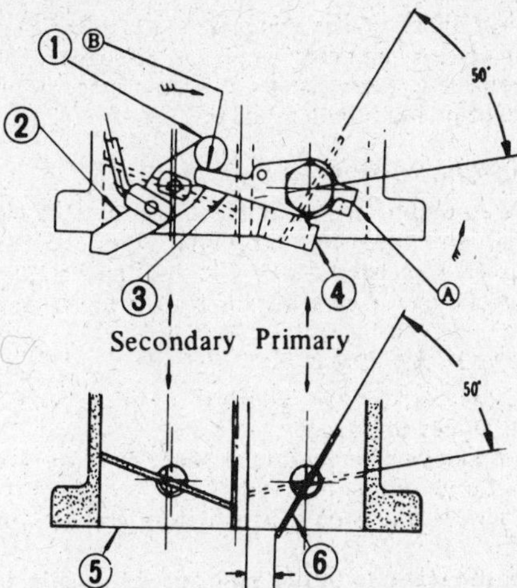

11.18 When adjusting the throttle valve interlock opening, the gap between the throttle valve and the chamber wall should be set to the proper specification

1 Roller
2 Connecting lever
3 Return plate
4 Adjust plate
5 Throttle chamber
6 Throttle valve

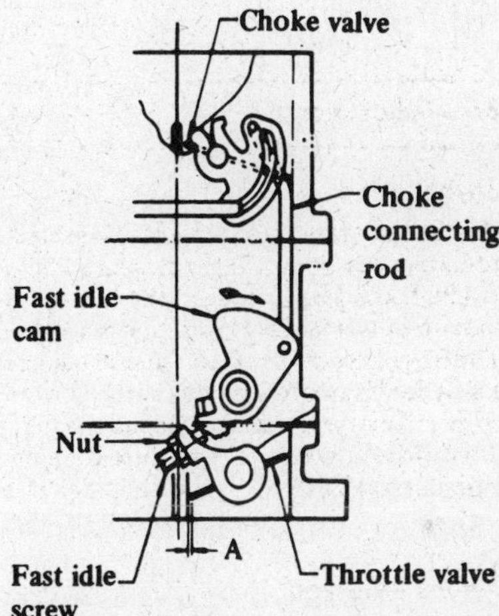

11.21 If the clearance is not as specified, turn the fast idle screw until the clearance is correct (1980 through 1983)

Fast idle

1980 through 1983 models

Refer to illustrations 11.20 and 11.21

19 Remove the carburetor from the engine, as described in Section 12.
20 Use a wire gauge (or drill bit) to measure the clearance A **(see illustration)** between the throttle valve and the carburetor bore, while the upper side of the fast idling screw is on the second step of the fast idling cam. Refer to the Specifications for the proper clearance.
21 If the clearance is not as specified, turn the fast idle screw until the clearance is set correctly **(see illustration)**.

1984 and 1985 models

Refer to illustration 11.23

22 Warm the engine and check that the idle rpm and ignition timing are adjusted properly.

4

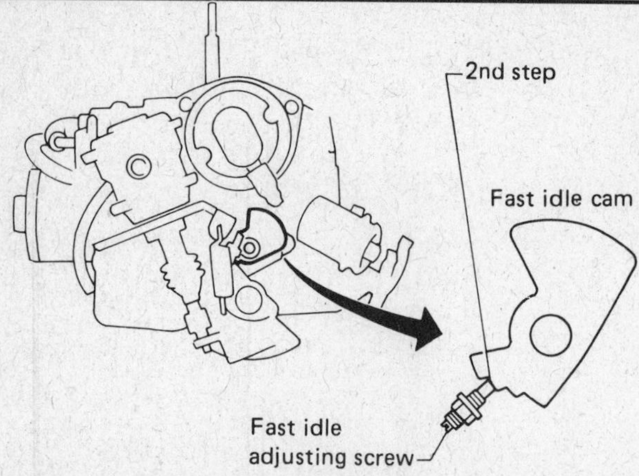

11.23 Make sure that the adjusting screw is on the 2nd step of the cam as shown when setting fast idle speed on later model carburetors (1984 and 1985)

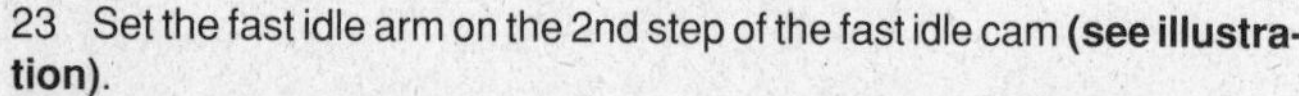

11.27 Accelerator pump location

23 Set the fast idle arm on the 2nd step of the fast idle cam **(see illustration)**.
24 Connect a tachometer to the engine following the manufacturer's instructions.
25 Check that the fast idle rpm is as specified in the Specifications section at the front of this chapter.
26 If adjustment is required, turn the fast idle adjustment screw.

Accelerating pump

Refer to illustration 11.27

27 Perform a visual check of the accelerating pump for any sign of fuel leakage **(see illustration)**. If any is found, the gasket must be replaced with a new one.
28 While looking down the carburetor barrel, turn the throttle valve by hand and make sure fuel is injected through the nozzle. A flashlight may be helpful in checking this. If this is not occurring, the carburetor will have to be disassembled to correct the problem. Refer to Section 12.

Anti-dieseling solenoid valve

29 This valve should be checked if the engine continues to run-on after the ignition switch has been turned off, or if the engine does not continue running while at idle.
30 With the engine running at idle, disconnect the wire leading to the anti-dieseling solenoid. If the engine does not stop running, perform the following check.
31 Use a voltmeter or test light to check the wiring connector to be sure that there is voltage when the ignition switch is On. If current is reaching the valve the solenoid valve assembly should be replaced as a unit. If current is not reaching the valve, refer to the testing procedures for the fuel shut-off system described in Chapter 6.

Altitude compensator (1981 California models and all 1982 models only)

32 The altitude compensator is designed to operate above an altitude of 1969 ft (600 m). It is not adjustable and if defective must be replaced with a new one. The hoses are color-coded as to the fittings they are attached to on the unit.
33 If the compensator is operating at low altitudes, the following symptoms should be noticed: hesitation and stumble when started, surging while cruising at about 50 mph (80 kmh), stumbling when accelerating from 50 to 70 mph (80 to 112 kmh), or poor acceleration at full throttle.
34 If the compensator is not working at higher altitudes, the following symptoms may be experienced: engine speed does not increase in correct response to depression of the accelerator, hesitation or stumbling when starting, poor acceleration at full throttle or when smooth running at partial throttle. These depend upon the altitude of the vehicle.
35 The compensator is checked by disconnecting the inlet and outlet hoses and blowing air through them. If this is done at a low altitude and air flows through smoothly, the unit is defective and must be replaced. If the test is performed at a higher altitude and air does not flow through smoothly, the unit should be replaced with a new one.

12 Carburetor – removal, overhaul and installation

Refer to illustrations 12.7 and 12.11

Warning: *Gasoline is extremely flammable, so extra precautions must be taken when working on any part of the fuel system. Make sure the engine is cool. Don't smoke or allow open flames or bare light bulbs near the work area. Also, do not work in a garage if a natural gas-type appliance with a pilot light is present.*

1980 through 1983 models

1 Remove the air cleaner.
2 Disconnect the fuel and vacuum lines from the carburetor, being sure to mark them as to their installed locations. Immediately plug all lines to prevent the entry of dirt.
3 Disconnect the accelerator cable from the carburetor.
4 Disconnect all wires attached to the carburetor, again taking note as to where they connect.
5 Remove the nuts that attach the carburetor to the intake manifold and lift off the carburetor. Be sure you do not drop any parts into the intake manifold, as the manifold may then have to be removed.
6 Once it's determined that the carburetor needs adjustment or an overhaul, several options are available. If you're going to attempt to overhaul the carburetor yourself, first obtain a good quality carburetor rebuild kit (which will include all necessary gaskets, internal parts, instructions and a parts list). You'll also need some special solvent and a means of blowing out the internal passages of the carburetor with air.
7 Because the vehicles covered by this book are primarily fuel injected (all Canadian vehicles and 1984 US models are equipped with carburetors) and because carburetor designs are constantly modified by the manufacturer in order to meet increasingly more stringent emissions regulations, it isn't feasible for us to do a step-by-step overhaul of each type. You'll receive a detailed, well illustrated set of instructions with any carburetor overhaul kit; they will apply in a more specific manner to the carburetor on your vehicle. An exploded view of the typical carburetors are included here **(see illustrations)**.
8 Another alternative is to obtain a new or rebuilt carburetor. They are readily available from dealers and auto parts stores. Make absolutely sure the exchange carburetor is identical to the original. A tag is usually attached to the carburetor. It will aid in determining the exact type of carburetor you have. When obtaining a rebuilt carburetor or a rebuild kit, take time to make sure that the kit or carburetor matches your application exactly.

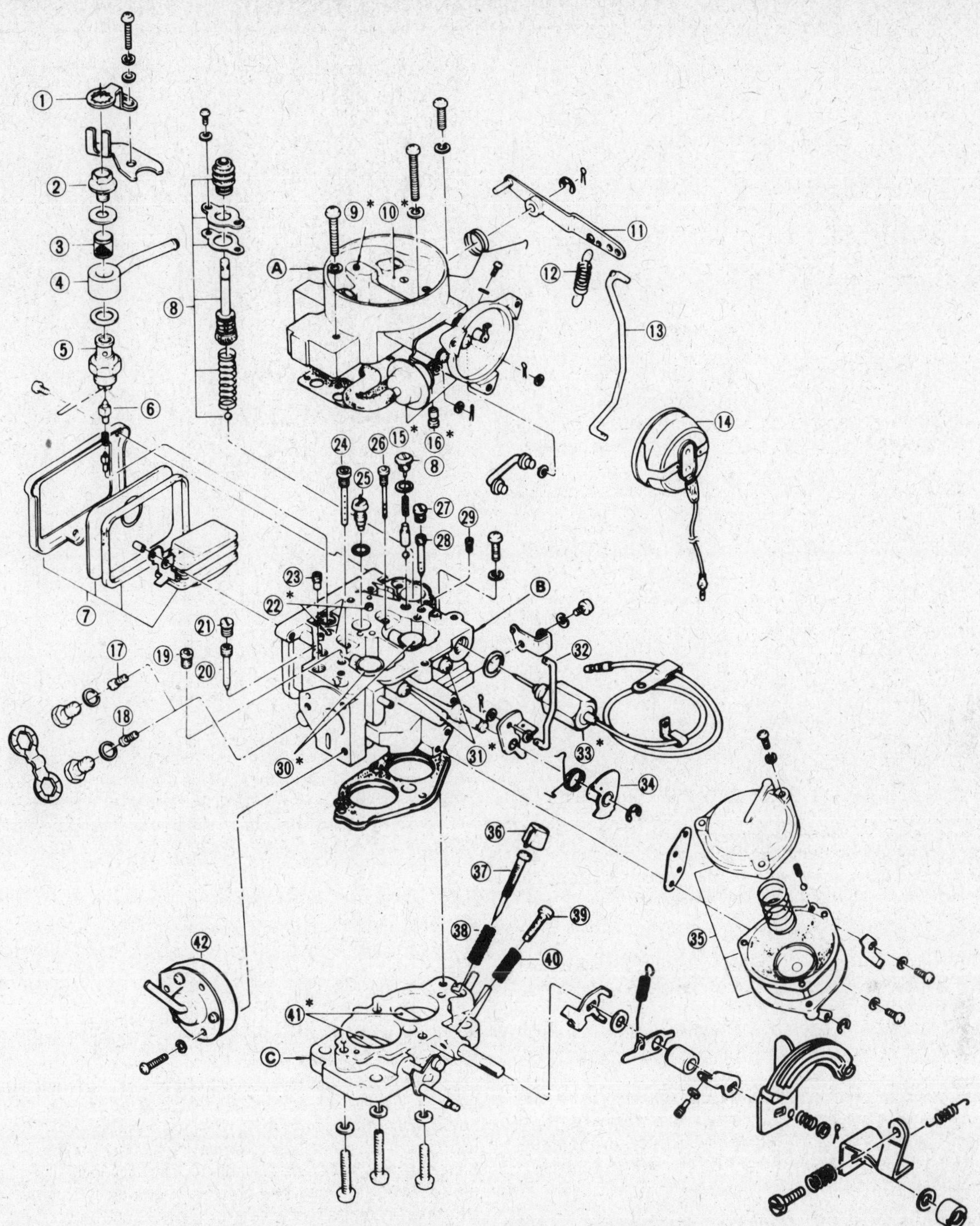

12.7 Typical early model carburetor — exploded view

1 Lock lever
2 Filter set screw
3 Fuel filter
4 Fuel nipple
5 Needle valve body
6 Needle valve
7 Fuel chamber parts
8 Accelerating pump parts
9* High-speed enricher air bleed
10* Choke valve
11 Accelerating pump lever
12 Throttle return spring
13 Accelerating pump rod
14 Automatic choke cover
15* Automatic choke body and vacuum break diaphragm
16* Enricher jet
17 Primary main jet
18 Secondary main jet
19 Secondary slow air bleed
20 Secondary slow jet
21 Plug
22* Air bleed
23 Coasting jet
24 Secondary main air bleed
25 Power valve
26 Primary main air bleed
27 Plug
28 Primary slow jet
29 Primary slow air bleed
30* Primary and secondary small venturi
31* Venturi stopper screw
32 Choke connecting rod
33 Anti-dieseling solenoid valve
34 Fast idle cam
35 Diaphragm chamber parts
36 Idle limiter cap
37 Idle adjusting screw
38 Idle adjusting screw spring
39 Throttle adjusting screw
40 Throttle adjusting screw spring
41* Primary and secondary throttle valves
42 Bypass air control unit

A Choke chamber
B Center body
C Throttle chamber

***Do not remove**

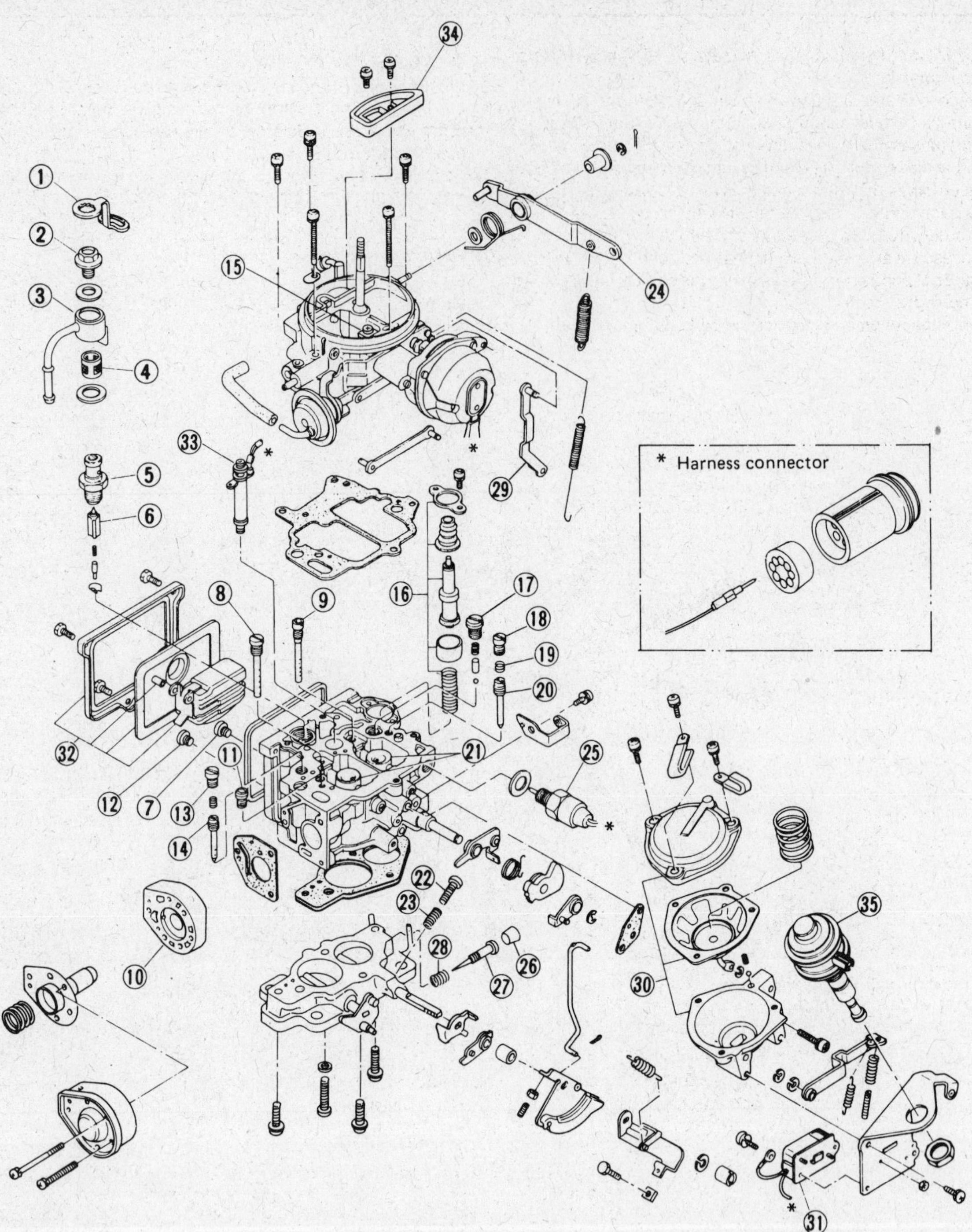

12.11 1984 and 1985 model carburetor — exploded view

1 *Lock plate*
2 *Filter set screw*
3 *Fuel nipple*
4 *Fuel filter*
5 *Needle valve body*
6 *Needle valve*
7 *Primary main jet*
8 *Secondary main air bleed*
9 *Primary main air bleed*
10 *B.C.D.D.*
11 *Secondary slow air bleed*
12 *Secondary main jet*
13 *Plug*
14 *Secondary slow jet*
15 *Idle compensator*
16 *Accelerating pump parts*
17 *Plug for accelerating mechanism*
18 *Plug*
19 *Spring*
20 *Primary slow jet*
21 *Primary and secondary small venturi*
22 *Throttle adjusting screw*
23 *Throttle adjusting screw spring*
24 *Accelerating pump lever*
25 *Anti-dieseling solenoid valve*
26 *Blind plug*
27 *Idle adjusting screw*
28 *Idle adjusting screw spring*
29 *Choke connecting rod*
30 *Diaphragm chamber parts*
31 *Throttle valve switch*
32 *Flat*
33 *Air-fuel ratio solenoid*
34 *Air vent cover*
35 *Dash pot*

Seemingly insignificant differences can make a large difference in the performance of your engine.

9 If you choose to overhaul your own carburetor, allow enough time to disassemble the carburetor carefully, soak the necessary parts in the cleaning solvent (usually for at least one-half day or according to the instructions listed on the carburetor cleaner) and reassemble it, which will usually take much longer than disassembly. When disassembling the carburetor, match each part with the illustration in the carburetor kit and lay the parts out in order on a clean work surface. Overhauls by inexperienced mechanics can result in an engine which runs poorly or not at all. To avoid this, use care and patience when disassembling the carburetor so you can reassemble it correctly.

10 Installation is the reverse of the removal procedure.

1984 and 1985 models

11 Only minor changes have been made to the later model carburetor, and therefore most of the information above will apply. An exploded view of the 1984/1985 carburetor has been included here for your convenience **(see illustration)**.

13 Electronic Fuel Injection (EFI) system – general information

Refer to illustrations 13.1a and 13.1b

Note: *The diagrams show the components typical of 1990 and later models. When performing procedures in this Chapter, refer to the proper photograph for the location of components.*

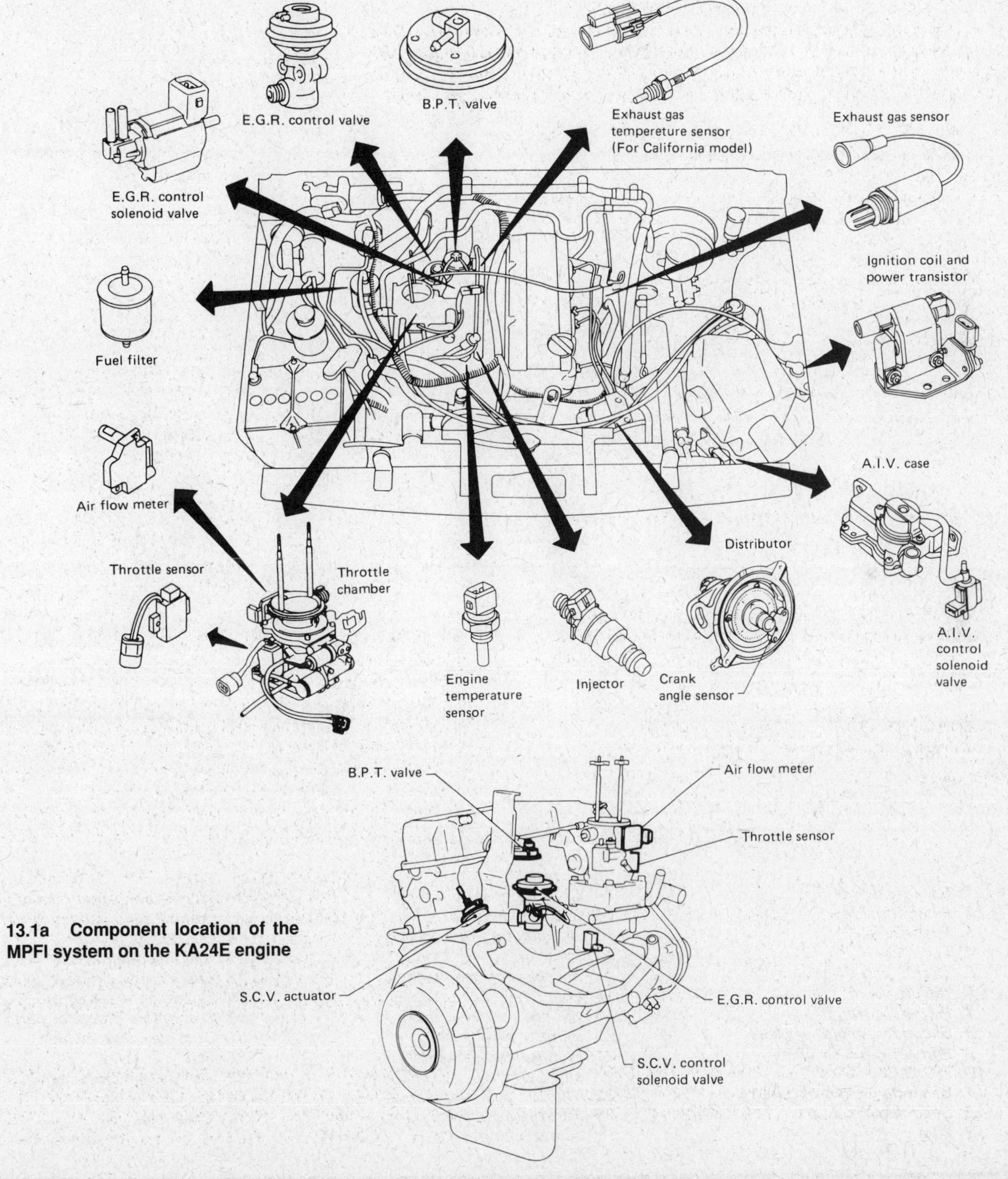

13.1a Component location of the MPFI system on the KA24E engine

R.H. cylinder head
#3
Detonation sensor
Front
L.H. cylinder head
#4
SEF807J

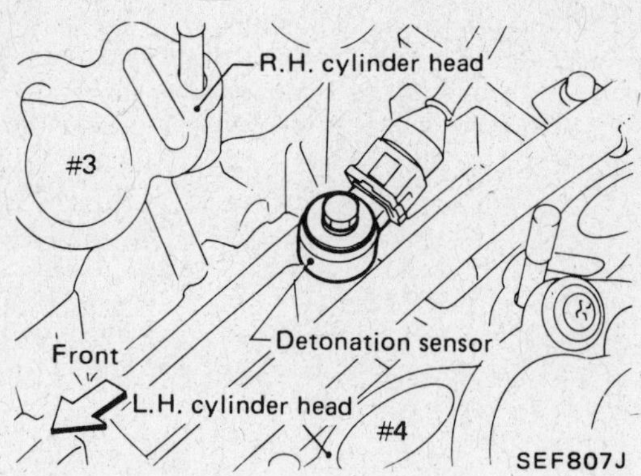

13.1b Component location of the MPFI system on the V6 engine

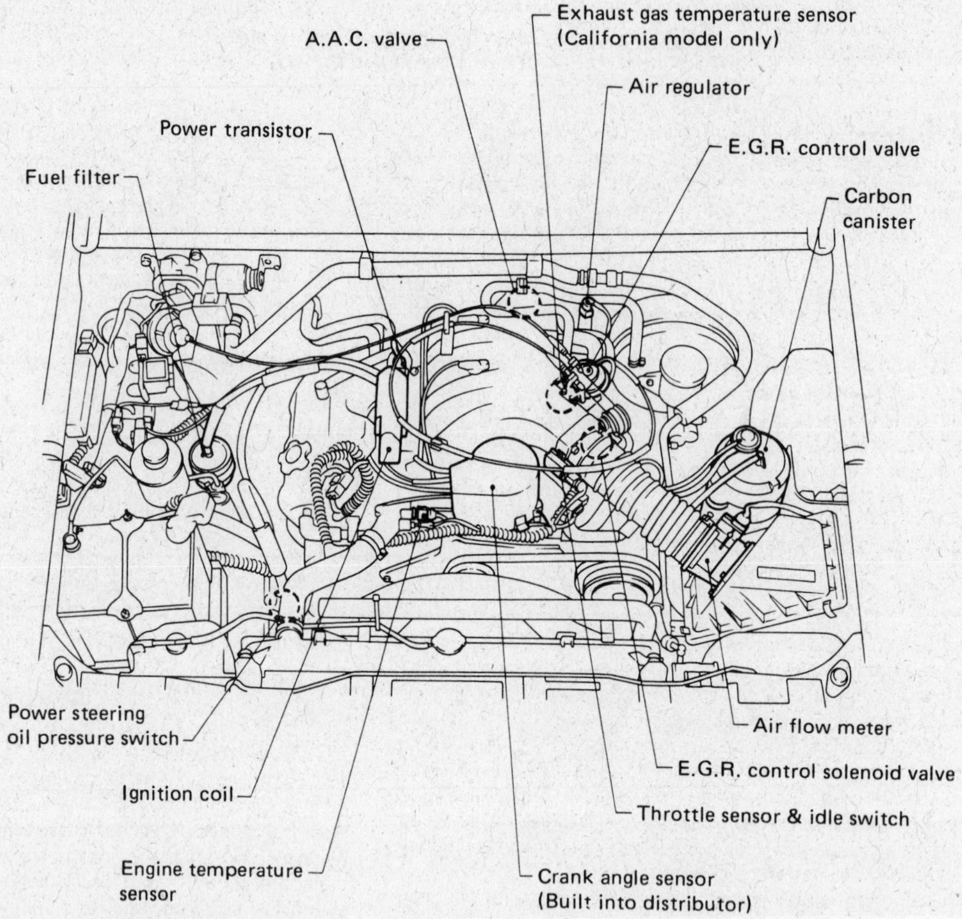

Exhaust gas temperature sensor
(California model only)
A.A.C. valve
Air regulator
Power transistor
E.G.R. control valve
Fuel filter
Carbon
canister
Power steering
oil pressure switch
Air flow meter
E.G.R. control solenoid valve
Ignition coil
Throttle sensor & idle switch
Engine temperature
sensor
Crank angle sensor
(Built into distributor)

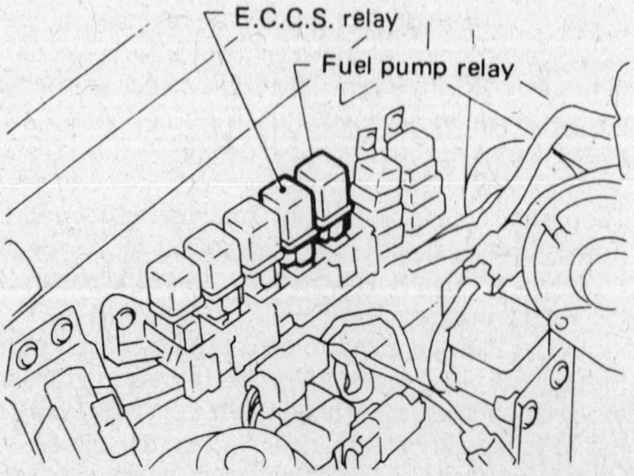

E.C.C.S. relay
Fuel pump relay

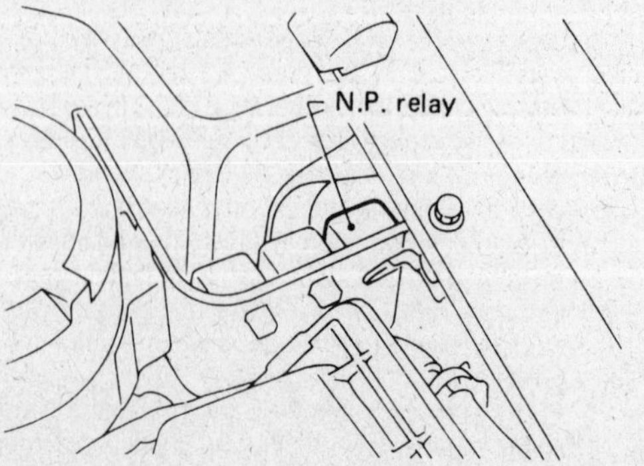

N.P. relay

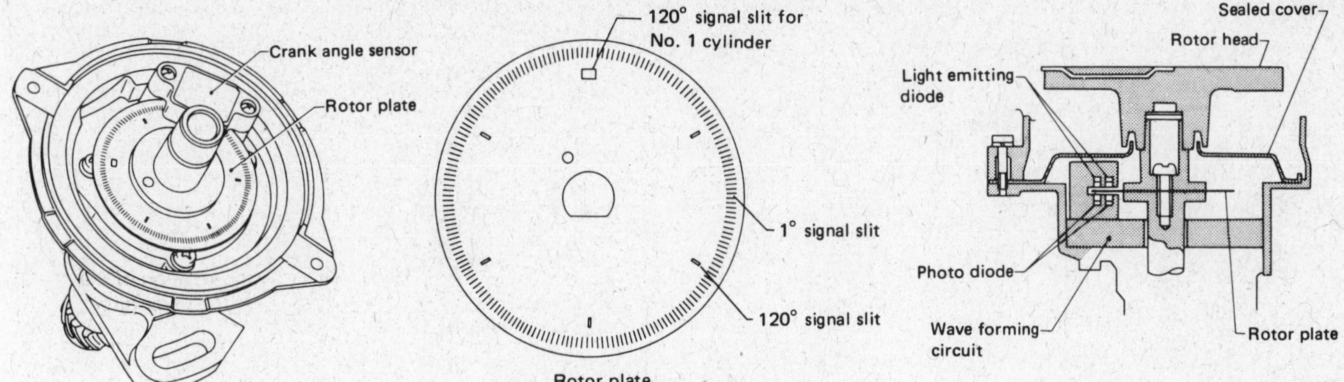

14.2a The crank angle sensor is the main signal sensor for the ECCS

14.2b The rotor plate has 360 slits to indicate engine speed and six slits for crank angle signal

14.2c Light passes through the slits in the rotor plate, sending signals in the form of on-off pulses to the control unit

The engines in later vehicles use an Electronic Fuel Injection (EFI) fuel system. They are equipped with either throttle body injection (TBI) or multi point fuel injection (MPFI). Electronic fuel injection provides optimum mixture ratios, and this, together with the immediate response characteristics of the fuel injection, permits the engine to run on the weakest possible fuel/air mixture. This vastly reduces the exhaust gas toxic emission. The fuel system is interrelated with and works in conjunction with the emissions control and exhaust systems covered in Chapter 6. Thus, some elements that relate directly to the fuel system are covered in that Chapter.

The EFI system consists of three subsystems: The fuel flow system, the air flow system and the electrical signaling system. The various components that make up the entire EFI system are detailed in Section 14.

Fuel from the tank is delivered under pressure by an electric fuel pump. The amount of fuel to be injected is determined by the injection pulse duration as well as by a pressure difference between fuel pressure and intake manifold vacuum pressure. The Electronic Concentrated Control System (ECCS) control unit controls only the injection pulse duration. For this reason, the pressure difference between the fuel pressure and intake manifold vacuum pressure must be maintained at a constant level. Since the intake manifold vacuum pressure varies with engine operating conditions, a pressure regulator is placed in the fuel line to regulate the fuel pressure in response to changes in the intake manifold pressure. Where manifold conditions are such that the fuel pressure could be beyond that specified, the pressure regulator returns surplus fuel to the tank.

An injection of fuel occurs once every rotation of the engine. Because the injection signal comes from the control unit, all injectors operate simultaneously and independent of the engine stroke (MPFI only). Each injection supplies half the amount of fuel required by the cylinder, and the length of the injection period is determined by information fed to the control unit by various sensors included in the system.

Elements affecting the injection duration include: Engine rpm, quantity and temperature of the intake air, throttle valve opening, temperature of the engine coolant, intake manifold vacuum pressure and amount of oxygen in the exhaust gases.

Because the EFI system operates at high fuel pressure, any leak can affect system efficiency and present a serious fire risk. Also, since the intake air flow is critical to the operation of the system, even a slight air leak will cause an incorrect air/fuel mixture. **Note:** *Certain precautions should be observed when working on the EFI system:*

a) Do not disconnect either battery cable while the engine is running.
b) Prior to any operation in which the fuel line will be disconnected, the high pressure in the system must first be eliminated. This procedure is described in Section 4. Disconnect the negative battery cable to eliminate the possibility of sparks occurring while fuel is present.
c) Prior to removing any EFI component, be sure the ignition switch is Off and the negative battery cable is disconnected.
d) The EFI wiring harness should be kept at least four inches (10 mm) away from adjacent harnesses. This includes a CB antenna feeder cable. This is to prevent electrical pulses in other systems from interfering with EFI operation.
e) Be sure all EFI wiring connections are tight, clean and secure, as a poor connection can cause extremely high voltage surges in the ignition coil which could drain the IC circuit.
f) The accelerator should Not be depressed prior to starting the engine. Immediately after starting, do not rev the engine unnecessarily.

The electric fuel pump uses relays, located in the engine compartment, that are designed so that should the engine stop (causing the alternator to turn off and the oil pressure to drop), the fuel pump will cease to operate.

Some basic checks of the EFI components are included in this Chapter. However, the complexity of the system prevents many problems from being accurately diagnosed by the home mechanic. If a problem develops in the system which cannot be pinpointed by the checks listed here, it is best to take the vehicle to a dealer service department to locate the fault.

4

14 ECCS components – general information

Multi point fuel injection (MPFI) system

Refer to illustrations 14.2a, 14.2b, 14.2c, 14.3, 14.4, 14.5, 14.6, 14.8, 14.9, 14.10, 14.11, 14.12, 14.14, 14.15, 14.16, 14.17, 14.18, 14.19, 14.20, 14.21 and 14.22.

ECCS control unit

1 The Electronic Concentrated Control System (ECCS) control unit, also known as the Engine Control Unit (ECU), is a microcomputer with electrical connectors for receiving input/output signals and for power supply, inspection lamps and a diagnostic mode selector. The control unit regulates the amount of fuel that is injected, as well as the ignition timing, idle speed, fuel pump operation and the feedback of the mixture ratio.

Crank angle sensor

2 The crank angle sensor could be regarded as the right hand to the ECCS control unit, as it is the basic signal sensor for the entire ECCS system. It monitors the engine speed, piston position and it sends signals to the ECCS control unit for control of the fuel injection, ignition timing, idle speed, fuel pump operation and the EGR function **(see illustrations)**.

The crank angle sensor has a rotor plate and a wave forming circuit. The assembly consists of a rotor plate with 360 slits representing 1-degree signals (engine speed signal) and six slits for 120-degree signals (crank angle signal). Light emitting diodes (LED) and photo diodes are built into the wave forming circuit.

In operation, the signal rotor plate passes through the space between the LED and photo diode and the slits in the signal rotor plate intermittently cut off the light sent to the photo diode from the LED. This causes an alternating voltage and the voltage is converted into an on/off pulse by the wave forming circuit. The on/off signal is sent to the control unit for processing.

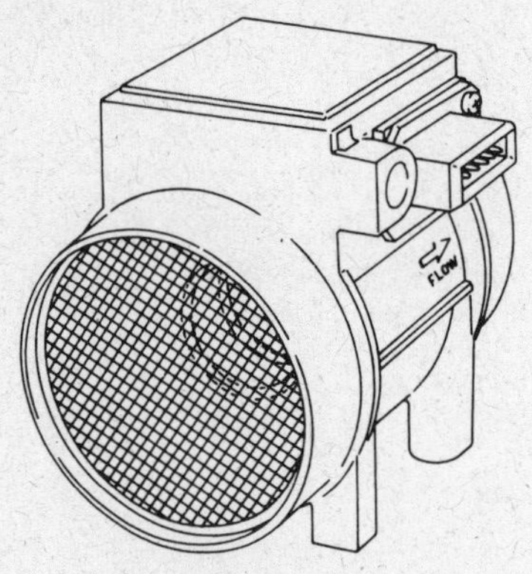

14.3 The air flow meter measures the mass flow rate of intake air

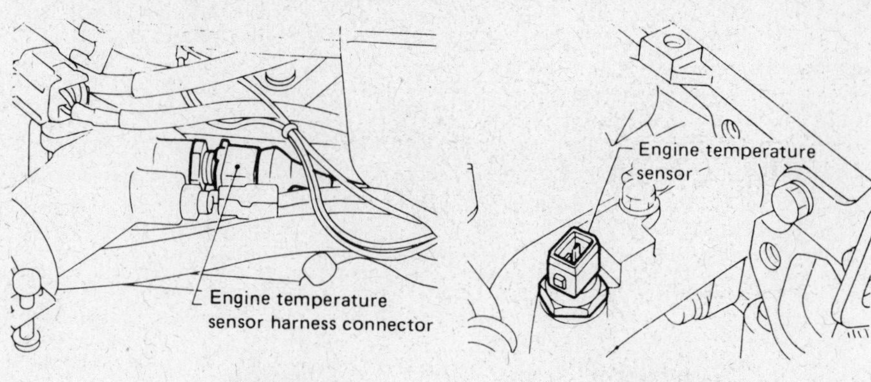

14.4 The engine temperature sensor is located in the cylinder head inlet housing

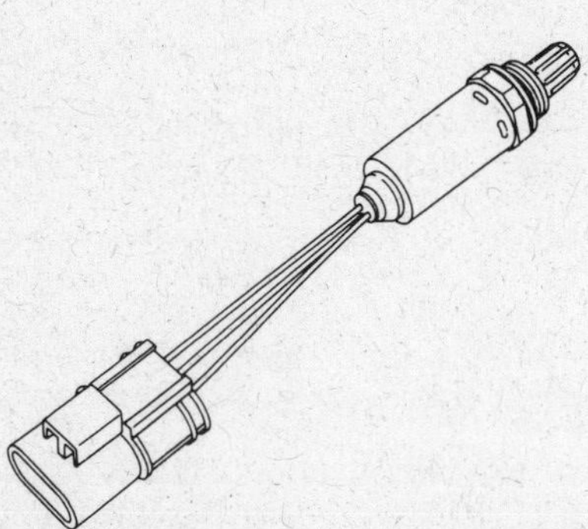

14.5 The exhaust gas sensor monitors the quantity of oxygen in the exhaust gas

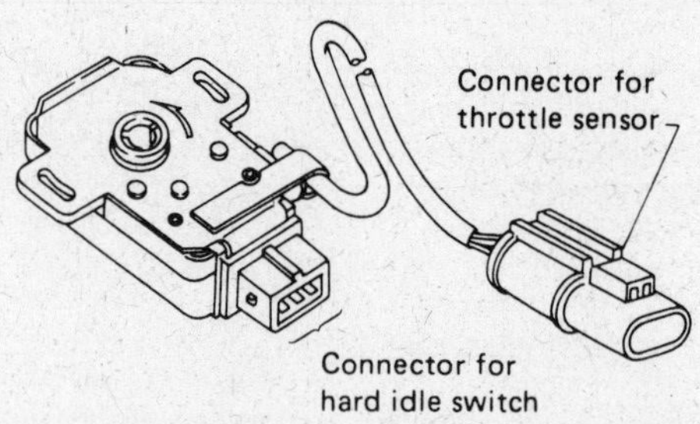

14.6 The throttle switch informs the control unit when the accelerator is at idle, and on electrically controlled automatic transmission equipped models it informs the control unit when the throttle is wide open

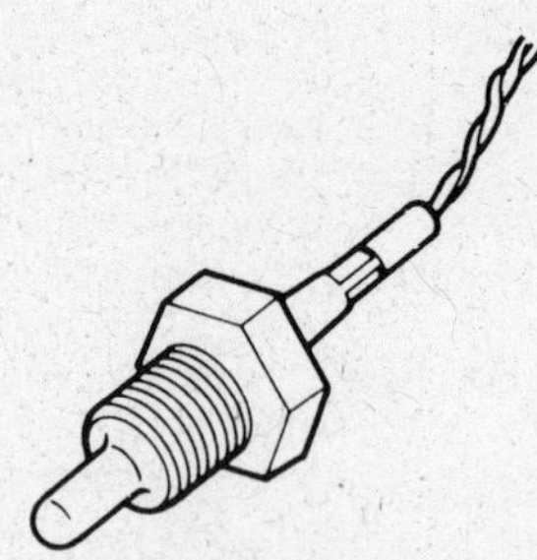

14.8 The exhaust gas temperature sensor lets the ECCS control module know the temperature of the exhaust

Air Flow meter

3 The air flow meter measures the mass flow rate of intake air. The control circuit emits an electrical output signal which varies in relation to the amount of heat dissipated from a hot wire placed in the stream of intake air **(see illustration)**.

Engine temperature sensor

4 The engine temperature sensor detects the changes in the coolant temperature and transmits the signal to the ECCS control unit **(see illustration)**.

Exhaust gas sensor

5 Mounted in the exhaust manifold, the exhaust gas sensor monitors the quantity of oxygen in the exhaust gases **(see illustration)**.

Throttle valve switch

6 The throttle valve switch is attached to outside of the throttle chamber and actuates in response to accelerator pedal movement. The switch is equipped with two contacts, one for idle and the other for full throttle contact. The idle contact closes when the throttle valve is positioned at idle and opens when it is at any other position. The full throttle contact is used for electronically controlled automatic transmissions only **(see illustration)**.

Vehicle speed sensor

7 The vehicle speed sensor provides a vehicle speed signal to the ECCS control unit. Two types of speed sensors are employed, depending upon the type of speedometer installed. Needle type speedometer models utilize a reed switch, which is installed in the speedometer unit and transforms vehicle speed into a pulse signal which is sent to the control unit. The digital type speedometer consists of an LED, photo diode, shutter and wave forming circuit.

Exhaust gas temperature sensor (California models only)

8 The exhaust gas temperature sensor monitors the exhaust gas temperature and transmits the information to the E.C.U. The information is used to control the mixture of the air and fuel **(see illustration)**.

Detonation sensor

9 Attached to the cylinder block, the detonation sensor is capable of sensing engine knock conditions. Any knocking vibration from the cylinder block is applied as pressure to the piezoelectric element. This pressure is then converted into a voltage signal which is delivered as output to the control unit **(see illustration)**.

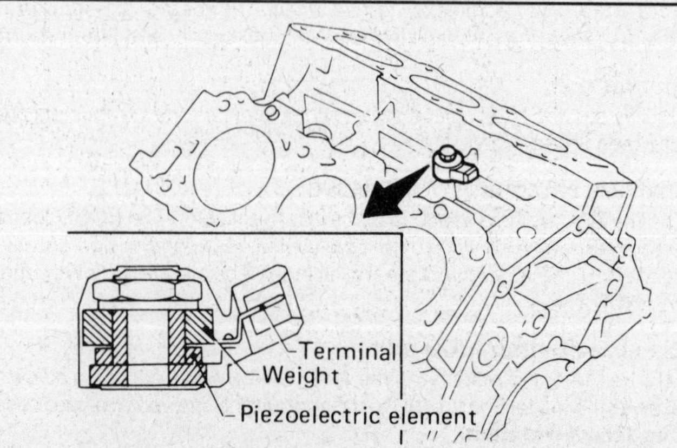

14.9 A detonation sensor is installed on the engine block of later models to sense engine knock conditions

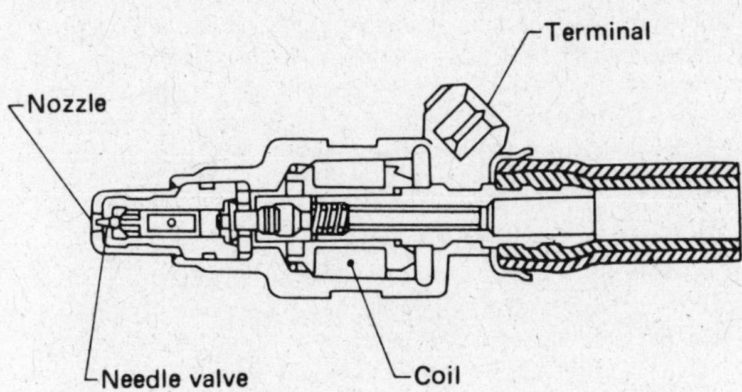

14.10 **The fuel injector receives a signal from the control unit and the needle valve opens to inject fuel into the intake manifold – the amount of fuel injected is determined by the pulse duration**

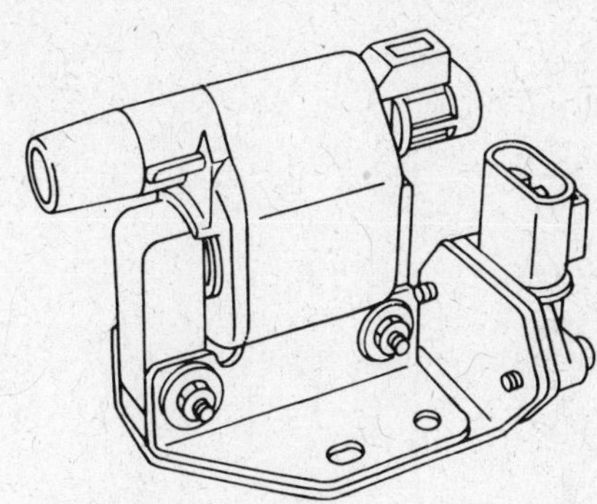

14.11 **The ignition signal is amplified by the power transistor, which triggers the proper high voltage in the secondary circuit**

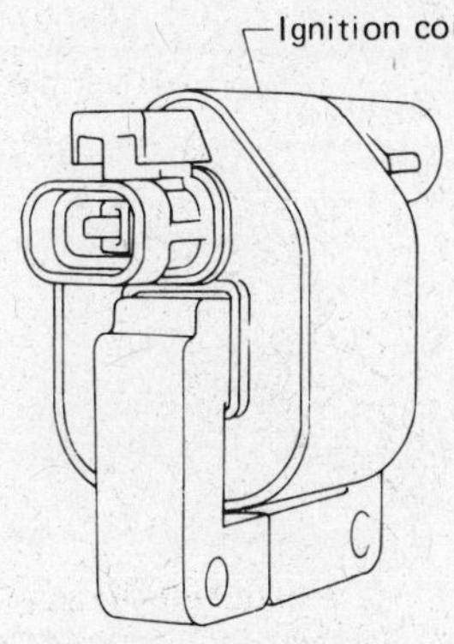

14.12 **The ignition coil**

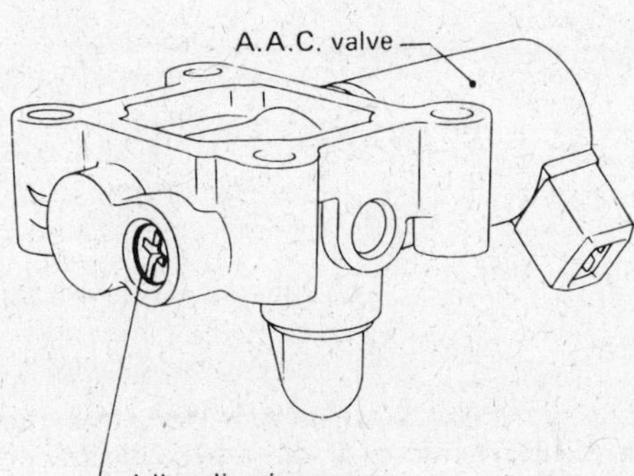

14.14 **The IAA unit is a combination of the AAC valve and the idle adjusting screw. This unit can be preset to control idle speed**

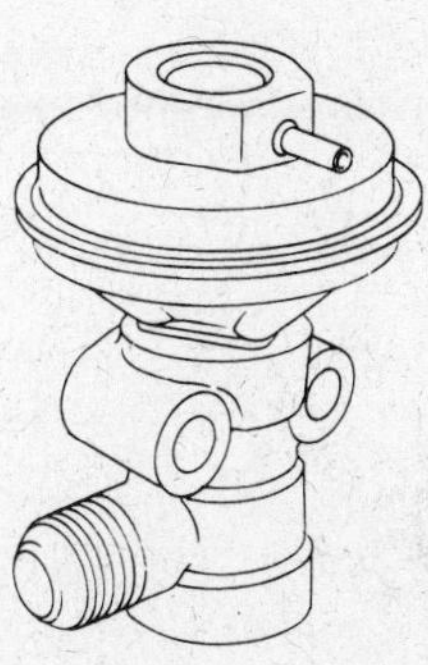

14.15 **The EGR valve controls the amount of exhaust gas to be circulated into the intake manifold**

Fuel injector

10 The fuel injector supplies each cylinder with fuel. The injector is a small, precision solenoid valve. As the ECCS control unit outputs an injection signal to each fuel injector, the coil built into the injector pulls the needle valve back and fuel is sprayed through the nozzle into the intake manifold. The amount of fuel injected is controlled by the ECCS control unit by injection pulse duration **(see illustration)**.

Power transistor

11 The ignition signal from the ECCS control unit is amplified by the power transistor, which connects and disconnects the coil primary circuit to induce the proper high voltage in the secondary circuit **(see illustration)**.

Ignition coil

12 The molded type ignition coil provides spark for the combustion process **(see illustration)**.

Auxiliary air control (AAC) valve

13 The AAC valve is attached to the intake collector. The ECCS control unit actuates the AAC valve by an on/off pulse. The longer the on-duty signal is left on, the larger the amount of air that will be allowed to flow through the AAC valve.

Idle air adjusting (IAA) unit

14 The IAA unit is made up of the AAC valve and idle adjusting screw. It receives the signal from the ECU and controls the idle speed at the preset value **(see illustration)**.

EGR control valve

15 The EGR control valve controls the quantity of exhaust gas circulated to the intake manifold through movement of the taper valve connected to the diaphragm, to which vacuum is applied in response to the opening of the throttle valve. **Note:** *When installing the EGR guide tube, be careful of its direction. The outlet faces the rear of the engine. Otherwise the distribution efficiency of the exhaust gas will be reduced* **(see illustration)**.

EGR control solenoid valve

16 The EGR control solenoid valve cuts the intake manifold vacuum signal for EGR control. The solenoid valve actuates in response to the on/off signal from the ECCS control unit. When the solenoid is off, a vacuum signal from the intake manifold is fed into the EGR control valve. As the control unit outputs an on signal, then the coil pulls the plunger downward, and cuts the vacuum signal **(see illustration)**.

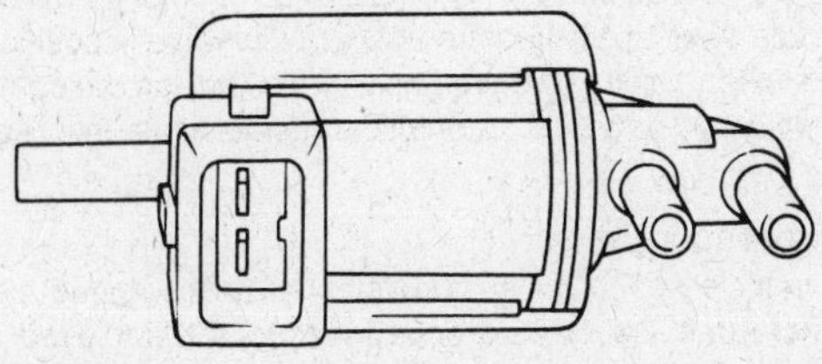

14.16 **The EGR control solenoid valve controls the vacuum to the EGR valve**

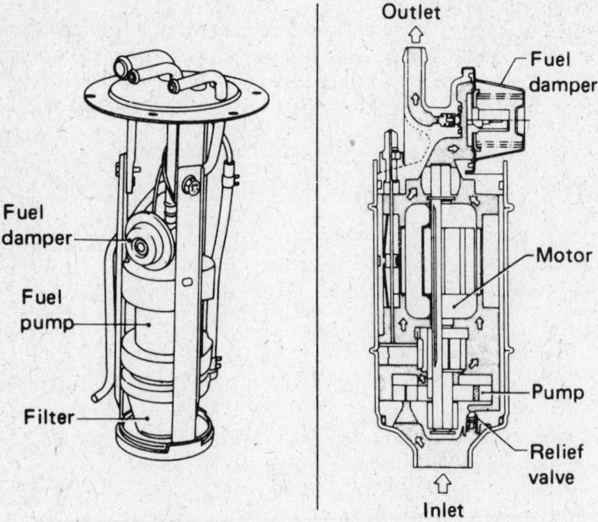

14.17 The fuel pump is a wet type pump, where the vane rollers are directly coupled to an electric motor which is submerged in fuel

Fuel pump

17 The fuel pump, which is located in the fuel tank, is a wet type pump where the vane rollers are directly coupled to a motor which is filled with fuel **(see illustration)**.

Air regulator

18 The air regulator gives an air bypass when the engine is cold to allow fast idle during warm-up. A bimetal heater and rotary shutter are built into the air regulator. When the bimetal temperature is low, the air bypass post is open. As the engine starts and electric current flows through a heater, the bimetal begins to rotate the shutter to close off the bypass port. The air passage remains closed until the engine is stopped and the bimetal temperature drops **(see illustration)**.

Air induction valve (AIV) (KA24E engine only)

19 The air injection valve sends secondary air to the exhaust manifold by means of a vacuum caused by exhaust pulsation in the exhaust manifold. When the exhaust pressure is below atmospheric pressure (vacuum), secondary air is sent to the exhaust manifold. When the exhaust pressure is above the atmospheric pressure the reed valve will prevent the secondary air from being sent back to the air cleaner **(see illustration)**.

AIV control solenoid valve (KA24E engine only)

20 The AIV control solenoid valve controls an intake manifold vacuum signal for the air induction valve. The solenoid valve actuates in response to the on/off signal from the ECCS control unit. When the solenoid is Off the vacuum signal from the intake manifold is cut. As this happens the control unit outputs an On signal and the coil pulls the plunger downward, feeding the vacuum signal to the AIV control valve **(see illustration)**.

Power steering oil pressure switch

21 The power steering oil pressure switch is attached to the power steering high pressure tube and detects the power steering load and sends the load signal to the E.C.U. The information is used to control the idle system under various conditions **(see illustration)**.

Air temperature sensor

22 The air temperature sensor controls ignition timing when the temperature of the intake air is extremely high in order to prevent knocking **(see illustration)**.

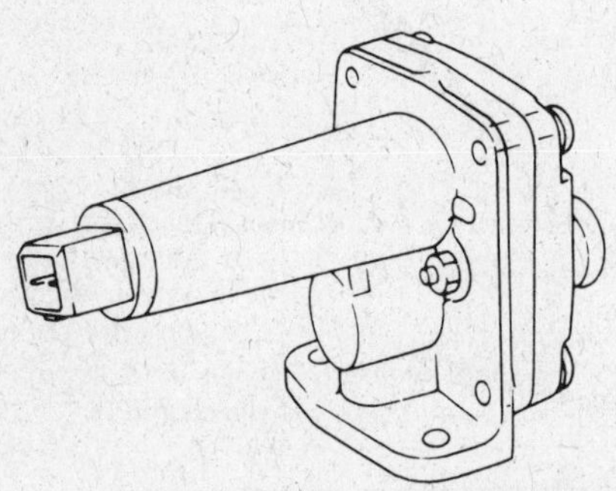

14.18 The air regulator bypasses air around the throttle valve into the air intake collector when the engine is cold to provide fast idle during warm-up

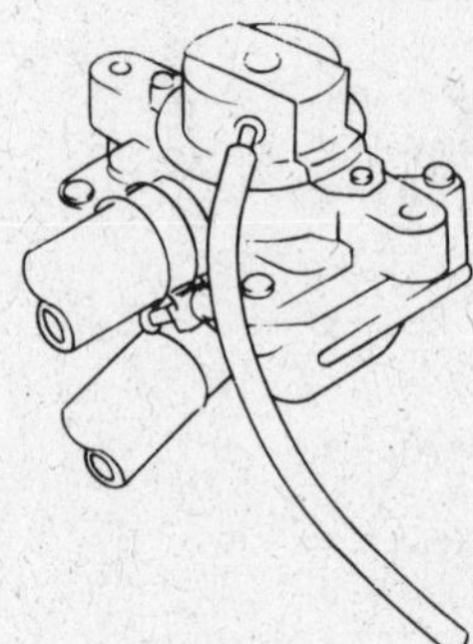

14.19 The air induction valve sends secondary air to the exhaust manifold

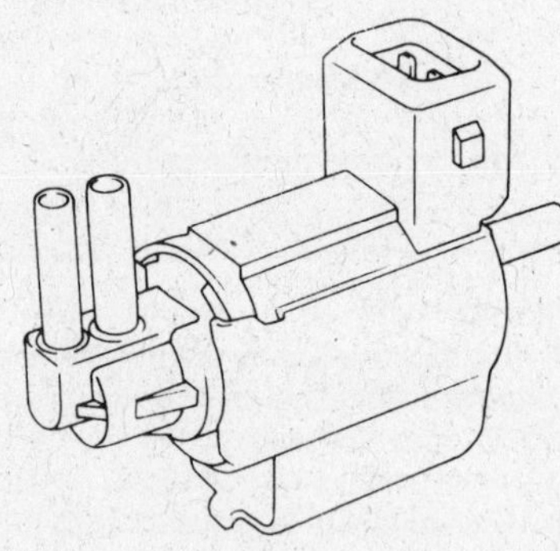

14.20 The AIV control solenoid valve controls the intake manifold vacuum signal to the air induction valve

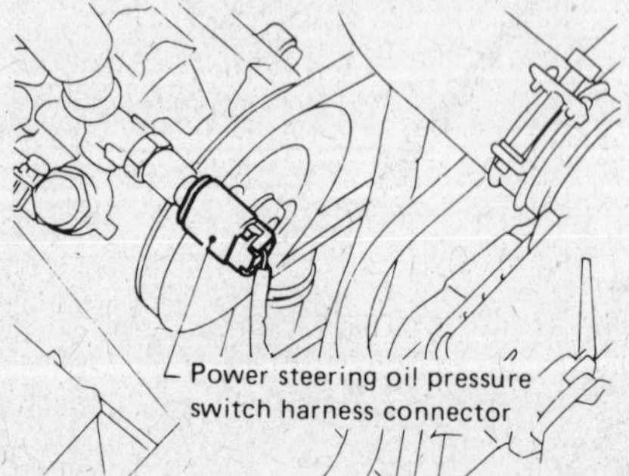

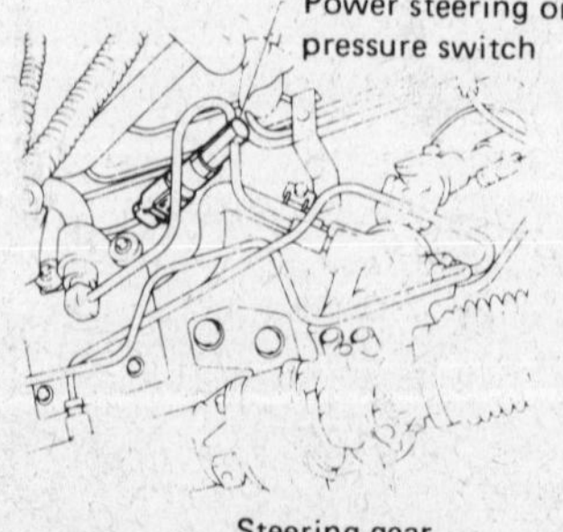

14.21 The power steering oil pressure switch relays information to the ECU to control the idle in various conditions

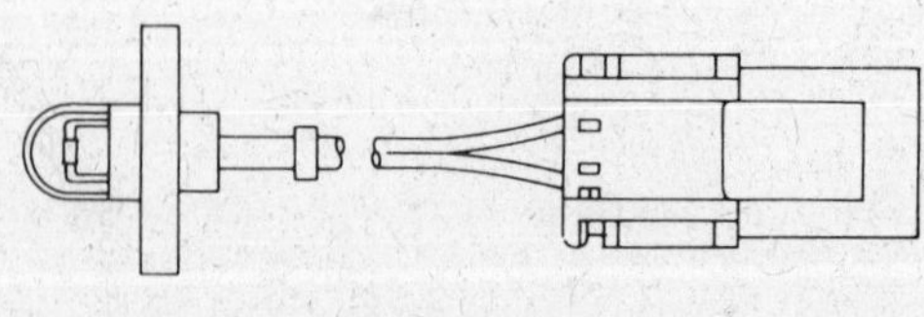

14.22 The air temperature sensor controls ignition timing when the temperature of the air is very high

Throttle body injection (TBI) system

Refer to illustrations 14.23a, 14.23b and 14.23c

23 The throttle body fuel injection system (TBI) is an electronically controlled system with one or two fuel injectors mounted in the throttle body. The electronic control unit (ECU) controls the amount of fuel that is injected into the combustion chamber by varying the pulse time that the fuel injectors stay "on". Many of the components of the TBI system are similar to the components equipped on the MPFI system **(see illustrations)**.

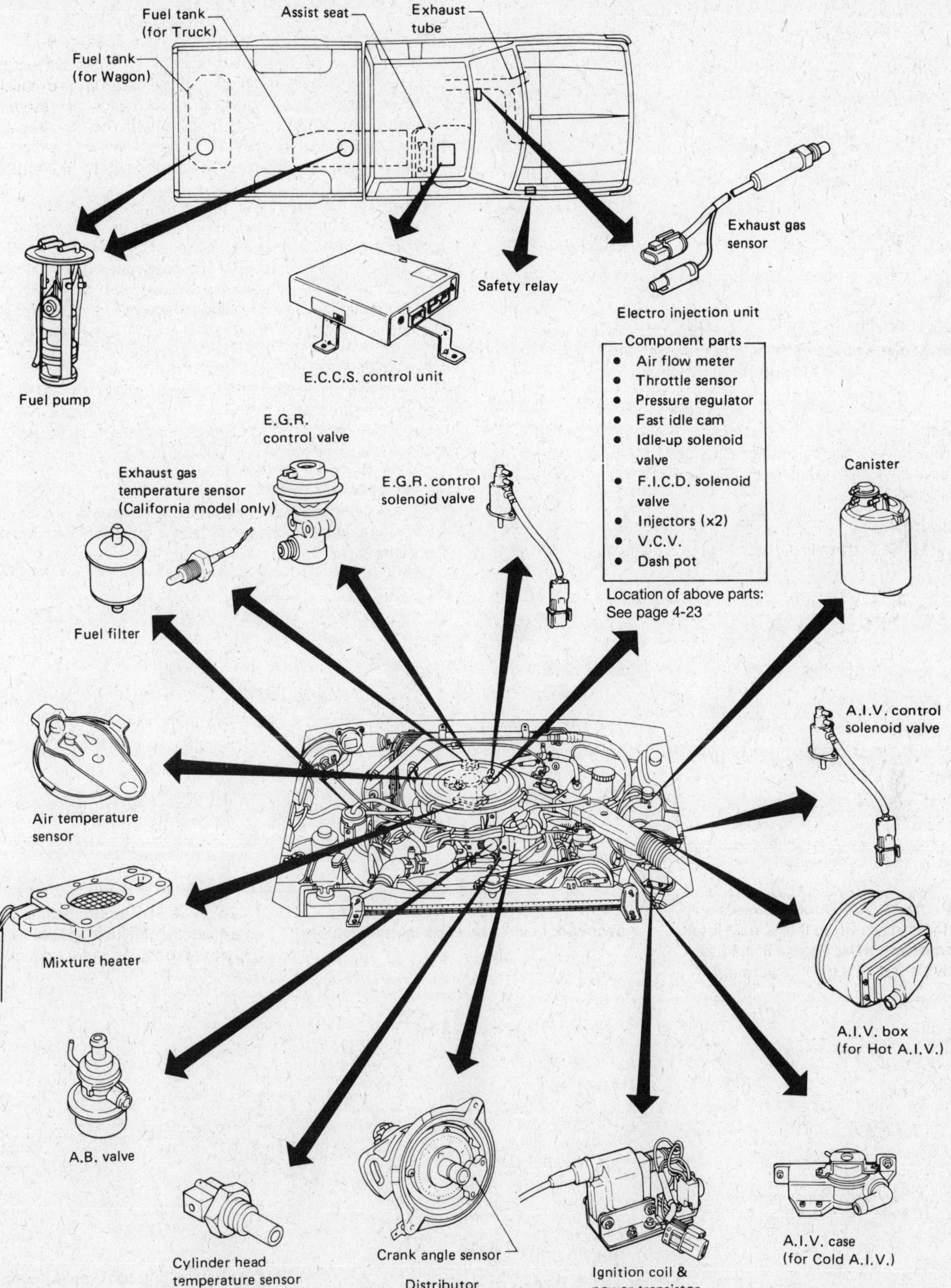

14.23a Location of the fuel injection components on the TBI four cylinder engines

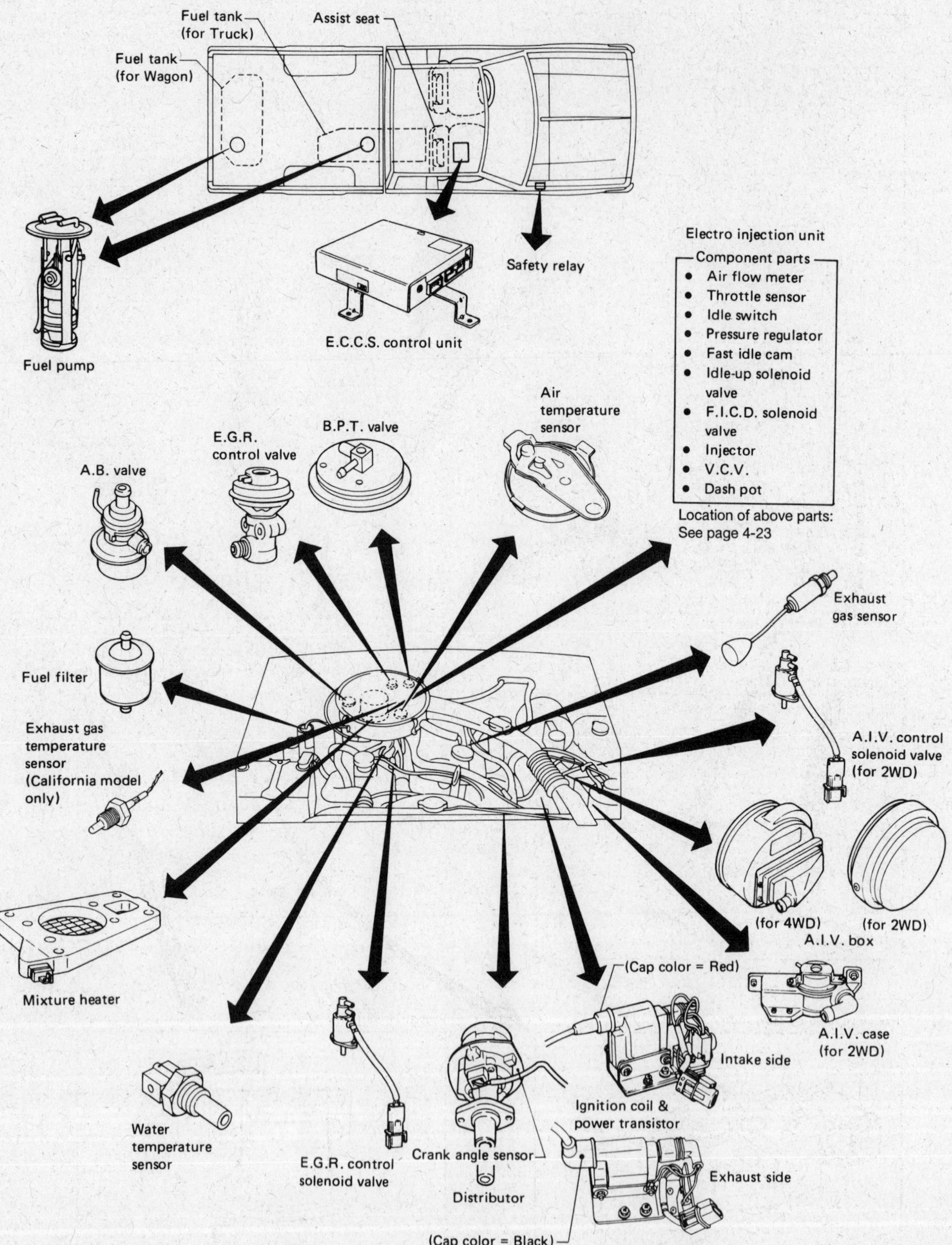
Fuel tank
(for Truck)
Assist seat
Fuel tank
(for Wagon)
Fuel pump
E.C.C.S. control unit
Safety relay
Electro injection unit
Component parts
• Air flow meter
• Throttle sensor
• Idle switch
• Pressure regulator
• Fast idle cam
• Idle-up solenoid valve
• F.I.C.D. solenoid valve
• Injector
• V.C.V.
• Dash pot
Location of above parts:
See page 4-23
Air temperature sensor
B.P.T. valve
E.G.R. control valve
A.B. valve
Exhaust gas sensor
Fuel filter
Exhaust gas temperature sensor (California model only)
A.I.V. control solenoid valve (for 2WD)
(for 4WD)
(for 2WD)
A.I.V. box
Mixture heater
(Cap color = Red)
A.I.V. case (for 2WD)
Intake side
Ignition coil & power transistor
Water temperature sensor
E.G.R. control solenoid valve
Crank angle sensor
Distributor
Exhaust side
(Cap color = Black)

14.23b Location of the fuel injection components on the V6 TBI engines

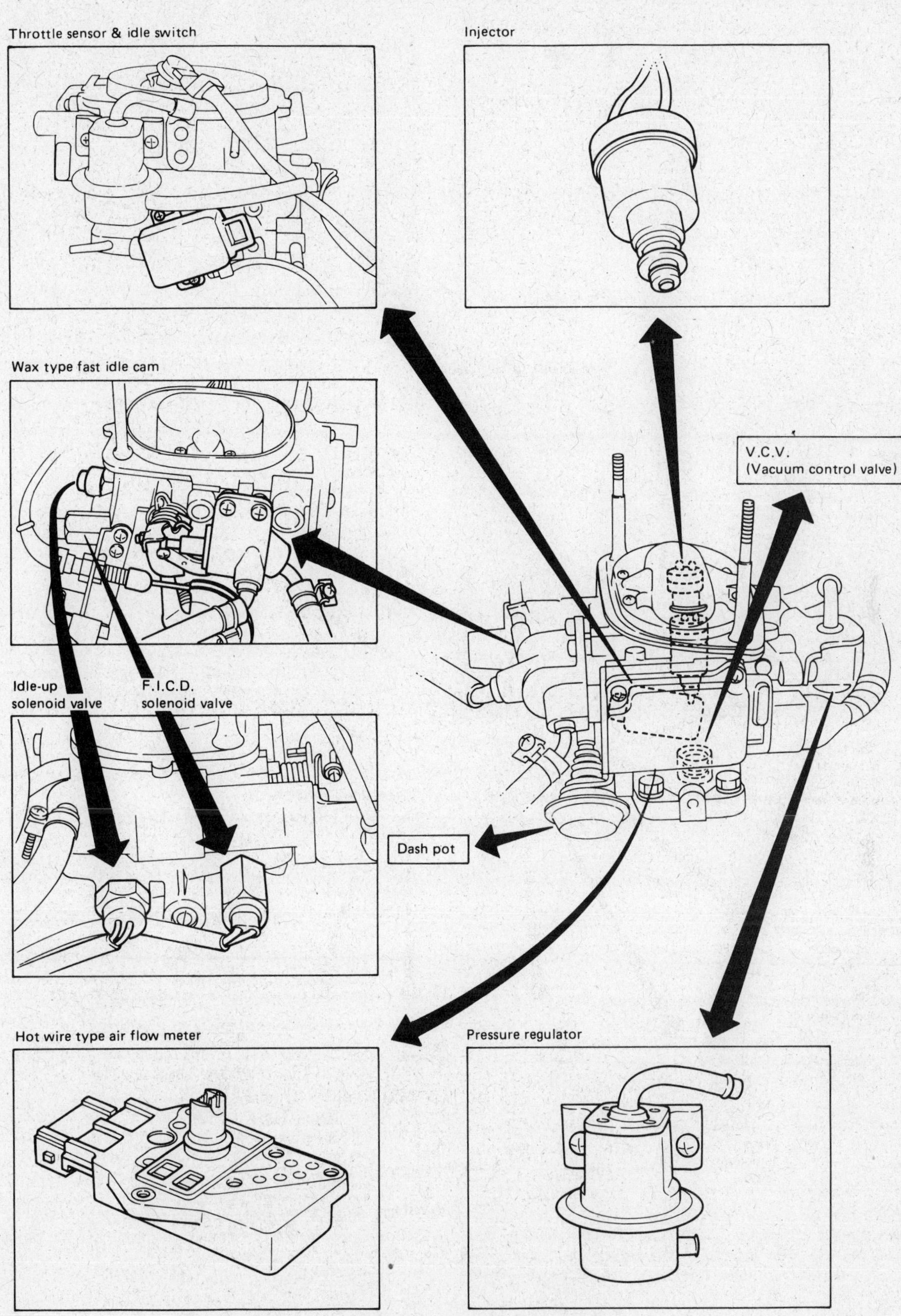

14.23c Throttle body details (1985 through 1989)

4

15.1 The fuel pump fuse should be clearly labelled at the fuse box

16.5b . . . unplug the connectors at the ends of the pigtail leads for the FICD solenoid valve, the idle-up solenoid valve and the injectors, detach the fuel hoses (arrows) from the pressure regulator (lower hose not shown), unplug the electrical connector (not shown – in back) to the throttle sensor and idle switch, remove all four throttle body mounting nuts and lift off the throttle body

15 Fuel pressure relief

Refer to illustration 15.1

1 Remove the fuse for the fuel pump **(see illustration)**.
2 Start the engine.
3 After the engine stalls, crank the engine two or three times.
4 Turn the ignition switch to Off.
5 After fuel system servicing is completed, replace the fuse.

16 Throttle body (TBI systems only) – removal and installation

Refer to illustrations 16.5a and 16.5b

Warning: *Gasoline is extremely flammable, so extra precautions must be taken when working on any part of the fuel system. Make sure the engine is cool. Don't smoke or allow open flames or bare light bulbs near the work area. Also, do not work in a garage if a natural gas-type appliance with a pilot light is present.*

Removal

1 Relieve the fuel pressure (see Section 14).
2 Detach the cable from the negative terminal of the battery.

16.5a To remove the throttle body, unplug the electrical connector to the air flow meter, detach the coolant hoses from the fast idle cam, detach the throttle cable and, if equipped, the ASCD (cruise control) cable (arrows), . . .

3 Drain approximately 1-1/8 quart of engine coolant (see Chapter 1).
4 Remove the air cleaner housing assembly.
5 Detach the electrical connectors for the throttle sensor, the idle switch, the injectors and the air flow meter **(see illustrations)**.
6 Detach the throttle cable from the throttle linkage (see Section 5 if necessary).
7 Detach the Automatic Speed Control Device (ASCD) cable, if equipped, from the throttle linkage (see Section 5 if necessary).
8 Detach the fuel hoses from the pressure regulator.
9 Detach the coolant hoses from the fast idle cam.
10 Remove the injection body-to-intake manifold mounting nuts.
11 Remove the injection body assembly and gasket from the manifold.

Installation

12 Installation is the reverse of removal. Tighten the throttle body mounting nuts to the specified torque. Make sure that all cables, wires and hoses are properly reattached.
13 Start the engine and make sure that there is no fuel leakage from the clearance between the injector cover and the throttle body. Stop the engine and make sure that the fuel vapor sprayed on the throttle valve is not dripping (if it is, there is a leak). Also be sure that the engine is idling steadily at the specified rpm. After the engine is warmed up, add approximately 1-1/8 quart of engine coolant (see Chapter 1 if necessary).

17 Fuel injector – replacement

Throttle body injection (TBI) system

Refer to illustrations 17.3, 17.4, 17.5a, 17.5b, 17.6, 17.7a, 17.7b, 17.7c, 17.9a, 17.9b, 17.9c, 17.12 and 17.14

Warning: *Gasoline is extremely flammable, so extra precautions must be taken when working on any part of the fuel system. Make sure the engine is cool. Don't smoke or allow open flames or bare light bulbs near the work area. Also, do not work in a garage if a natural gas-type appliance with a pilot light is present.*

1 Relieve the fuel pressure (see Section 14).
2 Remove the throttle body (see Section 15).
3 Remove the seal rubber and the injector harness grommet from the injection body **(see illustration)**.
4 Remove the injector cover **(see illustration)**.
5 With the throttle valve kept fully open, carefully tap the bottom of the fuel injector with a hollow bar **(see illustration)**. **Note:** *The hollow bar must have an inside diameter of no less than 0.217-inches* **(see illustration)**. Be careful not to damage the injector nozzle tip. If the tip is deformed by the bar during removal, the injector must be replaced.

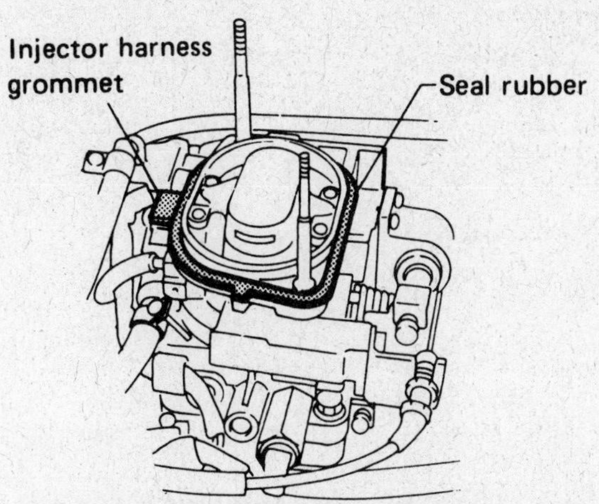

17.3 Remove the seal rubber and the injector harness grommet from the throttle body

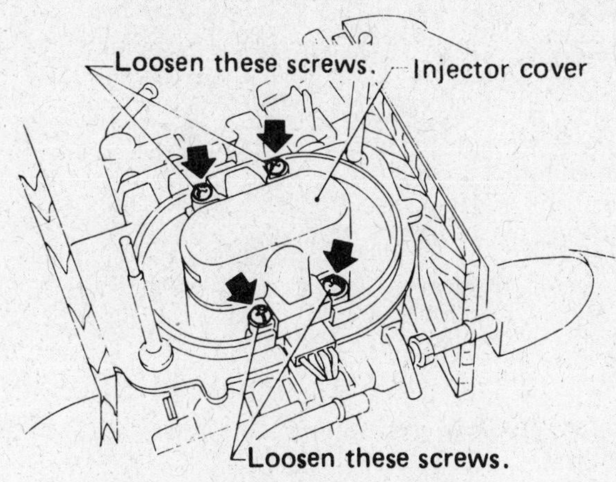

17.4 Remove the injector cover screws (arrows) and detach the injector cover

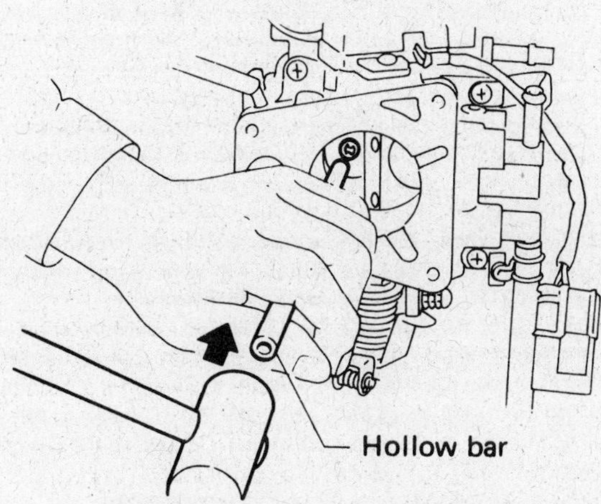

17.5a With the throttle valve fully open, tap the bottom of the injector with a hollow bar as shown

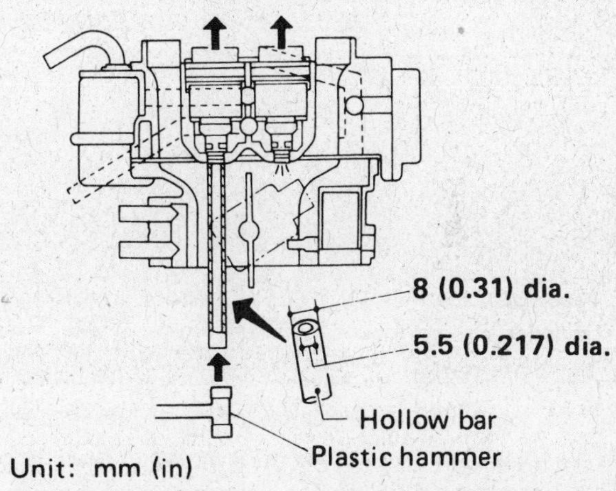

17.5b Make sure that the hollow bar has an inside diameter of at least 0.217-inches (so it doesn't damage the injector nozzle)

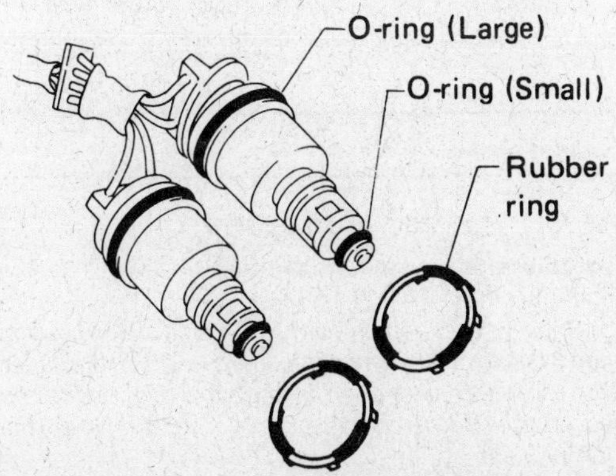

17.6 Every time you remove the injectors, replace the large and small O-rings and the rubber ring with new ones – be sure to apply some silicone oil to the O-rings when installing them

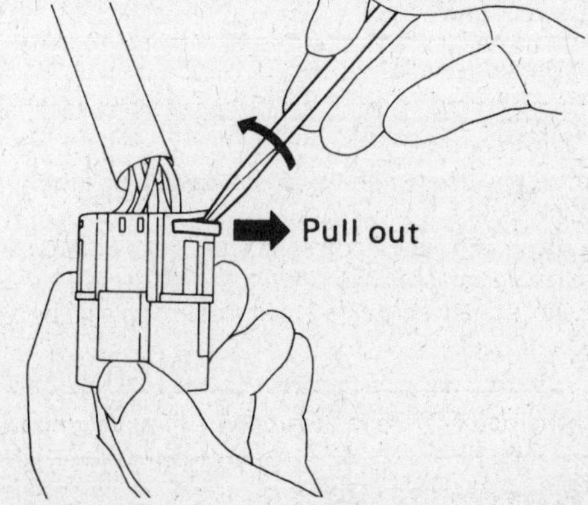

17.7a Before unplugging the terminal from the harness connector, remove the retainer – the best way to get the retainer out is to pry it loose with a small screwdriver, pick or scribe

6 If you are simply removing a leaking injector that is otherwise okay, remove the old large and small O-rings and the rubber ring **(see illustration)** and install new ones. Be sure to apply some silicone oil to both of the new O-rings when installing them on the injector. Then proceed to Step 12.

7 If you are replacing a faulty injector, disconnect the harness of the bad injector from the harness connector and remove it as follows:

a) Remove the terminal retainer **(see illustration)**.
b) With a small screwdriver, tilt the lock tongue and, at the same time,

4

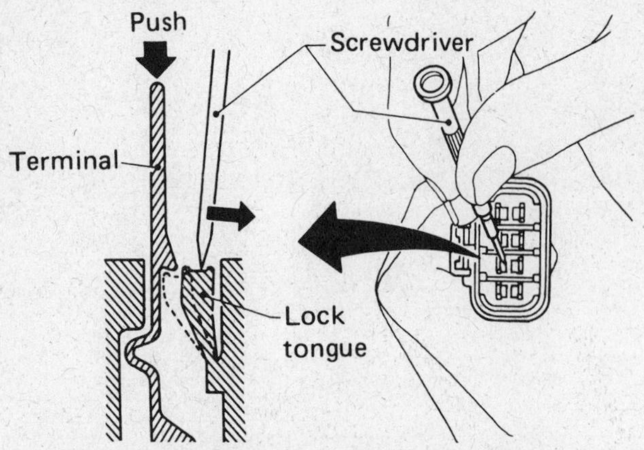

17.7b To get a terminal out of the connector, tilt the tongue lock with a small screwdriver, pick or scribe as shown and simultaneously push out the terminal

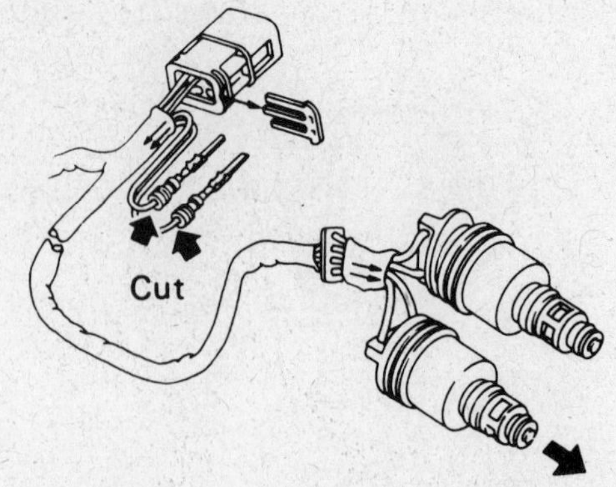

17.7c To detach the harness of a bad injector from the main fuel injector harness, cut the two wires at the boots as shown (arrows), then pull the wires through the harness tube and the grommet and discard the injector

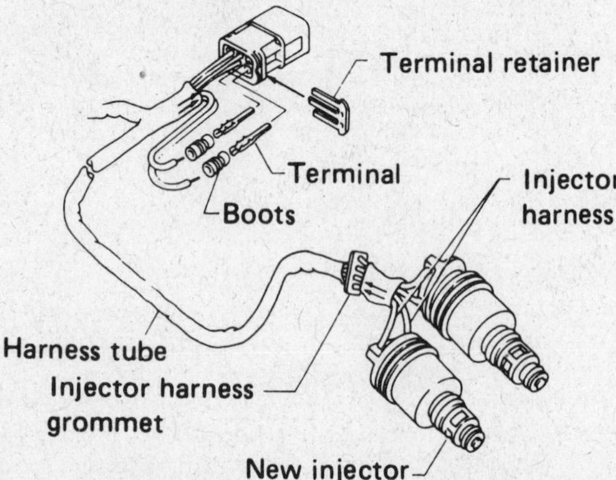

17.9a To attach a new injector to the harness, thread the two wires through the grommet and the tube, then crimp the boots and terminals into place on the ends of the wires

push out the terminal **(see illustration)**. **Caution:** *When extracting a terminal, do not pull the wire harness. Always push the tip of the terminal. Be careful not damage or spill gasoline on the seal boot unless you intend to replace it with a new one.*

c) Cut the wire boots as indicated **(see illustration)**. **Caution:** *Before cutting either wire, be sure you are cutting the wires for the injector you intend to replace by referring to the accompanying charts in Step 9.*

8 Push the harness of the new injector through the injector harness grommet and the harness tube. **Note:** *The harness grommet should be replaced with a new one every time it is removed.*

9 Attach the boots and terminals to the harness with terminal pliers, then, referring to the accompanying chart, plug the harness terminals into the connector **(see illustrations)**. **Caution:** *Be extremely careful when connecting the terminals to the connector. Pay attention to the harness colors and terminal numbers and positions. Otherwise, the injector(s) will be damaged.*

10 Push the terminal retainer back into the connector.

Actuator	Terminal No.	Harness color
Injector A ⊕	①	G
Injector A ⊖	②	W
Injector B ⊕	③	B
Injector B ⊖	④	R
F.I.C.D. solenoid valve ⊕	⑤	B
F.I.C.D. solenoid valve ⊖	⑥	B
Idle-up solenoid valve ⊕	⑦	B/W
Idle-up solenoid valve ⊖	⑧	B/W

A harness color of service part (injector)

Injector ⊕ : G/W

Injector A: Connect to terminal No. ①

Injector B: Connect to terminal No. ③

Injector ⊖ : Y/W

Injector A: Connect to terminal ②

Injector B: Connect to terminal ④

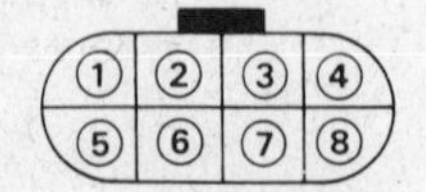

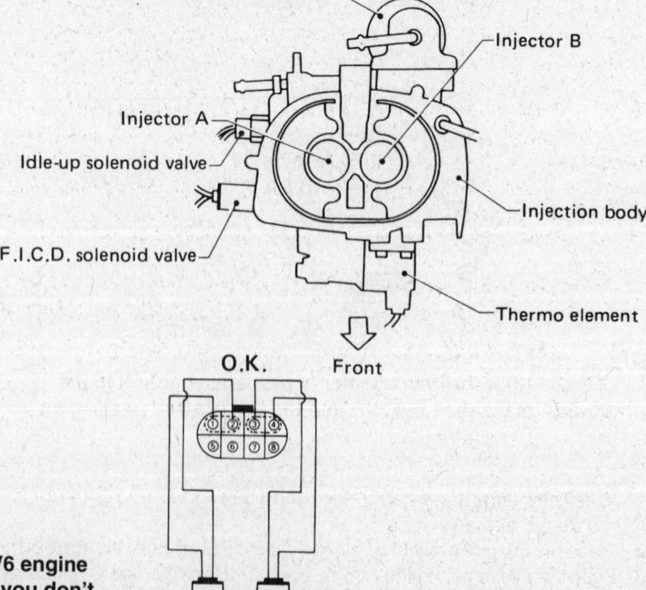

17.9b Refer to the chart above when installing a new injector on a V6 engine (VG30i) and 1987 and later four-cylinder (Z24i) engines to ensure that you don't mix up the terminal numbers and the wire colors – the diagrams in the middle and at the bottom are provided so that you won't confuse either the injector number or the wire-to-terminal connections

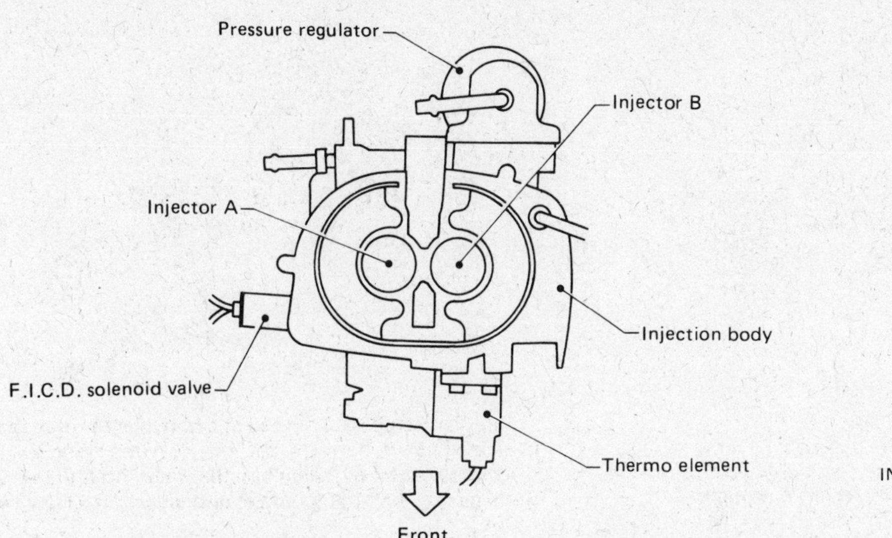

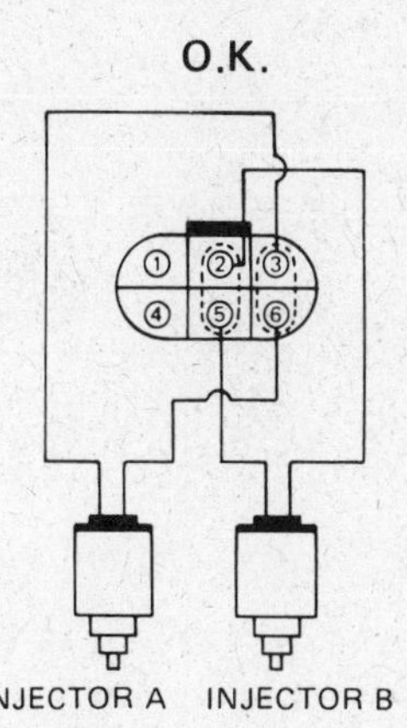

Actuator	Terminal No.	Harness color
Injector A ⊕	③	W
Injector A ⊖	⑥	G
Injector B ⊕	②	R
Injector B ⊖	⑤	L
F.I.C.D. solenoid valve ⊕	①	B/W
F.I.C.D. solenoid valve ⊖	④	B

A harness color of service part (injector)

Injector ⊕ : G/W Connect terminal No. ② or ③

Injector ⊖ : Y/W Connect terminal No. ⑤ or ⑥

17.9c Refer to the chart above when installing a new injector on a 1986 and earlier four-cylinder engine (Z24i) to ensure that you don't mix up the terminal numbers and the wire colors – the diagrams in the middle and at the bottom are provided so that you won't confuse either the injector number or the wire-to-terminal connections

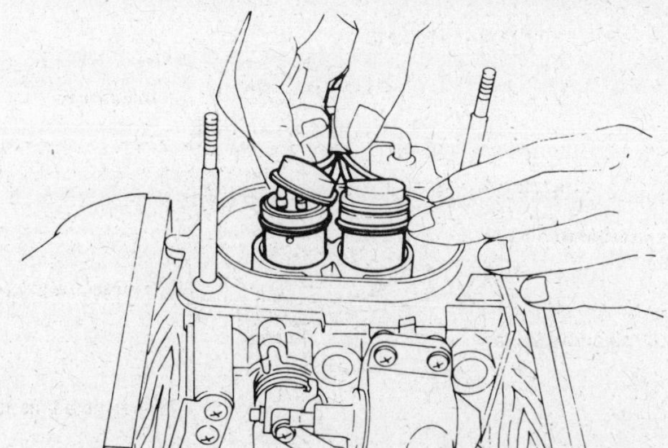

17.12 After the new injector is properly attached to the harness, place the injectors into the throttle body as shown

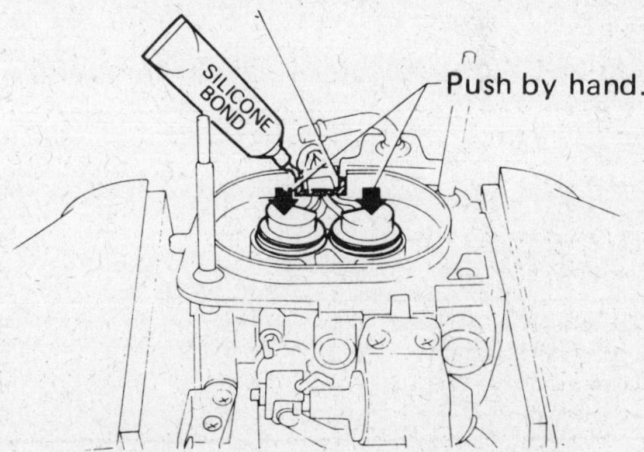

17.14 Apply silicone bond to the injector harness grommet, then push the grommet into place

11 Install new large and small O-rings and a new rubber ring on the injector (see Step 6 above).

12 Place the injector assembly into the injection body **(see illustration)**.

13 Push the injectors into the throttle body by hand until the O-rings are fully seated. Invert the injection body and make sure that the injector tips are properly seated.

14 Apply some silicone bond to the injector harness grommet **(see illustration)**.

15 Install the injector cover. Be sure to use locking sealer on the screw threads. Tighten the screws in a criss-cross pattern to ensure proper seating of the injector and cover.

16 Attach the seal rubber to the top face of the injection body with silicone bond. **Caution:** *Be sure to apply some silicone bond to the bottom of the seal rubber so that the rubber adheres to the throttle body. Do not reinstall the air cleaner housing assembly until this silicone bond has hardened.*

17 Install the throttle body on the intake manifold (see Section 15).

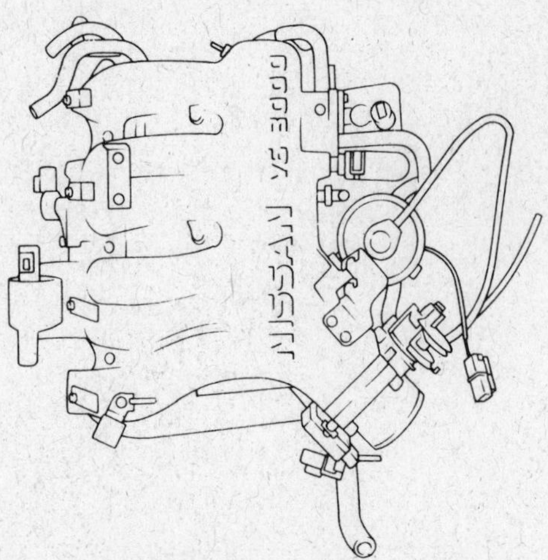

17.22 Intake air collector on the V6 engine

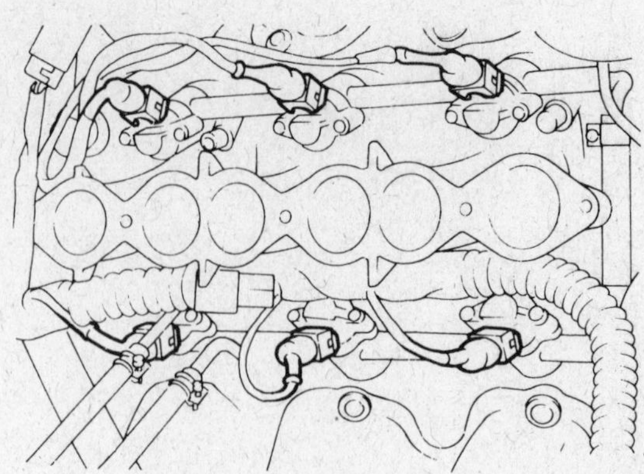

17.25 Disconnect the electrical connectors from the injectors (V6 engine shown)

18 Have the mixture ratio feedback system inspection performed by a dealer service department to make sure that there is no fuel leakage at the injector top seal (this procedure requires several special, expensive tools and is beyond the scope of the home mechanic).

Multi point fuel injection (MPFI) systems

Refer to illustrations 17.22, 17.25 and 17.27.

19 Relieve the fuel pressure (see Section 15)

20 Disconnect the negative cable at the battery.

21 Drain the coolant from the system (see Chapter 1).

22 Disconnect the spark plug wires at the plugs, remove the distributor cap and move the wire assembly out of the work area.

22 On the front of the intake air collector, carefully mark all lines and hoses and remove the throttle cable, throttle sensor and throttle valve switch, throttle cable brackets and all other vacuum lines and electrical connectors **(see illustration)**.

23 On all V6 engines, remove the bolts and lift the intake air collector from the manifold.

24 Remove the fuel feed hose and the return hose from the injector fuel tube assembly.

25 Remove the injector harness connectors **(see illustration)**.

26 Remove the injector fuel tube assembly. **Note:** *When disconnecting the fuel lines place a rag around the connection to catch any leaking fuel.*

27 Remove each of the injector retaining bolts and lift off the injector assembly **(see illustration)**.

28 If any of the individual injectors are to be replaced, determine the injector to be replaced and carefully remove it from the fuel tube.

29 To install the new injector, wet the new o-rings with gasoline and press the injector assembly into the fuel tube assembly.

30 Install the tube assembly.

31 Install and tighten the hold-down bolt for each injector **(see illustration)**.

32 Connect all the injector electrical connectors.

33 Clean all traces of old gasket material from the air intake collector and intake manifold. Install a new gasket and set the intake collector in place, routing the rear side wiring harness up on top of the collector.

34 Route the front side wiring harness along the collector.

35 Install the head bolts that secure the collector to the intake manifold. Tighten the bolts to the torque listed in this Chapter's Specifications.

36 Connect the EGR tube to the air intake collector.

37 Connect all electrical connectors and vacuum/fuel hoses that were disconnected during removal.

38 Connect all wiring harness hold-down straps to the collector.

39 Install the air regulator (see Section 12).

40 The remainder of installation is the reverse of removal.

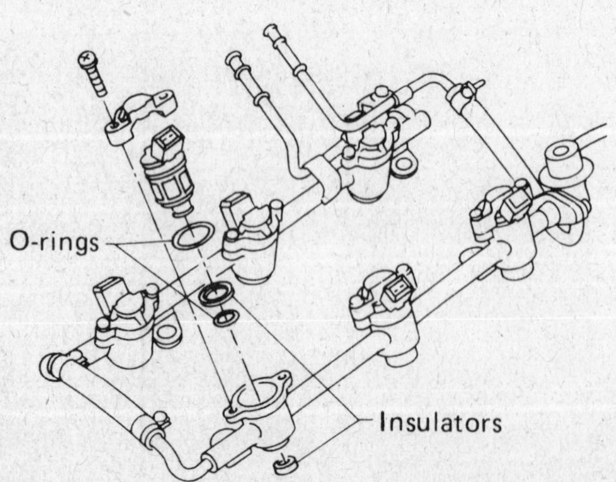

17.27 Each injector is bolted to an individual fuel tube assembly

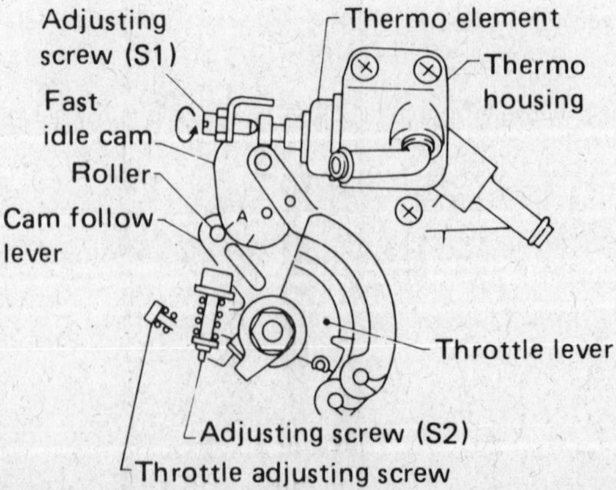

18.2 Before checking the fast idle adjustment clearance, make sure that the alignment mark stamped on the fast idle cam meets the center of the roller installed on the cam follow lever – if it doesn't, adjust the fast idle cam by turning the S1 adjusting screw (if it can't be brought into proper adjustment, replace the thermo element)

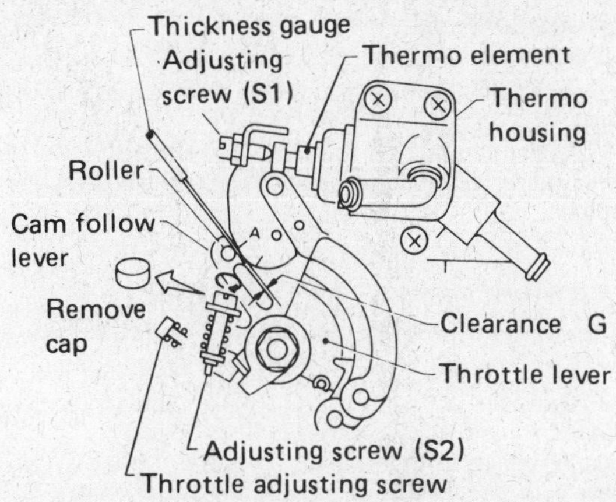

18.3 If clearance G between the roller and the fast idle cam is not as specified, correct it by turning the S2 adjusting screw (make sure that the engine has been sufficiently warmed up before making this adjustment)

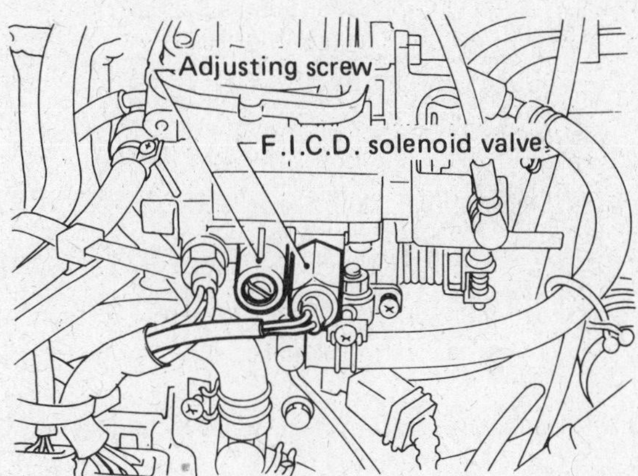

18.7 Adjust the idle speed by turning the adjusting screw next to the FICD solenoid valve

18 Fuel injection system – adjustments

TBI systems

Fast idle inspection and adjustment

Refer to illustrations 18.2 and 18.3

1 Warm up the engine to its normal operating temperature.

2 Make sure that the alignment mark stamped on the fast idle cam meets the center of the roller installed on the cam follower lever. If it doesn't, correct the location of the fast idle cam by turning the S1 adjustment screw **(see illustration)**. If it can't be properly adjusted, replace the thermo element.

3 Check clearance "G" between the roller and the fast idle cam **(see illustration)** and compare your reading to the specified clearance. If it's out of adjustment, correct it by turning the S2 adjusting screw until the clearance is as specified. **Note:** *Make sure that the engine has been warmed up when adjusting clearance "G."*

Fast Idle Control Device (FICD) inspection and adjustment

Refer to illustrations 18.7 and 18.8

4 Warm up the engine to its normal operating temperature.

5 Check the idle speed (see Chapter 1) and compare your reading to the specified idle speed.

6 Turn the air conditioner switch on and check the idle speed again. Compare your reading to the idle speed specified with the A/C on.

7 If the idle speed is out of adjustment, adjust it by turning the adjusting screw **(see illustration)**.

8 If the FICD solenoid valve does not work, check the harness and the solenoid valve **(see illustration)** as follows:

a) Disconnect the 8-pin connector.
b) Check the power supply through the harness with the ignition switch on and the air conditioner switch on.
c) Check the electric continuity of the solenoid valve.

9 If the solenoid valve has no continuity in spite of a proper power supply, replace it with a new one. **Note:** *Be sure to use a new washer with the new solenoid valve and tighten the valve to the specified torque.*

Dash pot inspection and adjustment

Refer to illustration 18.11

10 Warm up the engine to its normal operating temperature. The idle speed of the engine must be properly adjusted (see Chapter 1).

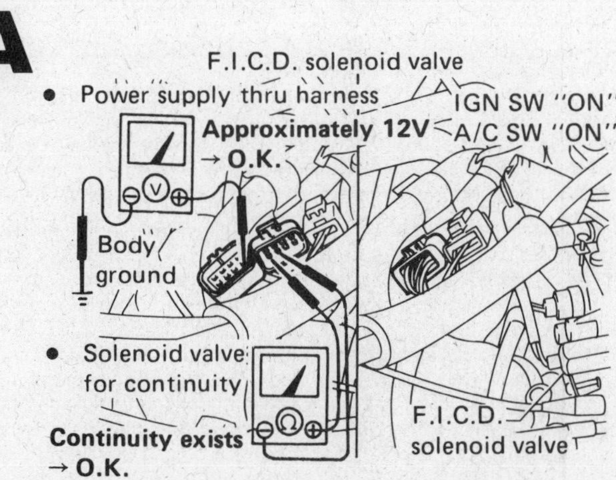

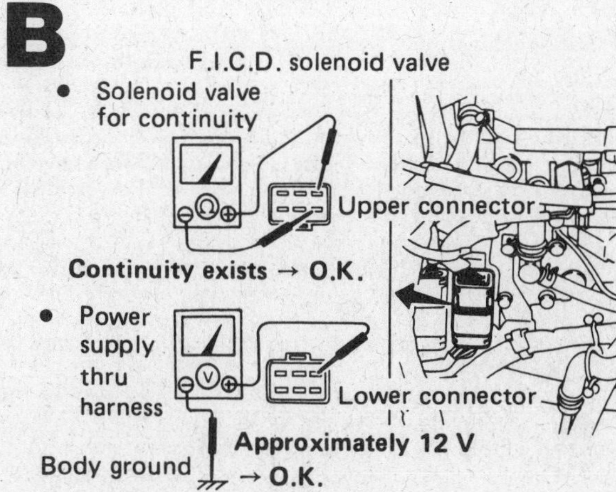

18.8 To check the FICD solenoid valve (A is the V6; B is the four) for continuity, unplug the 8-pin connector and check the power supply through the harness with the ignition and A/C turned on, then check the electrical continuity of the valve itself

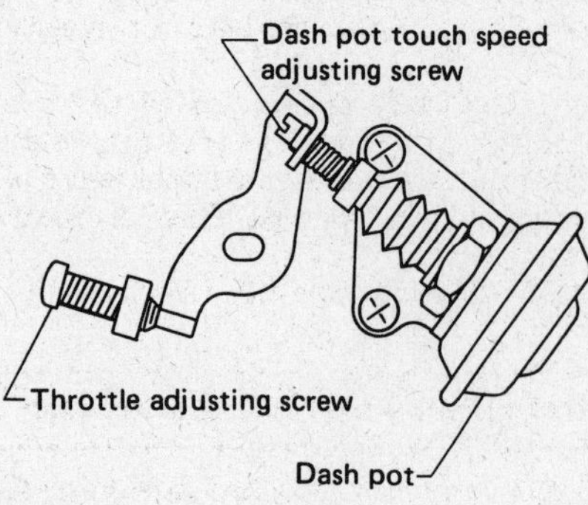

18.11 Adjust the dash pot touch speed by turning the adjusting screw

11 Turn the throttle valve by hand and read the engine speed when the dash pot just touches the adjusting screw **(see illustration)**. Compare your reading to the specified dash pot touch speed.
12 If the touch speed is out of specification, adjust it by turning the adjusting screw.

Idle-up solenoid valve inspection

Refer to illustration 18.13

13 Disconnect the 8-pin connector **(see illustration)** and check it for continuity.
14 If there is no continuity, replace the valve with a new one. Be sure to use a new washer with the new valve and tighten the new valve to the specified torque.

Multi point fuel injection (MPFI) systems

Fast idle inspection and adjustment (KA24E engines)

Refer to illustrations 18.17, 18.18, 18.19 and 18.20

15 Start the engine and warm it up until normal operating temperature is reached.
16 Stop the engine and remove the air cleaner.
17 Make sure the mark (Q) on the fast idle cam is pointing to the roller center **(see illustration)**.
18 Adjust the idle screw **(see illustration)** until the top of the cam faces the center of the lever roller.
19 Measure the clearance (G) between the roller and the top of the fast idle cam **(see illustration)**. Refer to the specifications listed in this chapter.
20 If the clearance is incorrect, adjust the clearance using the adjusting screw (B) **(see illustration)** until the specified clearance is obtained.

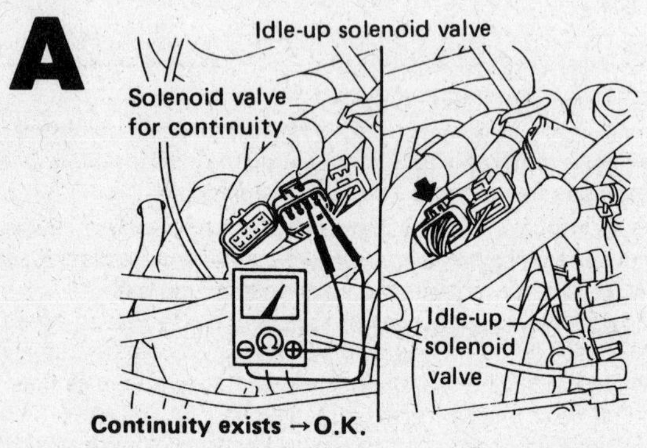

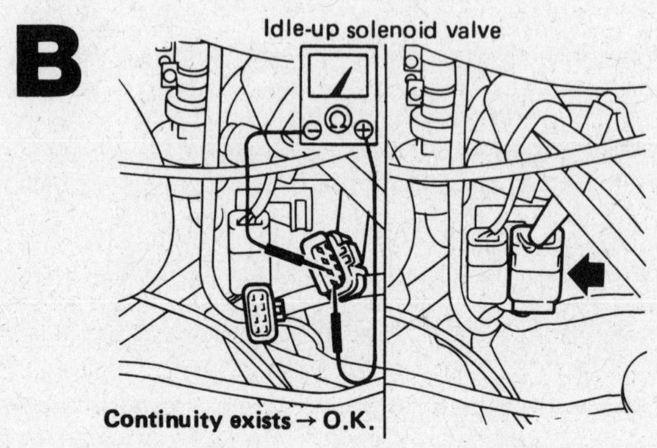

18.13 To check the idle-up solenoid valve, disconnect the 8-pin connector and check the valve for continuity as shown (A is the V6; B is the four)

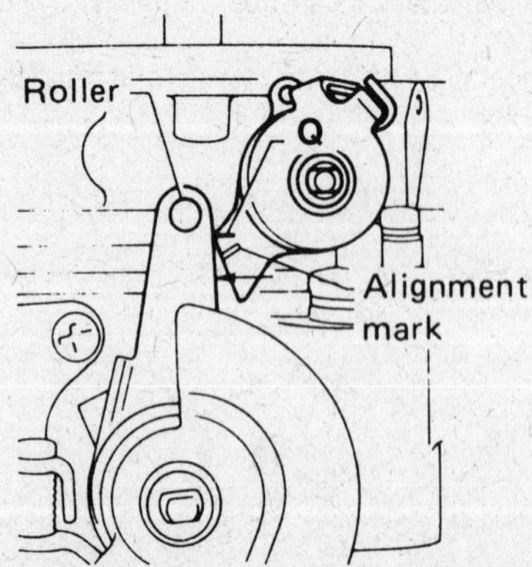

18.17 Be sure to measure from the tip (Q) of the fast idle cam to the roller. DO NOT use the alignment mark

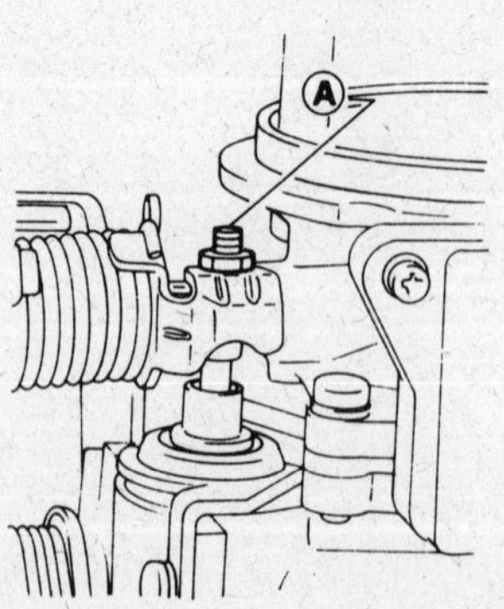

18.18 Loosen the locking nut and adjust the screw (A) to pivot the fast idle cam

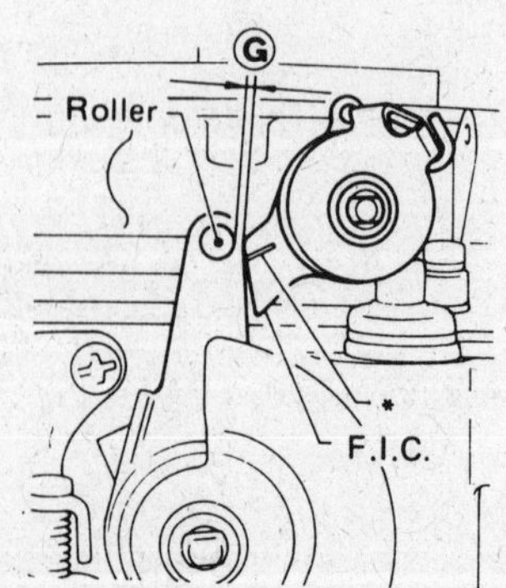

18.19 Measure clearance G from the roller to the tip of the fast idle cam

19 Fuel system – cleaning

Warning: *Gasoline is extremely flammable, so extra precautions must be taken when working on any part of the fuel system. Make sure the engine is cool. Don't smoke or allow open flames or bare light bulbs near the work area. Also, do not work in a garage if a natural gas-type appliance with a pilot light is present.*

1 With time it is likely that sediment will collect in the bottom of the fuel tank. Condensation, resulting in rust and other impurities, will usually be found in the fuel tank of any vehicle more than three or four years old. The following procedure should be performed to eliminate foreign material or contaminated fuel from the fuel system.

2 Disconnect the negative battery cable from the battery.

3 Drain and remove the fuel tank as described in Section 19.

4 Remove the fuel filter as described in Chapter 1. If the filter is clogged, replace it with a new one.

5 Remove the fuel tank gauge unit from the fuel tank as described in Section 20.

6 Disconnect the fuel inlet line at the fuel pump and clean the line out by applying air pressure through it in the direction of the fuel flow.

7 Use low air pressure to clean the pipes on the tank unit.

8 Refer to Section 21 for additional information regarding the cleaning of the fuel tank.

20 Fuel tank – removal and installation

Refer to illustration 20.3

Warning: *Gasoline is extremely flammable, so extra precautions must be taken when working on any part of the fuel system. Make sure the engine is cool. Don't smoke or allow open flames or bare light bulbs near the work area. Also, do not work in a garage if a natural gas-type appliance with a pilot light is present. Any repairs to the fuel tank or filler neck should be carried out by a professional who has experience in this critical and potentially dangerous work. While performing any work on the fuel tank, be sure to have a CO2 fire extinguisher on hand and wear safety glasses.*

1 Disconnect the negative battery cable from the battery.

2 Remove the drain plug from the bottom of the fuel tank **(see illustrations 4.1a and 4.1b)** and drain the fuel into an approved gasoline container.

3 From the top of the fuel tank, disconnect the fuel filler hose, fuel outlet hose, air ventilation hose, breather hose, fuel return hose and the wiring connector leading to the fuel tank gauge unit **(see illustration)**. Immediately plug all openings to prevent the entry of dirt.

4 If equipped, remove the fuel tank protector shield mounted in front of the tank.

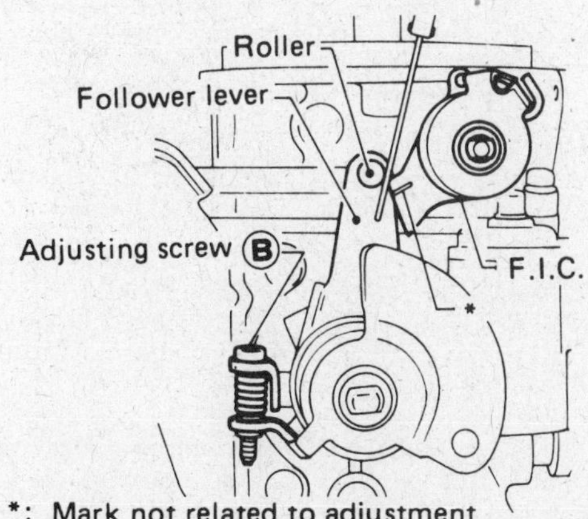

18.20 Adjust the throttle valve by turning adjusting screw B

5 While supporting the tank using either a jack or with the help of an assistant, remove the fuel tank mounting bolts and carefully lower the tank from the truck.

6 It is recommended that the tank be cleaned out immediately after removal, especially if it is to be worked on or stored. Refer to Section 21.

7 Before installing the tank make sure that all traces of dirt and corrosion are cleaned from it. If the tank is rusted internally however, it should be replaced with a new one.

8 Installation is the reverse of the removal procedure.

21 Fuel tank gauge unit – removal and installation

Warning: *Gasoline is extremely flammable, so extra precautions must be taken when working on any part of the fuel system. Make sure the engine is cool. Don't smoke or allow open flames or bare light bulbs near the work area. Also, do not work in a garage if a natural gas-type appliance with a pilot light is present. While performing any work on the fuel tank be sure to have a CO2 fire extinguisher on hand and wear safety glasses.*

1 Disconnect the negative battery cable.

2 Disconnect the wires leading to the fuel tank gauge unit.

3 Remove the fuel tank as described in Section 19.

4 Remove the gauge unit lock plate by using a hammer and brass punch to turn it clockwise. **Warning:** *Don't use a screwdriver or punch made from any material other than brass. They could cause sparks which could cause an explosion!*

5 Lift the gauge unit from the tank, and cover the tank opening to prevent the entry of dirt.

6 Installation is the reverse of the removal procedure.

22 Fuel tank – cleaning and purging

Warning: *Never perform repair work on the tank involving heat or flame without first carrying out the following procedure.*

1 Drain and remove the fuel tank as described in Section 19.

2 Remove the fuel tank gauge unit as described in Section 20.

3 Turn the tank over and empty out any remaining fuel.

4 If repair work needs to be done to the fuel tank that does not involve any heat or flame, the tank can be satisfactorily cleaned by running hot water into it and letting it overflow out the top for at least five minutes. This method, however, does not remove gas vapors.

5 If repair work involving heat or flame is necessary, have it done by an experienced professional. The following, more thorough procedures should be used to remove fuel and vapors from the tank for storage or transportation to a repair facility.

6 Fill the tank completely with tap water, agitate vigorously and drain.

7 Add a gasoline emulsifying agent to the tank according to the manufacturer's instructions, refill with water, agitate approximately 10 minutes and drain.

8 Flush to overflowing once again with water for several minutes and drain.

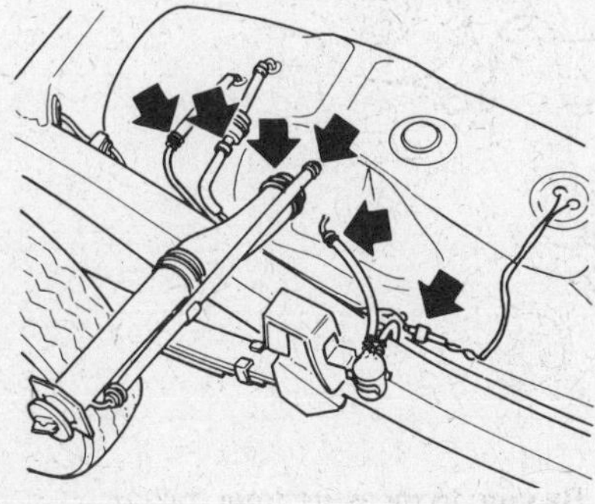

20.3 Locations of the tank hose and wiring connections on a typical fuel tank (arrows)

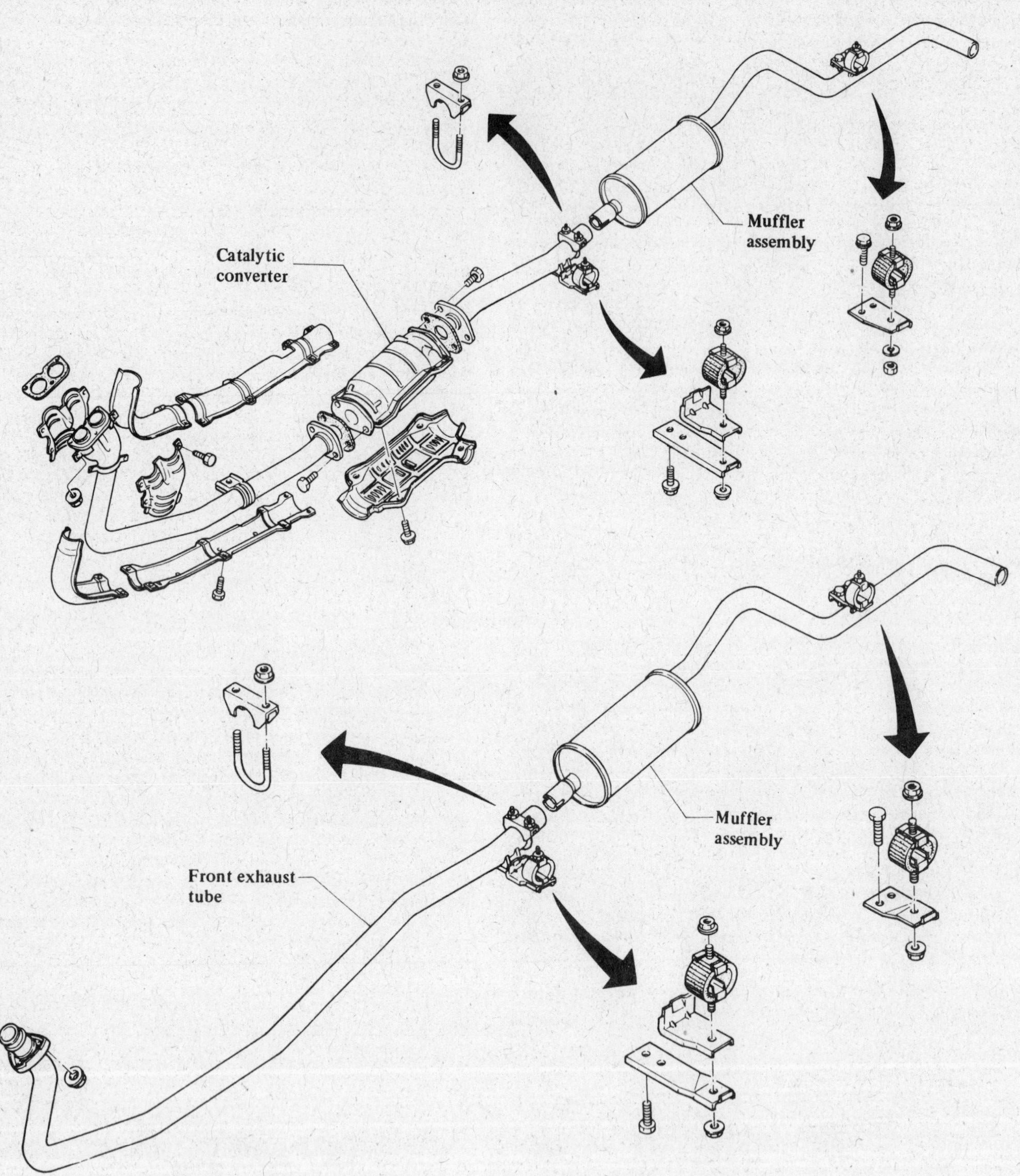

25.5a Typical exhaust system used on carburetor equipped vehicles (bottom – 1980 Canadian models; top – all others)

23 Exhaust system – general information

The exhaust system consists of the muffler, catalytic converter and exhaust pipes, and includes four main pieces; the front exhaust pipe which attaches to the exhaust manifold, the catalytic converter, the center tube and the muffler/tailpipe assembly. **Note:** *1980 Canada models use a two piece exhaust system consisting only of the front exhaust pipe and the muffler/tailpipe assembly.*

The catalytic converter is attached to both the front exhaust pipe and the center tube by mounting bolts. The muffler is attached to the center tube by a clamp and is welded to the tailpipe.

The interior of the catalytic converter is a honeycomb-like design that is coated with platinum and rhodium. When these elements interact with the hydrocarbon (HC), carbon monoxide (CO) and oxides of nitrogen (NOx) in the exhaust, it causes reactions to occur that convert the CO to CO2 (carbon dioxide), the HC to CO and H20 (water), and reduces the NOx.

Since lead and phosphorus additives in gasoline can poison the converter's catalytic elements, thus rendering it ineffective in altering the gases' toxic elements, only unleaded fuel should be used in the vehicle.

Periodic maintenance of the converter is not required, but it has a limited working life after which it must be replaced. This is usually at intervals of around 30,000 miles (48,000 km).

In order to accurately test the functioning of the converter, a CO tester is needed. For this reason, we recommend you take the vehicle to a Nissan dealer or other qualified shop to have the converter tested.

If, through physical damage, the use of leaded fuels or because its active elements have been depleted, the catalytic converter is rendered ineffective, it must be replaced as a unit.

Caution: *It should be noted that since the internal chemical conversions occur between the 600-degrees and 1200-degrees F, the converter operates at a very high temperature. Before performing any work on or near the converter be sure it has cooled sufficiently to avoid serious burns.*

When replacing any exhaust system parts, be sure you allow enough clearance from all points on the body to avoid overheating the floor pan and possibly damaging the interior carpet and insulation.

The entire exhaust system is attached to the body with mounting brackets and rubber hangers. If any one of the parts is improperly installed, excessive noise and vibration will be transmitted to the body.

Regular inspection of the exhaust system should be made to keep it at maximum efficiency. Look for any damage or mispositioned parts, open seams, holes, loose connections, excessive corrosion or other defects which could allow exhaust fumes to seep into the vehicle.

24 Exhaust system check

Because inspection of the exhaust system is part of the routine maintenance schedule, refer to Chapter 1 for this procedure.

25 Front exhaust pipe – removal and installation

Refer to illustrations 25.2a and 25.2b

1 Raise the front of the vehicle and support it on jackstands.

2 Remove the lower catalytic converter shield and protector (if equipped) **(see illustrations)**.

3 Using a piece of thick wire, secure the catalytic converter to the underside of the vehicle.

4 Remove any insulating shields mounted to the front exhaust pipe. Then disconnect the bracket that attaches the pipe to the body.

5 Loosen , but do not remove the two bolts attaching the front exhaust pipe to the catalytic converter. If the bolts are corroded and cannot be easily broken loose, penetrating oil and tapping with a hammer may help.

6 Remove the bolts that attach the front exhaust pipe to the exhaust manifold. Again, penetrating oil and tapping may be necessary.

7 Now, while supporting the front exhaust pipe, remove the two bolts holding the pipe to the converter, and lift out the pipe.

4

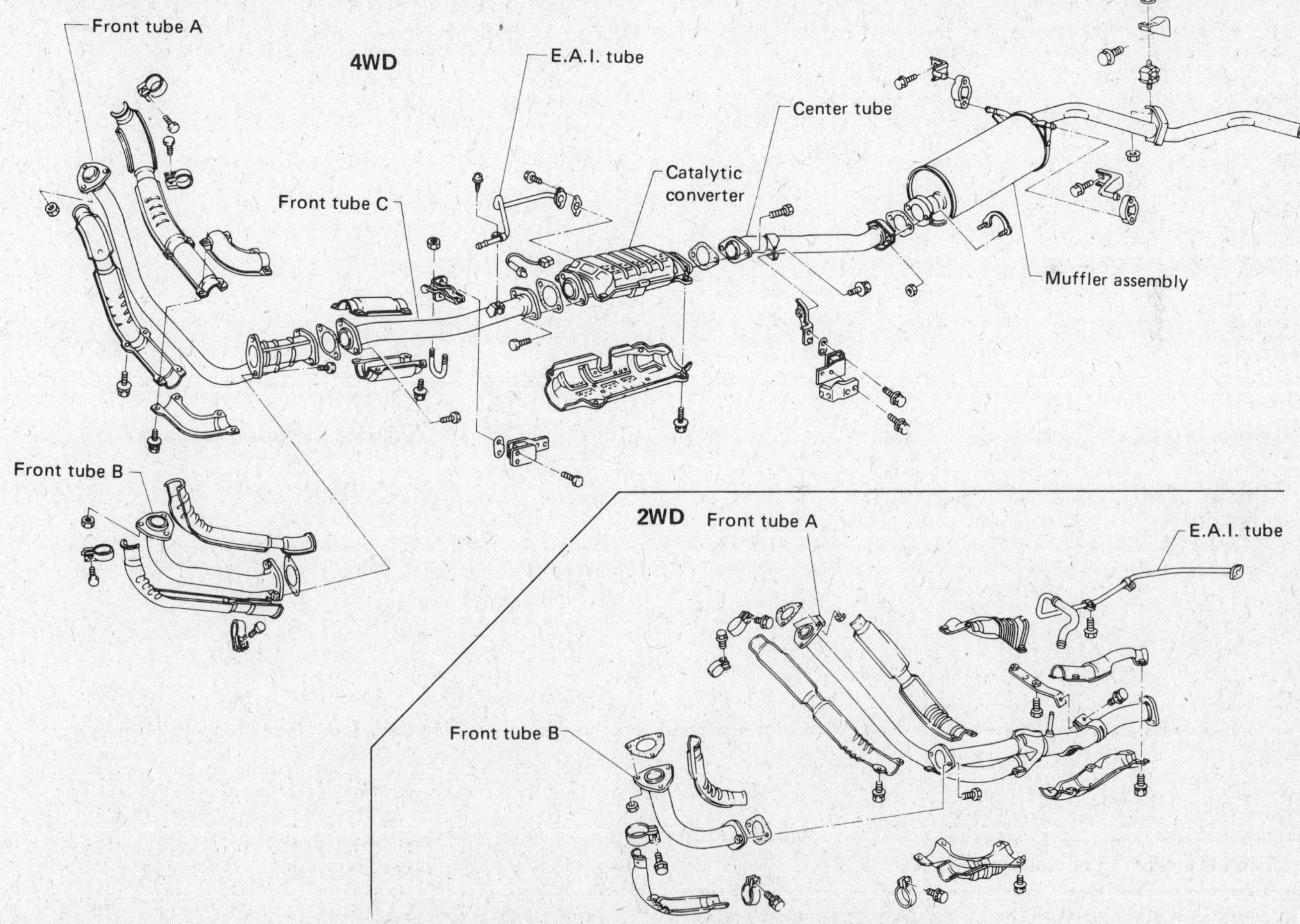

25.2b Typical exhaust system used on fuel injected vehicles

8 Installation is the reverse of the removal procedure. **Note:** *Be sure to use new gaskets between the front exhaust pipe and the exhaust manifold, and the front exhaust pipe and the catalytic converter. Also, before installing the bolts that attach these parts, apply an anti-seize compound to the threads.*

26 Catalytic converter – removal and installation

1 Raise the front of the vehicle and support it on jackstands.
2 Remove the lower catalytic converter shield and protector (if equipped).
3 Using a piece of strong wire, secure the center pipe to the driveshaft.
4 While supporting the catalytic converter, break loose, but do not yet remove the four converter mounting bolts that attach the converter to the front exhaust pipe and center pipe. If the bolts are corroded and cannot be easily broken loose, penetrating oil and tapping with a hammer may help.
5 While supporting the catalytic converter, remove all four mounting bolts, and remove the converter from the vehicle.
6 Installation is the reverse of the removal procedure. **Note:** *Be sure to use new gaskets during installation. Also, before installing the mounting bolts, apply anti-seize compound to the threads.*

27 Muffler/tailpipe assembly – removal and installation

1 The muffler is welded to the tailpipe, and both pieces are designed to be replaced as a unit. However, if either piece needs replacing, but the other is in good condition, a muffler shop will be able to cut off the muffler or tailpipe and weld on a new one without having to replace both pieces. The cost of this procedure, though, may offset the savings realized as a result of not replacing the entire assembly.
2 Raise the rear of the truck and support it on jackstands.
3 Remove the U-bolt clamp that secures the muffler to the center pipe.
4 Lightly tap all around the connection with a hammer to break up the internal sealant.
5 With a soft-faced hammer, tap on the front end of the muffler while pushing it backwards until the muffler is disengaged from the center pipe.
6 Remove the bolts attaching the tailpipe mounting bracket to the frame and lift the assembly out.
7 Installation is the reverse of the removal procedure. **Note:** *To ensure that no exhaust leaks occur at the muffler-to-center tube connection, an exhaust sealant should be used during installation. Follow the directions supplied with the sealant.*

28 Center exhaust pipe – removal and installation

1 Remove the muffler/tailpipe assembly as described in Section 26. 2 Remove the mounting nuts that attach the center pipe bracket to the frame.
3 Remove the bolts that attach the center pipe to the catalytic converter. If they are difficult to break loose, penetrating oil and tapping with a hammer may help. The center pipe can then be lifted out.
4 Installation is the reverse of the removal procedure. **Note:** *Be sure to use a new gasket between the center pipe and catalytic converter during installation. Also, before installing the mounting bolts, apply anti-seize compound to the threads.*

Chapter 5 Engine electrical systems

Contents

Specifications

Ignition system

Distributor

Direction of rotation	Counterclockwise
Air gap (1980 through 1985 models)	0.3 to 0.5 mm (0.012 to 0.020 in)

Ignition coil

Primary voltage	12-volts
Primary resistance at 68-degrees F (20-degrees C)	
1980	0.84 to 1.02 ohms
1981 through 1983	1.04 to 1.27 ohms
1984 and 1985	
Z24 engine	1.05 to 1.27 ohms
Z20 engine	0.84 to 1.02 ohms
1986 on	0.8 to 1.0 ohms
Secondary resistance at 68-degrees F (20-degrees C)	
1980	8.2 to 12.4 K ohms
1981 through 1983	7.3 to 11.0 K ohms
1984 and 1985	
Z24 engine	8.4 to 12.6 K ohms
Z20 engine	8.3 to 12.6 K ohms
1986 on	7.6 to 11.4 ohms
Distributor cap insulation resistance (1986 on)	Over 50,000 ohms
Spark plugs	See Chapter 1

Starting system

Starter motor

Minimum brush length	
US	12 mm (0.470 in)
Canada	11 mm (0.430 in)
Cranking voltage (minimum)	9.6 volts
Cranking current (maximum)	
Four-cylinder engine	150 amps
V6 engine	200 amps
No load current (maximum)	
Gear reduction starter	100 amps
Non-gear reduction starter	60 amps

Charging system

Alternator

Regulated output voltage	14.4 to 15.0 Volts
Minimum brush length	
1980	7.5 mm (0.290 in)
1981 through 1985	7.0 mm (0.280 in)
1986 on	Over 6.0 mm (0.240 in)

1 Ignition system – general information

In order for the engine to run correctly, it is necessary for an electrical spark to ignite the fuel/air mixture in the combustion chamber at exactly the right moment in relation to engine speed and load. The ignition system is based on feeding low tension (LT) voltage from the battery to the coil, where it is converted to high tension (HT) voltage. The high tension voltage is powerful enough to jump the spark plug gap in the cylinders many times a second under high compression pressures, providing that the system is in good condition and that all adjustments are correct.

The ignition system is divided into two circuits; the low tension circuit and the high tension circuit.

The low tension (sometimes known as the primary) circuit consists of the ignition switch, ignition and accessory relay, the primary windings of the ignition coil(s), the transistorized IC ignition unit, the pickup assembly in the distributor and all connecting wires.

The high tension circuit consists of the high tension or secondary windings of the ignition coil(s), the heavy ignition lead from the center of the coil to the center of the distributor cap, the rotor, the spark plug wires and spark plugs.

The distributor used on 1980 through 1985 vehicles is a pulse-triggered, transistor-controlled, inductive discharge unit in which the contact points of a conventional distributor are replaced by a control module and magnetic pick-up assembly.

The system functions in the following manner. Low tension voltage fed to the coils is changed into high tension voltage by the magnetic pick-up in the distributor. When the ignition switch is turned on, current flows through the primary circuit. A reluctor on the distributor shaft is aligned with the magnetic stator element of the pick-up assembly within the distributor housing, and as it turns it induces a low voltage in the pick-up coil. When the teeth on the reluctor and the magnets in the stator line up, a signal passes to the IC ignition unit which opens the coil's primary circuit. When the primary circuit is opened by the transistor unit, the magnetic field built up in the primary winding collapses and induces a very high voltage in the secondary winding. The high voltage current then flows from the coil, along the heavy ignition lead, to the carbon brush in the distributor cap. From the carbon brush, current flows to the distributor rotor which distributes the current to one of the terminals in the distributor cap. The spark occurs while the high tension voltage jumps across the spark plug gap. This process is repeated for each power stroke of the engine.

The system features a long spark duration and the dwell period automatically increases with engine speed. This is desirable for firing the leaner mixtures provided by the emissions control systems.

The IC ignition unit used in 1981 through 1983 models is located inside the distributor, while the IC unit used in 1980 models is attached to the outside of the distributor housing.

Because the four-cylinder engine used in 1981 and later models uses two spark plugs for each cylinder, the ignition system utilizes two ignition coils. Both are located on the left side of the engine compartment. The upper coil works in conjunction with the exhaust plugs, while the lower one works with the intake plugs. 1980 models use a conventional set-up with one spark plug per cylinder and one ignition coil.

The distributor used on all models is equipped with both mechanical and vacuum advance mechanisms. The mechanical governor mechanism compresses two weights which move out from the distributor shaft due to centrifugal force as the engine speed increases. The weights are held in position by two light springs, and it is the tension of the springs which is largely responsible for the correct spark advancement.

The vacuum control consists of a diaphragm, one side of which is connected via a small-bore tube to a vacuum source, and the other side to the magnetic pick-up assembly. Vacuum in the intake manifold, which varies with engine speed and throttle opening, causes the diaphragm to move, which, in turn, moves the magnetic pick-up assembly, advancing or retarding the spark. The distributor vacuum advance is controlled by the Spark Timing Control System, and is explained in detail in Chapter 6.

Because vehicles manufactured after 1986 are equipped with ECCS (see Chapter 6), the distributor used on these models differs in design and function from earlier distributors. A crank angle sensor inside the distributor on all four-cylinder (Z24i), KA24E engines and V6 (VG30i) engines monitors engine speed and piston position, then sends a signal to the ECCS control unit (ECU). The ECU uses this signal to determine ignition timing, fuel injector duration and other functions. The crank angle sensor assembly consists of a rotor plate, a "wave forming" circuit, a light emitting diode (LED) and a photo diode.

The rotor plate, which is attached to the distributor shaft, is in the base of the distributor housing. There are 360 slits machined into the outer edge of the rotor plate. These slits correspond to each degree of crankshaft rotation. Within this outer row of slits is a series of either four or six slightly larger slits corresponding to each cylinder in the four-cylinder or V6 engine, respectively. In the distributor for the four cylinder engine, these slits are spaced 180 degrees apart; on the V6 distributor, they are spaced 120 degrees apart. On both the four cylinder and V6 distributors, the slit for the number one cylinder is slightly larger than the slits for the other cylinders.

The wave forming circuit is positioned underneath the rotor plate. A small housing attached to one side of the wave forming circuit encloses the upper and lower outer edges of the rotor plate. A light emitting diode (LED) is located in the upper half and a photo diode is located in the lower half of the small housing. When the engine is running, the LED emits a continuous beam of light directly at the photo diode. As the outer edge of the rotor plate passes through the housing, the slits allow the light beam to pass through to the photo diode, but the solid spaces between the slits block the light beam. This constant interruption generates pulses which are converted into on-off signals by the wave forming circuit and sent to the ECU. The ECU uses the signal from the outer row of slits to determine engine speed and crankshaft position. It uses the signal generated by the inner, larger slits to determine when to fire each cylinder. This information is then relayed to the coil which builds secondary voltage and sends it to the distributor cap in the conventional manner, where it is distributed by the rotor to the appropriate cylinder.

Warning: *Because of the higher voltage generated by the electronic ignition system, extreme caution should be taken whenever an operation is performed involving ignition components. This not only includes the distributor, coil, control module and ignition wires, but related items which are connected to the system as well, such as the plug connections, tachometer and any testing equipment. Consequently, before any work is performed such as replacing ignition components or even connecting test equipment, the ignition should be turned off or the battery ground cable disconnected. Never disconnect any of the ignition HT leads when the engine is running or the transistor ignition unit will be permanently damaged.*

2 Ignition system – testing

Refer to illustrations 2.7a, 2.7b, 2.8a, 2.8b, 2.9a, 2.9b, 2.11a, 2.11b, 2.11c, 2.12a, 2.12b, 2.12c, 2.13, 2.14 and 2.15

Warning: *Never touch the spark plug or coil wires with your bare hand while the engine is running or being cranked. Even insulated parts can cause a shock if they are moist. Wear dry, insulated gloves or wrap the part in dry cloth before handling.*

1 If the engine will turn over but will not start, the first check of the ignition system should be to visually inspect the condition of the spark plugs, spark plug wires, distributor cap and rotor as described in Chapter 1. Also check the distributor air gap as described in Section 3.

2 If these are all in good condition, and the plug wires are secure in their connections, the next check should be to see if current is flowing through the high tension circuit and causing spark at the plugs.

a) Turn the ignition switch to the Off position.
b) Disconnect the wiring connector leading to the anti-dieseling solenoid valve connector to cut off fuel from the engine.
c) Disconnect the ignition coil wire from the distributor cap and hold it approximately 3/16 to 1/4-inch (4 to 5 mm) from a clean metal area of the engine. Have an assistant crank the engine over and check if a spark occurs between the coil wire and the engine. In systems with two ignition coils, check both coil wires in this manner.
d) If a spark occurs, the ignition system is okay, and the problem lies in another system. If no spark occurs, or occurs intermittently, proceed with further ignition system tests.

3 In order to accurately diagnose problems in the ignition system, a voltmeter which measures in the 0 to 20 volts DC and 0 to 10 volts AC ranges, and an ohmmeter which measures in the 0 to 1000 ohms and 0 to 5000 ohms ranges are needed.

4 If possible, start the engine and let it run about 5 to 15 minutes with the hood closed to bring all components to normal operating temperature. Turn off the engine.

5 Checking the battery voltage with no load:

a) With the ignition key in the Off position, connect a voltmeter so the positive lead is on the positive battery terminal and the negative lead is on the negative battery terminal.

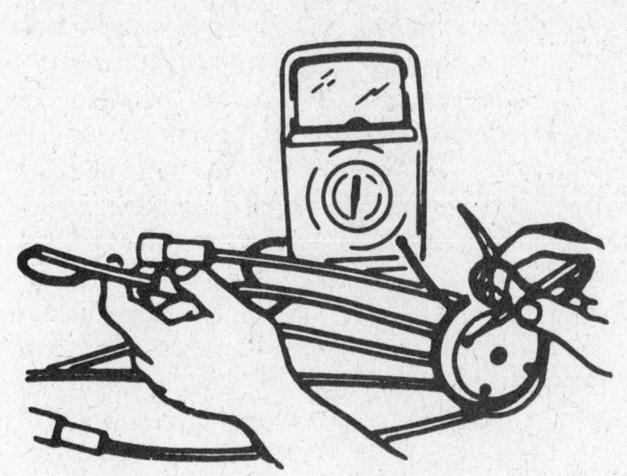

2.7a Plug wire resistance is checked by connecting one ohmmeter lead to the spark plug end of the wire and the other lead to the corresponding distributor cap inner terminal

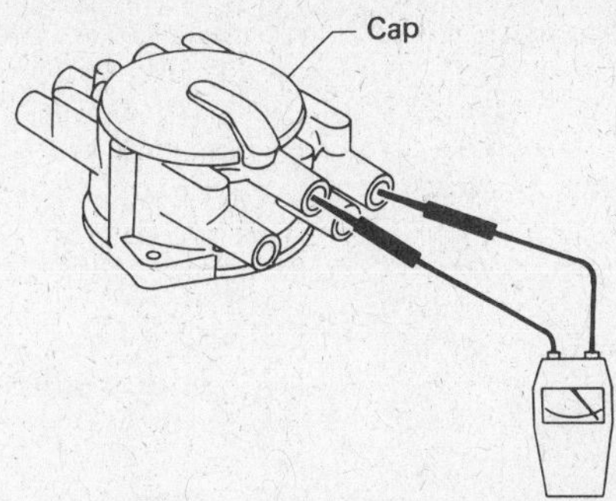

2.7b To check the distributor cap resistance on 1986 and later models, connect one ohmmeter lead to the coil terminal and the other lead to the terminal for each spark plug wire (since there are two spark plugs for each cylinder on four-cylinder engines, be sure to check both terminals)

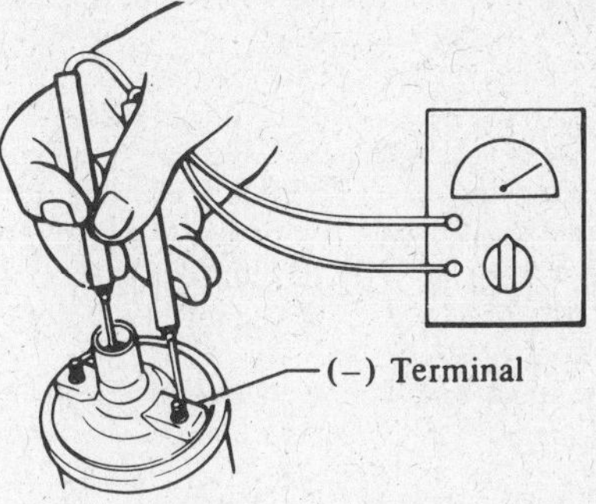

2.8a Place one ohmmeter lead inside the coil high tension terminal and touch the other to the (-) terminal to check the secondary resistance of the coil on 1980 through 1985 models

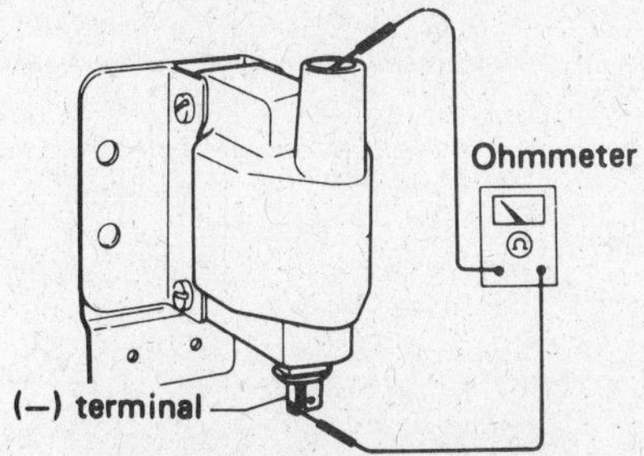

2.8b To check the secondary resistance of the coil on 1986 and later models, place one ohmmeter lead inside the coil high tension terminal and touch the other to the (-) terminal

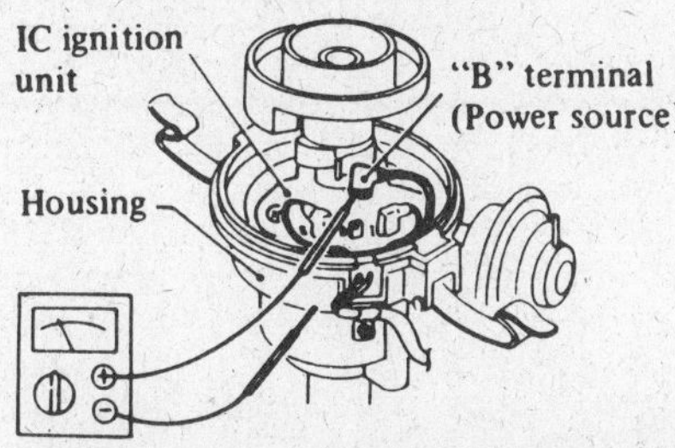

2.9a The power supply circuit on 1980 through 1985 models with a dual ignition system is checked by connecting the positive lead of the voltmeter to the B terminal on the IC ignition unit in the distributor and grounding the negative lead to the outside of the distributor body

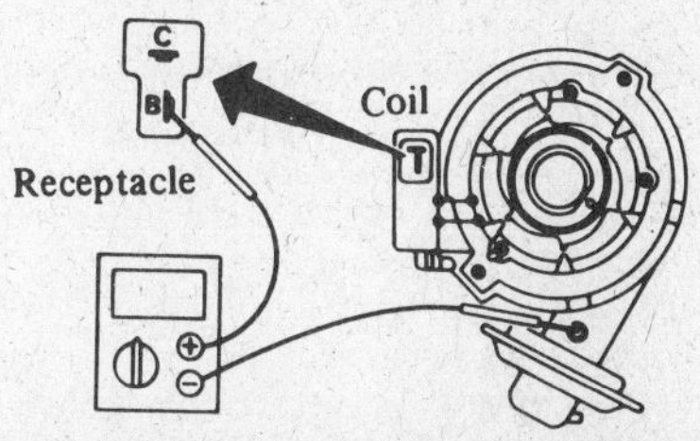

2.9b To check the power supply circuit on 1980 through 1985 models with a single ignition system, connect the positive lead of the voltmeter to the B connection and ground the negative voltmeter lead to the outside of the distributor body

5

b) Note the reading on the voltmeter. If the reading is between 11.5 volts and 12.5 volts, the battery is okay and you should proceed to Step 7.

c) If the reading is below 11.5 volts, the battery is insufficiently charged. It should be brought to a full charge either by running the engine or by using a battery charger. If the vehicle has been used on a regular basis and there is no obvious cause for the battery to be discharged (such as leaving the lights on), then the condition of the battery, charging system and starting system should be checked as described in this Chapter or Chapter 1.

6 Checking the battery voltage while the engine is cranking:

a) Leave the voltmeter connected to the battery as in the previous test.

b) Disconnect the ignition coil wire(s) from the distributor cap and ground it to the engine.

c) Have an assistant crank the engine over for about 15 seconds and note the reading on the voltmeter.

d) If the voltage is more than 9.6 volts, the battery is okay and you should proceed to Step 8. If the voltage is below 9.6 volts, the battery is insufficiently charged. Refer to Step 6.

7 Checking the distributor cap and secondary (spark plug) wires:

a) Disconnect the spark plug wires from the plugs.

b) Disconnect the ignition coil wire(s) from the coil(s).

c) Remove the distributor cap, with spark plug and coil wires still attached.

d) Connect an ohmmeter so that one lead is inserted in the spark plug end of one of the plug wires and the other lead is contacting the inner distributor cap terminal that the wire is connected to **(see illustration)**.

e) If the reading on the ohmmeter is less than 30,000 ohms, the cap terminal and wire are okay.

f) If the reading is more than 30,000 ohms, the resistance is too high. Check the cap and wire individually and replace the appropriate part.

g) Repeat this test on each of the spark plug and coil wires.

h) Check the cap and rotor for dust, carbon deposits and cracks. On 1986 through 1988 models, measure the insulation resistance between the electrodes at the coil and spark plug towers **(see illustration)**. If the reading is below specification, replace the cap.

8 Checking the ignition coil secondary circuit:

a) With the ignition key in the Off position, connect the ohmmeter so that one lead is contacting the center high tension wire connector and the other lead is contacting the negative coil terminal **(see illustrations)**.

b) If the reading is within the specified range, the secondary coil windings are okay.

c) If the ohmmeter reading is not within specification, replace the ignition coil (on systems with dual ignition coils be sure to test each coil).

9 Checking the power supply circuit at the distributor (1980 through 1985 models):

a) On dual ignition systems, connect the positive lead of the voltmeter to the B terminal on the IC ignition unit in the distributor **(see illustration)**. **Note:** *When performing this or any of the following tests, it is not necessary to disconnect the wiring connector when hooking up the voltmeter or ohmmeter, providing they have probes that can be inserted into the rear of the connector.*

b) Ground the negative voltmeter lead to the outside of the distributor body.

c) On single ignition systems, connect the positive voltmeter lead to the B connection. Ground the negative voltmeter lead to the distributor as shown **(see illustration)**.

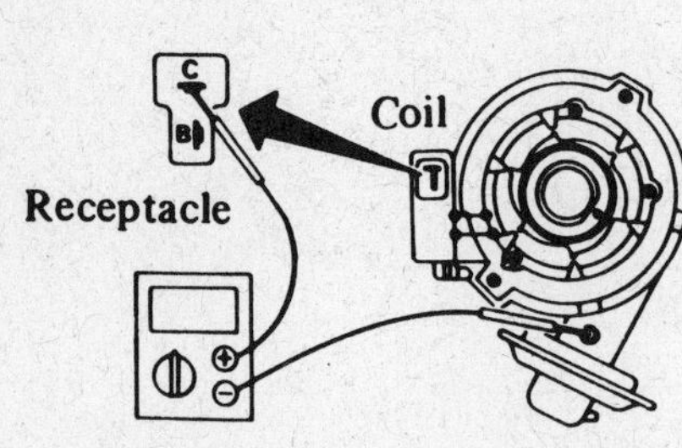

2.11a Connect the positive lead of the voltmeter to the C terminal on the IC unit and ground the negative lead to the outside of the distributor body to check the ignition primary circuit on 1980 through 1985 models with a single ignition system

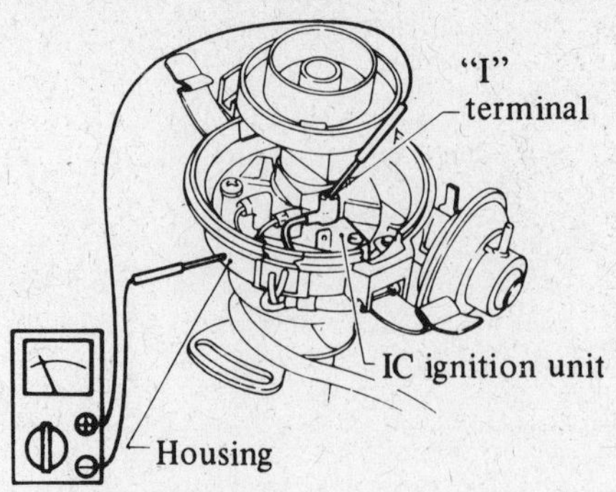

2.11b To check the ignition primary circuit on 1980 through 1985 models with dual ignition systems, connect the positive lead of the voltmeter to the I terminal on the IC unit and ground the negative lead to the outside of the distributor body . . .

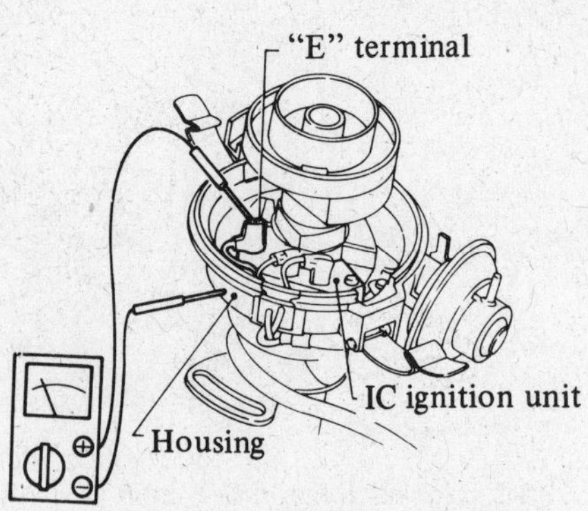

2.11c . . . and, if your reading is between 11.5 and 12.5 volts, reconnect the positive voltmeter lead to the E terminal on the IC unit and take another reading

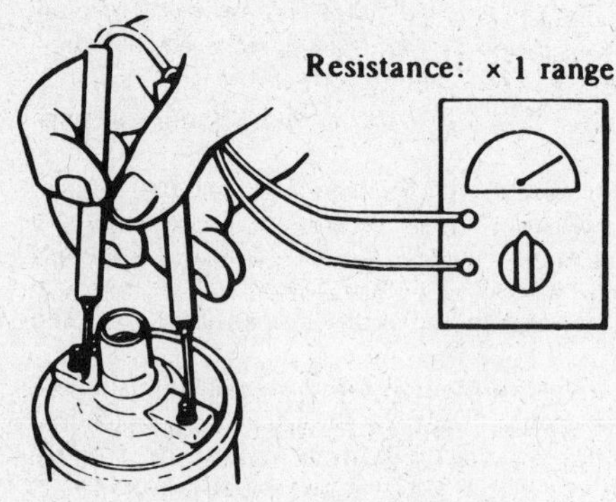

2.12a To check ignition coil primary circuit resistance on 1980 through 1985 models, connect the ohmmeter leads to the positive and negative terminals of the coil as shown (be sure to set the ohmmeter to the 1X range)

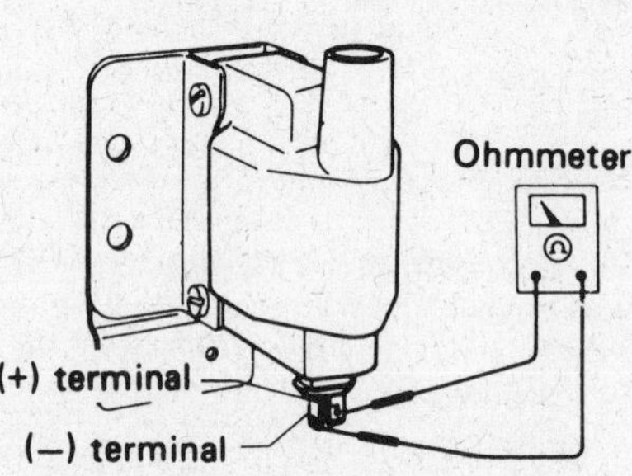

2.12b To check ignition coil primary circuit resistance on 1986 and later models, connect the ohmmeter leads to the positive and negative terminals of the coil as shown (be sure to set the ohmmeter to the 1X range)

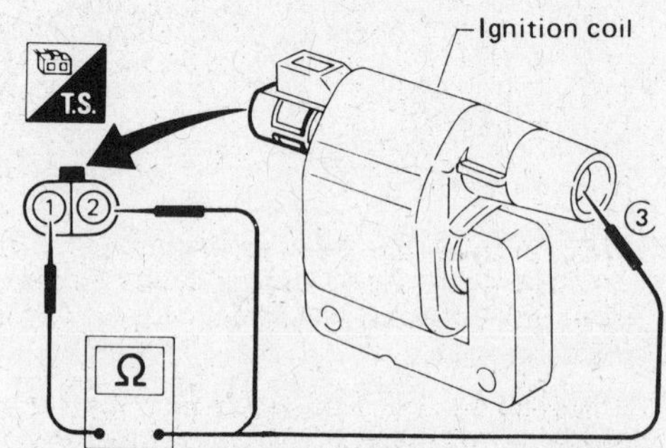

2.12c On 1990 and 1991 coils, check the resistance value between terminals 1 and 2. It should be 0.7 to 1.0 ohms. Then check the resistance between terminals 1 and 3. It should be 10,000 ohms.

d) Turn the ignition key to the On position and note the voltmeter reading.
e) If the reading is between 11.5 and 12.5 volts, the power supply circuit is okay. If the reading is below 11.5 volts, inspect the wiring between the ignition switch and the IC unit for damage or loose or dirty connections.

10 Checking the power supply circuit while the engine is being cranked (1980 through 1985 models):
a) Ground the coil secondary wire(s) to the engine.
b) Connect the voltmeter as in Step 9.
c) Have an assistant crank the engine over for about 15 seconds and note the reading on the voltmeter.
d) If the reading is less than one volt below the battery cranking voltage (measured in Step 6) and is greater than 8.6 volts, the circuit is okay.
e) If the reading is more than one volt below the battery cranking voltage and/or is below 8.6 volts, inspect the wiring between the ignition switch and the IC unit for damage or loose or dirty connections.

11 Checking the ignition primary circuit (1980 through 1985 models):
a) On single ignition systems, connect the voltmeter so the positive lead is connected to the C terminal on the IC unit and the negative lead contacts the distributor as shown **(see illustration)**. Turn the ignition key to the On position and note the voltmeter reading. If the reading is between 11.5 and 12.5 volts, the circuit is okay. Proceed to Step 13. If it is less than 11.5 volts, proceed to Step 12.
b) On dual ignition systems, connect the voltmeter so the positive lead contacts the I terminal on the IC unit, and the negative lead contacts the outside of the distributor body **(see illustration)**. Turn the ignition key to the On position and note the voltmeter reading. If less than 11.5 volts is shown, proceed to Step 12. If between 11.5 and 12.5 volts is shown, reconnect the positive voltmeter lead to the E terminal on the IC unit **(see illustration)** and, with the ignition key still On, take another voltmeter reading. If between 11.5 and 12.5 volts is shown again, the circuit is okay. Proceed to Step 13. If less than 11.5 volts is shown on this reading, proceed to Step 12.

12 Checking the ignition coil primary circuit:
a) With the ignition key in the Off position and the ignition coil wire removed from the coil, connect an ohmmeter (set in the 1x range) between the positive and negative terminals on the ignition coil **(see illustrations)**.
b) If the ohmmeter reading is within the specified range the coil is okay. On 1980 through 1985 models the ignition switch and the wiring between the ignition switch, the coil and the IC unit should be checked for damage, or loose or dirty connections.
c) If the ohmmeter reading is not within these specs, the ignition coil should be replaced.

Note: *In dual ignition systems, be sure to test both ignition coils.*

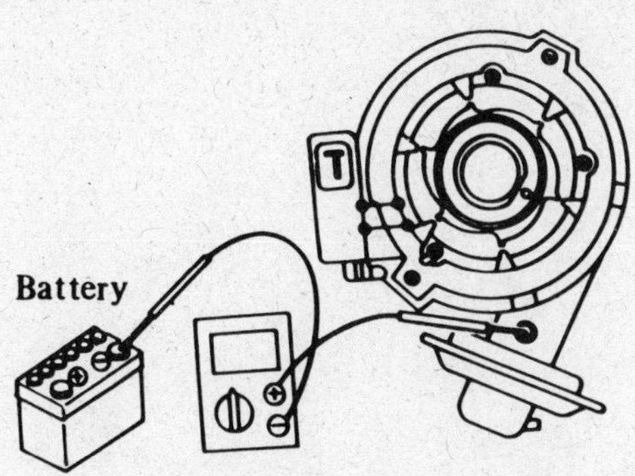

2.13 To check the IC unit ground circuit on 1980 through 1985 models, connect a voltmeter lead to the negative battery terminal and the positive lead to the outside of the distributor housing as shown

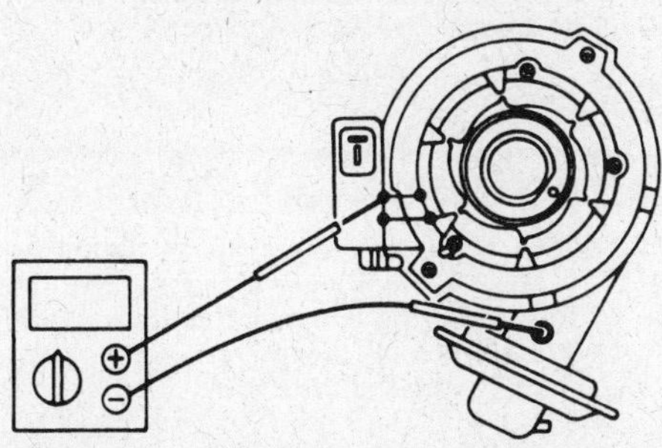

2.15 To check the pick-up coil output on 1980 through 1985 models with a single ignition system, connect a voltmeter (set on the low AC volt scale) between the indicated points

13 Checking the IC unit ground circuit (1980 through 1985 models):

a) Remove the ignition coil wire(s) from the distributor cap and ground it to the engine.
b) Connect a voltmeter negative lead to the negative battery terminal, and the positive lead to the distributor as shown **(see illustration)**.
c) Have an assistant crank the engine over for about 15 seconds and note the voltmeter reading.
d) If more than 0.5 volts is shown, check the grounding of the distributor, the wiring between the battery and the chassis ground and the negative battery cable connection.
e) If the reading shows 0.5 volts or less on dual ignition systems, the IC unit should be replaced.
f) If 0.5 volts or less is shown in single ignition systems, further checks are needed. Proceed to Step 14.

14 Checking pick-up coil resistance (1980 through 1985 models):

a) For this check the engine should be at normal operating temperature.
b) With the ignition switch in the Off position, connect an ohmmeter (set in the 100x range) as shown **(see illustration)** and note the reading.
c) If the reading is substantially above or below 400 ohms, inspect the pick-up coil and its wiring for damage, or loose or dirty connections.

15 Checking pick-up coil output (1980 through 1985 models):

a) The engine should be at normal operating temperature.
b) Connect a voltmeter (set on the low AC volt scale) between the indicated points **(see illustration)**.
c) Disconnect the ignition coil wire from the distributor cap and, using a jumper wire, ground it to the engine. Have an assistant crank the engine over for about 15 seconds and observe the movement of the voltmeter needle.
d) If the needle is steady, check the physical condition of the pick-up coil and reluctor for damage. Also check the wiring between the pick-up coil and the IC unit for damage, or loose or dirty connections.
e) If the needle wavers while the engine is being cranked, and there is still no spark being produced, replace the IC unit.

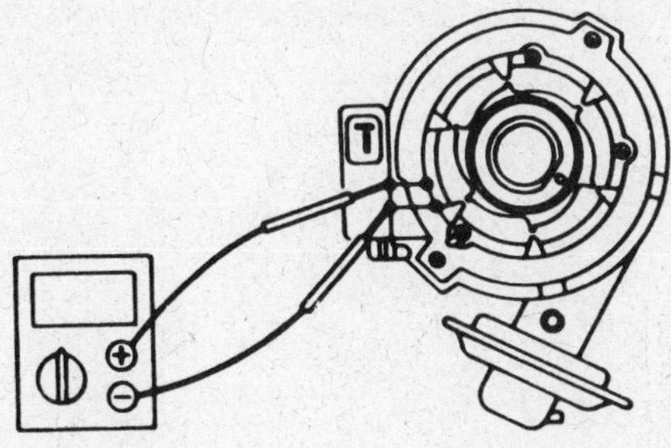

2.14 Pick-up coil resistance on 1980 through 1985 models with a single ignition system is checked by connecting a voltmeter (set at the 100X range) between the indicated points

3 Distributor air gap — check and adjustment (1980 through 1985 models)

Refer to illustration 3.4

Note: *To ensure that the ignition system functions correctly, the air gap (distance between the pick-up coil and reluctor) must be maintained as specified. To do this, proceed as follows:*

1 Disengage the two spring retaining clips and remove the cap from the distributor.

2 Remove the rotor from the end of the distributor shaft.

3 Position one of the raised segments of the reluctor directly opposite the pole piece protruding from the pick-up coil. This is best carried out by removing the spark plugs (to relieve compression) and rotating the crankshaft by using a ratchet and socket on the crankshaft bolt at the front of the engine.

4 Using feeler gauges, measure the gap between the pole and the reluctor segment **(see illustration)**. It should be 0.3 to 0.5 mm (0.012 to 0.020-inch). If the air-gap requires adjustment, loosen the pick-up coil retaining screws and move the coil in the required direction.

5 When the correct air-gap has been obtained, tighten the pick-up coil retaining screws and install the rotor and the distributor cap.

5

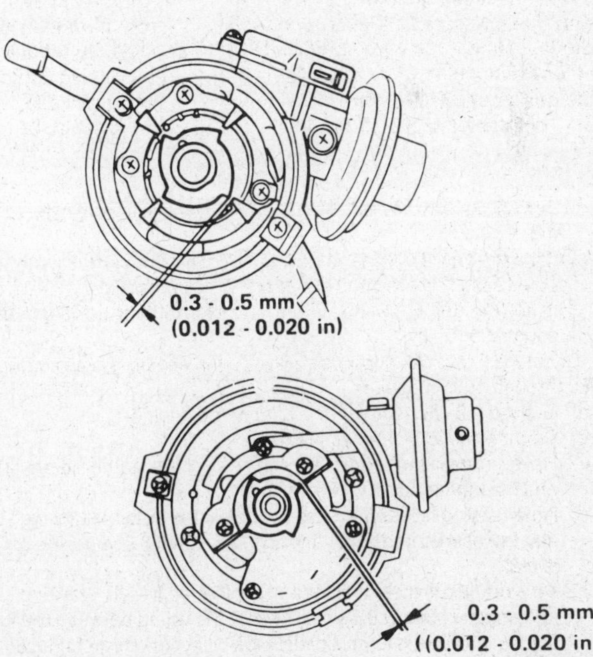

3.4 To check the distributor air gap, position one of the raised segments of the reluctor directly opposite the stator magnet (pole piece) protruding from the pick-up coil and, using a feeler gauge, measure the gap between them (1980 model — top; 1981 through 1985 models — bottom)

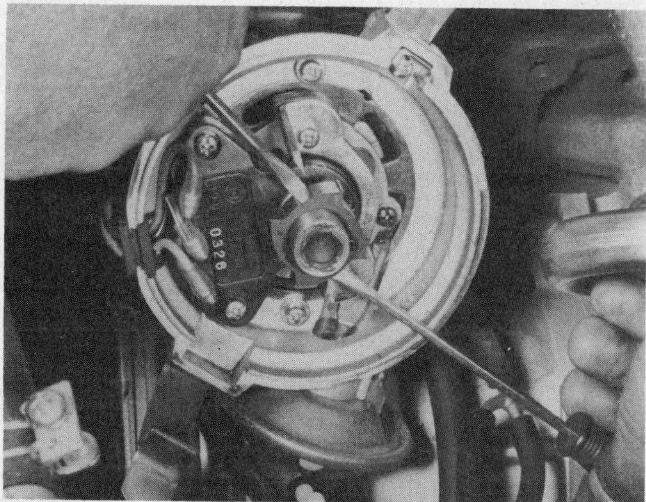

4.6 To remove the reluctor from the distributor on 1981 through 1985 models, pry it off with a pair of screwdrivers (be careful not to damage the teeth of the reluctor)

4.7 To remove the IC unit from the distributor on 1981 through 1985 models, remove both screws (A), detach all three wires and lift the IC unit off – to remove the stator and magnet (pick-up assembly), remove the screws (B) and lift it out

4 IC ignition unit – removal and installation (1980 through 1985 models)

1980 models

1 The IC ignition unit used on these models is located on the outside of the distributor body and is removed by unplugging the wiring connector, removing the mounting screws and disconnecting the wires leading to the pick-up assembly **(see illustration 8.5)**.
2 Installation is the reverse of the removal procedure.

1981 through 1985 models

Refer to illustrations 4.6 and 4.7

3 Remove the ignition coil wires from the distributor cap.
4 Remove the distributor cap from the distributor and secure it out of the way.
5 Remove the bolt on the side of the rotor and remove the rotor from the distributor shaft.
6 Using two screwdrivers, pry the reluctor off the distributor shaft **(see illustration)**. Be careful not to damage the teeth of the reluctor.
7 Remove the three wires from the IC ignition unit **(see illustration)**.
8 Remove the two screws retaining the IC ignition unit to the distributor and lift it out.
9 Installation is the reverse of the removal procedure. **Note:** *The reluctor can be installed by pressing it back onto the distributor shaft. The pin in the reluctor should be lined up with the flat spot in the distributor shaft.*

5 Stator and magnet (pick-up assembly) – removal and installation (1980 through 1985 models)

1980 models

1 Disconnect the ignition coil wire from the top of the distributor cap.
2 Remove the distributor cap from the distributor and position it out of the way.
3 Pull the rotor off the distributor shaft.
4 Using two screwdrivers (one on either side of the reluctor), carefully pry the reluctor from the distributor shaft. Be careful not to damage the teeth on the reluctor **(see illustration 8.5)**.
5 Remove the screws retaining the stator and magnet to the distributor breaker plate and lift them off.
6 Disconnect the distributor wiring harness and lift out the pick-up coil assembly.
7 Installation is the reverse of the removal procedure. When installing the reluctor, be sure the pin is lined up with the flat side of the distributor shaft. Also, before tightening the stator, check and adjust the air gap as described in Section 3.

1981 through 1985 models

8 Remove the ignition coil wires from the distributor cap.
9 Remove the distributor cap from the distributor and secure it out of the way.
10 Remove the bolt on the side of the rotor and remove the rotor from the distributor shaft.
11 Using two screwdrivers (one on either side of the reluctor), pry the reluctor off the distributor shaft. Be careful not to damage the teeth of the reluctor **(see illustration 4.6)**.
12 Remove the screws retaining the stator and magnet to the breaker plate and lift them off **(see illustration 4.7)**.
13 Installation is the reverse of the removal procedure. **Note:** *the reluctor can be installed by pressing it back onto the distributor shaft, but be sure the pin in the reluctor is lined up with the flat side of the distributor shaft. Also, before tightening the stator, check and adjust the air gap as described in Section 3.*

6 Distributor – removal

Refer to illustrations 6.3, 6.6a and 6.6b

1 Remove the ignition coil wire(s) that lead to the distributor from the coil(s).
2 Remove the distributor cap from the distributor and position it out of the way.
3 Mark the rotor in relationship to the distributor housing **(see illustration)**.
4 Disconnect the wires or wiring connector leading to the IC ignition unit (1980 through 1985 models) or the crank angle sensor (1986 through 1988 models).
5 Remove the vacuum line from the vacuum advance canister (1980 through 1985 models only).
6 Mark the position of the distributor adjusting bolt **(see illustration)**, remove the two distributor mounting bolts **(see illustration)** and lift out the distributor. **Note:** *Do not loosen the distributor adjusting bolts on 1981 through 1985 models.*

6.3 Before removing the distributor, be sure to mark the relationship of the rotor to the distributor body to ensure that the two components are correctly aligned when reinstalled (earlier distributor shown)

6.6a Before removing the distributor, be sure to mark the adjusting bolt to ensure that the distributor is installed in the same spot

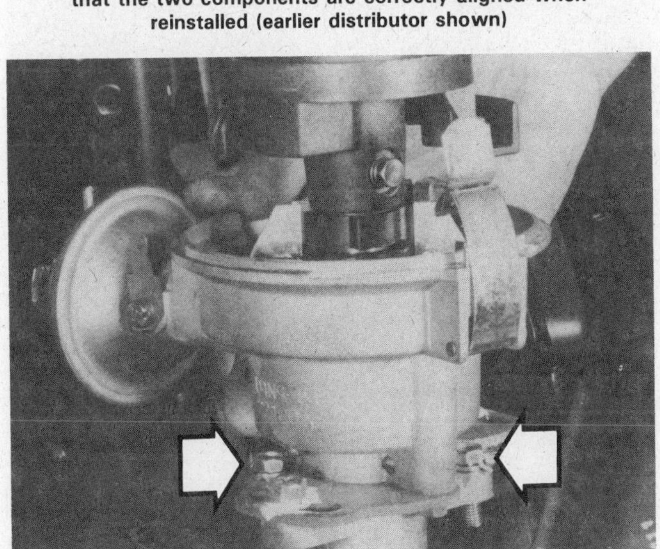

6.6b To remove the distributor on 1981 through 1985 models, unscrew the two bolts (arrows) but don't loosen the adjusting bolts

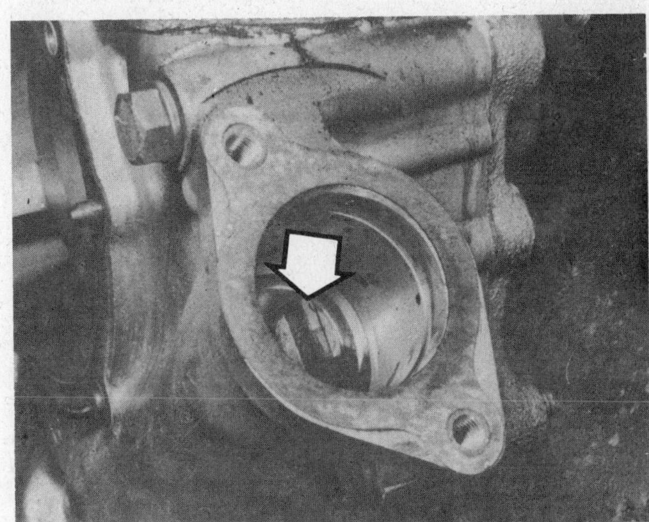

7.9 If the number one piston is at Top Dead Center (TDC), the protruding tooth (arrow) of the distributor drive spindle should be almost vertical (tilted slightly in a counterclockwise direction) and offset toward the front of the engine

7 Distributor — installation

Refer to illustration 7.9

If the crankshaft was not turned after removal

1 Position the rotor exactly as it was when the distributor was removed.

2 Lower the distributor down into the engine. To mesh the groove in the bottom of the distributor shaft with the drive spindle (which turns the distributor shaft), it may be necessary to turn the rotor slightly.

3 With the base of the distributor all the way down against the engine block and the mounting screw holes lined up, the rotor should be pointing to the mark made on the distributor housing during removal. If the rotor is not in alignment with the mark, repeat the previous Steps.

4 Install the distributor hold-down bolt(s) and tighten them securely.

5 Connect the vacuum line to the vacuum advance canister (if equipped).

6 Reconnect the wires to the IC unit (1980 through 1985 models) or crank angle sensor (1986 through 1988 models).

7 Reinstall the distributor cap and connect the ignition coil wire(s).

8 Check the ignition timing as described in Chapter 1.

If the crankshaft was turned after removal

9 Position the number one piston to TDC, referring to Chapter 2, if necessary. On 1980 through 1985 models check that the number one piston is on the compression stroke by noting the position of the distributor drive spindle. The protruding tooth should be almost vertical (tilted slightly in a counterclockwise direction) and offset toward the front of the engine **(see illustration)**.

10 Temporarily install the distributor cap on the distributor. Note where the number one spark plug terminal inside the cap is located in relation to the distributor body, and make a mark on the outside of the body at this point.

11 Remove the distributor cap again. Turn the rotor until it is aligned with the mark. In this position it should be firing the number one spark plug.

12 Proceed with installation as detailed in Steps 2 through 8. Disregard the rotor mark references in Step 3.

8 Distributor – disassembly and reassembly

1980 models

Refer to illustration 8.5

1 Remove the distributor from the vehicle as described in Section 6.
2 Remove the distributor cap.
3 Pull off the rotor.
4 Disconnect the wiring connector leading to the IC unit.
5 Remove the screws **(see illustration)** and lift out the stator and magnet assembly.
6 Remove the screws retaining the vacuum canister and lift it off.
7 Using two screwdrivers, one on either side of the reluctor, carefully pry it off the distributor shaft. Be careful not to damage the reluctor teeth.
8 Drive the roll pin out of the reluctor.
9 Remove the pick-up coil assembly.
10 Remove the breaker plate set screws and lift out the breaker plate assembly.
11 Using a suitable punch, drive the knock pin from the collar and pull off the collar.
12 Pull the rotor shaft assembly and drive shaft out through the top of the distributor.
13 Mark the relative position of the rotor shaft and driveshaft. Remove the packing from the top of the rotor shaft, remove the rotor shaft set screw and separate the two shafts.
14 Mark the relationship of one of the governor springs to its bracket. Also mark the relationship of one of the governor weights to its pivot pins.
15 Carefully unhook and remove the governor springs.
16 Remove the governor weights. A small amount of grease should be applied to the weights after removal.
17 Reassembly is the reverse of the disassembly procedure with the following notes:

a) Be sure to correctly align all positioning marks made during disassembly so that all parts are assembled in their original position.
b) When installing the reluctor on the shaft, drive the roll pin into the reluctor so that its slit is positioned toward the outer end of

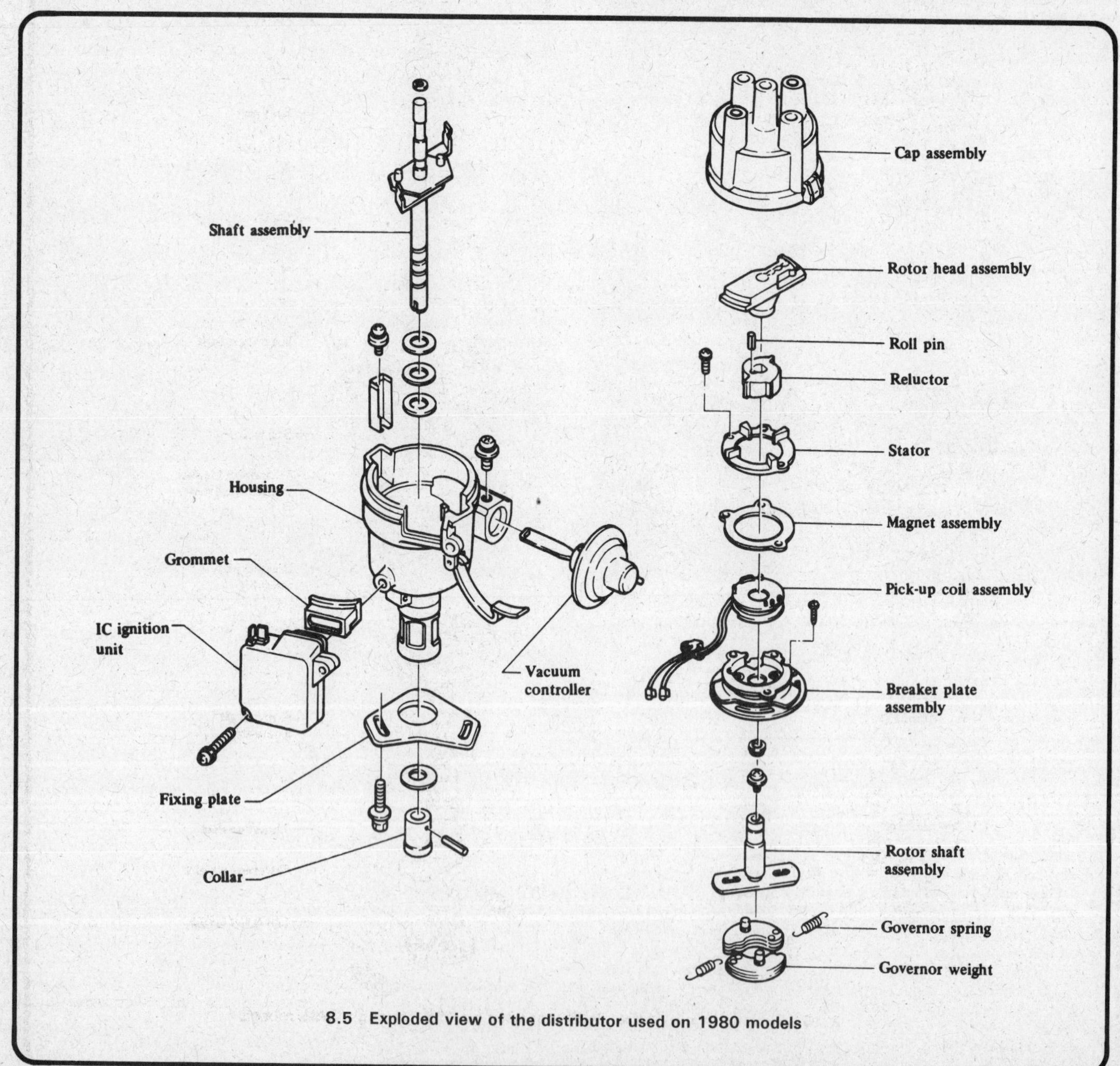

8.5 Exploded view of the distributor used on 1980 models

the shaft. Always use a new roll pin.

c) Before installing the IC unit onto the distributor body, make sure the mating surfaces of both the IC unit and the distributor are clean and free from dirt or moisture. This is very important.

d) Before tightening the stator plate, adjust the air gap as described in Section 3.

1981 through 1985 models

Refer to illustrations 8.20, 8.25 and 8.28

18 Remove the distributor from the engine as described in Section 6.

19 Remove the distributor cap.

20 Remove the bolt **(see illustration)** and lift off the rotor.

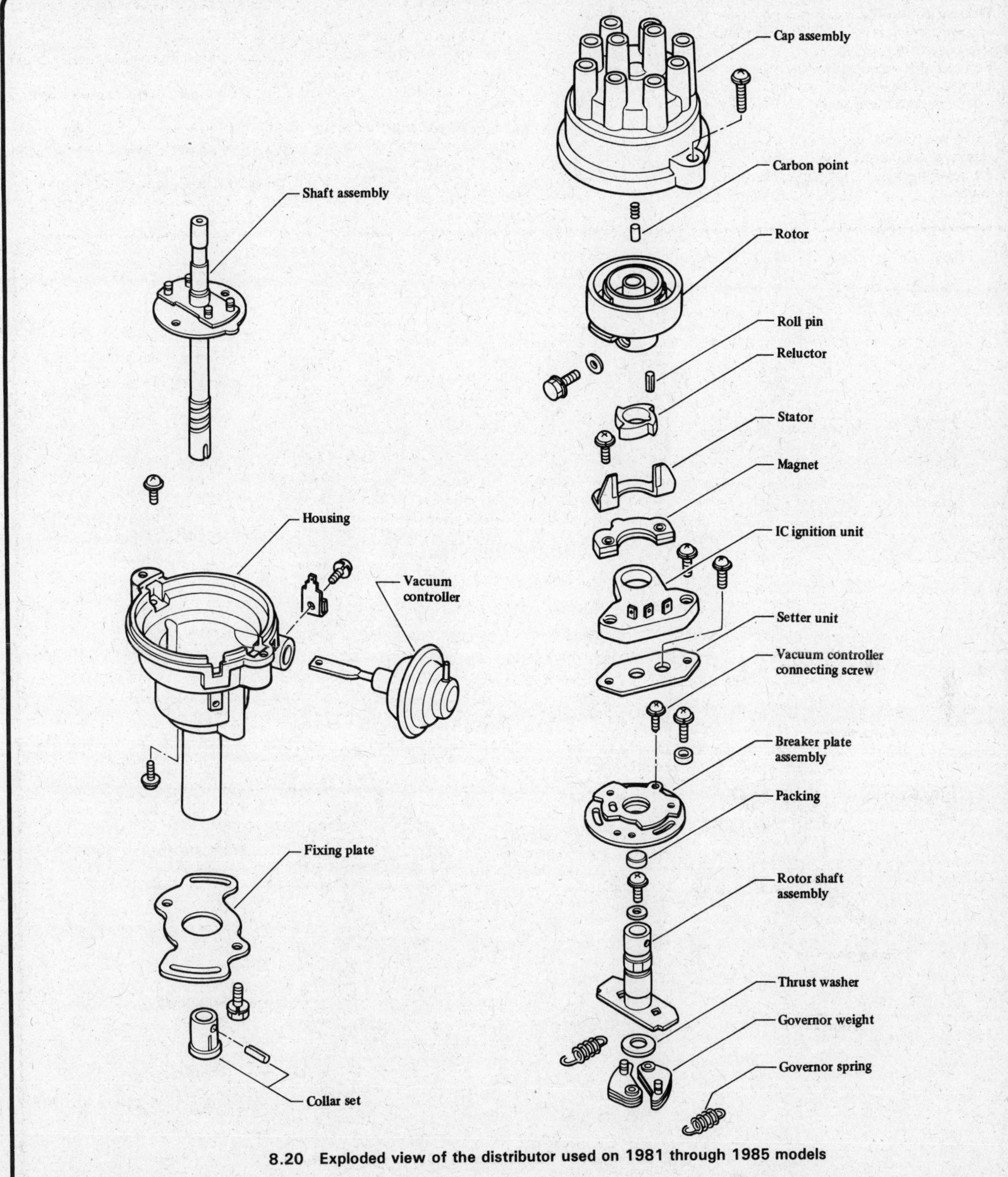

8.20 Exploded view of the distributor used on 1981 through 1985 models

5

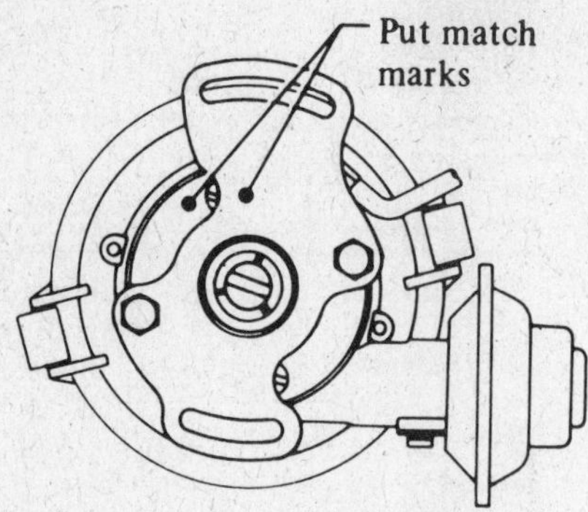

8.25 Before removing the breaker plate assembly, mark the relationship of the fixing plate to the distributor housing

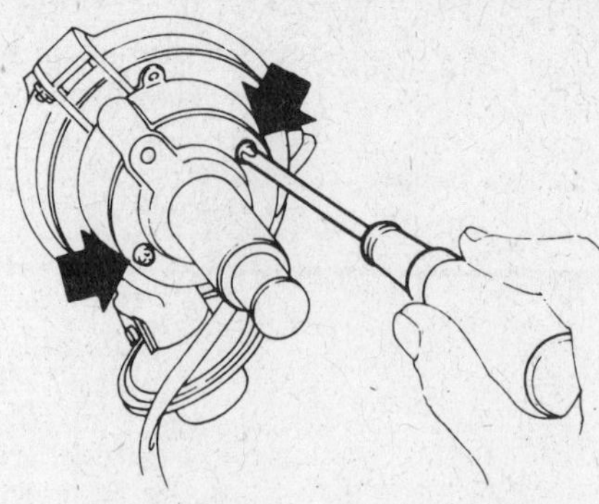

8.28 To remove the distributor shaft bearing retainer from the housing, remove the retainer screws (arrows) and lift off the retainer

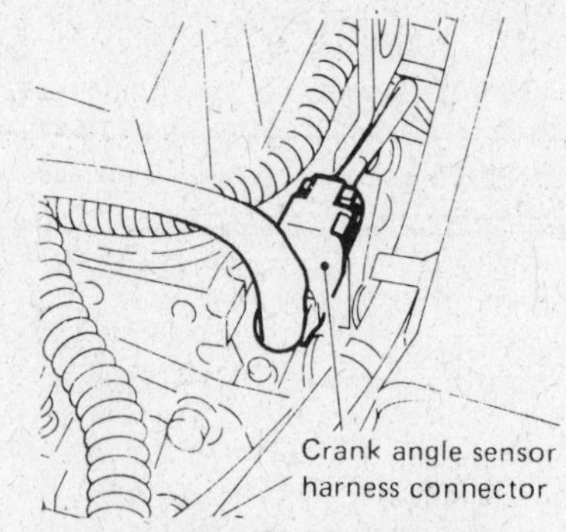

9.4a Location of the crank angle sensor harness connector (KA24E engine shown)

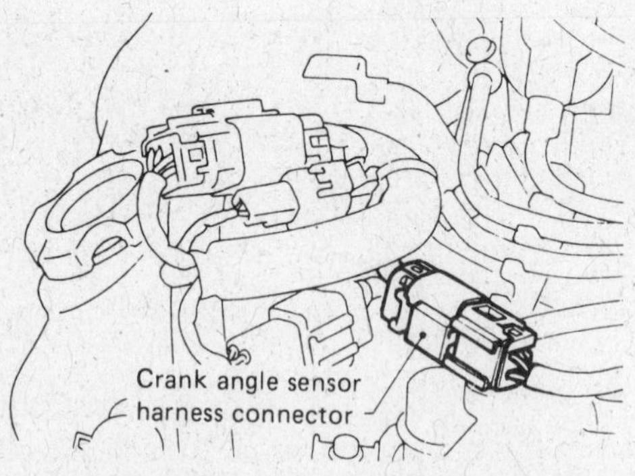

9.4b Location of the crank angle sensor harness connector (V6 engine shown)

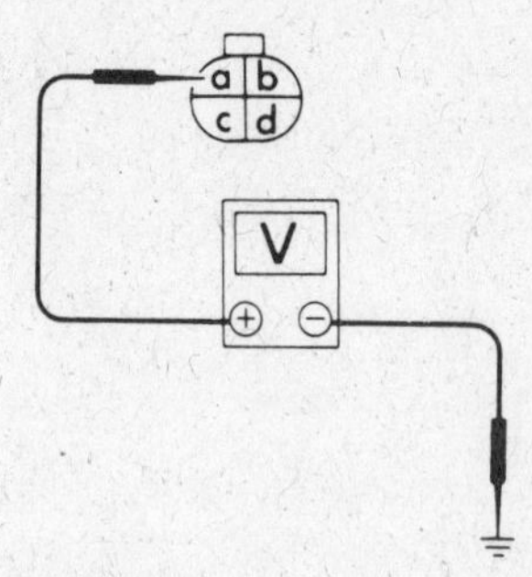

9.5 Check for voltage at terminal A with the ignition key ON. There should be battery voltage.

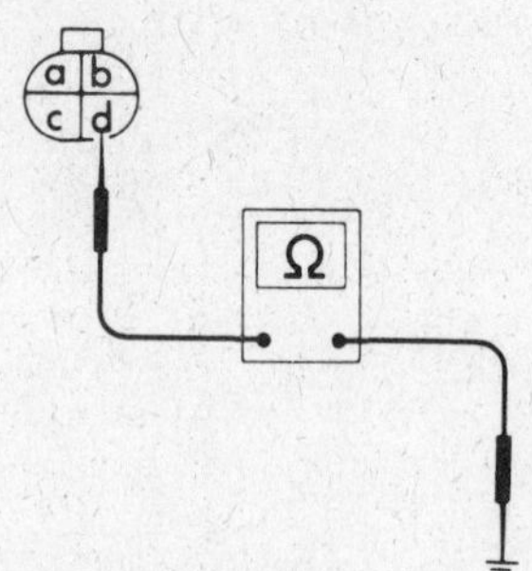

9.6 Check for continuity at terminal D with the ignition key OFF. There should be continuity

21 Using two screwdrivers, one on either side of the reluctor, carefully pry it off the distributor shaft. Be careful not to damage the reluctor teeth.

22 Remove the IC unit retaining screw and lift out the IC unit and setter unit.

23 Remove the stator attaching screws and lift out the stator and magnet.

24 Remove the screws that retain the vacuum canister and lift it off.

25 Mark the relationship of the fixing plate to the distributor housing **(see illustration)**, then remove the breaker plate assembly.

26 Remove the fixing plate.

27 Using a suitable punch, drive the pin from the collar and pull off the collar.

28 Remove the screws attaching the bearing retainer to the housing **(see illustration)** and lift the retainer off.

29 Pull the rotor shaft assembly and driveshaft out through the top of the distributor.

30 Mark the relative position of the rotor shaft and driveshaft. Remove the packing from the top

of the rotor shaft, remove the rotor shaft set screw and separate the two shafts.

31 Mark the relationship of one of the governor springs to its bracket. Also mark the relationship of one of the governor weights to its pivot pins.

32 Carefully unhook and remove the governor springs.

33 Remove the governor weights. A small amount of grease should be applied to the weights after removal.

34 Reassembly is the reverse of the disassembly procedure with the following notes:

- a) Be sure to correctly align all positioning marks made during disassembly so that all parts are assembled in their original positions.
- b) When installing the reluctor on the shaft, drive the roll pin into the reluctor so that its slit is positioned toward the outer end of the shaft. Always use a new roll pin.
- c) Before tightening the stator plate, adjust the air gap as described in Section 3.

1986 and later models

35 The D6P84-01 V6 engine and D4P84-04 four-cylinder engine distributors used on 1986 and later vehicles cannot be rebuilt. If the crank angle sensor, rotor plate, wave forming circuit, etc. malfunction, the entire assembly must be replaced.

9 Crank angle sensor – check

Refer to illustrations 9.4, 9.5 and 9.6

1 Use the self diagnosis mode (see Section 14 in Chapter 6) to pinpoint any problems in the vehicle's fuel system.

2 If the ECU flashes 1 red flash and 1 green flash then the crank angle sensor circuit is malfunctioning. Continue the checks as described below. If the self diagnostic code isn't displayed, the sensor/circuit is functioning properly.

3 Depending on the symptom, the crank angle sensor and its related circuit have several items that must be checked in order to pinpoint the exact problem.

4 Disconnect the crank angle sensor wire harness connector **(see illustrations)** and turn the ignition switch ON.

5 Check the voltage between terminal A and ground **(see illustration)**. There should be battery voltage.

6 Turn the ignition switch OFF and check for continuity between terminal D and ground **(see illustration)**.

7 If the tests are correct, have the ECU and the harness checked by a dealership service department or other professional auto repair shop.

10 Ignition coil – removal and installation

1 Remove the coil wire leading from the distributor cap.
2 Remove the dust boot.
3 Remove the nuts and detach the primary wires from the coil.
4 Remove the screws that hold the coil bracket to the body and detach the coil.
5 If the coil must be removed from the bracket, loosen the bracket screws until the coil can be pulled out.
6 Installation is the reverse of the removal procedure. **Note:** *On pre-1986 models with two ignition coils, the one with the orange plug controls the spark plugs on the intake side, while the coil with the black plug controls the spark plugs on the exhaust side.*

11 Starting system – general information

The function of the starting system is to crank the engine. This system is composed of a starting motor, solenoid and battery. The battery supplies the electrical energy to the solenoid, which then completes the circuit to the starting motor which does the actual work of cranking the engine.

Models sold in the US use a non-reduction gear type of starter motor. On this starter, the solenoid is mounted on top of the starter motor. When the ignition switch is operated, the solenoid's gearshift lever moves the starter drive pinion gear into engagement with the teeth on the flywheel.

Models sold in Canada are equipped with a reduction gear type of starter. This starter operates in a similar manner to the type described above except that in order to offset extremely low temperatures, increased rotating torque is provided through a reduction gear located between the armature and pinion gear.

An overrunning clutch is installed on both types of starter motors to transmit the driving torque and to prevent the armature from overrunning when the engine fires and starts.

The solenoid and starting motor are mounted together at the rear right side of the engine. No periodic lubrication or maintenance is required for the starter system components.

The electrical circuitry of the vehicle is arranged so that the starter motor can only be operated on automatic transmission models when the lever is at P or N. **Caution:** *Never operate the starter motor for more than 30 seconds at a time without pausing to allow it to cool for at least two minutes.* Excessive cranking can cause overheating, which can seriously damage the starter.

12 Starting system – check

1 If the starter motor does not rotate when the switch is operated on an automatic transmission equipped model, make sure that the shifter is in the N or P position.
2 Check that the battery is well charged and all cables, both at the battery and starter solenoid terminals, are clean, free from corrosion and secure.
3 If the starter motor can be heard spinning but the engine is not being cranked, then the overrunning clutch in the starter motor is slipping and the assembly must be removed from the engine and replaced.
4 Often when the starter fails to operate, a click can be heard coming from the starter solenoid when the ignition switch is turned to the Start position. If this is heard, proceed to Step 12.
5 Disconnect the ignition wire from the solenoid terminal. Connect a test light between this lead and the negative battery terminal.
6 Have an assistant turn the key, and note whether the test light comes on or not. If the light comes on proceed to Step 12.
7 If the test light does not come on, connect a voltmeter (set on the low scale) between the positive battery terminal and the bayonet connector at the solenoid. The ignition wire should be connected.
8 Disconnect the ignition coil wire(s) from the distributor cap and ground it to the engine, so the engine will not start.
9 Have an assistant attempt to crank the engine over and note the reading on the voltmeter. If less than 1.5 volts is shown, there is an open circuit in the starter and it should be replaced with a new or rebuilt unit.
10 If the voltmeter shows more than 1.5 volts, connect a jumper wire between the positive battery terminal and the S terminal on the solenoid.
11 Turn the ignition switch to the Start position and listen for a click from the solenoid. If there still is no click and the starter does not turn, both the solenoid and starter are defective and should be replaced. If a click is heard and the starter turns, then there is an open circuit in the ignition switch, inhibitor switch or relay (on automatic transmission equipped models) or in the wires or connectors.
12 If a click is heard while the ignition switch is turned to the Start position in Step 4, or if the starter turns at all, then the starter current should be tested. Disconnect the positive battery cable at the starter.
13 Connect an ammeter (set on the 500A range) between this cable and its terminal on the starter.
14 Remove the ignition coil wire(s) from the distributor cap to keep the engine from starting.
15 Have an assistant attempt to crank the engine and note the reading on the ammeter and the speed at which the starter turns.
16 If the ammeter reading is less than specified and the starter speed is normal, the starter is okay and the problem lies elsewhere.
17 If the reading is less than specified but the starter motor speed is slow, proceed to Step 22.
18 If the ammeter reading is more than specified, reinstall the ignition coil wire in the distributor cap.
19 Have an assistant start the engine but hold the key in the Start position so that the starter motor doesn't stop operating. Note the ammeter reading. (Do not allow the starter motor to turn for more than 30 seconds at a time).
20 If the ammeter reading is less than specified and the starter turns fast, then the problem is a mechanical one such as a tight engine. Make sure that the engine oil is not too thick, and check for other causes of resistance within the engine.
21 If the ammeter reading exceeds the specified no load current the starter is shorted and must be replaced with a new one.
22 If the ammeter reading in Step 15 is less than specified, but the starter turns slowly, test for a voltage drop in the starter positive circuit.
23 Connect a voltmeter (set on the low scale) so the positive lead is on the positive battery post (or cable) and the negative lead is connected to the M solenoid terminal (this is the terminal with the braided copper strap leading to the starter motor).
24 Remove the ignition coil wire(s) from the distributor cap and ground them on the engine.
25 Have an assistant attempt to crank the engine over and note the reading on the voltmeter. If less than one volt is shown, proceed to Step 28.
26 If more than one volt is shown, connect the negative voltmeter lead to the B solenoid terminal (this is the terminal which connects to the battery).
27 Have an assistant crank the engine and note the reading on the voltmeter. If more than one volt is shown, then the problem is a bad connection between the battery and the starter solenoid. Check the positive battery cable for looseness or corrosion. If the reading indicated less than one volt, then the solenoid is defective and should be replaced.
28 If the voltmeter test in Step 25 shows less than one volt test for a voltage drop in the starter ground circuit.
29 Connect the negative lead of the voltmeter (set on the low scale) to the negative battery terminal and hold the positive voltmeter lead to the starter housing. Be sure to make a good connection.
30 Have an assistant crank the engine and note the voltmeter reading. If the reading shows more than 0.5 volts, then there is a bad ground connection. Check the negative battery cable for looseness or corrosion. Also check the starter motor ground connections and the tightness of the starter motor mounting bolts.
31 If the voltmeter reading shows less than 0.5 volts, return to Step 7 and follow the procedure outlined there.

13.2 Typical starter motor assembly on an earlier (pre-1986) model four-cylinder engine, mounted at the lower right rear side of the engine- be sure to detach all the wires from the solenoid terminals before removing the starter

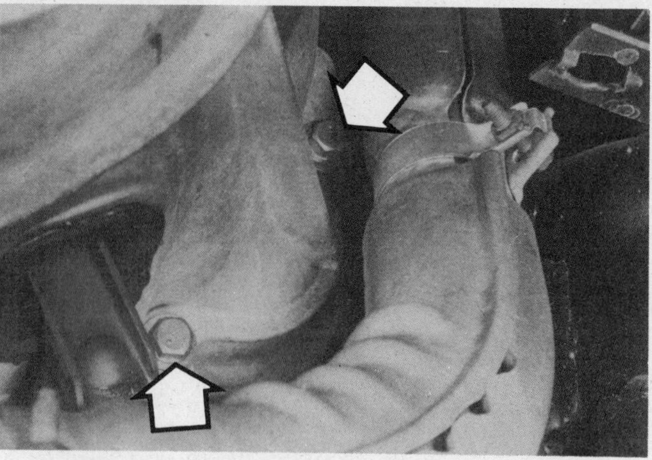

13.3 V6 engine starter mounting bolts (arrows) – the starter is mounted on the right (passenger) side of the engine

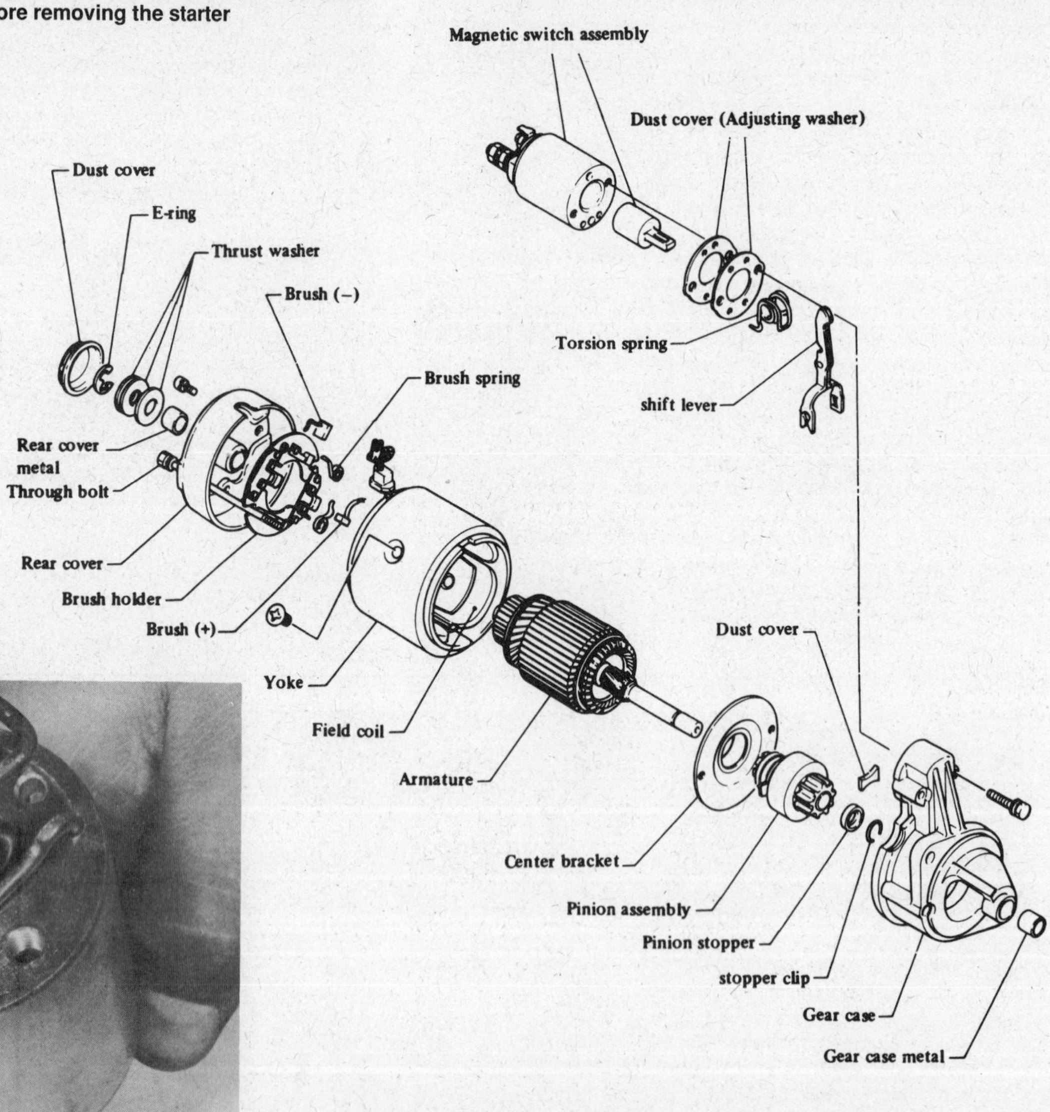

Magnetic switch assembly
Dust cover (Adjusting washer)
Dust cover
E-ring
Thrust washer
Brush (–)
Torsion spring
Brush spring
shift lever
Rear cover metal
Through bolt
Rear cover
Brush holder
Brush (+)
Yoke
Field coil
Armature
Dust cover
Center bracket
Pinion assembly
Pinion stopper
stopper clip
Gear case
Gear case metal

15.3a Exploded view of a typical non-reduction gear starter motor and solenoid assembly used on earlier vehicles

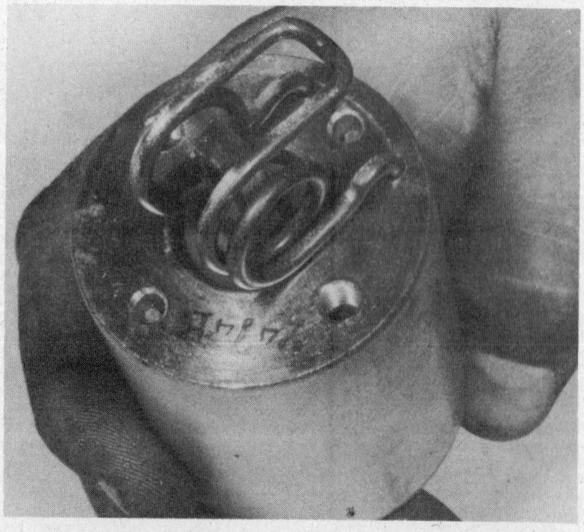

14.4 Assemble the solenoid as shown before installing it on the motor – make sure the solenoid plunger is engaged with the starter motor shift lever

13 Starter motor – removal and installation

Refer to illustrations 13.2 and 13.3

1 Disconnect the negative battery cable from the battery. On models equipped with a V6 engine, raise the vehicle and support it on jackstands.
2 Remove the wires from the starter solenoid **(see illustration)**. Label the wires and terminals to prevent confusion during installation.
3 Remove the starter motor mounting bolts **(see illustration)**.
4 Lift out the starter motor and solenoid.
5 Installation is the reverse of the removal procedure.

14 Starter solenoid – removal and installation

Refer to illustration 14.4

1 Remove the starter motor as described in Section 12.
2 Remove the nut that holds the braided copper strap to the solenoid.
3 Remove the two mounting screws and detach the solenoid from the starter motor.
4 Installation is the reverse of the removal procedure. **Note:** *During installation be sure to engage the solenoid plunger with the starter motor shift lever* **(see illustration)**.

15 Starter motor – brush replacement

Non-reduction gear starter

Refer to illustrations 15.3a, 15.3b, 15.3c and 15.8

1 Remove the starter motor (see Section 13).
2 Remove the starter solenoid (see Section 14).
3 Remove the rear dust cover from the starter motor **(see illustrations)**.
4 Remove the E-ring and thrust washer.
5 Remove the two brush holder set screws from the rear plate.
6 Remove the two through bolts from the rear of the starter.
7 Remove the rear cover.

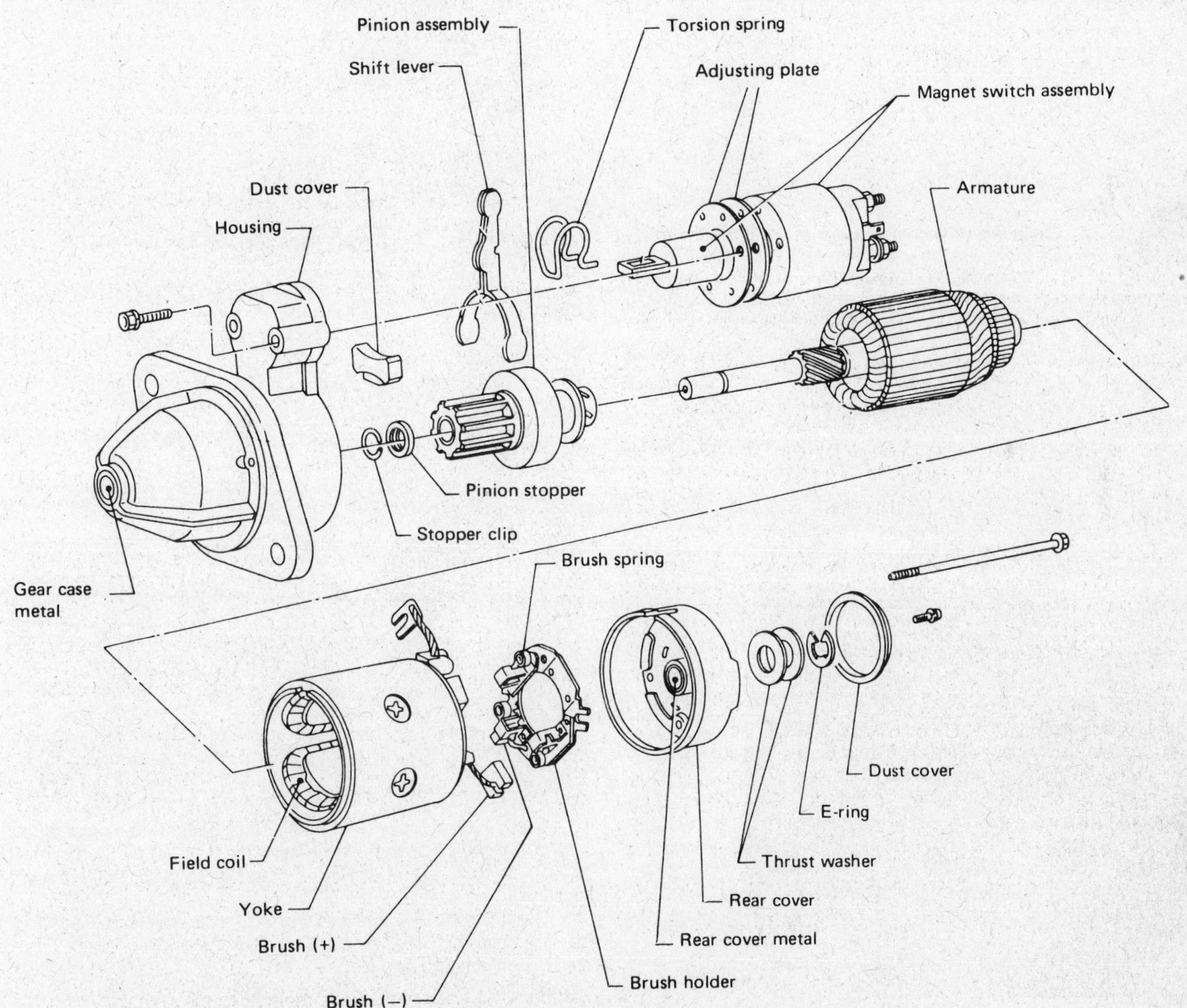

15.3b Exploded view of a typical non-reduction gear starter motor and solenoid assembly used on 1986 and later 2WD vehicles with a four-cylinder engine

5

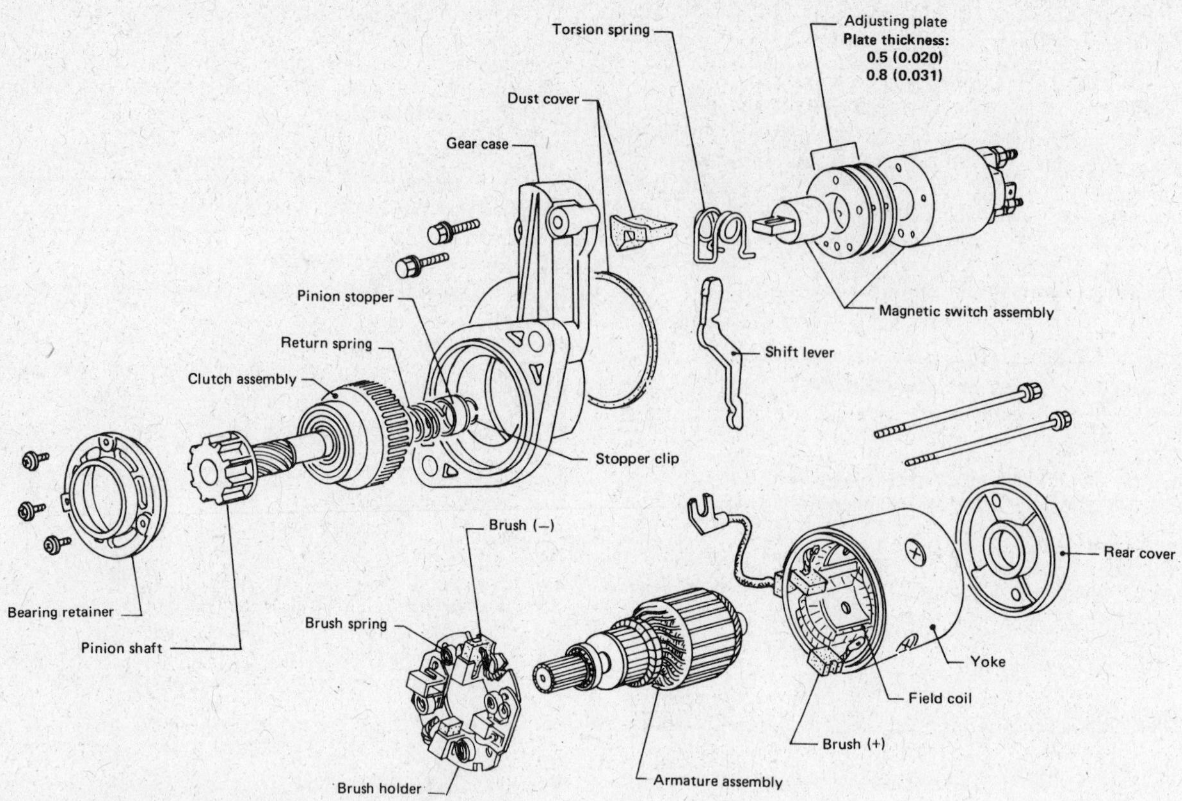

15.3c Exploded view of a typical non-reduction gear starter motor and solenoid assembly used on 1986 and later 4WD vehicles with a four-cylinder engine

15.8 The brushes on non-reduction gear starter motors are attached to the brush holder by springs and to the yoke with solder joints

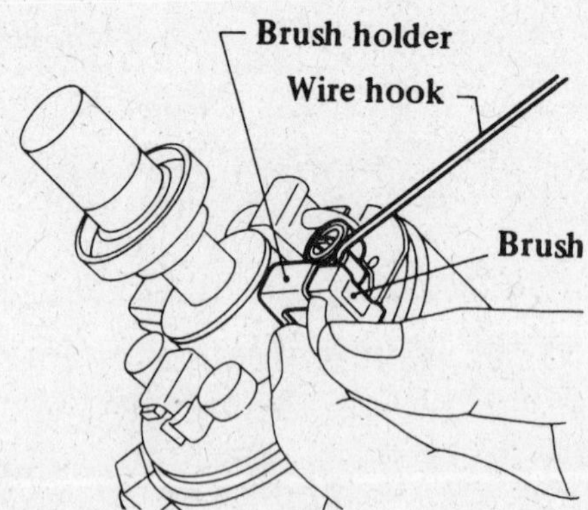

15.16 To remove the brush springs from a typical brush holder, hold the brush springs aside and slide the brushes out

8 Lift the brush holder plate and disconnect the springs **(see illustration)**. Remove each of the brushes from the holder plate by disengaging them from their springs. Measure the length of the brushes. If they are 12 mm (0.47-inch) or shorter they should be replaced with new ones.

9 Use a soldering gun to remove the old brushes and to attach new brushes.

10 Assembly is the reverse of the above procedure.

Reduction gear starter

Refer to illustrations 15.13a, 15.13b and 15.16

11 Remove the starter as described in Section 12.

12 Remove the solenoid as described in Section 13.

13 Remove the through bolts **(see illustrations)** by unscrewing them and drawing them out through the rear.

14 Remove the rear cover from the starter motor. Be careful not to damage the O-ring.

15 Remove the yoke, armature and brush holder as an assembly from the center housing. Be careful not to knock the brushes, commutator or coil against any adjacent part.

16 Lift the brush springs and remove the brushes from the brush holder **(see illustration)**.

18 Use a soldering gun to remove the brushes from the yoke and solder

17 Measure the length of the brushes. If they are shorter than the specified length they should be replaced with new ones.

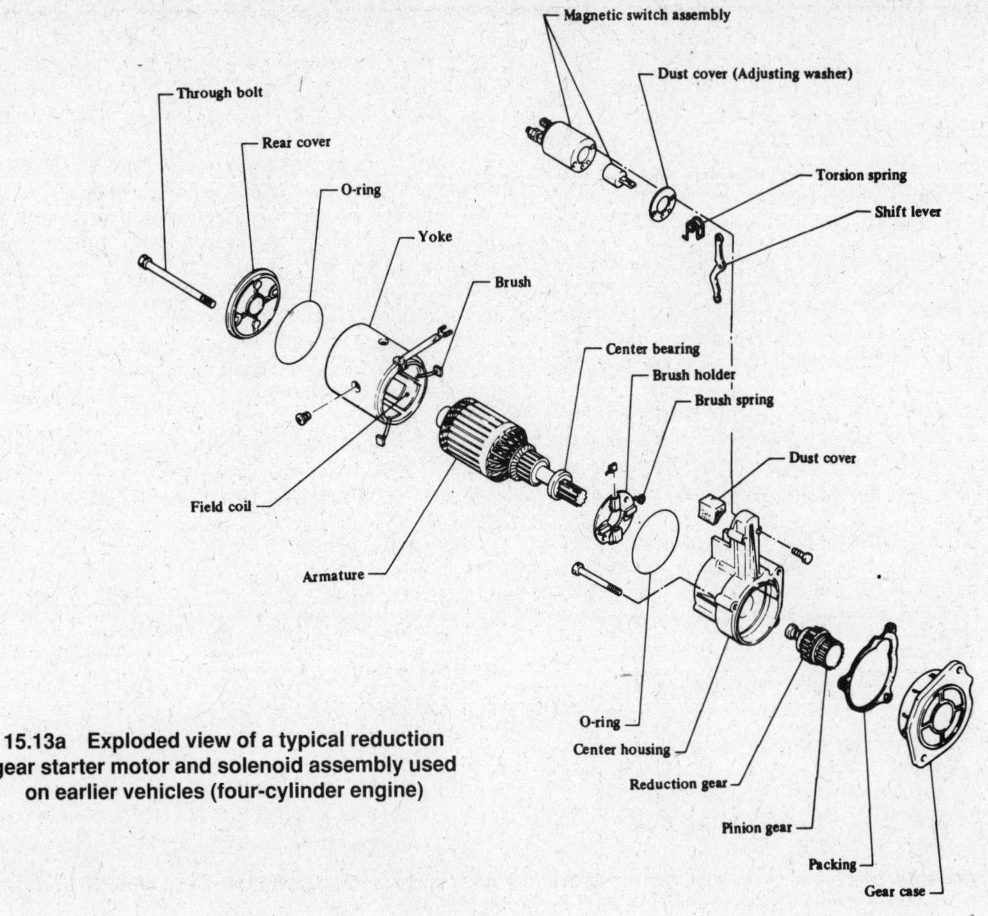

15.13a Exploded view of a typical reduction gear starter motor and solenoid assembly used on earlier vehicles (four-cylinder engine)

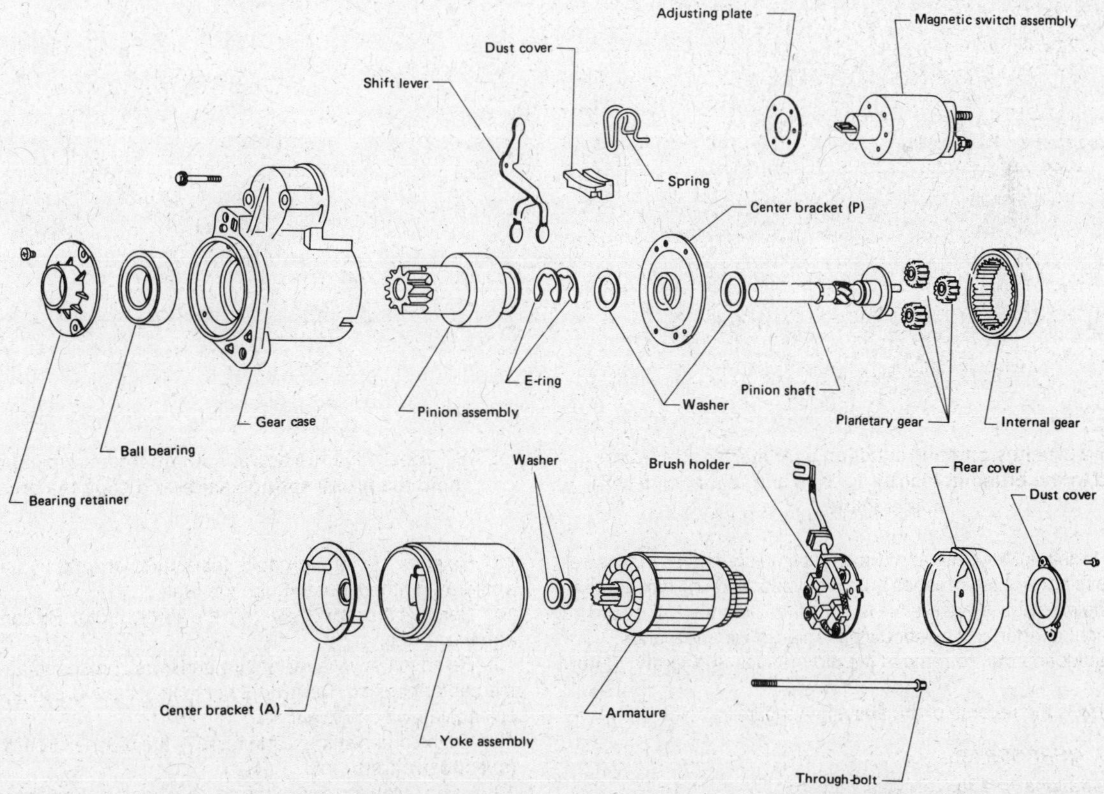

15.13b Exploded view of a typical reduction gear starter motor and solenoid assembly used on the V6 engine

new brushes on.
19 Reassembly of the starter motor is the reverse of the disassembly procedure.

16 Charging system – general information

The charging system consists of the alternator, the voltage regulator and the battery. These components work together to supply electrical power for the engine ignition, lights, radio, etc.

The alternator is turned by a drivebelt at the front of the engine. When the engine is operating, voltage is generated by the alternator to be sent to the battery for storage.

The alternator uses a solid-state regulator mounted inside the alternator housing. The purpose of the voltage regulator is to limit alternator voltage to a pre-set value, preventing power surges, circuit overloads, etc., during peak voltage output. The regulator voltage setting cannot be adjusted.

The charging system does not ordinarily require periodic maintenance. The drivebelts, electrical wiring and connections should, however, be inspected during normal tune-ups.

17 Alternator – maintenance and special precautions

1 Alternator maintenance consists of occasionally wiping away any dirt or oil which may have collected on it.
2 Check the tension of the drivebelt (refer to Chapter 1).
3 No lubrication is required, as alternator bearings are sealed for the life of the unit.
4 Take extreme care when making circuit connections to a vehicle equipped with an alternator and observe the following precautions: When making connections to the alternator from a battery, always match correct polarity. Before using electric-arc welding equipment to repair any part of the vehicle, disconnect the wiring from the alternator and disconnect the positive battery terminal. Never start the engine with a battery charger connected.

18 Charging system – check

1 When an alternator problem is suspected, always make sure that the battery is fully charged before proceeding. If necessary, have it charged from an outside source. Refer to Chapter 1.
2 Visually inspect all wires and connections to make sure they are clean, tight and in good condition.
3 A 30-volt voltmeter is necessary to accurately test the charging system.
4 Turn the ignition switch to the On position and check that the alternator warning light in the instrument cluster lights. If it does, proceed to Step 7.
5 If the warning light does not come on, check that the warning light bulb is not burned out. To do this, disconnect the SL connector at the rear of the alternator and ground the L lead wire with a jumper wire. These terminals should be identified on the rear cover of the alternator. Turn the ignition switch to the On position and check the warning light. If the warning light is still off, a burned out bulb or loose connection between the alternator and the warning light is indicated.
6 If the light comes on, the bulb is in good condition, and a faulty alternator or regulator is indicated. To determine which, reconnect the SL connector and ground the brushes to the alternator body by using a short section of wire as shown in Fig. 20.12. Turn the ignition switch On and check the warning light. If the light comes on, the voltage regulator is faulty. If the light remains off, the alternator is defective. Replace either component by referring to the appropriate Section of this Chapter.
7 If the warning light does come on with the ignition switch in the On position, start the engine and allow it to idle. The light should go out. If it remains on, even dimly or as a flicker, a faulty alternator is indicated. Replace it with a new or rebuilt unit.
8 Slowly increase the engine speed to 1500 rpm and maintain it at that speed.
9 Turn the headlights on and again check the alternator warning light. If it remains off, proceed to Step 11.
10 If the warning light comes on dimly, lower the engine speed to normal idle speed. Connect the voltmeter between the B and L terminals and measure the voltage. If more than 0.5 volts is shown the alternator needs replacing. If less than 0.5 volts is shown, the unit is okay.
11 If the warning light remains off when the lights are turned on, maintain the engine speed at 1500 rpm and measure the voltage at the B terminal. Be sure the S terminal is correctly connected.
12 If more than 15.5 volts is shown, the IC regulator is defective, and should be replaced.
13 If the voltage reading is between 13 and 15 volts, lower the engine speed to its normal level.
14 Turn the headlights on and check the alternator warning light in the dash. It should remain off. If the light comes on, a defective alternator is indicated and it should be replaced.

19 Alternator – removal and installation

Refer to illustration 19.3

1 Disconnect the negative battery cable from the battery.
2 For clearance on pre-1986 2WD models and all 1986 and later models, raise the front of the vehicle and support it securely on jackstands.
3 On pre-1986 4WD models, either remove the mud flap in the right wheel well or tape it up out of the way **(see illustration)**.

19.3 To gain access to the alternator on pre-1986 4WD vehicles, tape the rubber mud flap out of the way

4 Clearly label then detach all wires from the rear of the alternator.
5 Refer to Chapter 1 and remove the drivebelt.
6 Remove the adjusting and mounting bolts.
7 The alternator can now be separated from the engine. On pre-1986 2WD models, it can be lowered out from underneath, while on pre-1986 4WD models it can be taken out through the right wheel well. On 1986 and later models the alternator is removed from below.
8 Installation is the reverse of the removal procedure.

20 Alternator voltage regulator and brushes – replacement

1980 models

Refer to illustrations 20.2, 20.10 and 20.12

1 Remove the alternator from the vehicle as described in Section 18.

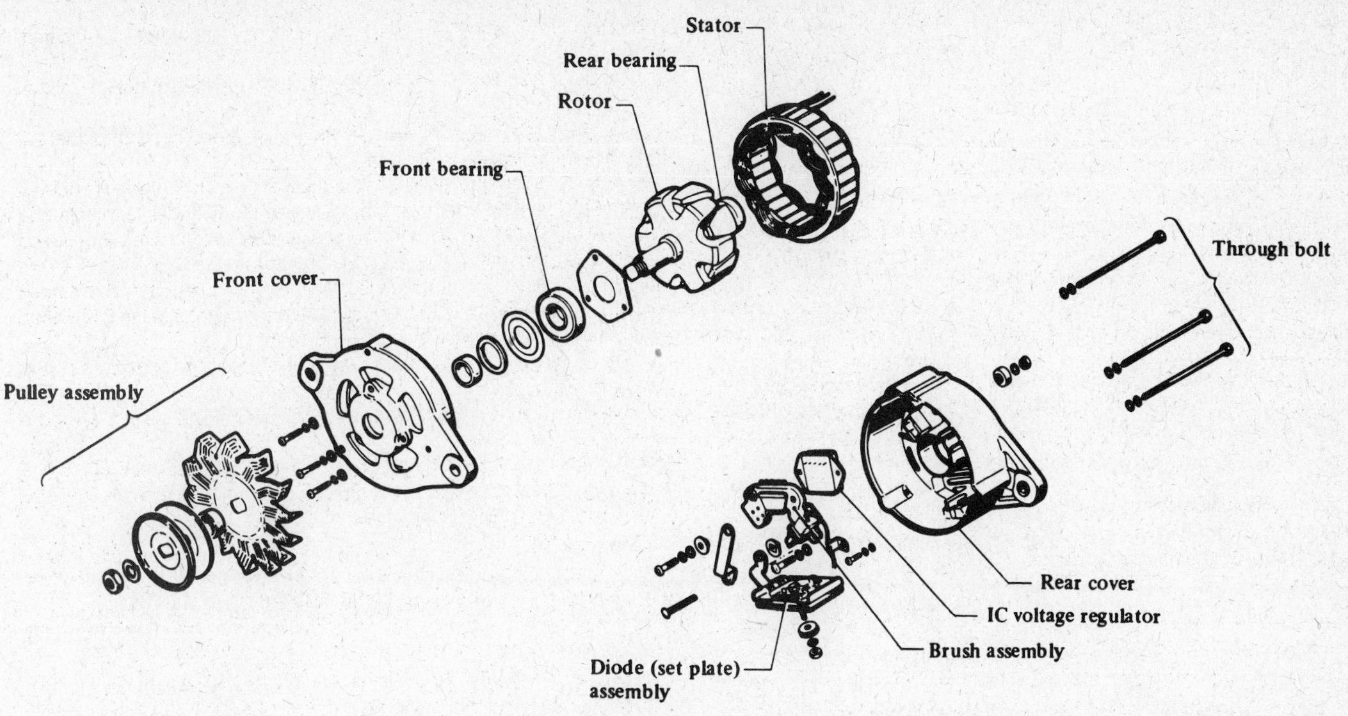

20.2 Exploded view of a typical alternator used on all 1980 models

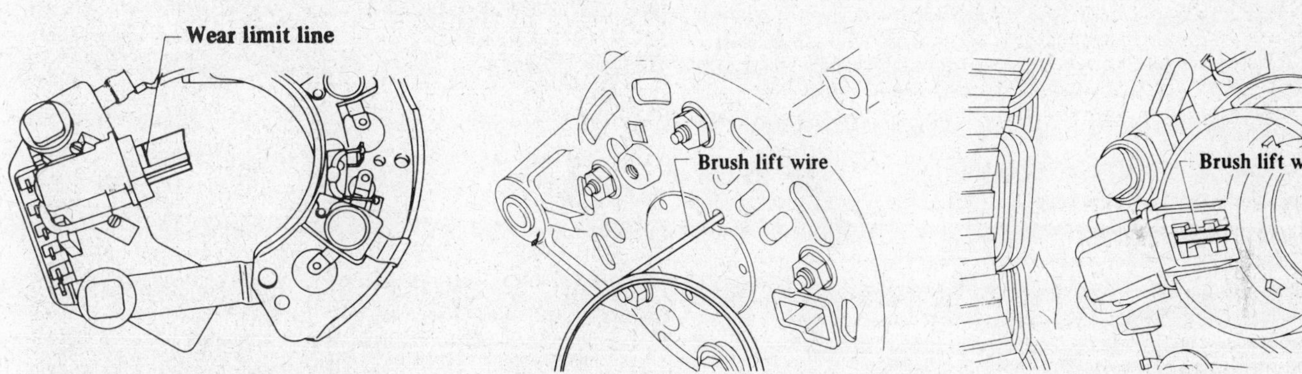

20.10 The quickest way to check for brush wear is to note how close the brush has worn to the limit line

20.12 During reassembly of the front and rear alternator covers, the brushes must be retained by a stiff wire inserted through the hole as shown

2 Remove the four through-bolts from the rear cover **(see illustration)**.
3 Separate the front cover/rotor assembly from the rear cover/stator assembly by lightly tapping the front bracket with a soft-faced hammer.
4 Disconnect the wire connecting the diode set plate to the brush at the brush terminal by heating it with a soldering iron.
5 Disconnect the diode set plate from the side face of the rear cover.
6 Remove the nut securing the battery terminal bolt.
7 Partially lift the diode set plate together with the stator coil from the rear cover. Remove the screw connecting the diode set plate to the brush.
8 Separate the rear cover, together with the stator coil and diode and remove the brush and IC regulator.
9 Check for free movement of the brush and make sure the holder is clean and undamaged.
10 Check for brush wear either by noting the brush wear limit line **(see illustration)** or by measuring the length of the brush and comparing it to the wear limit in the Specifications at the beginning of this Chapter. If the brush is worn beyond either limit, it must be replaced with a new one.
11 If the voltage regulator is defective, it and the brush assembly should be replaced as one unit.
12 Reassembly of the alternator is the reverse of the disassembly procedure, with the following notes:

a) Soldering of the stator coil lead wires to the diode assembly should be done as quickly as possible to prevent excessive heat from building up around the diode assembly.
b) When installing the diode A terminal, be sure the insulating bushing is correctly installed.
c) Before joining the front and rear covers together push the brush in the rear cover up with your fingers and hold it there **(see illustration)** by inserting a piece of stiff wire through the brush lift hole from the outside. After the front and rear covers have been joined, the wire can be removed by pushing the outside end toward the center of the alternator and pulling it straight out. If the wire is not removed in this way, the slip-ring sliding surface can be damaged.

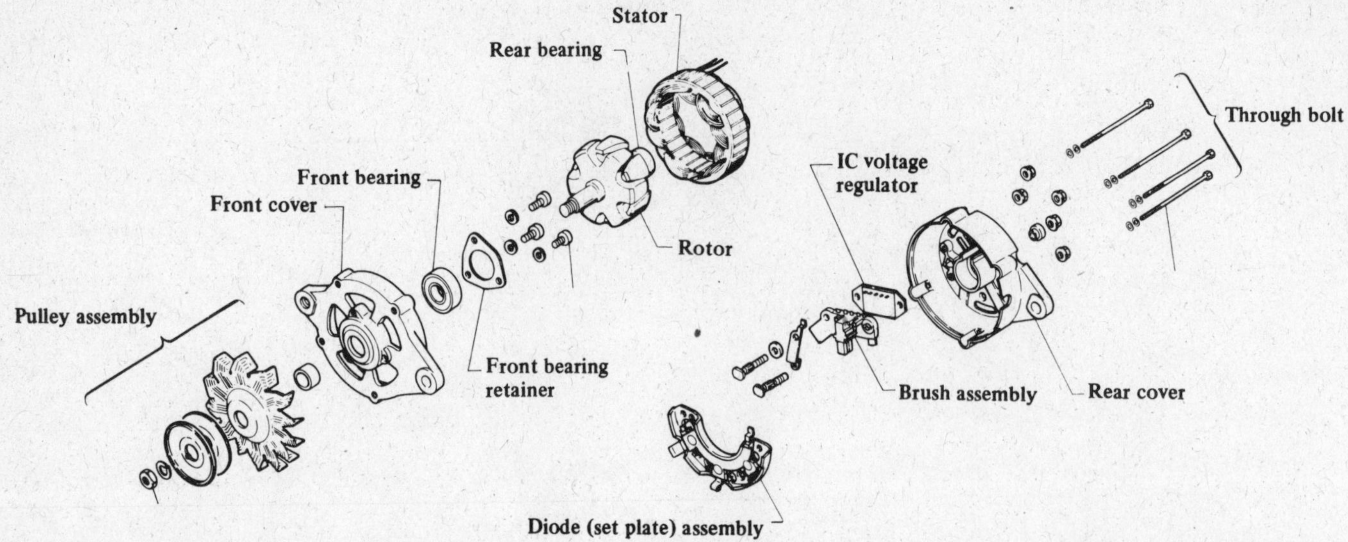

20.14 Exploded view of a typical alternator used on all 1981 and later models (dust cover used on later units not shown)

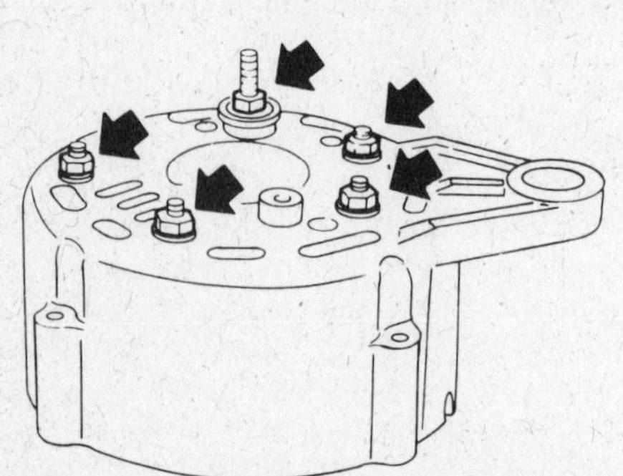

20.16 The stator assembly is attached to the alternator rear cover by five nuts on all 1981 and later models

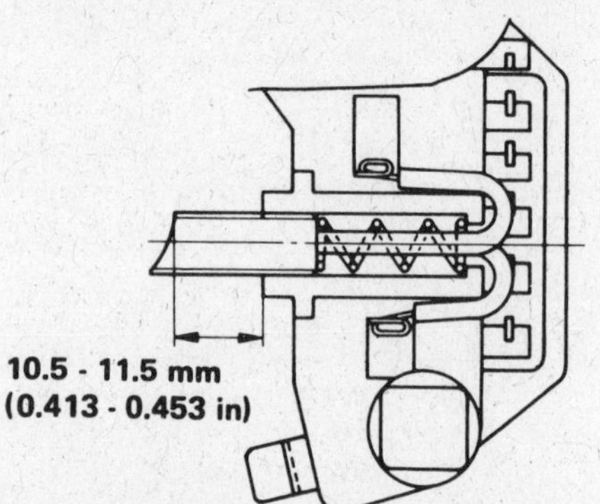

20.17a Before soldering the new alternator brush, make sure it's positioned as shown

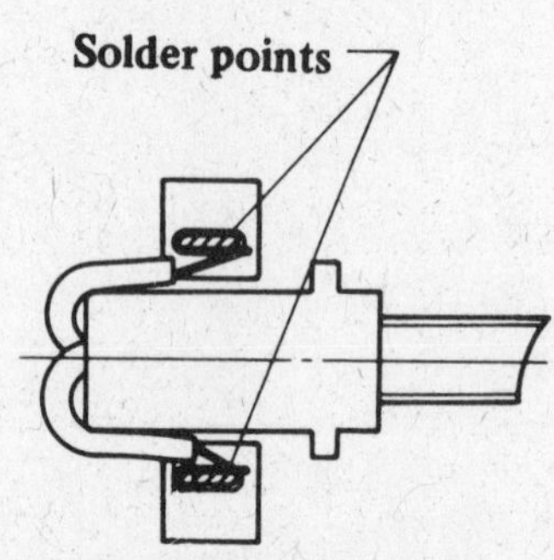

20.17b Solder the alternator brush lead wires to the outside of the terminal at the indicated points

1981 and later models

Refer to illustrations 20.14, 20.16, 20.17a, 20.17b and 20.18

13 Remove the alternator from the vehicle as described in Section 18.

14 Remove the four through bolts from the rear cover **(see illustration)**.

15 Separate the front cover/rotor assembly from the rear cover/stator assembly lightly tapping the front bracket with a soft-faced hammer. **Note:** *The rear covers on 1986 and later alternators are protected by a dust cover, attached by a pair of screws and a nut, which must be removed before disassembling the alternator.*

16 Remove the five stator assembly retaining nuts from the rear of the rear cover **(see illustration)**, then lift out the stator assembly.

17 Check the length and operation of the brushes as described in Steps 9 and 10, and replace them if necessary. **Note:** *Before soldering the brush lead wires, position the brush so that it extends about 7/16-inch (11 mm) from its brush holder* **(see illustration)**. Then coil the lead wire 1-1/2 times around the terminal groove, and solder the outside of the terminal **(see illustration)**. Be careful not to let solder adhere to the insulating tube as this could weaken and crack the tube.

18 If the IC voltage regulator needs to be replaced, use the following procedure: **Note:** *Do not remove the regulator unless it is being replaced with a new one.*

a) Disengage the regulator from the diode assembly by removing both the rivet and the solder **(see illustration)** that attaches them. This is made easier by using a soldering gun to disconnect the stator coil lead wires from the diode assembly.
b) To separate the regulator from the brush holder, remove the terminal's solder and, with a pair of pliers, take out the attaching bolts.
c) When installing the new regulator, place it on the brush holder and press-fit the bolts into place using a hand press or by carefully tapping them in.
d) Resolder all connections and install a new rivet. Stake the rivet following installation.

19 Reassembly of the alternator is the reverse of the disassembly procedure, following the special notes listed in Step 12.

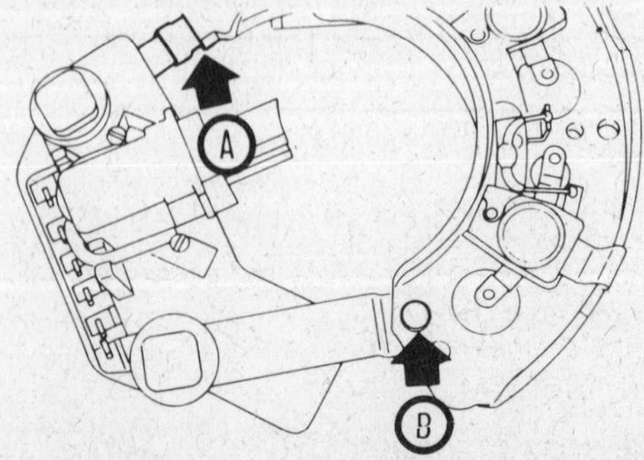

20.18 On 1981 and later alternators, the regulator/brush assembly is soldered (A) and riveted (B) to the diode assembly

6

Chapter 6 Emissions control systems

Contents

Specifications

General

Air regulator resistance	70 ohms
Exhaust gas sensor resistance	85.3 ± 8.5 K-ohms
Engine temperature sensor resistance (approximate values)	
At 68-degrees F	2.3 to 2.7 K-ohms
At 122-degrees F	680 to 1000 ohms
At 176-degrees F	300 to 330 ohms

Torque specifications

Torque specifications	Ft-lbs
Air gallery flare nuts	40
Air pump EGR exhaust tube nut	29
Thermal vacuum valve (maximum)	16

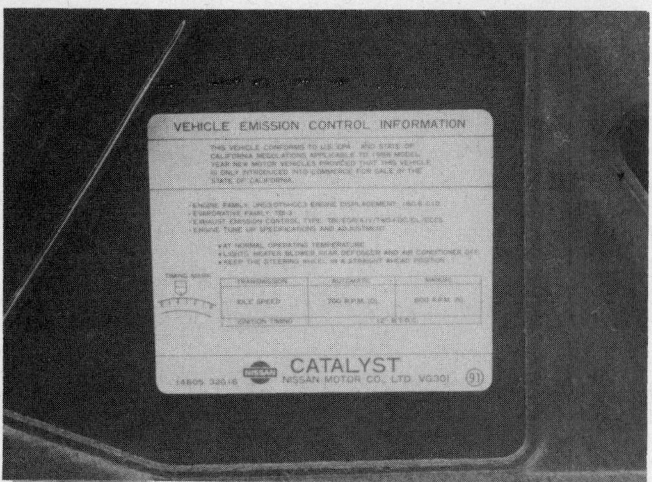

1.5a If there's a discrepancy between the information provided in this Chapter and the actual devices under the hood of your vehicle, the Vehicle Emission Control Information (VECI) label, located on the underside of the hood, should always be considered the final authority

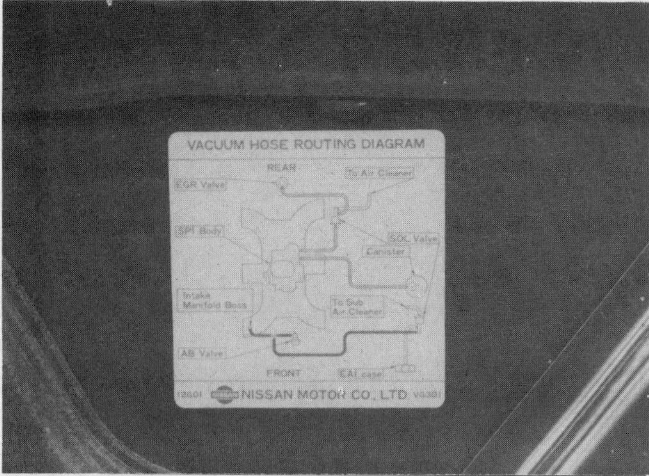

1.5b If there is any doubt regarding the routing of vacuum hoses as provided in this Chapter, the vacuum hose routing diagram label, located on the underside of the hood, will give you the most accurate routing schematic for your vehicle

1 General information

Refer to illustrations 1.5a, 1.5b, 1.5c and 1.5d

As smog standards have become more stringent, the emissions control systems developed to meet these requirements have not only become increasingly more diverse and complex, but are now designed as integral parts of the operation of the engine. Where once the antipollution devices used were installed as peripheral "add-on" components, the present systems work closely with such other systems as the fuel, ignition and exhaust systems. All vital engine operations are controlled by the emissions control system.

Because of this close integration of systems, disconnecting or not maintaining the emissions control systems, besides being illegal, can adversely affect engine performance and life, as well as fuel economy.

This is not to say that the emissions systems are particularly difficult for the home mechanic to maintain and service. You can perform general operational checks, and do most (if not all) of the regular maintenance easily and quickly at home with common tune-up and hand tools. **Note:** *The most frequent cause of emissions problems is simply a loose or broken vacuum hose or wire, so always check hoses, wires and connectors before performing major repairs.*

While the end result from the various emissions systems is to reduce the output of pollutants into the air (namely hydrocarbons (HC), carbon monoxide (CO), and oxides of nitrogen (NOx), the various systems function independently toward this goal. This is the way in which this Chapter is divided.

Note: *Always refer to the Vehicle Emission Control Information (VECI) label* **(see illustration)** *for specific information regarding emissions components on your vehicle.* Similarly, always use the vacuum hose routing diagram **(see illustration)** as the final word regarding hose routing for your particular vehicle.

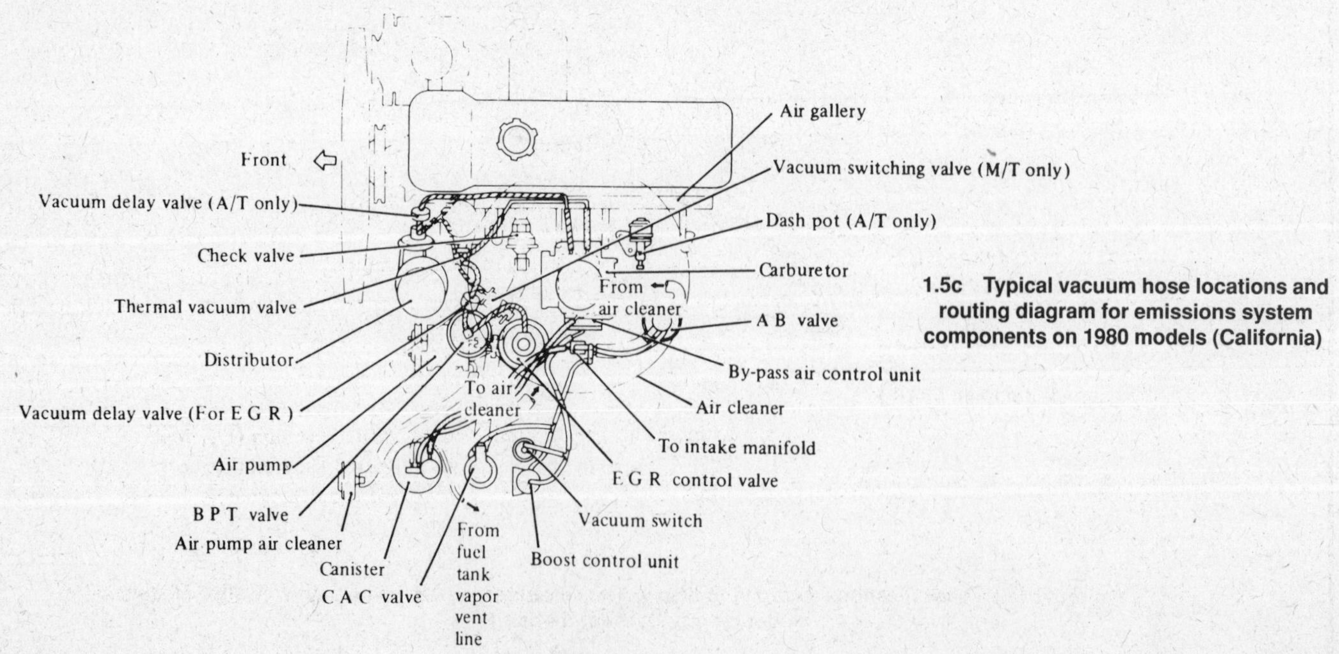

1.5c Typical vacuum hose locations and routing diagram for emissions system components on 1980 models (California)

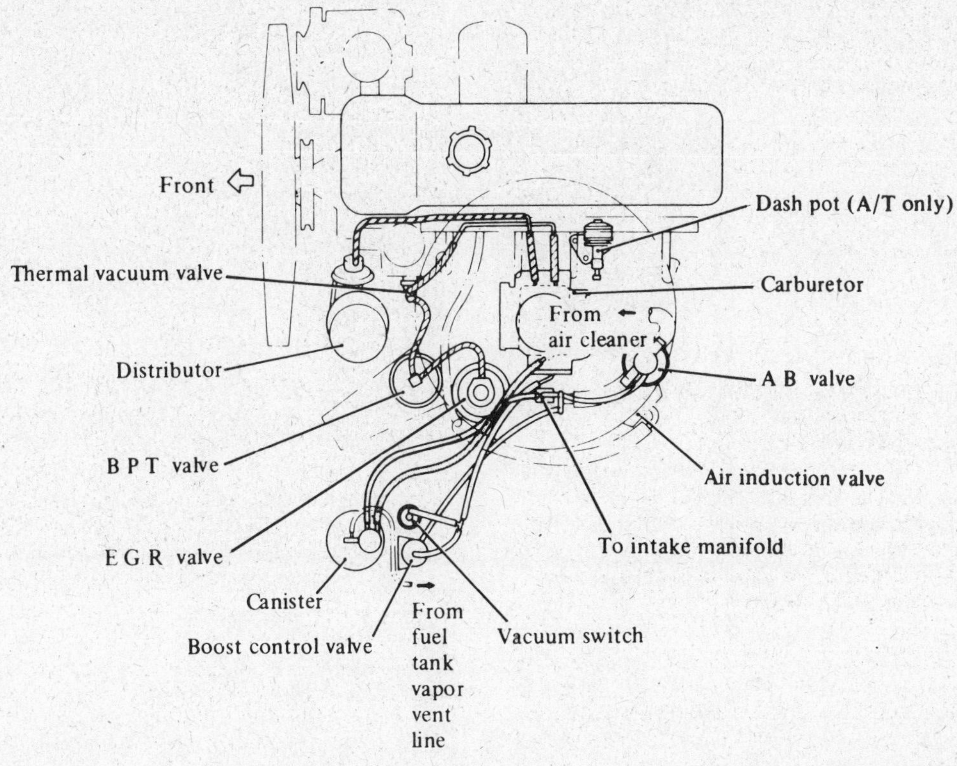

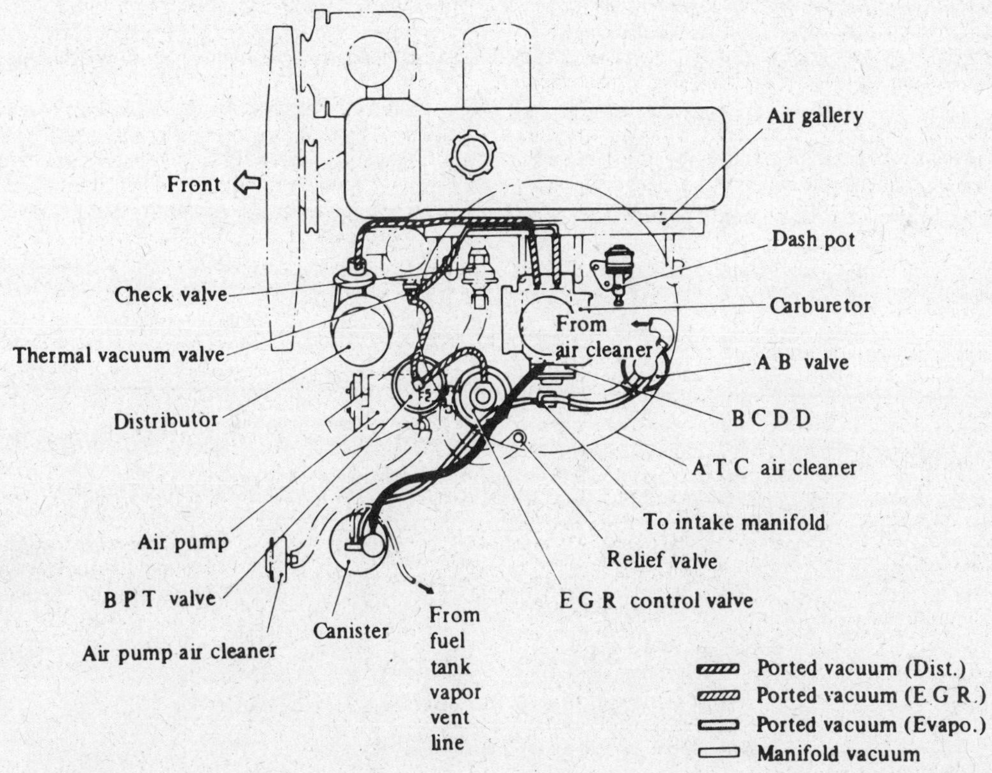

1.5c Typical vacuum hose locations and routing diagram for emissions system components on 1980 models (Federal – top; Canada – bottom)

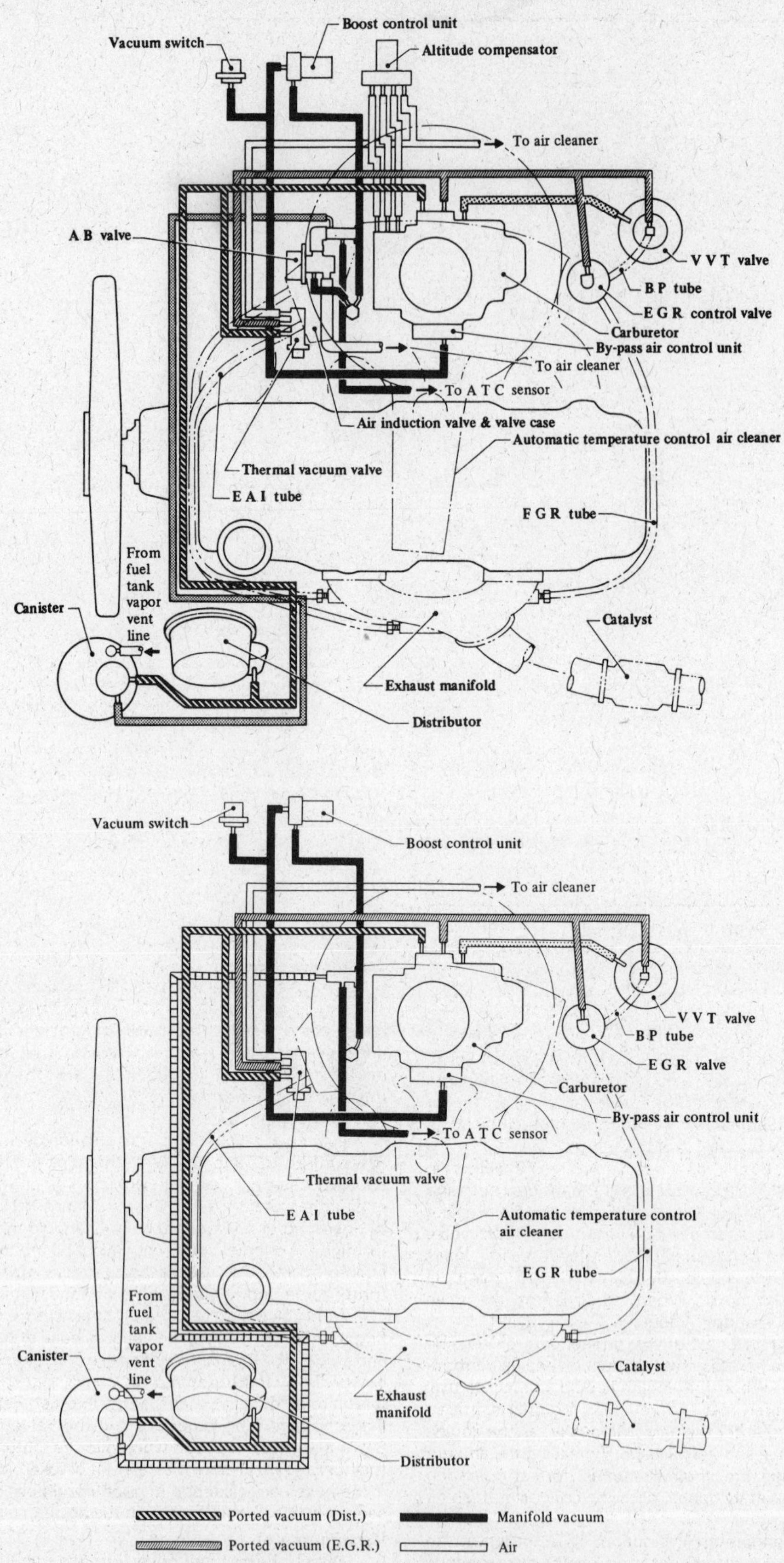

1.5c Typical vacuum hose locations and routing diagram for emissions system components on 1981 through 1985 models (California – top; Federal and Canada – bottom)

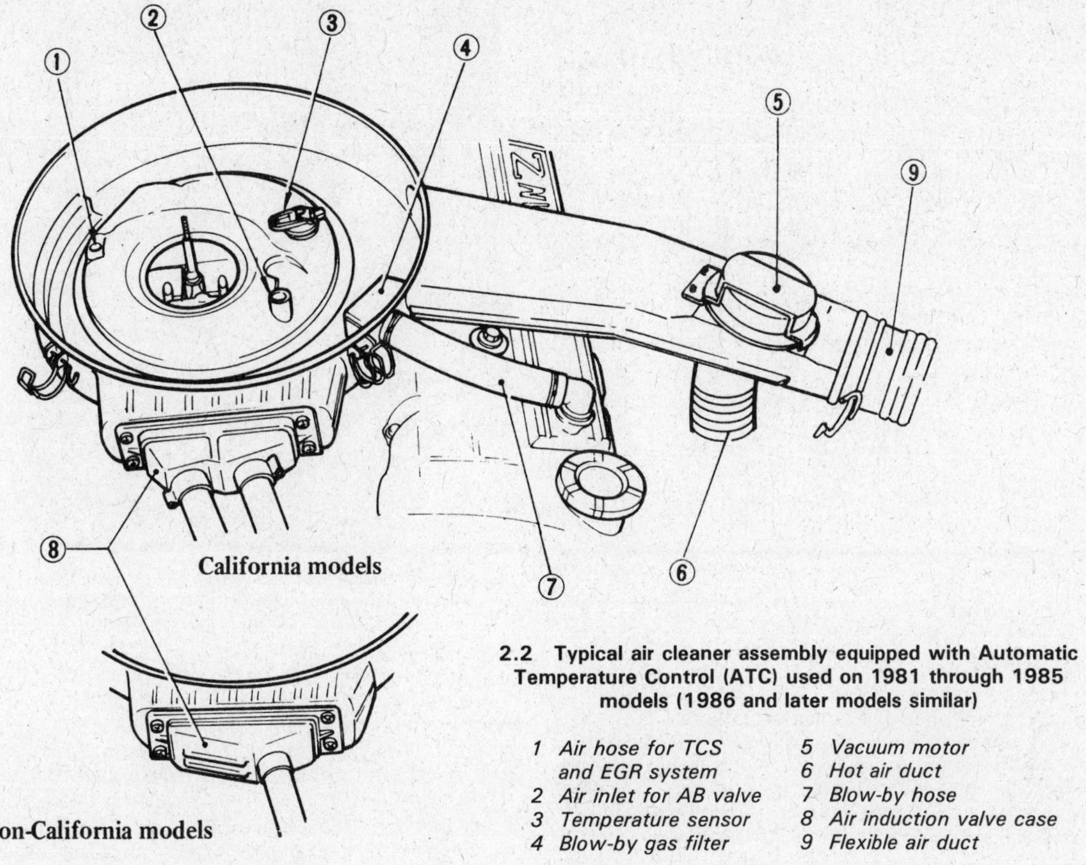

2.2 Typical air cleaner assembly equipped with Automatic Temperature Control (ATC) used on 1981 through 1985 models (1986 and later models similar)

1 Air hose for TCS and EGR system
2 Air inlet for AB valve
3 Temperature sensor
4 Blow-by gas filter
5 Vacuum motor
6 Hot air duct
7 Blow-by hose
8 Air induction valve case
9 Flexible air duct

2 Automatic Temperature Control (ATC) system

Refer to illustration 2.2

General description

1 The Automatic Temperature Control (ATC) system improves engine efficiency and reduces hydrocarbon emissions during the initial warm-up period of the engine by maintaining a controlled air temperature into the carburetor. Temperature control of the incoming air allows leaner carb and choke calibrations and helps prevent carburetor icing in cold weather.

2 The system **(see illustration)** uses an air control valve located in the snorkel of the air cleaner housing to control the ratio of cold and warm air into the carburetor. This valve is controlled by a vacuum motor which is, in turn, modulated by a temperature sensitive air bleed valve or temperature sensor in the air cleaner. This air bleed valve closes when the intake air temperature is cold, thus allowing intake manifold vacuum to reach the vacuum motor. When the air is hot, the valve opens, thus closing off the manifold vacuum.

3 It is during the first few miles of driving (depending on outside temperature) that this system has its greatest effect on engine performance and emissions output. When the engine is cold, the air control valve blocks off the air cleaner inlet snorkel, allowing only warm air from the exhaust manifold to enter the carb. Gradually, as the engine warms up, the valve opens the snorkel passage, increasing the amount of cold air allowed in. Once the engine reaches normal operating temperature, the valve completely opens, allowing only cold, fresh air to enter.

4 Because of this cold-engine-only function, it is important to periodically check this system to prevent poor engine performance when cold, or overheating of the fuel mixture once the engine has reached operating temperatures. If the air cleaner valve sticks in the 'no heat' position, the engine will run poorly, stall and waste gas until it has warmed up on its own. A valve sticking in the 'heat' position causes the engine to run as if it is out of tune due to the constant flow of hot air to the carburetor.

Checking

Temperature sensor

5 With the engine off, note the position of the air control valve inside the air cleaner snorkel. If the vehicle is equipped with an air duct on the end of the snorkel, it will have to be removed prior to this check. If visual access to the valve is difficult, use a mirror. The valve should be down, meaning that all air would flow through the snorkel and none through the exhaust manifold hot-air duct at the underside of the air cleaner housing.

6 Now have an assistant start the engine and continue to watch the valve inside the snorkel. With the engine cold and at idle, the valve should close off all air from the snorkel, allowing heated air from the exhaust manifold to enter the air cleaner intake. As the engine warms to operating temperature the valve should move, allowing outside air through the snorkel to be included in the mixture. Eventually, the valve should move down to the point where most of the incoming air is through the snorkel and not the exhaust manifold duct.

7 If the valve did not close off snorkel air when the cold engine was first started, disconnect the vacuum hose at the snorkel vacuum motor and place your thumb over the hose end, checking for vacuum. If there is vacuum going to the motor, check that the valve and link are not frozen or binding in the air cleaner snorkel. Replace the vacuum motor if the hose routing is correct and the valve moves freely.

8 If there was no vacuum going to the motor in the above test, check the hoses to make sure they are not cracked, crimped or disconnected. If the hoses are clear and in good condition, replace the temperature sensor inside the air cleaner housing.

Vacuum motor

9 Detach the vacuum hose from the vacuum motor and connect a vacuum tester in its place.

10 Apply vacuum to the motor. At –10.0 kPa (–75 mm-Hg or –2.95 in-Hg) the valve should begin to open. At over –22.0 kPa (–165 mm-Hg or –6.5 in-Hg) the valve should be fully open.

11 If the vacuum motor does not perform as described it should be replaced.

Component replacement

Temperature sensor

12 Using pliers, flatten the clip that retains the vacuum hose to the sensor.
13 Disconnect the hoses from the sensor.
14 Carefully note the position of the sensor. The new sensor must be installed in exactly the same position.
15 Remove the clip from the sensor tube and remove the sensor from the air cleaner. **Note:** *The gasket between the sensor and air cleaner is bonded to the air cleaner and should not be removed.*
16 Install the new sensor with a new gasket in the same position as the old one.
17 Press the retaining clip on the sensor. Do not damage the control mechanism in the center of the sensor.
18 Connect the vacuum hoses and install the air cleaner on the engine.

Vacuum motor

19 Remove the screws that attach the vacuum motor retainer to the air cleaner.
20 Turn the vacuum motor to disengage it from the air control valve and lift it off.
21 Installation is the reverse of the removal procedure.

3 Idle compensator

Refer to illustrations 3.7 and 3.8

General description

1 The idle compensator is a bimetal thermostatic valve which is designed to route air directly from the air cleaner to the intake manifold. This compensates for abnormal mixture enrichment which can occur at high outside air temperatures when idling. 1980 models use a dual-valve unit, with each valve calibrated to open (allowing the air into the intake manifold) at a different temperature range. The number 1 valve opens between 140 to 158°F (60 to 70°C) while the number 2 valve opens between 158 to 194°F (70 to 90°C). The idle compensator on these models is located inside the air cleaner.
2 The idle compensator on 1981 through 1984 US and 1981 through 1985 Canadian models is a single valve unit and is attached directly to the carburetor. The unit opens at approximately 127° F (53°C).

Checking

(1980 US and Canadian models)

3 A faulty idle compensator is suspected if the idling becomes erratic. To check it, make sure the engine is cold and remove the air cleaner lid.
4 Disconnect the hose that leads to the compensator and attempt to suck air through it. When the engine is cold, no air should pass through. If it does, replace the idle compensator. **Note:** *Check both valves individually by holding the other closed with your finger while checking.*
5 Next replace the air cleaner lid, close the hood, then start the engine and allow it to reach normal operating temperature.
6 With the engine fully warmed up, open the hood again and remove the air cleaner lid.

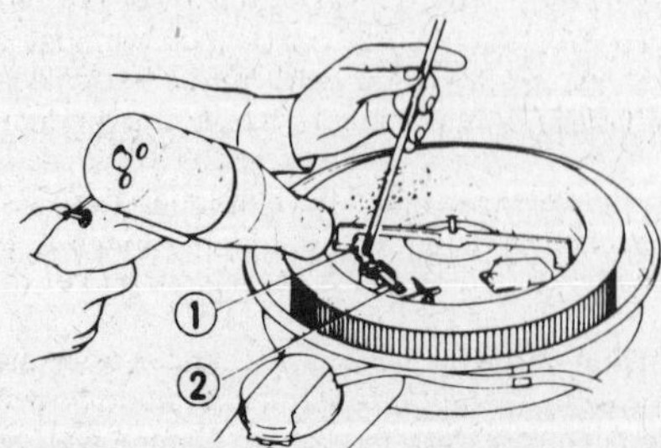

3.7 To check the operation of the idle compensator on 1980 through 1984 models, hold a thermometer next to the compensator while directing a hot air gun at it — if the compensator is in good condition, a hissing sound will be heard as each valve reaches its opening temperature (1980 model, with no. 1 bi-metal [1] and no. 2 bi-metal [2] valves, shown; 1981 and later models have one valve)

3.8 On 1981 through 1984 US models (and 1981 through 1985 Canadian models), the idle compensator and by-pass air control valve (arrows) are located on the carburetor

7 While holding a thermometer next to the idle compensator, direct a hot air gun at the compensator **(see illustration)**. If the compensator is in good condition a hissing sound will be heard as each valve reaches its opening temperature. If they do not open as described, replace the unit with a new one.

1981 through 1984 US and 1981 through 1985 Canadian models

8 Because the idle compensator on these models is mounted integrally with the carburetor **(see illustration)**, the only effective method of checking it is to remove it from the carburetor. Visually check that the valve is in its closed position when cold. Then, while holding a thermometer alongside it, direct a hot air gun at it to bring it up to its opening temperature. Watch to be sure the bimetal valve opens at its correct temperature. If not, replace it with a new one.

Replacement

1980 US and Canadian models

9 Remove the air cleaner top plate.
10 Disconnect the air hose from the unit.
11 Remove the screws that retain it to the air cleaner and lift it off, along with its gasket.
12 Installation is the reverse of removal. **Note:** *If replacing the compensator, be sure the new one has the same identification number as the old one.*

1981 through 1984 US and 1981 through 1985 Canadian models

13 Remove the air cleaner.
14 Remove the idle compensator cover screws and cover, then lift out the compensator and gasket.
15 Installation is the reverse of the removal procedure. **Note:** *If replacing the unit, be sure the new one has the same identification number as the old one.*

4 Positive Crankcase Ventilation (PCV) system

Refer to illustration 4.2

General description

1 The positive crankcase ventilation, or PCV system, as it is more commonly called, reduces hydrocarbon emissions by circulating fresh air through the crankcase. This air combines with blow-by gases, or gases blown past the piston rings during compression, and the combination is then sucked into the intake manifold to be reburned by the engine.
2 This process is achieved by using one air pipe running from the air cleaner to the rocker arm cover, a one-way PCV valve located on

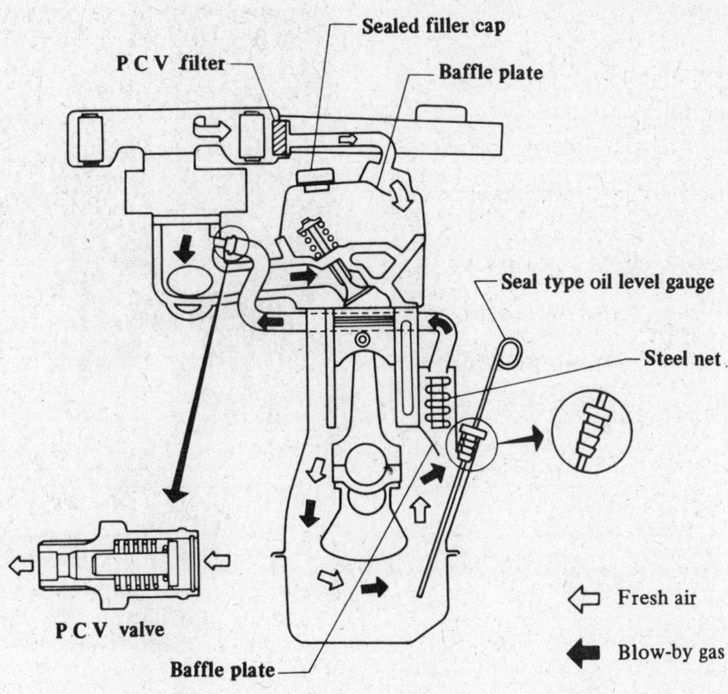

4.2 The Positive Crankcase Ventilation (PCV) system used on 1981 through 1985 models

the side of the intake manifold and a second air pipe running from the crankcase to the PCV valve **(see illustration)**.

3 During the partial throttle operation of the engine, the vacuum created in the intake manifold is great enough to suck the gases from the crankcase, through the PCV valve and into the manifold. The PCV valve allows the gases to enter the manifold, but will not allow them to pass in the other direction.

4 The ventilating air is drawn into the rocker arm cover from the air cleaner, and then into the crankcase.

5 Under full-throttle operation, the vacuum in the intake manifold is not great enough to suck the gases in. Under this condition the blow-by gases flow backwards into the rocker arm cover, through the air tube and into the air cleaner, where it is carried into the intake manifold in the normal air intake flow.

Checking

6 The PCV system can be checked for proper operation quickly and easily. This system should be checked regularly as carbon and gunk deposited by the blow-by gases will eventually clog the PCV valve and/or system hoses. When the flow of the PCV system is reduced or stopped, common symptoms are rough idling or reduced engine speed at idle.

7 To check for proper vacuum in the system, disconnect the rubber air hose where it exits the air cleaner.

8 With the engine idling, place your thumb lightly over the end of the hose. You should feel a slight pull of vacuum. The suction may be heard as your thumb is released. This will indicate that air is being drawn all the way through the system. If a vacuum is felt, the system is functioning properly.

9 If there is very little vacuum or none at all, at the end of the hose, the system is clogged and must be inspected further.

10 With the engine still idling, disconnect the rubber hose from the PCV valve. Now place your finger over the end of the valve and feel for a suction. You should feel a relatively strong vacuum at this point. This indicates that the valve is good.

11 If no vacuum is felt at the PCV valve, remove the valve from the intake manifold. Shake it and listen for a clicking sound. That is the rattle of the valve's check needle. If the valve does not click freely, replace it.

12 If a strong vacuum is felt at the PCV valve, yet there is still no vacuum during the test described in Step 8, then one of the system's vent tubes is probably clogged. Both should be removed and blown out with compressed air.

13 If, after cleaning the vent tubes, there is still no suction at the air pipe, there is a blockage in an internal passage possibly at the baffle plate and steel net inside the crankcase. This requires disassembly of the engine to correct.

14 When purchasing a new PCV valve, make sure it is the proper one for your vehicle. An incorrect PCV valve may pull too much or too little vacuum, possibly causing damage to the engine.

6

5 Exhaust Gas Recirculation (EGR) system

Refer to illustrations 5.13, 5.18a, 5.18b, 5.19, 5.34 and 5.40

General description

Overview (all models)

1 This system is used to reduce oxides of nitrogen (NOx) emitted from the exhaust. Formation of these pollutants take place at very high temperatures; consequently, it occurs during the peak temperature period of the combustion process. To reduce peak temperatures, and thus the formation of NOx, a small amount of exhaust gas is taken from the exhaust system and recirculated in the combustion cycle.

2 Slightly different EGR systems are used in the model years 1980.

3 In addition, within each system various EGR valves are used according to the transmission used and the altitude the vehicle is expected to be operated at. For replacement, the EGR valve can be identified by the part number stamped on the recessed portion at the top of the valve.

4 Because a malfunctioning EGR system can severely affect the performance of the engine, it is important to understand how each system works in order to accurately troubleshoot it. Common engine problems associated with the EGR system are: rough idling or stalling when at an idle, rough engine performance upon light throttle application and stalling on deceleration.

1980 models

5 The EGR system used on all 1980 models incorporates an EGR valve, a back-pressure transducer (BPT) valve and one thermal vacuum valve (TVV). In addition, California models also use a vacuum delay

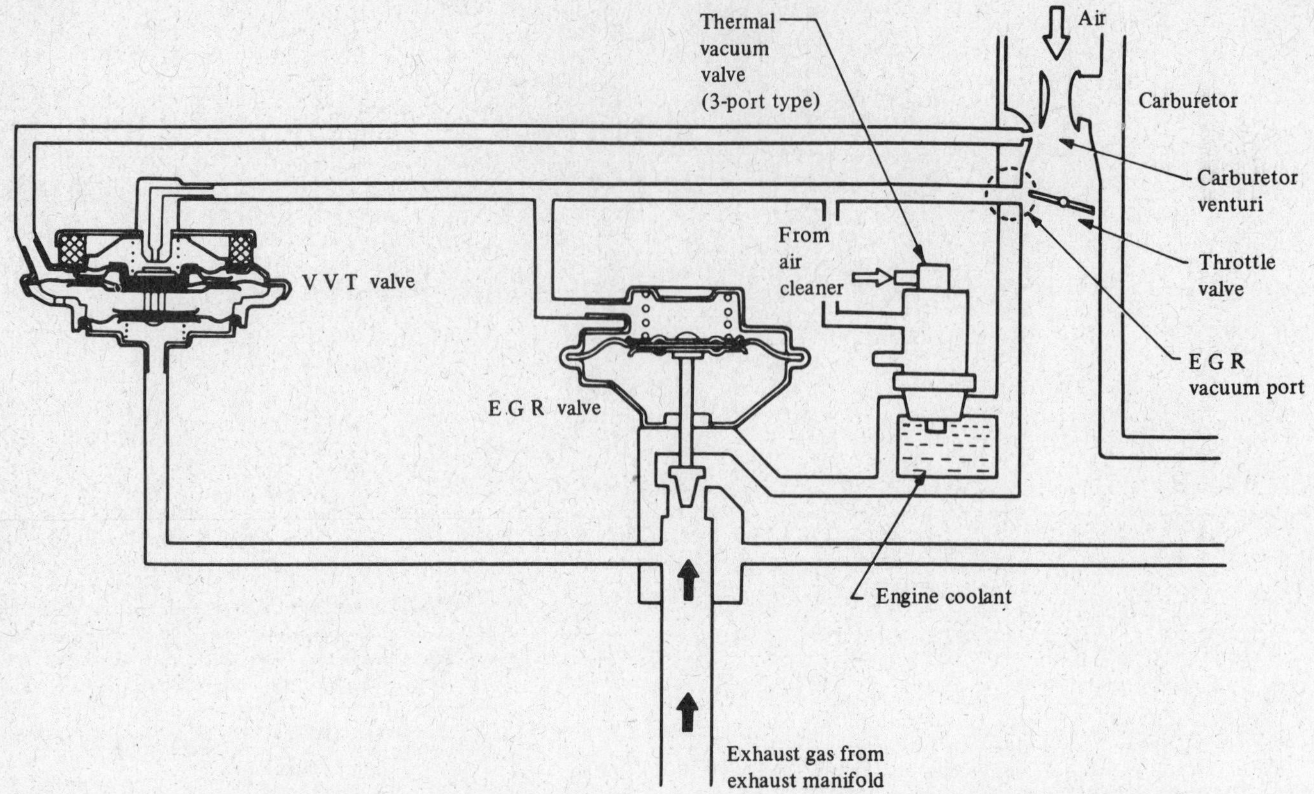

5.13 Schematic for the EGR system used on 1981 through 1984 models (except 1984 California vehicles)

valve installed in the vacuum line between the BPT valve and the TVV.

6 The heat of any EGR system is the EGR valve, which controls the flow of exhaust gases into the intake manifold for reburning. Under normal conditions the EGR valve is closed, which prevents the passage of exhaust gases into the intake manifold. The bimetal type TVV and the BPT valve are incorporated into the system to control the opening of the valve so that it will open only at the optimum time.

7 The direct vacuum signal that opens the valve comes from the throttle valve of the carburetor. This vacuum signal is only great enough to open the EGR valve during mid-range throttle positions. At idle and at full throttle, the vacuum signal lessens and the EGR valve will close again.

8 The TVV is placed into the vacuum signal line between the carburetor and the EGR valve, and is designed so that it will not allow the vacuum signal to reach the EGR valve until the engine coolant temperature reaches 122 ° F (50 degrees C), or normal operating temperature. This prevents the EGTR system from leaning out the rich fuel/air mixture needed during cold engine operation.

9 The BPT valve is tapped into the vacuum signal line after the TVV,and allows an air bleed to take place in the line until it is closed. This air bleed, when present, keeps the vacuum pressure low, thus preventing the EGR valve from opening.

10 The BPT valve is also connected by an air line to the lower portion of the the EGR valve , which opens it up to the exhaust pressure coming from the exhaust manifold. When this pressure reaches a predetermined point, it will overcome the spring-loaded diaphragm in the BPT valve, and close off the valve. The closing of the valve stops the air bleed in the signal line, and thus allows the vacuum signal to reach and open the EGR valve.

11 The vacuum delay valve, used on California models, is a one-way valve designed to prevent an abrupt escape of vacuum from the vacuum signal line to the EGR valve, thus increasing the length of the EGR valve operation. It allows air to pass freely toward the intake manifold but severely limits the amount allowed to pass toward the EGR valve. The brown side of the valve should always be toward the TVV.

12 The conditions, then, for the EGR valve to open in this system are: 1) the engine coolant must be 122° F (50 degrees C or higher), 2) the gas pressure in the exhaust manifold must be great enough to close the BPT valve, and 3) the throttle must be in a mid-range position.

1981 through 1984 models (except 1984 California)

13 The EGR system used on these models **(see illustration)** is similar to the one described above with a couple of principal differences. The thermal vacuum valve (TVV) used in this system is designed to permit an air bleed in the EGR vacuum signal line when open and therefore must be closed before the EGR valve can open. This TVV is calibrated to stay open until the engine coolant reaches 140°F (60°C). At this point the valve's wax sensor will expand and seal off the air leak.

14 Another major difference is that a venturi vacuum transducer (VVT) valve is used in place of the BPT valve. Like the TVV, the VVT valve also permits an air bleed through it, and therefore must be closed before the EGR valve can open. The VVT valve can be closed by either one of two ways. One method, as with the BPT valve in the 1980 system, is if the exhaust gas back-pressure becomes great enough, this pressure will cause the valve to close. The VVT valve also has a vacuum signal line from the carburetor venturi. A great enough vacuum at this point will also cause the VVT valve to close.

15 Therefore, with this system, the conditions that must be met for the EGR valve to open are: 1) the throttle valve must be in the mid-range position, 2) the engine coolant temperature must be at least 140°F (60°C) 3) either the exhaust back-pressure or the venturi vacuum pressure must be great enough to close the VVT valve.

1984 California, all 1985 and 1986 four-cylinder engine models only

16 Though basically similar to previous designs, the EGR system on 1984 California models, all 1985 models and 1986 vehicles powered by four-cylinder engines is equipped with a back-pressure transducer (BPT) valve instead of a venturi vacuum transducer (VVT). This BPT, which is identical in design and operation to the BPT used on 1980 models, contains a diaphragm activated by exhaust pressure. This diaphragm, in turn, regulates the amount of vacuum applied to the EGR control valve. Thus, the amount of recirculated exhaust gas varies with the operating condition of the engine.

1987 and 1988 four-cylinder and 1986 and later V6 engine models

17 The latest version of the EGR system is under the control of the Electronic Concentrated Control System (ECCS) control unit (ECU). Utilizing inputs from the crank angle sensor, cylinder head temperature sensor and the throttle sensor, the ECU computes engine speed, engine temperature and throttle valve position, respectively. The ECU inter-

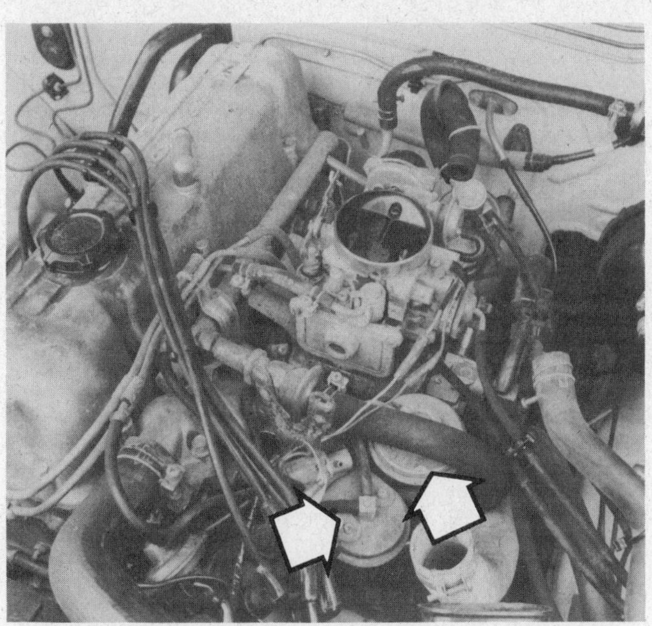

5.18a On 1980 models, the EGR valve (arrow) is located in front of the carburetor and the BPT valve (arrow) is located next to the EGR valve

5.18b On 1986 and later models with a V6 engine, the EGR valve (arrow) is located behind the throttle body and is mounted on the intake manifold

prets this data and sends a signal to the EGR control solenoid valve, which controls the EGR valve. Basically, anytime the engine is being started, engine temperature is low, the engine is idling, engine speed is high (more than 3200 rpm) or the engine speed is low (under 900 rpm), the EGR control solenoid valve is "on" and the EGR system is turned off. At all other times, the EGR control solenoid is off and the EGR is on.

Checking

EGR valve

18 Locate the EGR valve mounted at the front of the intake manifold on 1980 models, or at the rear of the intake manifold on 1981 and later models **(see illustrations)**.

19 Place your finger under the EGR valve and push upward on the diaphragm plate **(see illustration)**. The diaphragm should move freely from the closed to the open position. If it doesn't, replace the EGR valve.

20 Now start the engine and run at idle speed. While the engine is still just beginning to warm up, again push upward on the EGR diaphragm with your finger. If the valve or adjacent accessories are hot, wear gloves to prevent burning your fingers. When the diaphragm is pressed (valve open to recirculate exhaust), the engine should lose speed, stumble or even stall. If the engine did not change speed, the exhaust gas pipe leading to the EGR valve should be checked for blockage.

21 If equipped with a BPT valve, bypass it by connecting a hose directly between the TVV (or vacuum delay valve) and the EGR valve. If equipped with a VVT valve, disconnect the vacuum signal line from the valve and securely plug the hose.

22 Now allow the engine to reach normal operating temperature. Have an assistant depress the accelerator slightly and hold the engine speed constant above idle at about 2000 to 2500 rpm.

23 Pull off the vacuum signal line at the EGR valve and check that the diaphragm plate moves downward, accompanied by an increase in engine speed.

24 Reinstall the vacuum signal line to the valve and the diaphragm plate should move upward with a decrease in engine speed.

25 If the diaphragm did not move, make sure the engine was at operating temperature. Repeat the test if in doubt.

26 If the diaphragm still does not move, your next check would be that the vacuum is reaching the EGR valve. Pull off the vacuum hose at the valve, and with the engine running and accelerator slightly pressed, check for vacuum at the end of the hose with your thumb. If there is vacuum, replace the EGR valve with a new one. If there is no vacuum signal, follow the vacuum hose to its sources, inspecting

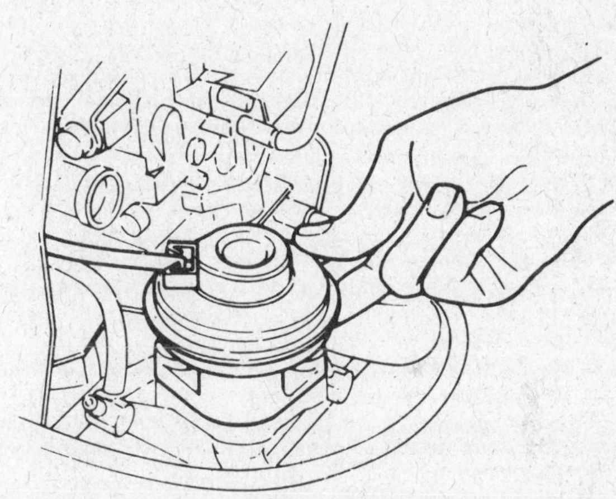

5.19 To check the EGR valve, place your fingers under the valve and feel for free movement of the diaphragm by pushing up — be sure to wear gloves if there is any danger of being burned by hot components near the EGR valve

for any cracks, breaks or blockage in the lines. Also check that the TVV and vacuum delay valve (if equipped) are working properly.

BPT valve

27 Disconnect both vacuum hoses from the top of the valve.

28 Remove the valve from the engine as described elsewhere in this section.

29 Plug one of the upper fittings and connect a hose to the other.

30 Attempt to suck air through the hose. If air cannot be sucked through the hose, the valve is stuck closed and should be replaced.

31 Next, connect a hand air pump to the fitting at the bottom of the valve.

32 While applying air pressure to the valve again attempt to suck air through. If you can, the valve is stuck closed and should be replaced. **Note:** *If an air pump is not available, the same effect can be achieved by attaching a hose to the bottom fitting and having an assistant blow air into the valve in order to close it.*

33 Before reconnecting the exhaust pressure line to the bottom of the valve, make sure the line is not clogged by blowing air into it.

5.34 The VVT valve (above) and the EGR valve (below) are located behind the carburetor on 1981 and 1982 models

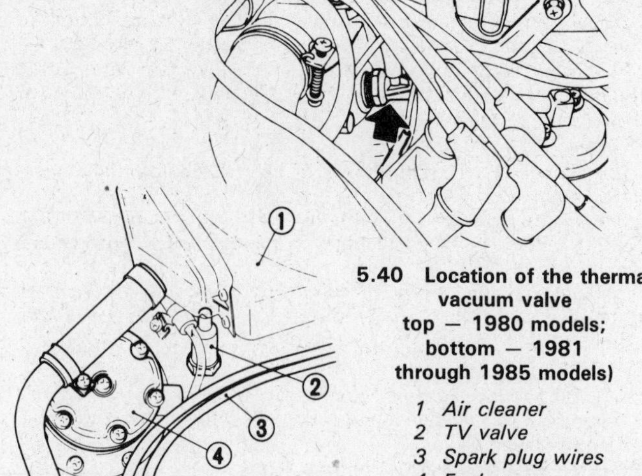

5.40 Location of the thermal vacuum valve top – 1980 models; bottom – 1981 through 1985 models)

1 Air cleaner
2 TV valve
3 Spark plug wires
4 Fuel pump

> **Note:** *Carbureted version shown – on 1986 fuel injected models with a four-cylinder engine, the TVV is mounted on the front side of the intake manifold.*

VVT valve

34 Follow the vacuum signal hose from the top center of the valve, and disconnect it at its first connection **(see illustration)**.

35 Attempt to suck air through the hose. If air cannot be sucked through the hose, the valve is stuck closed and should be replaced.

36 Disconnect the exhaust back-pressure hose from the bottom of the valve and connect a hand air pump to the fitting. While applying air pressure to the valve, again attempt to suck through the vacuum signal hose. This time you should not be able to suck air through. If you can, the valve is defective and should be replaced. If an air pump is not available, the same effect can be achieved by connecting a hose, the same diameter as the one removed, to the fitting and having as assistant blow into it to close the valve.

37 Before reconnecting the exhaust pressure hose to the bottom of the valve, make sure the line is not clogged by blowing air into it.

38 Next, disconnect the venturi vacuum hose from the top side of the valve, and connect a vacuum pump to the fitting. While applying vacuum to the valve, once again attempt to suck air through the vacuum signal hose. If you are able to draw air through, the valve is stuck open and should be replaced.

39 Before reconnecting the venturi vacuum hose, make sure it is not clogged by blowing through it. Then follow it along its entire length checking that there are no cracks, or other leaks.

Thermal vacuum valve (TVV)

40 To check for proper functioning of the thermal vacuum valve, start with a cold engine. On 1980 models, disconnect the vacuum line from the BPT valve, or vacuum delay valve, if equipped **(see illustration)**. On 1981 and 1982 models, first disconnect the vacuum hose from the top center of the VVT valve and plug it. Then disconnect the vacuum signal line from the EGR valve.

41 Now start the engine and, with your thumb, feel if any vacuum is coming through the line. If vacuum is reaching the valve immediately after starting the engine, the TVV should be replaced.

42 Now wait for the engine to reach normal operating temperature (above 122°F for 1980 models and above 140° for 1981 and 1982 models) and, again, feel for vacuum at the end of the hose. If no vacuum is present at the end of the hose, first check that the hoses are not clogged. Then, if all lines are clear, replace the TVV with a new one.

43 Another method of testing the TVV is with it off the engine. With the engine cold, remove the TVV complete with hoses attached to it. On 1981 and 1982 models, clamp the hose shut that's attached to the lower fitting of the valve. Attempt to suck air through the vacuum hose attached to the lower fitting (1980 models) or the middle fitting (1981 and 1982 models). While the valve is cold (room temperature) the TVV on 1980 models should be closed, preventing you from drawing air through it. On 1981 and 1982 models it should be open, allowing air to be drawn through.

If this is not the case, replace the valve.

44 Now put the valve in a pan and submerge it in water. Do not let the water get into the hoses or the inside of the valve. Heat the water until its temperature is above 122°F (1980 models or 140°F (1981 and 1982 models). Now attempt to such air through it as before. At this point the valve on 1980 models should be open, while on 1981 and 1982 models, it should now be closed. If the valve does not function in this manner and the hose is not clogged or split, replace the valve with a new one.

Vacuum delay valve

45 Remove the valve, noting its installed direction. Blow through the valve from the EGR valve side. Air should flow freely through the valve. Now blow through the other side (brown side). The flow should be restricted. If this is not the case, replace the valve.

EGR vacuum cut solenoid valve (1986 and later 1988 V6 and 1987 and 1988 four-cylinder models)

46 Because a portion of the test for normal operation of the EGR vacuum cut solenoid valve involves an EGR circuit test and an ECU input/output test, both of which require special diagnostic equipment, checking the solenoid is beyond the scope of the home mechanic. Additionally, all computer-controlled emission devices and systems are protected by a Federally mandated extended warranty (check with your dealer to find out the details of the coverage on your vehicle) and unauthorized tampering with any of these devices or systems could void the warranty.

Component replacement

EGR passage (1980 models)

47 Disconnect the EGR exhaust tube by loosening the retaining nut.

48 Disconnect all hoses from the EGR passage, noting how they are installed.

49 Remove the EGR passage mounting bolts and lift it off.

50 Clean the mating surfaces of the EGR passage and the intake manifold, removing all traces of old gasket material.

51 Installation is the reverse of the removal procedure. **Note:** *Be sure to use a new gasket.*

EGR valve (1981 and later models)

52 On 1981 and later models disconnect the EGR exhaust tube by loosening the retaining nut.

53 Disconnect the vacuum hose from the top of the valve.

54 Remove the EGR valve mounting nuts and lift it off.

55 Clean the mating surfaces of the EGR valve and intake manifold or EGR passage, removing all traces of old gasket material.

56 Installation is the reverse of the removal procedure. **Note:** *Be sure to use a new gasket. Also, when replacing the EGR valve, be sure the new one is the same type as the old one.*

BPT valve

57 Disconnect the vacuum signal hoses from the top of the BPT valve.

58 Remove the screws that hold the valve to the bracket, and lift off the valve.
59 Disconnect the exhaust back-pressure hose from the bottom of the valve, and remove the valve from the engine compartment.
60 Installation is the reverse of the removal procedure. **Note:** *When replacing the valve, be sure the new valve has the same type number stamped on it as the old one.*

VVT valve

61 Disconnect all hoses from the VVT valve. Be sure to label them as to their location.
62 Remove the two screws that hold the valve to the bracket, then lower the valve from the bracket and remove it from the engine compartment.
63 Installation is the reverse of the removal procedure. **Note:** *When replacing the VVT valve be sure the new valve has the same type number stamped on it as the old one.*

Thermal vacuum valve

64 Drain about one quart of coolant from the radiator.
65 Disconnect the vacuum hoses from the switch, noting their positions for reassembly.
66 Using a wrench, remove the switch.
67 When installing the switch, apply thread sealer to the threads, being careful not to allow the sealant to touch the bottom sensor.
68 Install the switch and tighten it to the specified torque.

6 Air induction system

Refer to illustrations 6.2, 6.7a. 6.7b, 6.10, 6.13 and 6.20

General description

1 The purpose of the air induction system is to reduce hydrocarbons in the exhaust by drawing fresh air directly into the exhaust manifold. The fresh, oxygen-rich air helps complete combustion of the unburned hydrocarbons before they are expelled as exhaust. All 1981 and 1982 models are equipped with this system, as well as 1980 US Federal and Canada heavy-duty models.

2 The components of this simple system include an air filter and a one-way reed valve, both of which are located in a case attached to the air cleaner, one or two (depending upon model) EAI tubes connecting the valve case with the exhaust manifold, and an anti-backfire (AB) valve on Type A systems. All 1980 models and 1981 and 1982 California models use the Type a system while 1981 and 1982 US Federal and Canada models use the Type B system, which uses no AB valve. Type A (California) and Type B (Federal and Canada) systems on all 1983 and 1984 vehicles use an AB valve. 1985 through 1988 vehicles are all equipped with identical systems with an AB valve. 1986 and later models are also equipped with an Air Induction Valve (AIV) vacuum cut solenoid valve **(see illustration)**, which regulates vacuum in accordance with signals from the ECU.

3 The opening and closing of the exhaust valves creates vacuum pulses which draw in fresh air through the filter and valve assembly. The reed valve only admits air to be drawn into the manifold, and prevents exhaust back-pressure from forcing the gases back out. In some systems, this fresh air entering the exhaust manifold can cause back-firing during deceleration due to an over rich fuel mixture. The AB valve, which is actuated by intake manifold vacuum, corrects this by routing additional air (from the air cleaner) into the intake manifold during deceleration.

Checking

4 The simplicity of the system makes it a very reliable one which seldom causes problems. Periodic checks should be made, however, of the condition of the components to be sure there are no leaks or cracks in the system. Always make a visual check of the hoses and tubes for bad connections, looseness, kinks or deterioration before checking the AIV components.

5 Two simple functional tests can be performed to ensure that the system is operating properly. Disconnect the rubber hose(s) from the metal EAI tube(s). For the first test, attempt to suck air through the rubber hose, and then attempt to blow air through the hose. The reed valve should allow you to suck air through the hose but prevent you from blowing it back through. If you are able to blow air through the hose then the valve is defective and should be replaced. If you are not able to suck air in, then check for a clogged air filter or hose. If this is not the case, then replace the valve.

6 For the second test, start the engine and allow it to idle. With the engine idling hold your hand over the open end of the metal EAI tube(s). There should be a steady stream of air being sucked into it. Have an assistant apply throttle and as the engine gains speed the suction should increase. If this does not happen, either there are leaks or blockage in the tubes.

7 To test the AB valve, first remove the air cleaner and disconnect the rubber hose from the AB valve **(see illustrations)**. Start the engine

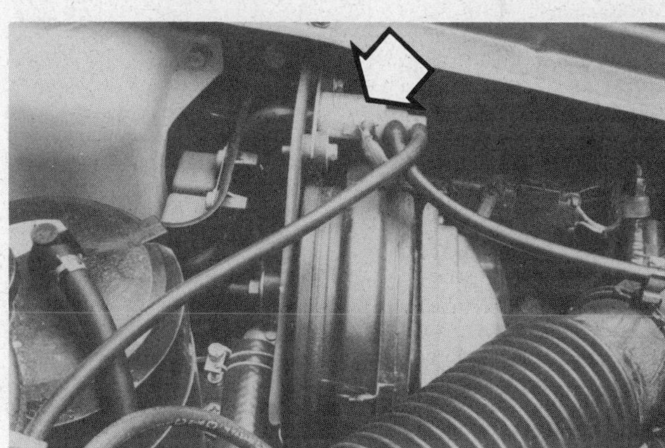

6.2 The Air Induction Valve (AIV) vacuum cut solenoid valve (arrow) regulates the vaccuum signal to the AIV system in accordance with an electrical signal from the ECU

6.7a The AB valve on 1981 and 1982 models is located in front of the carburetor

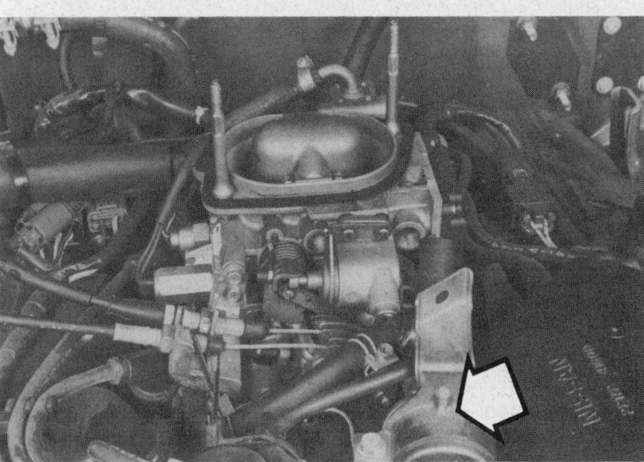

6.7b The AB valve on 1986 and later vehicles is located on the intake manifold in front of the throttle body

6.10 The AIV case for the reed valve is isolated from the AIV box for the filter on 1986 and later vehicles – to remove the reed valve, unscrew the Phillips screws, lift up the top half of the case and pry out the reed; to remove the case, detach the vacuum hose, loosen the mounting nuts and slide the rubber insulators out of the slotted mounting brackets

and allow it to reach normal operating temperature. When the engine is thoroughly warmed up, have an assistant run the engine at about 3000 rpm while you hold a finger near the AB valve outlet fitting. Have your assistant abruptly let off the accelerator so that the engine quickly returns to idle. As this happens, you should feel a pull or suction at the AB valve fitting. If so, the valve is functioning normally. If not, it should be replaced with a new one.

Component replacement

Air induction valve and filter

8 Refer to Chapter 1 for this procedure.

Air induction valve case

9 The rubber hose(s) are clamped to the valve case. Only if the valve case or hose(s) need to be replaced separate from the other, cut the clamps(s) that secure the two together, and separate them.

10 If you have a pre-1986 vehicle, remove the four screws that attach the valve case to the air filter housing. Newer vehicles have a separate AIV case **(see illustration)** located in the left front corner of the engine compartment. To remove it, clearly label and detach all hoses, then remove all mounting bolts.

11 Disconnect the rubber hose(s) from the metal air tube(s).

12 Check the reed valve for breakage, cracks or deformation. Check the "stopper" for looseness and tighten if necessary. Pry the reed valve out of the valve case and replace it if necessary.

13 Installation is the reverse of the removal procedure. Be sure the reed valve is reinstalled with the reeds facing in the proper direction **(see illustration)**. **Note:** *If the rubber hose(s) has been removed from the valve case, hose clamps should be used to secure them together.*

EAI tubes

14 Remove the screws that attach the valve case to the air cleaner.

15 Unscrew the nut that attaches each tube to the exhaust manifold. Due to the high temperature in this area, these nuts may be difficult to loosen. Penetrating oil applied to the threads of these nuts may help.

16 Remove the bolt that secures the tubes in their bracket and lift the assembly off. The valve case and hoses can then be removed from the tubes.

17 Before installing, apply a coat of anti-seize compound to the threads of the large end nuts.

18 Installation is the reverse of the removal procedure.

AB valve

19 Remove the air cleaner.

20 Disconnect the hoses and vacuum line from the valve **(see illustration)** and remove it.

21 Installation is the reverse of the removal procedure.

6.13 When installing a new reed valve, make sure that the reeds are facing the proper direction or the system won't function properly – also make sure that the "stopper" (arrow) is screwed on tightly

6.20 To remove the AB valve on 1986 and later V6 equipped vehicles, remove the air cleaner housing and detach the pipe on the underside of the air cleaner from the short fat hose attached to the rear of the AB valve (arrow), then detach the vacuum line (arrow) on top and the air hose (arrow) on bottom

7 Air injection system

Refer to illustrations 7.1, 7.25, 7.34 and 7.37

General description

1 This is a method of injecting air (generated in an external compressor) into the exhaust manifold in order to reduce hydrocarbons and carbon monoxide in the exhaust gas by providing conditions favorable for recombustion. The system is composed of an air cleaner, belt drive air pump, check valve, anti-backfire valve, air gallery and the associated hoses. Models for use in California also have a combined air control (CAC) valve with an integral emergency air relief valve to prevent excessive temperature rise in the catalytic converter. Canada models use a simpler relief valve which performs basically the same function **(see illustration)**.

2 Air drawn through the air pump air cleaner, compressed, and directed through the check valve to the air gallery and injection nozzles. During high speed operation, excessive pump pressure is vented to

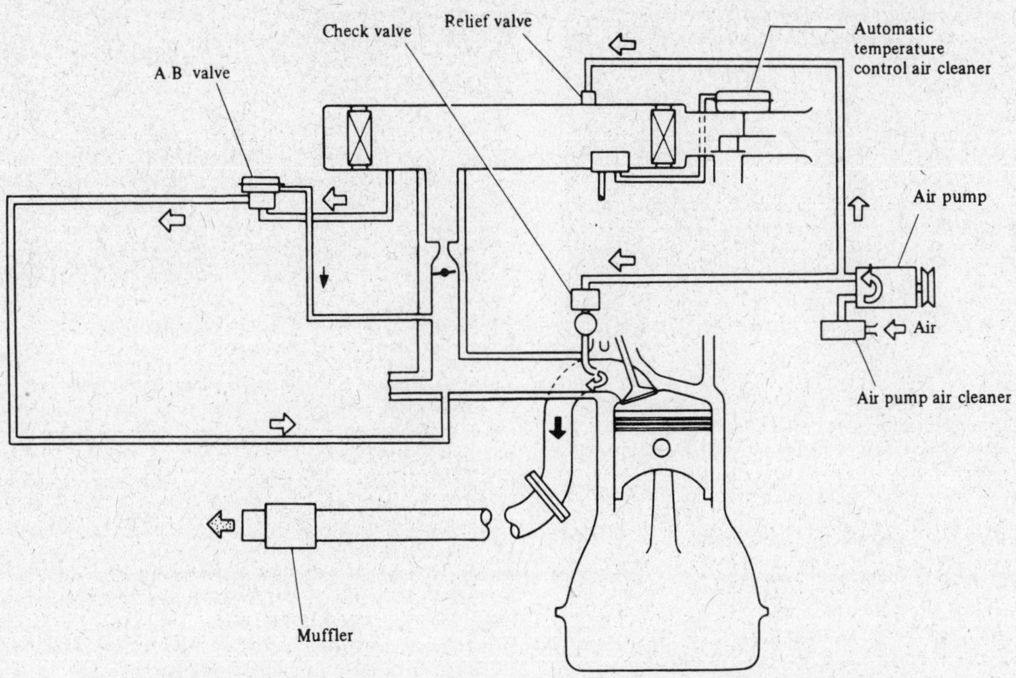

7.1 Diagram of the air injection system for 1980 California models – others similar

the atmosphere through the CAC valve or relief valve.

3 The check valve is installed in the delivery line at the injection gallery. The function of this valve is to prevent any exhaust gases from passing into the air pump should the manifold pressure be greater than the pump injection pressure. It is designed to close against the exhaust manifold pressure should the air pump fail as a result, for example of a broken drivebelt.

4 During deceleration, intake manifold vacuum opens the anti-backfire valve to allow fresh air to flow into the intake manifold. This ensures that the combustion cycle is more effective and reduces the amount of unburned gases exhausted.

5 On California models, the CAC valve opens when the combined air pump pressure and intake manifold vacuum reach a predetermined level as happens during lightly loaded conditions. The air from the air pump is bled off to the air cleaner which means that the injection system is less effective, the exhaust gas temperature is lowered and the catalytic converter temperature can be maintained at the optimum operating temperature.

6 The relief valve used in Canada models bleeds air from the air pump when there is a prolonged condition of low manifold suction as happens during the high continuous speed operation. This nullifies the air injection system, reduces the exhaust gas temperature and prevents the catalytic converter from overheating.

7 The air injection system used on California heavy-duty models is a much more complex system, involving electronic components. For this reason, servicing of this system should be left to a dealer or other qualified mechanic.

Checking

8 Checking all hoses, air gallery pipes and nozzles for security and condition.

9 Check and adjust the air pump drivebelt tension as described in Chapter 1.

10 With the engine at normal operating temperature, disconnect the hose leading to the check valve.

11 Run the engine at approximately 2000 rpm and then let it return to idling speed, while watching for exhaust gas leaks from the valve. Where these are evident, replace the valve.

12 Check the operation of the air pump relieve valve by first disconnecting the hoses from the non-return valve and then removing the CAC valve from the hose connector. Plug the connector.

13 Run the engine at a steady 3000 rpm and place your hand on the air outlet of the emergency relief valve (California models). A definite air pressure should be felt. If it is not, replace the valve.

14 Now pull the vacuum hose from the air control valve. If air ejection ceases from the outlet nozzle, the valve is in good condition but if it persists, replace the valve (which must be faulty).

15 The anti-backfire valve (flame-trap) can be checked, when the engine is at normal operating temperature, by disconnecting the hose from the air cleaner and placing a finger over the end of the hose. Run the engine at about 3000 rpm and then return it to idling. During this action, a strong suction effect should be felt at the hose which indicates that the valve is working properly.

Component replacement

Air pump filter

16 Refer to Chapter 1.

Air pump

17 Remove the air hoses from the pump.

18 Remove the drivebelt from the pump, referring to Chapter 1, if necessary.

19 Remove all hoses from the pump.

20 Remove the mounting and adjusting bolts and lift the pump out.

21 If necessary, remove the pulley from the pump.

22 Installation is the reverse of the removal procedure.

Check valve

23 Remove the air cleaner.

24 Disconnect the air hose from the check valve.

25 Remove the check valve from the air gallery pipe, using two wrenches **(see illustration)**.

26 Installation is the reverse of the removal procedure.

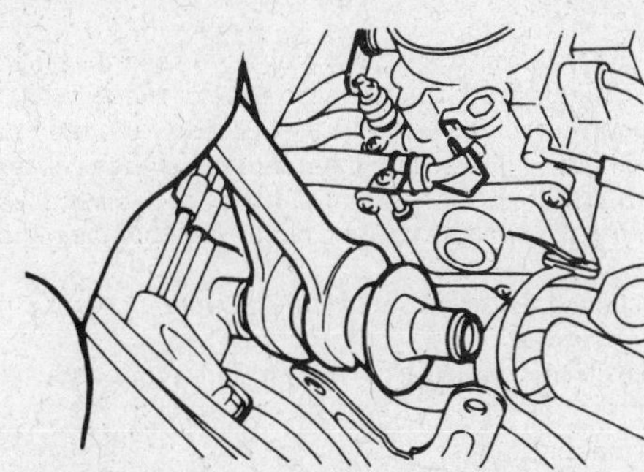

7.25 Two wrenches should be used to remove the air injection check valve from the air gallery pipe

6

Air gallery pipe and injection nozzles

27 Because of the likelihood of bending or damaging the pipes during removal, the pipes should not be removed unless they are already damaged and need replacing.
28 Remove the air cleaner.
29 Disconnect the hose from the check valve.
30 Disconnect or remove all lines and hoses that will interfere with removal of the air gallery assembly.
31 Apply penetrating oil to the nuts that attach the air gallery to the exhaust manifold, then loosen them until the gallery can be lifted out.
32 Lift out the injectors from the threaded openings in the exhaust manifold.
33 Installation is the reverse of the removal procedure. Be sure to tighten the air gallery nuts to their proper torque specifications.

AB valve

34 Locate the AB valve at the rear side of the air cleaner **(see illustration)**. The air cleaner may have to be removed for access.
35 Remove the air hoses from the valve and lift it out.
36 Installation is the reverse of the removal procedure.

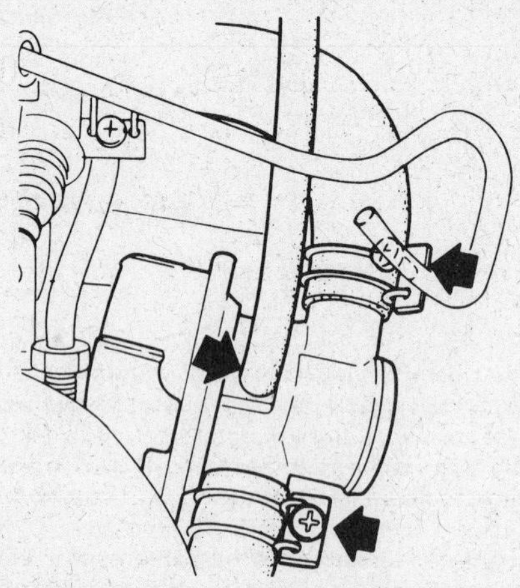

7.34 To remove the AB valve on 1980 models, detach the vacuum lines and air hoses

Relief valve

37 The relief valve **(see illustration)** is installed on the underside of the air cleaner. Disconnect the air hose from the valve.
38 Remove the screws that attach the relief valve to the air cleaner and detach it. If necessary to do this, remove the air cleaner.
39 Installation is the reverse of the removal procedure.

CAC valve

40 The CAC valve is located beneath the control device bracket.
41 Disconnect the air hoses and vacuum tube from the valve.
42 Remove the screws that secure the CAC valve and lift it out.
43 Installation is the reverse of the removal procedure.

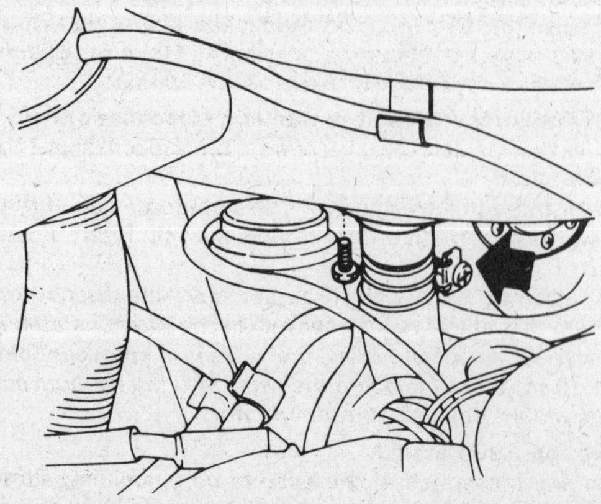

7.37 Location of the relief valve, mounted under the air cleaner on Canada models

8 Spark timing control system

Refer to illustrations 8.10, 8.12, and 8.30

General description

1 The spark timing control system is designed to control the distributor vacuum advance under varying conditions, in order to help reduce HC and NOx emissions, as well as to assure stable idling and good fuel economy.
2 Although the basic function of the system is the same in all models, the design of the system is somewhat different, depending upon year and model of the truck. These differences are noted in the following sub-sections. **Note:** *1980 US Federal and Canada models are not equipped with this system.*

1980 California models (with manual transmission)

3 The spark timing control system used on these models uses a vacuum switching valve to control the actuation of the distributor vacuum advance.
4 With this system, a vacuum signal line runs from the throttle valve to the distributor vacuum advance mechanism. Tapped into this line is a vacuum switching valve. When this valve is open it allows an air bleed through it, thus nullifying the vacuum signal coming from the throttle valve, and preventing it from reaching the distributor. When the vacuum switching valve is closed, it seals off the air bleed and allows the vacuum signal to affect the advance mechanism.
5 The opening and closing of the vacuum switching valve is controlled electrically by a switch on the transmission called the top gear switch. Located on the right side of the transmission, this switch is On (permitting current to pass through it) only when the transmission is shifted into the 4th or 5th gear positions.
6 The vacuum switching valve is designed so that it is open except when the top switch is On. Therefore the only time that the vacuum switching valve is closed, thus advancing the distributor, is when the transmission is in the 4th or 5th gear positions.

1980 California models (with automatic transmission)

7 The spark timing control system used on these models is an extremely simple one that uses a vacuum delay valve in the vacuum signal line running between the carburetor and the distributor's vacuum advance canister.
8 The in-line vacuum delay valve is essentially a one-way valve that restricts the flow of air toward the carburetor. This reduces the rate of the vacuum change reaching the distributor during periods of rapid acceleration, thus providing the vacuum advance unit some delay of time in responding.
9 Because of the one-way design of the valve, a decrease in vacuum at the carburetor (at idle or full throttle) is passed along in a normal manner to the distributor, thus de-activating the advance mechanism.

1981 through 1985 models

10 The system used on 1981 through 1985 models **(see illustration)** uses a thermal vacuum valve (TVV) to control the actuation of the advance mechanism in relation to engine temperature. This TVV is tapped into the vacuum signal line running between the throttle valve and the distributor. When the TVV is open it allows an air bleed in the vacuum signal line which prevents the vacuum from advancing the timing. Only when the TVV is closed, can the vacuum reach the advance mechanism.
11 The opening and closing of the valve is determined by the temperature of the engine coolant. The TVV used on California models is calibrated to be closed until the coolant temperature reaches 59°F (15°C). At this point it will stay open between 59° and 140° F (60°C). Above 140° it will close again. Therefore, the distributor is advanced while the engine is cold, in order to quickly warm up the engine. As the engine warms up, the vacuum signal is cut off, and the timing is retarded until the engine reaches its normal operating temperature, when it advances again. In addition, since the vacuum signal is taken from the throttle valve, at idle the vacuum is not great enough to advance the distributor, so the spark timing control system does not operate at all at idle.
12 Later model spark timing systems are also equipped with a vacuum control valve **(see illustration)** which is installed inline with the venturi vacuum line between the carburetor and the distributor. When the carburetor venturi vacuum exceeds the pre-set value, the air is bled to the distributor vacuum line, retarding the spark timing slightly.

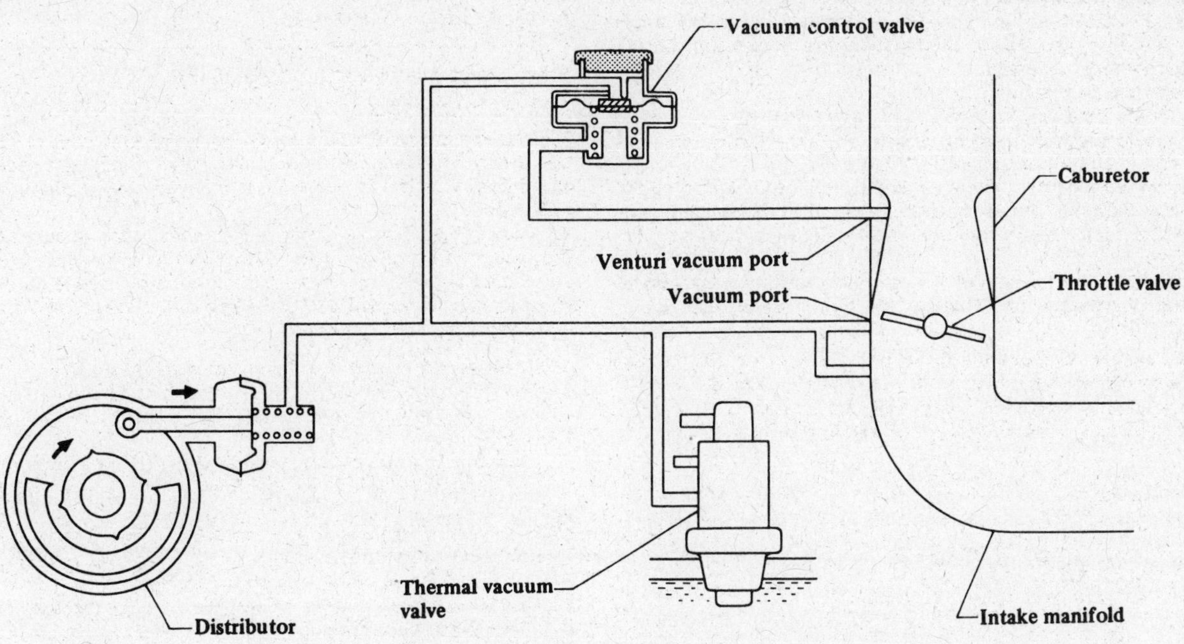

8.10 Diagram of the spark timing system for 1981 through 1985 models

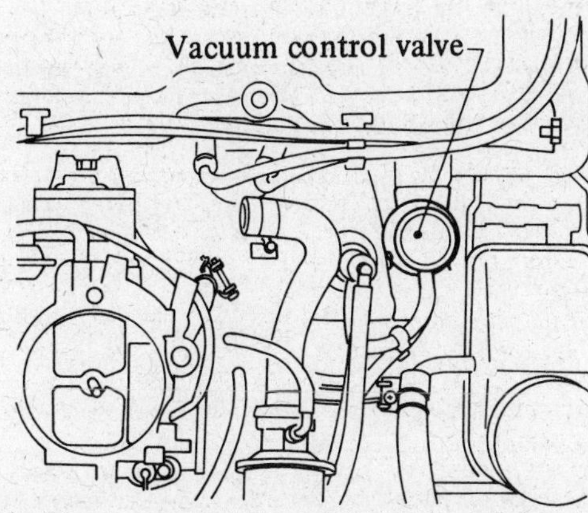

8.12 The vacuum control valve used on later spark timing systems is located on the intake manifold in front of the carburetor

Checking

1980 California models (with manual transmission)

13 Begin any check of this system by inspecting all lines and hoses, making sure they are properly connected and that there are no leaks or cracks.

14 Next the advance mechanism inside the distributor should be checked to be sure it is operating correctly. To do this, first remove the distributor cap so that the rotation of the timing plate can be observed. Next disconnect the vacuum line from the distributor, and connect a vacuum pump to the fitting. Apply vacuum pressure to the distributor and watch that the timing plate rotates inside. If the timing plate does not rotate, then there is a fault with the advance mechanism which must be corrected (refer to Chapter 5). If a vacuum pump is not handy, the same effect can be achieved by attaching a long rubber hose (the same diameter as the vacuum hose removed) to the fitting and sucking through it.

15 Reconnect the vacuum line to the distributor and reinstall the distributor cap.

16 Hook up a timing light according to the manufacturer's instructions.

17 Have an assistant start the engine and run the engine at about 2000 rpm. While checking the ignition timing with the timing light, have the assistant depress the clutch and then shift the transmission into each of the gears for a few seconds at a time. **Caution:** *Be sure the emergency brake is on and the wheels are securely blocked. Be sure the clutch remains fully depressed while the transmission is in gear to prevent the vehicle from moving. The spark timing should fully advance only when the transmission is shifted into 4th or 5th gear. In any other gear, the timing should remain at its original setting or only slightly advanced.*

18 If the timing is not operating as described above, the components of the system should be checked individually to locate the problem.

19 The vacuum switching valve is most easily tested by disconnecting the wires from it. Then with the timing light hooked up as before, run the engine at about 2000 rpm while you check the timing. Now use jumper wires to connect the valve's wires directly to the battery terminals, and with the engine again at 2000 rpm observe the timing. It should now be advanced from its former position. If not, make sure all vacuum lines are clear. If so, then replace the vacuum switching valve with a new one.

20 To test the top gear switch, locate it on the right side of the transmission and disconnect the wiring connector attached to it. Connect the leads of an ohmmeter or continuity tester to the switch leads. Then have an assistant shift the transmission through the entire gear range. The switch should show continuity only when the transmission is in the 4th or 5th gear positions. If not, replace the switch with a new one. switch with a new one.

21 As a final check that power is reaching the vacuum switching valve, disconnect the wires from the valve and connect the leads of a voltmeter or test light to them, and repeat the above test. If voltage is not indicated when the transmission is in the 4th or 5th gear positions, there is a loose connection or break in the wiring.

1980 California models (with automatic transmission)

22 Remove the vacuum delay valve from the vacuum signal line leading to the distributor.

23 Blow air through the valve from the carburetor side. If the air flows through without restriction, the valve is normal. If not, it needs to be replaced.

24 Next, attempt to blow air through it from the distributor (brown) side. If there is greater resistance than in the previous step (some air should escape the opposite side), the valve is in good condition. If not, replace it. **Note:** *When installing the valve into the vacuum line be sure the brown side is towards the distributor.*

1981 through 1985 models

25 Begin any inspection of the system by examining all hoses and wires to make sure they are properly connected and in good condition.

26 Next, the vacuum advance mechanism inside the distributor should be checked as described in Steps 14 and 15.

27 Hook up a timing light according to the manufacturer's instructions. With the engine cold, start the engine and have an assistant apply throttle to keep the engine running at about 2000 rpm. Immediately check the spark timing with the timing light. The needle in the coolant temperature gauge should be in the Cold position. If the outside temperature is below 59 °F the timing should retard as the engine begins to warm up.
28 Continue to run the engine at 2000 rpm and observe the spark timing while the engine warms up. You may wish to adjust the idle speed screw to maintain this engine speed. If the outside temperature was below 59 °F the timing should retard as the engine begins to warm up.
29 By the time the engine approaches normal operating temperature (the needle in the middle of the gauge), the spark timing should have advanced again. If this sequence does not take place, the TVV is suspect and should be replaced with a new one.
30 To check the vacuum control valve, detach the venturi vacuum hose from underneath the vacuum control valve. Connect a vacuum pump to the pipe for this hose **(see illustration)** and apply vacuum to the valve. If spark timing retards, the valve is functioning; if it doesn't, the valve is malfunctioning.
31 Detach the valve from the system and remove it. Note whether the distributor side of the valve is open or closed by attempting to suck air through the valve while applying vacuum to the valve in accordance with the following specified vacuum. Below 13.3 kPa (100 mm-Hg, 3.94 in-Hg), the distributor side of the valve should be closed; above these figures, it should be open. If the valve fails to perform as described, replace it.

Component replacement

32 The procedures for removing and installing a TVV is described in Section 5.
33 To replace the vacuum control valve, clearly label and detach the vacuum lines and unbolt the valve. Installation is the reverse of removal.

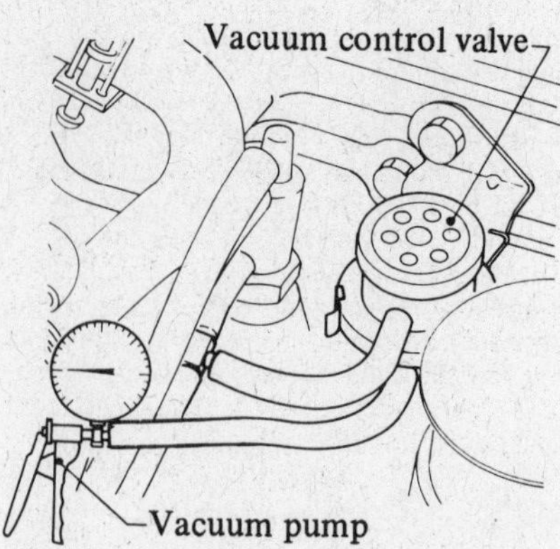

8.30 To check the operation of the vacuum control valve, detach the venturi vacuum line from underneath, hook up a vacuum pump and apply vacuum — the timing should be retarded

9 Evaporative Emission Control (EEC) system

Refer to illustrations 9.2, 9.3a, 9.3b, 9.6 and 9.8

General description

1 The evaporative emissions control system (EEC) is designed to prevent the release of hydrocarbons in the form of fuel vapor to the outside air.
2 This is achieved by venting the vapor in the fuel tank to a canister **(see illustration)** filled with activated charcoal, where the vapor is stored when the engine isn't running.
3 On top of this canister is a purge control valve **(see illustration)** with two hoses leading from it. The thicker hose is the purge hose, and runs directly to the intake manifold while the smaller hose is the vacuum signal line. Inside the purge control valve, are two holes. One, a very small hole, is called the constant purge orifice **(see illustration)** and is always open to the intake manifold. The second hole, a larger one directly in the center of the valve, is the main purge orifice and is normally covered by the valve's diaphragm.
4 When the engine is started, fresh air is drawn into the canister through an opening in the bottom. This fresh air picks up the stored vapors and carries them to the intake manifold. At idle, there is enough suction coming through the constant purge line to draw in a small amount of this air/vapor mixture through the constant purge orifice. The purge control valve, however, remains closed. As the engine speed increases, the manifold vacuum becomes great enough to open the diaphragm of the purge control valve, which allows the air/vapor mix-

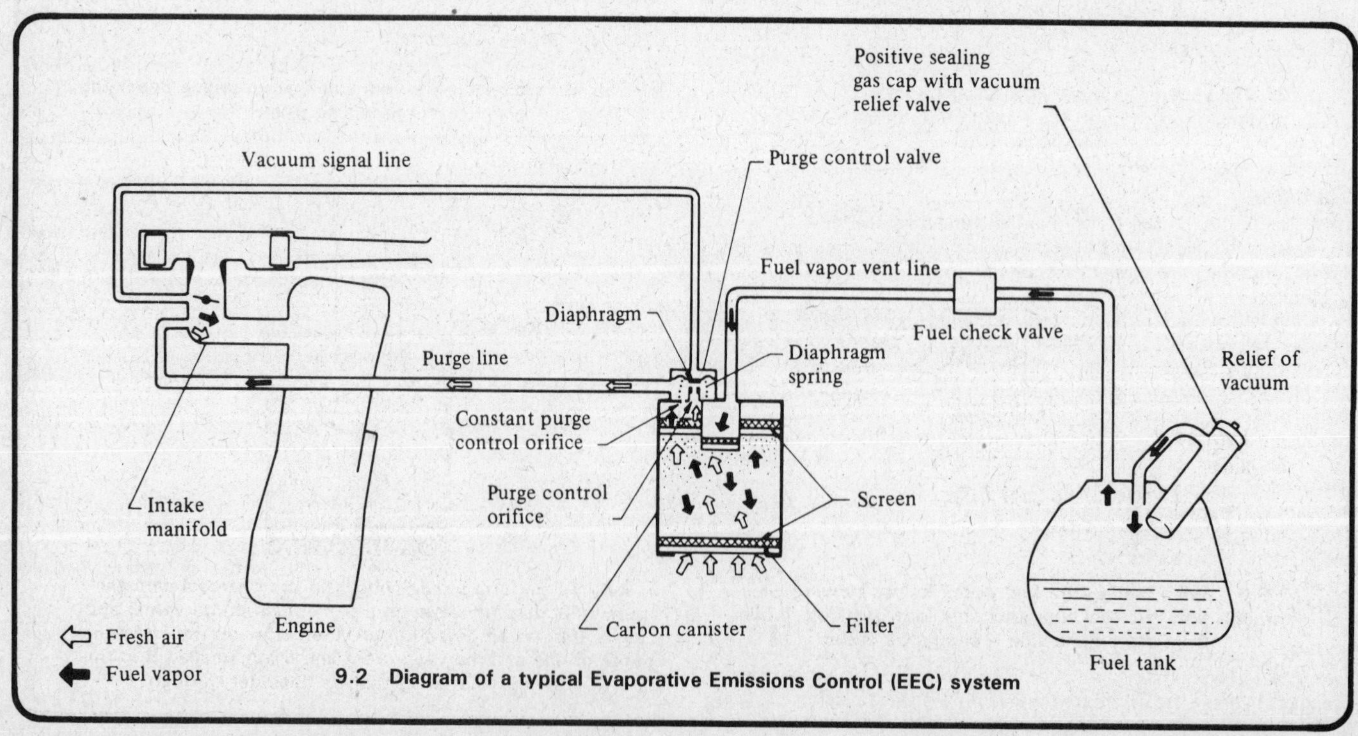

9.2 Diagram of a typical Evaporative Emissions Control (EEC) system

ture to be drawn in greater quantity to the intake manifold.

5 The operation of this system depends on maintaining a sealed fuel system. Therefore, a positive sealing gas cap is used which, under normal conditions, provides only a small vent to the outside air, and will open fully only if vacuum pressure within the fuel tank becomes too great. A vacuum relief valve is built into the gas cap.

6 A fuel check valve **(see illustration)** is located in the vent line between the fuel tank and the canister. When the engine is off, this valve allows the fuel vapor to bleed off into the canister when the pressure in the fuel tank reaches a certain level. When the engine is running, this valve allows outside air to be drawn into the tank from the canister. This effectively vents the tank so the fuel being drawn out for burning doesn't eventually cause a vacuum in the tank and produce vapor lock.

7 Other than the periodic replacement of the canister air filter detailed in Chapter 1, the EEC system normally requires no periodic attention. There are, however, a few components which should be checked once in a while to ensure proper operation of the system.

Checking

Carbon canister

8 To check the carbon canister **(see illustration)**, blow air through the pipe for the main purge orifice and verify that no air can get through. Then blow air through the purge control valve and the vapor vent line pipes and verify that air does get through. If the main purge orifice, purge control valve or vapor vent line do not check out, replace the canister (see Chapter 1).

Fuel tank vacuum relief valve

9 Remove the fuel filler cap. Wipe the valve housing clean. Try to suck air through the fuel tank side of the cap. A slight resistance accompanied by a "clicking" sound indicates that the valve is in good mechanical condition. The resistance, and clicks, should disappear as sucking continues. If the valve is clogged or if no resistance is evident, replace the cap.

Fuel check valve

10 Blow air through the connector on the fuel tank side. A significant resistance should be evident and some of the air should be directed toward the canister. Now blow air through the connector from the canister side. The air should be directed smoothly toward the fuel tank. If the fuel check valve does not perform as described, replace it.

Component replacement

11 Purchase a diaphragm kit.

12 Remove the three hoses from their fittings on top of the canister.

13 Release the retaining spring around the body of the canister and lift out of the engine compartment.

14 Pry off the top cover of the purge control valve.

15 Remove the diaphragm from the inside of the top cover.

16 Install a new diaphragm into the top cover, making sure the edge of the diaphragm is located in its groove all the way around the cover.

17 Replace the diaphragm spring and retainer with the new ones suppled with the diaphragm kit.

18 With the new spring and retainer in place, snap the valve cover back onto the canister.

19 Reinstall the canister.

20 Reconnect the three hoses, making sure they are in the proper locations.

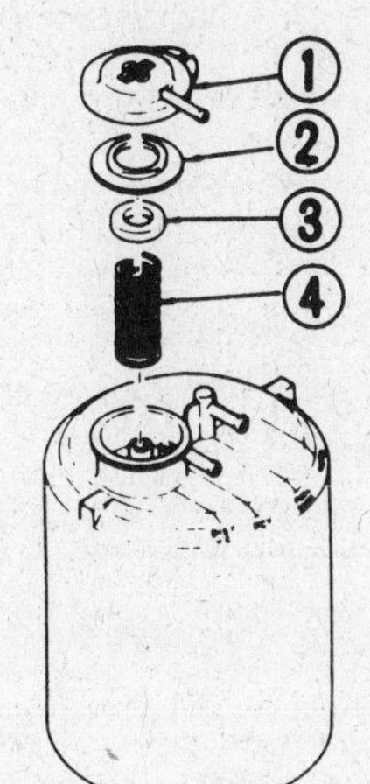

9.3a Components of typical charcoal canister purge control valve

1 Cover
2 Diaphragm
3 Retainer
4 Diaphragm spring

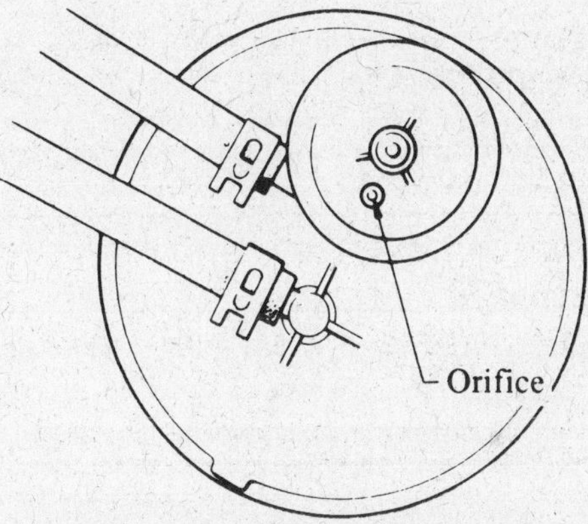

9.3b Location of the constant purge orifice under the purge control valve

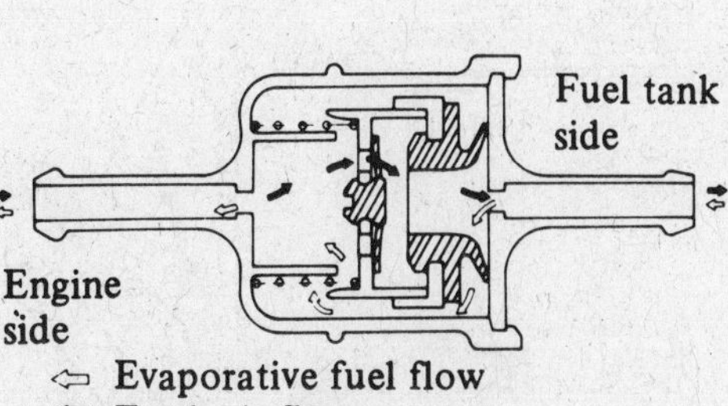

9.6 When testing the fuel check valve, blowing air through from the fuel side tank should be difficult, while from the engine side it should be easier

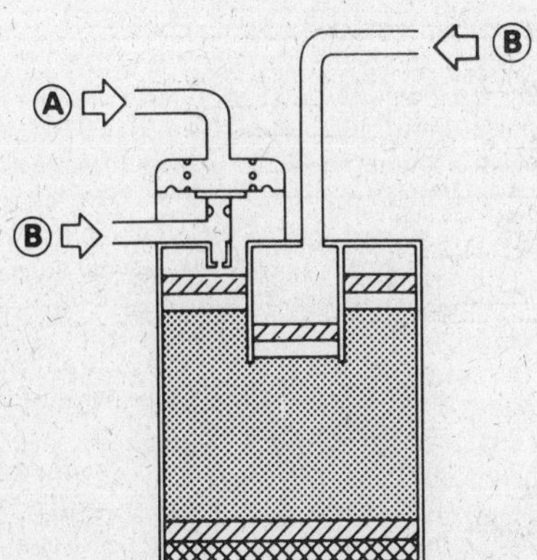

9.8 To perform a quick check of the charcoal canister purging apparatus, blow on pipe A (main purge valve) and verify that no air gets through, then blow on the constant purge orifice and the vapor vent line (both labelled B in this drawing) and verify that air does get through

6

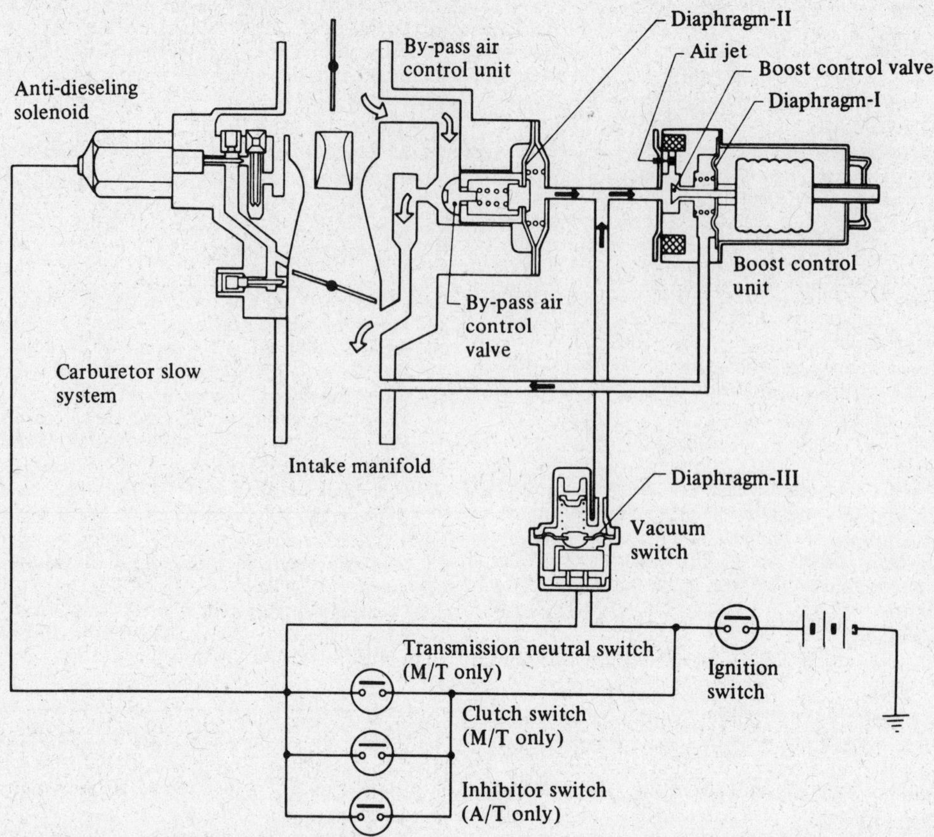

10.1 Diagram of a typical fuel shut-off system in a 1980 through 1983 model

10 Fuel shut-off system

Refer to illustrations 10.1, 10.5a, 10.5b, 10.6, 10.15 and 10.29

General description

1 The fuel shut-off system **(see illustration)** is used on all 1980 through 1985 models except 1980 Canada standard models. The purpose of this system is to reduce hydrocarbon emissions and to increase fuel economy during deceleration. This is achieved by actuating the anti-dieseling solenoid mounted to the carburetor during periods of deceleration, which shuts off the fuel flow in the carburetor slow system.

2 The actuation of the anti-dieseling solenoid is controlled by several other switches: the vacuum switch (on all models), the transmission neutral switch and clutch switch (on manual transmission models) and the inhibitor switch (on automatic transmission models). The anti-dieseling solenoid is actuated only when all of these switches are Off at the same time. If any one of them is On, the fuel shut-off system is not actuated.

3 The vacuum switch is located next to the charcoal canister on 1980 models and on the right hood ledge behind the windshield washer tank on 1981 through 1984 models (except California). This switch, which is connected by a vacuum hose to the boost control valve (described in Section 11), is normally On. Only during deceleration, when there is very high vacuum in the intake manifold, will the boost control valve transmit a vacuum signal to the vacuum valve which turns it Off until the vacuum is reduced again.

4 The clutch switch, used on manual transmission models, is mounted on a bracket at the upper part of the clutch pedal. Only when the clutch pedal is depressed is the clutch switch On.

5 A Neutral switch **(see illustration)** is used with manual transmission models and is located on the left side of the transmission. The inhibitor switch **(see illustration)** is used with automatic transmission models, and is also located on the left side. The Neutral switch is On, (permitting current to pass through it) only when the gears are in the Neutral position. The inhibitor switch is On only when the gears are in either the

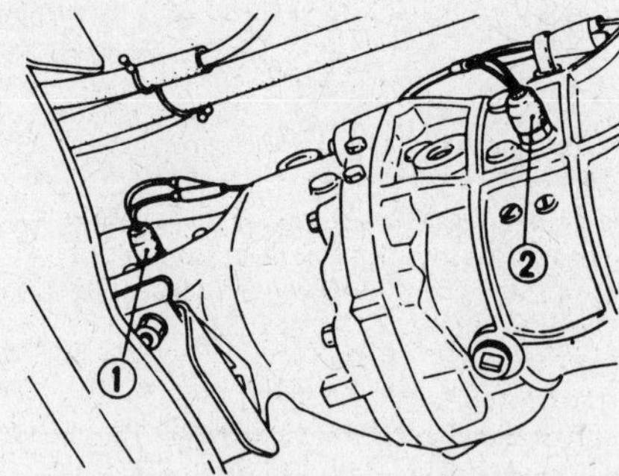

10.5a The manual transmission Neutral switch is located on the left side of the transmission

1 Neutral switch *2 Back up light switch*

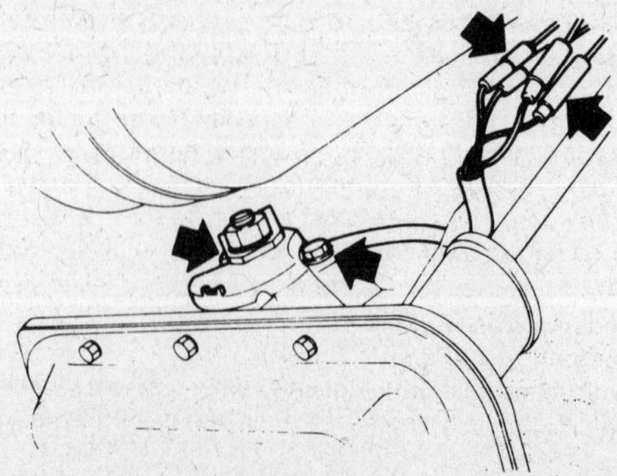

10.5b The automatic transmission inhibitor switch is located on the left side of the transmission

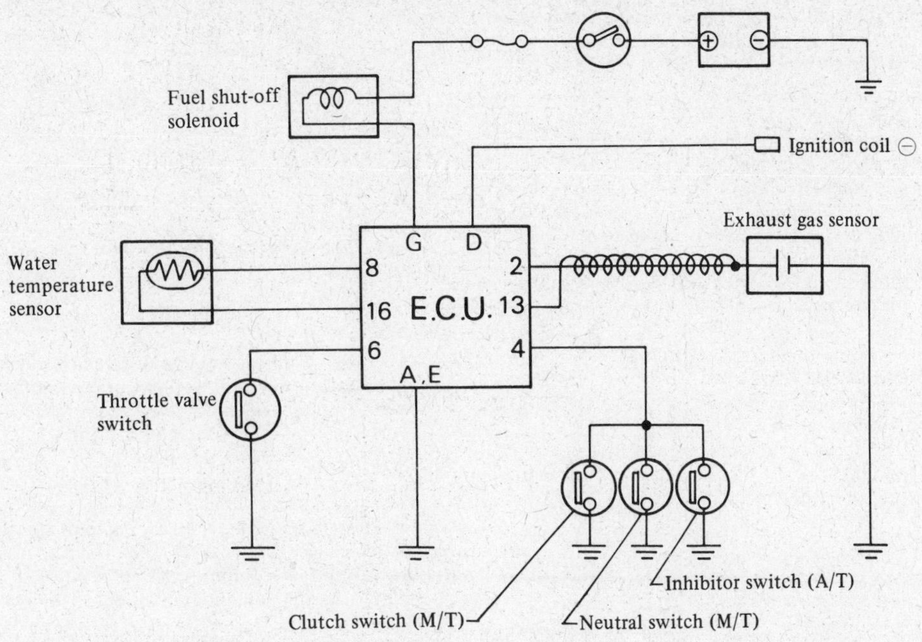

10.6 Diagram of a typical fuel shut-off system in a 1984 or 1985 vehicle

Neutral or Park positions. Therefore, the anti-dieseling solenoid is actuated (shutting off the slow system fuel flow) only during deceleration and when the transmission is in gear and the clutch pedal released.

6 The fuel shut-off system in 1984 California and all 1985 models is under ECU control **(see illustration)**. The neutral switch and clutch switch (manual transmission models) or inhibitor switch (automatic transmission models) still function similarly, but their signal(s) are sent to the ECU instead of through a vacuum switch to the anti-dieseling solenoid. And the anti-dieseling solenoid has been replaced by a fuel shut-off solenoid (essentially the same device).

Checking

Manual transmission models

7 Run the engine at an idle.

8 Disconnect the anti-dieseling solenoid valve assembly.

9 Connect a voltmeter to ground and to the harness side.

10 Connect the wire from the anti-dieseling solenoid valve directly to the (+) side of the battery.

11 Run the engine.

12 Disconnect the clutch pedal switch.

13 Push in the clutch pedal, shift to 4th gear and race the engine with no load. Keep the engine running at between 2500 and 3000 rpm, then quickly close the throttle valve. If the wiring is in good condition, the voltmeter should drop from 12 volts to zero volts instantly. If it doesn't, either the Neutral switch or the fuel-vacuum shut-off switch is out of order.

14 Reconnect the clutch pedal switch and disconnect the fuel shut-off vacuum switch connector.

15 Connect an ohmmeter to the vacuum switch **(see illustration)**. Increase the engine speed to between 2500 and 3000 rpm, then quickly shut the throttle valve. Check the continuity between terminals A and B and between A and C. If ''On-Off'' operation is normal the fuel shut-off vacuum switch is in good working order. **Note:** *Polarity between A and B should be reversed from that of A and C. Reconnect the fuel shut-off vacuum switch connector and repeat Step 13. If the voltmeter doesn't deflect immediately from 12 volts to zero volts, replace the Neutral switch.*

Automatic transmission models

16 Run the engine at an idle.

17 Disconnect the anti-dieseling solenoid valve connector. The engine should stop. If it doesn't, replace the anti-dieseling solenoid valve assembly.

18 Connect a voltmeter to ground and to the harness side.

19 Connect the wire from the anti-diesel solenoid valve directly to the (+) side of the battery.

20 Put the shifter into the P or N position.

21 Run the engine between 2500 and 3000 rpm, then shut off the throttle valve quickly. If the voltmeter doesn't drop from 12 volts to zero volts instantly, either the inhibitor switch or the fuel shut-off vacuum switch needs replacing.

22 Reconnect the harness to the anti-dieseling solenoid valve.

23 Disconnect the harness to the anti-dieseling solenoid valve.

24 Run the engine between 2500 and 3000 rpm and quickly close the throttle valve. This time check the continuity between A and B and between A and C. If the ''On-Off'' operation is normal, the fuel shut-off vacuum switch is in good working order. **Note:** *The polarity between A and B should be reversed from the polarity between A and C. Reconnect the fuel shut-off vacuum switch connector and repeat the test. If the voltmeter needle doesn't deflect immediately from 12 volts to zero volts, replace the inhibitor switch.*

25 The clutch, Neutral and inhibitor switches can be tested individually by disconnecting the wires and connecting a continuity tester to their wires. With the engine off but the ignition switch On, have an assistant shift the gear selector through the entire range of gears. The Neutral switch should show continuity only when the transmission is in Neutral.

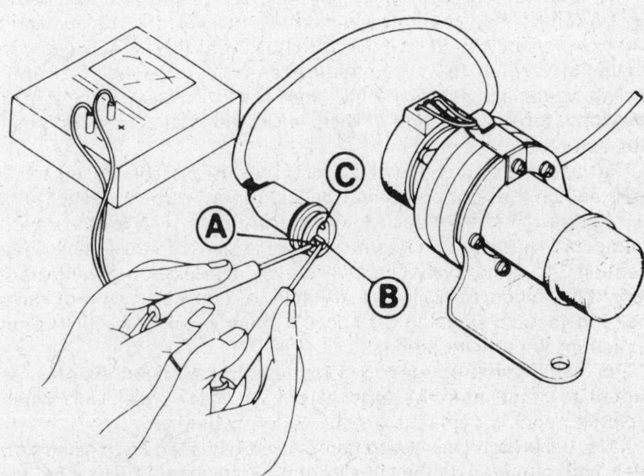

10.15 Refer to this connector terminal guide when checking continuity between the terminals of the vacuum switch in the fuel shut-off system

6

The inhibitor switch should show continuity only when the transmission is in Park (P) or Neutral (N). The clutch switch should show continuity only when the pedal is depressed. If this is not the case, the switch should be replaced.

1984 California and all 1985 models

26 Before performing the following test, visually check the fuel shut-off system. If any switches are broken, replace them.

27 If your vehicle is equipped with a manual transmission, unplug the Neutral switch harness connector; if your vehicle is equipped with an automatic transmission, unplug the inhibitor switch harness connector.

28 Start the engine and warm it up to its normal operating temperature.

29 To check the signal to either switch, locate the function check connector near the vapor canister **(see illustration)** and connect a voltmeter as shown.

30 Race the engine at above 2000 rpm and check connector voltage during deceleration. Above 1800 rpm, there should be zero voltage; between 1500 and 1800 rpm, there should be 12 volts; below 1500 rpm, there should be zero voltage.

31 If the indicated voltage at the connector is not as specified, further electrical checks must be performed on the ECCS system. These tests are beyond the scope of the home mechanic. Take the vehicle to a dealer service department.

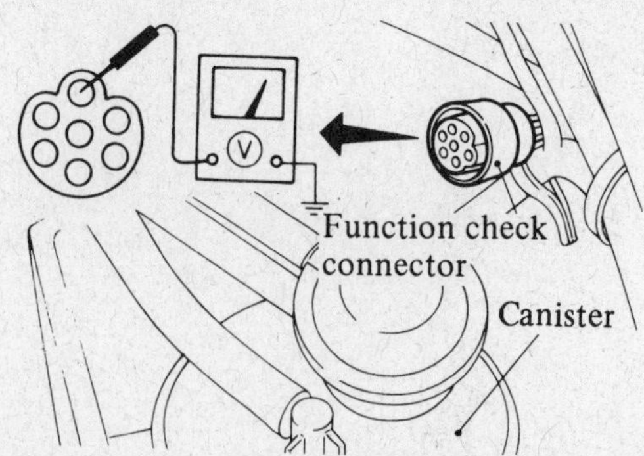

10.29 To check the signal to the Neutral or inhibitor switch, locate the function check connector near the vapor canister, unplug it and insert the probe of a voltmeter into the indicated terminal

11 Intake manifold vacuum control system

Refer to illustrations 11.9a, 11.9b and 11.14

General description

1 The intake manifold vacuum control system is used on all models except 1980 Canada standard models.

2 This system is designed to reduce the consumption of engine oil during deceleration, when there is extremely high vacuum in the intake manifold. Two components are used in the system: the boost control unit and the by-pass air control unit.

3 The boost control unit is mounted near the charcoal canister on 1980 models and on the right hood ledge behind the windshield washer tank on 1981 through 1984 models. It is designed to sense intake manifold vacuum. When the vacuum rises above a predetermined level, the unit opens, passing the vacuum signal onto the by-pass air control unit.

4 The by-pass air control unit is mounted in the carburetor, and consists of a spring and diaphragm. In its normal position, it is closed by spring pressure, plugging up an air by-pass passage in the carburetor. When the intake manifold vacuum rises and the boost control unit sends the vacuum signal on to the by-pass unit , the vacuum pulls back the diaphragm, overcoming the spring pressure and opening the air by-pass passage. This allows more air to flow into the manifold, thus reducing the high vacuum situation.

Checking

5 The boost control unit is easily checked by disconnecting the vacuum signal hose where it connects to the by-pass air control valve and holding your finger at the end of it. Have an assistant run the engine at about 2000 to 3000 rpm and then abruptly let off the accelerator completely . As this is done, you should feel a vacuum at the end of the vacuum hose.

6 If no vacuum is felt, inspect all connecting hoses for leaks or poor connections. Then disconnect the hose at the boost control valve that leads to the intake manifold and repeat the test at that one. If vacuum is felt here, but not in the first test, the boost control unit should be replaced with a new one.

7 Check the by-pass air control unit by removing it from the carburetor (as described below). Connect a hose to the fitting, and then suck through the hose. The valve plunger should retract into the unit when suction is applied. If not, the unit should be replaced.

8 Although the boost control unit is designed to be adjusted, this is not a routine operation and normally will be required only when a new unit is being installed. Because of the critical nature of this operation, it should be performed by a Nissan dealer service department or other qualified repair facility.

Component replacement

Boost control unit

9 Disconnect the vacuum hoses from the unit. Be sure to note where they are installed **(see illustrations)**.

10 Remove the unit's mounting bolts and lift it off its bracket.

11 Installation is the reverse of the removal procedure. **Note:** *If installing a new unit be sure it has the same model number and identifications marks as the old one.*

11.9a On 1980 models, the boost control valve and vacuum switch (arrows) are mounted next to the charcoal canister

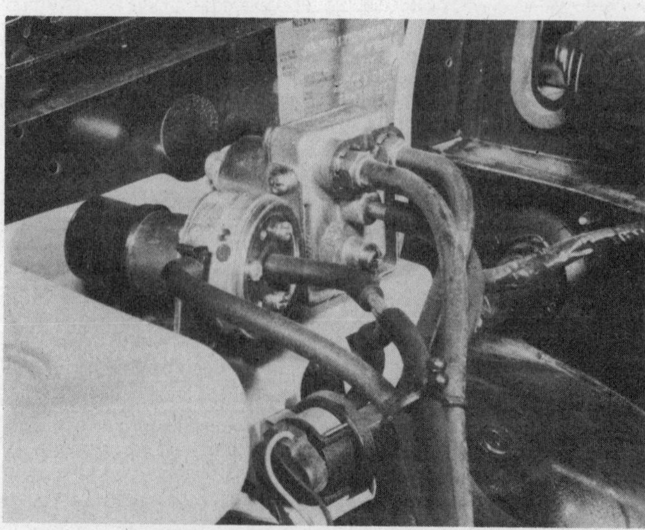

11.9b On 1981 and later models, the boost control valve, vacuum switch and altitude sensor are mounted together on the right side of the engine compartment

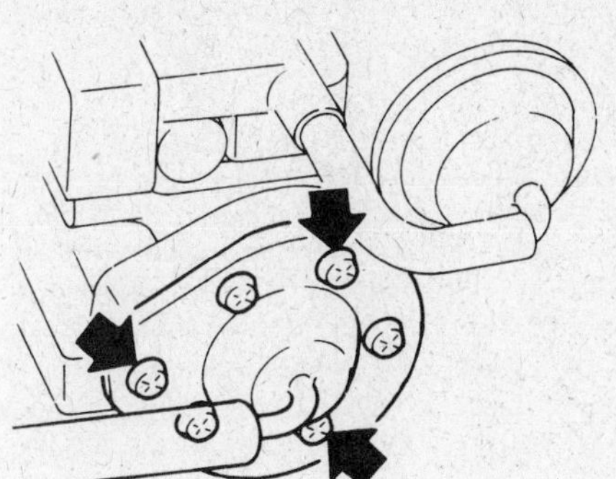

11.14 Location of the three by-pass air control valve mounting screws

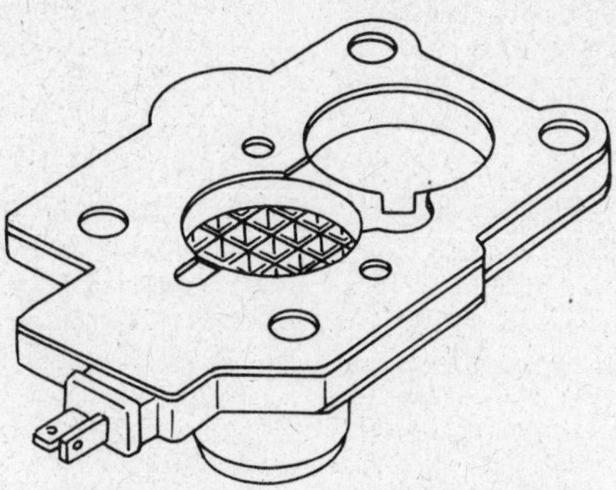

13.7 The mixture heater, located between the carburetor and the intake manifold, is an electrically heated device which improves driveability of the vehicle when cold by helping to vaporize the mixture

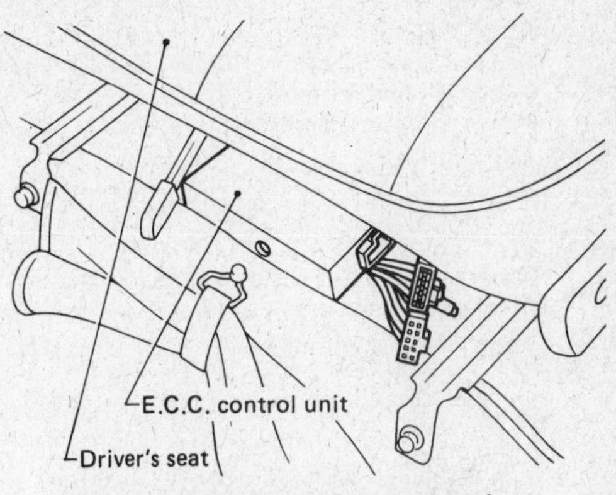

13.8 The Electronic Concentrated Control System control unit (ECU) is located underneath the driver's seat where it is safe from heat, moisture, vibration, etc. but still accessible for servicing

By-pass air control valve

12 Remove the air cleaner.

13 Disconnect the vacuum line from the unit.

14 Remove the three screws **(see illustration)** which attach the unit to the carburetor and lift it out.

15 Installation is the reverse of the removal procedure.

12 Boost Controlled Deceleration Device (BCDD)

General description

1 This device, used only on 1980 Canada models (except heavy duty), is designed to reduce emission of hydrocarbons during periods when the vehicle is coasting. The unit is installed in the carburetor and supplies extra air to the intake manifold in order to maintain the manifold vacuum at its correct operating pressure.

2 The unit incorporates two diaphragms, one to monitor the manifold vacuum and open the vacuum control valve, and the second to operate the air control valve according to the degree of vacuum transmitted through the vacuum control valve.

3 Operating pressure variations due to differences in operating altitudes are taken into account.

Removal and installation

4 The BCDD is easily removed by unscrewing its three mounting screws and lifting it off. The BCDD is not designed to be disassembled. If defective, it must be replaced as a unit.

5 Although the BCDD is designed to be adjusted, this is not a routine operation and normally will be required only when a new unit is being installed. Because of the critical nature of this operation, this should be performed by a Nissan dealer service department or other qualified repair facility.

13 Electronic Concentrated Control System (ECCS) (carburetor equipped vehicles)

Refer to illustrations 13.7 and 13.8

In 1984 the management of fuel and ignition functions in California vehicles was placed under the control of a microcomputer. In 1985 all vehicles were equipped with this system.

General description

1 The Electronic Concentrated Control System (ECCS) is basically a system of monitors which feed information to an electronic box. The system then directs a carburetor-mounted solenoid to control how much fuel is contained in the air/fuel mixture. In this way the engine will operate at optimum performance/emissions levels under all driving conditions.

2 The only time this system is not in operation (open-loop control condition), is when the engine is cold, when driving at high speeds or under a heavy load.

3 The system consists of the following sub-systems and components:

Spark plug switching control

4 This ECC sub-system is designed to cut out the firing of one of the spark plugs to each cylinder (there are two) under heavy load driving conditions. This reduces engine noise at those times.

5 This sub-system is not incorporated on Z20 engines. Also, it is not operational on certain models being used at high altitudes.

Fuel shut-off

6 This sub-system shuts off the fuel supply during deceleration, when the engine does not require fuel. This system does not operate when the engine is cold or under no-load conditions, where stalling could occur.

Mixture heating control

7 In order to improve the driveability of the vehicle when cold, a mixture heater **(see illustration)** has been built into the primary port of the carburetor insulator.

Control unit

8 The ECC control unit **(see illustration)** is a micro-computer mounted under the driver's seat. It is the 'brain' of the system and controls the operation of the system.

Air-fuel ratio control solenoid

9 This solenoid is mounted on the carburetor body and controls the flow of fuel into the carburetor. It operates continually during engine operation and gets its messages from the control unit.

Exhaust gas sensor

10 This sensor is mounted in the exhaust manifold and monitors the amount of oxygen in the exhaust gasses. It sends this information to the control unit for processing, ultimately altering the mixture at the carburetor to attain the optimum mixture. The exhaust gas sensor must be replaced periodically; see the Tune-up and maintenance information in this Supplement.

Water temperature sensor

11 This sensor, built into the water jacket of the intake manifold, monitors changes in water temperature. It then sends this information to the control unit.

Switches

12 There are various switches incorporated into the ECC system which also send information to the control unit.

13 The throttle valve switch is located at the carburetor and actuates in response to accelerator pedal movement. This switch sends signals to the control unit describing idle, part throttle or full throttle conditions.

14 The inhibitor/neutral switch detects the position of the transmission gear selector.

15 The clutch switch sends a signal to the control unit to indicate the clutch position (either depressed or released).

16 A vacuum switch located on the intake manifold detects full throttle or heavy load conditions and sends a signal to the control unit describing these low vacuum conditions.

Mixture heater

17 The mixture heater is situated on the primary side of the carburetor insulator and is electrically operated. As mentioned previously, it heats the air/fuel mixture under certain conditions to obtain optimum combustion.

Anti-dieseling solenoid

18 This solenoid is located on the carburetor and shuts off the supply of fuel under certain conditions to prevent engine dieseling.

Detonation sensor system (Z20 engine)

19 The function of this system is to sense engine 'knock' or detonation and then almost instantaneously alter the ignition to eliminate the condition.

20 The system consists of a detonation sensor attached to the cylinder block, a control unit and the necessary wiring between these two components and the ignition system distributor.

21 If problems with this system are suspected (usually due to excessive engine knock or poor running conditions) have the system inspected by a Nissan dealer.

Checking

22 Other than inspecting for obvious problems, such as hoses or wires being disconnected, the ECC system should be checked by a Nissan dealer service department.

14 Electronic Fuel injection (EFI) system – general diagnosis

General information

The Electronic Concentrated Control System (ECCS) controls the fuel injection system, the spark advance system, the self diagnosis system, the cooling fans etc. by means of the Engine Control Unit (ECU).

The ECU receives signals from various sensors which monitor changing engine operations such as intake air volume, intake air temperature, coolant temperature, engine RPM, acceleration/deceleration, exhaust temperature etc. These signals are utilized by the ECU to determine the correct injection duration and ignition timing.

The Sections in this Chapter include general descriptions and checking procedures, within the scope of the home mechanic and component replacement procedures (when possible). Before assuming the fuel and ignition systems are malfunctioning check the emission control system thoroughly (see Chapter 6). The emission system and the fuel system are closely interrelated but can be checked separately. The diagnosis of some of the fuel and emission control devices requires specialized tools, equipment and training. If checking and servicing become too difficult or if a procedure is beyond your ability, consult a dealer service department. Remember, the most frequent cause of fuel and emissions problems is simply a loose or broken vacuum hose or wire, so always check the hose and wiring connections first.

Note: *Because of federally mandated extended warranty which covers the emission control system components (and any other components which have a primary purpose other than emission control but have significant effects on emissions), check with your dealer about warranty coverage before working on any emission related systems. Once the warranty has expired, you may wish to perform some of the component checks and/or replacement procedures in this Chapter to save you money.*

Precautions

a) Always disconnect the power by either turning off the ignition switch or disconnecting the battery terminals before disconnecting EFI wiring connectors.
b) When installing a battery, be particularly careful to avoid reversing the positive and negative cables.
c) Do not subject EFI or emission related components or the ECCS to severe impact during removal or installation.
d) Do not be careless during troubleshooting. Even slight terminal contact can invalidate a testing procedure and even damage one of the numerous transistor circuits.
e) Never attempt to work on the ECU or open the ECU cover. The ECU is protected by a government mandated extended warranty that will be nullified if you tamper with it.
f) If you are inspecting electronic control system components during rainy weather, make sure water does not enter any part. When washing the engine compartment, do not spray these parts or their connectors with water.

Self diagnosis system

Note: *To access the code information on 1996 models, it is necessary to use a the GST (Generic Scan Tool) or the CONSULT scan tool and support test equipment. These tools are very expensive and are not recommended for use by the home mechanic. The flashing green and red LEDs on the control unit are no longer used on these models. If you suspect a problem with the emissions related components, have the system tested by a dealer service department or other repair shop.*

The self diagnosis is useful to diagnose malfunctions in major sensors and actuators of the ECCS system. There are five modes in the self diagnosis system.

1 **Mode I** – Exhaust gas sensor monitor – During a closed loop condition (when the engine is warm), the green inspection lamp turns ON indicating a lean condition or OFF for a rich condition. During an open loop condition (when the engine is cold) the green lamp remains ON or OFF.

2 **Mode II** – Mixture ratio feedback control monitor – During closed loop operation, the red inspection lamp turns ON and OFF simultaneously with the green inspection lamp when the mixture ratio is controlled within the specified value. During the open loop condition, the red lamp remains ON or OFF.

3 **Mode III** – Self diagnosis – This mode stores all malfunctioning diagnostic items in its memory. It will be stored in the ECU memory until the starter is operated fifty times, or until the power supply to the ECU is interrupted.

4 **Mode IV** – Switches ON/OFF diagnosis – During this mode, the inspection lamp monitors the idle switch portion of the throttle valve switch, the starter switch, vehicle speed sensor and other switches with an ON/OFF condition.

5 **Mode V** – Real time diagnosis – The moment the malfunction is detected, the display will be presented. This is the mode in which the malfunction can be observed during a road test, as it occurs.

Switching the modes – MPFI systems (1990 through1995)

Refer to illustration 14.1

Turn the ignition switch to the On position. Turn the diagnostic mode selector on the ECU fully clockwise **(see illustration)** and wait until the inspection lamps flash. Count the number of flashes to find which mode you are in, then turn the diagnostic mode selector fully counterclockwise.

When the ignition switch is turned off during diagnosis, in each mode, and then turned on again after the power to the ECU has dropped off completely, the diagnosis will automatically return to Mode I.

The CHECK ENGINE light on the instrument panel (California models only) comes on when the ignition switch is turned on or in Mode I when the emission system malfunctions (with the engine running).

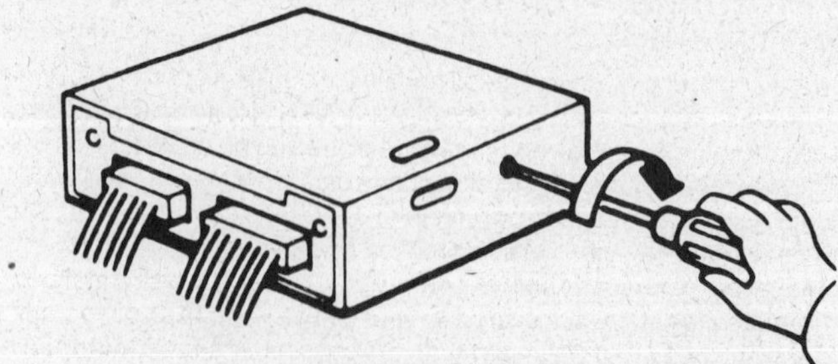

14.1 Turn the mode selector fully clockwise to begin the diagnostic procedure

Malfunctions related to fuel and emission control systems can be diagnosed using the self diagnostic codes of Mode III.

To start the diagnostic procedure, remove the ECU from under the passenger seat. Start the engine and warm it up to normal operating temperature. Turn the diagnostic mode selector on the ECU fully clockwise **(see illustration 14.1)**. After the inspection lamps have flashed 3 times, turn the diagnostic mode selector fully counterclockwise. The ECU is now in

Mode III. Check the trouble code chart for the particular malfunction.

After the tests have been performed and the repairs completed, erase the memory by turning the diagnostic mode selector on the ECU fully clockwise. After the inspection lamps have flashed 4 times, turn the mode selector fully counterclockwise. This will erase any signals the ECU has stored concerning a particular component.

SELF-DIAGNOSIS SYSTEM TROUBLE CODES (MODE III)

Display code	Malfunctioning component/circuit	Check/repair procedure
Code 11 (1 red flash, 1 green flash)	Crank angle sensor/circuit	Refer to Chapter 5 for the crank angle sensor check and replacement procedure.
Code 12 (1 red flash, 2 green flashes)	Air flow meter/circuit	The air flow meter source or ground circuit(s) may be shorted or open. Check the air flow meter.
Code 13 (1 red flash, 3 green flashes)	Engine temperature sensor	The sensor source or ground circuit(s) may be shorted or open. Check the temperature sensor/circuit(s) (Section 15).
Code 14 (1 red flash, 4 green flashes)	Vehicle speed sensor	The vehicle speed sensor signal circuit is open. This repair must be performed by a dealership service department.
Code 21 (2 red flashes, 1 green flash)	Ignition signal	The ignition signal in the primary circuit is not entered during engine cranking or running. This repair must be performed by a dealership service department.
Code 31 (3 red flashes, 1 green flash)	ECU control unit	The ECU input signal is beyond "normal" range. This repair must be performed by a dealership service department.
Code 32 (3 red flashes, 2 green flashes)	EGR Function	The EGR control valve does not operate (see Chapter 6)
Code 33 (3 red flashes, 3 green flashes)	Exhaust gas sensor	The exhaust gas sensor circuit is open (see Section 15)
Code 34 (3 red flashes, 4 green flashes)	Detonation sensor	The detonation circuit is open or shorted. This repair must be performed by a dealership service department.
Code 35 (3 red flashes, 5 green flashes)	Exhaust gas temperature sensor	The exhaust gas temperature sensor circuit is open or shorted circuit (see Section 15)
Code 41 (4 red flashes, 1 green flash)	Air temperature sensor	The air temperature sensor circuit is open or shorted circuit (KA24E engines only) (see Section 15)
Code 43 (4 red flashes, 3 green flashes)	Throttle sensor	The throttle sensor circuit is open or shorted. This repair must be performed by a dealership service department.
Code 45 (4 red flashes, 5 green flashes)	Injector leak	The injector(s) have fuel leaks (see Section 17).
Code 51 (5 red flashes, 1 green flash)	Injector circuit (V6 engine only)	The injector circuit is open. This repair must be performed by a dealership service department.
Code 55 (5 red flashes, 5 green flashes)	ECCS normal operation	

6

Switching modes – TBI systems

Refer to illustration 14.5

If the check engine light comes on while the engine is running (California vehicles only), or if the vehicle suddenly begins to run poorly, it may indicate that something is wrong with one of the engine emission components under ECU control. If this situation occurs, checking these devices will be impossible without expensive and sophisticated equipment. See your dealer and have the vehicle checked by a professional.

However, if you wish to determine the general area in which a malfunction is occurring before consulting with your dealer, you can do so yourself.

Take out the ECU from underneath the passenger seat. **Caution:** *Do not disconnect the harness connector from the ECU or you will erase any stored diagnostic codes.*

Turn the ignition switch to On. The red and green inspection lights on the ECU should come on.

Turn the mode selector on **(see illustration)**. The red and green inspection lights should flash repeatedly in the sequence shown in the chart.

Note that there are five possible modes. You are only concerned with Mode III (the self-diagnosis mode).

Turn the mode selector off immediately after the inspection lights flash three times.

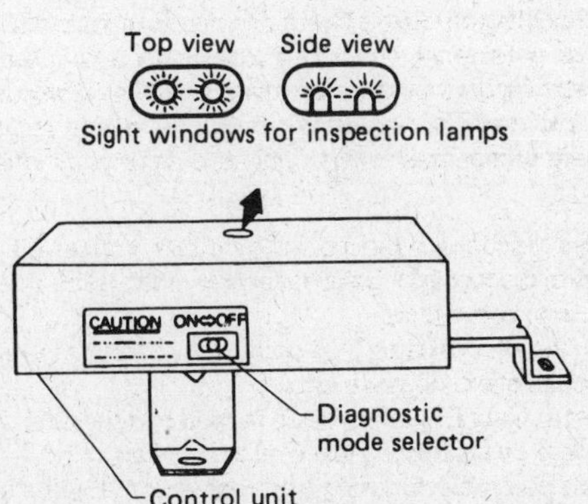

14.5 To activate the self-diagnostic function of the ECU, push the mode switch to the left – the red and green lights should begin flashing (models through 1995)

Now, count the number of times that the inspection lights flash. First, the red light flashes, then the green light flashes. The red light denotes units of ten, the green light denotes units of one. For example, if the red light flashes once and the green light flashes twice, the ECU is displaying the number 12, which indicates that the air flow meter is malfunctioning.

If the ignition switch is turned off at any time during a diagnostic readout in any mode, the diagnosis will automatically return to Mode I after the ignition is turned on again.

The stored memory or memories will be lost if, for any reason, the battery terminal is disconnected or if, after Mode III has been selected, Mode IV is selected.

To erase memory after the Mode III self-diagnosis codes have been noted and recorded, turn the diagnostic mode selector to On. After the inspection lamps have flashed four times, turn the diagnostic mode selector to Off.

Turn the ignition switch to Off.

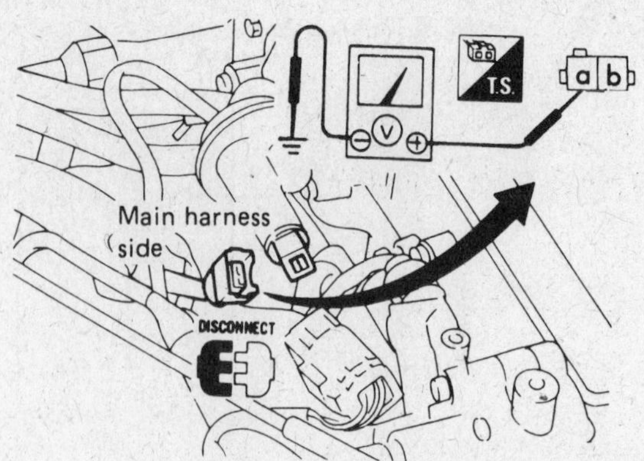

15.10 Attach the voltmeter positive lead to terminal A and ground the voltmeter negative lead

15 Air regulator (V6 engine only) – removal, check and installation

Note: *The air regulator is not incorporated into the Self Diagnosis system. Driveability and emission problems can be eliminated by checking the air regulator for proper operation.*

Refer to illustrations 15.10

Removal

1 Detach the hose from the end of the air regulator **(see illustration 13.1d** in Chapter 4).

2 Disconnect the electrical connector from the air regulator.

3 Remove the bolts and detach the air regulator from the air intake collector.

Check

4 Due to the complexity of the air regulator control system, the home mechanic is limited to a visual inspection of the valve's operation and resistance and voltage checks, which can be done with a multimeter. If voltage is available to the air regulator and the resistance is correct, but the valve doesn't close as the regulator warms up, take the vehicle to a dealer service department for diagnosis.

5 Look into the end of the regulator and note the position of the shutter. At a temperature of about 65 to 70-degrees F, the shutter should be covering about one-half of the port. At cooler temperatures, the opening will be larger.

6 Use jumper wires to apply battery voltage directly to the air regulator terminals. **Caution:** *One of the jumper wires should have an in-line fuse to avoid damage if the wires contact each other at the terminals.*

7 As the air regulator begins to heat up from the applied voltage, the shutter should close off the port (this should occur within five minutes). If it does, the air regulator is functioning correctly – proceed to Step 10.

8 If the shutter takes a very long time to close off the port, or if it doesn't close smoothly, use an ohmmeter to check the resistance of the air regulator by hooking the meter leads to the terminals. The correct resistance is listed in this Chapter's Specifications.

9 If the resistance is incorrect, replace the air regulator.

10 To check for power to the air regulator, attach a voltmeter positive lead to terminal A in the harness side of the connector and ground the voltmeter negative lead **(see illustration)**.

11 Turn the ignition switch on. The meter should indicate 12-volts (after 5-seconds the voltage will drop to zero). If 12-volts isn't indicated, the wire harness may have an open or short somewhere (such as a disconnected or broken wire).

12 Even if voltage is present at terminal A, the air regulator won't operate unless it is grounded through the ECU. If the regulator is good and there is power to it, check the ground wire from the regulator to the ECU for an open or short.

Installation

13 Installation is the reverse of removal, but be sure to use a new O-ring where the air regulator mates to the air intake collector.

16 Fuel pressure regulator and control solenoid – check and replacement

Warning: *Gasoline is extremely flammable, so extra precautions must be taken when working on any part of the fuel system. Do not smoke or allow open flames or bare light bulbs near the work area. Also, do not work in a garage if a natural gas type appliance with a pilot light is present.*

Check

1 The fuel pressure regulator control solenoid cuts the vacuum signal to the pressure regulator during hot start conditions, which will increase the fuel pressure to improve starting during these conditions.

2 If the fuel pressure regulator functions properly when a vacuum pump is connected to it but doesn't work properly when the vacuum control line is connected, check the pressure regulator control solenoid as follows.

3 Check the power source by disconnecting the electrical connector from the solenoid and turning the ignition switch to the On position. Check the voltage between terminals and ground. The voltmeter should read battery voltage.

4 Disconnect the fuel pressure regulator vacuum line and blow into it – air should pass through the valve when it is not energized.

5 If the fuel pressure control solenoid fails any of these tests, replace it.

Replacement

Fuel pressure regulator control solenoid

6 Disconnect the vacuum hoses, unplug the electrical connector and unbolt the solenoid.

7 Installation is the reverse of the removal procedure.

Fuel pressure regulator

Refer to illustration 16.10

8 Relieve the fuel system pressure (see Chapter 4).

9 Disconnect the negative cable at the battery.

10 Loosen the hose clamps and detach the two fuel hoses from the regulator **(see illustration)**. If there is any doubt as to which fittings the hoses are to be connected, mark them with pieces of tape.

11 Disconnect the vacuum line and fuel temperature sensor electrical connector (if equipped).

12 Loosen the hose clamp and disconnect the return fuel line from the underside of the regulator.

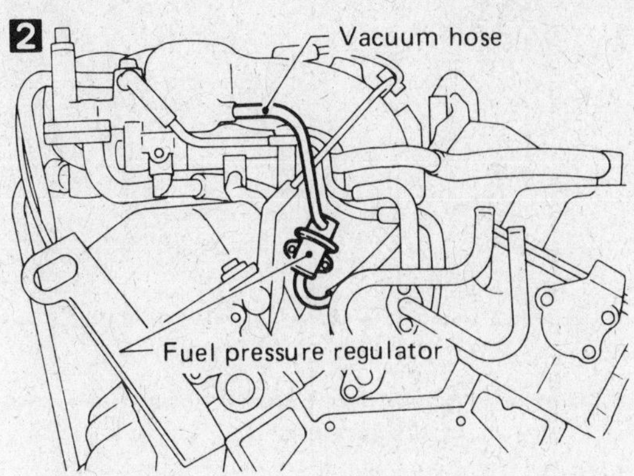

16.10 Location of the fuel pressure regulator on the V6 engine

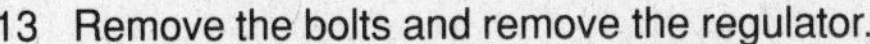

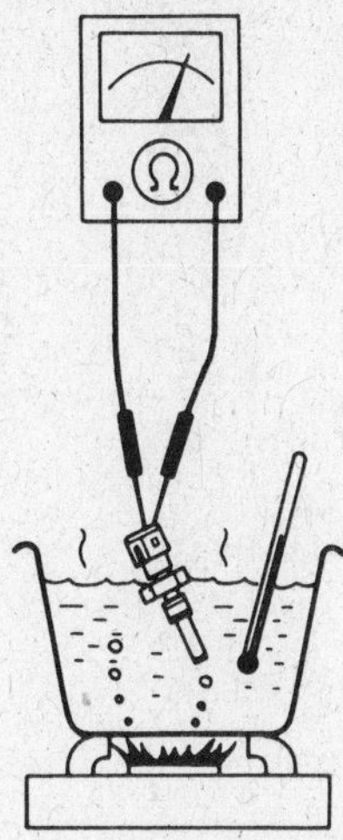

17.6 The cylinder head temperature sensor should decrease as the sensor is heated up

13 Remove the bolts and remove the regulator.
14 Installation is the reverse of the removal procedures. **Note:** *Wet the inside of the fuel lines with gasoline to facilitate hose installation.*

17 Information sensors

Engine temperature sensor – check and replacement

Refer to illustrations 17.6

Check

1 Use the self diagnosis mode (see Section 14) to pinpoint any problems in the vehicle's fuel system.
2 If the ECU flashes 1 red flash and 3 green flashes then the engine temperature sensor circuit is malfunctioning. Continue the checks as described below. If the self diagnostic code isn't displayed, the sensor/circuit is functioning properly.
3 Depending on the symptom, the engine temperature sensor and its related circuit have several items that must be checked in order to pinpoint the exact problem.
4 If the vehicle is impossible to start and there is a sound of partial combustion, disconnect the sensor electrical connector and crank the engine over. If the vehicle still does not start, check the resistance of the sensor.
5 Remove the cylinder head temperature sensor for testing **(see illustration 14.4** in Chapter 4).
6 Remove the sensor and place it in a pan of lukewarm water. Use a thermometer to monitor the temperature of the water. Use an ohmmeter to check the resistance value of the sensor **(see illustration)**.
7 Place the pan on a heat source (hot plate, stove etc.) and raise the temperature of the water. Carefully monitor the resistance values as the water temperature increases. If the values are not as listed in this Chapter's Specifications, replace the sensor.
8 If the resistance values are acceptable, check the continuity of the cylinder head temperature sensor circuit with an ohmmeter.
9 Installation is the reverse of removal

Exhaust gas temperature sensor – check

Refer to illustrations 17.13, 17.15 and 17.16

10 Use the self diagnosis mode (see Section 14) to pinpoint any problems in the vehicle's fuel system.
11 If the ECU flashes 3 red flashes and 5 green flashes then the exhaust gas sensor circuit is malfunctioning. Continue the check as described below. If the self-diagnostic code isn't displayed, the sensor/circuit is functioning properly.
12 Depending on the symptom, the exhaust gas sensor and its related circuit have several items that must be checked in order to pinpoint the exact problem.
13 If the vehicle drives poorly and surges while cruising, disconnect the exhaust gas temperature sensor electrical connector **(see illustration)** and drive the vehicle.
14 If the vehicle's driveability improves, replace the sensor.
15 If there is no improvement, disconnect the exhaust gas temperature sensor harness connector with the ignition switch ON, check voltage between terminal A **(see illustration)** and ground. It should be 5 volts.

6

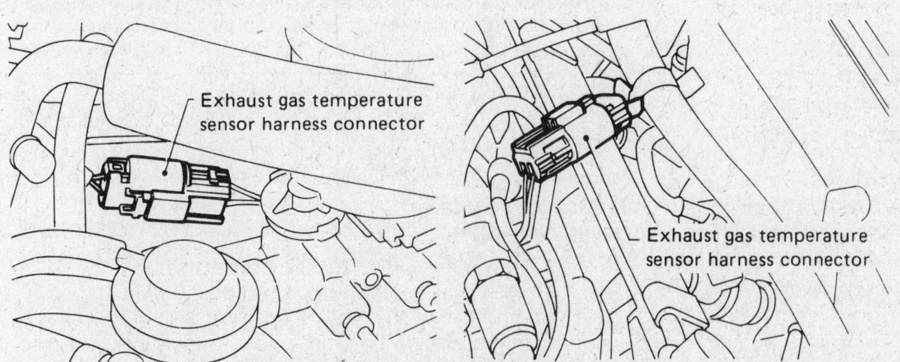

17.13 Location of the exhaust gas temperature sensor harness connector on the V6 and KA24E engine

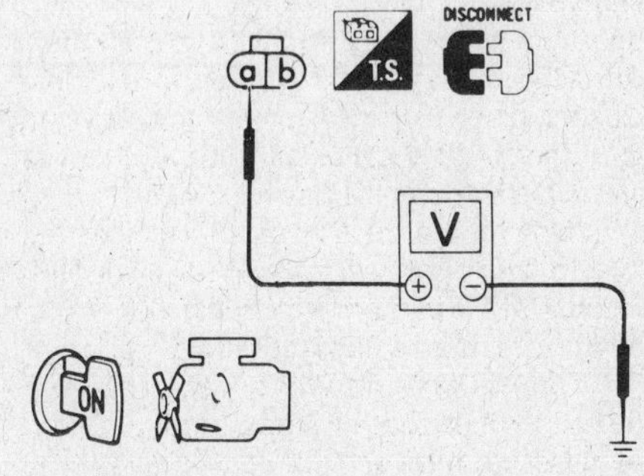

17.15 Check for voltage with the ignition key ON between terminal A and ground. It should be 5 volts.

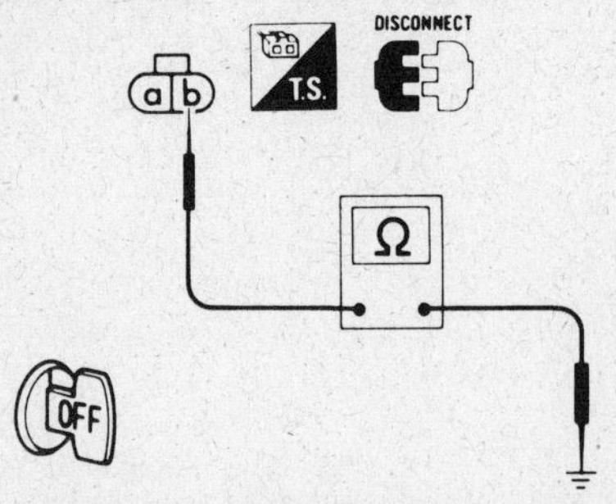

17.16 Check for continuity between terminal B and ground with the ignition key OFF

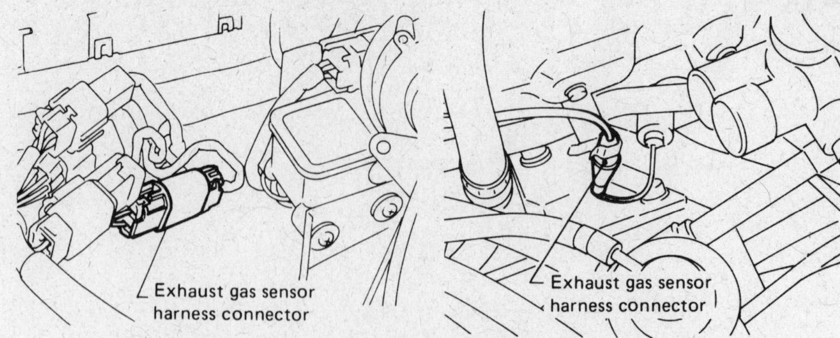

17.21 Location of the exhaust gas sensor harness connector on the V6 and KA24E engine

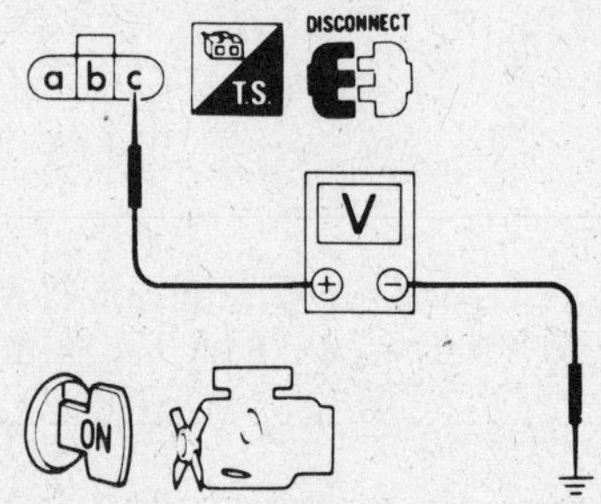

17.24 On V6 engines only, with the key OFF, the voltmeter should indicate battery voltage

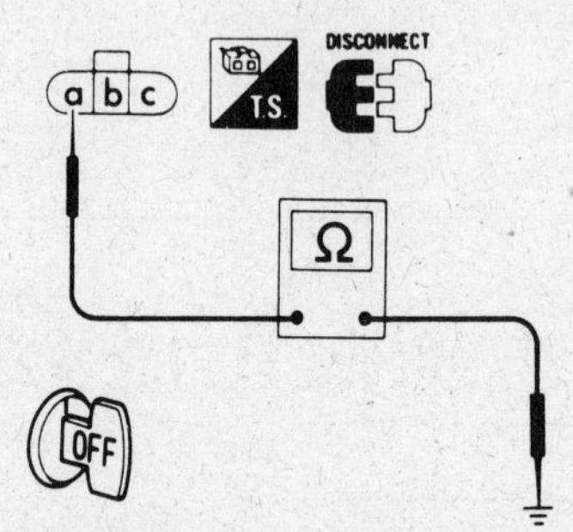

17.25 On V6 engines only, with the key OFF, check for continuity between terminal A and ground

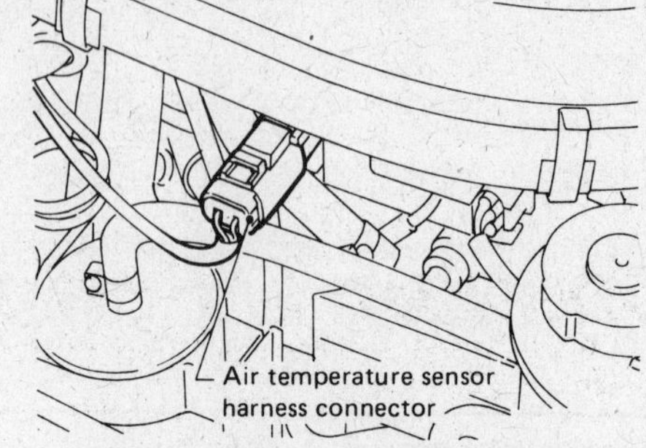

17.30a The air temperature sensor harness connector is located next to the air cleaner

16 Turn the ignition switch to the OFF position and check for continuity between terminal B **(see illustration)** and engine ground. The ohmmeter should indicate continuity.
17 If the test results are incorrect, replace the exhaust gas temperature sensor.

Exhaust gas sensor – check

Refer to illustrations 17.21, 17.24 and 17.25

18 Use the self diagnosis mode (see Section 14) to pinpoint any problems in the vehicle's fuel system.
19 If the ECU flashes 3 red flashes and 3 green flashes then the exhaust gas sensor circuit is malfunctioning. Continue the check as described below. If the self-diagnostic code isn't displayed, the sensor/circuit is functioning properly.
20 Depending on the symptom, the exhaust gas sensor and its related circuit have several items that must be checked in order to pinpoint the exact problem.
21 If the vehicle drives poorly and surges while cruising, disconnect the exhaust gas sensor electrical connector **(see illustration)** and drive the vehicle.
22 If the vehicle's driveability improves, replace the sensor.
23 If there is no improvement, run the engine at about 2,000 rpm's for about 2 minutes (under no load) and watch to make sure the green light on the ECU blinks ON and OFF.
24 On V6 engines only, turn the ignition key ON and disconnect the exhaust gas sensor harness connector and check voltage between terminal C **(see illustration)** and ground. It should be equal to battery voltage.
25 Turn the ignition switch to the OFF position and check for continuity between terminal A **(see illustration)** and engine ground. The ohmmeter should indicate continuity. **Note:** *On V6 engines the continuity is checked from terminal A to ground while on KA24E engines, the continuity is checked from terminal A to the ECU terminal number 19.*
26 If the test results are incorrect, replace the exhaust gas sensor.

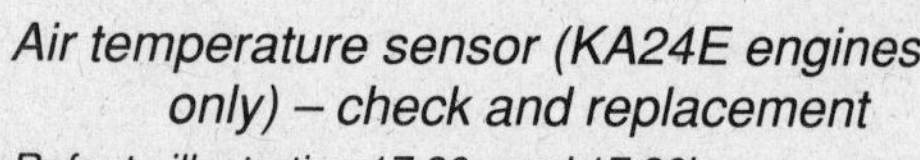

Air temperature sensor (KA24E engines only) – check and replacement

Refer to illustration 17.30a and 17.30b

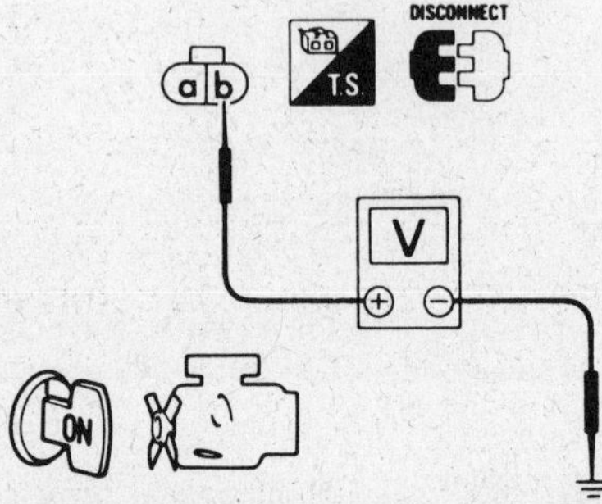

17.30b Check for voltage on terminal B and ground

Check

27 Use the self diagnosis mode (see Section 14) to pinpoint any problems in the vehicle's fuel system.
28 If the ECU flashes 4 red flashes and 1 green flash then the air temperature sensor circuit is malfunctioning. Continue the check as described below. If the self-diagnostic code isn't displayed, the sensor/circuit is functioning properly.
29 Depending on the symptom, the fuel temperature sensor and its related circuit have several items that must be checked in order to pinpoint the exact problem.
30 Disconnect the air temperature sensor harness connector **(see illustration)** and with the ignition key ON, check the voltage between the terminal B and ground **(see illustration)**. The voltage should be 5 volts.
31 If the voltage test is correct, check the continuity of the fuel temperature sensor circuit between terminal A and ground. Continuity should exist.
32 Check the resistance of the air temperature sensor on the harness connector. When the temperature of the sensor is low (68 degrees F) the resistance should be 2,100 to 2,900 ohms. When the temperature is warm (176 degrees F), the resistance should be 270 to 380 ohms.

Replacement

33 Remove the air temperature sensor from the air cleaner housing.
34 Installation is the reverse of removal.

Chapter 7 Part A Manual transmission

Contents

Specifications

F4W71B and F4W71C 4-speed transmission

Baulk ring/gear clearance	
Standard measurement	0.0472 to 0.0630 in (1.20 to 1.60 mm)
Wear limit	0.031 in (0.787 mm)
Gear backlash service limit	0.002 to 0.004 in (0.05 to 0.10 mm)
Gear end play	
1st gear	0.013 to 0.015 in (0.32 to 0.39 mm)
2nd gear	0.005 to 0.007 in (0.12 to 0.19 mm
3rd gear	0.005 to 0.014 in (0.13 to 0.37 mm)

FS5W71B 5-speed transmission

Baulk ring/gear clearance	
All except 5th gear	
Standard measurement	0.0472 to 0.0630 in (1.20 to 1.60 mm)
Wear limit	0.031 in (0.787 mm)
5th gear	
Standard measurement	0.0394 to 0.0551 in (1.00 to 1.40 mm)
Wear limit	0.020 in (0.51 mm)
Gear backlash service limit	0.002 to 0.004 in (0.050 to 0.10 mm)
Gear end play	
1st gear	0.0126 to 0.015 in (0.32 to 0.39 mm)
2nd gear	0.0047 to 0.0075 in (0.12 to 0.19 mm
3rd gear	0.0051 to 0.0146 in (0.13 to 0.37 mm)
5th gear	0.0126 to 0.019 in (0.32 to 0.50 mm)
Reverse idler gear	0.002 to 0.020 in (0.05 to 0.50 mm)

FS5W71C 5-speed transmission

Baulk ring/gear clearance	
All except 5th gear	
Standard measurement	0.0472 to 0.0630 in (1.20 to 1.60 mm)
Wear limit	0.031 in (0.787 mm)

FS5W71C 5-speed transmission (continued)

5th gear (thru 1987)	
Standard measurement	0.0394 to 0.0551 in (1.00 to 1.40 mm)
Wear limit	0.020 in (0.51 mm)
5th gear (thru 1988 on)	
Standard measurement	0.0472 to 0.0630 in (1.20 to 1.60 mm)
Wear limit	0.0315 in (0.80 mm)
Overdrive gear (1990 to 1991)	0.0472 to 0.0630 in (1.20 to 1.60 mm)
Gear end play	
1st gear	0.0122 to 0.0161 in (0.31 to 0.41 mm)
2nd gear	0.0043 to 0.0083 in (0.11 to 0.21 mm
3rd gear	0.0043 to 0.0083 in (0.11 to 0.21 mm)
5th gear	
Thru 1987	0.0126 to 0.0154 in (0.32 to 0.39 mm)
1988 on	0.0094 to 0.0161 in (0.24 to 0.41 mm)
Overdrive (1990 and 1991)	0.0094 to 0.016 in (0.24 to 0.41 mm)

FS5R30A 5-speed transmission

Gear end play	
All except reverse main gear	0.0091 to 0.0130 in (0.23 to 0.33 mm)
Reverse main gear	0.0130 to 0.0169 in (0.33 to 0.43 mm)
Reverse idler shaft end play	0.0118 to 0.0209 in (0.30 to 0.53 mm)

Torque specifications

	Ft-lbs
Transmission-to-engine bolts	
1980 through 1985	32 to 43
1986 on four-cylinder engine	
upper bolts	29
two lower bolts	18
V6 engine	29
Check ball plug	14 to 18
Clutch operating cylinder	22 to 30
Front cover-to-transmission case bolt	12 to 15
Rear extension-to-transmission case	
F4W71B/C and FS5W71B/C	12 to 15
FS5R30A	23 to 31
Mainshaft locknut (F4W71B/C and FS5W71B/C)	101 to 123
Countershaft locknut (F4W71B/C and FS5W71B/C)	72 to 94

1 General information

These models are equipped with 4- and 5-speed transmissions, of two different designs. The FS5W71B and FS5W71C 5-speed and its 4-speed variation, the F4W71B and F4W71C are available in both the 720 and later D21 models. The 5-speed FS5R30A transmission was introduced in 1986 with the D21 models.

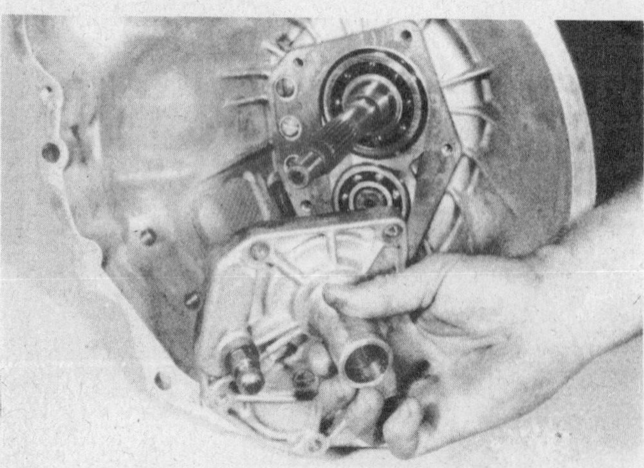

2.3 The transmission front cover is located in the clutch housing

2 Oil seals – replacement

Refer to illustrations 2.3, 2.4 and 2.10

Front oil seal

1 Remove the transmission as described in Section 3.
2 Remove the release bearing as described in Chapter 8.
3 Remove the bolts that retain the transmission front cover to the

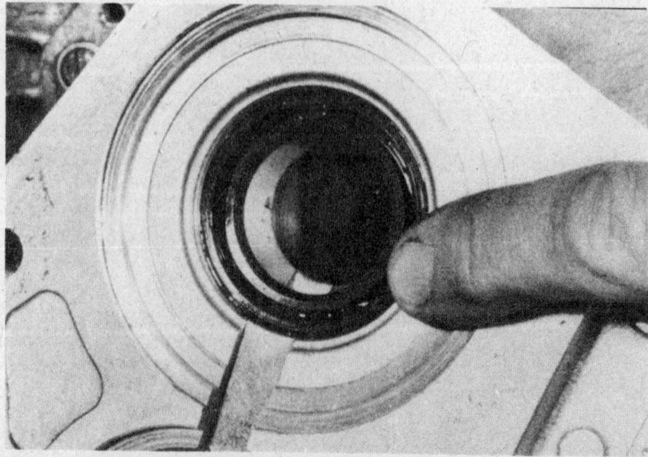

2.4 The front transmission oil seal is located in the front cover and can be pried out with a screwdriver

case and lift off the cover **(see illustration)**.
4 Being careful not to nick or damage the front cover, pry out the front oil seal from the cover **(see illustration)**.
5 Drive the new seal into position in the cover using an appropriate sized socket.
6 Apply a light coat of gear oil to the seal lips and the main drive shaft, and then reinstall the front cover.
7 Reinstall the components removed in the reverse order of removal.

Rear oil seal

8 Remove the driveshaft as described in Chapter 8 (2WD) or 9 (4WD).
9 On later models it may be necessary to remove the dust cover for access to the oil seal.
10 Being careful not to damage the output shaft of the transmission housing, use a screwdriver to pry out the old seal **(see illustration)**.
11 Apply a coat of gear oil to the lips of the new seal and drive it into place using an appropriate sized socket.
12 Reinstall the driveshaft.

2.10 The rear oil seal can be removed with the transmission still in the vehicle by prying it out with a screwdriver

3 Manual transmission – removal and installation

Refer to illustrations 3.5a, 3.5b, 3.11 and 3.18

1 Disconnect the negative battery cable from the battery.
2 Working inside the vehicle, disconnect the accelerator linkage.
3 Remove the console as described in Chapter 13.
4 Remove the rubber boot from the shift lever.
5 Place the shifter in the Neutral position. Then remove the E-ring and pin or snap-ring and lift out the shifter **(see illustration)**.
6 Jack up the vehicle and safety support its weight on suitable blocks or stands. Be sure the vehicle is high enough that the transmission can be slid out from underneath when removed.
7 Remove the front exhaust pipe.
8 On 4WD models, remove the front and primary driveshafts. Refer to Chapter 9, if necessary. Then support the front differential with a jack, and remove the rear crossmember support of the front differential. If additional clearance is needed in order to remove the transmission, remove the front differential as described in Chapter 9.
9 Remove the driveshaft, as described in Chapter 8. As this is done, plug or cover over the opening at the rear of the transmission to prevent leakage of oil.
10 Disconnect the wires from the back-up light switch, the top gear switch, the neutral switch and/or overdrive switch, as equipped.
11 Disconnect the speedometer cable **(see illustration)**. On 4WD models, the speedometer cable is attached to the transfer case.
12 Drain the oil from the transmission.
13 Unbolt and remove the clutch operating cylinder and tie it back out of the way. There is no need to disconnect the hydraulic line (further information can be found in Chapter 8).
14 Support the engine under the oil pan using a suitable jack and a block of wood as an insulator.
15 Place a second jack under the transmission.
16 Undo and remove the transmission mounting insulator securing nuts and the mount-to-frame bolts, and then lift the mount off.
17 Remove the starter motor from the bellhousing.

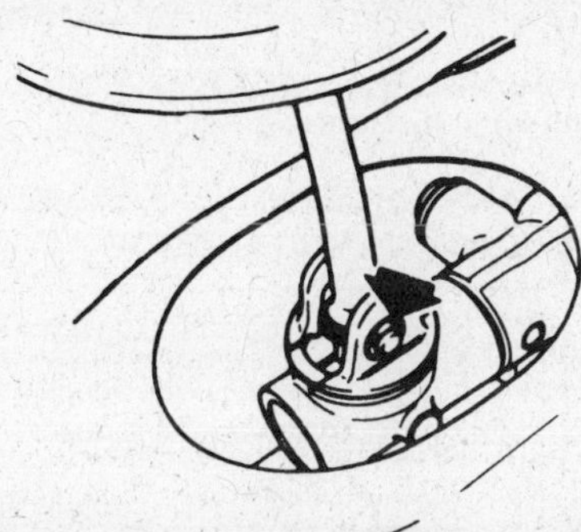

3.5a On earlier models the shift lever is retained with a pin (arrow)

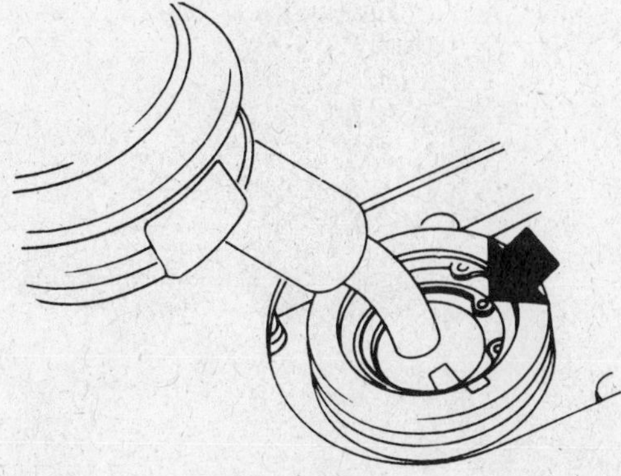

3.5b On later models a snap ring (arrow) retains the shift lever

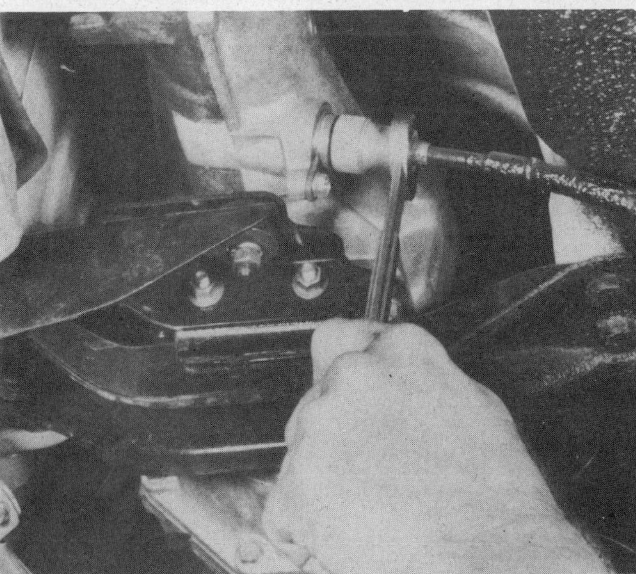

3.11 The speedometer gear is located on the transmission on 2WD models

18 Unscrew and remove the bolts which secure the clutch bellhousing to the engine crankcase **(see illustration)**.
19 Lower each of the two jacks simultaneously, until the transmission can be withdrawn to the rear and removed from underneath the vehicle. Do not allow the weight of the transmission to hang upon the input shaft while it is engaged with the splines of the clutch driven plate.
20 For details on repairing or overhauling a manual transmission, refer to Section 5 or 6 as appropriate.
21 Installation is a reversal of removal but smear a trace of grease on the input shaft splines, and the moving parts of the shift lever and striking rods. Also check if the clutch disc has been properly aligned as described in Chapter 8.
22 Check the clutch pedal free-travel and adjust if necessary (Chapter 1). Remember to fill the transmission with the correct grade and quantity of oil.

4 FS5W71B/FS5W71C 5-speed transmission – overhaul

Refer to illustrations 4.4, 4.5, 4.6, 4.7, 4.8, 4.9a, 4.9b, 4.10, 4.15a, 4.15b, 4.15c, 4.15d, 4.17a, 4.17b, 4.17c, 4.17d, 4.18, 4.38, 4.56, 4.84, 4.85 and 4.106

Note: *This procedure applies to transmissions manufactured prior to 1993 only. Due to the complexity of the 1993 and later transmissions, it's recommended that internal procedures be left to the dealer service department or repair shop.*

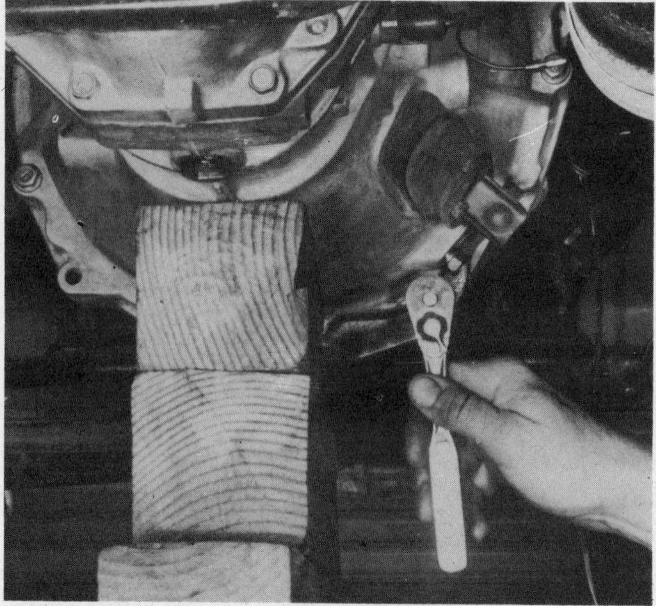

3.18 Support the transmission securely with blocks or a jackstand

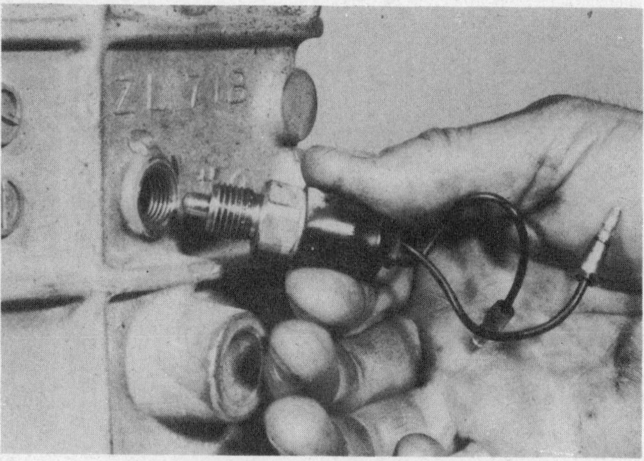

4.4 Electrical switches can be removed from the transmission by unscrewing them

Initial disassembly

1 With the transmission removed, thoroughly clean the exterior of the cases.
2 Remove the rubber dust boot from the withdrawal lever opening in the clutch bellhousing.
3 Remove the release bearing and hub together with the withdrawal lever (Chapter 8).
4 Remove the reverse light switch, neutral switch, top gear switch, and/or overdrive gear switch, as equipped **(see illustration)**.
5 On 2WD models, remove the screw that retains the speedometer gear to the rear extension housing and lift out the gear **(see illustration)**.
6 Pry off the E-ring from the stopper guide pin and drive out the pin **(see illustration)**.
7 Remove the return spring plug, and lift out the return spring and plunger **(see illustration)**.
8 Remove the two screws that retain the reverse check cover to the housing and lift out the reverse check sleeve **(see illustration)**.
9 Unscrew the bolts, and separate the rear extension housing from the main transmission case, using a soft-faced hammer **(see illustrations)**.

4.5 Remove the bolt and withdraw the speedometer gear assembly

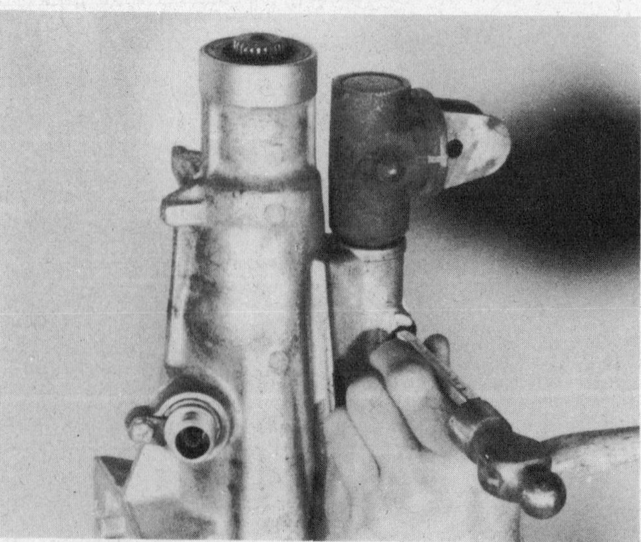

4.6 Use a punch to drive out the stopper guide

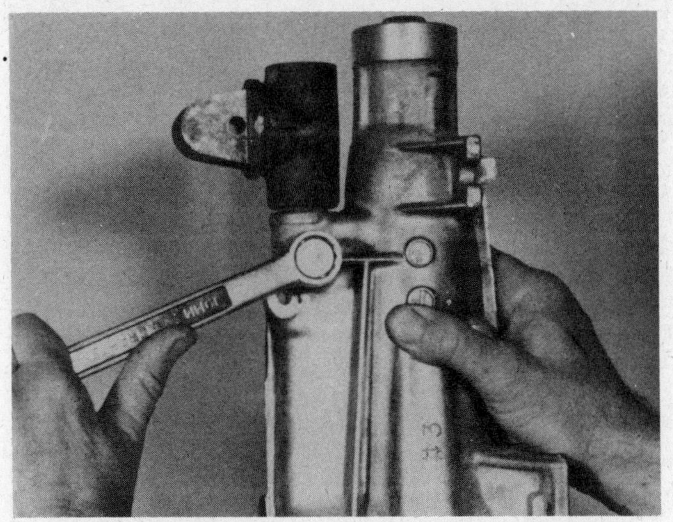

4.7 Use a wrench to unscrew the return spring plug

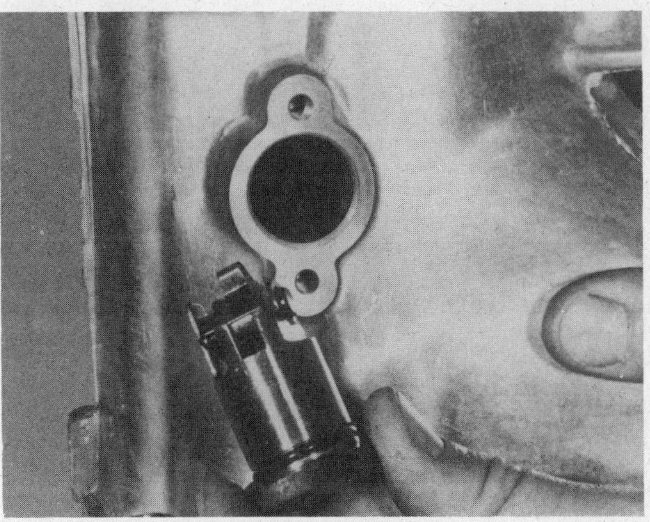

4.8 Remove the two bolts and withdraw the reverse check sleeve

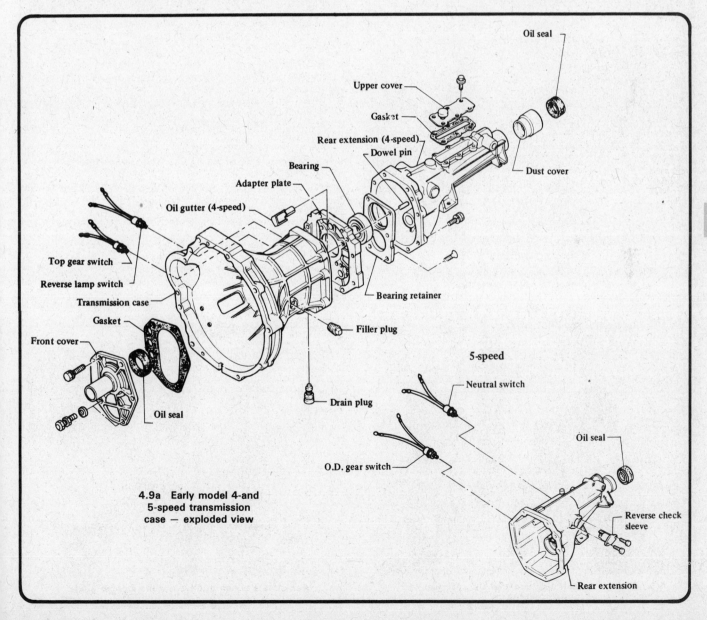

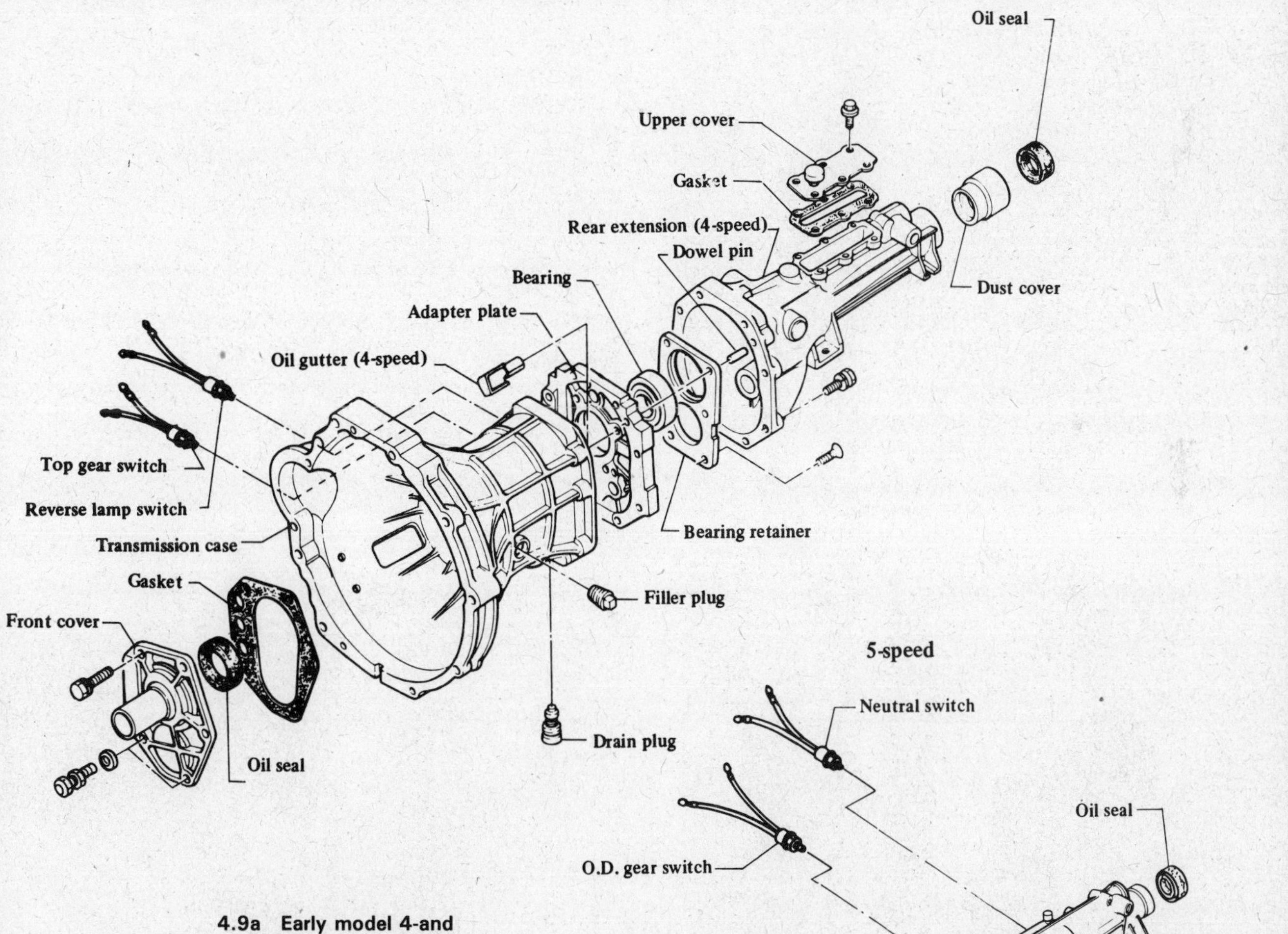

4.9a Early model 4-and 5-speed transmission case – exploded view

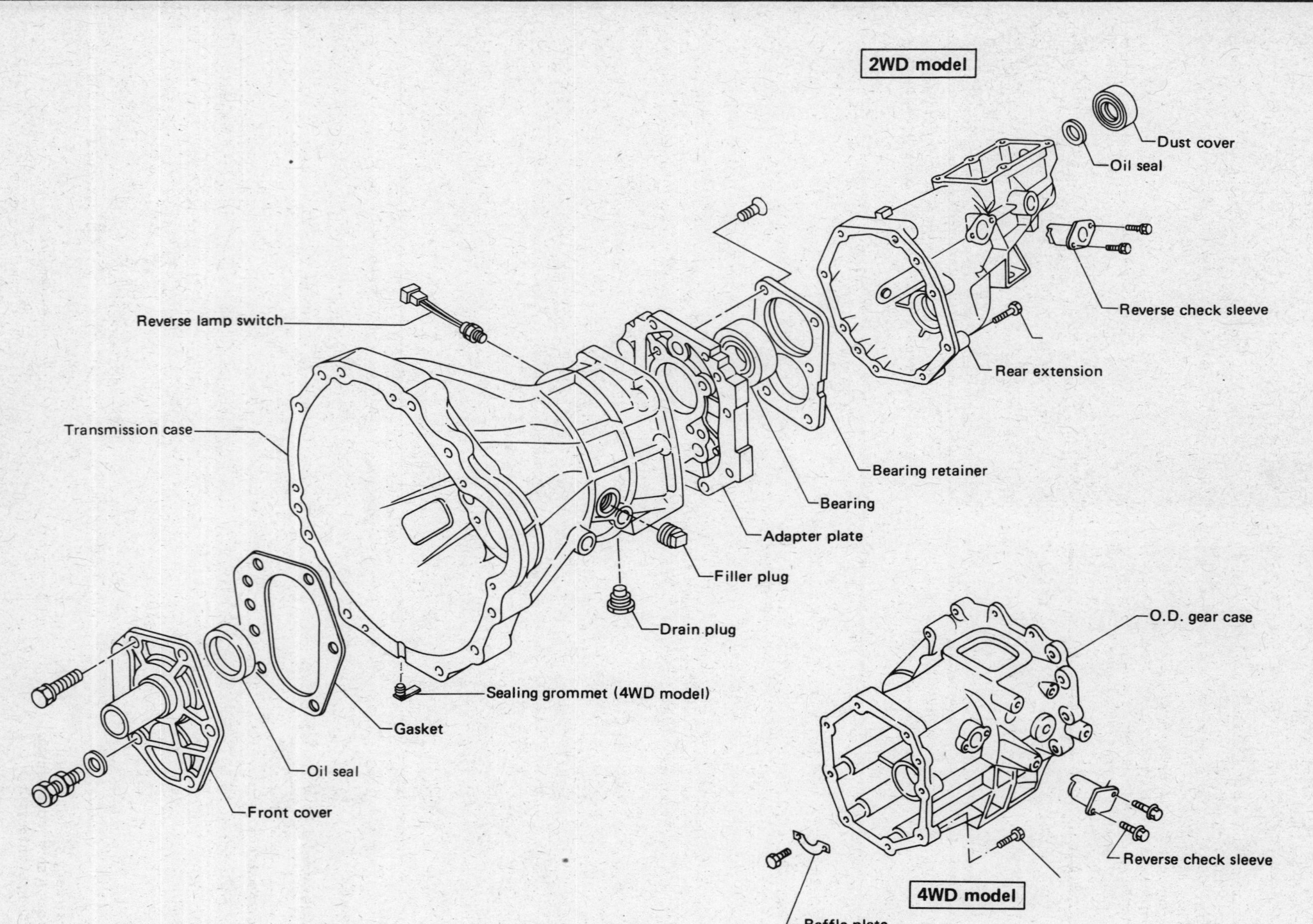

4.9b Later model 5-speed FS5W71B/C transmission case details

10 Unscrew and remove the front cover retaining bolts: remove the front cover and extract the countershaft bearing shim and the input shaft bearing snap-ring **(see illustration)**.
11 Drive off the one-piece bellhousing/transmission case from the adaptor plate.
12 Make up a suitable plate and bolt it to the transmission adaptor plate and then secure the support plate in a vise.
13 Drive out the securing pins from each of the shift forks, using a suitable thin drift **(see illustration)**.
14 Unscrew and remove the three detent ball-plugs.
15 Withdraw the selector rods from the adaptor plate **(see illustrations)**.
16 Catch the shift forks, and extract the balls and springs as the selector rods are withdrawn. The four smaller balls are the interlock balls.

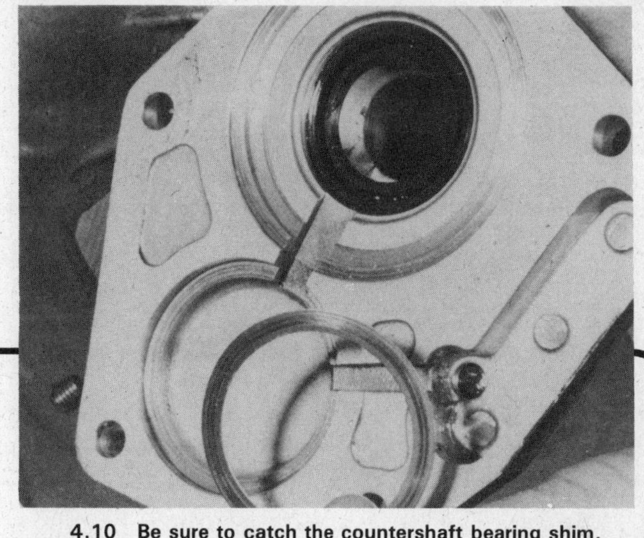

4.10 Be sure to catch the countershaft bearing shim, which will drop out when the front cover is removed

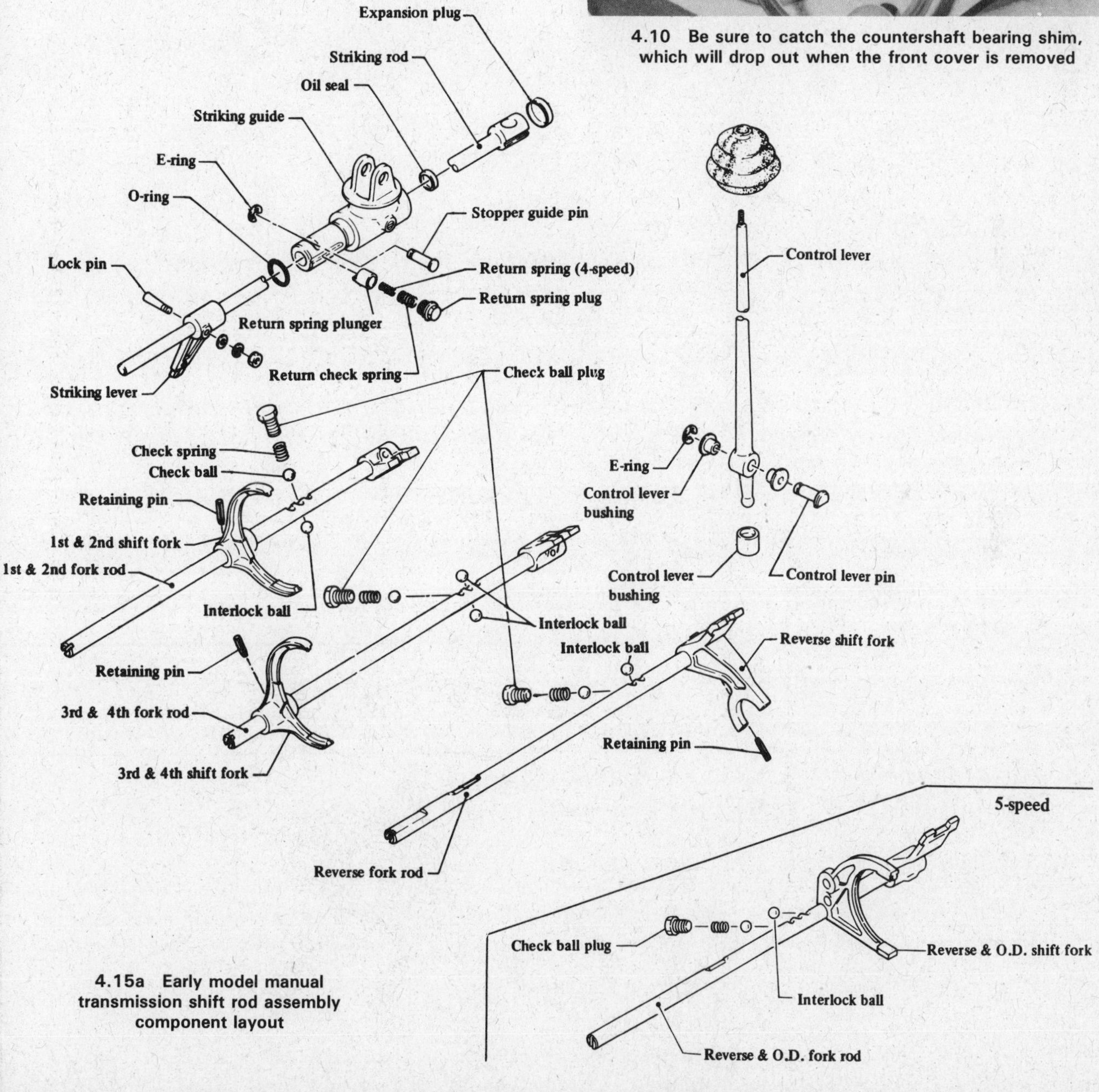

Expansion plug
Striking rod
Oil seal
Striking guide
E-ring
O-ring
Stopper guide pin
Lock pin
Return spring (4-speed)
Return spring plug
Return spring plunger
Return check spring
Striking lever
Check ball plug
Control lever
Check spring
Check ball
Retaining pin
1st & 2nd shift fork
1st & 2nd fork rod
E-ring
Control lever bushing
Control lever bushing
Control lever pin
Interlock ball
Interlock ball
Interlock ball
Reverse shift fork
Retaining pin
3rd & 4th fork rod
3rd & 4th shift fork
Retaining pin
Reverse fork rod
5-speed
Check ball plug
Reverse & O.D. shift fork
Interlock ball
Reverse & O.D. fork rod

4.15a Early model manual transmission shift rod assembly component layout

7A

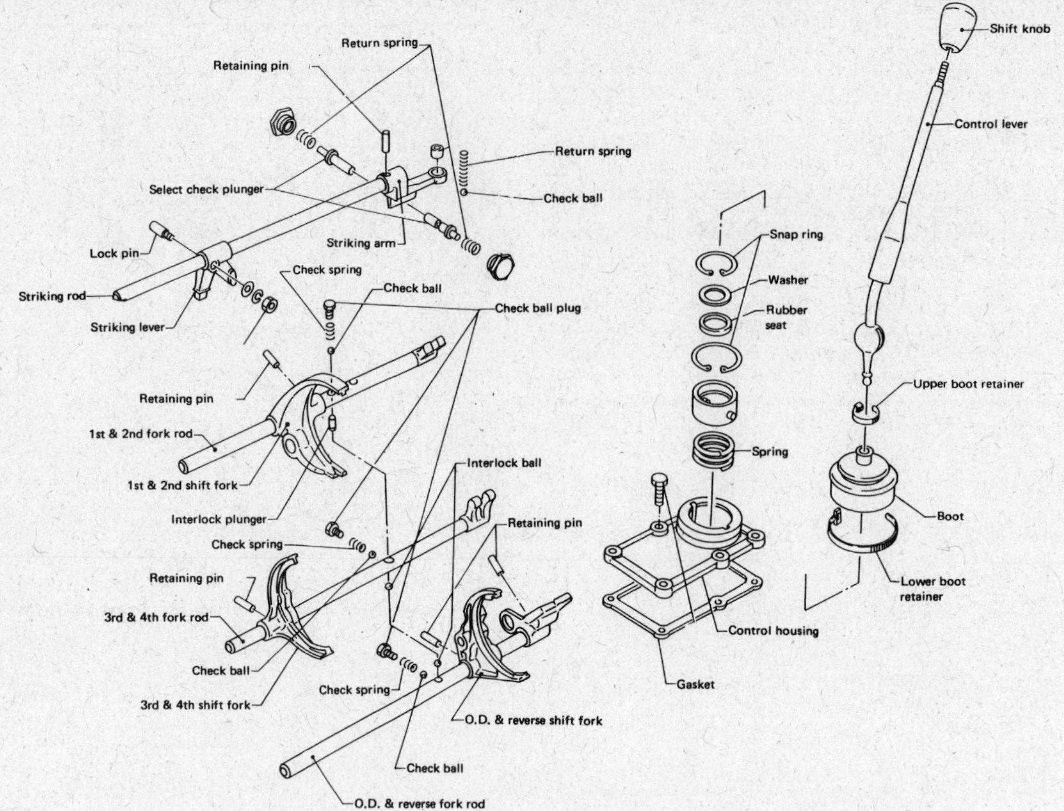

4.15b Later model (prior to 1993) manual transmission shift rod assembly component layout

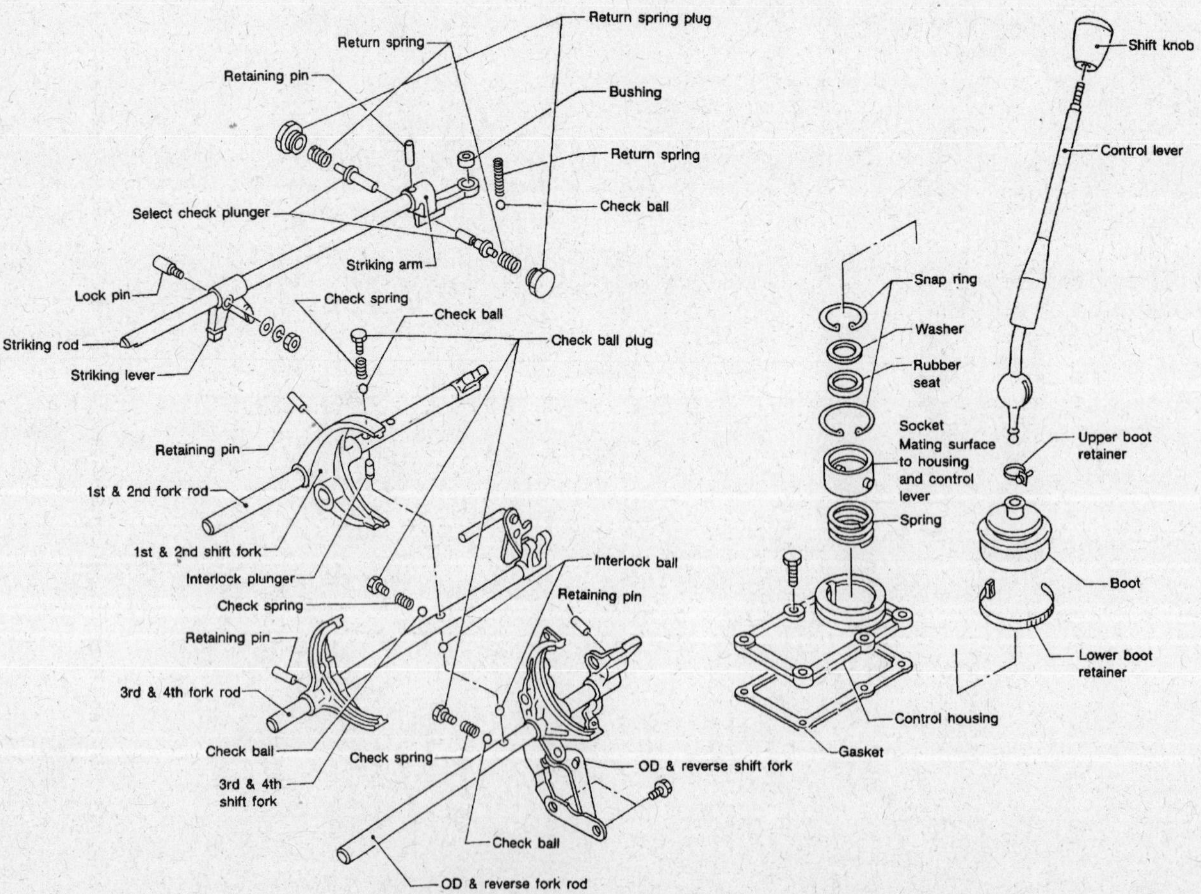

4.15c 1993 and later manual transmission shift rod assembly component layout (2WD models)

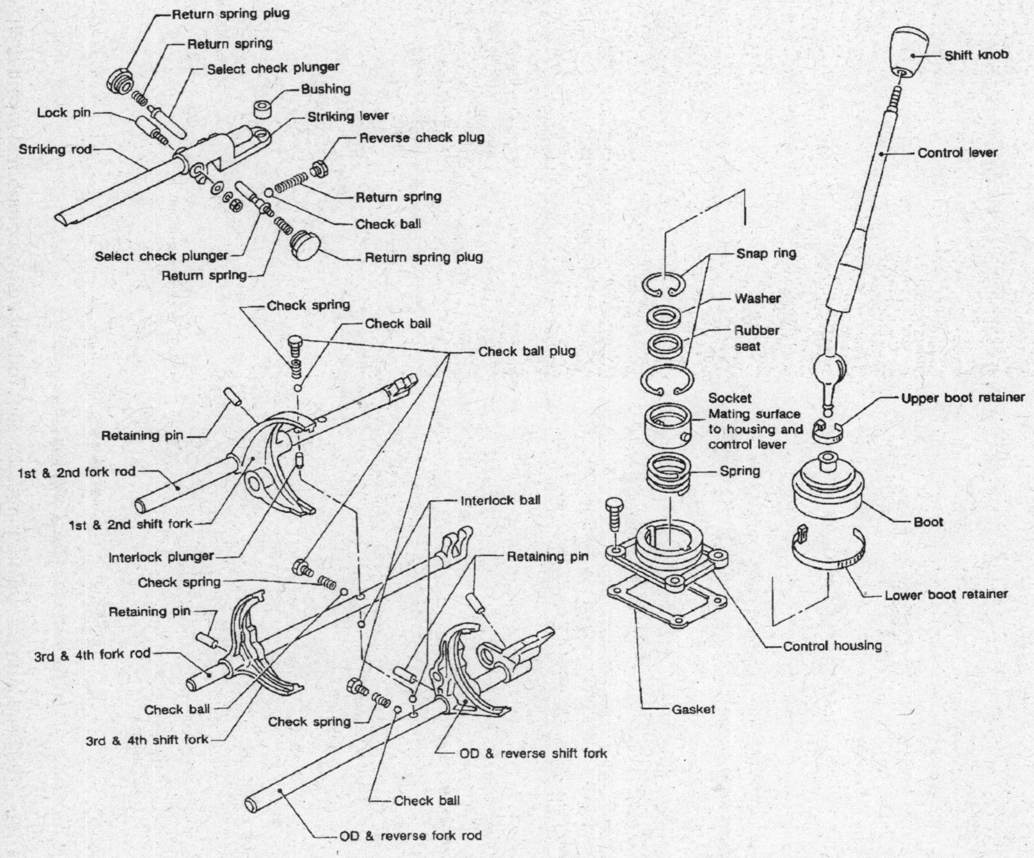

Return spring plug
Return spring
Select check plunger
Bushing
Lock pin
Striking lever
Striking rod
Reverse check plug
Return spring
Check ball
Select check plunger
Return spring plug
Return spring
Check spring
Check ball
Check ball plug
Retaining pin
1st & 2nd fork rod
1st & 2nd shift fork
Interlock ball
Interlock plunger
Retaining pin
Check spring
Retaining pin
3rd & 4th fork rod
Check ball
Check spring
3rd & 4th shift fork
OD & reverse shift fork
Check ball
OD & reverse fork rod
Shift knob
Control lever
Snap ring
Washer
Rubber seat
Socket
Mating surface to housing and control lever
Upper boot retainer
Spring
Boot
Lower boot retainer
Control housing
Gasket

4.15d 1993 and later manual transmission shift rod assembly component layout (4WD models)

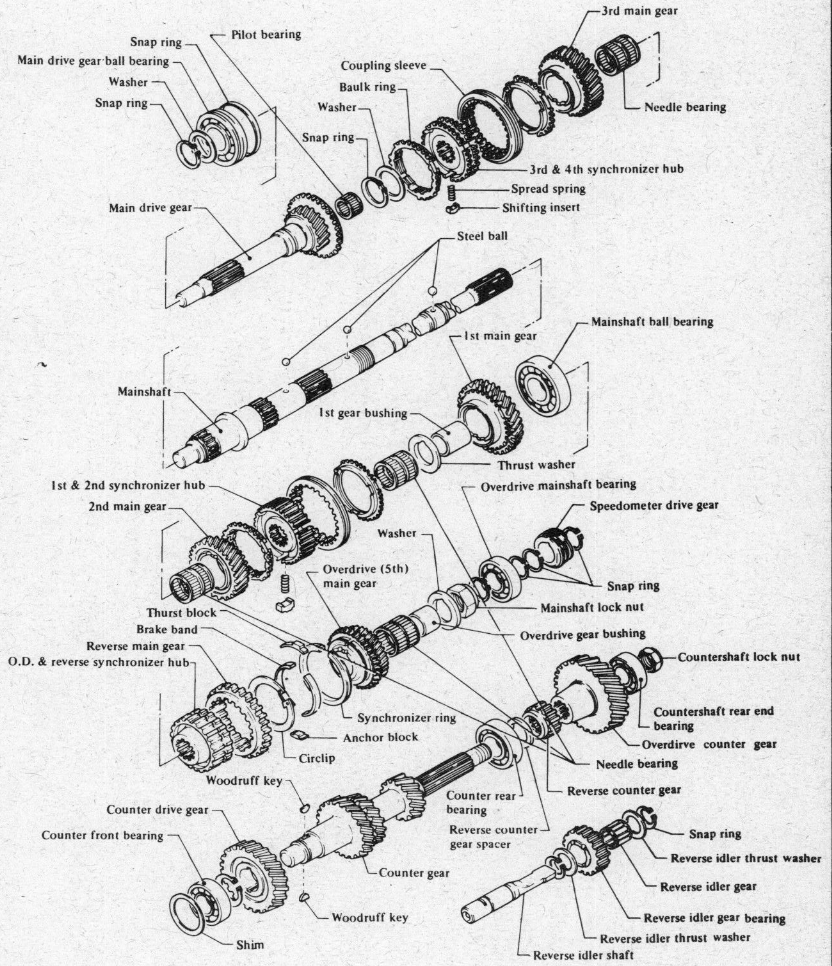

3rd main gear
Snap ring
Pilot bearing
Main drive gear ball bearing
Coupling sleeve
Washer
Baulk ring
Snap ring
Washer
Needle bearing
Snap ring
3rd & 4th synchronizer hub
Spread spring
Main drive gear
Shifting insert
Steel ball
Mainshaft ball bearing
1st main gear
Mainshaft
1st gear bushing
Thrust washer
1st & 2nd synchronizer hub
Overdrive mainshaft bearing
2nd main gear
Speedometer drive gear
Washer
Overdrive (5th) main gear
Snap ring
Thrust block
Mainshaft lock nut
Brake band
Overdrive gear bushing
Reverse main gear
O.D. & reverse synchronizer hub
Countershaft lock nut
Countershaft rear end bearing
Synchronizer ring
Anchor block
Overdirve counter gear
Circlip
Needle bearing
Woodruff key
Reverse counter gear
Counter rear bearing
Counter drive gear
Reverse counter gear spacer
Counter front bearing
Snap ring
Reverse idler thrust washer
Counter gear
Reverse idler gear
Woodruff key
Reverse idler gear bearing
Shim
Reverse idler thrust washer
Reverse idler shaft

4.17a 1980 model FS5W71B/C 5-speed transmission gears and shafts – exploded view

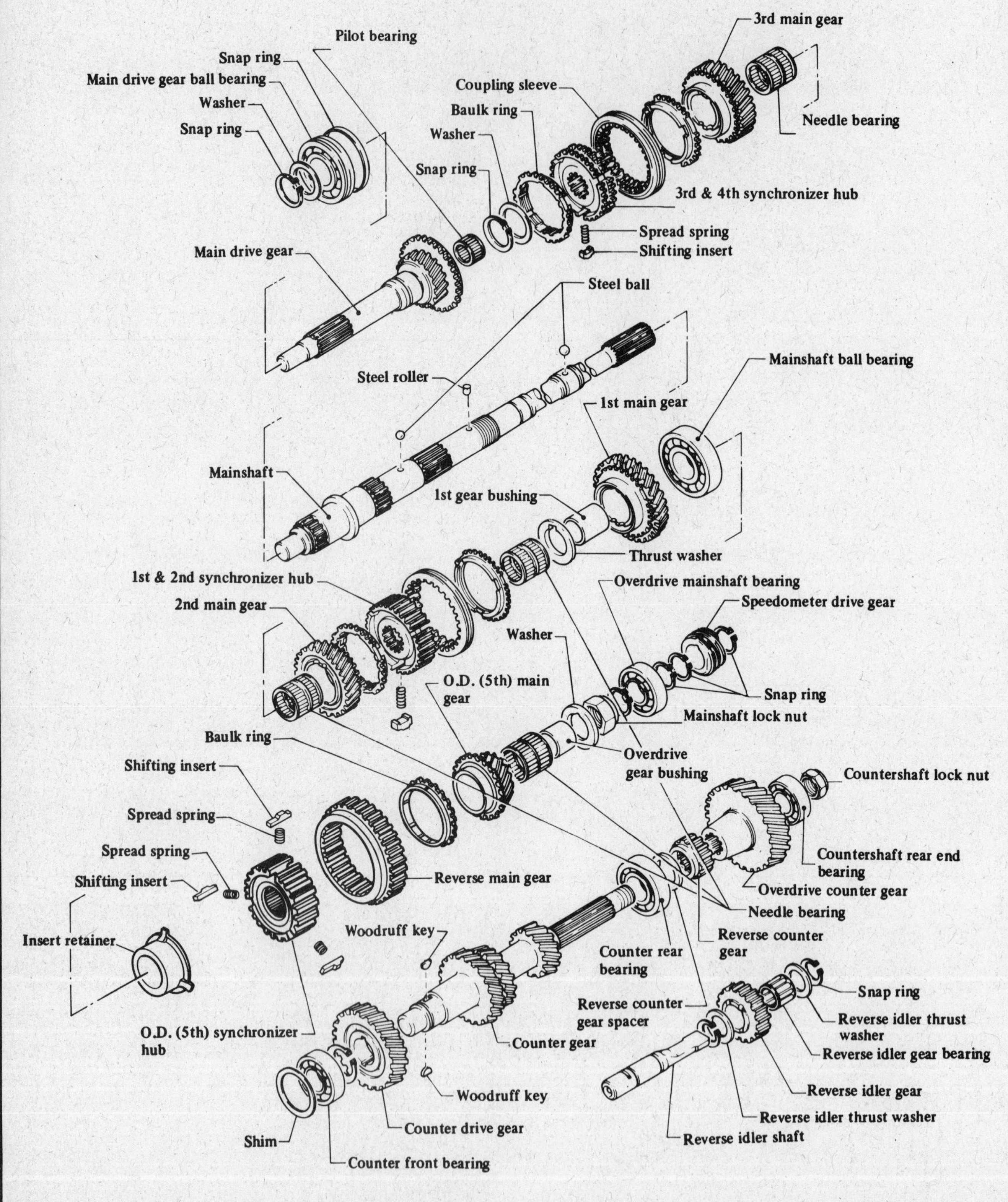

3rd main gear
Pilot bearing
Snap ring
Main drive gear ball bearing
Coupling sleeve
Washer
Baulk ring
Snap ring
Washer
Needle bearing
Snap ring
3rd & 4th synchronizer hub
Spread spring
Shifting insert
Main drive gear
Steel ball
Mainshaft ball bearing
Steel roller
1st main gear
Mainshaft
1st gear bushing
Thrust washer
1st & 2nd synchronizer hub
Overdrive mainshaft bearing
2nd main gear
Speedometer drive gear
Washer
O.D. (5th) main gear
Snap ring
Mainshaft lock nut
Baulk ring
Overdrive gear bushing
Shifting insert
Countershaft lock nut
Spread spring
Spread spring
Countershaft rear end bearing
Shifting insert
Reverse main gear
Overdrive counter gear
Needle bearing
Woodruff key
Insert retainer
Reverse counter gear
Counter rear bearing
Snap ring
Reverse counter gear spacer
Reverse idler thrust washer
O.D. (5th) synchronizer hub
Counter gear
Reverse idler gear bearing
Woodruff key
Reverse idler gear
Reverse idler thrust washer
Counter drive gear
Shim
Reverse idler shaft
Counter front bearing

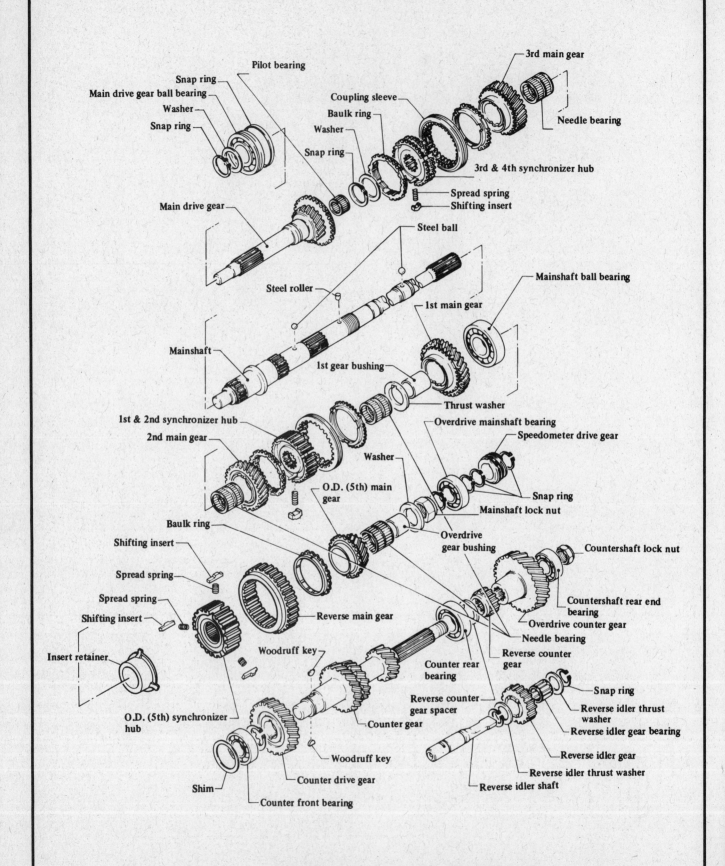

4.17b Later model (prior to 1993) FS5W71B/C 5-speed transmission gears and shafts – exploded view

4.17c 1993 and later 5S5W71/C five-speed transmission gears and shafts – exploded view

4.17d F4W71B/C 4-speed transmission gears and shafts – exploded view

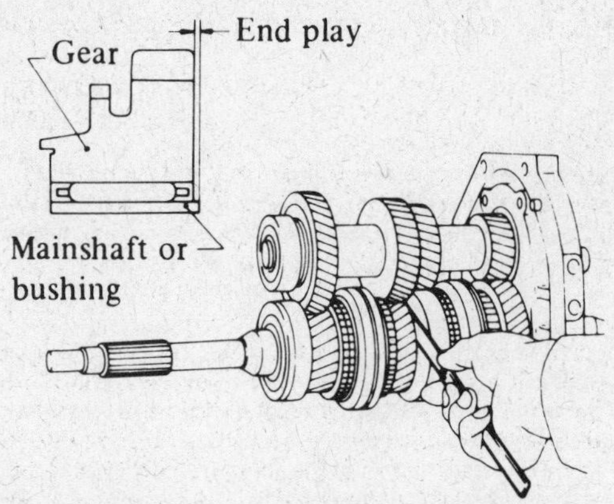

4.18 Measure the gear endplay before and after disassembling the transmission to check for wear and to make sure of proper assembly

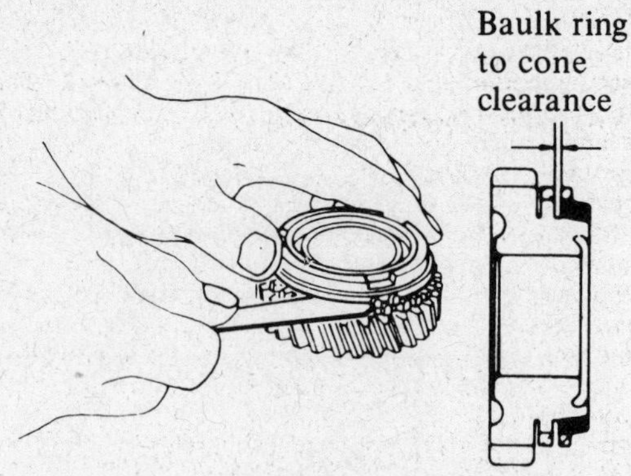

4.38 Check the baulk ring for wear by mating it with its gear and measuring the gap with a feeler gauge

17 At this point, inspect the gears and shafts for any wear, chipping or cracking **(see illustrations)**.

18 Also, use a feeler gauge between each mainshaft gear to determine the amount of gear endplay that exists **(see illustration)**. The standard end play is listed in the Specifications.

19 If the gear endplay is not within specifications or if the gears or shafts show signs of wear or damage, the gear assemblies should be disassembled and the defective parts replaced.

20 Lock the gears and draw the front bearing off the countershaft with a bearing puller.

21 Extract the now exposed snap-ring from the countershaft.

22 Withdraw the countershaft gear together with the input shaft. Take care not to drop the needle roller bearing which is located on the front of the mainshaft.

23 Extract the snap-ring from the front end of the mainshaft, followed by the thrust washer.

24 Withdraw 3rd/4th synchronizer unit followed by 3rd gear.

25 Both the mainshaft nut and the countershaft nuts are staked to prevent them from loosening. Use a hammer and punch to pull up the staked area.

26 Remove the reverse counter gear and spacer.

27 Use a gear puller to remove the countershaft overdrive gear and bearing.

28 Remove the countershaft nut. Once removed, this nut should not be reused.

29 Remove the snap-ring from the reverse idler shaft and remove the reverse idler gear.

30 Remove the snap-ring that retains the speedometer gear to the mainshaft, and remove the speedometer gear and steel ball.

31 Remove the other two snap-rings from behind the speedometer gear and withdraw the overdrive mainshaft bearing.

32 Drive out the staking on the mainshaft nut and remove it. Once removed, this nut should not be reused.

33 Remove the thrust washer, overdrive gear bushing, needle bearing, overdrive gear, reverse main gear, overdrive synchronizer assembly and insert retainer, as equipped.

34 Drive the mainshaft and countershaft assemblies simultaneously from the adaptor plate, using a soft-faced hammer.

Mainshaft

35 Carefully examine the gears and shaft splines for chipping of the teeth or wear and then dismantle the gear train into its component parts, replacing any worn or damaged items.

36 Examine the shaft itself for scoring or grooving, also the splines for twist, taper or general wear.

37 Examine the synchromesh units for cracks or wear or general looseness in the assembly and replace if evident, particularly if there has been a history of noisy gearshifts or where the synchromesh can be easily 'beaten'.

38 Press the baulk ring tight against the synchromesh cone and measure the gap between the two components. If it is less than specified, replace the components (refer to Specifications and accompanying illustration).

39 When reassembling the synchromesh unit, ensure that the ends of the snap-ring on opposite sides of the units do not engage in the same slot.

40 Begin assembly of the mainshaft by installing the 2nd gear needle bearing, 2nd gear and the baulk ring followed by the 1st/2nd synchromesh unit, noting carefully the direction of installation.

41 Now install the 1st gear baulk ring, needle bearing, steel ball, thrust washer, bushing and 1st gear. Be sure the steel ball is well greased when installed.

Countershaft

42 The countershaft front bearing was removed at the time of dismantling the transmission into major units.

43 The countershaft rear bearing was left in position in the adaptor plate.

44 Withdraw the countershaft drive gear and extract the two Woodruff keys.

45 Check all components for wear, especially the gear teeth and shaft splines for chipping. Reinstall the Woodruff keys and the snap-ring.

46 Reassembly is a reversal of dismantling.

Input shaft (main drive gear)

47 Remove the snap-ring and spacer.

48 Withdraw the bearing using a two-legged puller or a press. Once removed (by means of its outer race), discard the bearing.

49 Press the new bearing onto the shaft, applying pressure to the center race only.

50 Reinstall the washer.

51 Several thickness of snap-rings are available for the main input shaft bearing, as listed in the Specifications. Choose a size that will eliminate bearing endplay.

Oil seals

52 Pry out the oil seal from the rear extension and drive in a new one, with the seal lips facing inwards.

53 Reinstall the speedometer pinion sleeve O-ring seal.

54 Reinstall the oil seal in the front cover by prying out the old one and driving in a new one, with an appropriate sized socket.

Rear extension housing

55 Loosen the nut on the end of the striking rod lock pin, until it is half off the threads.

56 Using the nut as a guide, drive the lock pin from the striking rod with a punch **(see illustration)**.

57 Slide the striking lever from the striking rod, and withdraw the rod from the rear of the housing.

58 Check the rod and lever for wear or damage and replace if necessary. Replace the O-ring on the striking rod.

59 Inspect the bushing in the rear of the extension housing. If this bushing is worn or cracked, the entire rear extension housing must be replaced.

60 Reinstall the striking rod assembly by reversing the removal procedure.

Reassembly

61 Before beginning to reassemble the transmission, the mainshaft and countershaft adaptor plate bearings should be removed, examined and replaced if worn. To do this, unscrew the six screws which retain the bearing retainer plate to the adaptor plate. The use of an impact driver will probably be required for this operation.
62 With the bearing retainer plate removed, press the mainshaft and counter shaft bearings from the adaptor plate. Apply pressure only to the outer races of the bearings.
63 Check the bearings for wear by first washing them in clean solvent and drying with the air from a tire pump. Spin them with the fingers and if they are noisy or loose in operation, replace them with new ones.
64 Check that the dowel pin and oil trough are correctly positioned on the adaptor plate.
65 Tap the mainshaft bearing lightly and squarely into position in the adaptor plate.
66 Drive the reverse idler shaft into the adaptor plate so that 2/3 of its length is projecting rearwards. Ensure that the cutout in the shaft is positioned to receive the edge of the bearing retainer plate.
67 Install the bearing retainer plate and tighten the screws to the specified torque.
68 Stake each screw in two places to prevent them from loosening.
69 Tap the countershaft rear bearing into position in the adaptor plate.
70 Press the mainshaft assembly into position in the bearing in the adaptor plate. Support the rear of the bearing center track during this operation.
71 Press the countershaft assembly into position in the bearing in the adaptor plate. Again support the rear of the bearing center race during this operation.
72 Install the needle bearing, 3rd gear, baulk ring and the 3rd/4th synchromesh unit to the front of the mainshaft.
73 Install the thrust washer, and then choose a snap-ring from the sizes listed in the Specifications that will minimize endplay.
74 Insert the needle pilot bearing in its recess at the end of the input shaft.
75 Mesh the countershaft drivegear with the 4th gear on the input shaft. Push the drivegear and input shaft onto the countershaft and mainshaft simultaneously, but a piece of tubing will be needed to drive the countershaft gear into position while supporting the rear end of the countershaft.
76 Select a countershaft drivegear snap-ring from the sizes listed in the Specifications, so that the gear endplay will be minimized.
77 Using an appropriate sized socket, drive the front bearing onto the countershaft.
78 Install the reverse counter gear spacer onto the rear of the countershaft.
79 Install the snap-ring, thrust washer, needle bearing, reverse idler gear, reverse idler thrust washer and rear snap-ring onto the reverse idler shaft.
80 Onto the rear side of the mainshaft, install the insert retainer (if equipped), sychronizer assembly, reverse gear, overdrive gear bushing, needle bearing and baulk ring.
81 Install the reverse counter gear on the countershaft.
82 Mesh the overdrive gear with the overdrive counter gear and install them on their respective shafts with the overdrive gear on the mainshaft and the overdrive counter gear on the countershaft.
83 Apply grease to the steel ball and install it and the thrust washer onto the rear of the mainshaft.
84 Install a new locknut onto the rear of the mainshaft and torque it to specifications. **Note:** *In order to accurately tighten the nut to its torque specifications, a wrench adapter should be used as shown in the accompanying illustration. Used with the adaptor, the torque reading on the wrench will not be accurate and should be converted to the correct torque by referring to the chart shown* **(see illustration).**
85 Install the countershaft rear end bearing onto the countershaft **(see illustration).**

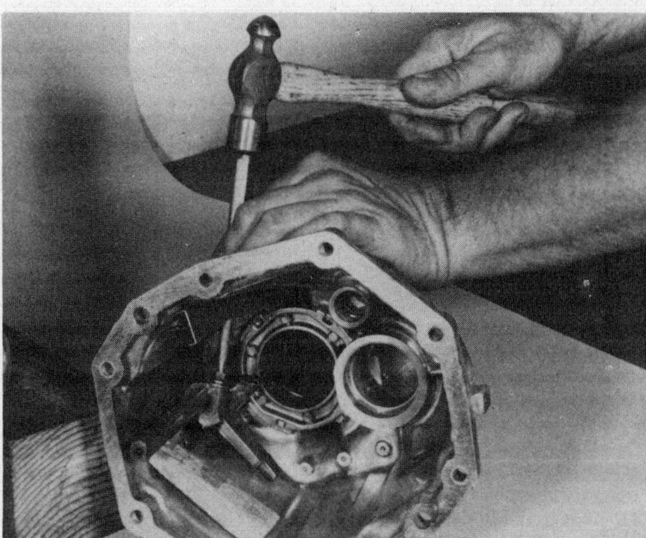

4.56 Use a hammer and long punch to drive out the striking rod lock pin

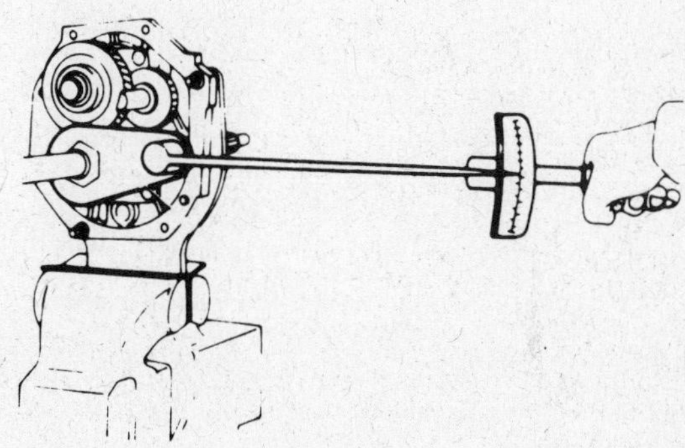

4.84 Lock the mainshaft shaft with an adapter such as the one shown before tightening the locknut with a torque wrench

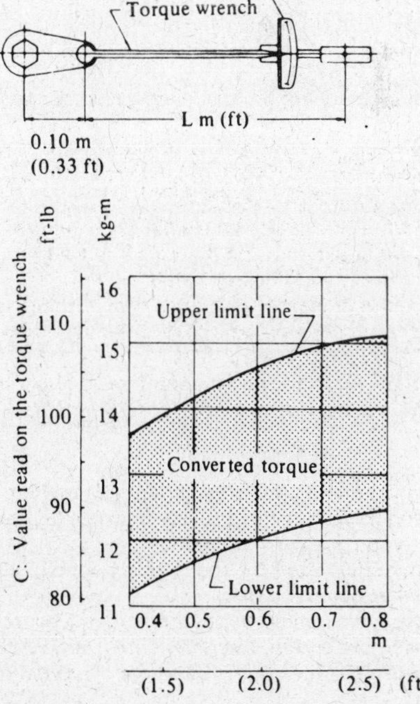

4.85 When tightening the mainshaft locknut, the true torque can be found by matching the torque reading on the wrench with the chart above

7A

86 Install the countershaft locknut and torque it to specifications.
87 Use a hammer and punch to stake both the mainshaft and countershaft lock nuts so they engage the groves in their respective shafts.
88 Once again measure the gear endplay, as described in Paragraph 18.
89 Fit a snap-ring onto the mainshaft and then install the overdrive mainshaft bearing.
90 Use a snap-ring from the sizes listed in the Specifications to eliminate endplay of the mainshaft rear bearing.
91 Install the next snap-ring, then grease the steel ball and install the ball and the speedometer drivegear onto the mainshaft. Finally install the last snap-ring.
92 Locate the 1st/2nd shift fork onto the 1st/2nd synchronizer unit, (the long end of the shift fork must be towards the countershaft). Now locate the 3rd/4th shift fork onto the 3rd/4th synchronizer unit, (the long end of the shift fork must be the opposite side to the 1st/2nd shift fork).
93 Locate the overdrive reverse shift fork onto the overdrive synchronizer so that the upper rod hole is in line with the 3rd/4th shift fork.
94 Slide the 1st/2nd selector rod through the adapter plate and into the 1st/2nd shift fork; align the hole in the rod with the hole in the fork and drive in a new retaining pin.
95 Align the notch in the 1st/2nd selector rod with the detent (check) ball bore, then install the detent (check) ball, spring and screw in the detent ball plug. Apply a little thread sealant to the detent ball plug.
96 Now invert the adapter plate assembly (hold the 3rd/4th and OD reverse shift forks in position) so that the check ball plug assembled at Paragraph 95, is lowermost. Drop two interlock balls into the 3rd/4th detent ball plug hole and, using a suitable thin probe, push them up against the 1st/2nd selector rod (if the adaptor plate is correctly positioned, the interlock balls will drop into position). Slide the 3rd/4the selector rod through the upper hole of the OD/reverse shift fork and the adaptor plate, ensuring that the interlock balls are held between this selector rod and the 1st/2nd selector rod, and into the 3rd/4th shift fork. Align the holes in the shift fork and selector rod and drive in a new retaining pin. Now install a detent ball, spring and detent all plug (with thread sealant applied) to the 3rd/4th detent ball plug bore. Ensure that the notch in the 3rd/4th selector rod is aligned with the detent ball plug before assembling the detent ball.
97 Drop two interlock balls into the remaining detent ball plug bore, ensuring that they locate against the 3rd/4th selector rod. Slide the overdrive/reverse selector rod through the overdrive reverse shift fork and into the adaptor plate. Ensure that the two interlock balls are held in position between the 3rd/4th selector rod and the overdrive/reverse selector rod, sliding the overdrive/reverse selector rod into the adaptor plate until the notch in the selector rod aligns with the detent ball plug bore. Insert the detent ball, spring and detent ball plug as before. Drive in a new retaining pin to retain the overdrive/reverse shift fork to the overdrive/reverse selector rod.
98 Finally, tighten the three detent ball plugs to the specified torque.
99 Thoroughly oil the entire assembly and check to see that the selector rods operate correctly and smoothly.
100 Clean the mating faces of the adaptor plate and the transmission casing and apply sealant to both surfaces.
101 Tap the transmission casing into position on the adaptor plate using a soft-faced hammer, taking particular care that it engages correctly with the input shaft bearing and countershaft front bearing.
102 Fit the outer snap-ring to the input shaft bearing.
103 Clean the mating faces of the adaptor plate and rear extension housing and apply gasket sealant.
104 Arrange the shift forks in their neutral mode and then lower the rear extension housing onto the adaptor plate so that the striking lever engages correctly with the selector rods.
105 Install the bolts which secure the sections of the transmission together and tighten them to the specified torque.
106 Measure the amount by which the countershaft front bearing protrudes from the transmission casing front face **(see illustration)**. Use feeler blades for this and then select the appropriate shims after reference to the following table:

Measurement	*Shim (thickness)*
0.1150 to 0.1185 in (2.92 to 3.01 mm) . . .	*0.0236 in (0.6mm)*
0.1189 to 0.1124 in (3.02 to 3.11 mm) . . .	*0.0197 in (0.5 mm)*
0.1228 to 0.1264 in (3.12 to 3.21 mm) . . .	*0.0157 in (0.4mm)*
0.1268 to 0.1303 in (3.22 to 3.31 mm) . . .	*0.0118 in (0.3mm)*
0.1307 to 0.1343 in (3.32 to 3.41 mm) . . .	*0.0079 in (0.2 mm)*
0.1346 to 0.1382 in (3.42 to 3.51 mm) . . .	*0.0039 in (0.1 mm)*

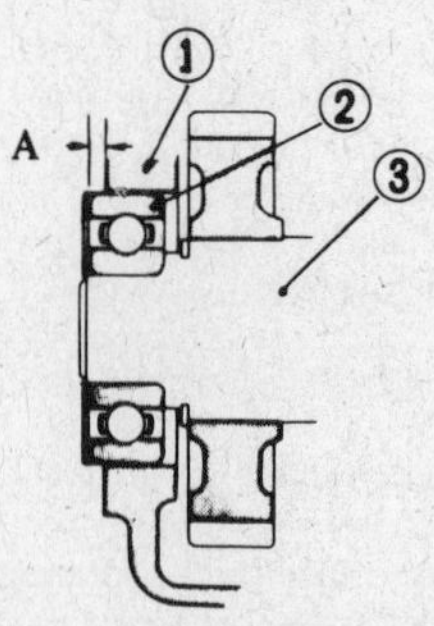

4.106 Measurement (A) for selection of the countershaft front bearing shim

1 Transmission case
2 Countergear front bearing
3 Countergear

107 Stick the shim in position using a dab of thick grease, then attach the front cover to the transmission case (within the clutch bellhousing) complete with a new gasket and taking care not to damage the oil seal as it passes over the input shaft splines.
108 Tighten the securing bolts to the specified torque, making sure that the bolt threads are coated with gasket sealant to prevent oil seepage.
109 Complete the reassembly by reversing the steps described in Paragraphs 1 through 8 of this Section.

5 F4W71B/F4W71C 4-speed transmission – overhaul

1 The overhaul procedure for the 4-speed transmission is basically the same as for the 5-speed transmission. The only differences are those noted below.
2 The following procedures should be used in place of Steps 17 thru 34 of Section 4.

a) Inspect the gears and shafts for any wear, chipping or cracking.
b) Use a feeler gauge between each mainshaft gear to determine the amount of gear endplay that exists. The standard endplay for each gear is listed in the Specifications.
c) If the gear endplay is not within specifications, or if the gears or shafts show signs of wear or damage, the gear assemblies should be disassembled and the defective parts replaced.
d) Lock the gears and using a suitable two-legged puller, draw the front bearing from the countershaft.
e) Extract the now exposed snap-ring from the countershaft.
f) Withdraw the countershaft gear together with the input shaft. Take care not to drop the needle roller bearing which is located on the front of the mainshaft.
g) Extract the snap-ring from the front end of the mainshaft, followed by the thrust washer.
h) Withdraw the 3rd/4th synchronizer unit, followed by 3rd gear.
i) Release the mainshaft nut and then loosen it.
j) Remove the mainshaft nut, the thrust washer and reverse gear.
k) Extract the snap-ring from the rear end of the countershaft and remove the reverse counter gear.
l) Drive the mainshaft and countershaft assemblies simultaneously from the adaptor plate, using a soft-faced hammer.

3 The following procedures should be used in place of Steps 78 thru 91 of Section 4.

a) To the rear of the mainshaft, install the reverse gear and the plain washer and screw on the nut, finger-tight.
b) Install the counter reverse gear on the countershaft and use a snap-ring from the thicknesses listed to give minimum endplay.
c) Install the reverse idler gear on the reverse idler shaft.
d) Tighten the mainshaft nut (after locking the gears) to the specified torque.
e) Stake the collar of the nut into the groove of the mainshaft.
f) Once again, measure the gear endplay, as described in Paragraph 2.

6 FS5R30A 5-speed transmission – overhaul

Refer to illustrations 6.3, 6.5, 6.6, 6.9, 6.16, 6.17, 6.19a, 6.19b, 6.35, 6.36, 6.37, 6.38, 6.39, 6.42, 6.43, 6.44 and 6.45

Initial disassembly

1 With the transmission removed (Section 3), thoroughly clean the exterior of the cases.

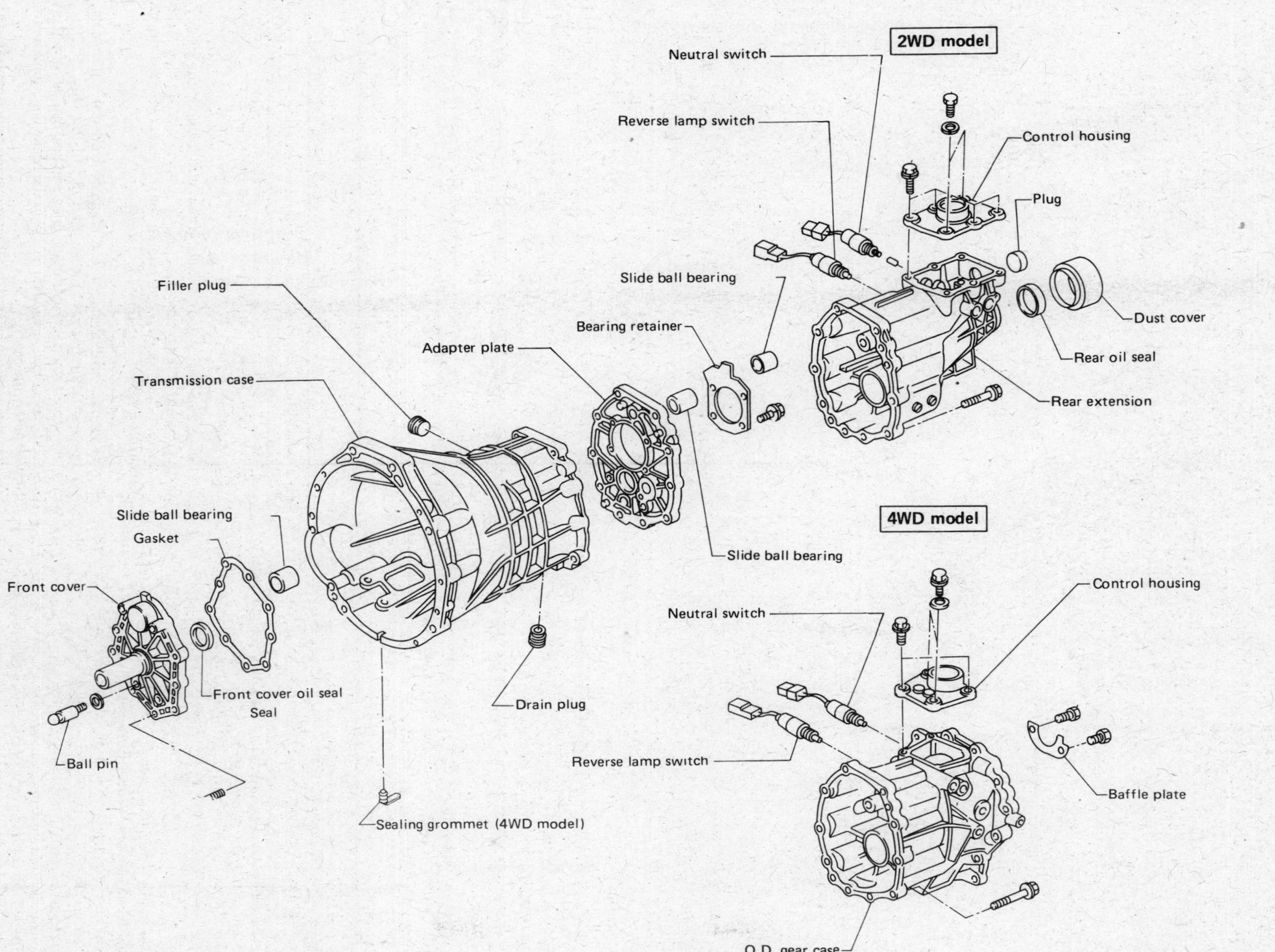

6.3 FS5R30A 5-speed transmission case details

O.D. & reverse fork rod
Check ball plug
Interlock stopper
O-ring
Retaining pin
Striking rod
Check spring
Check ball
Socket
Reverse shift fork
Retaining pin
Select check plug
Retaining pin
Select check spring
Select check plunger
1st & 2nd shift fork
Striking interlock
Striking lever
3rd & 4th shift fork
Stopper ring
Snap ring
Retaining pin
O.D. rod bracket
O.D. shift fork
O.D. fork rod
Control lever knob
Snap ring
Washer
Wave washer
Washer
Snap ring
Spring
Control lever
Upper boot retainer
Boot
Lower boot retainer
Control housing
Bushing
Return spring
Check ball
Reverse check sleeve
O-ring
Select check plug
Select check spring
Select check plunger
Striking arm
Guide plate

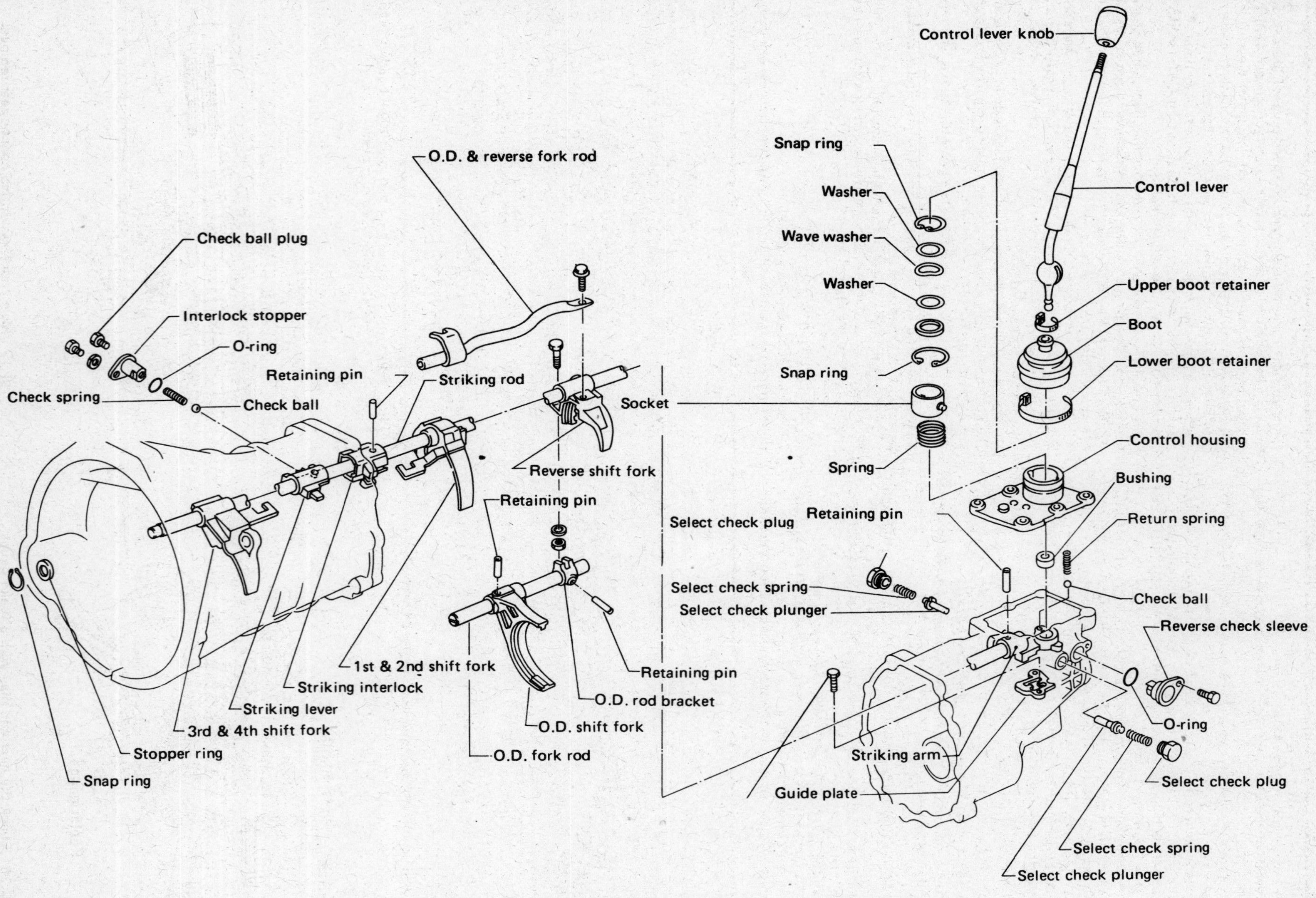

6.6 FS5R30A 5-speed transmission shift assembly details

2 Remove the clutch release assembly.
3 Unscrew the electrical switches from the transmission case **(see illustration)**.
4 With the transmission in Neutral, remove the clamp bolt and lift out the speedometer pinion.
5 Remove the bolts and use a screwdriver to pry the check ball plug, spring and interlock assembly out of the case **(see illustration)**.
6 Remove the shift control housing, return spring and check ball assembly **(see illustration)**.
7 Use a hammer and punch to drive out the striking arm roll pin.
8 Remove the bolts and use a soft faced hammer to tap on the case to separate the extension housing or overdrive gearcase.
9 Remove the bolts and separate the front cover from the case. Remove the stopper ring and use snap-ring pliers to remove the main bearing snap-ring **(see illustration)**.

Adapter plate and mainshaft disassembly

10 Place the case securely in a vise, using blocks of wood or cloth to protect the surface.
11 Remove the overdrive/reverse shift rod.
12 Drive out the striking lever roll pin, using a suitable punch and hammer.
13 Remove the striking rod, striking lever and interlock assembly from the adapter plate.
14 Remove the 1st/2nd, 3rd/4th and reverse shift forks.
15 Drive out the overdrive shift fork using a suitable punch and hammer and remove the rod and shift fork.
16 Use a feeler gauge to measure the gear end play **(see illustration)**. Compare the end play measurements to Specifications. Selective snap-rings (available from a dealer) are used to correct excessive end play. Inspect the mainshaft thrust washers for damage or wear.
17 Remove the reverse coupling sleeve and components from the main countershaft and countergear rear side **(see illustration)**.
18 Remove the rear mainshaft and countergear snap-rings.
19 Use a hammer and suitable punch to remove the C-ring holder and the mainshaft C-rings **(see illustrations)**.
20 Use a suitable gear puller tool to remove the countershaft gear rear bearing and then remove the reverse idler gear and thrust washers.
21 On 2WD models, use a puller tool to remove the mainshaft rear bearing.
22 Remove the reverse main gear, spacer and reverse synchronizer hub, using a puller tool. Remove the reverse gear needle bearings.
23 Use a puller tool to remove the reverse countergear, followed by the overdrive synchronizer.
24 Take the adapter plate to a suitable machine shop to have the mainshaft and countergear removed from the plate using a hydraulic press and suitable adapter tool.
25 Remove the 1st gear washer, steel ball and 1st gear and needle bearing from the mainshaft.
26 Have the 2nd gear, 1st gear bushing and 1st/2nd synchronizer pressed off the mainshaft.
27 Remove the front snap ring from the mainshaft.
28 Have the 3rd gear, the 3rd/4th synchronizer and the 3rd gear needle bearing pressed off the mainshaft.

Countershaft and gear disassembly

29 Remove the sub-gear snap ring.
30 Remove the sub-gear spring, sub-gear and the steel ball from the

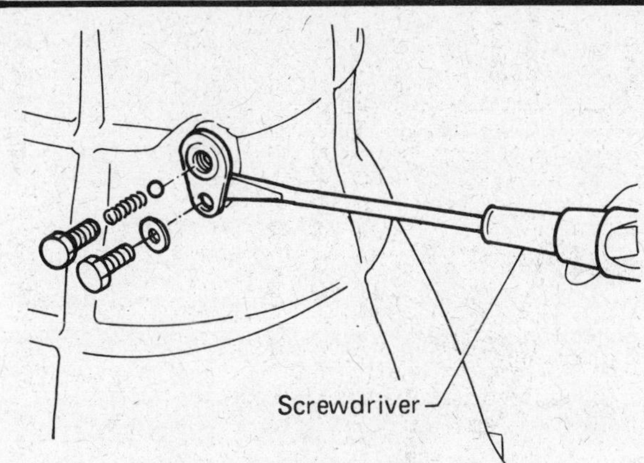

6.5 FS5R30A transmission interlock assembly removal details

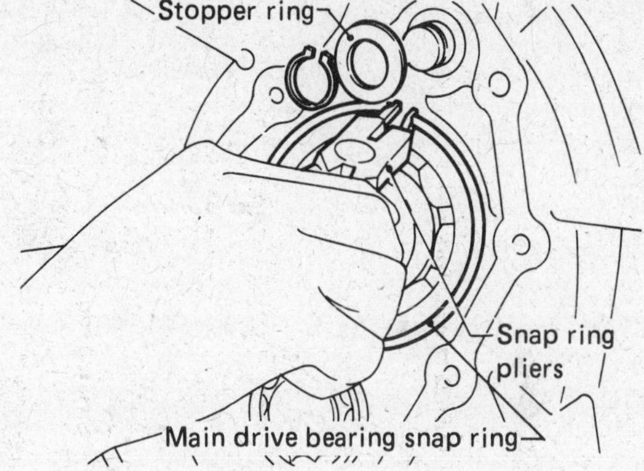

6.9 Remove the stopper ring and main drive bearing snap ring with snap ring pliers

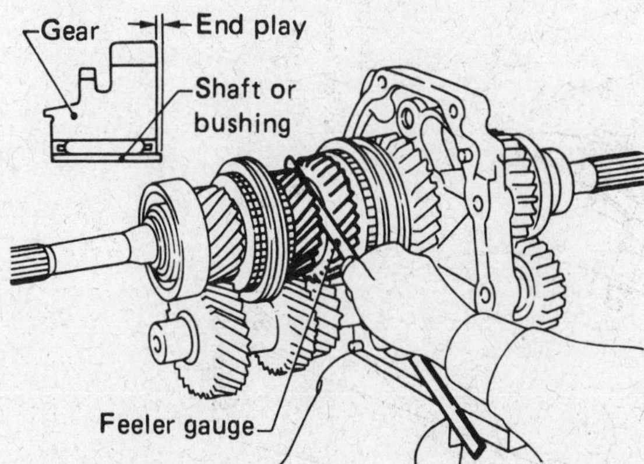

6.16 Check the gear end play with a feeler gauge

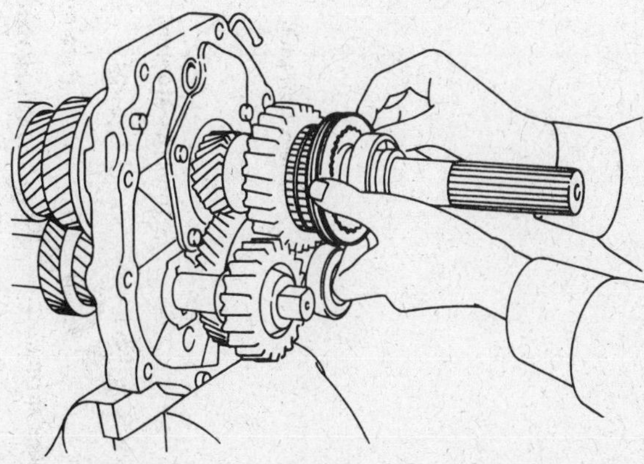

6.17 Main countershaft and countergear removal

7A

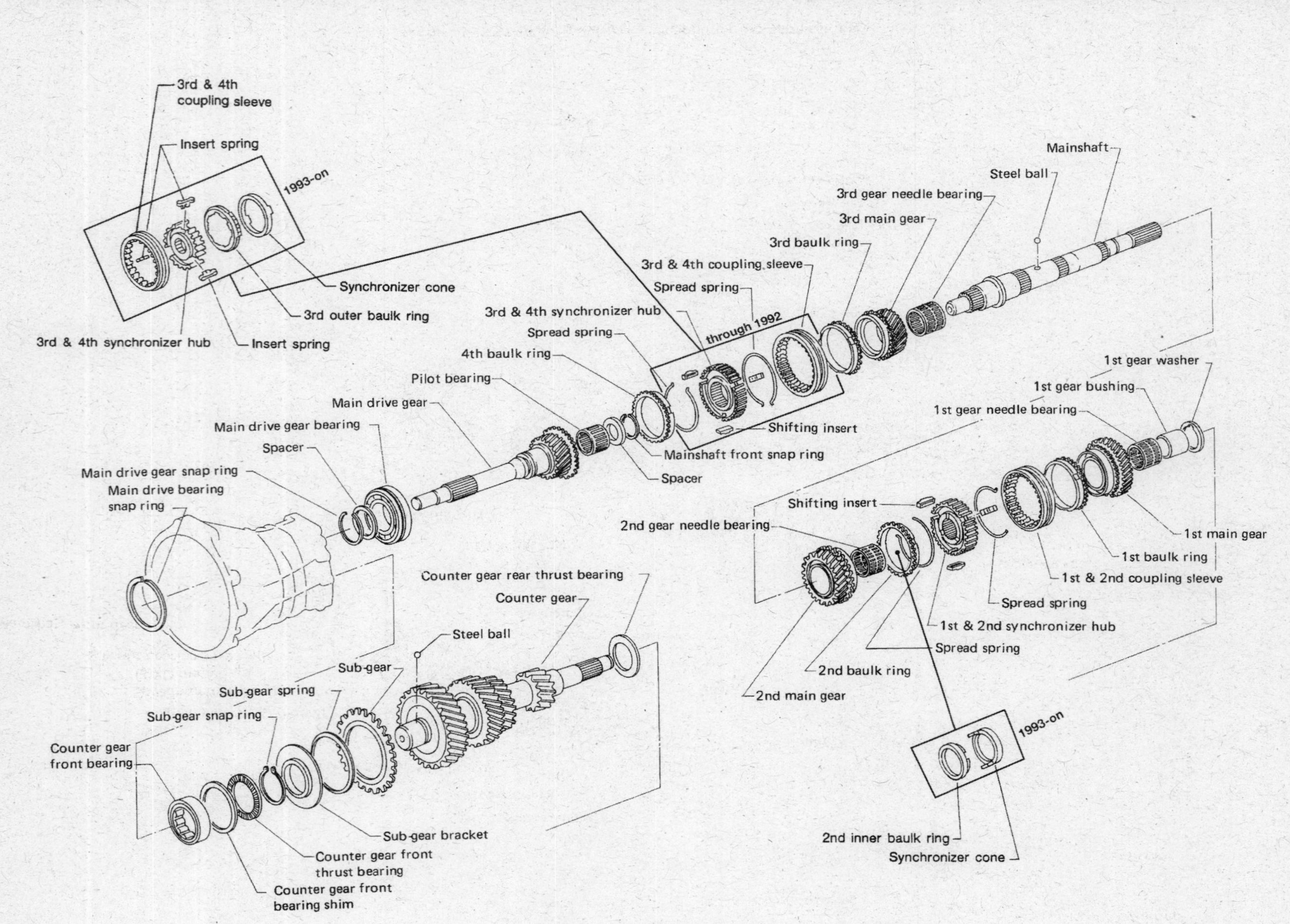

3rd & 4th coupling sleeve
Insert spring
1993-on
Synchronizer cone
3rd outer baulk ring
3rd & 4th synchronizer hub
Insert spring
Mainshaft
Steel ball
3rd gear needle bearing
3rd main gear
3rd baulk ring
3rd & 4th coupling sleeve
Spread spring
3rd & 4th synchronizer hub
through 1992
Spread spring
4th baulk ring
Pilot bearing
Main drive gear
Main drive gear bearing
Spacer
Main drive gear snap ring
Main drive bearing snap ring
Shifting insert
Mainshaft front snap ring
Spacer
1st gear washer
1st gear bushing
1st gear needle bearing
Shifting insert
2nd gear needle bearing
1st main gear
1st baulk ring
1st & 2nd coupling sleeve
Spread spring
1st & 2nd synchronizer hub
Spread spring
2nd baulk ring
2nd main gear
Counter gear rear thrust bearing
Counter gear
Steel ball
Sub-gear
Sub-gear spring
Sub-gear snap ring
Counter gear front bearing
Sub-gear bracket
Counter gear front thrust bearing
Counter gear front bearing shim
1993-on
2nd inner baulk ring
Synchronizer cone

6.19a FS5R30A 5-speed transmission mainshaft and related components — exploded view

C-ring holder
C-ring
Mainshaft rear snap ring
Mainshaft rear bearing
Mainshaft spacer
2WD
Reverse coupling sleeve
Reverse hub
Reverse gear needle bearing
Reverse main gear
4WD
Steel ball (2WD model)
Speedometer drive gear
(2WD model)
Front bearing snap ring
Reverse gear bushing
C-ring
Mainshaft front bearing
O.D. main gear
Mainshaft rear bearing
Mainshaft rear snap ring
O.D. baulk ring
C-ring holder
Reverse baulk ring
Counter gear rear snap ring
Spacer
O.D. coupling sleeve
Counter gear rear end bearing
O.D. counter gear
Reverse counter gear
Reverse cone
Insert spring
O.D. gear needle bearing
O.D. gear bushing
Reverse idler rear thrust washer
Counter gear rear
bearing
Reverse idler needle bearing
Reverse idler gear
Reverse idler front thrust washer
Reverse idler shaft
Retaining pin

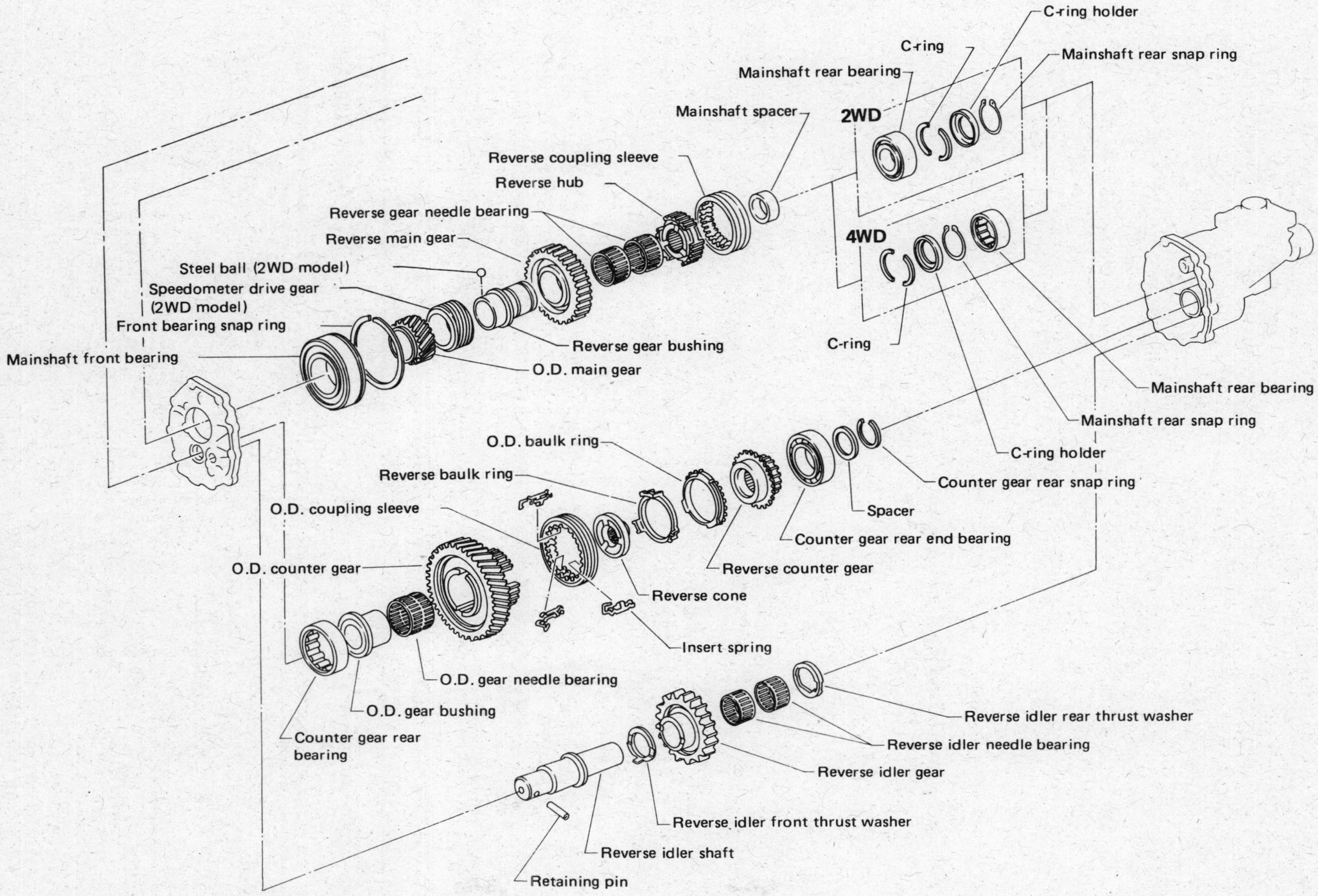

6.19b FS5R30A 5-speed transmission gear component layout

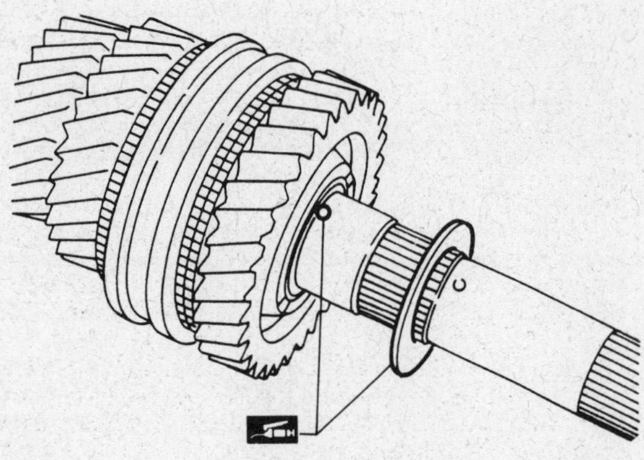

6.35 Lubricate the mainshaft with multipurpose grease at the points shown

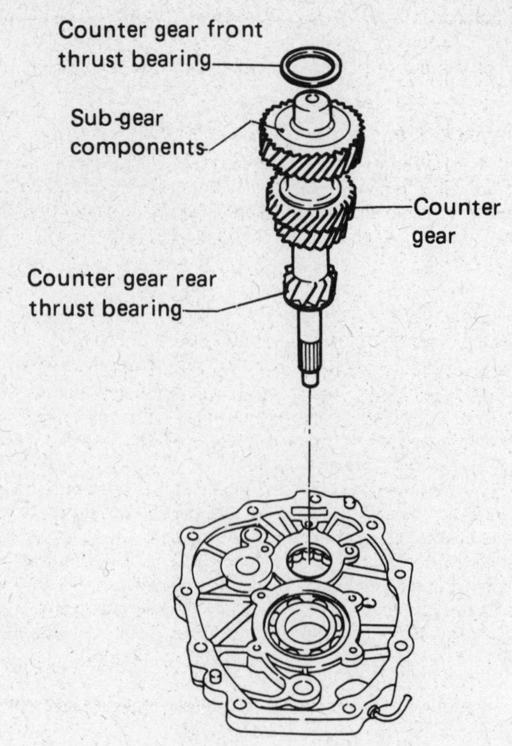

6.36 Countershaft installation details

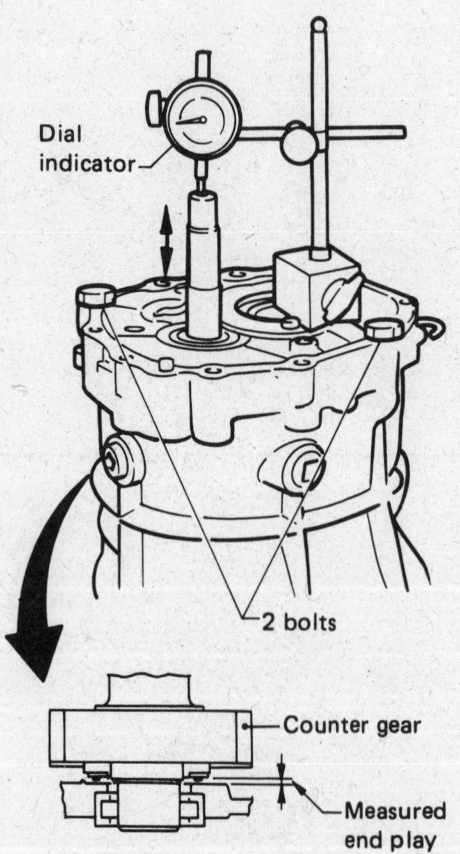

6.37 Use a dial indicator to check the countergear end play

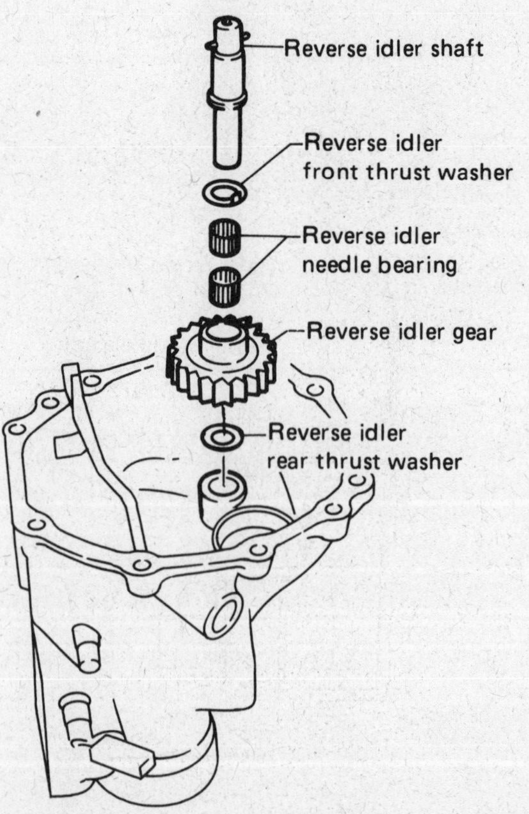

6.38 Reverse idler component layout

front of the countershaft. Installation is the reverse of removal.

Input shaft and gear disassembly

31 The input shaft and gear assembly is serviced as a unit and only the bearing is replaceable. If it is necessary to replace the bearing, remove the snap ring and spacer. Take the assembly to a properly equipped machine shop to have the old bearing pressed off and a new one installed.

Adapter plate and mainshaft reassembly

32 Have the 3rd/4th gear synchronizer, 3rd gear and needle bearing pressed on the shaft with a hydraulic press. Install the thickest selective snap ring which will fit in the groove. Check the snap ring clearance with a feeler gauge to make sure it does not exceed 0.004 inch (0.1 mm).
33 Have the 1st/2nd synchronizer, 2nd gear and needle bearing pressed on the mainshaft with a hydraulic press.
34 Have the 1st gear bushing and washer press on with a hydraulic press and then install the 1st gear and needle bearing.
35 Coat the steel ball and washer with petroleum jelly or multi-purpose grease and install on the mainshaft **(see illustration)**.
36 Assemble the countershaft and install it in the adapter plate **(see illustration)**.
37 Install the adapter plate on the transmission plate using 2 bolts. Install a dial indicator, set it a zero and then lift and release the countergear **(see illustration)**. Make a note of the reading and subtract 0.0039 to 0.0098 inch (0.10 to 0.25 mm) to determine the proper size countergear front bearing shim to be installed.
38 Install the reverse idler gear, needle bearing, thrust washers and shaft in the extension housing (2WD) or overdrive gearcase (4WD) **(see illustration)**.
39 Install a dial indicator on the front of the reverse idler shaft and use a ruler or straightedge **(see illustration)**. Set the indicator to zero, lift and release the idler shaft and measure the end play. The end play should be between 0.118 to 0.209 in (0.30 to 0.35 mm). If the end play is not within specification, replace the rear thrust washer with a new one.
40 Unbolt the transmission case from the adapter plate and place it securely in a vise, using blocks of wood or cloths to protect the surface.
41 Lubricate the surface of the countergear rear bearing with multipurpose grease and install the mainshaft partially on its front bearing in the adapter plate.
42 Install the countergear on the countergear rear bearing in the adapter plate and then push it upward on the upper roller of the bearing, using a screwdriver to seat the assembly **(see illustration)**.
43 Install the input shaft with the pilot bearing and spacer on the mainshaft **(see illustration)**.

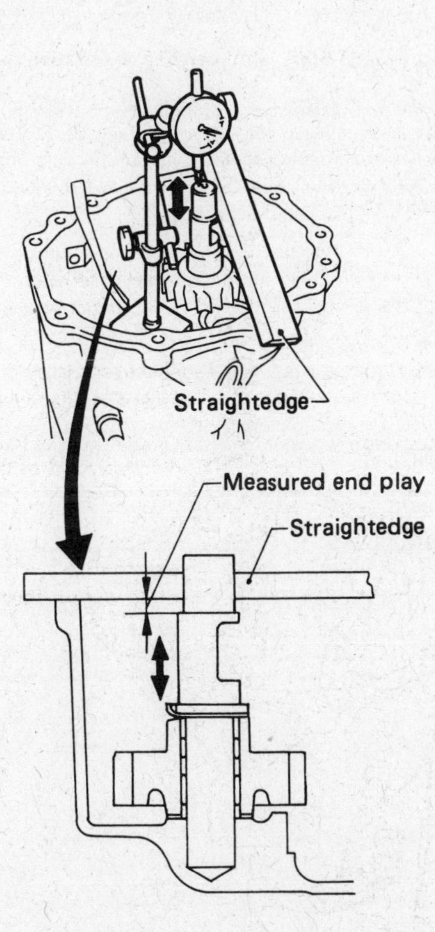

6.39 Checking the reverse idler shaft end play

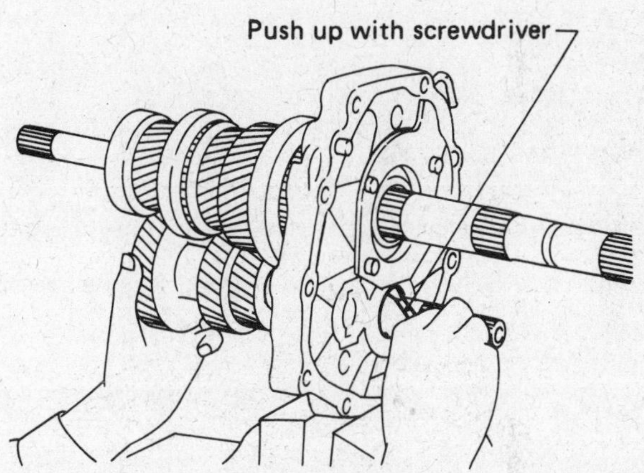

6.42 Use a screwdriver to seat the countergear assembly

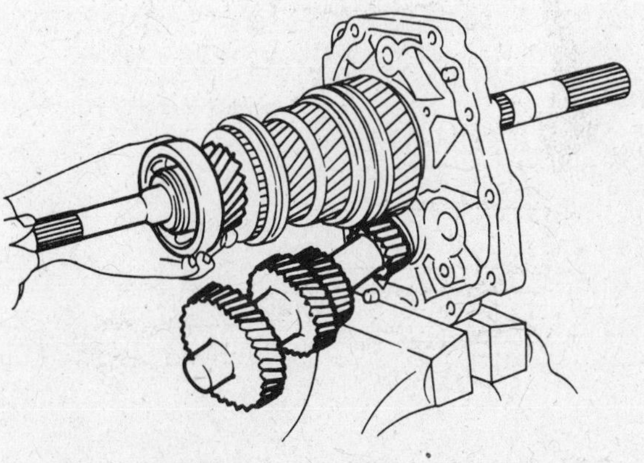

6.43 Installing the input shaft and pilot bearing on the mainshaft

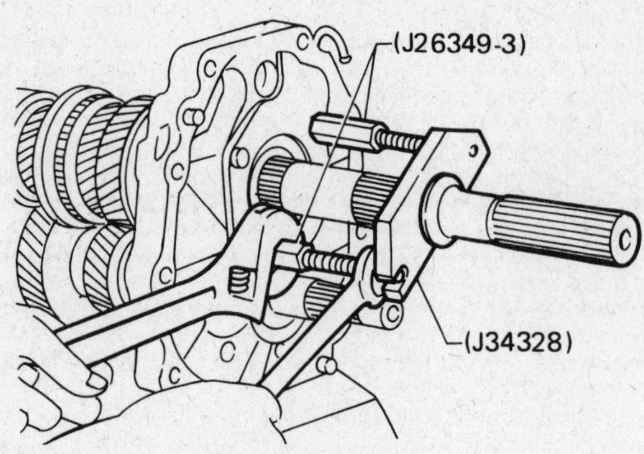

6.44 Special tools are required for countergear installation

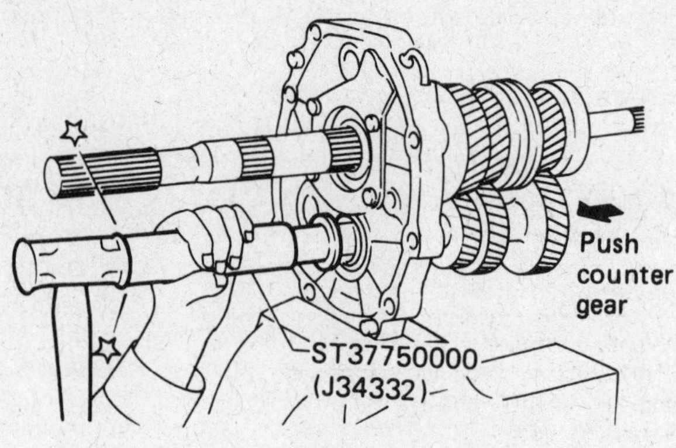

6.45 Push on the countergear while installing the bushing by tapping the installer with a hammer

44 Install tool J-26349-3 on the adapter plate with the C-ring and C-ring holder on the mainshaft and then install tool J-34328. Extend the tool to install the mainshaft and countershaft gear **(see illustration)**.
45 Install the overdrive gear bushing by tapping it in place with a hammer while pushing on the back of the countergear **(see illustration)**.
46 Install the overdrive gear.
47 Install the adapter plate complete with the gear assembly in the transmission case.
48 Install the overdrive gear needle bearing followed by the overdrive countergear and reverse idler shaft.
49 On 2WD models, install the reverse gear bushing with the speedometer gear drive.
50 Install the reverse cone.
51 Install the overdrive blocker ring on the overdrive countergear.
52 Install the reverse countergear, needle bearing, reverse main gear, reverse idler gear and thrust washer, followed by the reverse hub.
53 On 2WD models, install the mainshaft spacer and rear bearing.
54 Install the countershaft gear rear bearing.
55 Remove the adapter plate assembly from the transmission case and mount it in the vise again.
56 Install a new mainshaft C-ring and countershaft gear rear snap ring. With the proper ring installed, the groove clearance should not exceed 0.004 in (0.1 mm).
57 Install the reverse synchronizer assembly.
58 Measure the gear end play as described in Step 16.
59 Install the overdrive rod and shift fork, line up the rod and fork holes and install a new roll pin, using a hammer and suitable punch.
60 Install the 1st/2nd, 3rd/4th and reverse shift forks on their synchronizer grooves.
61 Install the striking rod to engage the shift forks, striker lever and interlock. Line up the rod and lever pin holes and install a new roll pin, using a hammer and suitable punch.

Transmission case assembly

62 Apply suitable sealant to the contact surfaces of the transmission case.
63 Install the adapter plate and gear assembly on the transmission case.
64 Coat the interlock check ball with multi-purpose grease and insert the check ball and spring in the interlock stopper.
65 Apply sealant to the plug threads, install the plug and tighten it to the specified torque.
66 Install the stopper ring and and secure it with a new main drive bearing snap ring.
67 Install the front cover, using a new gasket. Coat the threads of the bottom 3 cover bolts with sealer and install all of the front cover bolts. Tighten the bolts to the specified torque.
68 Apply suitable sealer to the contact surfaces of the adapter plate.
69 Install the extension housing (2WD) or overdrive housing (4WD) to the adapter plate with the striking arm.
70 Line up the pin holes and install a new roll pin in the striking arm, using a hammer and suitable size punch.
71 Install the control housing check ball and return spring (refer to illustration 6.6).
72 Apply sealer to the extension housing or overdrive gearcase mounting surfaces and install the control housing and bolts. Tighten the bolts to the specified torque.

Chapter 7 Part B Automatic transmission

Contents

Specifications

Model

1980 through 1985	3N71B
1986 on	
2WD with four-cylinder engine	L4N71B
2WD with V6 engine	E4N71B
4WD	
1987	L3N71B
1988	RE4R01A or RL4R01A

General

Driveplate maximum allowable runout	0.020 in (0.5 mm)
Torque converter installation distance A	
1980 through 1985	0.846 in (21.5 mm)
1986 through 1990	1.38 in (35 mm)
1991 and later	1.024 in (26.0 mm) or more
Recommended fluid	See Chapter 1
Fluid capacity	See Chapter 1

Torque specifications

	Ft-lbs
Torque converter-to-driveplate bolts	33
Converter housing-to-engine bolts	
All four-cylinder models and V6 models through 1990	33
1991 and later V6 models	
Upper 4 bolts	33
Lower 4 bolts	25
Inhibitor switch mounting bolts	4.3
Shift linkage locknut	
1980 through 1985	25
1986 on	
2WD floorshift	8
4WD floorshift	3.3 to 4.3
column shift	8

1 General information

The automatic transmission unit used on models manufactured between 1980 and 1985 is the type JATCO 3N71B, providing three forward ratios and one reverse. Later model (1986 through 1988) vehicles use a variety 4-speed automatic transmissions, depending on the engine used and whether 2WD or 4WD. Changing of the forward gear ratios is completely automatic in relation to the vehicle speed and engine torque output and is dependent upon the vacuum pressure in the manifold and the vehicle road speed to actuate the gear change mechanism at the precise time.

The automatic transmission unit used on 1990 and 1991 models is either a RL4R01A or a RE4R01A. These new and updated automatic transmissions are equipped with many features. An overdrive unit is built in as well as a lock-up torque converter to increase fuel mileage and efficiency. Also, they are equipped with a self-diagnosis system. The codes are accessed through the shift control and the ignition key. This system is handy for trained mechanics who can interpret the data to solve problems in the valve body or sensor circuits.

The transmission has six selector positions:

P Parking position which locks the output shaft to the interior wall of the transmission housing. This is a safety device for use when the vehicle is parked on an incline. The engine may be started with P selected and this position should always be selected when adjusting the engine while it is running. Never attempt to select P when the vehicle is in motion.

R Reverse gear.

N Neutral. Select this position to start the engine or when idling in traffic for long periods.

O Overdrive (if equipped). 4th gear is selected automatically once the overdrive switch (four-cylinder) is turned on or the power shift switch (V6 engine) is in the Auto position. Consult your owner's manual for guidelines for the proper use of overdrive.

D Drive, for all normal driving conditions.

2 Locks the transmission in second gear for wet road conditions or steep hill climbing or descents. The engine can be over-revved in this position.

1 The selection of this ratio above speeds of approximately 25 mph (40 kph) will engage second gear as the speed drops below 25 mph (40 kph) the transmission will lock into first gear. Provides maximum retardation on steep descents.

Due to the complexity of the automatic transmission unit, any internal adjustment or servicing should be left to a Nissan dealer, or other qualified transmission specialist. The information given in this Chapter is therefore confined to those operations which are considered within the scope of the home mechanic. An automatic transmission should give many thousands of miles of service provided normal maintenance and adjustment is carried out. When the unit finally requires major overhaul, consideration should be given to exchanging the old transmission for a factory reconditioned one, the removal and installation being well within the capabilities of the home mechanic as described later in this Chapter.

The routine maintenance chart in Chapter 1 calls for an automatic transmission fluid change once every 30,000 miles. This interval should be shortened to every 15,000 miles if the vehicle is normally driven under one or more of the following conditions: heavy city traffic, where the outside temperature normally reaches 90 °F or higher; in very hilly or mountainous areas; or if a trailer is frequently pulled. Refer to Chapter 1 for the proper procedures for checking and changing the automatic transmission fluid and filter.

The automatic transmission uses an oil cooler, located at the radiator, to prevent excessive temperatures from developing inside the transmission. Should the oil cooler need flushing or other servicing, take it to a dealer or radiator specialist.

If rough shifting or other malfunctions occur in the automatic transmission, check the following items first before assuming the fault lies within the transmission itself; the fluid level, the kickdown switch adjustment, manual shift linkage adjustment and engine tune. All of these elements can adversely affect the performance of the transmission.

Periodically clean the outside of the transmission housing as the accumulation of dirt and oil is liable to cause overheating of the unit under extreme conditions.

2 Shift linkage – adjustment

Refer to illustrations 2.3, 2.10a, 2.10b, 2.11, 2.13, 2.18 and 2.19

1980 through 1985 models

1 To check the manual shift linkage adjustment, move the shifter through the entire range of gears. You should be able to feel the detents

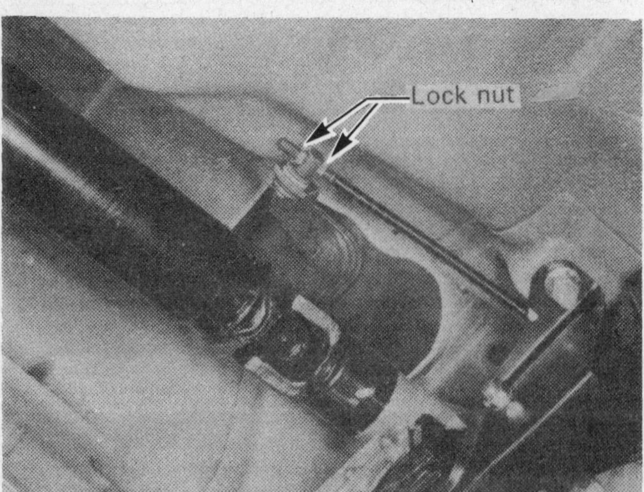

2.10a Manual shift linkage locknut location on 1986 and later 2WD (and 1986 and 1988 4WD) floor shift models

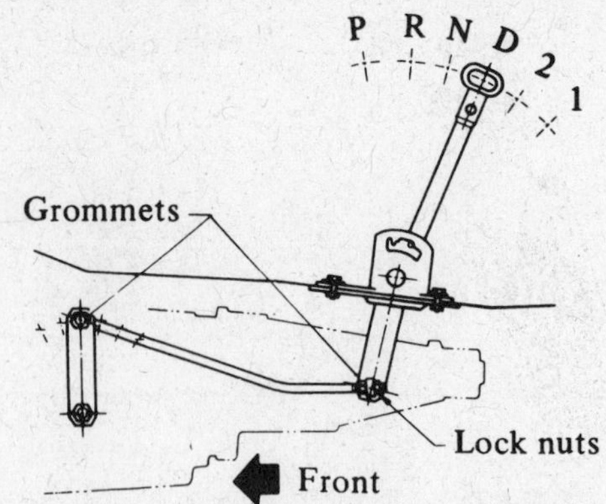

2.3 To adjust the manual shift linkage on pre-1986 models, place the shift lever in Drive, loosen the locknuts, move the shift lever so it's aligned with the D position, move the selector lever on the transmission so it's also aligned in the D position and tighten the locknuts

in each gear. If these detents are not felt or if the pointer is not properly aligned with the correct gear selection, the shift linkage should be adjusted in the following manner.

2 With the engine off, place the shift lever in Drive.

3 Working underneath the vehicle, loosen the locknuts **(see illustration)**.

4 Move the shift lever so that it is correctly aligned with the D position.

5 Move the selector lever on the transmission so that it is also correctly aligned in the D position.

6 Tighten the locknuts and recheck the levers. There should be no tendency for the selector rod to push or pull one rod against the other.

7 Again run the shifter through the entire range of gear positions. If there are still problems, the grommets that connect the selector rod with the levers may be worn or damaged and should be replaced.

1986 and later models

Floor shift models

8 Move the selector from the "P" range to the "1" range. You should be able to feel the detents in each range. If the detents cannot be felt, or the pointer indicating the range is improperly aligned, the linkage needs adjustment.

9 Place the selector lever in the "P" range.

10 Loosen the locknuts **(see illustrations)**.

2WD models

11 Tighten locknut X **(see illustration)** until it touches the trunnion pulling selector lever toward the "R" range side without pushing the button.

12 Back off locknut X 1/4 to 1/2 a turn and tighten it to the specified torque.

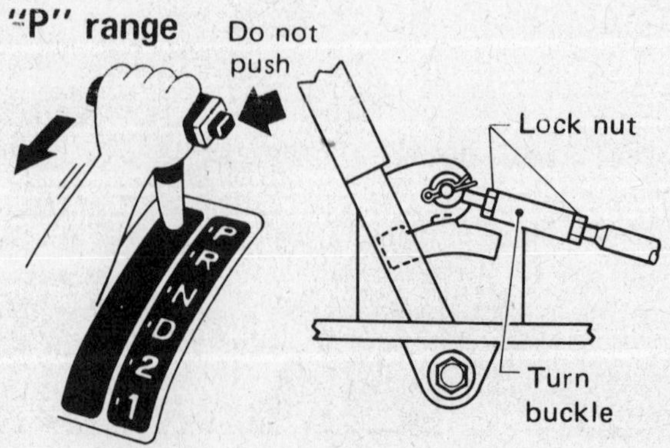

2.10b Manual shift linkage locknut location on 1987 4WD floor shift models

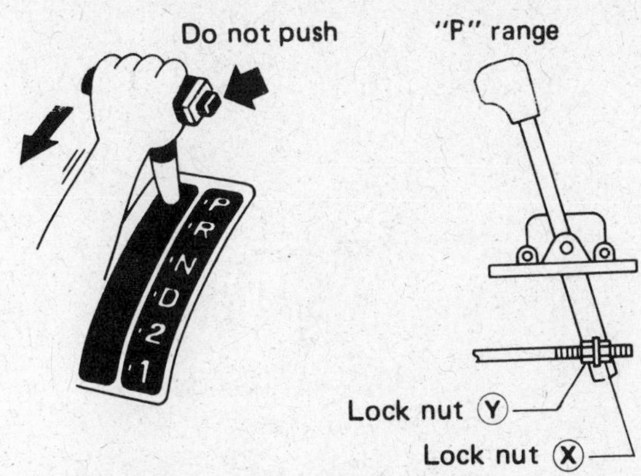

2.11 To adjust the manual shift linkage on 1986 and later 2WD (and 1986 and 1988 4WD) floor shift models, place the selector lever in the "P" range, loosen the locknuts, tighten locknut X till it touches the trunnion, back off locknut X 1/4 to 1/2 turn and tighten locknut Y to the specified torque

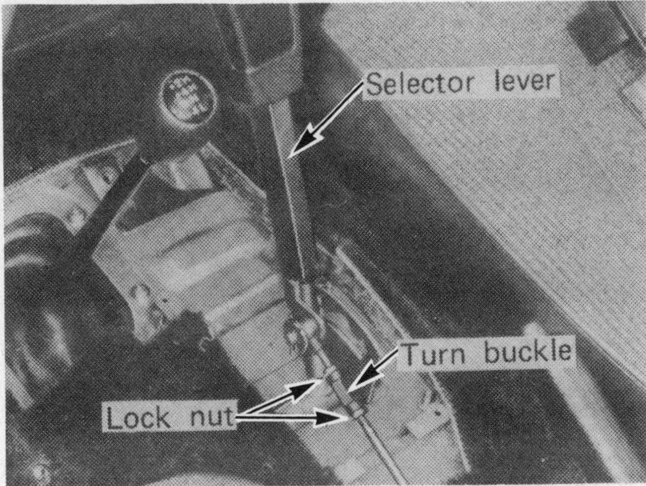

2.13 To adjust the manual shift linkage on 1987 4WD floor shift models, place the selector lever in the "P" range, loosen the locknuts, tighten the turnbuckle until it aligns with the inner cable, back off the turnbuckle one turn and tighten the locknuts to the specified torque

1987 and later 4WD models

13 Tighten the turnbuckle **(see illustration)** until it aligns with the inner cable, pulling the selector lever toward the "R" range side without pushing the button.

14 Back off the turnbuckle one turn and tighten the locknuts to the specified torque.

15 Move the selector lever from the "P" range to the "1" range. Make sure that the selector lever moves smoothly.

Column shift models

16 Move the shift lever from the "P" range to the "1" range. You should be able to feel the detents in each range. If the detents cannot be felt or the pointer indicating the range is improperly aligned, the linkage needs adjustment.

17 Place the shift lever in the "P" range.

18 Loosen the locknuts **(see illustration)**.

19 Tighten locknut A **(see illustration)** until it touches the trunnion, pulling the selector lever toward the "R" range side without pushing the button.

20 Back off locknut A two turns and tighten locknut B to the specified torque.

21 Move the control lever from the "P" range to the "1" range. Make sure that the control lever can move smoothly.

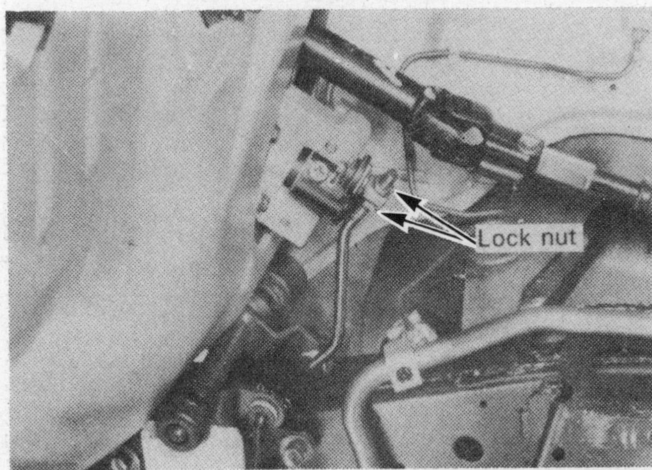

2.18 Manual shift linkage locknut location on 1986 through 1988 column shift models

3 Inhibitor switch — check and adjustment

Refer to illustrations 3.6, 3.8a, 3.8b, 3.8c and 3.8d

Check

1 The inhibitor switch performs two functions. It provides current to the back-up lights when the transmission is in the Reverse position. It also prevents the vehicle from being started in any gear position except Park or Neutral. If the back-up lights fail to operate, or if the vehicle will not start when the shifter is in the middle of the P or N positions, the inhibitor switch should be checked and, if necessary, adjusted.

1980 through 1985 models

2 Locate the inhibitor switch on the right side of the transmission and connect a continuity tester to the black and yellow wires.

3 With the engine off, but the ignition switch On, have an assistant run the gear shifter through the entire range of gear positions. The tester should show continuity through the switch only when the shifter is in the P or N positions.

4 Now connect the continuity tester to the red and black wires. With this arrangement the tester should show continuity through the switch only when the shifter is in the Reverse (R) position.

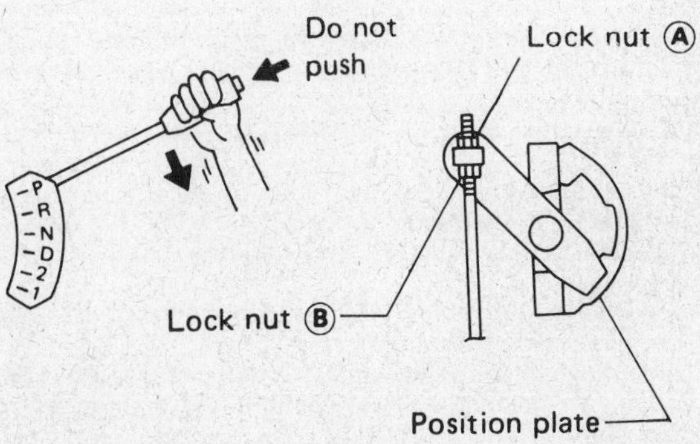

2.19 To adjust the manual shift linkage on a 1986 through 1988 column shift model, place the shift lever in the "P" range, loosen the locknuts, tighten locknut A until it touches the trunnion, back off locknut A two turns and tighten locknut B to the specified torque

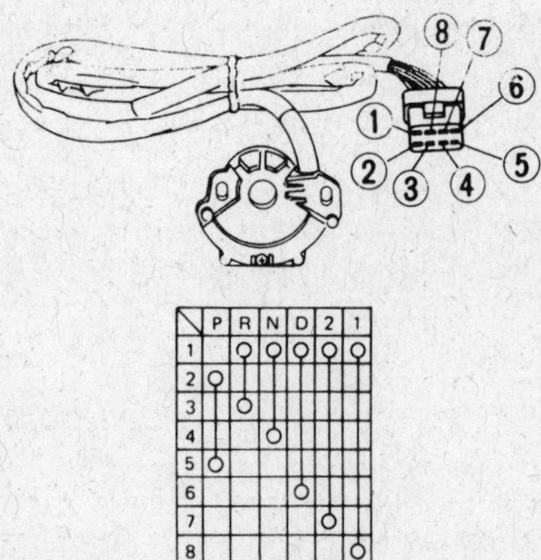

3.6 To check the continuity of 1986 and later inhibitor switches, unplug the harness connector and, using the accompanying chart, check the continuity between the indicated terminals in each drive range

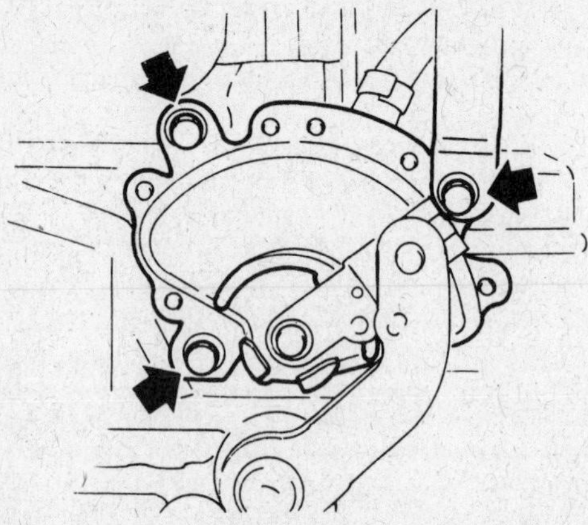

3.8b . . . loosen the inhibitor switch attaching bolts (arrows) – (1987/1988 4WD switch shown – other switch bolts are similar) . . .

1986 and later models

5 Disconnect the inhibitor switch harness at its electrical connector, then remove the switch.

6 Check continuity at the indicated terminals **(see illustration)** at each range. With the selector lever held in Neutral, turn the manual lever an equal amount in both directions to determine whether the current flow ranges are nearly the same (current normally begins to flow before the manual lever reaches an angle of 1.5° in either direction).

7 If current flow is outside the normal range, or if the normal flow range is out of specification, adjust the inhibitor switch as described above.

Adjustment

8 If the continuity tests did not give the results described above, the switch should be adjusted as follows:

a) Place the selector lever on the transmission in the Neutral (vertical) position.
b) On all switches except 1987 and 1988 4WD models, remove the screw **(see illustration)**.
c) Loosen the inhibitor switch attaching bolts **(see illustration)**.
d) Using an aligning rod or piece of wire **(see illustrations)** with a diameter of about 2 mm (0.079 in), align the screw hole with the hole in the rotor behind the switch, by moving the switch. Holding this alignment, retighten the inhibitor switch attaching bolts.
e) Remove the alignment rod or wire and install the screw.

9 With the switch adjusted, recheck it for continuity by repeating Steps 3 and 4. If the switch still does not function properly, replace it with a new one.

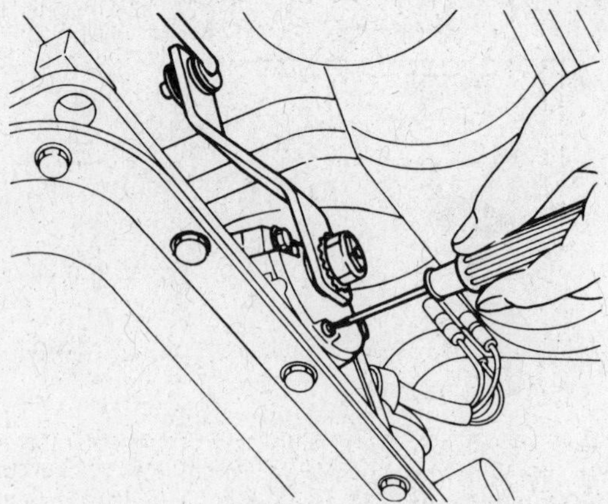

3.8a To adjust the inhibitor switch on any 2WD model, place the manual valve in Neutral (vertical position), remove the screw from the alignment hole (1987 and later switches have no alignment hole screw), . . .

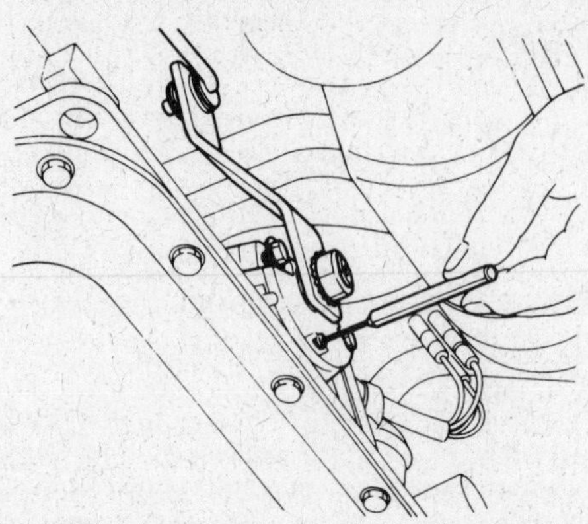

3.8c . . . and with an aligning rod or piece of wire (2 mm or 0.079-in diameter), move the switch until the pin falls into the hole in the rotor and tighten the attaching bolts equally

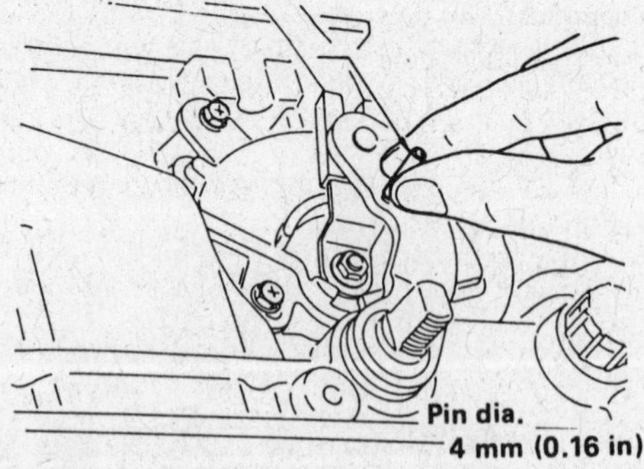

3.8d When adjusting inhibitor switches on 1987 and 1988 4WD models you must be able to insert a pin, rod or piece of thin wire though both the switch and the automatic transmission manual shift lever (make sure the lever is as vertical as possible)

4 Kickdown switch – adjustment

Refer to illustration 4.3

1 The kickdown switch, coupled with the downshift solenoid, causes the transmission to downshift when the accelerator pedal is fully depressed. This provides extra power when passing. If the transmission is not downshifting upon full throttle, the system should be inspected.

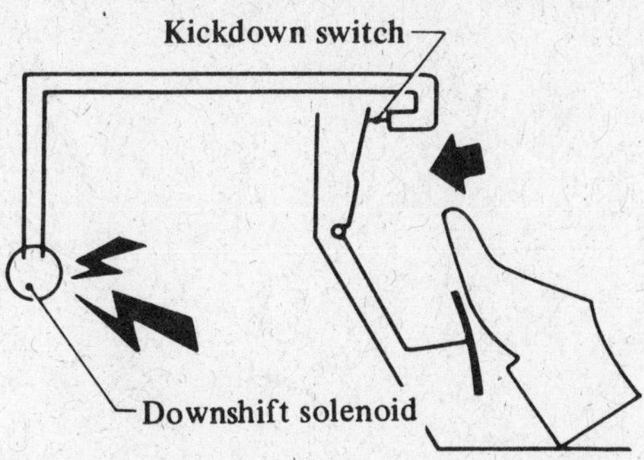

4.3 The kickdown switch for 1980 through 1985 transmissions, located at the upper post of the accelerator pedal, energizes the downshift solenoid when the accelerator pedal is fully depressed, providing extra power for passing — to check the switch, turn the ignition switch on (with the engine off), depress the accelerator pedal all the way and listen carefully for a click just before the pedal bottoms

2 With the engine off, but the ignition On, depress the accelerator pedal all the way and listen for a click just before the pedal bottoms.
3 If no click is heard, locate the kickdown switch at the upper post of the accelerator pedal **(see illustration)**. Loosen the locknut and with the pedal still depressed, extend the switch until it makes contact with the post and clicks. The switch should click only as the pedal bottoms. If it clicks too soon, it will cause the transmission to downshift on part throttle.
4 Tighten the locknut, and recheck the adjustment.
5 If the kickdown switch adjustment is correct but the transmission still will not downshift, check that current is reaching the switch, and with a continuity tester, check that the switch is passing current through it.
6 If the switch checks out okay, but the problem persists, take the vehicle to a dealer and have the downshift solenoid tested and replaced if necessary. Testing the kickdown circuits requires specialized equipment and is beyond the scope of the home mechanic.

5 Vacuum diaphragm rod — adjustment

Refer to illustration 5.4

1 The vacuum diaphragm and the length of its rod affect the shift patterns of the transmission. If the transmission is not shifting at precisely the right points, a different vacuum diaphragm rod may have to be installed.
2 Disconnect the vacuum hose from the vacuum diaphragm on the left inside of the transmission.
3 Remove the vacuum diaphragm.
4 Be sure the vacuum throttle valve is pushed into the valve body as far as possible and measure the distance L **(see illustration)** with a depth gauge.
5 Once this measurement is taken, use the chart below to determine the correct vacuum diaphragm rod length.

Measured depth L mm (in)	*Rod length mm (in)*
Under 25.55 (1.0059)	*29.0 (1.142)*
25.65 to 26.05 (1.0098 to 1.0256)	*29.5 (1.161)*
26.15 to 26.55 (1.0295 to 1.0453)	*30.0 (1.181)*
26.65 to 27.05 (1.0492 to 1.0650)	*30.5 (1.201)*
Over 27.15 (1.0689)	*31.0 (1.220)*

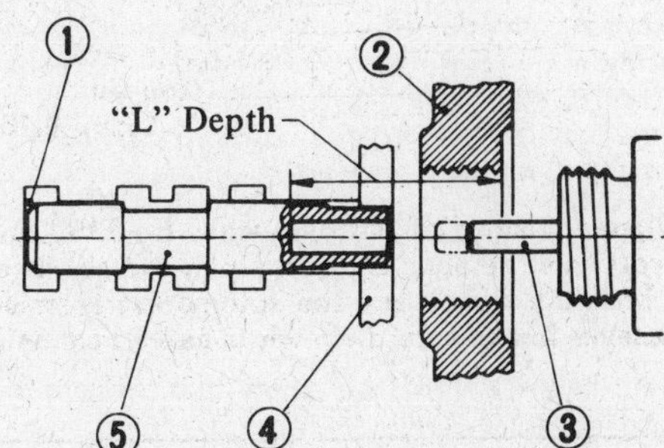

5.4 Refer to this illustration when adjusting the diaphragm rod

1 Note seated valve body
2 Transmission case wall
3 Diaphragm rod
4 Valve body side plate
5 Vacuum throttle valve

6 Rear oil seal — replacement

Refer to illustrations 6.2 and 6.3

1 Remove the driveshaft (Chapter 8). On 4WD models remove the transfer case (Chapter 9).
2 Being careful not to damage the output shaft or transmission housing, use a screwdriver to pry out the old seal **(see illustration)**.
3 Apply a coat of gear oil to the lips of the new seal and drive it into place using an appropriate sized socket **(see illustration)**.
4 Reinstall the driveshaft (Chapter 8) and, on 4WD models, the transfer case (Chapter 9).

6.2 Pry out the old oil seal with a screwdriver — be careful not to damage the seal bore (4WD model shown)

6.3 To install the new seal, coat the outside edge and the lips of the seal with gear oil and drive it into place with an appropriately sized socket

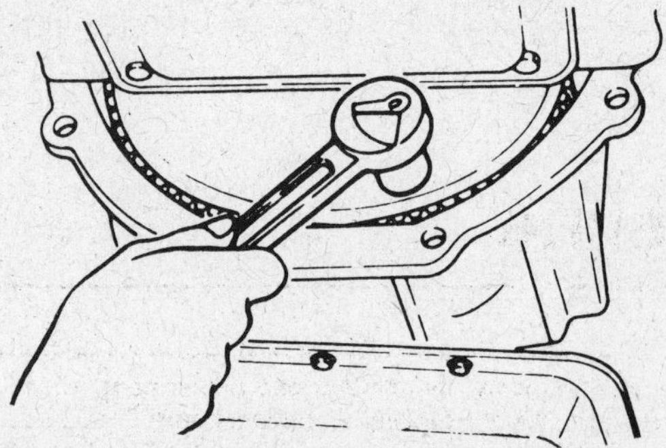

7.17 To remove the driveplate-to-torque converter bolts, turn the crankshaft and remove the bolts as they come into view at the bottom

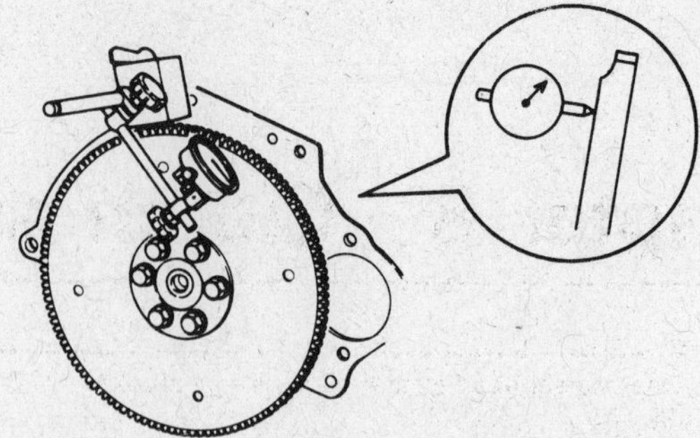

7.24 If you are replacing the torque converter, or it's removed for any reason, set up a dial gauge and measure driveplate runout – if the runout exceeds the specified allowable maximum, replace the driveplate

7 Automatic transmission – removal and installation

Refer to illustrations 7.17, 7.24, 7.25 and 7.27

Note: *Due to the complexity of the automatic transmission and the special equipment needed to service it, an automatic transmission overhaul is not practical for the home mechanic to perform. Considerable money can be saved however, by removing and installing the transmission yourself. Read through this Section to become familiar with the procedure and the tools needed for the job. The vehicle must be raised high enough so the transmission can be lowered and slid out from underneath.*

1 Prior to removal of the transmission, have the vehicle test driven and diagnosed by a qualified transmission specialist, so that he may determine the nature and cause of the problem.

2 Removal of the engine and automatic transmission as a combined unit is described in Chapter 2 of this manual. Where it is decided to remove the transmission leaving the engine in position in the vehicle, proceed as follows:

3 Disconnect the battery ground lead from the battery.

4 Drain the fluid from the transmission (Chapter 1).

5 Raise the vehicle to an adequate working height and support it securely on jackstands.

6 Remove the driveshaft (see Chapter 8). As this is done, plug or cover the opening at the rear of the transmission to prevent oil leakage.

7 Remove the front exhaust pipe (see Chapter 4).

8 Unplug the electrical connector to inhibitor switch.

9 Unplug the electrical connector to the downshift solenoid.

10 Disconnect the vacuum pipe from the vacuum capsule (if equipped) located just forward of the downshift solenoid.

11 Separate the selector lever from the selector linkage.

12 Disconnect the speedometer drive cable from the rear extension housing.

13 Disconnect the fluid filler tube. Plug the opening.

14 Disconnect the fluid cooler tubes from the rear extension housing.

15 Support the engine oil pan with a jack and use a block of wood to prevent damage to the surface of the oil pan.

16 Remove the cover from the lower half of the torque converter housing and driveplate and mark their positions in relation to each other for exact replacement.

17 Unscrew and remove the four bolts **(see illustration)** which secure the torque converter to the driveplate. Access to each of these bolts is obtained by rotating the engine slowly, using a wrench on the crankshaft pulley bolt.

18 Unbolt and withdraw the starter motor.

19 Support the transmission with a jack (preferably a trolley type).

20 Remove the bolts that secure the transmission mounting bracket to the transmission.

21 Remove the transmission mounting bracket from the body.

22 Unscrew and remove the transmission-to-engine securing bolts.

23 Lower the two jacks sufficiently to allow the transmission unit to be withdrawn from below and to the rear of the vehicle. The help of an assistant will probably be required due to the weight of the unit. If an automatic transmission is in need of minor repair, take it to a Nissan dealer or other qualified transmission specialist. If it is in need of a complete overhaul, it may be more economical to replace the old transmission with a rebuilt one.

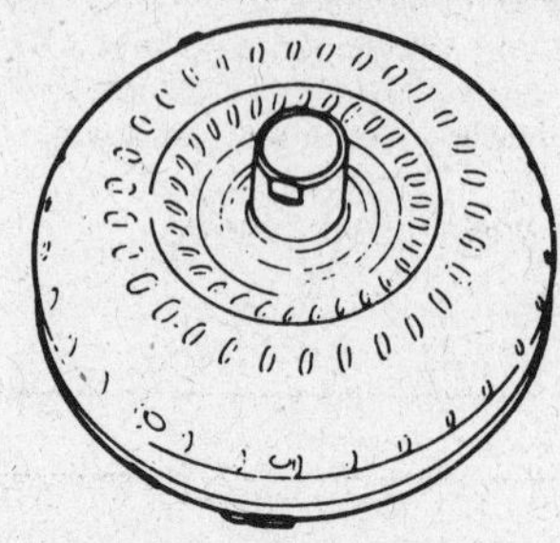

7.25 When installing the torque converter, be sure to align the notch in the converter with the flange in the transmission oil pump

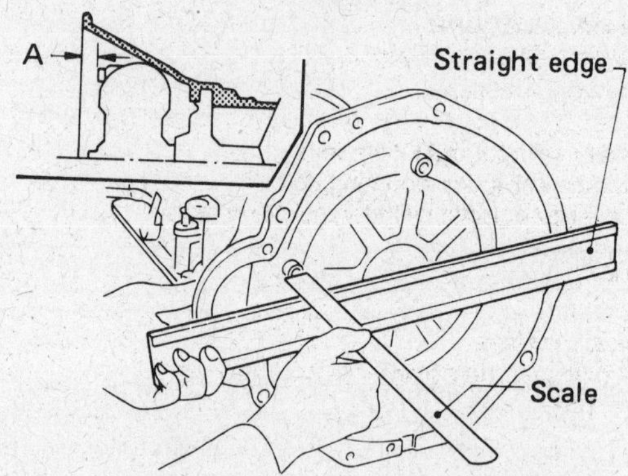

7.27 After installing the torque converter, measure distance "A" and compare your measurement with the specified distance for your transmission

24 If the torque converter is removed, measure the driveplate runout **(see illustration)**. If the runout exceeds the specified maximum allowable, replace the driveplate (see Chapter 2).

25 Installation is the reverse of removal but should the torque converter have been separated from the main assembly, ensure that the notch on the converter is correctly aligned with the corresponding one on the transmission oil pump **(see illustration)**.

26 When bolting the torque converter to the driveplate, be sure the marks made during removal are aligned.

27 After installing the torque converter to the transmission measure distance "A" **(see illustration)** to verify that the torque converter is correctly installed.

28 Tighten all bolts to the specified torque.

29 Once the converter is installed and the bolts are tightened rotate the crankshaft several times to make sure the transmission turns freely with no binding.

30 Refill the transmission with the correct grade and quantity fluid (see Chapter 1).

31 After reinstalling the transmission check the operation of the inhibitor switch and selector linkage and adjust as necessary.

Chapter 8 Clutch and driveline

Contents

Specifications

Clutch

Disc runout	0.040 in (1.0 mm)
Maximum unevenness of pressure plate diaphragm spring toe height	0.020 in (0.5 mm)

Torque specifications

	Ft-lbs
Pressure plate-to-flywheel bolts	
1980 through 1983	12 to 15
1984 on	16 to 22
Clutch master cylinder mounting bolts	6 to 9
Clutch operating cylinder mounting bolts	22 to 30
Damper cover-to-damper cylinder mounting bolts	3 to 4

Driveshaft

Runout limit	0.024 in (0.6 mm)
Journal axial play limit	0.008 in (0.2 mm)
Universal joint snap-ring sizes	
Through 1990	0.0587 in (1.49 mm)
	0.0598 in (1.52 mm)
	0.0610 in (1.55 mm)
	0.0622 in (1.58 mm)
	0.0634 in (1.61 mm)
	0.0646 in (1.64 mm)
	0.0657 in (1.67 mm)
	0.0787 in (2.00 mm)
	0.0795 in (2.02 mm)
	0.0803 in (2.04 mm)
	0.0811 in (2.06 mm)
	0.0819 in (2.08 mm)
	0.0827 in (2.10 mm)
	0.0835 in (2.12 mm)
1991 and later	0.0783 in (1.99 mm)
	0.0795 in (2.02 mm)
	0.0807 in (2.05 mm)
	0.0819 in (2.08 mm)
	0.0831 in (2.11 mm)
	0.0843 in (2.14 mm)
	0.0854 in (2.17 mm)
	0.0866 in (2.20 mm)

Torque specifications

	Ft-lbs
Driveshaft-to-differential bolts	
2WD	
1980 through 1985	17 to 24
1986 on	29 to 33
4WD – rear driveshaft (both ends)	58 to 65

8

Driveshaft (continued)

Torque specifications

	Ft-lbs
First shaft-to-second shaft flange bolts	
2WD	25 to 33
4WD	58 to 65
Center bearing locknut	
1980 through 1985 (2 and 4 wheel drive)	
flange type	181 to 217
nut-and-washer type	145 to 174
1986 on	
2WD	181 to 217
4WD	174 to 203
Center bearing bracket-to-frame bolts	12 to 16

Differential and rear axle

Drive pinion preload (with seal installed)	
H190A	9.5 to 13.9 in-lbs (1.1 to 1.6 Nm)
C200	9.5 to 14.8 in-lbs (1.1 to 1.7 Nm)
H233B	4.3 to 8.7 in-lbs (0.5 to 1.0 Nm)
Rear axle end play	
Models with rear drum brakes	0.0008 to 0.0059 in (0.02 to 0.15 mm)
Models with rear disc brakes	0 in (0 mm)
Rear axle housing end shim thicknesses	0.0020 in (0.05 mm)
	0.0028 in (0.07 mm)
	0.0039 in (0.10 mm)
	0.0059 in (0.15 mm)
	0.0079 in (0.20 mm)
	0.0197 in (0.50 mm)
	0.0394 in (1.00 mm)
Wheel bearing (hub) end play (dual tire models)	0.0031 in (0.08 mm) max.
Wheel bearing preload (with new grease seal)	4.6 to 8.2 lbs (20.6 to 36.6 N)

Torque specifications

	Ft-lbs
Drive pinion nut	
H190A and C200	94 to 217
H233B	145 to 181
Wheel bearing locknut (dual tire models)	123 to 145
Axleshaft-to-wheel hub (dual tire models)	42 to 55
Differential mounting bolts	16

1 Clutch – general information

Warning: *Dust produced by clutch wear and deposited on clutch components contains asbestos, which is hazardous to your health. DO NOT blow it out with compressed air and DO NOT inhale it. DO NOT use gasoline or petroleum-based solvents to remove the dust. Brake system cleaner should be used to flush the dust into a drain pan. After the clutch components are wiped clean with a rag, dispose of the contaminated rags and cleaner in a covered container.*

The clutch is located between the engine and the transmission and its main components are the clutch disc, pressure plate assembly, flywheel and release bearing. Other components which make up the hydraulically operated clutch system are the clutch pedal, clutch master cylinder, operating cylinder, clutch damper (1984 and later models) and release lever.

The clutch disc is sandwiched between the flywheel and the pressure plate and has a splined hub which engages and turns the transmission input shaft. When engaged, the pressure plate is held against the clutch disc by the spring pressure of its metal fingers and the clutch disc, in turn, is held against the flywheel.

The clutch pedal is connected to the clutch master cylinder by a short pushrod. The master cylinder and hydraulic reservoir are mounted on the engine side of the firewall in front of the driver.

Depressing the clutch pedal moves the piston in the master cylinder forward and forces hydraulic fluid through the clutch hydraulic pipe to the operating cylinder.

The piston in the operating cylinder moves forward and actuates the clutch release lever by means of a short pushrod.

The other end of the release lever, located inside the clutch housing is fork-shaped. This fork engages the clutch release bearing and forces the bearing against the pressure plate assembly's release fingers. When the fingers receive pressure from the release bearing they withdraw the mating surface of the pressure plate from the clutch disc, which disengages the clutch assembly from the flywheel.

As the friction linings on the clutch disc wear, the pressure plate automatically moves closer to the disc to compensate and eliminates the necessity for adjustment. **Note:** *Because access to the clutch components is difficult, any time either the engine or the transmission is removed, the clutch disc, pressure plate assembly and release bearing should be carefully inspected and, if necessary, replaced. Since the clutch disc wears the most, it should be replaced as a matter of course if there is any question about its condition.*

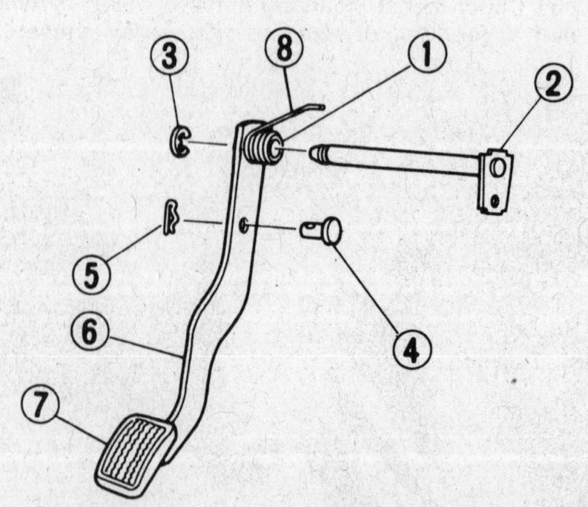

2.3a Clutch pedal mounting details – early models

1 Pedal bushing
2 Fulcrum pin
3 E-ring
4 Clevis pin
5 Snap pin
6 Clutch pedal
7 Pedal pad
8 Return spring

2 Clutch pedal – removal, installation and adjustment

Refer to illustrations 2.3a, 2.3b and 2.6

Removal

1 Disconnect the master cylinder pushrod from the pedal by prying off the snap pin and withdrawing the clevis pin.
2 Remove the stopper bolt or clutch switch from its bracket.
3 Pry off the E-ring from the fulcrum pin (early models). The fulcrum pin on later models is secured by a nut and washer **(see illustrations)**.
4 Remove the clutch pedal and the return spring.
5 Clean the parts in solvent and replace any that are damaged or excessively worn. The bushing in the pedal is press-fit, and if it's defective, the entire pedal must be replaced with a new one.

Installation

6 Installation is the reverse of the removal procedure. **Note:** *During installation, apply multi-purpose grease to the pedal boss, return spring and fulcrum pin. Also, when connecting the master cylinder pushrod to the pedal, smear a little grease on the clevis pin* **(see illustration)**.

Adjustment

7 Following installation, check the height and free play of the clutch pedal, and make adjustments as necessary as described in Chapter 1.

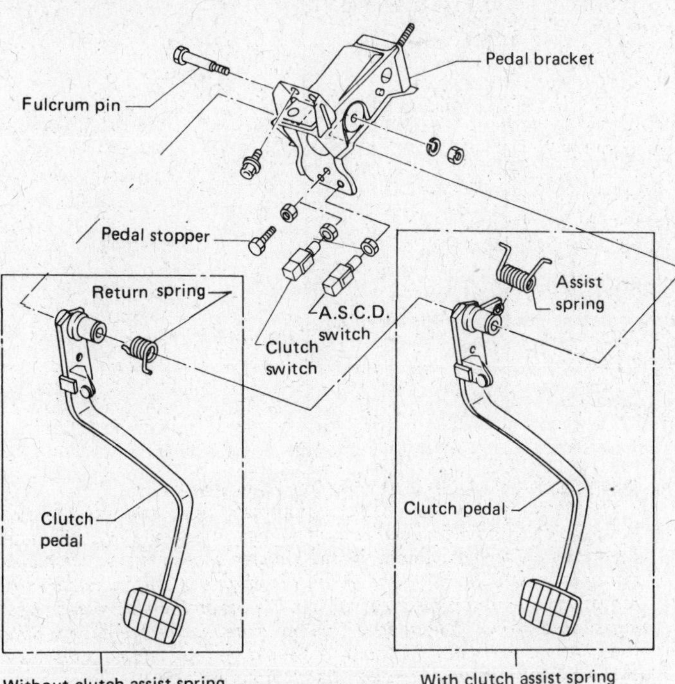

2.3b Clutch pedal mounting details – later models (left – four-cylinder engine; right – V6 engine)

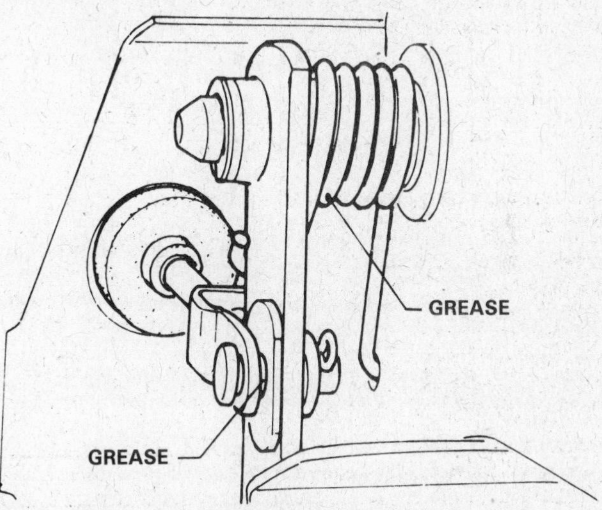

2.6 Grease should be applied to the points shown during installation of the clutch pedal

3 Clutch master cylinder – removal, overhaul and installation

Refer to illustrations 3.3, 3.5, 3.7 and 3.13

Caution: *Don't allow brake fluid to spill on painted surfaces of the vehicle, as damage to the finish will result.*

1 Disconnect the master cylinder pushrod from the clutch pedal.
2 Disconnect the fluid line from the master cylinder and drain the fluid into a container.
3 Remove the master cylinder flange mounting bolts and withdraw the unit from the engine compartment **(see illustration)**.
4 Drain any fluid from the reservoir and clean away all external dirt from the cylinder.
5 Peel back the flexible rubber boot at the end of the cylinder and pry out the stopper ring **(see illustration)**.
6 Remove the pushrod assembly from the cylinder.

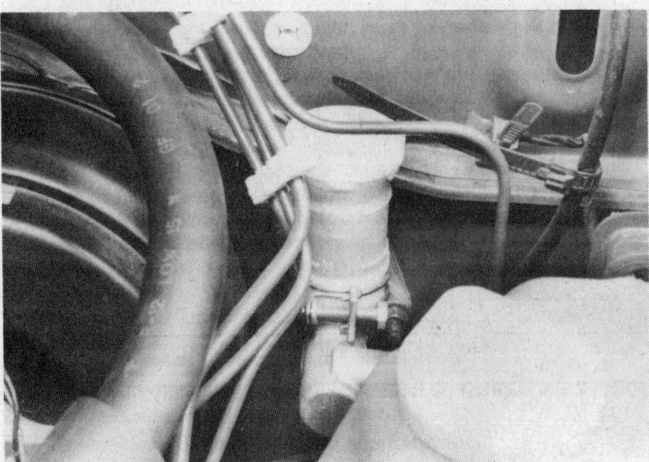

3.3 The clutch master cylinder is attached to the left side of the firewall

3.5 The stopper ring can be pried out with a narrow screwdriver

8

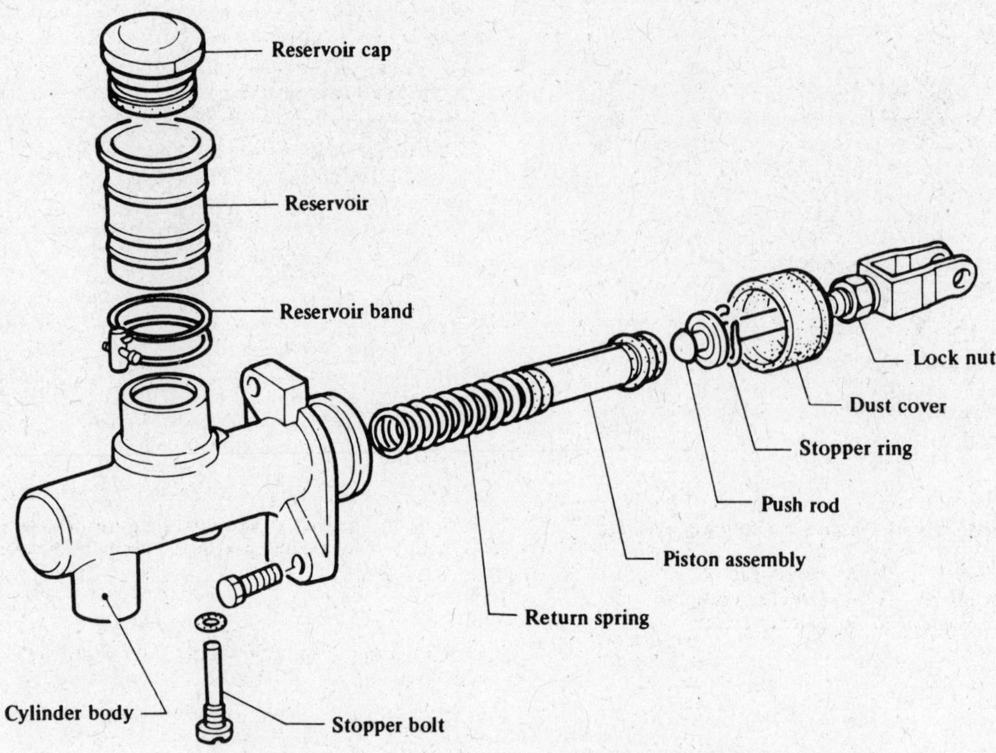

3.7 Exploded view of the clutch master cylinder components

7 Use a rod to depress the piston into the cylinder and hold it depressed while removing the stopper bolt from the bottom of the cylinder **(see illustration)**.

8 With the stopper bolt removed, the piston and spring assembly can be removed. **Note:** *The piston is not designed to be disassembled.*

9 Unless it's damaged, don't detach the reservoir from the cylinder body, as a new one will have to be installed if the old one is removed.

10 Examine the inner surface of the cylinder bore. If it's scored or exhibits bright wear areas, the entire master cylinder should be replaced.

11 If the cylinder bore is in good condition, obtain a clutch master cylinder rebuild kit, which will contain all of the necessary replacement parts.

12 Prior to installing any parts, first dip them in brake fluid to lubricate them. **Note:** *Don't use other solvents or lubricants.*

13 If the piston seals are not already mounted on the new piston supplied in the rebuild kit, use your fingers to manipulate them into their grooves. Be sure the lips face in the proper directions **(see illustration)**.

14 The installation of the parts in the cylinder is the reverse of the removal procedure.

15 Installation of the master cylinder is the reverse of removal, but check the pedal height and free play as described in Chapter 1, and bleed the hydraulic system (Section 6).

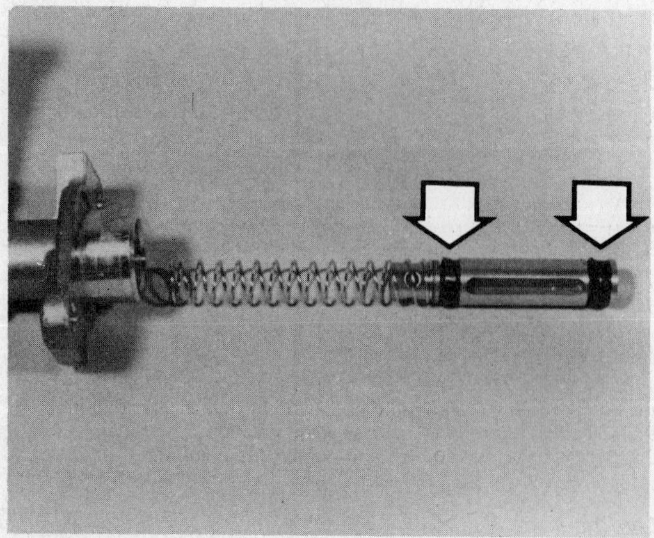

3.13 The lips on the piston seals (arrows) should face in the direction shown

4.5 The clutch operating cylinder is located on the right side of the clutch housing

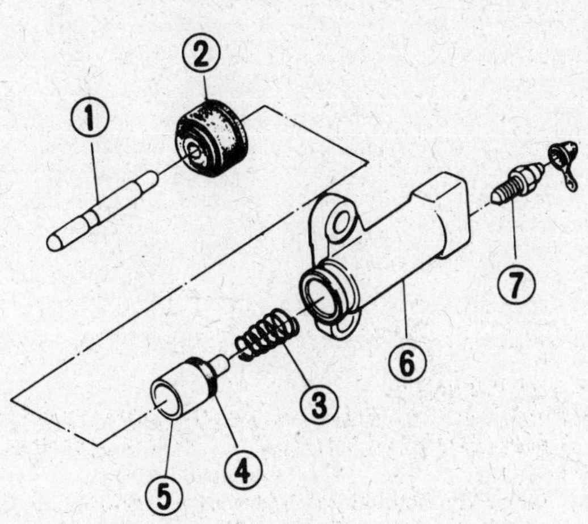

4.6 Exploded view of the clutch operating cylinder

1 Pushrod
2 Dust cover
3 Piston spring
4 Piston
5 Piston cup
6 Operating cylinder
7 Bleeder screw

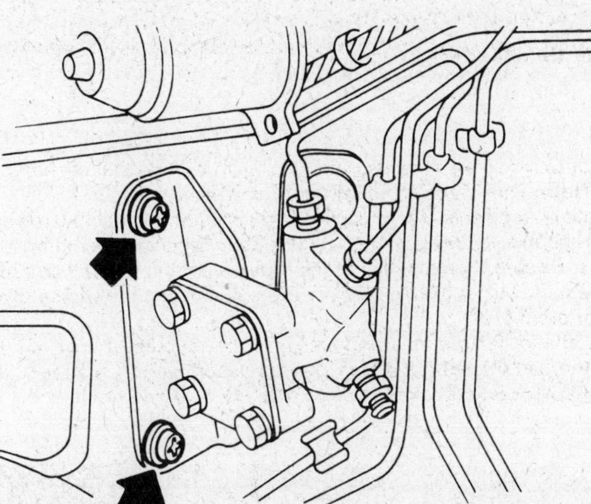

5.1 The clutch damper is attached to the firewall with two screws (arrows)

4 Clutch operating cylinder – removal, overhaul and installation

Refer to illustrations 4.5, 4.6 and 4.11

Removal

1 In order to prevent excessive loss of hydraulic fluid, when the operating cylinder hose is disconnected, remove the reservoir cap and place a piece of plastic wrap over the open reservoir. Then screw the cap back on. This will create a vacuum which will stop the fluid from running out of the open hose.
2 Loosen the clutch line flare nut at the bracket mounted on the body side member.
3 Remove the locking clip from the bracket and disengage the hose.
4 Remove the clutch hose from the operating cylinder.
5 Remove the two bolts which secure the operating cylinder to the clutch housing **(see illustration)**. The operating cylinder can now be removed.

4.11 The lip on the operating cylinder piston (arrow) should face in the direction shown

Overhaul

6 Pull off the dust boot and pushrod, then tap the cylinder gently on a block of wood to extract the piston and spring **(see illustration)**.
7 Remove the bleeder screw.
8 Examine the surfaces of the piston and cylinder bore for scoring or bright wear areas. If any are found, discard the cylinder and purchase a new one.
9 If the components are in good condition, wash them in clean brake fluid, remove the seal and discard it, noting carefully which way the seal lips face.
10 Obtain a repair kit which will contain all the necessary new items.
11 Install the new seal using only your fingers to manipulate it into position. Be sure the lip faces in the proper direction **(see illustration)**.
12 Dip the piston assembly in clean brake fluid before installing it and the spring in the cylinder.
13 Reinstall the bleeder screw.
14 Complete the reassembly by installing the pushrod and the dust cover. Be sure the dust cover is secure on the cylinder housing.

Installation

15 Installation is the reverse of removal but bleed the hydraulic system as described in Section 6.

5 Clutch damper – removal, overhaul and installation

Refer to illustrations 5.1, 5.3a and 5.3b

Removal

1 Using a flare nut wrench, disconnect the two hydraulic lines from the damper **(see illustration)**. Have plenty of rags available to mop up the spills and plug the lines after disconnection.
2 Remove the two screws and detach the damper.

Overhaul

Note: *Purchase a rebuild kit, which will contain all the necessary replacement parts.*

3 Remove the bolts and detach the cover. Remove the remaining parts, using the accompanying drawings for reference **(see illustrations)**.
4 Clean all parts with fresh brake fluid or denatured alcohol. *Do not use petroleum-based solvents.*
5 Check the cylinder bore and piston for score marks or rust. If any is found, the damper will have to be replaced with a new one.
6 Check the clearance between the cylinder bore and the piston. If more than 0.0059-inch (0.15 mm), either the piston or damper will have to be replaced with new parts to obtain the proper clearance.
7 During reassembly, dip the new piston cup, piston and cylinder in clean brake fluid. Use the new parts which came in the rebuild kit and pay close attention to the installed direction of all rubber parts.

Installation

8 Install the damper in the reverse order of removal.
9 Bleed the clutch system as described in Section 6.
10 Adjust the clutch pedal height and pedal free play, referring to the procedures in Chapter 1.

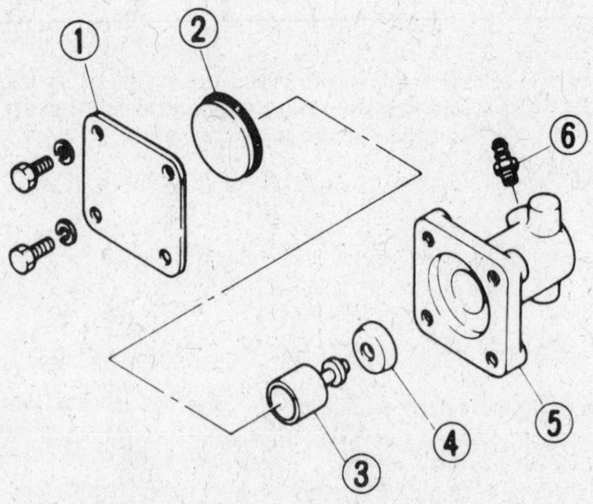

5.3a Exploded view of the clutch damper (early style)

1 Damper cover
2 Damper rubber
3 Piston
4 Piston cup
5 Cylinder
6 Bleeder screw

6 Clutch hydraulic system – bleeding

Caution: *Don't allow brake fluid to spill on painted surfaces of the vehicle, as damage to the finish will result.*

1 Bleeding will be required whenever the hydraulic system has been dismantled and reassembled and air has entered the system.
2 First fill the fluid reservoir with clean brake fluid which has been stored in an airtight container. Never use fluid which has drained from the system or has been bled out on a previous occasion, it may contain grit.

1980 through 1983 models

3 Fit a rubber or plastic tube over the bleeder screw on the operating cylinder and immerse the open end of the tube in a glass jar containing an inch or two of fluid.
4 Open the bleeder screw about half a turn and have an assistant quickly depress the clutch pedal all the way. Tighten the bleeder screw and then have the clutch pedal slowly released with the foot completely removed. Repeat this sequence of operations until air bubbles are no longer ejected from the open end of the tube beneath the fluid in the jar.
5 After two or three strokes of the pedal, check that the fluid level in the reservoir has not fallen too low. Keep it full of fresh fluid, otherwise air will again be drawn into the system.
6 Tighten the bleeder screw on a down stroke (do not overtighten it), remove the rubber tube and jar, top-up the reservoir and install the cap.
7 If the help of an assistant is not readily available, alternative 'one-man' bleeding operations can be carried out using a bleed tube fitted with a one way valve or a pressure bleed kit, both of which should be used in accordance with the manufacturer's instructions.

1984 and later models

8 Follow the above procedure, but before bleeding the operating cylinder the clutch damper must be bled.

7 Clutch components – removal, inspection and installation

Refer to illustrations 7.6, 7.7, 7.9 and 7.15

Warning: *Dust produced by clutch wear and deposited on clutch components contains asbestos, which is hazardous to your health. DO NOT*

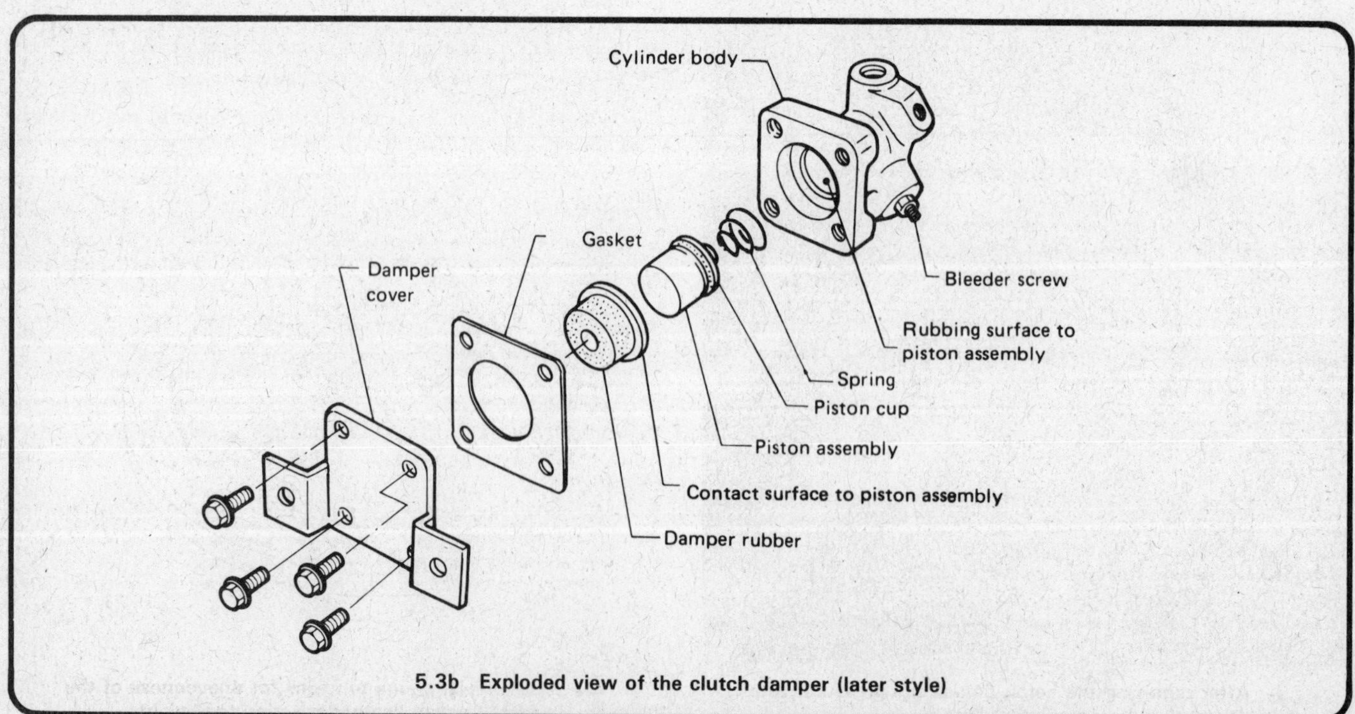

5.3b Exploded view of the clutch damper (later style)

blow it out with compressed air and DO NOT inhale it. DO NOT use gasoline or petroleum-based solvents to remove the dust. Brake system cleaner should be used to flush the dust into a drain pan. After the clutch components are wiped clean with a rag, dispose of the contaminated rags and cleaner in a covered container.

1 Due to the slow-wearing qualities of the clutch, it is not easy to decide when to go to the trouble of removing the transmission in order to check the wear on the friction lining. The only positive indication that something should be done is when it starts to slip or when squealing noises on engagement indicate that the friction lining has worn down to the rivets. In such instances it can only be hoped that the friction surfaces on the flywheel and pressure plate have not been badly worn or scored.

2 A clutch will wear according to the way in which it is used. Much intentional slipping of the clutch while driving — rather than the correct selection of gears — will accelerate wear. It's safe to assume, however, that the clutch disc will need replacement at about 40,000 miles (64,000 km).

3 Because of the clutch's location between the engine and transmission, the clutch cannot be worked on without removing either the engine or transmission. If repairs which would require removal of the engine are needed, the quickest way to gain access to the clutch is by removing the transmission, as described in Chapter 7.

4 With the transmission removed, but before removing the pressure plate assembly from the flywheel, check that none of the metal fingers on the pressure plate are distorted or bent. If any damage is evident the pressure plate will have to be replaced.

5 The pressure plate need not be marked in relation to the flywheel as it can only be installed one way due to the positioning dowels.

6 In a diagonal pattern, to keep from distorting the pressure plate, loosen the mounting bolts a little at a time until the spring pressure is relieved **(see illustration)**. If the flywheel begins to turn, insert a screwdriver through the starter motor opening and engage it in the teeth of the flywheel.

7 While supporting the pressure plate assembly, remove the bolts. Then remove the pressure plate and clutch disc **(see illustration)**.

8 Clean the pressure plate, flywheel mating surfaces and the bearing retainer outer surfaces to remove any oil and grease.

9 Examine the pressure plate surface where it contacts the clutch disc. This surface should be smooth, with no scoring, gouging or warping. Check the pressure plate cover and fingers for damage. Use a feeler gauge to measure the unevenness of the diaphragm spring to height and check that it is within the limit, as shown in the Specifications **(see illustration)**. If any fault is found with the pressure plate assembly it must be replaced as an entire unit.

10 Inspect the clutch disc for lining wear. Check for loose or broken rivets or springs. Because of the difficulty in reaching the clutch, if the friction plate lining is not at least 1/32-inch (0.8 mm) above the rivets, the disc should be replaced with a new one. If the lining material shows signs of breaking up or black areas where oil contamination has occurred, it should also be replaced. If there is any doubt at all, replace it.

11 Inspect the surface of the flywheel for rivet grooves, burnt areas or scoring. If the damage is slight, the flywheel can be removed and reconditioned using a lathe. If the damage is deep, the flywheel should be replaced. Check that the ring gear teeth are not broken, cracked or seriously burned. Refer to Chapter 2 for the flywheel removal procedure.

12 If any traces of oil are detected on the clutch components the source should be found and eliminated. If oil is coming from the center of the flywheel, this indicates a failure of the crankshaft rear oil seal (Chapter 2). Oil at the rear of the clutch assembly may indicate the need to replace the transmission input shaft seal (Chapter 7).

13 While servicing these clutch components, it's also a good idea to replace the release bearing at the same time. Refer to Section 8. Also check the pilot bushing for scoring and general wear, replacing it if necessary (Section 9).

14 Prior to installation, apply a light coat of moly-base grease to the splines of the transmission input shaft. Wipe off any excess grease.

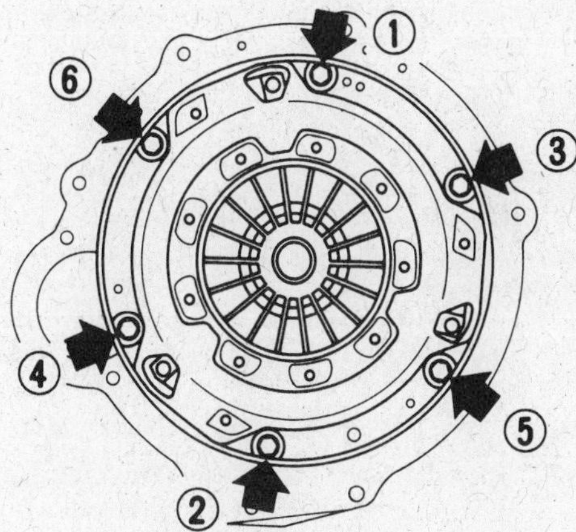

7.6 The pressure plate mounting bolts should be loosened and tightened in a criss-cross pattern, a little at a time, to avoid distorting the pressure plate

7.7 After removing the bolts, detach the pressure plate and clutch disc

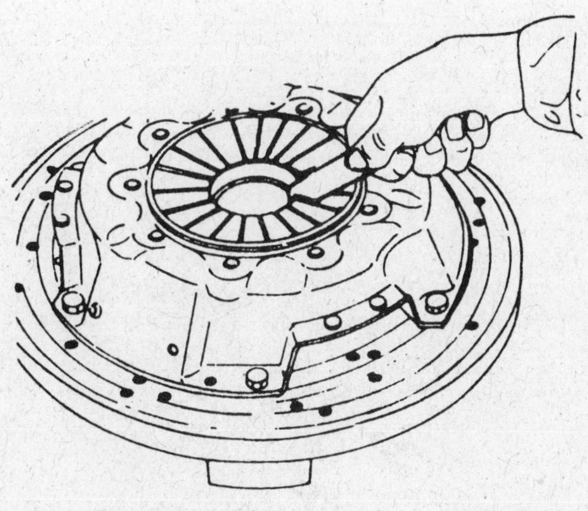

7.9 Use a feeler gauge to check for unevenness of the clutch cover diaphragm spring toe height

7.15 Before tightening the pressure plate mounting bolts it must be centered with an alignment tool (available at most auto parts stores) or an extension and socket as shown

15 To install the clutch, hold the disc and pressure plate together against the flywheel and insert an alignment tool through the center of them. Since the transmission input shaft must pass through the center of these components, they must be properly aligned during installation of the transmission. If an alignment tool is not available in an appropriate size, a socket on a ratchet extension will also work **(see illustration)**.

16 Locate the clutch pressure plate so that the cover engages with the dowels and install the mounting bolts. Tighten them in several steps, following a criss-cross pattern, until they are all at the specified torque **(see illustration 7.6)**.

17 Install the transmission.

8 Release bearing – replacement

Refer to illustrations 8.4, 8.6, 8.7, 8.9 and 8.11

1 The sealed release bearing, although designed for long life, is worth replacing at the same time that the other clutch components are being replaced or serviced.

2 Deterioration of the release bearing should be suspected when there are signs of grease leakage or the unit is noisy when spun with the fingers.

3 Remove the rubber dust boot which surrounds the withdrawal lever at the bellhousing opening.

4 Using a screwdriver, unhook and detach the retainer spring from the ball pivot in the bellhousing **(see illustration)**.

5 Remove the withdrawal lever.

6 The clutch release bearing and hub assembly can now be removed **(see illustration)**. **Note:** *Check that the withdrawal lever has not been cracked or bent. Slowly turn the front face of the release bearing, making sure it turns freely and without any noise. The release bearing is pre-lubricated and should not be washed in solvent. When a new clutch is installed, a new release bearing should always be used.*

7 If necessary, remove the release bearing from the hub with a two or three jaw puller **(see illustration)**.

8 Press on the new bearing, but apply pressure only to the center race.

9 Reassembly is the reverse of disassembly. Apply high temperature grease to the internal recess of the release bearing hub **(see illustration)**.

10 Also apply similar grease to the pivot points of the clutch withdrawal lever, the sliding surface of the bearing sleeve and the splines on the transmission main drive gear. **Note:** *Apply only a thin coat of*

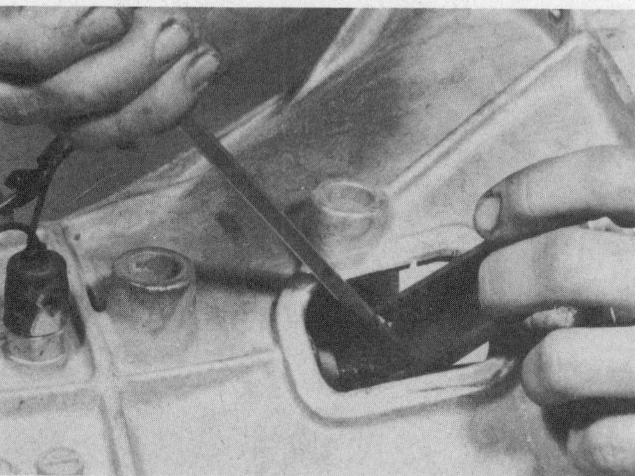

8.4 A screwdriver can be used to disengage the spring on the withdrawal lever from the ball pivot

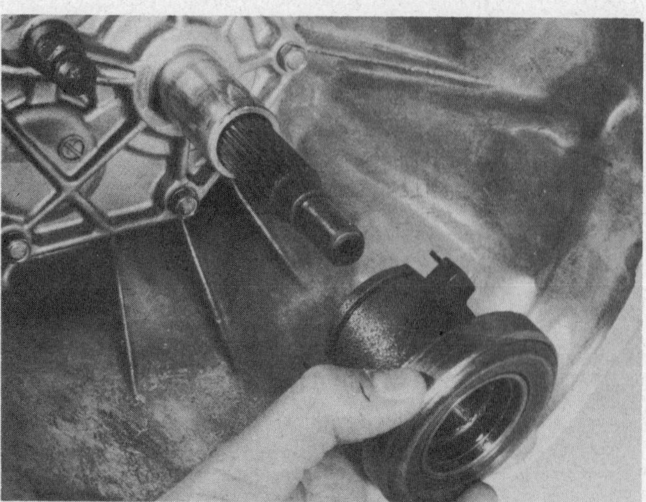

8.6 The release bearing and hub are removed from the input shaft as an assembly

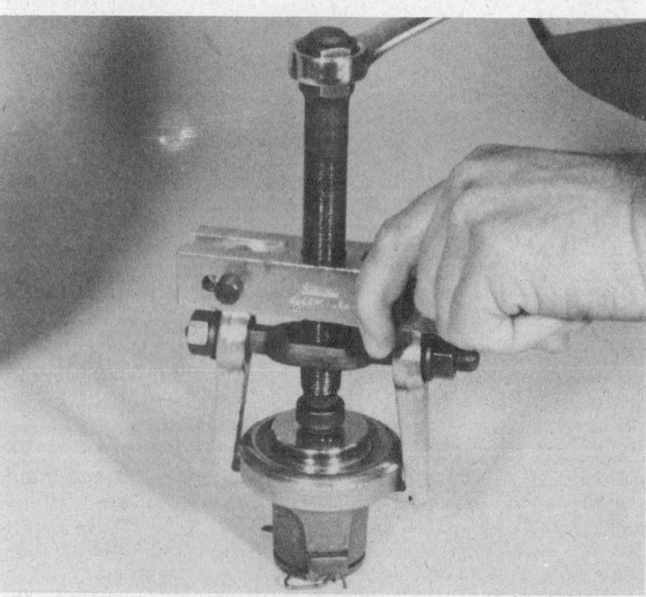

8.7 A puller is needed to separate the release bearing from the hub

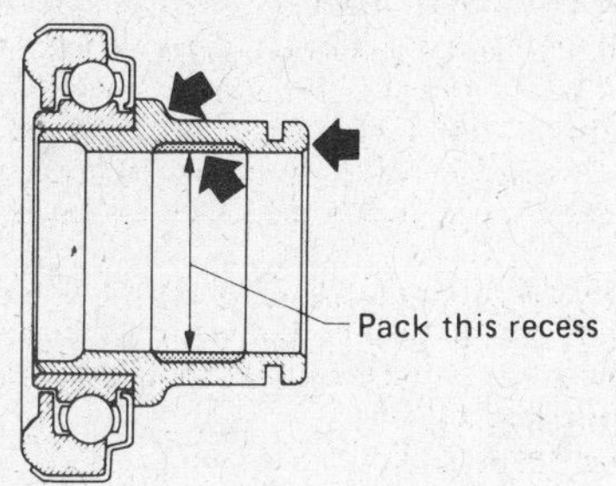

8.9 Pack the release bearing recess with grease and apply a thin coat of grease to the points indicated by arrows

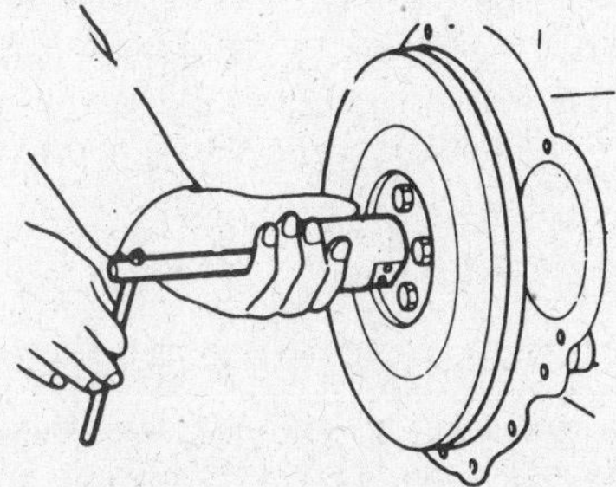

9.5 A special puller is available for removing the pilot bushing from the end of the crankshaft, . . .

grease to these points, as too much grease will run onto the friction plates when hot, causing damage to the clutch disc surfaces.

11 When installing the withdrawal lever to the release bearing, make sure the release bearing retaining spring ends are hooked over the ends of the withdrawal lever **(see illustration).**

9 Pilot bushing — replacement

Refer to illustrations 9.5, 9.9 and 9.10

1 The clutch pilot bushing is an oil impregnated bushing which is pressed into the rear of the crankshaft. Its primary purpose is to support the front of the transmission input shaft. The pilot bushing should be inspected whenever the clutch components are removed from the engine. Due to its inaccessibility, if you are in doubt about its condition, replace it with a new one. **Note:** *If the engine has been removed from the vehicle, disregard the following steps which do not apply.*

2 Remove the transmission (refer to Chapter 7 Part A).

3 Remove the clutch components (Section 3).

4 Using a clean rag, wipe the bushing clean and inspect for any excessive wear, scoring or obvious damage. A flashlight will be helpful to direct light into the recess.

5 Removal can be accomplished with a special puller **(see illustration)**, but an alternative method also works very well.

6 Find a solid steel bar which is slightly smaller in diameter than the bushing. Alternatives to a solid bar would be a wood dowel or a socket with a bolt fixed in place to make it solid.

7 Check the bar for fit — it should just slip into the bushing with very little clearance.

8 Pack the bushing and the area behind it (in the crankshaft recess) with heavy grease. Pack it tightly to eliminate as much air as possible.

9 Insert the bar into the bushing bore and hammer on the bar, which will force the grease to the backside of the bushing and push it out **(see illustration)**. Remove the bushing and clean all grease from the crankshaft recess.

10 Using an appropriate size socket or piece of pipe, drive the new bushing into the hole until the outer end of the bushing is 0.157-inch (4.0 mm) from the outside surface of the crankshaft flange **(see illustration).**

11 Reinstall the clutch assembly and transmission.

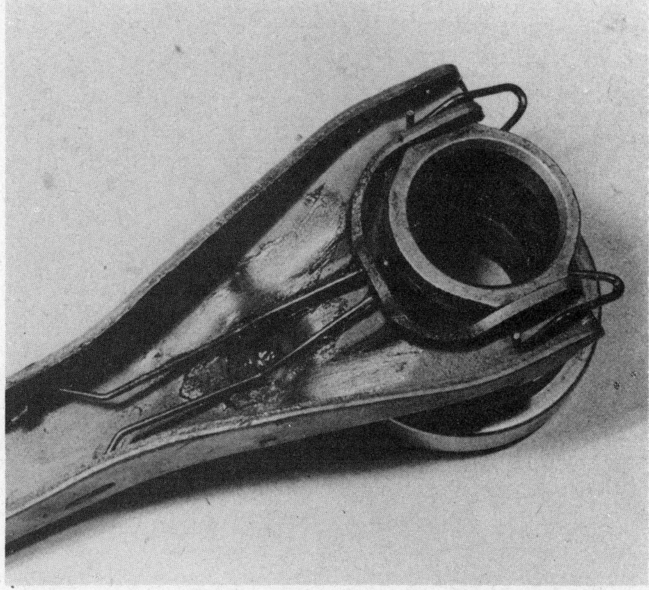

8.11 When properly installed, the withdrawal lever should be engaged with the release bearing spring

9.9 . . . or you can pack the recess behind the bushing with heavy grease and force it out hydraulically with a steel rod slightly smaller than the bore in the bushing — when the hammer strikes the rod, the bushing will pop out of the crankshaft

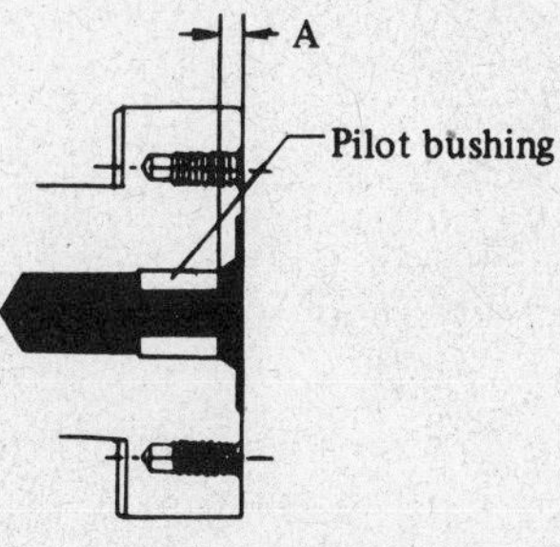

9.10 The pilot bushing must be recessed (distance A) 0.157-inch (4 mm)

8

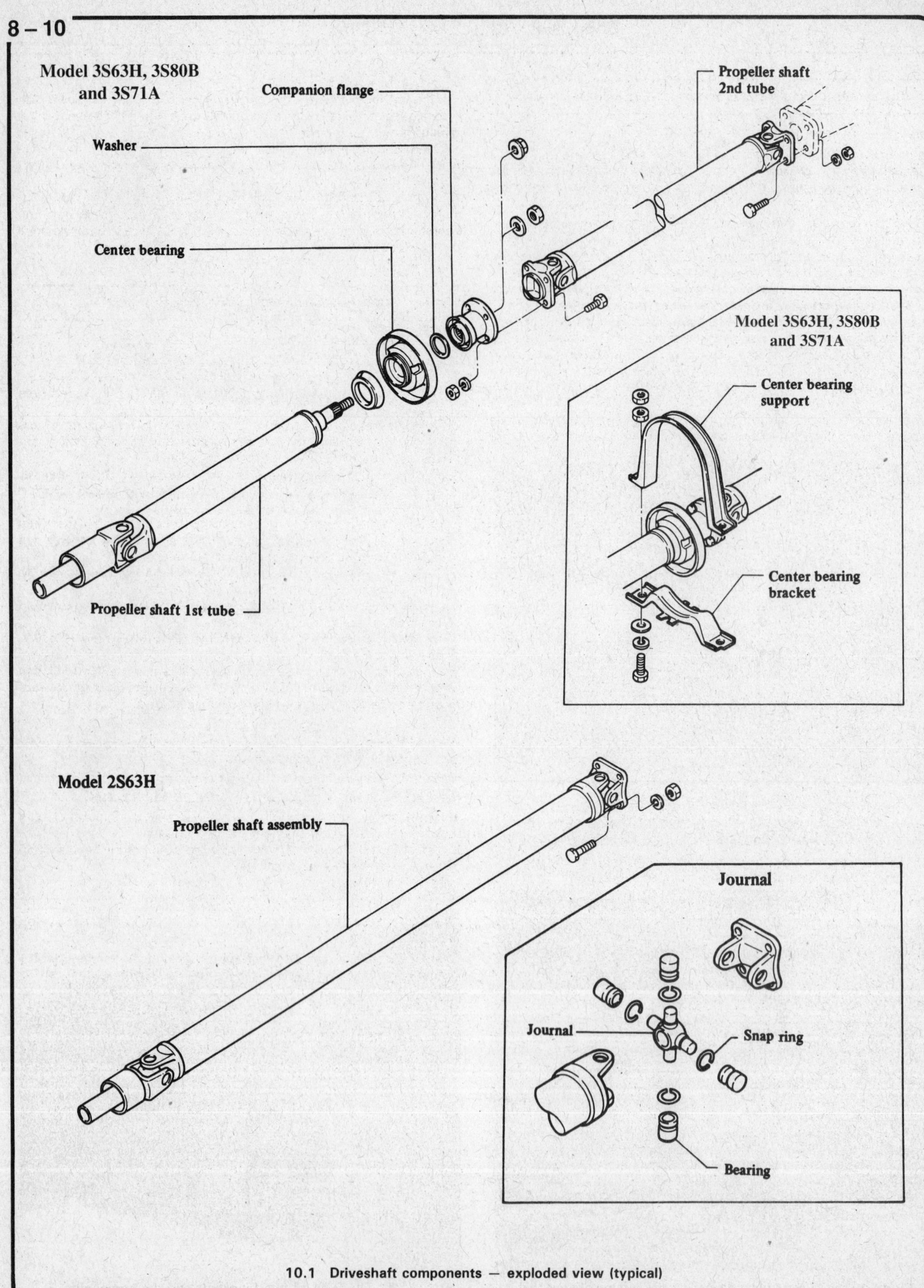

10.1 Driveshaft components — exploded view (typical)

10 Driveshaft, differential and rear axle – general information

Refer to illustration 10.1

Note: *The driveshaft, differential and rear axle information in this Chapter covers the components used on 2WD model pick-ups and the rear axle and driveshaft on 4WD models. For information on the other components used in 4WD models, refer to Chapter 9.*

Two different driveshafts are used, depending upon model. Regular bed models with a manual transmission use a one-piece driveshaft, which incorporates two universal joints, one at either end of the shaft.

All other models use a two-piece driveshaft, which incorporates a center bearing at the rear of the first shaft. This driveshaft uses three universal joints; one at the transmission end, one behind the center bearing and one at the differential companion flange. All universal joints are of the solid type, and can be replaced separately from the driveshaft.

The driveshaft is finely balanced during manufacture and whenever it is removed or disassembled, it must be reassembled and reinstalled in the exact manner and position it was originally in, to avoid excessive vibration.

The rear axle is a semi-floating type, having a 'banjo' design axle housing, which is held in proper alignment with the body by the rear suspension.

Mounted in the center of the rear axle is the differential which transfers the turning force of the driveshaft to the rear axleshafts, on which the rear wheels are mounted.

The axleshafts are splined at their inner ends to fit into the splines in the differential side gears; outer support for the shaft is handled by the rear wheel bearing.

Because of the complexity and critical nature of the differential adjustments, as well as the special equipment needed to perform the operations, we recommend any disassembly of the differential be done by a Nissan dealer service department or a repair shop.

11.2 The driveshaft rear flange and differential pinion flange should be marked prior to separation

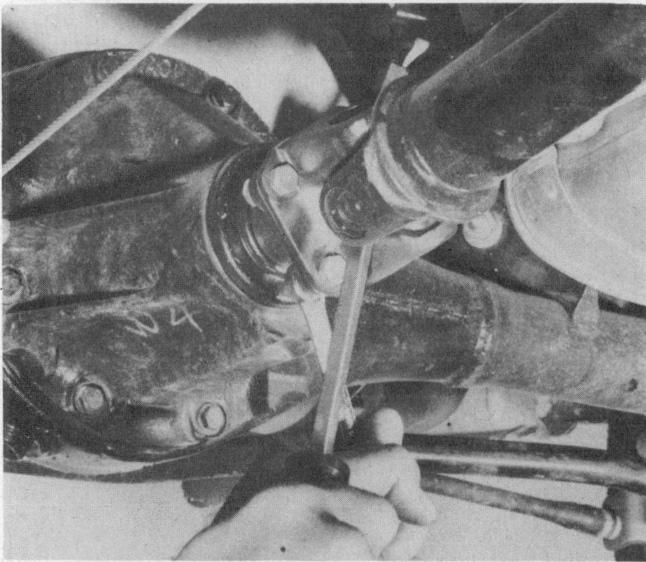

11.3 A screwdriver placed through the universal joint will keep the driveshaft from turning while removing the bolts

11 Driveshaft – removal and installation

Refer to illustrations 11.2 and 11.3

1 Raise the rear of the truck and support it on jackstands.
2 Mark the edges of the driveshaft rear flange and the differential pinion flange so that they can be realigned during installation **(see illustration)**.
3 Using a screwdriver placed through the rear universal joint to keep the shaft from turning, remove the four bolts that connect the rear flange with the pinion flange **(see illustration)**.
4 On two-piece type driveshafts, while supporting the driveshaft, remove the two bolts that attach the center bearing support bracket to the body.
5 Push the shaft forward slightly to disconnect the rear flanges. Then lower the shaft and carefully pull it to the rear until the forward end is withdrawn from the rear of the transmission.
6 While the driveshaft is removed, the rear of the transmission should be covered or plugged to prevent loss of oil.
7 If the driveshaft is removed, the rear of the transmission should be covered or plugged to prevent loss of oil.
8 If the driveshaft must be disassembled, refer to Section 12 or 13, as appropriate.
9 Installation is the reverse of the removal procedure. **Note:** *During installation make sure the marks on the rear flanges line up. Be sure to tighten the flange nuts to the specified torque.*

12 Center bearing – replacement

Refer to illustrations 12.2, 12.3, 12.5a, 12.5b, 12.6 and 12.11

1 Remove the nuts that secure the two halves of the support bracket together, and detach them from the driveshaft.
2 Mark the relationship of the companion flange to the front section of the driveshaft **(see illustration)**.

12.2 The front of the driveshaft and the companion flange should be marked (arrow) prior to separation

3 Using a long screwdriver placed through the center universal joint to keep the shaft from turning, remove the four bolts that attach the driveshaft to the companion flange **(see illustration)**.
4 Mark the companion flange in relation to the slot in the threaded shaft.
5 The center joint nut is staked to prevent it from working loose **(see illustration)**. To remove it, first use a punch to knock the staking back out, and unscrew it from the shaft. To keep the flange from turning, either obtain a special tool designed for this purpose, or one can be made using a flat steel bar and old bolts inserted through the flange holes. The bar should be drilled to match at least two of the flange holes **(see illustration)**.
6 Using a gear puller, remove the companion flange **(see illustration)**.
7 The center bearing can be removed from the front section of the driveshaft by using a hydraulic press and appropriate support plate. If a hydraulic press is not available, take the assembly to a machine shop or dealer service department to have the old center bearing pressed off and the new one installed.

12.3 Remove the companion flange bolts, using a screwdriver to keep the shaft from turning

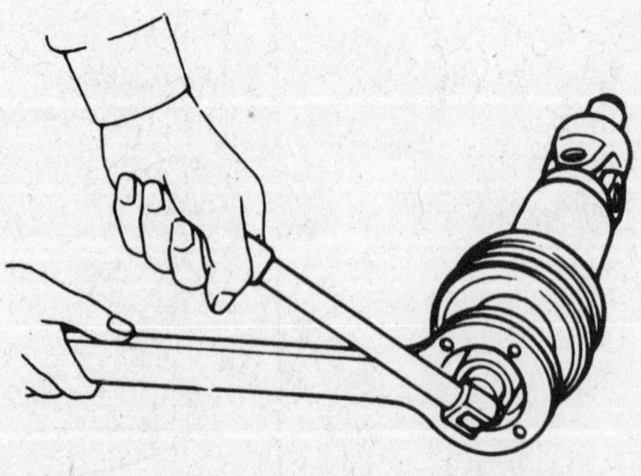

12.5b When removing the center bearing locknut, a tool must be fabricated to keep the driveshaft from turning

8 When the new bearing is pressed onto the shaft, make sure the letter F is facing the front of the vehicle.
9 Apply a coat of multi-purpose grease to the face of the center bearing and both sides of the washer, then insert the washer into the end of the center bearing.
10 Align the mark on the companion flange with the slot in the shaft and install the flange.
11 Install the locknut and tighten it to the specified torque **(see illustration)**. Stake the nut so it is engaged with the shaft's groove as before.
12 Align the marks on the companion flange and the center flange and install the attaching bolts.
13 The remainder of the reassembly is the reverse of the disassembly

12.5a The center bearing locknut is staked to keep it from working loose

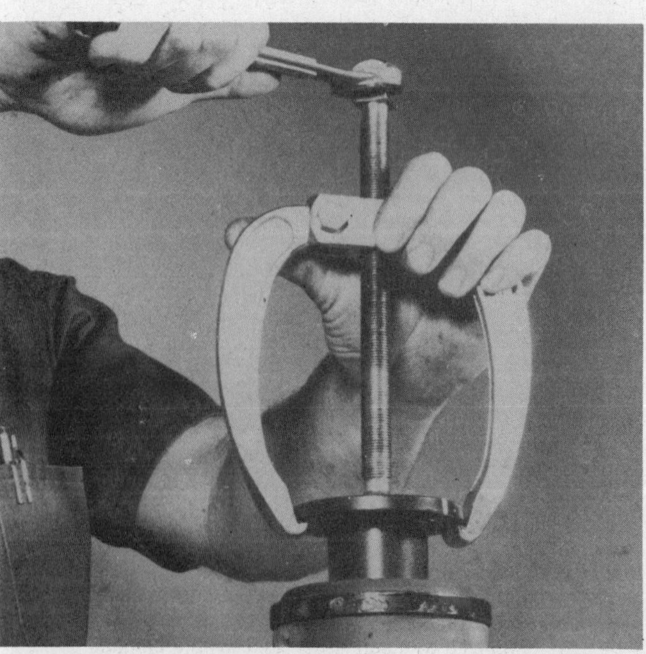

12.6 A puller is needed to separate the companion flange from the first shaft

procedure. **Note:** *Be sure the joint in the center bearing cushion rubber is facing up when the support bracket is installed.*

13 Universal joints — replacement

Refer to illustrations 13.2, 13.3 and 13.6

Caution: *The universal joints on certain models are not replaceable. Consult your parts supplier for parts availability before disassembling the driveshaft.*

Note: *Selective fit snap-rings are used to retain the universal joint spiders in the yokes. In order to maintain the driveshaft balance, you must use replacement snap-rings of the same size as originally used. Selective snap-rings are listed in the Specifications.*

1 Mark the relationship of all components so that they can all be installed in their original positions.

2 Clean away all dirt from the ends of the bearings on the yokes so the snap-rings can be removed with a small screwdriver **(see illustration)**. If they are very tight, tap the end of the bearing (inside the snap-ring) with a punch and hammer to relieve the pressure.

3 Once the snap-rings are removed tap the universal joints at the yoke with a soft-face hammer; the bearings will come out of the housing and can be removed easily **(see illustration)**.

4 Once the bearings are removed from each opposite journal yoke the journal can be easily disengaged.

5 In cases of extreme wear or neglect, it is possible that the bearing housings in the driveshaft, sleeve or flange will be worn so much that the bearings are a loose fit in them. In such a case, it will also be necessary to replace the worn component as well.

6 Installation is the reverse of the removal procedure. **Note:** *Be sure to grease the inner surface of the bearings prior to installing them. Also be sure to install the snap-rings in their proper positions as noted at the beginning of this Section* **(see illustration)**. *The difference in snap-ring thickness at opposite ends should not be more than 0.0024-inch (0.06 mm).*

14 Axleshaft, rear wheel bearing and oil seal — removal and installation

Single tire models

Refer to illustrations 14.6a, 14.6b, 14.7, 14.9, 14.10, 14.13, 14.16, 14.22 and 14.23

Removal

1 Raise the rear of the truck and support it on jackstands.

2 Remove the wheel and tire.

3 Remove the brake drum. Refer to Chapter 10, if necessary.

4 Disconnect the parking brake cable and brake line from the rear brake. Refer to chapter 10, if necessary.

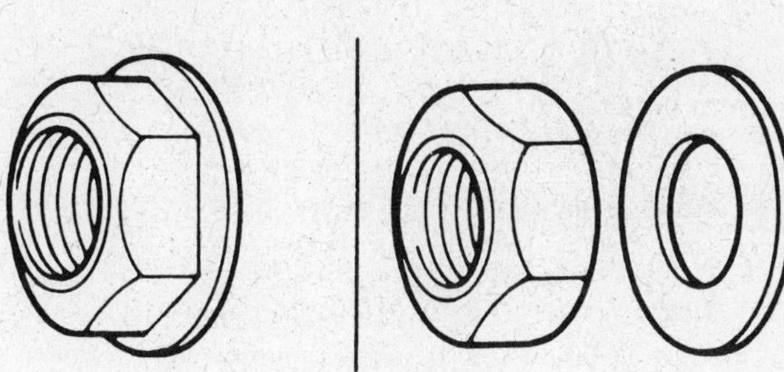

12.11 The two types of center bearing locknuts used on the two-piece driveshaft are the flange-type (left) and the nut-and-washer type (right) (each has a different torque value)

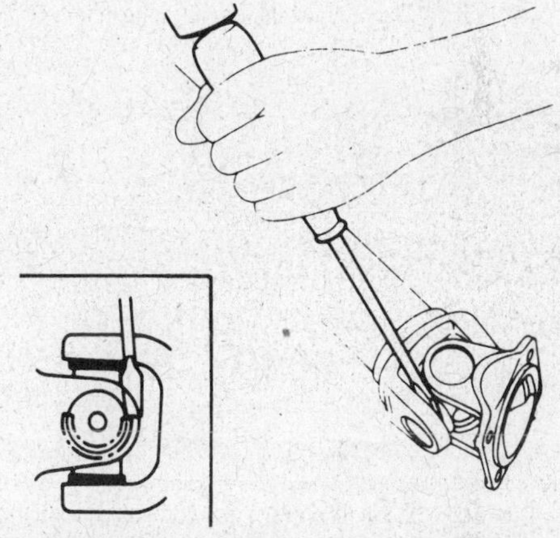

13.2 Remove the snap-rings from the U-joint bearings by tapping them off with a screwdriver and hammer

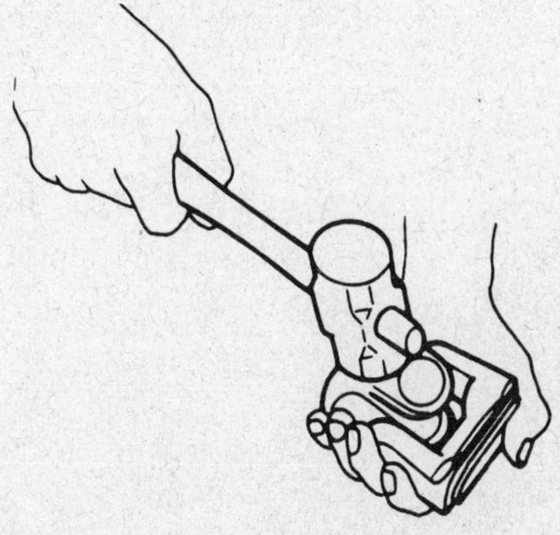

13.3 With the snap-rings removed, the bearings can be removed by tapping the yoke with a hammer

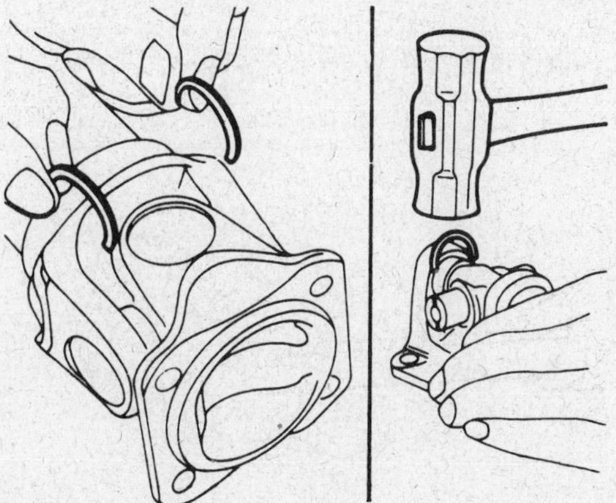

13.6 New snap-rings are installed by carefully tapping them into place

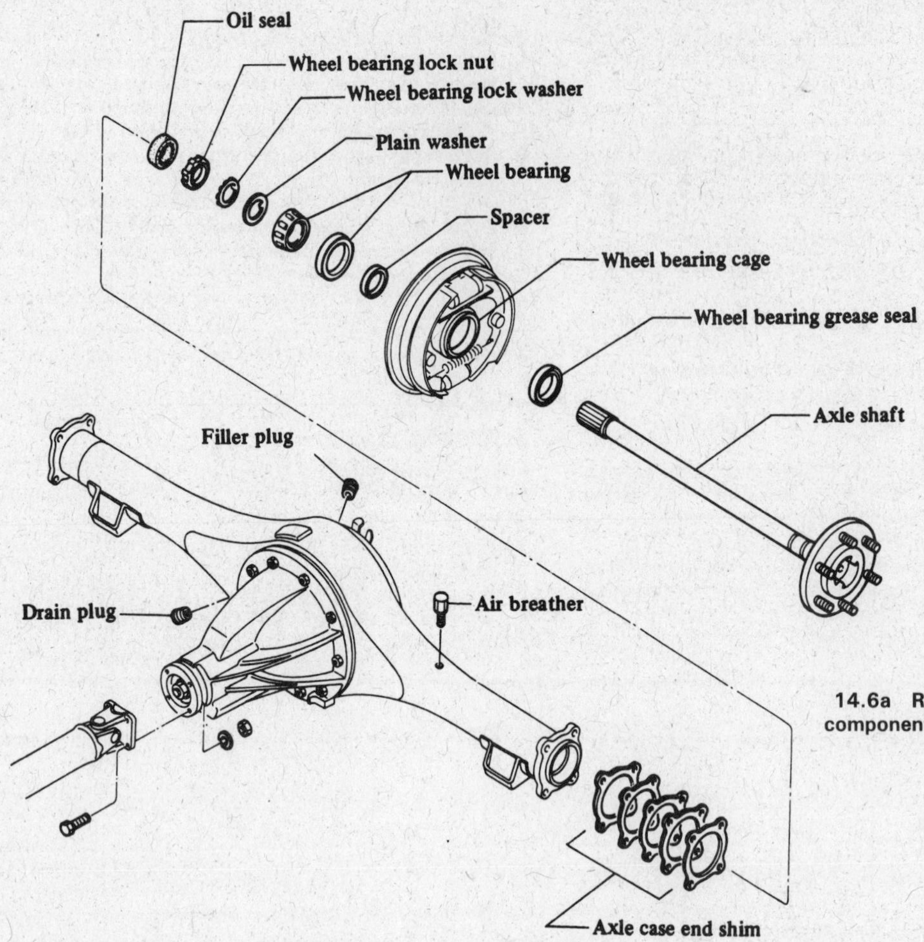

14.6a Rear axle and axleshaft components – single tire models

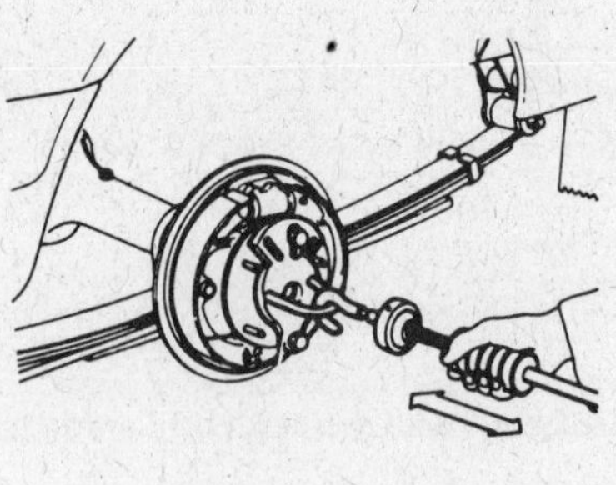

14.6b A rear axle adapter plate and slide hammer may be needed to remove the rear axleshaft assembly

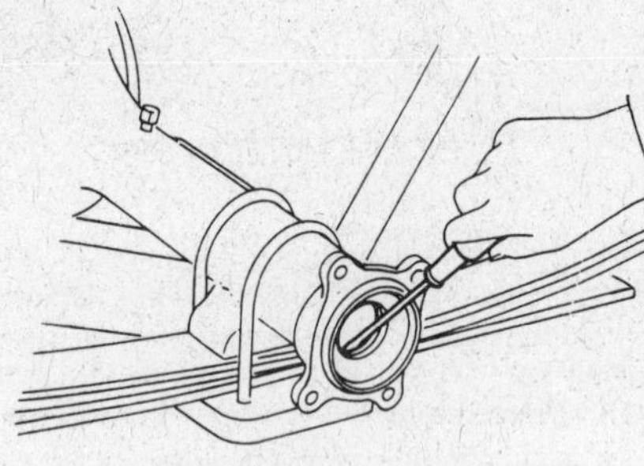

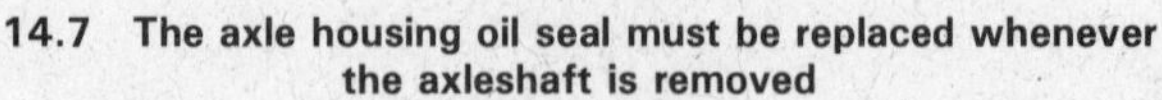

14.7 The axle housing oil seal must be replaced whenever the axleshaft is removed

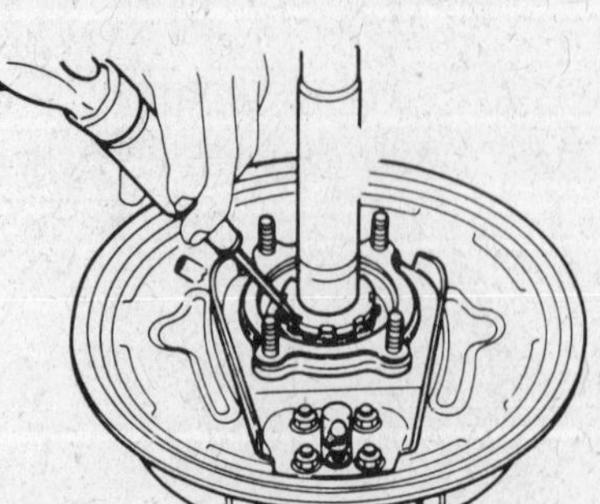

14.9 A punch or screwdriver can be used to unbend the tabs of the bearing nut lock washer

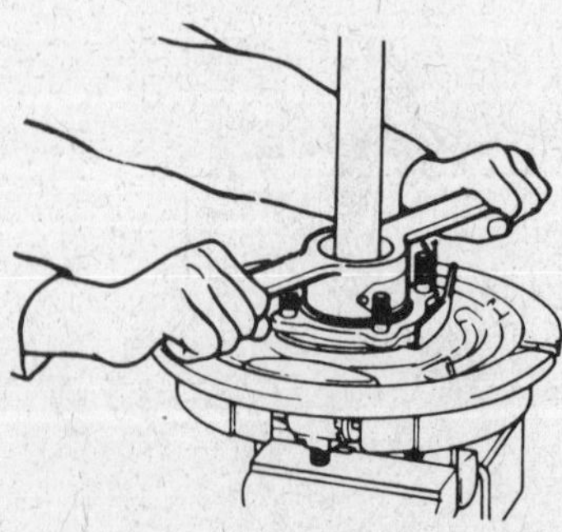

14.10 A ring wrench is needed to remove the wheel bearing locknut

5 Remove the brake backing plate mounting nuts.
6 The axleshaft, complete with the brake assembly, can now be pulled out from the rear axle **(see illustrations)**. If the axleshaft will not pull out by hand, a slide hammer can be attached to the wheel studs using an adapter plate.
7 Pry out the old oil seal from the end of the axle housing **(see illustration)**. This should always be replaced whenever the axleshaft is removed. A new seal can be installed by carefully tapping it in using an appropriate size socket.
8 Since the wheel bearing is press fit onto the axleshaft, its removal and installation will require the use of special tools and either a special puller or a hydraulic press. If the necessary equipment is not available, this operation should be left to a dealer or repair shop. If the equipment is available, proceed as follows.
9 Use a screwdriver to unbend the tabs of the bearing nut lock washer **(see illustration)**. The washer should always be replaced, once removed.
10 Using a ring wrench, remove the bearing locknut **(see illustration)**. The axleshaft will need to be secured in a vise to remove the nut. Use jaw protectors or blocks of wood to keep from damaging the axleshaft.
11 Using either a special puller designed for this purpose, or a hydraulic press equipped with the necessary supports, press the axleshaft out of the brake assembly and bearing cage.
12 Using a drift punch or screwdriver, drive the oil seal from the bearing case. Once removed, this oil seal must be replaced with a new one.
13 If the bearing outer race needs to be replaced (because it is pitted or scored), it can be tapped from the bearing cage using a brass drift punch **(see illustration)**. The outer race should be replaced whenever a new bearing is installed.

Installation

14 Begin installation by installing a new oil seal into the bearing case using an appropriate size socket. After installation of the seal, smear a light coat of grease between the seal lips.
15 Carefully tap a new outer race into place, again using a brass drift.
16 Install the spacer onto the axleshaft with the chamfered side of the spacer toward the axle flange **(see illustration)**.
17 Carefully tap the main bearing into place using a brass drift.
18 Install the washer and lock washer. Then install the bearing nut with the faced side toward the washer.
19 Bend the tabs of the lock washer over the nut to secure it in place.
20 Apply the wheel bearing grease to the wheel bearing and to the recess in the end of the axle housing.
21 Apply a coat of gear oil to the shaft splines, and a coat of wheel bearing grease to the lips of the axle housing oil seal.
22 Prior to installing the axleshaft, replace any removed shims in position on the axleshaft **(see illustration)**.
23 If both axleshafts have been removed, install the first one (either left or right). Then attach a dial gauge to the end of the shaft and measure the end play **(see illustration)**. The end play for the first axleshaft should be 0.012 to 0.035-inch (0.3 to 0.9 mm). If it is not, remove the shaft again and either add or subtract shims to obtain the proper end play. Shim sizes are listed in the Specifications.
24 If only one axleshaft was removed, or when installing the second one, the end play should be as listed in the Specifications.
25 The remainder of the installation procedure is the reverse of removal.

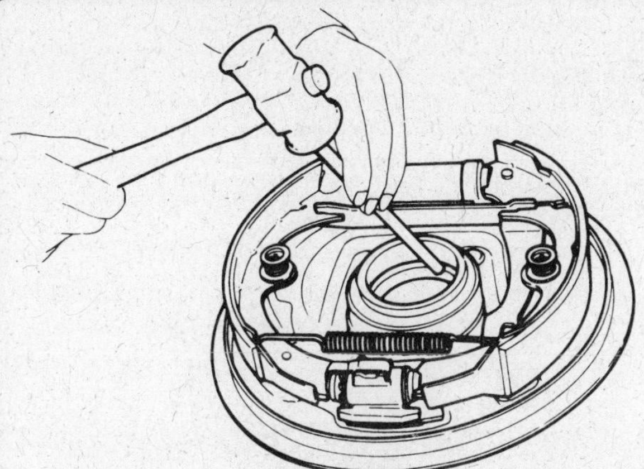

14.13 Drive the outer race from the cage with a brass drift punch

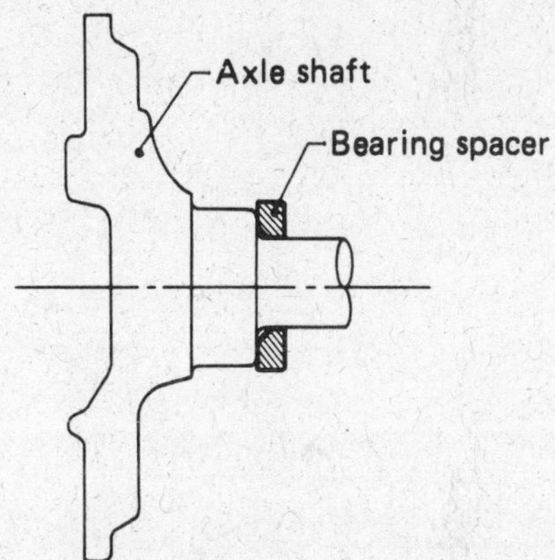

14.16 The chamfered inner diameter of the bearing spacer must face the axle flange

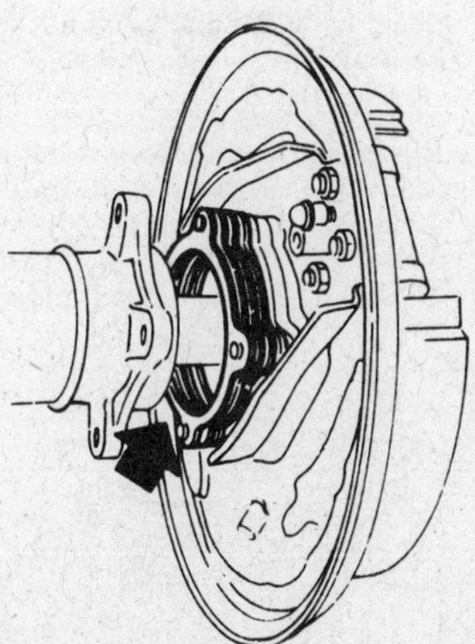

14.22 Shims are placed between the axle housing and the bearing retainer to adjust axle end play

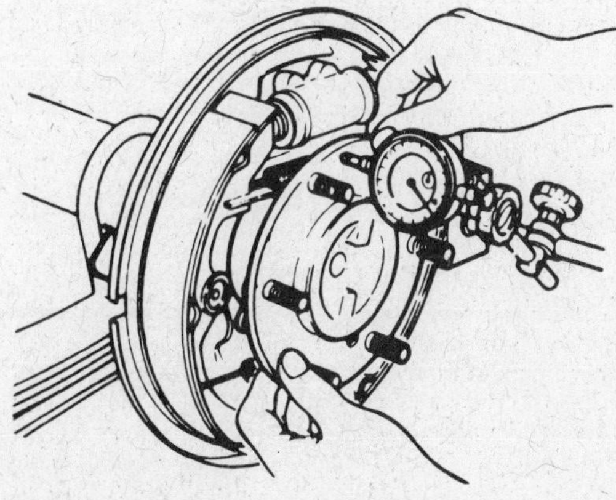

14.23 A dial gauge, attached to the ouside of the shaft, is used to measure the end play

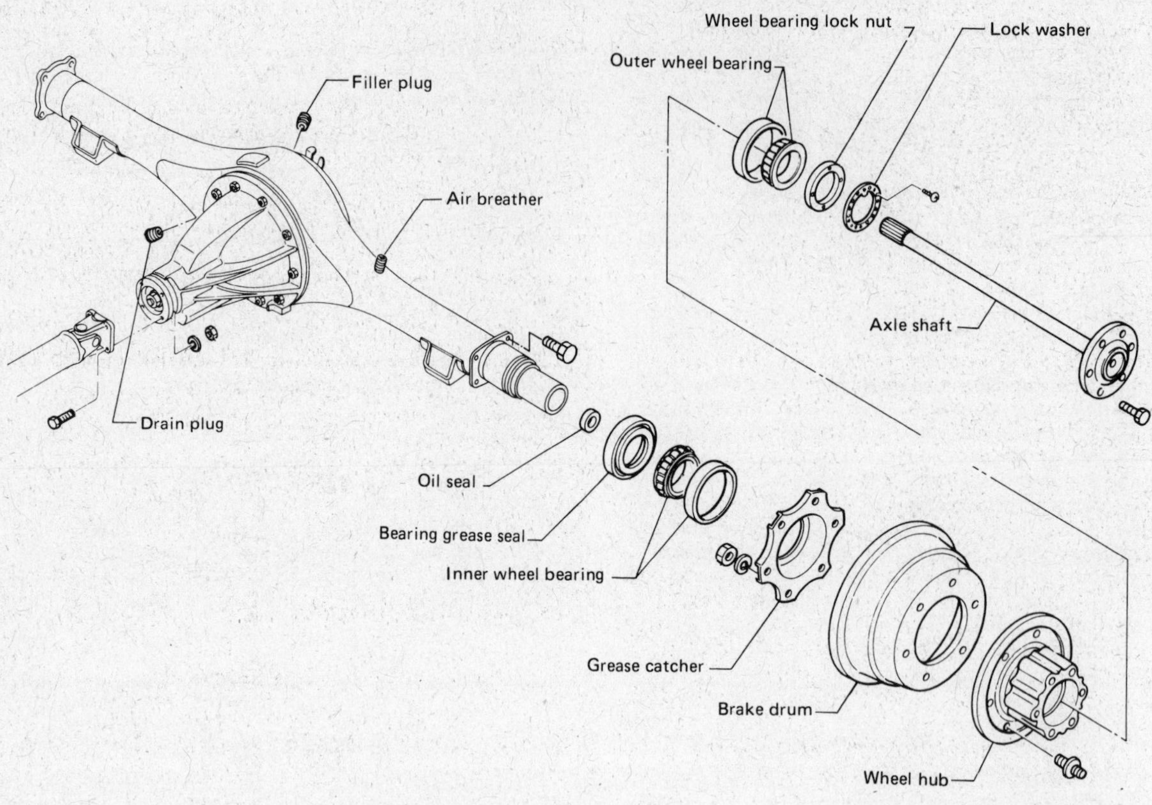

14.26 Rear axle and axleshaft components — dual tire models

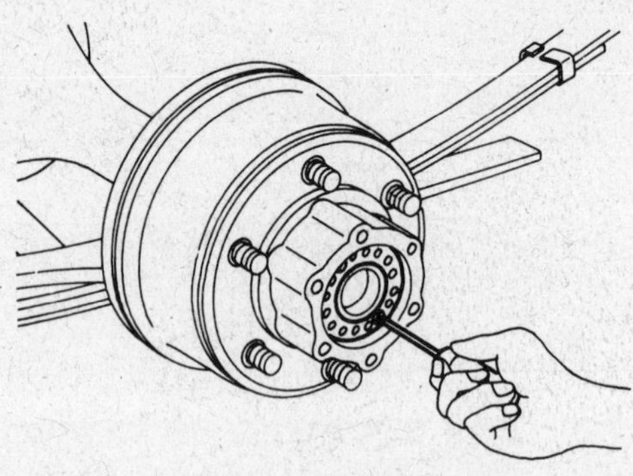

14.27 The lock washer is retained by a screw

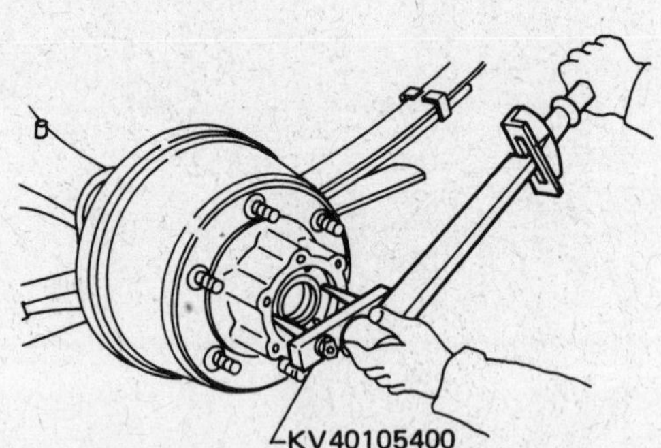

14.28 Remove the wheel bearing locknut. If this special tool cannot be obtained, one can be fabricated from two tight-fitting steel pins bolted through a flat metal bar. For installation purposes, drill and tap a hole between the two pins and install a large bolt. The tool can now accept a torque wrench.

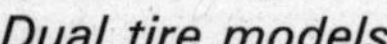

Dual tire models

Refer to illustrations 14.26, 14.27, 14.28, 14.30, 14.32, 14.34, 14.37, 14.41 and 14.42

Removal

26 Remove the six axle retaining bolts from the hub and pull the axle out of the housing **(see illustration)**.

27 Remove the lock washer retaining screw and the lock washer **(see illustration)**.

28 Remove the wheel bearing locknut. A special spanner type wrench (Nissan tool No.KV40105400) is required to loosen this nut **(see illustration)**.

29 Pull the hub and drum assembly out of the housing. Be careful not to let the outer bearing fall out of the hub.

30 Using a screwdriver, pry the oil seal from the housing **(see illustration)**.

31 Set the hub assembly upside-down on the workbench and pry the grease seal out of the hub using a large screwdriver. The inner bearing can now be removed.

32 Inspect the wheel bearings and races for cracks, bent cages, pitting, roughness or other signs of wear. If the bearings are to be replaced, it will be necessary to knock the outer races out of the hub, as the bearings/races come in matched sets. Using a brass drift punch and hammer, remove the bearing races **(see illustration)**.

Installation

33 Install a new oil seal in the housing. A socket or piece of pipe with an outside diameter slightly less than that of the seal can be used to drive the seal into position.

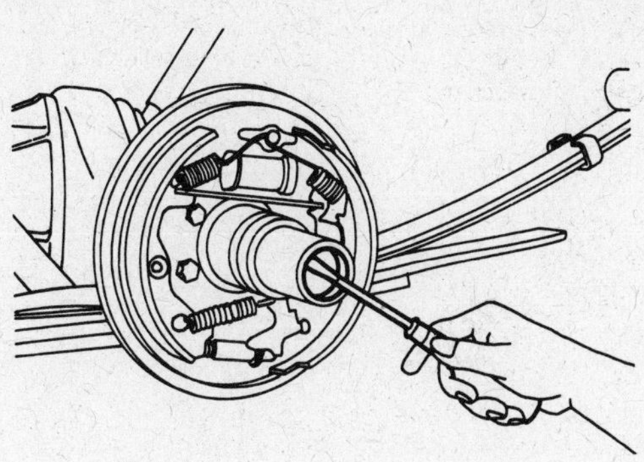

14.30 The axleshaft oil seal can be pried out of the axle housing with a screwdriver

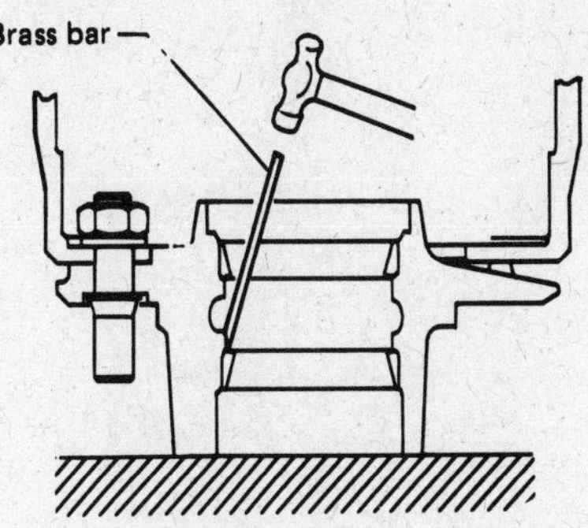

14.32 Remove the outer races from the hub with a brass bar and hammer

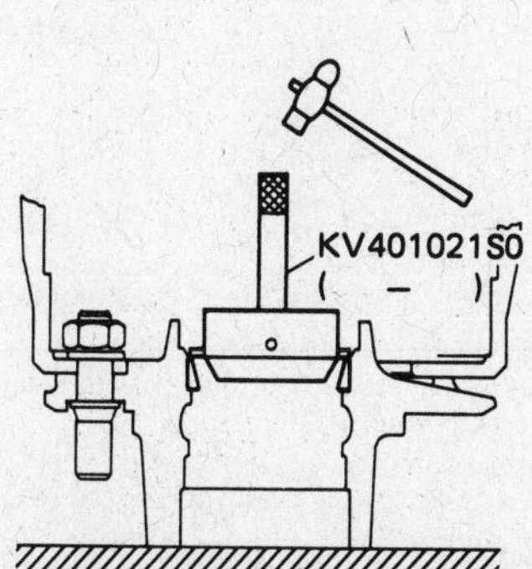

14.34 A bearing driver is the recommended tool for installing the new outer races

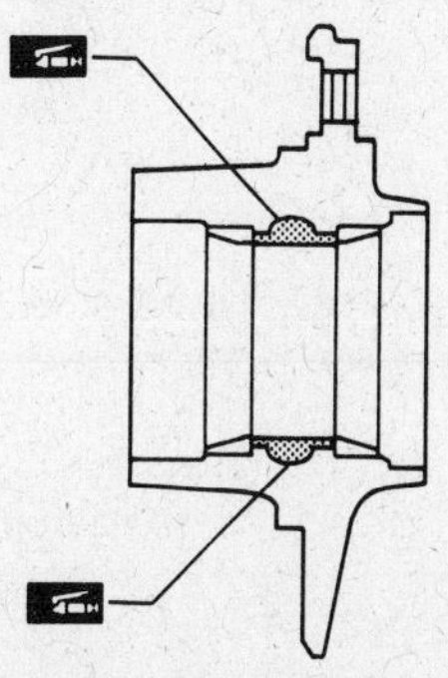

14.37 Fill the cavity between the races with high temperature wheel bearing grease

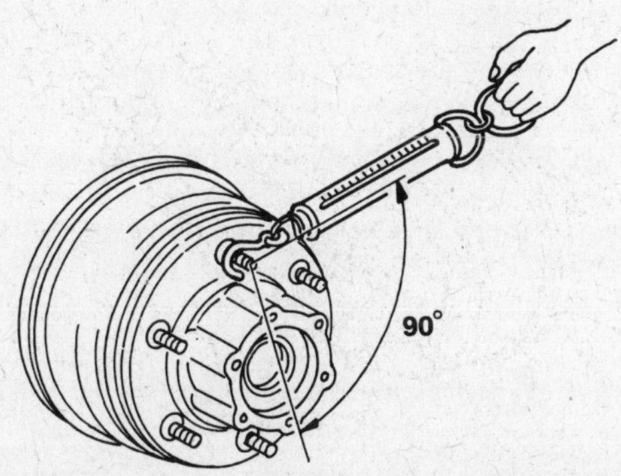

14.41 Use a spring scale to determine the rear wheel bearing preload; pull the hub through 90° of rotation while reading the scale, then compare the measurement with the Specifications

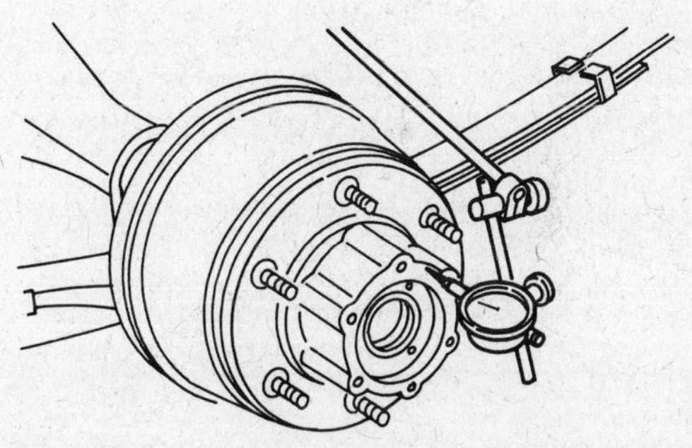

14.42 Position a dial indicator on the hub surface and move the hub in and out, noting the total end play reading

34 Use a bearing driver to install the new races in the hub **(see illustration)**. If such a tool is not available, an alternative method would be to use a block of wood and an old race as a driver, placed on top of the new race, then carefully tap the new race into the hub until it is seated.

35 If the bearings are to be re-used, thoroughly wash them in solvent. Dry the bearings off with compressed air, if available, then repack them with a high temperature wheel bearing grease. Be sure to also remove all traces of old grease from the hub.

36 New bearings must also be packed with high temperature wheel bearing grease.

37 Pack the inside of the hub and coat the races with the same grease **(see illustration)**.

38 Place the inner wheel bearing in the hub and install the grease seal. A block of wood can be used to drive the seal in evenly. Apply a thin coat of grease to the seal lip.

39 Install the outer wheel bearing in the hub and slide the assembly onto the housing. Install the wheel bearing locknut and tighten it to the specified torque.

40 Turn the the hub several times in both directions then retighten the locknut.

41 Check the wheel bearing preload with a spring scale **(see illustration)**. Loosen or tighten the locknut until the desired preload, as listed in the Specifications, is attained.

42 Using a dial indicator, measure the hub axial end play **(see illustration)**. It should not exceed the specified end play as listed in the

8

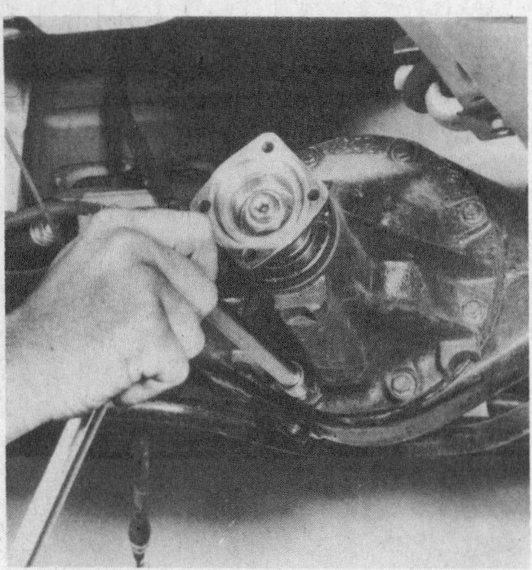

15.5 The differential mounting bolts should be loosened and tightened a little at a time in a criss-cross pattern

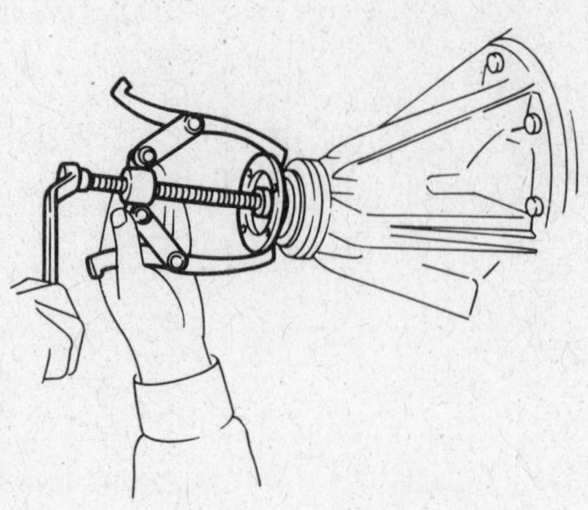

16.5 A two-jaw puller works well for removing the pinion flange

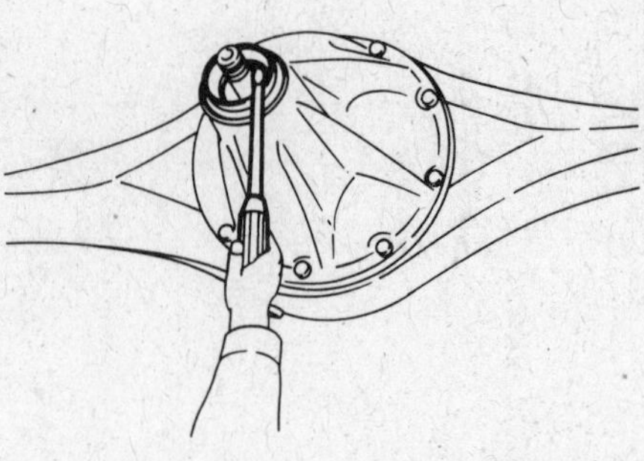

16.6 Pry the old pinion seal from the housing – be careful not to damage the pinion shaft

Specifications. If there is excessive end play, repeat the adjustment procedure.
43 Install the locknut, lock washer and screw.
44 Install the axle and tighten the bolts to the specified torque.

15 Differential – removal and installation

Refer to illustration 15.5

Note: *This procedure applies to differentials that can be removed as a complete unit ("pumpkin-type") only. Differentials which are mounted integrally with the rear axle should not be removed from the housing, as performing all of the critical adjustments after installation is beyond the scope of the home mechanic.*

1 Raise the rear of the truck and support it on jackstands.
2 Drain the oil from the differential.
3 Disconnect the rear of the driveshaft from the differential as described in Section 11, and position it out of the way.
4 Partially withdraw both axleshafts as described in Section 14, so they are disengaged from the differential.
5 Unscrew the differential housing mounting nuts evenly and in a criss-cross pattern **(see illustration)**, and lift the differential out of the rear axle.
6 The overhaul of the rear axle differential unit is not within the scope of the home mechanic, due to the specialized gauges and tools which are required. Where the unit requires servicing or repair, due to wear or excessive noise, it is most economical to exchange it for a factory reconditioned assembly.
7 Scrape all traces of old gasket material from the mating surface of the axle housing. Position a new gasket on the housing (use gasket sealant).
8 Installation is the reverse of the removal procedure. Be sure to tighten the bolts to the specified torque.
9 Following installation, fill the differential with the proper grade and quantity of oil (see Chapter 1).

16 Differential front (pinion) oil seal – replacement

Refer to illustrations 16.5 and 16.6

1 Place a container beneath the differential, then remove the drain plug and allow the oil to drain from the unit.Install the drain plug.
2 Raise the rear of the vehicle to obtain access to the unit, and support the frame and differential housing securely on jackstands or blocks.
3 Disconnect the rear end of the driveshaft as described in Section 11 and move the shaft to one side.
4 Hold the pinion flange by placing two inch (50 mm) long bolts through two opposite holes. Bolting them up tight, remove the self-locking nut while holding a large screwdriver or tire lever between the two bolts as a lever.
5 Using a puller, withdraw the pinion flange from the differential unit **(see illustration)**.
6 Remove the defective oil seal by driving in one side of it and levering it out **(see illustration)**.
7 Install the new oil seal after greasing the mating surfaces of the seal and the axle housing. The lips of the oil seal must face in. Using a large socket, carefully drive the new oil seal into the recess until the face of the seal is flush with the housing. Make sure that the end of the pinion is not moved during this operation.
8 Install the pinion flange, thrust washer and nut.
9 Again holding the pinion flange still with the screwdriver or tire lever, tighten the pinion nut until there is no axial play.
10 Once the pinion nut is tightened, use the wrench to turn the pinion shaft in both directions several times, to settle the bearing rollers. Then fit an inch-pound torque wrench over the pinion nut and slowly turn the pinion shaft, noting the amount of torque needed to begin turning the shaft. This is the drive pinion preload, and should be as specified. If the preload is below normal, tighten the pinion nut a little at a time until the proper preload is obtained. **Note:** *This preload is achieved by using a collapsible spacer within the differential. If the preload is set over the recommended specification the differential will have to be removed and the spacer replaced.*
11 The remainder of the installation is the reverse of the removal procedure.
12 Following installation, refill the differential with the proper grade and quantity of oil (see Chapter 1).

17 Rear axle assembly – removal and installation

Refer to illustrations 17.7a, 17.7b, 17.8 and 17.10

Removal

1 Raise the rear of the truck and support it under the body side members with jackstands.
2 Support the axle assembly under the differential with a moveable garage-type jack.
3 Remove the wheels and tires.
4 Disconnect the rear of the driveshaft from the differential as described in Section 11 and position it out of the way.
5 Disconnect the parking brake cables and brake lines from the rear brakes, as described in chapter 10. Plug the brake lines to prevent dirt from entering them.
6 Remove the lower shock absorber mounting nuts from both shocks and compress the shock bodies.

Leaf spring suspension

7 Remove the U-bolts and the U-bolt lower brackets from around the rear axle and leaf springs **(see illustrations)**.

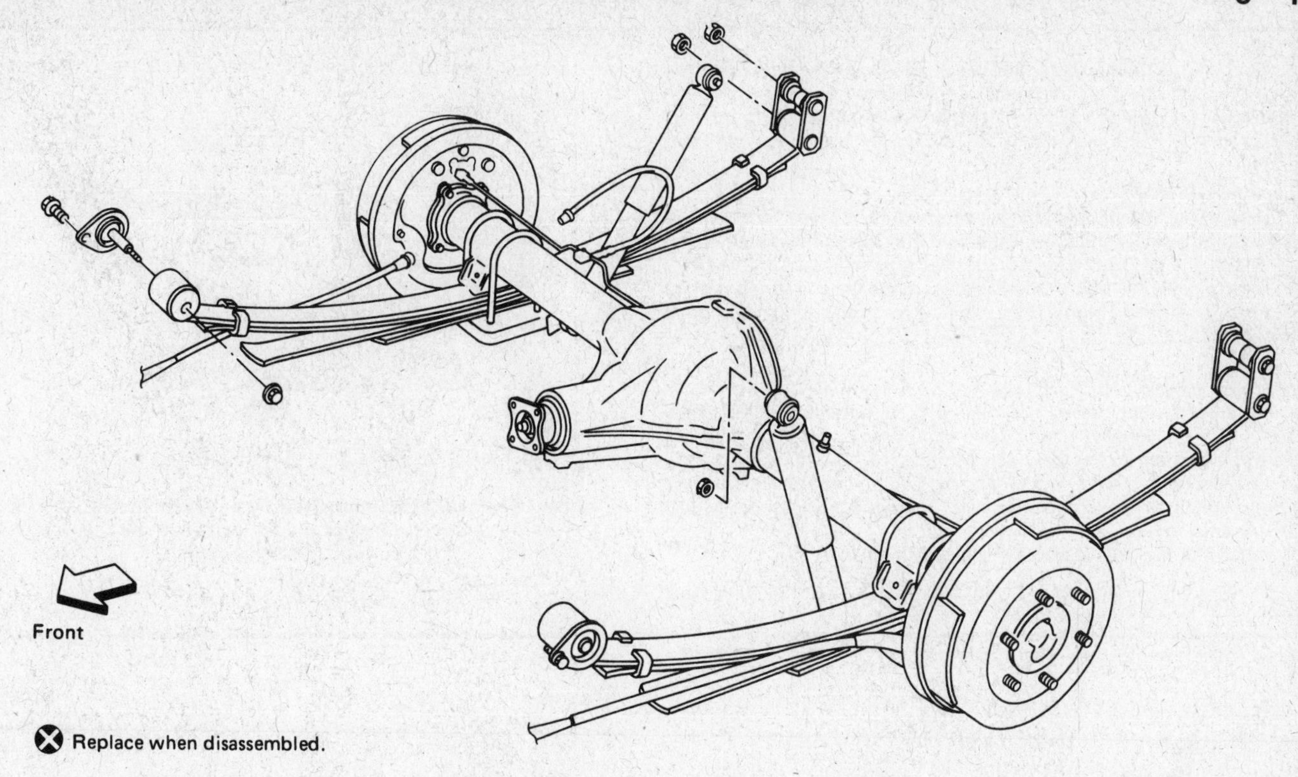

17.7a Rear axle mounting details – 2WD models

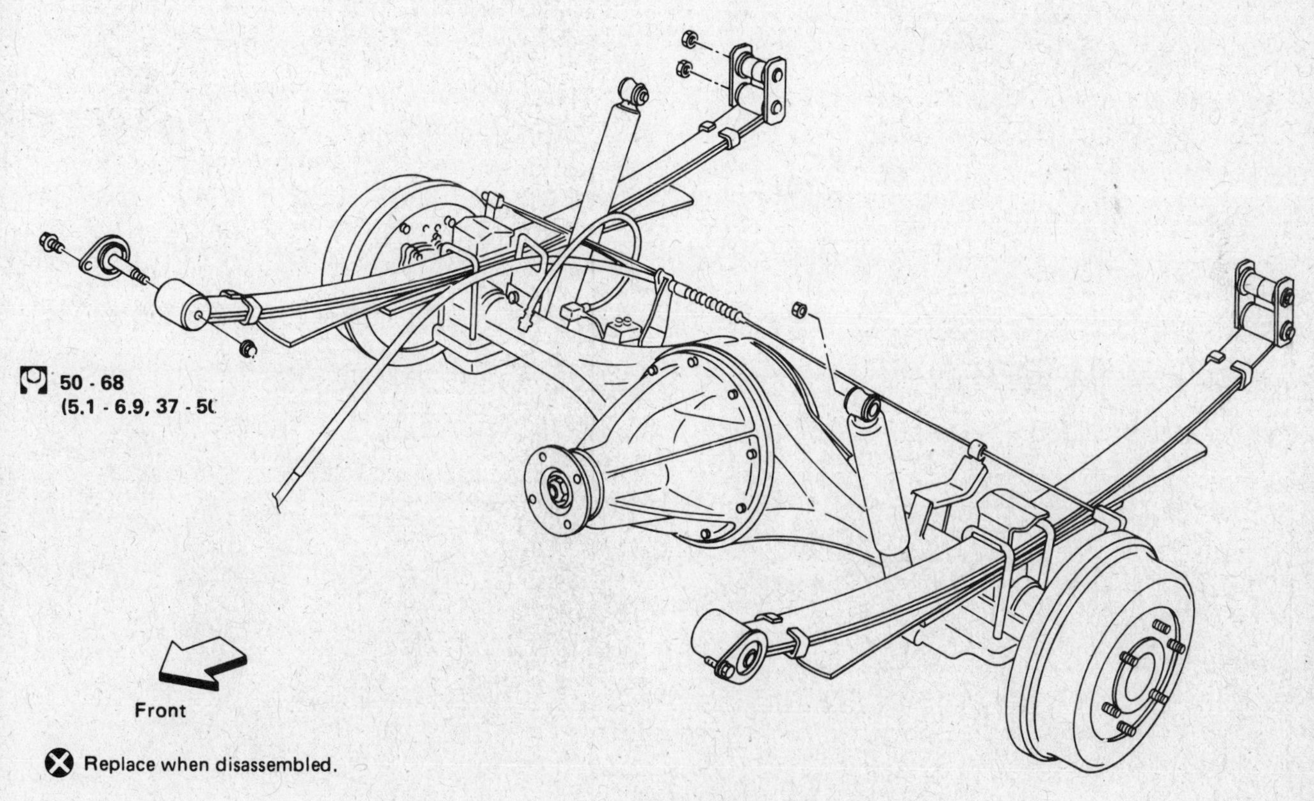

17.7b Rear axle mounting details – 4WD models

8 With an assistant helping to balance the axle on the jack, carefully move the jack sideways and remove the axle by passing it through the space above one of the leaf springs **(see illustration)**. On four wheel drive models, lower the axle assembly, as it is mounted below the leaf springs.

Coil spring suspension

9 Disconnect the stabilizer bar links from the body (see Chapter 11).
10 Unbolt the upper and lower links from the chassis **(see illustration)**.
11 Unbolt the panhard bar from the axle housing (see Chapter 11).
12 Slowly lower the axle assembly and remove the coil springs. Upon installation, refer to Chapter 11 for the correct coil spring installation procedure.

Installation (all models)

13 If the rear axle housing must be replaced, remove the rear brake assemblies, the axleshafts and related components and the differential and transfer them to the new axle.
14 Installation is the reverse of the removal procedure. Refer to the appropriate Chapters and Sections for installation of the individual components.
15 Bleed the brake system as described in Chapter 10.

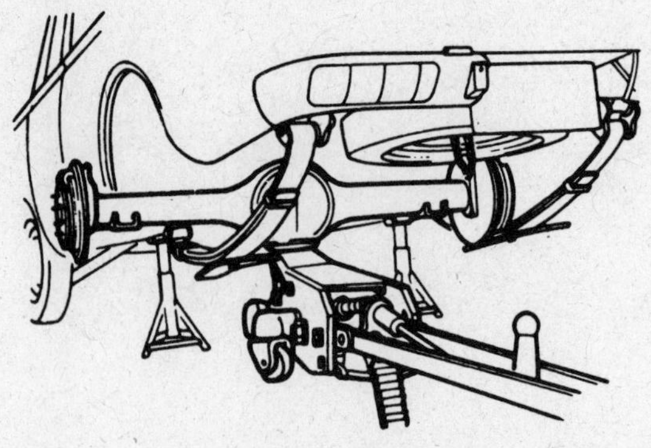

17.8 The rear axle, supported by a moveable jack, is most easily removed through the space above the rear leaf springs (2WD models)

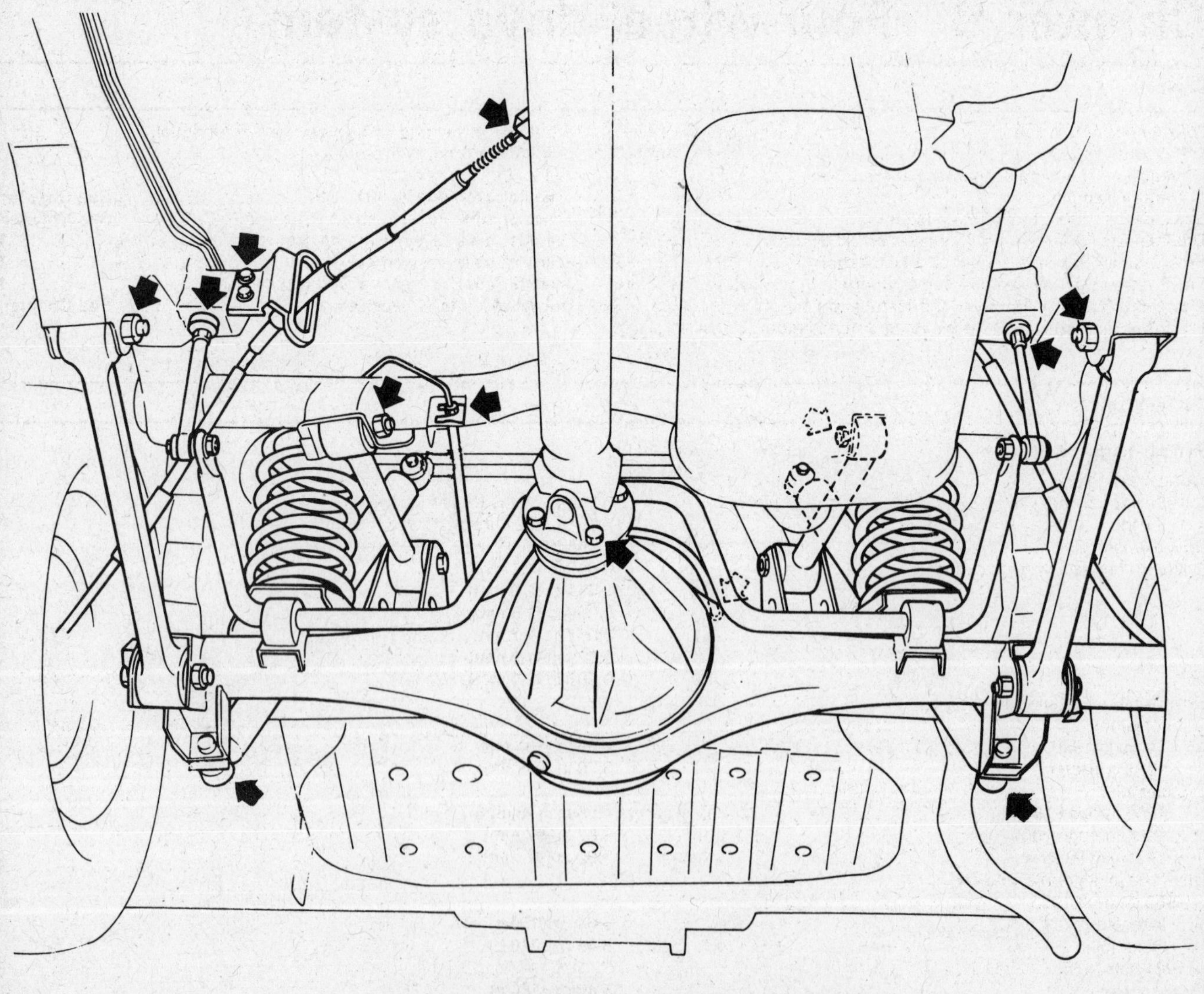

17.10 Rear axle mounting details – coil spring rear suspension

Chapter 9 Four-wheel drive system

Contents

Specifications

Front hub assembly

Wheel bearing preload
- 1980 through 1983 .... 0.5 to 2.2 ft-lbs (0.7 to 3.0 Nm)
- 1984 on .... 1.59 to 4.72 ft-lbs (2.15 to 6.4 Nm)

Driveaxle end play .... 0.004 to 0.012 in (0.1 to 0.3 mm)

Driveaxle end snap-ring thicknesses .... 0.043 in (1.1 mm)
0.051 in (1.3 mm)
0.059 in (1.5 mm)
0.067 in (1.7 mm)
0.075 in (1.9 mm)
0.083 in (2.1 mm)

Driveaxle boot installed length
- Inner joint ....
  - Through 1990 .... 4.06 in (103 mm)
  - 1991 and later .... 3.70 in (94 mm)
- Outer joint
  - 1980 through 1983 .... 4.65 in (118 mm)
  - 1984 through 1990 .... 3.82 in (97 mm)
  - 1991 and later .... 3.82 in (97 mm)

Driveaxle joint grease quantity
- 1980 through 1983
  - Inner joint .... 5.64 oz (160 g)
  - Outer joint .... 8.46 oz (240 g)
- 1984 and 1985
  - Inner joint .... 5.46 oz (160 g)
  - Outer joint .... 3.53 oz (100 g)
- 1986 on
  - Inner joint .... 7.76 oz (220 g)
  - Outer joint .... 5.64 oz (160 g)

Front hub assembly (continued)

Wheel bearing collar thicknesses

Number	Thickness
0	1.0996 in (27.93 mm)
1	1.1016 in (27.98 mm)
2	1.1035 in (28.03 mm)
3	1.1055 in (28.08 mm)
4	1.1075 in (28.13 mm)
5	1.1094 in (28.18 mm)
6	1.1114 in (28.23 mm)
7	1.1134 in (28.28 mm)
8	1.1154 in (28.33 mm)
9	1.1173 in (28.38 mm)
A	1.1193 in (28.43 mm)
B	1.1213 in (28.48 mm)
C	1.1232 in (28.53 mm)
D	1.1252 in (28.58 mm)

Driveshaft

Driveshaft runout limit	0.024 in (0.6 mm)
Journal axial play limit	less than 0.0008 in (0.02 mm)

Transfer case (1980 through 1985 only)

Gear end play	
High gear	0.0039 to 0.0079 in (0.10 to 0.20 mm)
Low gear	0.0039 to 0.0079 in (0.10 to 0.20 mm)
Coupling sleeve hub	0 to 0.0079 in (0 to 0.20 mm)
Coupling sleeve hub snap-ring selection thickness	0.051 in (1.3 mm)
	0.055 in (1.4 mm)
	0.059 in (1.5 mm)
	0.063 in (1.6 mm)
	0.067 in (1.7 mm)

Main gear front shim selection guide

Result of A + C – E	Shim thickness
0.0024 to 0.0059 in (0.06 to 0.15 mm)	None
0.0063 to 0.0098 in (0.16 to 0.25 mm)	0.0039 in (0.10 mm)
0.0102 to 0.0138 in (0.26 to 0.35 mm)	0.0079 in (0.20 mm)
0.0142 to 0.0177 in (0.36 to 0.45 mm)	0.0118 in (0.30 mm)
0.0181 to 0.0217 in (0.46 to 0.55 mm)	0.0157 in (0.40 mm)

Transfer case front shim selection guide

Result of B + D – F	Shim thickness
0 to 0.0051 in (0 to 0.13 mm)	None
0.0055 to 0.0091 in (0.14 to 0.23 mm)	0.0039 in (0.10 mm)
0.0094 to 0.0130 in (0.24 to 0.33 mm)	0.0079 in (0.20 mm)
0.0134 to 0.0169 in (0.34 to 0.43 mm)	0.0118 in (0.30 mm)
0.0173 to 0.0209 in (0.44 to 0.53 mm)	0.0157 in (0.40 mm)
0.0213 to 0.0248 in (0.54 to 0.63 mm)	0.0197 in (0.50 mm)

Front differential

Drive pinion preload (with oil seal)	
Four-cylinder engine	7.8 to 14.8 in-lbs (0.9 to 1.7 Nm)
V6 engine	10.0 to 15.2 in-lbs (1.13 to 1.72 Nm)

Torque specifications

	Ft-lbs
Wheel bearing locknut	
1980 through 1983	108 to 145
1984 on	58 to 72
Free running hub mounting bolts	18 to 25
Upper balljoint-to-upper link bolts	12 to 15
Lower balljoint-to lower link nuts	28 to 38
Knuckle arm-to-knuckle bolt	53 to 72
Brake caliper-to-bracket (or sliding pin)	16 to 23
Brake caliper bracket-to-knuckle	53 to 72
Driveaxle-to-differential bolts	
1980 through 1985	20 to 27
1986 on	25 to 33
Driveshaft-to-differential bolts	
1980 through 1985	25 to 33
1986 on	58 to 65
Driveshaft-to-transfer case bolts	
1980 through 1985	25 to 33
1986 on	58 to 65
Front differential drive pinion nut	
Four-cylinder engine	123 to 145
V6 engine	137 to 217

	Ft-lbs
Check ball plug	16
Transfer case companion flange nuts	
1980 through 1985	87 to 101
1986 on	166 to 239
Transfer case-to-transmission bolts	22 to 30
Wheel lug nuts	See Chapter 1

1 General information

Refer to illustrations 1.1a and 1.1b

The system used to direct power to all four wheels on 4WD models is an add-on system that works in conjunction with the standard 2WD components **(see illustrations).**

On 1985 and earlier models a short primary driveshaft exits the rear of the manual transmission and connects to the transfer case, which is mounted in the mid-section of the truck. 1986 and later vehicles are equipped with a transfer case that bolts directly to the rear of the transmission, eliminating the need for a primary driveshaft. The transfer case transmits the drive power to both the front and rear differentials through two other driveshafts (front and rear driveshafts).

The front differential is mounted below the engine oil pan. Connecting it with the front wheels are two driveaxles which turn the wheels when the truck is in the 4WD mode.

Free-running hubs are used which when unlocked (in the Free position) allow the front wheels to spin while the truck is in the 2WD mode without rotating the driveaxles and front differentials, thus reducing wear in these components. When the truck is switched to the 4WD mode, the hubs should then be locked to engage the wheels with the driveaxles. 1984 and later models are offered with automatic-locking front hubs, eliminating the need to get out and manually lock the hubs when the transfer case is placed in 4WD mode.

The rear differential and axle assembly are exactly the same as the 2WD components. For procedures relating to these components refer to Chapter 8.

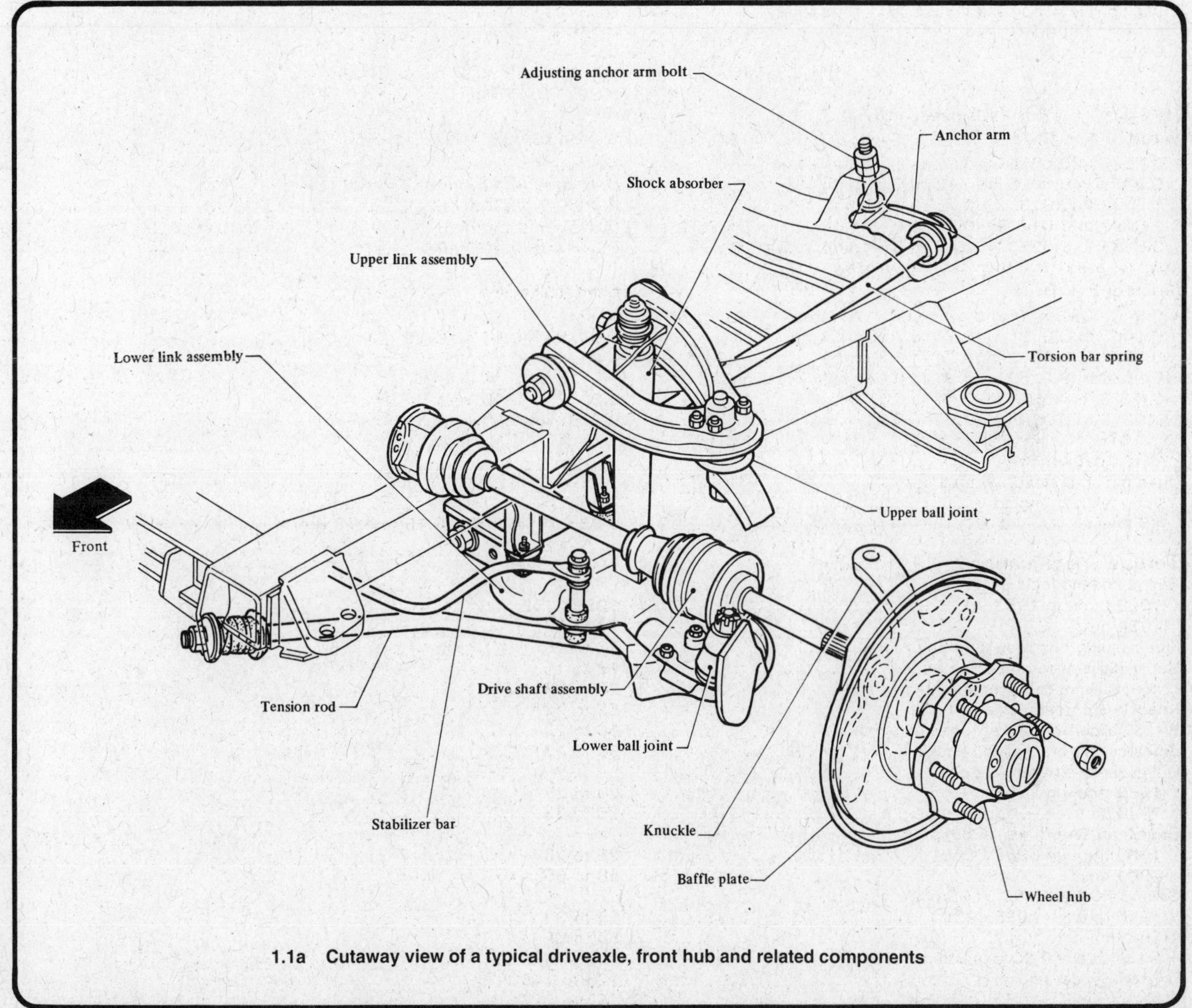

1.1a Cutaway view of a typical driveaxle, front hub and related components

9

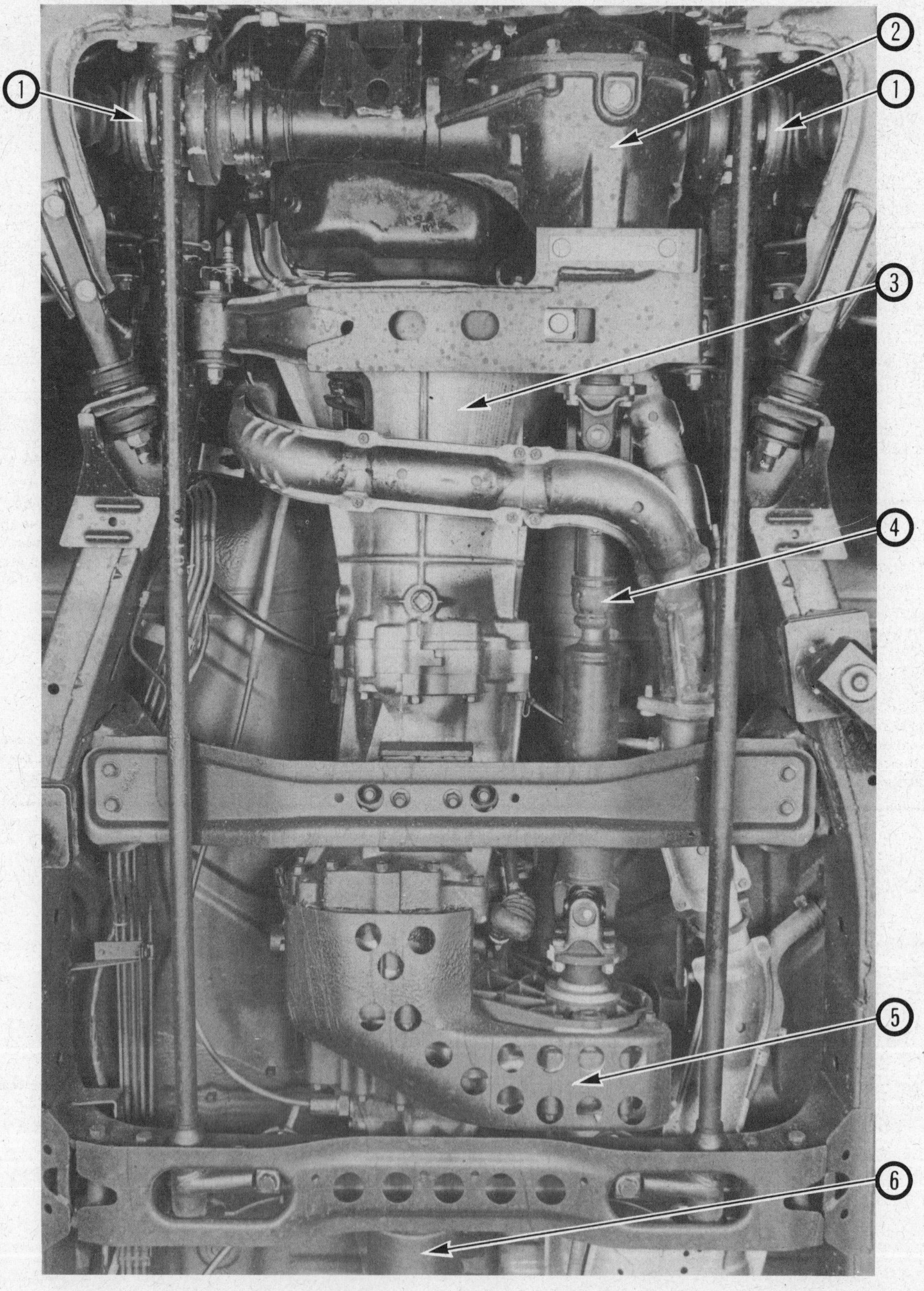

1.1b Underside view of the transmission and four wheel drive system (1986 and later models)

1 Driveaxle
2 Front differential
3 Transmission
4 Front driveshaft
5 Transfer case
6 Rear driveshaft

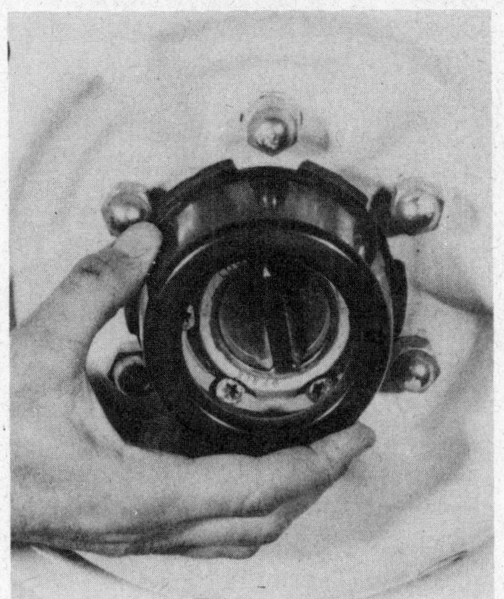
2.2 The free-running hub cover is removed by disengaging it from the wheel lug nuts

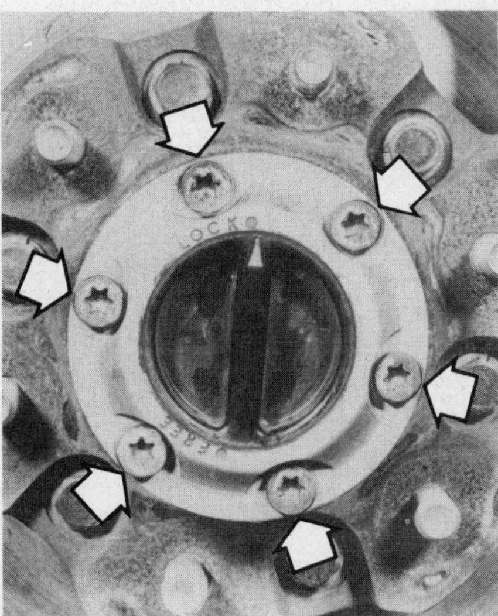
2.3 A Torx driver is needed to remove the free-running hub mounting bolts (arrows)

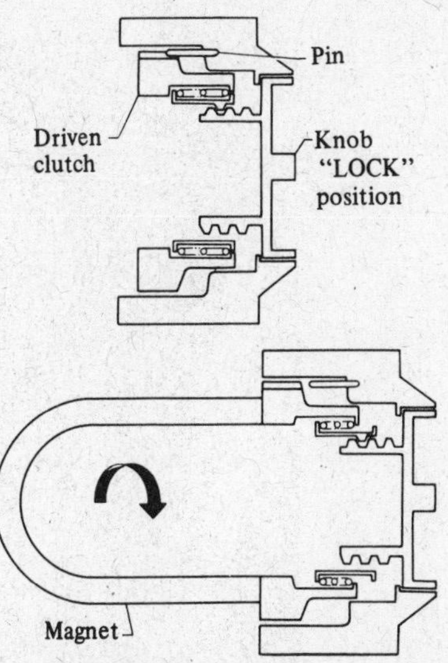

2.5 To remove the driven clutch from the free-running hub, use a magnet to pull it out and turn it clockwise

2 Free-running hub – removal and installation

Manual locking hub

Refer to illustrations 2.2, 2.3 and 2.5

1 Raise the front of the truck and support it on jackstands.
2 Twist the plastic hub cover to disengage it from the lug nuts **(see illustration)**, then remove the wheel and tire.
3 Remove the six hub assembly screws **(see illustration)**, and lift off the hub.
4 If the hub assembly needs to be disassembled, set the hub in the Lock position.
5 The driven clutch is retained in the hub case by a locking pin. To remove the clutch, use a magnet **(see illustration)** to draw the clutch out, then turn it clockwise to disengage and remove it.
6 Remove the lock pin from the hub case, if necessary.
7 When reassembling the hub assembly, first be sure the lock pin is in position. Then with the hub set in the Free position, screw the driven clutch counterclockwise into the hub case until it won't go any further. Turn it clockwise just until the indentations in the clutch are aligned with the bolt holes in the hub case.
8 Installation is the reverse of removal.

Auto-lock hub

Refer to illustrations 2.11, 2.12 and 2.13

9 Remove the wheel cap and the wheel.
10 Using a Torx wrench, remove the six bolts.
11 Carefully pull the hub off. The O-ring, spring and brake "A" **(see illustration)**, will come off as well. Make sure all parts are kept in the same order as they are removed to aid in reassembly.

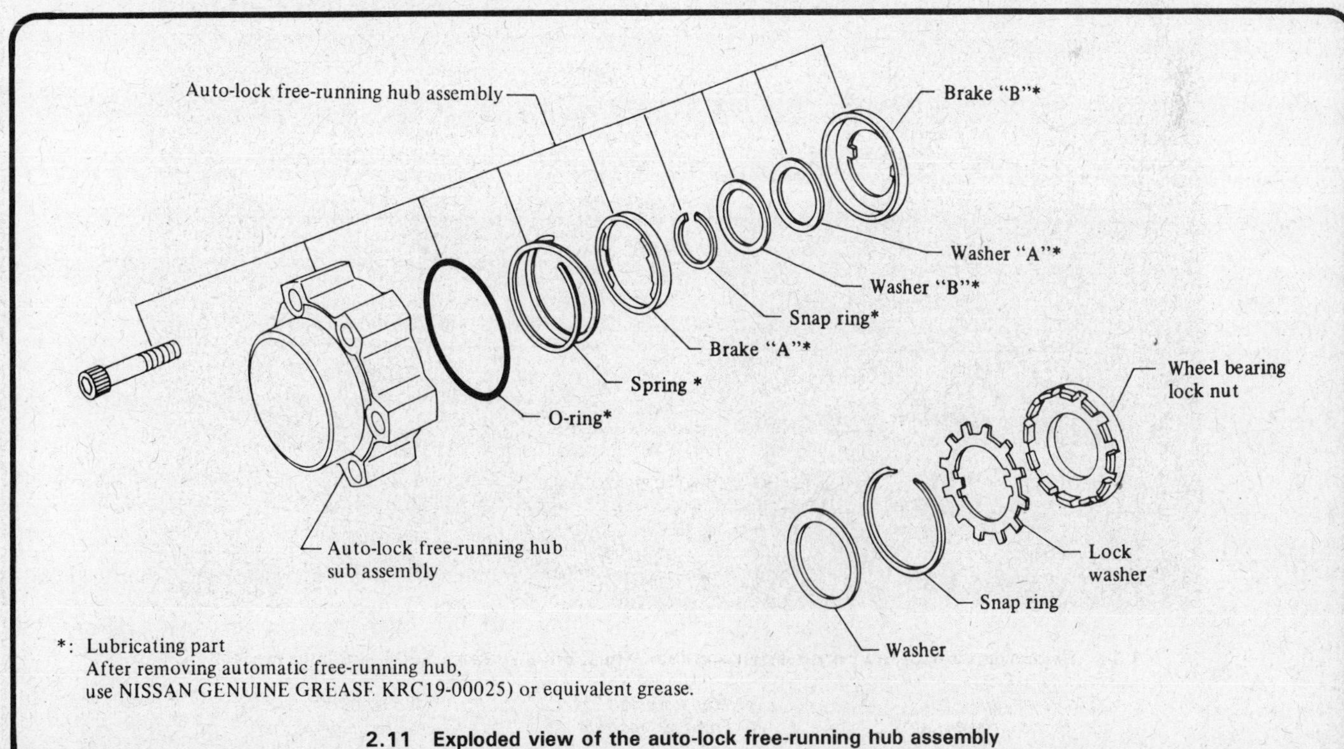

2.11 Exploded view of the auto-lock free-running hub assembly

9

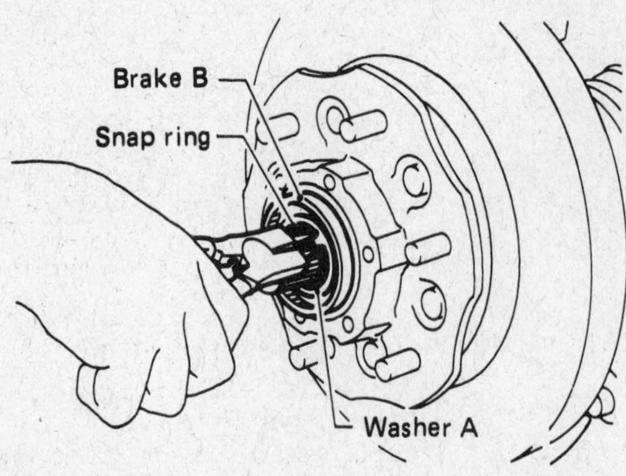

2.12 After removing the snap-ring, the remaining hub components can be removed

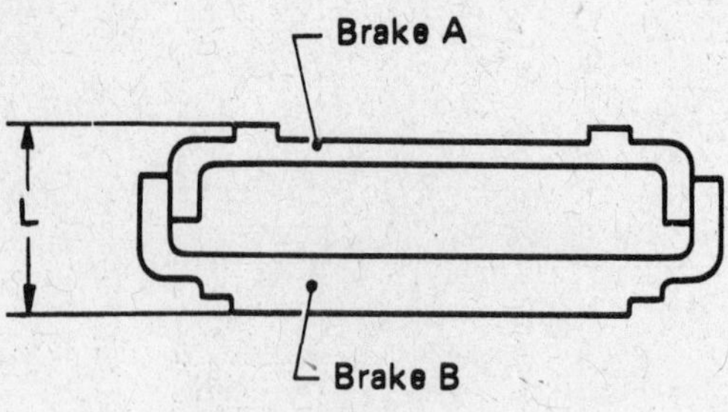

2.13 Place brake A into brake B and measure the thickness of the assembly – if the dimension is less than specified, replace brake A and B as a set

12 Remove the snap ring, various washers and brake "B" **(see illustration).**

13 Measure the thickness of brake "A" and "B" **(see illustration).** If the thickness is less than the specified limit, the brakes must be replaced as a set.

14 Installation is the reverse of removal. During reassembly, refer to illustration 2.11 and lubricate the designated parts with the recommended grease.

3 Driveaxle – removal and installation

Refer to illustrations 3.6, 3.15, 3.17a and 3.17b

Removal

1 Raise the front of the truck and support it on jackstands.
2 Remove the wheel and tire.
3 Remove the free-wheeling hub assembly (Section 2).
4 Remove the snap-ring from the end of the driveaxle spindle.
5 Slide off the drive clutch (manual locking hubs) or washer and brake "B" (auto lock hubs).
6 Remove the bolts that attach the driveaxle to the front differential **(see illustration).**
7 Remove the lower shock absorber mounting bolt.

1980 through 1985

8 Remove the front rubber rebound bumper, located above the lower link.

9 Remove the bolt attaching the stabilizer bar to the lower link, along with the grommets, washers and spacers. Keep the components in their proper order.

3.6 Put alignment marks on the driveaxle slide joint housing and the differential side shaft flange then remove the bolts

10 If removing the left driveaxle, turn the steering wheel all the way to the left. If removing the right driveaxle, turn the steering to the right.

11 Disconnect the driveaxle slide joint housing from the differential side shaft flange, then pull it out of the front hub. You might have to tap the end of the axle with a hammer and block of wood to free it from the hub splines.

1986 and later models

12 Remove the brake caliper and hang it out of the way with a piece of wire (see Chapter 10).

13 Disconnect the tie-rod end from the steering knuckle (see Chapter 11).

14 Support the lower link with a jack and raise it slightly. Remove the bolts and nuts securing the upper and lower balljoints to the upper and lower links, then carefully remove the knuckle and driveaxle as an assembly.

15 Mount the steering knuckle in a vise and tap the driveaxle out of the knuckle with a hammer and block of wood **(see illustration).**

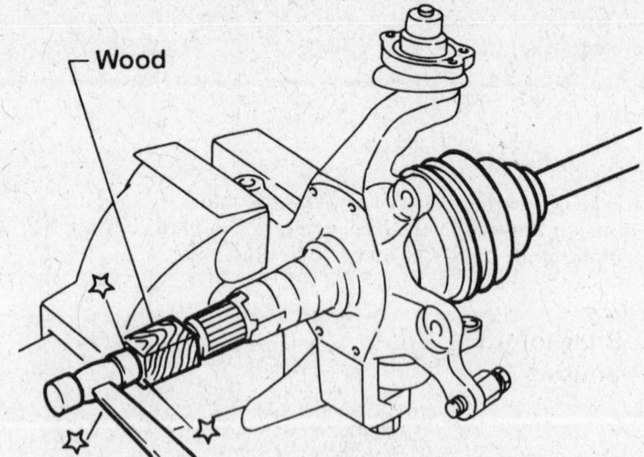

3.15 With the knuckle clamped in a vise, tap the driveaxle out using a block of wood to cushion the inpact

All models

16 If any defects exist in the shaft, rubber boots or joints, refer to Section 4 for disassembly.

Installation

17 Installation is the reverse of the removal procedure with the following notes.

a) Prior to installation, apply a coat of multi-purpose grease to the copper portion of the wheel bearing support **(see illustration).**
b) With the drive clutch reinstalled on the end of the driveaxle, set up a dial gauge **(see illustration)** to measure the axle end play. If it is not within the specified limits, select a snap-ring of an appropriate thickness (out of those listed in the Specifications) that will produce the correct end play.

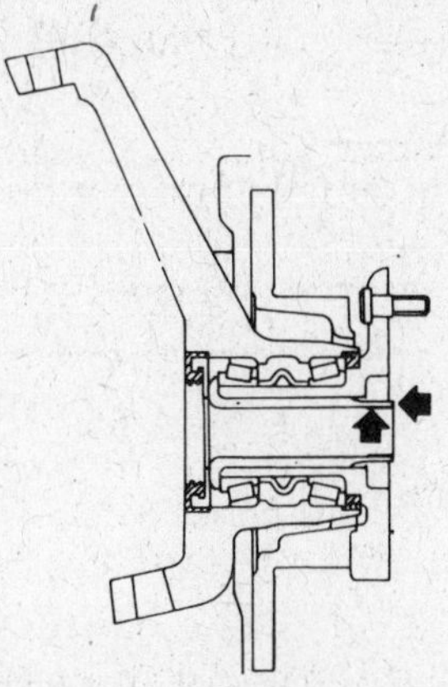

3.17a Prior to installing the driveaxle, apply grease (arrows) to the copper portion of the wheel bearing support inside the front hub

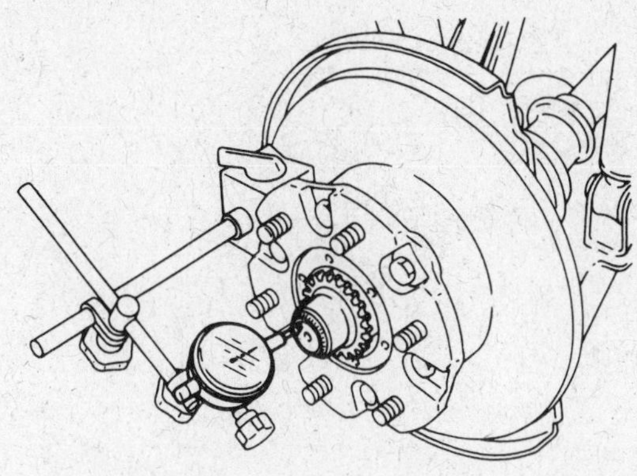

3.17b Measure the driveaxle end play with a dial indicator

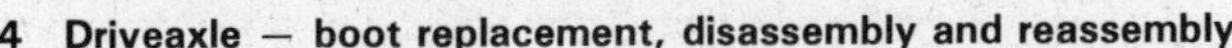

4 Driveaxle – boot replacement, disassembly and reassembly

Refer to illustrations 4.3a, 4.3b, 4.4a, 4.4b, 4.9, 4.12 and 4.15

Note: *A hydraulic press is needed for this operation.*

1 Remove the driveaxle as described in Section 3.

2 Secure the driveaxle in a vise using blocks of wood to prevent damage to the shaft.

3 Working from the differential side of the axle, unbend the securing tabs of the plug and lift it off along with the plug seal (early models). On later models, tap the joint housing to dislodge the seal **(see illustrations)**.

4 Remove both boot bands **(see illustrations)**.

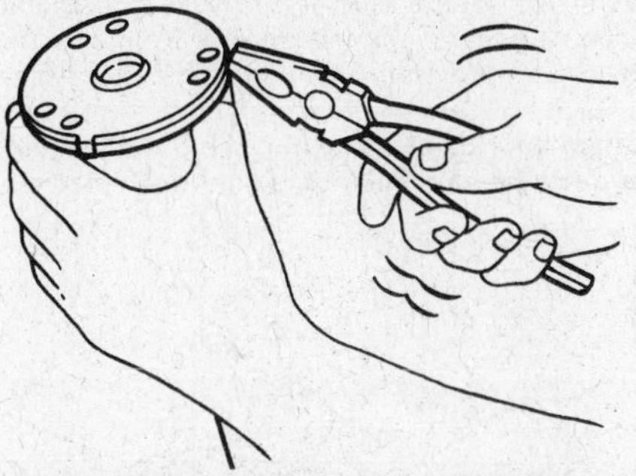

4.3a Bend the tabs of the slide joint housing end plug out, then remove the plug along with the seal (early style driveaxle)

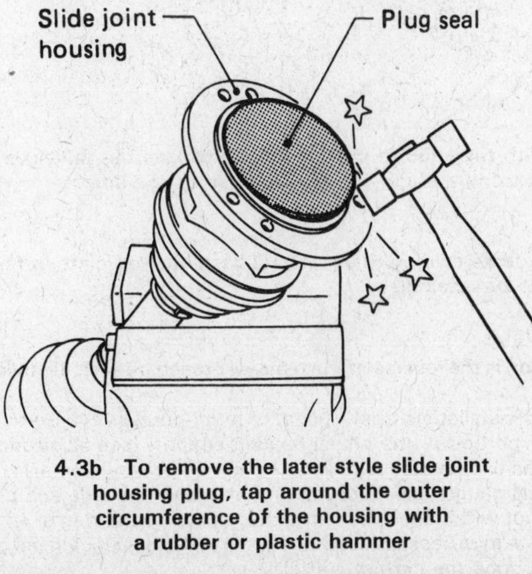

Slide joint housing
Plug seal

4.3b To remove the later style slide joint housing plug, tap around the outer circumference of the housing with a rubber or plastic hammer

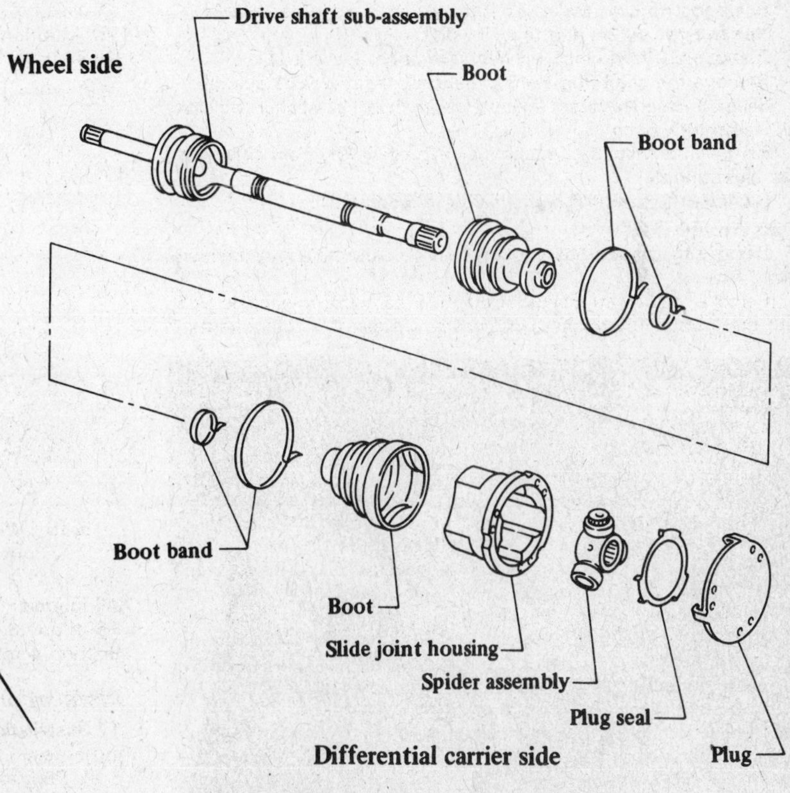

Drive shaft sub-assembly
Wheel side
Boot
Boot band
Boot band
Boot
Slide joint housing
Spider assembly
Plug seal
Differential carrier side
Plug

4.4a Exploded view of the driveaxle assembly components (1980 through 1985 models)

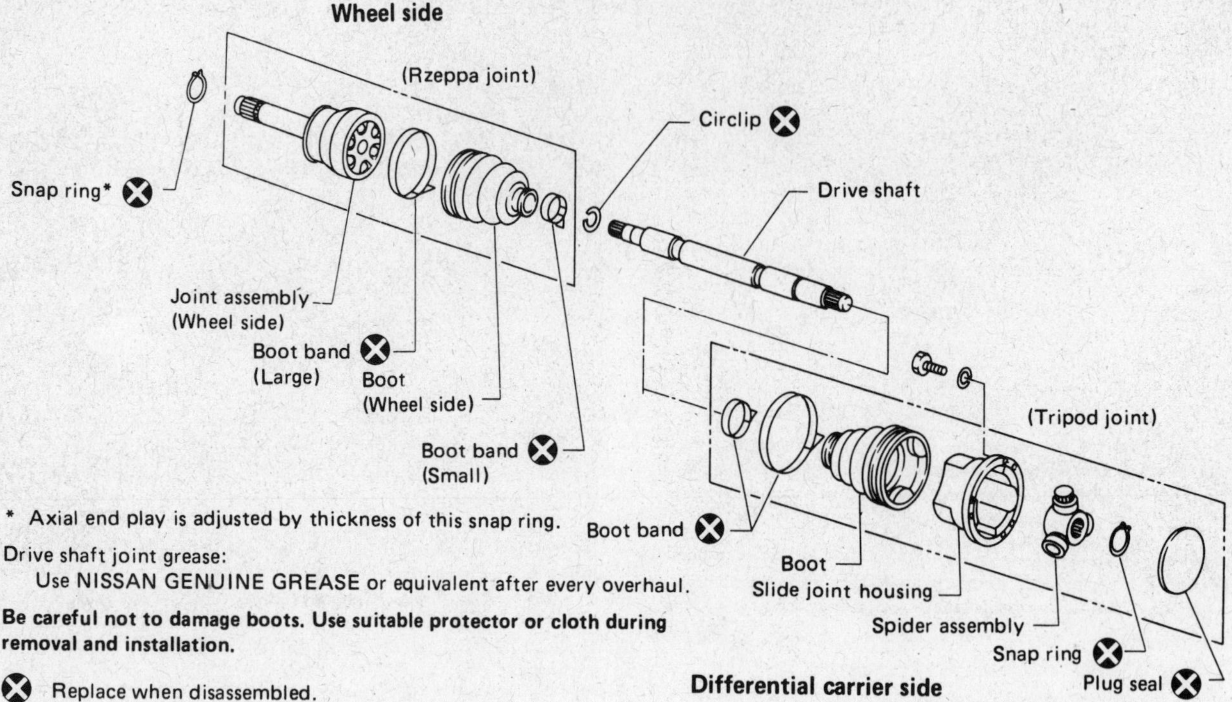

4.4b Exploded view of the driveaxle assembly components (1986 and later four-cylinder models, V6 models similar)

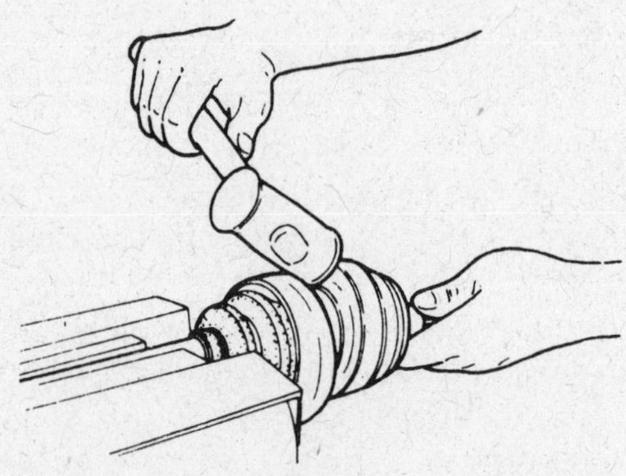

4.9 1984 and later models employ a removable outer CV (constant velocity) joint which can be removed by tapping it off of the shaft

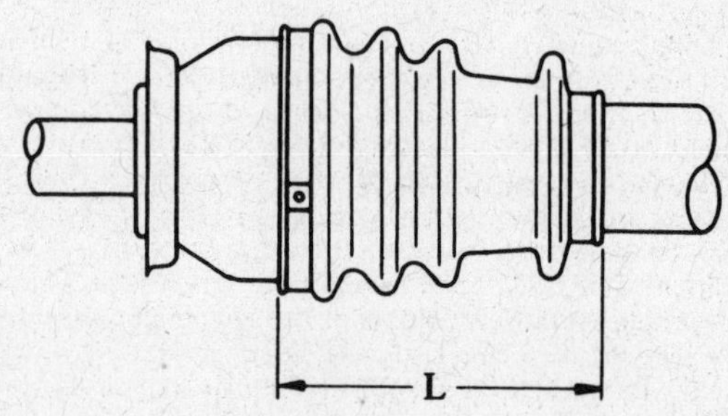

4.12 Before installing the small band, adjust the length of the joint (L) to the dimension listed in the Specifications

5 Move both the boot and the slide joint housing toward the wheel side of the axle.
6 Mark the installed position of the spider assembly on the shaft.
7 Using a press and support, press the axle out of the spider.
8 Remove the boot and slide joint housing from the shafts.
9 The outer (wheel side) joint on early models (1980 to 1983) is non-removable. If the wheel side boot must be removed, remove the boot bands and slide the boot off the inner end of the axle. The outer joint on later models (1984 on) can be removed from the driveaxle by gently tapping on it **(see illustration)**. Be sure to mark the relationship of the joint to the driveaxle before removing it. After the joint has been removed, remove the circlip from the shaft.
10 Clean all parts in solvent and inspect them for damage and excessive wear. The driveshaft/axle sub-assembly (early models), outer joint (later models) and spider assembly are not designed to be disassembled, and if defective must be replaced as a unit.
11 Begin assembly by packing the driveaxle sub-assembly (outer joint) with the specified amount of high quality multi-purpose grease.
12 Wrap tape around the shaft splines, slide the boot onto the shaft and install it over the sub-assembly (early models). Secure the boot with a new large band. Adjust the boot to the specified length **(see**

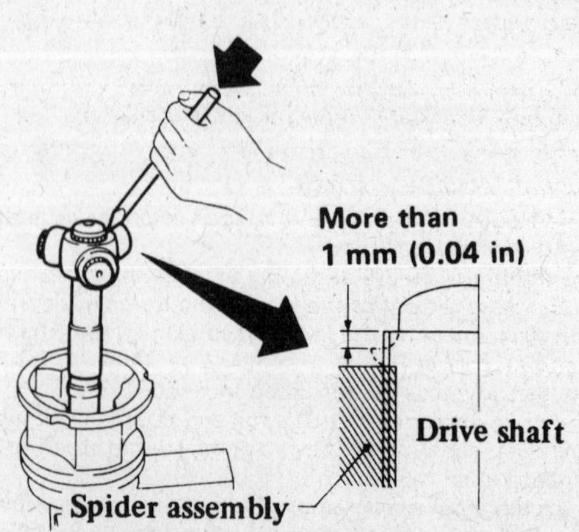

4.15 After installation of the spider assembly, the driveaxle should be staked as shown

5.6a The upper balljoint-to-upper link bolts

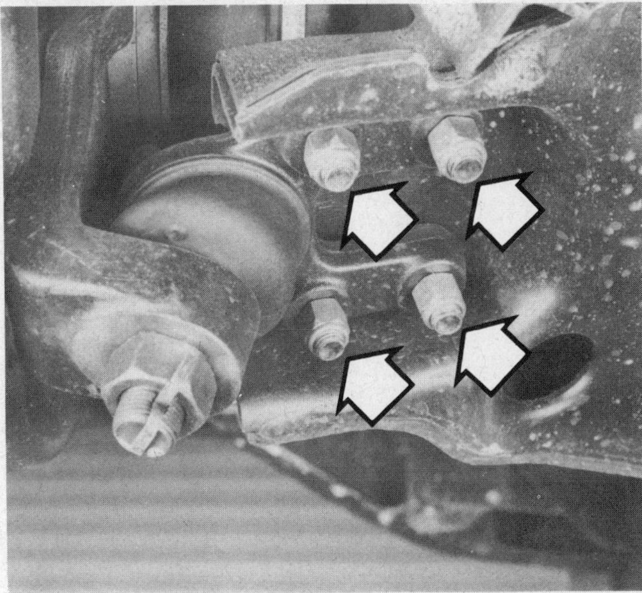
5.6b The lower balljoint-to-lower link bolts

illustration). Equalize the pressure in the boot by inserting a screwdriver blade under the boot (be careful not to damage the boot). Make sure it is not twisted or swollen and then install a new small band. On later models, slide the boot onto the shaft, install a new circlip, fill the outer joint with grease and carefully tap the joint onto the shaft. Install the bands.

13 Install the differential side boot, bands and slide joint housing on the shaft. Again be careful not to damage the boot on the shaft splines.

14 With the shaft secured between blocks of wood in a vise, install the spider on the end of the shaft, with the serration chamfer facing toward the shaft. **Note:** *If the used spider is to be installed be sure the marks made during removal line up. If a new spider is being installed, it should be aligned as close as possible to the one on the wheel side.*

15 With the spider assembly installed, use a punch or chisel to stake the serrations at the end of the shaft to secure the spider. The procedure should be done at two points which have not already been indented, and should be more than 1 mm deep **(see illustration)**.

16 Slide the slide joint housing and boot into position over the spider and pack them with the specified amount of high quality multi-purpose grease.

17 Secure the boot with a new large band.

18 Apply a coat of grease to the plug seal and install the plug. Secure them to the housing temporarily with three bolts and nuts and secure the plug by staking it in three places.

19 Set the boot to the specified length **(see illustration 4.12)** then equalize the pressure in the boot. Install a new small band.

5 Front hub and knuckle — removal and installation

Refer to illustrations 5.6a and 5.6b

1 Raise the front of the truck and support it on jackstands.

2 Remove the wheel and tire.

3 Remove the brake caliper assembly as described in Chapter 10. The caliper can be wired out of the way to the frame or other component without disconnecting the brake hose, eliminating the need for bleeding the brakes later on.

4 Remove the driveaxle as described in Section 3.

5 Loosen, but do not remove, the tie-rod end-to-steering knuckle arm nut. Using a puller, separate the tie-rod end from the steering knuckle arm (see Chapter 11).

6 The knuckle is most easily removed with the upper and lower balljoints attached. Place a jack under the lower link to support the torsion bar spring pressure. The jack must remain under the lower link during the entire procedure. Remove the bolts that attach both balljoints to the links **(see illustrations)**.

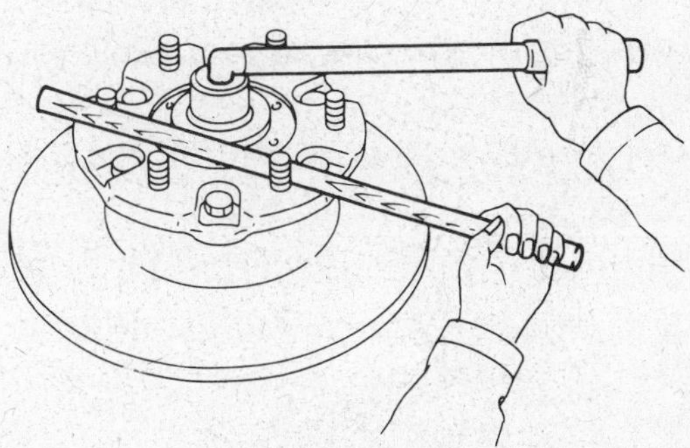
6.3 When removing the front wheel locknut, position a bar between the wheel studs to keep the hub from turning

7 The balljoints can now be separated from the links, and the knuckle and hub assembly lifted out. If the knuckle must be replaced, then the balljoints must be removed. This is done by loosening, but not removing, the balljoint nuts so they extend over the end of the stud. Use a puller or separating tool to disengage the balljoints from the knuckle. The nut should be left on the stud to prevent the upper or lower link from separating violently from the balljoint stud.

8 Installation is the reverse of the removal procedure. When reinstalling the driveaxle, be sure to adjust the axle end play as described in Section 3.

6 Front wheel bearing and grease seal — removal, installation and adjustment

Refer to illustrations 6.3, 6.4a, 6.4b, 6.6, 6.8, 6.14, 6.16 and 6.18

Removal

1 Remove the front hub and knuckle assembly as described in Section 5.

2 Using a screwdriver, unbend the lock plate tabs from around the locknut (early models). On later models remove the lock plate retaining screw.

3 Remove the locknut. To keep the hub from turning, place a pry bar between the wheel studs **(see illustration)**.

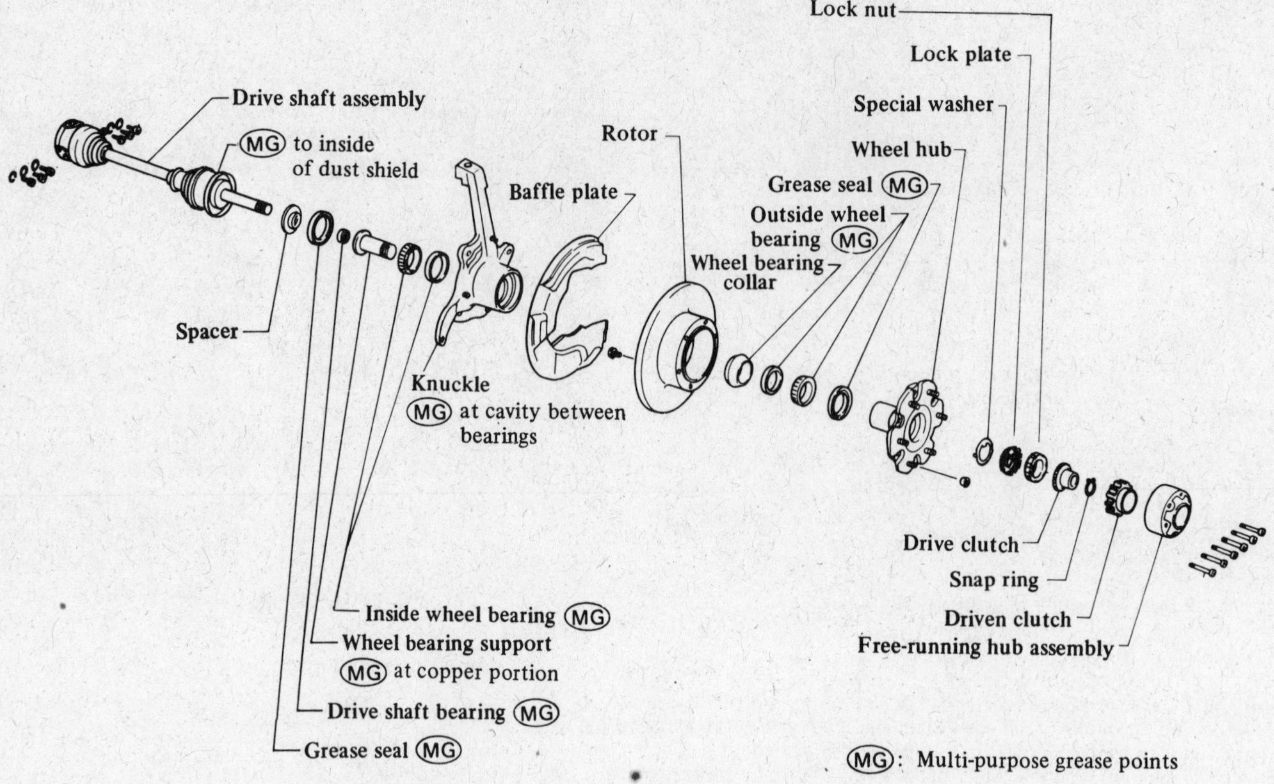

6.4a Exploded view of the driveaxle, front hub and knuckle assembly (1980 through 1984 models)

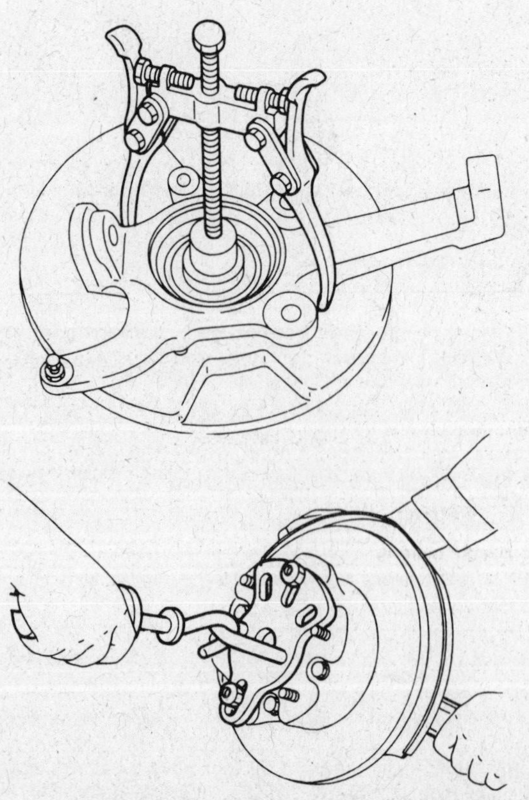

6.6 A puller or a slide hammer and adapter can be used to separate the knuckle from the front hub

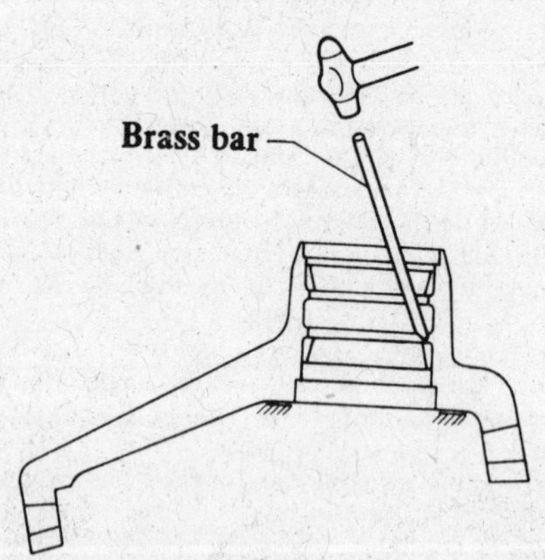

6.8 The inner bearing race can be removed from the knuckle by driving it out with a brass bar and hammer

4 Remove the lock plate and special washer **(see illustrations)**.

5 Remove the inner grease seal by prying it out with a screwdriver. Push the wheel bearing support out of the hub.

6 Separate the knuckle from the hub **(see illustration)**.

7 Lift out the wheel bearing collar.

8 Remove the inner wheel bearing by driving out the bearing race with a hammer and brass bar **(see illustration)**.

9 Remove the bolts that attach the rotor and hub and separate them. If they will not separate easily, refer to the rotor removal procedure in Chapter 10.

10 Tap the hub assembly on a wooden block to shift the position of the outer bearing.

11 Using a press and supports, press the outer bearing out of the hub. Also remove the grease seal.

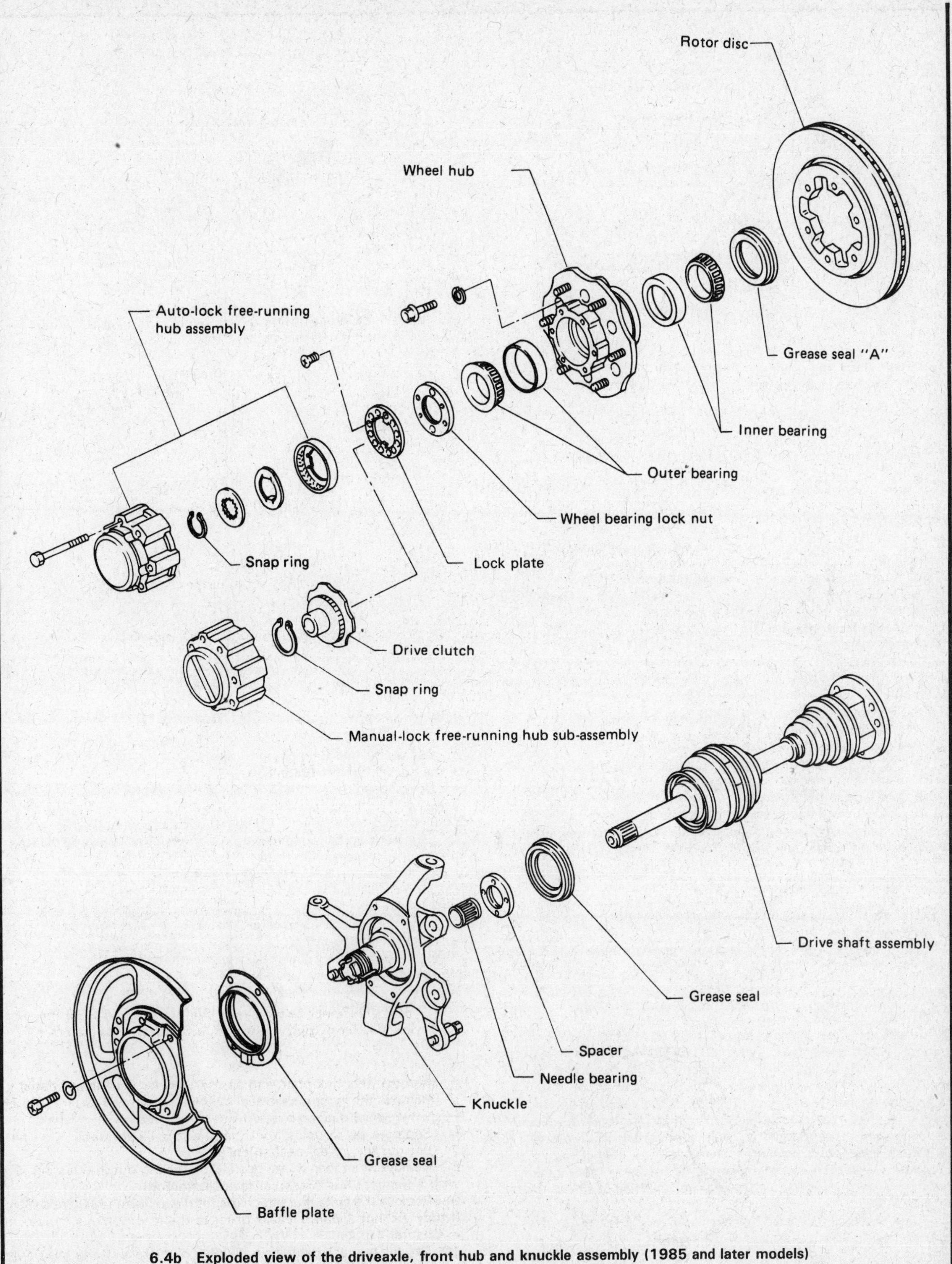

6.4b **Exploded view of the driveaxle, front hub and knuckle assembly (1985 and later models)**

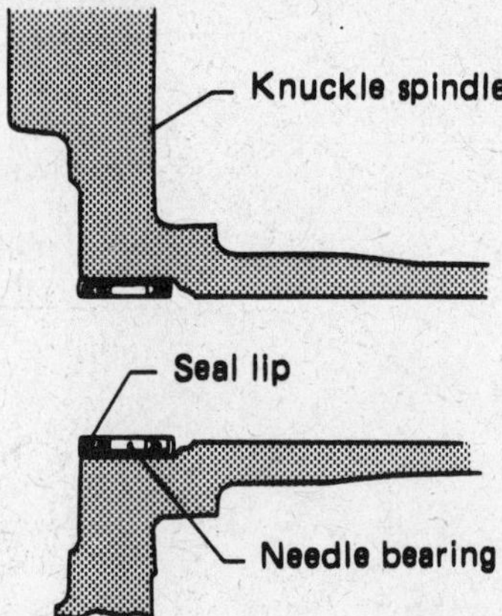

6.14 Pack the driveaxle bearing with grease and push it into the hub with the seal on the inner side of the knuckle

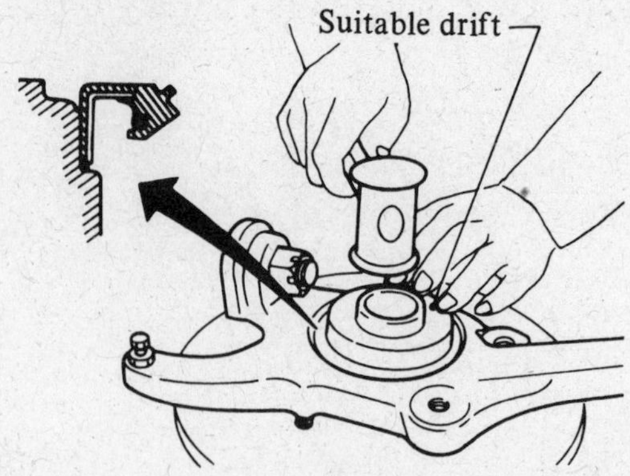

6.16 Use a seal driver or large socket to seat the inner seal in the hub — the open side of the seal must face down

12 Remove the driveaxle bearing from the wheel bearing support, using a brass bar, if necessary.
13 Clean all parts in solvent.

Installation

14 Begin installation by coating the driveaxle bearing with multi-purpose grease and installing it in the wheel bearing support, using a drift punch or large socket **(see illustration)**.
15 Using a large socket, install the outer bearing race in the knuckle.
16 Apply grease to the lip of the outer grease seal, then install it in the hub **(see illustration)**.
17 Install the outer wheel bearing and race in the hub.
18 Pack the outer bearing with the recommended grease and apply a coat of grease to the race. Install them together in the hub. Apply force only to the race when installing. Pack the center of the hub with the recommended grease **(see illustration)**.
19 Attach the rotor to the hub.
20 Reinstall the knuckle on the hub..
21 Install the bearing collar. If the collar is being replaced, install a collar of the same thickness as the old one (the stamped number on the collars will be the same).
22 Pack the inner bearing with grease and apply a coat of grease to the inner race, then, using a press, install the two together in the knuckle. Apply force only to the race when installing the bearing.
23 Install the special washer and lock plate. **Note:** *Always use a new lock plate (early models only).*
24 Install the locknut and tighten it to the specified torque.
25 Turn the hub in both directions several times to properly seat the wheel bearing.
26 Pack the lips of a new inner grease seal with grease and install it in the knuckle, being sure the lip faces in the proper direction.

Adjustment

1980 through 1983 models

27 Check the wheel bearing preload by installing a torque wrench over the locknut and slowly turning the hub clockwise, noting at what torque setting the hub begins to turn. Compare this to the wheel bearing preload listed in the Specifications. If the preload is not within this range, the bearing collar must be replaced with another one of a different thickness, as listed in the Specifications. **Note:** *If the measured preload is higher than specified, a thicker collar should be installed (indicated by a higher stamped number), while if the preload is lower than specified, replace it with a thinner collar (indicated by a lower stamped number. Change the collar thickness by only one number in either direction at a time.*
28 Once the proper preload has been achieved, bend the tabs of the lock plate up into the grooves of the locknut.

1984 and later models

Note: *A special tool is required to loosen and tighten the wheel bearing locknut. Do not attempt it without the special tool. Refer to Chapter 8 for instructions on fabricating an alternative tool if the recommended tool is not available.*

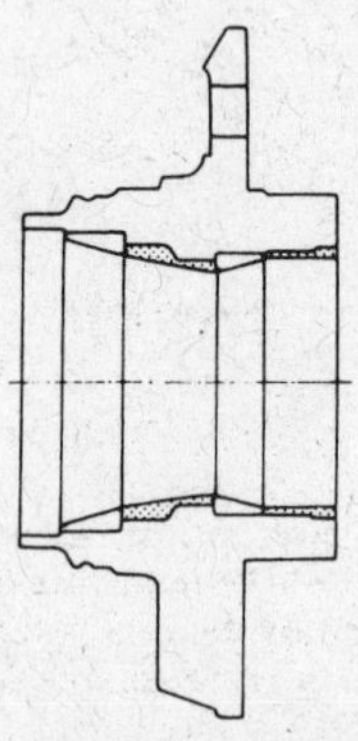

6.18 Pack the center of the hub (shaded area) with grease

29 Using a torque wrench and the special tool, tighten the locknut to the recommended torque.
30 Now loosen the locknut and check the end play, which should be zero.
31 Turn the wheel several times in both directions.
32 Connect a spring scale to the uppermost wheel stud and measure the force necessary to start the wheel hub in motion. Jot this number down, designating it A, for later reference.
33 Turn the wheel bearing locknut 15 to 30° and fit the lock plate onto the locknut.
34 Turn the wheel hub several times in both directions to properly seat the wheel bearings.
35 Hook up the spring scale again and measure the starting force now. Jot this number down, designating it B.
36 The wheel bearing preload is B minus A in the above checks.
37 Repeat the procedure until the proper preload is obtained.
38 Install the snap-ring in the locknut groove.
39 Install the remaining components in the reverse order of removal.

7 Driveshafts — removal and installation

Refer to illustration 7.9

Primary driveshaft

1 Raise the front of the vehicle and support it on jackstands. If necessary for clearance, remove the front driveshaft as described in the next sub-section.
2 Mark the positions of the driveshaft rear flange and the transfer case flange to be sure they are reinstalled in the same way.
3 Remove the flange bolts and separate the driveshaft from the transfer case.
4 Remove the transfer case as described in Section 11.

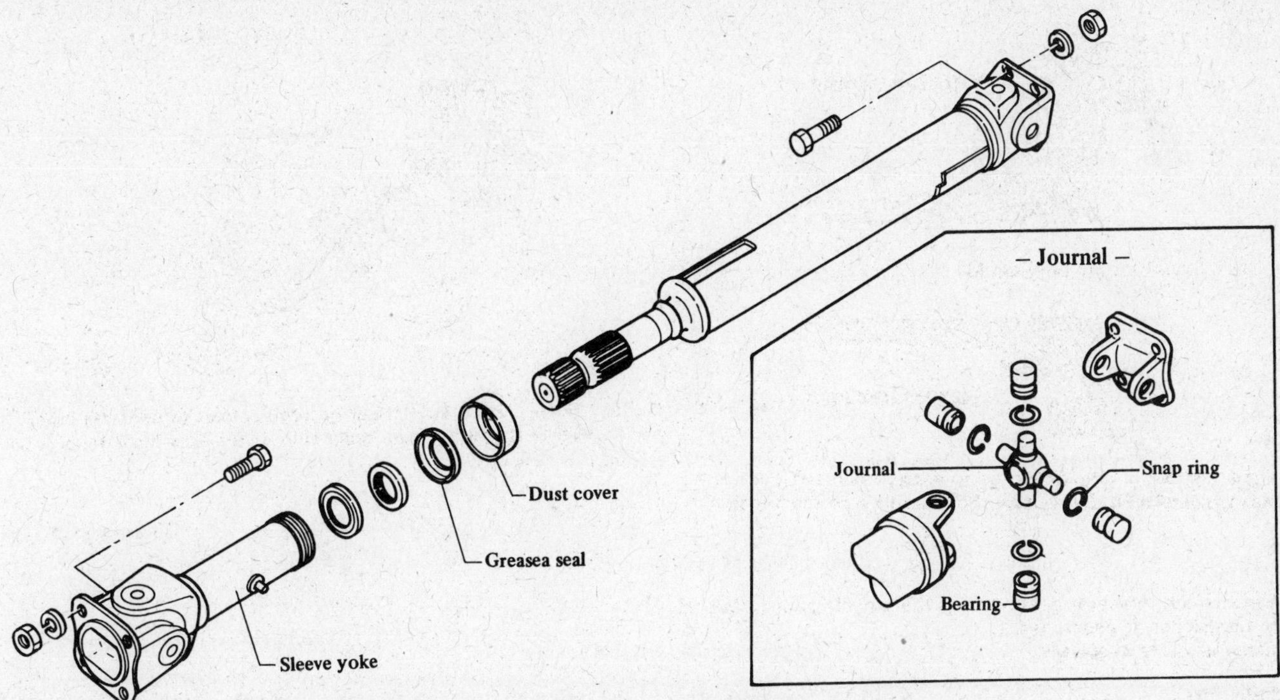

7.9 Exploded view of the front driveshaft and universal joint

5 Draw the primary driveshaft out of the rear of the transmission and immediately plug the end of the transmission to prevent loss of oil.
6 Installation is the reverse of the removal procedure, but be sure the flange marks made during removal are aligned.

Front and rear driveshafts

Note: *For 1986 and later model rear driveshaft removal and installation, refer to Chapter 8.*

7 Mark the positions of the driveshaft flanges on both the differential and transfer case.

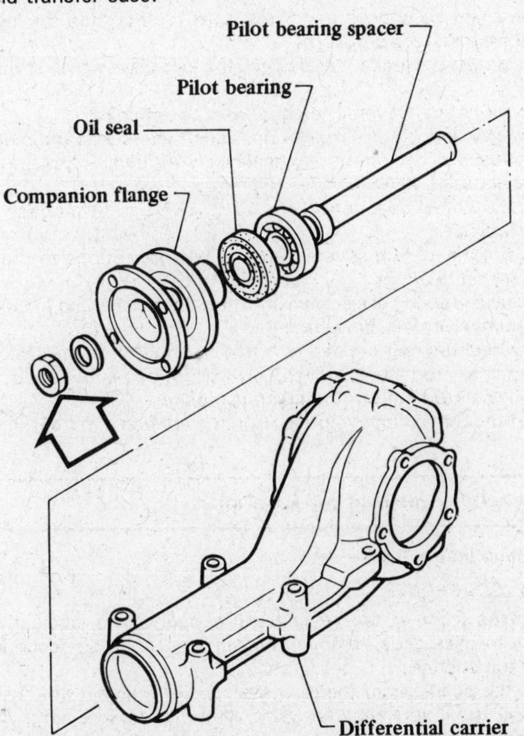

8.4 After removing the drive pinion nut (arrow), the companion flange and oil seal can be removed

8 Remove the mounting bolts at both ends and lower the driveshaft from the truck.
9 If necessary, the sleeve yoke can be separated from the driveshaft and the grease seal replaced **(see illustration)**.
10 Installation is the reverse of removal, but be sure the flange marks made during removal are aligned.

8 Front differential oil seals – replacement

Rear oil seal

Refer to illustrations 8.4 and 8.5

1 Remove the front differential drain plug and drain the oil into a container.
2 Raise the front of the truck and support it on jackstands. Be sure the parking brake is applied.
3 Disconnect the front driveshaft from the differential pinion flange. Refer to Section 7, if necessary.
4 Remove the drive pinion nut from the end of the shaft **(see illustration)**. To keep the flange from turning, two of the driveshaft mounting bolts can be reinstalled in the flange and a pry bar can be engaged between them.
5 Using a puller, remove the companion flange from the differential **(see illustration)**.

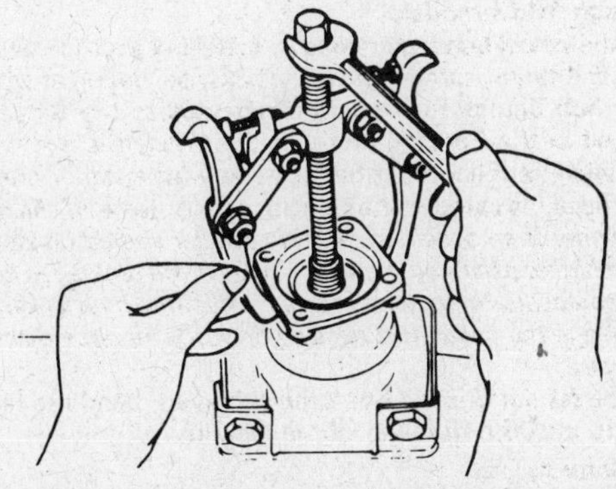

8.5 A puller should be used to remove the companion flange from the front of the differential

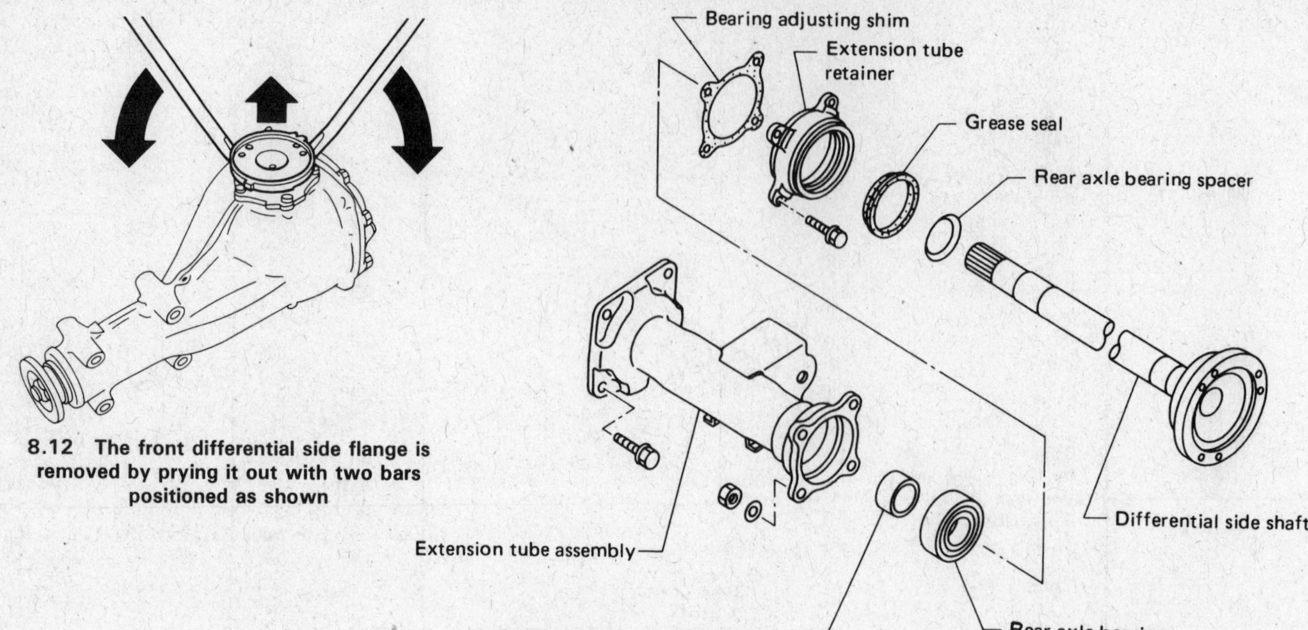

8.12 The front differential side flange is removed by prying it out with two bars positioned as shown

8.17 Exploded view of the differential side shaft, extension tube and related components

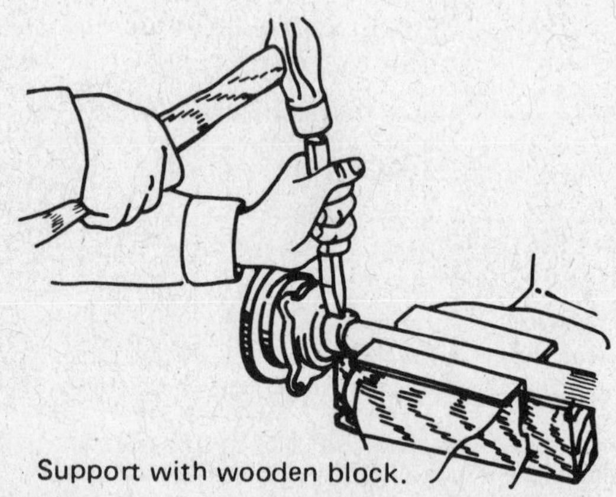

8.19 When chiseling the bearing collar off, be very careful not to damage the shaft

6 Use a screwdriver to pry out the oil seal. Be careful not to scratch or damage the seal bore surface of the differential.
7 Apply multi-purpose grease to the cavity between the oil seal lips of the new seal, then tap it into the differential using a large socket.
8 Install the companion flange and secure it by tightening the drive pinion nut to the proper torque.
9 Fit an in-lb torque wrench over the drive pinion nut and slowly turn it clockwise, noting at what torque the shafts begins to rotate. This is the drive pinion preload, and it should be checked against the Specifications. If the preload is not within the given range, tighten the nut a little at a time until the preload is correct. **Caution:** *This preload is achieved by using a collapsible spacer within the differential. If the preload is set over the recommended specification, the differential will have to be disassembled and the spacer replaced.*
10 The remainder of the procedure is the reverse of the removal procedure. Refer to Chapter 1 if necessary for filling the differential with oil.

Side oil seals

Left side (all years) and right side through 1985 models
11 Remove the driveaxle as described in Section 3.
12 Remove the side flange by prying it out with two bars **(see illustration)**.
13 Remove the side oil seal.

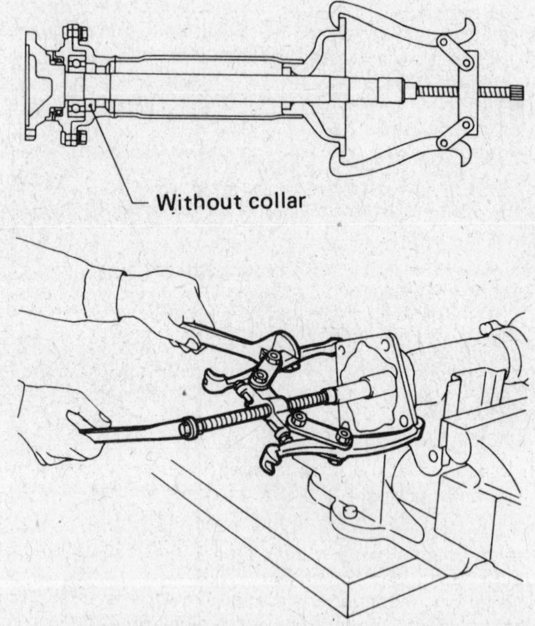

8.21 Reassemble the side shaft in the extension tube and press the shaft out of the bearing with a puller

14 Install the new seal in the differential with a large socket.
15 Apply grease to the cavity between the seal lips.
16 Reinstall the side flange and driveaxle.

Right side (1986 and later models)
17 Remove the four extension tube retainer bolts and pull the differential side shaft from the extension tube **(see illustration)**.
18 Mount the shaft in a vise. Place a block of wood on both sides of the shaft to prevent damage and a block of wood below the shaft to support it.
19 Using a cold chisel, cut the bearing collar off the axle **(see illustration)**.
20 Remove the four extension tube-to-differential carrier bolts and separate the extension tube from the carrier.
21 Reinstall the side shaft and retainer in the extension tube and in-

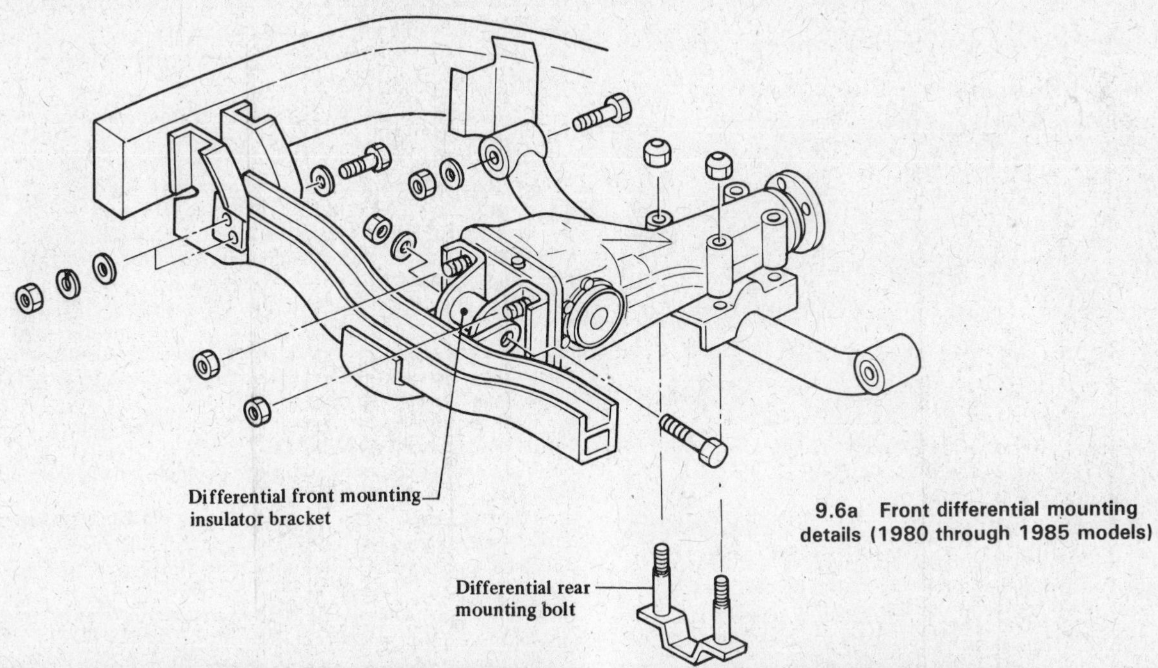

9.6a Front differential mounting details (1980 through 1985 models)

9.6b Location of the front differential forward mounting bolts (arrows) — 1986 and later models

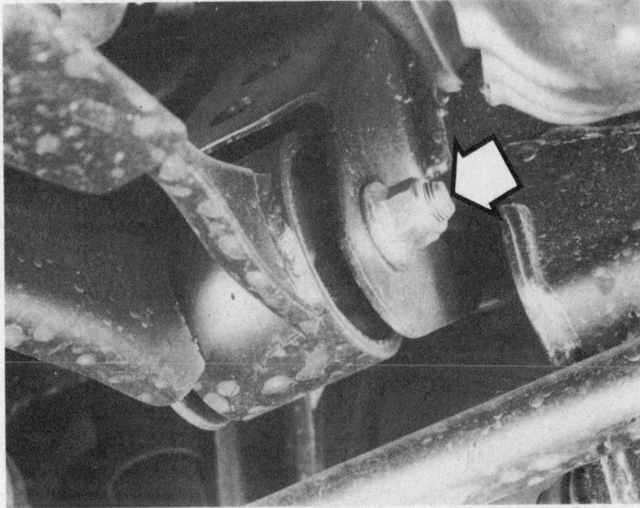

9.10 Remove the differential mounting member-to-frame bolts (the right side bolt is shown here)

9

stall the bolts. Using a two-jaw puller, push the side shaft out of the retainer and bearing **(see illustration)**.

22 Using a large screwdriver, pry the seal from the retainer. The new seal can be driven into the retainer with a block of wood or a socket with the same outside diameter as the seal.

23 Unbolt the retainer from the extension tube and place it on the side shaft. Slide the bearing onto the shaft, followed by a new collar. These must be pressed into position. If access to a hydraulic press is not available, take the assembly to a machine shop or Nissan dealer.

24 The remainder of the assembly is the reverse of the removal procedure.

9 Front differential — removal and installation

Refer to illustrations 9.6a, 9.6b and 9.10

1 Raise the front of the truck and support it on jackstands. Apply the parking brake or block the rear wheels.

2 Remove the drain plug and drain the oil from the differential into a container.

3 Disconnect the front driveshaft from the rear of the differential, referring to Section 7, if necessary.

4 Remove the bolts attaching the driveaxles to the differential and position them out of the way, hanging them with pieces of wire to avoid damaging the outer CV joints.

5 Position a jack under the differential to support it when the mounting bolts are removed.

6 Remove the differential mounting bolts at the front **(see illustrations)**.

1980 through 1985 models

7 Remove the mounting bolt brackets from the rear of the differential.

8 Remove the bolts that attach the crossmember, directly below the differential, to the frame and lift out the crossmember.

1986 and later models

9 Remove the engine mounting bolts and raise the engine with a hoist or a jack and block of wood under the oil pan.

10 Remove the differential mounting member-to-frame bolts **(see illustration)**. The mounting member will be removed along with the differential.

All models

11 Carefully lower the jack, then withdraw the differential from under the truck.

12 Installation is the reverse of the removal procedure.

10.2 Mark the relationship of the driveshaft to the transfer case companion flange before removing the bolts (this will ensure correct alignment of the shaft during installation)

10 Transfer case oil seals – replacement

Refer to illustrations 10.2 and 10.5

1 Raise the truck and support it on jackstands. Remove the transfer case rock guard and drain the oil.

2 Mark the position of the appropriate driveshaft flange in relation to the transfer case flange **(see illustration)**. Remove the bolts and disconnect the driveshaft.

3 Remove the locknut from the transfer case companion flange. To keep the flange from turning, reinstall two of the driveshaft mounting bolts and engage a pry bar between them.

4 Using a puller, remove the companion flange.

5 Carefully pry the oil seal out with a screwdriver, being sure not to scratch or damage the seal bore in the case **(see illustration)**. A block of wood placed between the screwdriver and case can provide additional leverage.

6 Lubricate the lip of the seal with gear oil and tap it into position with a socket or block of wood.

7 Place the companion flange into position. Install the locknut and tighten it to the specified torque.

8 Reinstall the driveshaft, being sure the flange marks made during removal are aligned.

9 Refill the transfer case with oil, referring to to Chapter 1 if necessary.

10 Reinstall the rock guard and lower the truck to the ground.

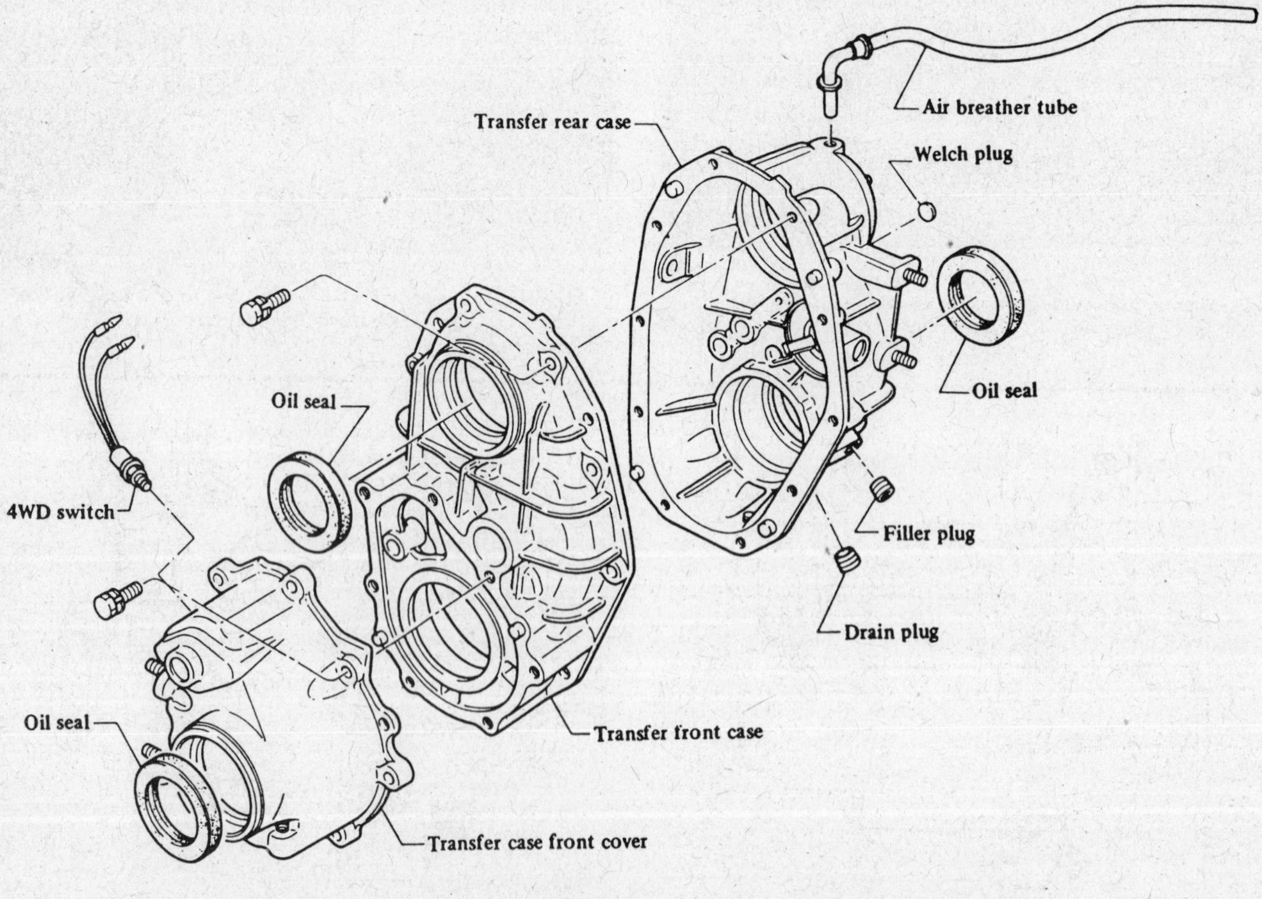

Air breather tube
Transfer rear case
Welch plug
Oil seal
Oil seal
4WD switch
Filler plug
Drain plug
Oil seal
Transfer front case
Transfer case front cover

10.5 Exploded view of the transfer case oil seals, cases and related parts

11 Transfer case – removal and installation

Refer to illustrations 11.7, 11.8, 11.11, 11.17 and 11.18

Removal

1 Disconnect the negative battery cable from the battery.
2 Raise the rear of the truck and support it on jackstands. Block the front wheels.
3 Remove the bolts that retain the transfer case rock guard to the body and detach it. Drain the oil from the transfer case.
4 Mark the positions of the driveshaft flanges contacting the transfer case. They must be reinstalled exactly as they are originally mounted.
5 Remove the bolts that retain the primary driveshaft to the transfer case.
6 Remove the front and rear driveshafts.
7 Disconnect the wire leading to the 4WD switch **(see illustration)**.
8 Disconnect the speedometer cable from the transfer case **(see illustration)**.

1980 through 1985 models

9 If necessary for clearance, remove the catalytic converter by referring to Chapter 4.
10 Position a jack under the transfer case to support its weight.
11 Loosen the bolts that secure the mounting insulators to the transfer case **(see illustration)**.
12 Moving to the interior, remove the rubber boot from around the transfer case shifter.
13 Remove the bolts that attach the mounting insulators to the frame and carefully lower the transfer case from the vehicle.
14 Slide the transfer case out and, if necessary, remove the mounting insulators from it.

1986 and later models

15 Remove the torsion bars (see Chapter 11).
16 Support the transmission with a jack and block of wood, then remove the crossmember from under the transfer case.

11.7 Unplug all electrical connectors (arrows) attached to wires leading to the transfer case

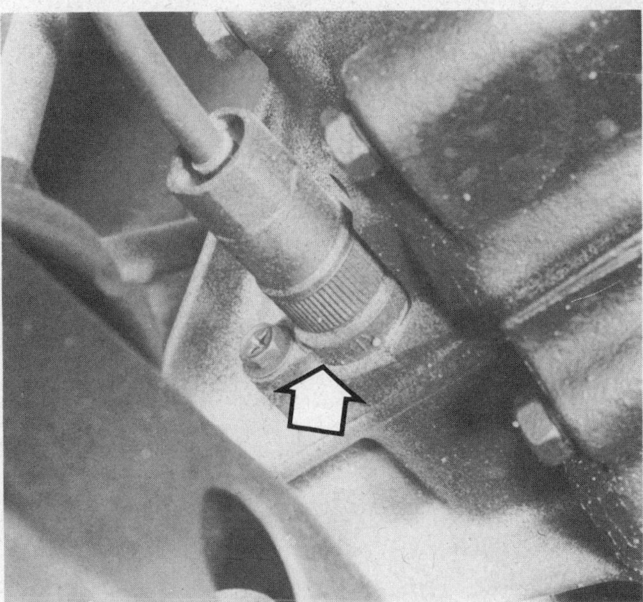

11.8 The speedometer cable attaches to the right rear of the transfer case (arrow)

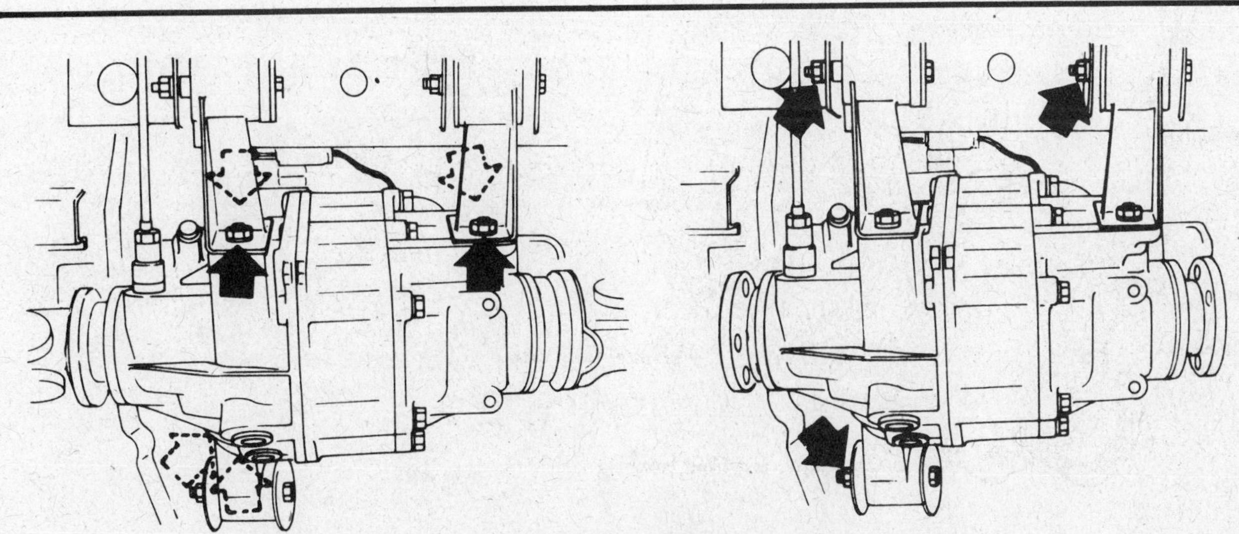

11.11 Location of the transfer case-to-bracket mounting bolts (left) and the bracket-to-frame mounting bolts (right) (1980 through 1985 models)

11.17 Peel back the boot to expose the transfer control lever rod-to-shift lever nut (arrow), remove the nut and slide the rod off of the stud

11.18 1986 and later transmission-to-transfer case bolts must be reinstalled in the same holes – the three lower bolts are longer than the others (not all can be seen from this angle)

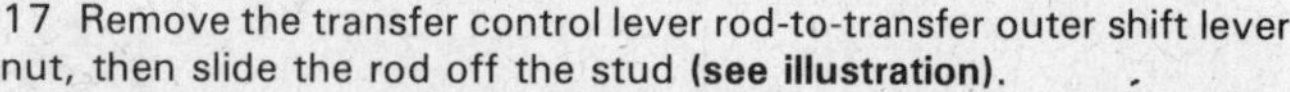

17 Remove the transfer control lever rod-to-transfer outer shift lever nut, then slide the rod off the stud **(see illustration)**.

18 Support the transfer case with a floor jack. Remove the transmission-to-transfer case bolts **(see illustration)** and slide the transfer case to the rear, disengaging it from the transmission. Carefully lower it to the ground.

19 Before installing the transfer case, apply a coat of sealer Nissan Part No. KP610-00250 or equivalent) to the mating surface of the transfer case (manual transmission equipped models only).

Installation

20 Installation is the reverse of the removal procedure, but be sure the driveshaft flange marks made during removal are aligned. If necessary, refer to Chapter 1 for refilling the transfer case with oil.

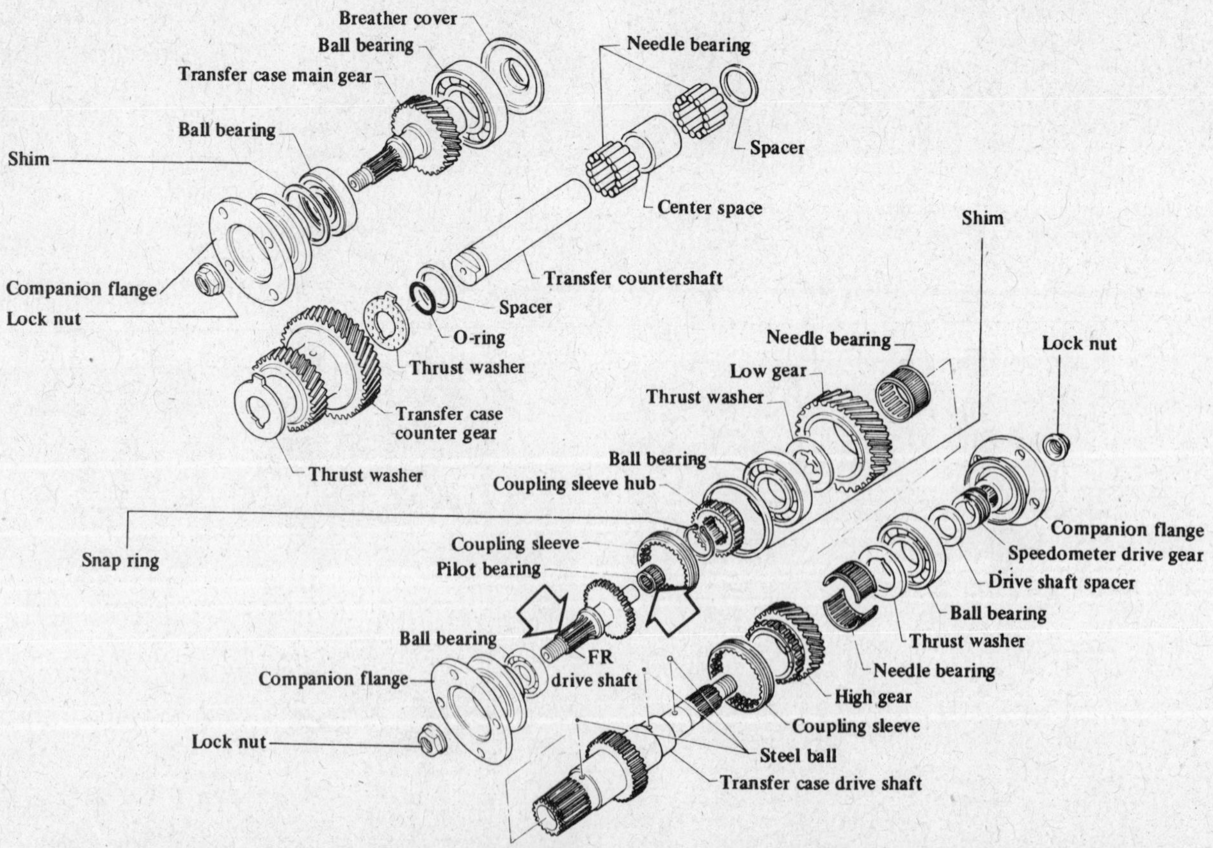

12.6 Exploded view of the transfer case gear assemblies (note the location of the FR driveshaft and pilot bearing)

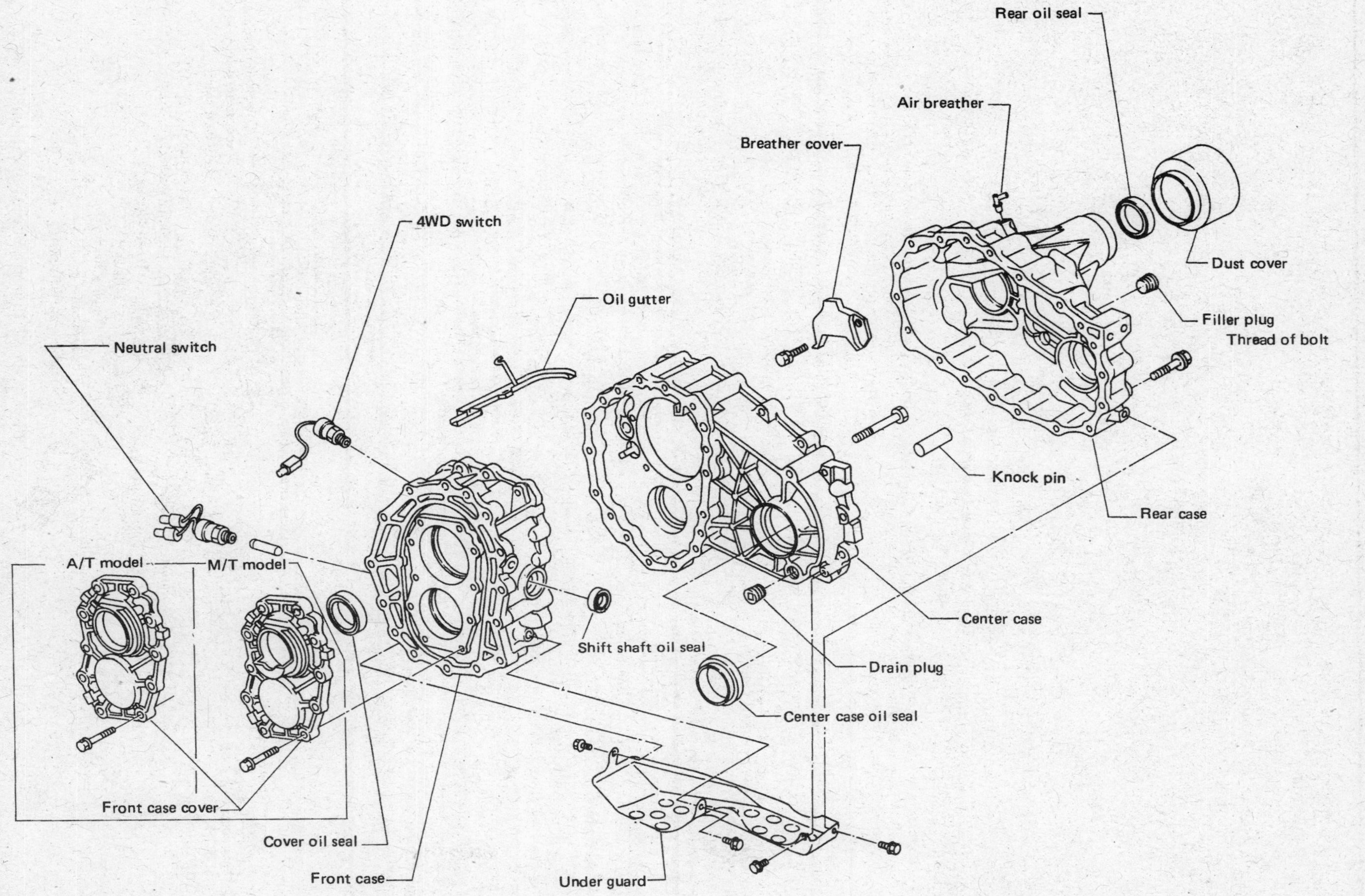

12.1 Exploded view of the TX10A transfer case

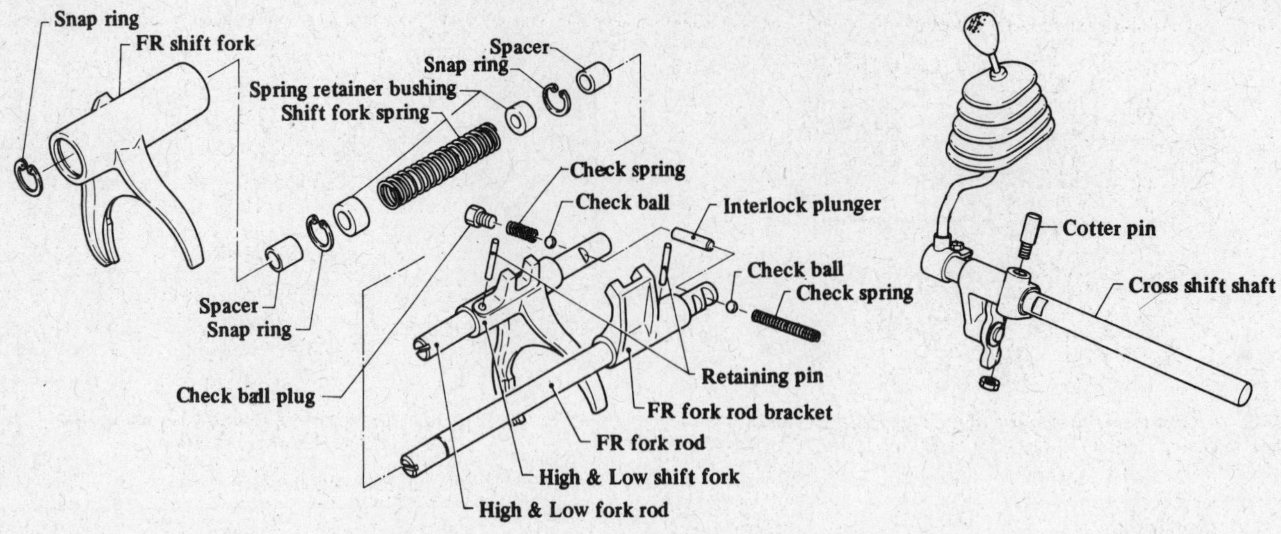

12.7 Exploded view of the transfer case forks and fork rods

12 Transfer case – overhaul

Refer to illustrations 12.6, 12.7, 12.14, 12.21, 12.27, 12.45, 12.59, 12.63, 12.80a and 12.80b

Note: *This procedure applies to vehicles manufactured from 1980 through 1985 only. Due to the complexity of the 1986 and later transfer case and the special tools required, it's recommended that internal repair procedures be left to a dealer service department or repair shop. Access to a hydraulic press is necessary for some steps in the following procedure.*

Forks and fork rods

1 With the transfer case removed from the vehicle, wipe off all dirt and grease from the exterior surfaces.

2 Shift the transfer case into the 4L and 2H positions, then remove the locknuts from the three companion flanges. To keep the flange from turning, reinstall two driveshaft mounting bolts into it and engage a pry bar between them.

3 Using a puller, remove the companion flanges.

4 Remove the 4WD switch.

5 Remove the front cover mounting bolts, and then remove the front cover by tapping it with a soft-faced hammer. If the front cover bearing must be replaced refer to Step 88.

6 Remove the FR driveshaft and pilot bearing **(see illustration)**.

7 Remove the snap-ring that retains the FR shift fork **(see illustration)**. Remove the shift fork assembly and spacer, together with the coupling sleeve.

8 Remove the snap-ring that retains the coupling sleeve hubs.

9 Draw out the coupling sleeve hub.

10 Remove the front case mounting bolts and then remove the front case by tapping it with a soft-faced hammer.

11 Remove the nut from the cotter pin. Tap the cotter pin out with a hammer.

12 Remove the cross shift shaft.

13 Remove the shift lever with the differential lever.

14 Remove the check ball plug located on the outside of the case, and remove the check spring and ball **(see illustration)**.

15 Using a punch, tap out the High and Low shift fork retaining pin.

16 Tap the rear end of the transfer case driveshaft assembly and remove it with the high and low shift fork and counter gear assembly. Be careful not to drop the needle bearings.

17 Pull out the main gear assembly.

18 Remove the transfer case front shim.

19 Remove the High and Low and FR fork rods, interlock plunger, steel ball and check spring.

20 Secure the FR fork rod in a vise, and tap out the retaining pin. The FR fork rod bracket can then be removed.

21 Insert an 8 mm bolt and nut through the FR shift fork. Tighten the nut to eliminate the shift fork spring tension, then remove the snap-ring with snap-ring pliers **(see illustration)**.

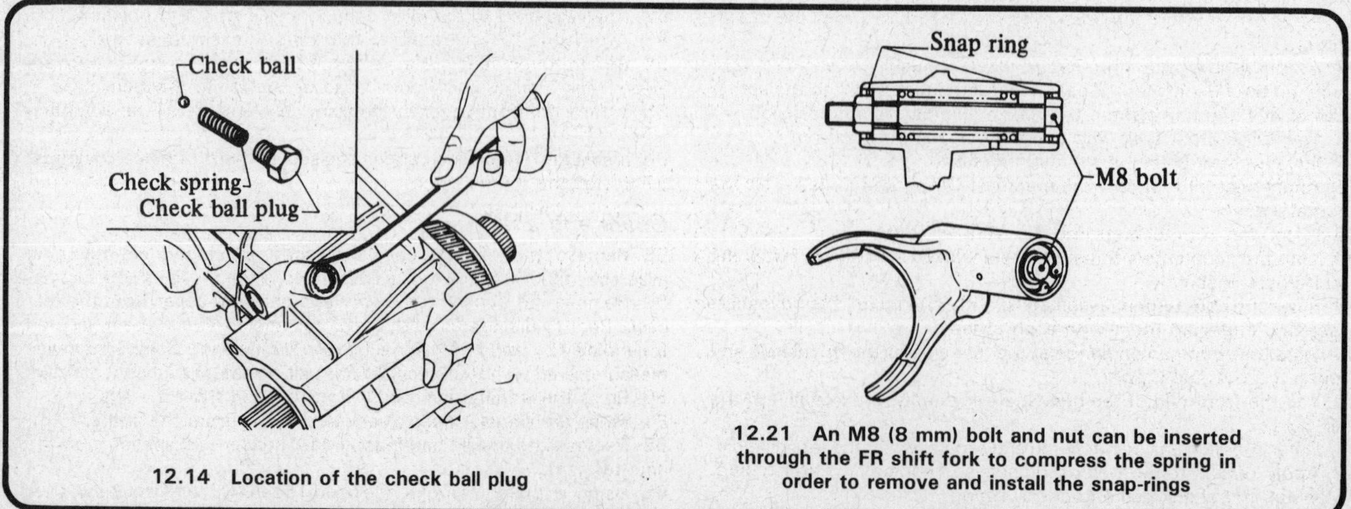

12.14 Location of the check ball plug

12.21 An M8 (8 mm) bolt and nut can be inserted through the FR shift fork to compress the spring in order to remove and install the snap-rings

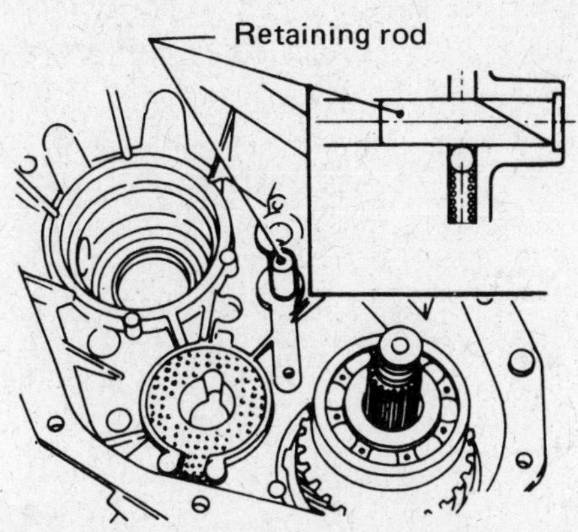

12.27 An appropriate size rod should be used to retain the check ball and steel ball before installation of the FR fork rod

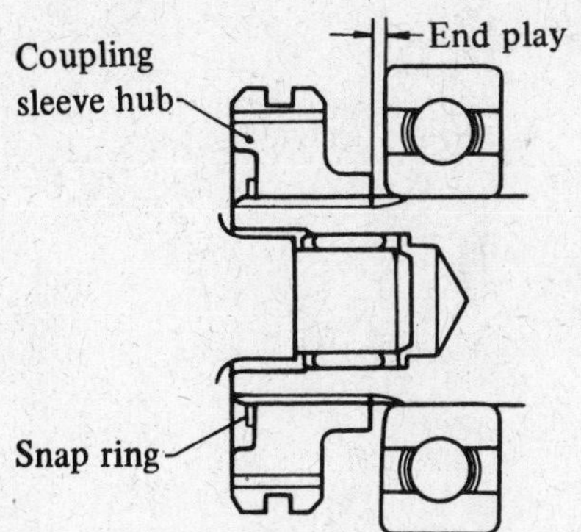

12.45 The coupling sleeve hub end play should be measured at the point shown

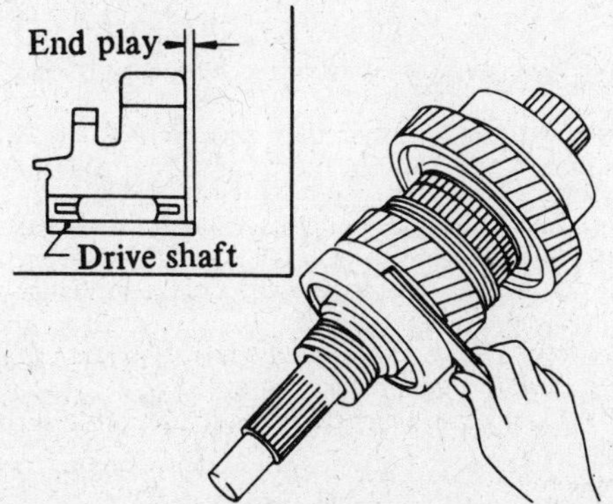

12.59 The gear end play of the transfer case driveshaft should be measured both before and after disassembly

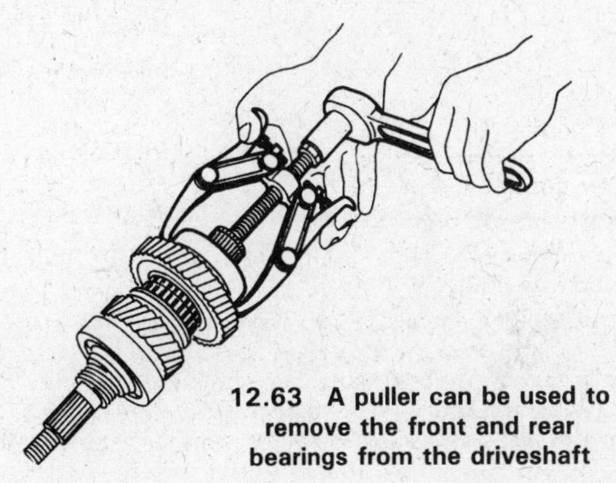

12.63 A puller can be used to remove the front and rear bearings from the driveshaft

22 Remove the spring retainer bushings and shift fork spring. Then separate them.
23 Clean all parts with solvent and carefully inspect them for scratches, damage and wear, replacing them as necessary.
24 Begin assembly by installing the breather cover, then install the transfer main gear assembly by tapping it into position.
25 Drive out the FR shift fork welch plug.
26 Install the check spring and steel ball in the hole in the rear case.
27 Insert a close fitting rod into the hole to retain the ball and spring **(see illustration)**.
28 Install the High and Low shift fork in the coupling sleeve.
29 With the FR fork rod in a vise, tap the retaining pin into position.
30 Install the FR fork rod by pushing the rod used to retain the ball and spring out of position. Then install the interlock pin.
31 Attach the FR fork rod bracket to the FR fork rod with the retaining pin.
32 Assemble the snap-ring, spring retainer bushings and shift fork spring on the FR shift fork. Again, insert an 8 mm bolt into the spring retainer bushing and tighten the nut to eliminate spring tension.
33 Install the other snap-ring and remove the bolt and nut.
34 Install a new O-ring in the countershaft.
35 Apply gear oil to a new countershaft O-ring and install it on the countershaft.
36 Install the countershaft into the transfer case.
37 With the countergear thrust washer installed in position, install the countergear assembly.
38 Raise the countergear assembly slightly and install the driveshaft assembly, engaging them with each other.
39 Install the companion flange at the rear side of the driveshaft and tighten the nut finger tight.
40 Tap the front end of the driveshaft assembly and install it in the rear case.
41 Install the High and Low fork rod and secure it with the retaining pin.
42 Apply sealant to the welch plug hole and reinstall the welch plug.
43 Install the check ball and check spring.
44 Apply sealant to the threads of the check ball plug and install it in position.
45 Install the coupling sleeve hub and measure the end play **(see illustration)**. A snap-ring of the appropriate thickness (as listed in the Specifications) should be used to retain the coupling sleeve hub, so the end play will be 0 to 0.0079-inch (0 to 0.20 mm).
46 Install the shift lever with the differential lever.
47 Install the cross shift shaft.
48 Apply grease to the thrust washer, main gear front and transfer case front shims and place them in position.
49 Be sure the mating surface of the front case is clean and apply sealant in a continuous bead around it.
50 Install the front case by tapping it into position.
51 Install the spacer, FR shift fork assembly with coupling sleeve and other spacer, and secure them with a snap-ring.
52 Apply gear oil to the pilot bearing and install it in position.
53 Attach the FR driveshaft to the transfer case driveshaft.
54 Be sure the mating surfaces of the front case and front cover are clean, then apply a continuous bead of sealant to the front case.
55 Attach the front cover to the front case and install the mounting bolts.
56 Install the companion flanges and secure them with new locknuts.
57 Install the 4WD switch.

Gears and shafts

58 Remove the transfer case driveshaft assembly, counter gear assembly, forks and fork rods as described in the previous sub-section.
59 Remove the transfer main gear and breather cover from the rear case. Prior to disassembly, the gear assemblies should be measured for end play by using a feeler gauge **(see illustration)**. Comparing these measurements with the Specifications will indicate the amount of wear.
60 Press the transfer main gear front bearing from the shaft.
61 Press the transfer main gear rear bearing from the shaft.
62 Remove the needle bearings, center spacer and spacer from the counter gear.
63 Using a puller, remove the front bearing from the Low gear assembly **(see illustration)**.

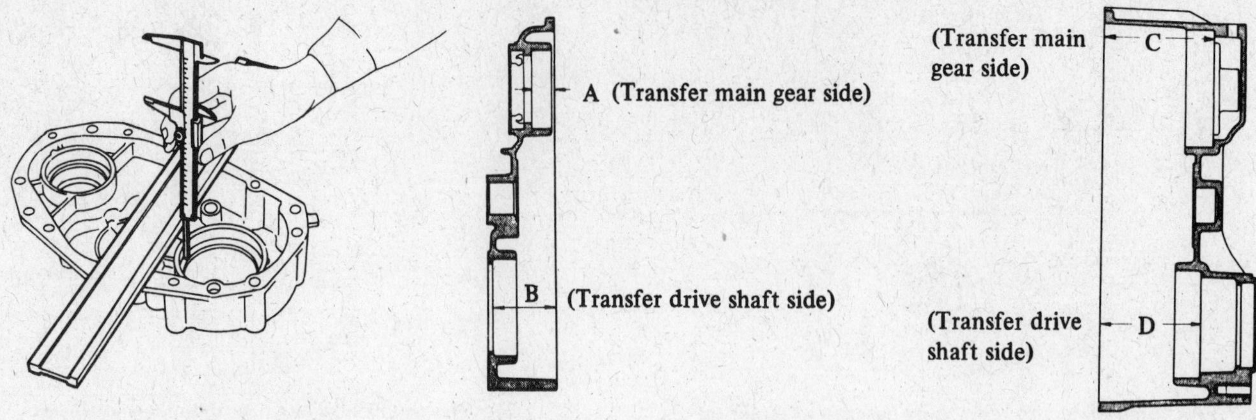

12.80a For proper shimming, the measurements shown above should be made for both the front and rear cases

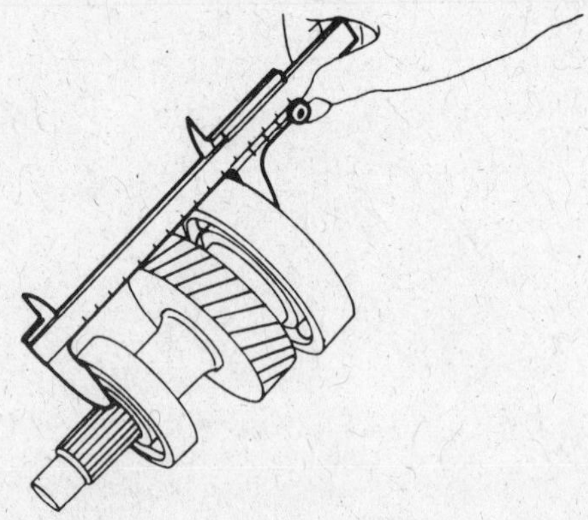

12.80b Measuring the distance between the bearing outer edges of both the main gear assembly (E) and driveshaft (F)

64 Remove the thrust washer and steel ball.
65 Remove the Low gear and needle bearing.
66 Press the speedometer worm gear off the High gear assembly.
67 Remove the spacer and steel ball.
68 Using a puller, remove the rear bearing from the High gear assembly.
69 Remove the thrust washer and steel ball.
70 Remove the High gear, needle bearings and coupling sleeves.
71 Clean all parts in solvent and inspect all gears for excessive wear, chips, cracks or other damage and replace as necessary.
72 Begin assembly of the High gear assembly by first applying gear oil to the needle bearings. Install them and the High gear onto the transfer case driveshaft.
73 Apply grease to the steel ball and thrust washer and attach them to the High gear.
74 Press the driveshaft rear bearing onto the shaft, being sure to hold the High gear with your hand to avoid dropping the thrust washer.
75 Install the driveshaft spacer.
76 Apply grease to the steel ball and install the ball and the speedometer worm gear.
77 Begin assembly of the Low gear assembly by applying gear oil to the needle bearing, then install the needle bearing, coupling sleeve and Low gear on the driveshaft.
78 Apply grease to the steel ball and thrust washer and attach them to the Low gear.
79 Press the driveshaft front bearing onto the shaft, being sure to hold the Low gear with your hand to avoid dropping the thrust washer. Again, measure the gear end play to be sure everything is installed properly.
80 Any time the thrust washer, any ball bearing, the driveshaft, transfer case main gear or either the front or rear case are replaced with new parts, the transfer case must be re-shimmed as described below:

a) Measure the distance between the outer part of both bearing bores and the edge of the front case, referring to those dimensions as A and B **(see illustration)** and jot down the measurements.
b) Measure the same distances in the rear case (referring to these measurements as C and D and jot them down also. When measuring C, be sure the breather cover is installed in its normal position.
c) Measure the distance between the outer edges of the bearings on the transfer main gear assembly. Mark this measurement E **(see illustration)**.
d) Measure the distance between the outer edges of the bearings of the transfer driveshaft, and mark this measurement F.
e) The correct main gear front shim is determined by adding the measurements A and C, and then subtracting E from the total. Jot down the result and refer to the Specifications for the proper shim thickness.
f) The correct transfer case front shim is likewise found by adding the measurements B and D, and then subtracting F from the total. Refer to the Specifications to find the proper shim thickness to use.
g) Once the correct shim thicknesses are found, install them in position.

81 Begin assembly of the transfer main gear and counter gear by pressing the transfer main gear front bearing onto the shaft.
82 Press the main gear rear bearing onto the shaft.
83 Install the breather cover, if not already done, and then install the transfer case main gear.
84 Apply grease to all needle bearings and spacers.
85 Install the center spacer on the counter gear, then assemble the needle bearings and spacers in the counter gear. After installing the needle bearings, apply a thick coat of grease to hold them in place.
86 Install the transfer case driveshaft assembly, forks and fork rods, referring to the previous sub-section.

Front cover bearing

87 Remove the front cover by referring to the *Forks and fork rods* sub-section.
88 Pry the oil seal out of the front cover.
89 Remove the snap-ring that retains the bearing.
90 Press the bearing out of the cover.
91 Installation is the reverse of removal.

Chapter 10 Brakes

Contents

Specifications

Disc brakes

Rotor maximum runout	
1980 through 1983	0.0059 in (0.15 mm)
1984 on	0.0028 in (0.07 mm)
Rotor maximum thickness variation (parallelism)	
1980 through 1983	0.0028 in (0.07 mm)
1984	0.0012 in (0.03 mm)
1985 on	0.0008 in (0.02 mm)

Disc brakes (continued)

Rotor minimum thickness	
1980 through 1983	0.413 in (10.5 mm)
1984 and 1985	0.787 in (20.0 mm)
1986 on	
CL25VA (2WD 4-cyl models)	0.787 in (20.0 mm)
CL25VD (all V6 and 4WD models)	0.945 in (24.0 mm)
AD14VB (rear disc brake rotor)	0.630 in (16.0 mm)

Drum brakes

Maximum inner drum diameter (also cast into the drum)	
1980 through 1983	10.06 in (255.5 mm)
1984 on	
LT26B (2WD except heavy duty)	10.30 in (261.5 mm)
DS25B, DS25C, DS25D (2WD HD and 4WD)	10.06 in (255.5 mm)
DS22 (dual tire models)	8.72 in (221.5 mm)
LT30A (1991 and later models)	11.67 in (296.5 mm)
Drum radial runout limit	
1980 through 1983	0.0047 in (0.12 mm)
1984	0.0012 in (0.03 mm)
1985 on	0.002 in (0.05 mm)
Drum out of round limit	
1980 through 1983	0.0006 in (0.015 mm)
1984	0.002 in (0.05 mm)
1985 on	0.0012 in (0.03 mm)
Drum maximum taper	
1980 through 1983	0.0008 in (0.02 mm)
1984 on	0.0016 in (0.04 mm)

Brake booster

Output rod length	
1980 through 1983	0.384 to 0.394 in (9.75 to 10.0 mm)
1984 and 1985	not adjustable
1986 on	0.4045 to 0.4144 in (10.275 to 10.525 mm)
Input rod length	
1980	7.09 in (180 mm)
1981 through 1983	10.83 in (275 mm)
1984 and 1985	10.10 in (256.5 mm)
1986 on	not adjustable

Torque specifications

	Ft-lbs
Caliper mounting bolts (1980 through 1983)	53 to 72
Yoke-to-cylinder body bolts (1980 through 1983)	12 to 15
Caliper-to-slide pin bolts (1984 on)	16 to 23
Torque member-to-knuckle bolts (1984 on)	53 to 72
Rear brake caliper guide pins (1988)	16 to 23
Torque member-to-rear axle case (1988)	40 to 47
Rotor-to-hub bolts	
1980 through 1983	33
1984 on	36 to 51
Brake hose-to-caliper union bolt	12 to 14
Brake pedal fulcrum pin nut	
Through 1990	6 to 8
1991 and later	12 to 16
Brake booster-to-firewall	
Through 1990	6 to 8
1991 and later	9 to 12
Master cylinder mounting nuts	6 to 8
Rear brake backing plate-to-axle	
Single tire models	39 to 46
Dual tire models	62 to 80
Wheel cylinder mounting nuts	
1980 through 1983	11 to 13
1984 through 1990	3.9 to 5.4
1991 and later	4.3 to 8.0

Torque specifications (continued)

	Ft-lbs
Load sensing valve mounting bolts	
Through 1990	5.8 to 8.0
1991 and later	12 to 15

1 General information

The braking system in the vehicles covered by this manual is a split system design. It incorporates two separate circuits; one for the front brakes and one for the rear brakes. With this system if one circuit fails, the other circuit will still function.

The master cylinder is designed for the split system and incorporates a primary piston for one circuit and a secondary piston for the other.

A vacuum booster unit is used which draws vacuum from the intake manifold to add power assistance to the normal brake pressure.

The Nissan load sensing valve (NLSV) is designed to prevent the rear wheels from locking under severe braking conditions. The valve operates by changing the front and rear brake fluid pressure distribution in response to vehicle loading.

The front wheels are equipped with disc brakes. These consist of a flat, disc-like rotor which is attached to the axle and wheel. Around one section of the rotor is mounted a stationary caliper assembly which houses two hydraulically-operated disc brake pads. On early models the inner pad is mounted to a piston facing the inner surface of the rotor, while the outer pad is mounted to a yoke and faces the outer surface of the rotor. Later models feature either a single or dual piston sliding caliper arrangement. When the brake pedal is applied, brake fluid pressure forces both pads against the rotor. The pressure and resultant friction on the rotor is what slows the wheel.

The rear brakes on some models use the conventional drum brakes of the dual-servo type. Other models employ a single action, leading/trailing shoe type with a pivot point at the bottom of each shoe. With either of these designs, fluid pressure from the master cylinder forces the rear wheel cylinder pistons outward, which in turn forces the brake shoes against the spinning brake drum attached to the rear wheel. The force of the brake shoes against the drum is what slows the wheel. The wheel cylinders contain two operating pistons which contact both brake shoes. Adjustment is automatic, occurring when the parking brake is applied. Some models are equipped with rear disc brakes, similar to the later style front disc brake.

The parking brake (handbrake) is cable operated from a dash mounted handle to the rear wheels.

After completing any operation involving the dismantling of any part of the brake system always test drive the vehicle to check for proper braking performance before resuming normal driving. When testing the brakes, perform the tests on a clean, dry, flat surface. Conditions other than these can lead to inaccurate test results. Test the brakes at various speeds with both light and heavy pedal pressure. The vehicle should brake evenly without pulling to one side or the other. Avoid locking the brakes, as this slides the tires and diminishes braking efficiency and control.

Tires, load and front end alignment are factors which also affect braking performance.

2 Disc brake pad – replacement

Refer to illustrations 2.2a, 2.2b, 2.3, 2.4, 2.8, 2.14a, 2.14b, 2.14c, 2.15, 2.17, 2.19 and 2.20

Note: *The following information applies to both front and rear (on vehicles so equipped) disc brakes.*

Warning: *Disc brake pads must be replaced on both wheels at the same time – never replace pads on only one wheel. Also, the dust created by the brake system contains asbestos, which is harmful to your health. Never blow it out with compressed air and don't inhale any of it. An approved filtering mask should be worn when working on the brakes. Do not, under any circumstances, use petroleum-based solvents to clean brake parts. Use brake cleaner or denatured alcohol only. When servicing the disc brakes, use only high quality, nationally recognized brand name pads.*

1 Loosen the wheel lug nuts, raise the front of the vehicle and support it securely on jackstands. Remove the wheel.

1980 to 1983

2 Remove the pad clip **(see illustrations)**.

3 While holding the springs in position, remove the two pad pins. Lift off the springs **(see illustration)**.

2.2a Use a screwdriver to pop the brake pad pin retaining clips out

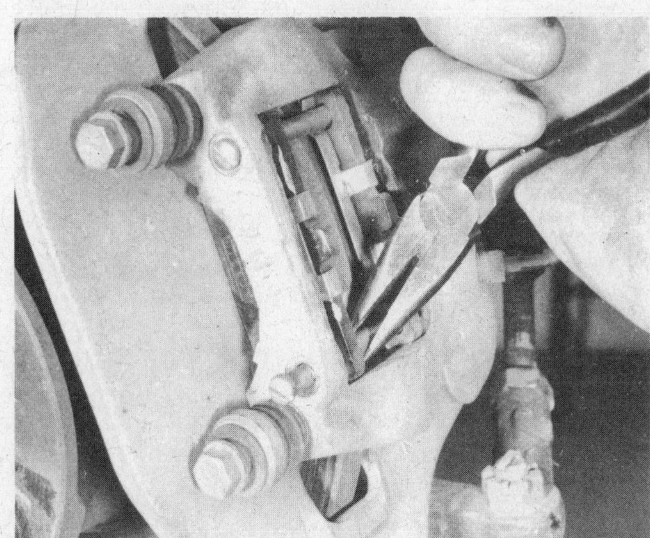

2.3 Pliers can be used to remove the pad pins

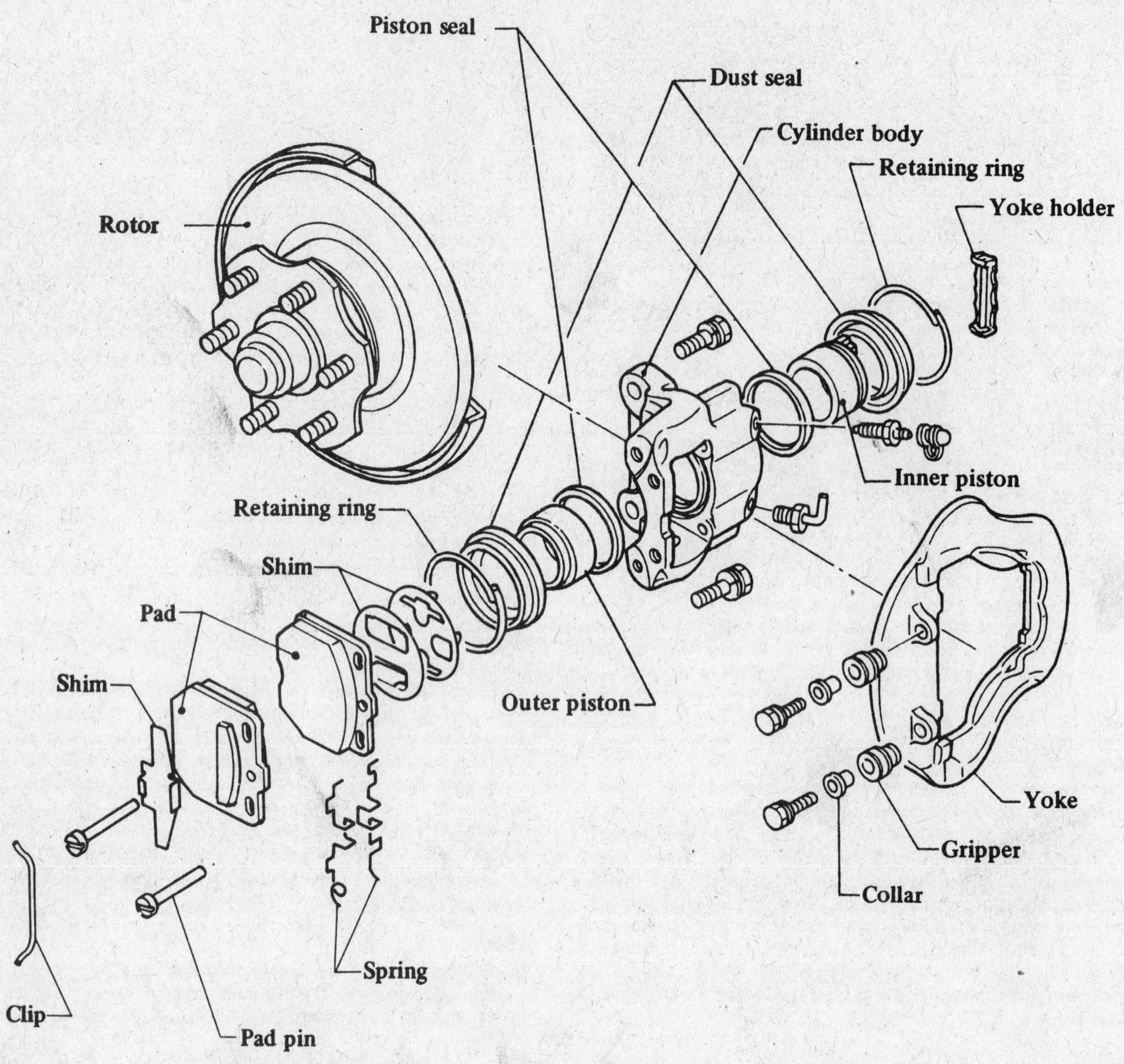

2.2b Exploded view of the front disc brake assembly (1980 through 1983)

4 Lift out the brake pads and any shims **(see illustration)**. **Note:** *After removing the pads, do not depress the brake pedal, as this will force the piston out of the cylinder.*

5 If the pads are glazed, damaged, fouled with oil or grease, or worn beyond their limit (see Specifications, Chapter 1), they should be replaced with new ones. **Note:** *Always replace all four pads on the axle (two in each brake assembly) at the same time, and do not mix different pad materials.*

6 Remove the cap on the brake master cylinder and siphon out a bit of the fluid in the reservoir.

7 Use a large screwdriver to carefully force the piston back into the caliper. Do not push it in too far, as damage will result. Slide the new inner pad into position.

8 Now use the screwdriver to slide the yoke outward to make room for the new outer pad **(see illustration)**.

9 Apply a light coat of grease to the pad pins.

10 While holding the springs in place, install the pad pins. Be careful not to get grease on the friction sides of the pads.

11 Install the pad clip.

12 Reinstall the wheel, lower the vehicle and tighten the lug nuts to the specified torque.

13 Check the fluid level in the master cylinder and add fluid as necessary. If none of the fluid hoses have been disconnected, there should be no reason to bleed the brakes. However, test the brakes carefully before putting the car in use.

1984 and later

14 Remove the lower cylinder to body slide pin bolt **(see illustrations)**.

2.4 Pliers can be used to remove the pads from the caliper

2.8 The yoke must be levered outward to install the outer pad

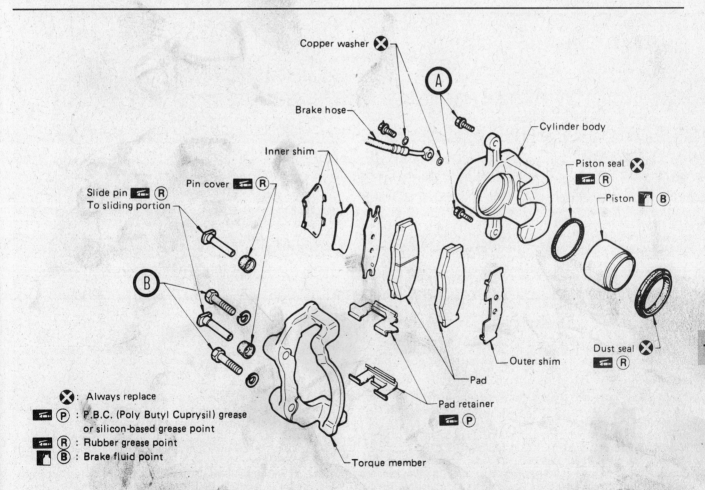

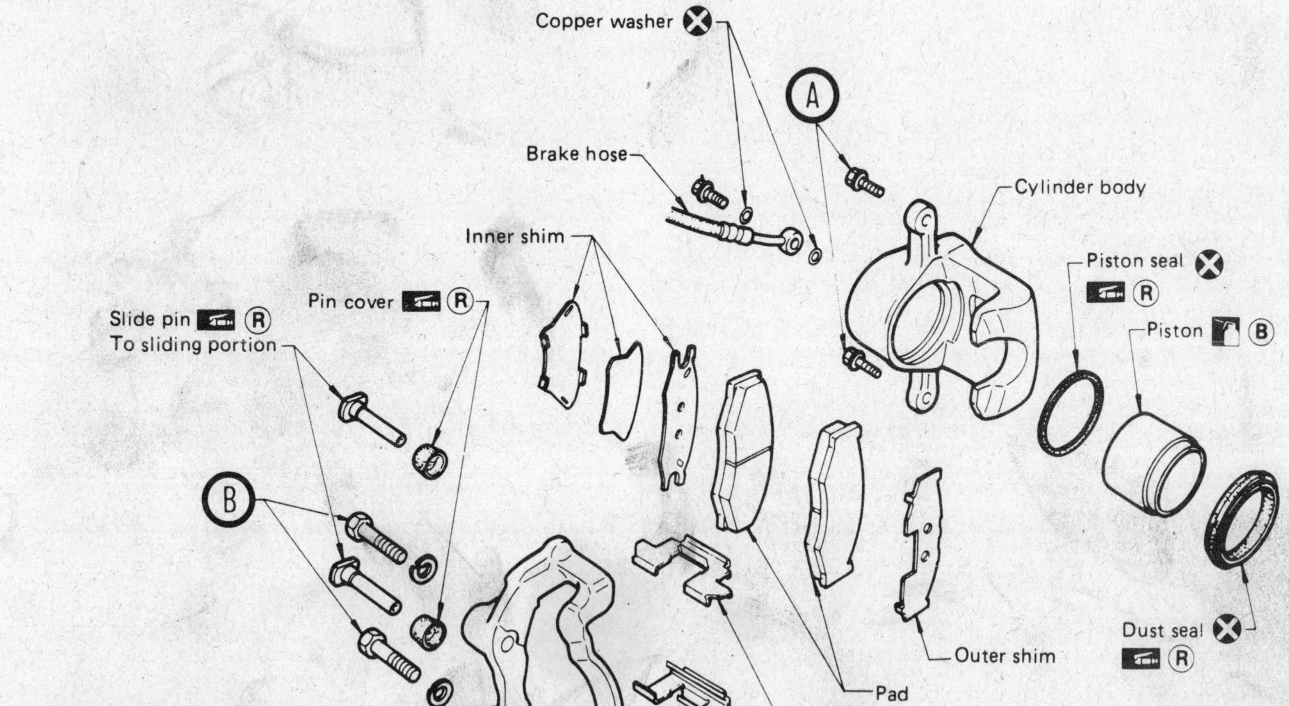

2.14a Exploded view of brake caliper used on later model four-cylinder, 2WD vehicles (CL28VA)

A Cylinder body-to-slide in bolts
B Torque member-to-knuckle bolts

10

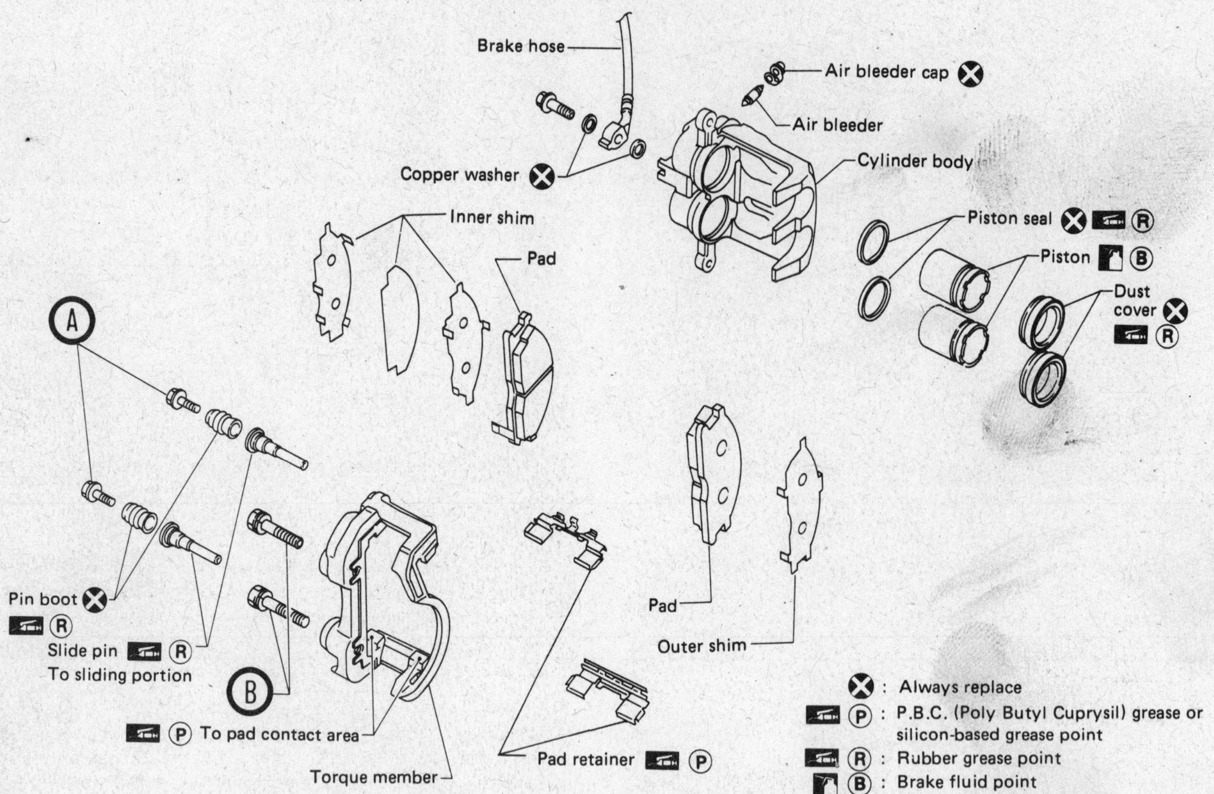

2.14b Exploded view of brake caliper used on later model V6, 4WD vehicles (CL28VD)

15 Swing the entire caliper assembly upward, allowing access to the brake pads **(see illustration)**.
16 Remove the pad retainers, the shims and the pads. Pay close attention to the position of each shim and retainer so that they can be reinstalled in their original locations.
17 Apply a small amount of silicon-based brake grease to the pad contact areas on the torque member **(see illustration)**.
18 Install the new inner pad and shims.
19 Rotate the caliper into position and use a long screwdriver or alignment tool to pull the caliper assembly to the outer side **(see illustration)**.
20 Raise the caliper and install the outer pad and shims, followed by the pad retainers **(see illustration)**.
21 Lower the caliper into position and install the lower cylinder body to slide pin bolt. Tighten the bolt to the specified torque.
22 Reinstall the wheel, lower the vehicle and tighten the lug nuts to the specified torque.
23 Check the fluid level in the master cylinder and add fluid as necessary. If none of the fluid hoses have been disconnected, there should be no reason to bleed the brakes. However, test the brakes carefully before putting the vehicle in use.

2.14c Remove the lower cylinder body-to-slide pin bolt . . .

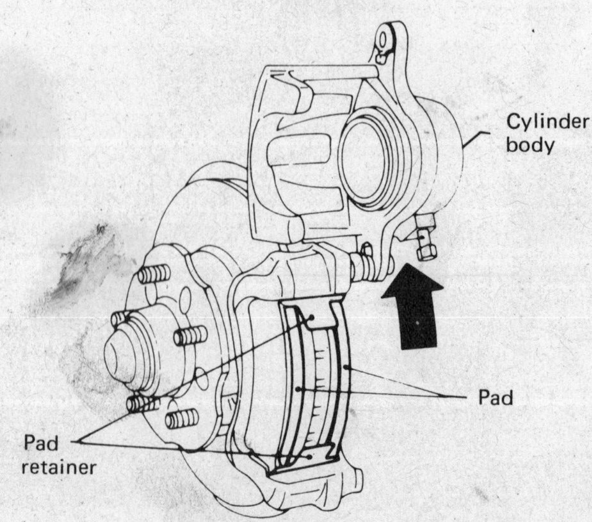

2.15 . . . then swing the caliper up to gain access to the brake pads

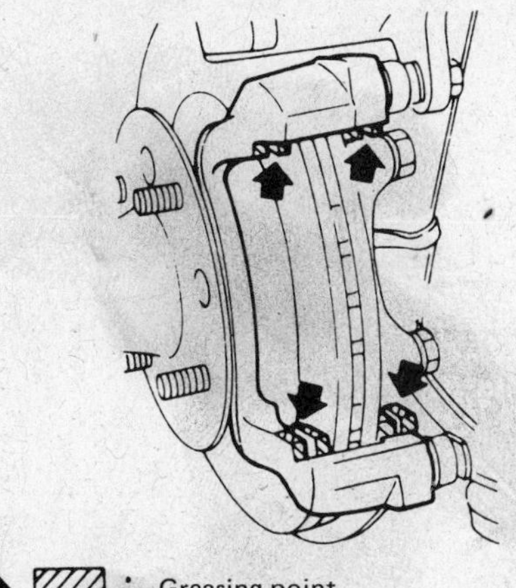

2.17 Apply silicon-based grease to these four points

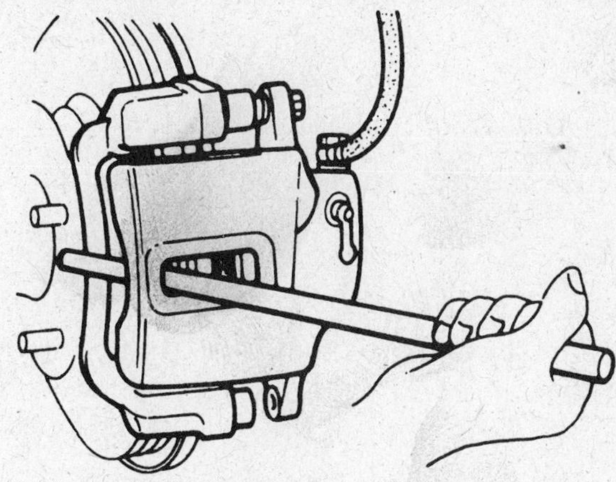

2.19 Use a large screwdriver or pry bar to move the caliper to the outside

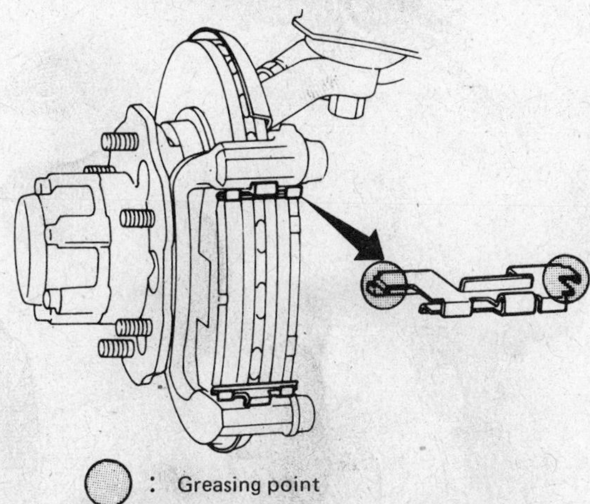

2.20 Apply a small amount of silicon-based grease to the ends of each retainer as shown

3 Disc brake caliper – removal, overhaul and installation

Refer to illustrations 3.2a, 3.2b, 3.6a, 3.6b, 3.8a, 3.8b, 3.10, 3.11, 3.20 through 3.27, 3.29, 3.33, 3.35 and 3.36

Removal

1 Remove the brake pads as described in Section 5.
2 On early style calipers, remove the brake tube and immediately plug the opening to prevent leakage of fluid and to keep foreign matter from entering the line **(see illustration)**. On later style calipers, remove the brake hose fitting bolt **(see illustration)**, disconnect the hose from the caliper and wrap a plastic bag tightly around the end of the hose to prevent excessive fluid loss or contamination.
3 Remove the two caliper mounting bolts (early style) or the upper cylinder body to torque member bolt (later style) and lift the caliper off the rotor.
4 Clean the outside of the caliper thoroughly with brake cleaner or denatured alcohol. Never use petroleum-based solvents.
5 Prior to disassembling the caliper, purchase a caliper overhaul kit.

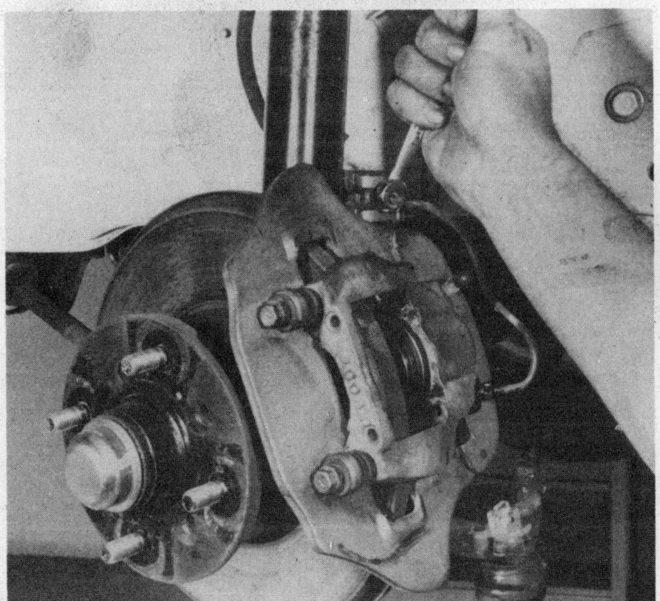

3.2a When disconnecting the front brake lines, plug the brake line openings immediately after disconnecting the line (early style caliper shown)

3.2b Remove the brake hose fitting bolt and separate the fitting from the caliper. Be sure to use new copper washers on each side of the fitting upon reassembly

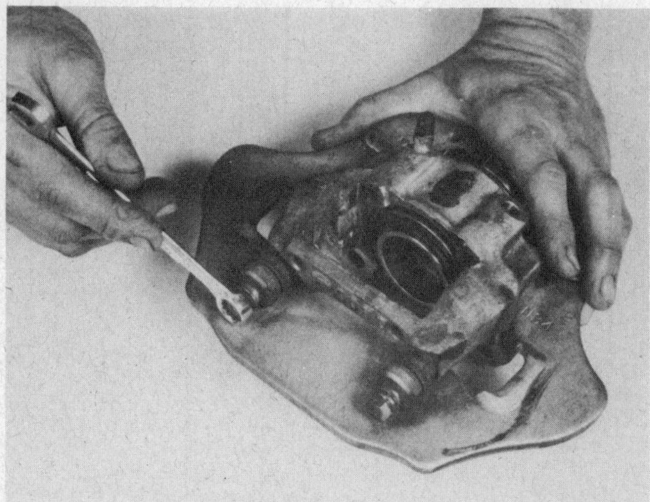

3.6a Removing the yoke-to-caliper bolts

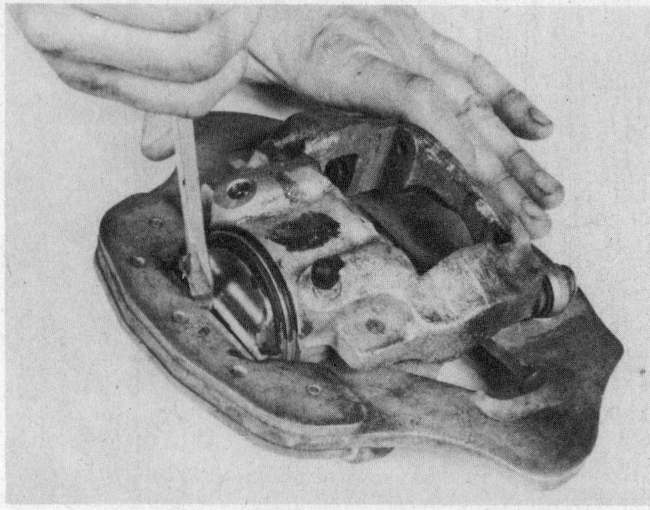

3.6b Use a screwdriver to pry the yoke holder off the yoke

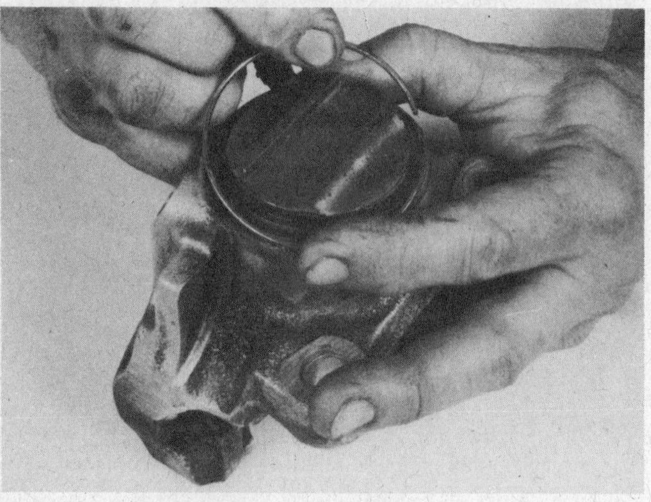

3.8a Remove the retaining ring from the inner piston dust seal

3.8b Remove the retaining ring from the outer piston dust seal

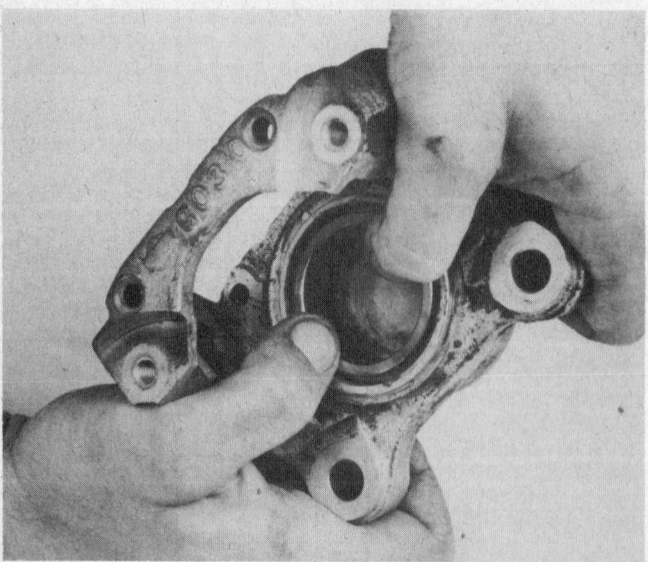

3.10 Both pistons are removed from the caliper by pushing on the outer piston

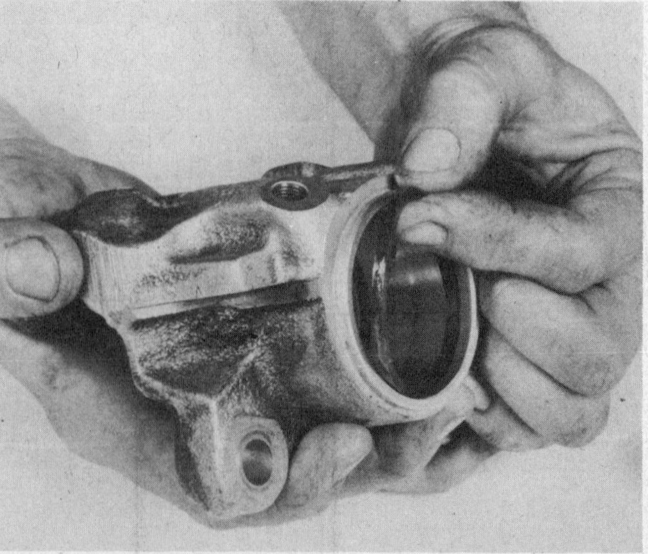

3.11 Remove the piston seal from the caliper bore. The use of a metal tool is not recommended, as it may scratch or gouge the bore

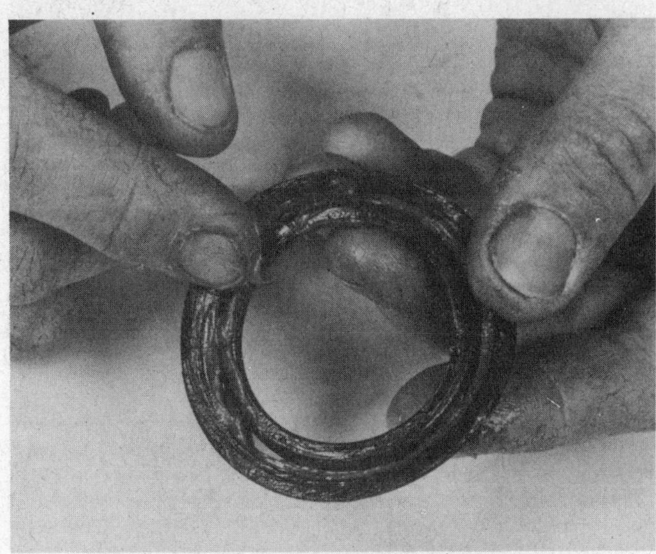

3.20 Apply silicon-based grease (usually supplied with the rebuild kit) to the inside of the dust seals prior to installation

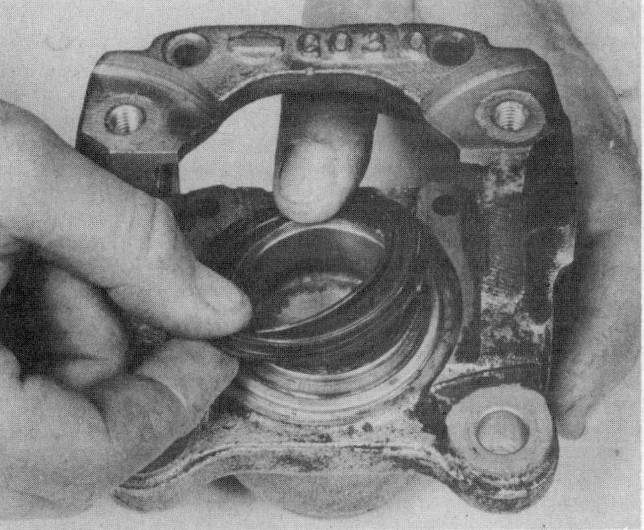

3.21 Installing the outer piston dust seal

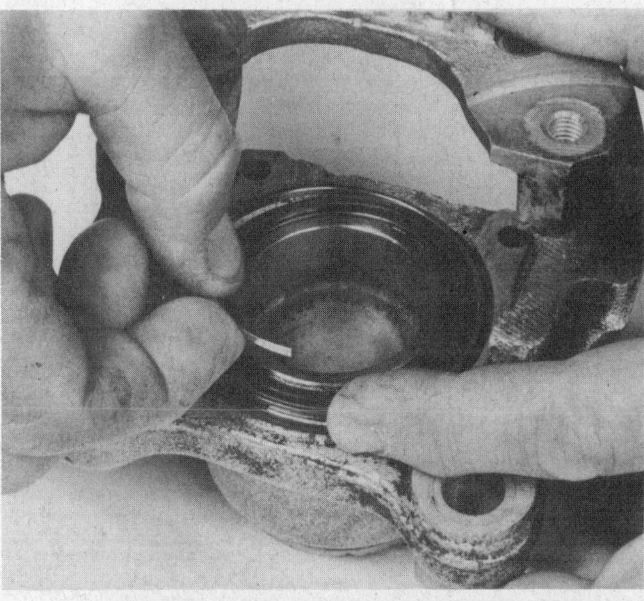

3.22 Install the retaining ring on the outer piston dust seal. Make sure it seats evenly around the entire circumference

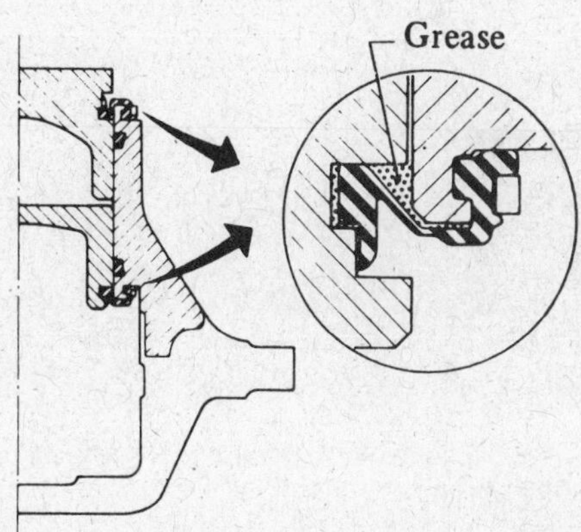

3.23 The disc brake pistons should be positioned as shown when installing the dust seals (apply grease to the seal grooves before installing)

1980 to 1983

6 Remove the two bolts that attach the caliper to the yoke **(see illustration)**. Use a flathead screwdriver to pry the caliper toward the outside of the yoke **(see illustration)**. This disengages the piston from the yoke.

7 Remove the caliper from the yoke.

8 Remove the yoke holder from the inner piston, then remove the dust seal retaining rings located on each side of the caliper **(see illustrations)**.

9 Remove the dust seals.

10 Push the pistons out of the caliper from the pad side **(see illustration)**.

11 Using a wooden or plastic dowel, remove the piston seals from the inside of the caliper bore **(see illustration)**.

12 Clean all of the metal parts in brake fluid or denatured alcohol. **Note:** *Never use mineral-based solvents, as this can cause the rubber seals to swell and possibly fail.*

13 Check the inside surface of the cylinder bore for any scoring, rust, nicks or other damage. If light scoring or rust is present it can be removed by polishing the bore with fine 600 grade emery cloth. If the damage is deep, the entire body will have to be replaced.

14 Check the yoke for cracks, excessive wear or other damage and replace it if necessary.

15 Inspect the piston for scoring, rust, nicks or other damage. The sliding surface of the piston is plated and cannot be polished with emery paper. If any defects are found, the piston must be replaced. If rubber grease is supplied with the overhaul kit, use it to lubricate the cylinder bore. Brake fluid can also be used for this purpose.

16 Install the two rubber seals into the grooves in the caliper bore. Lubricate the seals with rubber grease or brake fluid.

17 Lubricate the outer surfaces of both the pistons with either the rubber grease supplied with the overhaul kit or brake fluid.

18 Carefully insert each piston into its respective end of the bore. Be careful not to disturb the rubber seals inside the bore.

19 Press the outer piston into the bore so that the inner edge of the piston seal groove is in line with the inner edge of the caliper seal grooves.

20 If an orange grease is supplied with the overhaul kit, use it to fill the inner sealing surface of the outer dust seal **(see illustration)**. If no orange grease is supplied, use an approved silicone-base grease.

21 Install the dust seal so that it fits correctly into both the piston seal groove and the caliper seal groove **(see illustration)**.

22 Install the retaining ring securely around the dust seal **(see illustration)**.

23 Repeat the same procedure with the inner piston and inner dust seal.

3.24 Place the yoke holder into position on the inner piston

24 Press the yoke holder into its groove on the inner piston face **(see illustration)**.

25 Insert the caliper into position inside the yoke, making sure that the outer piston with yoke holder is properly aligned with the yoke. Place this assembly on a flat surface so that the outer piston is facing down and apply pressure to the inner piston to press the yoke holder onto the yoke **(see illustration)**. This can also be done with a hydraulic press if one is available.

26 Once the yoke holder is pressed onto the yoke, install the two mounting bolts that retain the yoke to the caliper housing. **Note:** *Before installing these bolts check the condition of the rubber boots and bushings, and if they are worn or otherwise damaged, replace them* **(see illustration)**. Tighten these bolts to the specified torque.

1984 and later

Note: *Although this procedure shows a single piston caliper overhaul, it also applies to the dual piston caliper.*

27 Position a wooden block or numerous shop rags in the caliper as a cushion, then use compressed air to remove the piston from the caliper **(see illustration)**. Use only enough air pressure to ease the piston out of the bore. If the piston is blown out, even with the cushion in place, it may be damaged. **Warning:** *Never place your fingers in front of the piston in an attempt to catch or protect it when applying com-*

3.25 To seat the yoke holder on the yoke, downward pressure must be applied to the inner piston

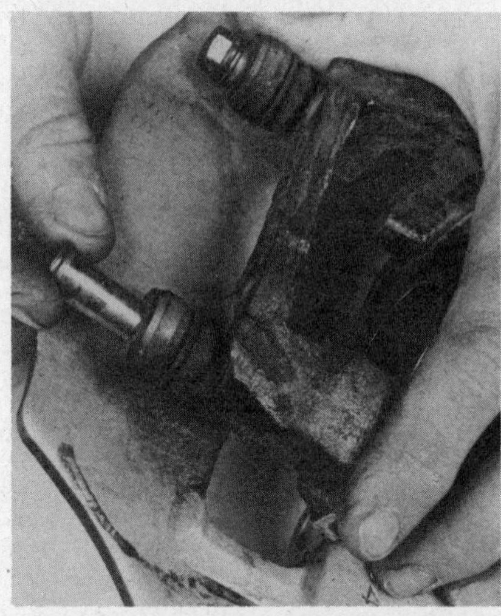
3.26 Before installing the yoke-to-caliper bolts, inspect the bushings and rubber boots. Lubricate the bushings with silicon-based grease

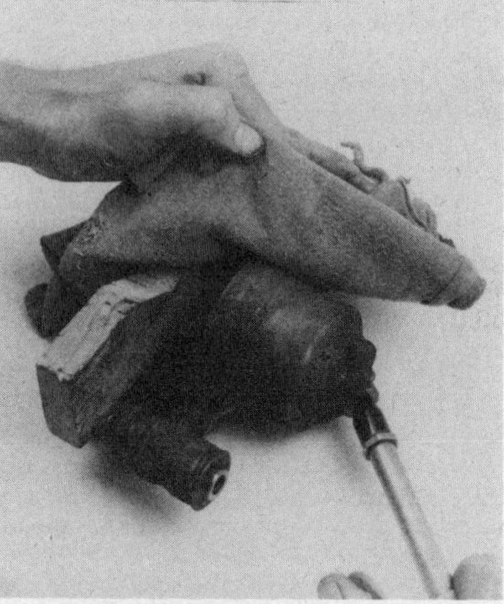
3.27 With the caliper padded to catch the piston, use compressed air to force the piston out of its bore. Make sure your hands or fingers are not between the piston and caliper

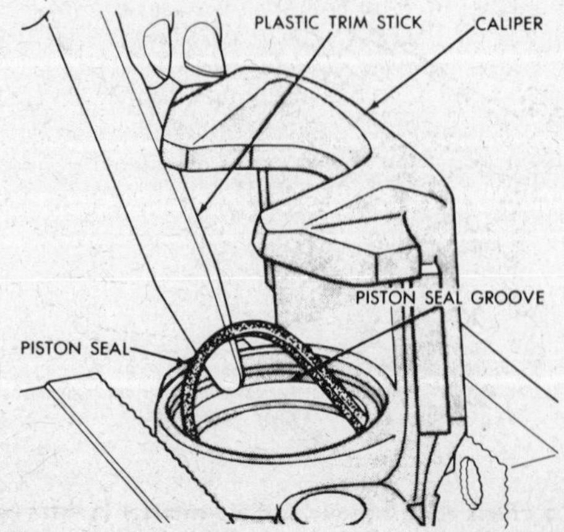

3.29 The piston seal should be removed with a plastic or wooden tool to avoid damage to the bore and seal groove

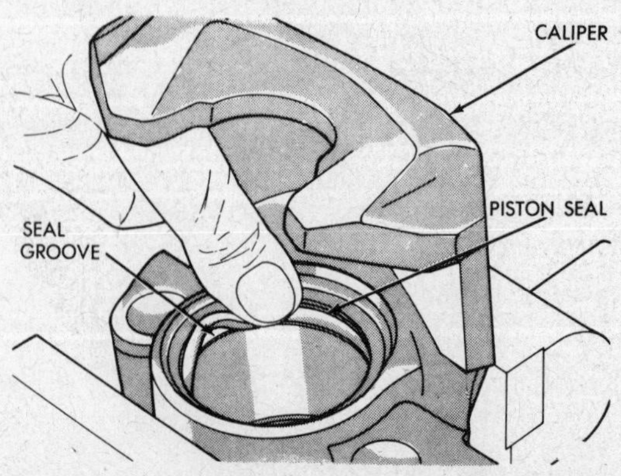

3.33 Start the new seal in the piston groove and push it in with your fingers (make sure it is not twisted)

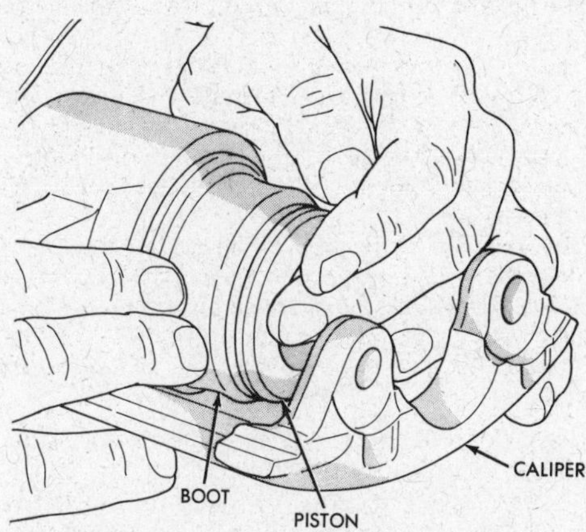

3.35 Install the piston and boot by hand only

pressed air, as serious injury could occur.
28 Carefully pry the dust boot out of the caliper bore.
29 Using a wood or plastic tool, remove the piston seal from the groove in the caliper bore **(see illustration)**. Metal tools may cause bore damage.
30 Remove the caliper bleeder valve, then remove the slide pins and covers from the caliper torque member (still attached to the steering knuckle). Discard all rubber parts.
31 Clean the remaining parts with brake cleaner or denatured alcohol then blow them dry with compressed air.
32 Carefully examine the piston for nicks and burrs and loss of plating. If surface defects are present, parts must be replaced. Check the caliper bore in a similar way. Light polishing with crocus cloth is permissible to remove light corrosion and stains. Discard the mounting bolts if they are corroded or damaged.
33 When assembling, lubricate the piston bores and seal with clean brake fluid. Position the seal in the caliper bore groove **(see illustration)**.
34 Lubricate the piston with clean brake fluid, then install a new boot in the piston groove with the fold toward the open end of the piston.
35 Insert the piston squarely into the caliper bore, then apply force to bottom the piston in the bore **(see illustration)**.
36 Position the dust boot in the caliper counterbore. Make sure that the boot seats in the bore properly **(see illustration)**.
37 Install the bleeder valve.
38 Lubricate the slide pins with silicone-based grease and install them into the torque member along with the new pin covers.
39 When reconnecting the brake hose fitting to the caliper, install new copper sealing washers on each side of the fitting.

4.3 Check the rotor surface for deep grooves and score marks (be sure to inspect both sides)

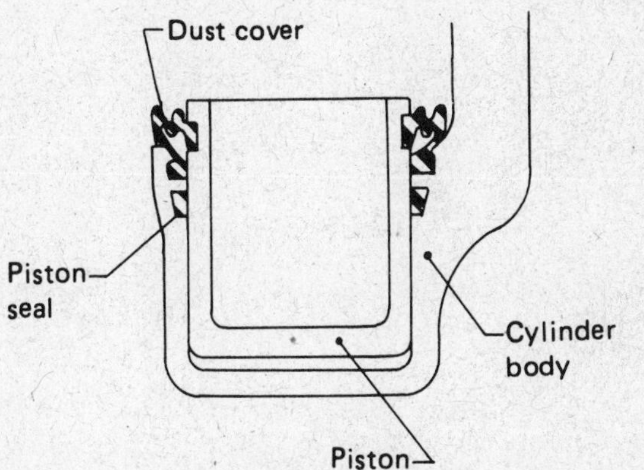

3.36 The dust cover (boot) must be seated squarely in the retaining groove

All models
40 Installation is the reverse of the removal procedure. Be sure to bleed the caliper as described in Section 13.

4 Front brake disc (rotor) – inspection, removal and installation

Refer to illustrations 4.3, 4.4a, 4.4b, 4.5a, 4.5b, 4.13a and 4.13b

Note: *For the brake disc/hub removal procedure for 4WD vehicles, refer to Chapter 9.*

Inspection

1 Loosen the wheel lug nuts, raise the vehicle and support it securely on jackstands. Remove the wheel.
2 Remove the brake caliper as outlined in Section 3. It is not necessary to disconnect the brake hose. After removing the caliper bolts, suspend the caliper out of the way with a piece of wire, then remove the torque member to knuckle bolts (later models).
3 Visually inspect the rotor surface for scoring or damage. Light scratches and shallow grooves are normal after use and may not always be detrimental to brake operation, but deep scoring – over 0.015 inch (0.38 mm) – requires rotor removal and refinishing by an automotive machine shop. Be sure to check both sides of the rotor **(see illustration)**. If pulsating has been noticed during application of the brakes, suspect rotor runout.
4 To check rotor runout, place a dial indicator at the center of the pad contact surface **(see illustration)**. Set the indicator to zero and turn the rotor. The indicator reading should not exceed the specified allowable runout limit. If it does, the rotor should be refinished by an

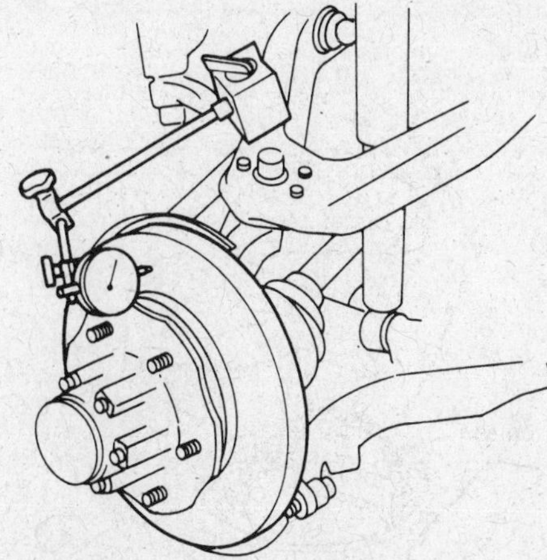
4.4a To check rotor runout, a dial indicator is attached to the caliper with the indicator touching the center of the contact area of the rotor. Turn the rotor through a complete revolution and note the indicator reading

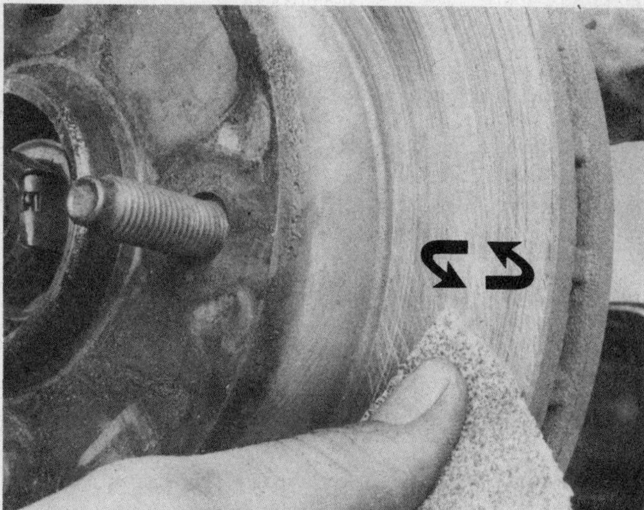

4.4b Using a swirling motion, remove the glaze from the rotor with medium grit sandpaper

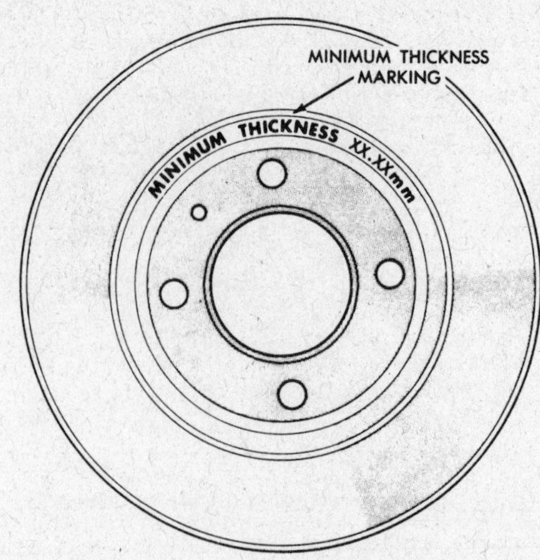

4.5a The disc can be resurfaced if the minimum thickness will not be exceeded

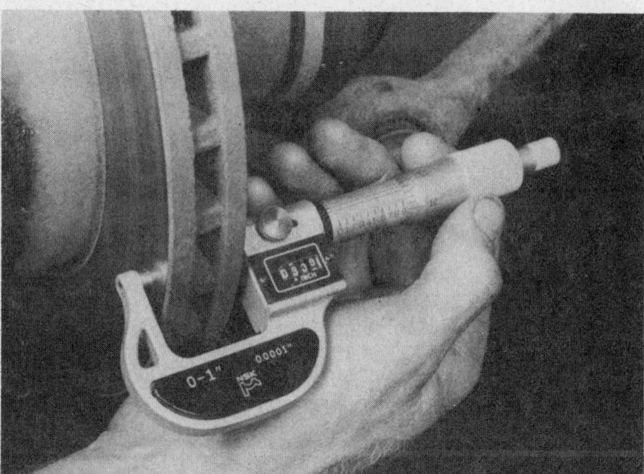

4.5b A micrometer is used to measure rotor thickness. Take measurements at several points around the rotor

automotive machine shop. **Note:** *It is recommended that the rotors be resurfaced regardless of the dial indicator reading, as this will impart a smooth finish and ensure a perfectly flat surface, eliminating any brake pedal pulsation or other undesirable symptoms related to questionable rotors. At the very least, if you elect not to have the rotors resurfaced, remove the glazing from the surface with medium-grit sandpaper using a swirling motion* **(see illustration)**.

5 It is absolutely critical that the rotor not be machined to a thickness under the specified minimum allowable rotor thickness. The minimum thickness is cast into the inside of the rotor **(see illustration)**. The rotor thickness can be checked with a micrometer **(see illustration)**.

Removal

6 Use a screwdriver to pry off the hub dust cap.
7 Remove the cotter pin.
8 Remove the adjusting cap.
9 Remove the wheel bearing nut and washer.
10 Remove the outer wheel bearing.
11 Remove the hub and rotor assembly.
12 If the rotor needs machining, remove the inner wheel bearing and grease seal.
13 If the rotor needs replacing it must be separated from the hub. First,

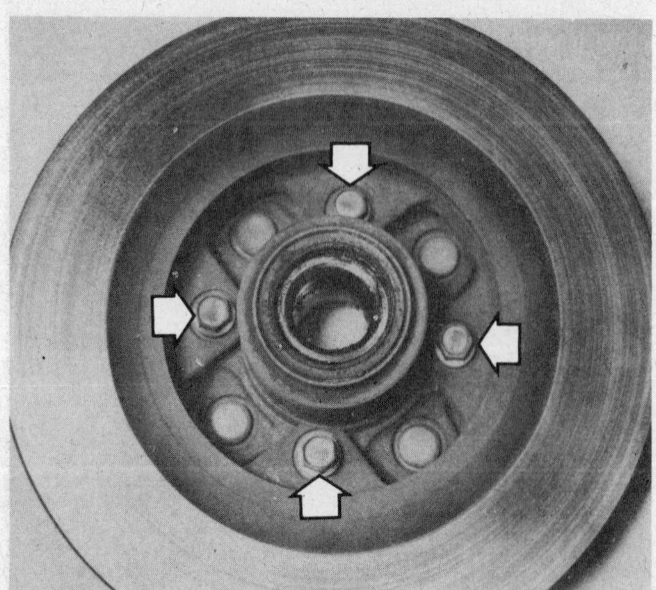

4.13a To separate the rotor from the hub, remove the four bolts attaching the two components . . .

4.13b . . . then lift the hub from the rotor. It may be necessary to tap the rotor from the hub

remove the bolts that secure the rotor to the hub **(see illustration)**. Then use a plastic hammer to tap along the outer edge of the hub until the hub can be removed from the rotor **(see illustration)**. Once the hub has been separated slightly, two flathead screwdrivers (one on each side) can be used to pry the two pieces apart. If the hub and rotor do not separate easily, apply penetrating oil where the two meet.

Installation

14 When attaching the rotor to the hub, position it on the hub and loosely install the bolts.
15 Tighten the bolts in a criss-cross pattern a little at a time until they are torqued to specs.
16 To complete the installation procedure, refer to Chapter 11 for re-packing the wheel bearings and installing the hub and rotor assembly onto the spindle.

5 Rear drum brakes — shoe replacement

Refer to illustrations 5.4, 5.6, 5.7a through 5.7g, 5.8, 5.15 and 5.16
1 Raise the rear of the truck and support it on jackstands. Be sure the parking brake is released.
2 Remove the rear wheel.
3 Back off the brake adjuster, referring to Chapter1, if necessary.
4 Remove the brake drum. If it is tight, use a soft-faced hammer and tap outwards at the circumference while rotating the drum. If the drum is tight, two 8 mm x 1.25 bolts can be inserted in the tapped holes in the drum and tightened evenly to draw the drum off **(see illustration)**.
5 Thoroughly clean the brake assembly with brake cleaner .
6 Use pliers or a brake spring tool to depress the anti-rattle spring and retainer and turn them 90° to remove them from the pin **(see illustration)**.
7 Remove both the brake shoe return springs attached to the lower part of the shoes on early models, or the upper return springs on later models **(see illustrations)**. Do not mix up the springs.

5.4 The brake drum can be forced from the hub by screwing the appropriate size bolts into the threaded holes provided for this purpose

5.6 The anti-rattle spring and retainer can be removed by depressing and turning them 90°

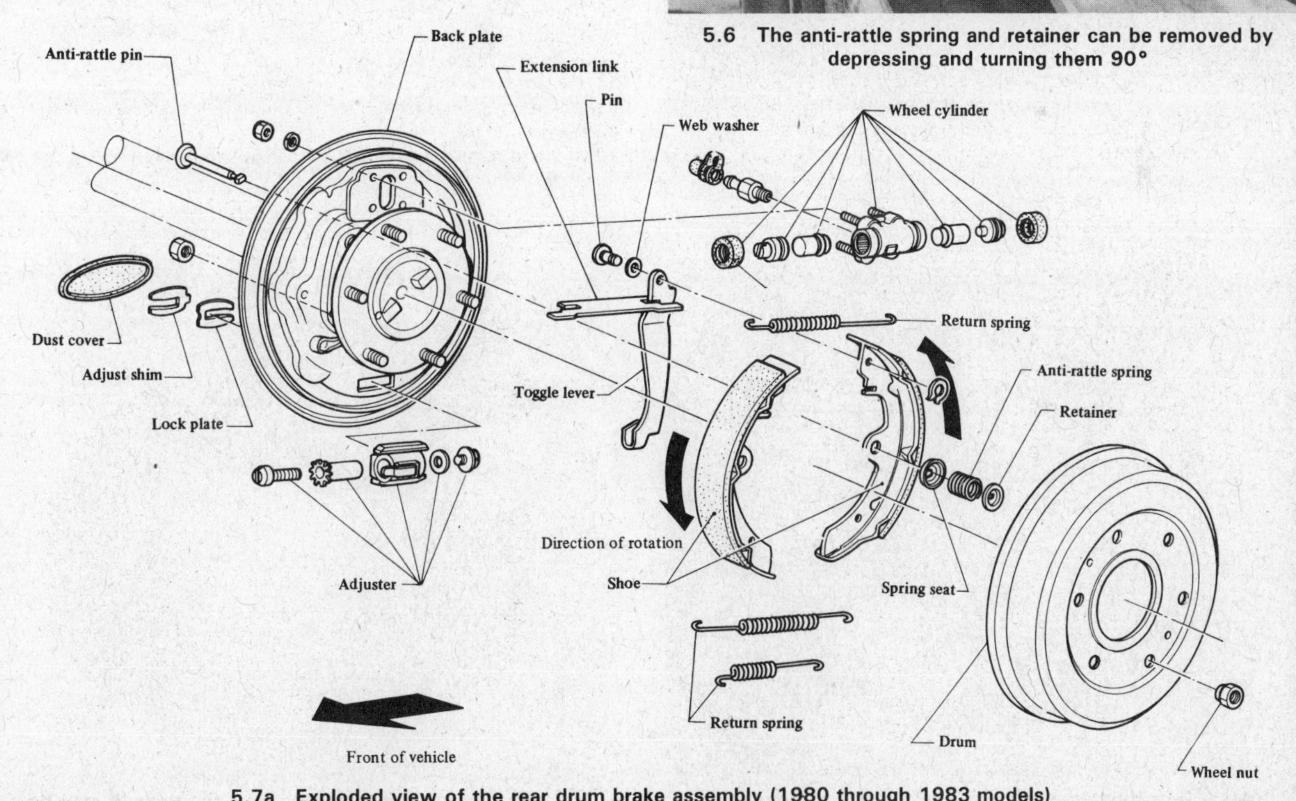

5.7a Exploded view of the rear drum brake assembly (1980 through 1983 models)

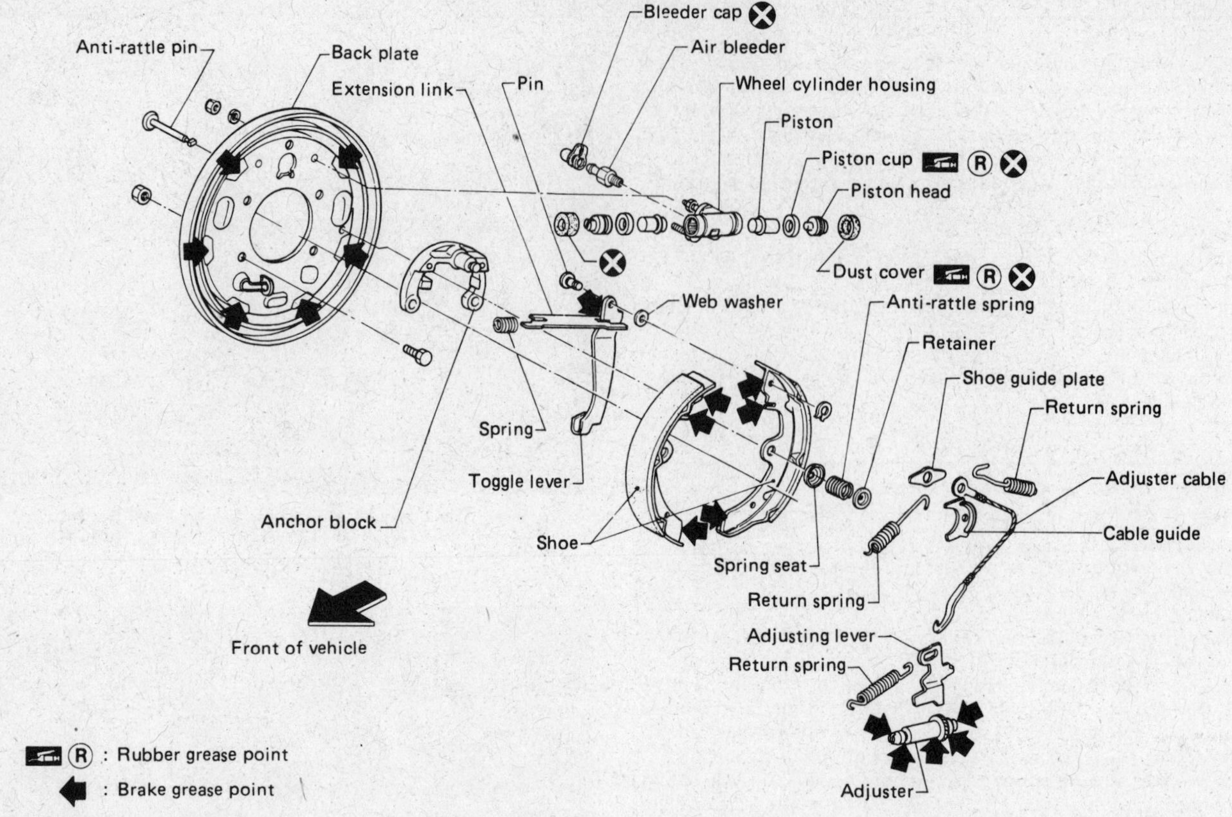

5.7b Exploded view of the rear drum brake assembly – 2WD and 4WD (1984 and 1985), 2WD V6 heavy-duty models (1986 on)

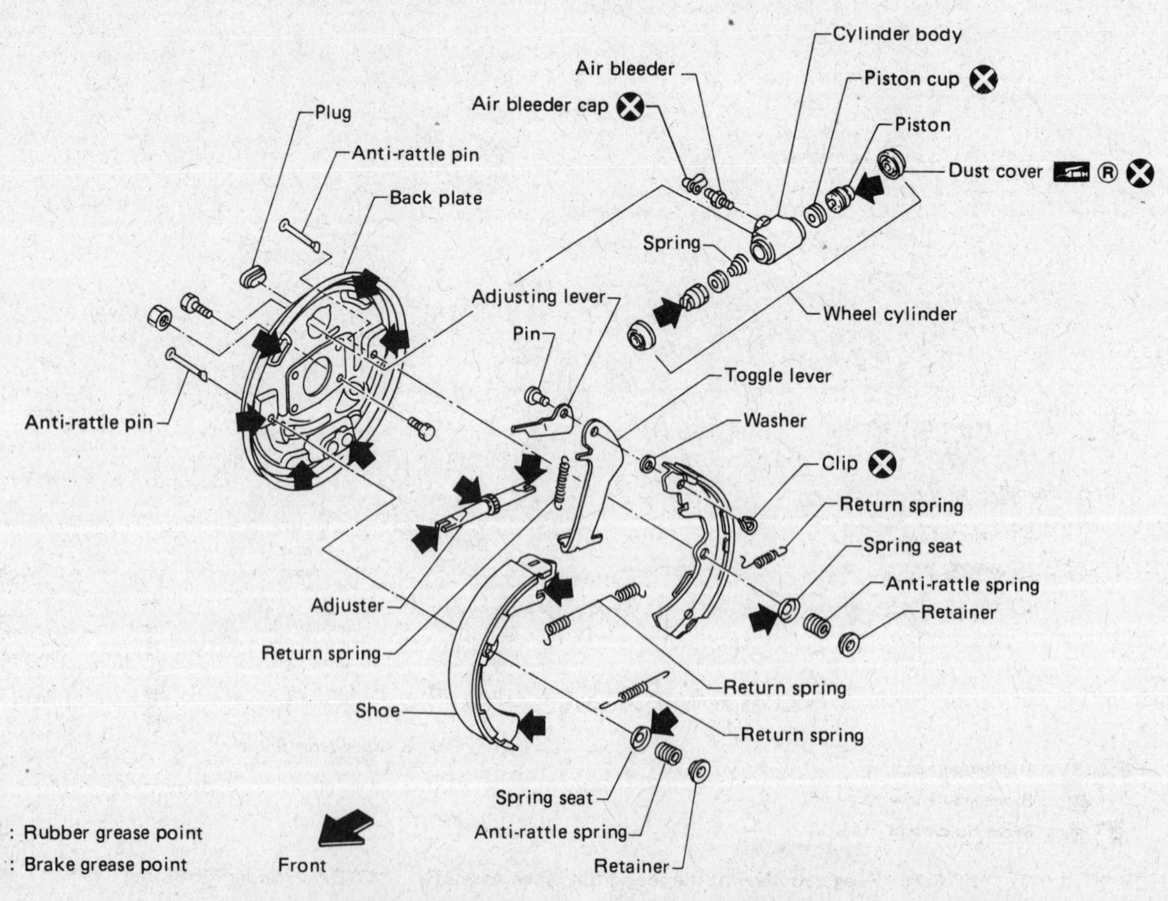

5.7c Exploded view of the rear drum brake assembly – 2WD four-cylinder and V6 truck (1986 on)

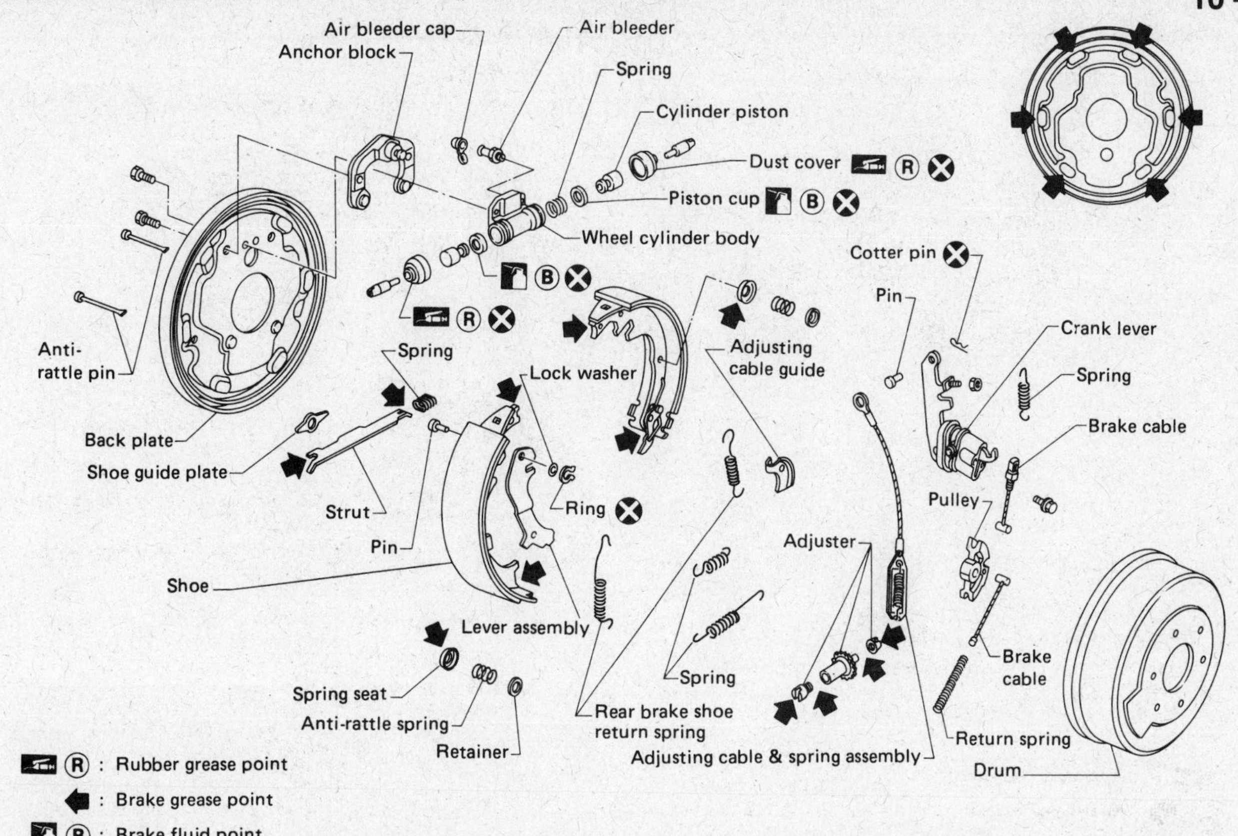

5.7d Exploded view of the rear drum brake assembly – 4WD truck (1986 on)

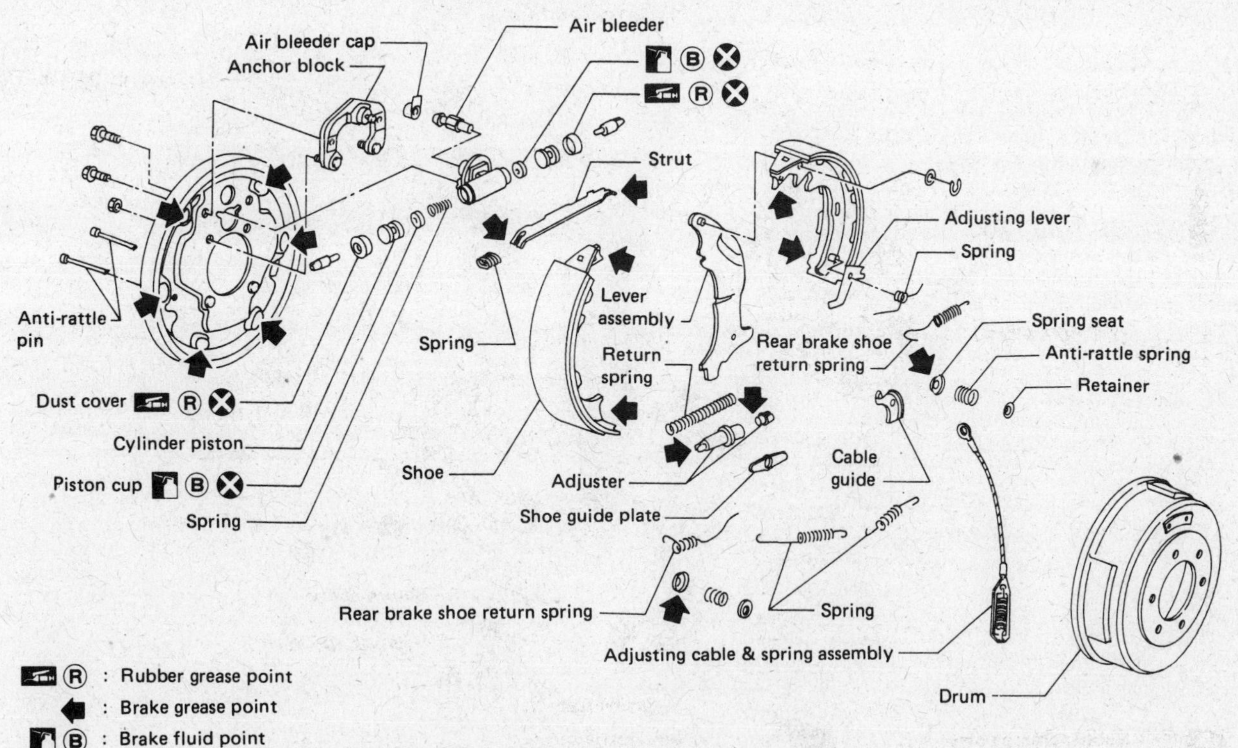

5.7e Exploded view of the rear drum brake assembly – 4WD Pathfinder (1986 on)

5.7f Locations of the lower brake shoe return springs (do not mix them up with the upper spring)

8 Spread the shoes apart slightly and remove the upper return spring (early models) and the extension link **(see illustration)**.
9 Carefully pry the shoes apart again, and remove them from the slots in the adjuster and wheel cylinder pistons. Note that the trailing (secondary) shoe must be detached from the lever by removing the clevis pin (early models). If the wheel cylinder pistons can be prevented from coming out, by using a rubber band or adhesive tape to hold them in position, it will not be necessary to bleed the brakes on completion.
10 Disconnect the parking brake cable from the lever.
11 Do not depress the brake pedal while the shoes are off, otherwise the pistons will be forced from the cylinder.
12 Check that the pistons are free to move in the cylinder, that the rubber dust covers are undamaged and in position, and that there are no hydraulic fluid leaks. **Note:** *If there are signs of fluid leakage or the wheel cylinders are to be overhauled for any reason, perform this operation now, before the new linings are installed. Refer to Section 10.*
13 Apply a little brake grease to the adjuster threads.
14 Prior to reassembly, smear a little brake grease on the platforms and shoe locations on the cylinder and adjuster. Do not allow any grease to come into contact with the linings or rubber parts.
15 When installing the shoes, install the upper and lower springs, then position the lower end of the rear shoe in the adjuster slot followed by the lower end of the front shoe. The shoes can then be spread and slotted into the wheel cylinder. Then the remaining parts can be installed **(see illustration)**.
16 Install the brake drum and wheel.
17 Adjust the brake and lower the vehicle to the ground. On later models adjustment can be carried out by operating the parking brake a few times. If there is any chance that air has entered the system, it is essential that it is bled, as described in Section 3.

6 Rear wheel cylinder – removal, overhaul and installation

Refer to illustrations 6.4 and 6.6

1 Obtain a wheel cylinder rebuild kit.
2 Remove the brake drum and shoes as described in Section 5.
3 Place a rag or drain pan under the backplate to catch any hydraulic fluid that may be expelled from the brake line or wheel cylinder.
4 Wipe the brake line connection at the rear of the wheel cylinder and unscrew the connector bolt (early models). Lift away the two washers, one each side of the connector. On later models unscrew the tube nut from the wheel cylinder **(see illustration)**.
5 Loosen and remove the four nuts and spring washers that secure the wheel cylinder to the backplate. Lift away the wheel cylinder.
6 To disassemble the wheel cylinder, first remove the two dust covers **(see illustration)**. Withdraw the two piston heads and then the pistons. Remove the seal from each piston noting which way it is installed.

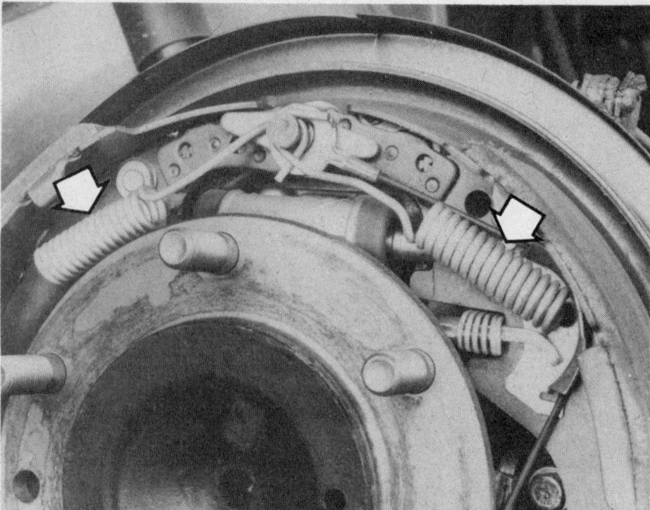

5.7g Location of the upper return springs, guide plate and adjuster cable

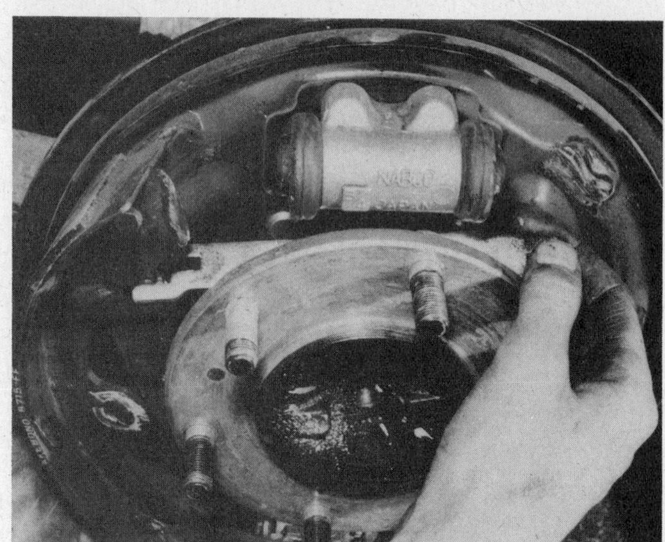

5.8 With the brake shoes spread apart, the strut can be lifted out or installed

7 Inspect the inside of the cylinder for score marks caused by impurities in the hydraulic fluid. **Note:** *If the wheel cylinder must be replaced, always ensure that the replacement is exactly identical to the one removed.*
8 If the cylinder is in good condition, thoroughly clean it out with clean hydraulic fluid.
9 Smear the new rubber seals with hydraulic fluid and install on the pistons, making sure that the lips face in when assembled.
10 Insert the pistons into the bore taking care not to roll the lip of the seal. Install the two pistons heads and then the dust covers.
11 Installation of the wheel cylinder is the reverse of the removal procedure. It will be necessary to bleed the hydraulic system, as described in Section 13.

7 Drum brake adjuster (1980 to 1983) – removal, inspection and installation

Refer to illustrations 7.4 and 7.5

1 Remove the brake drum and shoes as described in Section 5.
2 Press the adjuster firmly against the brake backplate, and remove the rubber cover, spring, lockplate and shim from the rear of the backplate.

2WD and 4WD (1984 and 1985), 2WD V6 heavy-duty models (1986 on)

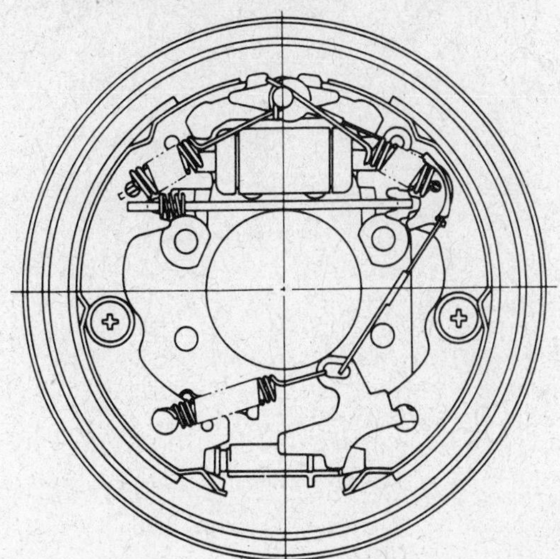

4WD truck (1986 on)

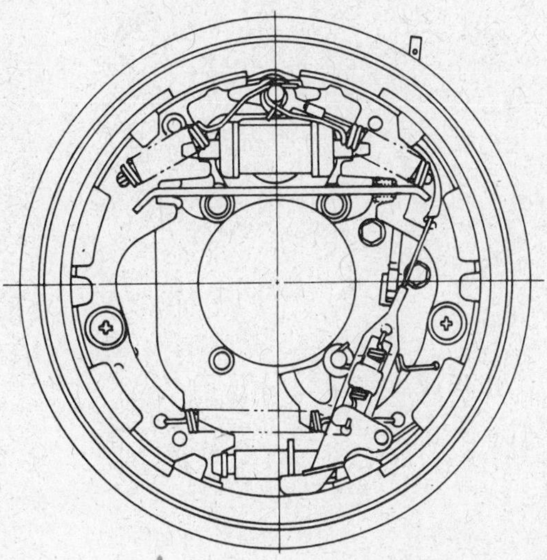

4WD Pathfinder (1986 on)

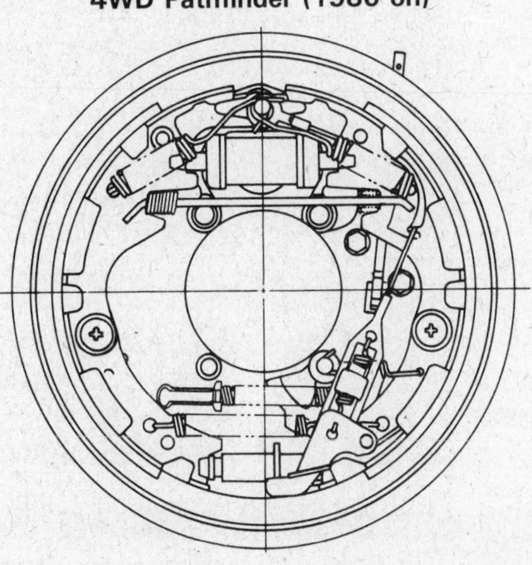

2WD four-cylinder and V6 truck (1986 on)

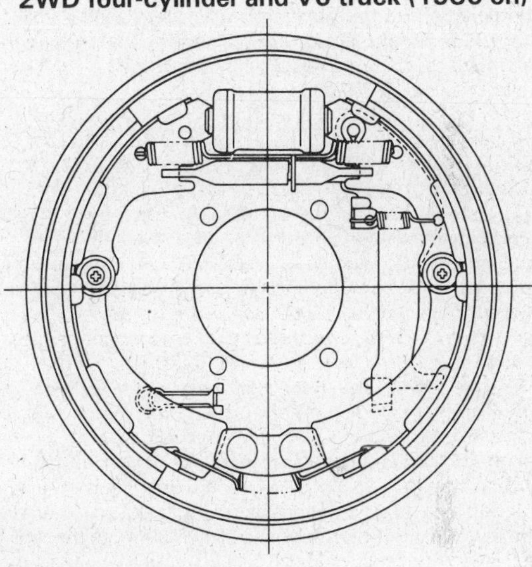

5.15 Drum brake component installation details (left-hand wheel shown)

5.16 The maximum drum diameter is cast into each drum

6.4 A flare nut wrench is recommended when loosening the hydraulic line (arrow) from the wheel cylinder

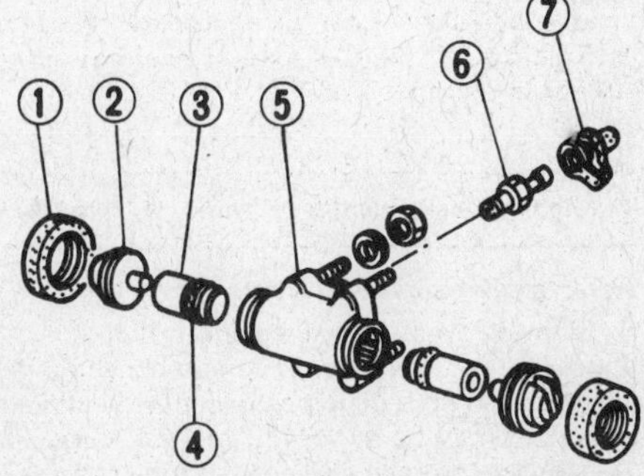

6.6 Exploded view of the rear wheel cylinder

1. *Dust cover*
2. *Piston head*
3. *Piston*
4. *Piston cup*
5. *Wheel cylinder housing*
6. *Bleeder screw*
7. *Bleeder cap*

7.4 When assembling the rear brake adjuster, grease should be applied to the areas indicated by arrows

3 Examine the parts for damage, corrosion and distortion, replacing them with new parts as necessary.
4 Reassemble the adjuster using a little brake grease on all the moving parts **(see illustration).**
5 Installation is the reverse of the removal procedure, but smear a little brake grease on the rubbing surface of the adjuster and in the backplate slot **(see illustration).**

7.5 When installing the adjuster, grease should be applied to the slot in the baffle plate

8 Rear brake disc (rotor) – inspection, removal and installation

Refer to illustrations 8.2 and 8.3

1 Inspect the rotor as described in Section 4 of this Chapter. Before checking rotor runout with a dial indicator, however, reinstall two lug nuts to hold the rotor against the axle flange.
2 Remove the caliper as described in Section 3, then remove the two torque member to rear axle case bolts **(see illustration).**
3 Pull the rotor from the axle flange. If the rotor is stuck and will not come off, apply penetrating oil around the wheel studs and allow it to soak in for a few minutes. Insert two bolts into the threaded holes in the center of the rotor and tighten them evenly, drawing the rotor from the axle **(see illustration).**
4 Installation is the reverse of the removal procedure. Be sure to tighten the torque member bolts and guide pins to the specified torque.

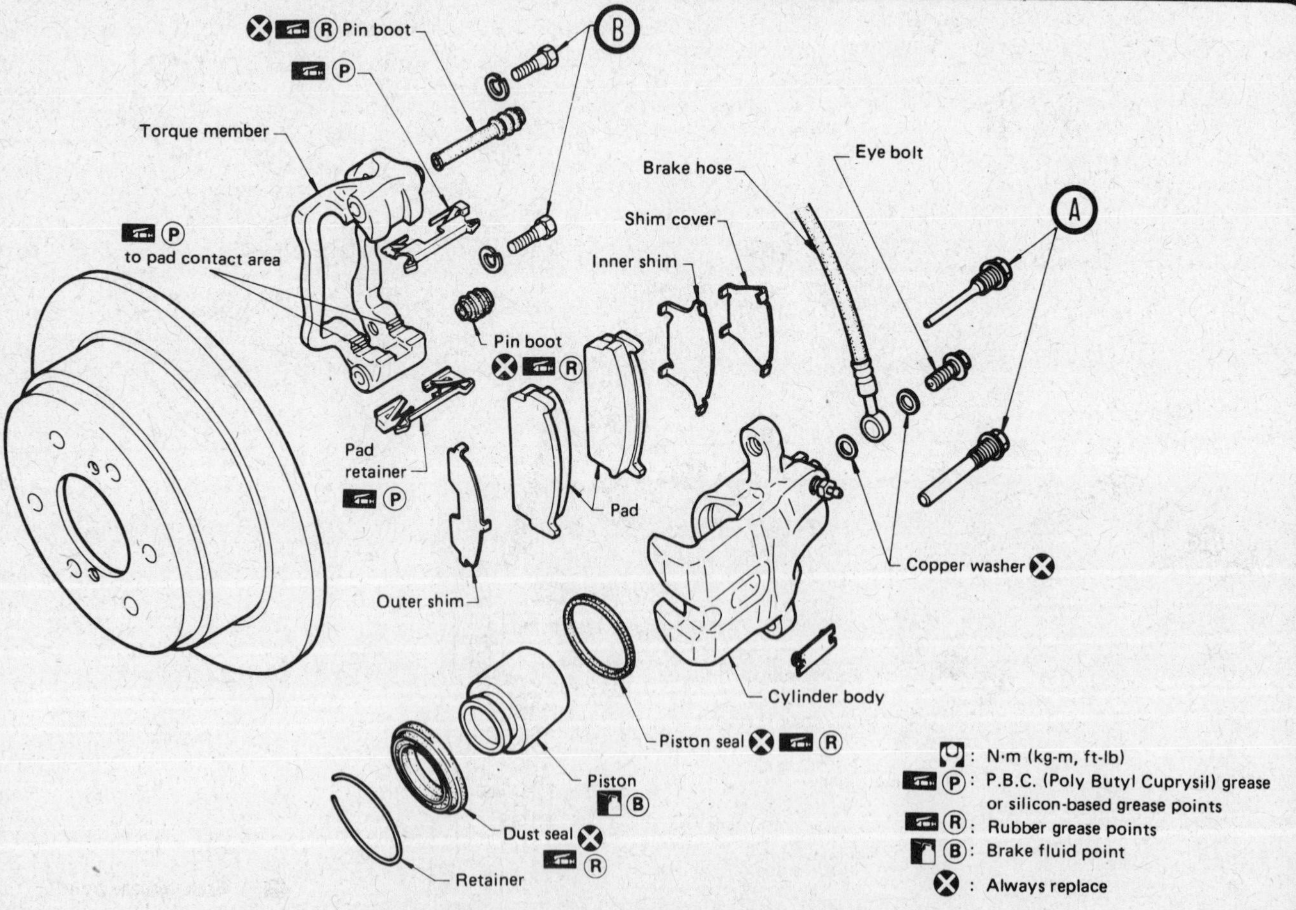

8.2 Exploded view of the rear disc brake assembly – 1988 and later Pathfinder models

A Guide pins *B Torque member-to-rear axle case bolts*

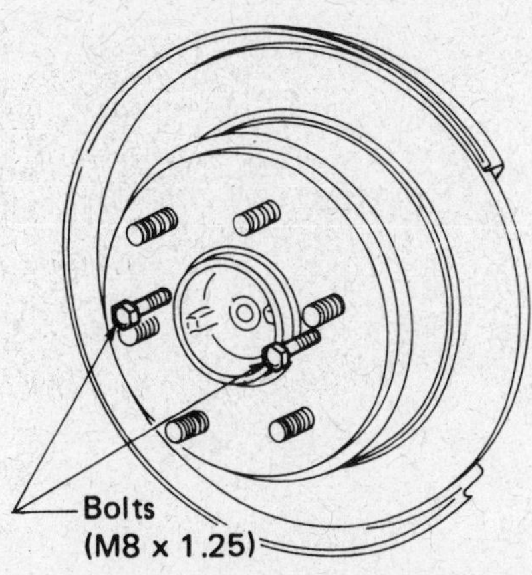

8.3 The brake disc can be forced from the axle flange by screwing the appropriate size bolts into the threaded holes provided for this purpose

9 Parking brake shoes (rear disc brake models) – removal and installation

Refer to illustrations 9.2, 9.3, 9.7 and 9.14

Warning: *Dust created by the brake system contains asbestos, which is harmful to your health. Never blow it out with compressed air and don't inhale any of it. An approved filtering mask should be worn when working on the the brakes. Do not, under any circumstances, use petroleum-based solvents to clean brake parts. Use brake cleaner or denatured alcohol only!*

Removal

1 Remove the brake disc following the procedure outlined in Section 8.

2 Using a pair of pliers, push down on the retainer, turn it 90° to disengage it from the anti-rattle pin then remove the anti-rattle spring and spring seat **(see illustration)**. Repeat this step to the other retainer and spring.

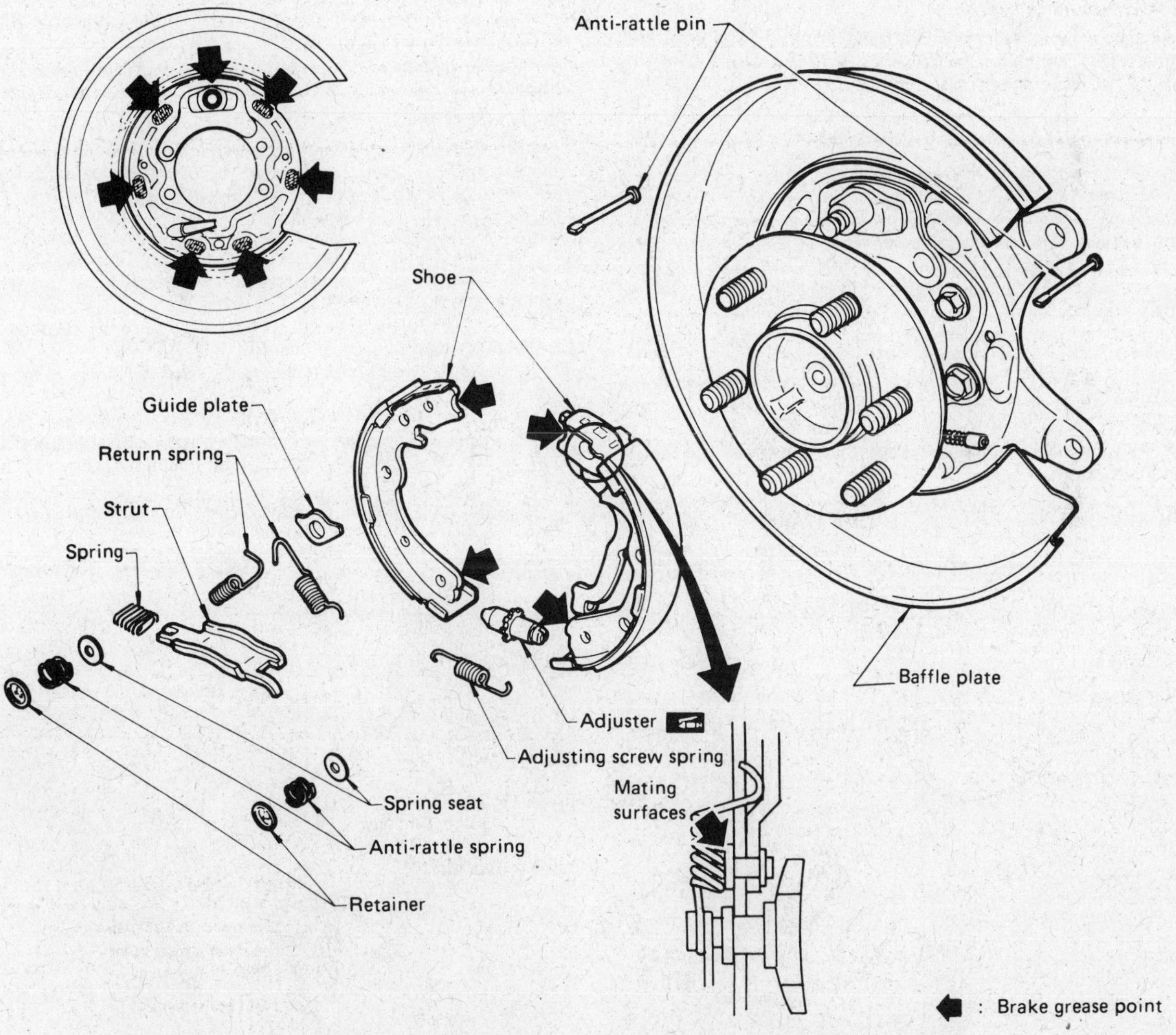

9.2 Exploded view of the rear parking brake assembly – rear disc brake models

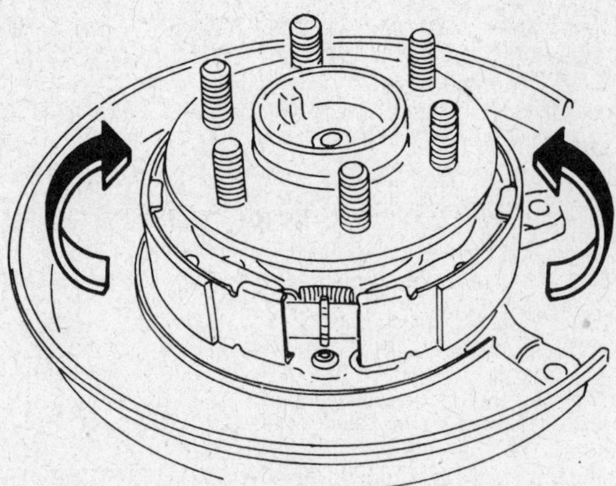

9.3 After the retainers and spring are removed, rock the shoes outward and remove the return springs

3 Rock the shoes out from the baffle plate **(see illustration)** and remove the two return springs, guide plate and strut.
4 Spread the shoes apart at the top and pull them out over the axle flange, then disconnect the parking brake cable from the lever.
5 Remove the adjusting screw spring and adjuster. Clean the adjuster with solvent and lubricate the threads with multi-purpose grease.
6 If replacing the shoes, transfer the parking brake lever to the new trailing shoe.

Installation

7 Connect the adjusting screw spring to the shoes and install the adjuster between the flat area at the bottom of each shoe. Make sure the slot on each end of the adjuster is properly engaged with the shoes.
8 Apply a thin coat of multi-purpose grease to the shoe contact areas on the baffle plate **(see illustration)**.
9 Connect the parking brake cable to the lever.
10 Spread the shoes apart and position them against the baffle plate. Place the parking brake strut between the two shoes with the ends of the strut in the proper notches.
11 Install the anti-rattle pins, spring seats, springs and retainers
12 Install the guide plate and return springs.
13 Place the rotor on the axle flange and install two lug nuts to hold the rotor in place during the adjustment procedure. Install the torque member and caliper.

Adjustment

14 Check to see that the parking brake is completely released. Remove the adjuster hole plug in the baffle plate and using a screwdriver, turn the adjuster wheel until the shoes touch the brake drum **(see illustration)**.

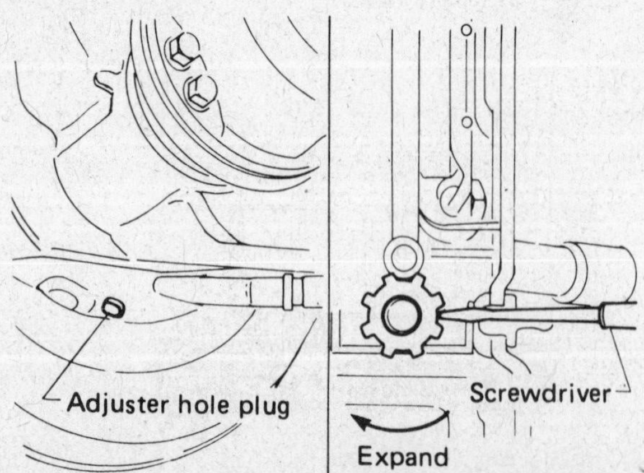

9.14 Remove the adjuster hole plug to access the adjuster. Turn the adjuster until the shoes touch the drum, then back off the adjuster 7 or 8 clicks

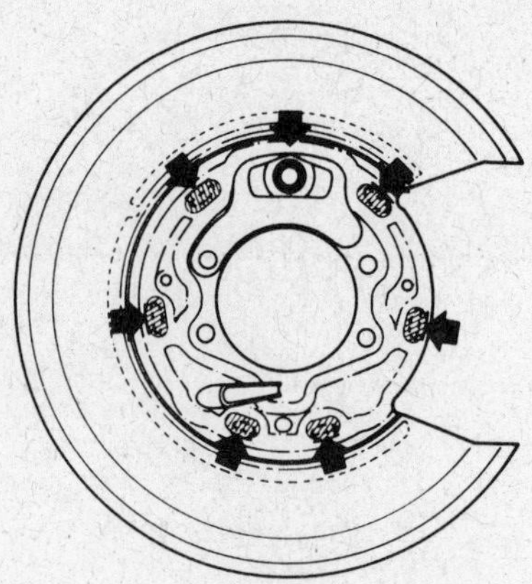

9.7 Apply a thin coat of grease to the points indicated (arrows)

15 Back off the adjuster wheel 7 or 8 clicks. turn the rotor to make sure there isn't any drag between the shoes and the drum.
16 Install the adjuster hole plug.

10 Master cylinder – removal, overhaul and installation

Refer to illustrations 10.3, 10.9a, 10.9b, 10.9c and 10.19

Caution: *Take care not to spill any brake fluid on the vehicle's painted surfaces, as it will damage it. Cover the fenders to protect the paint and clean up any spilled fluid immediately with plenty of water.*

Removal

1 Disconnect the negative battery cable from the battery.
2 Place newspaper or rags under the master cylinder to catch any leaking brake fluid.
3 Loosen the tube nuts securing the brake lines to the master cylinder **(see illustration)**.
4 Remove the two nuts that secure the master cylinder to the power brake booster unit.
5 Carefully lift the cylinder off its mounting studs, remove the brake lines from the cylinder, and immediately place your fingers over the holes to prevent leakage of fluid. Lift the cylinder out of the engine compartment.
6 Plug the fluid lines to prevent further leakage of fluid.

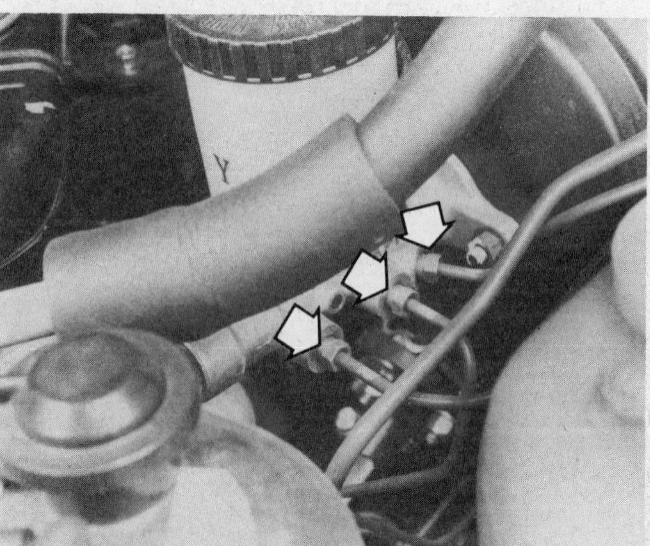

10.3 The use of a flare nut wrench is recommended when loosening the master cylinder tube nuts (arrows)

Overhaul

7 Obtain a master cylinder rebuild kit. **Note:** *The vehicles covered by this manual use one of the two different makes of master cylinder; either a Nabco or a Tokico. As there is no interchangeability of parts between the two models, be sure you get the appropriate rebuild kit for your vehicle.*

8 Clean away external dirt and then remove the reservoir caps and filters and empty out the fluid.

9 From the end of the master cylinder, pry out the stopper ring (early models) or pry off the stopper cap (later models). Then remove the stop washer (if equipped), the primary piston and the spring **(see illustrations)**.

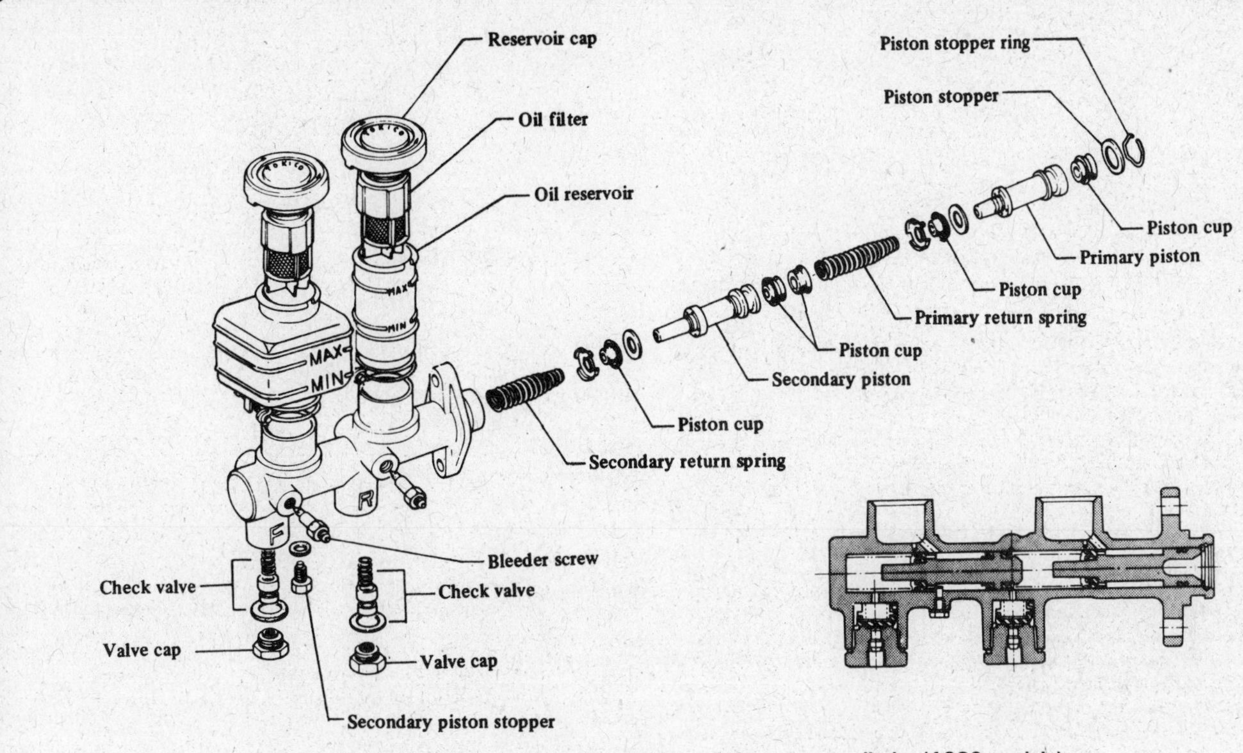

10.9a Exploded and cross sectional views of the master cylinder (1980 models)

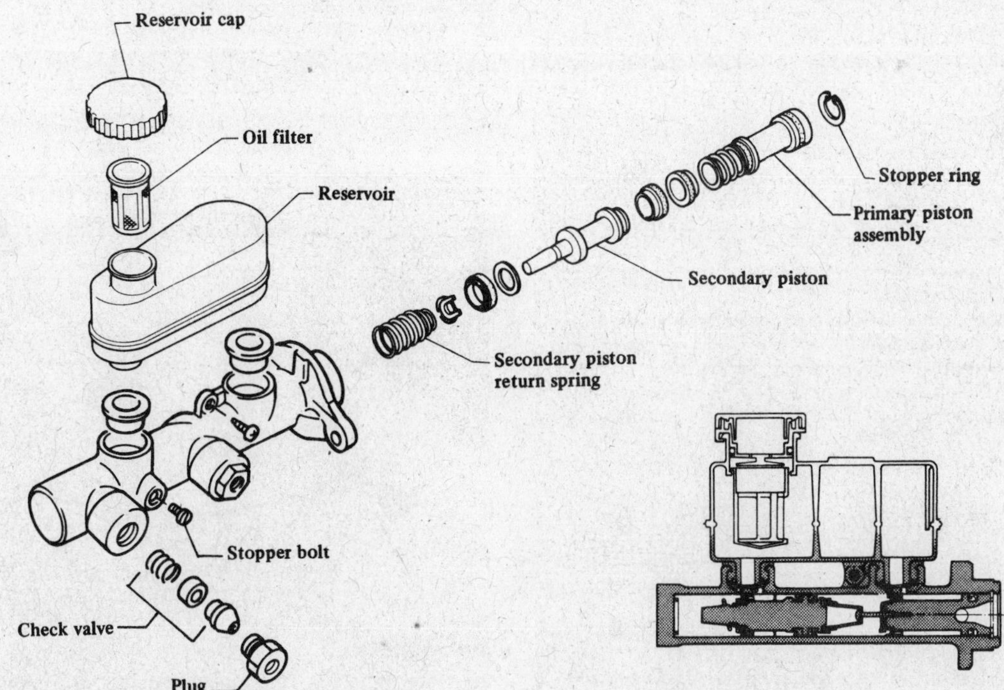

10.9b Exploded and cross sectional views of the master cylinder (1981 through 1985 models)

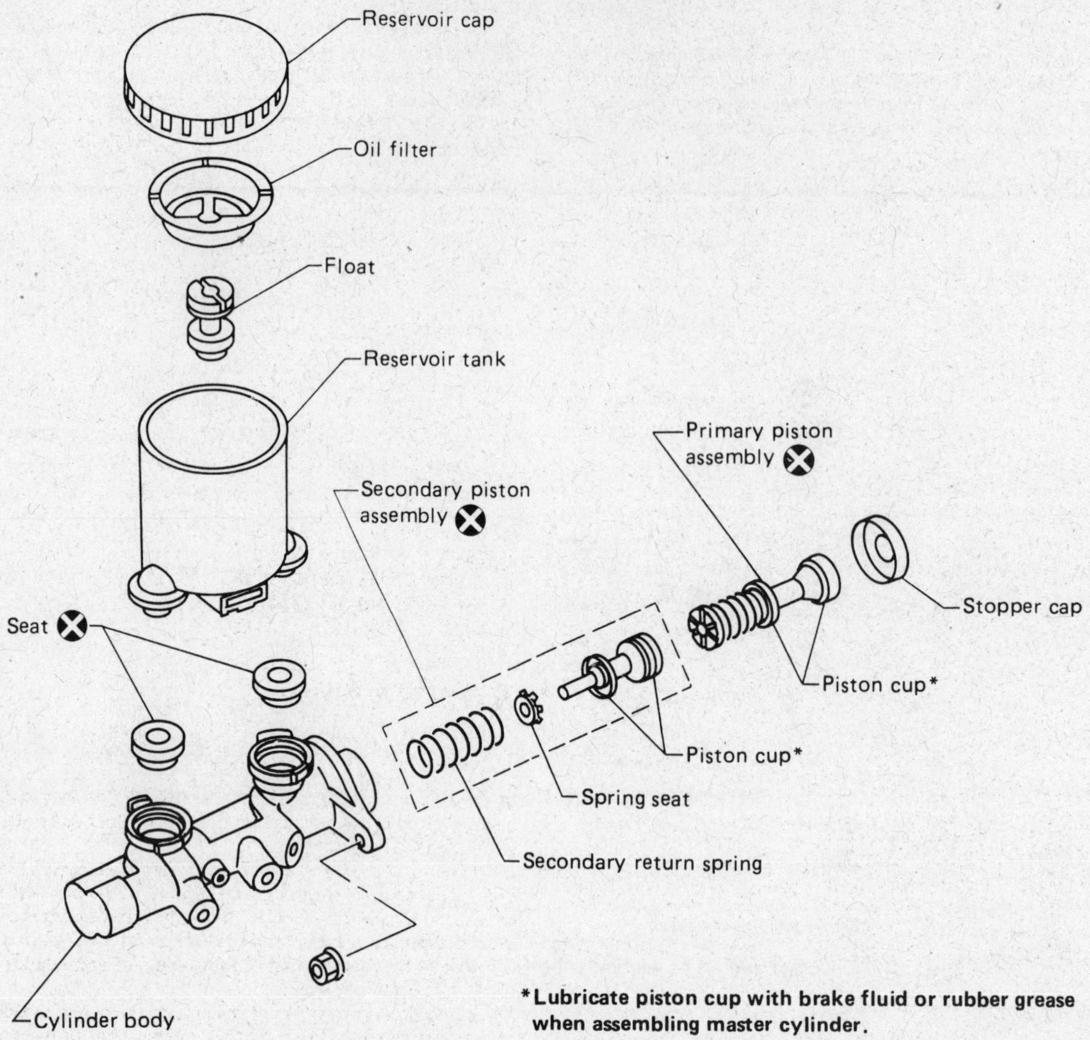

Reservoir cap
Oil filter
Float
Reservoir tank
Primary piston assembly
Secondary piston assembly
Stopper cap
Seat
Piston cup*
Piston cup*
Spring seat
Secondary return spring
Cylinder body

***Lubricate piston cup with brake fluid or rubber grease when assembling master cylinder.**

10.9c Exploded view of the master cylinder (1986 on)

10 Insert a rod to depress the secondary piston and then unscrew the stop screw from the master cylinder (early models). Release the rod and withdraw the secondary piston. On later models, invert the cylinder and tap it on a block of wood to eject the secondary piston assembly.
11 The check valve assemblies can be removed by unscrewing the check valve plugs (early models).
12 At this stage, inspect the surfaces of the pistons and cylinder bore for scoring or 'bright' wear areas. If these are evident, replace the complete master cylinder with a new or rebuilt unit.
13 Disassemble the piston and spring assemblies and remove all piston cups. **Note:** *The primary piston in 1981 and later models is not designed to be disassembled.*
14 Wash all components in clean hydraulic fluid or alcohol-nothing else.
15 Do not detach the reservoirs unless absolutely necessary.
16 Begin reassembly by manipulating the new seals into position using the fingers only. Be sure the seal lips are facing in the proper directions.
17 Dip all internal components in clean hydraulic fluid before re-assembly.
18 Install the secondary spring and piston assembly. Hold it depressed and screw in the stop screw (early models).
19 Install the primary spring and the primary piston assembly. Install the stop washer (if equipped) and the stopper ring. On later models bend the tangs of the stopper cap inwards **(see illustration)** then install it over the end of the master cylinder. Replace the stopper cap if it is deformed in any way.

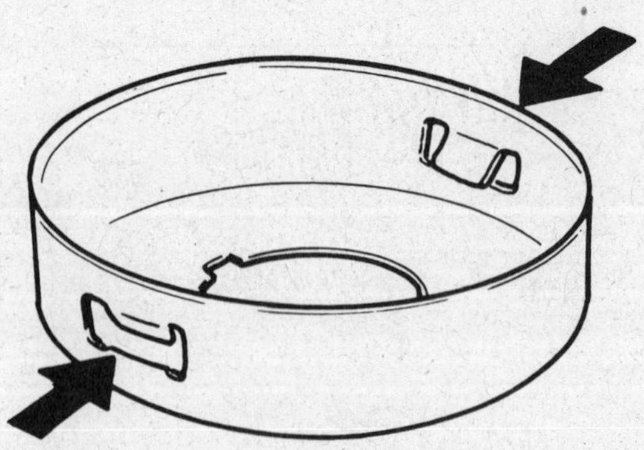

10.19 Before installing the stopper cap, bend the tangs inward

Installation

20 Note: Whenever the master cylinder is removed, the complete hydraulic system must be bled. The time required to bleed the system can be reduced if the master cylinder is filled with fluid and bench bled before the master cylinder is installed on the vehicle.
21 Insert threaded plugs of the correct size into the cylinder outlet

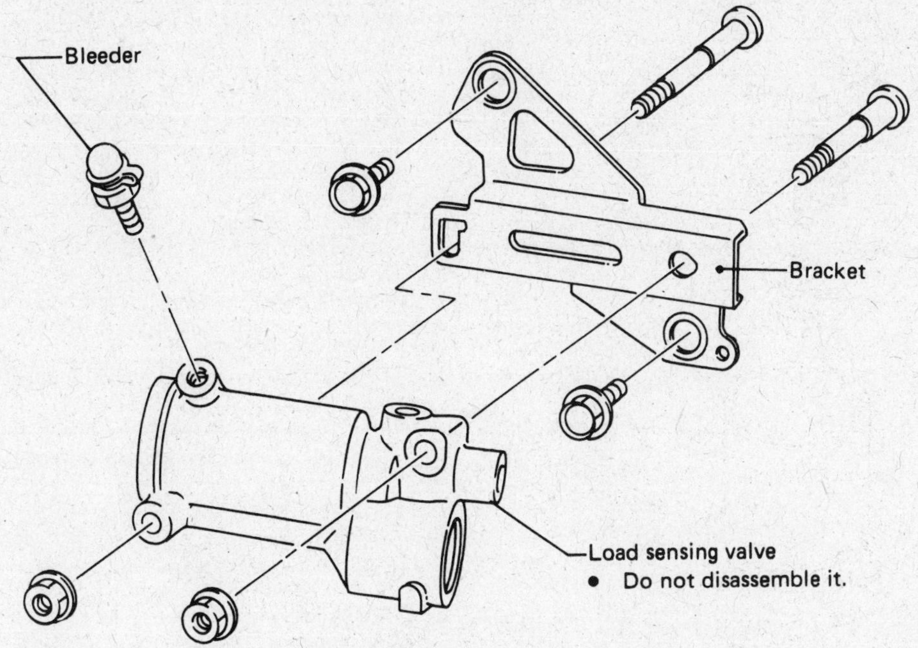

11.2a Mounting details of the load sensing valve (A-type)

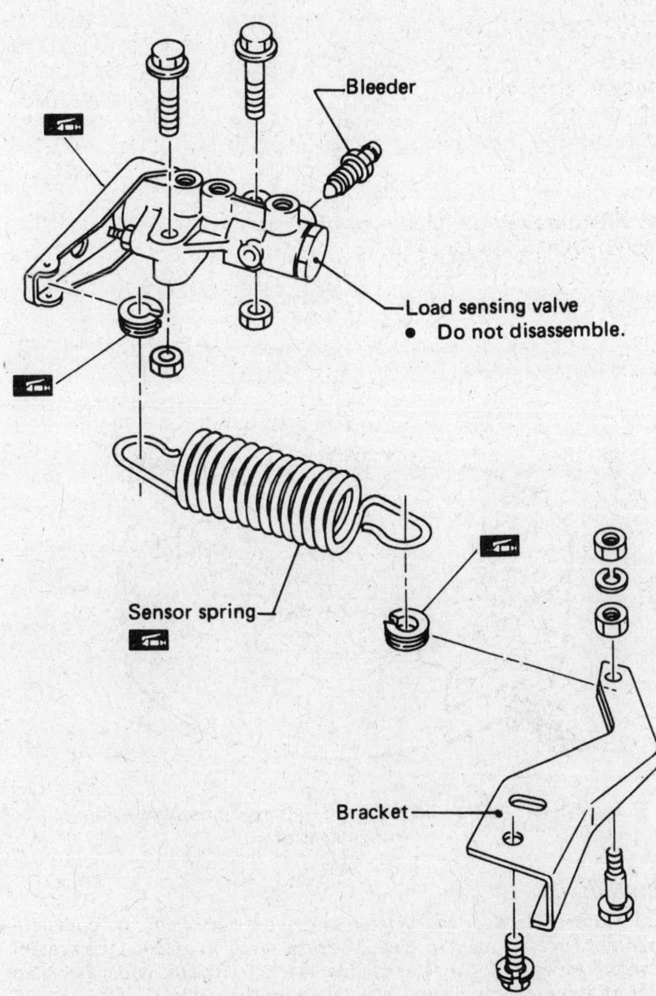

11.2b Mounting details of the load sensing valve (B-type)

holes and fill the reservoirs with brake fluid. The master cylinder should be supported in such a manner that brake fluid will not spill during the bench bleeding procedure.

22 Loosen one plug at a time and push the piston assembly into the bore to force air from the master cylinder. To prevent air from being drawn back into the cylinder, the appropriate plug must be replaced before allowing the piston to return to its original position.

23 Stroke the piston three or four times for each outlet to assure that all air has been expelled.

24 Since high pressure is not involved in the bench bleeding procedure, an alternative to the removal and replacement of the plugs with each stroke of the piston assembly is available. Before pushing in on the piston assembly, remove one of the plugs completely. Before releasing the piston, however, instead of replacing the plug, simply put your finger tightly over the hole to keep air from being drawn back into the master cylinder. Wait several seconds for the brake fluid to be drawn from the reservoir to the piston bore, then repeat the procedure. When you push down on the piston it will force your finger off the hole, allowing the air inside to be expelled. When only brake fluid is being ejected from the hole, replace the plug and go on to the other port.

25 Refill the master cylinder reservoirs and install the diaphragm and cover assembly. **Note:** *The reservoirs should only be filled to the top of the reservoir divider to prevent overflowing when the cover is installed.*

27 Carefully install the master cylinder by reversing the removal steps, then bleed the brakes at the wheel bleed valves.

10

11 Load sensing valve – removal and installation

Refer to illustrations 11.2a and 11.2b

1 Disconnect all brake lines from the valve, and immediately plug each one to prevent fluid leakage and dirt from entering the system.

2 Remove the bolts that attach the valve and valve bracket to the frame and lift them out **(see illustrations)**.

3 If the valve is to be replaced with a new one, remove it from its bracket. **Note:** *The load sensing valve is not designed to be disassembled, and if faulty should be replaced with a new or rebuilt unit.*

4 Installation is the reverse of the removal procedure.

5 Following installation, bleed the entire brake system as described in Section 13.

12 Brake lines – inspection and replacement

1 About every six months, the flexible hoses which connect the steel brake lines should be inspected for cracks, chafing of the outer cover, leaks, blisters, and other damage. These are important and vulnerable parts of the brake system and inspection should be complete. A light and mirror will prove helpful for a thorough check. If a hose exhibits any of the above conditions, replace it with a new one.

2 When it becomes necessary to replace steel lines, use only double-walled steel tubing. Never substitute copper tubing, as copper is subject to fatigue cracking and corrosion. The outside diameter of the tubing is used for sizing.

3 Some auto parts stores or brake supply houses carry various lengths of pre-fabricated brake line. Depending on the type of tubing used, these sections can either be bent by hand into the desired shape or must be bent in a tubing bender.

4 If pre-fabricated lengths are not available, obtain the recommended steel tubing and steel fitting nuts to match the line to be replaced. Determine the correct length by measuring the old brake line section and cut the new tubing to fit, leaving about 1/2-inch extra for flaring the ends.

5 Install the fittings onto the cut tubing and flare the ends using an ISO flaring tool.

6 Using a tubing bender, bend the tubing to match the shape of the old brake line.

7 Tube flaring and bending can usually be done by a local auto parts store if the proper equipment mentioned in paragraphs 5 and 6 is not available.

8 When installing the brake line, leave at least 3/4 in (19 mm) clearance between the line and any moving or vibrating parts.

13 Brake hydraulic system – bleeding

Refer to illustration 13.6

Caution 1: *Spilled brake fluid can damage the paint. Therefore, when using it, cover the fenders to protect the paint, clean up any spilled fluid immediately and wash with plenty of water.*

Caution 2: *On models equipped with anti-lock brakes (ABS), disconnect the negative cable from the battery before bleeding the brakes.*

1 Anytime any part of the brake system is disassembled or develops a leak, or when the fluid in the master cylinder reservoir runs low, air will enter the system and cause a decrease in braking performance. To eliminate this air the brakes must be bled using the procedure described in this Section.

2 If air has entered the system because the master cylinder has been disconnected, or the master cylinder reservoir has been low or empty of fluid, or if a complete flushing of the system is needed, all four brakes should be bled. If a brake line serving only one brake is disconnected, then only that brake has to be bled. Likewise, if any line is disconnected anywhere in the system, the brakes served by that line must be bled.

3 Before beginning, have an assistant on hand, as well as an ample supply of new brake fluid, an empty clear container such as a glass jar, a length of 3/16-inch plastic, rubber or vinyl tubing to fit over the bleeder valve and a wrench to open and close the bleeder valve. The vehicle may have to be raised and placed on jackstands for clearance.

4 If the vehicle is equipped with power brakes, remove the vacuum reserve in the system by applying the brakes several times.

5 Check that the master cylinder reservoir is full of fluid and be sure to keep it at least half full during the entire operation. If, at any point, the reservoir runs low of fluid, the entire bleeding procedure must be repeated. **Note:** *Do not mix different types of brake fluid, and do not re-use any old fluid, as this could deteriorate brake system components.*

6 On models so equipped, begin at one of the bleeder valves located on the master cylinder. On models where the master cylinder has no bleeder valves, begin with the load sensing valve, attached to the right frame rail, in front of the fuel tank **(see illustration)**. Loosen the bleeder valve slightly to break it loose then tighten it to a point where it is snug but can still be loosened quickly and easily.

7 Place one end of the tubing over the bleeder valve and submerge the other end in brake fluid in the container.

8 With your assistant sitting in the driver's seat, have him pump the brakes a few times to get pressure in the system. On the last pump have him hold the pedal firmly depressed.

9 While the pedal is held depressed, open the breather valve just enough to allow a flow of fluid to leave the valve. Watch for air bubbles to exit the submerged end of the tube. When the fluid flow slows after a couple of seconds, close the valve again and have your assistant release the pedal. If he releases the pedal before the valve is closed again air can be drawn back into the system.

10 Repeat Steps 8 and 9 until no more air is seen in the fluid leaving the tube. Then fully tighten the bleeder valve and proceed to the other master cylinder valve, the load sensing valve (if needed), the right rear wheel, the left rear wheel, the left front wheel, and the right front wheel, in that order, and perform the same operation. Be sure to check the fluid in the master cylinder reservoir frequently.

11 Refill the master cylinder with fluid at the end of the operation.

14 Power brake booster – general information and testing

1 A power brake booster unit is installed in the brake hydraulic circuit in series with the master cylinder, to provide assistance to the driver when the brake pedal is depressed. This reduces the effort required by the driver to operate the brakes under all braking conditions.

2 The unit operates by vacuum obtained from the intake manifold and is composed basically of a booster diaphragm and check valve. The servo unit and hydraulic master cylinder are connected together so that the servo unit piston rod acts as the master cylinder pushrod. The driver's braking effort is transmitted through another pushrod in the servo unit piston and its built-in control system. The servo unit piston does not fit tightly into the cylinder, but has a strong diaphragm to keep its edges in constant contact with the cylinder wall, assuring an air tight seal between the two parts. The forward chamber is held under vacuum conditions created in the intake manifold of the engine and, during periods when the brake pedal is not in use, the controls open a passage to the rear chamber so placing it under the vacuum conditions as well. When the brake pedal is depressed, the vacuum passage to the rea chamber is cut off and the chamber opened to atmospheric pressure. The following rush of air pushes the servo piston forward in the vacuum chamber and operates the main pushrod to the master cylinder.

3 The controls are designed so that assistance is given under all conditions and, when the brakes are not required, vacuum in the rear chamber is established when the brake pedal is released. All air from the atmosphere entering the rear chamber is passed through a small air filter.

4 Under normal operating conditions the power brake booster is very reliable and does not require overhaul except at very high mileage. In this case it is far better to obtain an exchange unit, rather than repair the original unit.

5 It is emphasized that the power booster assists in reducing the braking effort required at the foot pedal and in the event of its failure, the hy-

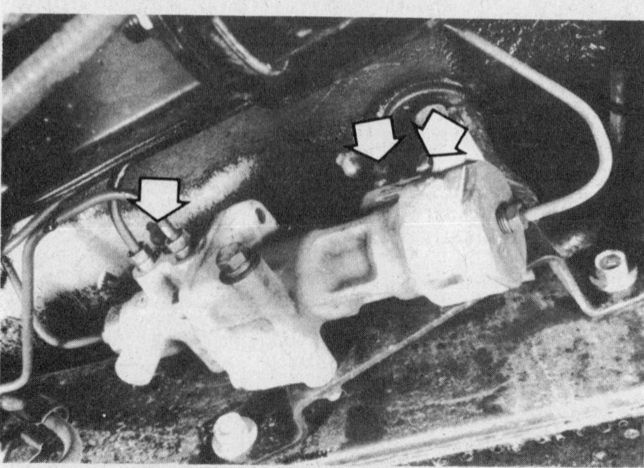

13.6 Locations of the three bleeder valves on the load sensing valve (arrows)

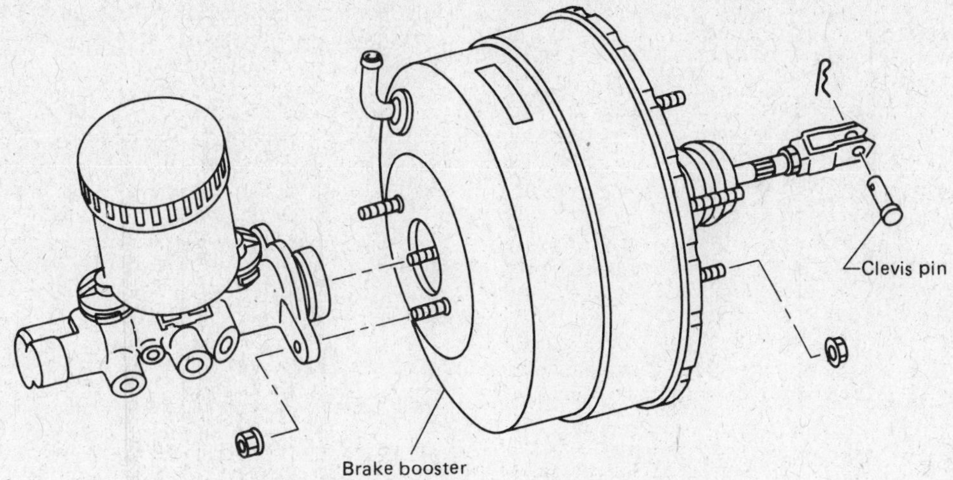

15.3 Power brake booster installation details

draulic braking system is in no way affected except that the need for higher pedal pressures will be noticed.

6 To check for satisfactory power booster operation, depress the brake pedal several times. The distance which the pedal travels on each depression should not vary.

7 Now hold the pedal fully depressed and start the engine. The pedal should move down slightly when the engine starts.

8 Depress the brake pedal, switch off the engine holding the pedal down for about 30 seconds. The position of the pedal should not change.

9 Restart the engine, run it for a minute or two and then turn it off. Depress the brake pedal firmly several times. The pedal travel should decrease with each application.

10 If the unit does not perform as indicated, locate the source of the problem by performing the following tests:

a) First, carefully inspect the condition of the vacuum hoses connecting the booster with the check valve, the check valve with the intake manifold, and the check valve with its other connections. If any holes, cracks or other damage is found replace the defective hoses.
b) Next, remove the check valve from the vacuum line. If a vacuum pump is available, apply 7.87 in Hg (26.7 kPa) of vacuum to the valve opening that leads to the servo unit. If a vacuum pump is not available, put your mouth to the opening and attempt to suck air through the valve. If the pressure on the pump drops more than 0.39 in Hg (1.3 kPa) in 15 seconds, or if you are able to suck air through the valve, the valve is defective and should be replaced.
c) Now blow air into the valve through the same opening as before. If the valve does not allow you to blow air into it, it is defective and should be replaced.
d) To test the power booster, connect a vacuum gauge between the unit and the check valve. Start the engine and slowly increase the engine speed. Shut off the engine when the vacuum reading reaches 19.69 in Hg (66.7 kPa) and observe the gauge. If the reading drops more than 0.98 in Hg 1/4 93.3 kPa) within 15 seconds after the engine has been shut off, the servo unit is defective and should be replaced.
e) One final test is to repeat the previous test with the brake pedal fully depressed. Again, if the vacuum leakage is greater than specified, replace the power brake booster.

15 Power brake booster – removal and installation

Refer to illustrations 15.3 and 15.5

1 Remove the master cylinder as described in Section 12.

2 Disconnect the vacuum line from the booster unit.

3 Working under the dash, disconnect the booster pushrod from the brake pedal by removing the clevis pin **(see illustration)**.

4 Remove the four retaining nuts from the booster unit's mounting studs. Return to the engine compartment and withdraw the unit from the vehicle.

5 Installation is the reverse of the removal procedure. **Note:** *Following installation, measure the length of the unit's pushrod and/or operating rod (depending on year)* **(see illustration)** before installing the master cylinder. If they are not as specified, adjust them. If the amount of the output rod adjustment exceeds 0.020 in (0.5 mm), replace the entire brake booster assembly, as it is worn beyond its service limits.

6 Bleed the entire brake system as described in Section 13.

7 Check the brake pedal height and free play and adjust them if necessary as described in Chapter 1.

16 Parking brake – adjustment

Refer to illustrations 16.4a and 16.4b

1 The parking brake does not need routine maintenance, but the cable may stretch over a period of time necessitating adjustment. Also, the parking brake should be checked for proper adjustment whenever the rear

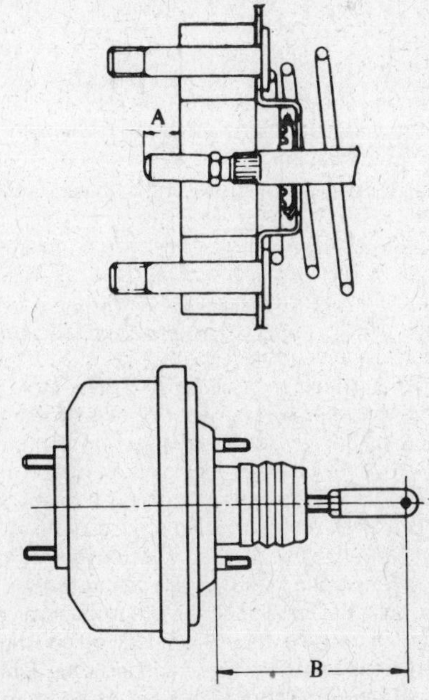

15.5 The output rod length (A) and/or the input rod length (B) of the brake booster should be adjusted (depending on the year model) to the measurements listed in the Specifications

10

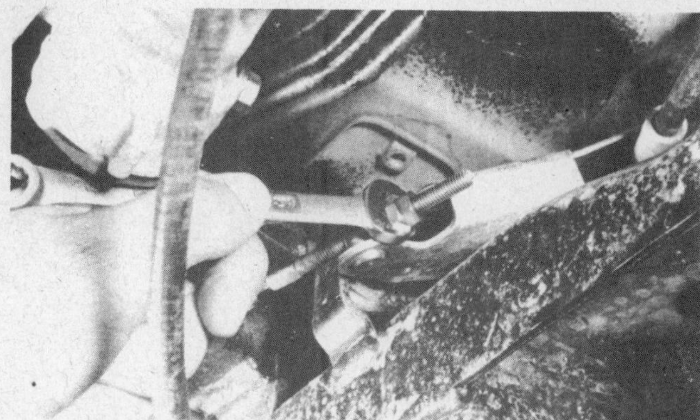

16.4a The parking brake adjuster is located on the right underside of the truck in front of the fuel tank (early 4WD model shown)

16.4b The parking brake on later models is adjusted by turning the cable nut (arrow)

brake cables have been disconnected.

2 While sitting in the driver's seat, pull back on the parking brake cable with heavy pulling force. When correctly adjusted, the lever should pull out 6 to 10 ratchet clicks. If the movement of the lever is shorter or longer than this, the cable needs adjustment.

3 For clearance, raise the rear of the vehicle and support it securely on jackstands.

4 Loosen the locknut at the parking brake cable adjuster **(see illustrations)**.

5 Turn the adjusting nut until the parking brake lever, when pulled,

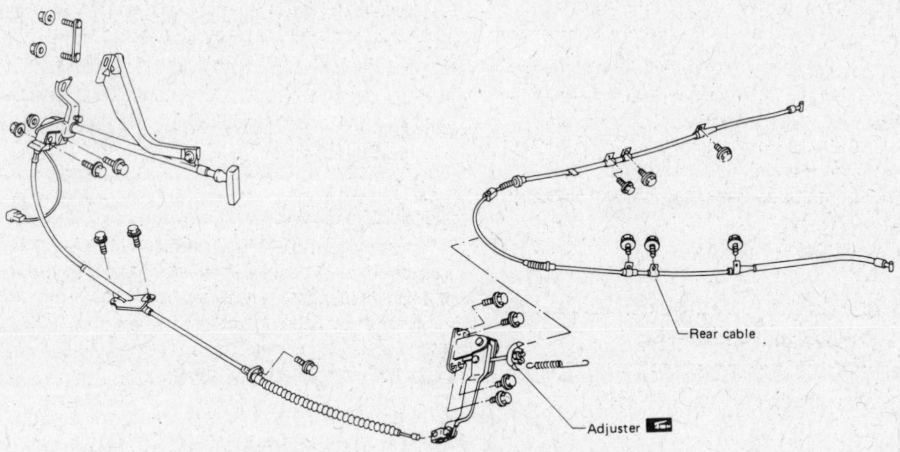

18.2a Parking brake handle and cable installation details – 2WD truck

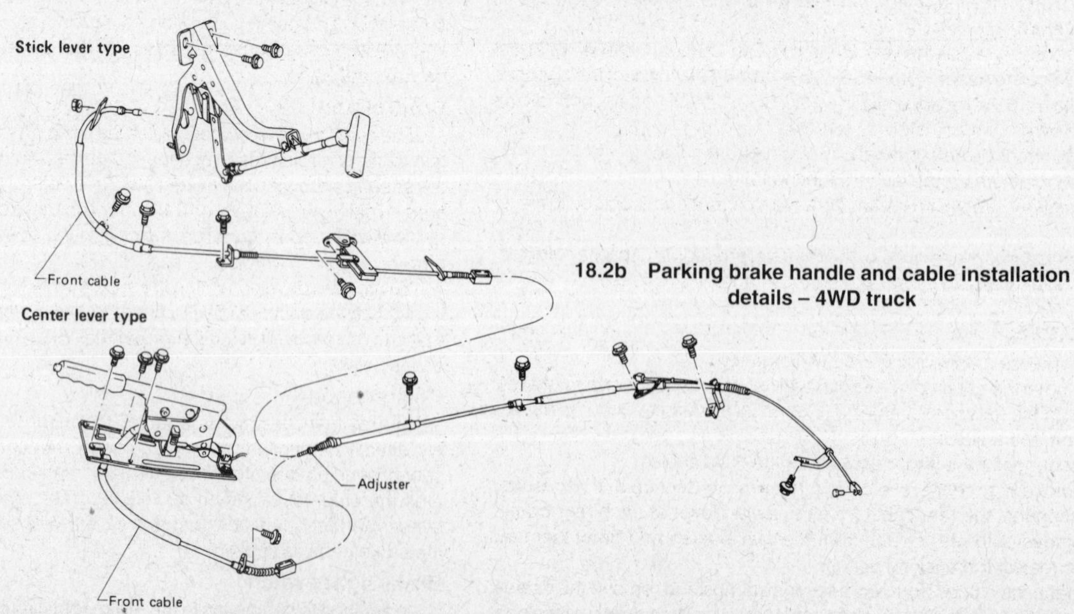

18.2b Parking brake handle and cable installation details – 4WD truck

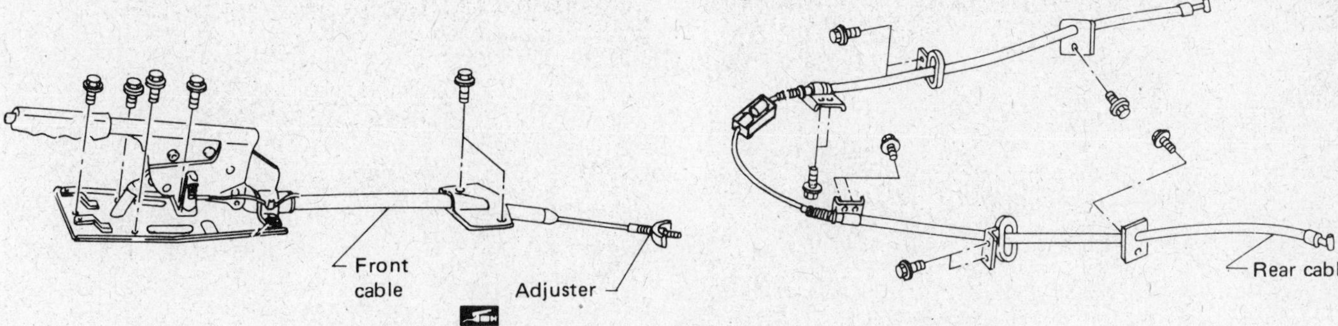

18.2c Parking brake handle and cable installation details – Pathfinder

moves the proper distance.
6 Retighten the lock nut.
7 Before lowering the vehicle, check that both rear wheels turn freely with the parking brake released and that there is no brake drag.

17 Parking brake control handle – removal and installation

1 Disconnect the wiring connector leading to the parking brake handle.
2 Disconnect the parking brake cable from the handle assembly by removing the clevis pin.
3 Remove the mounting bolts and screw that attach the control bracket to the firewall or the bolts that fasten the handle assembly to the floor.
4 Remove the spring retainer from the engine compartment side.
5 Lift out the control handle assembly.
6 Installation is the reverse of the removal procedure.

18 Parking brake cables – removal and installation

Refer to illustrations 18.2a, 18.2b and 18.2c

Front cable

1 Be sure the parking brake is fully released.
2 Disconnect the cable from the control handle by removing the clevis pin **(see illustrations)**.
3 If necessary, raise the rear of the truck and support it on jackstands.
4 Remove the parking brake adjusting nut and disconnect the opposite rear cable from the balance lever (4WD), or, on 2WD models, unhook the rear cable from the adjuster.
5 Disconnect the left rear cable from the front cable.
6 Remove the balance lever mounting bolts.
7 Detach all cable clamps and remove the front cable and balance lever.
8 Installation is the reverse of the removal procedure. Apply a little general-purpose grease to all sliding surfaces and pivot points.

Rear cable

9 Be sure the parking brake is fully released.
10 Remove the parking brake adjusting nut and disconnect the right rear cable from the balance lever (4WD), or on 2WD models unhook the rear cable from the adjuster.
11 Disconnect the left rear cable from the front cable.
12 Remove both rear brake drums, referring to Section 5, if necessary.
13 Disconnect the rear cable from the toggle lever at each rear brake.
14 Remove both rear cables from the rear brakes and draw them out from the rear of the backing plates.
15 Detach the cables from any securing clamps and remove the cables.
16 Installation is the reverse of the removal procedure. Apply a little general-purpose grease to all sliding surfaces and pivot points.

19 Brake light switch – removal and installation

1 The brake light switch is mounted on the brake pedal jacket just to the rear of the brake pedal.
2 Disconnect the wires leading to the switch.
3 Loosen the locknut.
4 Unscrew the switch from the bracket.
5 Installation is the reverse of the removal procedure. Note that the brake light switch controls the height of the brake pedal. Install the switch so that the brake pedal height is adjusted as described in Chapter 1.

20 Anti-lock Brake System (ABS) general information and code access

Description

The anti-lock brake system used on these vehicles controls the rear wheels only. It is designed to maintain vehicle maneuverability, directional stability and optimum deceleration under severe braking conditions on most road surfaces. It does so by monitoring the rotational speed of the rear wheels and controlling the brake pressure during braking. This prevents the wheels from locking up.

Components

Refer to illustration 20.2

Actuator assembly

The actuator assembly, which is mounted to the frame rail, consists of an isolation and dump valve. The valves operate by changing the brake fluid pressure in response to signals from the control unit **(see illustration on next page)**.

Control unit

The control unit is located under the dash on the right side. The function of the control unit is to accept and process information received from the speed sensor and brake light switch to control the hydraulic line pressure, avoiding wheel lockup. The control unit also constantly monitors the system, even under normal driving conditions, to find faults within the system.

If a problem develops within the system, the ANTI-LOCK or ABS warning light on the dashboard will illuminate. A diagnostic code will be stored that can be retrieved using the procedure listed under Accessing trouble codes below.

Rear sensor

The rear sensor, which is mounted to the front of the differential assembly, directly behind the companion flange, monitors rear wheel rotational speed, sending this information to the control unit. The control unit operates the actuator assembly to relieve brake system pressure when it senses sudden, dramatic changes in rear wheel rotational speed when the brake pedal is applied.

Brake light switch

In addition to its function in the brake light circuit, the brake light switch is used as part of the ABS system to send a signal to the control module,

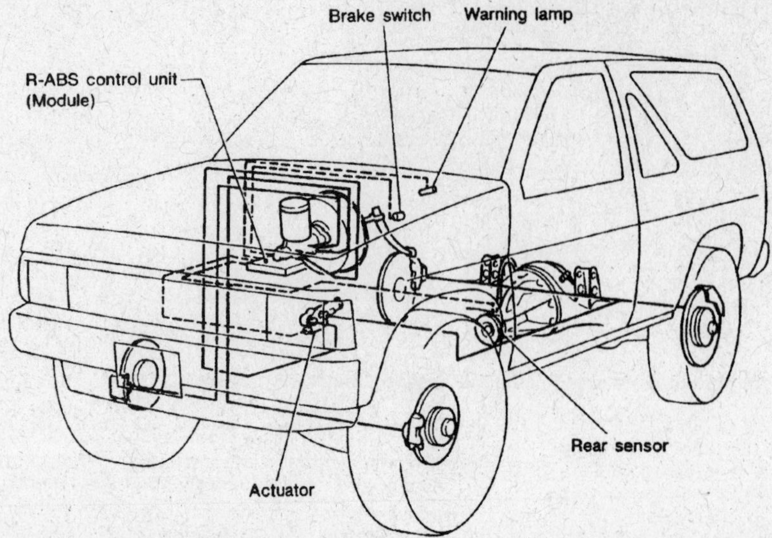

20.2 Locations of the ABS system components

indicating when the driver is depressing the brake pedal. Without this signal, the ABS system will not activate.

Diagnosis and repair

If the ANTI-LOCK or ABS warning light on the dash comes on and stays on, make sure there's no problem with the brake hydraulic system. If that's not the cause, the anti-lock system is probably malfunctioning. Although special test procedures are necessary to properly diagnose the system, the home mechanic can perform a few preliminary checks before taking the vehicle to a dealer service department.

a) Make sure the brakes, calipers and wheel cylinders are in good condition.
b) Check the electrical connectors at the control unit.
c) Check the fuses.
d) Follow the wiring harness to the speed sensor and brake light switch and make sure all connections are secure and the wiring isn't damaged.

If the above preliminary checks don't rectify the problem, first try to identify the area of trouble using the trouble codes listed below, then take the vehicle to a dealer service department.

Accessing trouble codes

Refer to illustrations 20.10a and 20.10b

If the ANTI-LOCK or ABS warning light on the dashboard comes on and stays on, there's a good chance that the control module has stored a trouble code that can help a service technician find the area of trouble in the system. **Caution:** *If the vehicle is in 4WD, the rear wheels will lock if the front wheels lock. This is because the front and rear axles are coupled mechanically through the transfer case. In this situation, the "Anti-Lock" warning light will come on, but the ordinary brakes will still function normally. This is not a malfunction. When the engine is re-started, the ABS will be reactivated and the warning light will go out.*

To access a trouble code, drive the vehicle over 25 mph for at least one minute (in 2WD if the vehicle is a 4WD model). Leave the engine running, then find the "Check" connector under the dashboard on the driver's side and ground Terminal 3 of the connector **(see illustrations)**.

The warning light will flash to indicate the trouble code (1 flash for a code 1, 2 flashes for a code 2, 3 flashes for a code 3, etc.). Refer to the accompanying chart to determine the failure indicated by the code. If there is more than one ABS system failure, only the first code recognized will be stored. After repairs are completed and the ignition key has been turned off, then on again, the memory is cleared and any other codes will be stored, one at a time, while the vehicle is being driven.

ABS system trouble code chart

Trouble code	Probable cause
2	Open in the actuator assembly isolation solenoid or circuit
3	Open in the actuator assembly dump solenoid or circuit
4	Actuator isolation solenoid blocked
5	Problem in the rear brake hydraulic circuit or faulty actuator assembly
6	Rear sensor operation erratic
7	Short in the actuator assembly isolation solenoid or circuit
8	Short in the actuator assembly dump solenoid or circuit
9	Open in the rear sensor or circuit
10	Short in the rear sensor or circuit
13, 14 or 15	Malfunction in the control unit or circuit

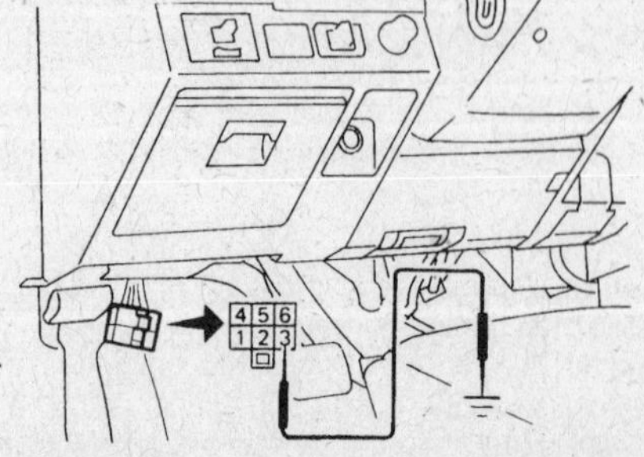

20.10a To retrieve a trouble code from the ABS control unit, ground Terminal 3 of the "check" connector with the engine running (1991 and 1993 models shown)

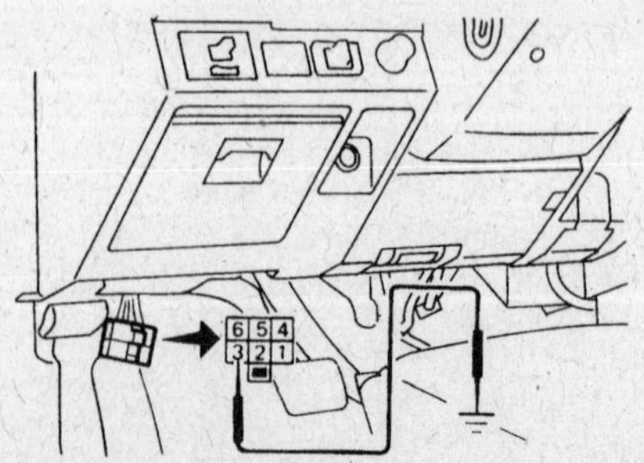

20.10b On 1992 models, Terminal 3 is in a different location in the "check" connector

Chapter 11 Steering and suspension systems

Contents

Specifications

Front suspension

Initial anchor arm setting	
1980 through 1983 (dimension A)	0.28 to 0.67 in (7 to 17 mm)
1984 (dimension G)	
left side	4.33 to 4.72 in (110 to 120 mm)
right side	5.12 to 5.51 in (130 to 140 mm)
1985	
2WD (dimension A)	1.46 in (37 mm)
4WD (dimension G)	
left side	3.74 in (95 mm)
right side	4.33 in (110 mm)
1986 on (dimension G)	
2WD	0.24 to 0.71 in (6 to 18 mm)
4WD	1.97 to 2.36 in (50 to 60 mm)
Secondary anchor arm bolt adjustment (dimension L)	
1980 through 1983	2.36 to 2.76 in (60 to 70 mm)
1984	
left side	2.72 in (69 mm)
right side	2.83 in (72 mm)
1985	
2WD	2.36 to 2.76 in (60 to 70 mm)
4WD	
left side	3.50 in (89 mm)
right side	3.86 in (98 mm)
1986 on	
2WD HD, Cab & Chassis and standard models	1.38 in (35 mm)
all other 2WD models	1.93 in (49 mm)
4WD	3.03 in (77 mm)
Vehicle ride height (dimension H)	
1980 through 1983	
2WD	4.88 to 5.08 in (124 to 129 mm)
4WD	5.28 to 5.47 in (134 to 139 mm)
1984	
2WD	
King Cab	4.45 to 4.61 in (113 to 117 mm)
Regular Cab	4.65 to 4.80 in (118 to 122 mm)
4WD	
King Cab	1.54 to 1.69 in (39 to 43 mm)
Regular Cab	1.73 to 1.89 in (44 to 48 mm)

Front suspension (continued)

Vehicle ride height (dimension H)	
1985	
2WD	5.04 to 5.20 in (128 to 132 mm)
4WD	2.09 to 2.24 in (53 to 57 mm)
1986 on	
2WD	4.25 to 4.65 in (108 to 118 mm)
4WD	1.61 to 2.01 in (41 to 51 mm)
Upper link spindle positioning	
Dimension A	
1980 through 1983	5.34 to 5.42 in (135.6 to 137.6 mm)
1984 and 1985	
2WD	5.34 to 5.42 in (135.6 to 137.6 mm)
4WD	4.33 in (110 mm)
1986 on	4.33 in (110 mm)
Dimension B	
1980 through 1983	1.114 in (28.3 mm)
1984 and 1985	
2WD	1.114 in (28.3 mm)
4WD	0.98 in (25 mm)
1986 on	1.26 in (32 mm)

Torque specifications	Ft-lbs
Upper balljoint-to-knuckle spindle	
1980 through 1983	58 to 72
1984 and 1985	
2WD	58 to 72
4WD	58 to 108
1986 on (all)	58 to 108
Upper balljoint-to-upper link	12 to 15
Upper link spindle-to-upper link	52 to 76
Upper link spindle-to-frame	80 to 108
Lower link to frame	80 to 108
Lower balljoint-to-lower link	
1980 through 1985	28 to 38
1986 on	35 to 45
Lower balljoint-to-knuckle spindle	
1980 through 1984 2WD, and all 1985	87 to 123
1980 through 1983 4WD	43 to 72
1986 on	87 to 141
Torque arm-to-lower link	
1980 through 1983	
inside	26 to 33
outside	20 to 27
1984 and 1985	
2WD	
inside	26 to 33
outside	20 to 27
4WD	66 to 87
1986 on	
2WD	37 to 50
4WD	
inside	33 to 44
outside	66 to 87
Tension rod-to-lower link	
1980 through 1985	33 to 44
1986 on	36 to 47
Tension rod-to-frame (all)	87 to 116
Compression rod-to-lower link	87 to 108
Compression rod to body	87 to 116

Rear suspension

Torque specifications	Ft-lbs
Leaf spring front pin nut	
1980 through 1985	37 to 50
1986 on	58 to 72
Leaf spring shackle nuts	
1980 through 1985	37 to 50
1986 on	58 to 72
Upper and lower link bolts (coil springs)	80 to 108
Panhard rod mounting bolts	
left side	
Through 1990	36 to 51
1991 and later	94 to 123
right side	80 to 108

Steering system

Manual steering gear

Sector shaft end play	0.0004 to 0.0012 in (0.01 to 0.03 mm)
Sector shaft shim thicknesses	0.0620 t0 0.0630 in (1.575 to 1.600 mm)
	0.0610 to 0.0620 in (1.550 to 1.575 mm)
	0.0600 to 0.0610 in (1.525 to 1.550 mm)
	0.0591 to 0.0600 in (1.500 to 1.525 mm)
	0.0581 to 0.0591 in (1.475 to 1.500 mm)
	0.0571 to 0.0581 in (1.450 to 1.475 mm)
	0.0768 in (1.95 mm)
	0.0787 in (2.00 mm)
	0.0807 in (2.05 mm)
Worm bearing preload	
1980 through 1983	3.5 to 5.2 in-lb (0.39 to 0.59 Nm)
1984 on	1.7 to 5.2 in-lb (0.20 to 0.59 Nm)
Steering gear preload (all years)	
New parts	7.4 to 10.9 in-lb (0.83 to 1.23 Nm)
Used parts	5.2 to 8.7 in-lb (0.59 to 0.98 Nm)
Steering linkage	
Standard side rod length	
2WD	
1980 through 1985	13.07 in (332 mm)
1986 on	13.54 in (344 mm)
4WD	
1980 through 1983	10.83 in (275 mm)
1984 and 1985	11.54 in (293 mm)
1986 and later	11.06 in (281 mm)

Torque specifications	Ft-lbs
Steering wheel nut	
1980 through 1985	29 to 36
1986 on	22 to 29
Jacket tube bracket-to-dash panel	
1980 through 1985	2.2 to 3.2
1986 on	6.5 to 10.1
Worm shaft to coupling	
1980 through 1983	29 to 36
1984 and 1985	11 to 16
1986 on	17 to 22
Ball stud nuts (all)	40 to 72
Side rod clamp nuts	
Through 1985	8 to 12
1986 through 1990	10 to 14
1991 and later	8 to 10
Side rod locknut (1984 and later)	58 to 72
Idler arm-to-frame bolts	
Through 1990	36 to 51
1991 and later	40 to 51
Idler arm nut	40 to 51
Steering gear-to-frame bolts	62 to 71
Steering gear arm (Pitman arm)-to-shaft nut	
Manual steering	
Through 1990	94 to 108
1991 and later	174 to 195
Power steering	101 to 130

1 Suspension system – general information

Refer to illustrations 1.1, 1.2a, 1.2b, 1.3 and 1.4

The front suspension system is an independent type using torsion bar springing. The main components are the upper and lower links, knuckle spindle, shock absorbers, tension rods, stabilizer bar and torsion bars **(see illustration)**.

Both links pivot on the frame on the inner end and are attached through balljoints to the knuckle spindle on the outer end. The knuckle spindle is attached directly to the front hub.

The front end of the torsion bar is attached to a torque arm which is mounted to the lower link. The rear end is attached to an anchor arm mounted directly to the frame. It is because of this arrangement that the links (and wheel and tire) are returned to their original positions after striking a bump. Adjustment of the torsion bar is by way of the anchor arm adjusting bolts.

The shock absorbers are conventional sealed hydraulic units, connected at the upper end to a bracket on the frame and at the lower end to the lower link. The double acting shock absorbers dampen both the initial upward force of striking a bump and the return force of the torsion bars. Some models use adjustable shock absorbers, controlled electrically from the driver's compartment.

Front and rear forces are controlled by tension rods (compression rods on 1984 and later 4WD models), and a front stabilizer bar is installed to control body roll in corners.

The rear suspension on some models uses semi-elliptic leaf springs, mounted on the ends to the frame and in the middle to the rear axle by way of U-bolts **(see illustration)**. On other models coil springs are used, located to the frame through upper and lower links and a panhard rod. A rear stabilizer bar is also used on these models **(see illustration)**. The rear shock absorbers are mounted between the axle and the frame. Like the front shock absorbers, the rear units are non-adjustable, nonrefillable and cannot be disassembled.

Never attempt to heat or straighten any suspension part, as this can weaken the metal or in other ways damage the part.

1.1 Front suspension and steering components

1 Steering knuckle
2 Upper balljoint
3 Upper link
4 Side rod
5 Idler arm
6 Stabilizer bar
7 Cross rod
8 Steering gear arm (Pitman arm)
9 Lower balljoint
10 Lower link
11 Shock absorber
12 Compression rod
13 Torsion bar

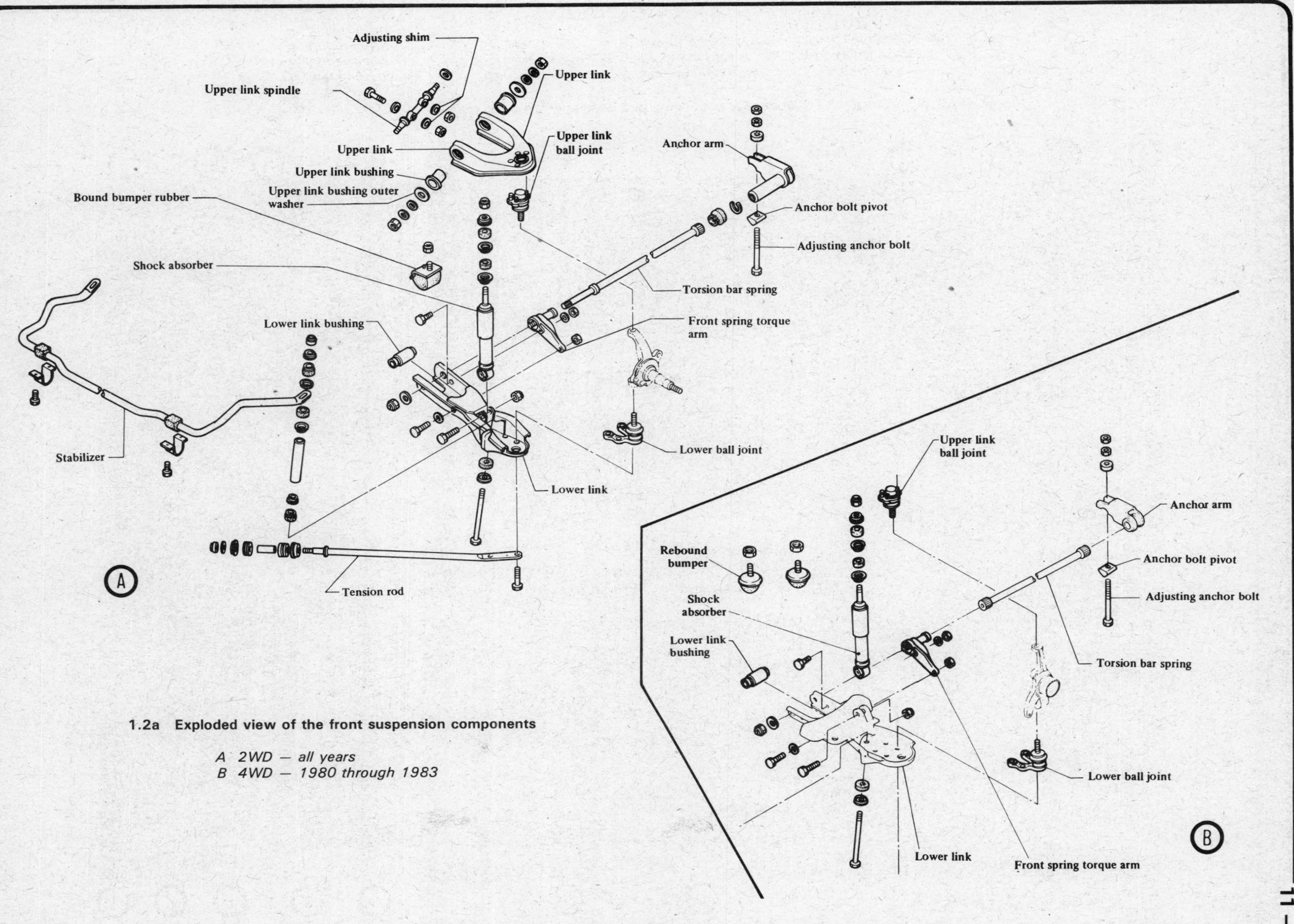

1.2a Exploded view of the front suspension components

A 2WD — all years
B 4WD — 1980 through 1983

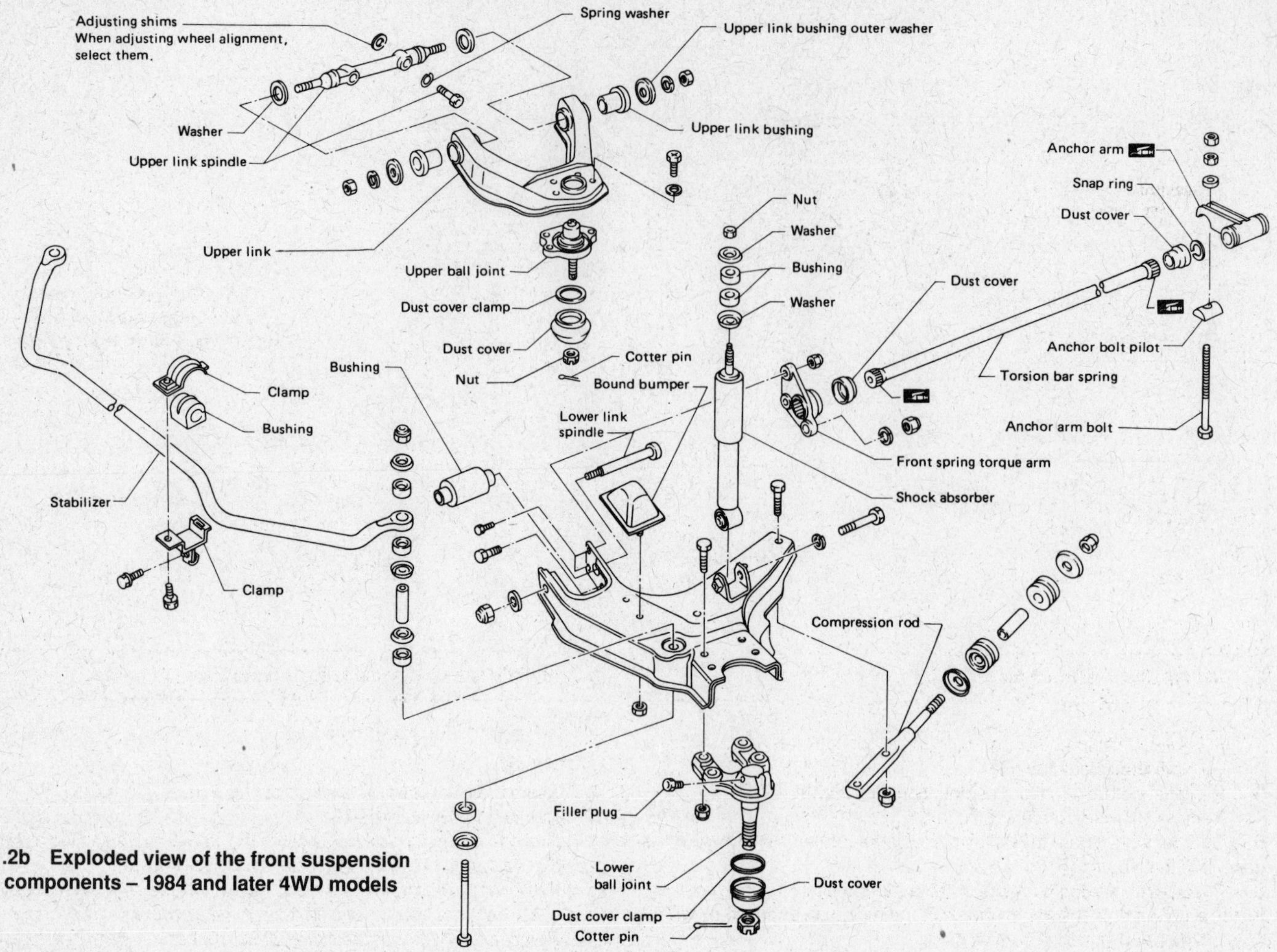

Adjusting shims
When adjusting wheel alignment, select them.
Spring washer
Upper link bushing outer washer
Washer
Upper link spindle
Upper link bushing
Anchor arm
Snap ring
Dust cover
Nut
Washer
Bushing
Washer
Upper link
Upper ball joint
Dust cover clamp
Dust cover
Torsion bar spring
Dust cover
Anchor bolt pilot
Cotter pin
Nut
Bound bumper
Bushing
Clamp
Bushing
Lower link spindle
Anchor arm bolt
Front spring torque arm
Shock absorber
Stabilizer
Clamp
Compression rod
Filler plug
Lower ball joint
Dust cover
Dust cover clamp
Cotter pin

1.2b Exploded view of the front suspension components – 1984 and later 4WD models

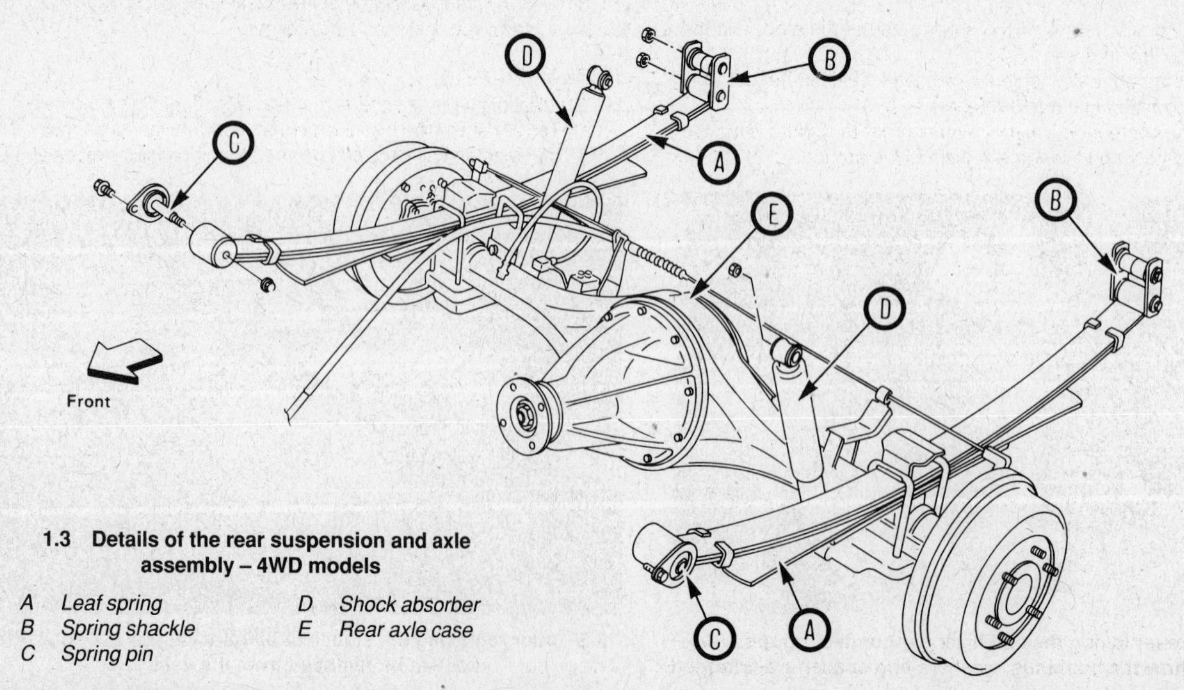

1.3 Details of the rear suspension and axle assembly – 4WD models

A Leaf spring
B Spring shackle
C Spring pin
D Shock absorber
E Rear axle case

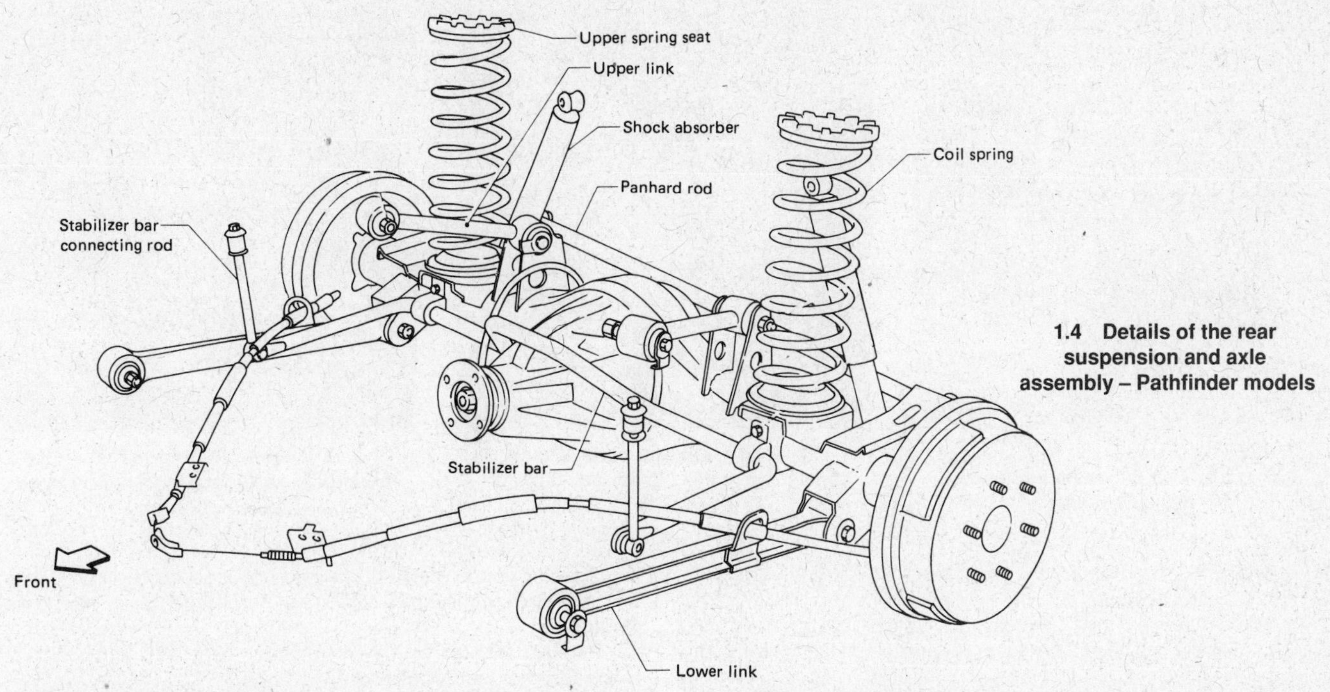

1.4 Details of the rear suspension and axle assembly – Pathfinder models

2 Wheel stud – replacement

1 Raise the vehicle and support it securely on jackstands.
2 Remove the wheel and tire.
3 Remove the brake caliper as described in Chapter 10.
4 Remove the rotor as described in Chapter 10.
5 On front wheels, the hub will have to be separated from the rotor as described in Chapter 10.
6 Position the stud to be replaced at either the 5 or 7 o'clock position. Install a lug nut onto the end of the stud and, using an appropriate wheel stud puller, press the stud from its seat.
7 Remove the lug nut, and then the stud.
8 With the stud hole at either the 5 or 7 o'clock position, insert the new stud in the hole, making sure the serrations are aligned with those made by the original bolt.
9 Place four flat washers over the outside end of the stud, and then thread a lug onto the stud.
10 Tighten the lug nut until the stud head seats against the rear of the hub. Then remove the lug nut and washers.
11 Reinstall the components in the reverse order they were removed.
12 Mount the wheel and lower the vehicle to the ground.

3 Stabilizer bar – removal and installation

Refer to illustrations 3.3 and 3.5

Removal

1 Raise the front of the vehicle and support it on jackstands.
2 Remove the splash shield.
3 Remove the upper nuts from both of the stabilizer connecting rods located at each end of the stabilizer bar **(see illustration)**.
4 Remove the rods from the bar and lower links, being sure to keep the bushings, washers and spacers in their installed order.
5 Remove the bolts that attach the stabilizer bar brackets to the frame and lift off the bar **(see illustration)**.
6 If the stabilizer bar bushings need to be replaced, simply spread them apart and slide them off the bar.
7 Inspect the stabilizer connecting rod bushings for cracking or any other damage and replace them as necessary.

Installation

8 Installation is the reverse of removal, with the following notes:
  a) The bar should be installed so that the white marks painted on the bar near the bushings can be seen from both sides of the vehicle.

3.3 Before removing the stabilizer bar connecting rod nut (arrow), note how the bushings, washers and spacer are arranged

3.5 After removing the stabilizer bar bracket bolts (arrow), the bar can be removed from the vehicle

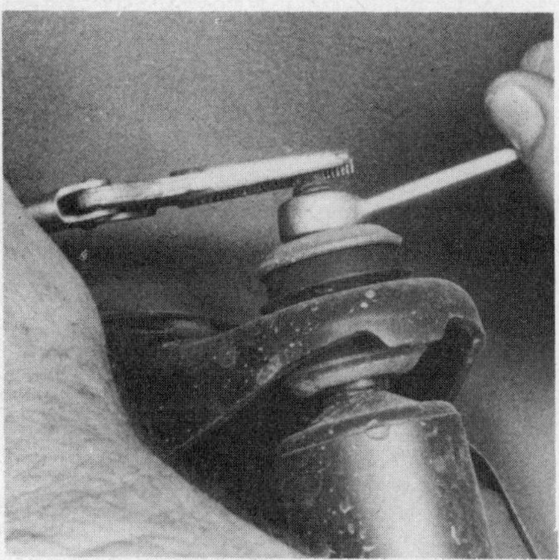
4.2 Hold the damper rod with a pair of locking pliers while loosening the nut with a wrench

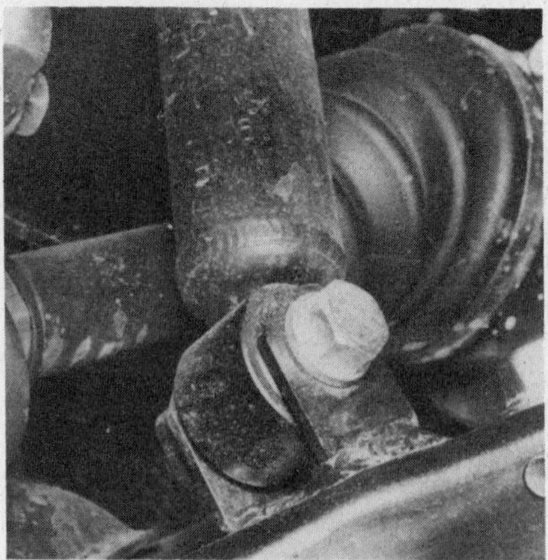
4.3 The lower end of the shock absorber is bolted to a bracket on the lower link

4.6 The lower end of the rear shock absorber is attached to the spring pad by a nut (arrow)

b) The connecting rod components should be installed in their original order and positions.
c) The stabilizer bar mounting bolts should not be fully tightened until the vehicle has been lowered to the ground and the full weight is on the wheels.

4 Shock absorbers – removal and installation

Refer to illustrations 4.2, 4.3, 4.6 and 4.7

Front

1 Turn the front wheel outward to allow access to the shock absorber. For additional clearance, remove the wheel and tire.
2 While holding the damper rod of the shock absorber to prevent it from rotating, remove the nut, washer and rubber bushing **(see illustration)**.
3 Remove the through-bolt at the lower end of the shock absorber **(see illustration)**.
4 Installation is the reverse of the removal procedure. Ensure that the bolt at the lower end is installed with its head towards the front of the vehicle.

Rear

5 Check the front wheels then raise the rear of the vehicle as high as possible so that it is supported on the axle tube. Be sure that adequate support is provided before starting work.
6 While holding the lower spindle of the shock absorber to prevent it from rotating, remove the nuts, washer and rubber bushing (early style). On later models, remove the nut from the stud on the lower spring pad **(see illustration)**.
7 Remove the nut from the mount at the upper end and detach the shock absorber **(see illustration)**.
8 Installation is the reverse of the removal procedure. Be sure that the weight is on the rear wheels before the mounting nuts are tightened.

4.7 The upper end of the rear shock absorber is attached to the frame stud by a nut (arrow)

5.2a Location of the torsion bar anchor bolts – 1980 through 1983 models

5.2b Location of the torsion bar adjusting bolt nut (arrow) – 1984 and later 4WD models

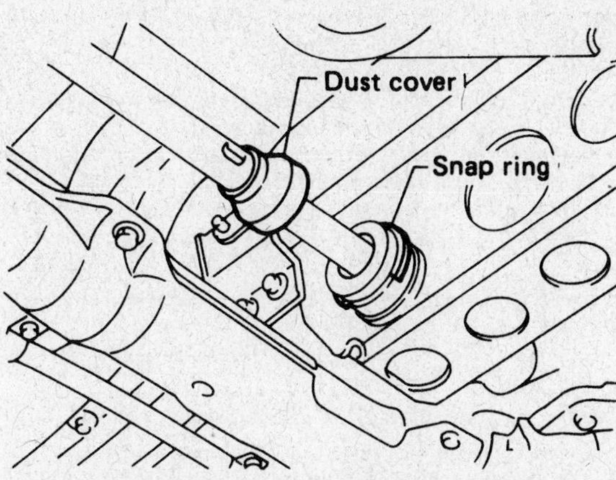

5.3 Slide the dust cover forward on the torsion bar to gain access to the anchor arm snap-ring

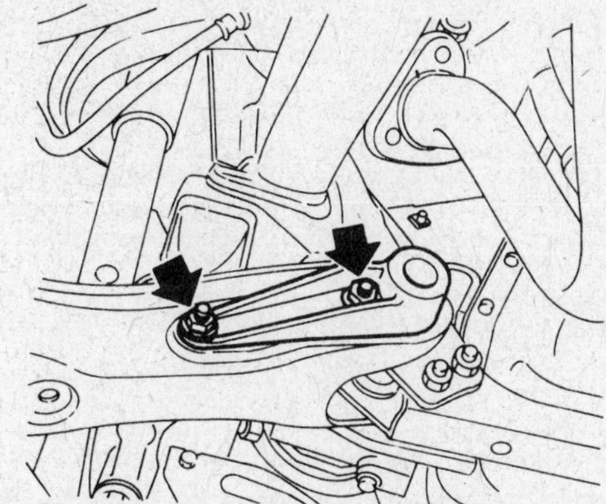

5.6 Location of the torque arm attaching nuts on the lower link (pre-1984 2WD models – others similar)

5 Torsion bar – removal and installation

Refer to illustrations 5.2a, 5.2b, 5.3, 5.6, 5.7, 5.11, 5.12, 5.13, 5.15, 5.16a and 5.16b

Removal

1 Raise the front of the vehicle and support it on jackstands.
2 Remove the adjusting nuts from the torsion bar anchor bolt and remove the anchor bolt **(see illustrations).**
3 Remove the dust cover and detach the snap-ring from the anchor arm **(see illustration).**
4 Pull the anchor arm off toward the rear of the vehicle (2WD models).
5 Withdraw the torsion bar toward the rear of the vehicle (2WD models).
6 Remove the torque arm from the lower link (2WD models) **(see illustration).**
7 On 4WD models, unbolt the torque arm from the lower link **(see illustration)** then remove the torsion bar and torque arm toward the front of the vehicle.
8 Check the torsion bar for excessive wear, twisting, bending or other damage. Also check the serrations of each part to be sure they are in good condition.

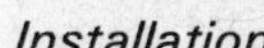

Installation

9 Begin installation by reinstalling the torque arm to the lower link (2WD models). Tighten the retaining bolts to the specified torque.
10 Apply a coat of grease to the serrations on the torsion bar, and then install the torsion bar into the torque arm (2WD models). On 4WD models, install the torsion bar and torque arm to the lower link and tighten the bolts to the specified torque. **Note:** *If both torsion bars are removed at the same time, be sure each is installed on the correct side of the vehicle. They are marked with a R (right) or L (left) on the end of the bar.*

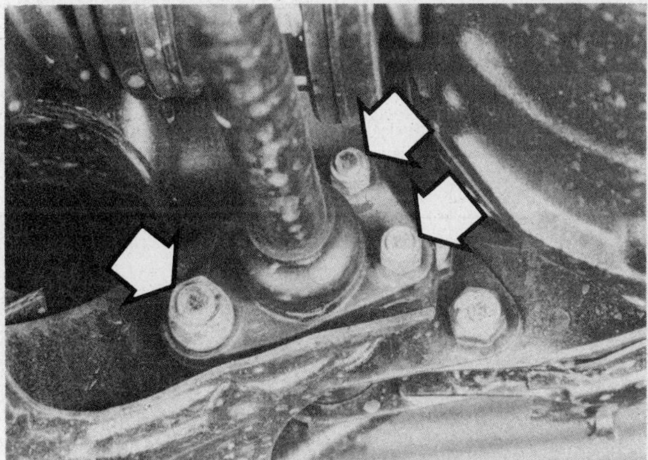

5.7 Location of the torque arm attaching nuts on the lower link (arrows) – late model 4WD

11 Install the anchor arm onto the rear of the torsion bar and install the anchor arm adjusting bolt and nuts (1980 to 1983). The correct initial positioning of the anchor arm should be set to the dimension given in the Specifications **(see illustration).**
12 On 1984 and later models raise the lower link until there is no clearance between the rebound bumper and the frame **(see illustration).**

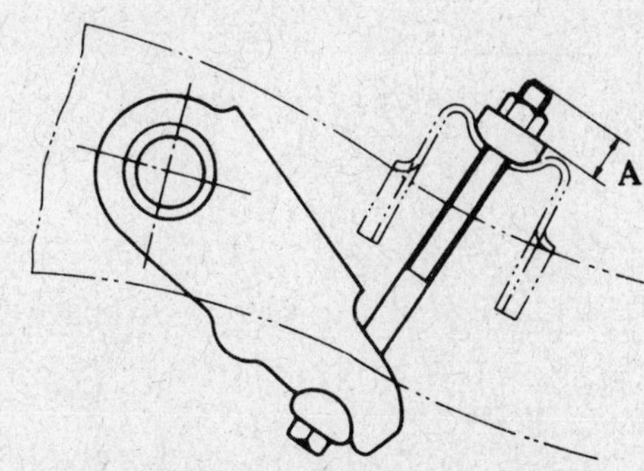

5.11 On 1980 through 1983 vehicles, measure the initial position of the torque arm (A) and adjust it to the dimension listed in the Specifications

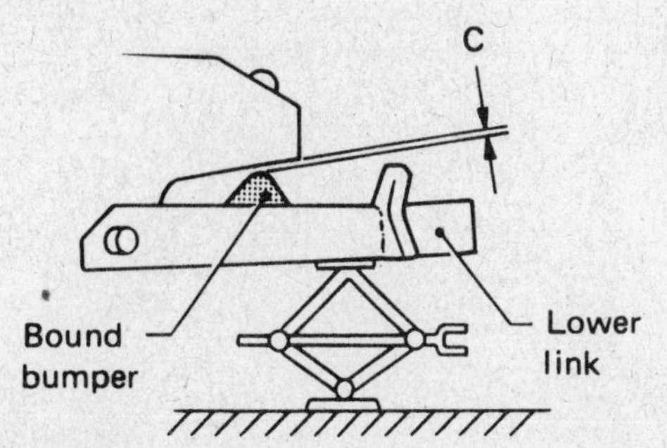

5.12 Prior to adjusting the initial torque arm setting on 1984 and later models, raise the lower link until the rebound bumper just contacts the frame

13 Install the anchor arm and adjust the initial torque arm setting to the dimension given in the Specifications **(see illustration)**.
14 Install the snap-ring to the anchor arm groove and slide the dust cover into position.
15 Turn the anchor arm nut until the anchor arm bolt protrudes the specified length **(see illustration)**.
16 Lower the vehicle to the ground and bounce it a few times to set the suspension. Measure the ride height at the points indicated **(see illustrations)**. If the dimension is not as specified, turn the anchor bolt adjusting nut until it is correct.
17 Drive the vehicle to an alignment shop and have the front end alignment checked, and, if necessary, adjusted.

6 Tension or compression rod – removal and installation

Refer to illustrations 6.2a, 6.2b, 6.3 and 6.6

1 Raise the front of the vehicle and support it on jackstands for clearance. Remove the splash shield, if equipped.
2 Remove the large nut from the end of the tension or compression rod and lift off the bushings and washer plates **(see illustrations)**.
3 Remove the bolts securing the rod to the lower link **(see illustration)**.
4 Remove the rod from the vehicle.
5 If both rods are being removed at once, be sure to note the marks referring to left and right for installation.
6 Installation is the reverse of the removal procedure. Be sure to install the bushings and washers in the proper direction **(see illustration) Note:** *Do not tighten the mounting bolts until the vehicle has been lowered to the ground and the full weight is on the wheels.*

7 Upper link and balljoint – removal and installation

Refer to illustrations 7.5a, 7.5b, 7.6a, 7.6b and 7.15

1 Raise the front of the vehicle and support it on jackstands.
2 Remove the wheel and tire.
3 Remove the upper shock absorber mounting nut and compress the shock absorber as much as possible.
4 Place a jack under the lower link to take the weight of the assembly.
5 Loosen, but do not remove, the upper balljoint nut. Using a suitable tool, separate the upper balljoint from the knuckle spindle **(see illustrations)**, then remove the nut.

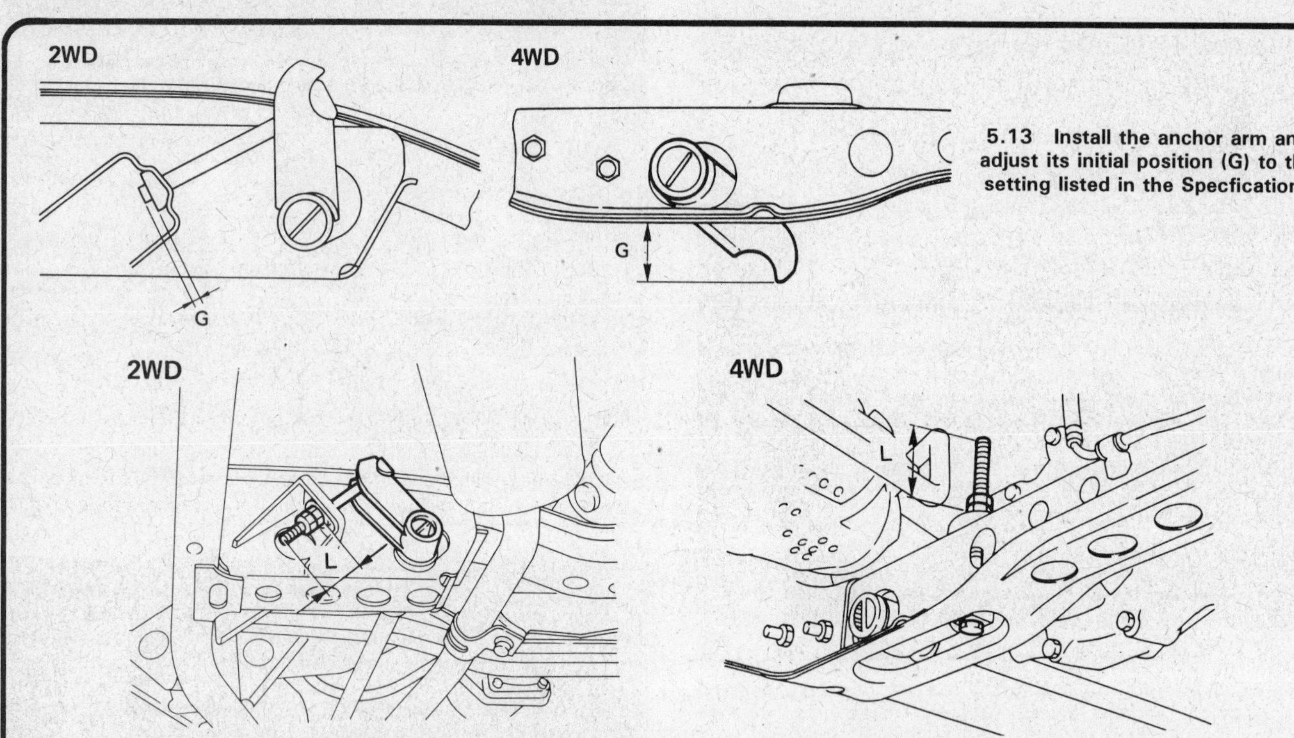

5.13 Install the anchor arm and adjust its initial position (G) to the setting listed in the Specfications

5.15 Turn the anchor arm nut until the exposed portion of the adjusting bolt reaches the correct length, as given in the Specifications

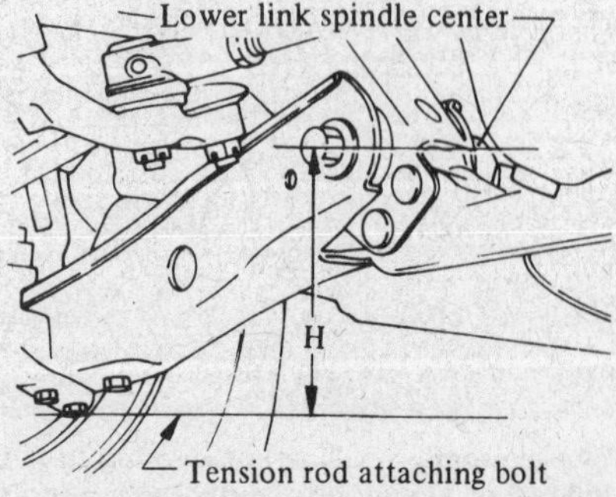

5.16a When checking the vehicle ride height, the measurement (H) should be taken at the points shown (1980 through 1983 4WD and all 2WD models)

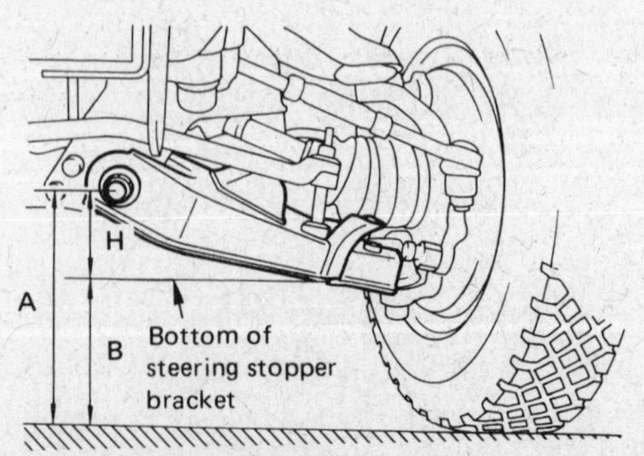

5.16b On 1984 and later 4WD models, check the vehicle ride height at distance H and adjust the torsion bar as necessary

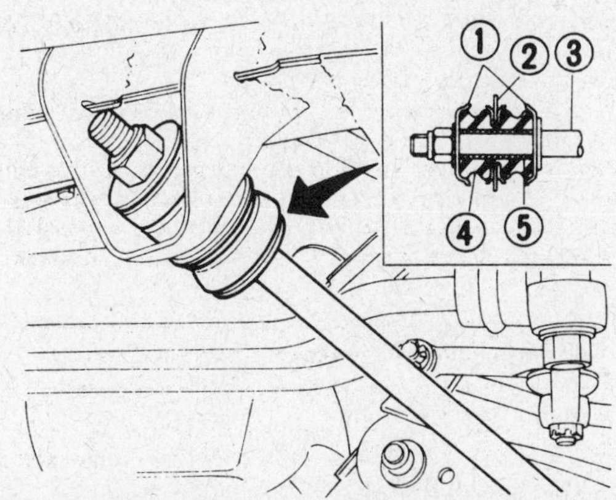

6.2a Tension rod, bushing and washer mounting details (1980 through 1983 4WD models and all 2WD models)

1 *Thrust washer*
2 *Frame*
3 *Tension rod*
4 *Bushing*
5 *Collar*

6.2b Compression rod-to-frame mounting details (1984 and later 4WD models)

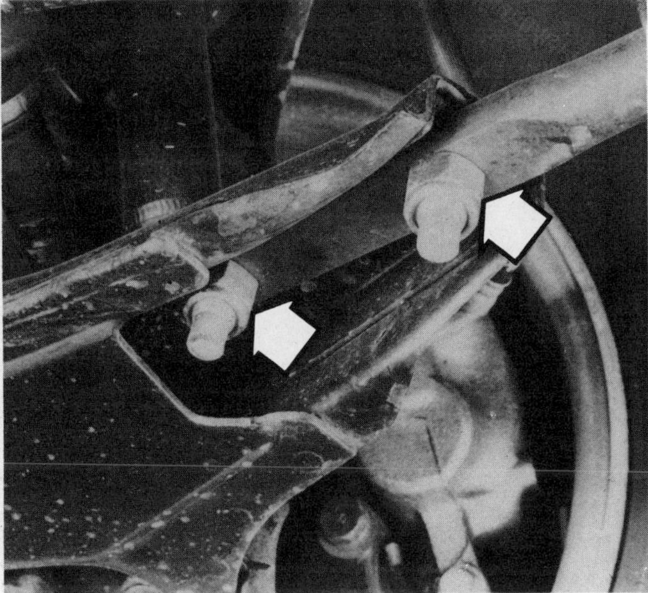

6.3 The compression rod is held to the lower link by two bolts

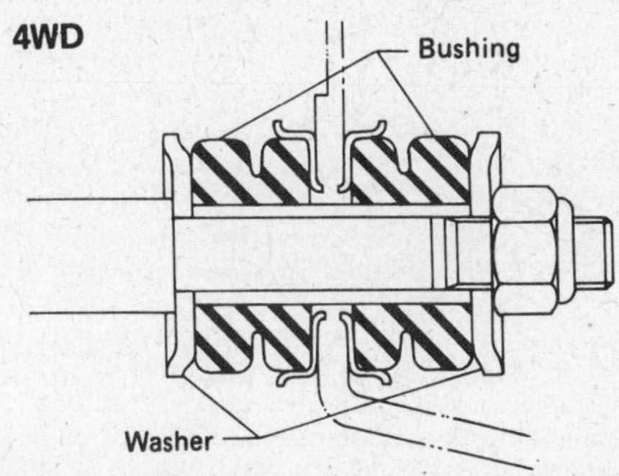

6.6 Correct positioning of the compression rod bushings and washers - note that the dished side of the washers faces out

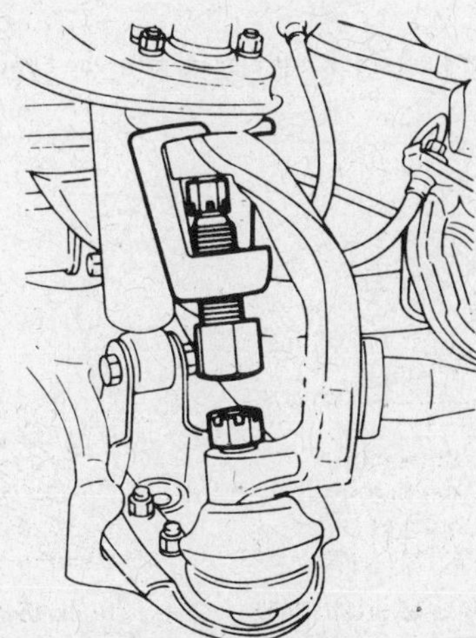

7.5a A special puller should be used to disengage the upper or lower balljoint from the knuckle spindle

7.5b An alternative balljoint separating tool can be fabricated out of a large bolt, nut, washer and socket, arranged as shown — when the nut is tightened against the socket, the bolt head (which should be held with a wrench to prevent it from turning) will push on the balljoint stud, breaking it loose from the knuckle

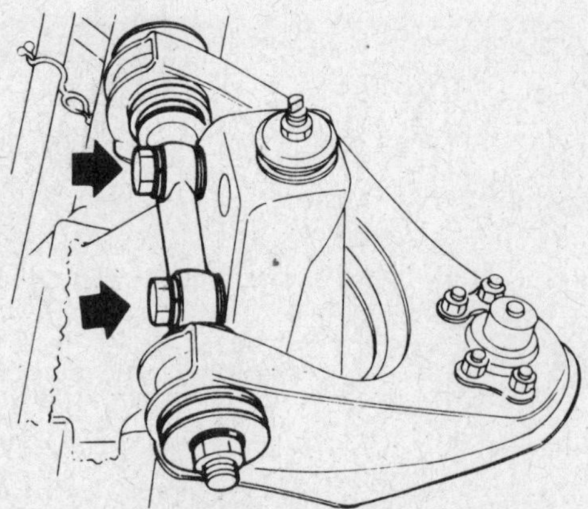

7.6a Location of the upper link spindle mounting bolts (1980 through 1984 models)

7.6b Location of the upper link spindle mounting bolts (1985 and later models)

6 Remove the bolts attaching the upper link spindle to the frame and lift out the complete upper link assembly, including any adjusting shims. Pay close attention to the number and position of all shims **(see illustrations)**.

7 The balljoint can now be removed from the upper link by removing the retaining nuts. The balljoint cannot be disassembled.
If it is defective, it must be replaced with a new one.

8 If the upper link bushings are hardened or cracked they must be replaced. This is done by removing the upper link spindle nuts on both ends of the upper link spindle and pressing the spindle from the link. A hydraulic press may be needed for this procedure.

9 To install new bushings, first apply a soapy water solution to one bushing. Then press it into the link until the bushing flange is up against the end of the link collar. Again, a hydraulic press may be needed for this procedure.

10 With one bushing installed, insert the link spindle and inner washers. Position the washers so their rounded edges are facing in.

11 Press in the other bushing in the same manner as the first.

12 Install the spindle nuts and snug them down.

13 Install the balljoint to the upper link.

14 Attach the upper link assembly to the frame by reinstalling the upper link spindle mounting bolts and shims. Be sure the shims are in their original positions and tighten the bolts to the specified torque.

15 After attaching the upper link to the frame, check the dimensions A and B **(see illustration)** to be sure the link is properly centered. Compare your measurements with the Specifications and adjust as necessary.

16 The remainder of the installation procedure is the reverse of removal. **Note:** *Do not fully tighten the upper link spindle nuts until the vehicle is lowered to the ground. Following installation, have the wheel alignment checked and adjusted as necessary.*

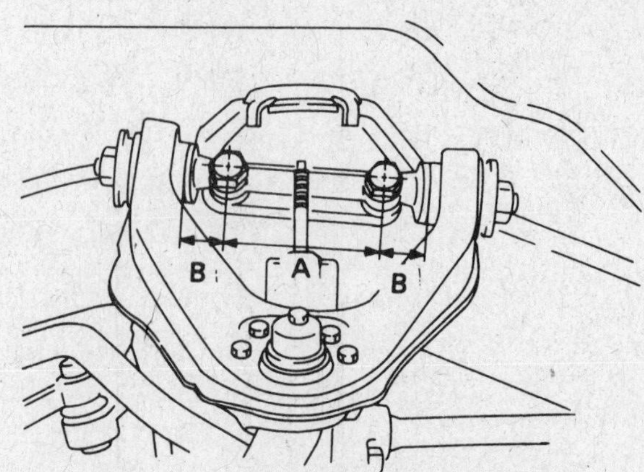

7.15 Check to be sure the upper link spindle is properly centered by measuring dimensions A and B – refer to the Specifications for the desired measurements

8 Lower link and balljoint – removal and installation

Refer to illustration 8.8

1 Raise the front of the vehicle and support it on jackstands.

2 Remove the wheel and tire.

3 Remove the torsion bar, as described in Section 5.

4 Disconnect the lower shock absorber mount from the lower link.

5 Remove the stabilizer bar connecting rod from the lower link.

6 Loosen, but do not remove, the lower balljoint nut and use a suitable tool to separate the lower link from the knuckle spindle. A two-jaw puller will work on 1984 and later 4WD vehicles. All other models must use a balljoint separator tool.

7 Disconnect the tension or compression rod from the lower link.

8 Remove the front lower link pivot nut **(see illustration)** and push the stud out through the rear.

9 Remove the torque arm from the lower link and lift the link away from the frame.

10 The balljoint can be removed from the link by removing the retaining bolts. The balljoint cannot be disassembled. If defective, it must be replaced with a new one.

11 If necessary, the lower link bushing can be removed from the frame

8.8 Location of the lower link nut (arrow)

9.3 Remove the lower shock absorber mounting nut (A) from the spring plate, then remove the four spring plate nuts (B)

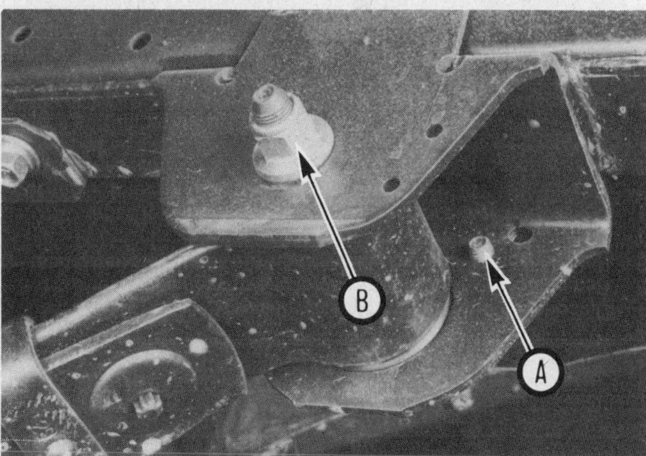

9.7 To remove the front spring pin, remove the locating bolt (A) then the pin nut (B) – push the pin out through the bushing

by tapping it out with a hammer and suitable size socket.

12 Installation is the reverse of the removal procedure. Be sure to tighten all the balljoint to lower link nuts, the balljoint stud to knuckle spindle nuts and the lower link pivot nut to the specified torque.

13 Following installation, lower the vehicle to the ground and check the ride height (refer to Section 5).

14 Have the wheel alignment checked, and adjusted as necessary.

9 Rear leaf spring – removal and installation

Refer to illustrations 9.3, 9.6 and 9.7

1 Raise the each of the vehicle and support it on jackstands.

2 Position a jack under the differential to take the weight of the rear axle.

3 Remove the lower shock absorber nut and disconnect the shock absorber from the spring plate. Remove the U-bolt nuts and lift off the U-bolts and plate **(see illustration)**.

4 On 4WD models, disconnect any parking brake rear cable clamps from the side of the side of the leaf spring being removed.

5 On 2WD models, raise the rear axle away from the leaf spring. On 4WD models, the rear axle must be lowered from the spring. In either case, be sure the axle is suitably balanced on the jack.

6 Remove the lower nut and loosen the upper nut from the rear spring shackle **(see illustration)**. Carefully drive out the lower bolt to free the rear end of the spring.

7 Remove the pin at the front end of the spring to permit the spring

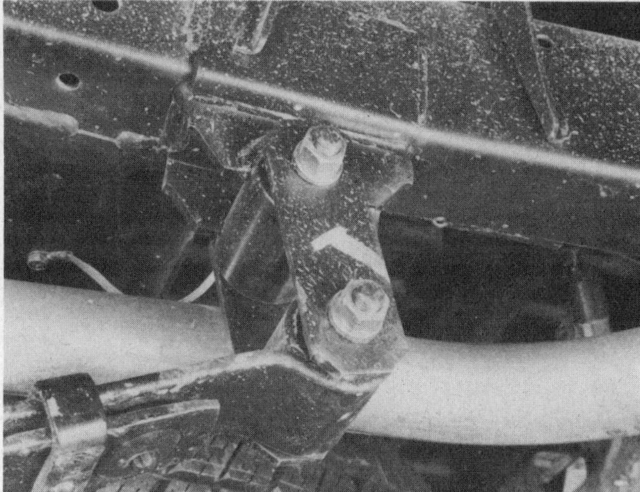

9.6 Loosen the upper shackle nut and remove the lower nut, then drive the lower bolt out of the shackle with a hammer and punch

to be removed **(see illustration)**.

8 Examine the spring for broken or distorted leaves; if any are found a replacement spring must be obtained. If the rubber bushings are damaged, they can be pressed out with a drift and spacer between the jaws of a vise. Coat new ones with a soap and water solution to simplify installation.

9 Installation of the spring is the reverse of the removal procedure, but ensure that the weight of the vehicle is on the wheels before the front pin nut, shackle nuts and shock absorber mounts are properly tightened.

10 Rear coil spring – removal and installation

Refer to illustrations 10.3 and 10.6

1 Raise the rear of the vehicle and support it securely on jackstands placed under the frame rails.

2 Support the rear axle with a floor jack placed under the differential.

3 Remove the lower shock absorber mounting nuts and slide the shock off the mounting pin **(see illustration on next page)**.

4 Lower the rear axle slowly, until the coil springs are fully extended.

5 Remove the coil spring and spring seats from the vehicle. Check the seats for cracking, hardness or other signs of deterioration and replace as necessary.

6 Installation is the reverse of the removal procedure. When installing the spring and the lower spring seat, make sure the direction marks face to the rear of the vehicle **(see illustration)**. Also, do not tighten the lower shock absorber mounting nuts until the vehicle is lowered to the ground.

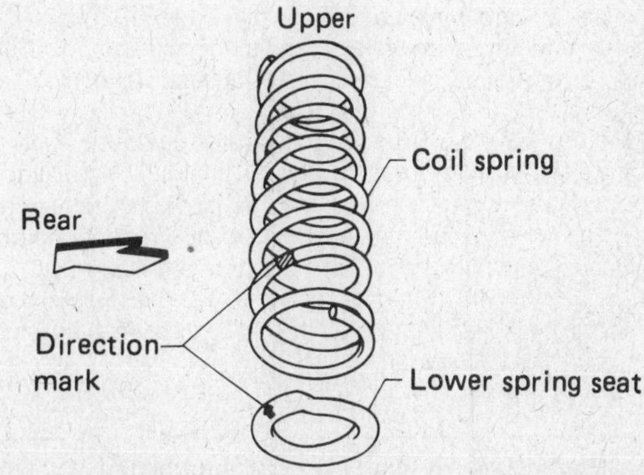

10.6 The tape on the spring and the directional mark on the lower spring seat must face toward the rear of the vehicle when installed

11

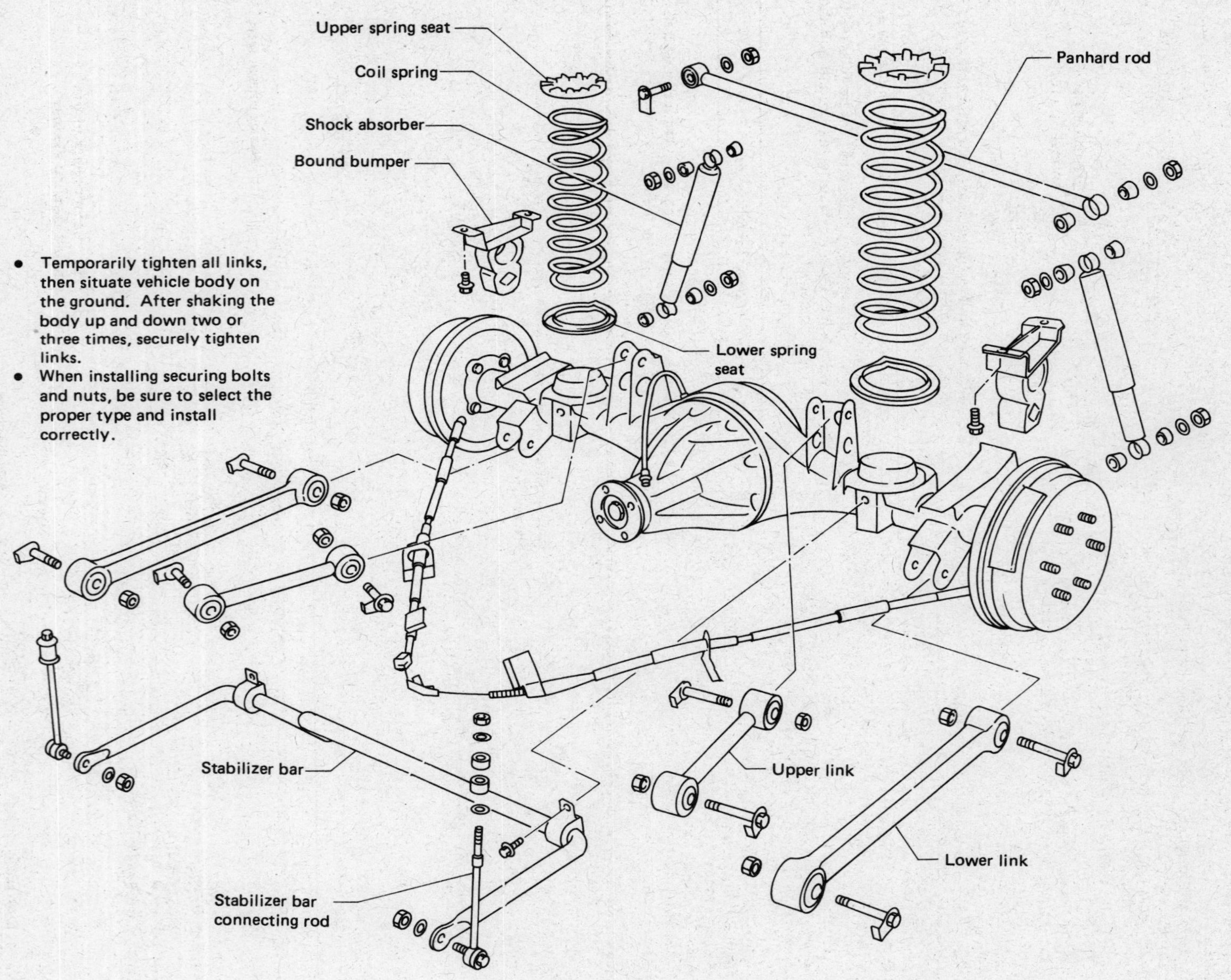

- Temporarily tighten all links, then situate vehicle body on the ground. After shaking the body up and down two or three times, securely tighten links.
- When installing securing bolts and nuts, be sure to select the proper type and install correctly.

10.3 Coil spring and rear suspension locating link components — exploded view

11 Rear suspension locating links – removal and installation

Note: *This procedure applies to the upper and lower links and the panhard rod. Remove only one link at a time unless removing the entire rear axle assembly.*

1 Raise the vehicle and support it securely on jackstands positioned beneath the frame rails.
2 Support the rear axle with a floor jack placed under the differential.
3 Remove the nuts from the ends of the link, then drive out the bolt through the bushing and bracket, if necessary. Remove the link from the vehicle.
4 Installation is the reverse of the removal procedure. Do not tighten the link nuts fully until the vehicle is lowered and resting at normal ride height.

12 Rear stabilizer bar – removal and installation

Refer to illustration 12.2

1 Raise the rear of the vehicle and support it on jackstands.
2 Remove the upper nuts from both of the stabilizer connecting rods located at each end of the stabilizer bar. Hold the connecting rod with a wrench to keep it from twisting **(see illustration)**.
3 Remove the rods from the bar and lower links, being sure to keep the bushings, washers and spacers in their installed order.
4 Remove the bolts that attach the stabilizer bar brackets to the rear axle case and lower the bar from the vehicle.
5 If the stabilizer bar bushings need to be replaced, simply spread them apart and slide them off the bar.
6 Inspect the stabilizer connecting rod bushings for cracking or any other damage and replace them as necessary.
7 Installation is the reverse of removal, with the following notes:

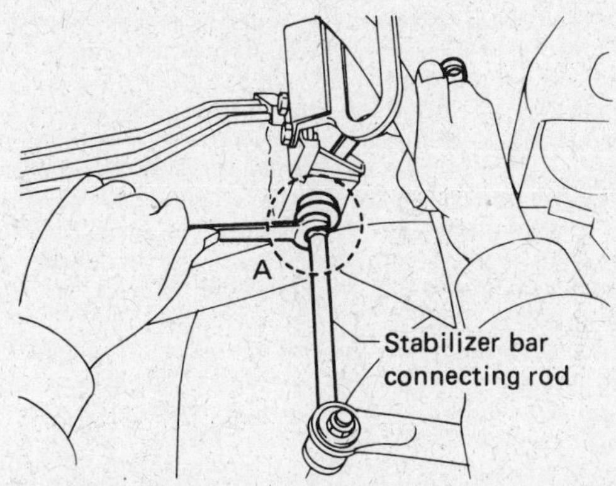

12.2 When removing the stabilizer bar connecting rod nut, hold it with a wrench to avoid twisting it

a) The connecting rod components should be installed in their original order and positions.
b) The stabilizer bar mounting bolts should not be fully tightened until the vehicle has been lowered to the ground and the full weight is on the wheels.

13 Steering system – general information

Refer to illustrations 13.1a and 13.1b

The steering system is of the worm and nut recirculating ball type. The components that make up the manual system are the steering

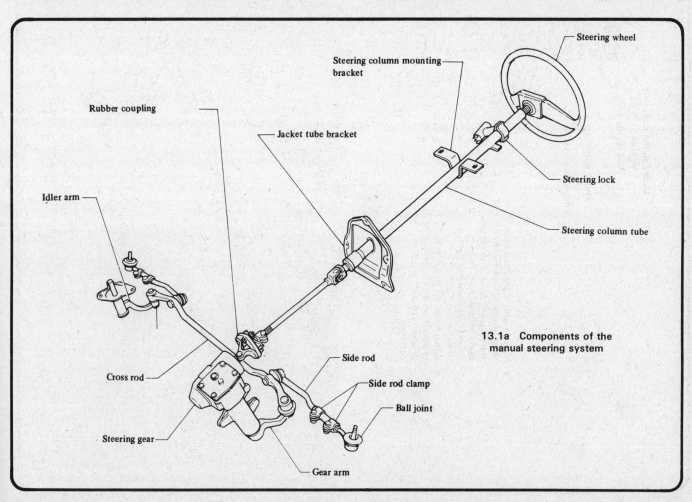

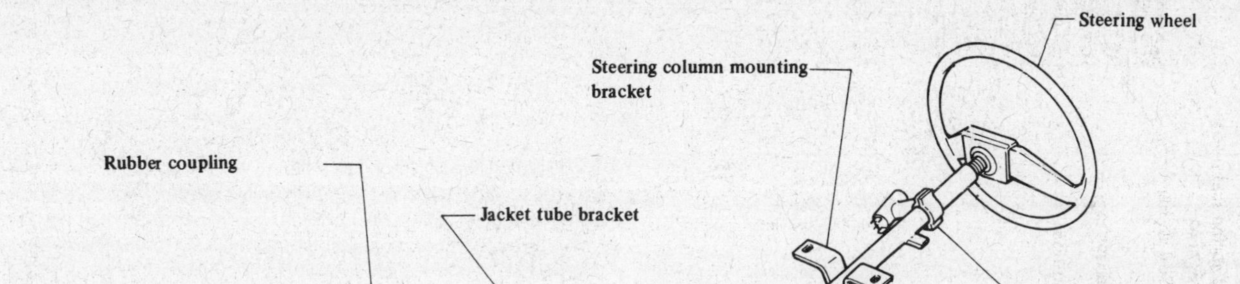

13.1a Components of the manual steering system

wheel, steering column, steering gear (steering box), and steering linkage assembly **(see illustrations)**. In addition to these the power steering system also uses a belt-driven oil pump with integrated reservoir tank to provide hydraulic pressure.

In a manual system, the motion of turning the steering wheel is transferred through the column to the wormshaft of the steering gear. Installed on the wormshaft is a free moving ball nut. Gear teeth on the ball nut are meshed with the teeth on the steering gear's sector shaft, which is directly connected to the linkage. It is through this ball nut and sector shaft that the circular motion of the steering wheel gets changed to the right and left of the linkage, and, in turn, the front wheels.

The power steering system operates in essentially the same way as the manual system except that the power steering gear assembly uses hydraulic pressure to boost the manual steering force.

If the power steering system loses its hydraulic pressure it will still function manually, though with increased effort.

The steering column is of the collapsible, energy-absorbing type, designed to compress in the event of a front end collision to minimize injury to the driver. The column also houses the ignition switch, steering column lock, headlight switch, turn signal control, headlight dimmer switch and windshield wiper control. On most models, the ignition and steering wheel can both be locked while the vehicle is parked to inhibit theft.

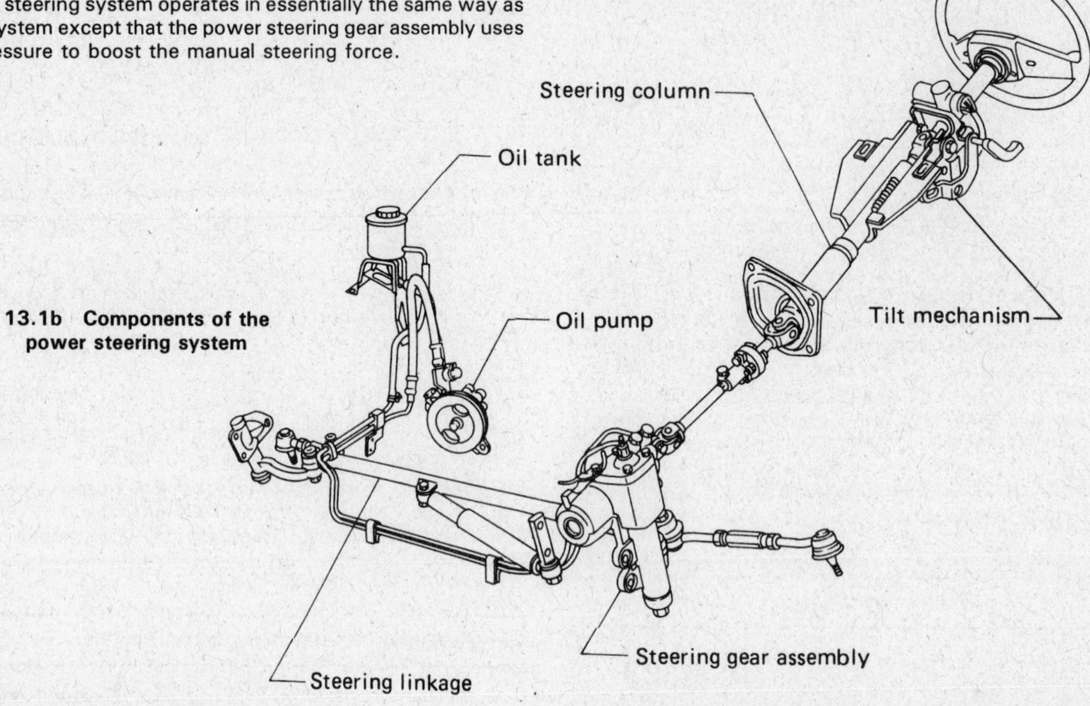

13.1b Components of the power steering system

14 Steering wheel – removal and installation

Refer to illustrations 14.3, 14.5, 14.6 and 14.7

Warning: *1996 models are equipped with a driver side airbag in the center of the steering wheel. Always disconnect the negative battery cable, then the positive battery cable and wait 10 minutes before working in the vicinity of the impact sensors, steering column or instrument panel to avoid the possibility of accidental deployment of the airbag, which could cause personal injury.*

1 Disconnect the negative battery cable from the battery.

2 On models so equipped, have the airbag disabled or removed from the steering wheel by an automotive repair facility or dealer service department.

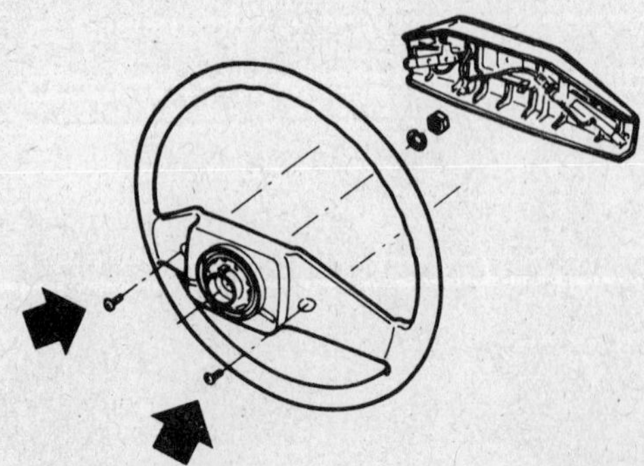

14.3 The horn pad on later models is retained with two screws

3 Grab the top of the center steering wheel pad and pull it off the steering wheel (early models) or remove the two screws from the back of steering wheel (later models prior to 1994) **(seeillustration)**. On 1994 models, insert a Phillips head screwdriver into the hole on the lower side of the spoke and remove the screw and clamp, then lift off the horn pad.

4 If equipped with a steering lock, be sure the steering wheel is in the unlocked position, and then remove the steering wheel nut.

5 Mark the position of the steering wheel in relation to the steering shaft **(see illustration)**.

14.5 Mark the relationship of the steering wheel to the shaft prior to removal

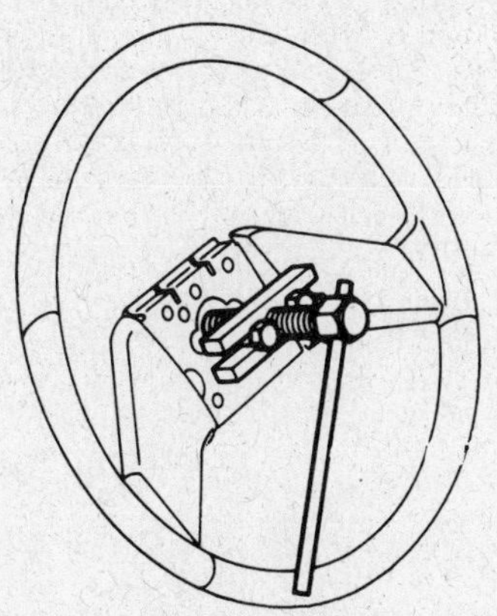

14.6 Use a puller to remove the steering wheel – do not hammer on the shaft!

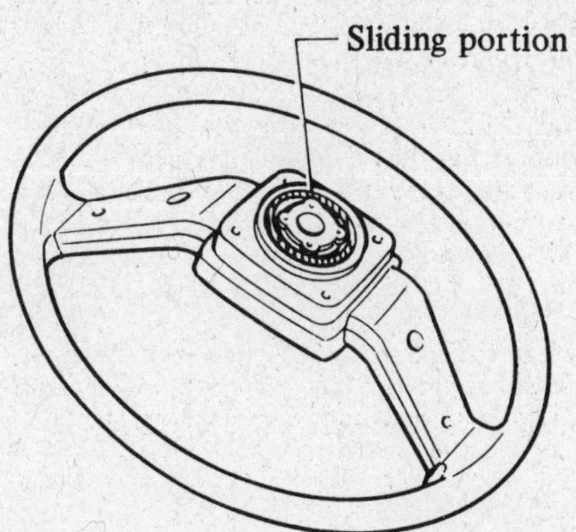

14.7 Prior to installing the steering wheel, a light coat of grease should be applied to the sliding surface of the horn contact

6 Note the two threaded holes in the steering wheel on either side of the shaft. Install an appropriate steering wheel puller into these holes, and remove the steering wheel **(see illustration)**. **Warning:** *Do not, for any reason, hammer on or strike the end of the shaft!*

7 Prior to installation, apply a light coat of grease to the sliding portion on the rear of the steering wheel **(see illustration)**.

8 Installation is the reverse of the removal procedure with the following note: When installing the steering wheel on the shaft be sure the alignment marks on the wheel and shaft match. Tighten the steering wheel nut to the proper torque and turn the wheel to check for drag.

15 Steering lock – removal and installation

Refer to illustration 15.7

Removal

1 Obtain two self-shear screws from your Nissan dealer, needed to reinstall the steering lock.

2 Remove the steering wheel as described in Section 14.

3 Remove the steering column cover.

4 The steering lock is secured to the steering shaft with two regular screws and two self-shear screws. Removing the shear screws will involve very careful drilling of the screws. Start by center punching the center of the screw. Select a drill that is about the diameter of the root of the thread. Very carefully, ensuring that the drill is square to the screw, drill out the center of the screw until a screw extractor can be used to remove the screw.

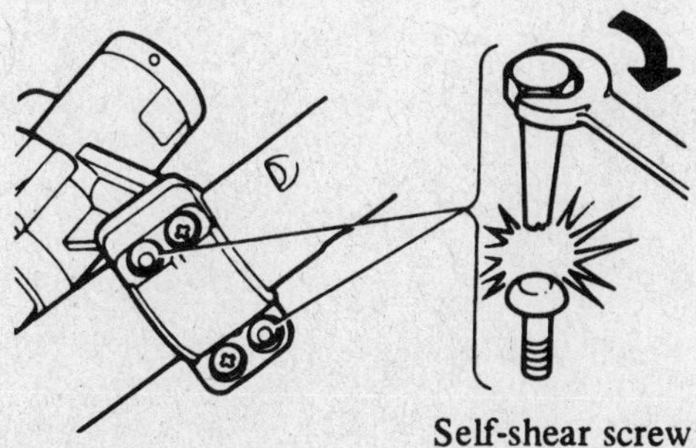

15.7 The self-shear screws are used in the positions shown to retain the steering lock to the column (early style) – later models use only two screws, both of them self-shearing

5 Remove the two regular attaching screws and disengage the steering lock from the shaft. Disconnect the ignition switch wires.

Installation

6 To install, align the mating surface of the steering lock with the hole in the steering column tube. Then loosely install the two regular attaching screws. Once the operation of the lock is checked using the key, these screws can be tightened.

7 Install the two self-shearing screws in their appropriate holes, making sure the top snaps off **(see illustration)**.

8 The remainder of the installation is the reverse of the removal procedure.

16 Steering gear – removal and installation

Refer to illustrations 16.1, 16.2a, 16.2b, 16.3 and 16.5

Removal

1 For clearance, remove the left front wheel and tire. Then either remove the rubber engine compartment side flap or tape it out of the way **(see illustration)**).

16.1 Access to the steering gear is gained by removing the left front wheel and rubber flap

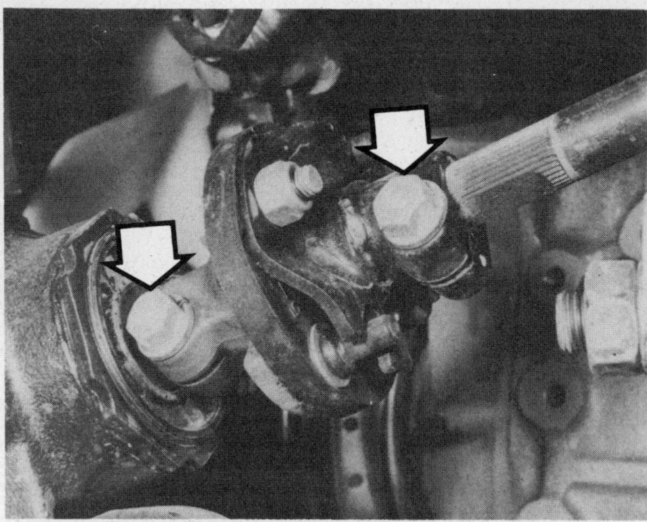

16.2a Location of the pinch bolts (arrows) of the steering column flexible coupling (manual steering models)

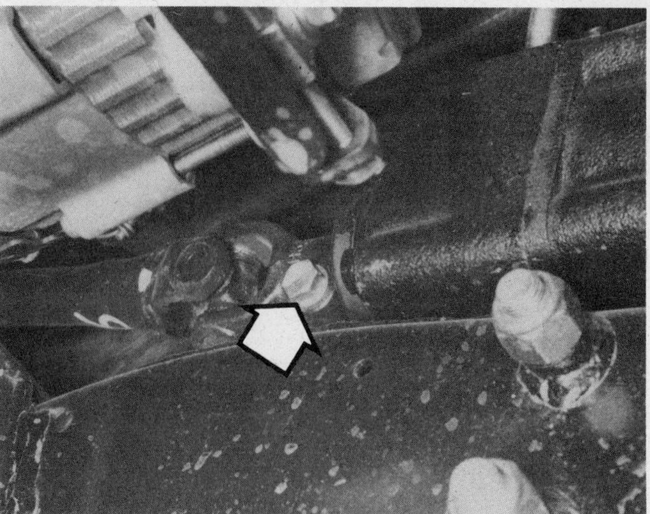

16.2b Location of the lower joint-to-steering gear pinch bolt (arrow) (power steering models)

2 Unscrew and remove the pinch bolt from the flexible coupling (early models) or remove the pinch bolt from the lower joint (later models) **(see illustrations)**.

3 Mark the relationship of the gear arm to the steering gear sector shaft. Unscrew the nut from the bottom of the steering sector shaft, remove the washer and then using a heavy duty puller, remove the gear arm **(see illustration)**.

4 On power steering models, place a suitable drain pan under the steering box hose connections, disconnect the hoses and allow the oil to drain from the hoses and steering box into the pan. Plug the open ends of the hoses and the open ports at the steering box.

5 Remove the steering gear mounting bolts and withdraw the gear out the left side **(see illustration)**.

Installation

6 Installation is a reversal of removal but observe the following points:

a) Before installing the pinch bolt that secures the coupling to the worm shaft, be sure the front wheels are in the straight- ahead position. Also be sure the steering wheel is properly positioned. The groove in the wormshaft should be aligned with the pinch bolt hole in the flexible coupling, and the pinch bolt should pass easily through. Tighten the mounting bolts and pinch bolts to the specified torque.

b) When installing the gear arm to the sector shaft make sure that the four master splines and grooves are aligned. Tighten the nut to the specified torque.

c) On power steering models, when installation is complete refill the oil pump reservoir with new oil of the correct grade and quantity. Bleed the air from the system as described in Section 20.

16.5 The steering gear mounting bolt nuts (arrows) are located on the inside of the left frame rail

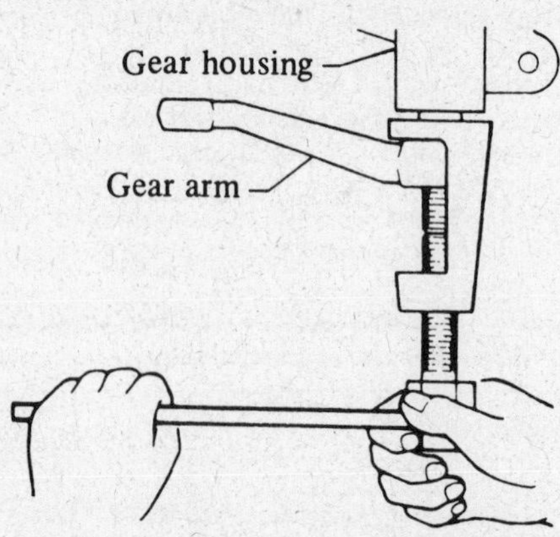

16.3 A puller should be used to separate the gear arm from the steering gear sector shaft

17 Steering gear (manual system) – overhaul

Refer to illustrations 17.2, 17.5, 17.6, 17.18, 17.20, 17.22 and 17.27

1 With the steering gear removed from the vehicle, unscrew the filler plug and drain the oil.

2 Release the locknut on the sector shaft adjuster screw and then extract the bolts which hold the sector shaft cover in position **(see illustration)**.

3 Turn the adjuster screw clockwise to wind it out of the cover and then remove the cover.

4 Withdraw the sector shaft and disengage the adjusting screw from it.

5 Using a special tool available from your Nissan dealer, remove the adjusting plug locknut **(see illustration)**.

6 Withdraw the worm gear assembly, complete with adjusting plug **(see illustration)**. **Note:** *Do not allow the ball nut to run down to either end of the worm or the ends of the ball guides may be damaged. If worn or damaged, the ball nut and worm must be replaced as an assembly.*

7 Do not attempt to remove the sector shaft needle bearings. If they are worn, the complete gear casing must be replaced.

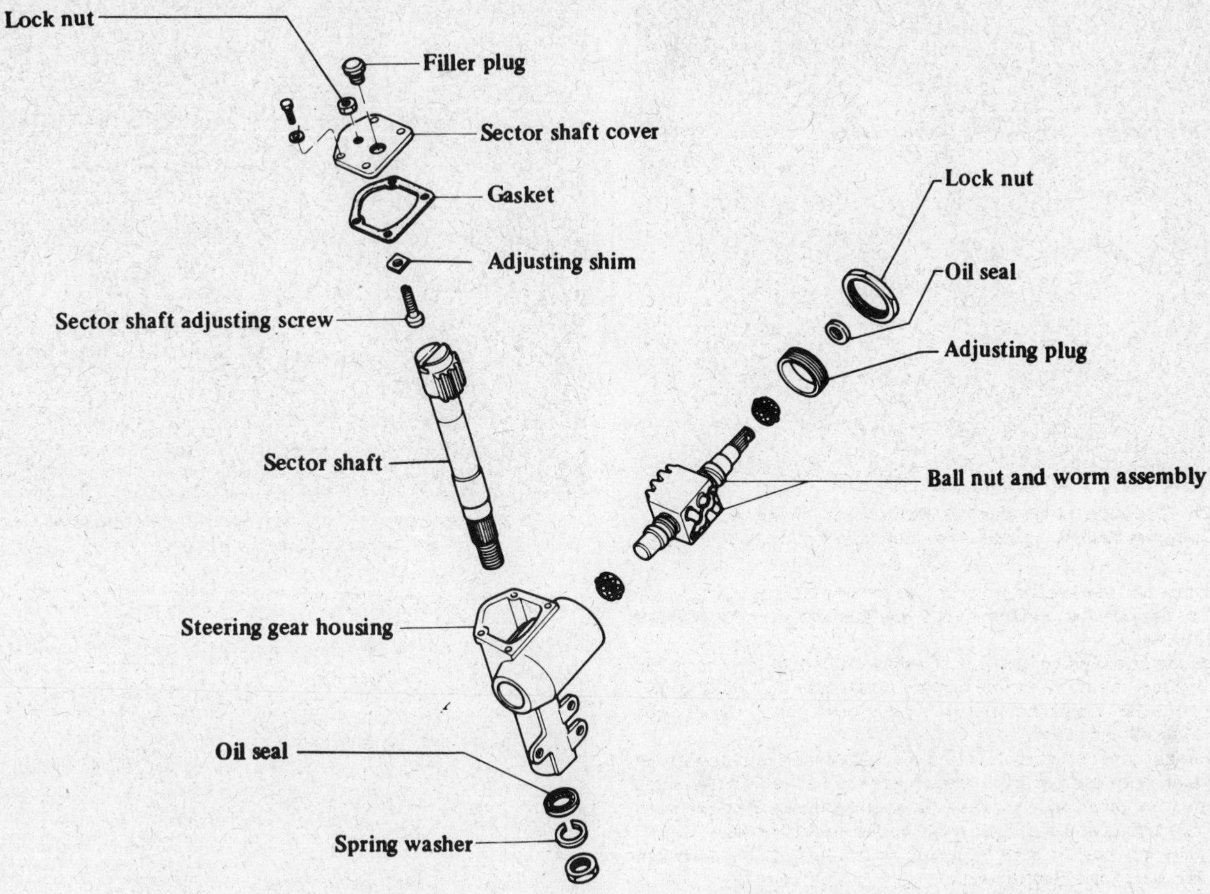

Lock nut
Filler plug
Sector shaft cover
Gasket
Adjusting shim
Sector shaft adjusting screw
Sector shaft
Steering gear housing
Oil seal
Spring washer
Lock nut
Oil seal
Adjusting plug
Ball nut and worm assembly

17.2 Components of the steering gear assembly (manual system) – exploded view

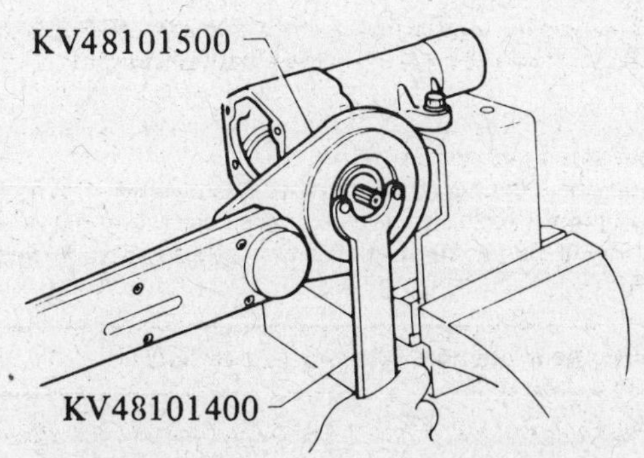

17.5 The adjusting plug and nut are most easily removed and installed with Nissan special tools

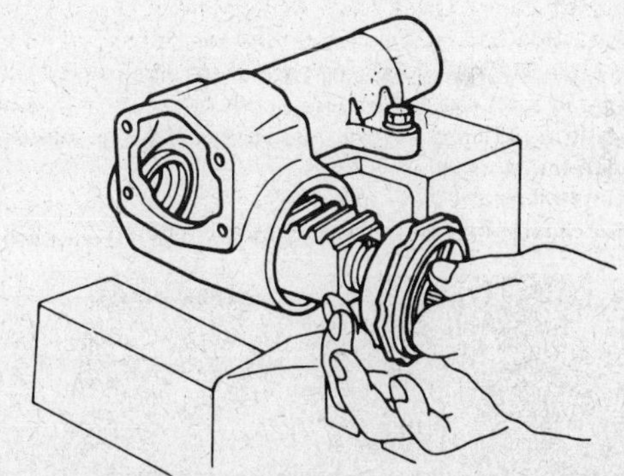

17.6 The worm gear should be removed and installed with the adjusting plug mounted on the shaft

8 Separate the adjusting plug from the worm assembly. Tap out the oil seal from the adjusting plug using an appropriate sized socket.
9 Pry out the oil seal from the bottom of the steering gear housing.
10 Wash all of the parts in clean solvent.
11 Carefully inspect the gear teeth on the sector shaft for any pitting, burrs, cracks or other damage.
12 Inspect the sector shaft splines for damage or distortion, replace the sector shaft if necessary.
13 Inspect the gear teeth of the ball nut and worm assembly for pitting, burrs, wear or other damage. Check also, that the ball nut rotates freely and smoothly on the worm gear. Check this by moving the ball nut to one end of the worm gear. Hold the worm gear upright until the ball nut moves down under its own weight. If the ball nut does not move freely over the entire stroke, replace the assembly. **Note:** *Be careful that you do not allow the ball nut to run down to the extreme ends of the worm gear teeth.*
14 Check that the worm bearing moves freely without any binding or noise. If necessary, replace the bearing and the outer race as a set.
15 During installation, lubricate all parts with oil prior to installing them. Also, use all new oil seals, installed so that the lettering on them is visible when viewed from the outside. Fill in the space between the seal lips with multi-purpose grease.
16 Install a new oil seal in the adjusting plug.
17 Install the adjusting plug onto the worm gear and install the assembly into the housing. Start the adjusting plug into its mating threads in the housing.

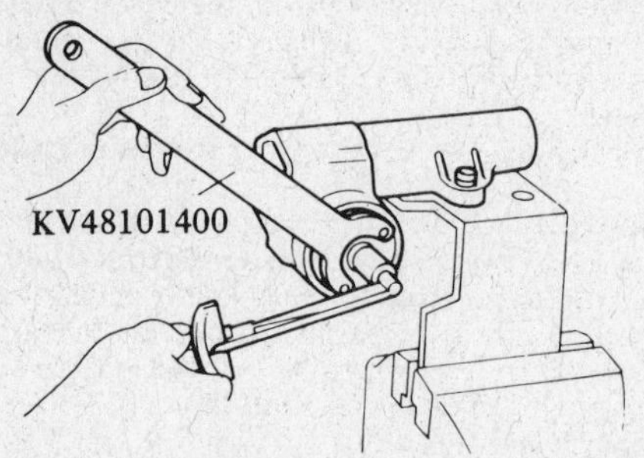

17.18 Measuring and adjusting the worm bearing preload

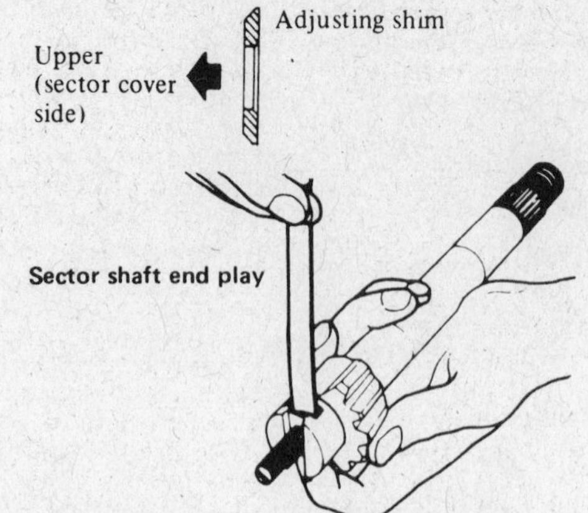

17.20 Feeler gauges can be used to measure the clearance between the adjusting screw and the sector shaft

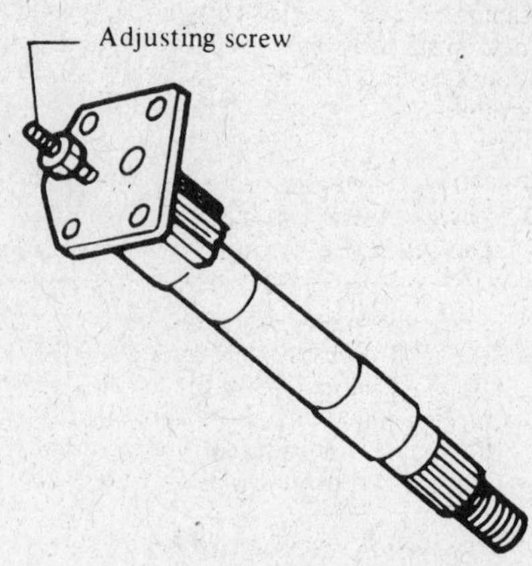

17.22 The sector cover adjusting screw and nut should be installed on the sector shaft prior to installing it in the steering gear housing

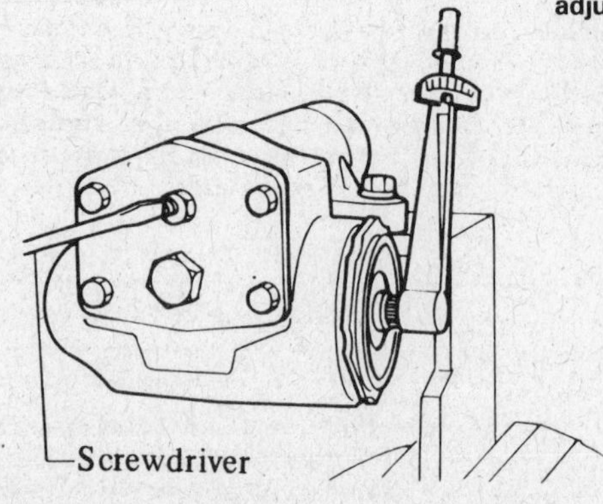

17.27 Turn the wormshaft with a torque wrench while turning the adjusting screw with a screwdriver – tighten the locknut when the force required to turn the wormshaft equals the desired preload

18 The worm bearing preload should now be adjusted. To do this, an adjusting plug tool and an in-lb torque wrench will be needed **(see illustration)**. Tighten the adjusting plug a little at a time until the torque required to start the worm rotating is as listed in the Specifications. To measure the torque, first turn the worm shaft a few turns in either direction to settle the bearings, then use the torque wrench. To get a good grip on the splines of the wormshaft, line an appropriate-sized socket with thin cardboard, and install it over the shaft.
19 Following adjustment of the worm bearing preload, apply a thread sealant to the threads of the adjusting locknut and install it on the adjusting plug. Be sure the plug does not turn while tightening the locknut, and afterwards recheck the worm bearing preload to ensure it is still within specs.
20 Insert the adjusting screw into the T-shaped groove in the end of the sector shaft. Using a feeler gauge, check the play between the bottom of the groove and the lower face of the adjusting screw **(see illustration)**. Use shims if necessary to provide the desired end play listed in the Specifications. Shims are available in several thicknesses; see the Specifications.
21 Install a new oil seal into the bottom of the gear housing.
22 Install the sector cover onto the sector shaft by turning the adjusting screw counterclockwise **(see illustration)**. Then loosely install the locknut onto the adjusting screw.
23 Coat both sides of a new sector cover gasket with gasket sealant and place it in position on the inside of the cover by passing it over the sector shaft.
24 Turn the wormshaft by hand until the ball nut is in the center of its travel, then install the sector shaft complete with adjusting screw. Make sure that the center tooth of the sector shaft engages with the center groove of the nut. Take great care not to cut or damage the lips of the oil seals during these operations.
25 Install the four sector cover bolts, and tighten them to the specified torque.
26 Pour the recommended amount of gear oil (see Specifications Section) into the steering gear, and install the filler plug.
27 Using an in-lb torque wrench on the wormshaft, as before, measure the steering gear preload, and adjust as necessary by turning the adjusting screw in the sector cover **(see illustration)**. The proper torque to start the worm shaft rotating should be as listed in the Specifications. As before, when measuring the torque, first rotate the wormshaft a few turns in both directions to settle the steering gear, then measure the preload with the steering gear in the straight-ahead position.
28 When the preload has been set, tighten the locknut, making sure the adjusting screw does not turn. Recheck the preload one last time to be sure it is still within specifications.

18 Power steering system – maintenance and adjustment

1 The hydraulic components used in the power steering system include a belt-driven oil pump with integrated reservoir tank, power steering gear assembly and connecting hoses and lines.
2 Normal maintenance of the power steering system consists mainly of periodically checking the fluid level in the reservoir, keeping the pump drivebelt tension correct and visually checking the hoses of any evidence of fluid leakage. It will also be necessary, after a system component has been removed, to bleed the system as described in Section 20.
3 If the operational characteristics of the system appear to be suspect, and the maintenance and adjustment mentioned in this Section is order, the vehicle should be taken to a Nissan dealer, who will have the necessary equipment to check the pressure in the system and the operational torque needed to turn the steering wheel. These two operations are considered beyond the scope of the home mechanic, in view of the high working pressure of the system and the special tools required.
4 If the checks mentioned in Step 2 prove that either the oil pump assembly or the steering gear assembly is at fault, a new or rebuilt pump or steering gear assembly will have to be purchased as it is not possible to overhaul them.
5 If there are oil leaks from the power steering gear assembly, individual oil seals can be replaced without replacing the entire assembly. But, once again, due to the critical nature of the assembly, this job should be done by a Nissan dealer or other qualified repair shop.
6 Drivebelt tension is adjusted by loosening the idler pulley locknut and turning the adjustment bolt as necessary. Refer to Chapter 1 for the proper procedure.
7 Excluding the oil pump, power steering gear and its associated

pressure hoses, the rest of the steering system components are identical to those used on the manual steering models. Servicing these components can be carried out by following the operations described in the relevant Sections of this Chapter.

19 Power steering pump and reservoir – removal and installation

1 If the power steering oil pump is found to be defective, both the oil pump and the reservoir tank should be replaced together.
2 Loosen the locknut on the idler pulley and turn the belt adjusting bolt counterclockwise to loosen the belt.
3 Remove the drivebelt from the power steering pump.
4 Loosen, but do not remove the hoses where they attach to the pump.
5 Remove the pump and reservoir tank mounting bolts and lift these components up as much as the hoses will allow. Place them in a shallow drain pan and disconnect the hoses, allowing the oil to drain into the pan.
6 Securely plug the ends of the hoses to prevent oil loss or dirt from entering the hose system.
7 If necessary, the drive pulley can be removed by unscrewing the retaining nut, and using a standard puller to withdraw the pulley from the shaft.
8 Installation of the oil pump assembly is a reversal of removal but before tightening the mounting bolts ensure that the correct drivebelt tension exists, as described in Chapter 1.
9 Once installation is complete, refill the pump reservoir with the correct grade and quantity of oil. If necessary, bleed the system as described in Section 20.

20 Power steering system – bleeding

Note: *Whenever a hose in the power steering hydraulic system has been disconnected, it is quite probable, no matter how much care was taken to prevent air from entering the system, that the system will need bleeding. To do this, proceed as described in the following paragraphs.*

1 First, ensure that the reservoir level is correct; if necessary, add fluid to bring the level to the mark on the dipstick. If necessary, refer to Chapter 1. If the vehicle has not just been driven, the power steering fluid should be brought up to operating temperature. This can be done by idling the engine and turning the steering wheel from left to right for about two minutes.
2 Raise the front end of the vehicle until the front wheels are just clear of the ground.
3 Quickly turn the steering wheel all the way to the right lock and then the left lock. Do not allow the lock stoppers to be struck with a bang. Try to gauge the end of the lock and only lightly touch the lock stoppers. This operation should be repeated about ten times.
4 Now check the reservoir fluid level again, as detailed in Step 1.
5 Start the engine and allow it to idle for a short time. Then stop it and check the fluid again.
6 Run the engine again for three to five seconds, then stop it and check the fluid level. Finally, turn the wheel lock-to-lock once more about ten times, and recheck the fluid level.
7 If the air bleeding is insufficient, the oil reservoir will be extremely foamy and the pump will be noisy. In this case, allow the foam in the reservoir to disperse, recheck the level again and repeat the entire bleeding process.
8 If it becomes obvious, after several attempts, that the system cannot be satisfactorily bled, there is quite probably a leak in the system. Have an assistant turn the wheel lock-to-lock a few times and then hold it for about five seconds at each stop. **Note:** *Do not hold the wheel at full lock for more than fifteen seconds at a time. Visually check the hoses and their connections for leaks. If no leaks are evident, the problem could be in the steering box itself and the only solution is to have the entire system checked by a Nissan dealer.*

21 Steering linkage – removal and installation

Refer to illustrations 21.2, 21.4, 21.5, 21.8, 21.10 and 21.12

1 The steering linkage is basically a system of rods that is designed to transmit the steering motion in the steering gear to the front wheels.
2 Included in this system is a cross rod, an idler arm, a gear arm and two side rods with inner and outer balljoints. The gear arm connects the steering gear to one end of the cross rod. The other end of the cross rod is connected to the idler arm, which is in turn bolted directly to the body. Each end of the cross rod is also connected to the front wheels by way of the side rods **(see illustration)**.

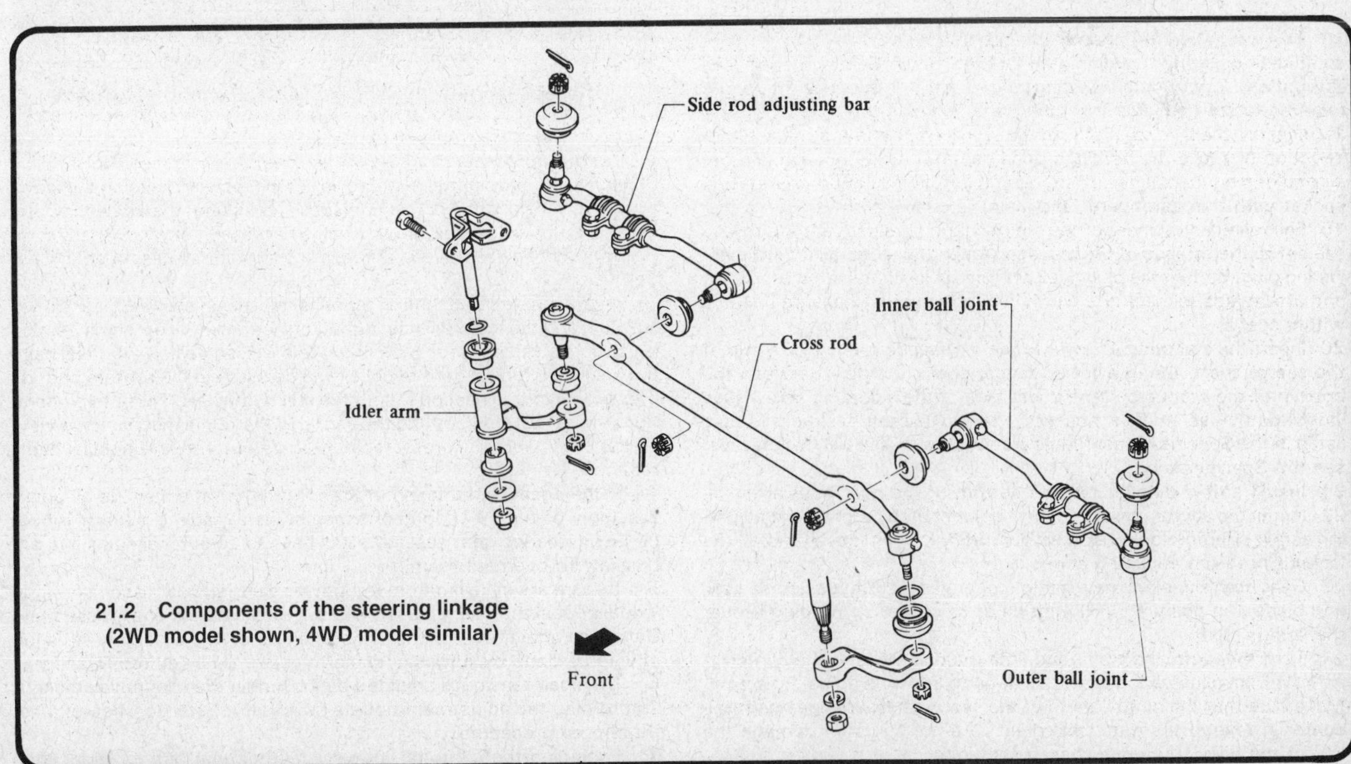

21.2 Components of the steering linkage (2WD model shown, 4WD model similar)

11

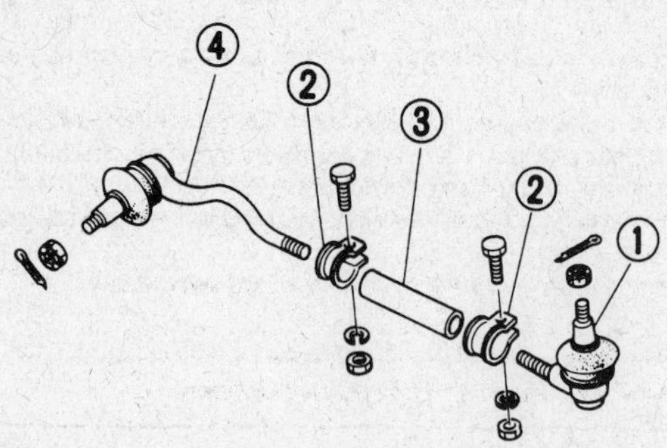

21.4 Exploded view of the side rod assembly components

1 Outer side rod assembly
2 Side rod clamp
3 Side rod adjusting tube
4 Inner side rod assembly

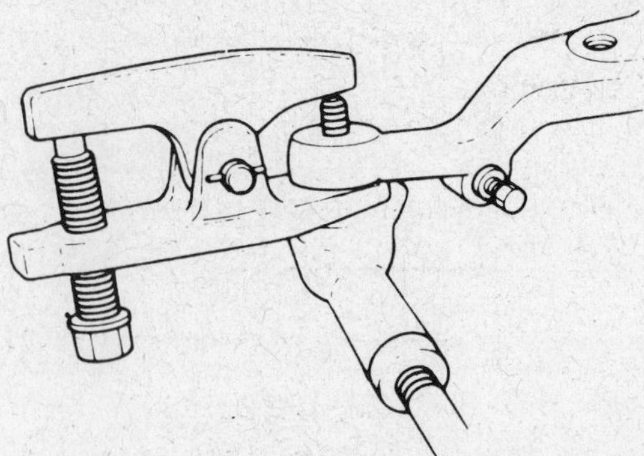

21.5 A special separator tool can be used to separate the ball stud from the knuckle arm – a two-jaw puller will also work

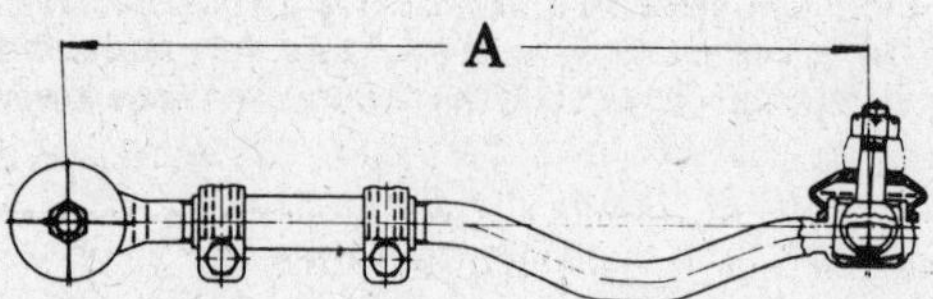

21.8 Standard adjustment of the side rods. Refer to the Specifications for the correct setting

21.10 Location of the idler arm assembly on the right side frame member

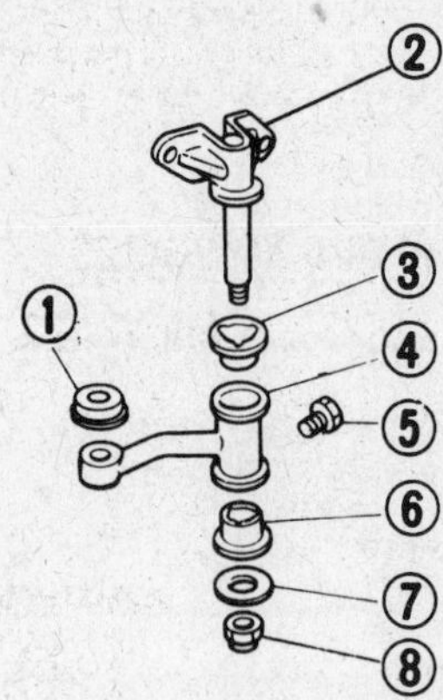

21.12 Components of the idler arm assembly

1 Dust cover
2 Idler bracket
3 Idler arm bushing
4 Idler arm
5 Filler plug
6 Idler arm bushing
7 Washer
8 Nut

3 The components of the steering linkage can be removed as a whole. Following any dismantling of the steering linkage, the front end alignment should be checked and adjusted, if necessary **Note:** *For each of the following procedures, the front of the vehicle should be raised and supported on jackstands. Following reinstallation of the components all nuts that are coupled with bushings should be left only finger-tight until after the vehicle has been lowered to the ground. Only when the full weight is on the wheels should these nuts be tightened to their specified torque.*

Side rod

4 Remove the cotter pins and locknuts on both ends of the side rod **(see illustration)**.

5 Using a special separator tool **(see illustration)** or a two-jaw puller, disengage the side rod from the knuckle arm and cross rod and lift it out.

6 Inspect the balljoint ends for excessive play or looseness and replace them if necessary.

7 If the side rod needs to be disassembled, first mark the points of adjustment by applying a dab of white paint on the adjusting clamps and center tube. Then loosen the adjusting bolts and unscrew the balljoint ends from the center tube.

8 Reassembly and installation is the reverse of the removal procedure. If the old side rod has been disassembled, be sure the adjustment is reset at the marks made during disassembly. If a new side rod is being installed, prior to installation, set the adjustment so the distance between the balljoint ends is as listed in the Specifications **(see illustration)**. Drive the vehicle to an alignment shop to have the alignment checked and, if necessary, adjusted.

Idler arm

9 Play in the idler arm assembly can be remedied by replacing the bushings.

10 Remove the bolts that secure the idler arm to the frame **(see illustration)**.

11 Swing the idler arm around into an accessible position. If the idler arm needs to be removed, remove the cotter pin and locknut that retain it to the cross rod. Then using an appropriate separating tool disengage the idler arm from the cross rod.

12 If only the bushings in the idler arm have to be replaced, first remove

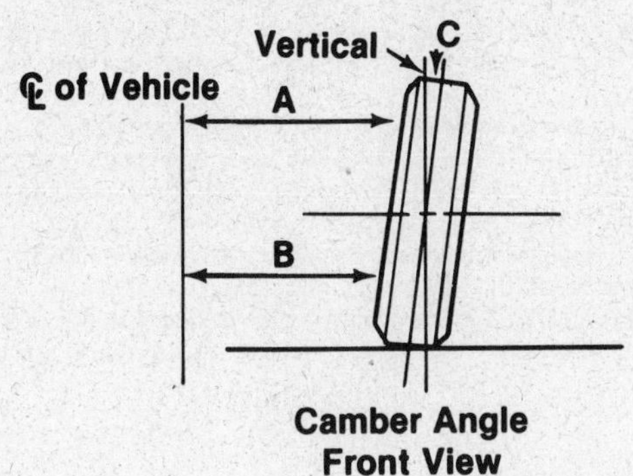

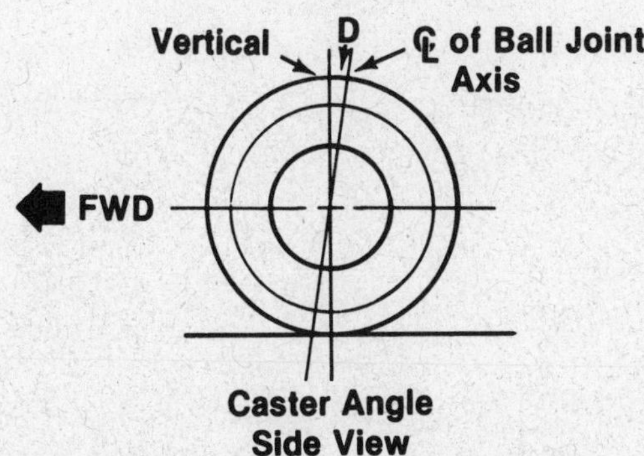

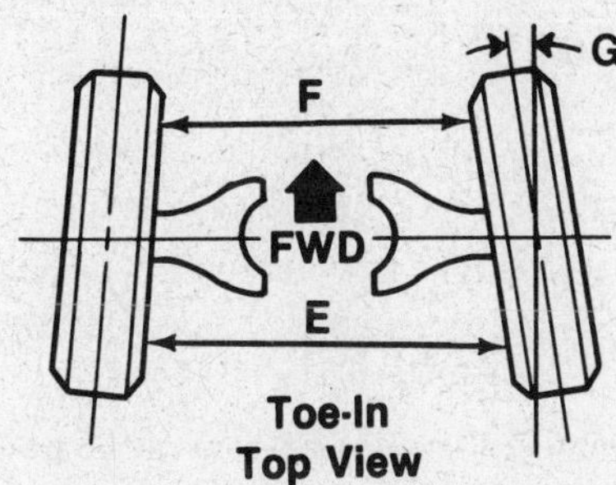

22.1 The three settings involved in a front end alignment are camber (top), caster (center) and toe-in (bottom) — the actual adjustment of these angles is beyond the scope of the home mechanic and must be performed by an alignment shop or service station

the lower nut and washer **(see illustration)**. Then lift the idler arm bracket off and remove the two bushings from it. Install new ones. Reassemble the idler arm.
13 Installation is the reverse of the removal procedure. Be sure to tighten all attaching nuts to the specified torque.

Cross rod

14 Remove the four sets of cotter pins and locknuts that retain the cross rod to the idler arm, gear arm and both side rods.
15 Using an appropriate separating tool, disengage the cross rod from each of these other components, and lift out the cross rod.
16 Inspect the bushings at each end of the rod for hardening or cracking and replace them if necessary.
17 Installation is the reverse of the removal procedure.

Complete linkage

18 To remove the steering linkage as a complete assembly, first remove the nut that retains the gear arm to the steering gear. Using an appropriate puller, disengage the gear arm from the steering gear shaft.
19 Remove the bolts that retain the idler arm to the frame, and lift the idler arm off.
20 Remove the cotter pins and locking nuts that retain the side rods to the steering knuckle arms. Then using an appropriate separating tool, disengage the side rods from the knuckle arms.
21 The entire steering linkage assembly can now be lowered from the vehicle.
22 Installation is the reverse of the removal procedure.

22 Front end alignment – general information

Refer to illustration 22.1

1 A front end alignment refers to the adjustments made to the front wheels so that they are in proper angular relationship to the suspension and the ground. Front wheels that are out of proper alignment not only affect steering control but also increase tire wear. The front end adjustments required on the vehicles covered in this manual are camber, caster and toe-in **(see illustration)**.
2 Getting the proper front wheel alignment is a very exacting process and one in which complicated and expensive machines are necessary to perform the job properly. Because of this, it is advisable to have a specialist with the proper equipment perform these tasks.

23 Wheels and tires – general information

Refer to illustration 23.1

1 All vehicles covered by this manual are equipped with metric-sized fiberglass or steel belted radial tires **(see illustration)**. The use of other size or type tires may affect the ride and handling of the vehicle. Do not mix different types of tires, such as radials and bias belted, on the same vehicle as handling may be seriously affected.
2 It is recommended that tires be replaced in pairs on the same axle, but if only one tire is being replaced, be sure it is of the same size,

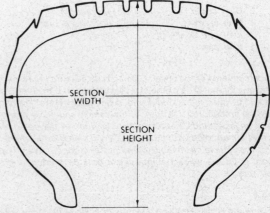

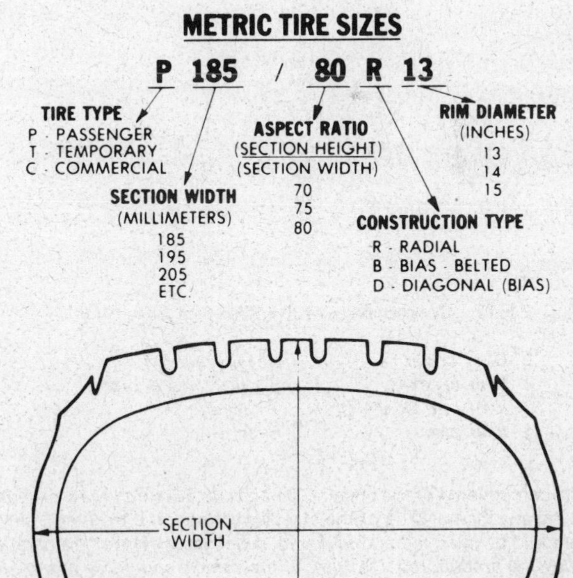

23.1 Metric tire size code

structure and tread design as the other.

3 Because tire pressure has a substantial effect on handling and wear, the pressure on all tires should be checked at least once a month or before any extended trips and set to the correct pressure. Tire pressure should be checked and adjusted with the tires cold (Chapter 1).

4 To achieve the maximum life of your tires they should be rotated at the intervals specified in Chapter 1.

5 Tires should be replaced when the tread is worn out. Correct tire pressures and driving techniques have an important influence on tire life. Heavy cornering, excessively rapid acceleration and sharp breaking increase tire wear. Extremely worn tires are not only very susceptible to going flat but are especially dangerous in wet weather conditions. Refer to Chapter 1 for tire inspection procedures.

6 The tire tread pattern can give a good indication of problems in the maintenance or adjustment of tires, suspension and front end components.

7 Wheels must be replaced if they are bent, dented, leak air, have elongated bolt holes, are heavily rusted, out of vertical symmetry or if the lug nuts won't stay tight. Wheel repairs that use welding or peening are not recommended, as this can weaken the metal.

8 Tire and wheel balance is important in the overall handling,braking and performance of the vehicle. Unbalanced wheels can adversely affect handling and ride characteristics as well as tire life. Whenever a tire is installed on a wheel the tire and wheel should be rebalanced.

Chapter 12 Body

Contents

Specifications

Torque specifications	Ft-lbs
Bumper bracket mounting bolts	
Through 1990	16
1991 and later	26 to 33
Bumper-to-bracket bolts	
Through 1990	16
1991 and later	9 to 12
Hood hinge-to-body bolts	
Through 1990	3.2
1991 and later	4 to 5
Door hinge mounting bolts	14 to 20
Seat mounting bolts	14 to 20
Seat belt anchor bolts	20 to 26
Rear gate hinge mounting bolts	
Through 1990	14
1991 and later	15 to 20
Rear bed mounting bolts	
Through 1990	44
1991 and later	14 to 17
Pathfinder liftgate retaining nut	15 to 20

1 General information

The Nissan 720 series pick-up is available in three basic body styles: the regular bed model (Li'l Hustler), long bed model (which uses the same cab with an extended bed) and the King Cab model (which uses the regular bed with an extended cab). Each of these is available in either the 2WD or 4WD version. In addition, various trim/luxury packages are available with certain models, which include the Deluxe, GL and Sports truck versions.

The Nissan D21 and Pathfinder body styles are similar in layout to the 720 series with the exception that the Pathfinder has a fixed station wagon style rear section.

The pick-up body consists of a separate cab and bed, both of which are bolted to a pressed steel, box-section frame. The only principle frame difference between pick-up models is the length of the regular bed model and the long bed/King Cab models.

Certain body panels which are particularly vulnerable to accident damage can be replaced by unbolting them and installing replacement items. These panels include the fenders, inner fender skirts, grille, front apron, bumpers, hood and rear gate. In addition, whether due to damage or for conversion reasons, the entire rear bed can be easily removed from the frame.

2 Maintenance — body and frame

1 The condition of your vehicle's body is very important, because it is on this that the second hand value will mainly depend. It is much more difficult to repair a neglected or damaged body than it is to repair mechanical components. The hidden areas of the body, such as the fender wells, the frame, and the engine compartment, are equally important, although they obviously do not require as frequent attention as the rest of the body.

2 Once a year, or every 12,000 miles, it's a good idea to have the underside of the body and the frame steam cleaned. All traces of dirt and oil will be removed and the underside can then be inspected care-

fully for rust, damaged brake lines, frayed electrical wiring, damaged cables and other problems. The front suspension components should be greased after completion of this job.
3 At the same time, clean the engine and the engine compartment using either a steam cleaner or a water soluble degreaser.
4 The fender wells should be given particular attention, as undercoating can peel away and stones and dirt thrown up by the tires can cause the paint to chip and flake, allowing rust to set in. If rust is found, clean down to the bare metal and apply an anti-rust paint.
5 The body should be washed as needed. Wet the vehicle thoroughly to soften the dirt, then wash it down with a soft sponge and plenty of clean soapy water. If the surplus dirt is not washed off very carefully, it will in time wear down the paint.
6 Spots of tar or asphalt coating thrown up from the road should be removed with a cloth soaked in solvent.
7 Once every six months, give the body and chrome trim a thorough waxing. If a chrome cleaner is used to remove rust from any of the vehicle's plated parts, remember that the cleaner also removes part of the chrome, so use it sparingly.

3 Maintenance – upholstery and carpets

1 Every three months remove the carpets or mats and clean the interior of the vehicle (more frequently if necessary). Vacuum the upholstery and carpets to remove loose dirt and dust.
2 If the upholstery is soiled, apply upholstery cleaner with a damp sponge and wipe it off with a clean, dry cloth.

4 Body repair – minor damage

See photo sequence

Repair of minor scratches

1 If the scratch is superficial and does not penetrate to the metal of the body, repair is very simple. Lightly rub the scratched area with a fine rubbing compound to remove loose paint and built up wax. Rinse the area with clean water.
2 Apply touch-up paint to the scratch, using a small brush. Continue to apply thin layers of paint until the surface of the paint in the scratch is level with the surrounding paint. Allow the new paint at least two weeks to harden, then blend it into the surrounding paint by rubbing with a very fine rubbing compound. Finally, apply a coat of wax to the scratch area.
3 If the scratch has penetrated the paint and exposed the metal of the body, causing the metal to rust, a different repair technique is required. Remove all loose rust from the bottom of the scratch with a pocket knife, then apply rust inhibiting paint to prevent the formation of rust in the future. Using a rubber or nylon applicator, coat the scratched area with glaze-type filler. If required, the filler can be mixed with thinner to provide a very thin paste, which is ideal for filling narrow scratches. Before the glaze filler in the scratch hardens, wrap a piece of smooth cotton cloth around the tip of a finger. Dip the cloth in thinner and then quickly wipe it along the surface of the scratch. This will ensure that the surface of the filler is slightly hollow. The scratch can now be painted over as described earlier in this section.

Repair of dents

4 When repairing dents, the first job is to pull the dent out until the affected area is as close as possible to its original shape. There is no point in trying to restore the original shape completely as the metal in the damaged area will have stretched on impact and cannot be restored to its original contours. It is better to bring the level of the dent up to a point which is about 1/8-inch below the level of the surrounding metal. In cases where the dent is very shallow, it is not worth trying to pull it out at all.
5 If the back side of the dent is accessible, it can be hammered out gently from behind using a soft-face hammer. While doing this, hold a block of wood firmly against the opposite side of the metal to absorb the hammer blows and prevent the metal from being stretched.
6 If the dent is in a section of the body which has double layers, or some other factor makes it inaccessible from behind, a different technique is required. Drill several small holes through the metal inside the damaged area, particularly in the deeper sections. Screw long, self tapping screws into the holes just enough for them to get a good grip in the metal. Now the dent can be pulled out by pulling on the protruding heads of the screws with locking pliers.
7 The next stage of repair is the removal of paint from the damaged area and from an inch or so of the surrounding metal. This is easily done with a wire brush or sanding disk in a drill motor, although it can be done just as effectively by hand with sandpaper. To complete the preparation for filling, score the surface of the bare metal with a screwdriver or the tang of a file or drill small holes in the affected area. This will provide a good grip for the filler material. To complete the repair, see the Section on filling and painting.

Repair of rust holes or gashes

8 Remove all paint from the affected area and from an inch or so of the surrounding metal using a sanding disk or wire brush mounted in a drill motor. If these are not available, a few sheets of sandpaper will do the job just as effectively.
9 With the paint removed, you will be able to determine the severity of the corrosion and decide whether to replace the whole panel, if possible, or repair the affected area. New body panels are not as expensive as most people think and it is often quicker to install a new panel than to repair large areas of rust.
10 Remove all trim pieces from the affected area except those which will act as a guide to the original shape of the damaged body, such as headlight shells, etc. Using metal snips or a hacksaw blade, remove all loose metal and any other metal that is badly affected by rust. Hammer the edges of the hole inward to create a slight depression for the filler material.
11 Wire brush the affected area to remove the powdery rust from the surface of the metal. If the back of the rusted area is accessible, treat it with rust-inhibiting paint.
12 Before filling is done, block the hole in some way. This can be done with sheet metal riveted or screwed into place, or by stuffing the hole with wire mesh.
13 Once the hole is blocked off, the affected area can be filled and painted. See the following sub-section on filling and painting.

Filling and painting

14 Many types of body fillers are available, but generally speaking, body repair kits which contain filler paste and a tube of resin hardener are best for this type of repair work. A wide, flexible plastic or nylon applicator will be necessary for imparting a smooth and contoured finish to the surface of the filler material. Mix up a small amount of filler on a clean piece of wood or cardboard (use the hardener sparingly). Follow the manufacturer's instructions on the package, otherwise the filler will set incorrectly.
15 Using the applicator, apply the filler paste to the prepared area. Draw the applicator across the surface of the filler to achieve the desired contour and to level the filler surface. As soon as a contour that approximates the original one is achieved, stop working the paste. If you continue, the paste will begin to stick to the applicator. Continue to add thin layers of paste at 20-minute intervals until the level of the filler is just above the surrounding metal.
16 Once the filler has hardened, the excess can be removed with a body file. From then on, progressively finer grades of sandpaper should be used, starting with a 180-grit paper and finishing with 600-grit wet-or-dry paper. Always wrap the sandpaper around a flat rubber or wooden block, otherwise the surface of the filler will not be completely flat. During the sanding of the filler surface, the wet-or-dry paper should be periodically rinsed in water. This will ensure that a very smooth finish is produced in the final stage.
17 At this point, the repair area should be surrounded by a ring of bare metal, which in turn should be encircled by the finely feathered edge of good paint. Rinse the repair area with clean water until all of the dust produced by the sanding operation is gone.
18 Spray the entire area with a light coat of primer. This will reveal any imperfections in the surface of the filler. Repair the imperfections with fresh filler paste or glaze filler and once more smooth the surface with sandpaper. Repeat this spray-and-repair procedure until you are satisfied that the surface of the filler and the feathered edge of the paint are perfect. Rinse the area with clean water and allow it to dry completely.
19 The repair area is now ready for painting. Spray painting must be carried out in a warm, dry, windless and dust free atmosphere. These conditions can be created if you have access to a large indoor work

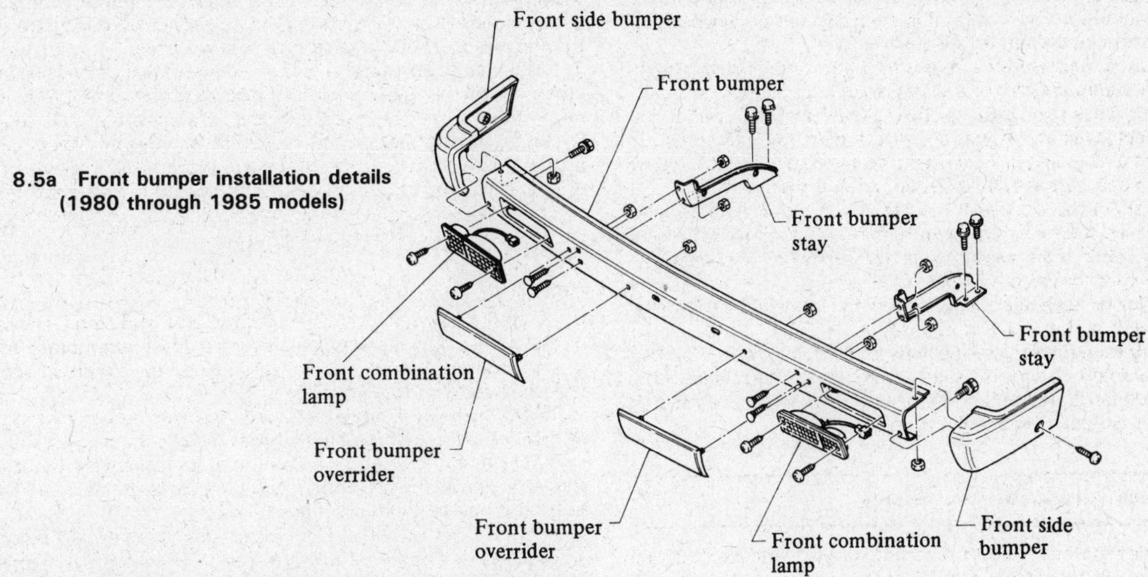

8.5a Front bumper installation details (1980 through 1985 models)

area, but if you are forced to work in the open, you will have to pick the day very carefully. If you are working indoors, dousing the floor in the work area with water will help settle the dust which would otherwise be in the air. If the repair area is confined to one body panel, mask off the surrounding panels. This will help minimize the effects of a slight mismatch in paint color. Trim pieces such as chrome strips, door handles, etc., will also need to be masked off or removed. Use masking tape and several thicknesses of newspaper for the masking operations.

20 Before spraying, shake the paint can thoroughly, then spray a test area until the spray painting technique is mastered. Cover the repair area with a thick coat of primer. The thickness should be built up using several thin layers of primer rather than one thick one. Using 600-grit wet-or-dry sandpaper, rub down the surface of the primer until it is very smooth. While doing this, the work area should be thoroughly rinsed with water and the wet-or-dry sandpaper periodically rinsed as well. Allow the primer to dry before spraying additional coats.

21 Spray on the top coat, again building up the thickness by using several thin layers of paint. Begin spraying in the center of the repair area and then, using a circular motion, work out until the whole repair area and about two inches of the surrounding original paint is covered. Remove all masking material 10 to 15 minutes after spraying on the final coat of paint. Allow the new paint at least two weeks to harden, then use a very fine rubbing compound to blend the edges of the new paint into the existing paint. Finally, apply a coat of wax.

5 Body and frame repair – major damage

1 Major damage must be repaired by an auto body/frame repair shop with the necessary welding and hydraulic straightening equipment.

2 If the damage has been serious, it is vital that the frame be checked for proper alignment or the vehicle's handling characteristics may be adversely affected. Other problems, such as excessive tire wear and wear in the driveline and steering may occur.

3 Due to the fact that many of the major body components (hood, doors, etc.) are separate and replaceable units, any seriously damaged components should be replaced rather than repaired. Sometimes these components can be found in a wrecking yard that specializes in used vehicle components, often at considerable savings over the cost of new parts.

6 Maintenance – hinges and locks

Every 3000 miles or three months, the door and hood hinges and locks should be lubricated with a few drops of oil. The door striker plates should also be given a thin coat of white lithium-base grease to reduce wear and ensure free movement.

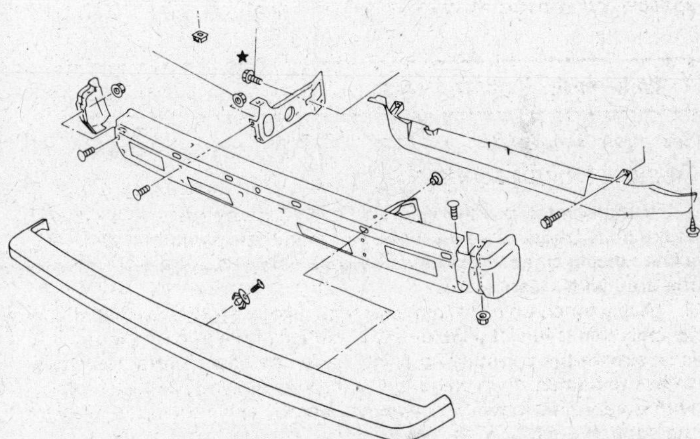

8.5b 1986 through 1988 model front bumper details

7 Windshield and fixed glass – replacement

1 Replacement of the windshield and fixed glass requires the use of special fast-setting adhesive/caulk materials and some specialized tools. It is recommended that these operations should be left to a dealer or a shop specializing in glass work.

8 Bumpers – removal and installation

Refer to illustrations 8.5a, 8.5b and 8.6

Refer to Fig. 13.1

1 Disconnect the negative battery cable from the battery.

2 Disconnect any wiring leading to the bumper.

3 On the front bumper, remove the bolts attaching the side bumpers to the fenders.

4 The bumper can be removed either by removing the nuts that attach the bumper to its bracket, or by removing the bolts that attach the bumper brackets to the body.

5 On the front bumper, the side bumpers and molding can be removed, if necessary, by simply removing the bolts that secure them to the bumper **(see illustrations)**.

6 On rear bumpers, disconnect any wiring, remove the bolts and lower the bumper **(see illustration)**.
7 Installation is the reverse of removal.

9 Grille – removal and installation

Refer to illustrations 9.2a, 9.2b and 9.3

1 Open the hood.
2 The grille is secured to the body by four retainers located along the top. With a screwdriver, simply turn the retainers until they line up with the grille mounting holes, and pull the top of the grille free. Then lift the grille straight up and out of its lower locating holes **(see illustrations)**.
3 Prior to installing the grille, remove the upper retainers from the body and fit them into the grille mounting holes **(see illustration)**. Then simply insert the lower locating tabs on the grille into their holes and press the upper retainers into place until they lock.
4 Close the hood.

10 Front apron – removal and installation

Refer to illustrations 9.2a and 9.2b

1 Remove the front bumper and grille as previously described in Sections 8 and 9.
2 Remove the apron mounting bolts and lift off the front apron.
3 Installation is the reverse of the removal procedure.

11 Cowl grille – removal and installation

Refer to illustration 11.3

1 Remove the hood as described in Section 14.
2 Remove both windshield wiper arms. Refer to Chapter 13, if necessary.
3 Remove the fastening screws that retain the cowl grille and lift it off **(see illustration)**.
4 Installation is the reverse of removal.

12 Front fender – removal and installation

1 Disconnect the negative battery cable from the battery.
2 Remove the front bumper as described in Section 9.
3 Remove the screws that retain the front fender protector and lift it out.
4 Disconnect the wiring leading to the side marker lamp.
5 Remove the screws that retain the front fender and lift it out.
6 If the fender is being replaced, remove the side marker lamp housing and install it on the new fender.
7 Installation is the reverse of the removal procedure.

13 Hood alignment

Refer to illustrations 13.3 and 13.4

1 To prevent engine compartment fumes from being pulled into the interior through the cowl vent, it is important that the hood be properly adjusted and sealed at the cowl area. Fore and aft adjustment of the hood is made by moving the hinge screws in their slots. Vertical adjustment of the front of the hood is made by adjusting the height of the screw-type rubber bumpers located at the front corners of the radiator support and the dovetail bolt, which is part of the hood latch assembly.
2 The hood is adjusted as follows: Scribe a line around the entire hinge plate to be repositioned. This will enable you to judge the amount of movement.

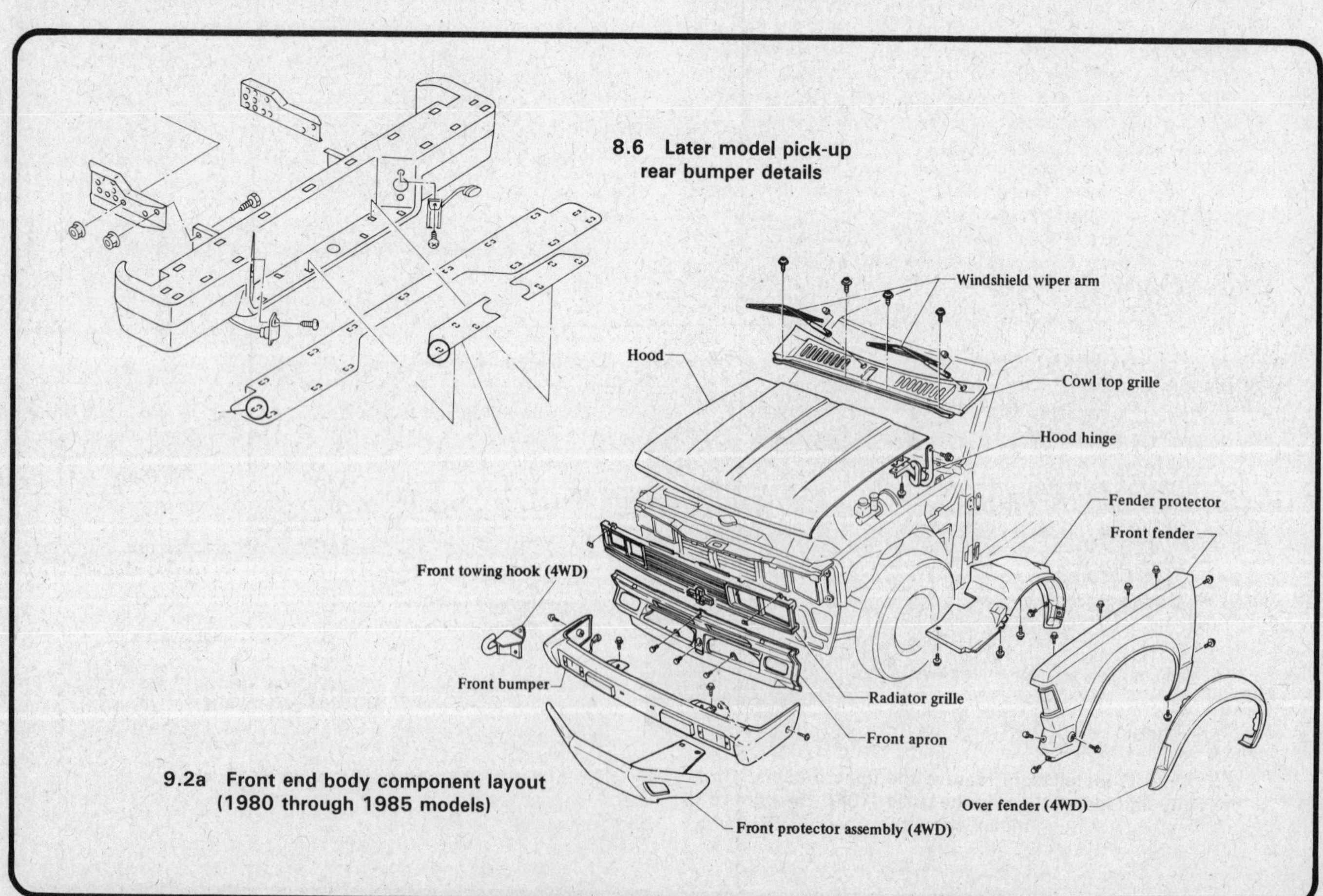

8.6 Later model pick-up rear bumper details

9.2a Front end body component layout (1980 through 1985 models)

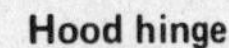

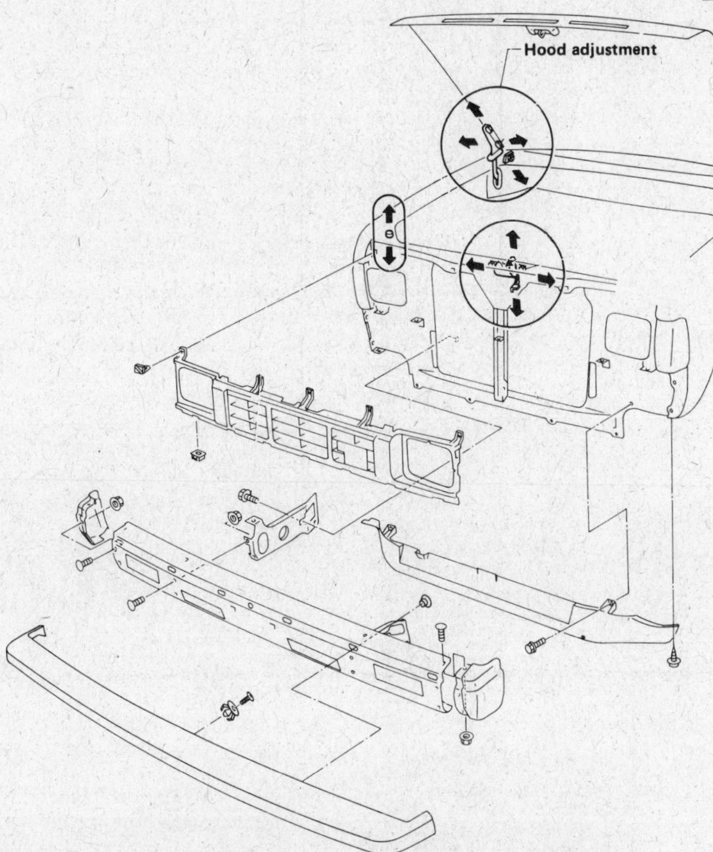

9.2b 1986 through 1988 models front body component layout and hood adjustment details

9.3 Prior to installation, remove the upper retainers from the body and install them in the grille (1980 through 1985 model shown)

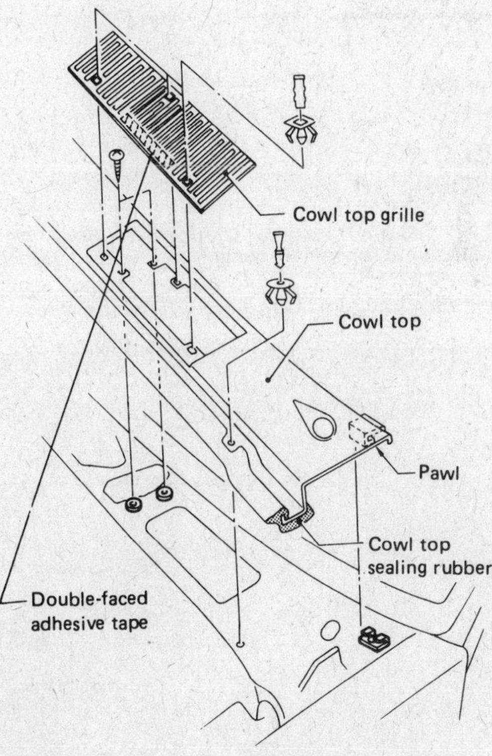

11.3 Later model cowl grille details

These photos illustrate a method of repairing simple dents. They are intended to supplement *Body repair - minor damage* in this Chapter and should not be used as the sole instructions for body repair on these vehicles.

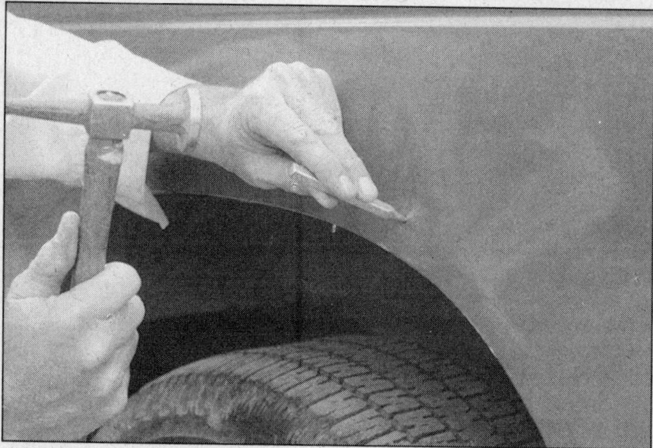

1 If you can't access the backside of the body panel to hammer out the dent, pull it out with a slide-hammer-type dent puller. In the deepest portion of the dent or along the crease line, drill or punch hole(s) at least one inch apart . . .

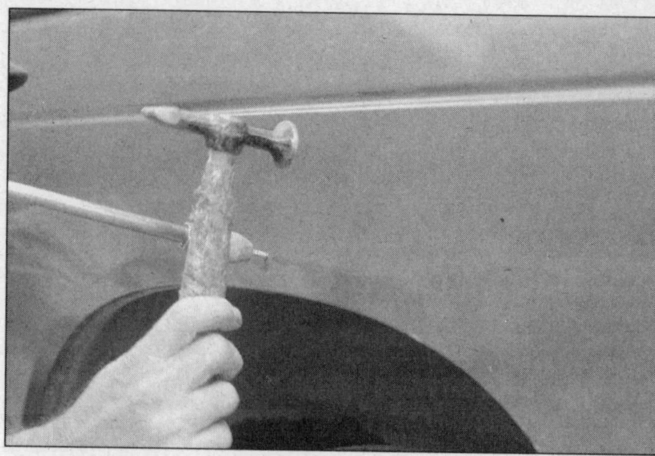

2 . . . then screw the slide-hammer into the hole and operate it. Tap with a hammer near the edge of the dent to help 'pop' the metal back to its original shape. When you're finished, the dent area should be close to its original contour and about 1/8-inch below the surface of the surrounding metal

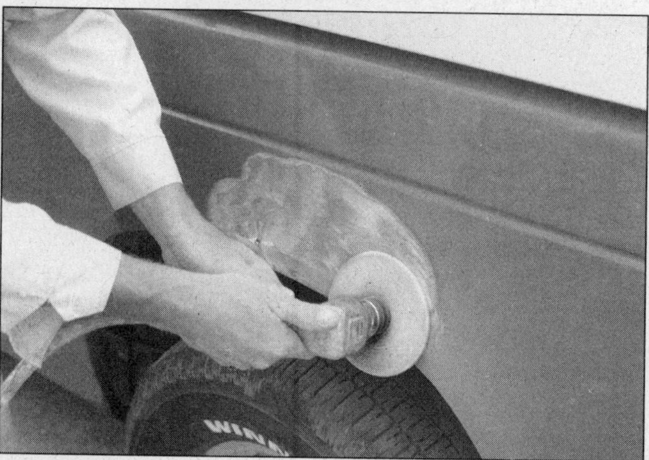

3 Using coarse-grit sandpaper, remove the paint down to the bare metal. Hand sanding works fine, but the disc sander shown here makes the job faster. Use finer (about 320-grit) sandpaper to feather-edge the paint at least one inch around the dent area

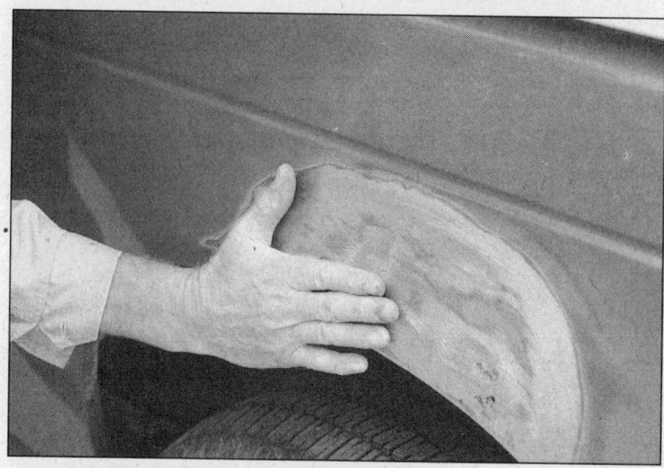

4 When the paint is removed, touch will probably be more helpful than sight for telling if the metal is straight. Hammer down the high spots or raise the low spots as necessary. Clean the repair area with wax/silicone remover

5 Following label instructions, mix up a batch of plastic filler and hardener. The ratio of filler to hardener is critical, and, if you mix it incorrectly, it will either not cure properly or cure too quickly (you won't have time to file and sand it into shape)

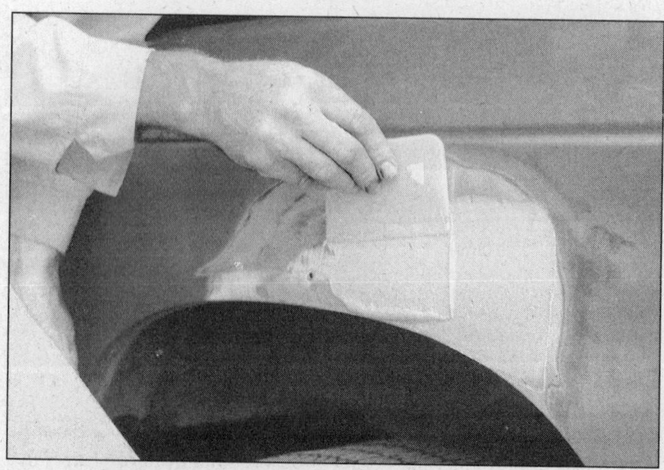

6 Working quickly so the filler doesn't harden, use a plastic applicator to press the body filler firmly into the metal, assuring it bonds completely. Work the filler until it matches the original contour and is slightly above the surrounding metal

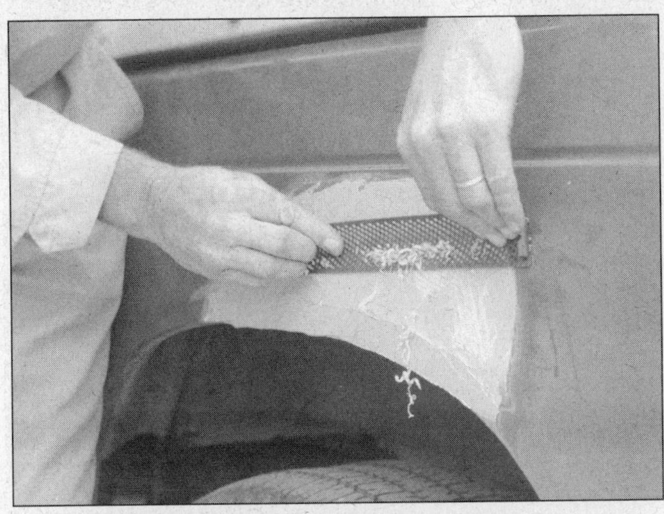

7 Let the filler harden until you can just dent it with your fingernail. Use a body file or Surform tool (shown here) to rough-shape the filler

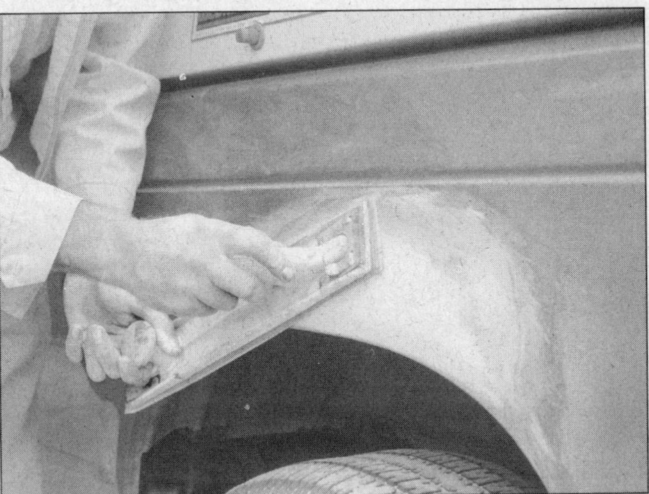

8 Use coarse-grit sandpaper and a sanding board or block to work the filler down until it's smooth and even. Work down to finer grits of sandpaper - always using a board or block - ending up with 360 or 400 grit

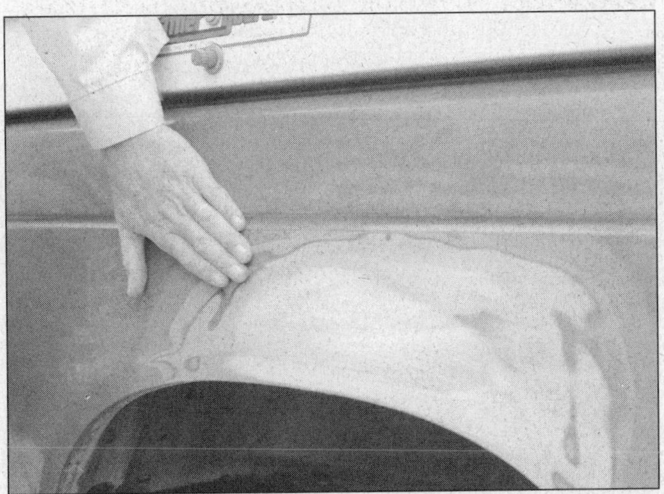

9 You shouldn't be able to feel any ridge at the transition from the filler to the bare metal or from the bare metal to the old paint. As soon as the repair is flat and uniform, remove the dust and mask off the adjacent panels or trim pieces

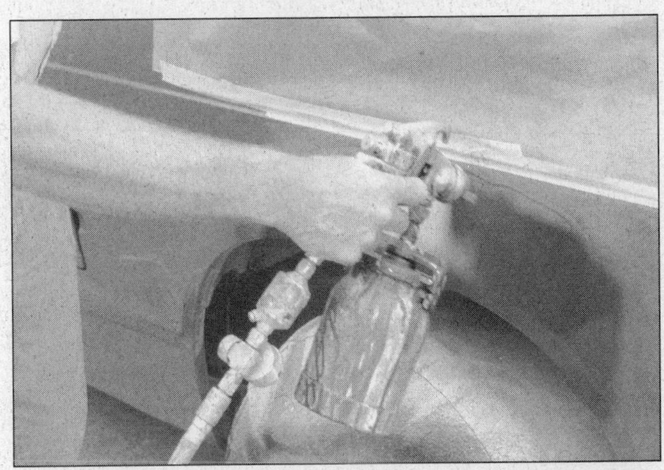

10 Apply several layers of primer to the area. Don't spray the primer on too heavy, so it sags or runs, and make sure each coat is dry before you spray on the next one. A professional-type spray gun is being used here, but aerosol spray primer is available inexpensively from auto parts stores

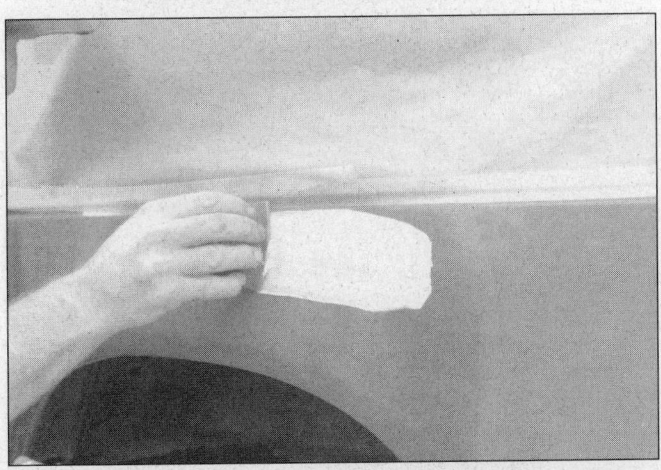

11 The primer will help reveal imperfections or scratches. Fill these with glazing compound. Follow the label instructions and sand it with 360 or 400-grit sandpaper until it's smooth. Repeat the glazing, sanding and respraying until the primer reveals a perfectly smooth surface

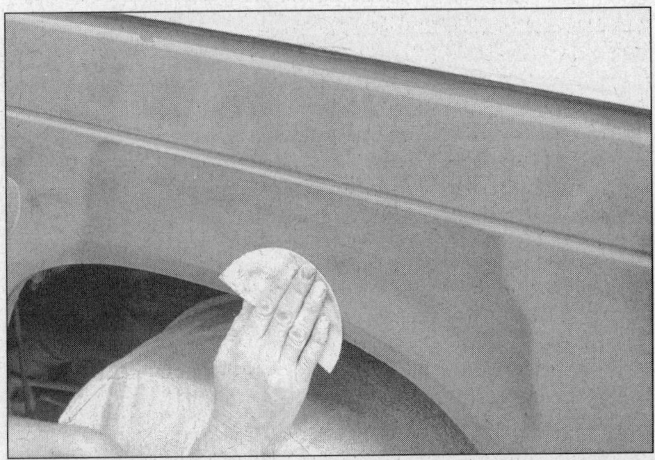

12 Finish sand the primer with very fine sandpaper (400 or 600-grit) to remove the primer overspray. Clean the area with water and allow it to dry. Use a tack rag to remove any dust, then apply the finish coat. Don't attempt to rub out or wax the repair area until the paint has dried completely (at least two weeks)

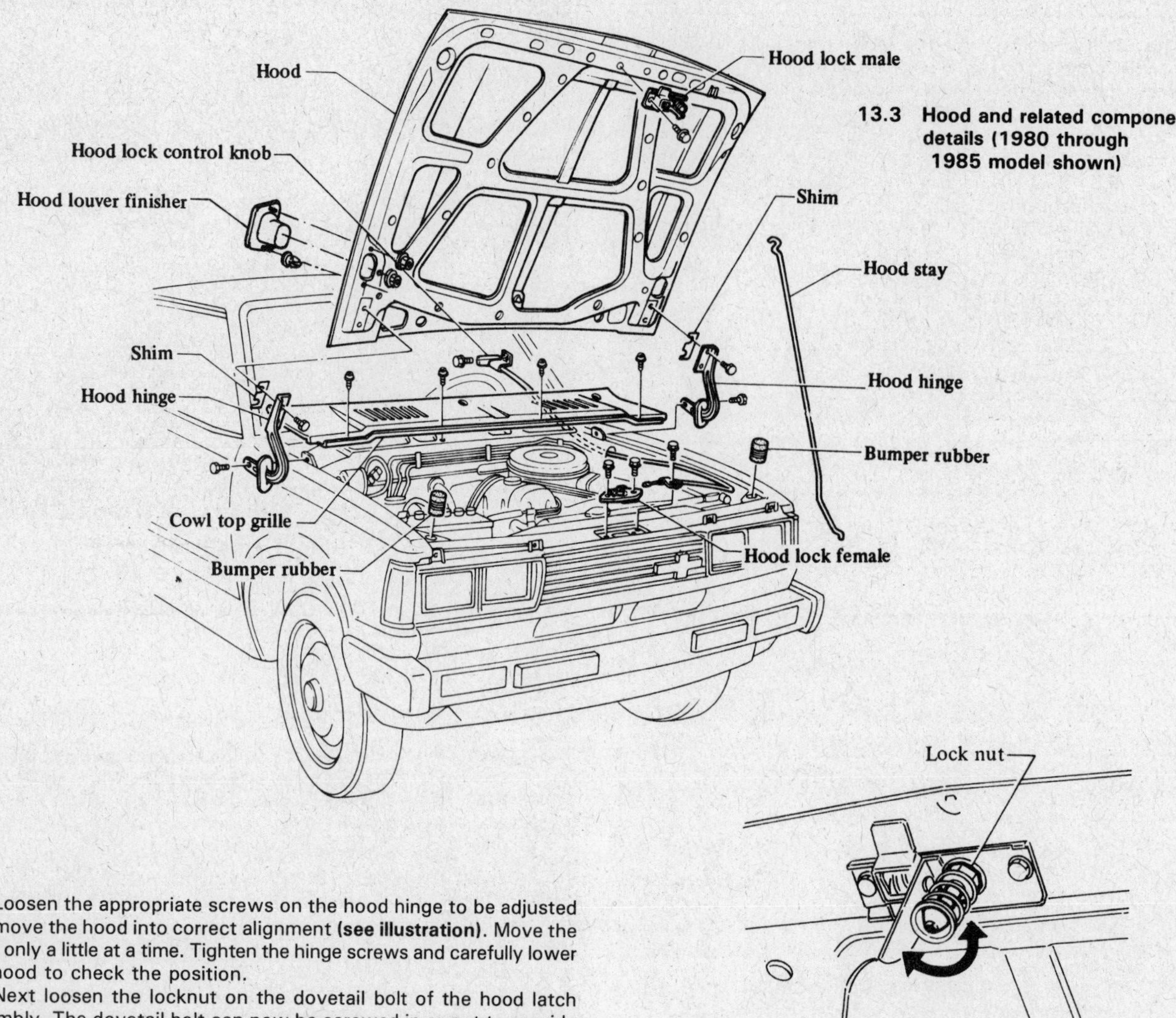

13.3 Hood and related component details (1980 through 1985 model shown)

3 Loosen the appropriate screws on the hood hinge to be adjusted and move the hood into correct alignment **(see illustration)**. Move the hood only a little at a time. Tighten the hinge screws and carefully lower the hood to check the position.
4 Next loosen the locknut on the dovetail bolt of the hood latch assembly. The dovetail bolt can now be screwed in or out to provide proper height at the front of the hood when it is closed **(see illustration)**. Once adjusted, retighten the locknut.
5 If necessary, the entire hood latch assembly can be adjusted forward and rearward as well as side-to-side to properly align with the hood lock in the radiator support. To do this, scribe a line around the hood latch mounting screws to provide a reference point. Then loosen them and reposition the latch assembly as necessary. Following adjustment, retighten the mounting bolts.
6 Finally adjust the hood bumpers on the radiator support so that the hood, when closed, is flush with the fenders.
7 The hood latch assembly, as well as the hinges, should be periodically lubricated to prevent sticking or jamming.

14 Hood – removal and installation

1 Raise the hood.
2 Use blankets or cloths to cover the cowl area of the body and the fenders. This will protect the body and paint as the hood is lifted free.
3 Mark the position of the hood on its hinges by outlining the hinge plate. This will greatly aid alignment when reinstalling.
4 While an assistant supports the hood, remove the hinge-to-hood screws on both sides and lift out the hinge shims.
5 Lift off the hood.
6 Installation is the reverse of the removal procedure.
7 Check the hood alignment and adjust if necessary as described in Section 10.

13.4 The front hood height is adjusted by turning the dovetail bolt in the hood latch assembly (1980 through 1985 model shown)

15 Hood latches – removal and installation

Refer to illustration 15.2

1 The hood latch assembly consists of two components: the latch (male) assembly located on the underside of the hood, and the lock (female) assembly located in the radiator support. The hood lock, to which the hood latch release cable is connected, incorporates the primary hood release mechanism and is not adjustable. The latch assembly incorporates the secondary hood release mechanism and its position can be adjusted to align with the hood lock.
2 To remove the hood latch assembly, first mark the position of the mounting bolts by scribing a circle around them. This will simplify alignment during installation. Then simply remove the mounting bolts **(see illustration)**.
3 To install the assembly, reverse the removal procedure, being sure to match the mounting screws up with their original position.
4 To remove the hood lock assembly from the radiator support, first remove the grille. Then simply remove the mounting screws, disconnect the release cable and lift it out.
5 Both the hood latch and lock assemblies should be lubricated periodically.

16 Hood latch release cable – removal and installation

1 The hood latch release cable is a one-piece assembly that includes the pull handle, control cable and flexible housing.
2 To remove it, raise the hood and disengage the cable from the hood lock at the radiator support. Take precautions to keep the hood from closing and locking while the cable is disconnected.
3 Disengage the cable from any retaining clips holding it to the body.
4 Moving to the vehicle's interior, remove the two screws that retain the handle bracket to the side panel.
5 Carefully withdraw the cable from the firewall.
6 Installation is the reverse of the removal procedure. When installing, check that the sealing grommet located where the cable passes through the firewall is in place.

17 Rear gate – removal and installation

Refer to illustrations 17.2a, 17.2b and 17.5

1 Open the rear gate.
2 Remove the bolts that attach the gate stays to the gate **(see illustrations)**.
3 Remove the bolts that attach the gate hinges to the body, remove any hinge shims and lift off the gate.
4 On Pathfinder models, prop the rear gate open, mark the bolts by

15.2 Later model hood latch bolt details

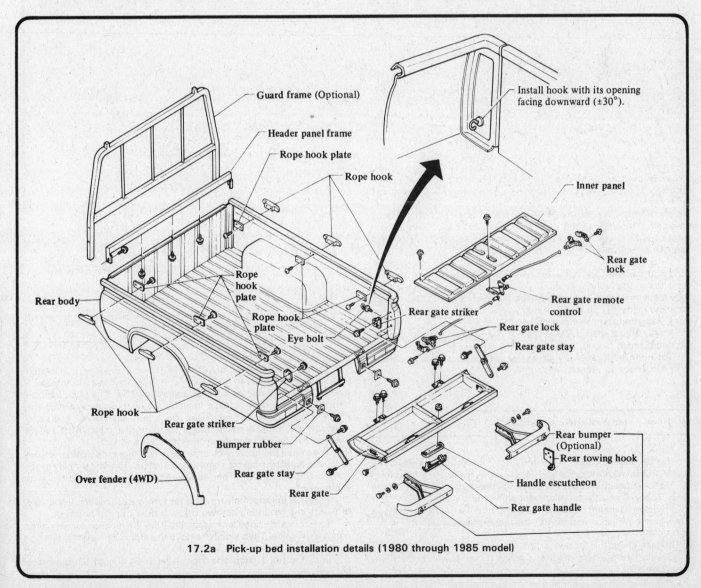

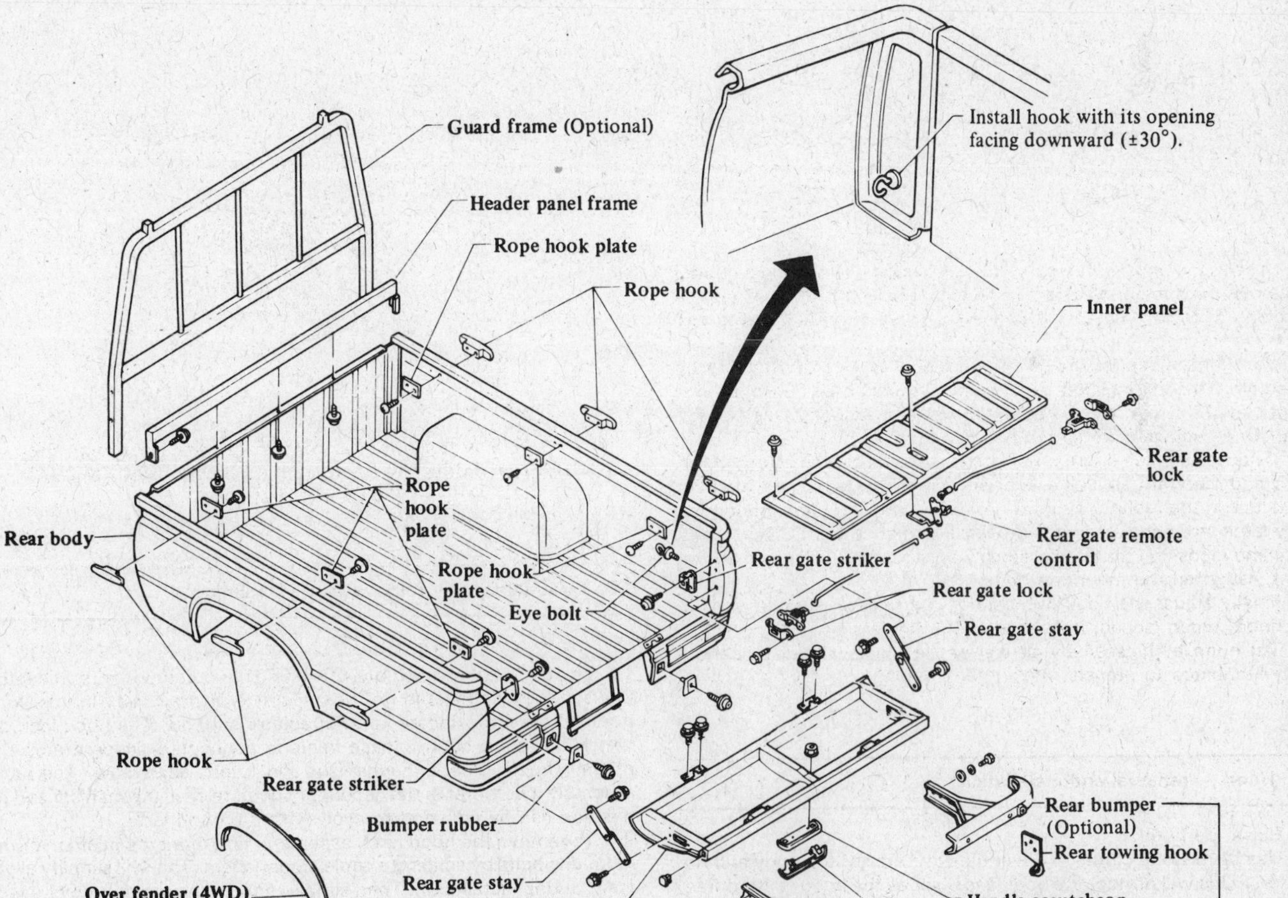

17.2a Pick-up bed installation details (1980 through 1985 model)

scribing around them and disconnect the prop struts.

5 Have an assistant support the rear gate, remove the nuts and lift the gate from the vehicle **(see illustration)**.

6 Installation is the reverse of the removal procedure. Be sure to replace the rear gate hinge shims in their proper positions.

18 Rear gate lock and lock control – removal and installation

Refer to illustration 18.5

1 Open the rear gate.

2 Remove the screws attaching the inner panel to the rear gate and lift it off.

3 Remove the entire lock control assembly by removing the bolts attaching the remote control assembly and gate locks to the rear gate. If necessary, the assembly can be disassembled after removal.

4 The rear gate handle can be removed by undoing the two retaining nuts and lifting it off.

5 On Pathfinder models, remove the liftgate trim panel. Disconnect the control rods, remove the retaining bolts and lift out the lock and control assemblies **(see illustration)**.

6 Installation is the reverse of the removal procedure.

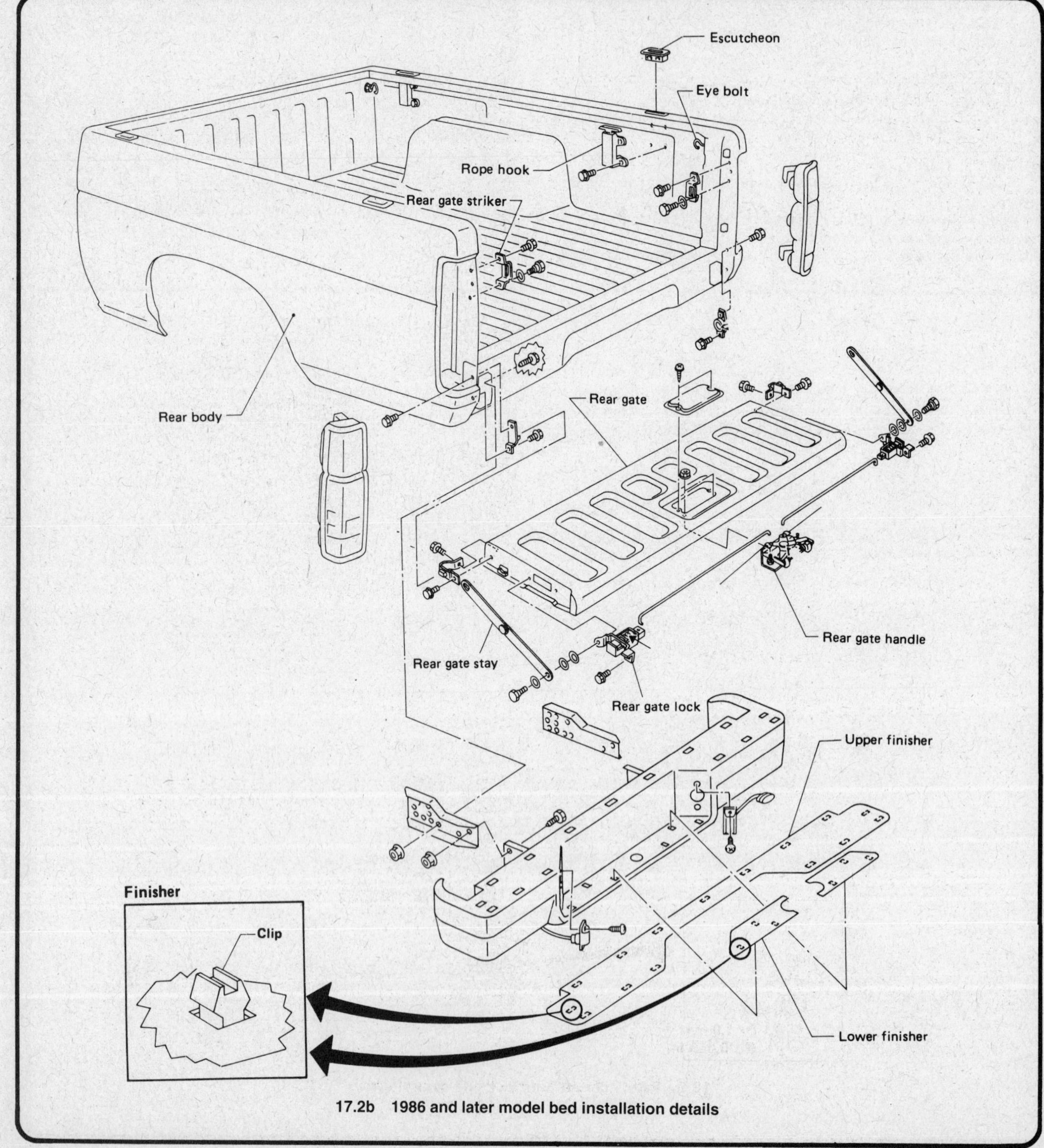

17.2b 1986 and later model bed installation details

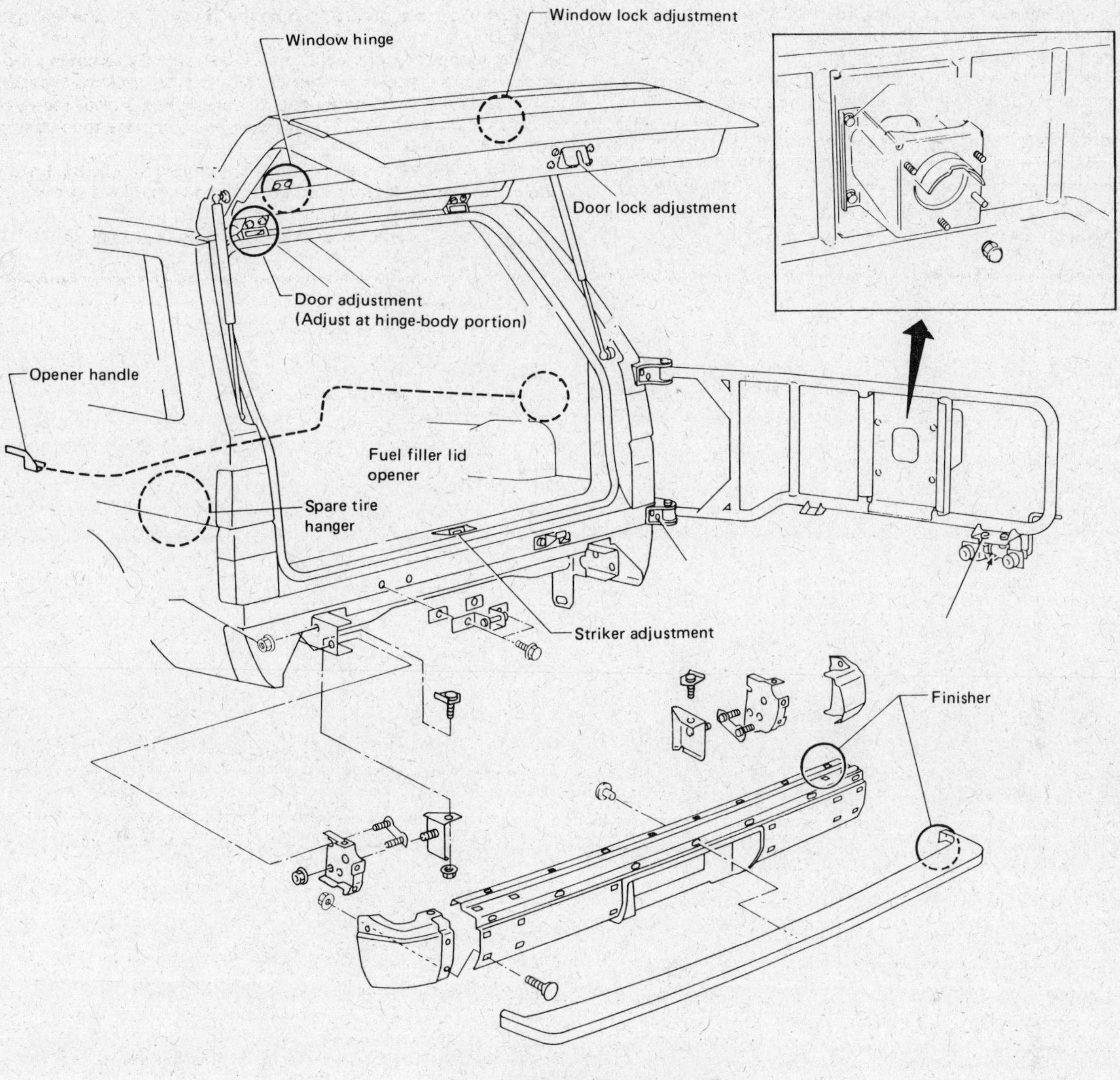

Window lock adjustment
Window hinge
Door lock adjustment
Door adjustment
(Adjust at hinge-body portion)
Opener handle
Fuel filler lid
opener
Spare tire
hanger
Striker adjustment
Finisher

17.5 Pathfinder lift gate details

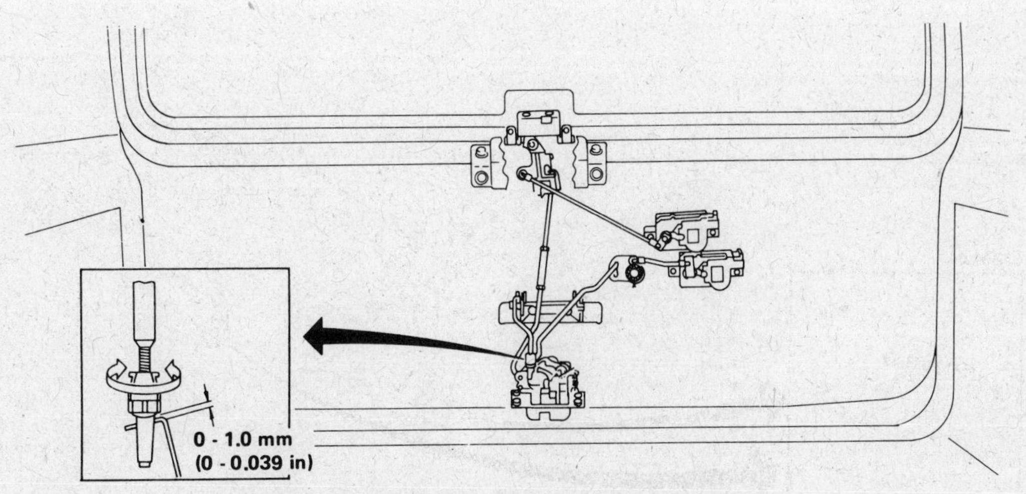

18.5 Pathfinder lift gate lock and control details

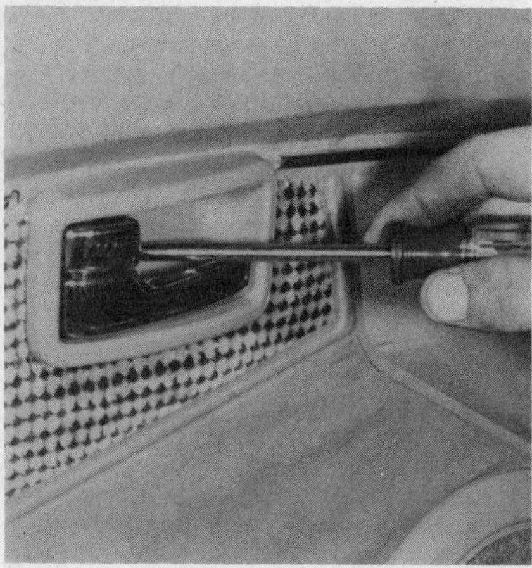

19.5 On most models, the interior door handle escutcheon is secured to the trim panel by one screw

19.6 The door trim panel is attached to the door by plastic clips

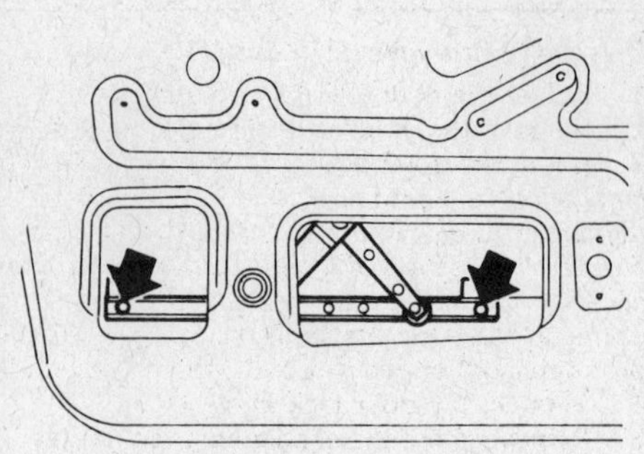

20.5 Window-to-regulator bolts (arrows) (1980 through 1985 models)

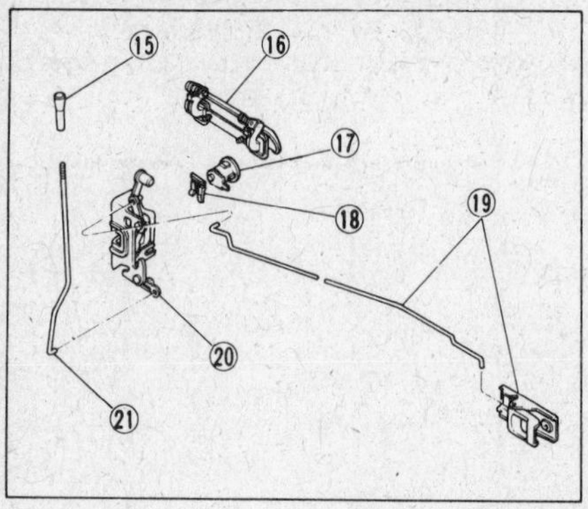

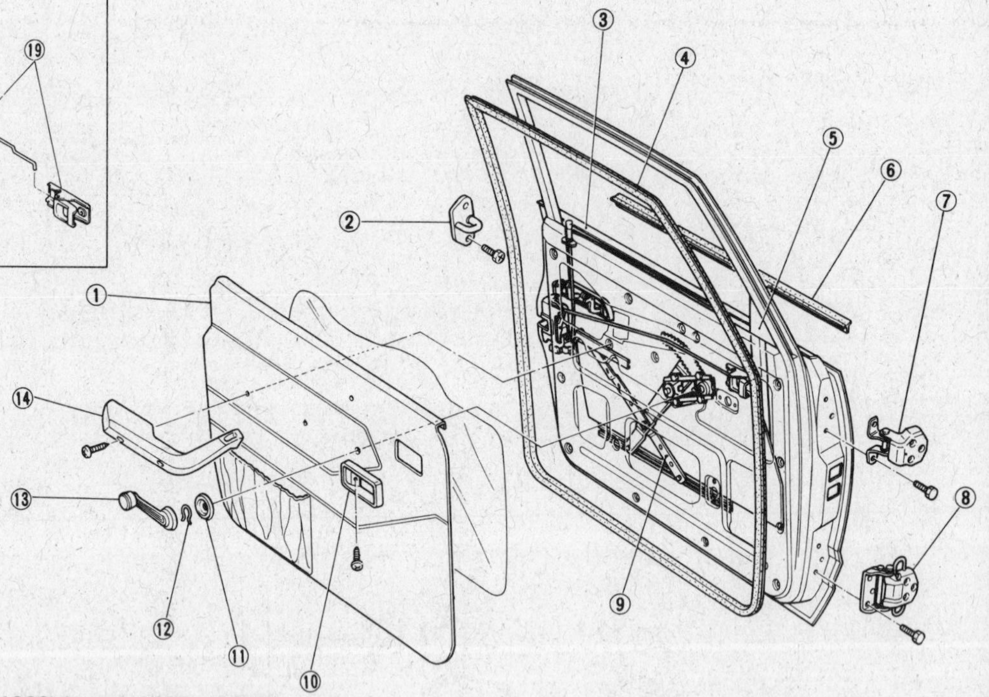

20.7a Door components (1980 through 1985 models)

1 Door trim panel
2 Door lock striker
3 Door
4 Weatherstrip
5 Lower sash
6 Outer side weatherstrip
7 Upper hinge
8 Lower hinge
9 Regulator assembly
10 Remote control escutcheon
11 Regulator seating washer
12 Retaining spring
13 Regulator door handle
14 Arm rest
15 Door lock knob
16 Outside handle
17 Door lock cylinder
18 Retaining clip
19 Remote control assembly
20 Door lock assembly
21 Door lock rod
22 Regulator
23 Door glass
24 Guide channel A
25 Guide channel B

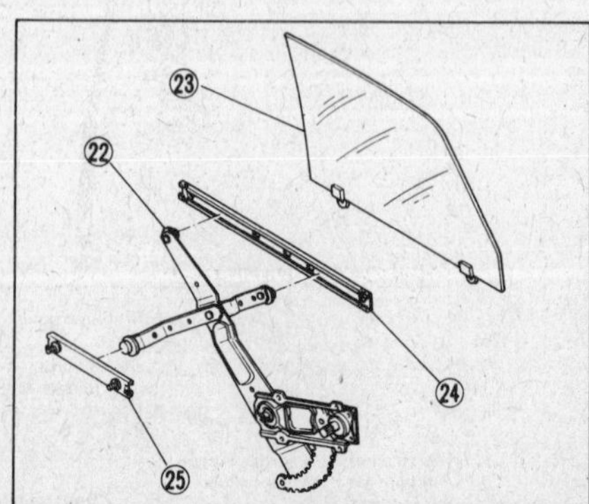

19 Door trim panel — removal and installation

Refer to illustrations 19.5 and 19.6

1 Lower the door glass completely.
2 Remove the screws that retain the arm rest to the trim panel.
3 Remove the window crank handle. The crank handle is held onto its shaft by a spring clip, requiring the use of a small hooked tool to remove it. Once can be fabricated out of a piece of coat hanger. With one hand, press the trim panel inward slightly to expose the shaft and clip, and with the other hand insert the tool behind the crank handle until you can hook the spring clip. Then pull the clip toward the handle knob and remove it. Lift off the crank handle and plastic washer.
4 Remove the door lock knob.
5 Remove the door handle escutcheon **(see illustration)**.
6 The trim panel is attached to the door with plastic retaining clips **(see illustration)**. To disengage these clips, insert a flat, blunt tool (like a screwdriver wrapped with tape) between the metal door skin and the trim panel. Carefully pry the door panel away from the door, keeping the tool close to the clips to prevent damage to the panel. Start at the bottom and work around the door toward the top. Once the retaining clips are pried free, lift the trim panel upward and away from the door.
7 Before installing the trim panel, check that all the trim retaining clips are in good condition and the sealing screen is correctly applied to the door.
8 Engage the top of the trim panel first and then position the panel correctly on the door. The shaft for the window winder can be used as a rough guide.
9 Press the retaining clips into their respective cups or holes in the door. Pressure can be applied with the palm of your hand or with a clean rubber mallet.
10 Complete the installation by reversing the removal procedure. To install the crank handle, first install the spring clip into its groove on the handle with the closed end facing the handle knob, align the handle with the one on the opposite door and push it onto its shaft until the spring clip clicks into place.

20 Door window and regulator — removal and installation

Refer to illustrations 20.5, 20.7a, 20.7b and 20.9

1 Remove the door trim panel as described in Section 16.
2 Using a flathead screwdriver, rotate the exterior door molding retaining clips 90 degrees and lift off and remove the molding.
3 Remove the plastic sealing screen.
4 Remove the lower sash.
5 Remove the bolts that attach the window to the regulator assembly **(see illustration)**.
6 Remove the glass from the door by pulling it upwards and away from the door.
7 If necessary, remove the regulator mounting bolts and remove the regulator through the large access hole **(see illustrations)**.
8 Prior to installing the regulator and guide channel, apply a light coat of lithium-based grease to all their sliding surfaces.

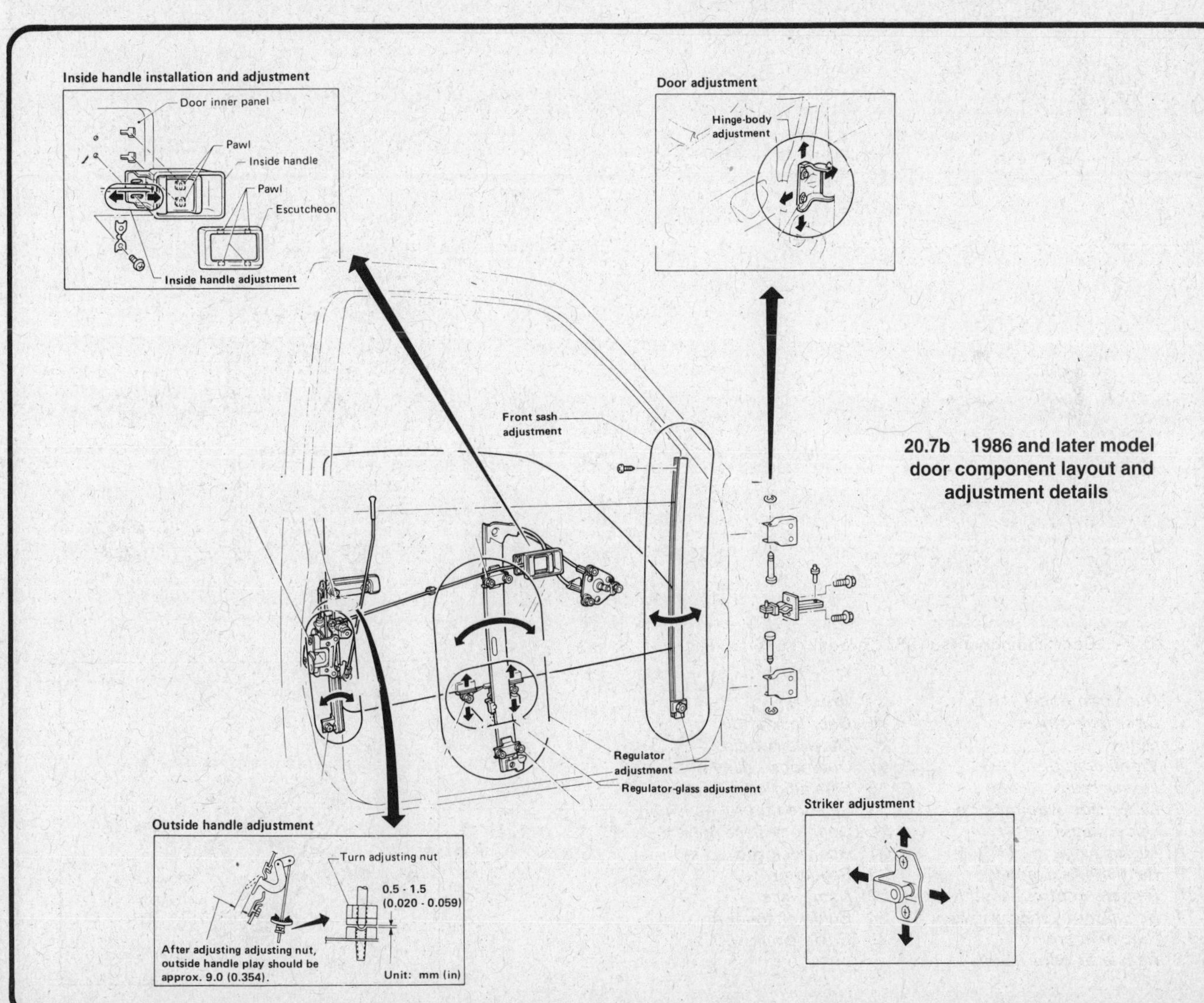

20.7b 1986 and later model door component layout and adjustment details

9 Installation is the reverse of the removal procedure. Following installation of the window, roll it up completely and use the following procedure to bring it into correct alignment.

a) The tilt of the window can be adjusted by loosening the channel B retaining nuts and moving the glass so that its upper edge is parallel with the upper sash **(see illustration)**. Following adjustment, retighten the retaining nuts.
b) To adjust the window in the fore-and-aft position, loosen the channel and door glass retaining bolts. Then adjust the glass so that its rear edge and upper rear corner are seated firmly in the rubber of the door frame. Following adjustment, retighten the retaining bolts.
c) To adjust the window's sliding resistance, loosen the front floor lower sash retaining bolts and slide the sash forward or backward so that the glass can be raised or lowered smoothly. Following adjustment, retighten the retaining bolts.

21 Door lock and lock control – removal and installation

1 Remove the door trim panel as described in Section 19.
2 Remove the plastic sealing screen, taking care not to tear it.
3 Disengage the interior handle rod from the connection at the door lock assembly.
4 Remove the screws that retain the interior handle assembly and lift it out.
5 Remove the retaining clip from the door lock cylinder and remove the cylinder.
6 Disengage the door lock rod from the door lock assembly.
7 Remove the three door lock assembly mounting screws, located on the outside rear of the door, and lift out the door lock assembly.
8 If necessary, remove the two nuts retaining the exterior handle and lift it out.
9 Installation is the reverse of removal. **Note:** *During installation, apply grease to the sliding surface of all levers and springs.*

22 Door – removal and installation

1 Either place a jack or stand under the door or have an assistant on hand to support it when the hinge bolts are removed. **Note:** *If a jack or stand is being used, place a rag between it and the door to protect the door's painted surfaces.*
2 Remove the hinge-to-door bolts and carefully lift off the door.
3 Installation is the reverse of removal.
4 Following installation of the door, check that it is in proper alignment and adjust it if necessary as follows:

a) Up-and-down and forward-and-backward adjustments are made by loosening the hinge-to-body bolts and moving the door as necessary. The inner fender protector will have to be removed in order to reach these bolts.
b) The door lock striker can also be adjusted both up-and-down and sideways to provide a positive engagement with the locking mechanism. This is easily done by loosening the securing bolts and moving the striker as necessary.

23 Swing-out side window – removal and installation

Refer to illustrations 23.3a, 23.3b and 23.3c

1 Remove the two screws retaining the catch handle bracket to the rear pillar.
2 Carefully pry off the hinge covers (if equipped) using a screwdriver. Take care not to damage the painted surfaces by placing a piece of rag between the screwdriver and the cover.
3 Remove the hinge securing nuts or screws and take out the side windows **(see illustrations)**.
4 If necessary, remove the weatherstripping from around the window opening.
5 Installation is the reverse of the removal procedure.

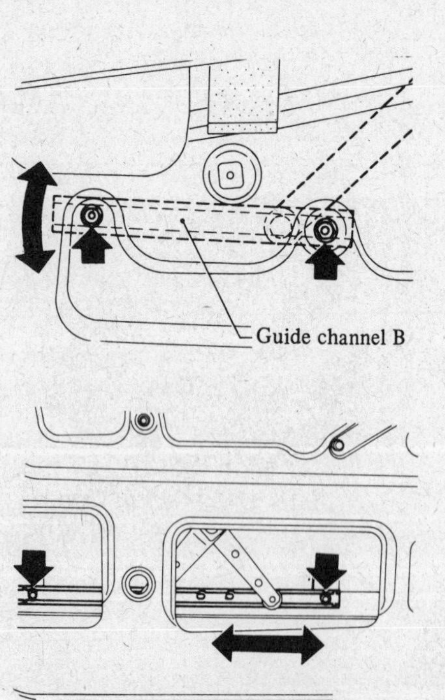

20.9 Location of the guide channel retaining nuts and bolts (1980 through 1985 models)

Top: Window tilt adjustment
Bottom: Window fore-and-aft adjustment

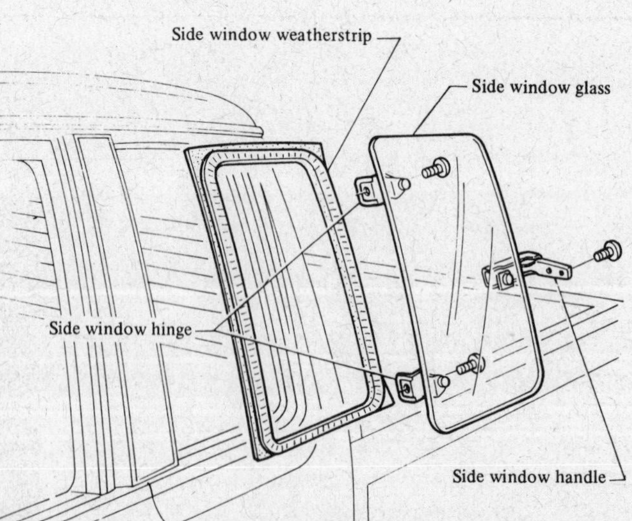

23.3a 1980 through 1985 King Cab swing-out side window details

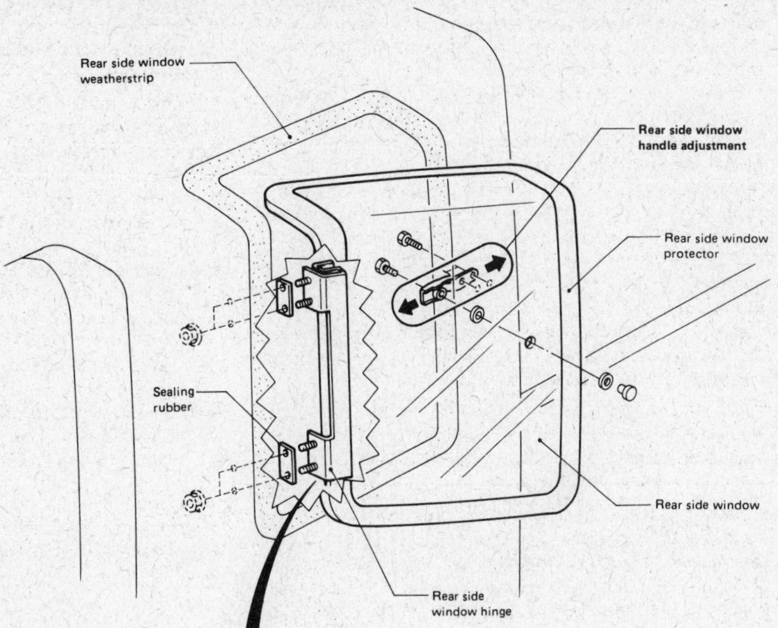

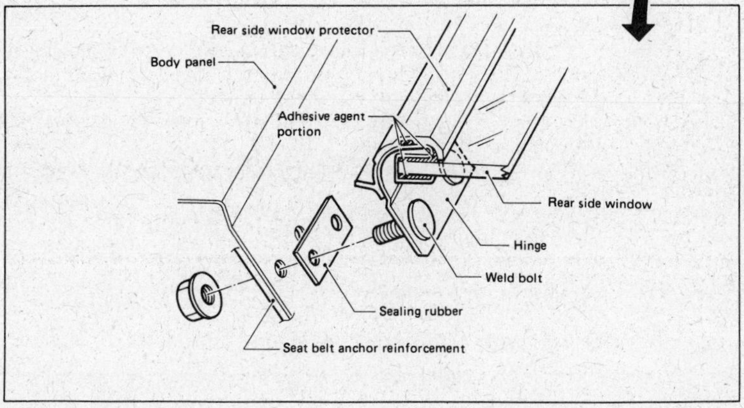

23.3b 1986 and later King Cab swing-out side window details

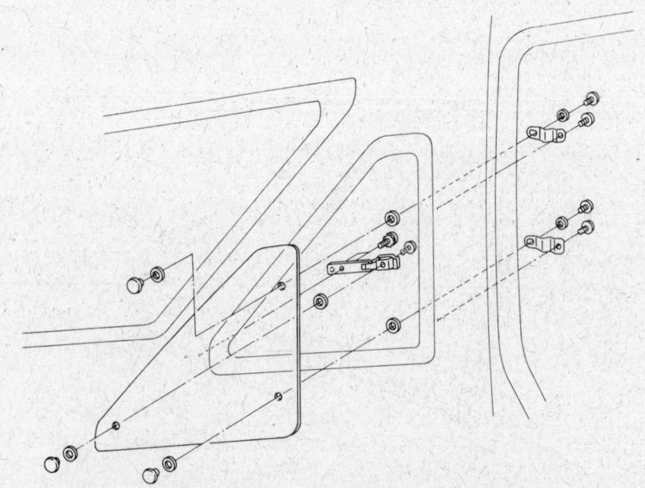

23.3c Pathfinder swing-out side window details

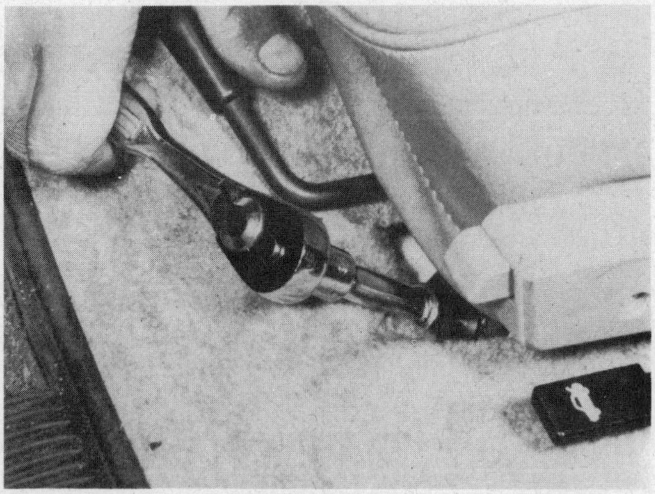

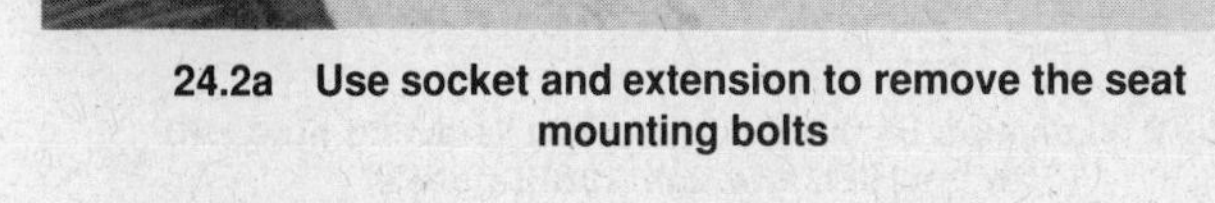

24.2a Use socket and extension to remove the seat mounting bolts

24 Seats – removal and installation

Refer to illustrations 24.2a, 24.2b, 24.2c and 24.2d

1 Slide the seat all the way forward and remove the rear mounting bolts.

2 Slide the seat all the way to the rear and remove the forward mounting bolts (see illustrations).

3 Lift out the seat.

4 Installation is the reverse of the removal procedure.

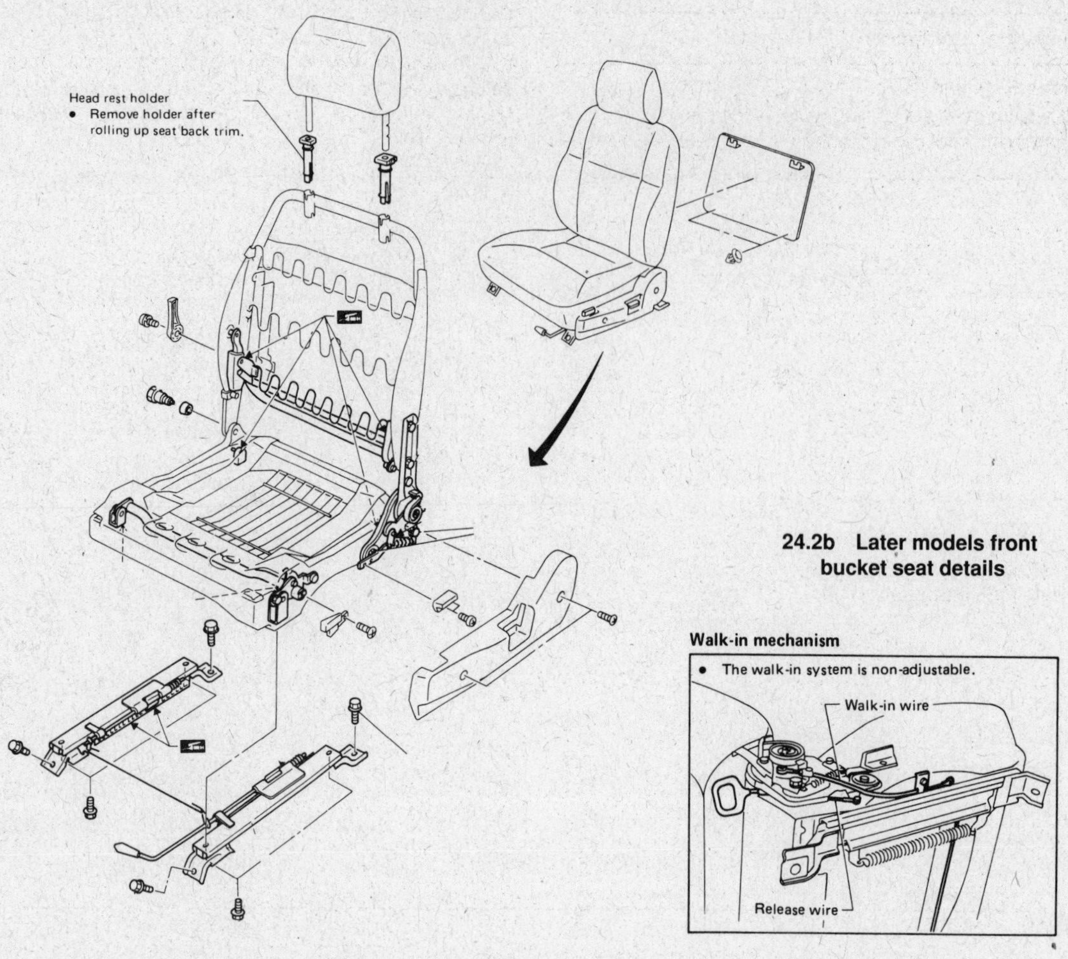
Head rest holder
• Remove holder after rolling up seat back trim.
Walk-in mechanism
• The walk-in system is non-adjustable.
Walk-in wire
Release wire

24.2b Later models front bucket seat details

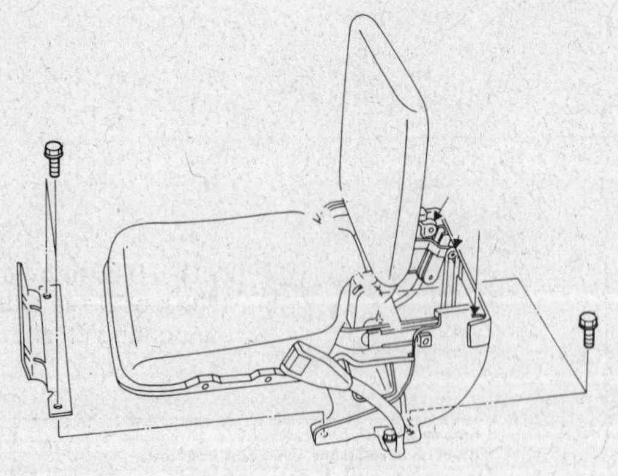

24.2c Jump seat details (1986 through 1988 model shown)

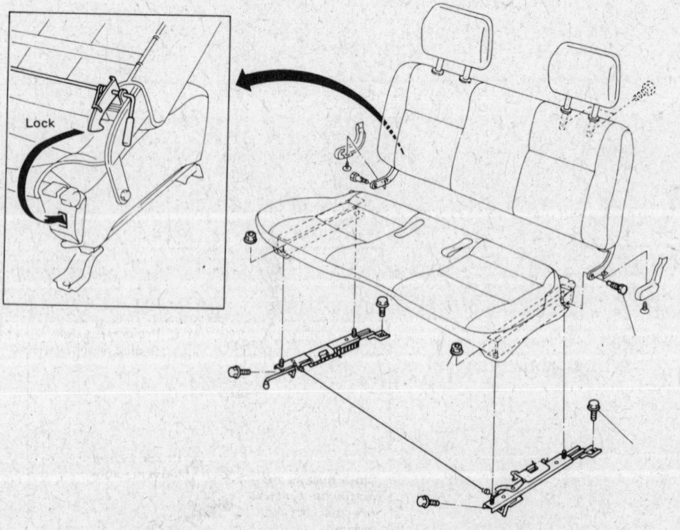
Lock

24.2d Later model front bench seat details

25 Seatbelts – general information

Refer to illustrations 25.1a and 25.1b

1 The seatbelt attachments are shown in the accompanying figure. If any component part of the seat belts is faulty, the complete belt must be replaced **(see illustrations)**. The same applies if the belts are strained in an accident.

2 To clean the belt webbing use only a soft bristle brush and a soap or detergent solution, then wipe off the surplus and allow to dry naturally. Never use bleach or chemical cleaners as these may cause the webbing to deteriorate.

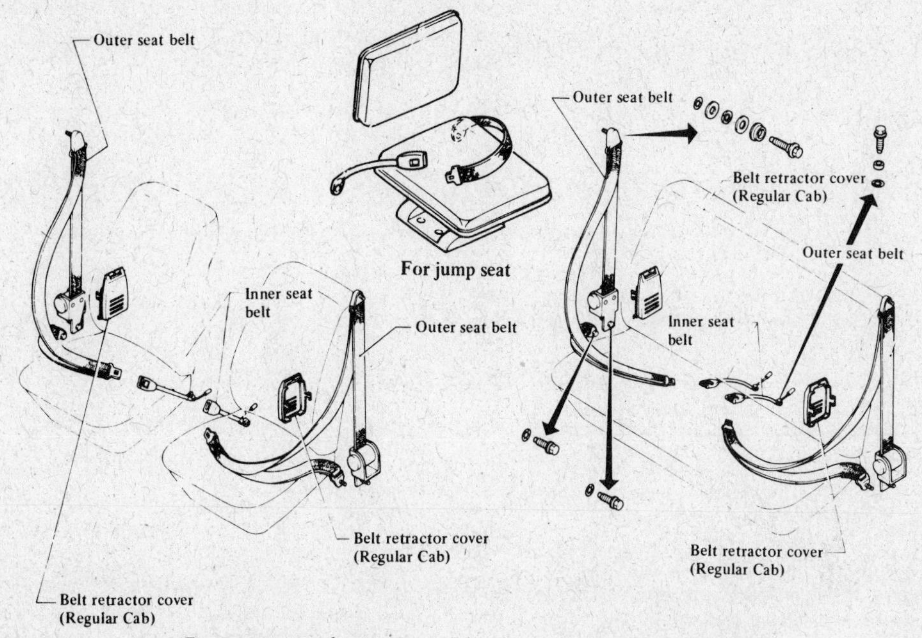

25.1a Seatbelt mounting details (1980 through 1986 models)

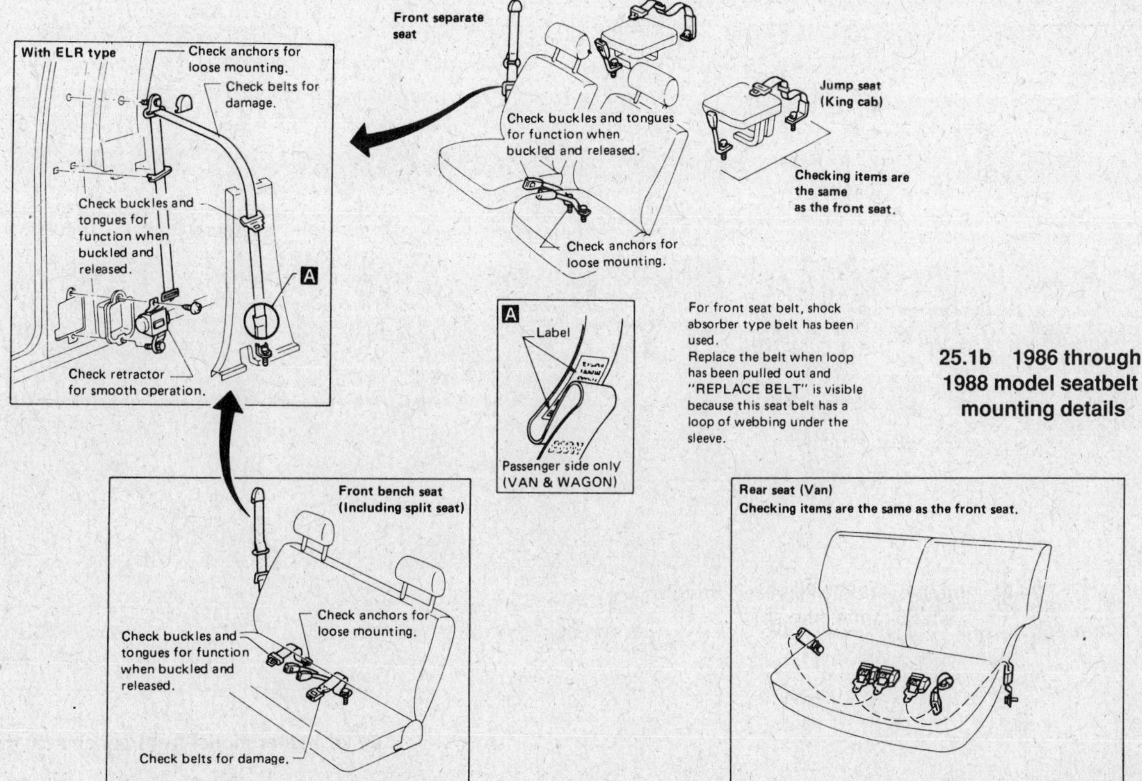

25.1b 1986 through 1988 model seatbelt mounting details

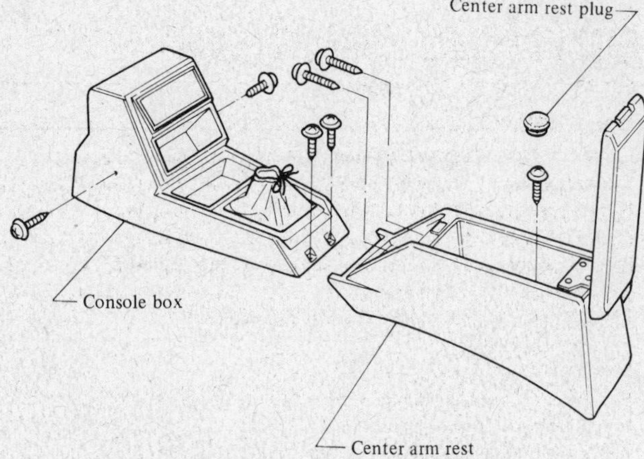

26.2a Center console installation details (1980 through 1985 models)

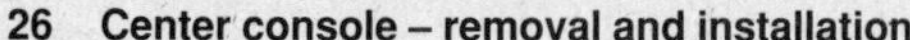

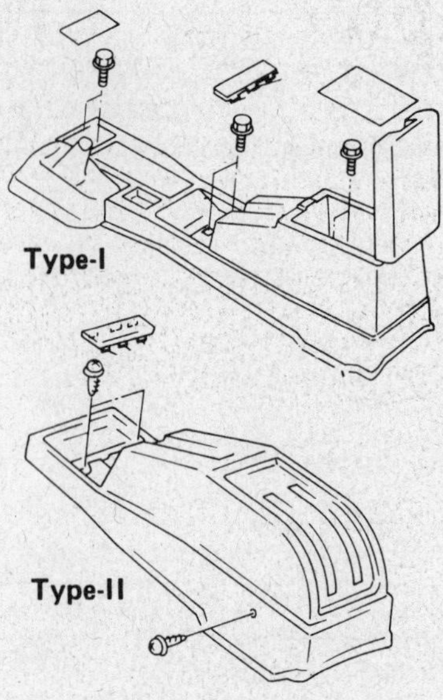

26.2b 1986 and later model console details

26 Center console – removal and installation

Refer to illustrations 26.2a and 26.2b

1 Raise the center arm rest cover and remove the plug from the bottom of the storage compartment (if equipped).

2 Remove the center arm rest mounting screws or bolts and lift the section out **(see illustrations)**.

3 Remove the console box mounting screws or bolts. Then lift the console box over the shift lever and out.

4 Installation is the reverse of removal.

27 Rear bed – removal and installation

Refer to illustrations 27.4, 27.5a and 27.5b

1 Disconnect the negative battery cable from the battery.

2 Apply the parking brake.

3 Disconnect the wiring leading to the taillights and license plate lamp.

4 Open the fuel filler access door and remove the fuel filler tube mounting screws **(see illustration)**.

5 Remove the bolts which attach the rear bed to the frame **(see illustrations)**. **Note:** *Be sure to take note of the installed order and position of the rubber grommets, washers and bushings for proper installation.*

6 The bed can be lifted off with the help of several assistants, or by attaching ropes to the rope hooks and lifting it off with a hoist.

7 Installation is the reverse of removal.

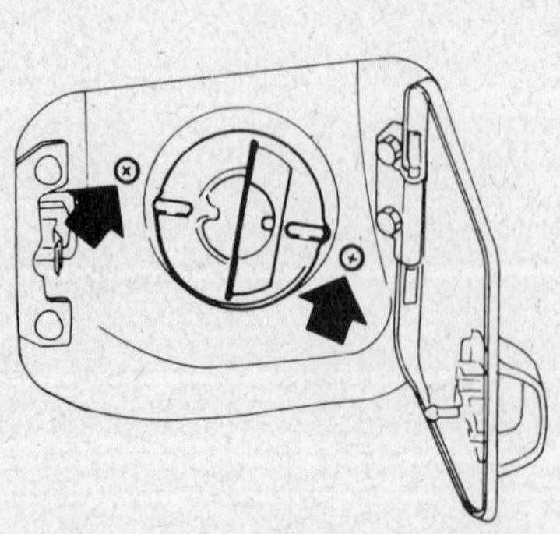

27.5 Location of the fuel filler tube mounting screws (1980 through 1985 model shown)

27.6a The bed mounting bolts are accessible from under the vehicle

27.6b Front bed mounting bolts (1980 through 1985 model shown)

Chapter 13 Chassis electrical system

Contents

Specifications

Bulbs

Application	Wattage	Type
Headlamp (sealed beam – 1980 through 1985)		
Inner – high	50	4651
Outer – high/low	40/60	4652
Halogen headlamp (1980 through 1985)		
Inner – high	50	H4651
Outer (type 2) – high/low	35/35	H4656
Headlamp (1986 on)		
Sealed beam	65/55	H6052
Halogen	65/35	H6054
Front combination lamp		
Turn signal	27	1156
Clearance (1980 and 1981)	5	–
Clearance (1982 on)	8	–
Side marker lamp (1980 and 1981)		
Front	8	–
Rear	8	–
Side marker lamp (1982 on)		
Front	5	–
Rear	3.8	–
Rear combination lamp		
Stop/tail	27/8	1157
Turn signal	27	1156
Back-up	27	1156
License plate lamp		
Interior lamp		
Except King Cab	5	–
King Cab	10	–
Combination meter		
Illumination lamp (1980 and 1981)	1.7	–
Illumination lamp (1982 on)	3.4	–
Warning lamp	3.4	158
Cigarette lighter illumination lamp	1.4	–
4WD oil pressure gauge illumination lamp	3.4	158
4WD voltmeter illumination lamp	3.4	158
4WD indicator lamp	3.4	158
Heater and A/C control panel illumination lamp	3.4	158
Radio illumination lamp	3.4	158
Selector lever illumination lamp (A/T models)	3.4	158
Rear window defogger switch indicator lamp	1.4	–
Rear window defogger switch illumination lamp	3.4	158

Fuses

1980

Circuit	Ampere rating
Headlight	20
Tail, license, clearance, side marker, illumination, interior light	10
Stoplight, hazard	15
Horn, clock	10
Radio, cigarette lighter	15
Wiper, washer, air conditioner, heater	15

Heater (with high-powered heater)	20
Warning lights, gauges, turn signal	15
Engine control	10

1981 on

Circuit	Ampere rating
Headlight	
Through 1990	10
1991 and later	15
Tail, license, clearance, side marker, illumination, interior light	
Through 1990	15
1991 and later	10
Stoplight	
Through 1990	15
1991 and later	10
Horn	10
Clock	10
Radio, cigarette lighter	15
Wiper, washer, air conditioner, heater	15
Heater	
Through 1990	20
1991 and later	15
Warning lights, gauges, turn signals	
Through 1990	15
1991 and later	10
Rear defroster	15
Engine control	15
Ignition coil	10

Fusible links

1980

Circuit	Color
Air conditioner circuits	Green
All load circuits	Red

1981 on

Circuit	Color
Headlight circuit	Green
Power supply (ignition/accessory at the fuse box)	Green
Power supply (battery at fuse box)	Black

Wiring harness color coding

Circuit	Base color
Starting and ignition systems	Black (B)
Charging system	White (W)
Lighting system	Red (R)
Turn signal and horn	Green (G)
Instrument system	Yellow (Y)
Others	Blue (L), Brown (Br) and Light green (Lg)
Grounding system	Black (B)

1 General information

This Chapter covers the repair and service procedures for various lighting and electrical components not associated with the engine, as well as general information on troubleshooting the various electrical circuits. Information on the battery, generator, distributor and starter motor can be found in Chapter 5.

The electrical system is of the 12-volt, negative ground type with power supplied by a lead/acid-type battery which is charged by the alternator.

Electrical components located in the dashboard do not use ground wires or straps, but rather use ground circuits which are integrated into the printed circuit mounted to the rear of the instrument cluster.

It should be noted that whenever portions of the electrical system are worked on, the negative battery cable should be disconnected to prevent electrical shorts and/or fires.

2 Electrical troubleshooting – general information

A typical electrical circuit consists of an electrical component, any switches, relays, motors, etc. relevant to that component and the wiring and connectors that connect the component to both the battery and the chassis. To aid in locating a problem in any electrical circuit, complete wiring diagrams of each model are included at the end of this Chapter. Also of benefit in locating specific circuits on the vehicle are wiring connector illustrations which identify all connectors used on the vehicle. These are also found at the end of this Chapter.

Before tackling any troublesome electrical circuit, first thoroughly study the appropriate diagrams to get a complete understanding of what makes up that individual circuit. Trouble spots, for instance, can often be narrowed down by noting if other components related to that circuit are operating properly or not.

If several components or circuits fail at one time, chances are the fault lies in the fuse or ground connection, as several circuits often are routed through the same fuse and ground connections. This can be confirmed by referring to the fuse box and ground distribution diagrams in this Chapter.

Often, electrical problems stem from simple causes, such as loose or corroded connections, a blown fuse or melted fusible link. Prior to any electrical troubleshooting, always visually check the condition of the fuse, wires and connections of the problem circuit.

If testing instruments are going to be utilized, use the diagrams to plan ahead of time where you will make the necessary connections in order to accurately pinpoint the trouble spot.

The basic tools needed for electrical troubleshooting include a circuit tester or voltmeter (a 12-volt bulb with a set of test leads can also be used), a continuity tester (which includes a bulb, battery and set of test leads) and a jumper wire, preferably with a circuit breaker incorporated , which can be used to bypass electrical components.

Voltage checks should be performed if a circuit is not functioning properly. Connect one lead of a circuit tester to either the negative battery terminal or a known good ground.

Connect the other lead to a connector in the circuit being tested, preferably nearest to the battery or fuse. If the bulb of the tester goes on voltage is reaching that point which means the part of the circuit between that connector and the battery is problem-free. Continue checking along the circuit in the same fashion. When you reach a point where no voltage is present, the problems lie between there and the last good test point. Most of the time the problem is due to a loose connection. Keep in mind that some circuits only receive voltage when the ignition key is in the Accessory or Run positions.

One method of finding shorts in a circuit is to remove the fuse and connect a test light or voltmeter in its place to the fuse terminals. There should be no load in the circuit. Move the wiring harness from side to side while watching the test light. If the bulb goes on, there is a short to ground somewhere in that area, probably where insulation has rubbed off of a wire. The same test can be performed on other components of the circuit, including the switch.

A ground check should be done to see if a component is grounded properly. Disconnect the battery and connect on lead of a self-powered test light such as a continuity tester to a known good ground. Connect the other lead to the wire or ground connection being tested. If the bulb goes on, the ground is good. If the bulb does not go on, the ground is not good.

A continuity check is performed to see if a circuit, section of circuit or individual component is passing electricity through it properly. Disconnect the battery, and connect one lead of a self-powered test light such as a continuity tester to one end of the circuit being tested, and the other lead to the other end of the circuit. If the bulb goes on, there is no continuity, which means the circuit is passing electricity through it properly. Switches can be checked in the same way.

Remember that all electrical circuits are composed basically of electricity running from the battery, through the wires, switches, relays,etc. to the electrical component (light bulb, motor, etc.). From there it is run to the body (ground) where it is passed back to the battery. Any electrical problem is basically an interruption in the flow of electricity from the battery or back to it.

3 Fuses – general information

Refer to illustrations 3.1a, 3.1b, 3.1c, 3.1d, 3.1e and 3.1f

The electrical circuits of the vehicle are protected by a combination of fuses and fusible links **(see illustrations)**.

The fuse box is located on the side panel underneath the dash or behind a panel on the dash cover on the left side of the vehicle. Access to the fuses is achieved by simply unsnapping the fuse cover.

Each of the fuses is designed to protect a specific circuit, as identified on the fuse cover.

If an electrical component has failed, your first check should be the fuse. A fuse which has "blown" can be readily identified by inspecting the curved metal element inside the plastic housing. If this element is broken the fuse is inoperable and should be replaced with a new one.

Fuses are replaced by simply pulling out the old one and pushing in the new one.

It is important that the correct fuse be installed. The different electrical circuits need varying amounts of protection, indicated by the amperage rating on the fuse. A fuse with too low a rating will blow prematurely, while a fuse with too high a rating may not blow soon enough to avoid serious damage.

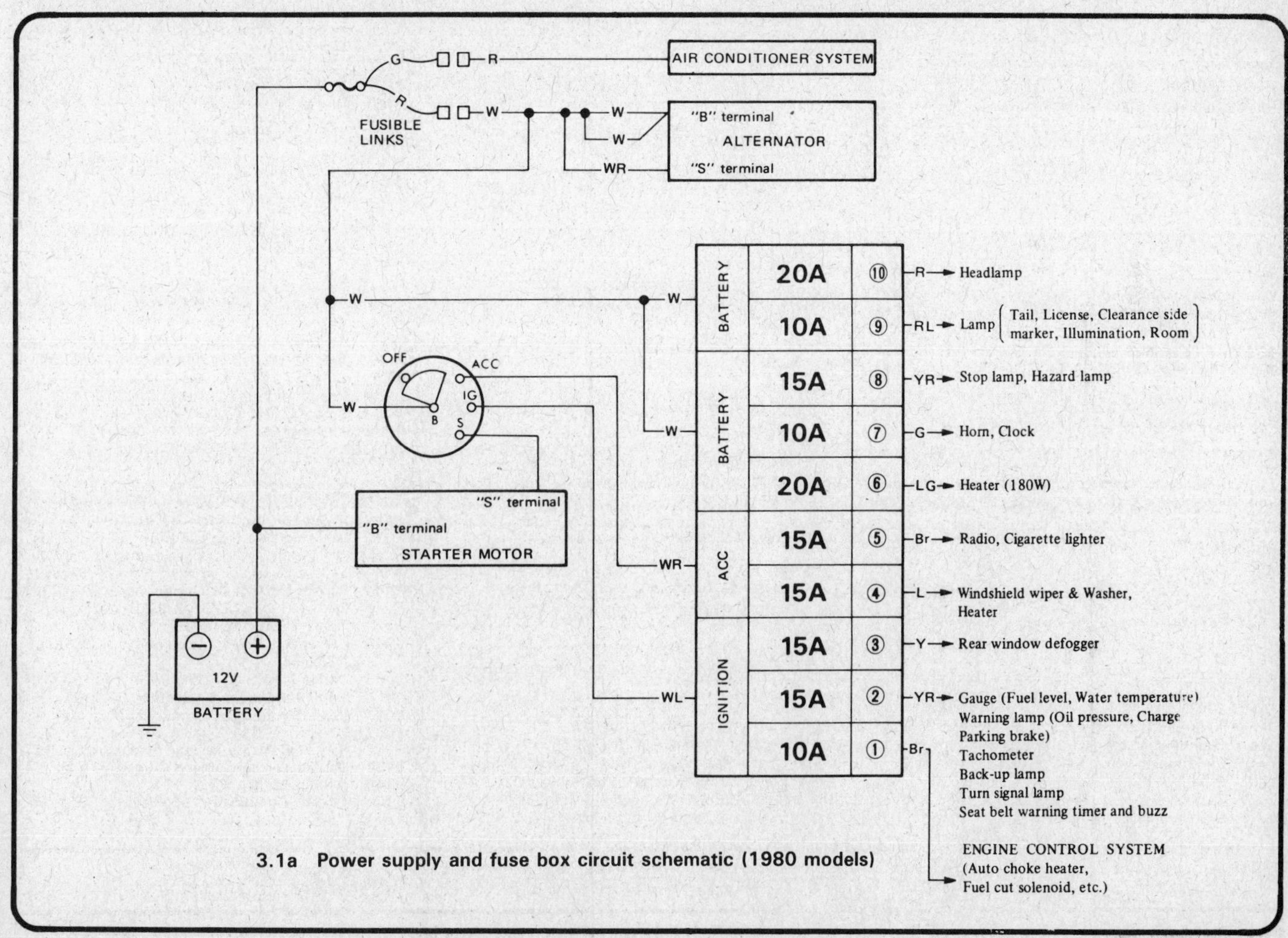

3.1a Power supply and fuse box circuit schematic (1980 models)

13

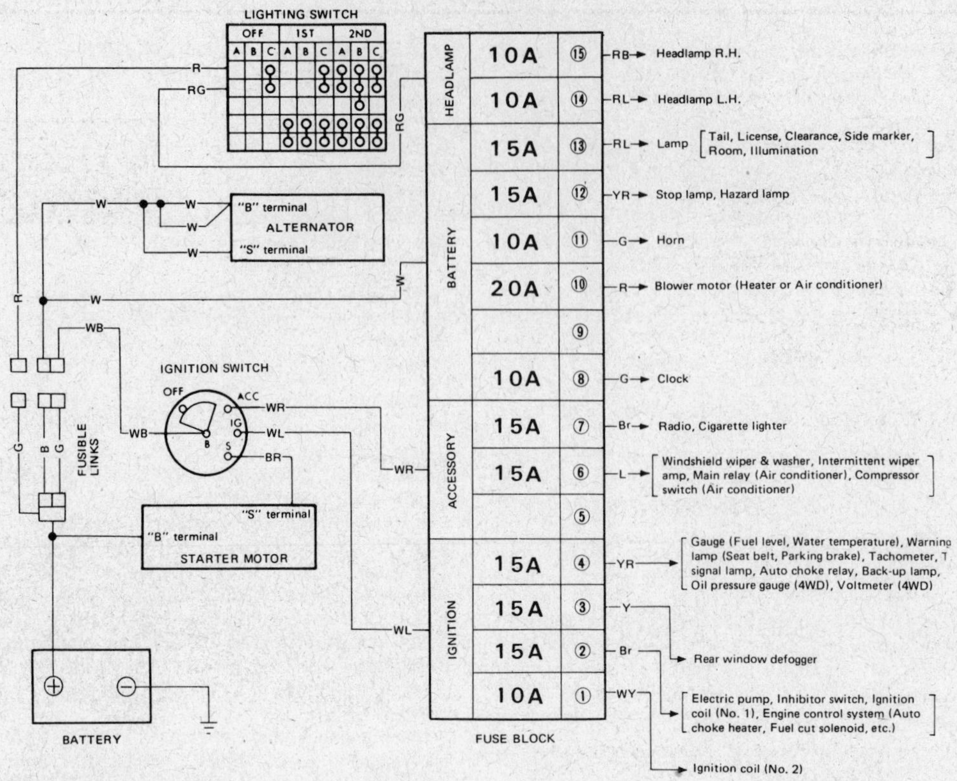

3.1b Power supply and fuse box circuit schematic (1981 through 1985 models)

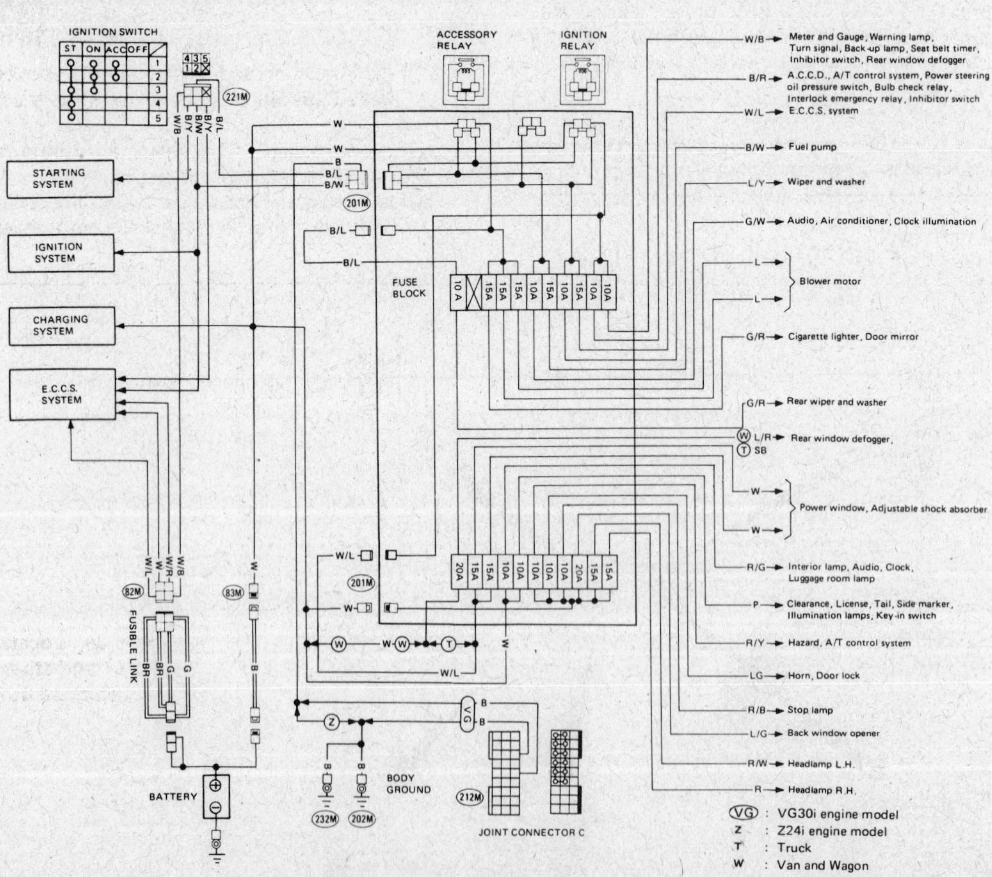

3.1c Power supply and fuse box circuit schematic (1986 and later models)

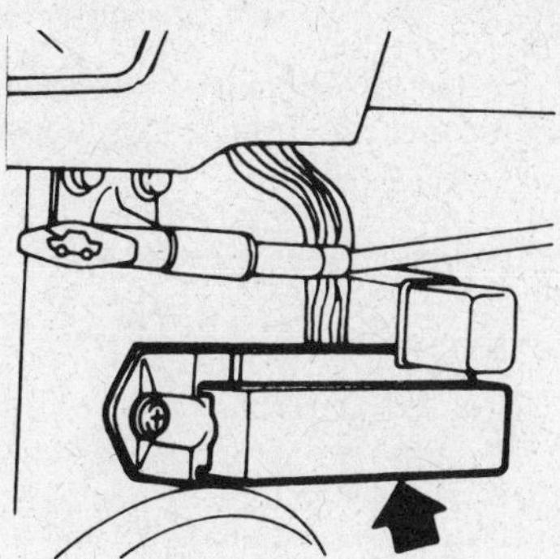

3.1d 1980 through 1985 model fuse box location (arrow)

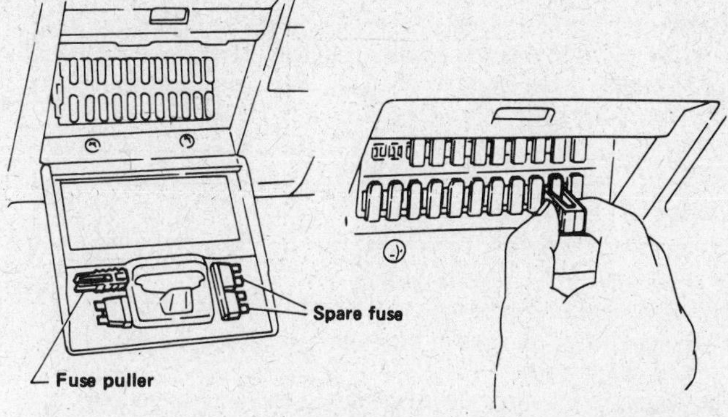

3.1e 1986 and later model fuse box details

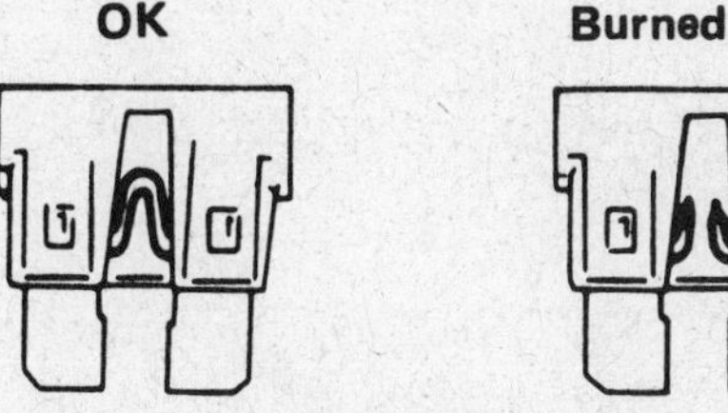

3.1f The type of fuse used on these models can be easily checked visually

At no time should the fuse by bypassed by using metal or foil. Serious damage to the electrical system could result.

If the replacement fuse immediately fails, do not replace it with another until the cause of the problem is isolated and corrected. In most cases this will be a short circuit in the wiring system caused by a broken or deteriorated wire.

4 Fusible links – general information

Refer to illustration 4.2

In addition to fuses, the wiring system incorporates fusible links for additional overload protection. These links are used in circuits which are not ordinarily fused, such as the ignition circuit.

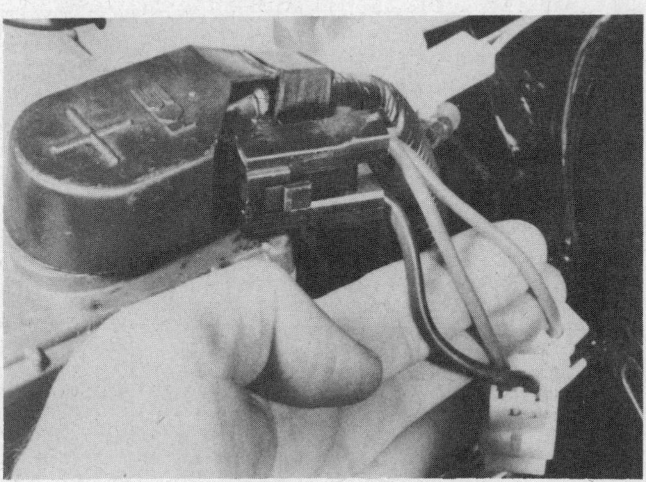

4.2 If the insulation on fusible link(s) is swollen, discolored or melted, the link has blown and should be replaced

The fusible links are located near the positive battery terminal, and are easily removed by unplugging the connectors at either end **(see illustration)**.

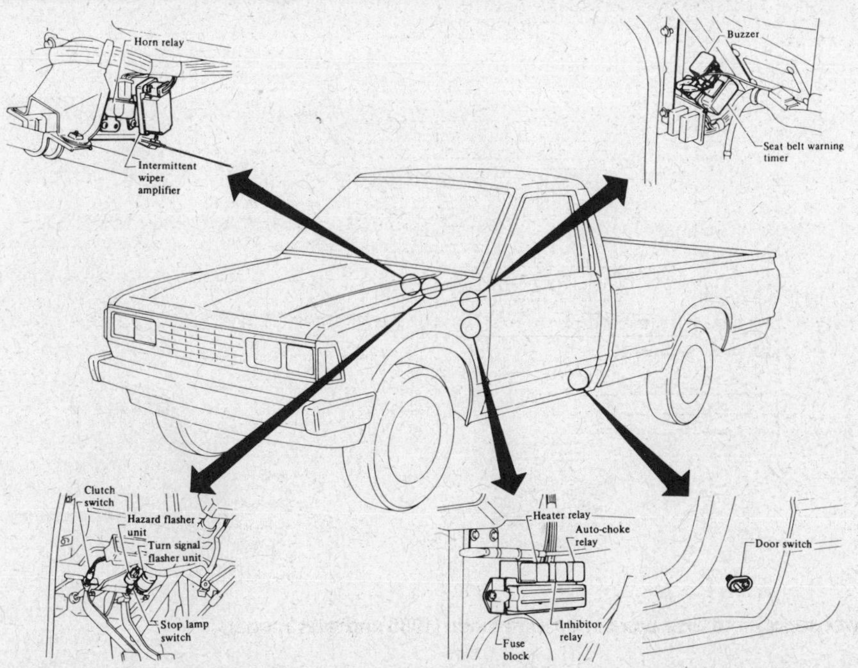

5.2a Locations of relays and other electrical components (1980 models)

If an electrical failure occurs in a circuit or group of circuits, and there are no blown fuses, check for a melted fusible link. If the link is melted, it should be replaced, but only after checking and correcting the electrical fault that caused it.

5 Relays – general information

Refer to illustrations 5.2a, 5.2b and 5.2c

Several electrical accessories in the vehicle use relays to transmit the electrical signal to the component. If the relay is defective, that component will not operate properly.

The various relays are grouped together in several locations under the dash for convenience in the event of needed replacement **(see illustrations)**.

If a faulty relay is suspected, it can be removed and tested by a Nissan dealer or other qualified shop. Defective relays must be replaced as a unit.

6 Switches – testing

Refer to illustrations 6.3a, 6.3b, 6.3c, 6.3d and 6.3e

1 All switches used in this truck can be easily tested for proper operation by using an ohmmeter or continuity tester. The wiring diagrams at the rear of this Chapter contain all the information necessary for testing each switch. In addition, the accompanying figure provides more information for testing the turn signal/horn switch and the heater/A/C fan switch.

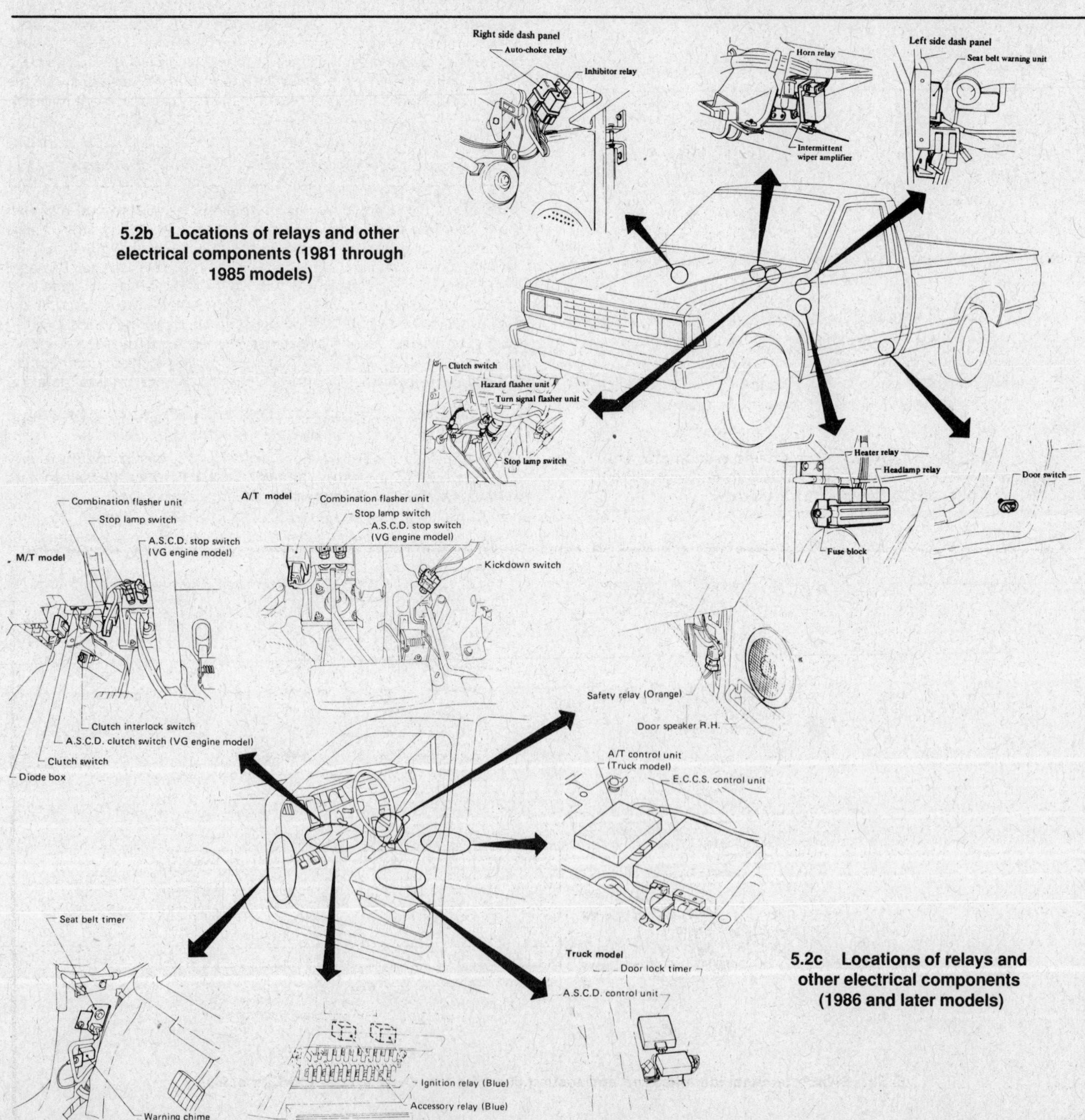

5.2b Locations of relays and other electrical components (1981 through 1985 models)

5.2c Locations of relays and other electrical components (1986 and later models)

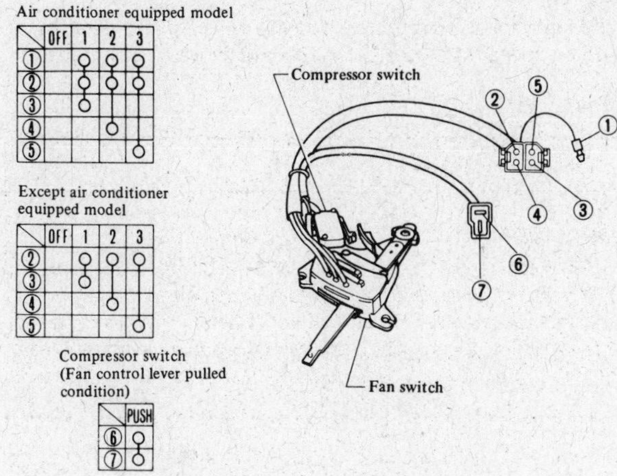

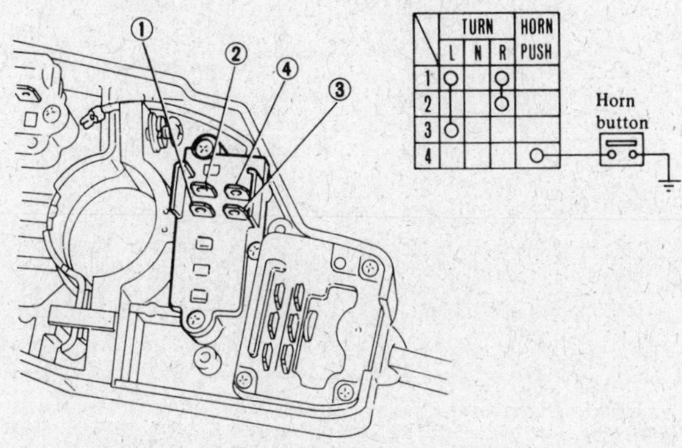

6.3a Switch terminal identification and testing chart for the turn signal/horn switch and heater/a/c fan switch (top) (1980 through 1982 models)

2 Simple on-off type switches, such as the parking brake switch, are the easiest to test. This kind of switch is either normally closed or normally open. Identify which type of switch you are testing by referring to the wiring diagram keys. Then disconnect the wires from the switch and connect the leads from the continuity tester or ohmmeter to the switch wires. Operate the switch in both the On and Off positions and note the result. When the switch is closed, continuity should exist (indicated by the continuity tester's bulb glowing or by the ohmmeter needle swinging away from the O mark). When the switch is open, no continuity should exist.

3 Switches that use multi-terminal connectors require a slightly different testing procedure. Each switch in the wiring diagrams is accompanied by a diagram which identifies the terminals of the switch's wiring connector **(see illustrations)**. Each switch is also accompanied by a chart that shows which terminals should display continuity in each switch position. Down the left side of the chart are the connector terminals and across the top are the various positions of the switch. The terminals between which continuity should exist in each switch position are indicated by small circles connected by lines. If the switch does not test out as shown in the chart, it should be replaced. Each position of the lighting switch is broken down into A, B and C positions. A is the upper position, B is the lower position and C is the pulled out position.

7 Turn signals and hazard flashers – general information

Small canister-shaped flasher units are incorporated into the electrical circuits for the directional signals and hazard warning lights. These are located under the dash and just above the steering column.

When the units are functioning properly, an audible click can be heard with the circuit in operation. If the turn signals fail on one side only and the flasher unit cannot be heard, a faulty bulb is indicated. If the flasher unit can be heard, a short in the wiring is indicated.

If the turn signal fails on both sides, the fault may be due to a blown fuse, faulty flasher unit or switch, or a broken or loose connection. If the fuse has blown, check the wiring for a short before installing a new fuse.

The hazard warning lamps are checked in the same manner as Paragraph 3 above.

When replacing either of these flasher units, it is important to buy a replacement of the same capacity. check the new flasher against the old one to be assured of the proper replacement.

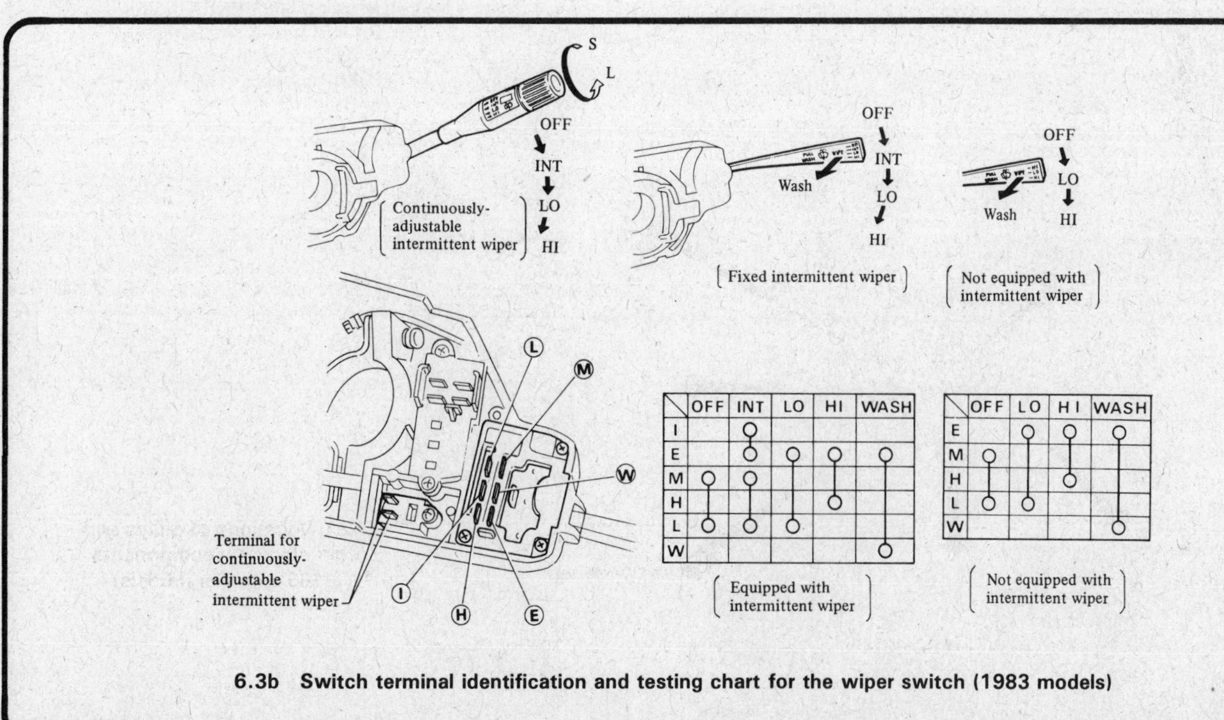

6.3b Switch terminal identification and testing chart for the wiper switch (1983 models)

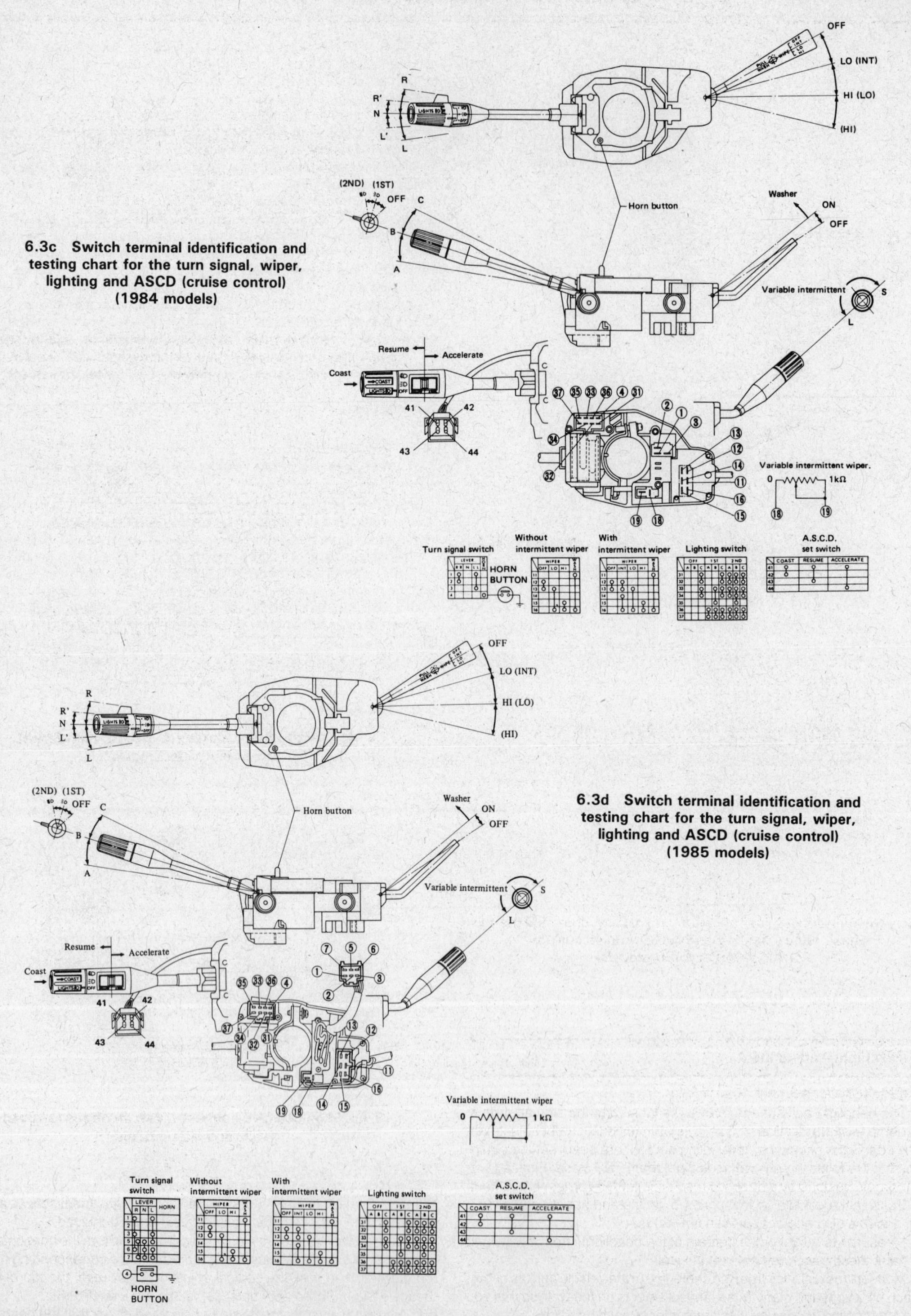

6.3c Switch terminal identification and testing chart for the turn signal, wiper, lighting and ASCD (cruise control) (1984 models)

6.3d Switch terminal identification and testing chart for the turn signal, wiper, lighting and ASCD (cruise control) (1985 models)

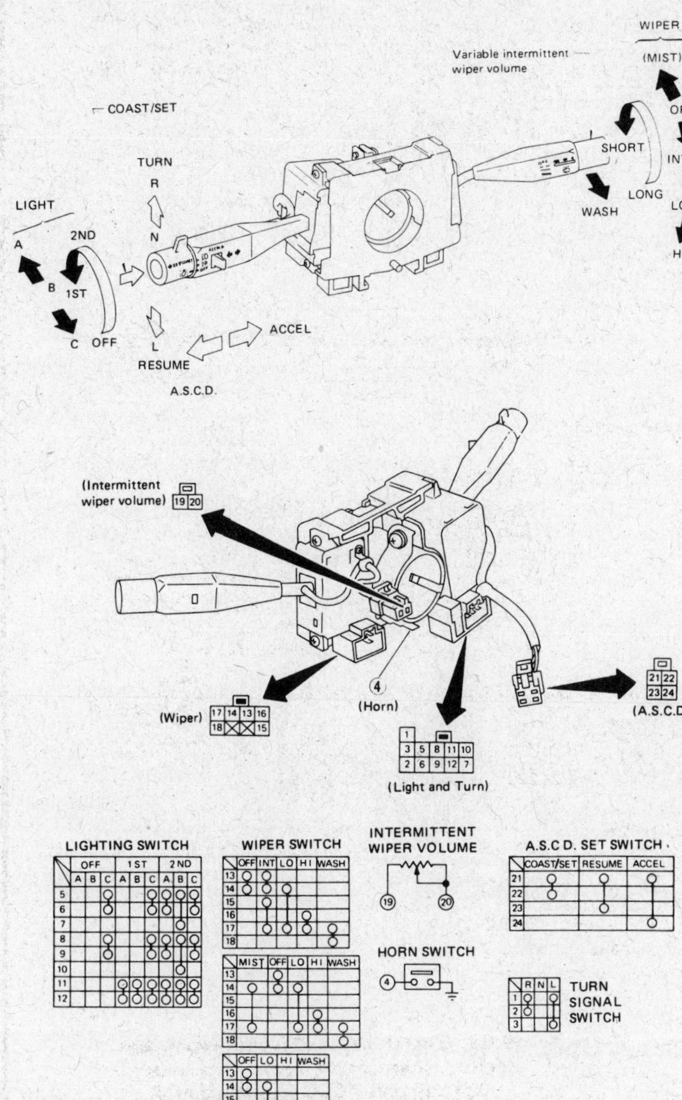

6.3e Switch terminal identification and testing chart for the turn signal, wiper, lighting and ASCD (cruise control) (1986 through 1988 models)

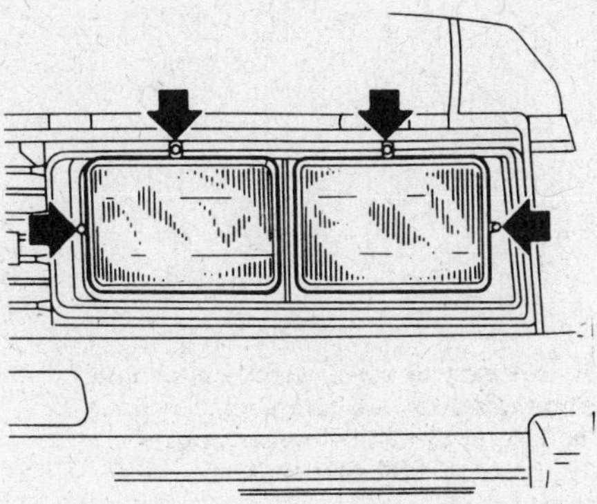

8.1a 1980 through 1985 model headlight adjustment screw locations (arrows); the top screws adjust the vertical movement, the side screws the horizontal movement

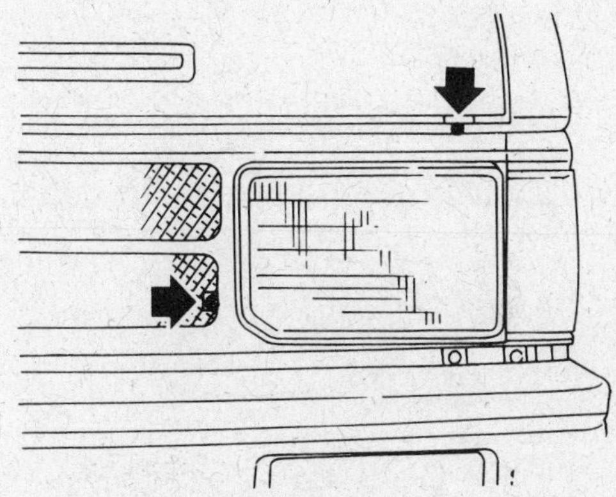

8.1b 1986 and later models low beam adjustment screw locations (arrows)

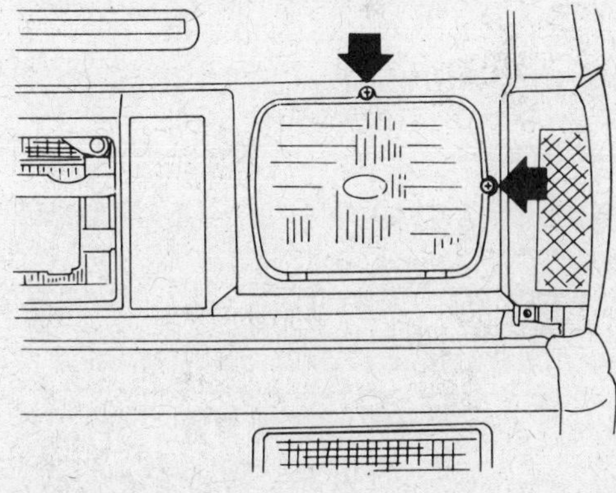

8.1c High beam adjustment screw locations (arrows) (1986 and later models)

8 Headlight – adjustment

Refer to illustrations 8.1a, 8.1b and 8.1c

1 The headlight adjustment screws are located to the side and top of each lamp **(see illustrations)**. Due to legal limitations, proper adjustment of the headlights should be done using appropriate beam setting equipment, but the following procedure will get them very close. Final adjustment should be done by a qualified mechanic with the proper equipment.

2 Position the vehicle on level ground, facing and at right angles to a wall, and at a distance of approximately 30 feet.

3 Measure the height of the centers of the headlights from the ground and mark these measurements on the wall.

4 Measure the distance from the centerline of the vehicle and the center of each headlight and mark these measurements on the wall, so that you have intersecting lines even with the center of each headlight.

5 On 1986 and later models, remove the headlight bezels. Adjustment is made on these models by first tightening the adjustment screws all the way and then loosening them until adjustment is achieved.

6 Turn on the regular beam of the headlights and turn the horizontal adjusting screws until each beam is centered with the corresponding marks on the wall. The, turn the vertical adjusting screw until the top of each beam is level with the horizontal centerline mark on the wall.

7 Bounce the vehicle on its suspension and check that the beams return to their original positions.

Headlight reflector
Glass envelope
Bulb
LOCK
PUSH to remove
Bulb socket
Electrical connector
Plastic base
UNLOCK
Bulb retaining ring

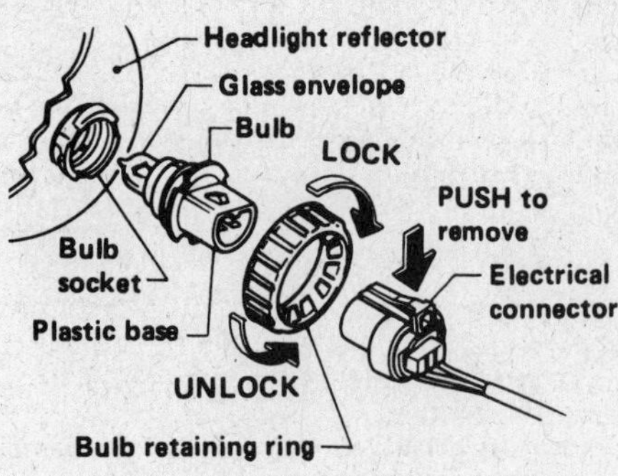

9.6 Halogen bulb-type headlight details

9 Headlight – removal and installation

Refer to illustration 9.6

Sealed-beam type

1 Remove the grille, referring to Chapter 13, if necessary.
2 Remove the headlight retaining ring.
3 Lift the headlight out and disconnect the wiring connector.
4 Installation is the reverse of removal.

Halogen bulb type

5 Disconnect the negative cable at the battery.
6 Unplug the electrical connector **(see illustration)**.
7 Rotate the bulb retaining ring counterclockwise until it unlocks and withdraw the bulb from the headlight reflector.
8 Installation is the reverse of removal.

10 Bulb – replacement

Refer to illustrations 10.2a, 10.2b and 10.3

1 The lenses of most lights are held on by screws, which makes it a simple procedure to gain access to the bulbs.
2 A few lights have their lenses held in by clips. On these, the lens can either be removed by unsnapping it by hand or, as with the interior overhead light, using a small screwdriver inserted in the rear to pry it off **(see illustrations)**.
3 Four different types of bulbs are used **(see illustration)**. Type A and B are removed by pushing in and turning counterclockwise. Type D simply unclips from its terminals and Type C simply pulls out of its socket.
4 To gain access to the instrument panel illumination light bulbs, the combination meter must be removed as described in Section 18.

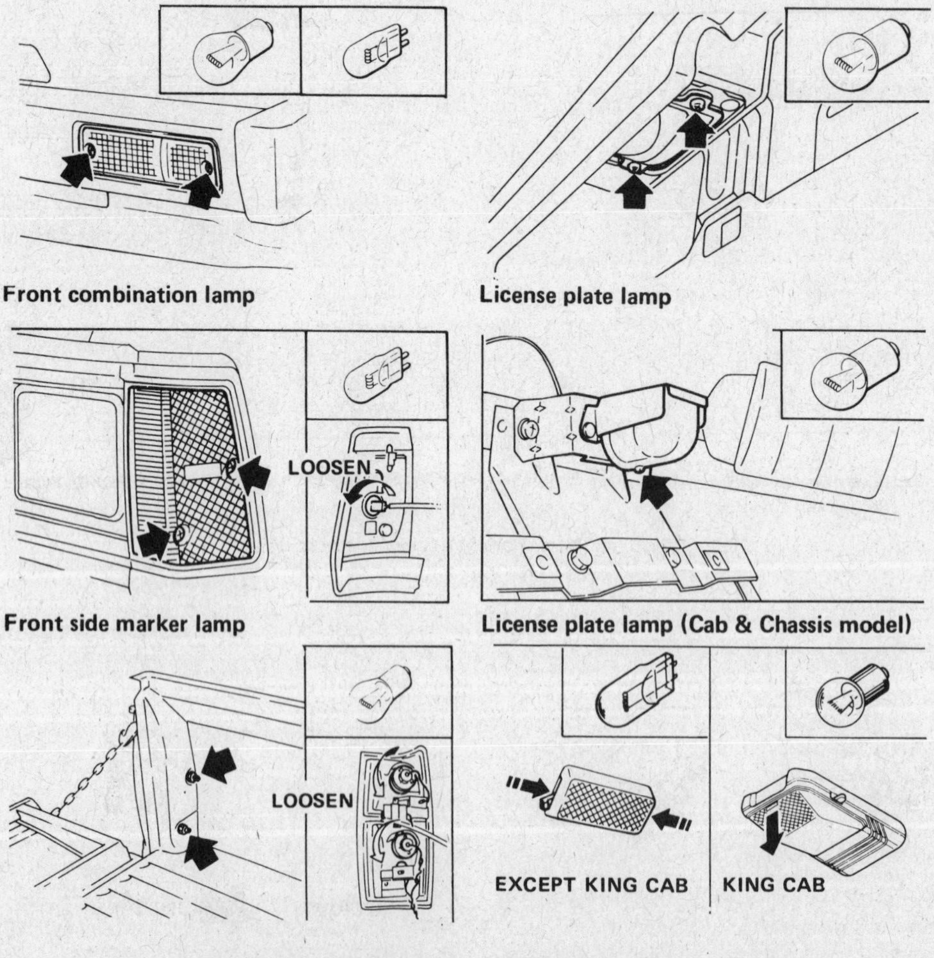

Front combination lamp
License plate lamp
LOOSEN
Front side marker lamp
License plate lamp (Cab & Chassis model)
LOOSEN
EXCEPT KING CAB
KING CAB

10.2a 1980 through 1985 model bulb replacement details

11 Horn – fault testing

1 Two horns are used, one with a low tone and the other with a high tone. They are both mounted behind the front bumper, one below either headlight. The horn switch is located in the steering wheel, and can be activated by pressing the center pad or, on some models, one of the side buttons. The pressing of one of the horn buttons grounds it against the metal frame of the steering wheel, which completes the electrical circuit and sounds the horns. The horn relay is located under the left side of the dash, above the steering column (see accompanying figure).
2 If the horn proves inoperable, your first check should be the fuse. A blown fuse can be readily identified at the fuse box.
3 If the fuse is in good condition, disconnect the electrical lead at one of the horns. Run a jumper wire from the positive battery terminal to the wiring terminal on the horn. If the horn does not blow, the fault lies in the grounding of the horn or the horn itself. Test the other horn also.
4 If the horn did sound in the previous test, this indicates that no current is reaching the horn. In most cases the problem will be in the horn relay. Other checks should include bent metal contacts in the horn switch assembly, or loose or broken wires in the system.

12 Horn – removal and installation

1 Disconnect the negative battery cable from the battery.
2 Remove the front combination light, positioned in front of the horn, from the front bumper.
3 Using a screwdriver inserted through the front combination light opening, remove the horn mounting screw and lower the horn.
4 Disconnect the wiring connector from the horn and lift it out.
5 Installation is the reverse of the removal procedure.

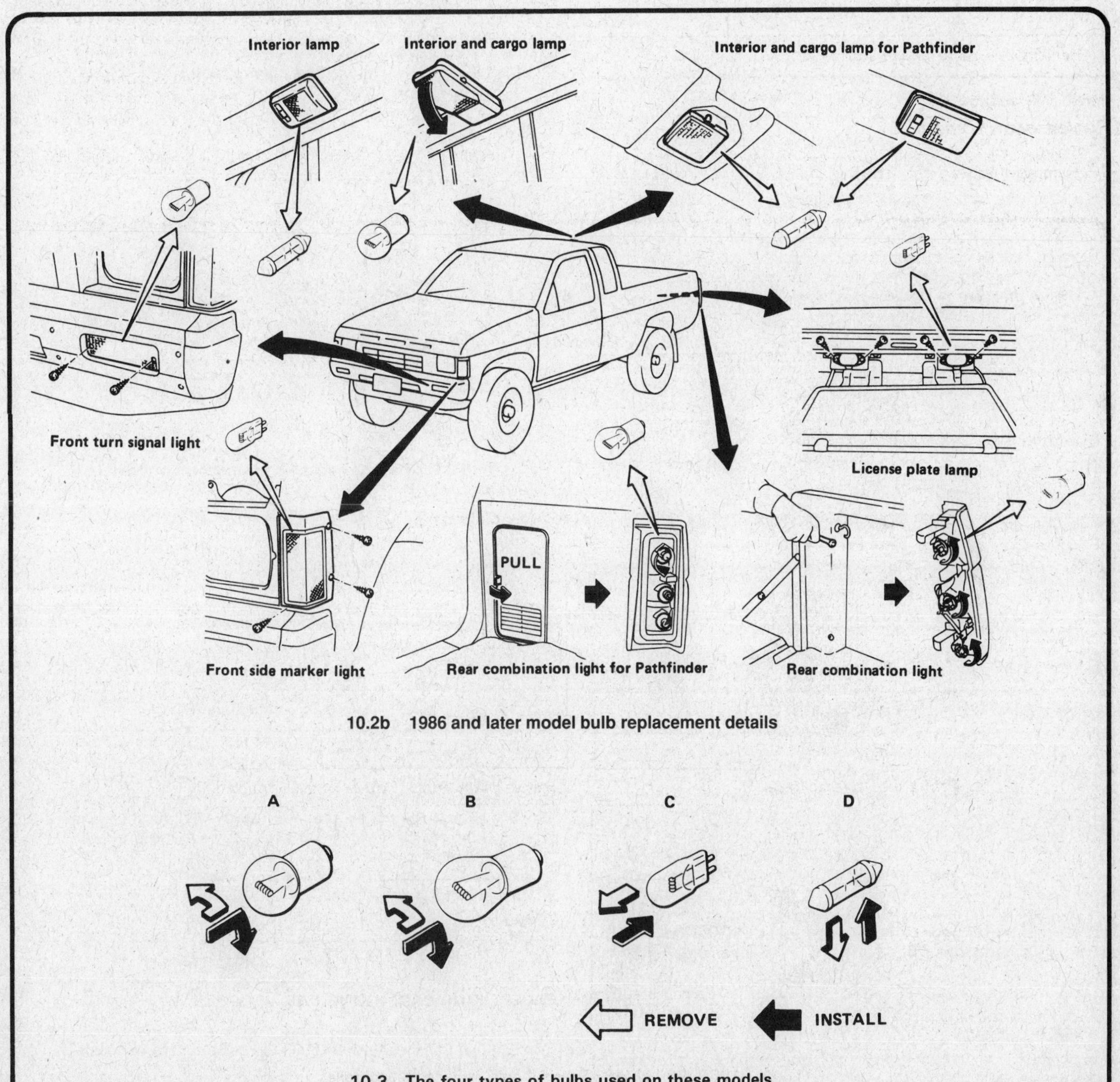

10.2b 1986 and later model bulb replacement details

10.3 The four types of bulbs used on these models

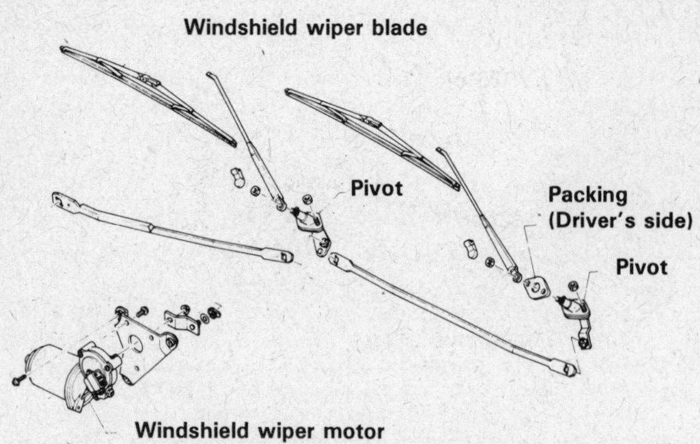

14.2a Windshield wiper system component layout (1980 through 1985 models)

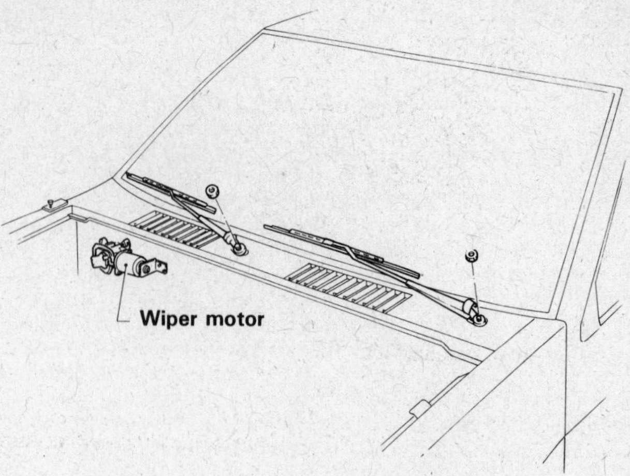

14.2b Windshield wiper system component layout (1986 and later models)

13 Windshield wiper system – general information

1 The windshield wiper consists of a wiper motor unit, link mechanism, wiper arms, blades and an intermittent amplifier.
2 The motor incorporates an auto-stop device and operates the wipers in three different stages: intermittent, low speed, and high speed.
3 The electrically operated windshield washer consists of a reservoir tank (with built-in motor and pump), washer nozzles and vinyl tubes used to connect the components.
4 The intermittent amplifier, which is located on the engine compartment relay mounting bracket, controls the intermittent operation of the wipers.
5 In the unlikely event of its failure, it is not possible to repair the amplifier and it must be replaced as an assembly.

14 Wiper motor – removal and installation

Refer to illustrations 14.2a and 14.2b

1 Remove the hood, referring to Chapter 13, if necessary.
2 Remove the windshield wiper arms **(see illustrations)**.
3 Remove the cowl (Chapter 11).
4 Remove the stop ring that retains the wiper linkage to the wiper motor.
5 Disconnect the wiring connector from the wiper motor.
6 Remove the wiper motor mounting screw and lift it out.
7 Installation is the reverse of removal.

15 Windshield washer – servicing

1 The washer fluid reservoir is located on the right side of the engine compartment. The washer pump is mounted under the fluid reservoir.
2 Normally the windshield washer requires no maintenance other than keeping the reservoir topped-up with water, to which a little windshield cleaning fluid can be added.
3 If the washer reservoirs or electric pump have to be placed individually, they may be separated after disconnecting the connecting pipes and leads.
4 When reconnecting the pump to the base of the reservoir, warm the reservoir by immersing it in hot water and use a solution of soapy water to lubricate the neck of the pump opening in the reservoir.

16 Steering column combination switch – removal and installation

Refer to illustration 16.5

1 Disconnect the negative battery cable from the battery.

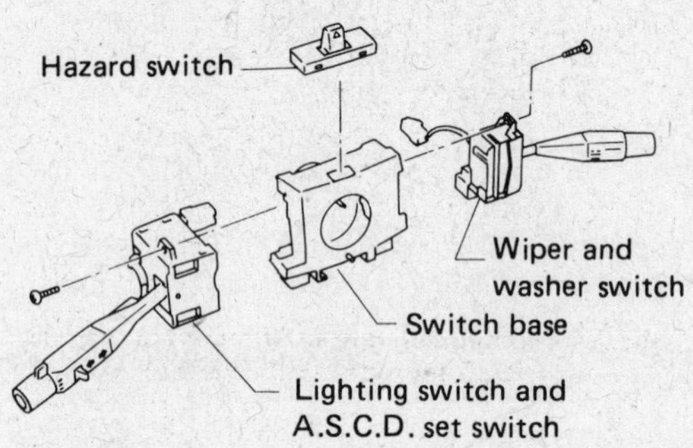

16.5 Typical later model combination switch details

2 Remove the steering wheel, referring to Chapter 12 if necessary.
3 Remove the steering column cover.
4 Disconnect the wiring connectors from the combination switch.
5 Loosen the combination switch retaining screw, and slide the switch off the steering column **(see illustration)**.
6 Installation is the reverse of removal.

17 Ignition switch – removal and installation

Refer to illustration 17.4

1 Disconnect the negative battery cable from the battery.
2 Remove the steering column cover from the steering column.
3 Disconnect the wiring connector from the ignition switch.
4 The ignition switch can now be removed **(see illustration)**. On models equipped with a steering lock, the ignition switch is attached to the lock by a retaining screw in the rear.
5 Installation is the reverse of removal.

18 Combination meter – removal and installation

Refer to illustrations 18.2, 18.3 and 18.5

1 Disconnect the negative battery cable from the battery.
2 Remove the screws that retain the cluster lid to the dash and lift it off **(see illustration)**.
3 Remove the screws that retain the combination meter to the dash **(see illustration)**.

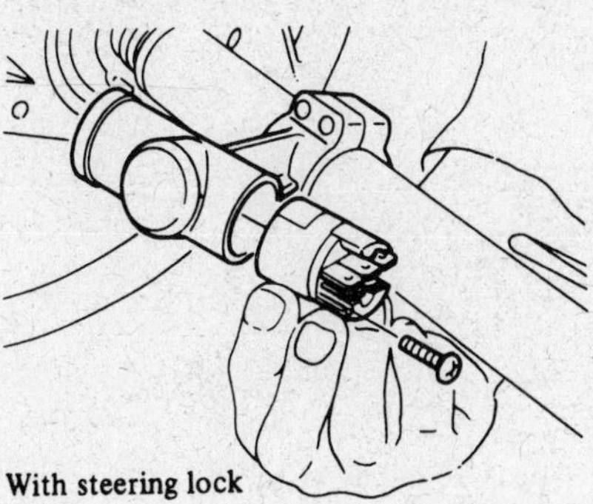

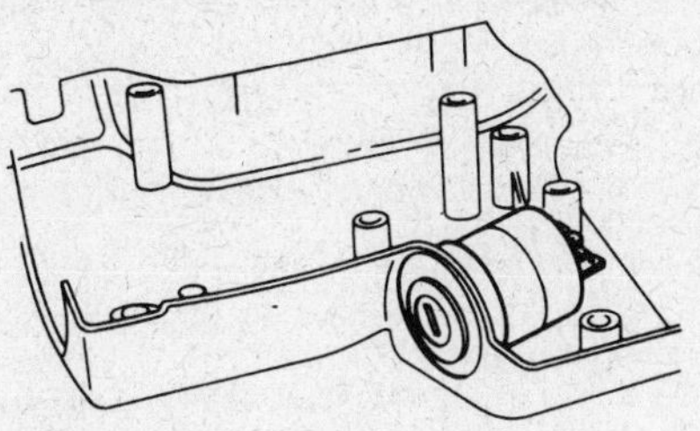

17.4 Typical ignition switch details (1980 through 1985 model shown)

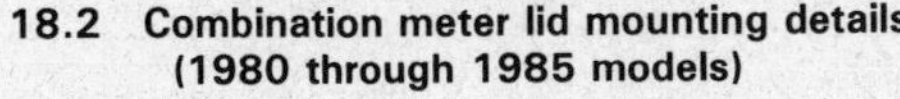

18.2 Combination meter lid mounting details (1980 through 1985 models)

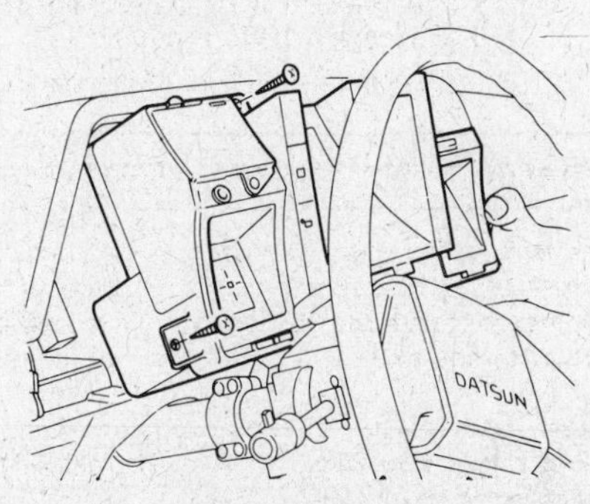

18.3 Combination meter mounting screw locations (1980 through 1985 models)

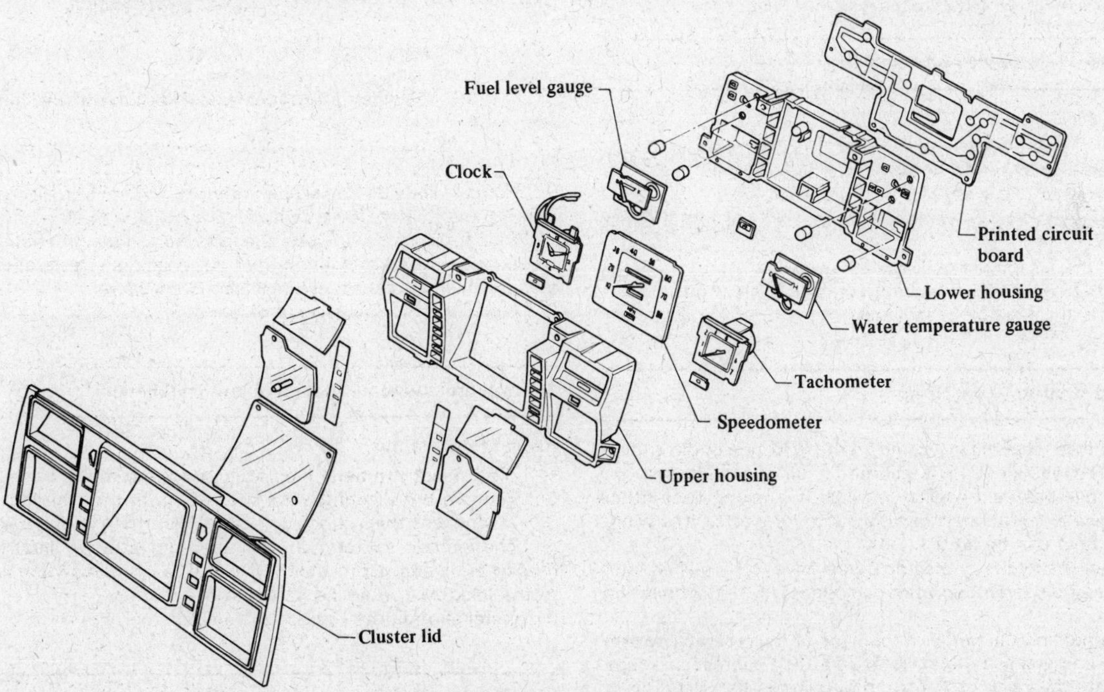

18.5 Typical combination meter — exploded view

4 Carefully pull the combination meter out from the dash far enough to disconnect the wiring and speedometer cable from its rear. Lift the combination meter from the dash.

5 The combination meter housing can be disassembled to allow access to the enclosed gauges and indicators by removing the retaining screws **(see illustration)**. The printed circuit board can be removed by removing the bulb sockets from the rear of the housing and then removing the retaining screws or clips. Be careful that you do not tear or damage the printed circuit board.

6 Installation is the reverse of removal.

19 Radio – removal and installation

Refer to illustrations 19.4 and 19.5

1 Disconnect the negative battery cable from the battery.
2 Remove the ash tray.
3 Remove heater-A/C control assembly as described in Chapter 3.
4 Working under the dash, remove the plug and the radio mounting screws **(see illustration)**.
5 Carefully pull the radio out from the dash and disconnect the wiring connector and antenna cable from the rear of the radio **(see illustration)**.
6 Installation is the reverse of removal.

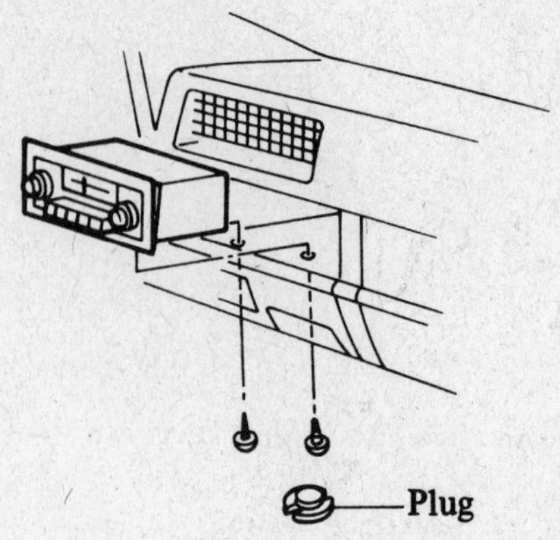

19.4 Typical radio installation details

20 Cigarette lighter – removal and installation

Refer to illustration 20.4

1 Disconnect the negative battery cable from the battery.
2 Disconnect the wires leading to the cigarette lighter.
3 Remove the lighter retaining nut from the back of the lighter assembly.
4 Pull the lighter assembly out from the front of the cluster. As this is done, the light bulb housing will also come off the back of the cluster **(see illustration)**.
5 Installation is the reverse of the removal procedure. When installing the components, be sure they are lined up properly by engaging the locating tabs in their respective slots.

21 Illumination control unit – removal and installation

1 Disconnect the negative battery cable from the battery.
2 Pull off the switch knob. On 1984 and later models, you must depress and rotate the knob before pulling it off.
3 Remove the ring nut.
4 Disconnect the wiring connector from the switch.
5 The switch can be removed from the rear of the instrument panel.
6 Installation is the reverse of removal.

22 Hazard warning switch – removal and installation

1 Disconnect the negative battery cable from the battery.
2 Remove the steering column cover.
3 Disconnect the wiring connector from the hazard warning switch.
4 Remove the screws that retain the hazard warning switch to the cover and lift off the switch.
5 Installation is the reverse of removal.

23 Rear window defogger switch – removal and installation

1 Disconnect the negative battery cable from the battery.
2 Using a small screwdriver, pry the switch out from its mounting location.
3 Disconnect the wiring connector from the switch and lift it out.
4 Installation is the reverse of removal.

24 Rear defogger grid – testing and repair

1 This option consists of a rear window with a number of horizontal elements that are baked into the glass surface during the glass forming operation.
2 Small breaks in the element system can be successfully repaired without removing the rear window.
3 To test the grids for proper operation, start the engine and turn on the system.
4 Ground one lead of a test lamp and lightly touch the other lead to each grid line.
5 The brilliance of the test lamp should increase as the probe is moved across the element from right to left. If the test lamp glows brightly at both ends of the grid lines, check for a loose ground wire for the system. All of the grid lines should be checked in at least two places.

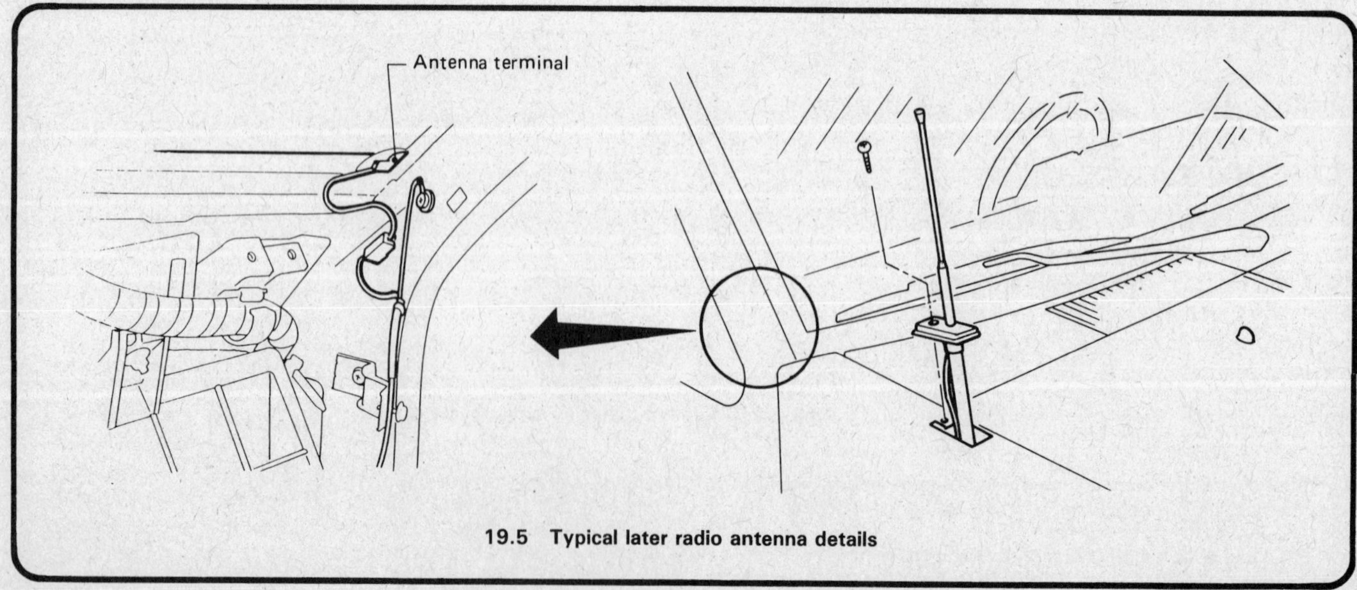

19.5 Typical later radio antenna details

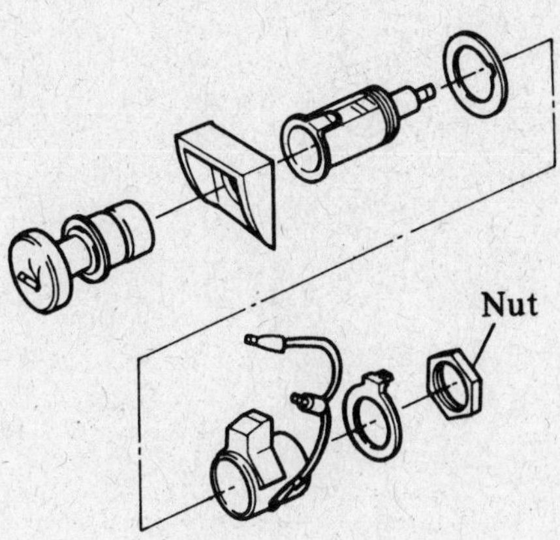

20.4 Typical cigarette light installation details

6 The materials needed to repair a breaking grid line include a conductive silver compound (available specifically for this purpose), a drawing pen, electrical tape, alcohol and cloth. Complete repair kits can also be obtained.
7 To repair a break, first turn off the system and allow it to de-energize for a few minutes.
8 Lightly buff the grid line area with a fine steel wool and then thoroughly clean the area with alcohol.
9 Use electrician's tape above and below the area to be repaired. The space between the pieces of tape should be the same width as existing grid lines. This can be checked from outside the vehicle. Press the tape tightly against the glass to prevent seepage.
10 Dip the pen in the silver and apply it at the break between the pieces of tape, overlapping the damaged area slightly on either end.
11 Carefully remove the tape. If a hot air gun is available, apply a constant stream of hot air directly to the repaired area. A heat gun set at 500- to 700-degrees Fahrenheit is recommended. Hold the gun about one inch from the glass for one to two minutes.
12 If the new grid line appears off color, tincture of iodine can be used to clean the repair and bring it back to the proper color. The mixture should not remain on the repair for more than 30 seconds.
13 Although the defogger is now fully operational, the repaired area should not be disturbed for at least 24 hours.

25 Airbag – general information

The 1996 models are equipped with the Supplemental Restraint System (SRS), more commonly known as an airbag. This system is designed to protect the driver in the event of a head-on or frontal collision up to 30-degrees of the centerline of the vehicle. It consists of an airbag inflator module in the center of the steering wheel, a crash zone sensor (4WD models), a diagnosis sensor unit and a spiral cable in the steering column.

On models equipped with an airbag, DO NOT remove the steering wheel without first having the airbag disabled or removed from the steering wheel by an automotive repair facility or dealers service department. Failure to do so can result in accidental deployment of the airbag and serious physical injury.

WIRING DIAGRAMS START
ON NEXT PAGE

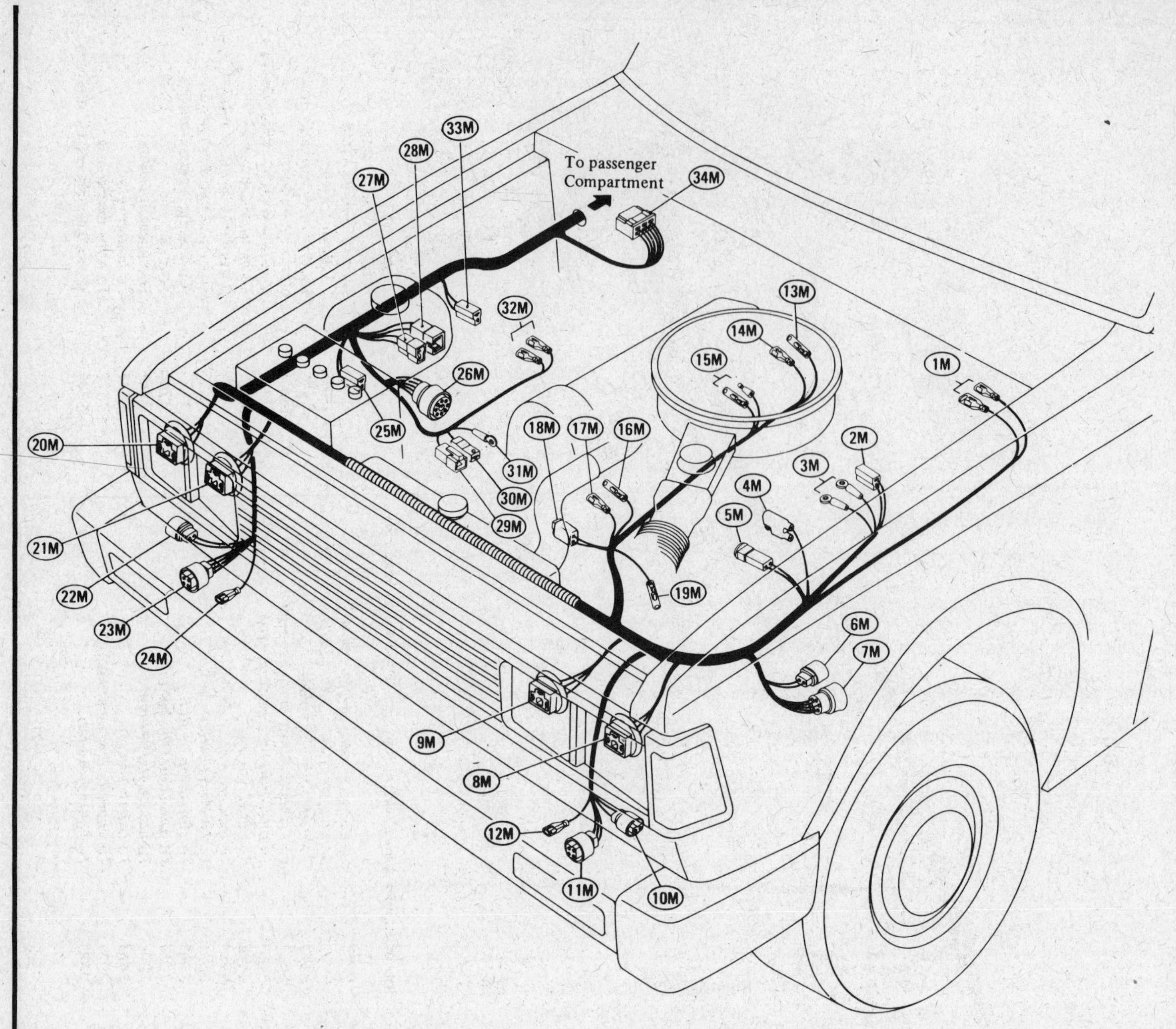

Identification of engine compartment wiring harness connectors (typical)

1M – *To magnet valve (FICD)*
2M – *To condenser*
3M – *To ignition coil*
4M – *To vacuum switching valve (Heavy duty for California models)*
5M – *To air control valve (Heavy duty for California models)*
6M – *To vacuum switch (US models)*
7M – *Check connector*
8M – *To left headlamp (Type-2)*
9M – *To left headlamp (Type-1)*
10M – *To left side marker lamp*
11M – *To left front combination lamp*
12M – *To horn Low*
13M – *To auto choke heater*
14M – *To fuel cut solenoid*
15M – *To vacuum cut solenoid (California models)*
16M – *To thermal transmitter*
17M – *To distributor earth point*
18M – *To distributor*
19M – *To air conditioner compressor*
20M – *To right headlamp (Type-2)*
21M – *To right headlamp (Type-1)*
22M – *To right side marker lamp*
23M – *To right front combination lamp*
24M – *To horn High*
25M – *To resistor (tachometer)*
26M – *To transmission harness 1S*
27M – *To transmission harness 3S*
28M – *To transmission harness 2S*
29M – *To fusible link (for air conditioner)*
30M – *To fusible link*
31M – *To ground*
32M – *To low pressure switch*
33M – *To windshield washer motor*
34M – *To wiper motor*

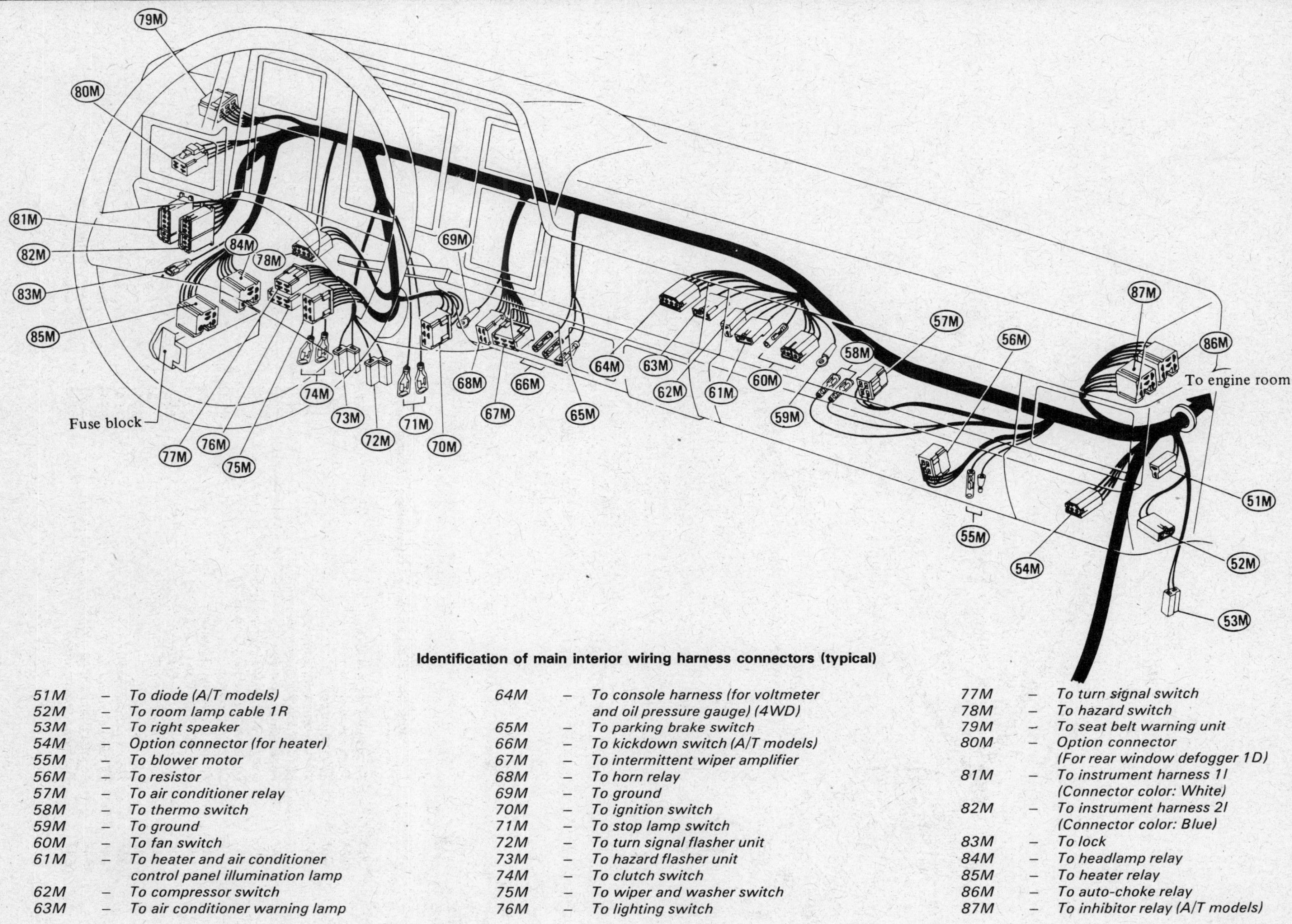

Identification of main interior wiring harness connectors (typical)

51M – To diode (A/T models)
52M – To room lamp cable 1R
53M – To right speaker
54M – Option connector (for heater)
55M – To blower motor
56M – To resistor
57M – To air conditioner relay
58M – To thermo switch
59M – To ground
60M – To fan switch
61M – To heater and air conditioner control panel illumination lamp
62M – To compressor switch
63M – To air conditioner warning lamp
64M – To console harness (for voltmeter and oil pressure gauge) (4WD)
65M – To parking brake switch
66M – To kickdown switch (A/T models)
67M – To intermittent wiper amplifier
68M – To horn relay
69M – To ground
70M – To ignition switch
71M – To stop lamp switch
72M – To turn signal flasher unit
73M – To hazard flasher unit
74M – To clutch switch
75M – To wiper and washer switch
76M – To lighting switch
77M – To turn signal switch
78M – To hazard switch
79M – To seat belt warning unit
80M – Option connector (For rear window defogger 1D)
81M – To instrument harness 1I (Connector color: White)
82M – To instrument harness 2I (Connector color: Blue)
83M – To lock
84M – To headlamp relay
85M – To heater relay
86M – To auto-choke relay
87M – To inhibitor relay (A/T models)

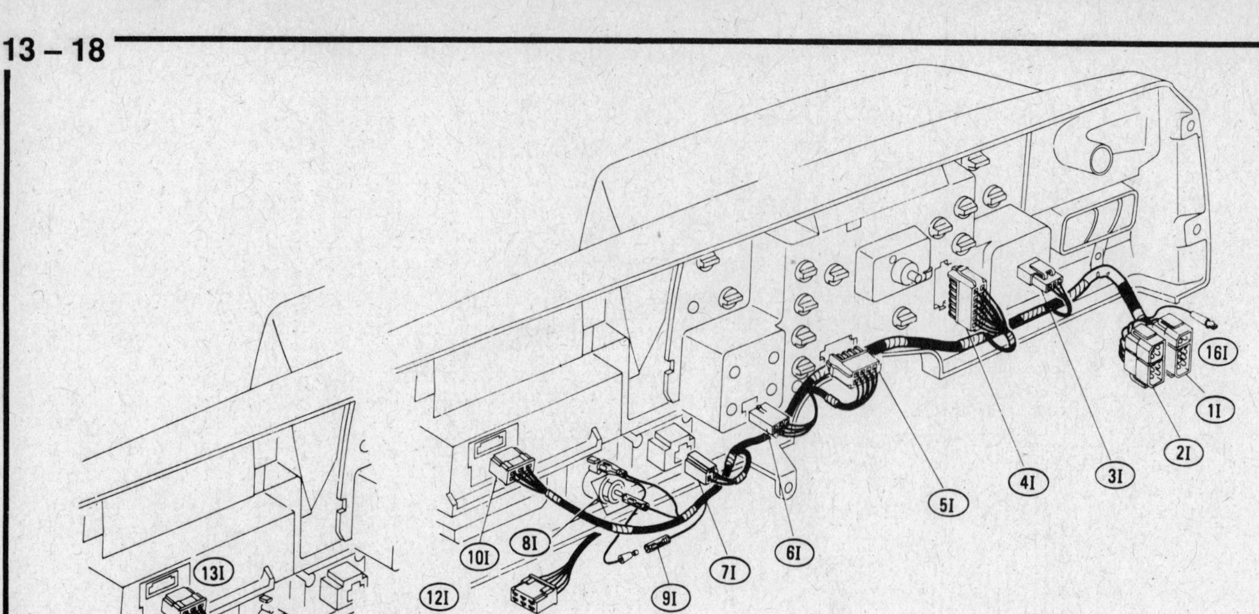

Identification of instrument cluster wiring harness connectors (typical)

11	–	*To main harness 81M (Connector color: White)*	*51*	– *To combination meter*	*111*	–	*To speaker harness*
21	–	*To main harness 82M (Connector color: Blue)*	*61*	– *To tachometer*	*121*	–	*To instrument harness*
31	–	*To clock*	*71*	– *To illumination control unit*	*131*	–	*To radio*
41	–	*To combination meter*	*81*	– *To cigarette lighter*	*141*	–	*To radio*
			91	– *To cigarette lighter illumination lamp*	*151*	–	*To left speaker*
			101	– *To radio*	*161*	–	*To mmain harness*

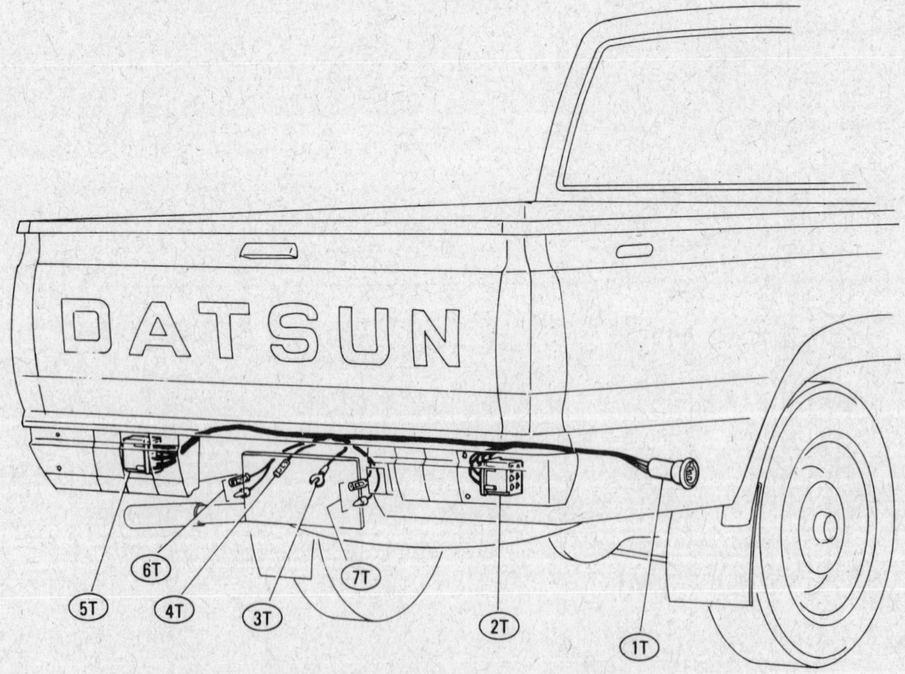

Identification of chassis wiring harness connectors

1C	–	*To main harness 102M*	*3C*	– *To tail harness 1T*	*5C*	–	*To electric fuel pump*
2C	–	*To fuel tank gauge unit*	*4C*	– *To transfer switch (4WD)*			

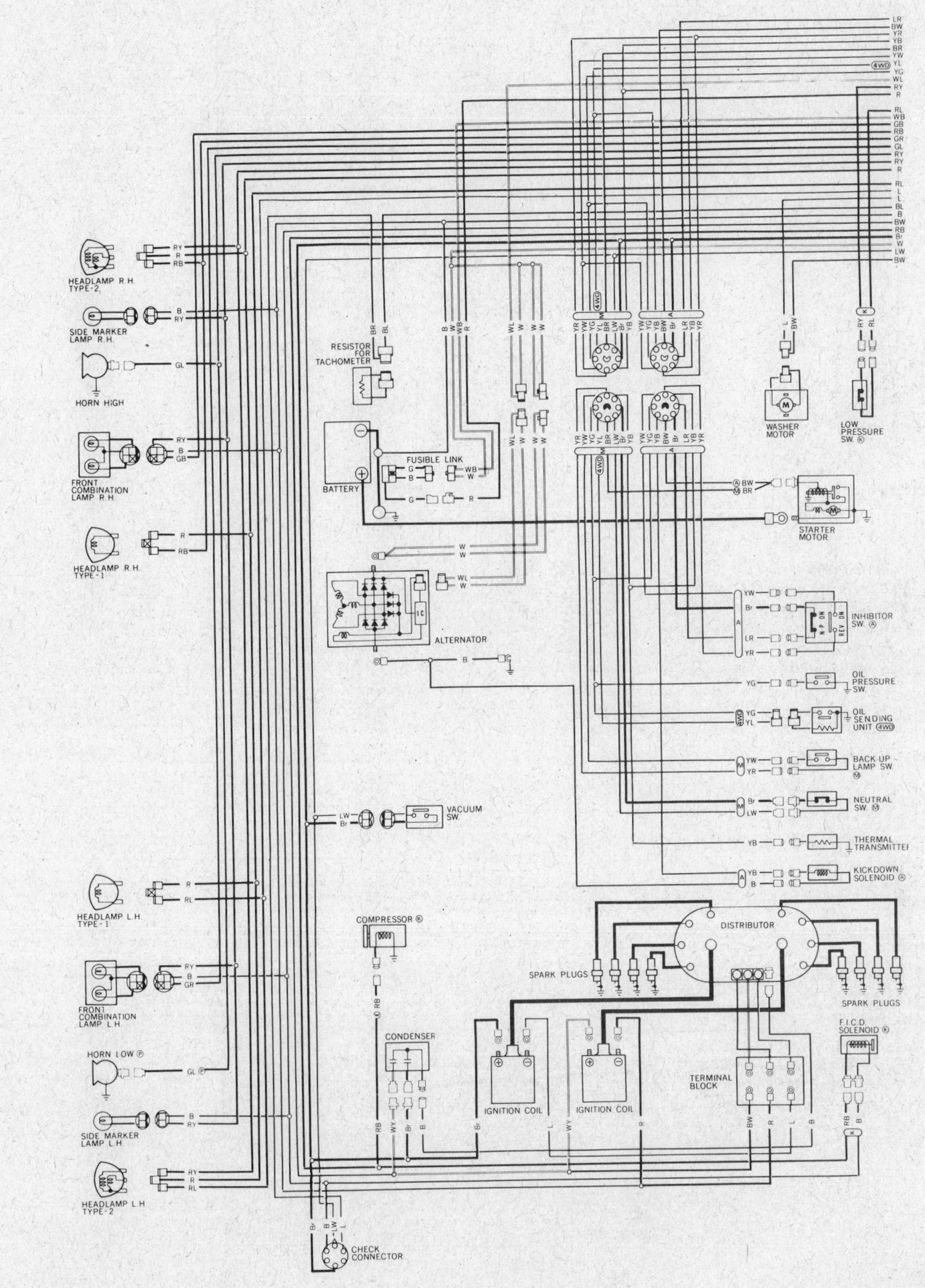

Typical chassis wiring diagram (1 of 3)

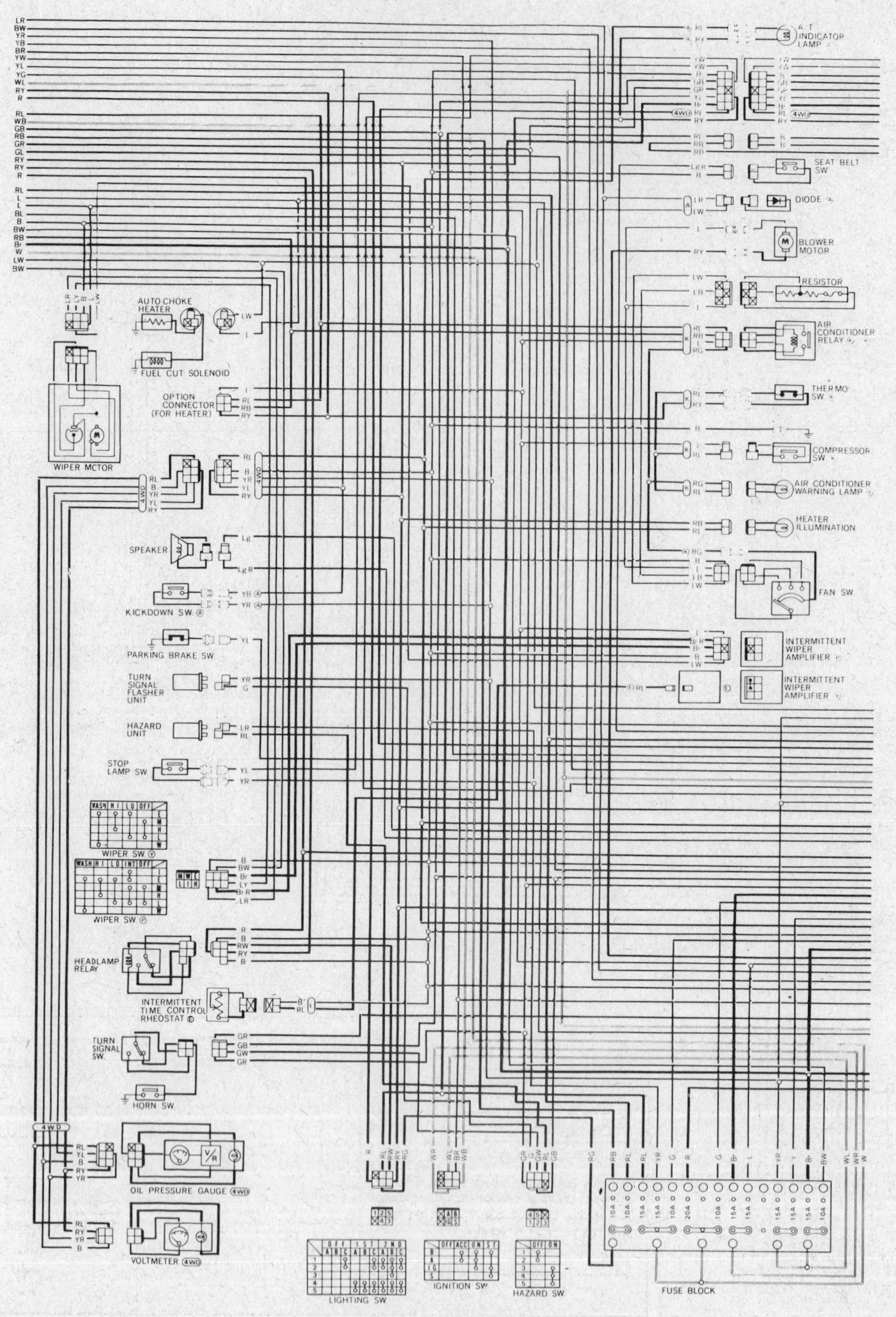

Typical chassis wiring diagram (2 of 3)

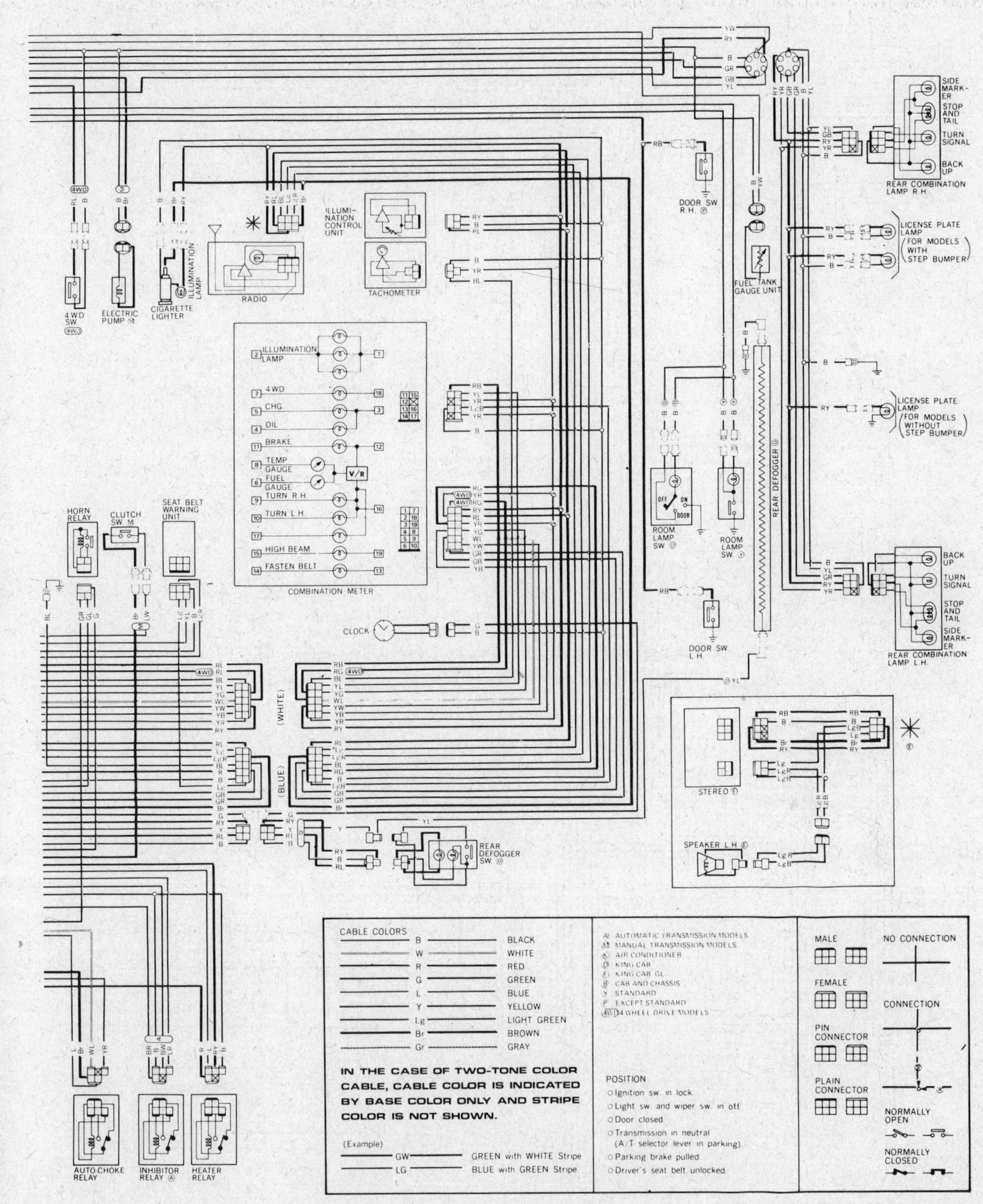

Typical chassis wiring diagram (3 of 3)

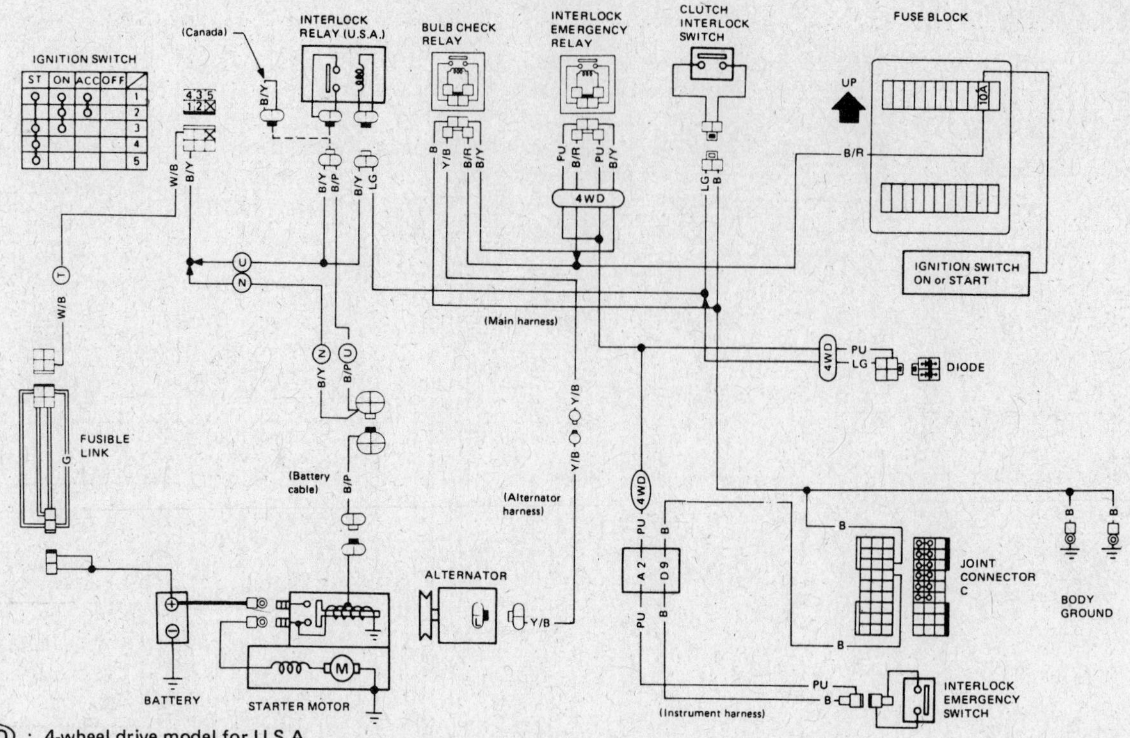

(4WD) : 4-wheel drive model for U.S.A.

(U) : For U.S.A., and E, 2WD SE model without A.S.C.D. and Van for Canada

(N) : Except (U) model

Starting system wiring diagram (manual transmission — late model)

(AS) : With A.S.C.D.

(WO) : Without A.S.C.D.

(2WD) : 2-wheel drive model

(4WD) : 4-wheel drive model

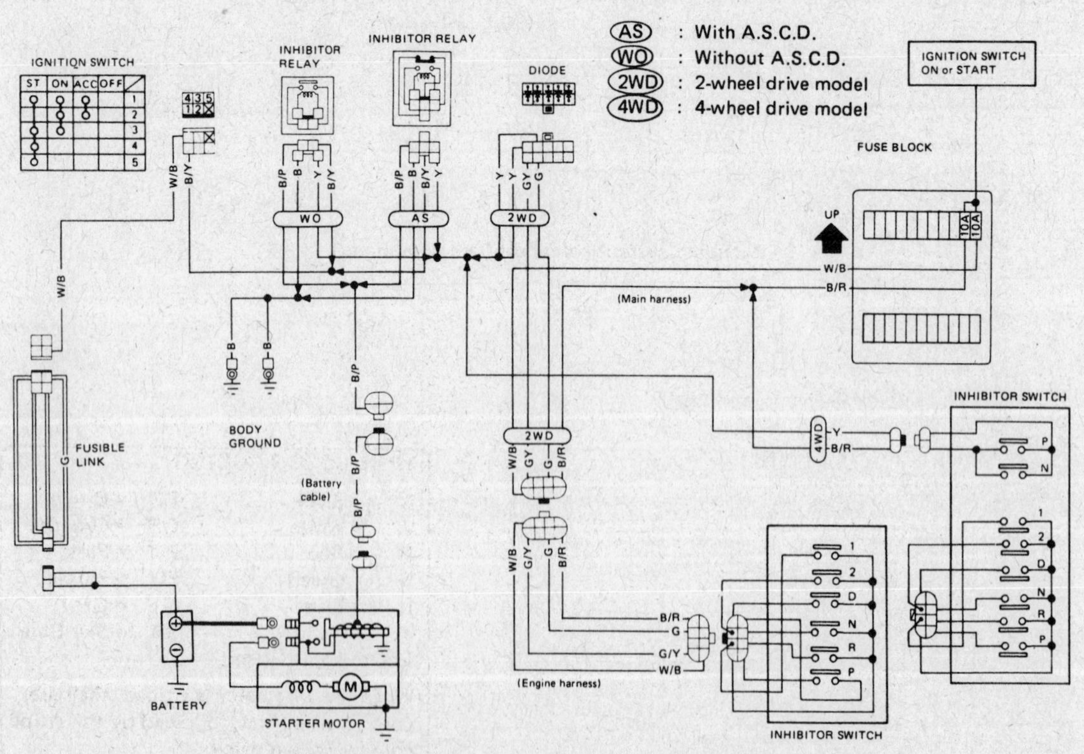

Starting system wiring diagram (automatic transmission — late model)

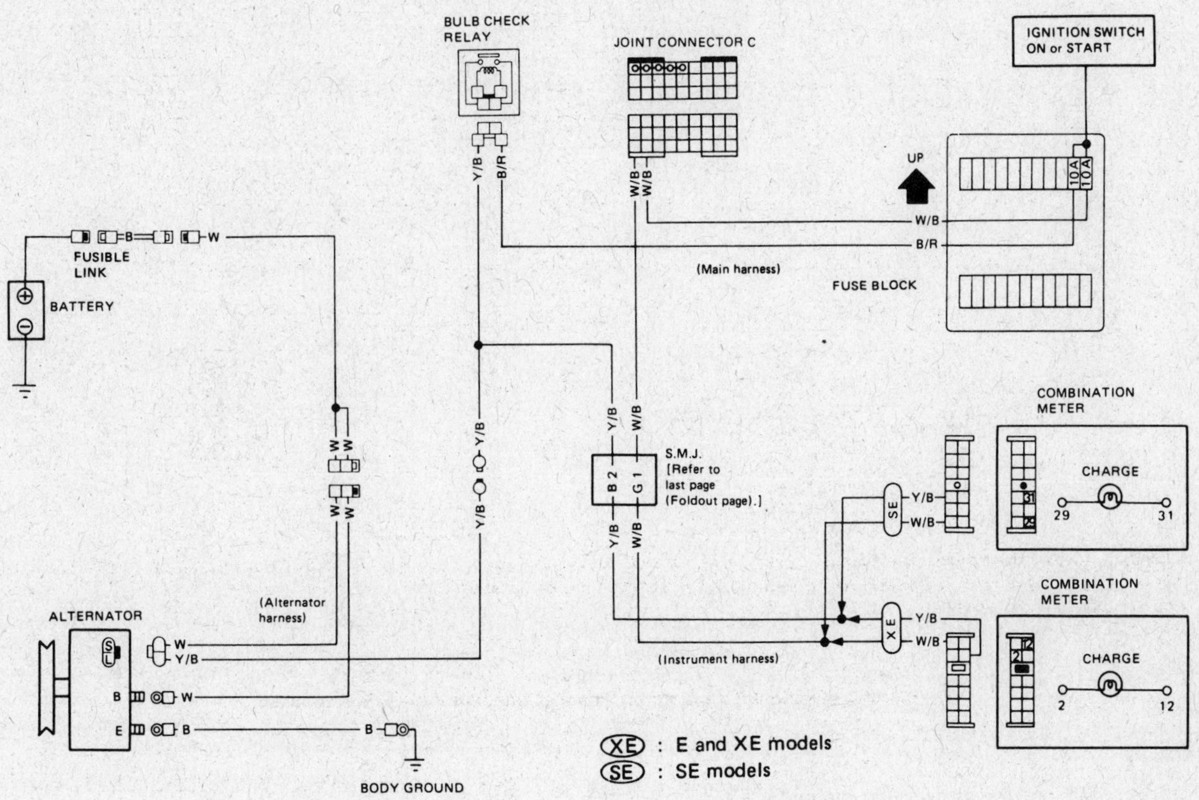

Charging system wiring diagram (late model)

WIRE COLOR CODING

B	= Black	BR	= Brown
W	= White	OR	= Orange
R	= Red	P	= Pink
G	= Green	PU	= Purple
L	= Blue	GY	= Gray
Y	= Yellow	SB	= Sky Blue
LG	= Light Green		

When the wire color is striped, the base color is given first, followed by the stripe color as shown below:

Example: L/W = Blue with White Stripe

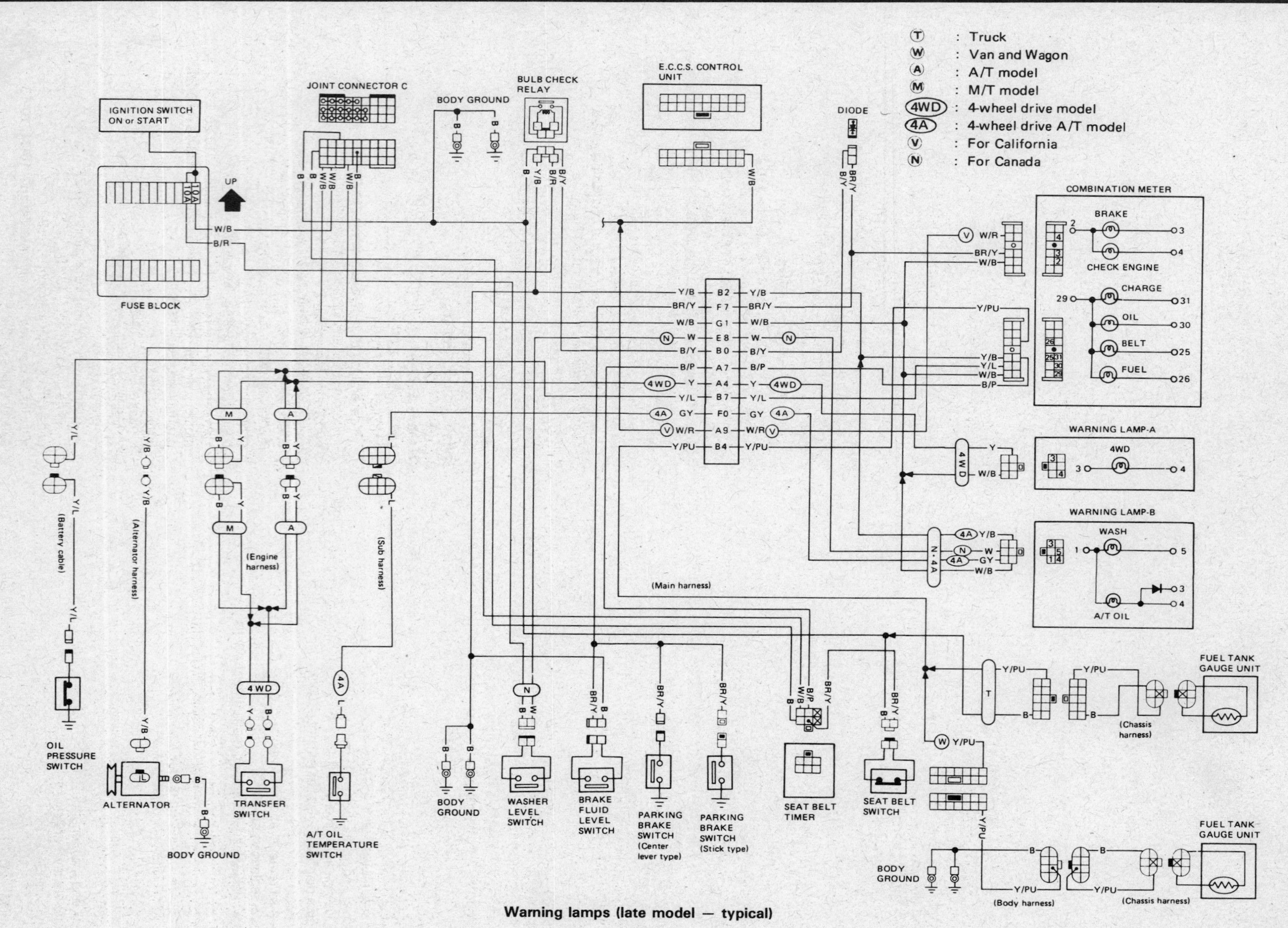

Warning lamps (late model — typical)

Index

C

D

E

F

G

H

I

J

L

T

U

V

W

Haynes Automotive Manuals

NOTE: New manuals are added to this list on a periodic basis. If you do not see a listing for your vehicle, consult your local Haynes dealer for the latest product information.

ACURA

*1776 **Integra** '86 thru '89 & **Legend** '86 thru '90

AMC

Jeep CJ - *see JEEP (412)*
694 **Mid-size models,** Concord, Hornet, Gremlin & Spirit '70 thru '83
934 **(Renault) Alliance & Encore** '83 thru '87

AUDI

615 **4000** all models '80 thru '87
428 **5000** all models '77 thru '83
1117 **5000** all models '84 thru '88

AUSTIN-HEALEY

Sprite - *see MG Midget (265)*

BMW

*2020 **3/5 Series** not including diesel or all-wheel drive models '82 thru '92
276 **320i** all 4 cyl models '75 thru '83
632 **528i** & 530i all models '75 thru '80
240 **1500 thru 2002** except Turbo '59 thru '77

BUICK

Century (front wheel drive) - *see GM (829)*
*1627 **Buick, Oldsmobile & Pontiac Full-size (Front wheel drive)** all models '85 thru '95 **Buick** Electra, LeSabre and Park Avenue; **Oldsmobile** Delta 88 Royale, Ninety Eight and Regency; **Pontiac** Bonneville
1551 **Buick Oldsmobile & Pontiac Full-size (Rear wheel drive)** **Buick** Estate '70 thru '90, Electra'70 thru '84, LeSabre '70 thru '85, Limited '74 thru '79 **Oldsmobile** Custom Cruiser '70 thru '90, Delta 88 '70 thru '85,Ninety-eight '70 thru '84 **Pontiac** Bonneville '70 thru '81, Catalina '70 thru '81, Grandville '70 thru '75, Parisienne '83 thru '86
627 **Mid-size Regal & Century** all rear-drive models with V6, V8 and Turbo '74 thru '87
Regal - *see GENERAL MOTORS (1671)*
Riviera - *see GENERAL MOTORS (38030)*
Skyhawk - *see GENERAL MOTORS (766)*
Skylark '80 thru '85 - *see GM (38020)*
Skylark '86 on - *see GM (1420)*
Somerset - *see GENERAL MOTORS (1420)*

CADILLAC

*751 **Cadillac Rear Wheel Drive** all gasoline models '70 thru '93
Cimarron - *see GENERAL MOTORS (766)*
Eldorado - *see GENERAL MOTORS (38030)*
Seville '80 thru '85 - *see GM (38030)*

CHEVROLET

*1477 **Astro & GMC Safari Mini-vans** '85 thru '93
554 **Camaro V8** all models '70 thru '81
866 **Camaro** all models '82 thru '92
Cavalier - *see GENERAL MOTORS (766)*
Celebrity - *see GENERAL MOTORS (829)*
24017 **Camaro & Firebird** '93 thru '96
625 **Chevelle, Malibu & El Camino** all V6 & V8 models '69 thru '87
449 **Chevette & Pontiac T1000** '76 thru '87
550 **Citation** all models '80 thru '85
*1628 **Corsica/Beretta** all models '87 thru '96
274 **Corvette** all V8 models '68 thru '82
*1336 **Corvette** all models '84 thru '91
1762 **Chevrolet Engine Overhaul Manual**
704 **Full-size Sedans** Caprice, Impala, Biscayne, Bel Air & Wagons '69 thru '90
Lumina - *see GENERAL MOTORS (1671)*
Lumina APV - *see GENERAL MOTORS (2035)*
319 **Luv Pick-up** all 2WD & 4WD '72 thru '82
626 **Monte Carlo** all models '70 thru '88
241 **Nova** all V8 models '69 thru '79
*1642 **Nova and Geo Prizm** all front wheel drive models, '85 thru '92
420 **Pick-ups '67 thru '87** - Chevrolet & GMC, all V8 & in-line 6 cyl, 2WD & 4WD '67 thru '87; Suburbans, Blazers & Jimmys '67 thru '91
*1664 **Pick-ups '88 thru '95** - Chevrolet & GMC, all full-size pick-ups, '88 thru '95; Blazer & Jimmy '92 thru '94; Suburban '92 thru '95; Tahoe & Yukon '95
831 **S-10 & GMC S-15 Pick-ups** '82 thru '93
*24071 **S-10 & GMC S-15 Pick-ups** '94 thru '96
*1727 **Sprint & Geo Metro** '85 thru '94
*345 **Vans - Chevrolet & GMC**, V8 & in-line 6 cylinder models '68 thru '96

CHRYSLER

25025 **Chrysler Concorde, New Yorker & LHS, Dodge** Intrepid, **Eagle** Vision, '93 thru '96
2114 **Chrysler Engine Overhaul Manual**
*2058 **Full-size Front-Wheel Drive** '88 thru '93
K-Cars - *see DODGE Aries (723)*
Laser - *see DODGE Daytona (1140)*
*1337 **Chrysler & Plymouth Mid-size** front wheel drive '82 thru '95
Rear-wheel Drive - *see Dodge (2098)*

DATSUN

647 **200SX** all models '80 thru '83
228 **B - 210** all models '73 thru '78
525 **210** all models '79 thru '82
206 **240Z, 260Z & 280Z** Coupe '70 thru '78
563 **280ZX** Coupe & 2+2 '79 thru '83
300ZX - *see NISSAN (1137)*
679 **310** all models '78 thru '82
123 **510 & PL521 Pick-up** '68 thru '73
430 **510** all models '78 thru '81
372 **610** all models '72 thru '76
277 **620 Series Pick-up** all models '73 thru '79
720 Series Pick-up - *see NISSAN (771)*
376 **810/Maxima** all gasoline models, '77 thru '84
Pulsar - *see NISSAN (876)*
Sentra - *see NISSAN (982)*
Stanza - *see NISSAN (981)*

DODGE

400 & 600 - *see CHRYSLER Mid-size (1337)*
*723 **Aries & Plymouth Reliant** '81 thru '89
1231 **Caravan & Plymouth Voyager Mini-Vans** all models '84 thru '95
699 **Challenger/Plymouth Saporro** '78 thru '83
Challenger '67-'76 - *see DODGE Dart (234)*
610 **Colt & Plymouth Champ (front wheel drive)** all models '78 thru '87
*1668 **Dakota Pick-ups** all models '87 thru '96
234 **Dart, Challenger/Plymouth Barracuda & Valiant** 6 cyl models '67 thru '76
*1140 **Daytona & Chrysler Laser** '84 thru '89
Intrepid - *see CHRYSLER (25025)*
*30034 **Neon** all models '94 thru '97
*545 **Omni & Plymouth Horizon** '78 thru '90
*912 **Pick-ups** all full-size models '74 thru '93
*30041 **Pick-ups** all full-size models '94 thru '96
*556 **Ram 50/D50 Pick-ups & Raider and Plymouth Arrow Pick-ups** '79 thru '93
2098 **Dodge/Plymouth/Chrysler** rear wheel drive '71 thru '89
*1726 **Shadow & Plymouth Sundance** '87 thru '94
*1779 **Spirit & Plymouth Acclaim** '89 thru '95
*349 **Vans - Dodge & Plymouth** V8 & 6 cyl models '71 thru '96

EAGLE

Talon - *see Mitsubishi Eclipse (2097)*
Vision - *see CHRYSLER (25025)*

FIAT

094 **124 Sport Coupe & Spider** '68 thru '78
273 **X1/9** all models '74 thru '80

FORD

10355 **Ford Automatic Trans. Overhaul**
*1476 **Aerostar Mini-vans** all models '86 thru '96
268 **Courier Pick-up** all models '72 thru '82
2105 **Crown Victoria & Mercury Grand Marquis** '88 thru '96
1763 **Ford Engine Overhaul Manual**
789 **Escort/Mercury Lynx** all models '81 thru '90
*2046 **Escort/Mercury Tracer** '91 thru '96
*2021 **Explorer & Mazda Navajo** '91 thru '95
560 **Fairmont & Mercury Zephyr** '78 thru '83
334 **Fiesta** all models '77 thru '80
754 **Ford & Mercury Full-size,** Ford LTD & Mercury Marquis ('75 thru '82); Ford Custom 500,Country Squire, Crown Victoria & Mercury Colony Park ('75 thru '87); Ford LTD Crown Victoria & Mercury Gran Marquis ('83 thru '87)
359 **Granada & Mercury Monarch** all in-line, 6 cyl & V8 models '75 thru '80
773 **Ford & Mercury Mid-size,** Ford Thunderbird & Mercury Cougar ('75 thru '82); Ford LTD & Mercury Marquis ('83 thru '86); Ford Torino,Gran Torino, Elite, Ranchero pick-up, LTD II, Mercury Montego, Comet, XR-7 & Lincoln Versailles ('75 thru '86)
231 **Mustang II** 4 cyl, V6 & V8 models '74 thru '78
357 **Mustang V8** all models '64-1/2 thru '73
*654 **Mustang & Mercury Capri** all models Mustang, '79 thru '93; Capri, '79 thru '86
*36051 **Mustang** all models '94 thru '97
788 **Pick-ups & Bronco** '73 thru '79
*880 **Pick-ups & Bronco** '80 thru '96
649 **Pinto & Mercury Bobcat** '75 thru '80
1670 **Probe** all models '89 thru '92
*1026 **Ranger/Bronco II** gasoline models '83 thru '92
*36071 **Ranger** '93 thru '96 & **Mazda Pick-ups** '94 thru '96
*1421 **Taurus & Mercury Sable** '86 thru '95
*1418 **Tempo & Mercury Topaz** all gasoline models '84 thru '94
1338 **Thunderbird/Mercury Cougar** '83 thru '88
*1725 **Thunderbird/Mercury Cougar** '89 and '96
344 **Vans** all V8 Econoline models '69 thru '91
*2119 **Vans** full size '92-'95

GENERAL MOTORS

*10360 **GM Automatic Transmission Overhaul**
*829 **Buick Century, Chevrolet Celebrity, Oldsmobile Cutlass Ciera & Pontiac 6000** all models '82 thru '96
*1671 **Buick Regal, Chevrolet Lumina, Oldsmobile Cutlass Supreme & Pontiac Grand Prix** front wheel drive models '88 thru '95
*766 **Buick Skyhawk, Cadillac Cimarron, Chevrolet Cavalier, Oldsmobile Firenza & Pontiac J-2000 & Sunbird** '82 thru '94
38020 **Buick Skylark, Chevrolet Citation, Olds Omega, Pontiac Phoenix** '80 thru '85
1420 **Buick Skylark & Somerset, Oldsmobile Achieva & Calais and Pontiac Grand Am** all models '85 thru '95
38030 **Cadillac Eldorado** '71 thru '85, **Seville** '80 thru '85, **Oldsmobile Toronado** '71 thru '85 **& Buick Riviera** '79 thru '85
*2035 **Chevrolet Lumina APV, Olds Silhouette & Pontiac Trans Sport** all models '90 thru '95
General Motors Full-size Rear-wheel Drive - *see BUICK (1551)*

GEO

Metro - *see CHEVROLET Sprint (1727)*
Prizm - *'85 thru '92 see CHEVY Nova (1642), '93 thru '96 see TOYOTA Corolla (1642)*
*2039 **Storm** all models '90 thru '93
Tracker - *see SUZUKI Samurai (1626)*

GMC

Safari - *see CHEVROLET ASTRO (1477)*
Vans & Pick-ups - *see CHEVROLET (420, 831, 345, 1664 & 24071)*

(Continued on other side)

** Listings shown with an asterisk (*) indicate model coverage as of this printing. These titles will be periodically updated to include later model years - consult your Haynes dealer for more information.*

Haynes Automotive Manuals (continued)

NOTE: New manuals are added to this list on a periodic basis. If you do not see a listing for your vehicle, consult your local Haynes dealer for the latest product information.

HONDA
351 **Accord CVCC** all models '76 thru '83
1221 **Accord** all models '84 thru '89
2067 **Accord** all models '90 thru '93
42013 **Accord** all models '94 thru '95
160 **Civic 1200** all models '73 thru '79
633 **Civic 1300 & 1500 CVCC** '80 thru '83
297 **Civic 1500 CVCC** all models '75 thru '79
1227 **Civic** all models '84 thru '91
*2118 **Civic & del Sol** '92 thru '95
*601 **Prelude CVCC** all models '79 thru '89

HYUNDAI
*1552 **Excel** all models '86 thru '94

ISUZU
*1641 **Trooper & Pick-up**, all gasoline models Pick-up, '81 thru '93; Trooper, '84 thru '91
Hombre - *see CHEVROLET S-10 (24071)*

JAGUAR
*242 **XJ6** all 6 cyl models '68 thru '86
*49011 **XJ6** all models '88 thru '94
*478 **XJ12 & XJS** all 12 cyl models '72 thru '85

JEEP
*1553 **Cherokee, Comanche & Wagoneer Limited** all models '84 thru '96
412 **CJ** all models '49 thru '86
50025 **Grand Cherokee** all models '93 thru '95
50029 **Grand Wagoneer & Pick-up** '72 thru '91 Grand Wagoneer '84 thru '91, Cherokee & Wagoneer '72 thru '83, Pick-up '72 thru '88
*1777 **Wrangler** all models '87 thru '95

LINCOLN
2117 **Rear Wheel Drive** all models '70 thru '96

MAZDA
648 **626** (rear wheel drive) all models '79 thru '82
*1082 **626/MX-6 (front wheel drive)** '83 thru '91
370 **GLC Hatchback (rear wheel drive)** '77 thru '83
757 **GLC (front wheel drive)** '81 thru '85
*2047 **MPV** all models '89 thru '94
Navajo - *see Ford Explorer (2021)*
267 **Pick-ups** '72 thru '93
Pick-ups '94 thru '96 - *see Ford Ranger (36071)*
460 **RX-7** all models '79 thru '85
*1419 **RX-7** all models '86 thru '91

MERCEDES-BENZ
*1643 **190 Series** four-cyl gas models, '84 thru '88
346 **230/250/280** 6 cyl sohc models '68 thru '72
983 **280 123 Series** gasoline models '77 thru '81
698 **350 & 450** all models '71 thru '80
697 **Diesel 123 Series** '76 thru '85

MERCURY
See FORD Listing

MG
111 **MGB** Roadster & GT Coupe '62 thru '80
265 **MG Midget, Austin Healey Sprite** '58 thru '80

MITSUBISHI
*1669 **Cordia, Tredia, Galant, Precis & Mirage** '83 thru '93
*2097 **Eclipse, Eagle Talon & Plymouth Laser** '90 thru '94
*2022 **Pick-up** '83 thru '96 **& Montero** '83 thru '93

NISSAN
1137 **300ZX** all models including Turbo '84 thru '89
*72015 **Altima** all models '93 thru '97
*1341 **Maxima** all models '85 thru '91
*771 **Pick-ups** '80 thru '96 **Pathfinder** '87 thru '95
876 **Pulsar** all models '83 thru '86
*982 **Sentra** all models '82 thru '94
*981 **Stanza** all models '82 thru '90

OLDSMOBILE
Achieva - *see GENERAL MOTORS (1420)*
Bravada - *see CHEVROLET S-10 (831)*
Calais - *see GENERAL MOTORS (1420)*
Custom Cruiser - *see BUICK RWD (1551)*
*658 **Cutlass** V6 & V8 gas models '74 thru '88
Cutlass Ciera - *see GENERAL MOTORS (829)*
Cutlass Supreme - *see GM (1671)*
Delta 88 - *see BUICK Full-size RWD (1551)*
Delta 88 Brougham - *see BUICK Full-size FWD (1551), RWD (1627)*
Delta 88 Royale - *see BUICK RWD (1551)*
Firenza - *see GENERAL MOTORS (766)*
Ninety-eight Regency - *see BUICK Full-size RWD (1551), FWD (1627)*
Ninety-eight Regency Brougham - *see BUICK Full-size RWD (1551)*
Omega - *see GENERAL MOTORS (38020)*
Silhouette - *see GENERAL MOTORS (2035)*
Toronado - *see GENERAL MOTORS (38030)*

PEUGEOT
663 **504** all diesel models '74 thru '83

PLYMOUTH
Laser - *see MITSUBISHI Eclipse (2097)*
For other PLYMOUTH titles, see DODGE.

PONTIAC
T1000 - *see CHEVROLET Chevette (449)*
J-2000 - *see GENERAL MOTORS (766)*
6000 - *see GENERAL MOTORS (829)*
Bonneville - *see Buick FWD (1627), RWD (1551)*
Bonneville Brougham - *see Buick (1551)*
Catalina - *see Buick Full-size (1551)*
1232 **Fiero** all models '84 thru '88
555 **Firebird** V8 models except Turbo '70 thru '81
867 **Firebird** all models '82 thru '92
Firebird '93 thru '96 - *see CHEVY Camaro (24017)*
Full-size Front Wheel Drive - *see BUICK, Oldsmobile, Pontiac Full-size FWD (1627)*
Full-size Rear Wheel Drive - *see BUICK Oldsmobile, Pontiac Full-size RWD (1551)*
Grand Am - *see GENERAL MOTORS (1420)*
Grand Prix - *see GENERAL MOTORS (1671)*
Grandville - *see BUICK Full-size (1551)*
Parisienne - *see BUICK Full-size (1551)*
Phoenix - *see GENERAL MOTORS (38020)*
Sunbird - *see GENERAL MOTORS (766)*
Trans Sport - *see GENERAL MOTORS (2035)*

PORSCHE
*264 **911** except Turbo & Carrera 4 '65 thru '89
239 **914** all 4 cyl models '69 thru '76
397 **924** all models including Turbo '76 thru '82
*1027 **944** all models including Turbo '83 thru '89

RENAULT
141 **5 Le Car** all models '76 thru '83
Alliance & Encore - *see AMC (934)*

SAAB
247 **99** all models including Turbo '69 thru '80
*980 **900** all models including Turbo '79 thru '88

SATURN
2083 **Saturn** all models '91 thru '96

SUBARU
237 **1100, 1300, 1400 & 1600** '71 thru '79
*681 **1600 & 1800** 2WD & 4WD '80 thru '89

SUZUKI
*1626 **Samurai/Sidekick &Geo Tracker** '86 thru '96

TOYOTA
1023 **Camry** all models '83 thru '91
92006 **Camry** all models '92 thru '95
935 **Celica Rear Wheel Drive** '71 thru '85
*2038 **Celica Front Wheel Drive** '86 thru '93
1139 **Celica Supra** all models '79 thru '92
361 **Corolla** all models '75 thru '79
961 **Corolla** all rear wheel drive models '80 thru '87
1025 **Corolla** all front wheel drive models '84 thru '92
*92036 **Corolla & Geo Prizm** '93 thru '96
636 **Corolla Tercel** all models '80 thru '82
360 **Corona** all models '74 thru '82
532 **Cressida** all models '78 thru '82
313 **Land Cruiser** all models '68 thru '82
*1339 **MR2** all models '85 thru '87
304 **Pick-up** all models '69 thru '78
*656 **Pick-up** all models '79 thru '95
*2048 **Previa** all models '91 thru '95
2106 **Tercel** all models '87 thru '94

TRIUMPH
113 **Spitfire** all models '62 thru '81
322 **TR7** all models '75 thru '81

VW
159 **Beetle & Karmann Ghia** '54 thru '79
238 **Dasher** all gasoline models '74 thru '81
96017 **Golf & Jetta** all models '93 thru '97
*884 **Rabbit, Jetta, Scirocco, & Pick-up** gas models '74 thru '91 & Convertible '80 thru '92
451 **Rabbit, Jetta & Pick-up** diesel '77 thru '84
082 **Transporter 1600** all models '68 thru '79
226 **Transporter 1700, 1800 & 2000** '72 thru '79
084 **Type 3 1500 & 1600** all models '63 thru '73
1029 **Vanagon** all air-cooled models '80 thru '83

VOLVO
203 **120, 130 Series & 1800 Sports** '61 thru '73
129 **140 Series** all models '66 thru '74
*270 **240 Series** all models '76 thru '93
400 **260 Series** all models '75 thru '82
*1550 **740 & 760 Series** all models '82 thru '88

TECHBOOK MANUALS
2108 **Automotive Computer Codes**
1667 **Automotive Emissions Control Manual**
482 **Fuel Injection Manual, 1978 thru 1985**
2111 **Fuel Injection Manual, 1986 thru 1996**
2069 **Holley Carburetor Manual**
2068 **Rochester Carburetor Manual**
10240 **Weber/Zenith/Stromberg/SU Carburetors**
1762 **Chevrolet Engine Overhaul Manual**
2114 **Chrysler Engine Overhaul Manual**
1763 **Ford Engine Overhaul Manual**
1736 **GM and Ford Diesel Engine Repair Manual**
1666 **Small Engine Repair Manual**
10355 **Ford Automatic Transmission Overhaul**
10360 **GM Automatic Transmission Overhaul**
1479 **Automotive Body Repair & Painting**
2112 **Automotive Brake Manual**
2113 **Automotive Detaiing Manual**
1654 **Automotive Eelectrical Manual**
1480 **Automotive Heating & Air Conditioning**
2109 **Automotive Reference Manual & Dictionary**
2107 **Automotive Tools Manual**
10440 **Used Car Buying Guide**
2110 **Welding Manual**
10450 **ATV Basics**

SPANISH MANUALS
98903 **Reparación de Carrocería & Pintura**
98905 **Códigos Automotrices de la Computadora**
98910 **Frenos Automotriz**
98915 **Inyección de Combustible 1986 al 1994**
99040 **Chevrolet & GMC Camionetas** '67 al '87 Incluye Suburban, Blazer & Jimmy '67 al '91
99041 **Chevrolet & GMC Camionetas** '88 al '95 Incluye Suburban '92 al '95, Blazer & Jimmy '92 al '94, Tahoe y Yukon '95
99042 **Chevrolet & GMC Camionetas Cerradas** '68 al '95
99055 **Dodge Caravan & Plymouth Voyager** '84 al '95
99075 **Ford Camionetas y Bronco** '80 al '94
99077 **Ford Camionetas Cerradas** '69 al '91
99083 **Ford Modelos de Tamaño Grande** '75 al '87
99088 **Ford Modelos de Tamaño Mediano** '75 al '86
99095 **GM Modelos de Tamaño Grande** '70 al '90
99118 **Nissan Sentra** '82 al '94
99125 **Toyota Camionetas y 4-Runner** '79 al '95

Over 100 Haynes motorcycle manuals also available

** Listings shown with an asterisk (*) indicate model coverage as of this printing. These titles will be periodically updated to include later model years - consult your Haynes dealer for more information.*

5-97

Haynes North America, Inc., 861 Lawrence Drive, Newbury Park, CA 91320 • (805) 498-6703